Lecture Notes in Computer Science 4282

Commenced Publication in 1973
Founding and Former Series Editors:
Gerhard Goos, Juris Hartmanis, and Jan van Leeuwen

Zhigeng Pan   Adrian Cheok
Michael Haller   Rynson W.H. Lau
Hideo Saito   Ronghua Liang (Eds.)

Advances in Artificial Reality and Tele-Existence

16th International Conference
on Artificial Reality and Telexistence, ICAT 2006
Hangzhou, China, November 29 – December 1, 2006
Proceedings

 Springer

Volume Editors

Zhigeng Pan
Zhejiang University, Hangzhou, China
E-mail: zhigengpan@gmail.com

Adrian Cheok
National University of Singapore, Singapore
E-mail: adriancheok@ntu.edu.sg

Michael Haller
Upper Austria University of Applied Sciences, Hagenberg, Austria
E-mail: haller@fh-hagenberg.at

Rynson W.H. Lau
University of Durham, Durham DH1 3LE, UK
E-mail: rynson.lau@durham.ac.uk

Hideo Saito
Keio University, Yokohama, Japan
E-mail: saito@ozawa.ics.keio.ac.jp

Ronghua Liang
Zhejiang University, Hangzhou, China
E-mail: rhliang@zjut.edu.cn

Library of Congress Control Number: 2006936898

CR Subject Classification (1998): I.2, H.5, H.4, H.3, I.3, I.4, J.3, J.5

LNCS Sublibrary: SL 3 – Information Systems and Application, incl. Internet/Web and HCI

ISSN   0302-9743
ISBN-10   3-540-49776-5 Springer Berlin Heidelberg New York
ISBN-13   978-3-540-49776-9 Springer Berlin Heidelberg New York

Springer is a part of Springer Science+Business Media

springer.com

© Springer-Verlag Berlin Heidelberg 2006
Printed in Germany

Typesetting: Camera-ready by author, data conversion by Scientific Publishing Services, Chennai, India
Printed on acid-free paper   SPIN: 11941354   06/3142   5 4 3 2 1 0

Preface

ICAT is the oldest international conference on virtual reality and tele-existence. ICAT 2006 not only looked for innovations in the technology itself, but also explored novel ways to transfer and express information and creative ideas to the society and people.

The 16th International Conference on Artificial Reality and Telexistence was held at the Zhejiang University of Technology, Hangzhou, P.R. China from November 29 to December 1, 2006. The main purpose of the conference is to provide opportunities for researchers and practitioners to present their research findings and exchange opinions on the development and use of such systems. The conference included plenary invited talks, workshops, tutorials, and paper presentation tracks.

The main conference received 523 submissions in total from 21 different countries, including China (mainland, Hong Kong, Taiwan), USA, UK, Germany, Austria, France, Australia, Canada, Korea, Japan, Malaysia, Mexico, etc., of which 138 papers were accepted for this volume and 11 papers were invited to submit extended versions for a special issue of *International Journal of Virtual Reality* (IJVR, 5(4)). The papers in this volume cover the topics including: Artificial Reality, VR, Telexistence, AR, Mixed Reality, Ubiquitous/Wearable Computing, Visual and Auditory Displays, Rendering Techniques, Architecture for VR, Immersive Projection Technology, Techniques for Modeling VR Systems, Virtual Heritage, Motion Tracking, Innovative Applications of VR, Haptics, Evaluation of VR Techniques and Systems, VR Interaction and Navigation Techniques, Artificial Life, Distributed and Collaborative VR Systems, VR Input and Output Devices, Virtual Medicine and Health Science, Human Factors of VR, Interactive Art and Entertainment.

The wide range of questions, ideas, concepts and applications discussed in the contributions of this volume reflect the vitality and engagement of the artificial reality and tele-existence communities and their neighboring disciplines. The current research situation in these areas demands interdisciplinary cooperation and mutual stimulation. With the strong support of Springer, the proceedings of ICAT this year were published in the *Lecture Notes in Computer Science* (LNCS) series.

November 2006

Zhigeng Pan
Adrian Cheok
Michael Haller
Rynson Lau
Hideo Saito
Ronghua Liang

Organization

Committee Listings

General Honorary Co-chairs
Deren Li (Wuhan University, China)
Susumu Tachi (University of Tokyo, Japan)

General Co-chairs
Zhigeng Pan (Zhejiang University, China)
Hideo Saito (Keio University, Japan)

Program Co-chairs
Adrain Cheok (Mixed Reality Lab, Singapore)
Michael Haller (University of Applied Sciences, Hagenberg, Austria)
Rynson W.H. Lau (University of Durham, UK)

Local Chair
Qingzhang Chen (Zhejiang University of Technology)

Local Vice-Chairs
Limin Men (Zhejiang Provincial Key Lab of Optic Fiber Communication Technology)
Huageng Wan (Zhejiang University)
Decai Huang (Zhejiang University of Technology)
Ronghua Liang (Zhejiang University of Technology)

Publicity Co-chairs
Ruigang Yang (The University of Kentucky)
Xiaohong Jiang (Zhejiang University)

Publication Chair
Li Li (Hangzhou Dianzi University)

Workshop Chair
Takuya Nojima (Japan Aerospace Exploration Agency)

Demo Chair
Masahiko Inami (the University of Electro-Communications)

Financial Co-chairs
Hui Gu (Zhejiang University of Technology)
Mingmin Zhang (Zhejiang University)

International Program Committee

Mark Billinghurst, New Zealand
Adrain Cheok, Singpore
Yukio Fukui, Japan
Michael Haller, Austria
Naoki Hashimoto, Japan
Larry Hodges, USA
Masa Inakage, Japan
Michael Jenkin, Canada
Fumio Kishino, Japan
Kiyoshi Kiyokawa, Japan
Frederick Li , UK
Tetsuro Ogi, Japan
Christian Reimann, Germany
Hideo Saito, Japan
Yoichi Sato, Japan
Daniel Thalmann, Switzerland
Toshio Yamada, Japan
Ruigang Yang, USA
Shunsuke Yoshida, Japan

Tony Brooks, Denmark
Gordon Clapworthy, UK
Kenji Funahashi, Japan
Soonhung Han, Korea
Wataru Hashimoto, Japan
Nicholas Holliman, UK
Shuichi Ino, Japan
Hiroyuki Kajimoto, Japan
Itaru Kitahara, Japan
Rynson W.H. Lau, UK
Robert Lindeman, USA
Kenichi Okada, Japan
Jeha Ryu, Korea
Kosuke Sato, Japan
Shamus Smith, UK
Ulrich Nlrichmann, USA
Hiroyuki Yamamoto, Japan
Hiroaki Yano, Japan
Hongbin Zha, China

Andreas Butz, Germany
Michael Cohen, Japan
Norihiro Hagita, Japan
Harold Thwaites, Malaysia
Michitaka Hirose, Japan
Yasushi Ikei, Japan
Yutaka Ishibashi, Japan
Myoung-Hee, Korea
Yoshifumi Kitamura, Japan
Gun Lee, Korea
Takeshi Naemura, Japan
Zhigeng Pan, China
Amela Sadagic, USA
Makoto Sato, Japan
Wookho Son, Korea
Greg Welch, USA
Ungyeon Yang, Korea
Naokazu Yokoya, Japan

Reviewer Listings

Song Aiguo
Congchen Chen
Adrain Cheok
Weilong Ding
Xianyong Fang
Kenji Funahashi
Soonhung Han
Hanwu He
Decai Huang
Yutaka Ishibashi
Xiaohong Jiang
Fumio Kishino
Rynson W.H. Lau
Hua Li
Ronghua Liang
Yongkui Liu
Takeshi Naemura
Yanjun Peng
Amela Sadagic
Yoichi Sato
Chengfang Song
Zheng Tan
Jianhua Tao
Huageng Wan
Qiang Wang
Yongtian Wang
Haihong Wu

Qing Xu
Bailing Yang
Hiroaki Yano
Zhengsheng Yu
Jiawan Zhang
Wei Zhang
Bingfeng Zhou
Mark Billinghurst
Dingfang Chen
Gordon Clapworthy
Xiumin Fan
Jieqing Feng
Hui Gu
Naoki Hashimoto
Michitaka Hirose
Yasushi Ikei
Michael Jenkin
Xiaogang Jin
Itaru Kitahara
Gun Lee
Li Li
Robert Lindeman
Jianfeng Lu
Tetsuro Ogi
Xujia Qin
Hideo Saito
Shamus Smith

Jizhou Sun
Bing Tang
Daniel Thalmann
Guoping Wang
Ruchuan Wang
Greg Welch
Lingda Wu
Xiaogang Xu
Ungyeon Yang
Zhiqiang Yao
Ruwei Yun
Maojun Zhang
Nailiang Zhao
Jiejie Zhu
Tony Brooks
Ling Chen
Michael Cohen
Jinglong Fang
Jun Feng
Norihiro Hagita
Wataru Hashimoto
Larry Hodges
Masa Inakage
Qingge Ji
Hiroyuki Kajimoto
Yoshifumi Kitamura
Fengxia Li

Zili Li
Yushen Liu
Xiaolan Luo
Kenichi Okada
Christian Reimann
Kosuke Sato
Wookho Son
Shusen Sun
Jie Tang
Harold Thwaites
Yangsheng Wang
Yigang Wang
Enhua Wu
Hui Xiang
Toshio Yamada
Ruigang Yang
Naokazu Yokoya
Hongbin Zha
Mingmin Zhang
XiangJun Zhao
Andreas Butz
Wei Chen
Guofu Ding
Tongzhu Fang
Yukio Fukui
Michael Haller
Gaoqi He

Nicholas Holliman	Jianfei Mao	Ulrich Neumann	Shunsuke Yoshida
Shuichi Ino	Zhigeng Pan	Jianming Wang	Yongzhao Zhan
Jinyuan Jia	Jeha Ryu	Zhaoqi Wang	Qiong Zhang
Myoung-Hee Kim	Makoto Sato	Fuli Wu	Wenting Zheng
Kiyoshi Kiyokawa	Mingli Song	Yongliang Xiao	
Xuelong Li	Zhengxing Sun	Hiroyuki Yamamoto	
Frederick Li	Yong Tang	Hongwei Yang	

Acknowledgements and Sponsoring Institutions

ICAT 2006 was sponsored by VRSJ (Virtual Reality Society in Japan) and was organized by:

- Zhejiang University of Technology
- VR Committee, China Society of Image and Graphics

However, ICAT 2006 owes its big success to the financial and organizational support of various institutions including:

- DEARC, Zhejiang University
- Computer Network and Multimedia Lab, Zhejiang University of Technology
- International Journal of Virtual Reality (IJVR)
- National Science Foundation of China

We would like to thank all of them for offering the opportunity to organize ICAT 2006 in a way that provided a diversified scientific and social program. Especially, we would like to thank all members of the International Program Committee and Organizing Committee for their great job in defining conference topics, reviewing the large number of submitted papers, and managing to put all the material together for this great event.

Table of Contents

Anthropomorphic Intelligent Robotics, Artificial Life

Augmented Reality/Mixed Reality

Distributed and Collaborative VR System

Haptics, Human Factors of VR

Innovative Applications of VR

Motion Tracking

Real Time Computer Simulation

Tools and Technique for Modeling VR Systems

Ubiquitous/Wearable Computing

Virtual Heritage, Virtual Medicine and Health Science

Virtual Reality

VR Interaction and Navigation Techniques

Gesture Recognition Based on Context Awareness for Human-Robot Interaction

Seok-Ju Hong, Nurul Arif Setiawan, Song-Gook Kim, and Chil-Woo Lee*

Intelligent Media Lab, Department of Computer Engineering,
Chonnam National University, Gwangju, Korea
Tel.: 82-62-530-1803
seokju@image.chonnam.ac.kr, arif@image.chonnam.ac.kr,
uaini@image.chonnam.ac.kr, leecw@chonnam.ac.kr

Abstract. In this paper, we describe an algorithm which can naturally communicate with human and robot for Human-Robot Interaction by utilizing vision. We propose a state transition model using attentive features for gesture recognition. This method defines the recognition procedure as five different states; NULL, OBJECT, POSE, Local Gesture and Global Gesture. We first infer the situation of the system by estimating the transition of the state model and then apply different recognition algorithms according to the system state for robust recognition. And we propose Active Plane Model (APM) that can represent 3D and 2D information of gesture simultaneously. This method is constructing a gesture space by analyzing the statistical information of training images with PCA and the symbolized images are recognized with HMM as one of model gestures. Therefore, proposed algorithm can be used for real world application efficiently such as controlling intelligent home appliance and humanoid robot.

Keywords: Gesture Recognition, Context Awareness, PCA, HMM.

1 Introduction

Recently, Human gesture analysis has received more attentions in computer vision field with applications in areas such as human friendly interfaces, intelligent surveillance, virtual reality, and so on. Especially, natural communication method between human and computer is becoming a key issue as intelligent interface techniques can be applied to home appliances. Human acquire the information over 80% from their eyes. And, we understand the human behavior using the temporal sequence of movement of human body automatically, and then to estimate some meanings of the temporal movement from previously trained and arranged motion data. Also, human uses non-linguistic method for their communication and it is better to make more natural communication with each other than using only linguistic method. However, it is very difficult to analyze temporal changes by computer, namely historical meaning of bodily motion

---

* Corresponding author.

Z. Pan et al. (Eds.): ICAT 2006, LNCS 4282, pp. 1–10, 2006.

automatically because a human body is a three-dimensional object with very complicated structure and flexibility. In early works, many researchers tried to measure the configuration of the human body with sensors attached to the joints of limbs and to recognize gesture by analyzing the variation of joint angles [3][4]. But, this requires the user to put on irritating devices, and it usually needs long cables connection from the devices to computers. So, it hinders the easy usage and embarrasses the user with unnatural dullness. Also, other algorithms use various markers attaching to the joints of a moving articulated body. With this reason, commercial products adopting the algorithm become very expensive and real-time processing can not be allowed.

To overcome these problems, video-based recognition techniques are proposed and it uses a set of video cameras and computer vision techniques to interpret gestures. One of the famous algorithms using global motion feature information is Motion History Image (MHI) method. In this method, the accumulation of object silhouettes is used to analyze the human motion [5]. Many other algorithms which use feature points or silhouette of body are proposed [6], but the methods have the generalization problems for recognition results. These systems have no problems in the case of recognizing the pre-trained gestures, but if the gestures are not defined previously, systems can not recognize or misunderstand the gestures. Moreover, because the human gestures can not be trained for all cases, it is easy to develop the restricted and system dependent algorithms.

To address these problems, we propose the gesture recognition algorithm using attentive features; probability of state, global and local motion and positional information. In this algorithm, the system classifies the situation of behaviors before recognizing the individual meaning of gestures. So, proposed algorithm can analyze the human gestures more precisely and it has a feature that can expand the application of recognition system. And we describe the algorithm which can automatically recognize human gesture without such constraints by utilizing three-dimensional features extracted from stereo images.

The paper structured as follows: Section 2 and 3 present a probabilistic state transition model and gesture interface system using the state transition model. And in Section 4.1, we explain Active Plane Model(APM) that the bodily region and features can be extracted from the stereo images. And in section 4.2, explain how the gesture model space is constructed by analyzing the statistical information of training images with the Principal Component Analysis (PCA) method. And then, section 4.3 presents how the sequential poses are classified into model gesture with Hidden Markov Model (HMM) algorithm. Finally, the paper is closed with mentioning the conclusion and further works in Section 5.

2   Overview

Before taking up the main subject, we need to define the terminology "context" clearly. According to the Cambridge dictionary, "context" is defined as the situation within which something exists or happens, and it also means that variation of circumstance or locational information of robot in engineering fields. In this paper, we define the "context" as intention of behaviors between human

Table 1. Definition of states

State	Definition
NULL	No object in view.
OBJECT	Something is moving, but it is not human.
POSE	Behavior is detected, and he/she is posturing.
Global Gesture	Behavior is detected, and he/she has a global motion.
Local Gesture	Behavior is detected, and he/she has a local motion.

and computer. This system uses only cameras for communication, and does not contain the situation using sound or any other sensors.

In this paper, we define the human gestures as five different states based on movement of subject. And then, we can represent the human gestures by continuous sequence of states, also we can understand intention of actor using the state information. And we present definition of five different states in Table 1.

In the first step, the system is trained with the image sequences. Through the training process, we can get the probability of state transition and the weights of feature vectors. And then, the system decides the state transition by using this information. Finally, we can apply the reasonable recognition algorithm to the system according to the context information.

3   Probabilistic State Transition Model

3.1   Feature Extraction and Training

In this paper, we use image features to decide a transition of state, and these image features are as follows:

f_1 : Motion information in image
f_2 : Locational information of subject
f_3 : Distance from subject
f_4 : Motion information of subject
f_5 : 3D trajectories of head and hands

The system can extract and track the subject's head and hands regions using skin tone every frame from stereo image. And then, we calculate three-dimensional depth information using this information and we can get the image features. The training image sequences include the state information, and system can be established the probabilistic model using these sequences. Through the training process, we can get the probabilities of each image features and its weights. Let the 5 image features is $f_i (i = 1,2,3,4,5)$, feature vector set F and its probabilities $P(F)$ can be denoted as equation (1).

$$F = \{f_1, f_2, f_3, f_4, f_5\} \tag{1}$$

$$P(F) = \prod_i P(f_i) \tag{2}$$

Also, if the set of states is $S_k(k = 1, 2, 3, 4, 5)$ conditional probabilities of feature vector set on each state are as follows:

$P(F|S_1)$: Prob. of set F on the NULL
$P(F|S_2)$: Prob. of set F on the Object
$P(F|S_3)$: Prob. of set F on the Pose
$P(F|S_4)$: Prob. of set F on the Global Motion
$P(F|S_5)$: Prob. of set F on the Local Motion

3.2   State Transition

We adopt Bayes' Theorem to decide transition between each state. First, the probabilities of set on the each state (a prior probability) are calculated from training process. And then, we can estimate the probabilities of transition to the each state (a posterior probability). Finally, the system is updated to the state information which has the maximum probabilities. The probabilities of transition with feature vector set F are denoted as equation (3). Also, the system adjusts the weights of features $w_i(i = 1, 2, 3, 4, 5)$ using the weight information as shown in equation (4).

$$P(S_k|F) = \frac{P(S_k)P(F|S_k)}{\sum_i P(S_i)P(F|S_i)} \qquad (3)$$

$$P(F') = \prod_i w_i P(f_i) \qquad (4)$$

If the feature vector set is extracted on the state S_j^t at time t, the probabilities of transition to each state is calculated using adjusted feature vector set F' and prior probabilities. And then, the system is updated to the state S_k^{t+1} which has the maximum probabilities as shown in equation (5).

$$k = \arg\max_j P(S_j^{t+1}|F') \qquad (5)$$

4   Gesture Recognition

The proposed recognition algorithm is marked by recognizing the gestures according to the situational information. It is easy to develop the restricted and system dependent algorithms, because all of human gestures can not be classified using only a small number of features. In this section, we propose the recognition system that can reduce limitations using context awareness.

4.1   Feature Extraction: Active Plane Model

In general, the scene includes a lot of objects in the background that may disturb gesture recognition. This background must eliminate because it is not need to processing information of gesture.

In this paper, we propose Active Plane Model(APM) that represent simultaneously gesture feature information and three dimensional depth information.

We use a simple foreground extraction method using depth information. First, detect a face region of the frontal person using skin tone, and then estimate the distance from the robot camera to the face by calculating stereo geometry. Finally, we can obtain the closer region of input images as the foreground. It is shown in Equation (6).

$$F(x,y) = \begin{pmatrix} 0 : D(x,y) > D_f + c \\ F(x,y) : D(x,y) \leq D_f + c \end{pmatrix} \tag{6}$$

In the equation, $F(x,y)$ is gray-level value of input image at position (x, y) of the corresponding disparity image, $D(x,y)$ is the distance from robot camera for each pixel, D_f is distance from camera to the face, and c is a constant value considering thickness of the body.

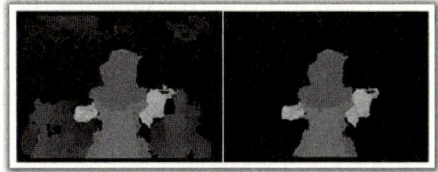

Fig. 1. Foreground extraction using depth information(Disparity Image)

The APM is characterized by that it can represent three dimensional depth information and two dimensional shape information at the same time. And you can see standardization model of APM in Fig. 2 and deformed APM examples in Fig. 3.

Fig. 2. Standardization of APM (Red rectangle of left side is the face region)

APM consist of several nodes connected to each other in grid shape and it is deformed by the shape and depth information. For the first step to deform the APM, we find the contour of foreground region. The contour is searched from the minimal rectangular boundary surrounding foreground region into center of rectangle.

If we find the contour, outer nodes of APM are fixed, then, inner nodes are moved to new location in order to keep the same distance between neighbor nodes. That means the inner nodes are rearrange by calculating the average

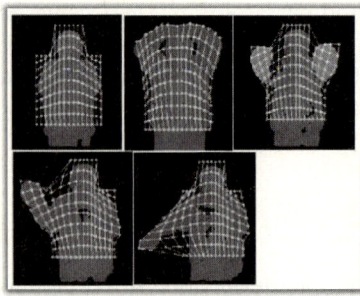

Fig. 3. Deformed APM examples(Normal, I Love You, Stop, Bye Bye, Point)

position between the most outer nodes as shown in equation (7). In equation (8), T expresses a suitable threshold distance. By adopting the criterion of equation (3), we can stop the deformation quickly.

$$N_i^{t+1} = \text{average position of neighbor nodes of } N_i^t \qquad (7)$$

$$N_i^{t+1} - N_i^t \leq T, \ (t \geq 0) \qquad (8)$$

Therefore, multi dimensional features are extracted for every frame by using the equation (9),

$$\begin{aligned} F_t &= \{N_1, N_2, ..., N_n\} \\ N_i &= \{x_i, y_i, z_i\} \\ (0 &\leq t \leq T, \ 1 \leq i \leq nT, \ n \geq 4) \end{aligned} \qquad (9)$$

Where F_t is a feature vector set at time t, N_i is i-th nodal position of APM, and n is the total number of APM nodes.

4.2   Pose Symbolization Using PCA

A common method for linear dimension reduction is Principal Components Analysis (PCA). The method is performed by applying eigenvalue decomposition on the covariance matrix of feature data. A small subset of resulting eigenvectors, covering a desired amount of the data variance from a new linear subspace for representing the data set. Extracted feature vector make projection of model gesture sequence into the gesture space in Fig. 4.

PCA is clearly capable of reducing the dimensionality of data sets with structure, but not necessarily suitable for finding spatio-temporal structure for several reasons. The method assumes that the underlying structure of the data is linear. Unless the underlying structure is linear, the resulting subspace will overestimate the reduced dimensionality and yield wrong principal components and reduced data that do not allow for the discovery of structure. The features extracted from an image sequence are multi dimensional and we can not solve the multi dimension problem easily. By subtracting the average vector c of the all features, as in equation (10), the new feature matrix X is obtained. The covariance matrix Q of gesture features can be obtained from equation (8). Then the PCA

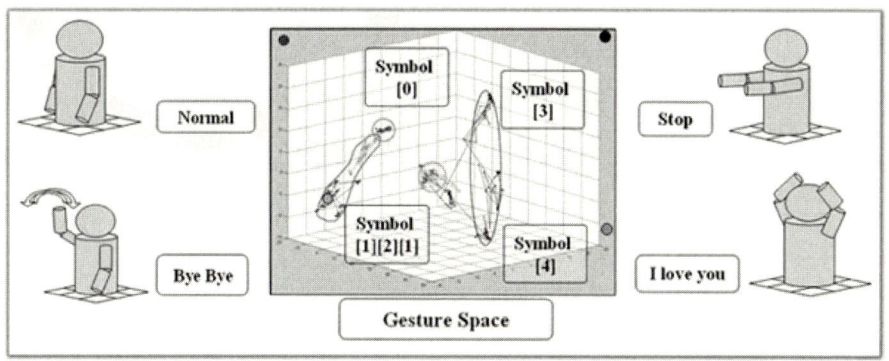

Fig. 4. Projection of model gesture sequence into the gesture space

is straight-forward requiring only the calculation of the eigenvectors satisfying equation (12).

$$c = (1/N) \sum_{i=1}^{N} x_i \tag{10}$$

$$X \cong [x_1 - c, x_2 - c, \cdots, x_N - c]^T \tag{11}$$

$$Q \cong XX^T \tag{12}$$

$$\lambda_i e_i = Q e_i \tag{13}$$

And as input feature, set x is subtracted from an average vector c and projected into the eigenspace as in equation (14).

$$p_i - [e_1, e_2, \cdots, e_k]^T (x_i \quad c) \tag{14}$$

Using the Principal Component Analysis, a small number of component vectors are chosen which can represent the whole space, and we call it dimension reduction.

4.3   Symbolic Gesture Recognition Using HMM

HMM is a stochastic process and also a probabilistic network with hidden and observable states. A time domain process demonstrates a Markov property if the conditional probability density of the current event, even though all present and past events are given, depends only on the j-th most recent events. If the current event depends solely on the most recent past event, then the process is a first order Markov process. The initial topology for an HMM can be determined by estimating how many different states are involved in specifying a sign. Fine tuning for this topology can be performed empirically. HMM λ is represented by the several parameters. The parameter a_{ij} indicates state transition probability of HMM changing from state i to state j. The parameter $b_{ij}(y)$ indicates that probability of that the output symbol y will be observable in the transition of state j from state i. And another parameter π_i presents the probability of the initial state. Learning of HMM is equal to estimating the parameters $\{\pi, A, B\}$ of a sequential symbolic data.

$$\xi_t(i,j) = \frac{P(s_t = i, s_{t+1} = j, Y|\lambda)}{P(Y|\lambda)} = \frac{\alpha_t(i)a_{ij}b_{ij}(y_{t+1})\beta_{t+2}(j)}{\sum\limits_{i=1}^{N}\sum\limits_{j=1}^{N}\alpha_t(i)a_{ij}b_{ij}(y_{t+1})\beta_{t+2}(j)} \tag{15}$$

$$\gamma_t(i) = \sum_{j=1}^{N}\xi_t(i,j) \tag{16}$$

In equation (15), $\xi_t(i,j)$ is the probability of being in state S_i at time t and in state S_j at time $t+1$, and $\gamma_t(i)$ is the probability of being state S_i at time t. Using equation (15) and (16) the gesture model can be estimated.

$$\overline{\pi_i} = \gamma_1(i) \tag{17}$$

$$\overline{a_{ij}} = \frac{\sum\limits_{t=1}^{T-1}\xi_t(i,j)}{\sum\limits_{t=1}^{T-1}\gamma_t(i)} \tag{18}$$

$$\overline{b_{ij}(k)} = \frac{\sum\limits_{t=1, s.t.y_t=k}^{T}\gamma_t(j)}{\sum\limits_{t=1}^{T}\gamma_t(j)} \tag{19}$$

Given the observation sequence [Y], the HMM model λ can be calculated using the forward variable $\alpha_t(i)$ and backward variable $\beta_t(i)$ with the following equating (20). This means that a symbol chain, namely an input image is recognized as a model which has the maximum value of equation (20).

$$P(Y|\lambda_i) = \sum_i\sum_j\alpha_t(i)a_{ij}b_j(y_{t+1})\beta_{t+1}(j) \tag{20}$$

5   Experimental Result

For the training and evaluation of the algorithm, we construct an image database about different gestures. The resolution of the image is 320 240 in pixels and capturing speed is about 10 frames per a second. We recorded six kinds of gesture image for ten different persons.

We made an experiment for recognizing gestures with test images. In the experiment an APM of 1510 in resolution was utilized, so that 450-dimensional feature vector was extracted for every frame. We used only five eigenvectors,

Table 2. Recognition rate for the test image

Gesture	Correct(%)	InCorrect(%)
Normal	98	Come here(2)
I love you	95	Normal (5)
Good bye	85	Normal (10), Come here (5)
Stop	80	Come here (20)
Come here	85	Normal (15)
Point	100	-
Average	90.5	-

and this low-dimensional vector can represent the whole gesture space well. We used six different HMMs for the six different gestures. The HMM parameters were estimated with the Forward-backward algorithm under assuming that each HMM had 6 states. "Good bye" and "Stop" gestures have recognition rates that are lower than the average rate respectively. We suppose that the gesture contain little motion or 3D information comparing to other gestures.

6   Conclusion

In this paper, we describe the gesture interface method using context awareness. We define five different states of behavior. In the training process, system can be established the probabilistic model from the pre-defined image sequences. And we can recognize the context of gestures and catch the intention of user by analyzing the state transition model. Also, we can apply the different recognition algorithms to the system according to the context information. And one novel gesture recognition method using 2D shape and 3D depth information simultaneously is proposed. The algorithm works very well since it is robust to shape and depth variation. There are many gesture recognition algorithms using visual information. However, most algorithms work under many restricted conditions. To eliminate such constraints, we have proposed Active Plane Model (APM) to recognize human gesture. This model comes from structured model approach instead of geometric feature model approach using edge or corners. Therefore, we can make a general model for recognition of human gesture in real world.

But, there are some problems in the case of being multiple persons in image because the system can not track user's head and hands regions. And motion can be occurred regardless of user's intention. However, efficient tracking algorithm can solve these problems, and selection algorithm of recognition target can improve the system. If these problems are solved, proposed algorithm can be used for controlling intelligent home appliances or humanoid robot more effectively.

Acknowledgment

This research has been supported by research funding of "Development of humanoid technology based on network, KIST, Korea, and Culture Technology Research Institute, Chonnam National University, Korea.

References

[1] Xia Liu, Kikuo Fujimura, "Hand gesture Recognition using depth data", AFGR, 2004. Proceeding 6th IEEE International Conference on, May 2004
[2] F. J. Huang and T. Chen, "Tracking of Multiple Faces for Human-Computer Interfaces and Virtual Environments", IEEE Intl. Conf. on Multimedia and Expo., July 2000
[3] Baihua Li; Holstein, H. "Articulated point pattern matching in optical motion capture systems", QinggangMeng; Control, Automation, Robotics and Vision, 2002. ICARCV 2002. 7th International Conference on , Volume: 1 , 2-5 Dec. 2002
[4] Yu Su; Allen, C.R.; Geng, D.; Burn, D.; Brechany,U.; Bell, G.D.; Rowland, R., "3-D motion system (datagloves):application for Parkinson's disease",Instrumentation and Measurement, IEEE Transactionson , Volume: 52 , Issue: 3 , June 2003
[5] James Davis, "Recognizing Movement using Motion Histograms", MIT Media Lab. Technical Report No. 487,March 1999
[6] Ross Cutler, Matthew Turk, "View-based Interpretation of Real-time Optical Flow for Gesture Recognition", Third IEEE International Conf. on Automatic Face and Gesture Recognition, 1998
[7] Ho-Sub Yoon; Byung-Woo Min; Jung Soh; Young-Iae Bae; Hyun Seung Yang, "Human computer interface for gesture-based editing system", Image Analysis and Processing, pp. 969 - 974, 1999

Evolving Creatures in Virtual Ecosystems

Nicolas Lassabe, Herve Luga, and Yves Duthen

Laboratoire IRIT-UT1, Université des Sciences Sociales (UT1) - Manufacture
de Tabacs - 21, Allée de Brienne - 31000 Toulouse, France

Abstract. In this article, we introduce the first steps of our 3D ecosystem project. We present the latest research on morphology, behavior and virtual environments of evolving creatures and we try to investigate future possibilities for improving more complex lifeforms in dynamic environment. We propose our model of an ecosystem which uses a new type of controller for evolving creatures based on classifiers. Our model comprises three different lifeforms: insects, plants and creatures based on a genetic coding and evolving by evolutionary methods. In the future, we intend to add more different lifeforms and more interactions. To focus on this aspect, we have chosen Breve an existing physic engine centered on artificial life simulation. In this article, we show the results of evolving creatures being able to crawl, to walk and to climb stairs.

1 Introduction

In this article, we will present the interests of combining different creatures in a complex environment. During the last years, many articles have been released about evolving creatures [4,10,13,16,19,20,24,25,26,27]. They often focus on the morphology and behavior of creatures without taking into account the complexity of the environment. In these cases creatures evolve without interaction between them, to optimize a preset fitness. Conversely, some simulations propose to model more complex environments with simpler creatures [32,33]. It is just recently that works presenting evolving creatures in ecosystem have been published [6]. In this article, we propose an architecture for a virtual ecosystem allowing the conjoint evolution of different kinds of creatures with natural selection. We will present works in progress and a new type of controller based on the classifiers. We will try to define what kind of interactions between the creatures allow the emergence of interesting adaptation strategies. To allow for the emergence of prey and predator like behaviors, species are differentiated by characteristics such as color, which control attraction and repulsion mechanisms within the ecosystem. Defensive mechanisms such as the ability for species to become poisonous to other species and corellation between color and poisonous nature have also been simulated to establish food chains. Such complex ecosystems will also enable us to study extinction and specification processes to which the species are subject.

2 Why Ecosystem?

The realization of an ecosystem can allow the generation of lifeforms able to adapt to a dynamic environment, the specification of species and the emergence

Z. Pan et al. (Eds.): ICAT 2006, LNCS 4282, pp. 11–20, 2006.

of life cycles. The interests of simulating such virtual ecosystems are numerous. In the field of biology, it could lead to a better understanding of the evolution and extinctions of species as well as of some mechanisms of life [1]. The evolution of morphology and behavior in relation to a specific environment has an interest in the design of robots and of their controllers [12,19,11]. A complex environment should generate adapted survival strategies during an evolution.

Interesting questions are whether different evolution scenarios can emerge from an identical initial environment and whether the environment complexity is a relevant criteria in the emergence of different survival strategies [2,22,23]. If that were the case, how does one evaluate complexity? What are the elements necessary for the emergence of complex life forms and behaviors? Is the use of a complex physics one of these elements or can biological complexity be supported by simpler physical models ? What is the importance of the interactions ? These are open questions which may be answered through experimentation with artificial ecosystems.

3   Related Work

There are many existing solutions for the representation of morphologies and controllers. Karl Sim's creatures certainly remain the most evolved [25,26]. He has realized evolutions bound by very few constraints and obtained a large diversity of creatures giving birth to crawling and swimming behaviors. Thereafter many works tried to reproduce these results, like the L-System creatures of Hornby [13] and Lipson's Golem project [19] with different approaches for the representation of morphologies and controllers. Their goals being to optimize 3D creatures in relation to a preset fitness inside a physics engine. Another approach to obtain more complex behavior is to optimize a set of 2D creatures in a virtual pool by means of natural selection [32]. Each creature has a quantity of energy and tries to survive looking for food in the environment. The advantage of this approach is that is possible to have many creatures. Komosinski tries to do the same thing in a 3D environment [16]. Recently, the project EvolGL [6] proposes to simulate a virtual world with worms. The evolving worms belong to herbivorous, carnivorous and omnivorous species and develop different strategies of survival. These works show that it is possible to distinguish two ways to optimize complex behavior evolving creatures: with a preset fitness or by means of natural selection. The works with a preset fitness continue to be improved with recents results like evolving flying creature [24] and evolving creatures for combat [20]. The works based on natural selection are becoming achievable and will certainly give more adaptive solutions and perspectives.

4   Proposition

4.1   Introduction

In this article, we propose a model of an ecosystem to evolve virtual lifeforms. The goal of our model is to provide more adapted and more complex strategies of

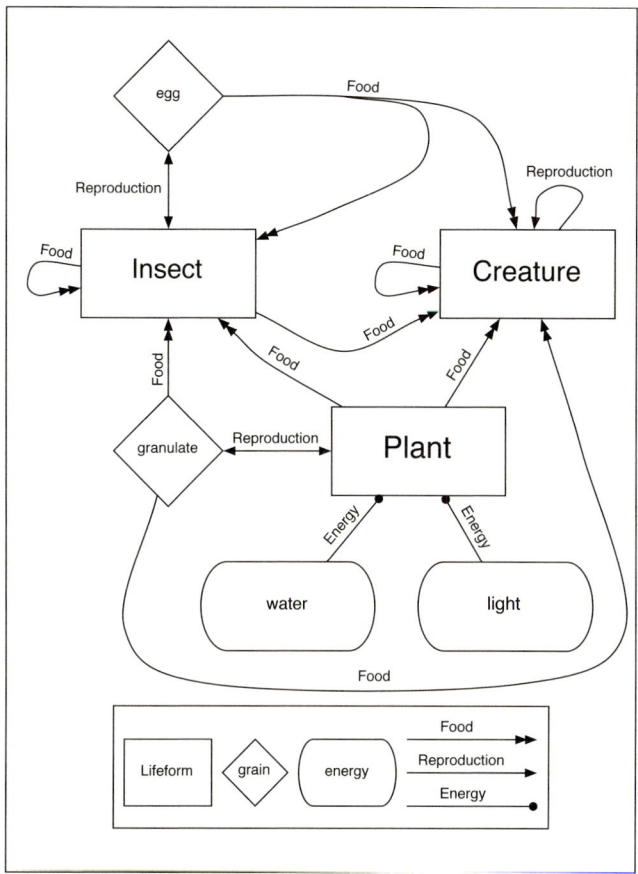

Fig. 1. Food chains and a part of the interactions between the elements of the environment

survival with a high interactivity between the different lifeforms. We do not want to focus on a specific representation of morphology or controller. The ecosystem must be capable of easily supporting different kind of lifeforms and manage their interactions. We would also like to allow the development of prey and predator strategies to obtain a complete food chain (Fig. 1). In this model, every lifeform has a quantity of energy provided by light or by food consumption. A creature dies when it does not have any energy left or when it is eaten by an another creature.

4.2   The Diet

The diet of a creature is coded by one its genes. Links in the food chain (Fig. 1) determine what a creature is allowed to eat : eggs, insects, plants, granulates, and another creatures like itself. The creature can eat five different kinds of foods. The links can be encoded in one of the creature's genes composed of five bits each representing one of the mentioned links. If a bit is set to 1, the creature is allowed to eat the corresponding food. For example the gene 01010, allows a creature to eat only insects and granulates. A creature is not allowed to eat another bigger than itself.

This interaction is not sufficient to enable the development of complex behaviors. Therefore we defined for each creature an attractive color define by another gene, a repulsive color and of course its own color. The combination of these four genes will allow the development of more complex strategies. A predator's color of attraction will evolve toward the color of other creatures which it can eat. One might think that the creatures will change colors very quickly from one generation to another leading to an unstable balance. However this does not happen because the successive crossings within a species guaranty a certain uniformity of the individuals within the species and an inertia making species variations slow and continuous. Another criteria differentiating species is their size. The reproduction process takes more time for the big creature than for the small ones. The strategy for a small species could be to develop a large population because they are more vulnerable.

4.3   The Concept of Poison

We also propose to introduce the concept of poison in our ecosystem. It could be a useful strategy of defense for the plants and the little creatures. The poison is represented by a gene of eight bits. The ability for creatures to eat another without being poisoned is based on whether its same eight bits are complementary. For example if the poison gene of a species is 0101110101, the complementary gene allowing for unharmful consumption will be 1010001010. We use the # character coding for both 0 and 1. The gene ########## protects again all the poisons but on the other hand, the creature's poison is inoffensive. When a creature eat another one, it gains energy due to food consumption but loses energy due to poisoning. To know the quantity of energy lost due to poisoning, we calculate what percentage of bits do not have the good complementary value. If none do, the eating creature dies. If it is half complementary, the creature loses fifty percent of its energy.

4.4   The Energy

The energy is necessary for the survival of all lifeforms. The creatures use it for their movements. If their movements are not effective, the creatures will not find food easily. The quantity of energy spent for movement depends on the size of the creature. For the plants, the energy is important to produce more seeds and have better chances of reproduction. The energy allows the plant to grow faster. A plant's energy collection is made by its leaves which collect the light transforming it in energy. If a plant grows faster, it needs more water. One of the strategies for the plants will be to find a good compromise between the number of leafs, the number of seeds produced and the quantity of water necessary for its survival.

4.5 Conclusion

With the concept of poison and attractive colors, we have the basis for a very complex environment. It could be interesting to study the evolution of the number of the species, their extinction and the evolution of their population sizes. If the process becomes stable, we will obtain ecosystem. An interesting observation could be to see if the same strategies appear from different simulations with different initializations. We can ask ourselves if slightly different initializations lead to different evolution scenarios. If the simulations are completely different after many generations with the same random initialization for the crossovers and the mutations, we can say that this environment is chaos determinist because the laws governing it are determinist.

It could be also interesting to measure the complexity of each creature and measure the degree of complexity necessary to generate complex auto-organization. If we do not obtain any auto-organization, we must find what are the missing criteria that prevent it to appear.

5 Environment and Architecture

5.1 Breve

The implementation of a physics engine is a difficult task requiring a full year of work. Our choice was therefore to use Breve [15], an engine based on ODE (Open Dynamic Engine), that is well suited for artificial life simulation. Our program is written in C++ and inserted in Breve in the manner of plugins. This way our program is not dependent of Breve and can be used like a library with another physics engine. Moreover Breve already implements a lot of useful functionalities like the quantity of light perceived by an object.

5.2 Morphology

There are three different lifeforms with a different representation for each (Fig. 1). The insect have a simple morphology, their characteristics which are subject to evolution are their color and their ability to fly or not. The plants use an L-system [18] representation (Fig. 2). Every plant has a number of leaves and seeds defined by its genotype and its environment. The creatures use a different morphology based on graphs like Karl Sims' creatures [25,26]. The morphology is not constant, we want to keep the ability of generating various lifeform inside the ecosystem. The morphology of our creatures (Fig. 3) is satisfactory for the moment, but we plan to broaden the types of joints between blocks and types of blocks defining the creatures' morphologies.

5.3 Controller

There are different controllers for each kind of lifeform. The insects have a preset behavior. They are attracted by some colors defined in their genes and flee some others. This way we hope to allow for the development of predator and prey

Fig. 2. Evolving trees represented by l-lsystem

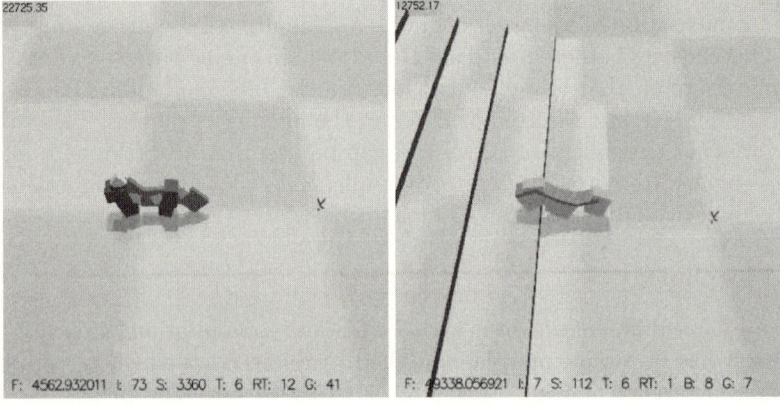

Fig. 3. Evolving creatures walking and climbing a stair

behaviors. For the moment, the plants and the trees do not have any behavior but we want to allow them to orient their leafs in further developments. For the creature, the controller use a classifier system. The controller needs to activate the articulations correctly (junction between the blocs). The signal to do this need to be continuous and must vary in time according to incoming sensors reception of information. This signal is generally a sine wave or a composition of periodical functions. It is imaginable to compose a signal from some preset patterns (Fig. 3). We have tried to do this in our work. The main problem is to conserve a continuity of the signal, while selecting the next adapted pattern. We start by defining a data base of random patterns. We have used one thousand generated patterns. The conditions for two appended patterns to compose a signal are the following:

- The patterns need to be defined between [-1,1] and their minimum and maximum too.
- If P_1 and P_2 are two patterns and if P_2 is append to P_1 it is necessary that:

$$\big(P_1(1) - P_2(-1)\big) < \varepsilon$$

  Here $\varepsilon = 0.01$
- The classifiers control the selection of patterns. The entries of the classifiers which define the information incoming from the environment are the sensors of the creature. According to the sensors' state, a set of rules pointing to patterns in the data base is triggered. The composed signal is used by the effectors controlling the muscles of the creature. If the resulting action is satisfactory, the rules used to generate that action are rewarded, else they are penalized. The advantages of this method lie in the fact that it is easy to enrich the used data base and obtain signals more complex than those obtained by simple primitive signal composition.

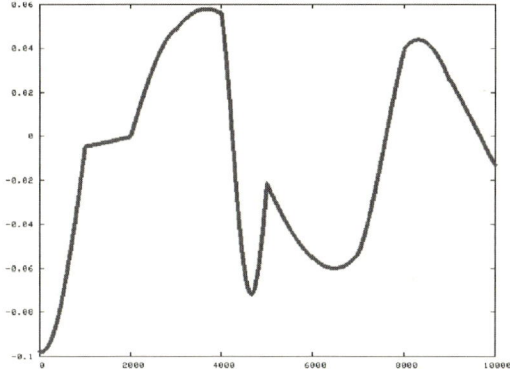

Fig. 4. Signal for a controller

6   Implementation

For the moment, the creatures and a good part of plants are implemented. An evolution of the creatures with a preset fitness based on the traversed distance has given some good results. For the final simulation, we will use Breve network implementation to deport all the calculations on different machines. The complete simulation will require a lot of computation and won't be computed on a single machine. Every lifeform is implemented in C++ in different plugins and these plugins are interfaced with Breve. We try to maintain a great facility in adding different lifeforms in order to get the broadest, most various and interesting results possible. We would like also to keep the possibility to use the plugings with another engine.

7   Results

In the experiments, we use a population of 100 individuals (creature) and the tournament selection is 3. The fitness maximizes the walked distance by a creature. After 100 generation and around 3h of computed time, the best creature is been able to walk, crawl or climb stairs [1].

8   Perspectives

The next steps for our project will be to implement and improve all the interactions between the different life forms, and also to confront the classifiers with more complex situations to see their adaptation capacity. Introducing an evolving language between the creatures could be interesting and allow a significant increase in the number of evolving strategies. It could be interesting to test the same ecosystem with a simple 2D representation and see what are the difference of results obtained. Concerning the controllers used, we plan to use the modular networks already tested in our chess engine to evaluate chess positions [3].

9   Conclusion

It is becoming possible to evolve a colony of evolving virtual creatures in a complex ecosystem with physics. The implementation of these ecosystems becomes essential to encourage the development of some adaptation strategies and to obtain more complex behaviors which were not possible in simple worlds. It will also allow to regroup evolving simulations, extinction simulations and others inside one application and therefore allow to observe the relations between them. We also show that it is possible to use classifiers as controllers and that this may in certain cases be a good alternative to the use of neural networks.

References

1. Abramson, G. (1997). Ecological model of extinctions Phys. Rev. E. 55, p 785.
2. Adami, C., Ofria, C., Collier, T. C. (2000). Evolution of Biological Complexity Proc. Nat. Acad. Sci (USA) 97.
3. Autones, M., Beck, A., Camacho, P., Lassabe, N., Luga, H., Scharffe, F. (2004). Evaluation of Chess Position by Modular Neural Network Generated by Genetic Algorithm. EuroGP 2004: 1-10.
4. Bongard, J. and Paul, C. (2000). Investigating Morphological Symmetry and Locomotive Efficiency using Virtual Embodied Evolution, From Animals to Animats: The Sixth International Conference on the Simulation of Adaptive Behaviour.
5. Bongard, J. and Pfeifer, R. (2001). Evolving Complete Agents using Artificial Ontogeny.

---

[1] A video of a part of the best creatures is on the Nicolas Lassabe's home page: http://www.irit.fr/~Nicolas.Lassabe/videos/icat2006.mov

6. Carbajal, S. G., Moran, M. B. and Martinez, F. G. (2004). EvolGL: Life in a Pond. Proc. of Artificial Life XI, ed. by Pollack, J., Bedau, M., Husbands, P., Ikegami, T. and Watson, R. A., p75-80.
7. Cliff, D. and Miller, G. F. (1996). Co-Evolution Of Pursuit And Evasion II Simulation Methods And Results, From animals to animats 4.
8. Conradie, A. and Miikkulainen, R. and Aldrich, C. (2002). Adaptive Control utilising Neural Swarming In Proceedings of the Genetic and Evolutionary Computation Conference.
9. Dellaert, F. and Beer, R. D., (1996). A Developmental Model for the Evolution of Complete Autonomous Agents. A developmental model for the evolution of complete autonomous agents. In [14], pages 393–401.
10. Eggenberger, P. (1997) Evolving morphologies of simulated 3d organisms based on differential gene expression, Evolving morphologies of simulated 3d organisms based on differential gene expression. In [10], page in press
11. Floreano, D. and Nolfi, S. (1999). Learning and Evolution. Autonomous Robots, 7(1), 89-113.
12. Floreano, D. and Mondada, F. (1994). Automatic Creation of an Autonomous Agent : Genetic Evolution of a Neural Network Driven Robot, From Animals to Animats 3. Proceedings of the Third International Conference on Simulation of Adaptive Behavior.
13. Hornby, G.S. and Jordan B. Pollack (2001) Evolving L-Systems To Generate Virtual Creatures
14. Hornby, G. S. and Pollack, J. B. (2002). Creating High-Level Components with a Generative Representation for Body-Brain Evolution. Artificial Life, 8:3.
15. Klein, J. (2002). Breve: a 3D simulation environment for the simulation of decentralized systems and artificial life. Proceedings of Artificial Life VIII, the 8th International Conference on the Simulation and Synthesis of Living Systems. The MIT Press.
16. Komosinski, M., (2000). The world of Framsticks: simulation, evolution, interaction, In: Proceedings of 2nd International Conference on Virtual Worlds, 214-224.
17. Koza, J.R. (1992). Genetic Programming. MIT Press.
18. Lindenmayer, A. (1968). Mathematical models for celluar interaction and development. Parts I and II Journal of theoritical biology. 18 280–315
19. Lipson, H. and Pollack J. B., (2000). Automatic Design and Manufacture of Artificial Lifeforms. Nature 406, pp. 974-978.
20. O'Kellym, M. J. T. and Hsiao, K. (2004). Evolving Simulated Mutually Perceptive Creatures for Combat. Proc. of Artificial Life XI, ed. by Pollack, J., Bedau, M., Husbands, P., Ikegami, T. and Watson, R. A., p111-118.
21. Funes, P. and Pollack, J. (1997). Computer Evolution of Buildable Object. Fourth European Conf. on Artificial Life, 358–367.
22. Seth, A.K. and Edelman, G.M. (2004). Environment and behavior influence the complexity of evolved neural networks. Adaptive Behavior, 12(1):5-21.
23. Seth, A. K. (1998). The Evolution of Complexity and the Value of Variability. Proc. of Artificial Life VI, ed. by Adami, C., Belew, R., Kitano, H., and Taylor, C. pp 209-218.
24. Shim, Y. S., Kim, S. J., and Kim, C. H., (2004). Evolving Flying Creatures with Path Following Behaviour. ALIFE IX: In Proceedings of 9th International Conference on the Simulation and Synthesis of Living Systems. pp.125-132.
25. Sims, K., (1994a). Evolving 3D morphology and behavior by competition. Proc. of Artificial Life IV, ed. by R. Brooks and P. Maes, pp. 28-39.

26. Sims, K. (1994b). Evolving Virtual Creatures. Proc. SIGGRAPH '94, pp. 15-22.
27. Taylor, T. and Massey, C. (2001). Recent Developments in the Evolution of Morphologies and Controllers for Physically Simulated Creatures,
28. Teo, J. and Abbass, H.A. (2002). Trading-Off Mind Complexity and Locomotion in a Physically Simulated Quadruped, Proceedings of the 4th Asia-Pacific Conference on Simulated Evolution And Learning, vol 2,776-780.
29. Terzopoulos, D., Tu, X. and Grzeszczuk, R. (1994). Artificial fishes: Autonomous locomotion, perception, behavior, and learning in a simulated physical world. Artificial Life, vol 1, 327-351.
30. Terzopoulos, D. and Grzeszczuk, R. (1995), Automated Learning of Muscle-Actuated Locomotion Through Control Abstraction, Computer Graphics, vol 29,63–70.
31. Ventrella, J. (1994). Explorations in the Emergence of Morphology and Locomotion Behavior in Animated Characters. Proceedings of the 4th International Workshop on the Synthesis and Simulation of Living Systems $Artificial Life IV$, pp. 436-441, MIT Press.
32. Ventrella, J. (1998a). Designing Emergence in Animated Artificial Life Worlds. Proceedings of the 1st International Conference on Virtual Worlds (VW-98), LNAI, Vol. 1434, pp. 143-155.
33. Ventrella, J. (1998b). Attractiveness vs. Efficiency: How Mate Preference Affects Locomotion in the Evolution of Artificial Swimming Organisms Proceedings of the 6th International Conference on Artificial Life (ALIFE-98), pp. 178-188, MIT Press.
34. Zaera, N., Cliff, D. and Bruten, J., (1996). Evolving collective behaviours in synthetic fish. From Animals to Animats 4: Proceedings of the Fourth International Conference on Simulation of Adaptive Behavior, p. 635-644.

The Application of Affective Virtual Human in Intelligent Web Tutoring System

Huiling Peng

Department of Information & Technology, Central China Normal University
Wuhan, 430079, P.R. China
phlhuangrong@gmail.com

Abstract. Aiming at the defects of the difficult emotional interaction of traditional Intelligent Web Tutoring System, based on the theory of artificial emotion of virtual human, an intelligent affective Web Tutoring System was presented in the paper. Second, the key module of the system was designed and the modeling on the Affective Virtual Human was carried out. Finally, the simulation command on it was made. The result showed this model coinciding with the emotion of human behaviors.

Keywords: Artificial Emotion, Virtual Human, Affective Computing, Intelligent Web Tutoring System.

1 Introduction

Traditional Intelligent Web Tutoring System can realize the intellectualized and personalized teaching on the cognitive level. Although it has this strongpoint, this system cannot apperceive students' emotion so as to fail to realize emotionally personalized education and timely communication. In fact, a real personalized teaching system should not only possess cognitive personalized teaching function, but also emotional personalized teaching function. So, how to set up an Intelligent Web Tutoring System with emotional teaching function to realize personalized internet teaching of the interaction of cognition and emotion is very significant in the field of study of Intelligent Web Tutoring System.

Based on the theory of Affective Computing of Virtual Human, the application of expression and gesture identification bring forward an emotional Intelligent Web Tutoring System, which can seize and identify every student's study expression, make emotional feedback according to different student's study emotion and give emotional guidance so as to realize personalized teaching of the mutual correspondence of cognition and emotion. Meanwhile, the key technology of this system--the model of Affective Virtual Human is accomplished.

2 The Integrated Structure and Function of Each Model of Intelligent Web Tutoring System for Affective Virtual Human

This system adopts B/S structure. A Video input device (camera) will be installed at each student's side to obtain video image of student's study expression. Students and

Z. Pan et al. (Eds.): ICAT 2006, LNCS 4282, pp. 21–27, 2006.
© Springer-Verlag Berlin Heidelberg 2006

teachers use The Tutoring System through user side's browser. The Tutoring System can obtain student's study information on cognition and emotion, through analysis of this information to instruct student's study process. The communication among students, teachers and the server of The Tutoring System proceed through Web Service. Its web system structure as Figure 1:

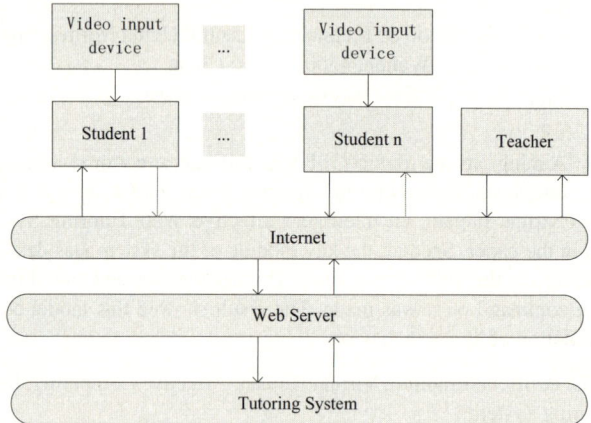

Fig. 1. Web system structure

Compared with traditional Intelligent Web Tutoring System, this system adds emotional model, including Affective Virtual Human and emotional instruction as well as video interface in the interaction modeling. Its web system structure as Figure 2 and the function of each model as follows.

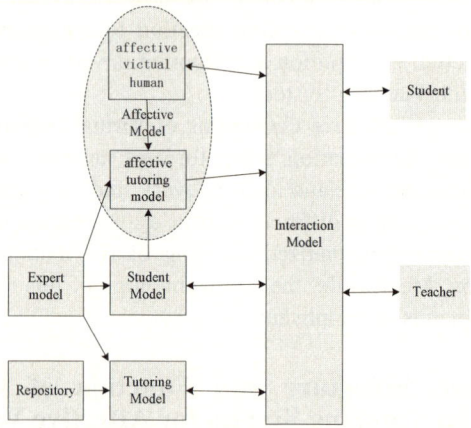

Fig. 2. System structure

Student Model: Keep record of initial knowledge level and study capability of each student and keep record of personality. It can ask and answer the history questions between students and system and make dynamic adjustment on each student's study progress circumstance.

Tutoring Model: Make intellectualized tutoring decision according to Student Model, judge student's study effect, put forward improvement method and advises etc.

Repository: Storage the due teaching subject domain and tutoring knowledge.

Interaction Model: Cognitive interface can understand natural language; realize the dialogue between human and machine in the common sense. Video interface can obtain student's study image.

Affective Model: Make affective identification and judgment according to the obtained student's study image by video interface and make feedback for student's emotion; meanwhile, make affective tutoring analysis according to student's study emotion, cognitive and personalized feature in the Student Model so as to provide personalized affective tutoring instruction.

3   The Design of the Key Module of the System and the Key Technology

3.1   The Design of Affective Model

3.1.1   The Design of Affective Virtual Human

Avatar is one type of virtual human, called as the embodiment of the real human, whose behaviors are controlled by real human. Using Avatar virtual human to denote student's virtual role in the web world, it can realize a personalized writing, voice and action, and can also talk with human beings through sound identification system on the terminal of the teacher, it will show student's Avatar.

First of all, video input devices Seize Video image of the student. Then the emotion was judged. Then the Affective Virtual Human recognizes the emotion and expresses its feeling. As a result, the teacher and the student can communicate with each other well. Figure 3 is the structure of Affective Virtual Human.

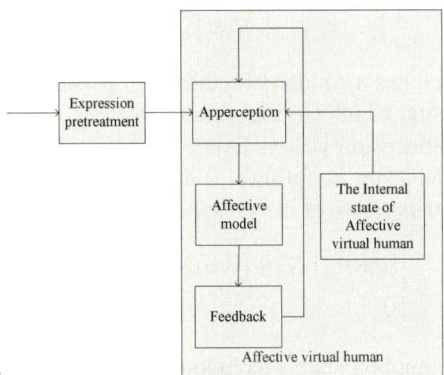

Fig. 3. The structure of Affective Virtual Human

3.1.2 The Design of Affective Tutoring Model

The affective tutoring model make affective tutoring analysis according to student's study emotion, cognitive and personalized feature in the Student Model and Mood teaching principle in Education psychology, and provide personalized affective tutoring instruction so as to adjust student's mood for better study.

3.2 The Affective Virtual Human Modeling

The Affective Virtual Human modeling is the key technology, so, this paper will put forward a method of Affective Virtual Human modeling. Detail introduction will be followed below.

3.2.1 The Affective Virtual Human

The Affective Virtual Human is a kind of virtual human with particular personality and capability of affective interaction (emotion recognition and expression), possessing a particular artificial emotion mathematic model, emotion recognition and expression way. It is the denotation of geometry and behaviors characteristics in virtual environment, research contents of multi-function apperception and affective computing and the concrete application of artificial psychology in the field of virtual reality.

3.2.2 The Personality and Emotion Model of the Affective Virtual Human

(1) The personality and emotion of the Affective Virtual Human
Every individual is an incessant entity. So, when we refer to the individual, we always indicate the comparative time t. It starts to exist on the moment t=0. L_t denotes an individual on the moment t. An individual has the state of personality and emotion. The personality is invariable, which has an initiate value on the moment t=0. The emotion is variable, which has an initiate value of zero on the moment t=0.

According to OCEAN model and PEN model, we can suppose that an individual is an n-dimension vector. Every dimension has a value between [0, 1]. The meanings of 0 and 1 are as follows: 0 denotes nonexistence of a dimension; 1 denotes the dimension having the biggest proportion. The denotation of personality is as follows:

$$\mathbf{P}^T = [\mu_1 \ K \ \mu_n], \forall \in [0,1] : \mu_i \in [0,1] \tag{1}$$

Emotion state, which has a similar structure with personality, is variable with time and is a series of emotion which has emotion intensity. e_t, which is the denotation of emotion state, is a n dimension vector. Every dimension has a value between [0, 1]. The meanings of 0 and 1 are as follows: 0 denotes nonexistence of a dimension; 1 denotes the max. The denotation of the vector is as follows:

$$e_t^T = \begin{cases} [\delta_1 k \delta_m], \forall i \in [0,m] : \delta_i \in [0,1] \text{if } t > 0 \\ 0 \qquad\qquad\qquad\qquad\quad \text{if } t = 0 \end{cases} \tag{2}$$

η_t denotes the past emotion states, including all the emotion states from the i=0 to i=t, as follows:

$$\eta_t = < e_0, e_1, K, e_t >\tag{3}$$

Based on the above model, personality L_t is defined as a 3D function of (P, m_t, e_t). p denotes personality, m_t denotes the mood and e_t denotes emotion state on the moment t. Emotion is not only One-dimensional, but also multi-dimensional. Every value of emotion is between [-1, 1]. Supposing emotion is a k-dimensional vector, it can be denoted as follows:

$$m_t^T = \begin{cases} [\theta_1 K \theta_k], & \forall i \in [-1,k] : \theta_i \in [-1,1] \text{ if } t > 0 \\ 0 & \text{if } t = 0 \end{cases}\tag{4}$$

λ_i denotes the past emotion state, including all the moods from the moment i=0 to i=t, as follows:

$$\lambda_t = < m_0, m_1, K, m_t >\tag{5}$$

(2) Emotion transferring

For each emotion, the definition of emotional information is the ideal emotional intensity changes. Emotional information has a value between [0, 1], which represented by the vector of ε, including changes of each m-dimension emotional intensity.

$$\varepsilon^T = [\delta_1 K \delta_m], \ \forall_i \in [1,m] : \delta_i \in [0,1]\tag{6}$$

There are two steps to transfer emotion. The first step is to change the mood, and the second is to change emotional state.

The functions of χ_m $(P, \eta_t, \lambda_t, \varepsilon)$ and V_m (P, η_t, λ_t) denote mood changes. $\chi_m (P, \eta_t, \lambda_t, \varepsilon)$ is decided by p, η_t, λ_t and ε. $V_m (P, \eta_t, \lambda_t)$ denotes internal changes of emotion (Enhancement or diminishment). New emotion is as follows:

$$m_{t+1} = m_t + \chi_m(p, \eta_t, \lambda_t, \varepsilon) + V_m(P, \eta_t, \lambda_t)\tag{7}$$

The functions of χ_e (P, η_t, ε) and V_e (P, η_t) denote mood state changes. χ_m $(P, \eta_t, \lambda_t, \varepsilon)$ is decided by p, η_t and ε. $V_m(P, \eta_t)$ denotes internal changes of emotion (Enhancement or diminishment). New emotion state is as follows:

$$e_{t+1} = e_t + \chi_e(P, \eta_t, \varepsilon) + V(P, \eta_t)\tag{8}$$

Emotion is decided by external function χ_e' $(P, \eta_t, \lambda_{t+1}, \varepsilon)$ and internal function V_e' $(P, \eta_t, \lambda_{t+1})$. χ_e' $(P, \eta_t, \lambda_{t+1}, \varepsilon)$ refers to the new and the past mood. V_e' $(P, \eta_t, \lambda_{t+1})$ also refers to the new mood. Therefore, the new emotion transferring is as follows:

$$e_{t+1}' = e_t + \chi_e'(P, \eta_{t+1}, \varepsilon) + V_e'(P, \eta_t, \lambda_{t+1})\tag{9}$$

4 Computer Simulation

The restriction condition that the experiment follows is that emotional changes of Affective Virtual Human begin with neuter character, then delay and decay for a certain extent, and finally go back to neuter character.

4.1   Feedback for Different Stimulus on the Same Model Parameters

In the initial emotional state [0 0 0], happiness, sorrow, surprise and neuter character are inputted in the experiment. The feedback is showed by figure 4:

stimulus	mapping in personality space
happiness	optimism
sorrow	Pessimism
surprise	optimism
neuter character	the usual mentality

Fig. 4. Feedback for different stimulus

4.2   Feedback for the Same Stimulus on Different Personality Model Parameters

In order to survey the feedback for the same stimulus on different personality model parameters, we select three different personalities: extroversion, introversion and the character between extroversion and introversion, and make them act on the same external stimulus: happiness. The feedback is showed as figure 5:

personality	the probability of emotional changes
extroversion	bigness
diffidence	smallness
the character between extroversion and diffidence	Somewhat between above

Fig. 5. Different feedbacks for the same stimulus

5   Conclusion

An intelligent affective Web Tutoring System is designed in this paper, which concerned student's affective changes. Then affective virtual human modeling is made. Finally a simulation is made on it. Testing results indicate that this model can realize emotional interaction of Affective Virtual Human. Since the emotional feedback of this model accord with the rule of human behaviors, so it's practicable and possesses a feature of flexible formation of different personalities.

Due to the short notice, many problems maybe exist in this system and more improvement and perfect are still required. Emotional modeling also needs further improvement and refinement as the development of artificial emotion.

References

1. Picard R. Affective Computing. Cambridge [M] . MA: MIT Press , 1997.
2. Yang Guoliang, Wang Zhiliang. A survey of affective modeling [J].Techniques of Automation and Applications,2004,23 (11).
3. Wilson I. Believable Autonomous Characters [D] . Dept of Artificial Intelligence, Univ of Westminster ,1996.
4. Goleman D. Emotional Intelligence [M] . [s. l.] :Bantam Books , 1995.
5. Xue W M,Wang ZL , Wei Z H. A new method for simulating human emotions [J] . Journal of University of Science and Technology: Beijing, 2003, 10(2):72 - 74.
6. Damasio A R. Descartes'Error: Emotion, reason and human brain [M]. New York: GrossetPPutnam Press, 1994.
7. Picard, Rosalind W. Toward computers that recognize and respond to user emotions [J]. IBM Systems Journal, 2001, 39(3 &4):705.

Extracting Behavior Knowledge and Modeling Based on Virtual Agricultural Mobile Robot

Xiangjun Zou[1,2], Jun Lu[1], Lufeng Luo[1], Xiwen Luo[1], and Yanqiong Zhou[2]

[1] The College of Engineering, South China Agriculture University, Guangzhou 510642
[2] Nanhua University, Hengyang, Hunan, 421001, China

Abstract. Aiming at complexity, unknown and uncertainty of picking object of agricultural intelligence mobile robot, extracting behavior knowledge and modeling based on the robot was put forward to help them obtain information effectively during operation, thereby to make decision for their behaviors. Firstly, behavior was studied based on picking behavior of the robot in virtual environment. Propose a behavior and method of extracting knowledge in virtual environment those are based on the association rules and, classify and express the entities such as robots, fruit trees and litchi, etc. Secondly, knowledge bases and models were built for reasoning. Thirdly, put forward for the first time to behavior knowledge classifies based on rough sets systematically, and classify the behaviors into obstacle-avoidance, picking, reasoning and fusion behavior to reduce redundant knowledge. Finally, an example for reasoning and simulation of the behavior was given. It realized picking behavior by message and route mechanism.

Keywords: Intelligence mobile robots, Behavior, Knowledge extraction, Uncertainty, Virtual environment.

1 Introduction

Agricultural intelligence mobile robots are unable to obtain certain knowledge information and make decision effectively and accurately during operation due to complexities, unknown and uncertainties of agricultural environment and its operating object. Therefore, knowledge modeling, uncertain reasoning and fusion of agricultural intelligence mobile robots' behavior have been the key technology and theory basis of simulation.

Researches on agricultural picking robots have been lasted for over 30 years. American scholars, Schertz and Brown, propose for the first time to adopt robots to harvest fruits and vegetables. Then, researches are developed among countries such as America, Canada, Holland, Japan, and UK etc. Japanese invented robots to pick tomatoes, cucumbers and Spanish invented robots to pick oranges [1]. And mobile robots were used to survey the crop to obtain its growth knowledge [2].

There are few agricultural robots in China, but things will be better. Researches on agricultural robots and their basic theories are begun to be recognized. South China Agricultural University has developed an operation platform that has machine vision, GPS (Global positioning system) and navigation control system [3], which provides a

Z. Pan et al. (Eds.): ICAT 2006, LNCS 4282, pp. 28–37, 2006.

mobile platform for agricultural mobile robots. Nanjing Agricultural University has researched on identification of the multi-resolution route in machine vision navigation. They hold the opinion that how to syncretize the priori knowledge to improve the identification ability of machine vision's mode is an important research content in this area [4]. Zhe Jiang University optimized the design of manipulator by optimizing the fruit picking manipulator and simulation experiment [5].

Now, the research of mobile robot concentrates its attention on vision, graphical processing, path selecting, motion of mechanism and simulation, and agronomists rarely research mobile robot's behavior decision and knowledge modeling.

But, behaviors of robot have been researched in the fields of industry and military. In the literature [6], the behavior control of robots which is based on the behavior control realized by artificial intelligence, was realized by the reasoning and fusion based on fuzzy rules and expert knowledge. In the literature [7], the process of uncertain knowledge and information is realized by the partial knowledge and the possibilistic logic approach. In the literature [8], as a robot, it has no a priori knowledge, has to explore a graph. So exploration method was studied on robot.

An example for picking litchi and longan in the south of China is given in the paper. It studies knowledge extraction and modeling, uncertainty reasoning and fusion of agricultural mobile robot's picking behaviors, presents the knowledge classification of robot's behaviors based on rough sets, classifies behaviors of the robot into obstacle-avoidance behavior, picking behavior, knowledge reasoning behavior and knowledge fusion behavior. By the attribute reduction of knowledge, treating behaviors as a design problem and the modified evidence theory [9], the uncertainty of reasoning and simulation can be solved, and the optimal behavior decision is obtained by reasoning and fusion.

2   Picking Object and Behavior Characteristics of Mobile Robots

2.1   Picking Object

The production of the litchi and the longan, which are specialties of the south of China, especially, the Guangdong accounts for about a third of that of the world. Generally, litchi trees are planted in gardens and on hillsides, and its fruits grow in Chains. Every year, in the season of picking, to complete the picking costs a great deal of manpower, its labor intensity is heavy and means of picking are rude, and mainly depends on people to climb the trees to pick litchi . The cost of picking accounts for about 50% to 70% of that of production. So, the agricultural robot which is a kind of automatic machines will take the place of handwork.

2.2   Behavior Characteristics of Agricultural Mobile Robots

There are more uncertainties with behavior decision of agricultural mobile robots. For example, the position of picking object and the size of litchi are uncertain, flexible and damageable, and the irregularity of road scene, the weather and the environment are uncertain and beastly. At the same time, when the robot is on working, its object may be covered by leaves and shadow, and its knowledge obtaining, vision and behavior decision will be interfered by noise, so, there are more uncertainties with the robot and its behavior control and decision. Through knowledge modeling of complex environment and behaviors of robots, the complex and uncertain problems can be classified and simplified, and behavior decision and simulation of the robot in virtual environment (VE) can be realized.

3 The Knowledge Extraction and Modeling of Robot's Picking Behavior

How to use a laconic mean to realize knowledge modeling and extraction is the key and also the difficulty to knowledge modeling of the robot's picking behavior in VE. The following analyzes the entities in VE and their behaviors at first, and then makes knowledge expression to them based on their association rules.

3.1 The Characteristics of the Entities and the Analysis of the Uncertain Problems

Picking behavior of the robot in VE is complex, the entities in this environment which can embody external characteristics of entities, are composed of some geometric entities and these entities such as ambient light and material and so on. Behaviors can embody both external characteristics and internal characteristics, and the state behavior that embodies external characteristics is the representation of the physical function of entities.

The picking behavior can be classified into static entity and dynamic entity. The dynamic entity, which is important to the reasoning and decision making of picking, is a result of the entity's state change.

Entities in virtual environment are primarily mechanism of robot, transportation mechanism of fruit, transducer, pick-up head, fruit tree, and fruit in chains, ground, weed, road-block, clouds, fog, sunlight and rain, etc. In the paper, these entities are classified into robot system, road, obstacle and climate. The knowledge about picking behavior should include the common sense needed by behavior decision, the characteristics of the growth of biology, the fruit, the agroclimate and the geography.

Generally, the knowledge about the static entities in virtual environment such as fruit tree, obstacle and climate, etc, is certain, but uncertain when the robot is on picking. For example, the size of the chain of fruit and the color are variable and sunlight varies randomly. So, there should be knowledge classification, expression and modeling to be done with knowledge extraction and robot can't make behavior decision validly without the good judgment of the variety of scene knowledge.

3.2 The Extraction and Expression of the Association Rules

In order to make reasoning of picking behavior easy and to simplify program structure, the association rules based on object is adopted. When to express behavior knowledge, the basic knowledge should be expressed by rules, the structure knowledge should be expressed by the object-oriented method, and then express the knowledge and structure knowledge about fact and rules in the form of example with the object-oriented method. The express method that is similar to man's way of thinking is easy for description, expression, abstraction, inheriting, organization and package. Next, the expression of robots' behavior function and virtual scene knowledge is discussed and is mapped to relation database to be stored, and, knowledge base is built in order to make the call and the management easy and efficient.

The association rules can make the asking of behavior knowledge of robot easy. If there is a rule set T {ti|i=1, 2... n }, the association rules will be used to study the influence which one item of T puts on another item [10].

Take the virtual scene of the picking behavior of the robot for example to explain how to make knowledge extraction and expression. In the scene, there are entities such as fruit trees, ground, and robots, etc.

The trees in a scene, which can be treated as a set, should include much information such as the tree's name, position, height, kind, fruit's size and color, etc.

If we input the key words litchi, type and color to ask the kind of the litchi in certain garden, we can get the information that 85% of litchis are reddish Fei Zixiao. The constrained association rule with a high reliability can be obtained by the algorithm for mining association rules. The rule can be expressed as following:

Identifiers 1, 2 Number attribute 1, attribute 2, attribute 3, and attribute 4, Conclusion, reliability.

When to plan behaviors preliminary, the knowledge that can help robot to make plan decision can be obtained by the Association Rules. For example, the system will give us the information about the matching of picking, scene, fruit tree and climate when to plan behaviors preliminary in computer-human-interaction virtual system. If the sensors obtain the information that the litchi is reddish, the value of reliability that is 0.85 will lead the system to search out the knowledge about the picking object matching with the value in knowledge base.

The common knowledge about picking behavior obtained from the knowledge base is as following:

```
LZ=1      # litchi tree
Varietal=2  # Fei Zixiao (a kind of litchi)
Color=3    # reddish
Mature=1   # maturity
CF=0.95    # reliability
```

The knowledge (including the position of manipulator) about the object of scene obtained by the sensor is as following:

```
LZ=1       # litchi tree
Varietal=2   # Fei Zixiao
Color=3     # reddish
High-Z=0.1   # the height of the object in direction Z
High-X=0.1   # the distance of the object in direction X
High-Y=0.1   #the distance of the object in direction Y
Action=1    # take action
CF=0.9
```

The upper two kinds of knowledge can be expressed in another form, as the following:

IF {LZ (I) =1 and I Varietal=2 and Color=3 then Mature=1}
IF {LZ (I) =1 and Color=3 and Mature=1 then Action=1}

The knowledge for decision can be obtained by the association rules.

The dynamic behavior of entities in VE is an expression of the function of the entity, a part of the function knowledge and expression of the structural state; so, the knowledge extraction of behavior knowledge is based on the expression of structure and function.

3.3 The Object Expression of Structure, Function and Behaviors of Virtual Robot Based on Rules

The paragraph studies how to express objects, classes and their attributes, operation, methods and relations. The association chart expresses their structure knowledge and behavior function, and the object chart can express three kinds of relationships [10].

(1) Association and linkage: association and linkage can express the relations between objects, classes and object and class. All the linkages in association connect to the objects of the same class.

(2) Summarization and inherit: The summarization expresses the inclusion relation between super class and subclass based on the view of super class. The inherit expresses the relation based on the share attribute, the operation principle, the view of subclass and that characterization and summarization are two different views of a same relation.

(3) Polymerization: treating an object as certain modules, expressing the object as an assemblage of these modules, modeling each module and then assembling these modules according to each other's relation. In the object model chart, the diamond represents the end point of polymerization relation. The structure and behavior function knowledge of robot expresses all kinds of association between entities such as the attributes of objects and classes and the operation by the hiberarchy of the chart and some symbols. An example of agricultural mobile robot for the expression of the knowledge model of the entities in VE is taken in the Fig 1.

In Fig 1, B- function is Behavior function, P- index is Performance index, O-principle is Operating principle, B-rules is Behavior rules; A –control is Auto control, F- control is Function control, S- control is Simulation control; Ob-location is Object location, O-avoidance is Obstacle-avoidance, D-making is Decision-making, P-behavior is Pick behavior.3-D is three-dimensional.

3.4 The Organization of the Behavior Design Knowledge Repository of Robots

Behavior design knowledge repository provides knowledge storage, management and maintenance for behavior function, motion, poses, target identification, picking and obstacle-avoidance behavior.

(1) The behavior knowledge object class mapping to the database table: Each kind of class maps to one table or many tables (a table also can be used in many classes). When simultaneously assigns the host key word, and supposes its value for none. Uses the SQL code to found and establishes the host key word index. Put the data type maps to the SQL level.

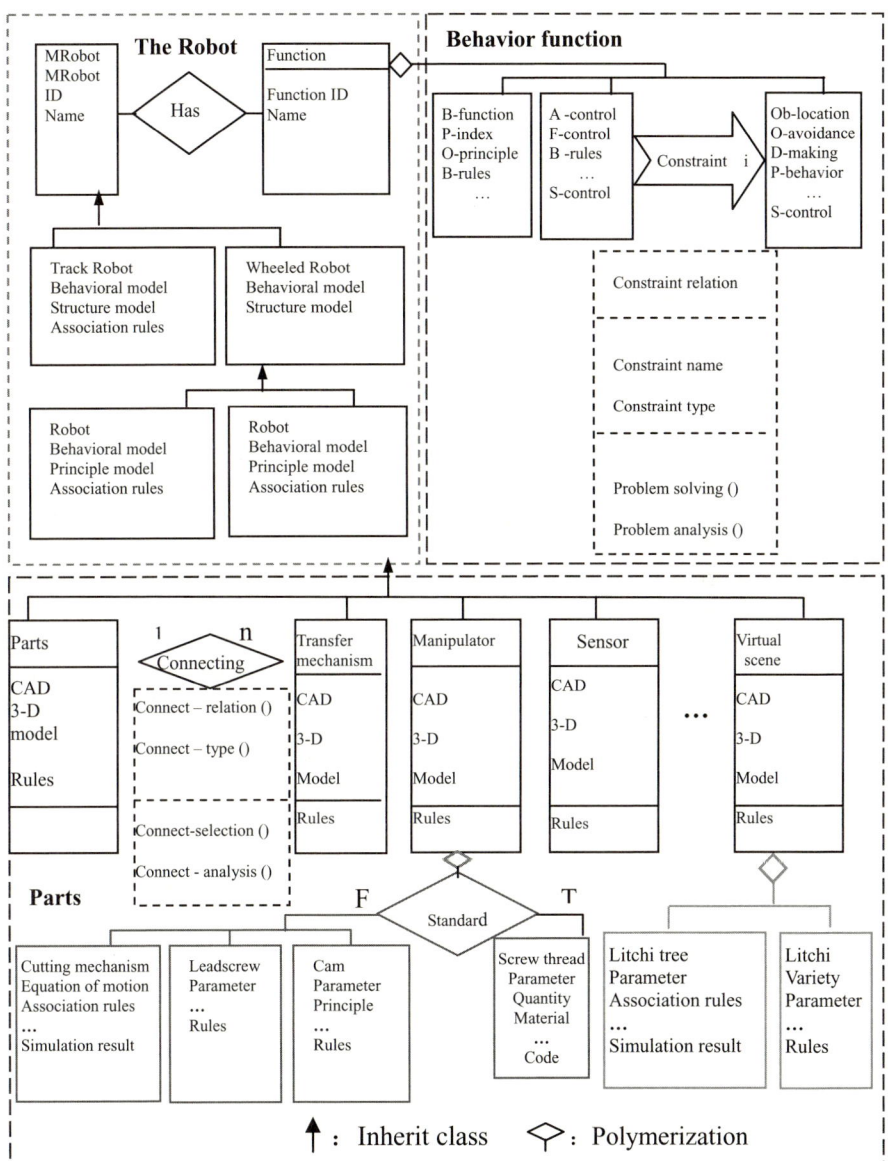

Fig. 1. The knowledge model of virtual mobile robot

(2) The association mapping to the table: Multi-association-to-multi-association maps to the tables, we need to satisfy the object's association relations. The class which correlative with the behavior knowledge object and the linking attribute of main key word are all became the attribute of the table. We know that the connection between two objects requests two objects mutually understand, which by the association characteristics.

(3) Summarization maps the table: Maps each subclass to a table, which causes the object marking to be preserved through using sharing ID. The logic relations of this expression are definitude. For example the MRobot's (a mobile Robot) table is allowed to summarize to the table's attribute names: MRobot ID, Track MRobot ID and Wheeled MRobot ID.

(4) The polymerization mapping to the table according to the above mapping rule, we can establish the polymerization mapping to the table.

(5) Mapping object structure to date table can put more object model's rules and semantics to the database and make the knowledge inquiring of intelligence mobile robot, the gaining behavior reasoning and fusion and the realization of decision making become easy.

3   Behavior Reasoning and Decision Based on Rough Sets Theory

Disposing the behavior problems of virtual robots as one kind of design problems, drawing up the design criterion, one solution based on the rough sets and the case was put forward to realize behavior design decision.

Knowledge extraction based on rough sets theory and object classification have common characteristics on method, that is to say both of them make classification according to the views by which human see the things. Knowledge classification is necessary while extracting property. One method is that, first of all, classify a type of knowledge (such as experience analogy, etc.) According to the characteristic of virtual robot's behavior attributes to obtain different division of the knowledge property, then classify again until the division meet the needs, and eventually, aggregate the classified information to obtain the property sets which we hope to extract.

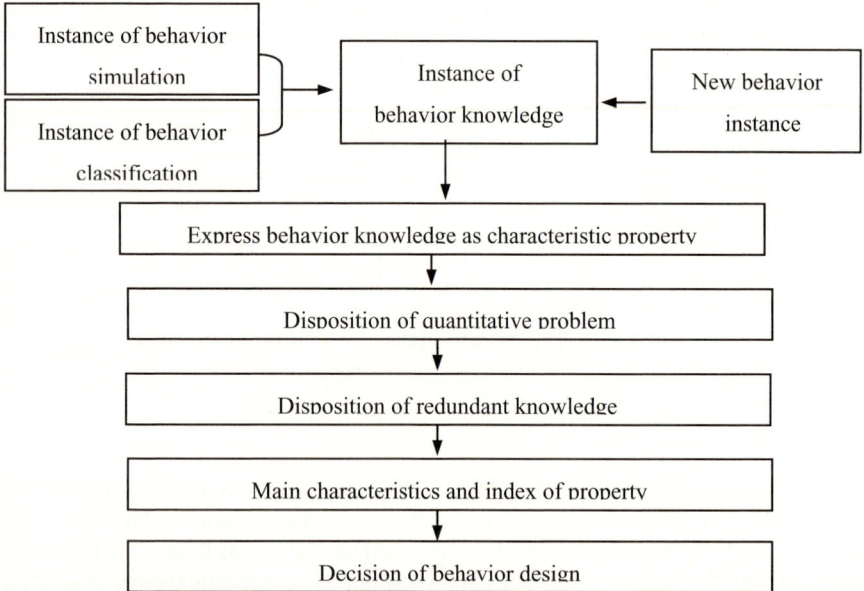

Fig. 2. The design process and searches of behavior instance based on rough sets

Behavior decision of the robot in complex environment is the decision knowledge based on uncertainty and multi-property. Analyzing the knowledge which has been classified, determining the degree of importance of characteristics, and establishing the decision-making table (including finding partial knowledge contrast), all of these, provide a basis to extract the key features of property, to build simple models of knowledge and reasoning models based on rough sets, thereby to achieve reasonable and certain design approach so as to fuse by similar matching and instance. Searches for the instance (in Fig 2) concludes the expression and conversion of the uncertain problems, the establishment of the decision table, the analysis of the importance of property and the establishment of index. Finally, make comprehensive evaluation by system similarities model and availability and solve the uncertain problem through the modified evidence theory to get the reasonable behavior decision.

4   Picking Behavior Realization of the Robot in VE

Picking behavior realization of the robot is realized by message and route mechanism on the platform of EON Studio 5.0 and VC++. Human-computer Interaction is realized by sensor, event driver and route mechanism. For instance, Fig 3 is a part of route mechanism on behavior realization of robot in VE and Fig 4 is a 3D dynamic simulation of picking process of agricultural mobile robot in VE.

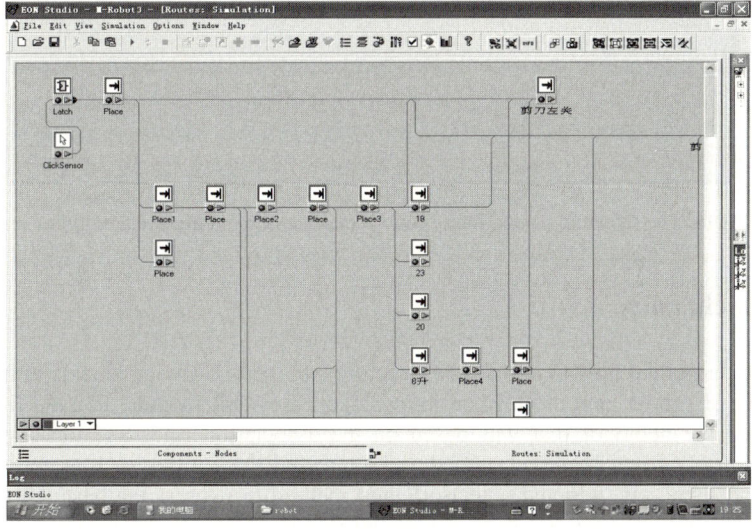

Fig. 3. The route mechanism of behavior control in virtual environment

In VE the elementary require of robot behavior is apperceiving environment by its sensors or effecting environment by operation and realizing interaction by communications. In software, sensors and data are defined as all kinds of equipments on VR such as data-gloves, keyboard mouse and so on. After functions are inputted, the inputting instructions from users are received, according to which the behavior is performed. In Eon Studio, the sensors have mostly Keyboard Sensor, Mouse Sensor, Box Sensor, Time Sensor and Click Sensor, etc, by which the system can receive inputting instructions and perform its behavior according to client's demands after the client send instructions.

The node in the system is an object with functions and data, which has different types. Generally, the data information of node concludes two aspects, the filed and the event. The final realization of action and interaction could be achieved by the transmission of message, which is the bridge of communication.

Fig. 4. The dynamic simulation of robot's picking process in virtual environment

5 Conclusions

The article studied how to extract the structure and the knowledge models of behavior function of robots, and established knowledge bases and models. For the first time proposed the behavior that was based on the association rules and the knowledge extraction of virtual scene, classified and expressed the entities such as robots, fruit trees and litchi, etc. adopted object-oriented method to express the basic knowledge, expressed the structure and behavior knowledge of robots based on the rough sets, treated the behavior problems of virtual robots as a design problems, developed design standards, solved the certain and uncertain problems of behavior decision, and realized the behavior decision by the rough sets and the case method. This paper took the behavior of agricultural mobile robots as an object to realize the knowledge modeling and simulation of the picking behavior of robot in VE.

Acknowledgments. This work was supported by (1).Natural Science Foundation of Guangdong, NO: 05006661. (2).Educational and Research Foundation of Hunan NO: 04B21. (3).the National Natural Science Foundation of Chine NO: 60574029. (4). the "211 Project" of South China Agriculture University.

References

[1] S. I. Cho, S. J. Chang; Y. Y. Kim; K. J. An.Development of a Three-degrees-of-freedom Robot for harvesting Lettuce Using Machine Vision and Fuzzy logic Control [J]. Biosystems Engineering. 2002. 82 (2): 143–149.

[2] Jun Qiao; Akira Sasao1; Sakae Shibusawa1 et al. Mapping Yield and Quality using the Mobile Fruit Grading Robot，Biosystems Engineering (2005) 90 (2), 135–142.

[3] Lou Xi-wen;Qu Ying-gang;Zhao Zuo-xi, Research and development of intelligent flexible chassis for precision farming, TRANSACTIONS OF THE CHINESE SOCIETY OF AGRICULTURAL ENGINEERING, 2005. 21(2): 83-85.(in Chinese)

[4] Zhou Jun;Ji Chang-ying, Multi-resolution Road Recognition for Vision Navigation, TRANSACTIONS OF THE CHINESE SOCIETY OF AGRICULTURAL MACHINERY, 2003.34（11）：120－124. (In Chinese)

[5] Liang X-feng, Experiments of Optimization and Simulation on Kinematics of a Tomato Harvesting Manipulator, TRANSACTIONS OF THE CHINESE SOCIETY OF AGRICULTURAL MACHINERY, 2005.36(7): 97-101.(in Chinese)

[6] Eugenio Aguirre, Antonio Gonz_alez，Fuzzy behaviors for mobile robot navigation: Design, coordination and fusion [J]. International Journal of Approximate Reasoning (S0888-613X). 2000. 25: 255-289.

[7] Claudio Sossai, Paolo Bison, Gaetano Chemello.Sequent calculus and data fusion [J]. Fuzzy Sets and Systems (S0165-0114).2001. 121: 371–395.

[8] Pierre Fraigniaud, David Ilcinkas, Guy Peer, Graph exploration by a finite automaton [J]. Theoretical Computer Science (S0304-3975). 2005. 345: 331–344.

[9] Zou Xiang-jun,Sun Jian,He Han-wu,Zheng De-tao,Zhang Ping, Research on Combination of Conflicting Evidences of Multi-Agent Decision in Virtual Environment, JOURNAL OF SYSTEM SIMULATION, 2006.18(4) :1010-1014(in Chinese)

[10] Zou Xiang-jun, Snu Jian ,Gu Bang-jun. Knowledge information extracting and modeling of virtual product design based knowledge，Modern Manufacturing Engineering.8 (2006): 6-8 (in Chinese).

Human Motion Interpolation Using Space-Time Registration*

Zhihua Chen[1,2], Lizhuang Ma[2], Yan Gao[2], and Xiaomao Wu[2]

[1] East China University of Science & Technology
201512, Shanghai, China
hualiczh0607@126.com, zhchen@cs.sjtu.edu.cn
[2] Department of Computer Science & Engineering, Shanghai Jiao Tong University,
200030, Shanghai, China

Abstract. Human motion interpolation plays an important role in virtual reality and human animation. In this paper, we propose a motion interpolation algorithm with space-time registration. Firstly, time registration based on motion cycles is used to seek the corresponding frames between input motions. Secondly, space registration based on analysis method is employed to align spatially the motion frames. Then the corresponding frames are interpolated according to the interpolation methods of transition and angles, respectively. Finally, we reconstruct the constraints of the resulting motion. Experimental results demonstrate that our algorithm succeeds in interpolating input motions to create new motions with new style.

1 Introduction

Motion interpolation is an important technique for blending different motions to create a new motion of new style. For example, the walk motion and run motion of human can be used to produce the jog motion by means of this technique [1, 2]. Motion interpolation has been applied to many areas including virtual reality, computer animation, digital entertainment, human machine interaction, etc.

In this paper, we study how to interpolate the parameters of human motion, and propose a new motion interpolation algorithm based on space-time registration. The algorithm consists of four steps, i.e., time registration, space registration, parameter interpolation and constraint reconstruction.

Firstly, we utilize the coordination and periodicity of movements of human joints, construct time registration function that is monotone and consistently increase, and then align temporally input motions. Our method can avoid the error of 'time reverse'.

Secondly, we spatially align the input motions. Considering that human usually move on a plane surface, we reduce human motion registration to the problem of 2D space registration, i.e., how to calculate the optimal solutions of 2D transition and rotation transformation. We introduce analytic method to deduce these solutions from a distance function. Our method reduces greatly the time that registration process costs.

---

* This paper is supported by National Science Foundation of China (No 60373070).

Z. Pan et al. (Eds.): ICAT 2006, LNCS 4282, pp. 38–47, 2006.

Thirdly, we interpolate the parameters of the corresponding frames of input motions. In this step, the interpolation of transitions of the root joints is executed, and then the interpolation of angles of all joints is implemented with quaternion technique.

Finally, fuzzy theory is introduced to constraint definition of resulting motion, and the constraints of resulting motion are reconstructed with IK (Inverse Kinematics) technique.

2   Related Works

Time Registration
Bruderlin et al use the method of signal processing to warp motion time [3]; Sloan et al align temporally input motions with weight average [4], but their method may result in 'time reverse'. Many researchers utilize human machine interaction to choose key time, and then implement time registration [1,5,6,7]. Despite their simplicity, their algorithms require user's intervention. Kovar implements time warping based on DP (dynamic programming) [8]. His method is automatic, however, it runs slowly.

Other than the former methods, our algorithm makes use of periodicity of human motions, warps the motion time, and automatically carries out time registration of input motions. Our method is rapid, and can avoid the error of 'time reverse'.

Space Registration
Kovar and Gleicher et al present coordinate frame alignment to implement space registration for motion frames [9, 10]. Lee et al define a distance function based on position and velocity of joints, but their function has its shortage. For two frames where motion poses are similar but motion coordinates are much different, the distance between frames by Lee's method are big.

We adopt the distance function that Kovar et al present [9,10] and deduce mathematically the optimal transformation. They firstly calculate spatial registration between all frames of input motions, and then implement time registration with DP method. However, our method is mainly different from their method. We carry out time registration based on motion cycles and then execute spatial registration between corresponding cycles of input motions. Our method greatly drops the computation cost.

Parameter Interpolation
Perlin and Winkin use weighed average method to interpolate Euler angles of two input motions [11,12]. Their methods fail to create smooth motion. Park et al propose a motion interpolation method based on RBF [1]. Unlike these methods, we divide motion data into two parts: spatial transition of root joint and Euler angles of all joints. We apply linear interpolation method based on motion velocity to the former, and apply quaternion interpolation method to the latter.

3   System Overview

The interpolation algorithm includes four steps: time registration, space registration, parameter interpolation and constraint reconstruction(Fig.1).

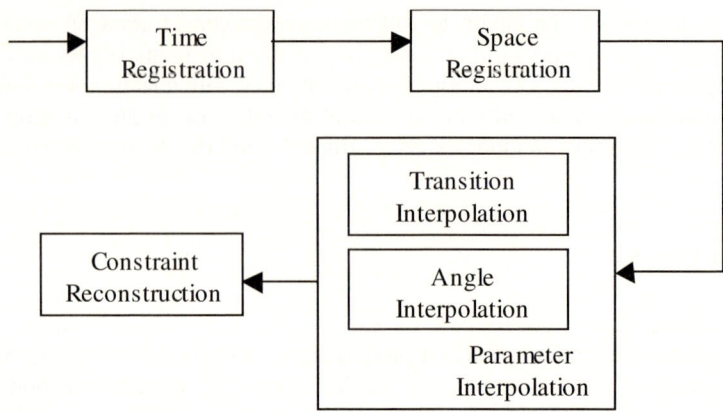

Fig. 1. The frame of the motion interpolation algorithm based on space-time registration

4 Time Registration

Motion Cycle

Human motion is of high cooperation and the movements of human joints interact. In practice, we can obtain experience from real life: some human motions such as the motions of human jog and run, share similar variety in joint movements. For example, the movements of limbs take on 'diagonal symmetry', i.e., human's left hand swings as similarly as his right foot, and human's right hand swings as similarly as his left foot. So we can compute the cycles of human motion according to the swing frequency of human's limb. The computation method is as follows:

1. According to the forward kinematics, use Euler angles of limb joint links to compute the transition function $\mathbf{p}_e(t)$ of end effectors of all input motions. The formula is as follows:

$$\mathbf{p}_{k,e}(t) = \mathbf{f}_F(\mathbf{A}_k(t)) \tag{1}$$

where the suffix k represents the k-th input motion, $\mathbf{A}_k(t)$ represents the Euler angle set of the k-th input motion, and $\mathbf{f}_F(\bullet)$ denotes the forward kinematics function.

2. Calculate the velocity function $\mathbf{v}_e(t)$ of End Effectors of human limbs. The formula is as follows:

$$\mathbf{v}_{k,e}(t) = \frac{d\mathbf{p}_{k,e}(t)}{dt} \tag{2}$$

3. Calculate the interval time set $\mathbf{T}_h$ of motion cycles. The formula is as follows:

$$\mathbf{T}_h = \left\{ t_i \mid \left\| v_{k,e}(t_i) \right\|_2 = 0 \right\} \tag{3}$$

4. Take out elements in sequence from $\mathbf{T}_h$ and then obtain motion cycles C_i:

$$C_i = \left\{ t_i, t_{i+1} \right\} \tag{4}$$

where $t_i \in \mathbf{T}_h$. In light of these motion cycles, we divide the human motion sequences into motion chips. Every motion chip lasts a motion cycle.

Time Registration

Time registration of two motion sequences can be simplified to correspondence between chips and correspondence between frames:

1.Correspondence between chips
Align in sequence motion cycles of input motions.
2. Correspondence between frames

After corresponding chips are obtained, we can seek corresponding frames in these chips. The computation formula is as follow (Fig.2):

$$\frac{f_i' - f_1'}{f_i - f_1} = \frac{f_2' - f_1'}{f_2 - f_1} \tag{5}$$

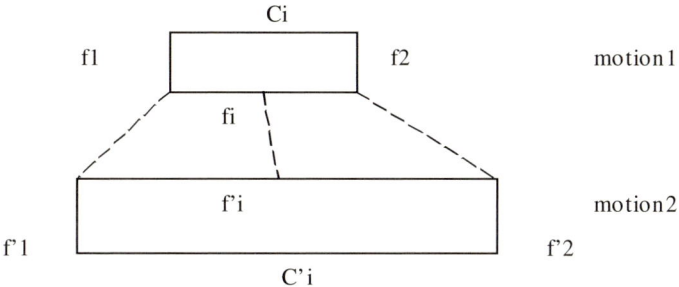

Fig. 2. Time corresponding between motion frames

where f_1 and f_2 represent the first frame and last frame of motion cycle C_i of input motion $\mathbf{m}_1(t)$, respectively. Similarly, f_1' and f_2' represent the first frame and last frame of motion cycle C_i' of input motion $\mathbf{m}_2(t)$, respectively.

Given an arbitrary frame f_i of motion cycle C_i of input motion $\mathbf{m}_1(t)$, its corresponding frame f_i' of motion cycle C_i' of input motion $\mathbf{m}_2(t)$ can be computed as follows:

$$f_i' = f_1' + \frac{f_2' - f_1'}{f_2 - f_1}(f_i - f_1) \tag{6}$$

5 Space Registration

After temporal registration, Input motions must be aligned spatially. Otherwise, There will be errors during interpolation resulting from the difference of human's positions.

In our registration method, spatial positions of all joints are calculated by means of forward kinematics, and then every joint of a motion frame can be represented as a point in 3D space. All joints of a motion frame form "point cloud". A distance function is introduced to define the difference of two motion frames, i.e., "two point cloud". In the end, we calculate the optimal rigid transformation to make the distance of two frames least and implement the spatial registration of human motions.

The distance between two frames is defined as follows:

$$f_d(\mathbf{m}(t_i),\mathbf{m}(t_j)) = \sum_{k=1}^{N} w_k \left\| \mathbf{m}(t_i) - \mathbf{T} \cdot \mathbf{R} \cdot \mathbf{m}(t_j) \right\|^2 \tag{7}$$

For simplification, we only consider that human moves on the plane surface. In this situation, spatial registration only requires 2D rigid transformation. Then Equation (7) is simplified as follows:

$$f_d(\mathbf{m}(t_i),\mathbf{m}(t_j)) = \sum_{k=1}^{N} w_k \left\| \mathbf{m}(t_i) - \mathbf{T}(X^*,Z^*) \cdot \mathbf{R}(\theta) \cdot \mathbf{m}(t_j) \right\|^2 \tag{8}$$

The distance between two frames is defined as the least value of the distance function under 2D transformation:

$$D(\mathbf{m}(t_i),\mathbf{m}(t_j)) = \min_{\theta,X^*,Z^*} f_d(\mathbf{m}(t_i),\mathbf{m}(t_j)) \tag{9}$$

The required transformation can be represented as:

$$\begin{cases} \theta = \arg\min_{\theta} f_d(\mathbf{m}(t_i),\mathbf{m}(t_j)) \\ (X^*,Z^*) = \arg\min_{(X^*,Z^*)} f_d(\mathbf{m}(t_i),\mathbf{m}(t_j)) \end{cases} \tag{10}$$

Then we try to calculate the value of θ and (X^*,Z^*). Suppose that two input motions are needed registration and denoted as $\mathbf{m}_1(t)$ and $\mathbf{m}_2(t)$。 The equations below can be obtained by using Equation (8) and (9):

$$D(\mathbf{m}(t_i),\mathbf{m}(t_j)) = \min_{\theta,X^*,Z^*} \sum_{k=1}^{N} w_k \left\| \mathbf{m}(t_i) - \mathbf{T}(X^*,Z^*) \cdot \mathbf{R}(\theta) \cdot \mathbf{m}(t_j) \right\|^2 \tag{11}$$

Equation (11) can be extended to:

$$D = \min_{\theta,X^*,Z^*} \sum_{k=1}^{N} w_k [(CX + SZ + X^* - x)^2 + (Y - y)^2 + (-SX + CZ + Z^* - z)^2] \tag{12}$$

Where $(x_j,y_j,z_j)^T$ and $(X_j,Y_j,Z_j)^T$ represent the j-th joint's coordinates of the i-th corresponding frame of $\mathbf{m}_1(t)$ and $\mathbf{m}_2(t)$, respectively.

Differentiate Equation (12):

$$\frac{\partial D}{\partial \theta} = 2 \sum w_k [S(xX + zZ - X^*X - Z^*Z) + C(X^*Z + zX - xZ - Z^*X)] \tag{13}$$

Let $\dfrac{\partial D}{\partial \theta} = 0$ and

$$\sum_k w_k x = \bar{x} , \sum_k w_k z = \bar{z} , \sum_k w_k X = \bar{X} , \sum_k w_k Z = \bar{Z} \tag{14}$$

Then we get the value of θ:

$$\theta == \arctan \frac{\sum_k w_k (xZ - zX) - (\bar{x}\bar{Z} - \bar{z}\bar{X})}{\sum_k w_k (xX + zZ) - (\bar{x}\bar{X} + \bar{z}\bar{Z})} \tag{15}$$

Similarly, we differentiate Equation (12) again:

$$\frac{\partial D}{\partial X^*} = 2\sum_k w_k (CX + SZ + X^* - x) \tag{16}$$

Alike, differentiate Equation (12) again and then we get:

$$X^* = \bar{x} - C\bar{X} - S\bar{Z} , \quad Z^* = \bar{z} + S\bar{X} - C\bar{Z} \tag{17}$$

6 Parameter Interpolation

6.1 Transition Interpolation

Given an arbitrary input motion $\mathbf{m}(t) = \{\mathbf{P}(t), \mathbf{A}(t)\}$, $\mathbf{P}(t)$ and $\mathbf{A}(t)$ represent transitions of root joint and angles of all joints, respectively. Parameter interpolation of transitions can be carried out according to Equation (18):

$$\mathbf{P}_b(t) = \sum_k w_k(t)\mathbf{P}_k(t) \tag{18}$$

Where $\mathbf{P}_k(t)$ represents the k-th input motion after space-time registration and $w_k(t)$ represents the weight of the k-th input motion.

6.2 Angle Interpolation

We convert Euler angles of human joints into quaternions, and then implement rotation interpolation by spherical linear interpolation. So the rotation interpolation of the j-th frame can be calculated:

$$\mathbf{A}_{b,j}(t) = slerp(\mathbf{A}_{1,j}, \mathbf{A}_{2,j}, w(t)) \tag{19}$$

Where $\mathbf{A}_{1,j}, \mathbf{A}_{2,j}$ are the rotation quaternions of the j-th frame of the first and second motion, respectively, and $slerp(\mathbf{E}_1, \mathbf{E}_2, w)$ represents interpolation function [5], w is the weight,

7 Constraint Reconstruction

The input motions are interpolated to create the target motion. However, it may break original constraints. So the step of constraint reconstruction is required. Ground-touch constraints are main considerations because they are the most important constraints of human motions.

We apply fuzzy mathematics method to the constraint state of the resulting motion. Suppose that $\mathbf{F}$ represent the set of all motion frames, $\mathbf{F}_c$ represent the set of the constrained frames, then:

$$S_k(t) = \begin{cases} 0, t \notin \mathbf{F}_c \\ 1, t \in \mathbf{F}_c \end{cases} \qquad (20)$$

Where $S_k(t)$ represent the constraint state function of the k-th input motion.

Let $S_b(t)$ represent the constraint state function of the resulting motion, then:

$$S_b(t) = \begin{cases} 0, 当 \hat{S}_b(t) < \lambda \\ 1, 当 \hat{S}_b(t) \geq \lambda \end{cases} \qquad (21)$$

Where λ is a threshold that is bigger than 0 and:

$$\hat{S}_b(t) = \sum_k w_k(t) S_k(t) \qquad (22)$$

After its constraint state is obtained, the resulting motion can be reconstructed by simple IK (inverse kinematics) method.

8 Results and Discussion

8.1 Experimental Results

Our experiments consist of two types of motion interpolation. The first type is standard interpolation (Figure 4), and the second is the interpolation with the specified path (Figure 5). All experiments can be run in real time in the condition of computer configuration: P4 2.4G, 512MB.

(a)   (b)

Fig. 3. The captured motions motion of run and walk are showed in (a) and (b)

We apply our algorithm for motion interpolation to the capture data of human motions. The captured motions include two kinds: human walk and run (Figure 3).

The standard interpolation results are showed in Figure 4. Figure (a) shows the result of Rose's interpolation algorithm that is without space-time registration. The hands of human character twitter abnormally. Figure (b) shows the result of our algorithm: run and walk motions are interpolated to create jog motion. In contrast to Rose's result, our result eliminate the error of abnormal twittering.

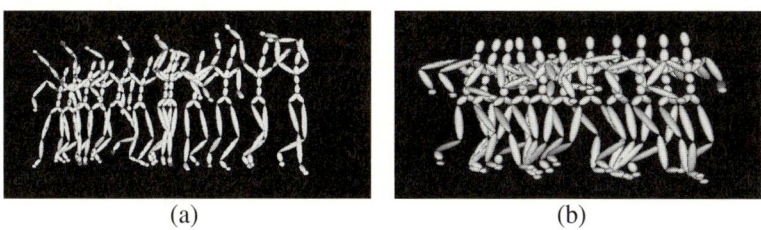

(a)   (b)

Fig. 4. The results of the motion interpolation algorithm. (a) The result of interpolation without space-time registration. (b) The result of our algorithm.

In some situations, the user hopes to specify the path of the interpolated motion. In order to create this motion, path correction must be add after motion interpolation. In our implementation, path correction includes two parts: location correction and orientation. Our interpolation result of run and walk motions is shown in Figure 5. The red curve indicates the path that user draws in advance.

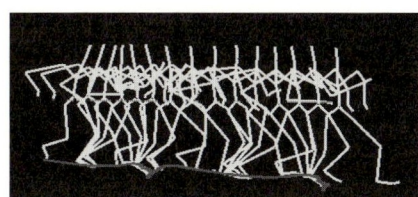

Fig. 5. The motion interpolation based on given path. Red curve shows the given path.

8.2 Discussion

Our time registration algorithm is based on motion cycles. Unlike many exiting methods [5,6,7], it requires no user's intervention. Furthermore, our algorithm is simple and runs in real time, other than Kovar's method based on DP. In addition, we overcome the error of 'time reverse' that red curve indicates (Figure 6).

Our method can greatly reduce the computation complexity of space-time registration. Suppose that the count of frames of two input motions are M and N, respectively, the computation complexity of Kovar's algorithm is $O(M \cdot N)$; In contrast, the computation complexity of our algorithm drops greatly down to $O(\frac{M}{l_1} \cdot \frac{N}{l_2})$ (l_1 and l_2 are the count of cycles of input motions, respectively).

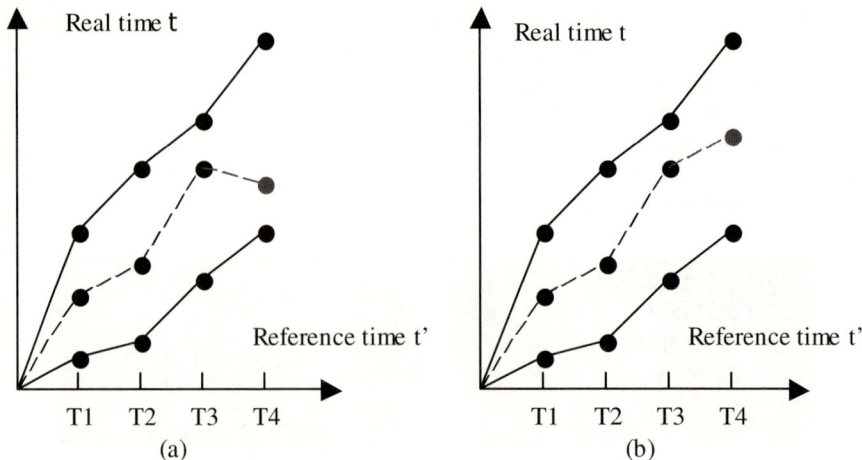

Fig. 6. The schematic diagram of the time registration step. (a) Principles of Sloan's algorithm; (b) Principles of our algorithm. Our algorithm overcomes the error of time reverse that red curve indicates.

9   Conclusion

In this paper, we propose a new algorithm for human motion interpolation based on space-time registration. The algorithm includes time registration, space registration, parameter interpolation and constraint reconstruction.

Experimental results demonstrate that our algorithm succeeds in interpolating input motions. Furthermore, our method can greatly reduce the computation complexity of space-time registration and can avoid the error of time reverse.

Reference

1. Park M. J., Choi M. G., Shin S. Y: Human motion reconstruction from inter-frame feature correspondences of a single video stream using a motion library. In Proc. of the 2002 ACM SIGGRAPH/Eurographics symposium on Computer animation. **ACM Press**(2002), 113-120.
2. Menardais S., Multon F., Kulpa R., Arnaldi B.: Motion blending for real-time animation while accounting for the environment. In Proceeding of Computer Graphics International (2004), 156- 159.
3. Bruderlin A., Williams L.: Motion signal processing. In Proc. of SIGGRAPH, ACM Press(1995), 97-104.
4. Sloan P., Rose C., Cohen M.: Shape by Example. In Proc. of 2001 Symposium on Interactive 3D Graphics , ACM Press(2001), 135 – 143.
5. Guo S., Robergé J.: A high-level control mechanism for human locomotion based on parametric frame space interpolation. In Proc. of the Eurographics workshop on computer animation and simulation(1996), 95—107.
6. Rose C., Bodenheimer B., Cohen M.: Verbs and Adverbs: Multidimensional Motion Interpolation. IEEE Computer Graphics and Applications(1998) 18(5), 32-41.

7. Park M., Shin S.: Example-based motion cloning. Computer animation and virtual worlds(2004), 15, 245-257.
8. Kovar L., Gleicher M.: Flexible Automatic Motion Blending with Registration Curve. In Proc. of Eurographics/SIGGRAPH Symposium on Computer Animation. ACM Press (2003), 214–224.
9. Kovar L., Gleicher M., Pighin F.: Motion Graphs. In Proc. of SIGGRAPH 2002, ACM Press(2002), 473-482.
10. Kovar L., Gleicher M.: Flexible Automatic Motion Blending with Registration Curve. In Proc. of Eurographics/SIGGRAPH Symposium on Computer Animation. ACM Press(2003), 214–224.
11. Perlin K.: Real time responsive animation with personality. IEEE Transactions on. Visualization and Computer Graphics (1995), 5-15.
12. Witkin A., Popovic Z.: Motion warping. In Proc. of SIGGRAPH, ACM Press(1995), 105-108.

Multi-stream Based Rendering Resource Interception and Reconstruction in D3DPR for High-Resolution Display

Zhen Liu, Jiaoying Shi, Hua Xiong, and Aihong Qin

State Key Lab of CAD&CG, Zhejiang University, 310027,HangZhou, PRC
{liuzhen, jyshi, xionghua, qinaihong}@cad.zju.edu.cn

Abstract. In order to bring Direct3D9 application to run on PC clusters for high-resolution display with no modification, we have firstly presented D3DPR parallel rendering system. According to multi-stream scene data organization and storage mode of Direct3D9, rendering resource has been classified as command stream, vertex stream, index stream and texture stream in D3DPR and the rendering resource interception and reconstruction becomes the most crucial problem. In this paper, above all we give an overview of D3DPR system architecture. Subsequently we bring forward multi-stream based rendering resource interception in D3DPR. In this section, we design DPGL, i.e. Direct3D9-based Parallel Graphics Library, through which the rendering information of Direct3D9 application can be converted into the above described rendering resource. Finally we focus on multi-stream based rendering resource reconstruction in D3DPR, through which the rendering command and scene data was reconstructed.

1   Introduction

With technological advances, large-high resolution displays are becoming prevalent in many fields, such as immersive virtual environment, command and control centers, geospatial imagery and video, scientific visualization, public information displays, vehicle design and so on [10]. Because standard computer monitors have remained at a resolution of around one million pixels, usually these high-resolution displays require the combination of several display devices into a single display environment, providing large physical size and high resolution by combining several images [11].

Traditionally, high-resolution display virtual environment has been driven primarily by powerful graphics supercomputers, such as SGIs Onyx System. Unfortunately, it comes at high cost. However the emergency of high-performance 3D commodity graphics cards has opened the way to use PC clusters for high-resolution display virtual environment.

In order to exploit the available and potential parallel rendering ability, we must take into account important design considerations associated with PC clusters rendering for high-resolution display system. These issues involve parallel

Z. Pan et al. (Eds.): ICAT 2006, LNCS 4282, pp. 48–57, 2006.

rendering library and interface, sorting in the rendering pipeline, task distributing, load balancing and network performance etc. Among them, the parallel rendering interface is a critical factor and determines whether the user could make use of the parallel system conveniently. Most research in parallel rendering field has focused on OpenGL interface. With respect that Direct3D has been developed rapidly and widely used in multimedia, entertainment, games, 3D animation and 3D graphics computation, it is imperious to develop a Direct3D interface to the users. We firstly presented D3DPR [9], a Direct3D9-based parallel rendering system, which is applied to high-resolution environment. It allows that Direct3D9 application can run on PC clusters with no modification. D3DPR parallel system has two type of logical node, one is Geometry Distributing Node (D-node), and the other is Geometry Rendering Node (R-node). Because Direct3D9 library is medium layer between Direct3D9 application and graphics hardware, the rendering resource interception on D-node of Direct3D9 application and reconstruction on R-node is the key problem of D3DPR. Compared with OpenGL, Direct3D9 provides COM-based interface and multi-stream scene data organization to the application. Therefore in this paper, we will research on multi-stream based rendering resource interception and reconstruction in D3DPR parallel system.

This paper is organized as Follows. The following section reviews the background and related work in parallel rendering. Section 3 describes multi-stream scene data organization and storage in Direct3D9. Section 4 gives an overview of D3DPR system architecture. Section 5 and section 6 explains rendering resource interception and reconstruction algorithm in D3DPR. Section 7 shows one experimental result. Finally in section 8, we will conclude our work and discuss future work.

2   Background and Related Work

2.1   Parallel Rendering Algorithm Classification

In 1994, Molnar et al. described a parallel rendering algorithm classification based on where the sort takes place in the translation from object coordinates to screen coordinates [1]. This is believed to be fundamental whenever both geometry processing and rasterization are performed in parallel. To summarize their classification scheme, parallel rendering algorithms fall into one of three classes: sort-first (early during geometry processing), sort-middle (between geometry processing and rasterization) and sort-last (after rasterization), shown as Fig. 1.

2.2   Popular PC Clusters Based Parallel Rendering System

Many famous universities and institutes, for instance Stanford, Princeton, UIUC and Zhejiang University etc, have devoted to the field of parallel rendering based on PC clusters, which supports high-resolution environment. A number of excellent systems have been produced. Stanford University Computer Graphics

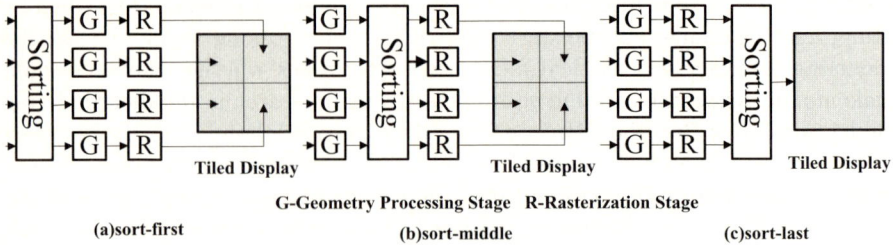

Fig. 1. Parallel Rendering Algorithms Classification

Lab designed WireGL [2] and its successor Chromium [3]. WireGL is the first sort-first graphics rendering system on PC clusters and is platform-independent to hardware. Chromium provides Stream Processing Unit (SPU) and can be configured to sort-first, sort-last and hybrid parallel graphics architecture.

Princeton University described four different systems to do parallel rendering [4].GL-DLL Replacement implements the OpenGL API in a fashion comparable to WireGL, although not as optimized. System-level Synchronized Execution (SSE) and Application-level Synchronized Execution (ASE) are comparable to the Aura [7] Multiple Copies renderer. The fourth renderer is not a really renderer but a virtual display (VDD) and is used for 2D (desktop) rendering. The integrated Systems Lab at University of Illinois at Urbana Champaign presented DGD (Distributed Graphics Database) [5], which provides the user with a scene graph interface and hides all parallel rendering related issues underneath it. Now DGD project has been renamed to Syzygy [6].

State Key Lab of CAD&CG in Zhejiang University has presented several PC clusters based parallel rendering systems for high-resolution display, such as AnyGL [13], MSPR [12] and D3DPR [9]. AnyGL is a hybrid sort-first and sort-last rendering system, which supports large scale geometry data distributing rendering with high scalability. MSPR is a retained-mode based multi-screen parallel rendering system that offers programmers OpenGL-like API. D3DPR provides completely transparent Direct3D9 application parallelization.

3   Multi-stream Scene Data Organization and Storage

In order to intercept rendering resource of Direct3D9 application on D-node and reconstruct them on R-node in D3DPR parallel rendering system, first of all we should focus on how the scene data are organized and stored in Direct3D9 application.

3.1   Multi-stream Scene Data

Direct3D9 library provides Vertex Buffer and Index Buffer for application to organize scene data. Vertex Buffer, represented by IDirect3DVertexBuffer9 interface, is sequential memory to store vertex data of scene, including position, normal, color, material, and texture coordinate etc. Index Buffer, represented by IDirect3DIndexBuffer9 interface, is sequential memory to store index information for addressing topological relationship of vertex data in the Vertex Buffer [8]. This manner that vertex data and index data are stored sequentially by Vertex Buffer and Index Buffer can be defined as stream-based scene data organization. Furthermore, if position, normal, color, material and texture coordinate property of vertex data was stored in different Vertex Buffer, this manner could be named for multi-stream scene data organization and each Vertex Buffer could be considered as one stream. But for once specific rendering, multiple Vertex Buffers could only correspond to one Index Buffer.

3.2   Multi-stream Scene Data Layout

Conceptually, the vertex declaration is a way of programming the vertex direct memory access (DMA) and tessellator engine of the Direct3D9 graphics pipeline. It expresses the stream-based data layout and the tessellator operation concisely. To address the complexity and extensibility of declaration in Direct3D9, vertex streams are now declared with an array of D3DVERTEXELEMENT9 structures. Each element of the array describes one vertex property, such as position, normal or texture coordinate. This is a new style of declaration that replaces the older style that uses flexible vertex format (FVF) codes [8].

3.3   Multi-stream Scene Data Storage

Multi-stream scene data organized by Vertex Buffer and Index Buffer has three layers storage mode in the memory space, i.e. system memory, AGP memory and video memory of graphics card [8]. Because AGP memory, as extension of video memory, is one part of system memory and AGP bus provides a high-bandwidth path from the graphics card to system memory, AGP memory enhances the potential storage capacity of graphics card to a certain extent. Therefore the scene data, which should be stored in video memory, now can be put into AGP memory. To summarize, multi-stream scene data organization manner, formed by the combination of Vertex Buffer and Index Buffer, and its three layers storage mode is one efficient approach to implement high-performance rendering making use of Direct3D9.

4   D3DPR Overview

D3DPR uses a cluster of PCs with high-performance graphics accelerators to drive an array of projectors. It consists of two types of logical nodes, Geometry Distributing Node (D-node) and Geometry Rendering Node (R-node), shown as Fig. 2. D3DPR allows existing Direct3D9 application to run on the parallel system without any modification. According to the multi-stream scene data organization, the rendering resource of Direct3D9 application can be classified as command stream, vertex stream, index stream and texture stream in D3DPR parallel rendering system. Through the rendering resource rendering interception

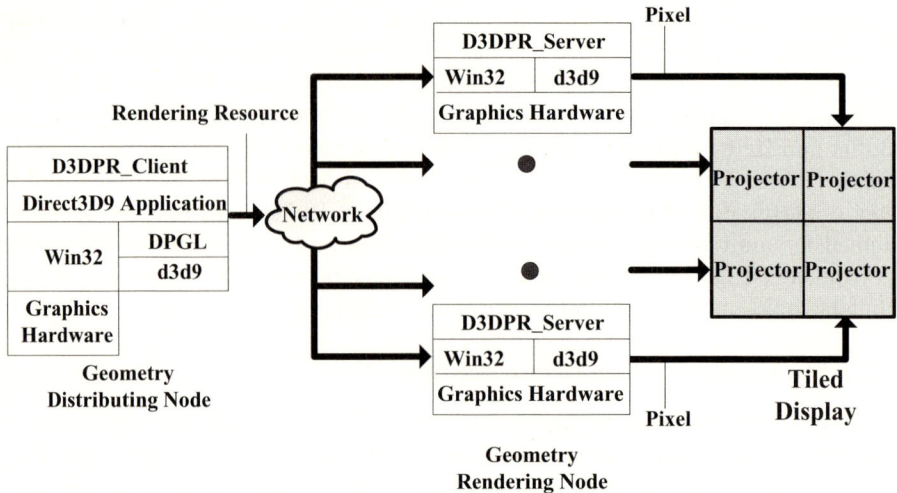

Fig. 2. D3DPR System Architecture

on D-node and rendering resource reconstruction on R-node, not only the details of network topology architecture, communication and synchronization that are related to network transmission, but also rendering resource interception, rendering resource reconstruction, data distribution strategy that are related to parallel rendering are hidden from the application. Therefore D3DPR is a completely transparent parallel rendering system that support Direct3D9 application parallelization and the tiled display environment can provide better immersion and reality to us.

5   Rendering Resource Interception in D3DPR System

As we known, Direct3D9 library is medium layer between Direct3D9 application and graphics hardware. And Direct3D9 application usually sets the current state of graphics rendering pipeline before it starts up the pipeline to render the scene by calling the "drawprimitive" method of "IDirect3DDevice9" interface. Consequently, if D-node intercepts all the render states of pipeline before its startup, it could obtain the rendering process of the application. Furthermore by intercepting from the corresponding stored memory space of vertex buffer, index buffer and texture buffer, i.e. from corresponding system memory, AGP memory or video memory, D-node could obtain the vertex stream, index stream and texture stream of Direct3D9 application. The intercepted command stream corresponds to the rendering process of application and the intercepted vertex stream, index stream and texture stream correspond to the scene geometry data of application. Although this method has eliminated the rendering resource computation, it can record the entire rendering resource of Direct3D9 application for parallel rendering.

In order to intercept the rendering resource of Direct3D9 application, we design DPGL, i.e. Direct3D9-based Parallel Graphics Library on D-node in D3DPR system. It is COM-based dynamic linked substitute library and has the same interfaces as Direct3D9 library. Because Direct3D9 library is the interface between Direct3D9 application and graphics rendering pipeline, so the substitute library DPGL can be considered as filter between Direct3D9 application and Direct3D9 library, which prevents Direct3D9 application from invoking Direct3D9 library. Through this method, DPGL can hide rendering resource interception and realize completely transparent parallelization for Direct3D9 application.

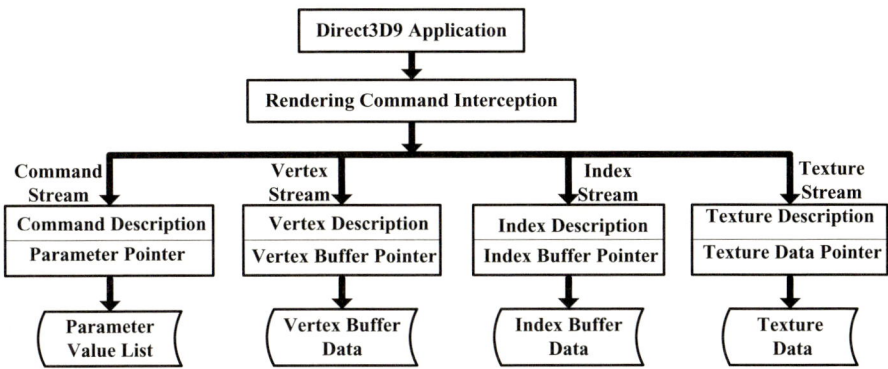

Fig. 3. D3DPR Rendering Resource Interception

Depicted as Fig. 3, when Direct3D9 application is executing on D-node in D3DPR, the rendering information of it can be converted into rendering resource described by the above four types of stream after the application routes through rendering command interception layer. The four types of stream could record the scene geometry data and rendering process of every frame of application. For each stream, DPGL should not only record the stream data, for instance parameter value list, vertex buffer data, index buffer data and texture data, but also record the description of each stream data, for instance command description, vertex description, index description and texture description. The purpose of the recorded description is to reconstruct the rendering resource on R-node in D3DPR system.

6 Rendering Resource Reconstruction in D3DPR System

For the purpose of accomplishing parallel rendering on R-node in D3DPR system, in the first place R-node should reconstruct the rendering command and scene data according to the rendering resource described by four types of stream received from the D-node, including command stream, vertex stream, index stream and texture stream.

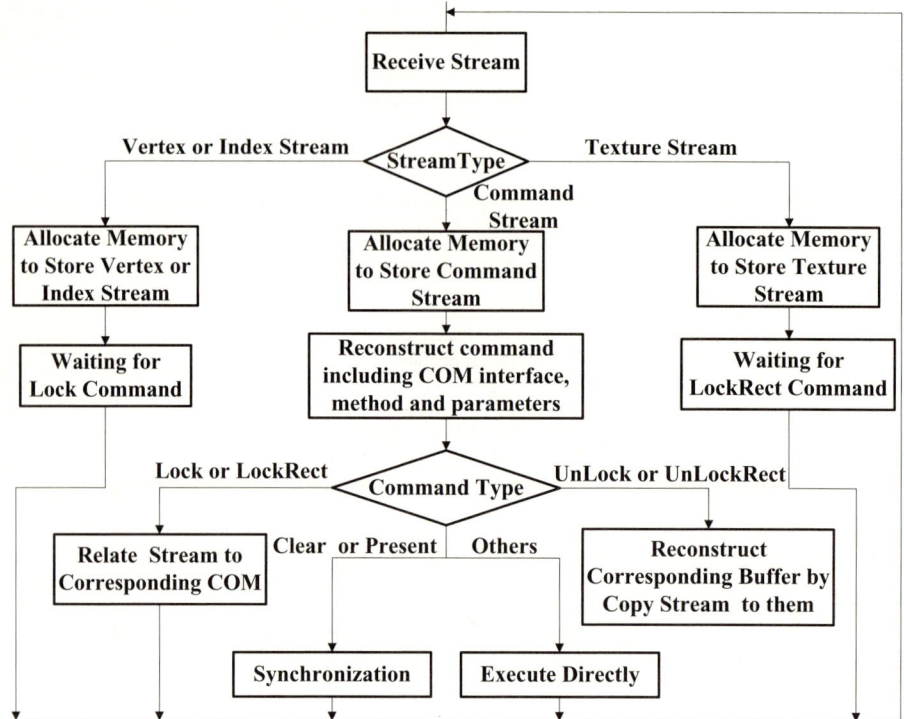

Fig. 4. D3DPR Rendering Resource Reconstruction

The reconstruction process is illuminated as Fig. 4. When the R-node having received stream from D-node, first of all it determines which type the stream belongs to. If it is vertex stream, index stream or texture stream, R-node will allocate temporary memory to store them and then wait for "Lock" method of corresponding interface. If it is command stream, R-node will reconstruct the rendering command, including COM interface, method and parameters according to the command description of rendering resource interception. Because the parameters can include COM interface, so R-node should also reconstruct them in the process. Subsequently R-node chooses which type the command attributes to. If it is Lock or "LockRect", R-node will relate the stream to the corresponding COM interface, i.e. IDirect3DVertexBuffer9, IDirect3DIndexBuffer9 or IDirect3DTexture9 and wait for "UnLock" or "UnLockRect" method. If it is "Clear" or "present", R-node should execute synchronization operation between all the R-node. And if it is others, R-node will execute the command directly. In the following performing process, R-node will reconstruct real IDirect3DVertexBuffer9, IDirect3DIndexBuffer9 or IDirect3DTexture9 by copying memory from the temporary space to the space that the reconstructed COM interface has created. Till now the above interface can represent the multi-stream scene geometry data in deed. After reconstructing all the rendering command and scene data, each R-node can render a sub-frustum of the original scene and all the R-node can be configured into single high-resolution display.

7   Experimental Result

Our experiment is performed on 5 PCs that are connected via 1000M Ethernet network. Each PC is configured as Table 1:

Table 1. PC configuration

CPU	Two Intel XEON 2.4GHz
Memory	Kingston 1G DDR Memory
Mainboard	Supermicro X5DAL-G, AGP8X graphics card data transmission
Graphics Card	NVIDIA Geforce FX5950
Switch	Enterasys N7, 1000MT
Network Card	Intel Pro 1000MT dual ports

In addition, we select "StencilMirror" application from Direct3D9 SDK. The sample uses stencil buffers to implement a mirror effect. In the sample, a watery terrain scene is rendered with the water reflecting a helicopter that flies above.

In our experiment, One PC is as D-node and fours PCs are as R-node. The D-node intercepts the rendering resource of StencilMirror application and the R-node reconstructs the rendering command and scene data. And each R-node is responsible for drawing a quarter scene of the application. Experimental result is shown as Fig. 5. Four projectors have tiled into high-resolution display virtual environment and the resolution has arrived at 2048*1536.

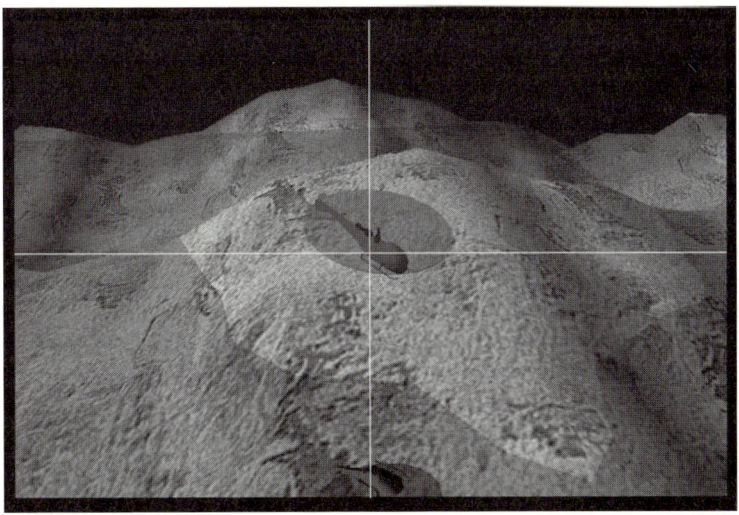

Fig. 5. High-Resolution Display of "StencilMirror" Application

8   Conclusions and Future Work

D3DPR is a Direct3D9-based parallel rendering system, which is applied to high-resolution display virtual environment. It allows Direct3D9 application to run on PC clusters with no modification. In order to accomplish the purpose, we focus on the rendering resource interception on D-node and reconstruction on R-node in this paper. It is the most crucial problem to implement D3DPR parallel rendering system. In Direct3D9, scene data is organized by multi-stream manner, so rendering resource of Direct3D9 application can be classified as command stream, vertex stream, index stream and texture stream. On D-node, we adopt COM-based dynamic linked substitute library DPGL to realize transparent interception of rendering resource. On R-node, we reconstruct the rendering command and scene data according to the received streams from D-node. Each R-node can render a sub-frustum of the original scene and all the R-node can be configured into single high-resolution display. Topics for further study include development of algorithms for improving the performance of D3DPR, including task decomposition, load balancing and communication overhead reduction etc.

Acknowledgements

This paper is supported by National Basic Research Program of China (Grant No:2002CB312105)and Key NSF Project on Digital Olympic Museum(Grant No: 60533080).

References

1. S.Molnar, M.Cox, and et al.:A Sorting Classification of Parallel Rendering. IEEE Computer Graphics and Applications, 14(4)23-32, July 1994
2. Greg Humphreys et al.:WireGL: A Scalable Graphics System for Clusters. In Proceedings of ACM SIGGRAPH 2001
3. Greg Humphreys et al.:Chromium: A Stream-Processing Framework for Interactive Rendering on Clusters. ACM Transactions on Graphics, vol 21(3), pp. 693-702, Proceedings of ACM SIGGRAPH 2002
4. K.Li, H.Chen, and et al.:Early Experiences and Challenges in Building and Using a Scalable Display Wall System. IEEE Computer Graphics and Applications, 20(4): 671-680, July/Aug, 2000
5. B.Schaeffer.:A Software System for Inexpensive VR via Graphics Clusters. http://www.isl.uiuc.edu/ClusteredVR/paper/DGDoverview.htm 2000
6. B.Schaeffer, C.Goudeseune.:Syzygy: Native PC Cluster VR", Proceeding of IEEE Virtual Reality, 2003
7. D.Germans, H.J.W. Spoelder, and et al.:VIRPI: A High-Level Toolkit for Interactive Scientific Visualization in Virtual Reality. Proc. Immersive Projection Technology/Eurographics Virtual Environments Workshop, Stuttgart, May 2001
8. Microsoft DirectX 9.0 Update (Summer 2003). http://www.microsoft.com/downloads
9. Zhen Liu et al.:D3DPR: A Direct3D-Based Large-Scale Display Parallel Rendering System Architecture for Clusters. ACSAC 2005, pp. 540 - 550, 2005

10. Tao Ni, Greg S. Schmidt, and et al.:A Survey of Large High-Resolution Display Technologies, Techniques, and Application. IEEE Virtual Reality 2006, March, 2006
11. Oliver G. Staadt, Justin Walker, and et al.:A Survey and Performance Analysis of Software Platforms for Interactive Cluster-Based Multi-Screen Rendering. In Proceedings of the Workshop on Virtual Environments 2003, pp. 261-270, Zurich, Switzerland, 2003, ACM Press
12. Chao Li, Zhefan Jin and Jiaoying Shi.: MSPR:A Retained-Mode Based Multi-screen Parallel Rendering System.The the 4th International Conference on Virtual Reality and its Application in Industry, Tianjin, P.R.China, 2003
13. Jian Yang, Jiaoying Shi, Zhefan Jin and Hui Zhang.: Design and Implementation of A Large-scale Hybrid Distributed Graphics System. Eurographics Workshop on Parallel Graphics and Visualization, Saarbruecken, Germany, 2002

VirtualPhonepad: **A Text Input Tool for Virtual Environments**

Jaewoo Ahn[1] and Kyungha Min[2,*]

[1] Mobience Inc., Seoul, Korea
[2] Sangmyung Univ., Seoul, Korea
Dept. of Digital Media, Sangmyung Univ., 7 Hongji-dong,
Jongro-gu, Seoul, 110-743, Korea
minkh@smu.ac.kr

Abstract. This paper presents an effective text input tool for virtual environments. The key idea of this paper is that we make use of the text input mechanism of mobile phones. We present a 3×3 keypad widget whose user interface is similar to the keypad of mobile phones, where each key on the widget has several characters. We present indexing schemes by which users locate the key on the keypad they want and selection schemes by which users choose the desired character from the characters on the keys of the keypad using diverse input devices.

1   Introduction

As applications of virtual reality are widening their influences over various areas rapidly, the number of virtual environments that need text input schemes is also increasing. For example, a user in a traditional building walkthrough application may want to send a message to other users, or a user in a virtual museum may want to ask a query about items he or she is looking at. In all these applications, a common requirement is a scheme that enables text input in virtual environments. Since the traditional keyboard is not available in these environments, it is not intuitive to develop text input schemes for virtual environments. In this paper, we present *VirtualPhonepad* scheme for text input in virtual environments. This scheme is developed by exploiting the text input scheme on mobile phones. Users who possess mobile phones send text messages using SMS (Short Message Service) applications on the phones. Most of the SMS applications on mobile phones from various vendors present simple text input mechanisms, which are intuitive to use. We analyze the mechanism of the text input of the SMS applications and design a similar text input scheme for virtual environments. Figure 1 illustrates the overview of the proposed *VirtualPhonepad* scheme. This paper is organized as follows. In Section 2, we briefly review related works, and we analyze the text input mechanism in the mobile phones in Section 3. We design the *VirtualPhonepad* in Section 4, and we implement the scheme in Section 5. In Section 6, we summarize this paper and suggest future work.

---

* Corresponding author.

Z. Pan et al. (Eds.): ICAT 2006, LNCS 4282, pp. 58–64, 2006.

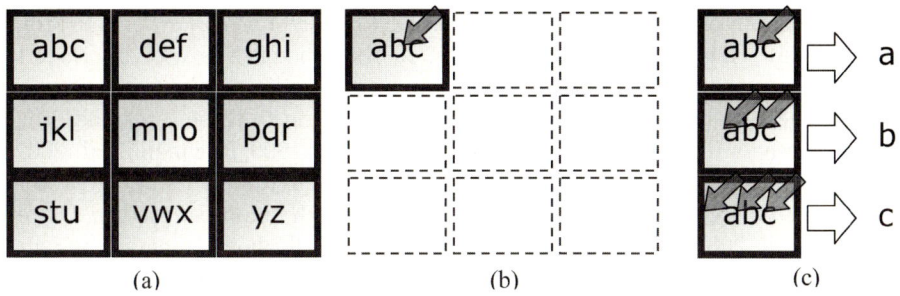

Fig. 1. Overview of the *VirtualPhonepad*: (a) User interface of the scheme, (b) Indexing a key that contains the desired character, (c) Selecting the character by pressing the key in appropriate number of times

2 Related Works

In virtual reality, several schemes have been proposed to introduce text input in immersive virtual environments. Poupyrev et. al. [Poupyrev et al. 1998] proposed a *virtual notepad*, which records characters written on a notepad in the virtual environment. This scheme enables users to leave a short hand written message in the virtual environment. This scheme, however, cannot be regarded as a text input scheme, since only the drawings of the characters written on the notepad are simply recorded and played back. Fels and Hinton [Fels & Hinton 1998] proposed *GloveTalkII* scheme that converts gestures into speech by recognizing the predefined gestures using neural nets. The hand gesture contains ten control parameters, which are combined to represent the context to express. The limitation is that the range of expressible contexts is limited and that it requires a reasonable exercise to use this scheme. Rosenberg and Slater [Rosenberg & Slater 1999] presented a *chording glove*, which interprets combinations of touches of fingers on a hard surface as a character. Even though this scheme can represent all the alphanumeric characters, users are required to memorize the correspondences between the characters and the chords of fingers. Bowman et. al. [Bowman et al. 2001] have presented a *virtual keyboard* implemented by a pinch glove and tested its usability over other text input schemes. This scheme presents an intuitive interface for the text input by displaying the keyboard in immersive virtual environments and selecting the characters on the keyboard by the interactions of the pinch glove. This scheme, however, suffers from the inefficiency of the input procedure. Shin and Hong [Shin & Hong 2006] presents the *Keypad glove* scheme for the text input in wearable computing environments. A data glove in one hand plays the role of keypad of a mobile phone by assigning each key to the corresponding finger segment on the glove, and the other hand plays the role of pressing the key. The difference from the selection step of the text input scheme in a mobile phone is that a character among the characters on a key is selected directly by assigning different indices to the three fingers of the other hand.

Frees et. al. [Frees et al. 2006] have presented *Connect The Dot* scheme for text input in immersive virtual environments. In the scheme, the user interface is composed of nine dots organized in 3×3 structure. Users input characters by connecting the dots in some predefined orders. In addition to these researches, several researchers [Thomas et al. 1998, Lindeman et al. 1999, Bowman et al. 2002] have tested existing text input schemes for virtual environments and wearable computing environments and compared them through empirical studies. Ogi et al. [Ogi et al. 2001] have exploited the interface of cell phone in navigating virtual environments. However, they didn't provide any text input schemes in their works.

3   Analysis of the Text Input Mechanism on Mobile Phones

The fundamental operation of the text input mechanism for alphabetic characters is to choose one of possible twenty six characters. When we use a device that has twenty six individual keys each of which is dedicated only to one alphabetic character such as a keyboard or a typewriter, the only operation required to enter a character is to locate the key that contains the desired character. Mobile devices whose small sizes do not support full-sized keyboard require some mechanisms that enable text input for the devices. The text input mechanisms developed for such devices can be classified into two categories: using keypads of limited keys or using character recognition techniques. Many mobile phones use the keypad-based mechanism and many PDA's use the recognition-based mechanism. We focus on the keypad-based mechanism used in mobile phones. In the keypad-based approach, each key on the keypad contains about three characters due to the limited number of keys. The basic philosophy of the text input operation in this approach is to separate the operation into two steps. The first step, which is denoted as indexing process, is to locate a key whose character set contains the desired character and the second step, which is denoted as selection process, is to select the desired character from the set. In most of the mobile phones, the selection process is commonly practiced by repeatedly pressing the key. For example, a user who wants to enter "A" indexes a key that contains the character set of "A B C" and presses it once, and a user who wants to enter "B" indexes the same key and presses it twice, and so on.

4   Design of *VirtualPhonepad*

4.1   Basic Concept

The *VirtualPhonepad* is designed by a combination of a widget and a text input scheme. The widget, which is similar to the keypad of mobile phones, is a 3×3 matrix of keys each of which contains several characters. Similar to the mechanism in mobile phones, the text input mechanism of *VirtualPhonepad* is composed of indexing the key whose character set contains the desired character and selecting the character from the character set.

4.2   Design of the Widget

The design strategy of the widget is to arrange 26 alphabet characters and a space character in 3×3 keypad. The configuration of the keys can be modified according to that of the keys on users' mobile phone. The benefit of the 3×3 structure over the 3×4 structure is that each key on 3×3 structure corresponds to the nine directions in two dimensional coordinate, which is a combination of (up, middle, down) and (left, center, right). This benefit extends the possible devices for text input even to joystick devices, whose only inputs are direction information.

4.3   Indexing

Indexing a key is implemented in two ways. One way is to trace the position of the device and identify the key whose position is occupied by the pointer of the device, and the other way is to recognize the direction of the input device and identify the key that is lying on the direction.

4.4   Selection

In the case of phones, the number of key presses within a predefined time interval selects a character on the key. For example, pressing a key that contains "A", "B", and "C" once selects "A", twice selects "B", and three times selects "C". This selection scheme is due to the limited input interface of phones. In this paper, we use two classes of selection schemes.

Single-button Device: The selection scheme for single-button devices is designed by the number of key presses. For this scheme, we assign a threshold value t_p to the time interval between the key presses for the selection. A subsequent press of a button within t_p denotes that it is for the current character selection. Similarly, a press not within t_p denotes that it is for the next character selection.

Multi-button Device: The selection scheme for multi-button devices can be designed by utilizing the multiple buttons. We assign different selection identifiers for the individual buttons or fingers on such devices. The selection schemes for the devices exploited in this paper are listed as follows:

  Data glove: When using a data glove, we assign the selection function to different fingers. For example, the index finger denotes the first character on the button, the middle finger denotes the second, and the ring finger denotes the third.

  Two-button mouse: When using a two-button mouse, the left-button click denotes the first character, the right-button click denotes the second, and simultaneous presses of left-button and the right-button denotes the third.

  Multi-button joystick: Similar to the case of a two-button mouse, combinations of buttons in the joystick can be used to select a character from the character sets on a button.

5   Implementation of *VirtualPhonepad*

Figure 2 illustrates the snapshots of *VirtualPhonepad*. We present a visual feedback by changing the color of the key and by displaying the selected character in bold-face.

We have tested *VirtualPhonepad* scheme in four different versions classified by the indexing scheme and the selection scheme. The indexing scheme is either to direct the key by a data glove or to position the key by a mouse, and the selection scheme is either to press the key with a button repeatedly within a predefined time interval (single-button) or to press the key with different buttons or combinations of the buttons (multi-button). We have grouped twenty subjects

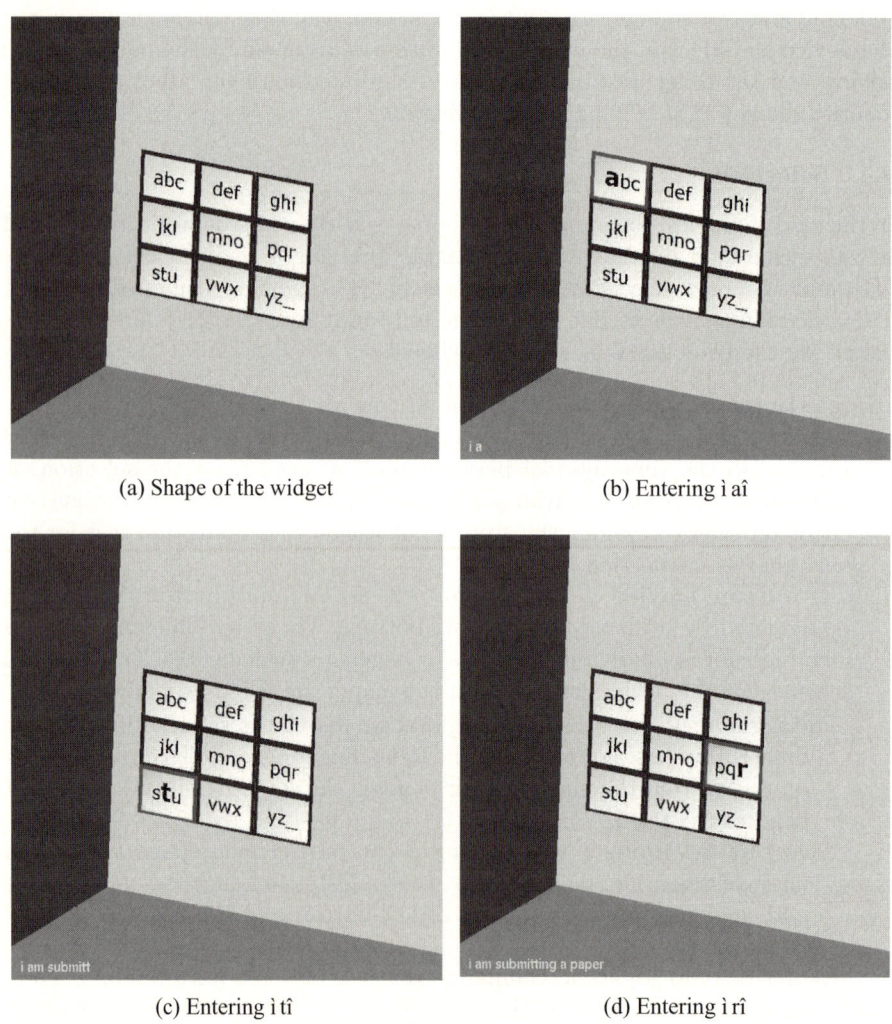

(a) Shape of the widget   (b) Entering ì aî

(c) Entering ì tî   (d) Entering ì rî

Fig. 2. Screen-shots of *VirtualPhonepad* scheme

	single-button	multi-button
directing	12.8 (15.3)	15.6 (19.2)
positioning	10.7 (13.1)	14.3 (17.5)

Fig. 3. Comparing performances of combining various selection schemes and indexing schemes. Note that single-button and multi-button are selection schemes and directing and positioning are indexing schemes. The number indicates words per minute.

into four different versions of the *VirtualPhonepad* and tested the scheme by entering five different sentences. We also have tested them at the final step by entering the first sentence again. The result is illustrated in Figure 3.

The test reveals that the combination of directing and multi-button makes the best performance. The number in parenthesis is the average performance for the re-entry of the first sentence. We have got an experimental argument that the most bottleneck of the text input process is the unfamiliarity of the character locations on the keypad. This argument is somewhat proved in that the performance of the input is improved as experiments are progressed, although it has limitations.

6   Conclusion and Future Work

In this paper, we have presented *VirtualPhonepad*, a text input scheme for virtual environments. The scheme is proved to be very powerful and robust in comparison to other text input schemes. The future research direction is to improve the scheme to include the numerics and symbols as well. We are going to find a new arrangement of the characters on the keypad so that it is familiar and intuitive to users for an improved text input tool in virtual environments.

References

[Bowman et al. 2001] Bowman, D. and Wingrave, D. and Campbell, J. and Ly, V.: Using Pinch Gloves for both Natural and Abstract Interaction Techniques in Virtual Environments. Proceedings of HCI International, 629–633, 2001.

[Bowman et al. 2002] Bowman, D. and Rhoton, C. and Pinho, M.: Text Input Techniques for Immersive Virtual Environments: an Empirical Comparison. Proceedings of the Human Factors and Ergonomics Society Annual Meeting, 2154–2158, 2002.

[Fels & Hinton 1998] Fels, S. and Hinton, G.: Glove Talkll: A Neural Network Interface which Maps Gestures to Parallel Formant Speech Synthesizer Controls. IEEE Transactions on Neural Networks, **9(1)**, 205–212, 1998.

[Frees et al. 2006] Frees, S. and Khouri, R. and Kessler, G.: Connecting the Dots: Simple Text Input in Immersive Environments, Proceedings of IEEE Virtual Reality, 25–29, 2006.

[Lindeman et al. 1999] Lindeman, R. and Sibert, J. and Hahn, J.: Towards Usable VR: An Empirical Study of User Interfaces for Immersive Virtual Environments, Proc. Of the SIGCHI '99, 64–71, 1999.

[Ogi et al. 2001] Ogi, T. and Yamamoto, K. and Yamada, T. and Hirose, M: Experience of Virtual World Using Cellular Phone Interface, Proceedings of IEEE PCM 2001, 32-39, 2001.

[Poupyrev et al. 1998] Poupyrev, I. and Tomokazu, N. and Weghorst, S.: Virtual Notepad: handwriting in immersive VR. Proceedings of the Virtual Reality Annual International Symposium, 126–132, 1998.

[Rosenberg & Slater 1999] Rosenberg, R. and and Slater, M.: A Chording Glove: A Glove Based Text Input Device, IEEE Transactions on Systems, Man, and Cybernetics, **29(2)**, 186–191, 1999.

[Shin & Hong 2006] Shin, J.H. and Hong, K.S.: Keypad gloves: glove based text input device and input method for wearable computers, Electronics Letters, **41(16)**, 15–16, 2006.

[Thomas et al. 1998] Thomas, B. and Tyerman, S. and Grimmer, K.: Evaluation of Text Input Mechanisms for Wearable Computers. Virtual Reality, **3(3)**, pp. 187-199, 1998.

An Animation System for Imitation of Object Grasping in Virtual Reality

Matthias Weber, Guido Heumer, Heni Ben Amor, and Bernhard Jung

VR and Multimedia Group
TU Bergakademie Freiberg
Freiberg, Germany
{matthias.weber, guido.heumer, amor, jung}@informatik.tu-freiberg.de

Abstract. Interactive virtual characters are nowadays commonplace in games, animations, and Virtual Reality (VR) applications. However, relatively few work has so far considered the animation of interactive object manipulations performed by virtual humans. In this paper, we first present a hierarchical control architecture incorporating plans, behaviors, and motor programs that enables virtual humans to accurately manipulate scene objects using different grasp types. Furthermore, as second main contribution, we introduce a method by which virtual humans learn to imitate object manipulations performed by human VR users. To this end, movements of the VR user are analyzed and processed into abstract actions. A new data structure called *grasp events* is used for storing information about user interactions with scene objects. High-level plans are instantiated based on grasp events to drive the virtual humans' animation. Due to their high-level representation, recorded manipulations often naturally adapt to new situations without losing plausibility.

1 Introduction

Achieving realistic body movement in virtual humans for interactive object manipulations is still a difficult task. Previous work in this field has led to two different approaches to realistic character animation: data-driven methods, using motion-capture data, and model-driven methods, synthesizing animations at runtime. Usually, the data-driven approaches suffer from limited adaptability to new situations, such as changing environments and different character proportions. Model-driven approaches on the other hand allow for high adaptability but suffer from an increasing number of control parameters. This normally results in a tedious trial-and-error process for finding an accurate set of parameters. Although one could hard-wire such parameters in a model-driven animation system, flexibility against modified objects or differently sized virtual humans would be lost as a consequence.

This paper follows a novel, imitation based approach to animation called *Action Capture* [1] which combines the strengths of data-driven and model-driven techniques. The interactions of a real user with the virtual environment are recorded, processed and abstracted, such that they can be adapted to new

Z. Pan et al. (Eds.): ICAT 2006, LNCS 4282, pp. 65–76, 2006.

situations. This allows for fast and easy recording of new animations without need for parameter optimization and, at the same time, also enables the flexible reproduction of interactions with scene objects.

While the generic conceptual framework for Action Capture including its relationships to the fields of imitation learning and robotics has been described elsewhere [1], this contribution focusses on the details of a specific implementation for imitation of object grasping by virtual humans. For this, a hierarchical control architecture for animation of virtual humans is realized. On the highest level of abstraction plans describe animations as sequences of object interactions. Plans instantiate goal-oriented behaviors to influence body movement. Behaviors use low-level motor programs to directly move the body's limbs. Additionally, for storing information about user interactions with scene objects a new data structure called *grasp events* is introduced. In turn, grasp events are converted into high-level plans in order to drive the virtual human's movement.

This imitation-based approach provides great ease-of-use when creating animations for object grasping. Taking full advantage of immersive VR, the animation process reproduces a human user's natural 3D interactions without the need for cumbersome retargetting of motion capture data or trial-and-error parameter optimization. After discussing related work, the remainder of this paper presents an operational system implementing the imitation-based approach to character animation.

2   Related Work

In order to enable a virtual human to manipulate other objects, it is of importance to specify different meaningful ways of interaction. An interesting approach to this was introduced by Kallmann and Thalmann [2]. The basic idea of the *smart object* approach is that each object "knows" the way an interaction with it should look like. Additionally, each object stores a number of parameters and other meta-data, that can be accessed and used by the virtual human. This meta-data has to be specified by the system developer when creating the objects and the world. Still, there is the question of how to synthesize an appropriate animation from this data. Early work on animation and control for manipulation and grasping was reported by Sanso and Thalmann [3]. Kuffner and colleagues [4] proposed the use of a path planner and inverse kinematics in order to plan a collision-free trajectory connecting an initial arm position with a goal position. In an extension of this algorithm [5] they were also able to bias the inverse kinematics algorithm towards natural-looking poses using a motion database. In contrast to this, the work of Douville et al. [6] describes a *behavioral* approach to motion synthesis. Here, different objects are grasped using specialized grasping behaviors and an *object specific reasoner*. The latter helps to break down the high-level plans into motions.

In many applications it is desirable to have a virtual human imitate the behavior of a real person while at the same time being subject to the physics of its own virtual environment. While this approach preserves the plausibility of the animation, it also demands for special algorithms which can abstract actions from raw motion capture data. Such algorithms have long been studied in the robotics and Artificial Intelligence literature; a survey on this topic was published by Jung et al. [1]. Pollard and Zordan [7] present an algorithm, which extracts a set of parameters from motion capture data. The parameters are in turn fed into a controller used for performing active and passive grasping.

The system presented in this paper combines several of the above ideas with a hierarchical architecture for animation synthesis. In contrast to previous work, the motion capture data is not only used for parametrizing particular controllers or behaviors. Instead, the motion is analyzed, abstracted and transformed into an intermediate representation. This allows the recorded action to be performed in different environments and settings.

3   Animation Synthesis

This section presents a hierarchical control architecture for interactive animation of virtual humans, with a particular focus on animating object manipulation tasks. The architecture is currently implemented as an extension of the VR system *Avango* [8]. In principle, however, it is independent of any particular VR software. At its core, the framework consists of hierarchically organized modules at three distinct levels: plans, behaviors, and motor programs.

Fig. 1 gives an overview of the control architecture. In general, the control flow for animation synthesis is as follows: High-level plans are abstract descriptions of action sequences. The selection and execution of plans can be triggered by issuing an appropriate command from Avango's integrated Scheme interpreter. Execution of a plan will instantiate several behaviors which in turn start one or more motor programs to control the basic movements of the virtual human, i.e. changing bone rotations of the virtual character's skeleton. Behaviors are notified about collisions occurring between body parts and scene objects, e.g. when grasping an object. They can decide if it is necessary to stop movement when collisions occur. Behaviors terminate when all motor programs finished. A plan stops when all behaviors were terminated.

Motor Programs. On the lowest level of the animation synthesis hierarchy, motor programs control the joint values of a virtual human's bones. The specification of a motor program defines different parameters, e.g. target joint values. Additionally a scope has to be defined, i.e. the set of bones influenced by its execution in the kinematic chain of the skeleton. Motor programs do not directly set joint values, but instead modify so-called motor states. A motor state represents the orientation of a bone at a certain time. After a motor program has calculated a new state, the state is passed to an arbiter component. As many motor programs may run in parallel, conflicts may occur when calculating motor states referring to the same bone. Conflicts are resolved by the arbiter through motor state priorities, which were set by associated motor programs. The arbiter then sets the consolidated joint values. This way resolution of conflicting bone movements occurs on a fine-granular motor state level rather than on the complete

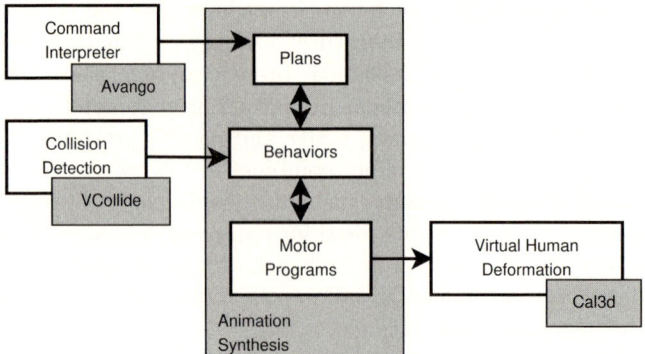

Fig. 1. Control architecture

scope of the motor program, i.e. set of influenced bones, or on the higher level of behaviors. Two types of motor programs are currently supported. One type interpolates motor states from current states to specified goal states, defining the end-posture for a part of the virtual human. The second type uses inverse kinematics to let a kinematic chain of arbitrary length reach a certain position.

Behaviors. Mid-level behaviors are used to accomplish certain sub-actions of object manipulations, like closing a hand or reaching for an object. To realize movements of the virtual human, they select and instantiate motor programs, that work directly on the kinematic chain of the virtual human. Behaviors are parametrized, allowing them to reactively adapt to changing virtual scenes. E.g. moving objects can be reached by only setting the object's name as a parameter and letting the behavior calculate where the object is currently located. There are currently four types of behaviors to accomplish different tasks: Open a hand, close a hand to grasp an object, reach a certain point or object, and move joints to a given end or rest posture. These behaviors can be adjusted with parameters like begin and end time or the object to interact with.

Plans. On the highest level, plans describe complete manipulation tasks, e.g. grasping an object, in a declarative fashion. They consist of plan steps, which can be executed either sequentially or in parallel. Plans are described in an XML-based language. Fig. 2 shows a simple example of such a plan description. Instantiating the plan `grasp-object` with the object `Ball-1`, the grasp port `ball-port`, the hand `RightHand` and the grasp type `spherical` as parameters results in selecting the plan out of a plan database and refining the plan by substituting variables in the plan with the parameters (variables in this example are `$OBJECT`, `$PORT`, `$HAND` and `$GRASPTYPE` respectively). It is not necessary for the triggering command to specify all parameters of a plan: For example, if just the target object of the grasp is specified, then suitable values for `$PORT`, `$HAND` and `$GRASPTYPE` will be automatically added, e.g. using default values or object annotations (see below for a description). In the example, first a parallel

```
<plan>
  <name>grasp-object</name>
  <parallel>
    <behavior>
      <type>Reach</type>
      <vh_name>Body</vh_name>
      <param name="object">$OBJECT</param>
      <param name="grasp-port">$PORT</param>
    </behavior>
    <behavior>
      <type>GraspOpen</type>
    </behavior>
  </parallel>
  <behavior>
    <type>GraspClose</type>
    <param name="grasp-type">$GRASPTYPE</param>
  </behavior>
</plan>
```

Fig. 2. Example for a plan: grasping an object

set of plan steps is instantiated for reaching the grasp port `ball-port` on the object `Ball-1` and for opening the hand. The type <`type`>, the name of the virtual character affected <`vh_name`>, and several parameters <`param`> can be specified for such behaviors. After reaching the object with an open and correctly oriented hand, the hand is closed (behavior type `GraspClose`) using a specified or automatically inferred grasp type from a grasp taxonomy. When the object is grasped, the plan finishes.

Annotated Objects. To support movement generation, semantically *annotated objects* are used in behaviors to, e.g. find a proper place on a chosen object to grasp. Grasp ports define positions on an object, where grasping is possible. Additionally, they describe the shape of the object at that position so it is possible to choose an appropriate hand shape for grasping. Annotated objects are akin to the concept of *smart objects* in literature (e.g. Kallman and Thalmann [2]), differing in the way that we do not explicitly describe behaviors in the objects. Annotated objects are represented in XML structures; see Fig. 3 as an example. In this example the object type `Ball` is defined. Besides a specified scale factor (`scale`), one grasp port with a spherical form (`type="SPHERICAL"`) is defined. The grasp port has a unique name `ball-port`, a certain position (`position`) and a radius (`radius`). Finally, the graphical model to load for the annotated object is specified.

Virtual Human Body and Hand Model. In skeletal animation, a virtual character's body is represented by a polygon mesh and a skeleton composed of bones. In our system, the virtual humans' skeleton structures are based on the joint hierarchy of the H-Anim standard (`http://www.hanim.org`). Every bone is

```
<annotated-object>
  <name>Ball</name>
  <scale>0.00595 0.00595 0.00595</scale>
  <grasp-port type="SPHERICAL">
    <name>ball-port</name>
    <position>0.0 0.0 0.0</position>
    <radius>5.775</radius>
  </grasp-port>
  <model>models/iv/ball2.iv</model>
</annotated-object>
```

Fig. 3. Example for an annotated object: A Ball

represented with a name and its orientation and translation relative to it's parent bone. Several virtual characters can populate a scene, acting independently of each other. Additionally, virtual characters can be composed of several independent articulated models. We use this method to integrate different models for body, right and left hand. In this way, the modelling of the virtual human's body is separated from the modelling of its hands. Thus, the hands, which are more complex to model, can be easily re-used with different bodies. Fig. 4 shows the skeletons of a virtual human and of the right hand.

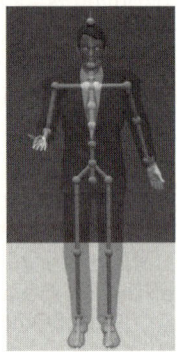 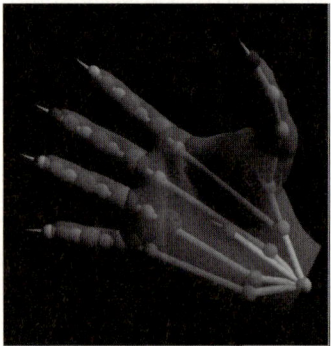

Fig. 4. Skeletons of virtual human and right hand

Since the focus of our animations is on object manipulation, particular effort has been put into a detailed virtual hand model. Just as the virtual character's body, the hand model is a skinned mesh, deformed by an underlying skeleton structure. Each finger consists of three segments/bones, with the proximal joints having two degrees of freedom (flexion and pivot) and the others only having one (flexion). Additionally, joint angle constraints are enforced, to permit natural looking movements only.

For interaction and collision detection with scene objects, the hand model has been fitted with spherical collision sensors (see Fig. 4). Currently, there is one sensor in the palm, one sensor in each finger segment and an additional one at each finger tip. These sensors fire collision events, as soon as they touch a scene object. This information is used by motor programs and behaviors to adjust the animation in turn to avoid intersection of the hand with the objects.[1]

Collision detection is currently implemented using VCollide [9]. For the visual part, to realize skeletal animation and mesh deformation according to the bone movements, the character animation library Cal3d (`http://cal3d.sourceforge. net`) is used.

4 Imitating Grasp Actions

In the previous section, the process of an autonomous movement generation for virtual character animation was described. Movement is triggered by instructing the virtual character to execute specific plans. In this section, we introduce an alternative method in which the virtual character learns to *imitate* object manipulations performed by a human VR user.

To this end, the interactions of the VR user with scene objects are analyzed and transformed to plans, that can be executed by virtual characters using the animation synthesis architecture described above. Animations are thus generated by recording and analyzing movement data from virtual reality input devices. Such devices could be, but are not limited to, optical position trackers and data gloves. The recorded data is processed to calculate certain features to describe a grasp. These features are hierarchically organized from low level features – describing low level data like the joint values of a human skeleton – to high level features, where the grasp is only described by a category belonging to a grasp taxonomy[2]. Low level features need no calculation when movement of a real human is analyzed. High level features achieve high abstraction of human movement by just providing grasp types and objects to grasp. Such a high abstraction makes it possible to adapt virtual human movement to changing scenes.

Fig. 5 gives an overview of the whole process of imitating grasp actions. The two parts, movement analysis with the focus on grasp event detection and movement synthesis for the reproduction of actions, will now be described.

4.1 Analyzing User Actions for Grasp Events

Analyzing movement data involves the following steps: segmentation of the hand movement, mapping of glove sensor values to joint rotation values and calculating grasp features out of the posture of the hand and the grasped object. This process

---

[1] A further use of the hand model is to support the interactions of human VR users with the virtual world, particularly for grasp analysis (see Sec. 4). Here, the user hand is projected into the virtual world to provide visual feedback to the user as well as to find contact points with scene objects during grasps. In this case, joint angles are deducted from data glove sensor input and then mapped directly to the joints of the virtual hand.

[2] Grasp taxonomies classify grasps into several categories, describing the features of a grasp, e.g. Cutkosky [10] or Schlesinger [11].

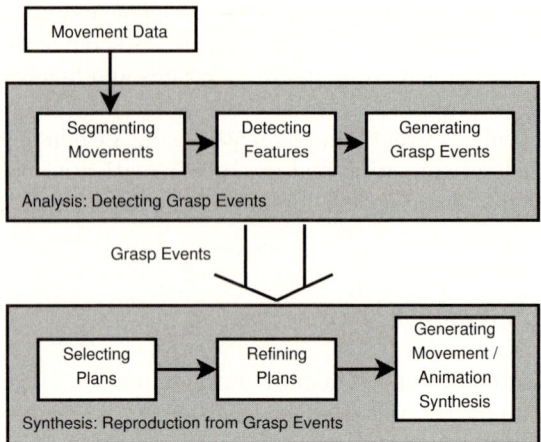

Fig. 5. Imitation process

is subject of other work and is not the focus of this paper. But the results are used to imitate human movement, especially in the domain of grasping objects.

A novel representation form is used to store the results: Grasp events. They contain grasp features, the grasp type and a time stamp. The time stamp defines when the grasp happened with respect to the time when the manipulation sequence began. Low level features include: joint values, contact points, grasped objects, and hand position. High level features denote the resulting category of a grasp w.r.t. a certain taxonomy. Grasp events can be stored in XML files for the purpose of later playback. An example for the structure of such an XML file is shown in Fig. 6.

4.2 Reproducing Actions from Grasp Events

To animate the virtual character and reproduce the recorded sequence of grasp events, the events have to be converted into executable plans. This is done in two steps (see the synthesis part of Fig. 5): First, a plan is selected, based on the received grasp events. As a simple example, this could be the plan `grasp-object` whenever events of type `grasp` are received. After that, the selected plan is refined by means of the features contained in the grasp events. Refinement is done by filling unspecified parameters of the plan with reasonable values. This can be done in a very simple way by providing the last value that was received for a parameter. Another conceivable possibility would be to use the information provided by grasp events and the actions that already took place for computing new parameters.

When only high level features, i.e. grasp taxonomy categories, are used to specify a grasp, a grasp database is used to look up the grasp type and retrieve features useful to generate a similar grasp by the virtual human. For now such useful features include the start and end postures of the grasp, see Fig. 7 for

```
<event-sequence>
  <event timestamp="3.895" type="grasp">
   <low-level>
    <joint-angle joint-id="r_index1">19.8306 -0.0865252 0.678805 0.729203
    </joint-angle>
    <contact-point joint-id="sensor_r_index1">
      <object>Ball-1</object>
      <pos>0.00730081 -0.0734563 0.0135953</pos>
    </contact-point>
    <object-ids> Ball-1 </object-ids>
    <hand-transform>0.0205884 0.211408 -0.97718 0
                    0.0805939 0.973855 0.212386 0
                    0.996533 -0.0831275 0.00301189 0
                    -0.1502 -0.626599 0.917001 1
    </hand-transform>
    <hand-side> right </hand-side>
   </low-level>
   <high-level>
    <taxonomy>schlesinger</taxonomy>
    <category>spherical</category>
   </high-level>
  </event>
  ...
</event-sequence>
```

Fig. 6. An XML example for grasp events

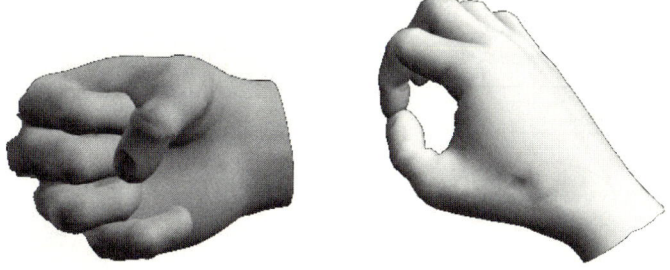

Fig. 7. Two end postures from the grasp database: cylindrical and tip

an example of end postures for the two grasp categories cylindrical and tip. In addition to this, finger groups are used for describing similar behaving fingers. Fingers in a finger group stop whenever one of the fingers stops, caused e.g. by collision detection. Unfilled parameters in a selected plan are then refined by using these features.

By execution of the refined plan, the virtual human performs the appropriate movement, using the framework described in Sec. 3. Behaviors, parametrized with the values computed by the refinement step, are instantiated, which use adequate motor programs to control virtual human movement.

5   Example

The whole process of movement generation by instruction will now be explained by considering the example of grasping a ball, as shown in Fig. 8. Grasps performed by a user are recorded and processed to generate a grasp event containing a spherical grasp for the ball Ball-1 with timestamp 3.895.

To grasp the ball Ball-1, an appropriate plan is selected and parametrized to convert the features into parameters of the plan. In this plan, parallel behaviors for reaching the grasp port of the object and for opening the hand are executed. After finishing these behaviors, a behavior for closing the hand, i.e. grabbing the object, is executed.

For reaching, the behavior will start a motor program that moves the virtual human's hand to the object's grasp port position using inverse kinematics. A scene information database is queried for information about the grasped object.

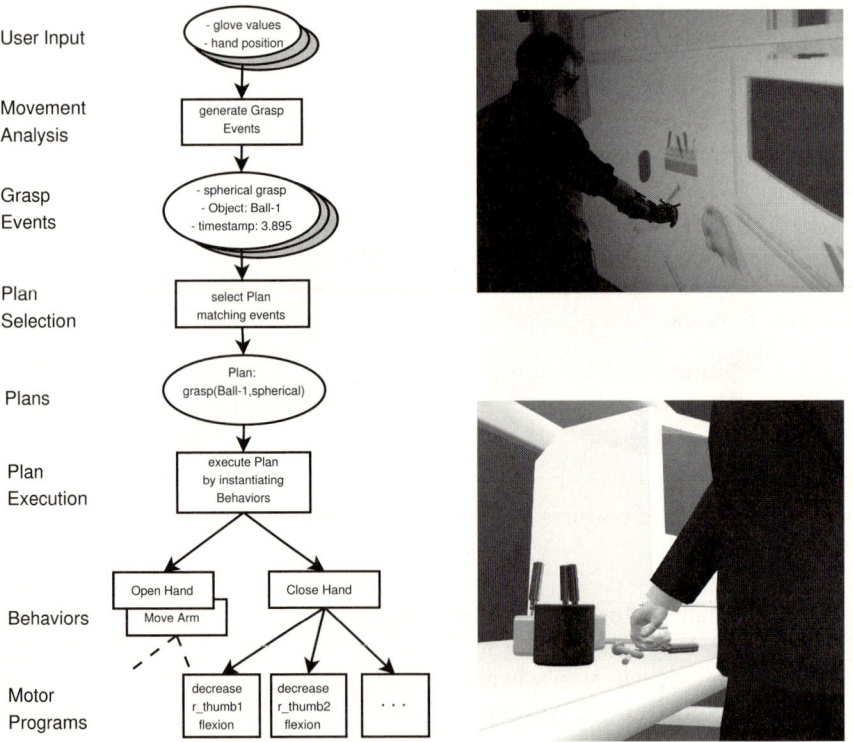

Fig. 8. Example: Imitation of grasping a ball

In this example, this would be an annotated object of type `ball` with a spherical grasp port for `Ball-1`.

Opening and closing of the hand will start motor programs that interpolate joint values to given goal motor states. These are goal angles for opening and closing the hand representing certain postures that describe an opened or closed hand respectively. When closing the hand, collision sensors are used to stop the movement of bones when fingers get contact with the annotated object.

6   Conclusion

We have presented a system for instructing virtual humans for the synthesis of virtual human-object interactions. A hierarchical three-level approach is used to generate accurate object manipulations from high-level commands. The system automatically instantiates behaviors and appropriate motor programs to control the virtual human.

Using this framework, grasps performed by a real human in a virtual environment can be imitated. For this, grasps are recorded, analyzed for grasp features, and stored as grasp events. The recorded grasp events are used to select and refine appropriate plans, which in turn trigger lower level behaviors. In this way, interactions between the human and the environment can be recorded and imitated. Due to their high-level representation, recorded manipulations often naturally adapt to new situations without losing plausibility.

In on-going work we are developing a more elaborate plan generator to create high level plans out of sequences of grasp events. With such plans it will further be possible to create a plan database containing several highly abstract representations of object manipulations in virtual environments. Additionally, we want to improve the refinement step for selecting plans. Missing parameters could, for instance, be computed based on predictors acquired through machine learning techniques. Learning could further be used for improved reproduction of different movement styles exhibited by different VR users.

Acknowledgments. The research described in this contribution is partially sponsored by the DFG (Deutsche Forschungsgemeinschaft) in the Virtual Workers project.

References

1. Jung, B., Ben Amor, H., Heumer, G., Weber, M.: From Motion Capture to Action Capture: A Review of Imitation Learning Techniques and their Application to VR-based Character Animation. In: Proceedings ACM VRST 2006, Cyprus. (2006)
2. Kallmann, M., Thalmann, D.: Direct 3D Interaction with Smart Objects. In: Proceedings ACM VRST 99, London. (1999)
3. Sanso, R.M., Thalmann, D.: A Hand Control and Automatic Grasping System for Synthetic Actors. Computer Graphics Forum **13**(3) (1994) 167–177
4. Kuffner, J., Latombe, J.: Interactive Manipulation Planning for Animated Characters. In: Proceedings of Pacific Graphics. (2000)

5. Yamane, K., Kuffner, J.J., Hodgins, J.K.: Synthesizing Animations of Human Manipulation Tasks. ACM Trans. Graph. **23**(3) (2004) 532–539
6. Douville, B., Levison, L., Badler, N.: Task-level Object Grasping for Simulated Agents. Presence **5**(4) (1996) 416–430
7. Pollard, N., Zordan, V.B.: Physically Based Grasping Control from Example. In: Proceedings of the ACM SIGGRAPH/Eurographics Symposium on Computer Animation. (2005)
8. Tramberend, H.: Avocado: A Distributed Virtual Reality Framework. In: Proceedings of IEEE Virtual Reality. (1999) 14
9. Hudson, T., Lin, M., Cohen, J., Gottschalk, S., Manocha, D.: V-COLLIDE: Accelerated Collision Detection for VRML. In: Proceedings of VRML'97. (1997)
10. Cutkosky, M.: On Grasp Choice, Grasp Models and the Design of Hands for Manufacturing Tasks. IEEE Trans. on Robotics and Automation **5**(3) (1989)
11. Schlesinger, G.: Der Mechanische Aufbau der Künstlichen Glieder. In Borchardt, M., et al., eds.: Ersatzglieder und Arbeitshilfen für Kriegsbeschädigte und Unfallverletzte. Springer-Verlag: Berlin, Germany (1919) 321–661

Generating Different Realistic Humanoid Motion

Zhenbo Li[1,2,3], Yu Deng[1,2,3], and Hua Li[1,2,3]

[1] Key Lab. of Computer System and Architecture, Institute of Computing Technology,
Chinese Academy of Sciences, Beijing 100080, P.R. China
[2] National Research Center for Intelligent Computing Systems, Institute of Computing
Technology, Chinese Academy of Sciences, Beijing 100080, P.R. China
[3] Graduate University of Chinese Academy of Sciences,
Beijing 100039, P.R. China
{zbli, dengyu, lihua}@ict.ac.cn

Abstract. Different realistic humanoid motion can be used in vary situations in animation. It also plays an important role in virtual reality. In this paper, we propose a novel method to generate different realistic humanoid motion automatically. Firstly, eigenvectors of a motion sequence is computed using principle component analysis. The principle components are served as "virtual joints" in our system. The number of "virtual joints" can be used to control the realistic level of motions. After given the "virtual joints" number, the actual joints' parameters of new motion are computed using the selected "virtual joints". The experiments illuminate that this method has good ability to generate different realistic level motions.

Keywords: PCA, DOF, Motion Capture.

1   Introduction

Humanoid motion plays an important role in games, movies etc. With its wildly use, different realistic motions are needed in many cases. Traditionally, in order to get a motion sequence, animators need to specify many key frames. However, creating these key frames is extremely labor intensive.

Motion capture technique is triumphantly used to produce motion scripts recently, which can get motion data from living human beings directly and expediently. Though motion capture lightens the burden of animators, it has two limitations: 1.people can only use the motion scripts recorded beforehand. 2. When the body proportion in animation is not suitable with the recorded body proportion; the data must be retargeted. These two limitations counteracted its using.

Humanoid motion is defined as the combination of a set of postures fi $(i=1, 2... n)$, each posture is represented by a set of degrees of freedom (DOF). The motion space is often high, generally fifty to sixty. For many behaviors, the movements of the joints are highly correlated; this makes it possible to change the movement reality through controlling the energy of motions.

The goal of making motion animation is reality, but at many situations such as in a cartoon system, people often need nonrealistic motions. In this paper, we present a method to generate different realistic level motions through selecting the dimensions

Z. Pan et al. (Eds.): ICAT 2006, LNCS 4282, pp. 77–84, 2006.

of motion space. The method could help people generate new nonrealistic motions from a given motion sequence.

The rest of this paper is organized as follows: Section 2 reviews the related work of human motion space reducing, which is the base of our work. In section 3, we described our method of generating different realistic humanoid motions. We give the experiment results in section 4. And finally in section 5, we conclude with a brief summary and discussion of future works.

2   Related Works

Automatically generating animations is an important problem and many good solutions have been proposed [1, 2, 3]. In the process of making animation, animators are often confused by the high motion dimensions because it's not easy to control the data in high dimension directly. Recently people find that the movements of the joints are highly correlated for many behaviors [4, 5]. These correlations are especially clear for a repetitive motion like walking. For example, during a walk cycle, the arms, legs and torso tend to move in a similar oscillatory pattern: when the right foot steps forward, the left arm swings forward, or when the hip angle has a certain value, the knee angle is most likely to fall within a certain range. And these relationships hold true for more complex motions as well [4]. Using the correlated information, we can reduce the dimensions of working space. It also means reducing energy of the motion space. And motion space reducing is the base of our work.

Degrees of freedom are correlated with each other, many research works are also benefited from the observation. Alla Safonova et al. [4] proved that many dynamic human motions can be adequately represented with only five to ten degrees of freedom. He used lots of motions with similar behavior to construct a low-dimensional space to represent well other examples of the same behavior. Arikan[6] used this observation to implement the compression of motion capture databases and got good compression results. Popovi'c and Witkin [7] showed that significant changes to motion capture data can be made by manually reducing the character to the degrees of freedom most important for the task. Howe and colleagues [8] published one of the earliest papers on using global PCA to reduce the dimensionality of human motion. They incorporated the reduced model into a probabilistic Bayesian framework to constrain the search of human motion. Sidenbladh and colleagues [9] reduced the dimensionality of the database using global PCA and then constrained the set of allowable trajectories within a high-dimensional state space. Pullen and Bregler[4] used this observation for motion synthesis/texturing and Jenkins and Mataric [10] used it for identifying behavior primitives.

There are many methods to reduce the dimensions like PCA, Kernel PCA [11], Isomap[12], Locally Linear Embedding[13] etc. These methods could implement linear or nonlinear dimension reduction. We attempts to apply these dimension reduction approaches to generate different realistic motions. With the dimension adding or reducing, we could get different realistic level motions. And these motions contain the basic intrinsic information of the original motion.

3 Proposed Method

For a motion animation sequence, we compute eigenvectors V $(v_1, v_2 \dots v_n)$ from the sequence. The principle components can be represented by the eigenvectors and their coefficients, which we named "virtual joints". Through controlling the number of "virtual joints", we could get different realistic level of humanoid motion sequences.

3.1 Motion Definition

Motion M is defined as the combination of a set of postures f_i $(i=1, 2\dots n)$, which is organized according time axis (fig.1). It could be a simple motion (such as walking, running) or a complex motion (such as playing basketball).

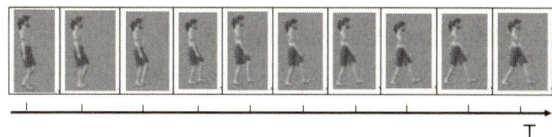

Fig. 1. Sketch map of motion definition

3.2 Different Realistic Motion Generating

After we got a motion sequence M, which might be represented by fifty or sixty DOF. It's hard for us to generate similar motions in such high dimension. PCA method is used to reduce the motion space.

3.2.1 Principal Component Analysis

Each frame f_i $(i=1, 2\dots n)$ saved in the captured file is a point of fifty or sixty dimension. Because joint movements of human body are highly correlated, we can synthesize some main measures from the DOF of human model. These measures contain the primary information of the motion. So we can use these measures to describe the captured motion data.

PCA method is useful to get such main measures. After gotten a motion capture file, we assume the frame length is n and the DOF of the human model is p. The data matrix can be represented as:

$$X = (x_1, \cdots, x_n)' = \begin{pmatrix} x_{11} & \cdots & x_{1p} \\ \vdots & \ddots & \vdots \\ x_{n1} & \cdots & x_{np} \end{pmatrix} \tag{1}$$

For PCA to work properly, we have to subtract the mean from each of the data dimensions. The mean subtracted is the average across each dimension.

$$\bar{x} = \frac{1}{n}\sum_{i=1}^{n} x_i = (\frac{1}{n}\sum_{i=1}^{n} x_{i1}, \dots, \frac{1}{n}\sum_{i=1}^{n} x_{ip})' = (\overline{x_1}, \dots, \overline{x_p})' \tag{2}$$

We select a jump motion sequence, which contains 300 frames. Firstly, we compute the eigenvectors of the motion using the method introduced in section 3. The number of "virtual joints" m we selected are 1,3,6,13,23,33,43,53 respectively. The relationship of "virtual joints" number and its energy containing percent is shown in table 1.

Table 1. The relationship of "virtual joints" numbers and the ratio of energy it containing

Number	1	3	6	13	23	33	43	53
Percent	41.9%	76.8%	91.7%	98.4%	99.8%	99.99%	≈ 100%	100%

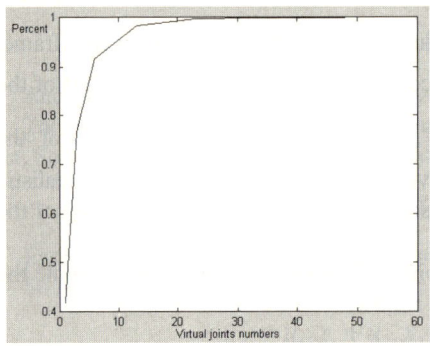 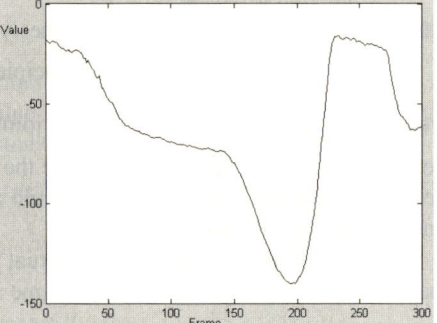

Fig. 2. Energy ratio chart   **Fig. 3.** The value of first "virtual joints"

The relationship of "virtual joints" numbers and the energy it containing is also shown in figure 2. When the "virtual joints" number changes from 6 to 53, the energy was not change greatly. In figure 3, we gave value of the first "virtual joints" changing according the frame numbers.

From the experiment results, we could see all of the motions containing the basically motion configuration. But they have different view realistic results. The results of motions generated using our method is shown in figure4. The figure also reflects the relationship of "virtual joints" and their realistic level. When we selected the number of "virtual joints" as 1, the motion we generated can be recognized as jump hazily; when the number of "virtual joints" up to 13, the motion is more like a mummy jump; when the number up to 53, we could get the original motion sequence. We could see it's a holistic method to generating humanoid motions.

From table 1 and figure 4, we could also derive that the details determined the reality of motions. Throwing away some details could help us get different realistic motions like cartoon motion etc.

5   Discussion and Future Works

Though generating realistic humanoid motion is important in animation and virtual reality, different level realistic humanoid motion is often required in many

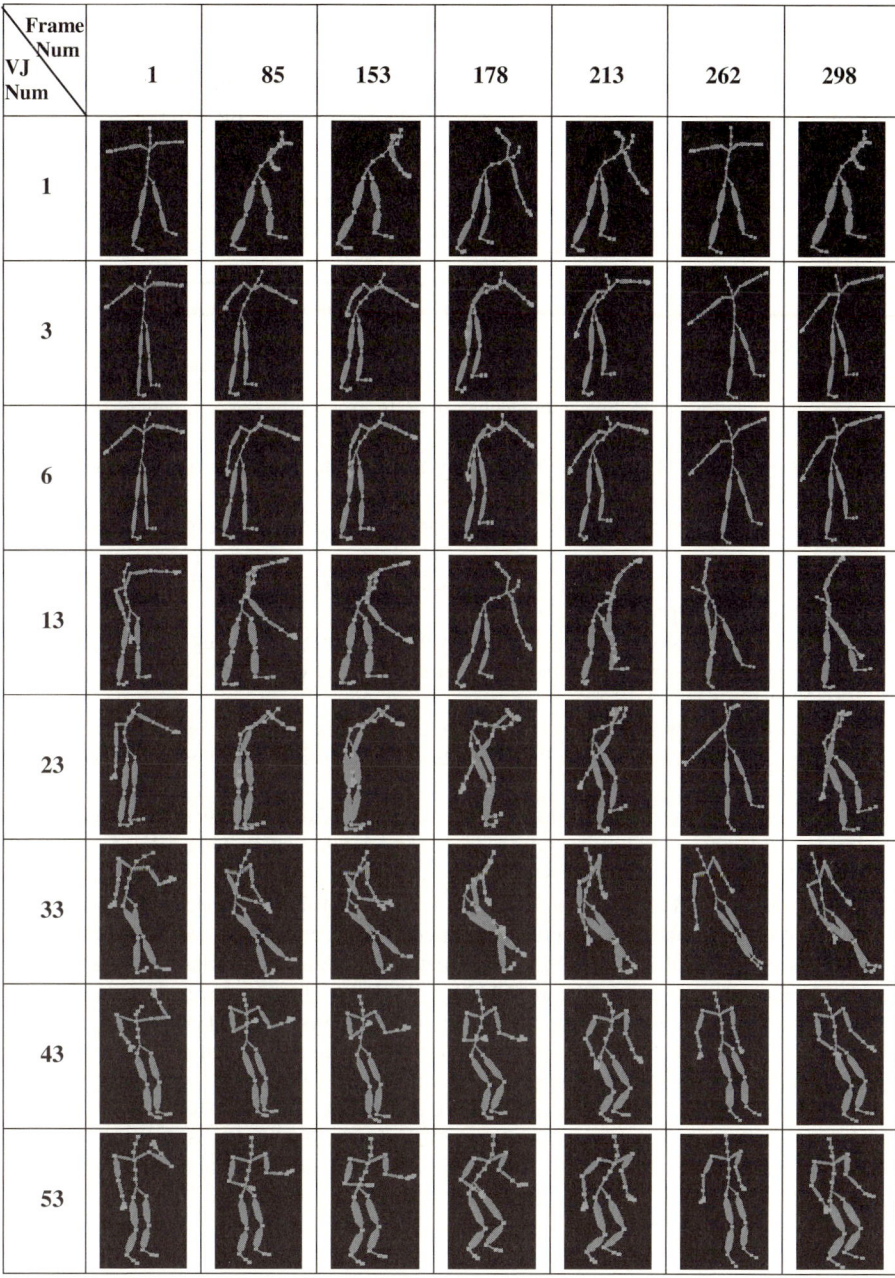

Fig. 4. The results of motion generating using different "virtual joints" numbers

applications. For example, cartoon motion is often used in many systems. We proposed a method to generate different level realistic humanoid motion automatically. This could help lighten the burden of animators and reuse the existed animation sequence.

In future work, we will try to use other dimension reducing methods to compute the "virtual joints". The relationship of "virtual joints" with different motion types and the motion details influence to motion reality are other aspects to be particularly studied in future.

Acknowledgements. This work was supported in part by National Natural Science Foundation of China (grant No: 60533090). The data used in this project was obtained from mocap.cs.cmu.edu. The database was created with funding from NSF EIA-0196217.

References

1. Wilkin. A. and Kass. H: Spacetime Constraints. In Proceedings of Siggraph88, 1988: 159-68
2. Shin. H. J, Lee. J, Gleicher. M. and Shin. S.Y. Computer puppetry: An importance based aproach. ACM Trans. On Graphics, 20(2), 2001: 67-94
3. Gleicher. M: Retargeting motion to new characters. In Proceedings of Siggraph98, 1998: 33-42
4. Pullen. K, and Bregler. C: Motion capture assisted animation: Texturing and synthesis. In Proceedings of Siggraph02, 2002: 501–508
5. Alla Safonova, Jessica K. Hodgins, Nancy S. Pollard: Synthesizing physically realistic human motion in low-dimensional, behavior-specific spaces. ACM Trans. On Graphics.23 (3), 2004:524-521
6. Okan Arikan: Compression of Motion Capture Databases. To appear in Siggraph 2006
7. Popovi ´c. Z., and Witkin A. P: Physically based motion transformation. In Proceedings of Siggraph 99, 1999:11–20
8. Howe. N, Leventon. M. and Freeman. W: Bayesian reconstruction of 3d human motion from single-camera video. In Advances in Neural Information Processing Systems 12. 1999:820-826.
9. Sindenbladh, H, Black. M. J., and Sigal, L: Implicit probabilistic models of human motion for synthesis and tracking. In European Conference on Computer Vision, 2002:784-800
10. Jenkins, O. C, and Mataric. M. J: Automated derivation of behavior vocabularies for autonomous humanoid motion. In AAMAS '03: Proceedings of the second international joint conference on Autonomous agents and multiagent systems, 2003:225–232
11. B. Scholkopf, A. J. Smola and K.-R. Muller: Nonlinear component analysis as a kernel eigenvalue problem. Neural Computation, 10(5), 1998:1299–1319
12. J. B. Tenenbaum, V. de Silva and J. C. Langford: A global geometric framework for nonlinear dimensionality reduction. Science, 290(5500), 2000:2319–2323
13. S. T. Roweis and L. K. Saul: Nonlinear dimensionality reduction by locally linear embedding. Science, 290(5500), 2000:2323–2326

Handheld AR for Collaborative Edutainment

Daniel Wagner[1], Dieter Schmalstieg[1], and Mark Billinghurst[2]

[1] Graz University of Technology Institute for Computer Graphics and Vision,
Inffeldgasse 16 Graz, 8010 Austria
{wagner, schmalstieg}@icg.tu-graz.ac.at
[2] University of Canterbury HIT Lab New Zealand
Private Bag 4800 Christchurch 8004 NZ
mark.billinghurst@canterbury.ac.nz

Abstract. Handheld Augmented Reality (AR) is expected to provide ergonomic, intuitive user interfaces for untrained users. Yet no comparative study has evaluated these assumptions against more traditional user interfaces for an education task. In this paper we compare the suitability of a handheld AR arts-history learning game against more traditional variants. We present results from a user study that demonstrate not only the effectiveness of AR for untrained users but also its fun-factor and suitability in environments such as public museums. Based on these results we provide design guidelines that can inform the design of future collaborative handheld AR applications.

Keywords: AR education, collaborative AR, usability studies.

1 Introduction

Augmented Reality (AR) interfaces have been developed for many application areas such as medicine, engineering and gaming. Recently, PDAs and cell phones have reached a level of performance where they can be used for mobile AR. With built-in cameras and 3D graphics chips, these handheld devices can readily be turned into video-see through magic lenses, providing an AR view of the user's real world.

In our ongoing work to build a handheld AR platform [1], we have targeted edutainment as a suitable application area for real world deployment of multi-user AR. Our efforts towards developing high-quality AR edutainment applications is driven by the belief that collaborative handheld AR can surpasses traditional media in user satisfaction, intensity of collaboration and learning efficiency.

Although edutainment AR applications are becoming more common, few studies have compared learning in an AR setting to more traditional educational tools. Research is needed to explore the educational value of mobile AR applications and inform the design of these interfaces. In this paper we present a user study comparing learning in a collaborative handheld AR environment to more traditional PC interfaces. This was done using an application, Virtuoso, that has similar gameplay across a handheld AR platform, desktop computer and a set of playing cards.

Z. Pan et al. (Eds.): ICAT 2006, LNCS 4282, pp. 85 – 96, 2006.

2 Related Work

Our work on handheld collaborative AR games in a museum is built on related work in handheld AR, collaborative AR, AR games, AR for museums, and comparative AR user studies. In this section we briefly review past work in these areas.

The Touring Machine [2] developed at Columbia University pioneered the concept of mobile AR almost 10 years ago. Since then, mobile AR interfaces have moved from cumbersome backpack computers to handheld AR devices. Initially these were tethered handheld AR displays such as Fitzmaurice's Chameleon [3] and Rekimoto's NaviCam [4] but in 2003 the first author developed the first fully self-contained handheld AR application [1]. Originally based on a PDA port of ARToolKit [6], this work has since then been extended into a full blown cross-platform version of *Studierstube* [7]. Most recently, mobile AR interfaces have been developed for cell phones by Möhring [8] and Henrysson [9].

Around the same time, Augmented reality as a collaboration tool emerged in a number of "shared space" systems [10][11][12][13] for face to face collaboration. Other work focuses on remote collaboration making use of multiple possibilities of mixed reality continuum [14] simultaneously [15][16].

AR as a new medium is attractive for education institutions such as museums. The incorporation of AR enhanced exhibits can range from a single high-performance AR display [17] to an entire exhibition realized using AR special effects [18]. Mobile AR technology can offer an attractive replacement for the traditional audio-tape tour guide. Tour guides are a recurring application theme for mobile AR research, partially because they show the strength of mobile AR, namely to present useful information registered to static locations in the real world, such as historic edifices. Some examples of outdoor AR guides are Situated Documentaries [19], ArcheoGuide [20], GEIST [21] and Signpost [22]. Work on mobile indoor AR has specifically targeted museums, for example the Guggenheim Bilbao museum [23] or Sweet Auburn [24].

As can be seen from the related work mobile AR interfaces have migrated from bulky backpacks to self contained handheld systems. Similarly the applications that people are using these systems for have evolved and more and more people are interested in educational use of AR technology. Despite this there have been few examples of user studies comparing education in a mobile AR setting to more traditional educational experiences. Our work is unique because it is the first paper that compares education with a handheld AR platform to more traditional tools. The application itself is also interesting as it provides one of the first examples of using handheld AR as a platform for producing educational content in a collaborative setting.

3 The Handheld AR Platform

We have created a component-based software architecture for the development of PDA-based handheld AR applications. This is the first feature-complete version of the *Studierstube* software framework that runs cross-platform on Windows, Linux and Windows CE. The technical details of the platform are beyond the scope of this paper, see [5] for more details. This section summarizes the key capabilities of the *Studierstube* framework for handheld devices.

Graphics and multimedia: OpenGL ES is an emerging standard for 3D graphics on embedded devices. Klimt[1] is a software library that executes OpenGL compliant software on top of a third party hardware OpenGL ES implementation or Klimt's own built-in software renderer. Using Klimt, it is possible to execute a high-level object-oriented scene graph library such as Coin[2]; we call this version Coin ES.

Tracking: We have developed ARToolKitPlus[3] as an optimized successor to the popular ARToolKit [6] marker tracking library. ARToolKitPlus shares the basic working principles with its ancestor, while the code has been rewritten in fixed point arithmetic and incorporates several novel computer vision algorithms. The resulting code tracks in real time on a high-end PDA (5ms per image on the Axim X51v).

Networking: Muddleware is a networking middleware loosely inspired by the idea of a Tuplespace. It provides state synchronization for multi-user applications, persistency and resource streaming.

Application framework: The *Studierstube* application manager coordinates the various system components mentioned above. It loads and executes concurrent applications.

4 Art History Application: Virtuoso

Using the Handheld AR framework we implemented an educational game called Virtuoso. Besides the AR version, the game was also implemented in Macromedia Flash on a desktop PC and as a paper game without any technology.

The players' objective in the Virtuoso game is to sort a collection of artworks according to their date of creation along a timeline – left means earlier and right means later. The timeline has a number of slots, each of which can hold exactly one artwork. Initially all slots are randomly filled with artworks. Each player can pick up one item from a slot and put it into another empty slot. If the desired target slot is full, the player can ask a team member to help by picking up the item in the target slot. When taking an item from the timeline, the player is provided with basic information about the item, such as its name and a brief description. The player can ask Mr. Virtuoso, the virtual arts expert, for more information about the item. The game ends when all items are correctly located on the timeline.

The art history application features an overall selection of 20 artworks from which the game master can select an arbitrary subset for play. The set of artworks covers a range from 20.000 BC to 2004 AD including pieces from western and eastern culture. We specifically created polygonal 3D models for each artwork. Most items are textured; some include audio or video features.

The PDA version of the Virtuoso game shows a video-see through AR scene. It runs on an arbitrary number of PDAs which are synchronized via WiFi using our Muddleware collaboration running on a hidden PC. Paper fiducial markers placed

---

[1] Klimt: open source 3D graphics library for mobile devices, http://studierstube.org/klimt
[2] Coin3D: open source scene graph renderer, http://www.coin3d.org
[3] ARToolKitPlus: http://studierstube.org/handheld_ar/artoolkitplus.php

along a wall are used to mark the slots of the timeline (Figure 1). Every marker can carry one artwork which is only visible on the player's PDA. A player can pick up any artwork from the wall onto her PDA, by clicking on the artwork on the display. Next she can drop it onto a free position on the wall by clicking on an empty marker on the display. While an item is located on the PDA, the player can access basic information about it such as its name. To get more information the player can place the object onto the desk of Mr. Virtuoso, an animated virtual 3D character who plays the game's arts expert (Figure 3). Mr. Virtuoso will then be prompted to provide his expertise on the subject through the use of text, audio playback and animation. The player can take back the artwork onto her PDA at any time. After an artwork is placed at its correct position, it cannot be moved again.

Besides the explanation from Mr. Virtuoso, the game engine can provide more explicit help by showing arrows pointing "left" and "right" next to the artwork if it should be placed earlier or later on the timeline (Figure 2). Furthermore, the game engine can display an item's date of creation when the item is placed at its correct location on the timeline.

Fig. 1. Using the AR PDA version

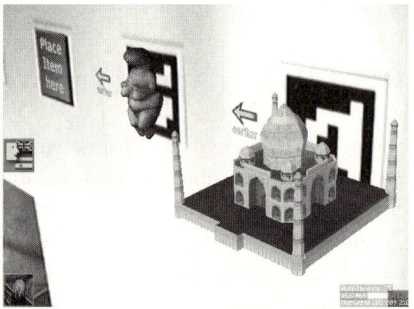

Fig. 2. Virtual arrows providing game hints

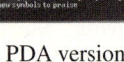

Fig. 3. PDA version

Fig. 4. PC version

Fig. 5. Paper version

The desktop PC version was programmed in Macromedia Flash (see Figure 4). Players can move artworks on the timeline displayed on the screen using drag and drop operations with the mouse. Consequently the PC version can only be operated by one player at the time. While this restricts the user interface of the game, it provides a more realistic example of typical PC-based edutainment application or museum installation. As usual, when an item is located at its final position its date of creation is displayed below of it and the item can no longer be moved. Moving an item to the left-top pane provides basic information, while the animated Mr. Virtuoso on the top-right pane provides detailed explanations in text and audio. Items can be directly dragged from one slot on the timeline onto another.

For the paper version of the game we printed pictures of the artworks on playing cards (Figure 5). On the front, the playing cards show the introductory text, while on the back more detailed descriptions by Mr. Virtuoso are provided. Players are only allowed to hold one playing card at a time and must only put it back into a free position. A human game master takes care that the game's rules are not violated. The game master will also reveal an item's date of creation when an item is located on its correct position on the timeline. So this version of the game has the same functional characteristics as the AR PDA and desktop PC versions.

5 Experimental Evaluation

We compared our collaborative AR application with the two non-AR variants of the game (the desktop PC and paper-based version). In the experiment participants were grouped into teams of four. In each game, players had to sort seven items on the timeline. After a team finished its task they filled out a questionnaire about the game they just played including detailed art history questions about the items they just arranged, and how they felt about the game interface. Then all teams moved on to another version of the game. After the participants played all three versions of the game they filled out another questionnaire asking to rank the conditions in several categories. The introductory instructions to the participants emphasized the focus on collaboration and the need to learn about the artwork items, more than completing the task as fast as possible. To further motivate cooperation between players, players were told, that the goal of the game was to get a high team score, rather than personal scores on the arts history questions they had to answer.

6 Results

There were 48 participants 26 female and 22 male, aged from 20 to 43. 25 people stated that they had never used a PDA before. The experiment lasted about one hour for each subject including introduction and a short finishing discussion. Data analysis was performed by using SPSS version 13 and the main effect was tested with repeated ANOVA. If a main effect was found, pair-wise post-hoc comparisons using the Bonferroni adjustment for multiple comparisons were performed. The questions the participants had to answer after each game can be grouped into four main categories: collaboration, easiness of the task, learning effect and fun factor. Subjects were asked to mark on a Likert scale of 1 to 7 how much they agreed or disagreed with a number of statements (1 = Strongly Disagree and 7 = Strongly Agree.

We asked two questions about the way people collaborated:

Q1: I collaborated intensively with my team members.
Q2: I knew exactly what the others were doing.

Table 1 shows the average results for each of these questions. Subjects felt that they collaborated more in the Paper and PDA versions; an ANOVA test found a significant difference for Q1 ($F(2,94)=3.94$, $P<0.023$) and a post-hoc comparison found a significant difference between the PC game and the other two variants. Similarly, an ANOVA for Q2 found a significant difference between how well subjects felt they knew what the others were doing: $F(2,94)=6,13$, $P<0.003$. A post-hoc comparison found a significant difference between the PDA condition and the PC and paper versions of the game.

Table 1. Average results on collaboration

Condition	Paper	PC	PDA
Q1	5.71	5.00	5.61
Q2	5.67	5.75	4.73

In the category *ease of the task* we asked the following five questions:

Q3: I always had a good overview of the timeline

Q4: I had sometimes problems with the user interface

Q5: The game was sometimes confusing

Q6: The user interface was easy to use

Q7: The task was easy to solve

Table 2 shows the average results. As can be seen, there is little difference for the conditions of the questions Q3, Q4 and Q5. An ANOVA test found significant differences for *Q6: The user interface was easy to use* ($F(2,94)=5.27$, $P<0.007$). A post-hoc comparison showed that the paper variant was rated significantly lower than the PC version and there was no difference between the PC and PDA conditions. For *Q7: The task was easy to solve*, ANOVA found significant differences ($F(2,94)=3.52$, $P<0.034$), and a post-hoc comparison showed that the PC version was rated significantly easier than the PDA version, but there was no significant difference between the other conditions.

Table 2. Average results for ease of use

Condition	Paper	PC	PDA
Q3	5.10	5.27	4.81
Q4	2.27	2.21	2.69
Q5	2.56	1.98	2.65
Q6	5.38	6.27	5.86
Q7	5.60	5.94	5.44

To measure if people felt a learning effect we asked the question:

Q8: I believe I learned something about those artworks

Performing an ANOVA on Q8 did not find any significant differences. The last group of questions we asked after each game was about how much people liked the game and how much it would fit into a museum setting:

Q9: I enjoyed playing the game
Q10: Playing the game was a great experience
Q11: This game would fit well into a museum exhibition
Q12: I would like to play this game in a museum

Figure 8 shows the average results for each of these questions. There were significant differences between the results for all of these questions. As can be seen for every question the PDA version scored highest while the paper version was rated lowest. An ANOVA was conducted and *Q9: I enjoyed playing the game* resulted in $F_{(2,94)}=5.472$, $P<0.006$. Post-hoc analysis found that the PDA version was rated significantly higher than the paper version. An ANOVA for *Q10: Playing the game was a great experience* resulted in $F_{(2,94)}=32.916$, $P<0.001$. Post-hoc analysis showed that the results for all three conditions were significantly different. For question *Q11: This game would fit well into a museum exhibition* the PC and PDA version got very similar ratings. An ANOVA ($F_{(2,94)}=25.713$, $P<0,001$) including a post-hoc analysis showed significant differences between the paper and the other two conditions but no differences between the PC and PDA conditions. Finally for *Q12: I would like to play this game in a museum*, an ANOVA resulted in $F_{(2,94)}=30.716$, $P<0.001$. Post-hoc analysis found all three versions of the game were significantly different.

In general subjects thought the PDA version provided a greater experience than the other two conditions and they would like to play this in a museum more than the other two games.

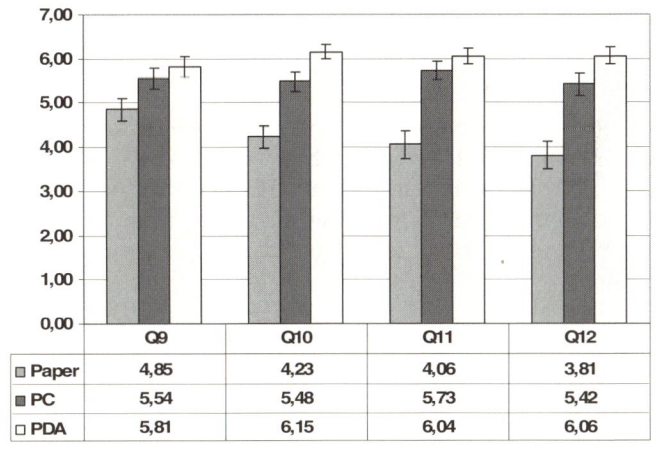

	Q9	Q10	Q11	Q12
▫ Paper	4,85	4,23	4,06	3,81
▪ PC	5,54	5,48	5,73	5,42
▫ PDA	5,81	6,15	6,04	6,06

Fig. 8. Average results for Questions Q9 – Q12

In addition, subjects were also asked to rank each of the conditions in order according to the following criteria. For each criteria 1 = lowest, 3 = highest.

R1: How easy the game was to play
R2: How much you learnt

R3: How good the overview of the timeline was
R4: How much you collaborated
R5: How much fun the game was
R6: How much the game would improve a museum exhibition

Table 3. Average results for rankings R1 and R2

Condition	Paper	PC	PDA
R1	1.89	2.25	1.86
R2	1.82	2.09	2.09

The rankings for *R1* and *R2* did not produce significantly different results. As can be seen in Table 3, all conditions were ranked very closely. However, for ranking *R3: How good the overview of the timeline was*, an ANOVA found $F(2,90)=4.723$, $P<0.011$. A post-hoc analysis showed that the PC and PDA conditions were significantly different giving the PC version the best score of overview of the timeline (see Table 4). Interestingly, ranking *R4: How much you collaborated*, resulted in exactly the opposite ratings. Here the PC version scored significantly lower, while the paper and PDA conditions were rated almost equally well. An ANOVA plus post-hoc comparisons resulted in $F(2,88)=4.006$, $P<0.022$ and found significant differences between the PC condition and the other two conditions.

Table 4. Average results for rankings R3 and R4

Condition	Paper	PC	PDA
R3	1.89	2.35	1.76
R4	2.15	1.67	2.13

Finally, *R5: How much fun the game was* and *R6: How much the game would improve a museum exhibition* produced the results shown in Table 5. An ANOVA found $F(2,92)=43.607$, $P<0.001$ for R5 and $F(2,88)=31.253$, $P<0.001$ for R6. For both R5 and R6 post-hoc comparisons showed that all results were significantly different resulting in the PDA version being ranked as the most fun and most appropriate for a museum exhibition.

Table 5. Average results for rankings R5 and R6

Condition	Paper	PC	PDA
R5	1.36	1.89	2.75
R6	1.36	2.00	2.64

7 Interviews

We interviewed the participants after each condition and several consistent themes emerged. For the paper version, subjects felt that they needed to organize themselves to prevent chaos, which was not a problem in the electronic versions of the game where strict rules were implicit. While many players said that it felt good to have a physical object in their hands they also added that the paper version was very "old school". In general subjects felt the paper version was less appealing.

Although most participants rated the PC version as providing the best overview of the timeline in the questionnaires, some participants complained that too many items crowded the screen which confused them. Interestingly, the same audio recordings for Mr. Virtuoso's voice-over was used in the PC and PDA version, but several users commented that the PC version's virtual character sounded more pleasing. We assume the reason for this is the low quality of the PDAs' built-in speakers. Subjects told us that collaboration was most difficult with the PC version because there was only one mouse to use and every action had to be first discussed with the other players. Players sitting more distant from the PC screen usually participated the least.

Some subjects said that the PDAs' touch-screens were more difficult to use than the mouse interface which is expected since most subjects had never used a PDA before, and people were afraid to break the PDA, especially due to the attached camera. All participants complained that Mr. Virtuoso should speak louder which is a well known problem with PDA speakers. Participants noted that the small screens could not be seen by the other players so collaboration was more difficult than with the paper version. Mr. Virtuoso was identified as a bottleneck for the game progress because other players would have to wait until Mr. Virtuoso had finished describing the artwork. People thought the user interface and the graphics in general were very appealing although some participants argued that it was difficult to explore the 3D artworks on the small screen. As most users had only minimal computer science experience, they were very excited due to the high-tech feeling of the PDA game and commented that the handheld AR concept was "innovative" and "ingenious".

8 Discussion

Although we tested three different game conditions, there was no difference in the educational outcomes. This could be because the learning task was essentially a memory task that wasn't dependent on effective collaboration or the ease of use of the interface. However, there were significantly different user subjective results as a consequence of the different characteristics of each condition.

One of the most obvious differences between the conditions is in how space was used. In both the AR PDA case and the paper interface the art pieces were spread out in physical space allowing the four users to work on the game in parallel. This shows one of the advantages of AR, namely that it allows virtual content to move from the screen and into the real world. In contrast, with the PC interface the users are working on a much smaller screen with only a single input device. In this case it was impossible for users to manipulate objects at the same time. Thus users felt that both the AR PDA interface and the paper version allowed them to collaborate more effectively than the PC interface.

Another key difference between the interfaces was in how much awareness they provided of what the others were doing. In the PC and paper versions all of the users could see all of the art pieces on the timeline at the same time. When a player moves a piece of artwork, everyone is aware of it. In contrast, in the AR PDA application, each of the users had a personal view of the virtual content, and unless they shared their PDA, they were not aware of which players had picked up which art pieces. One of the challenges of designing collaborative AR systems is providing independent views of virtual data while at the same time creating shared group awareness.

Despite the different interface conditions, there was not a significant difference in usability. Although the users had never used an AR PDA interface before, in general they found it relatively easy to use; as easy as using the mouse-based PC interface and manipulating real cardboard pictures. This is unusual for first time users of a novel interface, but is due to using an intuitive interface metaphor. In this case a magic lens metaphor in which the AR PDA becomes a virtual window on the real world. Users are able to view the virtual scene as easily as if they were using a real handheld lens.

Users ranked the PDA interface as the most enjoyable of the three conditions and the one that they would most like to see in a museum. The fun factor may be due to both the novelty and visually appealing nature of the AR interface. The AR condition provided 3D virtual imagery, animation, sound and text.

From these results we can infer several design guidelines for handheld AR interfaces that can inform future applications:

- Allow the user to experience the virtual content in space.
- Use an appropriate interface metaphor, such as a lens input metaphor.
- Seamlessly integrate 3D virtual imagery with animation, 2D images and text to create a multi-sensory experience.

In general, in a face to face collaborative AR interface, key elements of normal human face to face must be considered. This includes providing a mechanism for sharing user views to establish shared understanding, enabling users to work in parallel, and preserving the ability to share verbal and non-verbal face to face communication cues.

9   Conclusion and Future Work

In this paper we have described a handheld AR application developed for enhancing the museum experience, and a user study evaluating its effectiveness. This work is the first rigorous comparison of a handheld AR experience with more traditional PC desktop and paper-based applications. In general users felt that the AR PDA system provided the most fun of the three conditions and would most improve the museum experience.

Although these results are interesting and provide insight into designing AR museum experiences, the research is just beginning and there is a lot of future work that can be done.

First, other application areas for handheld AR should be explored, such as medicine, engineering and different games, among others. Each of these application areas have unique requirements that need to be designed for and evaluated in context.

Secondly, future user studies should use a wider range of analysis tools. In this experiment we have used subjective surveys, and interviews. In a collaborative setting, interesting analysis could also be performed on the language, gestures and group behaviour used, which can highlight more of the difference between collaborative process, rather than performance measures.

Finally, there are other devices than PDAs that could be used to provide AR experiences. It would be interesting to run a future experiment to compare user preferences and performance between AR experiences based on head mounted displays, PDAs and screen or projection based AR.

Acknowledgements

We would like to thank all participants for joining the user study and personnel at Graz University of Technology for helping organizing and executing the user study. Thanks go to the staff of Imagination Computer Services for helping in creating the 3D content. This project was funded in by part by Austrian Science Fund FWF under contract No. L32-N04 and Y193.

References

1. Wagner, D., Schmalstieg, D., First Steps Towards Handheld Augmented Reality, 7th International Conference on Wearable Computers (ISWC 2003), White Plains, NY, 2003
2. Feiner, S., MacIntyre, B., H¨ollerer, T., Webster, A.: A touring machine: Prototyping 3d mobile augmented reality systems for exploring the urban environment. Proceedings of the First International Symposium on Wearable Computers (ISWC), Cambridge, Massachusetts, USA (1997) 74–81
3. Fitzmaurice, G. W. Situated Information Spaces and Spatially Aware Palmtop Computers. Communications of the ACM, Vol.36, Nr.7, pp 38-49, July 1993
4. Rekimoto, J., Nagao, K. The World through the Computer: Computer Augmented Interaction with Real World Environments, User Interface Software and Technology (UIST '95), pp. 29-38, November 14-17, 1995
5. Wagner, D., Schmalstieg, D., Handheld Augmented Reality Displays, Proceedings of IEEE Virtual Reality 2006 (VR 2006), March 2006
6. Billinghurst, M., Kato, H., Weghorst, S. and Furness, T. A. A Mixed Reality 3D Conferencing Application. Technical Report R-99-1 Seattle: Human Interface Technology Laboratory, University of Washington, 1999
7. Schmalstieg, D., Fuhrmann, A., Hesina, G., Szalavari, Z., Encamao, L. M., Gervautz, M., and Purgathofer, W. The Studierstube augmented reality project. Presence - Teleoperators and Virtual Environments 11(1), 2002
8. Moehring, M., Lessig, C. and Bimber, O., Video See-Through AR on Consumer Cell Phones, International Symposium on Augmented and Mixed Reality (ISMAR'04), pp. 252-253, 2004
9. Henrysson, A., Billinghurst, M., Ollila, M. Face to Face Collaborative AR on Mobile Phones. International Symposium on Augmented and Mixed Reality (ISMAR'05), pp. 80-89, 2005
10. Schmalstieg, D., Fuhrmann, A., Szalavari, Z., Gervautz, M.: "Studierstube" - An Environment for Collaboration in Augmented Reality, Proceedings of Collaborative Virtual Environments '96, Nottingham, UK, Sep. 19-20, 1996
11. Poupyrev, I., Billinghurst, M., Weghorst, S. and Ichikawa, T., The Go-Go Interaction Technique: Non-Linear Mapping for Direct Manipulation in VR. Proceedings of ACM Symposium on User Interface Software and Technology (UIST '96), 1996

12. Rekimoto, J. TransVision: A Hand-held Augmented Reality System for Collaborative Design. Proceedings of Virtual Systems and Multi-Media (VSMM '96), Sept. 1996
13. Kiyokawa, K., Takemura, H., Yokoya, N., SeamlessDesign for 3D Object Creation, IEEE MultiMedia, ICMCS '99 Special Issue, Vol.7, No.1, pp.22-33, 1999
14. Milgram, P. Kishino, F., A Taxonomy of Mixed Reality Visual Displays, IEICE Transactions on Information Systems E77-D(12), pp. 1321-1329, 1994
15. Höllerer, T., Feiner, S., Terauchi, T., Rashid, G., and Hallaway, D. Exploring MARS: Developing Indoor and Outdoor User Interfaces to a Mobile Augmented Reality System. Computers and Graphics, 23(6), Elsevier Publishers, Dec. 1999, pp. 779-785, 1999
16. Kato, H., Billinghurst, M., Morinaga, K., Tachibana, K., The Effect of Spatial Cues in Augmented Reality Video Conferencing. HCI International 2001, New Orleans, LA, USA, 2001
17. Bimber, O., Fröhlich, B., Schmalstieg, D., and Encarnação, L.M. , The Virtual Showcase. IEEE Computer Graphics & Applications, vol. 21, no.6, pp. 48-55, 2001
18. Stapleton, C.B., Hughes, C.E., Moshell, J.M., MIXED FANTASY: Exhibition of Entertainment Research for Mixed Reality, CM International Symposium on Mixed and Augmented Reality (ISMAR 2003), pp. 354-355, Tokyo, Japan, 2003
19. Höllerer, T., Feiner, S., Pavlik, J., Situated Documentaries: Embedding Multimedia Presentations in the Real World, Proceedings of ISWC '99 (Third Int. Symp. on Wearable Computers), pp. 79-86, San Francisco, CA, 1999
20. Vlahakis, V., Ioannidis, N., Karigiannis, J., Tsotros, M., Gounaris, M., Stricker, D., Gleue, T., Daehne, P., Almeida, L., Archeoguide: An Augmented Reality Guide for Archaeological Sites, IEEE Computer Graphics and Applications, V.22 N.5, pp. 52-60, September 2002
21. Holweg D., Jasnoch U., Kretschmer U.: GEIST – Outdoor Augmented Reality in an Urban Environment. Computer Graphics Topics, pp. 5-6, June 2002
22. Reitmayr, G., Schmalstieg, D., Collaborative Augmented Reality for Outdoor Navigation and Information Browsing, Geowissenschaftliche Mitteilungen (Proc. 2nd Symposium on Location Based Services and TeleCartography), pp. 53-62, Vienna University of Technology, 2003
23. Grimm P., Haller M., Paelke V., Reinhold S., Reimann C., Zauner J., AMIRE - Authoring Mixed Reality, First IEEE International Augmented Reality Toolkit Workshop, Darmstadt, Germany, 2002
24. MacIntyre, B., Bolter, J.D., Moreno, E., Hannigan, B., Augmented Reality as a New Media Experience, International Symposium on Augmented Reality (ISAR 2001), New York, NY, 2001

VR-Based Simulation for the Learning of Gynaecological Examination*

Liliane dos Santos Machado[1] and Ronei Marcos de Moraes[2]

[1] Department of Informatics and [2] Department of Statistics
Universidade Federal da Paraíba, Cidade Universitária s/n
João Pessoa, PB 58059-900 Brazil
liliane@di.ufpb.br, ronei@de.ufpb.br

Abstract. Training is an effective way to acquire learning. Recently, virtual reality systems have been proposed and developed to provide training in medical procedures. This work presents the SITEG, a virtual reality simulator for education in the practice of gynaecological examinations. The SITEG offers a virtual environment where the user can practice the two steps present in a real exam and learn different stages of diseases like Herpes and Human papillomavirus. For that, the system integrates stereoscopic view and a haptic device to allow the identification of malignancies commonly found in this kind of examination. Attached to the simulator there is an assessment tool to classify the user training.

1 Introduction

Virtual Reality (VR) applications for medicine can be divided in three main groups: planning, assistance and training. Planning systems allow the study of specific cases. They use real information of the patient, as magnetic resonance or computerized tomographic imaging, to re-create a real situation and plan a procedure. Assistance systems are used to support a real procedure, adding or overlapping computer-generated images in a real situation. Finally, training systems are used to provide a realistic training environment. These systems aim the development of specific abilities of their user by the simulation of generic situations [1].

One of the challenges of VR systems for training is to provide realistic environments that re-create exactly what the physician experiment when performing a real procedure. For this reason, these systems incorporate several characteristics as 3D visualization by stereoscopic images, capture and processing of user movements, force-feedback according user interactions and deformation of the virtual organs manipulated [2]. In spite of the technological advances, to obtain a high-level degree of realism can require the utilization of expensive hardware, what could turn not viable the dissemination of the system.

---

* This work is supported by FINEP (Research and Projects Financing) under grant 01-04-1054-000 and CNPq (National Council for Scientific and Technological Development) under grant 506480/2004-6.

Z. Pan et al. (Eds.): ICAT 2006, LNCS 4282, pp. 97 – 104, 2006.

For medical education, applications based on VR are developed to the teaching of anatomy through three-dimensional atlas. By a 3D visualization of the anatomy, students also can understand important physiological principles. In the surgical simulation area, VR offers uncountable possibilities and uses computers for training, assessment and certification. Initially, the first simulators were limited due to the low graphical resolution and the lack of realistic devices for interaction. Nowadays, a generation of systems offers interactive models and incorporates haptic devices [3].

In 1998 was presented a simulator for the identification of pathologies in the prostate through palpation using a haptic device [4]. Previously, another simulator already allowed the identification of subcutaneous tumours by the use of a haptic device [5]. Recently, VR simulators have been developed for training in laparoscopy [6], arthroscopy [7] and many other specialties, as paediatric training of bone marrow harvest [8]. In the field of veterinary, applications based on VR for rectal touch of bovines [9] and identification of tumours in equines [10] were already developed for educational purposes.

Besides of the many systems for medical education or training, there is not any application related to the teaching of gynaecological examination and identification of cervix pathologies. Then, it was observed the possibility of use of VR technologies to help students to training the visual and the palpation phases of this examination.

We present the SITEG, a VR-based system to support the learning of the main pathologies related to cervical cancer and their stages.

2   The Gynaecological Examination

The gynaecological examination is one of the most important procedures for women health. It has significantly reduced the deaths caused by cervix cancer. The success of this examination is the detection of pathologies present in the cervix that can develop a cervix cancer. In this context, the Herpes and Human papillomavirus (HPV) are the pathologies most commonly related to the development of the cancerous cells [11].

A traditional gynaecological examination is composed by a visual phase and by a palpation phase. In the visual phase, the doctor uses a tool called speculum to observe the aspect of the vagina walls and cervix of the patient. Coloration and presence of lesions or warts are some of the features observed. After that, the doctor removes the speculum and performs a digital examination of the internal portion of the vagina and cervix. At this phase, no visual information is available and the doctor must feel the vagina and the cervix, to identify the presence of lumps or warts, and their tissues elasticity.

There are some problems related to the traditional method of training of the gynaecological examination. The first one is related to knowledge of the pathologies. Because there are different pathologies and several stages with different symptoms for each one, some cases are rare and sometimes do not occur during the medical residence of the students. A second problem is related to the palpation phase of the examination. In this phase, the student cannot know if the forces applied or if the structures are correctly touched, even if a physician assists him. This fact occurs because there is no visual information and the touch is the main sense used. Other problems can be related to the time necessary to perform the examination.

3 The SITEG

The SITEG – Interactive System for Training of Gynaecological Examination – is being developed to support the training of new doctors in performing gynaecological examinations. The system is a simulator that presents several pathologies related to the cervix cancer. As main objective, the SITEG can improve the abilities of new doctors in identifying a disease, allow them to know the several stages of the pathologies related to the cervix and improve their dexterity to perform a palpation examination in a patient.

The system was designed to be a tool for study and training. Due this, it contains two different modules. In the study module, the user can choose a specific disease and its stage and learn how it occurs. For the training, a diagnosis module can be used to observe a random-presented case. In this module, the user should perform the examination and provide a diagnosis by an assessment tool attached to the module.

Both study and diagnosis modules present a two-step simulation. Each step is responsible for simulating one of the phases of the real gynaecological examination (Fig. 1). The first step simulates the observing phase, when the doctor uses a device called speculum to observe the patient cervix. During the observation, the doctor should identify the colouring and general aspect of the cervix. In a real examination this step is also used to collect material to laboratory analysis. The second step simulates the palpation phase. In this phase it is not present the speculum and the doctor can see inside the patient body. So, he uses the finger to palpate the vagina wall and cervix to identify some anomaly.

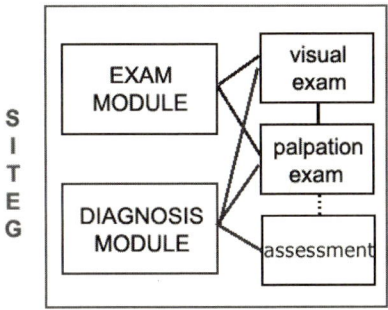

Fig. 1. Structure of SITEG modules

Once the touch is an important sense to learn how to perform the examination, there is the necessity of use of some interaction device to provide force-feedback to the SITEG user. This interaction device must allow an intuitive interaction. For that, it was chosen a haptic device based on a robotic-arm to allow 3D interaction and provide 3D force-feedback to the user (Fig. 2). Because the user interacts with a 3D world there is the necessity of stereoscopic visualization, possible with the use of shutter glasses.

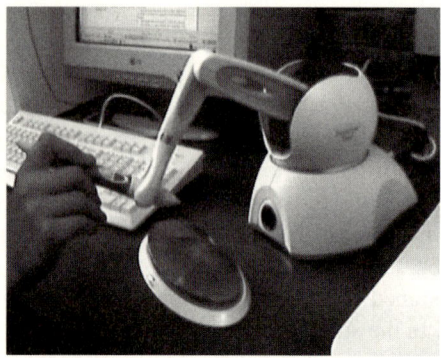

Fig. 2. Haptic device used in the SITEG

The presence of an assessment tools attached to the SITEG is necessary because the user cannot see what is happening during the palpation phase. He also did not know if is or is not correct the way he is performing the examination. Even if a teacher is observing the user (student), the teacher will not be able to know if the forces applied by the student during the palpation is appropriate or not. However, the simulator can collect these data and use them to provide a classification of the student examination and of his diagnosis.

3.1 Development

To develop the simulator a set of libraries called CyberMed [12] have been used. These libraries can deal with all requirements of the SITEG. CyberMed deals with several stereoscopic view modes, supports the use and operation of haptic devices, presents an assessment library and can read 3D models. It also allows the association of textures with the representation of the interaction device.

Once the real gynaecological examination presents two stages, the SITEG was developed to simulate these two stages separately. To do that, was necessary to define the body structures related to the procedure. Due to the fact that the examination occurs in a specific part of the body, were chosen four body structures to be presented in the simulator: the exterior female genital, the vagina duct, the cervix and the speculum. To modelling these objects was used the 3D modeller Blender (www.blender.org). The models were grouped to compose the graphical scene of the simulator, as shows Fig. 3. For the haptic scene, the model of the speculum is not used.

Together, the models integrate a 3D scene that offers a view similar to the one observed by the physician during a real examination. For this phase, the external genitals aperture was modelled smaller in order to do not provide internal visual information for the user. Similarly, the vagina duct has lower calibre and was modelled to be narrow. Its elastic property could be calibrated after for the palpation.

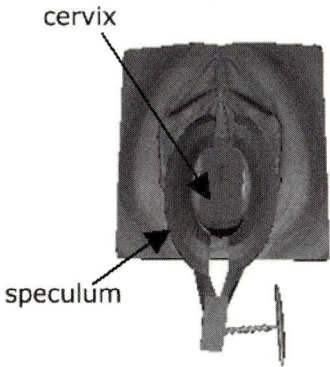

Fig. 3. The models developed grouped and positioned to observe the cervix

The models are read by the SITEG and used to construct two separated scenes. The visual scene is a graphical window divided in two columns. The left column shows the graphical scene while the right column presents a description about the disease (in the study module) or explains what the user should observe (in the diagnosis module). For the left column the user can choose the stereoscopic mode wanted. At this time, the SITEG support stereoscopic visualization using shutter glasses or coloured glasses (anaglyph mode).

Then, for the visual rendering a class from CyberMed will generate and control the visual scene. In this class the visual world dimensions are defined, the models are positioned inside it, as well as the light sources, the representation of the 3D device cursor and the textures and colours of the models (textures and colours are used to simulate the visual effect of the diseases). This class will perform all the visual rendering process and it will controls the routines of generation of the stereoscopic pairs and supervise all the interactive modifications that can be made in the scene. This class also will assign textures to the models to allow the simulation of different diseases. The objects are static in the SITEG but the user can manipulate the 3D interaction device in order to position a lamp for better observation of the structures. The lamp is not visible but its light can be noticed, a fact which helps in the observation of the scene.

For the implementation of the haptic simulation is necessary to attribute properties to the models in order to create a similar effect of the real tissues represented by them. The effects cannot be visually noticed and must be described by an expert according his experience when performing a real examination. The SITEG allows the calibration of the elasticity, roughness and density of each model.

The assessment tool of SITEG is composed by a database of assessment models used to classify the user in four classes of experience, according his interaction information collected during the simulation. The classes of performance are: beginner, regular, almost expert and expert.

The SITEG integrates three basic classes to provide a realistic simulation: a visualisation class, a touching class and an assessment class. However, it was necessary the definition of several other classes to: treat collision detection (when the interaction device collides with the models), generate the tactile effects and collect the interaction information used for assessment, among others. It runs on a PC under Linux and is been developed using C++, OpenGL and the CyberMed libraries.

4 Results

Actually the SITEG presents the simulation of four different diagnoses. Because HPV and Herpes are the diseases more commonly related to the cervix cancer, they were chosen for the first version. A normal and an inflammatory condition are the other

Table 1. Visual and tactile properties for the cases presented in SITEG

Case / Pathology	Cervix and Vagina Walls Coloration	Texture	Viscosity	Cervix Elasticity
Normal	rosy	similar to buccal mucous membrane	smooth	Similar to an orthopedic rubber
Herpes	white	spongy	soft bubbles	very soft
HPV	semi-transparent white	irregular	solid bubbles	very soft
Inflamed	red	similar to buccal mucous membrane	smooth	hard/tense

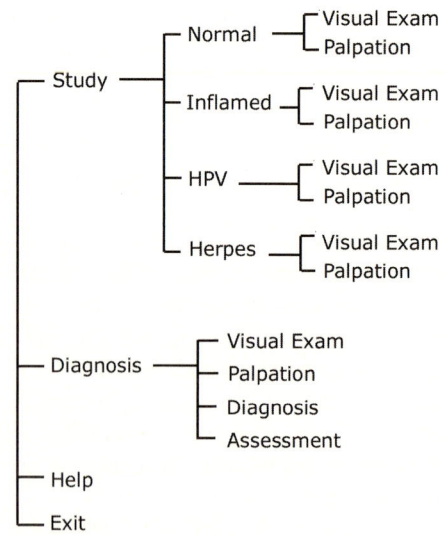

Fig. 4. The menu options of SITEG

two diagnoses present in the system. An expert described the properties associated to the models for each case, as shows Table 1. These properties were used to calibrate the system.

The user interface allows the choice of a study or diagnosis simulation. When the study module is selected a menu presents the cases available by the system and the user can select which one he wants to study and learn about. However, if the diagnosis module is selected, a random case will be presented and the user will need to perform the virtual examination to make his diagnosis. This diagnosis will be used, with the interaction information collected during the simulation, to classify the user performance. The Fig. 4 presents al menu options available in the SITEG.

To interact with the system the user manipulates a haptic device. During the visual examination it did not provide force-feedback and is used as a lamp to helps the viewing. In the palpation examination the device is represented by the texture of a finger and can touch the models.

5   Conclusions

This paper presents the design and implementation of a simulator for learning of gynaecological examination. The main advantage of a VR-based system for education in gynecological exam is to offer several diseases and stages for training without any risk or discomfort for students and patients. Besides, the student can learn about the different stages of diseases.

At this moment the system can simulate four different cases and integrates a study and a diagnosis module. It allows the use of SITEG so for study purposes as for training purposes. At this moment the system is been adapted to the VirtWall platform to allow its use in classroom [13].

Further works are related to the insertion of other diseases as well as the addition of stages for the diseases already present in the simulator.

Acknowledgments

The authors thank to Aldeni Sudário de Sousa and Daniel Faustino Lacerda de Souza for their support in the modelling, and to Milane Caroline de Oliveira Valdek for the medical support.

References

1. Burdea, G. and Coiffet, P. Virtual Reality Technology. Wiley (2003)
2. Satava, R. Medicine 2001: The King is Dead. VR Conf. Proc. (2000)
3. Satava, R. Surgical Education and Surgical Simulation. World J. Surg, 25-11 (2000) 1484-1489
4. Burdea, G., Patounakis, G., Popescu, V. and Weiss, R. Virtual Reality-Based Training for the Diagnosis of Prostate Cancer, IEEE Transactions on Biomedical Engineering, **46**-10 (1999) 1253-1260

5. Dinsmore, M., Langrana, N., Burdea, G. and Ladeji, J. Virtual Reality Training for Palpation of Subsurface Tumors. IEEE Int. Symp. on VR and App. (1997) 54-60

6. Voss, G. et al. Lahystotrain – Intelligent Training System for Laparoscopy and Hysteroscopy. Studies in Health Tech. and Inf., **70** (2000) 359-364

7. Mabrey, J. et al. Development of a VR Arthroscopic Knee Simulator. Studies in Health Tech. and Informatics, **70** (2000) 192-194

8. Machado, L. and Zuffo, M. Development and Evaluation of a Simulator of Invasive Procedures in Pediatric Bone Marrow Transplant. In Studies in Health Technology and Informatics, **94** (2003) 193-195

9. Baillie, S. et al. Validation of a Bovine Rectal Palpation Simulator for Training Veterinary Students. Studies in Health Technology and Informatics, **111** (2005) 33-36

10. Crossan, A., Brewster, S. and Glendye, G. A Horse Ovary Palpation Simulator for Veterinary Training. PURS 2000 Proc. (2000) 79-86.

11. Cotran, R.S., Kumar, V. and Collins, T. Robbins Pathologic Basis of Disease, 6th edition. W.B. Saunders Company (2000)

12. Machado, L. Campos, S., Cunha, I. and Moraes, R. CyberMed: VR for Medical Teaching. IFMBE Proc. **5**-1 (2004) 573-576

13. Moraes, R., Machado, L. and Souza, A. VirtWall: A Concept of Low-Cost Virtual Wall for Immersion in VR. Brazilian Symp. on VR (2003) 383-385

Visual Perception Modeling for Intelligent Avatars

Ronghua Liang[1], Tinan Huang[1], Meleagros Krokos[2], Jinglong Fan[3]

[1] College of Information Engineering, Zhejiang University of Technology,
Hangzhou,310032, P.R. China
[2] Dept. of Creative Technologies, University of Portsmouth, UK
[3] Computer School, Hangzhou Dianzi University,
Hangzhou 310018, P.R. China
rhliang@zjut.edu.cn

Abstract. Visual perception modeling for intelligent avatars can play subsidiary roles in controlling the behavior and animation of avatars in Intelligent Virtual Environments (IVE). We present a visual perception recognition model by integrating the color model, 3D object matching, sensors perception and path planning, therefore, it is quite useful for the avatar to make appropriate decisions in real-time in an IVE. In our approach, the 3D objects in the IVE are recognized and the moving directions of the avatar are obtained by using the avatar's perception viewpoint and sensor. The avatar's path planning employs our motion path synthesis proposed previously, called two-stage process synthesis. Experimental results show the efficiency and high prospect of our approach.

Keywords: Color model, sensor perception, visual perception, motion path synthesis.

1 Introduction

In IVE, one of the challenging research issues is that avatar has the ability of making decisions, visual perception and making appropriate response to the virtual environment. Human facial expressions play a critical role in creating believable avatars to populate virtual worlds. Unlike the off-line animator-intensive methods used in the special effects industry, real-time embodied agents are expected to exist and interact with us "live" by realistic-looking human expressions. There has been a large amount of research on off-line human face modeling and walking animation [1, 2]. The last few years have seen great maturation in understanding how to use computer graphics technology to portray 3D embodied characters or virtual humans in virtual environment [3, 4, 5].

Tu and Terzopoulos [6] did the pioneering work for life-like animation simulation by generating artificial fish. They simulated the real fish like locomotion in a virtual world. Fish behavior is controlled by fish life-characteristic, a sequence of behavior rule-base and an intender generator. Every time, the intender generator can create an intender regarding the outside environment and choose an appropriate behavior from the rule base. Norman Badler et al have done impressive work in this field [7,8]. They

Z. Pan et al. (Eds.): ICAT 2006, LNCS 4282, pp. 105–112, 2006.
© Springer-Verlag Berlin Heidelberg 2006

described a Parameterized Action Representation (PAR) [7] that allows an agent to act, plan, and reason about its actions or others. Besides embodying the semantics of human action, PAR is designed for building future behaviors into autonomous agents and controlling the animation parameters that portray personality, mood, and affect in an embodied agent. The controller for avatar consists of virtual sensors, working behavior sequence, and behavior hierarchy structure. The avatar's walking is designed according to the principle of plan and advice, the limitation is that the avatar didn't always walk along a specific path. Gratch et al [4, 9, 10] have shown some of this daunting subtlety in human behavior can be modeled by intelligent agents, from the perception of events in the world, to the appraisal of their emotional significance, through to their outward impact on an agent's behavior. They created general computational models to support characters that act in virtual environments, make decisions, but whose behavior also suggests an underlying emotional current.

We integrate two complementary approaches for the autonomous agent model and the avatar's realistic behavior modeling to visual perception and behavior modeling into a single unified system in IVE based on the system of human face reconstruction [1] and animation and IVES (Intelligence Virtual Environment System) [11] we developed previously. This paper focuses on visual perception modeling for the intelligent Avatar in IVE, and in another forthcoming article, we will present the behavior and expression modeling for the intelligent Avatar. The Avatar recognizes the 3D models and gets the location of models in the virtual world by using a color model and two sensors. Compared to the approaches mentioned above, the contributions of this paper is we present a simplified recognition model by integrated a color model and two sensors, therefore, it is quite helpful for the avatar to make decisions in real-time in IVE.

The rest of this paper is organized as follows: In section 2 our algorithm is outlined, the detailed description of the avatar's visual perception is given in section 3, the system implementation is presented in Section 4 and the related conclusions are summarized in Section 5.

2   Algorithm Outline

Our algorithm consists of five steps. The first step is the avatar's perception of objects in virtual environment using color model, the coarse recognition results in the first

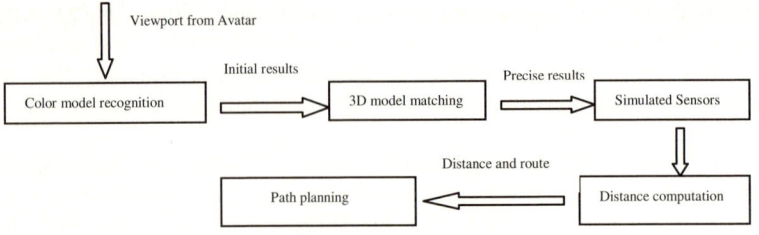

Fig. 1. Algorithm outline

step are then greatly improved by 3D model matching. The third step is to decide the moving directions for avatar, we use two sensors to calculate. The fourth step is to compute the distance between the Avatar and object, and the final step is the path planning for avatar to "walk" in IVE. The integrated algorithm is shown in Figure 1.

3   Visual Perception Modeling

All detailed five steps of visual perception are described in this section

3.1   Perception Mechanism of the Avatar

The perception of the avatar here is obtained by simulating the viewport as the avatar's eyes (for the reason of real-time rendering, the size of viewport is usually small, in our algorithm it is 64 by 64), and perception image and z-buffer of virtual world in avatar's eyes is acquired by rendering virtual world with the viewport. An example virtual environment is shown in Figure 2 (a), and the corresponding rendering image of avatar's viewport is shown in Figure 2(b).

The perception image acquired by the virtual human is not for rendering in computer screen, but for retrieving the 3D models. Therefore, there is not a procedure for texture and illumination while that is usually necessary in rendering a 3D model. Color is also very important for the perception image rendering, because color information can provide supplemented information for distinguishing different models when employing 3D model matching recognition (see the Section 3.2).

(a) Virtual world in avatar's eyes

(b) Avatar perception image represented by colour information and z-buffer in (a)

Fig. 2. Example of avatar perception

When rendering the avatar perception, we can get the z-buffer value which is used in the next section for modeling matching and simulation sensors. Therefore, 3D coordinate of the perception image pixel can be represented as follows.

$$q\_proj = \begin{bmatrix} -1.0 + 2*i/w \\ -1.0 + 2*j/h \\ z_{screen}/z_{max} \\ 1 \end{bmatrix}, \tag{1}$$

where $q\_world = q\_proj*(MP)^{-1}$, (i, j) is the 2D coordinate in the perception image, q_proj is the perspective coordinate, q_world is the world coordinate, w is the width of screen, h is the height of screen, Z_{screen} is screen z-buffer, and Z_{max} is a predefined value, P is the projection matrix, and M is the viewport matrix, respectively.

3.2 Recognition of Objects Based on Model Matching

As to the precise object matching, we present an approach of model matching with the aid of the avatar's perception. Model base consists of some models represented with 3D meshes, such models including TVs, buildings, tables, cars, and so on. All 3D objects in model base are denoted with $\mathbf{G}=\{\mathbf{T, F}\}$, where $\mathbf{T}=\{Tr_1,Tr_2,...Tr_k\}$ are triangular meshes, and $\mathbf{F}$ is the eigenvector function of triangular meshes denoted by s-dimension vectors, so $\mathbf{F}$: Tr_i->$\mathbf{f}_{mi}=(f_{i1}(Tr_1),f_{i2}(Tr_2),...f_{is}(Tr_k))$, where $f_i(Tr_i)$ is a two-dimension vector.

The model matching is an iterative process. If $\mathbf{G}'$ is assumed to be the target object, and $\mathbf{G}$ is its corresponding model in the model base, to match the 3D model in the model base can be summarized as the following steps:

1) Create the corresponding probability values $\mathbf{L}$ between $\mathbf{T}'$ in $\mathbf{G}'$, $\mathbf{T}$ in $\mathbf{G}$, and $\mathbf{L}=\{p_1,p_2,...p_k\}$, where $p_i=\{p_{i1},p_{i2}...,p_{ik}\}(i=0,1,2,...,k)$ denotes the matching probability values of the ith triangular meshes.

2) Define the optimization function for matching as follows:

$$E = \min \sum_{i=1}^{k}\sum_{j=1}^{k}((Tr_i - M \bullet Tr_j')p_{ij})^2 + \sum_{i=1}^{k}\sum_{j=1}^{k}\sum_{o=1}^{s}(\|f_{oi} - f_{oj}'\|p_{ij})^2 \tag{2}$$

$$\text{where} \quad M = \lambda \begin{bmatrix} \mathbf{R} & \mathbf{t} \\ \mathbf{0} & 1 \end{bmatrix} \tag{3}$$

is the transformation matrix of vertices, and $\mathbf{R}$ is translation vector and $\mathbf{t}$ is a rotation matrix and λ is the scale factor. M can be obtained by aligning 9 points manually in $\mathbf{G}$ and $\mathbf{G}'$. If a is a threshold value and $E< a$, $\mathbf{G}'$ can be recognized as $\mathbf{G}$.

3.3 Simulation Sensor

The simulation sensor is designed for helping the virtual human avoid the collision with barriers. In our approach, there are two sensors: object sensor (see Figure 3) and barrier sensor (see Figure 4), which help the virtual human walk freely in real time through the virtual world.

(1) Object sensor
The object sensor is used to decide the distance and angle between the virtual human and the object found according to the location and the orientation. The virtual human can walk directly to the object by using object sensor.

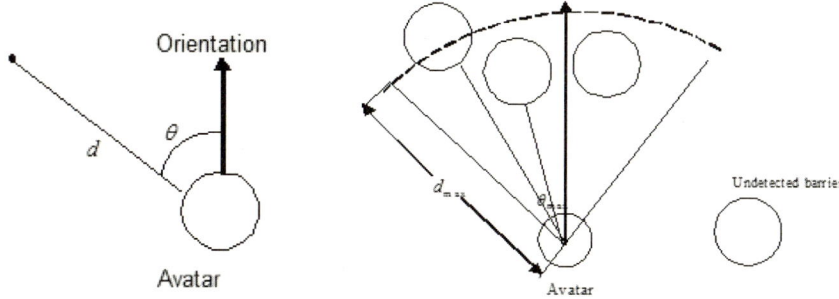

Fig. 3. Object Sensor   **Fig. 4.** Barrier Sensor

(2) Barrier sensor

The function of the barrier sensor is used for collision detection for the virtual human. Barrier sensor can be employed when the avatar meets the barrier in the range of its viewport in IVE. Barrier sensor is represented in Figure 4. The window of the sensor in Figure 4 is decided by (θ_{max}, d_{max}), where θ_{max} is the maximum rotation angle of the virtual human, and d_{max} is the maximum length of avatar's viewport. The barrier sensor can get a set of collision which represents all barrier objects for the avatar, and the next direction of the virtual human's walking can be decided by calculating the force field of the collision set.

The distance in the above two sensors can be computed in Section 3.4.

3.4 Distance Computation in Sensor with OBBtree

Although an Axis Aligned Bounding Box (AABB) is easily constructed to represent the object, an Oriented Bounding Box (OBB) [12] provides a better object approximation. An OBB is a bounding box that does not necessarily line up along the coordinate axes. OBB generation requires the following:

(1) the centroid of triangle i, $m_i = (p_i + q_i + r_i)/3$, where p_i, q_i and r_i are the vertices of triangle i, the centroid, μ, for one 3D object $\mu = \dfrac{1}{3n}\sum_{i=1}^{n}(p_i + q_i + r_i)$, where n is the number of triangles of one object in IVE.

(2) the 3×3 covariance matrix C, given by:

$$C_{j,k} = \frac{1}{3n}\sum_{i=1}^{n}\left[\overline{p}_i^{\,j}\overline{p}_i^{\,k} + \overline{q}_i^{\,j}\overline{q}_i^{\,k} + \overline{r}_i^{\,j}\overline{r}_i^{\,k}\right]$$

where n is the number of triangles, $\overline{p}_i = p_i - \mu$, $\overline{q}_i = q_i - \mu$ and $\overline{r}_i = r_i - \mu$. These last terms represent the vector from a vertex to the centroid. The approach uses a statistical technique, principal components analysis, that finds the best fit for 3 primary axes (the principal components) to minimize the square of the distance of each vertex from its centroid. As C is symmetric, its eigenvectors will be mutually orthogonal. Two of the three eigenvectors of the covariance matrix are the axes of maximum and of minimum variance. The normalized eigenvectors are used as a basis as they will tend to align the box with the geometry of a tube or a flat surface patch.. We find the extremal vertices along each axis of the basis, and size the bounding box, oriented with the basis vectors, to bound those extremal vertices.

The distance between the avatar and objects can be calculated by finding the length between the centroid of the object's OBB and the avatar's eye.

3.5 Path Planning

In our previous work [13], we presented a new motion generation technique, called motion path synthesis. The objective was to generate a motion for an intelligent avatar to move along a planned route using a pre-existing motion library. First, motion primitives each of which is defined as a dynamic motion segment were extracted from the motion library. Then a motion graph was constructed based on the motion primitives and their connectivities. Within this motion graph, the desired realistic motion for avatars can be synthesized through a two-stage process: search an optimal motion path within the motion graph, join the motion path and adapt it to the route. We construct a hierarchical directed graph as shown in Figure 5 to generate the motion path. The start motion primitive is selected as vertex V0. Let the number of all the motion primitives be n, we set the other vertices V_{ij} = MP_j , where V_{ij} is the jth vertex at level i, j $\in$ [1, n]. The weight of each edge is $-lgP(MP_{ki}|MP_{ki-1})-lgP(MP_{ki}|R,S_{ki})$, to be calculated in the runtime. According to this graph, the problem can be transformed to finding a shortest path. Because no evident end vertex exists and the number of vertices in the graph is infinite, the traditional Dijkstra algorithm can not be adopted directly. A revised Dijkstra algorithm was given in our previous work [13].

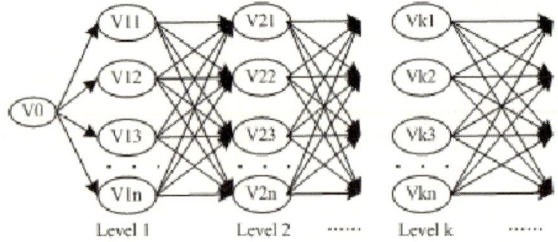

Level 1   Level 2   ······   Level k   ·······

Fig. 5. Hierarchical graph for motion path finding

4 Algorithm Implementation

The approaches aforementioned have been integrated into our IVE system (IVES), and all the approaches are implemented in real-time. In IVES, the user can interact with avatar with a friendly window interface. The frame rate in our IVES is about 20 fps, which meets the real-time-rendering requirement. The experimental system is implemented with Visual C++ 6.0 under Windows 2000. Most rendering employs DirectX 9 from Microsoft 3D rendering toolkit.

Figure 6 shows some demonstrations of our approach. In Figure 6(a), the Avatar walks along a specify route, and we track the whole route by showing its skeleton behind the Avatar. By visual perception modeling, the Avatar can recognize some objects and show some poses. Figure 6 (b) (c) (d) demonstrate the Avatar meets cars and two cylinder objects, respectively.

(a) Avatar walks along a specific route   (b) Avatar recognizes a car

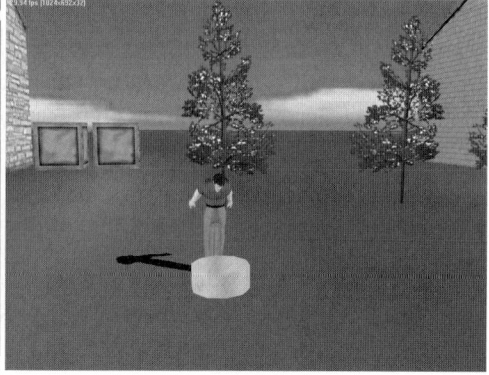

(c) Avatar recognize a object and shows a pose   (d) Avatar recognize a object and shows a pose

Fig. 6. Some experiments to verify our algorithm

5   Conclusions and Future Work

In this paper, we concentrate on the visual perception modeling for the intelligent Avatar. The visual perception modeling consists of five steps: color model, 3D object matching, sensors perception, distance computation and path planning. Experimental results verify the efficiency and high prospect of our approach. The future work mainly includes how to create more robust and complicated visual perception base.

Acknowledgments. This work was partly supported by key project from Zhejiang Provincial Natural Science Foundation of China grants Z603262.

References

1. Liang, R., Pan, Z., Chen, C.: New algorithm for 3D facial model reconstruction and its application in Virtual Reality. Journal of Computer Science and Technology. 19(4)(2004)501-509.
2. Zordan, V. B., Majkowska, A., Chiu, B.: Dynamic response for motion capture animation. ACM Transactions on Graphics (Proceedings of ACM SIGGRAPH). 24(3)(2005):697-701.
3. Blumberg, B. M., Galyean, T. A.: Multi-Level Direction of Autonomous Creatures for Real-Time Virtual Environments. Proceedings of SIGGRAPH. (1995) 47-54.
4. Gratch, J., Marsella, S.: A Domain-independent framework for modeling emotion. Journal of Cognitive Systems Research. 5(4)(2004) 269-306.
5. Treuille, A., Cooper, S., Popović, Z.: Continuum Crowds. ACM Transactions on Graphics (Proceedings of ACM SIGGRAPH 2006). 25(3) (2006) 1160 - 1168 .
6. Tu X., Terzopoulos, D.: Artificial Fishes: Physics, Locomotion, Perception, Behavior, Proceedings of SIGGRAPH. 28(3) (1994):43-50.
7. Badler, N., Allbeck, J., Zhao, L., Byun, M.: Representing and Parameterizing Agent Behaviors. Proc. Computer Animation, IEEE Computer Society, Geneva, Switzerland. (2002)133-143.
8. Allbeck, J., Badler, N.: Toward Representing Agent Behaviors Modified by Personality and Emotion, Workshop Embodied conversational agents - let's specify and evaluate them! AAMAS 2002, Bologna, Italy.
9. Gratch, J., Marsella, S.: Evaluating a computational model of emotion. Journal of Autonomous Agents and Multiagent Systems. 11(1)(2005)23-43.
10. Gratch, J., Marsella, S.: Some Lessons for Emotion Psychology for the Design of Lifelike Characters. Journal of Applied Artificial Intelligence. 19(3-4)(2005)215-233.
11. Liu, Z., Pan, Z., Zhang, M.: Behavior Animation of Virtual Human In Virtual Society. The twelfth International Conference on Artificial Reality and Telexistence(ICAT). (2002)186-187.
12. Gottschalk, S., Lin M., Manocha, D.: OBB-Tree: A Hierarchical Structure for Rapid Interference Detection, *Proc. SIGGRAPH.* (1996)171-180.
13. Liu, F., Liang, R.. Motion Path Synthesis for Intelligent Avatar. The 4th International Working Conference on Intelligent Virtual Agents (IVA), Kloster Irsee, Germany. LNAI 2792(2003)141–149.

Steering Behavior Model of Visitor NPCs in Virtual Exhibition

Kyungkoo Jun[1], Meeyoung Sung[2], and Byoungjo Choi[1]

[1] Dept. of Multimedia Systems Engineering
[2] Dept. of Computer Engineering
University of Incheon, Korea
{kjun, mysung, bjc97r}@incheon.ac.kr

Abstract. We propose *steering behavior* model to simulate virtual characters (NPC) which walk around in virtual exhibition environment and see exhibits one by one just like humans do. Steering behavior model of such environment has its significance in that it would raise the reality level of virtually recreated exhibition space such as museums or city area with points of attraction. However, currently available steering behavior models and techniques are improper to generate such behavior patterns. Our model is autonomous and individual–centric; virtual characters autonomously determine what exhibit they are going to see, in what order, at which view point, and how long, based on their personal preferences. We also describe the implementation of our model and provide the graphical results of simulations.

1 Introduction

We propose *steering behavior* model to simulate that visitor *Non–Player Characters (NPCs)* walk around autonomously in a virtual exhibition hall and see exhibits one by one just like humans do. NPC is a computer controlled virtual character which is mainly used in online games to raise the entertainment level as well as the reality of the virtual space. Steering behavior means the ability of NPCs to navigate around their world in a life-like and improvisational manner.

The research about the steering behavior modeling of NPCs in virtual environment draws more and more interest recently because of its wide applications [7]. Autonomously behaving NPCs are able to improve the reality experiences of virtual space; imagine two virtual cities, one is crowded with human–like behaving NPCs, while the other is empty. Another important application of NPCs is to study the social behavior during building emergency evacuations [8].

Steering behavior model of visitor NPCs has its significance in that it would raise the reality level of virtually recreated exhibition space such as virtual museums, art galleries, and busy city area with a number of points of attraction. As the number of such spaces increases, its necessity also rises. However, currently available steering behavior models and techniques are improper to generate such visitor behavior patterns because they are mainly focusing on the modeling of flocking of a large number of people, most of them are mindlessly wandering city

Z. Pan et al. (Eds.): ICAT 2006, LNCS 4282, pp. 113–121, 2006.
© Springer-Verlag Berlin Heidelberg 2006

area without purpose following a group leader, just like the notorious zombie characters. The most prominent deficiency of such models to simulate visitors is the lack of the capability to reflect individual properties.

We address this issue by proposing steering behavior model to simulate visitor NPCs in virtual exhibition. Our work presented in this paper makes the following contributions

- We propose individual–centric and autonomous steering behavior model, which is discussed in Section 2; NPCs with their own personal properties determine what exhibit they are going to see, in what order, at which view point, and how long, autonomously, based on their personal preferences.
- Our model is not computing intensive. It allows to increase the realism and, at the same time, satisfy the real time simulation constraints.
- We describe how to implement the proposed model in Section 3 and 4, thus able to provide insight how to incorporate the steering model into the systems.

2   Steering Behavior Model of Visitor NPCs

We propose steering behavior model of NPCs to simulate that visitor NPCs in a virtual exhibition hall appreciate exhibits one by one in order of the popularity of the exhibits and individual NPC's preference. The following assumptions are made about the visitor behaviors in exhibitions, e.g. museums and art galleries, to propose the NPC behavior model.

- Visitors have knowledge in advance about what exhibits are and where they are located.
- Visitors have their own preference which differs depending on exhibits.
- Visitors like viewing such exhibits first which they have preference to and which are closely located to them among many items.
- Visitors have tendency to appreciate exhibits at the location which is optimal for viewing in terms of angle and distance.
- Good locations for viewing exhibits are determined by both angle and distance from exhibits.
- Parameters determining how long visitors are going to stay for each exhibit are the visitors' preference to it, its own popularity, the fatigue level of visitors at the moment, and the optimality of visitors' view point.

We establish, based upon the aforementioned assumptions, three steering behavior models of visitor NPCs; the first model is to decide in which order visitors view exhibits, the second one is to determine at which view points visitors locate themselves, and the third one is how long visitors stop for viewing exhibits.

2.1   Visit Order Model

This model determines which one of exhibits a visitor NPC views first by judging from the visitor's preference to it, the exhibit's own popularity, and the distance from the visitor to the exhibit. Each visitor tags every exhibit with *order* value and views the exhibits in descending order of the order values. The order value O_{ve} assigned to an exhibit e by a visitor v is calculated as

$$O_{ve} = P_v * PP_e * (1/D_{ve}{}^2) \qquad (1)$$

where P_v is the preference of visitor v to exhibit e, PP_e is the popularity of exhibit e, and D_{ve} is the distance from v to e. This order value is linearly proportional to visitor's preference and exhibit's own popularity, while exponentially inverse proportional to distance. Intuitively, the distance has a more critical influence to the order than personal preference and popularity of exhibits. The implication of this model can be understood if we retrospect to our own experiences in exhibitions; we never rush to the most interesting exhibit at the beginning, instead we move toward it gradually viewing other tempting exhibits close to us first.

2.2   View Point Selection Model

Selecting the view point of exhibits is affected by both the angle and the distance between exhibits and visitors. People like, for example, seeing exhibits from the front rather than either the reverse or the side, and from a decent distance at which a good look at exhibits can be obtained. However, since there are only a few locations which satisfy both angle and distance constraints, it is common that visitors find second best locations when the surroundings of exhibits are crowded with other visitors.

The view point selection model assigns every exhibit the angle limits by two vectors, the minimum distance, and the maximum distance, and finds a list of

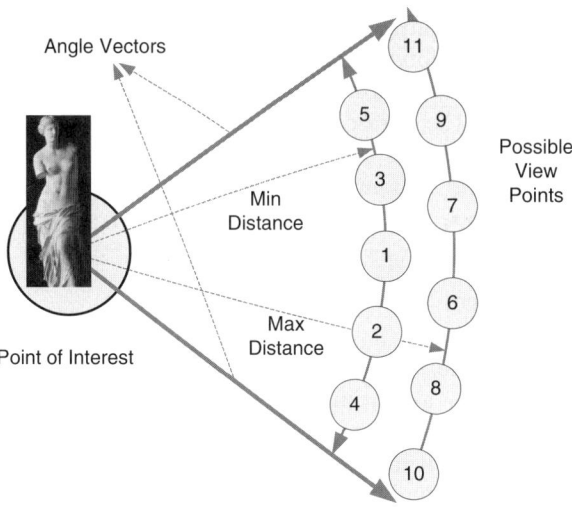

Fig. 1. View point selection model finds a list of possible view points

possible view locations of the exhibit. Figure 1 shows the procedure to calculate the candidate view locations. An exhibit is located at *point of interest*, the possible view points are represented as circles inside which numbers mean the optimality of the view locations; the lower number a location has, the more optimal view point it is. The best location is at the front and at the middle of two angle vectors, the second best locations are around the best location while maintaining the same distance from the point of interest, then next best locations are found at little bit far distance. The possible view points are located only between two angle vectors, and the nearer the location is to the point of interest, the more optimal it is. The algorithm to find the view points will be discussed in Section 3.

2.3   Appreciation Time Model

Parameters that determine the time during which visitors appreciate an exhibit are the popularity of the exhibit, visitors' preference, how optimal visitors' view point is, and the fatigue visitors feel. The appreciation time A_{ve} that a visitor v stay to see exhibit e is as

$$A_{ve} = P_v * PP_e * L_v * 1/logF_v \qquad (2)$$

where P_v is the preference of visitor v to exhibit e, PP_e is the popularity of exhibit e, L_v is the optimum degree of the view point of visitor v, and the F_v is the fatigue level that visitor v feels at the moment. The more optimal the view point of visitor v is, the higher value L_v has. The implication of this model is that visitors tend to stay longer as long as exhibits are popular, interesting to them, they are less tired, and at the better view points. We let the fatigue degree have little influence on the results by using its logarithmical value, because we believe, based on a heuristic ground, that people can somehow forget how they are tired when they are dealing with interesting subject.

We proposed in this section three steering behavior models. The mathematical equations used in the models are composed based on heuristics and our experiences, thus how good they are can be judged by how natural the movement of visitor NPCs is. We discuss the implementation of these models in Section 3, and present the results simulating the virtual exhibition space crowded with visitor NPCs in Section 4.

3   Implementation of Visitor NPCs

This section discusses the implementation of the proposed models in Section 2 and describes necessary algorithms in detail. We use the object oriented approach to realize the models. Implemented classes represent visitor, exhibit, and (exhibition) space as shown in Figure 2. We implement visitor by two classes; visitor class contains individual information such as preference, fatigue level, etc, and steering class is responsible for controlling visitor movement, e.g. seek, turn, avoid collision. Detailed description of basic steering behaviors can be found in

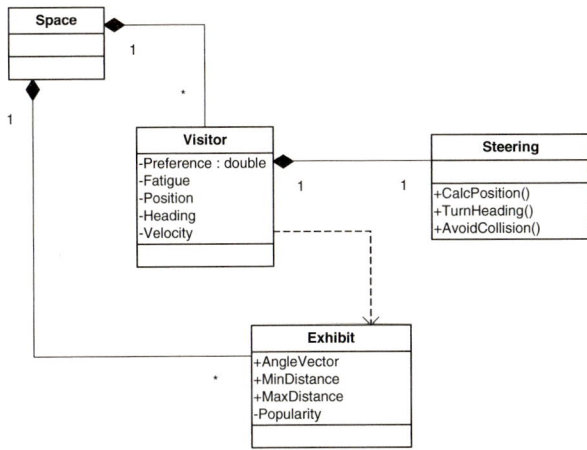

Fig. 2. UML class diagram of classes implementing the proposed models

[1]. We use exhibit class to store information about the geometric location of exhibits, popularity, and a list of view points. Space class provides visitor and exhibit with geometric space in which they reside and move around. This class also sets up walls limiting the exhibition area.

Steering class, in particular, implements a finite state machine which represents that visitor NPCs wander through exhibition hall and appreciate exhibits. The finite state machine consists of five states as shown in Figure 3. A visitor NPC is in STATE_SELECT_EXHIBIT at the beginning and selects an exhibit to see first according to the visit order model of Section 2. If no exhibit is left to visit, it changes its state to STATE_EXIT and ends its life cycle by exiting from the exhibition area. Otherwise, it changes to STATE_MOVE_TO_EXHIBIT. The visitor NPC, in this state moves toward a selected exhibit and avoids collision with obstacles and other visitors on the way. Once it reaches at a specified distance from the exhibit, its state is changed into STATE_SETTLE_DOWN and it tries to find a best view point to position itself to view the exhibit. If the best view point is already occupied by other visitors, it selects secondary best view point available based on the order how locations are optimal, moves toward it, and its state becomes STATE_APPRECIATE once it reaches the view point. It first decides in this state the how long it will stay at this exhibit by using the model Eq. 2 and stops until the appreciation time expires at which it goes into STATE_SELECT_EXHIBIT state to visit next interesting exhibit.

4   Simulation of Virtual NPCs

This section presents the graphical results of the simulation that applies the implementation of the proposed models to the steering behavior of virtual visitors wandering in an exhibition hall. Since the simulation focuses on the verification

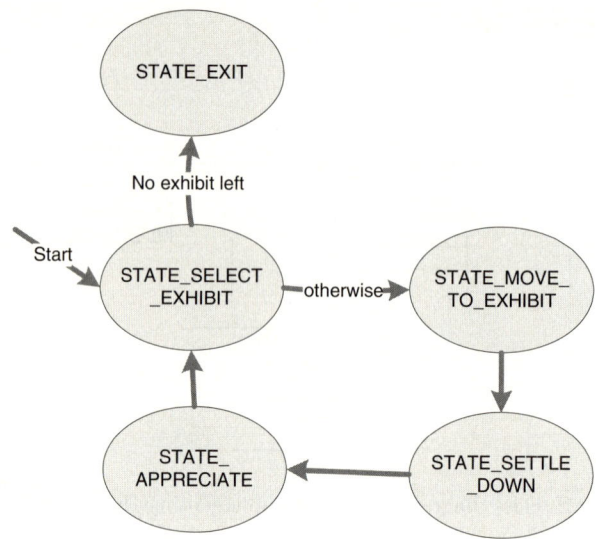

Fig. 3. Finite state machine controls visitor behavior

of the model implementation and aims at checking how similarly visitors walk around just as human visitors do, we configure the simulation environment with 2D graphic contents with very tersely simplified characters. Once we prove, however, that the models are effective to reproducing visitors' behavior, they can be easily employed with little modification to the systems equipped with more elaborate graphic capabilities.

The exhibition hall modeled in the simulation is the one that can be easily seen in museums or art galleries, and it is rendered in 2D graphics as shown in Figure 4. There are four exhibits rendered as squares, and each exhibit has its own popularity and parameters for possible view points as shown in Table 1. Figure 4(a) shows possible view points as filled circles that the exhibits can have. The exhibit at the top right corner has the longest view distance, while the one at the bottom left corner has the shortest.

Table 1. Properties of exhibits

Location	Popularity	View Angle	Optimal View Distance
Top/Left	30	60	90
Bottom/Left	10	60	70
Top/Right	50	60	110
Bottom/Right	60	60	80

Figure 4(b)(c)(d) show visitor NPCs as squares containing a circle, which is slightly biased to a side, representing the heading to which a visitor faces at

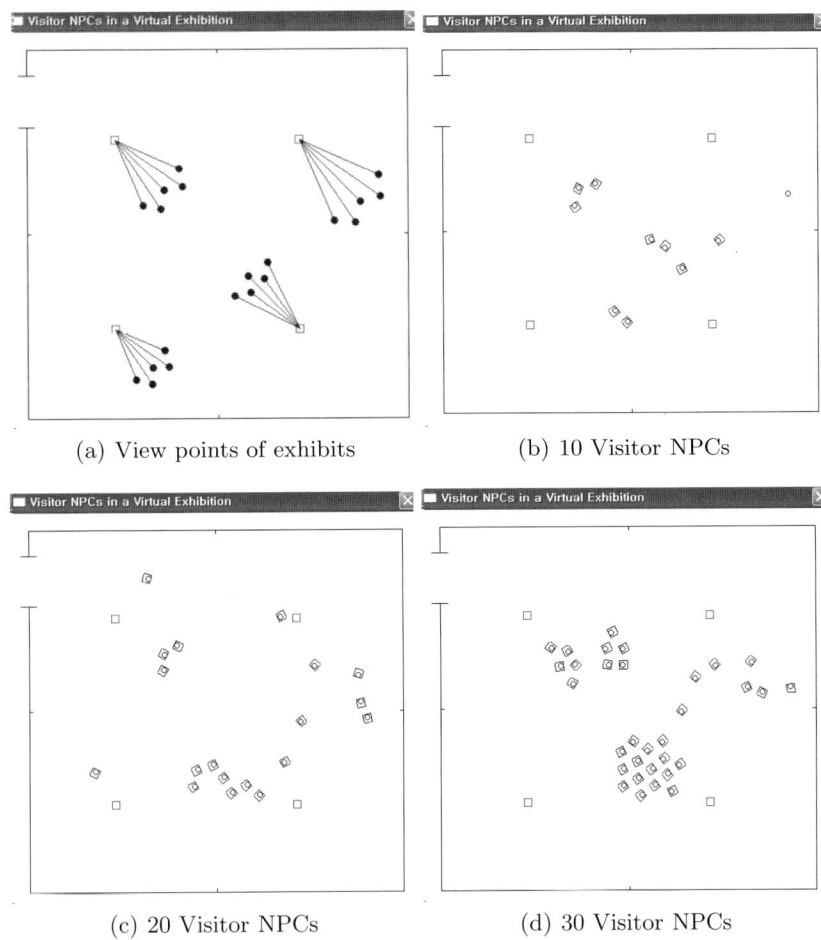

(a) View points of exhibits   (b) 10 Visitor NPCs

(c) 20 Visitor NPCs   (d) 30 Visitor NPCs

Fig. 4. Simulation of virtual visitors in exhibition

the moment. The visitors walk around the exhibition hall and stops for a while to see the exhibits as directed by the proposed models. We execute simulations several times each with different number of visitors: 10 in Figure 4(b), 20 in (c), and 30 in (d). As more visitors participate in the simulations, the exhibit at the top right corner, possessing the highest popularity, has the largest number of visitors around it, while the one at the bottom left corner, having the lowest popularity, has the least number of visitors.

5   Related Work

Since Reynolds [1] laid down a foundation for the steering behavior modeling, there have been a lot of research efforts in this field. Among them, our work builds upon the motivation endowed by the following bodies of research. Ashida [2] intended to improve individual features of NPCs, for example, its work added

subconscious actions such as walking stopped when feel sad so that there may
be a greater diversity of behaviors. In our work, we allow visitors to have their
own preference about exhibits, thus able to reproduce the individual behavior
pattern more realistically. Feurtey [3] collected a large number of crowd features,
e.g. the relation between the flow of pedestrians, the density of the area and the
speed, or the influence of the weather on the behavior. These data can help to
find what is significant in the way a crowd behaves so as to be able to incorporate
this into a model. Our model also try to integrate common features of visitors in
exhibition by retrospecting to our own personal experiences, but research about
this issue should be pursued more in our future work. Space syntax techniques
[4] have a long tradition in urban studies. In the context of cities, space syntax
aims at describing some areas in the sense of integration and segregation. A
location is more integrated if all the other places can be reached from it after
going through a small number of intermediate places. With such parameters,
the movement pattern in a city can be understood and predicted: for example,
the more a region has extensive visibility from the surrounding area, the busier
it will be. Some space syntax analysis results even show correlations between
predicted segregated areas and areas of high incidence of burglary. This space
syntax technique motivated us to assign popularity to exhibits, thus able to
realize that visitors gather around popular exhibits.

6   Conclusions

We proposed the steering behavior model of virtual visitors in exhibitions filled
with many exhibits and showed through a simulation that the proposed model
is able to reproduce the visitor behavior pattern. The model considers the popularity of exhibits, visitors' personal preferences, and other factors to decide in
what order visitor NPCs view exhibits, at what location and how long they appreciate the exhibits. We performed the simulation in 2D simplified graphical
environment; however, our models can be adopted in 3D environment with little
modification. In our future work, we plan to extend the models to add the visitor
group support since visitors rarely come to exhibitions alone.

Acknowledgement. This work was supported by the Brain Korea 21 Project
in 2006, by grant No. RTI05-03-01 from the Regional Technology Innovation
Program of the Ministry of Commerce, Industry and Energy and by grant of
the Korea Science and Engineering Foundation through Multimedia Research
Center at University of Incheon.

References

1. Reynolds, C. W., "Steering Behaviors for Autonomous Characters," in Proceedings
   of GDC 1999, pp. 763 - 782.
2. Koji Ashida, Seung-Joo Lee, Jan M. Allbeck, Harold Sun, Norman I. Balder, Dimitris Metaxas, "Pedestrians: creating agent behaviors through statistical analysis of
   observation data", Computer Animation, 2001.

3. Franck Feurtey, Takashi Chikayama, "Simulating the collision avoidance of pedestrians", Masters thesis, University of Tokyo, February 2000.
4. Bin Jiang, Christophe Claramunt, Bjorn Klarqvist, "An integration of space syntax into GIS for modelling urban spaces", JAG, Volume 2, Issue 3/4, 2000.
5. Woodcock, Steve, "Flocking: A Simple Technique for Simulating Group Behavior," Game Programming Gems, Charles River Media, 2002.
6. Shark Jaws, Atari Interactive, Inc.
7. P. Willemsen, J. Kearney, and H. Wang. "Ribbon networks for modeling navigable paths of autonomous agents in virtual urban environments", In Proceedings of IEEE Virtual Reality Conference, pages 79   86, March 2003.
8. X. Pan, C. Han, and K. Law, "A Multi-Agent Based Simulation Framework for the Study of Human and Social Behavior in Egress Analysis", ASCE Journal, 2005.

Scalable Architecture and Content Description Language for Mobile Mixed Reality Systems

Fumihisa Shibata, Takashi Hashimoto, Koki Furuno,
Asako Kimura, and Hideyuki Tamura

Graduate School of Science and Engineering, Ritsumeikan University
1-1-1 Nojihigashi, Kusatsu, Shiga 525-8577, Japan
fshibata@is.ritsumei.ac.jp

Abstract. We propose a new scalable architecture for mobile mixed reality (MR) systems and a content description language to be used in such architecture. Several architectures already exist to realize mobile MR systems, however, most of them are device specific. The architecture we propose here is able to accommodate a variety of devices, from mobile phones to notebook PCs. We have already designed a concrete specification for our architecture and content description language. We have also confirmed their viability by implementing several applications on various mobile devices.

Keywords: Mixed Reality, Augmented Reality, Scalable Architecture, Content Description Language, Mobile Computers.

1 Introduction

Outdoor application of augmented reality (AR) and mixed reality (MR) systems using mobile devices is expected to be a rich field [1]. Though there are some developments that implement AR/MR functionality on mobile phones and PDAs, their performance is inadequate [2]-[5]. In general, the main reason for this is that today's mobile devices have neither enough computational power nor memory.

These limitations could be eliminated soon. Mobile phones will become multifunctional, and we will soon have Ultra-Mobile PCs (UMPC). However, conventional desktop and laptop PCs probably may offer more performance than such UMPCs. AS a result, we need to consider frameworks that can overcome the performance differences between various mobile devices, instead of hastily attempting to implement AR/MR functions on a few low-performance devices. We must ensure that we accommodate future device developments, as well as existing performance differences between types and models of devices.

Based on these principles, we proposed a scalable architecture for various mobile MR systems and a core content description language "SKiT-XML." Our architecture is based on a client-server model that distributes the functionalities required to realize MR systems to the clients and a server. The architecture's design and implementation is explained in [6] and in the panel of [1].

Since then, our architecture has improved. Now, most of the primary functions have been implemented. We also tested the effectiveness of our scalable architecture

Z. Pan et al. (Eds.): ICAT 2006, LNCS 4282, pp. 122–131, 2006.

using various mobile devices and multiple applications. This paper provides an overview of the architecture and language as well as the applications used for confirmation.

In Section 2, we present related work. Section 3 describes our scalable architecture. In Section 4, we present our content description language, which describes information exchanged between the server and the clients. Section 5 presents the experimental results of three application types based on our architecture. Finally, Section 6 summarizes this paper and describes future directions.

2 Related Work

Some previous works in virtual and augmented reality have addressed a framework or a toolkit for developing VR/AR systems. MacIntyre and Feiner proposed a toolkit, called Columbia object-oriented testbed for exploratory research in interactive environments (COTERIE), which provides language-level support for building distributed virtual environments [7]. Feiner *et al.* also developed a Touring Machine [8] based on COTERIE. The Touring Machine is an application that provides information about Columbia's campus. COTERIE realized a shared, distributed database, and handles various trackers. Bauer and his colleagues proposed distributed wearable augmented reality framework (DWARF), which is a CORBA-based framework that allows rapid prototyping of distributed AR applications [9]. DWARF consists of reusable distributed services such as trackers, middleware to dynamically match these services, and extensible software architecture. Unfortunately, this work does not apply to mobile phones. Mobile phones with digital cameras are widespread and no other device seems to be an ideal candidate as a handy AR/MR platform. Although current mobile phones do not have sufficient CPU power to display videos and calculate camera parameters, AR/MR on mobile phones will be used in the near future. Accordingly, it is important for AR/MR frameworks to support mobile phones.

Miyamae *et al.* proposed a navigation platform for wearable AR/MR systems [10]. Miyamae's platform can address a wide variety of navigation scenarios, based on event, condition, and/or action-driven navigation systems. However, this platform is not versatile, as only navigation applications for wearable computers are assumed in this platform.

A software framework, Studierstube 4.0, was proposed in the Studierstube Augmented Reality Project [11][12]. This framework aims at creating a complete solution for AR on PDAs. Studierstube 4.0 is a cross-platform software framework that includes various components, such as graphics API, scene graph libraries, tracking middleware, multimedia playback tools, and so on. Wagner developed an application named "Signpost" based on this framework [13]. The application guides the user through a building by showing a map and an arrow, which indicates the direction. The framework mentioned in [13] supports not only a fully self-contained AR/MR system, but also a server-assisted AR/MR system. However, this framework cannot be applied in extremely limited devices such as mobile phones.

3 Scalable Architecture

3.1 Design Concept

There are varieties of mobile devices, ranging from mobile phones to notebook PCs, and there are significant performance gaps between them. For example, some contemporary notebook PCs have almost the same capability as desktop PCs. However, mobile phones used in Japan do not have enough memory and have many security limitations [14][15]. Accordingly, it is difficult to develop and run complex applications on such devices. It is assumed that these performance gaps will continue to exist in the future.

In order to absorb such performance gaps within the system, we decided to adopt a client-server model, allowing the server to compensate for low-performance clients.

In general, a mixed reality system is comprised of the following six modules:

(1) Camera Module
     The Camera Module captures raw images (real world scenes), on which virtual objects are superimposed, augmenting the user's perception.
(2) User-Interface Module
     This module is an interface for users. It can present users with raw images superimposed with MR information, and receives explicit input from users.
(3) Tracking Module
     The Tracking Module is one of the most important components of an MR system. This module detects the position and orientation of the client.
(4) Rendering Module
     The Rendering Module draws virtual objects with the correct distance, position, and orientation, based on the client's position and orientation.
(5) Content-Management Module
     This module manages the content database in the database system. The content database includes 3D graphic models, text annotations, and 2D images.
(6) Application Module
     The Application Module handles application-specific logic. It performs processes such as switching current contents based on the user's context, user position, and/or input from the user.

In addition to these modules, one additional module completes the client server/system.

(7) Client Management Module
     This module manages client information and user context.

3.2 System Architecture

In order to accommodate the performance gaps between various types of mobile devices, we distributed modules, one through seven, to the server and clients. Fig. 1 shows the system architecture. In this architecture, mobile devices are classified into three groups: light-load clients (LLCs), middle-load clients (MLCs), and heavy-load clients (HLCs).

LLCs are also called thin clients. For LLCs, the system places only the camera and the user-interface modules in client devices. All other functions are performed by modules on the server. Since the vision-based tracking method is used for LLCs, an LLC client has to communicate with the server each time it displays an image. Therefore, it is not suitable for continuous presentation of the MR images. However, since the client has only two modules, it is fairly easy to implement. For example, mobile phones of NTT DoCoMo, the most widely used phones in Japan, can run programs in an environment called "the i-αppli Runtime Environment." In this environment, only one i-αppli can run at a time because of security limitations [16]. In other words, when the camera function is used, i-αppli execution is interrupted and the actual photographing depends completely on the user—the application program cannot operate the shutter. This means that users have to press the shutter of the built-in camera to capture every scene. The process flow for LLCs stated before is assumed to be used in such limited environment.

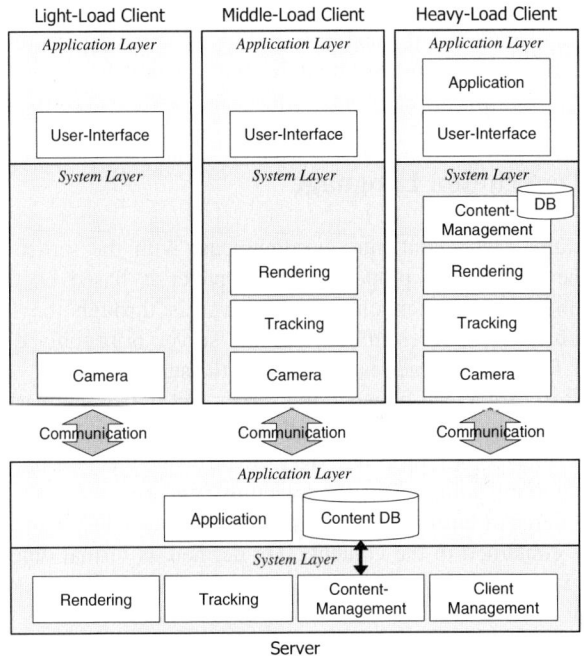

Fig. 1. The system consists of a server (the lower box) and clients (the upper boxes). Both the server and clients have two layers: *System* and *Application Layer.*

MLCs are clients that have tracking and rendering modules in addition to the camera and user-interface modules. MLCs detect and send position and orientation information to the server and receive local content related to the surrounding real world. It is possible to continuously present MR images by drawing MR information based on contents received from the server. However, since the application module on the server selects the contents to be sent to the client, the clients can only render images based on the contents sent by the server.

HLCs are self-contained clients that have all modules required to realize mixed reality themselves. Because of this, HLCs must be relatively high-performance devices. If the client is an HLC, a user can experience high-quality mixed reality in real time by wearing a head mounted display (HMD). HLCs store and manage perfectly duplicated copies of the server database. The HLC synchronizes the content database with the server, so that the database is always up to date. Since the database itself is on the HLC, the application module in the client can select the contents to be presented to the user.

However, the server must have all five modules, other than the camera and user-interface module, so that it can compensate for shortcomings of any client. The server responds to requests from clients by providing the required functionalities, based on the client type.

Both the server and clients have two layers: system and application layer. In any client, the camera and tracking modules are placed in the system layer, as they are shared by all applications. However, the application and user-interface modules reside in the application layer, because different applications use different modules. Reference implementations of modules placed in the application layer can be obtained. However, application-layer modules must be developed and installed by the developers.

4   Content-Description Language

In this architecture, each client must communicate with the server to display MR information. The architecture proposed in this paper is based on the client-server model; communication between client and server is through the HTTP protocol. Information exchanged between clients and the server is roughly divided into two groups: requests from clients and responses from the server.

The information exchanged between the server and the clients varies according to the client type, as shown in Fig. 2. SKiT-XML serves as the content-description language used in such communication. SKiT-XML is one instance of XML [17].

The most important point in this architecture concerns sharing identical content among various clients or terminals. Note that elements such as 3D graphic models and text annotations contained in the contents, are defined as virtual objects. The clients have to display identical motion of virtual objects to the users even when the objects change over time.

Two kinds of motion of virtual objects are to be considered: shape changes of an object, and movement of an object within the environment. Note that it is impractical to describe all object position and orientation parameters for each frame. Therefore, we describe parameters of each object at a specified timing, assuming that each client's system time is synchronized with the server. We call the parameter list the Sequence, and the sequence is used to represent object motions. In the sequence, the states of objects between one parameter set and the next are obtained by linear interpolation. The same method is used for animation description in scalable vector graphics (SVG) [18].

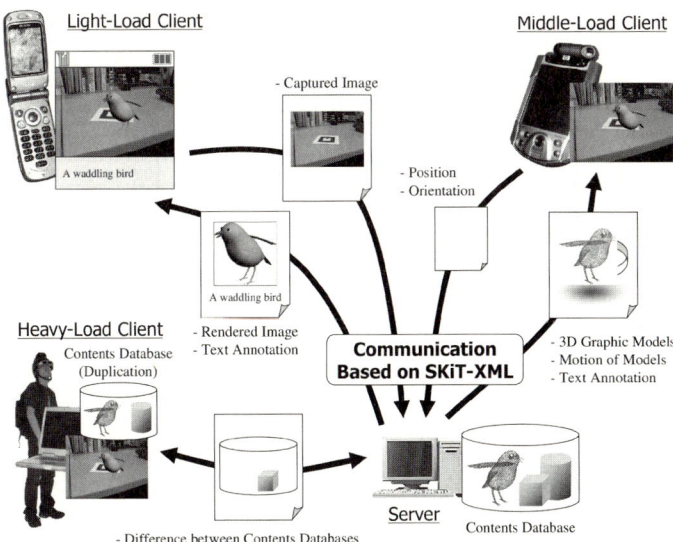

Fig. 2. Information exchanged between the server and the clients differs according to the client type. The LLC sends a captured image to the server and receives a rendered image and text annotations. The MLC sends its position and orientation and receives 3D graphics models, motion of the models, and text annotations. The HLC synchronizes the content database with the server.

All sequences of the virtual objects are stored in the server's content database. The application module changes the records in the content database according to the user's context, or while interacting with the user.

When we describe contents in the way shown above, the following data exchange is required, depending on the client type.

- LLC sends a camera image to the server in order to detect its position and orientation. The server renders the contents at that time, based on the corresponding sequence, and sends the rendered image to the client.
- MLC sends its position and orientation to the server. The server returns a sequence of virtual objects surrounding the client.
- HLC checks periodically for any changes in the server's content database. The server returns SQL statements used to change the contents in the database, to the client.

5   Experimental Results

We examined the effectiveness of our architecture by installing the system on various terminals. Table 1 shows specifications of clients and the server used in these experiments.

Table 1. This table shows the hardware specifications of the clients and the server used in these experiments

Hardware	Type	Resolution	Graphics Chip	Camera	Network
Dell Precision 450	Server	----	nVIDIA Quadro FX500	----	----
NTTDoCoMo SH901iC	LLC	QVGA	----	Built-in	Packet Network
Sharp Zaurus SL-6000W	LLC, MLC	VGA	----	CE-AG06	IEEE 802.11b
HP iPAQ h5550	MLC	QVGA	----	FlyCAM-CF1.3	IEEE 802.11b
Xybernaut MA-V	MLC, HLC	SVGA	ATI RAGE Mobility-M	CMS-V13	IEEE 802.11g
Sony VAIO Type U	MLC, HLC	SVGA	Intel 855GM	CMS-V13	IEEE 802.11g
Dell Precision M60	MLC, HLC	SVGA	nVIDIA Quadro FX Go1000	CMS-V13	IEEE 802.11g

5.1 Hidden Cable Viewer

An application called "Hidden Cable Viewer" was developed and installed on the server and the clients. The application visualizes cables hidden beneath the panels of a free-access floor, so that re-arrangement of such cables is possible.

The objective area consists of 4×6 panels, each 50 cm square. Beneath the panels are power and LAN cables. The ARToolKit [19] is used as a tracking mechanism, and 12 cm square markers are respectively placed on each tile. The ARToolKit is used only to ensure solid and stable positioning and we do not recommend using such markers.

Fig. 3 shows an example application. LLCs and MLCs of multiple types offered the expected performance.

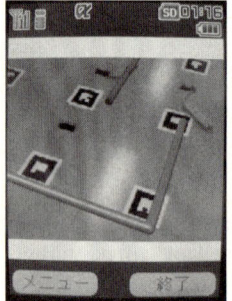 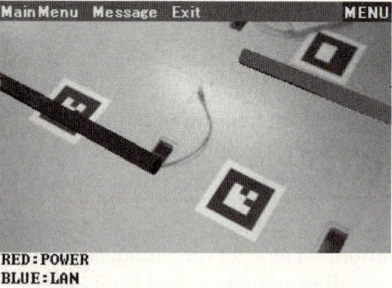

RED: POWER
BLUE: LAN

Fig. 3. The left figure is a screenshot of SH901iC, which is implemented as an LLC. The right figure is a screenshot of iPAQ h5550, which is implemented as an MLC.

When the shutter is pressed on an LLC, it sends the image taken by the camera to the server. The server computes client's position and generates MR information, which is then returned to the client. The client, then, displays the returned MR image. It takes approximately 15 seconds for the SH901iC mobile phone and 3 seconds for SL-6000W PDA to display an MR image to the user from the moment the shutter is pressed. Note that most of this time is spent in communication.

Since an MLC can detect position and orientation, it does not need to send an image to the server. It sends only the required position and orientation information. Similarly, the server can return only wiring information to the client. This reduces the communication load, allowing a movie-like presentation. The user can change the direction of the PDA and can see MR images for that direction with only a small delay.

5.2 Navigation System

Another application we used to examine our architecture is an MR-based navigation system. In this system, a user follows a path to a goal by following a flapping virtual bird. The system provides navigation at cross points, switching modes to show an arrow indicating the direction to go.

Fig. 4 shows sample images of this application. A bird at the center of the screen flies by changing position and orientation. This motion is described by the sequence explained in Section 3. A Precision M60 is used as a client. Its screen shows images from a USB CMOS camera with the superimposed virtual bird. This is an HLC, and the system ran at approximately 20 fps (frames per second). ARToolKit provided solid and stable position information.

Fig. 4. The left figure is a screenshot of a Precision M60, which is implemented as an HLC. A fluttering bird guides the user to his/her destination. The right figure is a screenshot of VAIO Type U, which is implemented as an MLC. A user heading and an annotated image of a room are displayed.

5.3 Campus Guide System

We also tested our architecture by implementing the Campus Guide System. Fig. 5 shows examples. Since position and orientation detection by the ARToolKit cannot be applied outdoors, we adopted a gyro-aided, dead-reckoning module (Gyro-DRM-III) and an inertial-based 3-DOF sensor (InertiaCube3), to build the tracking module. Since Gyro-DRM-III only detects positions within one foot, we obtained positions between each step by linear interpolation of the detected positions. The tracking module integrates the output of Gyro-DRM-III and InertiaCube3, which provides full 360-degree tracking in all axes. The error of Gyro-DRM-III is within 5 m for 100 m, and is not accurate enough. However, it is possible to use it in applications such as in outdoor guide system.

The system frame rate is nearly 25 fps. The frame rate is mainly dependent on the performance of the USB camera. When a USB CCD camera is used (Buffalo BWC-C35H01/SV), the frame rate is 28 fps. However, the USB CCD camera is slightly unstable.

Fig. 5. These figures are screenshots of a Precision M60, which is implemented as an HLC. Annotations are displayed in front of the corresponding buildings.

6 Conclusion

In this paper, we proposed a scalable architecture that can accommodate various types of mobile devices to realize AR/MR functionality, and described the results of its implementation in actual applications. These results show that the significance of our scalable architecture will increase as mobile devices evolve.

Though it is out of the scope of our concept, one problem to be resolved is building a stable tracking method for outdoor use. We used Gyro-DRM-III as a position detection device, however, the results indicated that it did not have the required accuracy. Many researchers are working on sensing devices for outdoor use. We believe that our application- and sensor-independent architecture can play a great role in outdoor use also when this research is expanded.

Acknowledgement

This research was partially supported by a Grant-in-Aid for Scientific Research (B), of the Ministry of Education, Culture, Sports, Science and Technology, No.17200039, 2005. The authors would like to thank Dr. Ryuhei Tenmoku for fruitful discussions.

References

[1] Handheld Augmented Reality, Proc. of 4th IEEE and ACM Int. Symp. on Mixed and Augmented Reality, pp.xix–xxi, 2005.

[2] J. Fruend, C. Geiger, M. Grafe, and B. Kleinjohann: The Augmented Reality Personal Digital Assistant, Proc. of 2nd Int. Symp. on Mixed Reality, pp.145–146, 2001.

[3] D.Wagner and D.Schmalstieg: First Steps towards Handheld Augmented Reality, Proc. of 7th IEEE Int. Symp. on Wearable Computers, pp.127–135, 2003.

[4] W. Pasman and C. Woodward: Implementation of an Augmented Reality System on a PDA, Proc. of 2nd IEEE and ACM Int. Symp. on Mixed and Augmented Reality, pp.276–277, 2003.

[5] M. Möhring, C. Lessig, and O. Bimber: Video See-through AR on Consumer Cell-phones, Proc. of 3rd IEEE and ACM Int. Symp. on Mixed and Augmented Reality, pp.252–253, 2004.

[6]   F. Shibata, A. Kimura, T. Hashimoto, K. Furuno, T. Hiraoka, and H. Tamura: Design and Implementation of General Framework of Mixed Reality Systems Applicable to Various Mobile and Wearable Platforms, Transactions of the Virtual Reality Society of Japan, Vol.10, No.3, pp.323–332, 2005(in Japanese).

[7]   B. MacIntyre and S. Feiner: Language-level Support for Exploratory Programming of Distributed Virtual Environments, Proc. of 9th ACM Symp. on User Interface Software and Technology, pp.83–94, 1996.

[8]   T. Höllerer, S. Feiner, T. Terauchi, G. Rashid, and D. Hallaway: Exploring Mars: Developing Indoor and Outdoor User Interfaces to a Mobile Augmented Reality System, Computers and Graphics, Vol.23, No.6, pp.779–785, 1999.

[9]   M. Bauer, B. Bruegge, G. Klinker, A. MacWilliams, T. Reicher, S. Riß, C. Sandor, and M. Wagner: Design of a Component-based Augmented Reality Framework, Proc. of 2nd IEEE and ACM Int. Symp. on Augmented Reality (ISAR '01), pp.45–54, 2001.

[10] M. Miyamae, T. Terada, Y. Kishino, S. Nishio, and M. Tsukamoto: An Event-driven Navigation Platform for Wearable Computing Environments, Proc. of 9th IEEE Int. Symp. on Wearable Computers (ISWC 2005), pp.100–107, 2005.

[11] Studierstube Augmented Reality Project Homepage, http://studierstube.icg.tu-graz.ac.at/

[12] D. Schmalstieg, A. Fuhrmann, G. Hesina, Z. Szalavari, L. M. Encarnação, M. Gervautz, and W. Purgathofer: The Studierstube Augmented Reality Project, PRESENCE - Teleoperators and Virtual Environments, Vol.11, No.1, pp.33–54, 2002.

[13] D. Wagner and D. Schmalstieg: First Steps towards Handheld Augmented Reality, Proc.of 7th Int. Symp. on Wearable Computers (ISWC 2003), pp.127–135, 2003.

[14] NTT DoCoMo, Let's make i-mode contents: i-αppli, http://www.nttdocomo.co.jp/english/p_s/i/make/java/index.html

[15] KDDI au, EZfactory, http://www.au.kddi.com/ezfactory/index.html (in Japanese)

[16] NTT DoCoMo, i-αppli Content Developer's Guide for DoJa-3.0, 2003.

[17] Extensible Markup Language (XML) 1.0 (Third Edition), http://www.w3.org/TR/REC-xml/

[18] Scalable Vector Graphics (SVG) 1.1 Specification, http://www.w3.org/TR/SVG11/

[19] H. Kato, M. Billinghurst, I. Poupyrev, K. Imamoto, and K. Tachibana: Virtual Object Manipulation on a Table-top AR Environment, Proc. of Int. Symp. on Augmented Reality, pp.111–119, 2000.

A Novel Sound Localization Experiment
for Mobile Audio Augmented Reality Applications

Nick Mariette

Audio Nomad Group, School of Computer Science and Engineering
University of New South Wales, Sydney, Australia
nickm@cse.unsw.edu.au

Abstract. This paper describes a subjective experiment in progress to study human sound localization using mobile audio augmented reality systems. The experiment also serves to validate a new methodology for studying sound localization where the subject is outdoors and freely mobile, experiencing virtual sound objects corresponding to real visual objects. Subjects indicate the perceived location of a static virtual sound source presented on headphones, by walking to a position where the auditory image coincides with a real visual object. This novel response method accounts for multimodal perception and interaction via self-motion, both ignored by traditional sound localization experiments performed indoors with a seated subject, using minimal visual stimuli. Results for six subjects give a mean localization error of approximately thirteen degrees; significantly lower error for discrete binaural rendering than for ambisonic rendering, and insignificant variation to filter lengths of 64, 128 and 200 samples.

1 Introduction

Recent advances in consumer portable computing and position sensing technologies enable implementation of increasingly sophisticated, light-weight systems for presenting augmented reality (AR) and mixed reality (MR) environments to mobile users. Greater prevalence of this technology increases the potential for more common usage of AR/MR as a form of ubiquitous computing for information and entertainment applications. Furthermore, audio-only AR/MR applications allow for less encumbered use than visual AR/MR applications, since the output device is a set of headphones, which are less intrusive and more familiar to the general public than visual devices such as the head mounted display (HMD).

The concept of audio augmented reality, proposed at least as early as 1993 [1], is to present an overlay of synthetic sound sources upon real world objects that create aural and/or visual stimuli[1] [2]. Also in 1993, even before the completion of the Global Positioning System (GPS), the concept was proposed to use GPS position tracking in a personal guidance system for the visually impaired, by presenting the user with

---

[1] In this paper, the augmentation of real *visual* stimuli with virtual sound will be considered audio AR, although existing definitions of AR and MR are not clear with regards to cross-sensory stimuli for the real and virtual components of the user's environment [2].

Z. Pan et al. (Eds.): ICAT 2006, LNCS 4282, pp. 132–142, 2006.
© Springer-Verlag Berlin Heidelberg 2006

virtual sound beacons to guide their travel [3]. Since then, several outdoor, GPS-based audio AR implementations have been built as fairly bulky packages, for example, backpack-based systems [4], [5], or roll-around cases [6]. In 2001-2004, the indoors LISTEN project [7], had high resolution, sub-decimetre tracking, and further reduced the worn system to passive tracking signal emitters and headphones, with remote tracking and spatial audio rendering. A substantial collection of these projects and other relevant literature is reviewed in [8].

With cheap digital compasses, powerful portable computers, lightweight consumer GPS receivers (and soon, Galileo European Satellite Navigation System receivers), implementation of affordable portable outdoors audio AR systems is possible. Potential applications include personal tourist guides, location-based services and entertainment, or even navigation for the visually impaired. However, despite this burgeoning potential, little evaluation has occurred on the usability and perceptual performance afforded by these systems. Subjective testing of mobile audio AR systems has often been limited to simply verifying functionality. Some examples of evaluations in the literature are discussed in the next section.

In a separate field of research, the human ability to localize real and synthetic spatial sounds has been extensively studied via laboratory-based perceptual experiments, yielding fine-grained results on the effects of many factors. These experiments tend to neglect ecological factors relevant to the audio AR situation, where the creative content designer intends synthetic sounds to be perceived as co-incident with real audible and visible objects in uncontrolled environments. In AR, as in the real world, with simultaneous, distracting ambient stimuli from other foreground and background objects, it is important that people can maintain direct or peripheral awareness of aural and visual object positions while moving.

The present experiment is designed to evaluate perception quality afforded by practical mobile audio AR systems, such as "Campus Navigator" – a tour guide demonstrator being built by the Audio Nomad research group[2]. Firstly, the experiment verifies that a pedestrian user can localize synthetic binaural spatial audio in relation to real stationary visible objects, and indicate their judgment by walking. Secondly, it examines binaural rendering factors' effects on localization errors, informing software design decisions that balance perceptual performance with limited speed of portable computing. Further, the experiment controls for the effects of latency and accuracy of position and orientation information by using static, pre-rendered spatial audio stimuli with a mobile subject response method. Finally, validation of the novel response method, by cross checking results against similar laboratory experiments, sets precedence for using similar response methods in future AR audio localization experiments.

2   Background

Few examples of sound localization research incorporate ecological validity to the AR setting by including interaction via body translation motions (not just head-turns), and/or multimodal stimuli. In 1993, Cohen et al [1] presented a very early AR study

---

[2] http://www.audionomad.com

verifying two subjects' ability to successfully co-localize a virtual binaural sound source with a real sound source received via telepresence from a robot-mounted dummy head. Since then, limited evaluation has occurred for many audio AR projects, up to and including the sophisticated LISTEN project of 2001-2004 [7]. Following, is a brief discussion of selected experiments with quantitative evaluations.

Cheok et al [9] used a visual AR environment to assess 3D sound's impact on depth and presence perception, and audio/visual search task performance, showing all three performance indicators improved using 3D sound. Ecological validity to the mobile, outdoors AR setting is limited due to the HMD visuals and tethered position and head orientation tracking, confined to a 3x3 metre area. Also, the performance metrics of depth judgment rate, task performance time and questionnaire results do not compare easily with traditional sound localization experiments.

Härmä et al [8] described the use of their wearable augmented reality audio (WARA) system for "preliminary listening tests". The subject is seated in a laboratory with stationary head position, and is requested to indicate whether a test signal was virtual or originated from a loudspeaker placed out of sight. Results showed subjects could not discriminate between virtual and real sound sources, with audio rendering using individualized head related impulse responses (HRIRs). Relevance to mobile AR is limited by lack of subject interaction via head-turns or position translation.

Walker and Lindsay [10] presented an investigation of navigation efficiency with respect to waypoint beacon capture-radius in an audio-only virtual environment. The use of navigation performance tasks to study the effect of rendering system factors was novel, yet relevance to mobile AR is limited due to only implementing the auditory modality, the lack of subject motion interaction, and a purely virtual environment. Yet, subject tasks might be successfully transferred to mobile AR studies.

Loomis [3] presents the subjective sound localization research most relevant to the mobile AR setting, based on the Personal Guidance System for the visually impaired. One study examines distance perception [11], using a novel outdoors subjective method of "measurement of perceived distance using perceptually directed action", whereby subjects' judgments were indicated via the open-loop spatial behaviour of pointing at the perceived location of the auditory image while moving. Loomis' research bears strong relevance to the present work, although to best of the author's knowledge the study of angular localization has not occurred.

Having discussed applied AR studies incorporating 3D sound, we will briefly address relevant laboratory-based research on fundamental human sound localization ability. Experiments are often designed for precision with respect to specific, often artificial factors (e.g. stimuli frequency spectrum), rather than ecological validity to a particular application environment. Three relevant research topics are: studies on localization precision, multimodal stimuli, and head-turn latency.

Localization precision afforded by binaural 3D sound rendering methods may be compared to baseline localization ability of about one degree minimal audible angle (MAA) in the horizontal plane [12]. This research provides a basis for expected performance, subjective experimental methods and associated performance measures such as mean localization error or response time to localize brief sound stimuli.

Strauss and Buchholz [13] compared localization error magnitudes for amplitude panning and first order ambisonic rendering methods to a six-channel hexagonal speaker array. With head movements permitted (allowing more accurate localization due to the closed perception-action feedback loop), the mean localization error was 5.8 degrees for amplitude panning (AP) and 10.3 degrees for ambisonic rendering (Ambi). Without head movements, mean errors were 15.8 degrees (AP) and 18.5 degrees (Ambi). The present study uses virtual amplitude panning and ambisonic rendering for binaural output, by replacing speakers with convolution by HRIR pairs.

One multimodal aspect is the "ventriloquist effect" [14], identified as a visual bias on sound localization during simultaneous presentation with visual objects. Larsson et al [15] also noted higher level cognitive effects of improved presence, focus, enjoyment and faster completion of navigation tasks for virtual visual environments augmented with correlated auditory stimuli. These results inform the decision to trial the visual/motile response method in the present experiment. Future experiments will investigate how multimodal perception might mitigate system latency limitations.

System latency to head-turns is known to affect localization ability for real-time binaural spatial audio. Brungart et al [16] discovered that system head-turn latency is detectable above 60-80 milliseconds for a single sound source, or above 25ms when a low-latency reference sound is present, as per the case of virtual sound sources augmenting real sources. The present study notes this result by using an experimental design that controls for position/orientation latency effects to isolate the rendering method effects. Using static pre-rendered virtual sources and requiring subjects to respond by moving relative to a static visual reference object, the experiment exhibits infinite latency to head orientation and position. Future experiments will re-introduce latency, studying its effects on localization and task performance in AR settings.

3   Experimental Procedure

The experiment was performed in a flat, open, grassy space, in clear weather conditions during daylight hours. To date, six volunteers (all male, aged in their 20s) have performed the experiment. Subjects wore/carried a system comprised of: a set of headphones; a position tracking system mounted at the centre back of the waist; and a portable computer running custom experiment software that displayed a graphical user interface, played sound stimuli and logged user positions.

The positioning system, a Honeywell DRM-III [17], combines an inertial navigation system (INS), a GPS receiver, pedometer, digital compass and barometric altimeter (that can all be individually activated/deactivated), with optional Kalman filtering and a serial RS232 interface. Stated INS position accuracy is 2-5% of distance traveled and the compass is accurate to within one degree. A feasibility study by Miller [18] using the DRM-III, suggests that positioning accuracy varies significantly according to usage factors such as stride length variation. We executed a preliminary performance test, obtaining the most accurate positioning for small distances (tens of metres) by using only the INS and digital compass. It was also necessary to request subjects to move only in the direction their torso was facing, never sideways, only changing direction by on-the-spot rotation.

Other equipment included Sennheiser HD485 headphones (an economical, open backed, circumaural design) and a Sony Vaio VGN-U71 touch-screen handheld computer with a Pentium M processor, running Windows XP Service Pack 2. Present experiment software is not computationally taxing, however this powerful portable platform will be necessary for future experiments employing real-time binaural rendering. The DRM-III interfaced to the Vaio with a Keyspan USB-Serial interface.

3.1 Subject Task and Instructions

The experiment configuration (Fig. 1) used a camera tripod as the visual reference object, placed at the end of a straight, fifteen-metre *reference line* from the *base position*. Each subject listened to 36 binaural stimuli and responded to each by walking forward until the tripod position corresponded to the perceived auditory image position. For example, if the sound seemed to be located 45 degrees to the *right*, the subject walked to the *left* until the tripod was positioned 45 degrees to their right. Subjects were asked to keep their heads parallel to the reference line when making localization judgments, achieving this by fixing their gaze on a distant object past the tripod in the direction of the reference line. Subjects were also asked to judge source distance, and advised that all stimuli matched a tripod position in front of them – thereby avoiding the occurrence of front-back confusions.

The experiment user interface is simple, with only two buttons (Fig. 2). For each stimulus, the subject begins at the base position, facing the tripod, and clicks the green (first) button to start the sound. The stimulus plays for up to 50 seconds, during which the subject walks to match the tripod position with the perceived auditory image position. Clicking the red (second) button stops the stimulus, and the subject returns to base, ready for the next sound. After the final stimulus, the subject records a walk from the base position to the tripod, capturing a reference track.

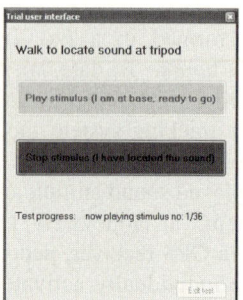

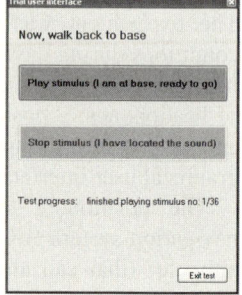

Fig. 1. Experiment layout with base position, tripod and 15m reference line

Fig. 2. Graphical interface used by the subject to run the experiment

Experiment software resets the INS position when the green *play* button is clicked and records the subject's position 4 times per second until the red *stop* button is clicked. For each subject, stimuli order is randomized, avoiding bias effects such as progressive fatigue during the experiment.

For each test, 37 position log files are recorded, representing 36 stimuli tracks and one reference track. The stimuli play order is also recorded. Subsequent data analysis is performed in Matlab using several custom scripts.

3.2   Binaural Stimuli and Factors

A single, mono white noise sample was processed in Matlab into 36 binaural stimuli, each created using a different combination of three factors: azimuth angle, filter length and rendering method. The process used HRIRs taken directly from subject number three in the CIPIC database [19]; the subject chosen arbitrarily due to lack of literature recommending a single preferable set.

Filter length was chosen because a tradeoff exists between the need for fast computation (requiring shorter filters), and high rendering quality (requiring longer filters). An optimal rendering system would use the shortest possible filters that don't significantly affect perceptual performance. Three different HRIR filter lengths were obtained: the 200-sample originals and new 128 and 64-sample versions, created by truncating the tail using a rectangular window.

Two rendering methods were used: discrete binaural rendering and a virtual ambisonic method. Discrete rendering simply convolved the source audio with the appropriate left and right-ear HRIRs of each length and azimuth angle. The virtual ambisonic method, adapted from [20], multiplied the source by a panning vector to become a four-channel b-format signal, subsequently decoded via a twelve-channel "virtual speaker array" of twelve HRIR pairs, resulting in the final binaural output.

Rendering method was a focal point because ambisonic rendering is more computationally efficient, scaling at a much lower rate per sound source than discrete rendering. However, localization accuracy afforded by first-order ambisonic rendering is expected to be lower than for discrete rendering [13].

Ambisonic rendering requires a constant computation load equivalent to five HRIR convolutions to convert the b format signal into binaural, with only four additional multiply-accumulate (mac) operations per sound source to create the b-format signal. In comparison, discrete rendering requires two HRIR convolutions per sound source, with two mac operations to mix in each additional source.

A further ambisonic advantage is that the intermediate b-format signal can be easily rotated relative to listener head-orientation at a stage between mixing mono sources to b-format and rendering to binaural. A distributed rendering architecture becomes possible where many sources are mixed to b-format on a powerful, capacious server, the b-format streams wirelessly to a computationally limited portable device that rotates it with head-turns, and renders to binaural as close as possible (with lowest latency) to the orientation sensor. Since perceptual quality is significantly affected by latency to head-turns [16], the ambisonic method is preferable if it has insignificant effects on localization ability.

Each combination of factors (three HRIR filter lengths and two rendering methods) was used once to generate stimuli at six azimuth angles: -65, -35, -15, 10, 25 and 45 degrees from the median plane. Stimuli were amplitude normalized across, but not within, rendering methods. Nevertheless, stimuli amplitude should only affect distance perception, which is not analyzed in this paper.

4 Results Analysis and Discussion

Each subject's raw track data was imported into Matlab and matched to corresponding stimuli factors using the play order record.   For each stimulus, perceived direction and localization errors are calculated and tabulated with respect to subject, stimulus azimuth, filter length and rendering method.

Fig. 3 shows all six subjects' raw tracks, rotated for display so the reference track runs due north, from the base position to the tripod. We can see that movement style is fairly individual to each subject, some honing their localization in a piece-wise manner, correcting many times (e.g. subject 1), while others choose a single direction at the outset and walk until they achieve localization (e.g. subject 5).   Subject 4 appears to have made gross position misjudgments (or misunderstood instructions), having crossed from one side of the reference line to the other for two localizations.

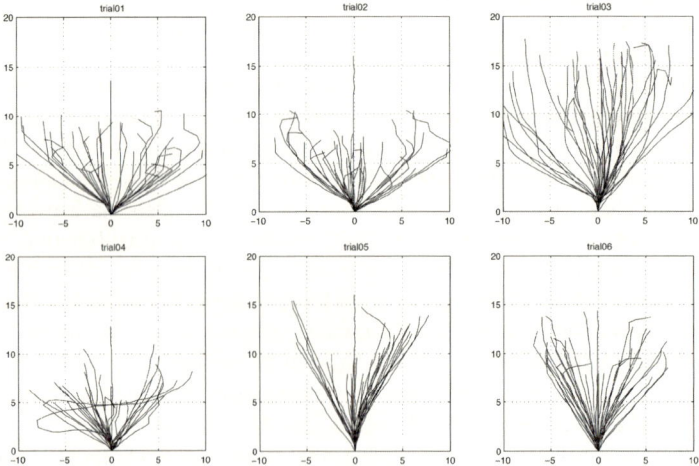

Fig. 3. Raw position tracks for each subject (both x and y axes in metres)

For each subject's set of raw tracks, we assume the tripod to be located exactly 15 metres from the base point, in the reference track direction.   Thus the perceived distance and direction of each localization judgment can be calculated as a vector from each recorded stimulus track terminal to the assumed tripod position. We know that every recorded track includes INS positioning errors, but the actual reference line is a measured 15 metres.   While the recorded reference track length may not be precisely 15m, assuming the tripod position avoids summing INS positioning errors for stimulus and reference tracks, which are likely to be uncorrelated due to different types of movements that created them.   Thus the recorded reference track is used for its angular heading and as a basic reality check for correct tracking.

A one-way ANOVA test across subjects, with a post-hoc multiple comparison using Tukey's Honestly Significant Difference (HSD) (Fig. 4) showed that Subject 3 had significantly different mean absolute azimuth error from all other subjects ($F(5,190)=8.1$, $p<0.001$).   With Subject 3's data removed, the same tests (now for $p<0.05$) show no significant difference between remaining subjects (Fig. 5).

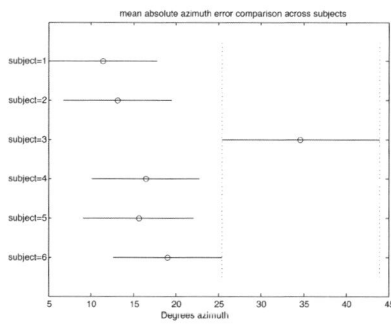

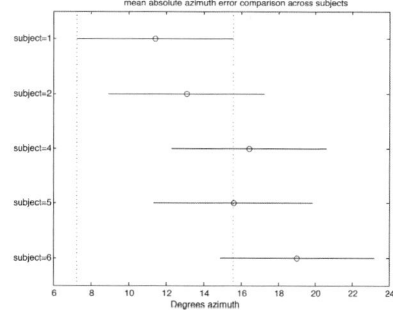

Fig. 4. Multiple comparison test of mean absolute azimuth error for six subjects. Five subjects have significantly different marginal means to Subject 3 ($p<0.001$).

Fig. 5. Multiple comparison test of mean absolute azimuth error for five subjects after removing Subject 3. No subjects have signify-cantly different marginal means ($p<0.05$).

Cross-checking with notes taken during the experiment, Subject 3 mentioned a high rate of front-back confusions and did not follow instructions to keep the tripod positioned in front (necessary to control for this type of confusion). Tracks in Fig. 3 confirm that Subject 3 often moved to the far end of the reference line. Due to this significant difference, Subject 3's results are removed from all subsequent analyses.

Next, we present scatter plot analyses of the remaining subjects' perceived azimuth, across single factors (Fig. 6), and factor pairs (Fig. 7). The ideal response would be points on a diagonal line, with perceived and actual azimuth values matching exactly. The results show more accurate localization for discrete rendering than ambisonic rendering, and a general agreement between perceived and intended azimuth for all factors, verifying that all subjects achieved some degree of correct localization using the novel mobile, multimodal response method.

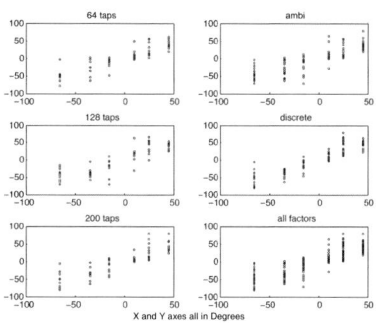

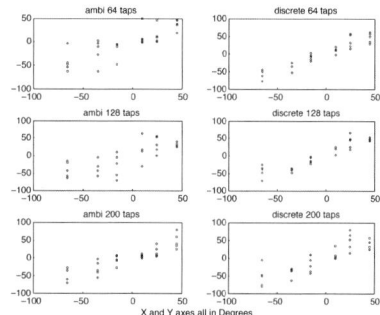

Fig. 6. Scatter plot analysis of perceived azimuth by single factors for all subjects: filter length on left; rendering method and all factors on right. X-axis is intended azimuth, Y-axis is perceived azimuth, both in degrees.

Fig. 7. Scatter plot analysis of perceived azimuth by paired factors for all subjects: filter length varies top to bottom; rendering method varies left to right. X-axis is intended azimuth, Y-axis is perceived azimuth, both in degrees.

Fig. 8 presents a three-way ANOVA test of mean absolute azimuth error for the 5 remaining subjects, across factors of azimuth (a reality check), rendering method and filter length.   Significant effects are observed due to azimuth ($F(5,152)=3.16$; $p<0.01$); render method ($F(1,152)=6.84$; $p<0.01$); and interaction between render method and filter length ($F(2,152)=3.66$; $p<0.05$). For reference, "ambi render?" is a label for rendering method, set to 1 for ambisonic, 0 for discrete rendering. The question arises why azimuth significantly affects the mean azimuth error, even though it has insignificant effect in combination with any other factor, as should be expected.

Analysis of Variance					
Source	Sum Sq.	d.f.	Mean Sq.	F	Prob>F
azimuth	2405.8	5	481.15	3.16	0.0096
ambi render?	1039.6	1	1039.61	6.84	0.0098
filter length	189.2	2	94.6	0.62	0.5382
azimuth*ambi render?	1064	5	212.8	1.4	0.2276
azimuth*filter length	1253.3	10	125.33	0.82	0.606
ambi render?*filter length	1113.2	2	556.61	3.66	0.028
Error	23116.3	152	152.08		
Total	30152.6	177			

Fig. 8. Multi way ANOVA test of mean azimuth error for 5 remaining subjects, across factors: azimuth, render method and filter length

A post-hoc multiple comparison test using Tukey's HSD (Fig. 9) reveals that only stimuli at -65 degrees azimuth have a significant effect on mean absolute azimuth error ($p<0.05$). This is the greatest absolute angle, so the larger mean error might be explained by these stimuli requiring the most subject movement, causing greater position tracking errors. This angle also positions the tripod furthest into the subjects' peripheral vision, maximizing the likelihood of aural/visual localization mismatch. No other stimulus angle has a significant effect on mean absolute azimuth error, so we shall accept this reality check to hold.

A final post-hoc multiple comparison test using Tukey's HSD (Fig. 10) shows the significant effect of rendering method on mean absolute azimuth error, ($p<0.05$).

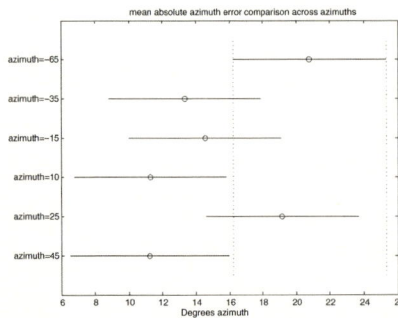

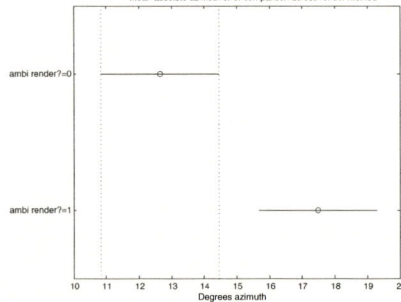

Fig. 9. Multiple comparison of mean azimuth error across azimuths, for 5 subjects. Two groups have marginal means significantly different from azimuth = -65 ($p<0.05$).

Fig. 10. Multiple comparison of mean azimuth error across rendering methods, for 5 subjects. "ambi render?=0" is discrete rendering, "ambi render?=1" is ambisonic rendering. They have significantly different marginal means ($p<0.05$).

Results show a mean absolute azimuth error of 13 degrees for discrete rendered stimuli, versus approximately 17.5 degrees for ambisonic rendered stimuli. These values correspond closely to results of Strauss and Buchholz' experiment for subjects seated in a laboratory, localizing sounds rendered to a hexagonal speaker array [13]. For subjects with unrestricted head movements, their experiment produced a mean azimuth error of 5.8 degrees for amplitude panning and 10.3 degrees for ambisonic rendering. Amplitude panning is equivalent to discrete binaural rendering for sounds aligned to the speaker directions, indicating a relevance to these results. Error magnitude differences between the Strauss and Buchholz results and the present results might be attributed to: use of non-individualized HRIRs, INS position tracking errors and the subject response method being less precise. Nevertheless, our novel methodology is validated by a reasonable mean absolute azimuth error of 13 degrees, with discrete panning affording better localization than ambisonic panning.

5   Conclusion

Preliminary results are presented for an outdoors sound localization experiment using static, pre-rendered binaural stimuli to study the effect of HRIR filter length and ambisonic or discrete binaural rendering on angular localization errors. A novel response method was employed, where subjects indicated the perceived sound source location by walking to match the auditory image position to a real visual object.

Results for 5 subjects show a mean absolute azimuth error of 13 degrees for discrete rendering – significantly better than 17.5 degrees error for ambisonic rendering. This variation according to rendering method compares well with other researchers' results for static laboratory experiments. HRIR filter lengths of 64, 128 and 200 samples show no significant effect on azimuth error.

The results validate the novel outdoors experiment and subject response method designed to account for multimodal perception and subject interaction via self-motion, both often ignored by traditional sound localization experiments. Thus, the novel methodology presented can be considered more ecologically valid for studying perceptual performance afforded by mobile audio AR systems.

Acknowledgments. Audio Nomad is supported by an Australian Research Council Linkage Project with the Australia Council for the Arts under the Synapse Initiative.

References

1. Cohen, M., Aoki, S., and Koizumi, N. Augmented Audio Reality: Telepresence/AR Hybrid Acoustic Environments. in IEEE International Workshop on Robot and Human Communication. (1993).
2. Milgram, P. and Kishino, F., A Taxonomy of Mixed Reality Visual Displays. IEICE Transactions on Information Systems, (1994). E77-D(12).
3. Loomis, J.M. Personal Guidance System for the Visually Impaired Using GPS, GIS, and VR Technologies. in VR Conference. (1993). California State University, Northridge.
4. Holland, S., Morse, D.R., and Gedenryd, H. AudioGPS: Spatial Audio in a Minimal Attention Interface. in Proceedings of Human Computer Interaction with Mobile Devices. (2001).

5. Helyer, N. (1999-2001), Sonic Landscapes Accessed: 22/8/2006
6. http://www.sonicobjects.com/index.php/sonicobjects/more/sonic_landscapes/
7. Rozier, J., Karahalios, K., and Donath, J. Hear & There: An Augmented Reality System of Linked Audio. in ICAD 2000, Atlanta, Georgia, April 2000. (2000).
8. Olivier Warusfel, G.E. LISTEN - Augmenting Everyday Environments through Interactive Soundscapes. in IEEE VR2004. (2004).
9. Härmä, A., et al. Techniques and Applications of Wearable Augmented Reality Audio. in AES 114TH Convention. (2003). Amsterdam, The Netherlands.
10. Zhou, Z., Cheok, A.D., Yang, X., and Qiu, Y., An Experimental Study on the Role of Software Synthesized 3D Sound in Augmented Reality Environments. Interacting with Computers, (2004). 16: p. 989.
11. Walker, B.N. and Lindsay, J. Auditory Navigation Performance Is Affected by Waypoint Capture Radius. in ICAD 04 - The Tenth International Conference on Auditory Display. (2004). Sydney, Australia.
12. Loomis, J.M., Klatzky, R.L., and Golledge, R.G., Auditory Distance Perception in Real, Virtual and Mixed Environments, in Mixed Reality: Merging Real and Virtual Worlds, Ohta, Y. and Tamura, H., Editors. (1999): Tokyo. p. 201-214.
13. Grantham, D.W., Hornsby, B.W.Y., and Erpenbeck, E.A., Auditory Spatial Resolution in Horizontal, Vertical, and Diagonal Planes. Journal of the Acoustical Society of America, (2003). 114(2): p. 1009-1022.
14. Strauss, H. and Buchholz, J., Comparison of Virtual Sound Source Positioning with Amplitude Panning and Ambisonic Reproduction. The Journal of the Acoustical Society of America, (1999). 105(2): p. 934.
15. Choe, C.S., Welch, R.B., Gilford, R.M., and Juola, J.F., The "Ventriloquist Effect": Visual Dominance or Response Bias? . Perception & Psychophysics, (1975). 18: p. 18, 55-60.
16. Larsson, P., Västfjäll, D., and Kleiner, M. Ecological Acoustics and the Multi-Modal Perception of Rooms: Real and Unreal Experiences of Auditory-Visual Virtual Environments. in International Conference on Auditory Display. (2001). Espoo, Finland.
17. Brungart, D.S., Simpson, B.D., and Kordik, A.J. The Detectability of Headtracker Latency in Virtual Audio Displays. in International Conference on Auditory Display. (2005). Limerick, Ireland.
18. Point Research, DRM-III Oem Dead Reckoning Module for Personnel Positioning. (2002): Fountain Valley, California.
19. Miller, L.E., Indoor Navigation for First Responders: A Feasibility Study. (2006), National Institute of Standards and Technology.
20. Algazi, V.R., Duda, R.O., Thompson, D.M., and Avendano, C. The CIPIC HRTF Database. in Proc. 2001 IEEE Workshop on Applications of Signal Processing to Audio and Electroacoustics. (2001). Mohonk Mountain House, New Paltz, NY.
21. Noisternig, M., Musil, T., Sontacchi, A., and Höldrich, R. A 3D Real Time Rendering Engine for Binaural Sound Reproduction. in International Conference on Auditory Display. (2003). Boston, MA, USA.

A Tangible User Interface for Remote Collaboration System Using Mixed Reality

Yuichi Bannai[1,2], Hidekazu Tamaki[2], Yuji Suzuki[2],
Hiroshi Shigeno[2], and Kenichi Okada[2]

[1] Canon Inc.
[2] Department of Computer Science and Informatics, Keio University

Abstract. In this paper we propose a remote collaboration system mediated by the tangible object held by each user. The process and result of interaction with the object are depicted through overlapped CG images using mixed reality and is shared between users. This system enables the user to interact with the object naturally via touch. We implemented a pointing function to the object, and conducted an experimental evaluation to investigate the effectiveness of this function. The result shows the pointing task was accomplished correctly within a practical length of time. Finally, we describe the applicability of our concept to the field of remote communication mediated by tangible objects.

1 Background

Many remote collaboration systems, such as a video conferencing system using 2D video data[12], and a virtual reality (VR) system handling 3D avatars and virtual objects, have been developed. Since shared data in these systems are displayed on a 2D monitor and manipulated through a graphical user interface, it is impossible to manipulate real objects directly in a real space where the user exists.

Shared view[6] captures a video image from the head-mounted camera, which an operator wears, and sends the image to the monitor in an instructor site. Since the screen of the monitor is captured by another camera at the same time, when the instructor points to the screen with his hand, the image of the monitor overlapped with his hand is transmitted to the operator's head-mounted display. As a result, the operator receives the instructor's message by the instructor's hand overlapped on the scene he is viewing. Shared view is an asymmetric system in terms of function and system configuration.

Augmented reality (AR) and mixed reality (MR), which enables virtual objects to be merged with the real world, have been applied to remote collaboration systems such as Real World Teleconferencing[1], Studierstube[9], and 3-D Live[8]. For example, 3-D Live is an AR video conferencing system where an observer can see the collaborator rendered from the observer's viewpoint. The system generates a 3-D video avatar by the images from multiple cameras surrounding the collaborator using the shape from silhouette algorithm. The video avatar is

Z. Pan et al. (Eds.): ICAT 2006, LNCS 4282, pp. 143–154, 2006.
© Springer-Verlag Berlin Heidelberg 2006

superimposed on the observer's real space and gives the impression the collaborator is truly part of the scene. However, this system is uni-directional, i.e., the observer can see the collaborator, but not vice versa.

When we construct a symmetric MR system between remote sites, we must consider the handling of real objects. The easiest way to do this is to represent the real object in a remote site as a virtual object in the local space, and vice versa. The other way is to use tangible replicas (objects of the same size and shape) as seen in Psybench[2]. Psybench synchronizes distributed objects to provide a generic shared physical workspace across distance. It is constructed from two augmented and connected motorized chessboards. Positions of the chess pieces on a ten-by-eight grid are sensed by an array of membrane switches. The pieces have magnetic bases so they can be moved using an electromagnet placed on a 2-axis positioning mechanism under the surface. Although the system provides a symmetrical tangible user interface between the remote sites, the actuator mechanism is needed to move real objects in each site.

We propose a symmetric MR collaboration system mediated by the tangible replicas where the users hold and interact with them. Since the results and process of the interaction overlap the replica as the virtual objects using mixed reality, the user wearing a HMD can share the information of the object and collaborate with the counterpart. The system also provides a tangible user interface enabling user's sense of touch.

2   Related Work

In the following text, we list some collaboration systems using real objects between the remote sites.

Actuated Workbench[6] attempts to overcome Psybench's limitations, i.e., motion of the object is limited to a straight line; orientation of the object cannot be controlled; and only one object can move at a time. In this system, the real objects can be moved on only the 2-D board.

In-Touch[2] is a tele-haptic communication system consisting of two hand-sized devices with three cylindrical rollers embedded within a base. The rollers on each base are haptically coupled such that each one feels like it is physically linked to its counterpart on the other base. To achieve simultaneous manipulation, In-Touch employs bilateral force feedback technology, with position sensors and high precision motors. Although it is interesting that the system provides a means for expression through touch, it is not supposed to support a specific cooperative work.

RobotPHONE [10]is a communication system via the real object, i.e., a robot modeled after a Teddy bear with the same technology as in In-Touch. When the user moves the bear's left hand, the left hand of the remote bear follows the action. RobotPHONE intends the remote users to share the feeling of each other.

In these two systems, there is merit in the tangible user interface, which enables users to manipulate the objects intuitively via touch. On the other

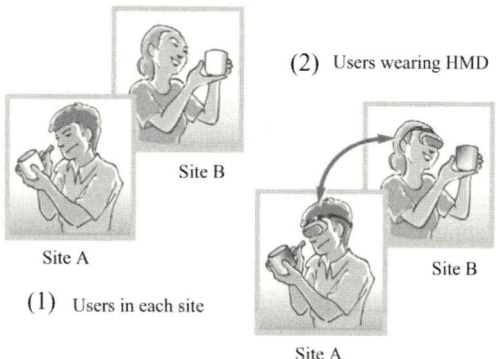

Fig. 1. An example of remote collaboration using tangible replicas

hand, two systems have drawbacks: a magnetic or mechanical actuator is needed, motion of the objects is limited, and moreover, unexpected motion of the object may occur by the counterpart's manipulation due to the lack of awareness information.

From the viewpoint of the multi-modal interface, a tactile channel can be added to enhance the existing voice communication channel.

ComTouch[3] is a device that augments remote voice communication with touch by converting hand pressure into vibrational intensity between users in real-time. Five input devices located on fingertips first detect the pressure of the finger; then five vibrators, located on the lower portion of the hand, pulsate when receiving the pressure signal. The experimental study shows users developed an encoding system similar to that of Morse code, as well as three new uses: emphasis, mimicry, and turn-taking.

Since a message from the tactile channel as non-verbal information is abstract and limited, it is difficult to convey the information necessary for the work only with the tactile channel.

3   Remote Collaboration Using Real Objects

3.1   Tangible Replicas

It is assumed a user in each location holds a real object the same size, shape, and material as a target object for a remote cooperative work. We define this object as a tangible replica. Figure 1 shows an example of remote collaboration using tangible replicas. Users A and B existing in different sites have the tangible replica of a plain white mug. Each user wearing a head-mounted display (HMD) can paint texture on the cup with his stylus. A line is drawn as a CG object on the surface of the replica where the stylus touched. Users A and B can draw and erase it moving the replicas independently; the results of operation are displayed and shared between the users.

We assume the 3D model of the replica is known beforehand, and location and orientation parameters of the HMD, the stylus, and the replica, are measured in real time. As the relative position between the HMD and the replica changes during the operation, the texture data from the user's viewpoint is continually updated. Although texture data and pointer information are shared, no information related to the replica (i.e., location, orientation, and motion data) passes between users. Therefore, user B's replica and its view are not affected by the motion of user A's replica, and vice versa.

It is a main feature of the system that users have the ability to share the virtual object, a result of mutual interaction to each replica, while maintaining consistency of each user's view.

3.2   World and Object Coordinate Systems

In an MR system, a world coordinate system is set in real space, with real and virtual objects represented using coordinates. When we construct a remote MR system, we set each of the worlds coordinate systems W_a in site A, and W_b in site B independently, as shown in Figure 2. The system manages the virtual objects and its update data such that the shared object can maintain the same parameters in each site and consistency within the system.

We introduced an object coordinate system based on the replica in addition to the world coordinate system to construct the model described in Section 3.1. It is not necessary to use world coordinates for the replica and the stylus, because absolute coordinates are not important. What is important is the relative position between the replicas and the stylus. Therefore, we create the object coordinate system of the replica in each site, and represent the relative position as location parameters of the virtual objects and the stylus, in the coordinate system based on the replica.

This system is especially effective if the replica is a portable object rather than one fixed on a table, because the latter can be managed in the world coordinate system.

3.3   Replicas in Object Coordinate Systems

Virtual objects overlapping on the replica are displayed in the object coordinate system of the replica. These objects, such as textures, move along with the replica when moved by the user. Since it is necessary for the position parameters to be shared between the sites, the parameters of the manipulated object in site A are sent to site B; the objects are simultaneously displayed using the same parameters in the object coordinate system of site B. Figure 2 shows the relationship of the coordinate systems between the sites. The virtual object S_a is expressed by $S_{ma} = [x_{ma}, y_{ma}, z_{ma}, 1]^t$, where S_{ma} is a set of location parameters in the object coordinate system of site A, whereas S_{wa} is a set of location parameters in the world coordinate system of site A. Transformation from object coordinates to world coordinates is calculated by $S_{wa} = M_a S_{ma}$

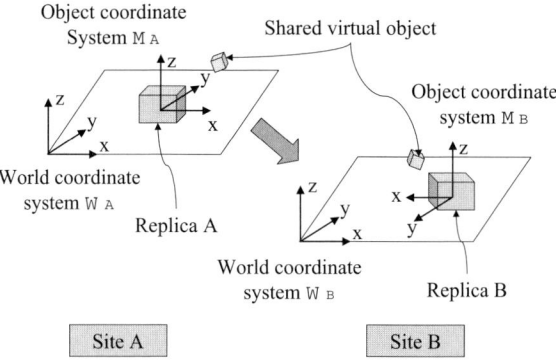

Fig. 2. World coordinate system and Object coordinate system

using modeling transformation matrix M_a, where M_a is a 4 x 4 homogeneous matrix.

Since the virtual objects are managed based on the world coordinates in each site, we calculate the location parameters of the object coordinates by transforming $S_{ma} = M_a^{-1}S_{wa}$, where M_a^{-1} is the inverse matrix of M_a. Since the virtual object is shared at the same object coordinates in each site, we can set $S_{ma} = S_{mb}$, where S_{mb} is the object coordinates in site B. After receiving S_{mb} from system A, the system in site B transforms S_{mb} to S_{wb} (the world coordinates in site B) using $S_{wb} = M_b S_{mb}$, where M_b is the modeling transformation matrix of site B, and displays the object at S_{wb}.

3.4   Synchronization of Shared Virtual Objects

Users in each site can move the replica independently. This means the world coordinates of the shared object are changed frequently even when the object coordinates of the object are not. On the other hand, the object coordinates may be changed by user interaction. At this time, the object coordinates of the other site must be updated immediately.

To accomplish this, we use the virtual object management table shown in Table 1 that stores the shared virtual objects that can change the state. When the state of an object changes, the flag is set and the other corresponding data in Table 1 is updated. This data is sent to the other site and the flag is reset by the background loop program that checks the update periodically. The system of the receiver site updates the object data for display of the object. This process is executed periodically in each site in order to synchronize the shared object.

Since the shared object may be manipulated by more than one user simultaneously, the object is controlled under the following four states.

1. No user can manipulate
2. Only user A can manipulate

Table 1. Virtual objects management Table

Virtual Object ID
Virtual Object Name
Flag
Type of Change
Amount of Change

3. Only user B can manipulate
4. Every user can manipulate

For example, when user A accesses the object whose state is State 4, the state of the object transits to State 2. User B cannot manipulate the object during State 2. The state changes to State 4 when user A finishes the manipulation of the object. The pointer of each user is controlled exclusively, at all times, by its owner.

3.5 View Management

In order to overlap virtual objects on the replica correctly, it is necessary to get the 3D model of the replica first. Using the position and orientation data from a magnetic sensor, we overlapped the transparent 3D model onto the replica so that rendering could be completed by the CG system (Open GL). As a result, the user can see the replica and other virtual objects with maintaing consistency with the real world.

4   System Configuration and Features

4.1   System Configuration

Figure 3 shows the system configuration. The video see-through HMD, which is Canon VH2002, is equipped with a pair of NTSC video cameras and a pair of VGA LCDs. Its horizontal view angle is 51 degrees and its weight is 450g. A sensor receiver made by FASTRAKR®that is attached on the HMD and the stylus get 6DOF parameters of its position and orientation. The same type of receiver is also fixed on the replica.

MR Platform[11] generates the CG image from the viewpoint of HMD using the parameters from the sensor receivers. A marker registration for HMD that compensates for sensor registration error is made in order to precisely overlap the CG image onto the real object. Two video boards within the PC capture the video output from the right and left camera and send the composed image of video and CG to the right and left display monitor respectively. The specifications of the PC are as follows: CPU=Pentium4 3.4GHz (PC1), Pentium4 2.4GHz(PC2); RAM=1GB; Graphics board=nVIDIA GeForce4; OS=Red Hat Linux9.

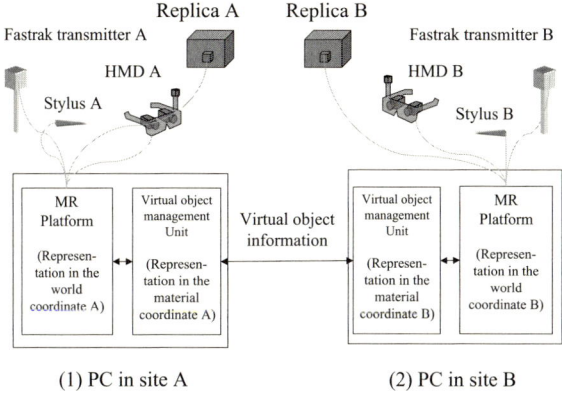

Fig. 3. System configuration

The system configuration is symmetrical between sites A and B shown in Figure 3. The handling of virtual objects in each site is managed by the MR Platform, while synchronization is controlled by Virtual object management units using Table 1.

4.2   Features of the System

Main features of this system are as follows:

– The user can move the replica freely using the sensation of touch. The motion of the replica dose not affect the replica of the counterpart. It is assumed the replica is rigid and no deformation is made.
– The user can paint drawings on the replica as well as point to it with his stylus. The stylus is handled as an exclusive object and is displayed as a CG pointer in the counterpart site. As a result, the user can recognize both his own and his counterpart's pointers.
– The pointer image provides only awareness for the counterpart. The pointer moves in the following cases.
  • when the counterpart moves either his stylus or replica, or moves both of them at the same time;
  • when the user moves his replica.

The motion of the pointer is observed by the user as a composition vector of motion, created by his own replica, and by the counterpart's pointer and replica. The user cannot recognize whether the counterpart is moving the pointer or the replica but is able to recognize the change of relative position between pointer and replica.

5   Evaluation

The purpose of the evaluation experiments is to investigate the following problems:

- Can the pointer movement and pointing position be recognized correctly, since the motion is displayed as a composition of vector images of three movements described above?
- How efficient is the object coordinate system (i.e. where the user can handle the replica as a portable object) compared with the world coordinate system (i.e. used in the conventional MR system where the replica is fixed on the table) when involved in pointing tasks?

5.1   Conditions of Experiments

Twelve subjects (10 males and 2 females, aged from 20 to 25) were divided into six pairs. One became an indicator and the other one played the role of responder in the pointing task and wore the HMD. Both systems of the indicator and responder were set in the same room. Each workspace was partitioned so the other subject could not see it. Communication between the subjects was made via voice.

The replica used in the experiments was a 12x12x12cm cube whose surface was divided into a 3x3 mesh (4x4cm square). The numbers from 01 to 45 generated by CG were randomly overlapped on the mesh of the surfaces except the bottom. The average frame rate of the HMD display was 26.3 frames/sec; no delay was observed during the experiments.

5.2   Experiment 1: Mutual Pointing

The experiment aimed to investigate whether or not mutual pointing is accomplished correctly; i.e., can the indicator point the target as he wishes and can the responder correctly read the number highlighted by the indicator. Each subject pointed to an arbitrary number with his stylus in one hand while holding the replica in the other.

The responder, who sat in front of the table, responded the number by moving his replica so he could trace the pointer. The indicator let the responder answer by saying "OK" when he pointed to the number. When he heard the answer from the responder, the subjects changed role. This task was repeated five times. The total time was measured. In the screenshot of Figure 4, the right pointer is local and the left pointer is remote.

The result of 60 pointing trials by six pairs showed the average time from pointing to response was 3.6 sec, with a standard deviation was 0.33 sec; the correct answer rate was 100%. We observed the responder could trace the pointer and correctly determine the number without trouble even the motion of the pointer was displayed as a composition vector of three movements.

Fig. 4. Screenshot of Experiment 1

Fig. 5. Screenshot of Experiment 2 in world coordinate system

5.3   Experiment 2: Comparison Between the Coordinate Systems

Since the pointing task in Experiment 1 was accomplished successfully, we conducted another experiment comparing the pointing and response time between the world coordinate system and the object coordinate system. In this experiment, the role of a pair of subjects was fixed: one was an indicator while the other was a responder.

The indicator pointed to a number on each of five surfaces of the cube except the bottom surface (i.e., he pointed to five places). The other conditions were similar to those of Experiment 1 mentioned earlier. In the world coordinate system, both the indicator and the responder had to move their upper body in order to see the numbers on the back surfaces of the cube since the replica was fixed on their tables in front of them.

The subjects in the case of the world coordinate system saw the screen shown in Figure 5. The cube was fixed on the table facing three surfaces in the view. The pointing time was taken as the duration from the time when the indicator began to point to the time when he said "OK" soon after fixing his pointer. The response time was measured as the end of the pointing to the time when the responder said the number. We first recorded the task during the experiment in order to get a precise time and then again while watching the video after the experiment.

Figure 6 shows the average time per point of pointing and response. The average pointing time of the world coordinate system was 3.7 seconds (standard deviation (sd): 1.4 sec), while that of the object coordinate system was 2.7 sec (sd: 0.6 sec). The average response time of the former system was 2.0 sec (sd: 0.6 sec) and that of the latter system was 1.6 sec (sd: 0.4 sec). The correct answer rate was 100% in each case. In the world coordinate system, the responder, as well as the indicator saw the back surfaces either while standing or in a half-sitting posture.

5.4   Consideration

We tested the difference of average pointing time and response time between the two systems by Student's $t - test$. The T value of the pointing time was $Tp = 2.25 > T(22, 0.05)$, and that of the response time was $Tr = 2.07 >$

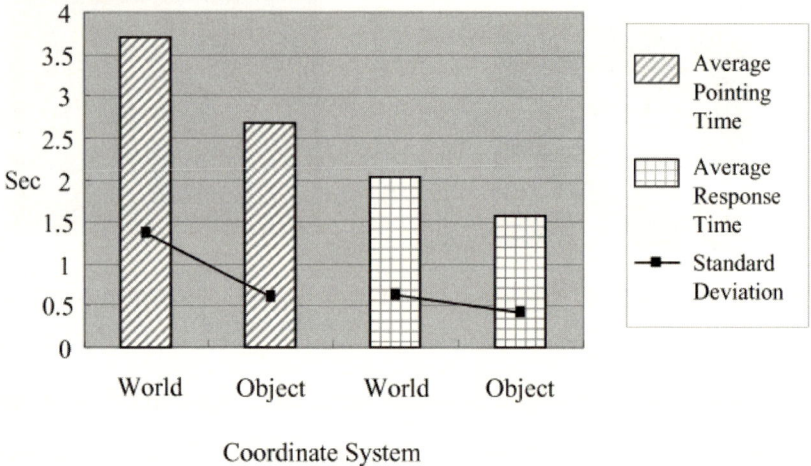

Fig. 6. Pointing time and response time in each system

$T(22, 0.05)$. We then found the difference of the average time between the two systems as significant at the 5% level. Standard deviation in the pointing time for the object coordinate system was lower than that of the world coordinate system. The reason for this may be due to the two different cases used in the world coordinate system: the case where the subject had to physically move in order to see the surface, and the other case where he did not have to move while viewing the front surface. From the results of the two experiments, we derived the following facts.

- When users are participating in the collaboration task using the tangible replicas, each user can recognize the pointed position correctly in the object coordinate system that represents the relative position between the replica and the pointer.
- When the replica is a portable object, the user can accomplish the pointing task more efficiently in the object coordinate system than in the world coordinate system.

6   Future Works

6.1   Generalization of Virtual Objects

Although virtual objects, such as textures, associated with the replica are displayed along the motion of the replica, the virtual objects independent of the replica are displayed as a composite vector of the three motions described above. In the latter case, the user might have the trouble seeing the virtual objects such as the viewpoint or body of the counterpart if they move frequently and in a wider range than the user expected. Therefore, it is necessary to study the display method of such information.

6.2   Generalization of Tangible Objects

The number of tangible objects that can be shared simultaneously is limited to one in the proposed system. It is very difficult to handle more than two tangible objects since the relative position of the two objects must be changed by a mechanism, such as an actuator when either of object moves (i.e., relative position is changed). As a practical solution, users can pick one object from group of objects by negotiating the target objects, and handling one by one.

Another point is to relax the restriction of the replica such that tangible objects of different size and/or shape can be handled. For example, we can share objects with the same shape but different size. Even when the objects have a different shape, users can share them by the proposed method in this paper if the point on the object corresponds to that on the other object.

6.3   Applicability

1. Design and prototyping
    The drawing of a designer and the prototypical mockup of an engineer may be shared as tangible objects, since points of the drawing can be mapped to those on the surface of the mockup, and vice versa.
2. 3D entertainment
    The game in a co-location space where many players manipulate a 3D object can be extended to a remote system where each user holds the replica of the 3D object.
3. Education system
    A teacher and a student in remote sites possess the same notebook or text-book as a replica, where each person can point to or annotate the virtual drawings on the book if the page and position/orientation of the book is being measured in real time.
4. Networked awareness
    There are some systems that enable transmission of awareness information from a remote user via real objects. Lovelet[4] is such a system. Users can feel the temperature of their counterpart via a watch that measures and reproduces temperature. Another awareness information could be displayed on the object using mixed reality.
5. Communication mediated by real objects
    Many user interfaces using real objects linked with other media (e.g., text linked by voice data[5]) have been proposed in recent years. As we see further progress in ubiquitous computing technologies, communication media (communication tools) are expanding to other common objects around us. We predict a trend where many collaboration systems will be mediated by real objects adding visual information using mixed reality.

7   Conclusions

We proposed a symmetric MR collaboration system that enables users to share the process and the result of interaction with the object using tangible replicas.

This system offers users a feeling of touch via the replica and enables natural interaction. Shared objects are managed in both the object coordinate system based on the replica and the world coordinate system.

Results of experiments showed the pointing task could be accomplished correctly within a practical time and the material coordinate system was more efficient than the world coordinate system when the user manipulated portable objects.

Although there exist some limitations of the tangible objects in the present system, we believe mixed reality is one of the best approaches to the remote communication system mediated by real objects.

References

1. Billinghurst M., Kato H.: Real world teleconferencing, *CHI '99 Late breaking results*, pp. 194–195, (1999).
2. Brave S., Ishii H., Dahley A.: Tangible interfaces for remote collaboration and communication, *CSCW '98 Proceedings*, pp. 169–178, (1998).
3. Chang, A. O'Modhrain S., Jacpb R., Gunther E., Ishii H.: CoMTouch: Design of a vibrotactile communication device, *DIS '02 Proceedings* , pp. 312–320,(2002).
4. Fujita H. and Nishimoto K.: Lovelet: A Heartwarming Communication Tool for Intimate People by Constantly Conveying Situation Data, *CHI '04 Late breaking results: Poster*, pp. 1553, (2004).
5. Klemmer S. R., Graham J., Wolff G. J., Landay A. J.: Books with Voices: Paper Transcripts as a Tangible Interface to Oral Histories, *CHI '03 CHI letters5(I)* , ACM Press pp. 89–96, (2003).
6. Kuzuoka H.: Spatial workspace collaboration: A sharedview video support system for remote collaboration capability, *CHI '92 Proceedings*, pp. 533–540, (1992).
7. Pangaro G., Aminzade D.M., Ishii H.: The actuated workbench: Computer controlled actuation in tabletop tangible interface spatial workspace collaboration: *UIST '02 Proceedings*, pp. 181–190, (2002).
8. Prince S., Cheok A.D., Farbiz F., Williamson T., Johnson N., Billinghurst M., Kato H.: 3-D Live: Real time interaction for mixed reality, *CSCW '02 Proceedings*, pp. 364–371, (2002).
9. Schmalstieg D., Fuhrman A., Hesina G.: Bridging multiple user interface dimensions with augmented reality, *ISAR '00 Proceedings*, pp. 20–29, (2000).
10. Sekiguchi D., Inami M., Kawakami N., Tachi S.: The design of internet-based RobotPHONE, *ICAT '04 Proceedings*, pp. 223–228, (2004).
11. Uchiyama S., Takemoto K., Sato K., Yamamoto Y., Tamura H.: MR Platform: A basic body on which mixed reality applications are built, *ISMAR '02 Proceedings*, pp. 246–253, (2002).
12. Watabe K., Sakata S., Maeno K., Fukuoka H., Ohmori T.: Distributed Multiparty Desktop Conferencing System: MERMAID, *CSCW '90 Proceedings*, pp27-38, (1990).

Multi-sensor Data Fusion Based on Fuzzy Integral in AR System

Yan Feng[1], Yimin Chen[1], and Minghui Wang[2]

[1] School of Computer Engineering and Science, Shanghai University, Shanghai, 200072
[2] School of Mathematical Science, Qufu Normal University, Qufu, 273165
fywmh@163.com

Abstract. In this paper, a data fusion model, based on the notion of fuzzy integral is presented to combine the results of multiple tracking sensors in augmented reality (AR). According to the application characteristic in AR, the tracking range and the tracking error have been chosen to act as evaluation factors. A method for dynamically assigning weighting factors, using the comprehensive performance evaluation of individual sensors is also proposed. The fuzzy integral approach can release the user's burden from tuning the fusion parameters. Experiments demonstrate that our fusion algorithm prominently improve the tracking precision, consequently to enhance the third dimension of AR system.

Keywords: Fuzzy Integral, Data Fusion, Target Locating, Augmented Reality.

1 Introduction

Augmented reality (AR) is a new developing technology based on virtual reality, and has attracted more and more attention in recent years. It enhances the real world by superimposing computer generated information on top of it [1]. The moving target in AR should be tracked correctly to fuse the real and virtual scenes perfectly. So tracking-registration is a key technology in AR.

In our AR system, only magnetic trackers were used originally. But with its improvement and considering the tracking range and precision, we now added stereo-vision sensors. Therefore, a certain algorithm is necessary to fuse the sensors data effectively.

2 Related Work

2.1 Information Fusion

With the development of sensor technology, more and more systems begin to adopt multi-sensor data fusion technology to improve their performances. Multi-sensor data fusion is a kind of paradigm for integrating the data from multiple sources to synthesize new information, so that the whole is greater than the sum of its parts.

Z. Pan et al. (Eds.): ICAT 2006, LNCS 4282, pp. 155 – 162, 2006.

Though the concept of data fusion is not new, as a technique, it is new. In recent years, various theories and approaches have been developed for it. Kalman Filter is often used to obtain more accurate estimation of the target in the low level fusion [2]. The methods for high level decision-making include Bayesian reasoning [3], the Dempster-Shafer structure [4], neural networks [5] and fuzzy logic [6].

2.1 Applications of Fuzzy Integral

Sugeno introduced fuzzy measures and fuzzy integrals [7] in last century. A wide range of applications of fuzzy integrals have been reported since a few years ago. These applications include the combination of classifiers for handwritten word and character recognition [8], quality assessment [9], buried land mine detection [10], systems modeling [11] and Image Retrieval [12].

In previous work, such as the combination of classifiers, data fusion based on fuzzy integral mostly studies the data coming from heterogeneous sensors. In this paper, a new data fusion for homogeneous sensors is presented.

The rest of this paper is organized as follows: In the next section, we introduce the two tracking systems in our AR environment. Section 4 presents the concepts of fuzzy integrals. The proposed fusion algorithm based on fuzzy integrals is described in Section 5. Section 6 gives the experimental results. Finally, Section 7 discusses the drawback of our algorithm and some of the directions our future work will take.

3   The Tracking System in AR

The whole tracking system includes two parts, magnetic sensors and visual sensors. Fig.1 shows their layout in the magic-room (the interactive environment of our AR).

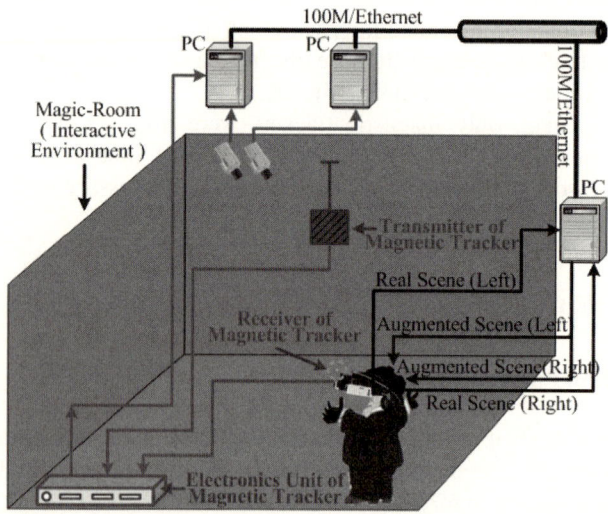

Fig. 1. Our Tracking system in AR

The magnetic sensors we chose is FASTRAK tracking system produced by Polhemus Incorporated, composed of transmitter, receiver and electronics unit. The transmitter is fixed on the center of ceiling, and the receiver is fixed on the video see-through HMD (head-mounted display).

The visual tracking system is composed of two CCD cameras (LCH-P49A), two video capture cards (10Moons SDK-2000) and a set of artificial signs. We fixed the two CCD cameras on the ceiling, and fixed the artificial signs on the HMD. In order to improve the real-time quality of tracking, we introduced parallel processing technique, that is to say, two computers respectively process the images coming from the two CCD cameras, which can attain the rate of 25 frames /second.

The above two tracking systems all have their deficiencies. On one hand, metallic objects located near the transmitter or receivers may adversely affect the performance of the magnetic sensors. On the other hand, ambient brightness or barriers may affect the performance of the visual sensors. Therefore their respective repeated-locating-accuracy is unsatisfactory. In addition, the two tracking systems have different tracking range, and all have complicated nonlinear error. So, it's necessary to fuse the two systems together to compensate each other.

4 Fuzzy Measures and Fuzzy Integrals

4.1 Fuzzy Measures

Let X be an arbitrary set, and $P(X)$ represents the power set of X. A set function $g: P(X) \rightarrow [0, 1]$ with the following properties is a fuzzy measure:

1. Boundary: $g(\varnothing) = 0$, $g(X) = 1$;
2. Monotonicity: $g(A) \leqslant g(B)$, if $A \subseteq B$;
3. Continuity: if $A_1 \subset A_2 \subset \cdots \subset A_i$, $A_i \in X$, then $g\left(\bigcup_{i=1}^{\infty} A_i\right) = \lim_{i \to \infty} g\left(A_i\right)$.

A Sugeno fuzzy measure is called g_λ-fuzzy measure if it satisfies the following additional condition:

$$g_\lambda (A \cup B) = g_\lambda (A) + g_\lambda (B) + \lambda\, g_\lambda (A)\, g_\lambda (B) . \tag{1}$$

where $A, B \subseteq X$, $A \cap B = \varnothing$, $\lambda > -1$ and $\lambda \neq 0$.

For a finite set $X = \{x_1, x_2, \cdots, x_i\}$ and $g(X) = 1$, the value of λ can be uniquely determined by the following equation:

$$1 + \lambda = \prod_{i=1}^{n}\left(1 + \lambda g^i\right) . \tag{2}$$

where $g^i = g_\lambda(\{x_i\})$ is called fuzzy density.

4.2 Fuzzy Integral

Let X be an arbitrary set, and $h: X \rightarrow [0, 1]$ be a fuzzy subset of X. The fuzzy integral over X of the function h with respect to a fuzzy measure g is defined as:

$$\int_X h(x) \circ g(\cdot) = \sup_{E \subseteq X} \left[\min \left(\min_{x \in E} h(x), g(E) \right) \right] = \sup_{\alpha \in [0,1]} \min \left[\alpha, g(H_\alpha) \right] . \tag{3}$$

where $H_\alpha = \{x \mid h(x) \geqslant \alpha\}$.

For the finite case, suppose $h(x_1) \geq h(x_2) \geq \ldots \geq h(x_n)$. (If it is not be satisfied, reorder X so that this relation holds.) Then the fuzzy integral e of function h with respect to a fuzzy integral g can be computed by

$$e = \max_{i=1}^{n} \left[\min \left(h(x_i), g(A_i) \right) \right] . \tag{4}$$

where $A_i = \{x_1, x_2, \cdots, x_i\}$.

Note that when g is a Sugeno measure, the values of g (A_i) can be computed recursively by

$$g\ (A_1) = g(\{x_1\}) = g^1 . \tag{5}$$

$$g\ (A_i) = g^i + g(A_{i-1}) + \lambda g^i g(A_{i-1}), \ 1 < i \leq n . \tag{6}$$

The parameter λ can be determined by equation (2).

Thus the calculation of the fuzzy integral with respect to a g_λ-fuzzy measure would only require the fuzzy densities.

5 Fusion Algorithm Based on Fuzzy Integral

5.1 The Choice of Evaluation Factors

The two tracking systems have different tracking range and all have complicated nonlinear error. Our intension is mainly to improve the tracking accuracy and compensate the tracking range each other, so we chose the tracking error and the tracking range as the evaluation factors, that is to say, the finite set $X = \{x_1, x_2\}$, x_1 denotes tracking error, x_2 denotes tracking range.

5.2 The Design of Index Functions

The magnetic tracking system uses electro-magnetic fields to determine the position of a remote object. The technology is based on generating near field, low frequency magnetic field vectors from a transmitter, and detecting the field vectors with a receiver. According to this principle of work, we concluded that its tracking range and error are equivalent in three directions. Let $[-R_x', R_x']$, $[-R_y', R_y']$, $[-R_z', R_z']$ be the tracking range in x, y, z, and $\left(x', y', z'\right)$ be the returned data from sensors, then $R_x' = R_y' = R_z'$. In addition, the system will provide the specified accuracy when the receiver is located within a certain separation from the transmitter, and operation with farther separation is possible with reduced accuracy. Therefore, we defined $h(x_1)$ and $h(x_2)$ as follows:

$$h(x_1) = \begin{cases} 1 - \dfrac{16x'^2}{5R_x'^2}, & |x'| \in \left[0, \dfrac{1}{4}R_x'\right] \\ \dfrac{4}{5} - \dfrac{64x'^2 - 4R_x'^2}{75R_x'^2}, & |x'| \in \left[\dfrac{1}{4}R_x', R_x'\right] \\ 0, & |x'| \in \left[R_x', +\infty\right) \end{cases}, \quad h(x_2) = \begin{cases} 1, & |x'| \in \left[0, \dfrac{1}{4}R_x'\right] \\ 1 - \dfrac{16x'^2 - R_x'^2}{15R_x'^2}, & |x'| \in \left[\dfrac{1}{4}R_x', R_x'\right] \\ 0, & |x'| \in \left[R_x', +\infty\right) \end{cases}$$

The above two functions defined the evaluation indexes of magnetic tracking system in x direction. On account of its operating characteristic, we defined the same index functions in y and z as in x.

For the binocular vision tracking system, its principle of work is different from the magnetic tracking system. It recognizes the visual marks from left and right 2D images, and then calculates the 3D locations with calibration parameters of the cameras and a certain algorithm. Its tracking range and error in three directions are not equivalent, which is different from the magnetic system. Let [- R_x'', R_x''], [- R_y'', R_y''], [0, R_z''] be the tracking range in x, y and z, and (x'', y'', z'') be the returned data of visual sensors. Here $R_x'' \neq R_y'' \neq R_z''$. We defined $h(x_1)$ and $h(x_2)$ as follows:

$$h(x_1) = \begin{cases} \dfrac{9}{10} - \dfrac{3x''^2}{10R_x''^2}, & |x''| \in \left[0, R_x''\right] \\ 0, & |x''| \in \left(R_x'', +\infty\right) \end{cases}, \quad h(x_2) = \begin{cases} 1, & |x''| \in \left[0, R_x''\right] \\ 0, & |x''| \in \left(R_x'', +\infty\right) \end{cases}$$

The above two functions defined the evaluation indexes in x direction. On account of its operating characteristic, we defined the same function $h(x_2)$ in y and z as in x. As for $h(x_1)$, we defined the same function in y as in x. Because visual sensors usually have bigger measurement error in depth than in x and y, we defined $h(x_1)$ in z direction as follows:

$$h(x_1) = \begin{cases} \dfrac{7}{10} - \dfrac{2z''^2}{5R_z''^2}, & |z''| \in \left[0, R_z''\right] \\ 0, & |z''| \in \left(R_z'', +\infty\right) \end{cases}$$

5.3   The Assignment of Weighting Factors

We adopted g_λ fuzzy measures. For the two evaluation factors x_1 and x_2, their importance degree are denoted as $g_\lambda(x_1)$ and $g_\lambda(x_2)$, namely g_1 and g_2.

Let $g(\{x_1\})=g_1$, $g(\{x_2\})=g_2$, $g(\{x_1+x_2\})= g(\{x_1\}) + g(\{x_2\})=1$.

Considering the characteristic of AR system, we finally set $g_1=0.7$ and $g_2 = 0.3$.

Suppose e_1, e_2 are respectively the comprehensive evaluation results of the two tracking systems, and t_1, t_2 are weighting factors.

Let $t_1 = e_1 /(e_1+ e_2)$, $t_2 = e_2 /(e_1+ e_2)$.

In this way, the weighting factors can be assigned dynamically.

our future work, we'll further improve on the algorithm and try to find a better method of selecting fuzzy density.

Acknowledgements. This research is supported by the University Student Science Pioneer-Enterprise Foundation of Shanghai Municipal Commission (No.PY-2005-10).

References

1. Azuma R T. "A survey of augmented reality" [J], *Tele-operators and Virtual Environments*, 1997, 6(4), pp. 355-385.
2. Ferrante, J., "A Kalman filter-based radar track data fusion algorithm applied to a select ICBM case", *Proceedings of IEEE Conference on Radar*, 26-29 Apr. 2004, pp. 457-462.
3. C. Coue, T. Fraichard, P. Bessiere and E. Mazer, "Multi-sensor data fusion using Bayesian programming: an automotive application", *Proceedings of IEEE Conference on Intelligent Robots and Systems*, 30 Sept.-5 Oct. 2002, pp. 141-146.
4. Basir, O., Karray, F., Hongwei Zhu, "Connectionist-based Dempster-Shafer evidential reasoning for data fusion", *IEEE Transactions on Neural Networks*, 2005, 16(6), pp. 1513-1530.
5. Chiping Zhang, Pingyuan Cui, Yingjun Zhang, "An Algorithm of Data Fusion Combined Neural Networks with DS Evidential Theory", *Proceedings of 1st International Symposium on Systems and Control in Aerospace and Astronautics*, 19-21 Jan. 2006, pp. 1141-1144.
6. Payeur, P., "Fuzzy logic inference for occupancy state modeling and data fusion", *Proceedings of IEEE International Symposium on Computational Intelligence for Measurement Systems and Applications*, 29-31 Jul. 2003, pp. 175-180.
7. M. Sugeno, "Fuzzy measures and fuzzy integrals: a survey", *Fuzzy Automata and Decision Processes*, Amsterdam, The Netherlands: North-Holland, 1977, pp. 89-102.
8. Beiraghi, S., Ahmadi, M., Shridhar, M., Ahmed, M.S., "Application of fuzzy integrals in fusion of classifiers for low error rate handwritten numerals recognition", *Proceedings of 15th International Conference on Pattern Recognition*, 3-7 Sept. 2000, vol.2, pp. 487-490.
9. Junli Li, Gang Chen, Zheru Chi, Chenggang Lu, "Image coding quality assessment using fuzzy integrals with a three-component image model", *IEEE Transactions on Fuzzy Systems*, 2004, 12(1), pp. 99 – 106.
10. P. D. Gader, J. M. Keller, and B. N. Nelson, "Recognition technology for the detection of buried land mines" , *IEEE Transactions on Fuzzy Syst.*, Feb. 2001, vol. 9, pp. 31-43.
11. Cadenas, J.M., Garrido, M.C., Hernandez, J.J., "Fuzzy integral in systems modeling", *Proceedings of IEEE International Conference on Systems, Man and Cybernetics*, 5-8 Oct. 2003, vol.4, pp. 3182-3187.
12. Junli Li, Zheru Chi, Gang Chen, "Image Retrieval Based on Sugeno Fuzzy Integral", *Proceedings of the Third International Conference on Image and Graphics*, 18-20 Dec. 2004, pp. 160-163.

AR Baseball Presentation System with Integrating Multiple Planar Markers

Yuko Uematsu and Hideo Saito

Graduate School of Science and Technology, Keio University, Yokohama, Japan
{yu-ko, saito}@ozawa.ics.keio.ac.jp

Abstract. This paper presents "On-line AR Baseball Presentation System", which is a vision-based AR application for entertainment. In this system, a user can watch a virtual baseball game scene on a real baseball field model placed on a tabletop through a web-camera attached to a hand-held LCD monitor. The virtual baseball scene is synthesized from an input history data of an actual baseball game. Visualizing the input history data can help the user to understand the contents of the game. For aligning the coordinate of the virtual baseball game scene with the coordinate of the real field model, we use multiple planar markers manually distributed into the real field model. In contrast with most of AR approaches using multiple markers, we do not need any manual measurement of the geometrical relationship of the markers, so that the user can easily started and enjoy this system.

1   Introduction

Augmented Reality(AR)/Mixed Reality(MR) is a technique for overlaying virtual objects onto the real world. AR has recently been applied to many kinds of applications including entertainment, such as [1,2,3,4]. In this paper, we propose "AR Baseball Presentation System" which allows a user to watch a virtual baseball game at any place in the real world via a web-camera attached to a hand-held LCD-monitor with moving around the real world. For example, as shown in Fig. 1, the user can observe the virtual baseball game on the table-top where a real baseball field model is placed. The virtual baseball game scene is synthesized with 3D CG players and overlaid on the field model in the real world. In this proposed system, the virtual game played on the field model is the replayed game of the actual game. When the history data of the actual game, such as web-site, is input, the same game is replayed on the real field model by 3D virtual players. In contrast with just reading such 2D web-site, observing the 3D game will be a big help for the user to understand the game history.

For such AR applications, registration of virtual objects with real images is a significant issue. Therefore many approaches have been studied before such as sensor-based approach, vision-based approach and hybrid approach, etc. Especially the vision-based registration does not require any special devices except cameras, so a lot of methods have been proposed. This kind of approach can be categorized into marker-based approach and using natural features approach.

Z. Pan et al. (Eds.): ICAT 2006, LNCS 4282, pp. 163–174, 2006.

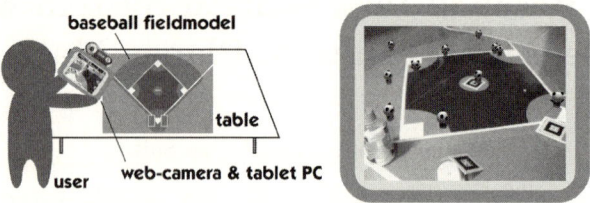

Fig. 1. AR Baseball Presentation System

Using natural features, the augmentation is naturally realized [5,6,7]. However, it is not easy to construct a robust on-line system because exact recognition of natural features in real-time is hard task and registration jitters are often caused. It is also true that only few features are available for registration in the real world. Since AR-based applications have to work in real-time and on-line, we focus on marker-based approach.

As a marker-based approach, "AR-Toolkit" [8] is very popular tool for simple implementation of an on-line AR system [9,10,11]. The simplest way is using one marker like [9], however, the camera's movable area is limited to the area where the camera (user) can see the marker in the frame. Moreover, when the marker cannot be recognized properly because of a change in its visibility, the registration of virtual objects is getting unstable.

Using multiple markers can solve such problems. In order to use multiple markers, however, it is necessary to know geometrical arrangement of the markers, such as their positions and poses, in advance [12,13,14,15,16]. In [12], they need the position and pose of a square marker and the position of a point marker in advance. In [13], they proposed marker-less registration method by setting up a learning process. In the learning process, the markers' geometrical information is required for learning the markers.

In most cases, the task for measuring of the multiple markers' arrangement is manually implemented. However such a task is very time-consuming and not sufficiently accurate. Kotake et al. [17] proposed a marker-calibration method combining multiple planar markers with bundle adjustment. Although they do not require a precise measurement of the markers, they need a priori knowledge of the markers such as qualitative information to compute markers' geometrical information from a set of images by bundle adjustment, *e.g.* multiple markers are coplanar.

We have already proposed Multi-Markers based On-line AR System [18]. In this system, multiple planar markers like AR-Toolkit are placed at arbitrary positions and poses in the real world. These markers can be used for the registration without manual measurement task because of introducing the registration method using arbitrary multiple planes [19]. In this registration method, geometrical prior-knowledge about the planes is not required because the geometrical arrangement of the planes is automatically estimated via 3D projective space defined by projective reconstruction of two images. Therefore, in this proposed system, the markers can be placed at arbitrary positions and poses on the field model. The user can freely move around wide area. Moreover the system can work at video-rate. It is suitable for AR entertainment applications.

2 System Overview

Fig. 2 shows overview of the proposed system. Multiple markers are distributed inside and outside of the baseball field model which is placed on the tabletop in the real world. The markers can be placed at arbitrary positions and poses without measuring the arrangement of them. The image of the tabletop field model is captured with a web-camera attached to a LCD monitor and displayed on the monitor. The user watches the field model and the virtual baseball game the web-camera and the LCD monitor.

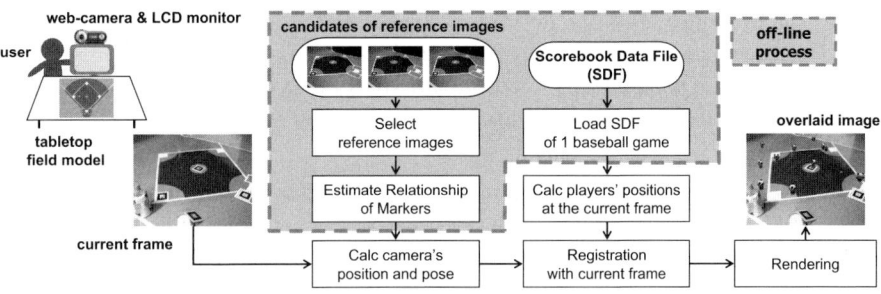

Fig. 2. Overview of Proposed System

This system can be divided into off-line and on-line process. At the off-line process, first, a game history data file of a baseball game called "Scorebook Data File" (SDF) is prepared and loaded. In this file, history of game results are described play-by-play. Next, the field model is captured by the moving web-camera for some seconds to estimate the markers' arrangement automatically. The above processes are executed once in advance.

At the on-line process, the three steps are repeated on-line: (1) synthesizing the baseball game scene while 1 play according the input data, (2) computing the camera's position and pose at the current frame, and (3) overlaying virtual players onto the field model. At the first step, when one line of the SDF is read out, the positions of the players and the ball at every frame while 1 play are computed according to the data to render them on the field model. At the second step, the camera's rotation and translation are estimated using the markers in the current frame. At the final step, the virtual baseball scene, such as the players and the ball synthesized with CG, is overlaid onto the tabletop field model.

Using this system, the user can see the virtual baseball game from favorite view points with the web-camera and LCD monitor. Because the arrangement of the markers does not need to be measured, the markers can be placed in a wide area, and the camera can also move around in wide area.

3   Replay Baseball Game by 3D Virtual Players

3.1   Input Scorebook Data File

The game played on the field model is the replayed game of the actual game which is reproduced according to input data file called "Scorebook Data File" (SDF). As shown in Fig. 3, the game history of the actual game is described play-by-play in the SDF. "1 play" means the actions of the players and the ball from the moment that the pitcher throws the ball to the moment that the ball returns to the pitcher again. It is about for 15 to 30 seconds. The actions of the players and the ball in 1 play are described on one line in the SDF. The former part of the line represents the actions of the fielders and the ball, while the latter part describes the actions of the offensive players. This file is loaded in starting the system and is sequentially read out line-by-line at every 1 play. In this way, the actions of the baseball scene are described in the SDF.

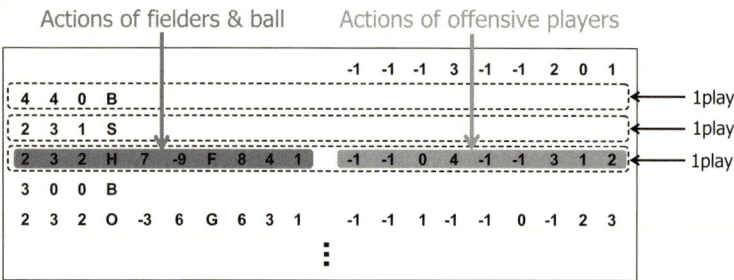

Fig. 3. Scorebook Data File (SDF)

3.2   Actions of Offensive Players

Offensive players indicate a batter, runners, and players who are waiting in the bench. Each player belongs to one of the six states as shown in Fig. 4(a). The batter is in the batter's box, so its state is "0", third runner is "3", and the waiting players are "-1". In SDF, the destination state to which every player changes in each play is sequentially recorded. When one line of the file is read out, the destination of each player is decided according to the data like Fig. 4(b). Then the game scene that 3D players are moving from the present state to the destination state while 1 play is created with CG.

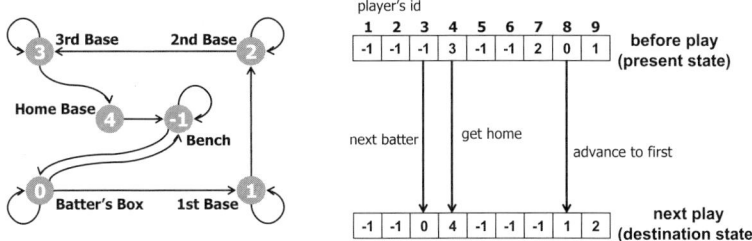

(a) State transition of offensive play- (b) Example of Scorebook Data File for
ers   offensive players

Fig. 4. Actions of the offensive players

3.3 Actions of Fielders and Ball

In contrast to the offensive players who are just moving from present state to
destination while 1 play, the fielders are doing some actions while 1 play, such
as moving around the field and throwing and catching the ball, etc. Therefore
only the action of the ball is described in the SDF. Fielders move to catch the
ball according to the action of the ball. The action of the ball while 1 play is
described as shown in Fig. 5

Fielders basically stay own positions. First, the ball is thrown by the pitcher
and hit to the position which is described in part D of Fig. 5. Then the player
whose position number is described in the fist of part E moves to the position of
part D to catch the ball. After catching the ball, the player throws the ball to
the next player whose position number is described next. The next player moves
to the nearest base and catches the ball. After the same iterations, finally, the
ball is thrown to the pitcher.

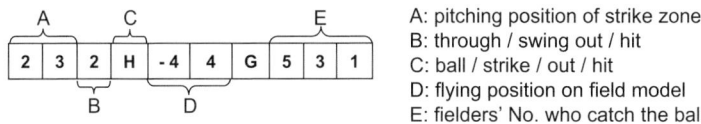

A: pitching position of strike zone
B: through / swing out / hit
C: ball / strike / out / hit
D: flying position on field model
E: fielders' No. who catch the ball

Fig. 5. Scorebook Data File of the fielders and the ball

4 Multi-markers Based Registration

In this section, we explain the algorithm of registration method in the Multi-
Markers Based On-line AR System [18]. This algorithm is based on [19].

This registration method can be divided into two stages. At the first stage,
the geometrical relationship of the markers is automatically estimated. For the
estimation, a 3D projective space, which is a 3D virtual space, is defined by

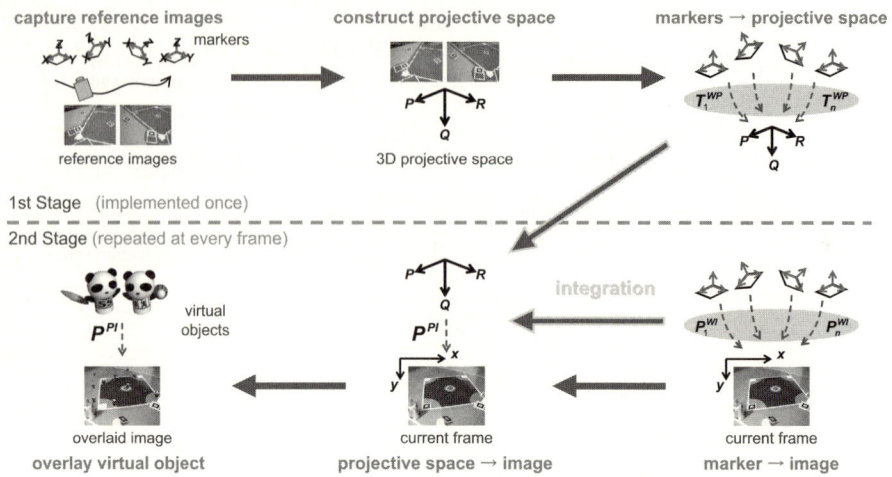

Fig. 6. Overview of the Registration Method

projective reconstruction of two reference images. The reference images are automatically selected from some candidate images. The geometrical relationship of the markers is represented as a transformation matrix called T_i^{WP} between each marker i and the projective space. These transformation matrices are computed once in advance. At the second stage, a projection matrix P_i^{WI} from each marker i to the input image. Those projection matrices and the transformation matrices which are computed at the first stage are integrated into a projection matrix P_i^{PI} by eq. (1) respectively, which is based on each marker i and projects the projective space to the input image.

$$P_i^{PI} = P_i^{WI} \left(T_i^{WP}\right)^{-1} \tag{1}$$

Moreover those P_i^{PI} are integrated into one projection matrix P^{PI} by least-square method. Then virtual objects described in the projective space coordinate system are overlaid onto the input image by using the projection matrix. These processes of the second stage are performed at every frame.

4.1   3D Projective Space

A 3D projective space is used for estimation of the geometrical arrangement of multiple planes placed at arbitrary positions and poses. The projective space is defined by projective reconstruction of two images which are captured from two different view points and called reference images. As shown in Fig. 7, a 3D space P-Q-R is defined as a 3D projective space, which is projected to the reference image A and B by following equations.

$$\left[u_A v_A 1\right]^\top \simeq P_A \left[P\ Q\ R\ 1\right]^\top, \qquad \left[u_B v_B 1\right]^\top \simeq P_B \left[P\ Q\ R\ 1\right]^\top \tag{2}$$

$$P_A = [\mathbf{I} \,|\, \mathbf{0}], \qquad\qquad P_B = \left[-\frac{[e_B]_\times F_{AB}}{\|e_B\|^2} \,|\, e_B \right] \qquad (3)$$

where, $[u_A, v_A, 1]^\top$ and $[u_B, v_B, 1]^\top$ are homogeneous coordinates of 2D points in the reference images, and $[P, Q, R, 1]^\top$ is also homogeneous coordinates of a 3D point in the projective space. F_{AB} is a F-matrix from the image A to B, e_B is an epipole on the image B, and $[e_B]_\times$ is the skew-symmetric matrix [20].

Since the projective space is defined by projective reconstruction of the reference images, the accuracy of F_{AB} is important. F_{AB} is computed from the projection matrix which is computed from the markers by using the algorithm of [8]. Therefore the accuracy of F_{AB} is depending on the accuracy of marker detection. In this system, two reference images which have most accurate F_{AB} are automatically selected. The details will be described in next section.

4.2 Automatic Selection of Reference Images

The projective space is defined by the projective reconstruction of two reference images. Therefore the F-matrix between the reference images is important to construct the accurate projective space. We introduce automatic selection algorithm of the reference images. The detail is shown in Fig. 8.

First, the object scene is captured for a few seconds by a moving camera. This image sequence becomes the candidates of the reference image. When two images are selected from the candidate images, projection matrices based on the markers which exist in the selected reference images are computed by using the algorithm of [8]. Here, P_{A_i} and P_{B_i} are the projection matrices which project marker i to the selected reference image A and B, respectively. Using each pair of the projection matrices, a F-matrix based on marker i is computed as following equation,

$$F_{AB_i} = [e_{B_i}]_\times P_{B_i} P_{A_i}^- \qquad (4)$$

where, $P_{A_i}^-$ represents the pseudo inverse matrix of P_{A_i} [20]. Then one F-matrix is selected as F_{AB} which has the smallest projection error:

$$error = m_B{}^\top F_{AB_i} m_A \qquad (5)$$

where, m_A and m_B are corresponding points in the selected reference images.

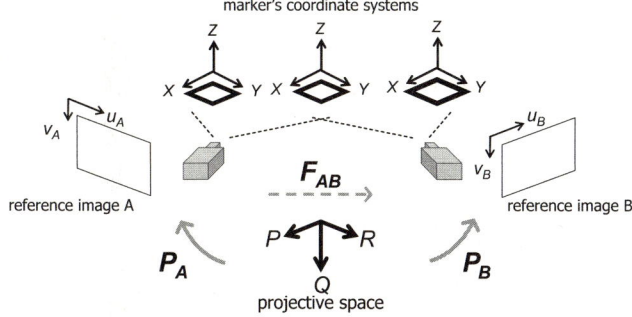

Fig. 7. Projective 3D space defined by projective geometry of the reference images

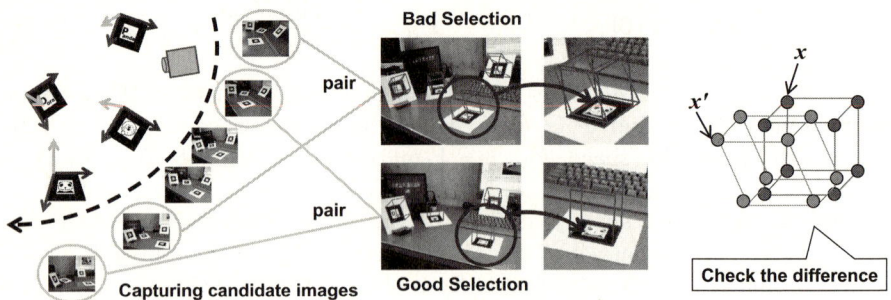

Fig. 8. Automatic selection of the reference images

When a projective space is temporarily constructed by the selected F_{AB} from eq. (3), T_i^{WP} between each marker i and the projective space is computed. Then P_i^{PI} are computed and integrated into one projection matrix P^{PI}. Then we compare these two projected coordinates x_i, x_i':

$$x_i = P_{B_i} X_W, \qquad\qquad x_i' = \left(P^{PI} T_i^{WP}\right) X_W \qquad (6)$$

Although these two coordinates should be equal, if the combination of the two reference images is not reasonable, they will be different. In such case, we return to the phase of selecting a pair of temporary reference images. We iterate these processes until every difference of x_i and x_i' based on plane i becomes smaller than a few pixels. In the experiments in Sec.5, we decide the threshold as 3 pixels.

5 Experimental Results

We have implemented AR Baseball Presentation System. A user watches a table-top baseball field model thorough a web-camera (ELECOM UCAM-E1D30MSV) attached to a LCD monitor. The resolution of the captured image is 640×480 pixels. Multiple planar markers are distributed inside and outside the field model. In this case, one of the markers must be put on one of the bases in order to determine relationship between the field model and the markers. The other markers can be placed at arbitrary positions and poses. In these experiments, we use four markers and place one of them on the third base. A Scorebook Data File of a baseball game is manually prepared in accordance with sec. 3.1. 3D models of virtual objects, such as players and a ball, are renderd with OpenGL.

First, the user places the baseball field model on the tabletop and distributes the markers. Next the object scene is captured with moving around the field model for 100 frames as candidates of the reference images. Inside of the system, the best pair of the reference images is automatically selected from the candidate images. Then the projective space is constructed by the selected reference images. The geometrical relationship of the markers is also estimated. These automatic

┌─ User's Operations ──┐

1. **Arrangement**
   Place field model and multiple markers at arbitrary positions and poses;
2. **Capturing**
   Capture the object scene as candidates for two reference images;
3. **Input**
   Input Scorebook Data File;
4. **Observation**
   Start system and observe game with moving around;

└──┘

processes take about 60 seconds. After the automatic preparations, the user inputs a Scorebook Data File and starts the system. The virtual baseball game begins on the field model and the user can watch the game from favorite view point with moving around the real world.

Fig. 9 presents a baseball game: team RED vs. team WHITE. In this situation, team WHITE is in the field and team RED is at bat. The bases are loaded and 4th batter of team RED is in the batter's box. The batter hits safely to left, and then all runners move up a base. Team RED gets a score. In this experiment, frame rate of AR presentation is about 10 fps with a desktop PC (OS:Windows XP, CPU:Intel Pentium IV 3.6GHz). Thus user can see the baseball game at video-rate without feeling any discomfort.

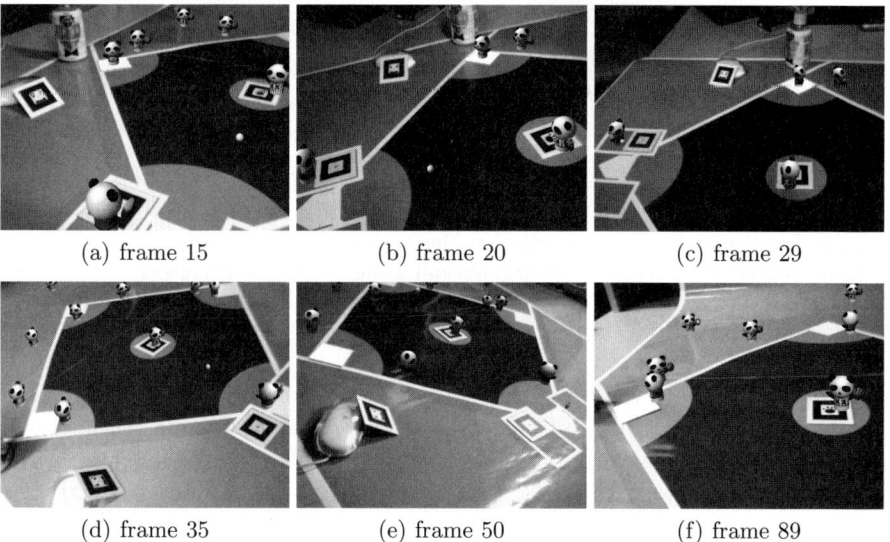

(a) frame 15   (b) frame 20   (c) frame 29

(d) frame 35   (e) frame 50   (f) frame 89

Fig. 9. Example of play: 4th batter of team RED sends a hit to left with the bases loaded and scores a goal

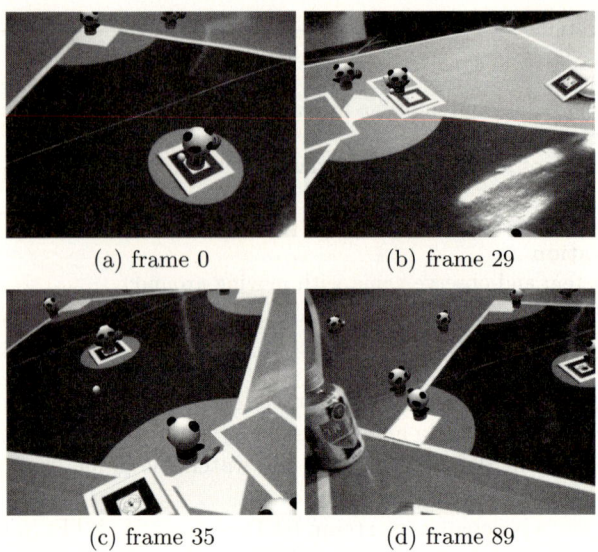

(a) frame 0   (b) frame 29

(c) frame 35   (d) frame 89

Fig. 10. Closeup views of the same scenes as Fig. 9 from different view points

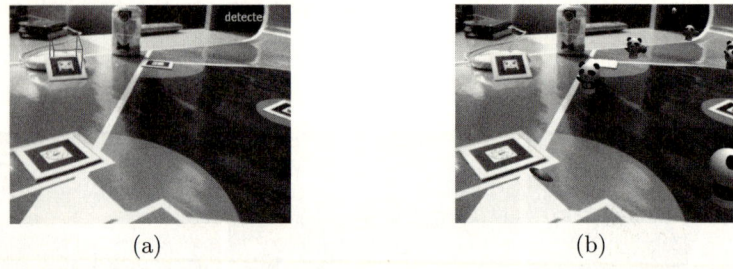

(a)   (b)

Fig. 11. Most of the markers which face to the same directions as the tabletop cannot be detected; The marker which faces to different direction is detected successfully. (a) Marker detection: The red cube on the marker represents detected marker. (b) Augmented view: Virtual objects are overlaid using the detected marker.

Fig. 10 shows some closeup views of the same scene. Since these images are captured from closeup view points, only a few markers can be captured in the field of view, and the captured markers are different in every frame. Even though particular markers are not continuously captured over the frames, the virtual players and the ball can correctly registered onto the real tabletop field with the same world coordinate. This means that the consistency of the geometrical relationship between the camera and the virtual objects is kept properly, although the geometrical arrangement of the markers is unknown.

In Fig. 11, the angle of the camera relative to the tabletop is too small to detect the markers lying on the tabletop plane. One marker is placed at different pose from the ground plane and the other markers are placed on the ground plane. In such a case, the markers which face to the same directions as the tabletop plane cannot be recognized because of the angle of the camera. If all the markers have to be on the same plane, it even fails recognition for most of the markers. In our registration method, however, the markers can face to various directions like Fig. 11 because the markers can be placed at arbitrary positions and poses. The marker with the red cube is placed at different pose from the ground plane, so that this marker can be detected even in the case that the markers on the tabletop plane are not detected. Therefore, the registration can be stably continued even if the user moves the camera to any view point. This is a big advantage of the proposed system for applying to entertainment AR applications.

6   Conclusion

We have presented AR Baseball Presentation System based on multiple planar markers. On-line AR System using multiple markers placed at arbitrary positions and poses is extended to the AR application so that a baseball game can be presented on the tabletop field model in the real world according to an input game history data of the game. Multiple markers can be placed anywhere without knowledge about their geometrical arrangement, so extra effort, such as measuring geometrical relationship of the markers, is not necessary in advance. Since such measurement is not needed, the directions of the markers' faces are also free. Making the markers face to various directions allows keeping the registration accurate. Moreover the proposed system can be performed at video-rate.

References

1. Cheok, A.D., Fong, S.W., Goh, K.H., Yang, X., Liu, W., Farbiz, F.: Human pacman:a mobile entertainment system with ubiquitous computingand tangible interaction over a wide outdoor area. Personal and Ubiquitous Computing **8**(2) (2004) 71–81
2. Klein, K., Drummond, T.: Sensor fusion and occlusion refinement for tablet-based ar. In: Proc. of the ISMAR. (2004) 38–47
3. Henrysson, A., Billinghurst, M., Ollila, M.: Virtualobject manipulation using a mobile phone. In: Proc. of the ICAT. (2005) 164–171
4. Haller, M., Mark Billinghurst, J.L., Leitner, D., Seifried, T.: Coeno-enhancing face-to-face collaboration. In: Proc. of the ICAT. (2005) 40–47
5. Neumann, U., You, S.: Natural feature tracking for augmented reality. IEEE Trans. on Multimadia **1**(1) (1999) 53–64
6. Simon, G., Fitzgibbon, A., Zisserman, A.: Markerless tracking using planar structures in the scene. In: Proc. of the ISAR. (2000) 120–128
7. Chia, K.W., Cheok, A., Prince, S.J.D.: Online 6 DOF augmented reality registration from natural features. In: Proc. of the ISMAR. (2002) 305–313
8. Billinghurst, M., Cambell, S., Poupyrev, I., Takahashi, K., Kato, H., Chinthammit, W., Hendrickson, D.: Magic book: Exploring transitions in collaborative ar interfaces. Proc. of SIGGRAPH 2000 (2000) 87

9. Prince, S., Cheok, A.D., Farbiz, F., Williamson, T., Johnson, N.., Billinghurst, M., Kato, H.: 3d live: Real time captured content for mixed reality. In: Proc. of the ISMAR. (2002) 7–13
10. E.J.Umlauf, Piringer, H., Reitmayr, G., Schmalstieg, D.: ARLib: The augmented library. In: Proc. of the ART02. (2002) TR–188–2–2002–10
11. Claus, D., Fizgibbon, A.W.: Reliable automatic calibration of a marker-based position tracking system. In: Proc. of the WACV. (2005) 300–305
12. Kato, H., Billinghurst, M., Poupyrev, I., Imamoto, K., Tachibana, K.: Virtual object manipulation on a table-top ar environment. In: Proc. of the ISAR. (2000) 111–119
13. Genc, Y., Riedel, S., Souvannavong, F., Akinlar, C., navab, N.: Marker-less tracking for ar: A learning-based approach. In: Proc. of the ISMAR. (2002) 295–304
14. Foxlin, E., Naimark, L.: Miniaturization, calibration & accuracy evaluation of a hybrid self-tracker. In: Proc. of the ISMAR. (2003) 151–160
15. Foxlin, E., Naimark, L.: Vis-traker: A wearable vision-inertial self-tracker. In: Proc. of Virtual Reality. (2003) 199–206
16. Foxlin, E., Altshuler, Y., Naimark, L., Harrington, M.: Flighttracker: A novel optical/inertial tracker for cockpit enhanced vision. In: Proc. of the ISMAR. (2004) 212–221
17. Kotake, D., Uchiyama, S., Yamamoto, H.: A marker calibration method utilizing a priori knowledge on marker arrangement. In: Proc. of the ISMAR. (2004) 89–98
18. Uematsu, Y., Saito, H.: Ar registration by merging multiple planar markers at arbitrary positions and poses via projective space. In: Proc. of ICAT2005. (2005) 48–55
19. Uematsu, Y., Saito, H.: Vision-based registration for augmented reality with integration of arbitrary multiple planes. In: 13th International Conference on Image Analysis and Processing (ICIAP2005), LNCS 3617. (2005) 155–162
20. Hartley, R., Zisserman, A.: Multiple View Geometry in computer vision. CAMBRIDGE UNIVERSITY PRESS (2000)

An Efficient 3D Registration Method Using Markerless Image in AR-Based CNC Machining Simulation

Z.Y. Ma, Y.P. Chen, C.M. Yuan, and Z.D. Zhou

School of Mechanical Engineering,
Huazhong University of Science and Technology, China

Abstract. In this paper we present a model-based approach for the real-time recognition and registration for augmented reality applications. It does not need any artificial markers to track the target. What the system need is the 3D model of target and some representative learning images. The most contribution of our work is that we put forward an idea of transferring the construction of correspondent point pairs between model and real scenes to the calculation of the affine matrix between a pair of 2D images. Our method is based on a two-stage process. In the first stage, a set of features is learned from the training images. The second stage matches the learned features with that obtained from the real scenes. If the target is recognized, the final correspondences used for registration are built with the help of the calculated affine matrix. The system is robust to large viewpoint changes and partial occlusions. And in the premise of stability assurance, the system has a good performance in reducing the computation burden.

Keywords: Model-based recognition; markerless tracking; features matching; augmented reality.

1 Introduction

During the past few years, rapid progress in several key areas has enabled the development of information system using augmented reality [1] (AR) technology. It provides us new perspectives for a lot of application areas [2], such as medical, manufacturing and maintenance, annotation and visualization, robot path planning, entertainment, and military aircraft. The tracking technique plays an important role in AR system. It determines the positioning accuracy of the virtual objects in real scenes directly. The trackers should calculate the projection matrices of the virtual objects relative to the real scenes in real time. Through those matrices, the virtual scenes can be overlapped in real scenes in a proper way to output the mixture scenes. Briefly, the main function of trackers is to keep synchronous and harmonious between the objects in the real scenes and the virtual objects generated by the computer. It is the focal and hard problem for a long time in AR technique researches that how to raise the registration accuracy while the speed of registration is satisfied.

Existing tracking methods in the literature are of two types: those that sensor-based and those that image-based. In the view of fundamental principle, the sensor-based trackers have been used include mechanical, photoelectric, inertial, ultrasonic,

Z. Pan et al. (Eds.): ICAT 2006, LNCS 4282, pp. 175 – 184, 2006.

GPS, hybrid, infrared and electromagnetic [2]. The main advantages of those sensors are their real-time performance. The main disadvantages are the deficiency of accuracy or huge volume or expensive price or sensitive to disturbance. However, image-based techniques have some advantages over sensor-based tracking techniques, as they do not need expensive devices to obtain high accuracy and can minimize system registration error. The two main disadvantages of Image-based techniques are that the heavy computing burden in image recognition and registration and the various influence from the circumstances.

In some image-based AR applications, several markers are manually placed on some joint locations. In this way, the computation efficiency of the pose estimation can be improved remarkably through processing and recognizing those markers in the video stream. The typical representation of this method is the ARToolkit [3]. The use of markers increases robustness and reduces computational requirements. However, their use can be very complicated, as they are subject to severe limitations in some areas such as partial occlusions or illumination changes. There may be some problems when using marker in some fields such as manufacturing. It is not always possible to install markers on machine as they may hinder the motion and furthermore they can be occluded during tool motion. Fortunately, with the development of recent computer vision, the performances of image-based techniques have been improved greatly. Direct use of scene features for tracking instead of the markers is much desirable, especially when certain parts of the workspace do not appropriate to use markers. This paper presents a method of markerless image-based tracking which robust to partial occlusions. It is based on a two-stage process. In the first stage, a set of features is learned from a series of training images. The second stage uses these learned features to estimate the affine matrix between the learning image and the real one. Once that matrix is verified, the correspondent point list used for the calculation of final projective transformation will be built.

This paper is organized as follows. In Section 2, we first review related work, and then we explicit some important details about our approach in section 3. Section 4 is the results and conclusions. In Section 5 we point out future work in our plan.

2 Related Work

It is very similar to the marker-based approach searching for 2D/3D correspondences by using natural features instead of artificial ones. Computer vision based methods provide the best accuracy, and represent the currently most developed approach. In the related literature, the most common geometric features used in pose estimation are often interest points, intersection lines, ellipses, arcs, corners, or a combination of these different features. By these features, we can form 2D/2D or 2D/3D correspondences for pose estimating.

In the methods of features extraction, we can distinguish between routine and special according to its surface has some obvious features or is smooth. If the target has some distinguished features, such as corners point, peaks, and grooves. They can be easily found. In the previous work, some object recognition systems are designed to work on isolated and unoccluded targets. This will be a serious disadvantage if these systems run in practice, because real scenes contain clutter and occlusion. From another point of view, feature extraction is an important issue that determines the system reliability. Consequently, any recognition system designed to work in real world should satisfy the following requirements as much as more:(1) Be resistant to cluttered backgrounds; (2) Handle partial occlusions; (3) Work well on highly textured objects; (4) Be invariant to the changes of illumination or scale or viewpoint; (5) Tolerate few errors in the correspondences or remove spurious matches; (6) Reduce the computational burden for real-time applications.

In order to obtain excellent features, much work have been done in computer vision fields. Some Approaches use sample 2D features such as corners or edges [4], which make them resistant to partial occlusions and cluttered backgrounds. As long as enough features are obtained and matched, the object can still be detected. Spurious matches can be removed by enforcing geometric constrains, such as epipolar constrains between different views or full 3D constrains if an object model is available [5]. Scale-invariant feature can be obtained by using the Harris detector [6], or by considering local optima of pyramidal difference-of-Gaussian (DOG) filters in scale-space [7]. In another literature, an affine invariant point detector has been proposed by Mikolajczyck et al. to handle larger viewpoint changes, but it increases computation burden due to its iterative estimation [8]. Baumberg uses a variant of the Fourier-Mellin transformation to achieve rotation invariance [9]. Lepetit has put forward an interesting approach to avoid jitter and drift during tracking. He merges the information of subsequent frames with that of off-line calibrated reference images [10]. Genc provides useful criteria of stable features [11]. Comport uses edge features instead of points [12].

In computer vision, the purposes of recognizing maybe are inspection, grasping or object avoidance. As for applications in our system, we augment the CNC machining simulation into the real working environment. The virtual workpiece is located according to the result of recognition and pose estimation of real clamps. In other words, the goal of the recognition is to implement initial installation of the controlled virtual models. The models should be registered to the real targets in real workspace at first. When simulation works, the virtual machining system composed of those controlled models begins to process the virtual workpiece to verify machining codes and provide feedback information. So it is the emphasis discussed in this article that how to efficiently recognize and register some mechanical parts such as clamps in clutter background. And it is also the base of our work.

3   Experimental Setup

We have preliminarily implemented the registration work described in the previous section. The experiment consists of series of works. For example, establishing the 3D model of target to obtain the actual coordinates of all possible feature points, forming 2D learning image group by selecting appropriate viewpoints and detecting features to build pseudo-correspondences list and advanced features list, obtaining features from the input video image and classifying the real image according different viewpoint, matching advanced features between the learning image and the real one, calculating the affine and projection matrix, and drawing the virtual image overlapping the real image. In the experiment we take the mechanical part, such as a clamp that used for fixed the workpiece, as the recognized target to describe the details of our implementation and the choices that we have made. Because many mechanical parts are regular polyhedrons consisted of some line segments and regular curves, the method proposed in our experiment has certain reference meanings for the recognition and registration of this kind of objects. One real image with a clamp obtained from the video is shown in figure 1. In order to reducing the computational burden, we have taken some steps such as offline preprocessing and getting the interval images from the input video if the system allows.

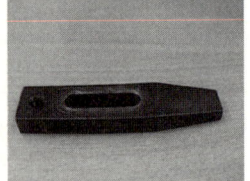

Fig. 1. One original real 2D image from the video

3.1 Feature Description

All features we can get from the image are categorized into three types by their information. One is the original feature, which includes corners and center points of ellipses. There are many ways to locate corners in the original image directly, such as Harris corner detector and SUSAN corner detector. However, center points of ellipses or circles or arcs are the feedback of primary feature detection. Original features are used to form correspondent pairs.

In the image, other simple geometry features are also easily detected, such as lines and ellipses, and circle is handled as a special case of ellipse. Then we get some unit areas environed by some lines or ellipses, which we called primary features. The ways of area composition may be like this: areas environed only by lines, by a single ellipse, by ellipses or by lines and ellipses. Other lines or curves that cannot environ areas are ignored. This kind of features is used for further composition of advanced features.

Advanced features are some three-element units describe two primary features and their relation. The admitted relations between the two line-environed areas are inclusion, overlapping edge. The ones between the two ellipse-environed areas are inclusion but not concentricity, inclusion and concentricity, separation. The structure of three-element unit are given as below:

Triple:	Primary feature	Primary feature	Relation

The advanced features are used to find target in real image. If the target is recognized, at least three correspondences come from the advanced features matches are obtained to calculate the affine matrix between the learning image and the real one.

3.2 Offline Preprocessing

In the offline stage, we have the following works to do.

At first, we establish the 3D model of the target, and take the corner labeled '1' as the origin to set up the coordinate system that shown in figure 2. With these dimensions, it is easy to obtain all the original features' (a_1, a_2, ..., a_n) coordinates of the clamp.

Secondly, we select a small set of ideal images representing the scene of the target from different viewpoints to construct the 2D learning image group. Every target to be recognized has its correspondent ways to build learning image group mainly according to their appearances. In this case, as the clamp is a convex polyhedron and the camera is placed on the skew upward side of the target, the viewpoint can be placed on eight positions (labeled as 'A', 'B', ..., 'H') shown in figure 3. Moreover, we found the set of corners with viewpoint 'E', 'F', 'G' and 'H' is a subset of those with viewpoint 'A', 'B', 'C' and 'D'. So, at last the learning images group in the system only includes 4 special members as shown in figure 4.

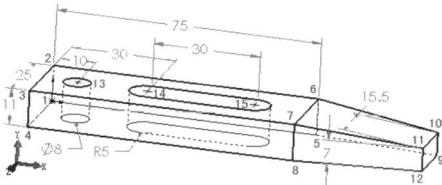

Fig. 2. 3D model of a clamp with corner labels and dimensions

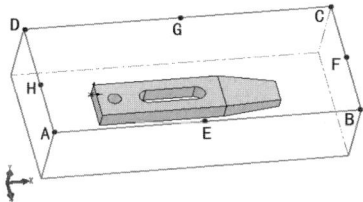

Fig. 3. Choose viewpoint in model space to obtain learning image group

Fig. 4. The learning images group we selected consist of images with the viewpoint 'A', 'B', 'C' and 'D'

As the 2D learning image group has established, all the original and advanced features in each learning image should be figured out. The extraction of corners and that of line segments or ellipses are two independent procedures. As for corner, improved Harris detector is an appropriate choice. To ensure the key corners to be detected, we have to reduce the threshold of the detector. This may bring many pseudo-corners, but it doesn't matter.

On the other hand, before primary features extraction, some preprocessing work should be done, such as graying the image, extracting contour, making binary-state, removing isolated points by median filter and thinning. In simplified binary-state contour image, Hough Transformation (HT) is a good method for detecting lines. The result of HT is the list of lines with parameters of their start and end points and rate of slope. As for ellipse, it needs five parameters to determine its shape and position. The plane ellipse equation with five parameters can be described as follows:

$$\frac{[(x - x_0) \cdot \cos \theta - (y - y_0) \cdot \sin \theta]^2}{a^2} + \frac{[(x - x_0) \cdot \sin \theta + (y - y_0) \cdot \cos \theta]^2}{b^2} = 1. \quad (1)$$

Where $x0$ and $y0$ specify the center point of ellipse; a and b are the length of long axes and short one; θ is the angle between the long axis and horizontal line. All those parameters are used to judge the relations between ellipses. When we get five points in a curve to obtain all the parameters, equation (1) can be written in a simplified form to be solved by matrix transformation. The simplified equation of ellipse can be expressed like this:

$$Ax^2 + Bxy + Cy^2 + Dx + Ey + 1 = 0. \qquad (2)$$

We sampled five pixels equidistantly on the continuous curve whose length is greater than the threshold. After coefficients of equation (2) are resolved, we have to resample another five pixels on the same curve to verify the validity of those coefficients. If it is qualified, the exact ellipse parameters (x_0, y_0, a, b, θ) can be calculated by equation (1). As a result, we get the list of ellipses with shape and position parameters.

In primary features extraction, any curves except lines and ellipses are ignored. With these lines and ellipses, it is easy to obtain the areas environed by them. Before edge tracking to generate areas, we have to polymerize some endpoints of line segments. If the terminals of some lines are near enough, the lines are deemed to intersect at that terminal. On the other hand, all intersection points among all lines and ellipses are calculated. They are saved respectively as the appendages of lines and ellipses. The lines without any intersection point will be deleted. Then, we select a line and take the intersection nearest to the left endpoint or just the left endpoint as the starting point to track the edge. When the next intersection is met, the leftmost adjacent element is selected to continue the tracking. If it comes back to the starting point, an area is generated. If cannot, but the number of elements that have been tracked is more than three, we joint the beginning and the end to generate an area. Otherwise, another line is selected to repeat the above work until the ergodic processes of all lines are completed. Till now, we have got all the primary features and the relation of overlapping edge between areas. The relations between the two ellipse-environed areas are easy to calculate, as all parameters of ellipses are known. The relation-judgment between two polygons, in a general way, is obtained through ray method, which has been well researched in Computer Graphics.

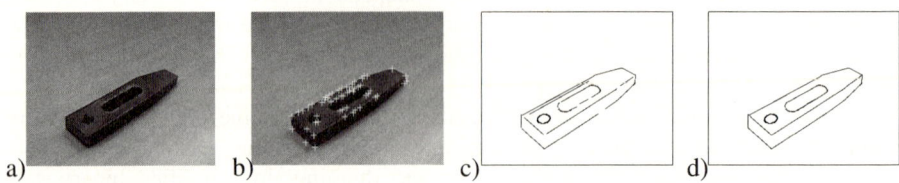

a)   b)   c)   d)

Fig. 5. The feature extraction results of a learning image. a) A learning image without processing; b) Corners extraction using Harris detector with threshold=1000, although there are many pseudo-corners, we get eight valid corners; c) Line segments and ellipses extraction using Hough Transformation, all isolated points and small lines and other curves are ignored; d) The primary features we get finally, after connecting collinear line segments, polymerizing all the near endpoints of line segments and removing isolated lines. Advanced features are obtained according to the relations between those primary features.

Once all feathers we needed are extracted, we manually select the valid original feathers ($b_1, b_2, \ldots, b_n$) in learning image to match those in 3D model to build the pseudo-correspondences list $\{(a_1, b_1), (a2, b_2), (\ldots), (a_n, b_n)\}$. And according to each learning image, we have got all the three-element units to build the advanced features list. The extraction results of all features we needed are given in figure 5.

3.3 Online Recognition and Registration

After all the offline work has been completed, we can begin the main topic—recognition and registration. When a real image in video frame sequence is obtained, advanced features in that are extracted just as the same way described in offline stage. They are compared with those in the advanced features list of each learning image one by one. If it is found in the list of one learning image, the counter of that learning image increases by one. At last, the learning image with maximal count is chosen as the suitable intermediate matching image. On the contrary, if the maximal count is less than the threshold, it shows the recognition fails and the work will be repeated with the next frame image. Besides selecting the right intermediate image from group, the advanced feature matching has another goal—obtaining at least three correspondent points between the learning image and the real one. The center points of ellipses and the endpoints of overlapping edges are the best ones to form the correspondent point pairs. They are used for calculating the 2D affine matrix (M_A) between learning image and real one. The matrix M_A has taken the most influencing factors into account, such as rotation, scale, translation, shear and reflection. The equation of 2D affine transformation between the correspondences composed of the point (u_i, v_i) in learning image and the point (x_j, y_j) in real image can be written as:

$$\begin{bmatrix} u_i \\ v_i \\ 1 \end{bmatrix} = \begin{bmatrix} m_{11} & m_{12} & m_{13} \\ m_{21} & m_{22} & m_{23} \\ 0 & 0 & 1 \end{bmatrix} \cdot \begin{bmatrix} x_j \\ y_j \\ 1 \end{bmatrix}. \tag{3}$$

If the number of the correspondent point pairs is more than three, the least-squares solution is appropriate to calculate the affine matrix M_A. Now we wonder if there are enough evidences to proof the existence of the target in the real image. As for polyhedron, the borderline of target is often used as appropriate evidence. We transform each line segment and ellipse in the real image into the learning image space by the affine matrix M_A, and compare the parameters of the transformed element with those of every element in the learning image. If the error is allowed, that element is marked as verified. If enough elements are verified, the target is deemed to be in the real image.

And next, if the target is confirmed to be in the real image, the original features will be extracted through Harris detector with the same condition of detecting the learning image. At the same time, the manually selected corners (b_1, b_2, ..., b_n) in intermediate learning image are transformed into real image space, which are marked as b_1', b_2', ..., b_n'. Then, we look for the nearest original features within the t-neighborhood of each transformed corners in the real image. The corners (c_1, c_2, ... , c_k) obtained from the t-neighborhood of transformed corners are used for replacing the selected corners (b_1, b_2, ... , b_k) to regenerate the actual-correspondences list $\{(a_1,c_1), (a_2,c_2), (...), (a_k,c_k)\}$ ($k \geq 6$). This list includes the final correspondent point-pairs between the 3D model and the real image. They are just what we want to calculate the projection matrix.

It is supposed that the valid corners (u_j, v_j) in the real image and the corresponding actual coordinates (x_j, y_j, z_j) on the 3D model are matched. By the methods mentioned in the Computer Vision, it is easy to get the projection matrix M_P of real image. The projection equation can be described as follows:

$$
\begin{bmatrix} s \cdot u_j \\ s \cdot v_j \\ s \end{bmatrix} = \begin{bmatrix} c_{11} & c_{12} & c_{13} & c_{14} \\ c_{21} & c_{22} & c_{23} & c_{24} \\ c_{31} & c_{32} & c_{33} & 1 \end{bmatrix} \begin{bmatrix} x_j \\ y_j \\ z_j \\ 1 \end{bmatrix}.
\tag{4}
$$

Equation (4) can be represented in the matrix form where X is the column vector of unknowns and B is the column vector of image corner coordinates:

$$
A_{2 \times 11} \cdot X_{11 \times 1} = B_{2 \times 1} .
\tag{5}
$$

Where:

$$
A = \begin{bmatrix} x_j, & y_j, & z_j, & 1, & 0, & 0, & 0, & 0, & -x_j u_j, & -y_j u_j, & -z_j u_j \\ 0, & 0, & 0, & 0, & x_j, & y_j, & z_j, & 1, & -x_j v_j, & -y_j v_j, & -z_j v_j \end{bmatrix} ;
$$

$$
X = \begin{bmatrix} c_{11}, & c_{12}, & c_{13}, & c_{14}, & c_{21}, & c_{22}, & c_{23}, & c_{24}, & c_{31}, & c_{32}, & c_{33} \end{bmatrix}^T ;
$$

$$
B = \begin{bmatrix} u_j, & v_j \end{bmatrix}^T .
$$

Since each corresponding corner gives two such equations, at least six pairs of corresponding corners are needed to compute all the unknowns. The equation with all correspondences can be given like this:

$$
A_{2n \times 11} \cdot X_{11 \times 1} \approx B_{2n \times 1} \ (n \geqslant 6) .
\tag{6}
$$

In equation (6), X is the projection matrix with 11 unknowns and B is the obtained corner coordinates in image. Since equation (6) is an over determined system, a least-squares solution is appropriate. We suppose B' is the predicted coordinates by the projection matrix $X_{11 \times 1}$. We want to minimize the residual between B and B'. Because the residual vector $R = B - B' = B - AX$ is orthogonal to the column space of matrix A. so there is $A^T \cdot R = 0$. Replace R with $B - AX$, we can get $A^T A X = A^T B$. $A^T A$ is symmetric and positive definite, so it has an inverse, which can be used to solve for

$$
X = \left(A^T A \right)^{-1} A^T B .
\tag{7}
$$

Because the interval between the two adjacent frames is very short, it is naturally considered that the "movement" of corner is continuous. So when the next frame comes, there are two ways to obtain the actual-correspondences list. One is just as the above describes, beginning with extracting advanced feathers and recognizing until the final matching points list is generated. This way has the advantage of high reliability but consuming more computation time. The other way is to make full use of the position information of corners in the previous frame. We look for the corners that are nearest in the s-neighborhood of the matched corners in previous frame, and replace the old 2D image corners with the new ones if they are found. By this means, we have reconstructed the actual-correspondences list for new frame image to make the above procedure iteratively working. This way reduces much computation burden, which leads to high speed of registration. But, on the other hand, it may cause failing in reconstruction of correspondences list. And once it happens, the failure will be gone down to the next. So an appropriate strategy is needed that how to make use of the two methods alternately.

4   Results and Conclusions

As a result of our work, a virtual wire frame or solid is superimposed on the real image at the location specified by projection matrix transformation. The recognizing and registration system was implemented in VC++ 6.0 on a PIV 1.7GHz Processor with 256MB of main memory, and 30fps with video (320×280 pixels). The final augmented results of some frame images from the video are presented in figure 6. The experimental results showed that the method is quite robust even in the presence of moving objects.

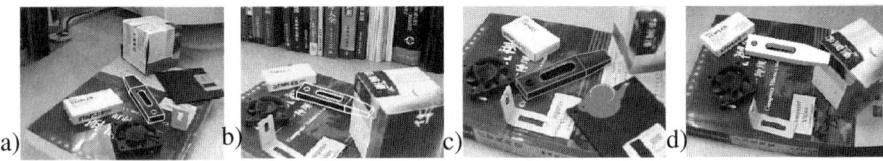

Fig. 6. Some augmented results taking from an experimental video. a) A wire frame model is projected onto the recognized target in a cluttered background; b) Another registered case under partial occlusions; c) Besides the target registration, an additional teapot is drawn in a fixed position relative to the clamp; d) Compared to the wire frame model, the solid model is registered under partial occlusions.

In this paper, we have proposed an approach to build the actual correspondences list for registration based on advanced features matching. It is coincident with the way that human recognize an object. The system first learns the advanced features contained in the target in the selected ideal learning image. This training step results in a set of advanced features hash tables. Then we count the advanced features obtained from the real image according to the tables to determine the intermediate learning image and calculate the 2D affine matrix between them, by which the system obtains the actual correspondences list to calculate the final projection matrix.

The most contribution in our work is that we transfer the hardest work in correspondences forming to the calculation of the affine matrix between a pair of 2D images. The difference differ form former markless tracking is that we avoid the heavy computation in finding correspondent points. In our approach, the traditional corner detection takes the secondary place in this approach. Moreover, we have reduced the threshold of the detector to ensure the key corners to be detected. The main effort is put into the extraction and matching of the advanced features to indirectly build the actual correspondences list. Because we need at least six pairs of correspondent points to calculate the projection matrix but only three or two (if the effects of shear and reflection are ignored) pairs to get the affine matrix. The ways that we build correspondences list by advanced features decreases the blindness and computation burden, but raise the reliability of system.

5   Future Work

The most difficult work in augmented reality system is not the calculation of projection matrix, but the establishment of the actual-correspondences list. If there is a deviation in the list, it may cause incorrect projection matrix and unsuccessful registration. So the most crucial problem in our work is the matching of advanced features and the calculation of the 2D affine matrix between the learning image and the real one. Because the target in our example is just a regular geometric entity, we define some simple primary and advanced features. For the recognition and registration of more complex objects, it is necessary to expand the definitions of available advanced features and explore the rapid and efficient extraction methods of them.

References

1. R. T. Azuma (1997), A survey of augmented reality, Presence: Teleperations and Virtual Environments. Vol. 6, No. 4, pp. 355-385.
2. R. T. Azuma (2001), Y. Baillot, R. Behringer, S.Feiner, S. Julier and B. MacIntyre, Recent advances in augmented reality, IEEE Computer Graphics and Application, Vol. 21, No. 6, pp. 34-47.
3. Hiroshima Kato, Mark Billinghurst, Ivan Poupyrev. ARToolKit Manual[M]. Version 2.70 . Human Interface Technology Laboratory, University of Washington. http://www.hitl. washington.edu/artoolkit/. 2005.7
4. F. Jurie (1996). Solution of the Simultaneous Pose and Correspondence Problem Using Gaussian Error Model. Computer Vision and Image Understanding, 73(3):357–373.
5. N. Allezard, M. Dhome, and F. Jurie (2000). Recognition of 3d textured objects by mixing view-based and model-based representations. In International Conference on Pattern Recognition, pages 960–963, Barcelona, Spain.
6. C.G. Harris and M.J. Stephens (1988), A combined corner and edge detector, in Fourth Alvey Vision Conference, Manchester.
7. David G. Lowe (1999). Object recognition from local scale-invariant features. In International Conference on Computer Vision, pages 1150–1157.
8. K. Mikolajczyk and C. Schmid (2002). An affine invariant interest point detector. In European Conference on Computer Vision, pages 128–142. Springer, Copenhagen.
9. Adam Baumberg (2000). Reliable feature matching across widely separated views. In Conference on Computer Vision and Pattern Recognition, pages 774–781.
10. Lepetit, V., Vacchetti, L., Thalmann, D. and Fua, P (2003). Fully Automated and Stable Regis-tration for Augmented Reality Applications. In Proc. Second IEEE and ACM International Symposium on Mixed and Augmented Reality.
11. Genc, Y., Riedel, S., Souvannavong, F. and Navab, N. Markerless tracking for aug-mented reality: A learning-based approach. In Proc. International Symposium on Mixed and Augmented Reality, 2002
12. Comport, A.I., Marchand, E., and Chaumette, F. A real-time tracker for marker-less augmented reality. In Proc. Second IEEE and ACM International Symposium on Mixed and Augmented Reality, Tokyo, Japan, pp. 36-45, 2003

Shared Design Space: Sketching Ideas Using Digital Pens and a Large Augmented Tabletop Setup

Michael Haller[1], Peter Brandl[1], Daniel Leithinger[1], Jakob Leitner[1], Thomas Seifried[1], and Mark Billinghurst[2]

[1] Digital Media, Upper Austria University of Applied Sciences, Austria
[2] HITLabNZ, University of Canterbury, New Zealand
coeno@fh-hagenberg.at

Abstract. Collaborative Augmented Reality (AR) setups are becoming increasingly popular. We have developed a collaborative tabletop environment that is designed for brainstorming and discussion meetings. Using a digital pen, participants can annotate not only virtual paper, but also real printouts. By integrating both forms of physical and digital paper, we combine virtual and real 2d drawings, and digital data which are overlaid into a single information space. In this paper, we describe why we have integrated these devices together in a unique way and how they can be used efficiently during a design process.

1 Introduction

In recent years, Augmented Reality applications have been developed for many different platforms, such as mobile phones and handheld devices and also tabletop environments. Kiyokawa et al. describe the communication behaviors in a tabletop collaborative AR interface setup and they present several ways to improve the face-to-face collaboration by using AR [1]. In this paper, we describe a novel tabletop AR environment suitable for enhancing face to face collaboration, especially in the design process.

Designers and people who are discussing and brainstorming usually work in a studio surrounded with sketches, which are either pinned on a wall or placed on large surfaces. Currently, new sketches are mainly created directly on paper on the drafting table before developing a digital mock-up model on the computer. With new technology if may be possible to enhance this process. Blinn [2] postulates that the creative process is a two-phase process: firstly, moving from chaos to order and secondly, from ideation to implementation. Most computer-based design tools are primarily focussed on the second phase, and there is limited support for digital tools where people can play with ideas in a free form manner. Digital tabletop setups would be an ideal interface for sketching out a crude version of an idea. In the creative process, people still prefer using paper and large tables to capture their ideas. Therefore, the table still remains the main interaction device during the creative process. Augmented with virtual elements, a tabletop setup becomes an ideal input and output device around which people can share a wide range of verbal and non-verbal cues to collaborative effectively (cf. figure 1).

In this paper, we describe the combination of different hardware devices that can be combined to develop an AR-based tabletop environment for creating efficient applications [3]. Now, that it is technically possible to develop large augmented surfaces, it is

Z. Pan et al. (Eds.): ICAT 2006, LNCS 4282, pp. 185–196, 2006.
© Springer-Verlag Berlin Heidelberg 2006

Fig. 1. (a) Participants can either interact with the interactive table either using tablet PCs or digital pens. (b) The collaboration mode allows to sketch the same document.

important to conduct research on the different types of collaborative AR applications that are ideally suited for these types of tabletop setups and to present "user interface guidelines" for developing these applications. In the next section, we review related work on tabletop collaboration environments. Next, we present our system, focusing on hardware and design decisions. Section 3 focuses on interaction techniques. From the early user feedback, we conclude with design guidelines for collaborative tabletop AR systems and directions for future research.

2   Related Work

Early attempts at computer enhanced face-to-face collaboration involved conference rooms in which each participant had their own networked desktop computer that allowed them to send text or data to each other. However, these computer conference rooms were largely unsuccessful partly because of the lack of a common workspace [4]. An early improvement was using a video projector to provide a public display space. For example the Colab room at Xerox PARC [5] had an electronic whiteboard that any participate could use to display information to others. The importance of a central display for supporting face-to-face meetings has been recognized by the developers of large interactive commercial displays (such as the SMARTBoard DViT). In traditional face-to-face conversation, people are able to equally contribute and interact with each other and with objects in the real world. However with large shared displays it is difficult to have equal collaboration when only one of the users has the input device, or the software doesn't support parallel input. In recent years, Stewart et al. coined the term Single Display Groupware (SDG) to describe groupware systems which support multiple input channels coupled to a single display [6]. They have found that SDG systems eliminate conflict among users for input devices, enable more work to be done in parallel by reducing turn-taking, and strengthen communication and collaboration. In general traditional desktop interface metaphors are less usable on large displays. For example, pull down menus may no longer be accessible, keyboard input may be difficult, and mouse input may require movement over large distances. A greater problem is that traditional desktop input devices do not allow people to use free-hand gesture or object-based interaction as they normally would in face-to-face collaboration. Researchers such as Ishii [7] have explored the use of tangible object interfaces for tabletop collaboration, while Streitz et al. [8] use natural gesture and object based interaction in their i-Land smart space. Regenbrecht et al. extend the idea of tangible user interfaces and demonstrates the benefits in novel video conference system [9]. In many interfaces there is a shared projected display visible by all participants; however, collaborative spaces can also support private data viewing. In Rekimoto's Augmented Surface's interface [10] users are able to bring their own laptop computers to a face-to-face meeting and drag data from their private desktops onto a table or wall display area. They use an interaction technique called hyper-dragging which allows the projected display to become an extension of the user's personal desktop.

In the next section, we describe our AR tabletop system which combines these features. Unlike previous work, our system benefits from the following features:

– Seamless combination of both real and virtual data combined with augmented content,
– Intuitive data exchange using multiple (heterogeneous) devices based on natural and easy-to-use metaphors,
– Adapted and modified interaction methods (e.g. improved hyper-dragging for objects, Pick-and-Drop etc.), and
– Detailed discussion of what customers expect while using such a system. From the first meetings with our customers, we achieved a couple of interesting ideas which somehow diverge from the requirements seen by the developers.

3   System Overview

Our interface consists of four ceiling and a wall mounted projector showing data on a table surface (Interactive Table) and on an adjacent wall (Interactive Wall). All ceiling projectors are connected to a single display computer (cf. figure 2). Users can sit at the table and either connect their own laptop and/or tablet PC computer to the display server or interact directly with the table using digital pens. There is no limit as to how many clients can connect simultaneously to the system, and the amount of co-located participants depends on the space around the table. In our case, typically more than 5 participants are involved in a meeting, where one of the participants usually leads the session.

The tracking is realized by using large Anoto[1] patterns and digital pens from Maxell. Anoto-based pens are ballpoint-pens with an embedded camera that tracks the movements simultaneously (cf. figure 2). The pen has to be used on a specially printed paper with a pattern of tiny dots. Each paper sheet is unique and has its ID. The pen with its inbuilt infrared (IR) camera tracks the dots of the paper to retrieve both the ID of the paper and the position relative to the upper left corner of the paper. All required

---

[1] www.anoto.com

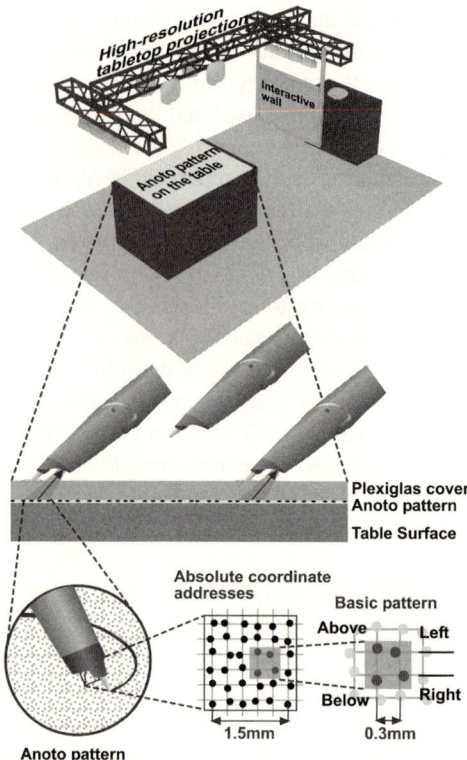

Fig. 2. The system consists of an interactive table and an interactive wall. The tracking on the table is realized using digital pens which can track the tiny dots of the Anoto pattern. To protect the Anoto pattern, we put a Plexiglas cover, which however, does not interfere the accurate tracking results.

informaion can then be sent in real-time to the PC using Bluetooth. Usually, the digital pens are used in combination with real printouts and real notebooks. However, we use this technology for tracking the users' movements and interactions on the whole table surface. To do this we put two A0-sized Anoto-patterns under the Plexiglas cover placed on the table (cf. figure 2). This allows us to track users' gesture input while holding the digital pen. Once the user touches the table with the pen, the camera tracks the underlying Anoto paper. Images projected onto to the table do not interfere with the tracking. Since every digital pen has its own personal ID, we can easily identify who is interacting with the interface without any additional hardware requirements (e.g. capacity measurement on the chairs [11]). Notice that the pens are also pressure sensitive which allows additional functionalities (i.e., for a better control in a sketching/drawing application).

We also allow real paper to be used in the interface. Real paper is socially well-accepted in meetings and does not interfere with the face-to-face collaboration. In design meetings, participants often have to handle paper documents and drawings. Paper also has the advantage that it gives a fast and quick overview, provides a high resolution surface and is easy to carry. However, it can be difficult to transfer sketches on paper into digital applications. In our AR tabletop interface, we augment real paper with projected virtual graphics [12]. Participants can make annotations on the real content that is combined with digital content projected on top of the paper surface. The paper itself is tracked by using ARTag [13] markers, printed on each piece of paper.

Whenever a sketch is finished, it can be presented to the audience by moving it to the Interactive Wall. For the Interactive Wall setup we use a 60" diffuse Plexiglas display surface with special qualities for rear-projection. The anti-reflex surface homogeneously distributes the light to achieve a balanced image. A single camera tracking solution provides the interaction data for the sketch presentation. An IR pass filter that is applied to the camera avoids interferences with the projected image. As the tracking is done via shadows in the IR spectrum, IR lights are needed to provide a homogeneous illumination in front of the screen. Touching the screen with one hand, the user can scroll through the sketches. A timeline on top provides a map-like overview that can also be used to navigate in a fast-forward style. Using both hands activates the zoom mode on screen, changing the distance between the hands affects the zoom-level accordingly. Notice that Anoto pens cannot be used on the interactive wall due to technical limitations: Althouth the embedded IR camera can track the graphite ink even on transparent surfaces (e.g. a pattern printed on a transparent foil), the rear-projected light interferes the tracking results.

4   Interaction Techniques

In this section, we mainly focus on novel interaction techniques we used in our project. We also present the different interaction possibilities and highlight why we have chosen the individual interface metaphors that we use. During a face-to-face brainstorming process, we can identify the following main tasks, which require adequate interaction techniques:

- Data Creation and Selection,
- Data Transfer, and
- Data Manipulation.

4.1   Data Creation and Selection

Usually, in the design process participants already have some sketches, notes, or drawings they want to share. On the tabletop system, users have two methods for data sharing, depending on the device they are using. If they have already some sketches on their private devices (e.g. tablet PC, laptop), the user can use traditional desktop tools for data creation. They can also create new sketches on the table using real/virtual paper and the digital pen. By observing users, we noticed that people preferred using the digital pen more; especially for sketching quick ideas. In fact, our system allows a seamless combination of digital and real content, where the augmented content has mainly be picked up from the table's surface. Thus, the table becomes a storage pool of digital content,

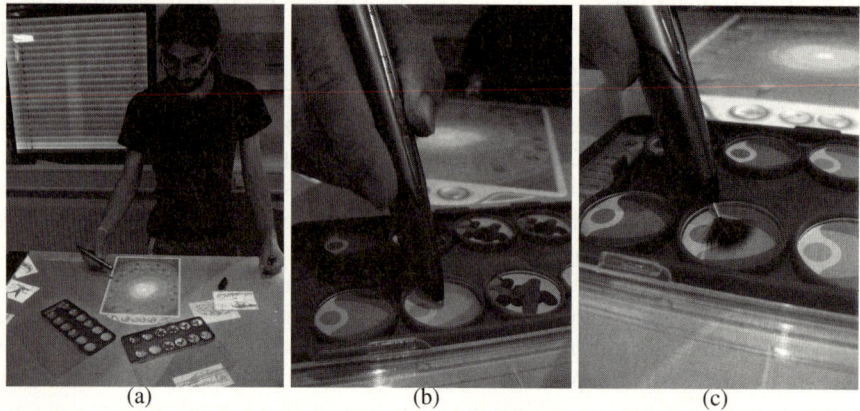

Fig. 3. Shared Design Space Interaction. (a) Designers can choose different color from a tangible interface (b) and sketch directly on the private workspace. (c) Optionally, users can also use pens with different caps.

where participants can share data. It is still a challenging task in which way the content initially comes onto the table. As mentioned before, we use additional devices, where the content can be moved smoothly to the table by hyper-dragging [10]. In the early phase, we did also experiments with a 1-degree of freedom (dof) menu, which was directly projected on the table surface (cf. figure 4).

After drawing an ink-rectangle with the pen, users get the 1-dof menu with additional digital content available. The user can interact by clicking with their pen on the special control elements (check boxes), which are printed on the real paper sheet. We used a default directory, which was browsed and shown in the menu. Once the corresponding geometry has been selected (again the user has to select the corresponding checkbox

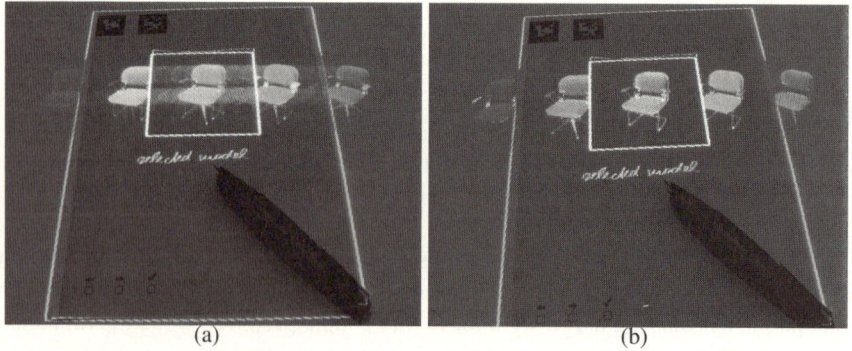

Fig. 4. 1-degree of freedom menu for selecting different 3d geometries

on the paper), the printout can be moved including the augmented content (e.g. videos). Notice that people can also select 3d geometries simultaneously (cf. figure 4).

4.2   Data Transfer

In interfaces that contain multiple displays, an important research question is how to transfer data from one source to the other. In our setup, users sitting around the Interactive Table can move notes to the Interactive Wall by touching special control elements, projected onto the table surface and using the digital pen (cf. figure 5).

Fig. 5. Special control elements projected on the table surface allow to share the sketches, but also to transfer them to the Interactive Wall

As noticed by Rekimoto in [14], people often have to transfer data from one device to another - especially in an augmented tabletop environment. In most cases, the traditional interaction metaphors (e.g. drag-and-drop) fail and more natural and quick data transfer metaphors have to be found.

In our setup, participants have three different possibilities of moving data from one screen to another depending on the device they are using (i.e. wireless presenter, personal device (e.g. laptop, tablet PC), and the Maxell pen).

4.3   Moving Data with the Laptop PC (Hyper-Dragging)

In our setup, all participants around the table can quickly re-arrange the content on the table using their personal devices and the user's mouse attached to their own devices. Therefore, users can click on a virtual image on their laptop computer desktop and drag it. Once the mouse reaches the edge of the physical display, the content appears on the table connected by a virtual line to the center of the desktop (cf. figure 6). Dragging with the mouse continues to move the note across the table.

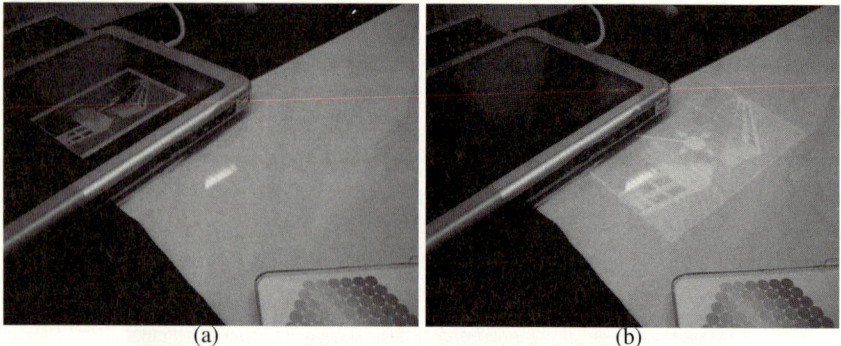

Fig. 6. Using the hyper-dragging metaphor allows an easy-to-use transfer of data between two devices (e.g. tablet PC and tabletop desk)

Participants can create new content on their private device and then move it to the public space. However, the direct interaction with content on the table surface is in many ways more natural that using mouse cursor input. In pilot studies people expected to be able to interact with their images once they were on the table surface and were surprised when this was initially not possible. We found that some people preferred using a device rather than interacting with their fingers. For this reason we added support for input from the Anoto digital pen.

4.4   Moving Data with the Digital Pen (Pick-and-Drop)

The combination of both real and virtual data requires a novel metaphor for data transfer. Instead of using the Drag-and-Drop metaphor, which is mainly used in 2d-based

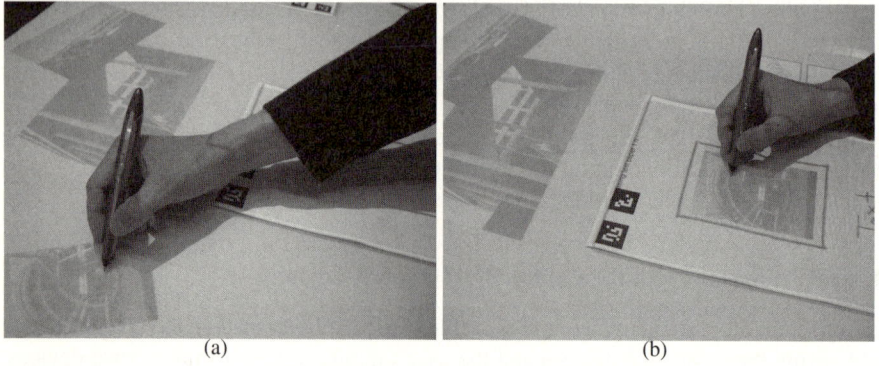

Fig. 7. Pick-and-Drop. Users can pick (a) an object from the interactive table to drop it (b) onto the real paper.

GUI applications, Rekimoto proposed the Pick-and-Drop metaphor [14]. It is more natural if users can manipulate and insert data in a computer environment as if it would be a real, physical object. In our setup, users can pick-up digital data from the table (e.g. video, images, 3d geometry) and drop-it on the real paper by using the digital pen. Once the users pick an object, the digital pen tracks the underlying Anoto paper.

Once the user taps a digital object on the interactive table, our content manager automatically binds it (virtually) to the pen (cf. figure 7). Whenever the user moves the same pen onto the real paper, the manager transfers the data to the server that displays it on the interactive table. During our first tests, we recognized two reasons that the Pick-and-Drop metaphor is more convenient than the Drag-and-Drop interaction. Firstly, our pens did not have additional buttons, which would have been necessary for realizing the Drag-and-Drop metaphor. Secondly, large movements on the table can be really uncomfortable and time-consuming, and are not required in the Pick-and-Drop metaphor. Robertson et al. presents improved Drag-and-Drop metaphors for wall-size displays for multiple data sets that could be integrated in the future [15].

4.5   Moving Data on the Interactive Wall

Once the digital data has been sent to the interactive wall, participants can move the data with users' gestures. We noticed during our first tests with end-users that the interactive wall is mainly used for presenting intermediate results. We also noticed that in most cases one person (mostly the coordinator of a session) stands up and presents the results to other participants.

4.6   Data Manipulation

On the interactive table, people can just move the sketches and perform simple transformations, such as translating, scaling, and rotating. Once participants want to manipulate the data sheet, they have to move it to private space (either to the personal tablet PC by hyper-dragging or to the personal workspace, as depicted in figure 3a).

An easy-to-use sketching tool allows the creation of simple strokes which are layered either onto the virtual data or onto the real printout (cf. [16][17]). The colors and brush strokes can be changed by using different tangible tools (e.g. the color chooser as depicted in figure 3). Again, the tiles of the color palette are printed with the special Anoto pattern. As mentioned before, users can also integrate virtual content (i.e., 2d images, movies, or 3d geometries) into the printout and/or the virtual paper. Not surprisingly, people also expect to have the possibility to transform the geometry or to start and/or stop a projected video. The ultimate goal would be that people draw their own control elements onto the paper and control the virtual content accordingly.

4.7   Group Interaction

Using a collaborative interactive table means sharing information and working together. Often, in traditional meetings, people have neither enough hard-copies nor enough space for the large sketches (e.g. CAD sketches). Group interaction often becomes difficult and in many cases it is hard for user to see where their colleagues are pointing to. Moreover, the manual annotations (mainly done with markers or pens) cannot be stored digitally. Figure 1b depicts a scenario where both users are working on the same paper sheet. All modifications are sent from the digital pen through Bluetooth to the server and the individuals' view of the projected comments is updated accordingly. The "shared desktop", which is embedded as a window in front of the collaborators, becomes a WYSIWIS (What You See Is What I See) window and all participants can see the same thing.The content control is mainly left to social norms. Discussing with participants, they have not felt the need to explicitly lock modification control over data objects, because they could always see who was attempting to modify their objects. However, it is important that users can identify who is manipulating each object (e.g. by using different colors).

5   Implementation

A system overview is presented in figure 2, which depicts the most important components. The system is written in C++ based on OpenGL for rendering the virtual content and on ClanLib for rendering the graphical user interface. The advantage of the ClanLib library is that the system is based on top of OpenGL and can therefore be combined easily with the basic rendering system of the 3d graphics library. In addition, we used the component model of the ClanLib library for the inter-component communication and the network extension for the communication between the clients and the server. The tracking of the markers attached on the printout was performed by the ARTag tracking library. The real-time tracking of the Maxell pen was implemented in C# by using Maxell's Streaming API. Moreover, we use an in-house library for recognizing the axis-aligned rectangles drawn on the paper. The tracking on the rear-projection screen is mainly based on both the JazzUp library and OpenCV.

6   Conclusions and Future Work

In this paper, we presented the results of combining different easy-to-use interaction metaphors in a tabletop setup using digital pens and paper. Previous research demonstrated that AR technology can be used to enhance face-to-face collaboration in a natural way. The first results were strongly influenced by the first informal tests with our customers. The setup incorporates multiple devices and novel interaction metaphors to create an easy-to-use environment. The installation offers a cooperative and social experience by allowing multiple face-to-face participants to interact easily around a shared workspace, while also having access to their own private information space and a public presentation space combining both virtual and real sketches. The project is different from typical screen-based collaboration, because it uses advanced interface technologies to merge the person and task space. It is also uses multiple display surfaces to support private, group and public data viewing and interaction. The Anoto-based pen allows an ideal interface for interacting with both the real and virtual paper. Special control elements, projected on the desk, allow to share the own work for further discussion with the participants. Moreover, we included intuitive and natural objects (e.g. color palette etc.) and combined the real paper with digital content. We also investigated adequate and intuitive interaction metaphors for data movement (e.g. hyper-dragging, pick-and-drop etc.) and demonstrated their usage in the tabletop setup. We have also shown that the simultaneous use of the digital pen for the printout and for the interaction on the interactive table makes a lot of sense. The Anoto pattern used for tracking the users' movements seems to be an ideal configuration for similar tabletop applications.

Currently, we are starting with a formal evaluation. The main goal is to find out how the participants are using the real paper and in which sense they benefit from the augmented annotations. Finally, we also want to find out, in which sense a centralized data placement differs from a replicated note (cf. [18]). In a centralized design, participants only see one copy on the table. This often causes orientation and viewing problems by the participants who are sitting on the opposite of the table. Moreover, people have often problems, if one person is pointing to an object. To address these limitations, we also implemented the replicated view, where everybody can get the same view projected onto the personal paper sheet. Moreover, everybody can edit the paper simultaneously. In which sense traditional meetings will be influenced by a simultaneous interaction, will be investigated in a next user-study.

Acknowledgements

This research is funded in part by the Austrian FFG consortium (FHplus framework, no. 811407) and voestalpine Informationstechnologie. We also thank both Maxell and Anoto for their support. Finally, we thank our "Office of Tomorrow" team for providing inspirational ideas and constructive support for our work.

References

[1] Kiyokawa, K., Billinghurst, M., Hayes, S.E., Gupta, A., Sannohe, Y., Kato, H.: Communication behaviors of co-located users in collaborative ar interfaces. In: ISMAR '02: Proceedings of the International Symposium on Mixed and Augmented Reality (ISMAR'02), Washington, DC, USA, IEEE Computer Society (2002) 139

[2] Blinn, J.: The ultimate design tool. IEEE Computer Graphics and Applications **10**(6) (1990) 90–92

[3] Haller, M., Billinghurst, M., Leithinger, D., Leitner, J., Seifried, T.: Coeno, enhancing face-to-face collaboration. In: ICAT '05: Proceedings of the 15th International Conference on Artificial Reality and Telexistence. (2005)

[4] Kori M. Inkpen, P.: Adapting the Human-Computer Interface to Support Collaborative Learning Environments for Children. PhD thesis, UBC (1997)

[5] Stefik, M., Foster, G., Bobrow, D.G., Kahn, K., Lanning, S., Suchman, L.: Beyond the chalkboard: computer support for collaboration and problem solving inmeetings (reprint). (1988) 335–366

[6] Stewart, J., Bederson, B.B., Druin, A.: Single display groupware: A model for co-present collaboration. In: CHI. (1999) 286–293

[7] Ishii, H., Ullmer, B.: Tangible bits: Towards seamless interfaces between people, bits and atoms. In: Proceedings of CHI. (1997) 234–241

[8] Streitz, N., Tandler, P., Mller-Tomfelde, C., Konomi, S.: Roomware: Towards the next generation of human-computer interaction based on an integrated design of real and virtual worlds. In Carroll, J., ed.: Human-Computer Interaction in the New Millenium. Addison-Wesley (2001) 553–578

[9] Regenbrecht, H., Lum, T., Kohler, P., Ott, C., Wagner, M., Wilke, W., Mueller, E.: Using augmented virtuality for remote collaboration. Presence: Teleoper. Virtual Environ. **13**(3) (2004) 338–354

[10] Rekimoto, J., Saitoh, M.: Augmented surfaces: a spatially continuous work space for hybrid computing environments. In: CHI '99: Proceedings of the SIGCHI conference on Human factors in computing systems, New York, NY, USA, ACM Press (1999) 378–385

[11] Dietz, P., Leigh, D.: Diamondtouch: a multi-user touch technology. In: UIST '01: Proceedings of the 14th annual ACM symposium on User interface software and technology, New York, NY, USA, ACM Press (2001) 219–226

[12] Newman, W., Wellner, P.: A desk supporting computer-based interaction with paper documents. In: CHI '92: Proceedings of the SIGCHI conference on Human factors in computing systems, New York, NY, USA, ACM Press (1992) 587–592

[13] Fiala, M.: Artag, a fiducial marker system using digital techniques. In: CVPR '05: Proceedings of the 2005 IEEE Computer Society Conference on Computer Vision and Pattern Recognition (CVPR'05) - Volume 2, Washington, DC, USA, IEEE Computer Society (2005) 590–596

[14] Rekimoto, J.: Pick-and-drop: a direct manipulation technique for multiple computer environments. In: UIST '97: Proceedings of the 10th annual ACM symposium on User interface software and technology, New York, NY, USA, ACM Press (1997) 31–39

[15] Robertson, G., Czerwinski, M., Baudisch, P., Meyers, B., Robbins, D., Smith, G., Tan, D.: The large-display user experience. IEEE Comput. Graph. Appl. **25**(4) (2005) 44–51

[16] Ishii, H., Ben-Joseph, E., Underkoffler, J., Yeung, L., Chak, D., Kanji, Z., Piper, B.: Augmented urban planning workbench: Overlaying drawings, physical models and digital simulation. ISMAR (2002) 203

[17] McGee, D.R., Cohen, P.R., Wu, L.: Something from nothing: augmenting a paper-based work practice via multimodal interaction. In: DARE '00: Proceedings of DARE 2000 on Designing augmented reality environments, New York, NY, USA, ACM Press (2000) 71–80

[18] Morris, M.R., Paepcke, A., Winograd, T., Stamberger, J.: Teamtag: exploring centralized versus replicated controls for co-located tabletop groupware. In: CHI '06: Proceedings of the SIGCHI conference on Human Factors in computing systems, New York, NY, USA, ACM Press (2006) 1273–1282

AR Table Tennis: A Video-Based Augmented Reality Sports Game

Jong-Seung Park[1], TaeYong Kim[2], and Jong-Hyun Yoon[1]

[1] Department of Computer Science & Engineering, University of Incheon,
177 Dohwa-dong, Incheon, 402-749, Republic of Korea
{jong, jhyoon}@incheon.ac.kr
[2] Graduate School of Advanced Imaging Science, Multimedia and Film, Chung-Ang
University, 17 HukSuk-dong, Seoul, 156-756, Republic of Korea
kimty@cau.ac.kr

Abstract. Interactions in augmented reality systems are based on human gestures rather than classical input devices. Due to the instability
of the current gesture recognition technologies, the previous development processes of augmented reality games have introduced many ad
hoc methods to handle the shortcomings, and the game architectures
have become highly irregular and inefficient. This paper describes an
efficient development methodology for gesture-based augmented reality
games through prototyping a table tennis game with a gesture interface.
We also verify the applicability of the prototyping mechanism by implementing and demonstrating the augmented reality table tennis game
played with real rackets wherein the implementation requires the real-
time tracking of real rackets to allow fast movements and interactions
without delay.

1 Introduction

Computer games have driven very rapid technological development over the past
several years. Many 3D games are extremely realistic and sophisticated. However,
most games tie the players to the monitors and control devices away from their
real environments. Recently, several novel augmented reality (AR) games have
appeared to provide immersive 3D gaming environments. AR games attempt to
integrate the gamers' real environment into the game environment. They let the
players perceive and act in their real environment. Augmented reality technologies
allow game designers to create novel exciting games starting from a real physical
environment. Testbeds for AR tabletop gaming have also been proposed to explore
the possibilities of realistic and interactive game interfaces [1].

The gesture interface is a powerful tool for the interactions in AR games. In
recent years, vision-based gestural interfaces have been proposed. However, in
the field of gesture recognition, it is very difficult to understand hand gestures,
mainly due to the large degrees of freedom (DoF) of the hand configuration
[2]. The stability and accuracy of gesture recognition methods determine the
applicability of the gesture interface to AR games.

Z. Pan et al. (Eds.): ICAT 2006, LNCS 4282, pp. 197–206, 2006.

The uses of AR technologies in computer gaming have been presented in sports computer game genres. One of the most strong points of AR games is that games built in AR can blend physical aspects and mental aspects to enhance existing classical game styles [3]. A virtual tennis game was developed on a virtual environment connecting an egocentric head mounted display system with an exocentric fishtank system [4]. Their system uses a head mounted display and a motion tracker without using sports instruments.

A table tennis game is a kind of a sports game involving the use of a paddle. Ball-and-paddle games are popular and the well-known games in this genre are tennis games, pong-like games, and breakout style games. These games employed physics for the paddle and ball interactions as well as collisions with the walls and bricks of the game. Some paddle game applications use real balls and real rackets [5][6]. On the other hand, other applications use real rackets without real ball [7]. Theoretically-based taxonomies of interactive entertainment genres indicate that the table tennis game is one of the most interactive game among various computer game genres[8]. From the reason, we choose table tennis game as a testbed of our AR game prototyping.

Real world sports games are strongly physical and players are free to use their whole physical bodies. AR games could also be physical as real world games. Moreover, the same content can be injected seamlessly into the real world [3]. However, current AR devices are indisposed and are not ready to such AR games. Physical interactions are significantly limited by input devices, such as paddle trackers in table tennis games. In a vision-based gestural interface, hand poses and specific gestures are used as commands. Naturalness of the interface requires that any gesture should be interpretable [2]. It also requires that intended gestures should be discriminated from accidental hand motions. The intended gestures would activate corresponding instructions to the interface system. Computer vision algorithms for interactive graphics applications need to be robust and fast. They should be reliable, must work for different people, and must work against unpredictable backgrounds.

An important property of AR applications is that the application context restricts the possible visual interpretations and the user exploits the immediate visual feedback to adjust their gestures [9]. The consideration makes the problem much easier. Moreover, the high-level knowledge is seldom required for most sports games. The minimum level of knowledge could be extracted by a simple and fast method not discarding the naturalness of the interface. These cues motivate us to investigate a development methodology of a versatile gesture interface for AR games.

2   Prototyping AR Table Tennis

We implemented an augmented reality table tennis game called *AR Table Tennis*. A table tennis game is a game involving the use of a racket. In our AR table tennis game, we use only a real racket but we do not require any real ball and table in playing. The ball and the table are virtually created and inserted into a

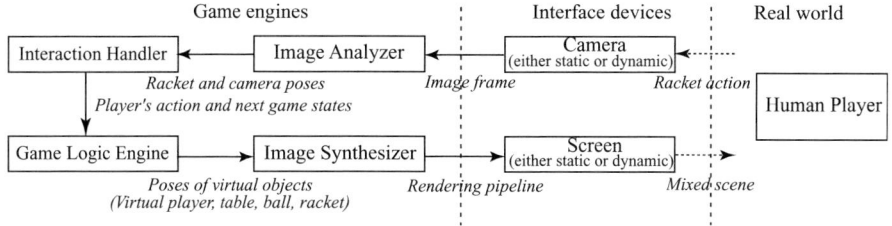

Fig. 1. System block diagram of the AR table tennis

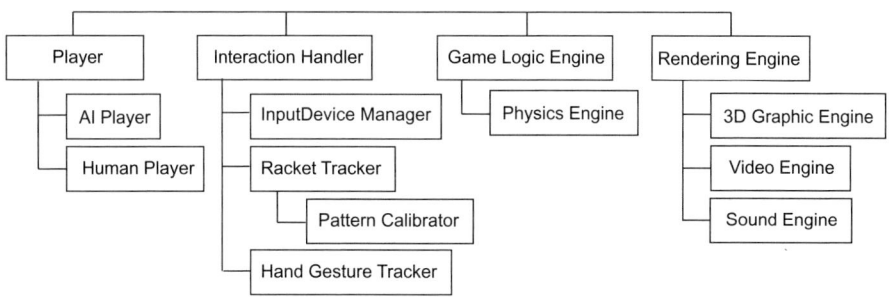

Fig. 2. System modules of the AR table tennis game

real scene. The system block diagram of the AR table tennis is shown in Fig. 1. The racket action of a human player is captured by a camera and the image frame is transmitted to an image analyzer. The image analyzer estimates the racket position and direction by detecting and tracking several racket attributes. An interaction handler accepts the action of the human player and invokes a game logic engine to compute a new game status. The game logic engine evaluates all game physics and determines new states of all virtual objects. The new attributes of virtual objects are sent to an image synthesizer to compose virtual objects with the real image. The image synthesizer renders all virtual objects and shows a mixed scene onto screen.

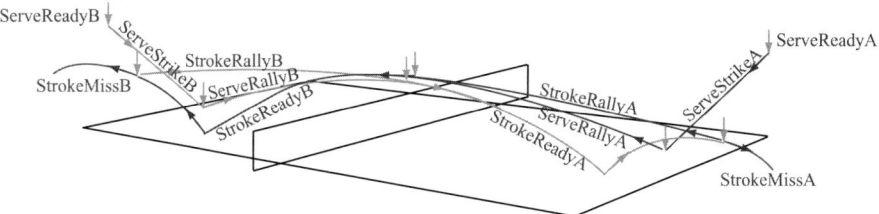

Fig. 3. The game status is determined by the ball position

Our game system has several functionally separated modules and the modules are shown in Fig. 2. The *Player* module controls the status of each player according to the game rules. The *Interaction Handler* manages all interactions with the human player. It includes the *Racket Tracker* to identify the racket action of the human player. The *Game Logic Engine* provides realistic physical simulation. We do not try to build a perfect physical model but to create a physically realistic gaming environment. Most physics things can be easily approximated assuming Newtonian physics and rigid bodies. The *Rendering Engine* composes the updated virtual objects on the video frame.

In a game play, a score point is commenced by the player serving the ball. The player in a service must hit the ball such that it bounces once on the near half of the table, and then bounces at least one time on the far half. During play, if a player conducted errors, score points are awarded to the opponent. Common errors include not hitting the ball after it has bounced on the near side, having the ball bounce on the near side after hitting it, and causing the ball not to bounce on the far half. The game status is determined by the status of the ball. We introduce 12 states, 6 states for each side, as shown in Fig. 3. The six states for the right side player are *ServeReadyA*, *ServeStrikeA*, *ServeRallyA*, *StrokeReadyA*, *StrokeRallyA*, and *StrokeMissA*. When there is a failure to make a service or a return made by the opponent, a point is awarded to the opponent. The current state of the ball discriminates all the possibilities.

It is simple to implement the game scenario since it requires just a small set of geometric models and strategies. The most difficult problem in the game development is the fast and stable racket motion recognition. We have developed a fast detection and tracking module for paddle motions and have applied to the table tennis game.

3   Recognizing Human Actions

Human interactions in augmented reality applications are based on real world human motions. An AR game requires a recognition method for human actions

Fig. 4. A player playing table tennis at the virtual court

Fig. 5. Real-time racket position tracking by filtering the racket surface color

in game playing to accept the player responses to the game world. We have investigated a fast hand motion detection and gesture classification method that should be applicable to sports games. Great emphasis has been placed on the processing speed and the stability of the responses. We subdivided the interaction techniques into three categories, bare-hand interaction, real paddle interaction, and marker-attached paddle interaction. For each interaction category we developed a recognition module and applied it to our prototype.

A player strokes the virtual ball with a real racket by looking at the virtual ball displayed on a monitor or a HMD. The player can see herself in the virtual space on a monitor screen or on a stereoscopic head-mounted display.

3.1   Type 1: Recognizing Bare Hand Actions

In the interactions with bare hands we first filter skin color regions and determine the candidate image location of a hand. Then, we detect and track the skin regions. The intended hand motion is inferred based on the trajectories of the moving regions in a short time interval. A robust recognition of hand motions in an arbitrary unprepared environment is a very difficult problem since there are too many varying factors such as spatially and temporally varying illumination conditions, confusing backgrounds, and irregular motions.

In the AR table tennis game, the game logic engine evaluates all collisions between the virtual ball and other virtual objects such as a virtual table top with net. The real video stream is horizontally flipped and it is shown at the player side to allow the player to see oneself as shown in Fig. 4. A user can hit the virtual ball with the hand motions. We found that it is very hard to improve the recognition accuracy for the hand gestures since there are a lot of variations in hand gestures and also in the surrounding environment.

3.2   Type 2: Recognizing a Real Paddle

A more practical approach is using a real racket instead of human hands. Contrary to human hands, rackets are rigid objects and have less degree of freedoms

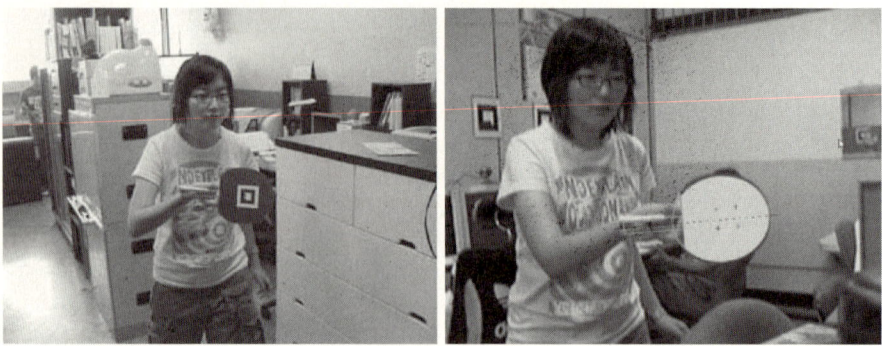

Fig. 6. The racket tracking by detecting the marker attached to the racket face

in their shapes. In the interactions with a real racket, we filter the red color region and determine the racket location. A table tennis racket is covered in a red-colored rubber. Finding red-colored pixels can be simply done by checking the hue component in the hue-saturation-value color space. Note that the hue component is hardly affected by the lighting conditions and the racket region filtering is robust to the illumination. To locate the racket position, we filter racket-colored pixels and count the number of pixels in two directions of the image coordinate system. The number of pixels in the racket color range is counted along both the horizontal and the vertical directions and the counts along the two directions are stored in two separate arrays. The image location of the racket is given by seeking the peak points at the arrays. This technique is robust even for the case when some racket-like regions exist around the real racket.

A user can hit the virtual ball with a table tennis racket. The game player manipulates the virtual ball in 3D space by means of a red colored table tennis racket in the video camera field of view. Fig. 5 shows the racket tracking by filtering the racket surface color. In the figure, the pixels of the racket color are marked in magenta and the estimated center of the racket position is drawn in green.

3.3   Type 3: Recognizing a Marker-Attached Real Paddle

Though the racket detection using the color filtering is fast and robust to the illumination, it provides the position of the racket only in the image coordinate system. To recover the racket position in a 3D space, more complicated approaches are required. A widely used approach is using a known visual marker within the field of view of the camera. Many augmented reality applications use black and white fiducial markers for both the fast and easy detection of features and the direct computation of camera poses. Using a marker-attached racket, we can utilize further information for the racket poses in the 3D space such as the position and orientation of the racket relative to the camera. We attach a marker on the racket face and detect the marker during the game playing as

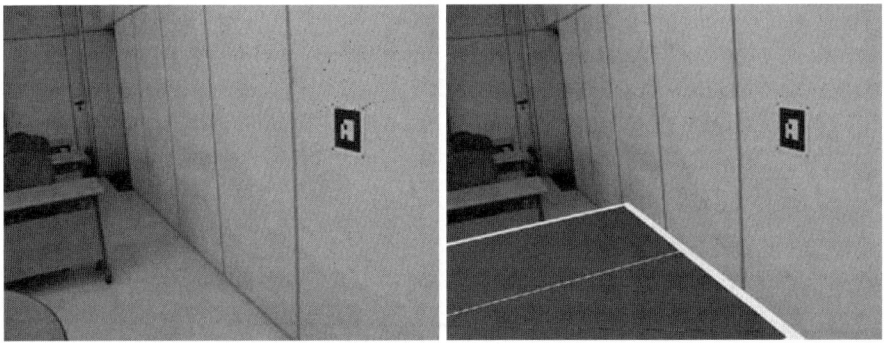

Fig. 7. Positioning the virtual table relative to the marker on the wall

shown in Fig. 6. The right figure shows the detected racket poses overlapped on the marker-attached racket. The identified racket face is marked in yellow color together with the marker corners and the marker orientation.

4   Implementing Game Components

4.1   Simulating Physics

In real games, a ball can fly up to 175km/h over the table, which means the ball passes the table within a tenth second. The conventional frame rate of a cheap off-the-shelf video camera is only up to 30 frames per second. Ball trajectory analysis is nearly impossible and we should depend on the ball detection result from a single frame.

We implemented a simple physics engine that is responsible for the dynamics of the table tennis ball. Common dynamics are the stroking, flying, and bouncing of the ball. The time-dependent location of the ball is computed using the Newtonian physics. In the case where the acceleration is constant we can express the position as a function of time using the fact that the average acceleration and instantaneous acceleration have the same values. The position function for a constant acceleration $\mathbf{a}$ can be written as

$$\mathbf{x}(t) = \mathbf{x}_0 + \mathbf{v}_0(t - t_0) + \frac{1}{2}\mathbf{a}(t - t_0)^2 , \qquad (1)$$

where $\mathbf{x}_0$ and $\mathbf{v}_0$ are the initial position and the initial velocity at t_0, respectively. The fourth-order Runge-Kutta method, the most often used integration method, provides highly accurate numerical solutions of Eq. (1).

The interesting property of table tennis is spin. Advanced players can apply spins of up to 150 revolutions per second and can hit a ball off the racket at around 50 meters per second. Although it will be slow down a little due to air resistance, the ball flies very fast. The ball will drop due to gravity only about 2cm during the time it takes to cross the table. So if the ball is hit at the same

Fig. 8. Game playing in the moving camera environment

height as the top of the net, it will be physically impossible to hit the ball at this speed and still land the ball on the opponent's court. It gets worse as the ball gets lower, since the ball must be hit upwards to get over the net. The ball could only be hit at full speed and power if the ball was high enough to draw a virtually straight line between the ball and a point on the opponent's side of the table, without the net getting in the way. Spin allows players to hit a table tennis ball hard when the ball is below the net. By putting heavy topspin on the ball, one can hit the ball fast in an upwards direction, but the topspin pulls the ball down onto the other side of the table. There are endless varieties of spin and the sheer amount of spin available to a table tennis player and these sets the table tennis sports apart from all other racket sports. The ability to vary the spin and deceive your opponent is crucial to success in table tennis. This fact suggests that allowing the skill of spin to the human player increases the level of excitement in playing.

4.2   Composing Virtual Objects

When using a marker-attached real racket, we can estimate the position and orientation of the racket relative to the camera. It means that, even when the camera is moving, we can put a virtual object at the same location in the 3D

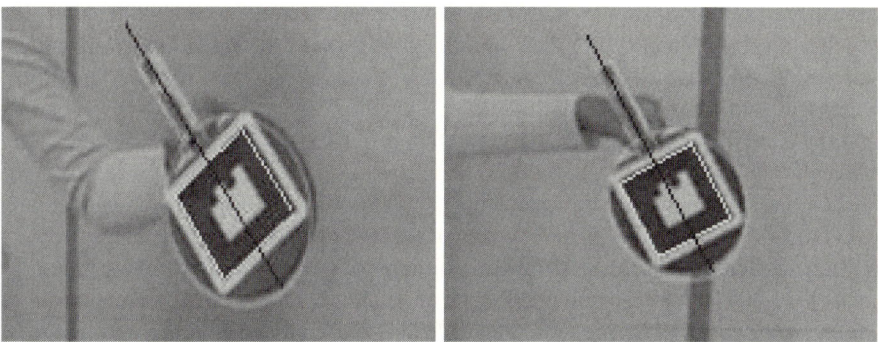

Fig. 9. The estimated racket position and orientation

space corresponding to the real world. We attach another marker on the real environment and utilize the marker to compute the relative position and orientation of the camera. In our experiment, we attached a marker on the wall as shown in Fig. 7. We detect the marker and estimate the camera pose. The right figure shows the mixture of a virtual table. The red lines in the right figure shows the predefined room structure that was rendered using the estimated camera pose. The marker on the racket face is also tracked to obtain the racket pose relative to the camera. Fig. 8 shows the input scenes (the left side) and mixed scenes (the right side) in the moving camera environment. Fig. 9 shows the estimation result of the racket pose.

The experiments were performed on a 2.6GHz Pentium 4-based system. The frame size is fixed to 320×240. The overall rendering speed is about 17 frames per second for *Type 1* and *Type 2* interactions and about 12 frames per second for *Type 3*. Red color pixel filtering and histogram accumulation provide candidate positions of the racket. Though much complicated and accurate analysis is possible, it is just a trade-off between time and cost. Our simple and fast implementation of racket detection has worked pretty well in most cases. The overall physics and rendering speed for the game is over 75 frames per second. Due to the limit of our camera capability, the frame rate is limited by 30 frames per second. Thus, actual paddle movement is reflected to the virtual paddle position at the frame rate.

5   Conclusion

This paper presented implementation details of an AR sports game by focusing on a cost and time efficient development methodology. The prototyped implementation is an augmented reality table tennis game with a gesture interface, where interactions are based on human gestures rather than classical input devices.

It is simple to implement the game scenario since it requires just a small set of rules, geometric models, and strategies. The most difficult problem is the fast and stable racket motion recognition. We have developed a fast detection and tracking module for paddle motions and have applied to the table tennis game.

We classified the three different ways in recognizing actions of the human player and compared the applicability. The implementation requires the real-time tracking of real rackets to allow the fast movements and interactions without delay. Though much complicated and accurate analysis is possible by introducing a time-consuming estimation procedure, it is just a trade-off between time and cost. Our simple and fast implementation of racket detection has worked pretty well in most cases. In our AR application, the player can exploit the immediate visual feedback to adjust their gestures and, hence, the prompt rough response is more important than the slow accurate feedback.

Acknowledgements. This work was supported in part by grant No. RTI05-03-01 from the Regional Technology Innovation Program of the Ministry of Commerce, Industry and Energy(MOCIE) and in part by the Brain Korea 21 Project in 2006.

References

1. Nilsen, T., Looser, J.: Tankwar tabletop war gaming in augmented reality. In: Proceedings of 2nd International Workshop on Pervasive Gaming Applications. (2005)
2. Pavlovic, V., Sharma, R., Huang, T.S.: Visual interpretation of hand gestures for human-computer interaction: A review. IEEE Transactions on Pattern Analysis and Machine Intelligence **19**(7) (1997) 677–695
3. Nilsen, T., Linton, S., Looser, J.: Motivations for augmented reality gaming. In: Proceedings Fuse 04, New Zealand Game Developers Conference. (2004) 86–93
4. Asutay, A., Indugula, A., Borst, C.: Virtual tennis: a hybrid distributed virtual reality environment with fishtank vs. hmd. In: IEEE International Symposium on Distributed Simulation and Real-Time Applications. (2005) 213–220
5. Govil, A., You, S., Neumann, U.: A video-based augmented reality golf simulator. In: ACM Multimedia 2000. (2000) 489–490
6. Ishii, H., Wisneski, C., Orbanes, J., Chun, B., Paradiso, J.: Pingpongplus: Design of an athletic-tangible interface for computer supported cooperative play. In: Proceedings of Conference on Human Factors in Computing Systems (CHI '99). (1999) 394–401
7. Woodward, C., Honkamaa, P., Jappinen, J., Pyokkimies, E.: Camball - augmented virtual table tennis with real rackets. In: Proc. ACE 2004. (2004) 275–276
8. Aitkin, A.L.: Playing at Reality: Exploring the potential of the digital game as a medium for science communication. PhD thesis, Institution The Australian National University (2005)
9. Freeman, W.T., Anderson, D.B., Beardsley, P.A., Dodge, C.N., Roth, M., Weissman, C.D., Yerazunis, W.S., Kage, H., Kyuma, K., Miyake, Y., ichi Tanaka, K.: Computer vision for interactive computer graphics. IEEE Computer Graphics and Applications **18**(3) (1998) 42–53

Enhancing Immersiveness in AR-Based Product Design[*]

Taejin Ha[1], Yeongmi Kim[2], Jeha Ryu[2], and Woontack Woo[1]

[1] GIST U-VR Lab,
[2] GIST HMCI Lab,
Gwangju, 500-712, Korea
{tha, kym, ryu, wwoo}@gist.ac.kr

Abstract. Recently, various AR-based product design methodologies have been introduced. In this paper, we propose technologies for enhancing the immersive realization of virtual objects, where, by adapting tangible objects we can provide touch sensation to users. A 3D model of the same scale overlays the whole area of the tangible object so the marker area is invisible. This contributes to enhancing immersion. Also, the hand occlusion problem when the virtual objects overlay the user's hands is partially solved, providing more immersive and natural images to users. Finally, multimodal feedback also creates better immersion. In our work, both vibrotactile feedback through page motors and sound feedback are considered. In our scenario, a game-phone model is selected, by way of proposed augmented vibrotactile feedback, hands occlusion-reduced visual effects and sound feedback are provided to users. These proposed methodologies will contribute to a better immersive realization of the conventional AR system.

Keywords: AR-based Product Design, Hands Occlusion, Tangible Object, Interaction using Hands, Vibrotactile.

1 Introduction

In general, when customers buy an electronic product, they consider several criteria, such as price, maker, durability, operating time, design etc. Among these, contemporary product design has become an increasingly important consideration for prospective customers. As a response to these consumer demands, product design cycles are getting shorter. Therefore rapid product design methodologies are necessary to keep up with these trends. Generally mock-up models in product design are based on 3D models in CAD. This enables customers to experience the product before production, and designers can obtain direct feedback on colours or position of buttons from customers. However, as the product design cycle becomes shorter, the process related to the mock-up model design and its reproduction should also be significantly reduced.

In the conventional desktop-based product design environment, users inspect virtual objects through a monitor in a fixed position, using a mouse or a keyboard to

---

[*] This research is supported by the UCN Project, the MIC 21C Frontier R&D Program in Korea, ICRC and RBRC at GIST.

Z. Pan et al. (Eds.): ICAT 2006, LNCS 4282, pp. 207–216, 2006.

model virtual objects. In that situation, view space is in a monitor and interaction space is constructed through a mouse or a keyboard on the table. This can cause unnatural interaction because each space is not collocated. To compensate for the above problem, AR-based design methodologies have been introduced [1-3]. In this case, the user is usually wearing an HMD and can interact with virtual objects in a real environment. This enables collocation between view space and interaction space, and therefore a more intuitive interaction is possible.

However, several problems exist in applying AR technology to product design. First of all, usually an augmented virtual object has no physical entity so we can not touch the virtual object, and this reduces immersion. Phantom devices [4] can be one method for touching virtual objects but this requires fixed positions and users can only touch objects through the end effecter of a pen. Second, an augmented virtual object can occlude users' hands because virtual objects just overlay the whole marker area (e.g. the tangible object). This may cause visually awkward images and it also can reduce immersion or naturalness. Also hand segmentation is difficult under changing lighting conditions. Lastly, in terms of interaction, conventional AR applications mainly focus on visual feedback. The most augmented objects do not provide any tactile feedback even though providing tactile cues is helpful for generating their presence. Touch sensations and auditory sensations are also necessary for better immersion.

In our proposed AR-based product design, users can interact with virtual objects which are overlaid on tangible objects. By registering the nonphysical virtual object to the physical tangible object on a corresponding scale, better immersion can be achieved. The virtual object can have a physical entity, thus reducing the gap between virtual environments and real environments. Second, in order to reduce the hand occlusion phenomenon under changing lighting conditions, our method extracts convexes of tangible objects, and then estimate an unobservable underlying probability density function only in that convex area through the "Kernel Density Estimation" [5]. The peaks and valley of the histogram are then calculated to establish the thresholds for segmenting the hand object. Lastly, to provide multimodal feedback to users, visual, sound and vibration feedback is provided through a vibration module embedded in the tangible object which reacts when events occur.

In application, we implemented the immersive modeling test bed for the functionality test of a game-phone. Users are able to control cars in racing game by grasping and tilting a tangible object If the car collides with a wall then vibration and sound feedback are provided for better immersion, enabling multimodal feedback. The proposed methodologies in this paper will contribute to improvements in conventional AR-based product design.

Section 2 provides the detailed algorithm, and section 3 addresses implementation and shows the experiment results of our proposed method. Finally we present conclusions and future work in section 4.

2   Enhancing Immersiveness in AR-Based Product Design

Users wearing a 3D HMD on their head interact with virtual objects by grasping a tangible object. This tangible object is a mock-up model of a game-phone. Multiple fiducial markers are attached to provide 3D information. A 3D model is overlaid on the whole area of the tangible object excluding the hands area. Also vibrotactile feedback and sound feedbacks are provided to the users according to the event.

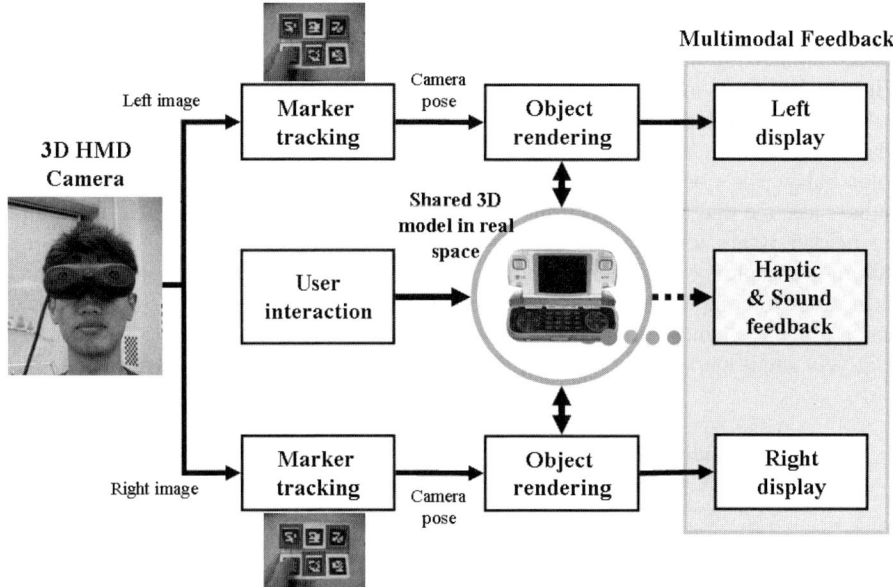

Fig. 1. Overall system

2.1 Tangible Object Design

Conventionally, users can not touch a virtual object because it has no physical presence or entity. However, by using tangible objects, users experience a touch sensation. In our work, diverse tangible objects and interaction methodologies are designed. Basically, multiple markers are attached to a tangible object so that the virtual object can be augmented when at least one marker is detected. It is necessary that several markers are hidden by hands when the user grasps the tangible object. The designed tangible object is a game-phone [6] which has a folder-type structure, as shown in Figure 2 (b) which is based on the CAD model in Figure 2 (a).

(a)   (b)

Fig. 2. (a) A CAD model (b) A folder-type Mock-up model

2.2 Reduction of the Hand Occlusion Problem

In existing AR applications using the ARToolKit, augmented virtual objects can occlude with the user's hands because virtual objects just overlay the marker area as shown in Figure 6. This can cause visually awkward augmented images and also reduce immersion or naturalness [7]. Especially, the hands occlusion problem is critical when users interact with the augmented virtual objects by using their hands.

To reduce the hand occlusion problem [3], skin pixels are extracted through the adaptive threshold, but some of the parameters need to be manually set. Also, if the color balance is not correct, skin pixels can not be extracted properly. In [8], the authors assume that the marker's pattern information is already known and the size of the marker is greater than that of their hands. If the marker is small, the marker's pattern is complex, or the rotation angle is increased, then noise will also increase.

In order to compensate for the above problems, we propose the following method which enables hands segmentation under changing lighting conditions, with a relatively small marker area and in real-time.

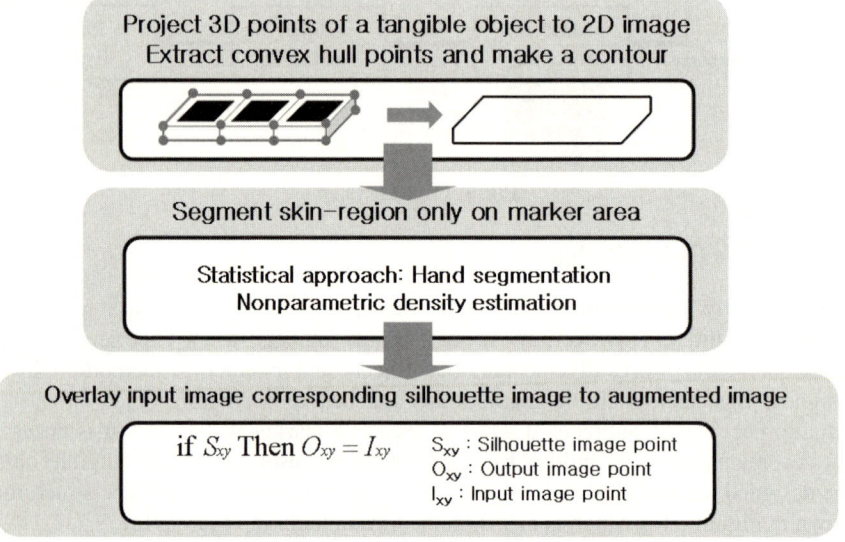

Fig. 3. Three steps for reducing the hands occlusion phenomenon

In the first step, by processing only the hands area on the tangible object, we can reduce the redundant time needed to process an entire image and thus improve processing speed. To do this, the 3D outer points of the tangible object are projected to a 2D image as shown in the upper part of Figure 3, and then the convex hull points are extracted by using the 3 coins algorithm [9]. From these points, contours (upper surface, bottom surface) are extracted and segment skin-regions only on this area.

In the second step, we apply the statistical approach to segment hand objects from the area of the tangible object. The hue and saturation components of the HSV color space are used to minimize the sensitivity of lighting. Through "Kernel Density

Estimation" using "Parzen Windows"[10], we can estimate an unobservable underlying probability density function, based on observed data. In the histogram, the x-axis is divided into bins of length h. The probability of a sample x in a bin is estimated as follows.

$$p \approx k_N / N \qquad (1)$$

Where N is the total number of samples, and k_N is the number of samples in a bin. The corresponding probability is approximated by the frequency ratio. This approximation converges to the true P as N -> ∞. The corresponding pdf value is assumed constant throughout the bin and is approximated by

$$\hat{P}(x) \equiv \hat{P}(\hat{x}) \approx \frac{1}{h}\frac{k_N}{N}, \qquad |x - \hat{x}| \le \frac{h}{2} \qquad (2)$$

Where $\hat{x}$ is the midpoint of the bin and $\hat{p}(\hat{x})$ is the amplitude of the histogram curve. The x-axis is divided into bins of length h. Let x_i, i = 1, 2, ..., N, be the available feature vectors and define the function φ(x) (4). The function is equal to 1 for all points inside the unit centered at the origin and 0 outside it. Then equation (2) can be rephrased as (3). We consider a window with the length of h centered at x, the point where the pdf is to be estimated. The summation equals k_N. That is, the number of points falling inside this window. Then the pdf estimates results from dividing k_N by N and the respective length h.

$$\hat{P}(x) = \frac{1}{h}\left(\frac{1}{N}\sum_{i=1}^{N}\Phi\left(\frac{x_i - x}{h}\right)\right) \qquad (3)$$

$$\Phi(x_i) = \begin{cases} 1 & for\, |x_i| \le 1/2 \\ 0 & otherwise \end{cases} \qquad (4)$$

The peaks of distributions should be detected. The first peak can be easily found in the histogram, being the bin with the largest value. The second peak is then detected by multiplying the histogram values by the square of the distance from the first peak [11]. This is the peak that is not close to the maximum. So, if the largest peak is at level j in the histogram, select the second peak as (6). The maximum value of the peaks is 256. The valley between the distributions is calculated by equation 6. From this data, threshold values are decided and segmentation is executed.

$$\underset{0 \le k \le 255}{\arg\max}\left\{((k - j)^2 histogram[k])\right\} \qquad (5)$$

$$if(j > k) \quad then \quad \underset{k \le i \le j}{\arg\min}\left\{histogram[i]\right\}$$
$$else \quad \underset{j \le i \le k}{\arg\min}\left\{histogram[i]\right\} \qquad (6)$$

In the last step, the extracted hand objects are overlaid again on the augmented virtual objects. In order to achieve this, a processor is added to the pipeline of existing ARToolKik. If pixels in the silhouette image exist, corresponding input pixels are overlaid on the augmented virtual object again. As a result, users interacting with augmented virtual objects by hand will experience better immersion and more natural images.

$$If\ S_{xy}\ exists$$
$$then\ A_{xy} = R_{xy}$$

(7)

Where S_{xy} is the silhouette image coordinates, A_{xy} is the augmented image coordinates and R_{xy} is the input image coordinates respectively.

2.3 Multimodal Feedback Focused on the Vibrotactile Feedback

In order to provide immersive interaction, multisensory feedback combining visual and auditory effects is used. However, the importance of haptic feedback is increased in manipulation and exploration tasks. David Feygin, et al. explained the role of haptics in training [12] and Miriam Reiner emphasised the need of haptic feedback to provide better realism [13].

There have been some attempts to combine tactile feedback into augmented reality. Working with urban planning workspaces, V. Buchmann, et al. used buzzers mounted on gloves so that users were able to feel the vibration when their hand was in contact with AR models of city blocks [14]. Thus they could provide immersive interactions to users.

In our game application scenario (e.g. the racing game), if a player collides with a wall, a vibration is generated and an explosive sound is played. A vibrotactile module is inserted into the tangible object as shown in Figure 4. A wireless communication module (Bluetooth:ADCODE-300) for a vibrotactile module was used. Pancake style vibrators were selected due to their similarity to real vibrating motors in real cellular phones. The vibration module can be controlled at seven levels. 0 is the lowest level and 6 is the highest level of intensity. If the car is on the road, then the 2~3 levles is applied, but if the car collides with a wall or other cars, the 6 step of intensity is applied.

Therefore sight, touch and auditory senses are provided to the users simultaneously, resulting in better immersion as the users interact with virtual objects in the augmented reality.

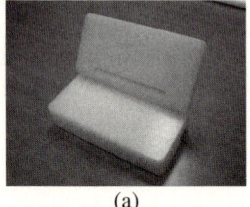   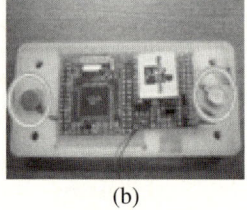

(a)   (b)

Fig. 4. (a) A tangible object (b) Inner part of tangible object

3 Implementation and Experiment Result

3.1 Experiment Environment

In our system, we used a 3D video see-through HMD of VRmagic corporation [15]. Cameras were attached on the positions of each eye. The frame rate was 30 (f/s) and resolution was 640*480 pixels. The two input images from cameras were processed in Dell Corp.'s workstation (e.g. 650MT). An output image was resized to 800*600 to display on LCD in HMD. We referenced the OpenCV version 5.0 beta [16] and ARToolKit version 2.70 beta [17] libraries. The experiment environment was an indoor complex background. As shown in Figure 5, the user wearing the HMD interacts with the virtual object by grasping a tangible object. This tangible object is a mock-up model of a game-phone to which fiducial markers are attached . The user sees a virtual game-phone through the HMD.

(a)   (b)

Fig. 5. (a) the user wearing the HMD (b) the user can interact with a tangible object

3.2 Hands Object Segmentation

Figure 6 (a-c) represent input images and Figure 6 (a'-c') show contours (upper surface, bottom surface). Processing only the hands area on this area, reduces the redundant time needed to process an entire image.

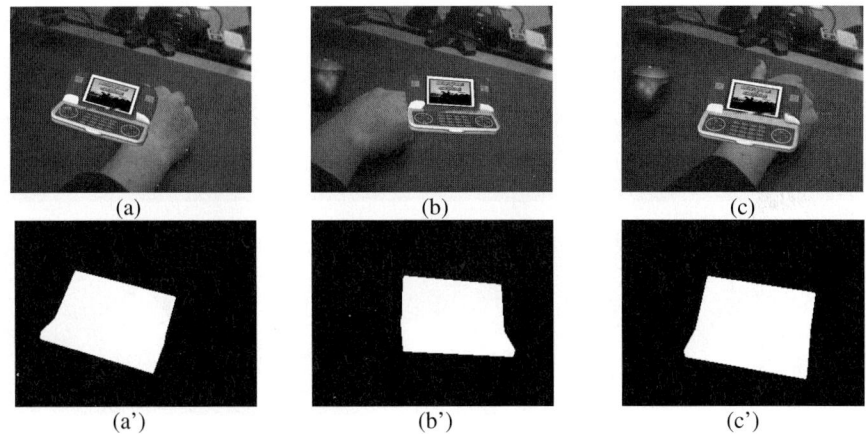

(a)   (b)   (c)

(a')   (b')   (c')

Fig. 6. (a-c) Hand occluded images (a'-b') Extract convexes (the upper side and bottom side of a convex)

Through "Kernel Density Estimation" using "Parzen Windows", we can estimate unobservable underlying probability density function, based on observed data. Figure 7 (a-c) shows the histograms of the pixels in hands objects corresponding with the images of Figure 6 (a'-c'). We can see the variances of distributions according to the area of hands objects. Figure 7 (a'-c') shows the results of "Kernel Density Estimation".

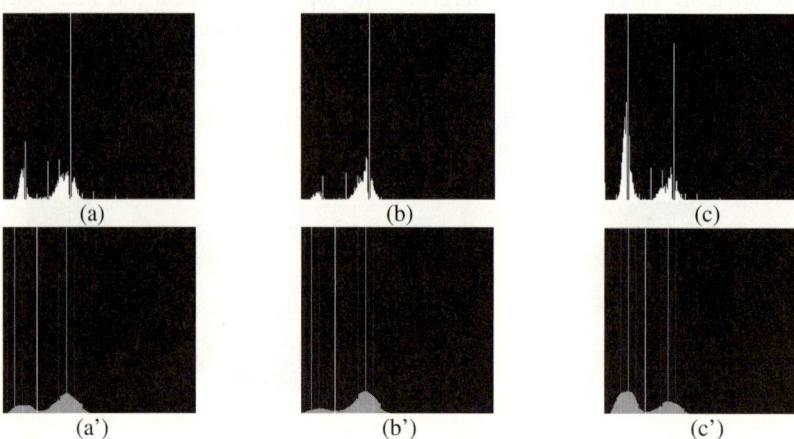

Fig. 7. (a-c) Histograms corresponding the Figure 6. (a'-c') Results of "Kernel Density Estimation".

Our method partially solves the hand occlusion problem, providing better immersive and more natural images to the users when they interact with virtual objects by hands. Also hands object segmentation under various lighting condition is possible, as shown in Figure 8 (a'-c').

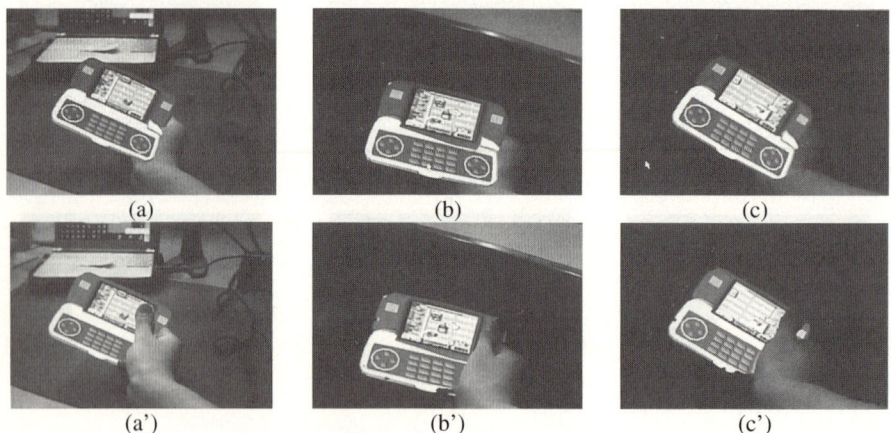

Fig. 8. Hands object segmentation under various lighting conditions

3.3 Game Scenario

Figure 9 shows the racing game in action. The users can obtain multimodal feedback with a virtual game-phone using the tangible object. The users can control the car by tilting the tangible object in the direction of x, z axis. If a player collides with a wall, vibration feedback is generated and an explosive sound is played.

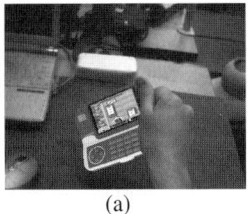
(a)

(b)

Fig. 9. Game control by tilting the tangible object

4 Conclusion and Future Work

In this paper, we proposed methodologies for better immersion and interaction in AR-based product design. By adapting the tangible object touch sensations can provide to the users. Also we have partial solved the hand occlusion problem, providing more immersive or natural images to the users. We improve user interaction with tangible objects by multimodal feedback, focusing on vibrotactile feedback.

Using the proposed methodologies, we realized our immersive model in a game-phone, where users control cars in a racing game by tilting a tangible object. The proposed methodologies contribute to the immersive realization of the conventional AR system.

In future work, we will add other cues for more robust hands segmentation such as edge and geometry relations of hands models. Also we are considering interaction with virtual objects using fingertips by exploiting 3D depth information and the augmentation by exploiting points tracking of a tangible object, even though all of markers are not detected.

References

[1] Klinker, G., Dutoit, A.H. Bauer, M. Bayer, J. Novak, V. Matzke, D, "Fata Morgana - a presentation system for product design", ISMAR 02, 30 Sept.-1 Oct. 2002, pp. 76 - 85

[2] Fiorentino, M. de Amicis, R. Monno, G. Stork, A., "Spacedesign : A Mixed Reality Workspace for Aesthetic Industrial Design", ISMAR 02, 30 Sept.-1 Oct. 2002, pp. 86 – 318

[3] Woonhun Lee, Jun Park "Augmented Foam: A Tangible Augmented Reality for Product Design", Woohun Lee, Jun Park, ISMAR 05, 5-8 Oct. 2005, pp. 106 – 109

[4] Phantom device, http://www.sensable.com/products/phantom_ghost/phantom.asp

[5] "An introduction to kernel density estimation", http://www.maths.uwa.edu.au/~duongt/seminars/intro2kde/

[6] LG-KV 3600, http://www.cyon.co.kr/good/product/product_view1.jsp?product_id=165

[7] Gun A. Lee, Claudia Nelles, Mark Billinghurst, Gerard Jounghyun Kim, "Immersive Authoring of Tangible Augmented Reality Application", ISMAR 04, 2-5 Nov. 2004 Page(s):172 - 181

[8] Shahzad Malik, Chris McDonald, Gerhard Roth, "Hand Tracking for Interactive Pattern-based Augmented Reality", ISMAR 02, 30 Sept.-1 Oct. 2002 Page(s):117 - 126

[9] Avis, D. and Toussaint. An optimal algorithm for determining the visibility of a polygon from an edge. IEEE Trans. Comput. 30, 910-914

[10] Sergios theodoridis and konstantinos koutroumbas, "Classifiers based on Bayes decision theory", Book of Pattern recognition, Elsevier academic press

[11] J. R. Parker, "Advanced methods in grey-level segmentation", algorithms for image processing and computer vision, Wiley

[12] David Feygin, Madeleine Keehner, Frank Tendick, "Haptic Guidance: Experimental Evaluation of a Haptic Training Method for a Perceptual Motor Skill", Proceedings of 10th International Symposium in Haptic Interfaces for Virtual Environment and Teleoperator Systems (Haptics 2002), Orlando, FL, pp. 40-47, March, 2002.

[13] Miriam Reiner, "The Role of Haptics in Immersive Telecommunication Environments", IEEE TRANSACTIONS ON CIRCUITS AND SYSTEMS FOR VIDEO TECHNOLOGY, VOL. 14, NO. 3, MARCH, 2004.

[14] Buchmann, S. Violich, M. Billinghurst, "A. Cockburn. FingARtips: gesture based direct manipulation in Augmented Reality", In Proceedings of the 2nd international conference on Computer graphics and interactive techniques in Australasia and SouthEast Asia (Graphite 2004). 15-18th June, Singapore, 2004, ACM Press, New York, New York, pp. 212-221.

[15] VRmagic, http://www.vrmagic.com/index_e.html

[16] Intel OpenCV Library, http://www.intel.com/research/mrl/research/opencv/

[17] ARToolKit, http://www.hitl.washington.edu/ARToolKit

Personal Information Annotation
on Wearable Computer Users
with Hybrid Peer-to-Peer Communication

Koji Makita, Masayuki Kanbara, and Naokazu Yokoya

Nara Institute of Science and Technology,
8916–5 Takayama, Ikoma, Nara, 630–0192, Japan

Abstract. This paper proposes a wearable annotation overlay system which can correctly annotate dynamic users of wearable computers. To provide users with the newest annotation information, a network shared database system for wearable AR systems has been proposed. With the database, a wearable annotation overlay system which can dynamically annotate users of wearable systems has been investigated. In conventional systems, since dynamic users' position is transmitted to wearable AR systems via a shared database server, it is difficult to overlay annotations at a correct position because of low frequency of updating and delay of client-server communication. In this paper, we propose a new effective method for wearable AR systems to obtain dynamic users' positions by using hybrid peer-to-peer(P2P). In experiments, annotations on dynamic users have been proven to be overlaid correctly enough to show where users are.

1   Introduction

With an advancement in computing technologies, a wearable computer can be realized[1]. Therefore, many wearable augmented reality(AR) systems have been investigated for displaying location-dependent annotation information[2-7]. At the same time, the concept of network shared database system for wearable AR systems has been proposed[8] in order to efficiently provide users with newest information. Furthermore, a wearable annotation overlay system which can annotate dynamic users of wearable systems has been developed with the network shared database[9].

Fig.1 shows an example of wearable annotation overlay system which can annotate dynamic users of wearable computers. The system has possibilities of new effective applications. Some examples are mentioned in the following.

- When we want to find our acquaintances in a crowd of people, wearable AR systems can show us where our acquaintances are.
- In case of emergency, we can easily and fastly find a policeman or a medical doctor around us by using wearable AR systems.

Z. Pan et al. (Eds.): ICAT 2006, LNCS 4282, pp. 217–227, 2006.

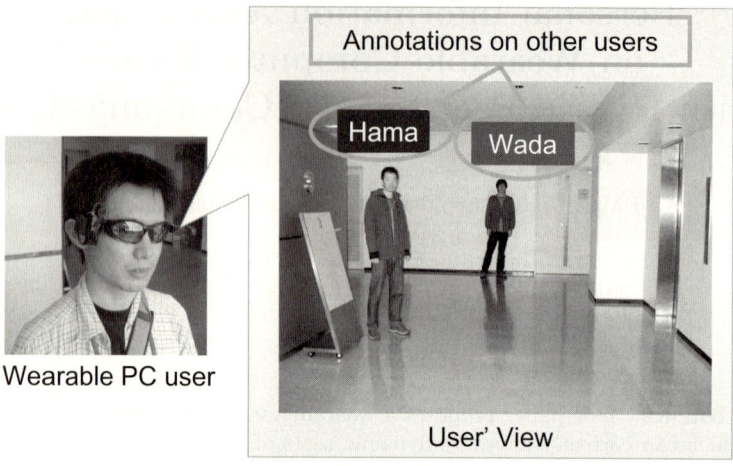

Fig. 1. An example of annotation overlay system which can annotate dynamic users of wearable systems

To annotate dynamic users of wearable systems in a multi-user environment, a user's computer needs to obtain annotation information of other users in real-time. At present, a network-shared annotation database via a wireless network is usually prepared and annotation information of users is managed by the annotation database in a server. Thus wearable annotation overlay systems obtain annotation information and position of users from the database. Therefore, it is difficult to overlay annotations of dynamic users on the correct position in AR images because of the low frequency of updating information and communication delay. In the case that there are displacements of annotations, it is difficult for users to recognize correspondences between annotations and dynamic users of wearable systems. Therefore, the conventional framework works well only when there are a limited number of clients around.

High frequency of updating and low communication delay make it possible for annotation overlay systems to overlay annotations of dynamic users at correct position. If the system can correctly overlay annotations of dynamic users, the system might be suitable for much broader range of applications because the system can work well in the crowds of people. The purpose of the present study is to construct a new effective method for wearable AR systems to obtain dynamic users' positions. To realize high frequency of updating and low communication delay, we use both client-server communication and hybrid P2P. In the method, a client system transmits its position to the server at some intervals. The client system also transmits its position using P2P to other client systems by request from the server.

This paper is structured as follows. Section 2 describes the proposed method for wearable AR systems to obtain dynamic users' positions. In Section 3, experimental results with a prototype system are described. Finally, Section 4 describes summary and future work.

2 Annotation Overlay to Dynamic Users with Hybrid P2P

2.1 Overview of the Framework

To overlay annotation information of dynamic users, two types of data below are usually needed.

1. Users' personal information
2. Users' positions

For example, in Fig.1, users' names are needed as personal information and users' positions are needed to overlay annotations on correct positions. Since these data are updated successively, client systems have to obtain the latest data in order to annotate to dynamic users. Users' personal information is acquired once in a while. On the other hand, users' positions are updated in real time. Thereby, client systems can overlay annotations by obtaining users' personal information at regular intervals. However, users' positions must be consecutively obtained with a small communication delay. If a server provides client users' positions, time lag which arises from a delay of client-server communication is not small. Furthermore, the server must send and receive all of the users' positions continuously in real-time. In this case, loads of the server and the network are generally high. To solve these problems, we employ hybrid P2P communication for obtaining users' position from other clients. However, since we have to consider a network limit and marginal performance of user's system, it is difficult to send and receive multiple users' positions by only using P2P.

Because of this situation, we install a database server which can be accessed with a wireless network and the database manages annotation information. The server is shared by multiple users of AR systems and has two functions below.

1. Providing multiple users' personal information and positions
2. Management of timing of starting and stopping P2P communication

Since the database contains personal data of multiple users, we have to carefully consider the security and privacy issue. In this study, we apply existing network-shared database design[8] to the database which manages multiple users' personal information and positions. Moreover, the database manages user's ID and IP address to control P2P communication. In Section 2.2, the outline of the proposed system is described. Section 2.3 describes how to update and obtain annotation information by client-server communication. Section 2.4 describes how to obtain dynamic users' positions.

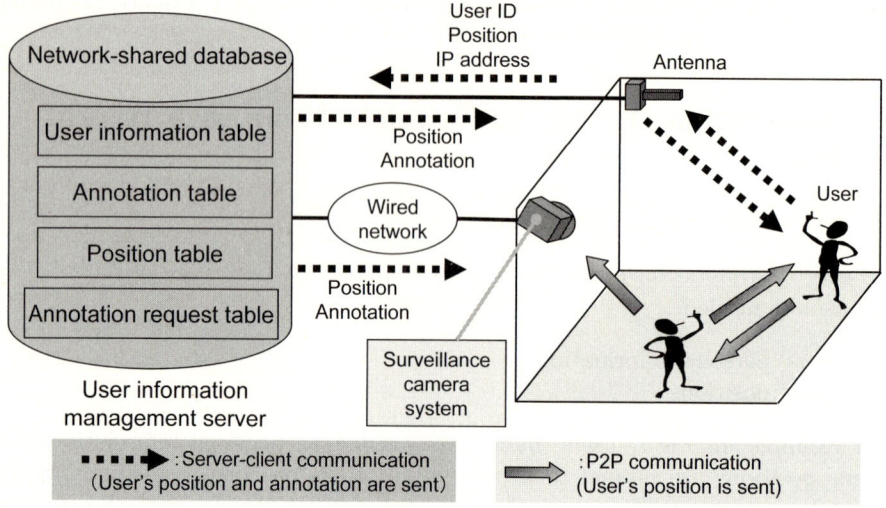

Fig. 2. Outline of proposed annotation overlay system

2.2 Outline of the Proposed System

Fig.2 shows an outline of the proposed annotation overlay system. The proposed system consists of a user information management server and two types of client systems. Components of client systems and the database in the server are described in detail in the following.

– Client systems
 In this study, we assume an environment where there are multiple users of wearable AR systems which can access network and obtain the position and orientation of the user's viewpoint. We assume two types of client AR systems; wearable AR system and fixed surveillance camera system. Wearable AR system can be applied into a communication tool between multiple users. On the other hand, fixed camera system can be applied into a security camera system.

 Client systems request annotation information by transmitting request packet to the server. After obtaining annotation information, the systems create AR images.
– User information management server
 Personal information and position of users are managed by network-shared database in the user information management server. The server has a user information table, an annotation table, and a position table. Tables 1, 2, and 3 show sample lists of information. The server also has an annotation request table. Table 4 shows a sample list of data. The data in Table 4 means that there are five users in an area, and client A has requested annotation information of clients B and D.

Table 1. User information table

ID	Password	Group	IP adress
User A	aaa	Group A	163.221.···
User B	BBBB	Group D	163.221.···
User C	cCcC	- - -	163.221.···

Table 2. Annotation table

ID	Annotation ID	Authorization
User A	A001	User B, C
User B	B001	User C
User C	C001	Group A

2.3 Updating and Obtaining Annotation Information by Client-Server Communication

Each client system has specific ID and communicates with the server in a certain interval. Each wearable AR system automatically sends its specific ID, IP address, and position to the server via a wireless network. On the contrary, the fixed camera system only sends its ID and IP address because its position is fixed in the real world. Position table is updated by the positions sent from wearable AR systems. In the case that a user of wearable AR system wants annotation information, the system sends a request to the server. Annotation request table is updated by request of client systems.

User information management server generates the P2P transmission list as shown in Table 5. The P2P transmission list is generated for each system. Destination addresses of client systems are included in the P2P transmission list. The P2P transmission list is updated by using data of table 1, 2, 3, and 4. Each client system automatically obtains the P2P transmission list in a certain interval and

Table 3. Position table

ID	X	Y	Z	Updated time
User A	0.2	1.0	1.1	19:00:00
User B	-3.2	15.3	1.2	19:39:11
User C	3.6	8.8	1.0	19:54:53

Table 4. Annotation request table

Dst(*) ID R. S(**)	A	B	C	D	E
Client A		O	×	O	×
Client B	O		×	×	O
Client C	O	×		O	×
Client D	O	O	×		×
Client E	O	×	×	×	

Table 5. P2P destination list

Dst(*) ID	Dst(*) address
User B	163.221.····
User D	163.221.····
User E	163.221.····

Dst(*) : Destination

R. S(**) : Request sender

refers to the list in order to transmit its position to other clients. For example, if the list shown in Table 5 is for client A, the system of client A continuously transmits its position to systems of clients B, D, and E.

2.4 Obtaining Dynamic User's Position

This section describes a procedure of obtaining users' positions. The procedure consists of nine processes as shown in Fig.3, which shows an example of the case client A requests annotation information of client B. Each process in Fig.3 is described in detail in the following.

1. Request-transmission for users' positions
   First, client A requests annotation information of client B. Every client system is always able to transmit a request to the server. The request is transmitted with an user ID as well as a password of request sender(client A).
2. Client authentication
   The server checks the user ID and the password to authenticate the validity of the client system. Only if the ID and the password are successfully authenticated by the server, we go to the next step.
3. Checking of obtaining annotation authorization
   The server checks that client A is given permission for obtaining annotation information of client B. Only if client A is given permission by client B, we go to the next step.
4. Update of annotation request table
   The annotation request table is updated by the server with the request. Table 4 shows that client A has requested annotation information of clients B and D.
5. Generation of P2P transmission list
   The server generates a P2P transmission list for each client system. Table 5 indicates that client A has to transmit its position to clients B, D, and E by P2P communication. The server generates the P2P transmission list considering the specification of client systems and network environment.

6. Determination of doing P2P transmission
   The server checks the P2P transmission list for client B. If client A is in the list, we go to Step 7. Otherwise, we go to Step 9.
7. Position-transmission instruction
   In this step, the server orders client B to send its position to client A by P2P communication.
8. Position-transmission by client system
   Client B is ordered to transmit its position by receiving a P2P transmission list. In this case, since client A is included in the list, client B starts transmitting its position to the system of client A by P2P communication.
9. Position-transmission from server
   If client A is not included in a P2P transmission list, the server starts transmitting the position of client B to the system of client A.

When client A wants to stop obtaining annotation information, client A requests the server to stop transmission. This stop-transmission is implemented in a similar way of obtaining user's position.

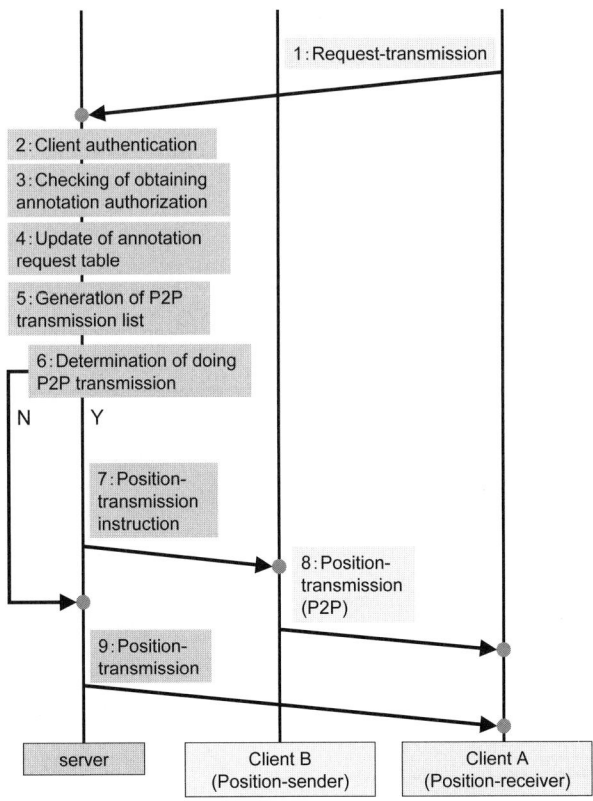

Fig. 3. A procedure of obtaining user's position via P2P communication

3 Experiments

3.1 Experimental Environment

We have carried out some experiments using the proposed method in our campus where users of wearable AR systems can use a wireless LAN. Fig.4 illustrates the experimental environment. We have developed a network-shared database of annotation information in a user information management server and set up one fixed camera system on the ceiling. The fixed camera system consists of a video camera and a standard PC. The user information management server and the video camera system use a wired LAN. We have also set up invisible visual markers on the ceiling for wearable computer users to estimate their position and orientation[7]. The area where user's wearable system can estimate its position and orientation is about 15m   3.5m. In experiments, three wearable system users exist in the environment. Users' positions are estimated by their wearable systems and are transmitted to the location server every 1 second. Wearable systems and the video camera system obtained the annotation information and users' positions and generated annotation overlay images. Fig.5 illustrates a hardware configuration of the wearable augmented reality system which is used in these experiments. Table 6 shows hardware configurations of the location server and the video camera system.

To generate annotation overlay images, position and orientation of the camera are needed. In experiments, the wearable system estimates the position and orientation of the user's viewpoint by using the conventional marker-based registration method[7]. On the contrary, the position and orientation of the video camera is estimated in advance.

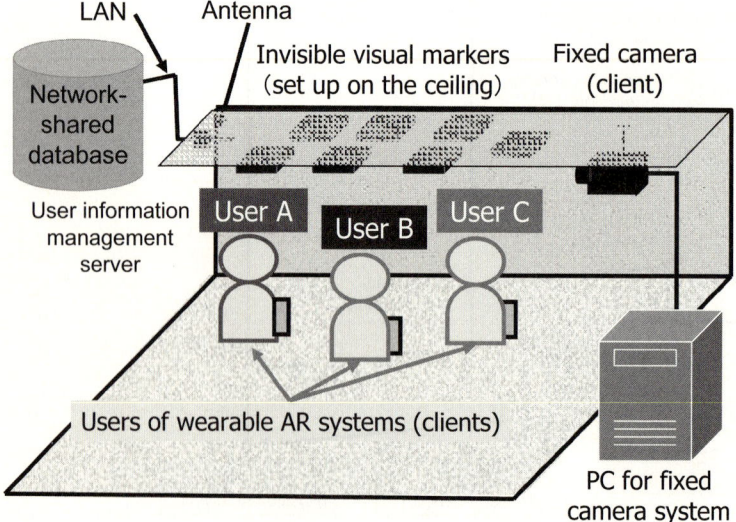

Fig. 4. Experimental environment

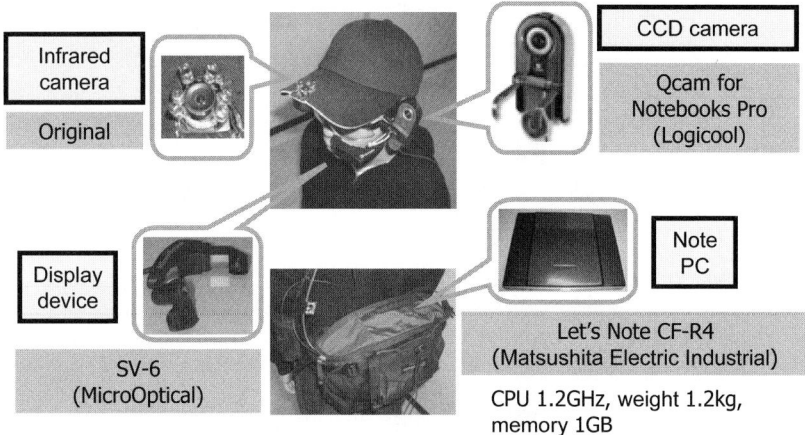

Fig. 5. Hardware configuration of wearable AR system

Table 6. Hardware configuration of server and fixed camera system

	Hardware	specification
Server	PC	CPU:Pentium 3 1.2GHz 512MB memory 100Mbps Ethernet
Fixed camera system	PC	CPU:Pentium D 3.0GHz 3.25GB memory 1Gbps Ethernet
	camera	DCR-TRV900(Sony) 640×480 pixels

3.2 Annotation Overlay by Fixed Camera System

Fig.6 shows examples of annotation overlay images generated by the fixed video camera system. In the augmented images, translucent circles are overlaid on wearable system users' infrared cameras to indicate the positions of annotated users. The size of the circle is proportional to the distance of the fixed video camera system to a user. Users' personal information are also shown on the corners of the images. Figs.6 (a) through (c) show the annotation overlay images when the users' positions are obtained from the user information management server. Figs.6 (d) through (i) show the annotation overlay images when the users' positions are directly transmitted from users by using P2P communication. From Figs.6 (a) through (c), it is clear that the translucent circles are misaligned. This is because users' position table in the server is updated at approximately every second. On the other hand, the translucent circles in Figs.6 (d) through (i) are correctly overlaid on users' infrared cameras. In this case, users' positions are directly transmitted from users at about 10 times per second.

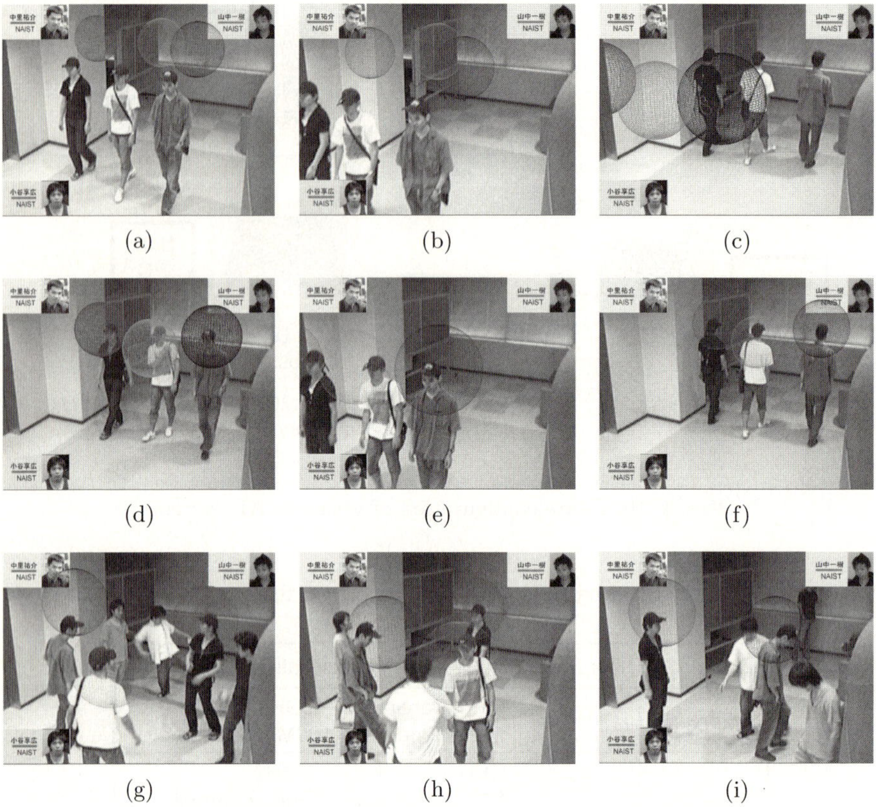

(a)   (b)   (c)

(d)   (e)   (f)

(g)   (h)   (i)

Fig. 6. Overlay images generated by fixed camera system

3.3   Annotation Overlay by Wearable Computer Systems

Fig.7 shows the annotation overlay images generated by a wearable computer system. In this experiment, three wearable computer users are walking in the area and their position and orientation are transmitted to one another at about 10 times per second. The method of showing annotations is same as the previous

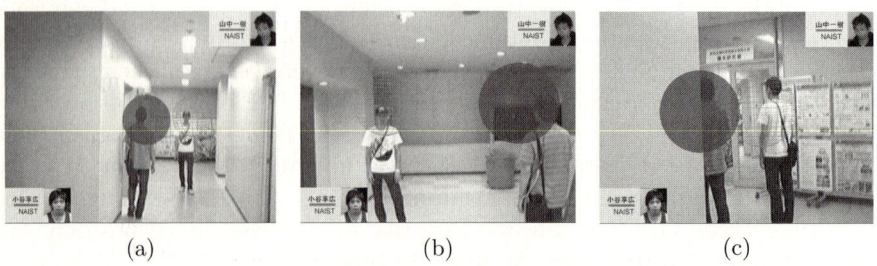

(a)   (b)   (c)

Fig. 7. Overlay images generated by wearable AR system

experiment. As shown in Fig.7, the translucent circles are correctly overlaid on users' infrared cameras. Through this experiment, we have confirmed that wearable computer systems can generate appropriate annotation overlay images by using P2P communication and show where other users are.

4   Summary

This paper has proposed a new method for annotating dynamic users of wearable AR systems to intuitively indicate other users' positions in user's view. Users of this annotation overlay system can see annotations on dynamic users and can correctly recognize where other users are. We have shown the feasibility of the method through the demonstration with experiments in our campus. In the future, we should further investigate the optimal management of P2P communication considering the specification of wearable computers and wireless network.

Acknowledgments

This research was supported in part by Strategic Information and Communications R&D Promotion Programme (SCOPE) of Ministry of Internal Affairs and Communications of Japan.

References

1. S. Mann: "Wearable Computing: A First Step Toward Personal Imaging," IEEE Computer, Vol.30, No. 2, 2002.
2. S. Feiner, B. MacIntyre, T. Höllerer, and A. WebsterF "A Touring Machine: Prototyping 3D Mobile Augmented Reality Systems for Exploring the Urban Environment", Proc. 1st Int. Symposium. on Wearable Computers, pp. 74-81, 1997.
3. R. Azuma: "A Survey of Augmented Reality," Presence, Vol. 6, No. 4, pp. 355-385, 1997.
4. B. H. Thomas, V. Demczuk, W. Piekarski, D. Hepworth, and B. Gunther: "A Wearable Computer System with Augmented Reality to Support Terrestrial Navigationh, Proc. Int. Symposium. on Wearable Computers, pp. 168-171, 1998.
5. R. Tenmoku, M. Kanbara, and N. Yokoya: "Annotating user-viewed objects for wearable AR systems", Proc. IEEE and ACM Int. Symposium. on Mixed Augmented Reality(ISMAR 05), pp. 192-193, 2005.
6. M. Kourogi, T. Kurata, and K. Sakaue: "A Panorama-based Method of Personal Positioning and Orientation and Its Real-time Applications for Wearable Computers", Proc. 5th Int. Symposium. on Wearable Computers, pp. 107-114, 2001.
7. Y. Nakazato, M. Kanbara, and N. Yokoya: "Wearable augmented reality system using invisible visual markers and an IR camera", Proc. IEEE Int. Symposium. on Wearable Computers, pp. 198-199, 2005.
8. K. Makita, M. Kanbara, and N. Yokoya: "Shared annotation database for networked wearable augmented reality system", Proc. 5th Pacific Rim Conf. on Multimedia, Vol. 3, pp. 499-507, 2004.
9. R. Tenmoku, A. Anabuki, M. Kanbara, and N. Yokoya: "Annotation of Personal Information on Wearable Users Using Shared Database", Proc. Meeting on Image Recognition and Understanding 2005, pp. 1598-1599, 2005. (in Japanese)

An Initialization Tool for Installing Visual Markers in Wearable Augmented Reality

Yusuke Nakazato, Masayuki Kanbara, and Naokazu Yokoya

Nara Institute of Science and Technology,
8916–5 Takayama, Ikoma, Nara, 630–0192, Japan

Abstract. It is necessary to precisely measure pose (position and orientation) of a user in order to realize an augmented reality (AR) system with a wearable computer. One of major methods for measuring user's pose in AR is visual marker-based approach which calculates them by recognizing markers pasted up on the ceilings or walls. The method needs 3D pose information of visual markers in advance. However, much cost is necessary to calibrate visual markers pasted up on the ceiling in a wide environment. In this paper, an initialization tool for installing visual markers in wearable AR is proposed. The administrator is assisted in installing visual markers in a wide environment by the proposed tool. The tool calibrates alignment of visual markers which exist in the real environment with high accuracy by recognizing them in the images captured by a high-resolution still camera. Additionally, the tool assists the administrator in repairing the incorrect pattern of marker using a wearable AR system.

1 Introduction

Recently augmented reality (AR) system using a wearable computer has received a great deal of attention as a method for displaying location-based information in the real world[1]. To realize a wearable AR system, the exact pose (position and orientation) of the user is required. Especially in indoor environments, since a GPS cannot be used, various localization methods have been investigated[2,3,4,5]. User's pose is sometimes estimated by recognizing visual markers pasted up on the ceilings or walls whose poses are known[6,7,8]. We have proposed a localization method with an infrared camera and invisible visual markers consisting of translucent retro-reflectors as shown in Fig.1[9]. The method can realize indoor localization without impairing the scenery in a wide environment. In the visual marker-based approach such as in [9], the alignment information of visual markers, which is 3D poses of markers located in real environment, is needed in advance.

In this paper, we focus on initialization methods of visual markers for wearable AR system. The initialization of visual markers means calibration of their alignment in advance. The simplest method is calibration by hand using a ruler and others, although the accuracy of calibration results is low. Another method

Z. Pan et al. (Eds.): ICAT 2006, LNCS 4282, pp. 228–238, 2006.
© Springer-Verlag Berlin Heidelberg 2006

(a) Invisible visual markers   (b) Invisible visual markers with a flash

Fig. 1. Positioning infrastructures with invisible visual markers placed on the ceiling. Though it is difficult to perceive the markers, these can be captured clearly with a flash.

using a laser rangefinder can calibrate the poses of visual markers with high accuracy. However the laser rangefinder is an expensive instrumentation in general. Furthermore, these methods need much labor to calibrate the poses of visual markers in a wide environment. On the other hand, the calibration methods using images of visual markers have been proposed[10,11,12]. Baratoff, et al have proposed a semiautomatic image-based calibration method requiring only minimal interaction[10]. Maeda, et al have calibrated all visual markers by capturing markers which include one reference marker automatically[11]. These methods can work online, however the calibration results of markers' poses do not have high accuracy, because the pose of marker is usually estimated based on propagation with some low resolution images. When a large number of visual markers are installed as positioning infrastructures for user's localization, the calibration of visual markers with high accuracy is generally required. In this case, the offline calibration tool for wearable AR system is useful.

We focus on high accuracy calibration of visual markers' poses used as positioning infrastructures. This paper proposes an initialization tool which assists on administrator in installing visual markers. First, the administrator sets up visual markers on the ceilings or walls and then captures images of visual markers by a high-resolution still camera. Secondly, the proposed tool generates alignment information of visual markers by recognizing visual markers on the images captured by the administrator. Finally, the tool assists the administrator in repairing duplicate patterns of visual markers using a wearable AR system. Because such patterns of visual markers placed in the neighborhood sometimes cause failure of user localization. However, it is difficult to confirm such incorrect pattern from a large number of visual markers by human beings. In particular, when the invisible visual markers as shown in Fig.1 are used, the task is more difficult because the markers are invisible. Therefore, the tool provides the administrator with images containing indication of repairing markers using a wearable AR system.

This paper is structured as follows. Section 2 describes an initialization tool for visual marker-based localization. In Section 3, experiments of infrastructure

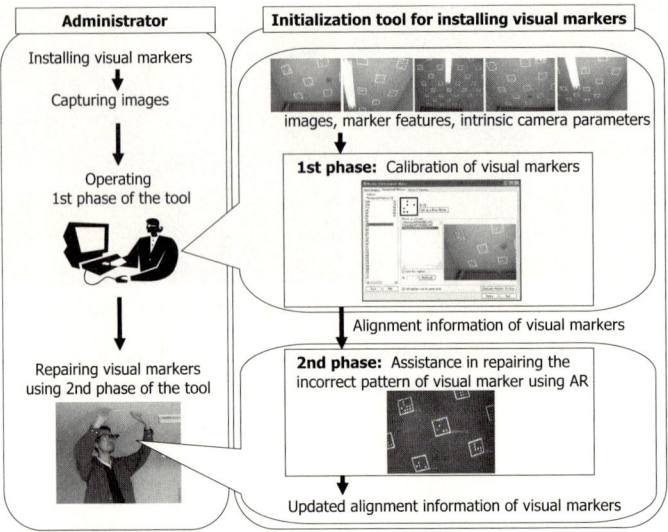

Fig. 2. Flow diagram of initialization tool of visual markers

initialization with the proposed tool are described. Finally, Section 4 gives conclusion and future work.

2　Initialization Tool for Installing Visual Markers

In this section, the proposed initialization tool is explained in detail. The overview of the proposed tool is illustrated in Fig.2. First, visual markers are installed as positioning infrastructures and then high-resolution images of visual markers are captured by the administrator. Secondly, the tool calibrates poses of visual markers by using captured images and outputs calibration results as alignment information. Finally, using the calibration results, the tool provides the administrator with augmented images in order to repair incorrect patterns of visual markers.

This tool consists of two phases: the first phase is concerned with calibration of visual markers and the second phase is to assist in repairing incorrect markers using a wearable AR system. In the first phase, poses of visual markers are calibrated from high-resolution images of markers. The administrator inputs (1) intrinsic camera parameters (focal length, pixel size, center of image, radial distortion factor coefficient), (2) features of visual marker (frame length and width, pattern size), and (3) images of visual markers. The tool estimates poses of visual markers, and outputs this information as alignment information of visual markers. In the second phase, the tool assists the administrator in repairing incorrect patterns of markers using alignment information of visual markers generated in the first phase. The tool provides the administrator with overlaid images containing indication of repairing visual marker and then outputs updated alignment information of visual markers. Sections 2.1 and 2.2 explain about the first and second phases, respectively.

2.1 First Phase: Calibration of Visual Markers

In this section, the first phase of initialization tool is described.

Overview of First Phase of Initialization Tool. In the first phase, the alignment information of visual markers is generated. This phase uses three forms as shown in Figs. 3,4, and 5: an input, a confirmation, and an output forms. Fig.3 illustrates the input form. The administrator inputs intrinsic camera parameters, visual marker features, and images of visual markers. Then the administrator

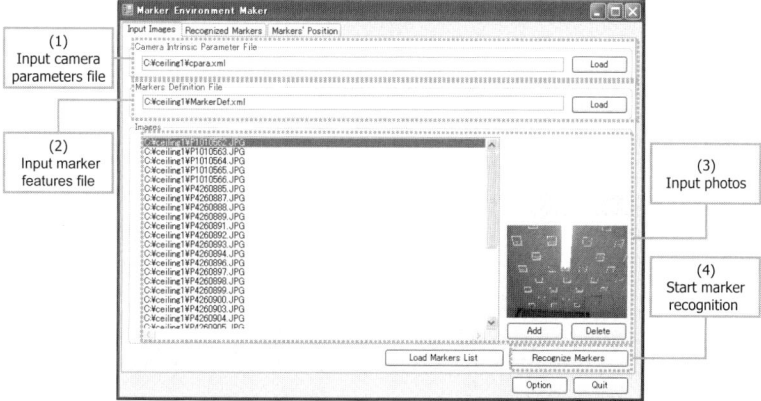

Fig. 3. Input form in the first phase

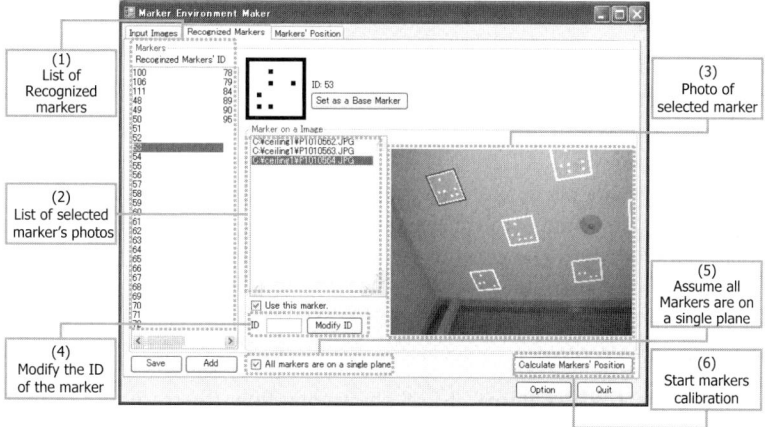

Fig. 4. Confirmation form in the first phase

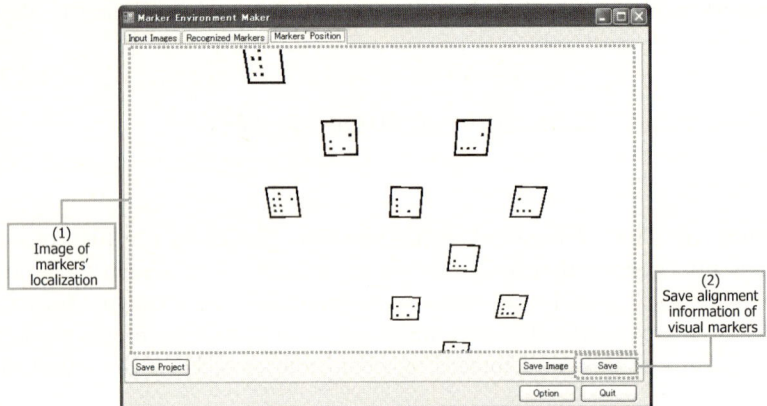

Fig. 5. Output form in the first phase

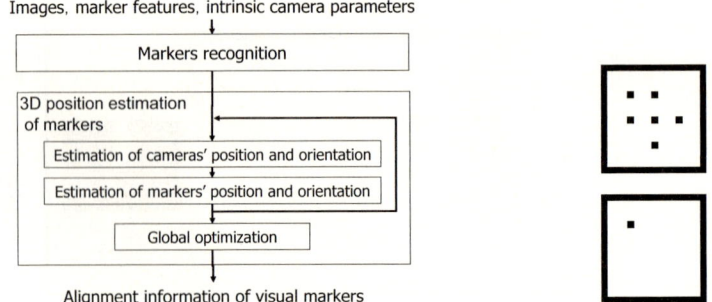

Fig. 6. Flow diagram of visual marker calibration

Fig. 7. Instances of markers

dictates to start recognition of visual markers, and switches to the confirmation form. In the confirmation form shown in Fig.4, the administrator confirms result of marker recognition. If misrecognized or duplicate visual markers exist, the administrator modifies this field(Fig.4. (4)). Furthermore, if it is supposed that all visual markers are on a single plane, the administrator sets a flag on this field(Fig.4. (5)). Then the administrator dictates to start calibration of visual markers, and switches to the output form. Fig.5 illustrates the output form. The form shows an image on which the calibrated visual markers are drawn and then the tool outputs the alignment information of visual markers. This information is used in the second phase.

Visual Markers Calibration. Fig.6 shows the flow diagram of the process of visual markers calibration in the first phase. First, visual markers in each image in the input form are recognized. Secondly, one recognized visual marker is set the 3D pose as a reference marker. Poses of cameras capturing the reference visual marker are estimated. Then, position and orientation of visual markers are estimated by estimated poses of the cameras. Finally, the poses of the visual markers are optimized all over the images. The details of these processes are described below.

Marker Recognition. We employ invisible visual markers[9] which consist of grid points showing their IDs as shown in Fig.7. In the process of marker recognition, edges are detected from the input image using canny operator [13], then contours of marker are retrieved. The area of original image corresponding to the contour is binarized using a threshold which is determined by the discriminant analysis method[14]. Four vertices of a square as a visual marker are detected from the area, and its ID is recognized. The four vertices and centroids of grid points in the marker are used as feature points in the process of 3D pose estimation of markers described below.

3D Pose Estimation of Markers. First, one recognized visual marker is given its 3D pose as a reference marker; vote that the reference marker determines the origin of the world coordinate system. Next, using a Sato's method[15], pose of camera capturing the reference marker are estimated. Then, poses of other markers captured by camera known 3D position and orientation are estimated. Using the estimated poses of markers, unestimated poses of cameras are estimated. These processes of pose estimation of camera and visual markers are iterated until all the markers' poses are determined. In the iteration process, visual markers captured by multiple images, which has a large reprojection error, are considered as those with duplicate patterns. The reprojection error is defined as the sum of squared distances between detected positions of marker's feature points in the image and projected positions of marker's feature points in the world coordinate system. The poses of duplicate visual markers are estimated individually. These visual markers with duplicate patterns are candidates for repairing in the second phase. Finally, 3D poses of cameras and visual markers are globally optimized so as to minimize the sum of reprojection errors all over the images.

2.2   Second Phase: Assistance in Repairing Incorrect Markers Using AR

In the second phase, our tool assists the administrator in repairing incorrect patterns of markers using a wearable AR system. The administrator equips a wearable computer, an HMD and an IR camera with IR-LEDs in order to capture the invisible visual markers as shown in Fig.8. The tool uses alignment information of visual markers generated in the first phase, and provides the administrator with images containing indication of repairing markers as shown in Fig.8. The administrator's view images are overlaid with IDs and contours of recognized markers. If incorrect visual markers such as duplicate or lacked patterns of markers exist in the administrator's view, the tool provides the administrator images with the repaired pattern of marker. In case of Fig.8, the administrator has modified ID No. 289 to No. 32. When the pattern of marker is repaired by the administrator, the tool updates alignment information of visual markers.

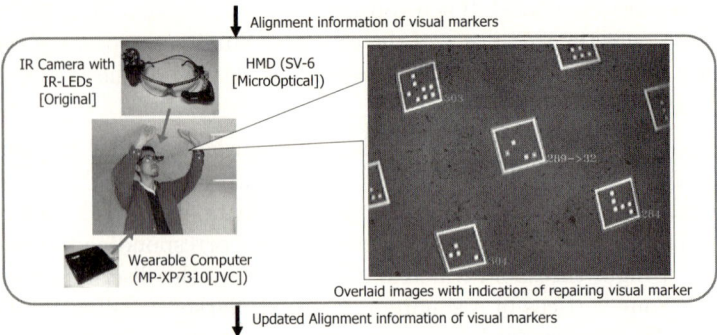

Fig. 8. Overview of the second phase

3   Experiments

First, we evaluated the accuracy of estimated position of visual markers in the first phase. In this experiment, invisible visual markers were set up on the ceiling. The size of the marker was 16cm. These markers are arranged at intervals of 60cm on the ceiling plane. The 20 images captured by a digital still camera "OLYMPUS C-5050ZOOM" were used as shown in Fig.9. The size of these images was 2560×1920 pixels. The intrinsic camera parameters were estimated by Tsai's method [16] in advance. Since the visual markers were set up along pattern of ceilings, the grand truths of the visual marker poses were calibrated manually. When it is assumed that all markers are not located on the single plane (no co-planar constraint), the projected points to 2D plane of estimated positions of visual markers' four vertices are shown in Fig.10(a). Fig.10(b) shows

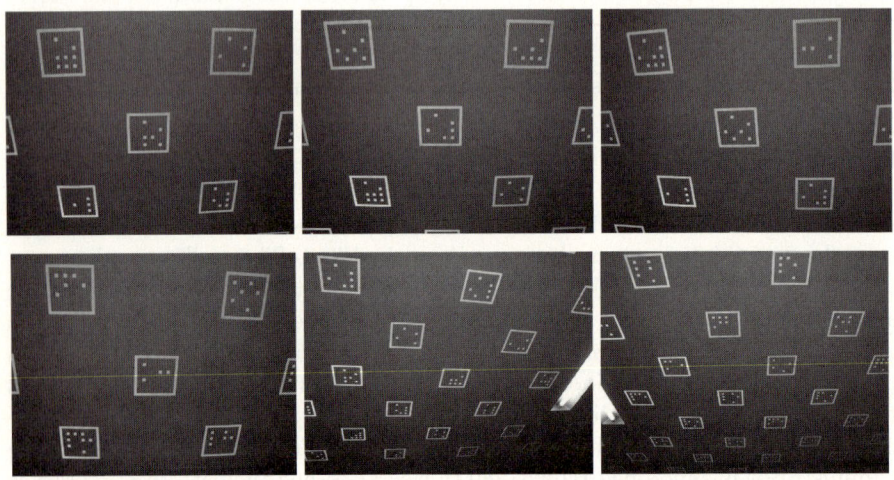

Fig. 9. Examples of input images (2560×1920 pixels)

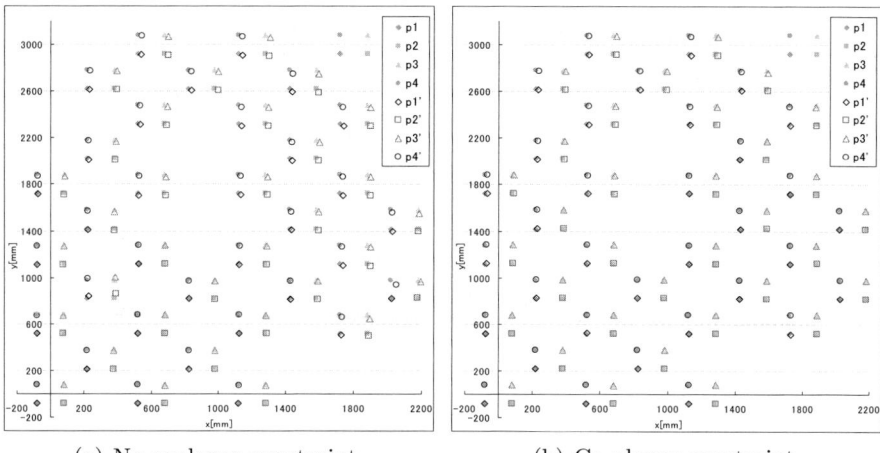

(a) No-coplanar constraint.   (b) Co-planar constraint.

Fig. 10. Results of marker calibration (pn:true position, pn':estimated position)

Table 1. Average and standard deviation of marker calibration errors

	no co-planar constraint			co-planar constraint		
	x	y	z	x	y	z
average of absolute error[mm]	9.9	11.6	16.9	6.0	3.7	0.0
standard deviation of error[mm]	7.7	9.7	13.6	5.2	4.6	0.0

estimated markers' positions when it is assumed that all markers are located on the single plane (co-planar constraint). In these figures, p1, p2, p3 and p4 show true positions of visual marker's four vertices, and p1', p2', p3' and p4' show corresponding estimated positions. The average of absolute errors of markers' positions and standard deviation of errors are shown in Table 1. In this experiment, we used a note PC (Pentium M 1.6GHz, Memory 512MB). When the no co-planar constraint is assumed, it took about 173 seconds for calibration of the markers, and reprojection error was about 1.5 pixels. When the co-planar constraint is assumed, the processing time of marker calibration was about 75 seconds, and reprojection error was about 1.7 pixels. From Table 1, we confirmed that the average error of estimated position was about 6mm and 17mm in case of co-planar constraint and no co-planar constraint, respectively. In user localization, when we use a camera whose angle is 90 degrees and resolution is 640 × 480 pixels and then the user captures the visual markers on the ceiling 1.2m away, the marker's position error of 6mm corresponds to the error of about 1.6 pixels on the image. We can conclude that the accuracy obtained is sufficient for user's localization. Most visual markers were captured in about 3 images; however some markers were captured only one time. These markers caused some errors.

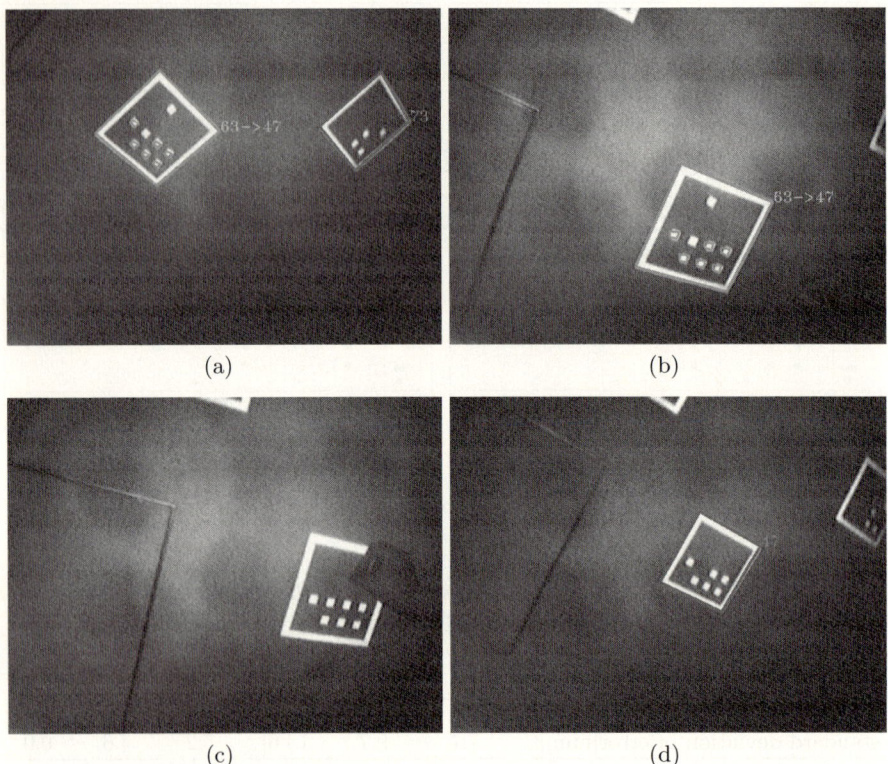

Fig. 11. Augmented images. These images are overlaid with IDs and repaired pattern of marker. The administrator modified the duplicate pattern of No.63 to No.47 according to the indications given in these images.

In the experiment of the second phase, we confirmed that proposed tool was able to assist in repairing the patterns of markers. Fig.11 shows augmented images with which the administrator is provided repairing the marker. From the result of the first phase, it was understood that No.63 is duplicated. Thus the administrator modified the pattern to No.47 according to the indications given in augmented images.

4   Conclusions

This paper has proposed an initialization tool for installing visual markers in wearable AR. In order to construct an environment for visual marker-based localization, the tool calibrates pose of visual markers by using images of markers captured by high-resolution still camera. Furthermore, the tool assists the administrator in repairing incorrect patterns of markers by presenting augmented images. In experiments, we have confirmed that the proposed tool is able to estimate poses of markers with the high accuracy of about 6 mm when the co-planar constraint is assumed. We have also confirmed that the tool is able to assist in repairing incorrect patterns of markers using a wearable AR system. In future work, we should carry out experiments of infrastructure initialization of visual markers in a wide area. In order to calibrate poses of visual markers which have some errors with more high accuracy, we will indicate the additional positions at which the images should be taken using wearable AR system.

Acknowledgments

This research was supported in part by Strategic Information and Communications R&D Promotion Programme (SCOPE) of Ministry of Internal Affairs and Communications of Japan.

References

1. Höller, T., Feiner, S., Terauchi, T., Rashid, G., Hallaway, D.: Exploring mars: Developing indoor and outdoor user interfaces to a mobile augmented reality system. Computers and Graphics **23**(6) (1999) 779–785
2. Kourogi, M., Kurata, T.: Personal positioning based on walking locomotion analysis with self-contained sensors and wearable camera. Proc. 2nd IEEE/ACM Int. Symp. on Mixed and Augmented Reality (ISMAR 03) (2003) 103–112
3. Tenmoku, R., Kanbara, M., Yokoya, N.: A wearable augmented reality system using positioning infrastructures and a pedometer. Proc. 7th IEEE Int. Symp. on Wearable Computers (ISWC'03) (2003) 110–117
4. Vacchetti, L., Lepetit, V., Fua, P.: Combining edge and texture information for real-time accurate 3D camera tracking. Proc. 3rd IEEE/ACM Int. Symp. on Mixed and Augmented Reality (ISMAR 04) (2004) 48–57
5. Oe, M., Sato, T., Yokoya, N.: Estimating camera position and posture by using feature landmark database. Proc. 14th Scandinavian Conf. on Image Analysis (SCIA2005) (2005) 171–181
6. Thomas, B., Close, B., Donoghue, J., Squires, J., De Bondi, P., Piekarski, W.: First person indoor/outdoor augmented reality application: Arquake. Personal and Ubiquitous Computing **6**(1) (2002) 75–86
7. Kalkusch, M., Lidy, T., Lnapp, M., Reitmayr, G., Kaufmann, H., Schmalstieg, D.: Structured visual markers for indoor pathfinding. Proc. 1st IEEE Int. Augmented Reality Toolkit Workshop (ART'02) (2002)
8. Naimark, L., Foxlin, E.: Circular data matrix fiducial system and robust image processing for a wearable vision-inertial self-tracker. Proc. 1st IEEE/ACM Int. Symp. on Mixed and Augmented Reality (ISMAR2002) (2002) 27–36
9. Nakazato, Y., Kanbara, M., Yokoya, N.: A localization system using invisible retro-reflective markers. Proc. IAPR Conf. on Machine Vision Applications (MVA2005) (2005) 140–143
10. Baratoff, G., Neubeck, A., Regenbrecht, H.: Interactive multi-marker calibration for augmented reality applications. Proc. 1st IEEE/ACM Int. Symp. on Mixed and Augmented Reality (ISMAR2002) (2002) 107–116
11. Maeda, M., Habara, T., Machida, T., Ogawa, T., Kiyokawa, K., Takemura, H.: Indoor localization methods for wearable mixed reality. Proc. 2nd CREST Workshop on Advanced Computing and Communicating Techniques for Wearable Information Playing (2003) 62–65

12. Zauner, J., M. Haller, A.: Authoring of mixed reality applications including multi-marker calibration for mobile devices. Proc. 10th Eurographics Symp. Virtual Environments (EGVE2004) (2004) 87–90
13. Canny, J.: A computational approach to edge detection. IEEE Trans. Pattern Analysis and Machine Intelligence **8**(6) (1986) 679–698
14. Otsu, N.: A threshold selection method from gray-level histograms. IEEE Trans. Systems, Man, and Cybernetics **SMC-9**(1) (1979) 63–66
15. Sato, T., Kanbara, M., Yokoya, N.: 3-D modeling of an outdoor scene from multiple image sequences by estimating camera motion parameters. Proc. 13th Scandinavian Conf. on Image Analysis(SCIA2003) (2003) 717–724
16. Tsai, R.Y.: An efficient and accurate camera calibration technique for 3D machine vision. Proc. IEEE Conf. on Computer Vision and Pattern Recognition (1986) 364–374

Increasing Camera Pose Estimation Accuracy Using Multiple Markers

Jong-Hyun Yoon, Jong-Seung Park, and Chungkyue Kim

Department of Computer Science & Engineering, University of Incheon,
177 Dohwa-dong, Nam-gu, Incheon, 402-749, Republic of Korea
{jhyoon, jong, ckkim}@incheon.ac.kr

Abstract. If the geometry of a marker is known and camera parameters are available, it is possible to recover a camera pose. The transformation between a camera and a marker is defined relative to the local coordinate system of the marker. This paper proposes a real-time camera tracking method using multiple markers while the camera is allowed to move freely in a 3D space. We utilize multiple markers to improve the accuracy of the pose estimation. We also present a coordinate registration algorithm to obtain a global optimal camera pose from local transformations of multiple markers. For the registration, a reference marker is automatically chosen among multiple markers and the global camera pose is computed using all local transforms weighted by marker detection confidence rates. Experimental results show that the proposed method provides more accurate camera poses than those from other methods.

1   Introduction

The methods of camera motion estimation are classified into a marker-based approach and a feature-based approach. The feature-based methods do not use specific markers and have an advantage that they do not need the preparation of markers. In other side, there are some shortcomings that the camera pose estimation is frequently unstable and inaccurate since it heavily depends on the accuracy of the feature extraction and tracking result. The feature-based methods require a relatively large number of feature points, hence they are slower than the marker-based methods. Our approach falls into the marker-based approach for the reason that real-time interactive augmented reality applications require a fast and stable camera tracking.

Among the various kinds of markers, the most commonly used types are planar markers. Different planar patterns are attached to the markers to distinguish the multiple markers. Once the camera pose is recovered, the virtual objects can be easily synthesized to the captured image frame.

Many previous studies have focused on reducing the recovered camera pose errors[1][2]. Ababsa[3] proposed a method based on tracking calibrated 2D fiducials in a known 3D environment. When a camera is calibrated, the distortion factor is available and it can be used to increase the camera pose accuracy. Efficient calibration methods are readily available[4]. Camera motion recovery without a camera calibration has also been presented[5]. Besides the consideration

Z. Pan et al. (Eds.): ICAT 2006, LNCS 4282, pp. 239–248, 2006.

of the camera distortion factor, camera pose errors are affected by environment variables such as occlusion and lighting. Skrypnyk introduced a method to reduce such errors[6]. As well as the user's viewpoint, the positions of light sources can be considered for a seamless registration. Kanbara used a marker and a mirror ball to estimate the relationship between the real and virtual worlds and the positions of light sources[7].

In this paper, we propose a fast and reliable camera pose estimation method using multiple markers. Our approach is different from previous works in the sense that our method is adaptive to the number of detected markers. If there is at least one accurate detected marker in a frame, a reliable camera pose estimation is guaranteed even when there also exist erroneous markers in the frame. In the next section, we describe the related works about fast and stable camera tracking using markers. Section 3 presents our proposed method based on multiple markers. Section 4 describes experimental results of our method for real video frames. Finally, we conclude with an overall evaluation and summary in Section 5.

2   Marker-Based Camera Tracking

For the realization of practical augmented reality systems, marker-based camera pose estimation methods have been actively investigated. Using a single marker, the transformation between the marker and the camera can be calculated and the camera motion can also be estimated by the marker transform. However, the single marker tracking has several limitations. It cannot be applied to the camera motion recovery if the marker is not visible, which is commonly occurred when a camera is moved freely in a wide space. A solution for such a problem is using multiple markers to cover a wide area.

The purpose of our research is to develop an accurate algorithm to track the camera motion using multiple markers whose positions are known in the real environment[8]. Uematsu proposed a multi-marker registration method in a projective space[9]. In the algorithm, a projective matrix is computed for each plane to relate it to the real world. The projection matrices are computed from the coordinate systems that are defined by the planes without geometrical relationship to each other. Then, all the projection matrices are merged into a single transformation matrix via the projective 3D space. Zauner proposed a mixed reality application using multiple markers and applied it to a mobile device[10]. The method assumed that the geometry between markers are known in advance. To detect multiple markers, the algorithm uses a simple reference marker that has the highest confidence value among detected markers. To improve the accuracy and stability, the average filter and the linear regression filter methods are used. The average filter reduces the errors of estimated values for input image sequences. The linear regression filter considers the history of the tracking results. Via the linear regression filter, the estimated marker transformation becomes more stable.

2.1   Camera Tracking Using a Single Marker

ARToolkit and ARTag are two most representative methods that detect a planar marker and calculate the relation between the marker and the camera. ARToolkit is the representative marker tracking system and it is the widely used method for a fiducial marker system in AR. There are some steps to calculate the relationship between the marker and the camera. First, the input image is converted to a binary image by the grey scale thresholding. Then, four outline segments of marker's square are extracted from the binary image.

The square region for each detected marker is found by the binary image analysis. For each marker, the pattern inside the square is captured and compared with pre-defined pattern templates to identify the type of the detected marker. If the captured pattern is matched to one of the predefined templates, the corresponding pattern number is assigned to the detected marker. After the marker detection, the 3D position and the orientation of the marker is computed[11]. The rotation matrix is calculated using the line segments and the translation matrix is computed using the four corner points of the marker that are the intersections of the line segments. The transformation matrix $\mathbf{T}_m^c$ from the marker coordinate system to the camera coordinate system consists of the 3×3 rotation matrix $\mathbf{R}$ and the 3×1 translation vector $\mathbf{t}$. The estimation error of $\mathbf{T}_m^c$ can be reduced by the iterative optimization process minimizing the differences between the detected corner points and the projections of the marker vertices.

The ARTag is an extension of the ARToolKit. Its marker is a combination of special planar patterns[12]. ARTag finds four outlines of the rectangular marker using an edge detection method. The marker detection in ARTag is more robust in illumination than that in ARToolKit since ARTag uses edge detection instead of binary thresholding. Each detected marker is identified using its corners and inner grid cells. An ARTag marker is a 10×10 grid rectangle and the inner pattern is a 6×6 grid rectangle of black-and-white cells. The inner pattern is sampled to determine whether each grid cell corresponds to zero or one. Then, we could obtain the marker identification number.

2.2   Camera Tracking Using Multiple Markers

This section explains a typical multi-marker registration method based on the works by Uematsu[9] and Zauner[10]. The registration method by Uematsu estimates extrinsic parameters of the camera and aligns virtual objects according to the parameters[9]. The method uses the relationship between the projective space and the reference image. A projection matrix $\mathbf{P}_i$ that relates the ith marker coordinate system to the input image is computed by the planar homography for each marker. The subscript i is the marker identification number. The transformation matrix $\mathbf{T}_i^{WP}$ is a 4×4 symmetric matrix and it relates the ith marker's coordinate system with the projective space. A point in the world space $\mathbf{X}_W$ and the corresponding point in the projective space $\mathbf{X}_P$ are related by $\mathbf{X}_P \simeq \mathbf{T}_i^{WP} \mathbf{X}_W$. Using the projection matrix $\mathbf{P}_i$ and the transformation matrix $\mathbf{T}_i^{WP}$, we could compute another transformation $\mathbf{T}_i^{PI}$ that relates the projective space to each image by $\mathbf{T}_i^{PI} = \mathbf{P}_i \left(\mathbf{T}_i^{WP} \right)^{-1}$. After obtaining all the transformation matrices, all $\mathbf{T}_i^{PI}$ are merged into the transformation matrix $\mathbf{T}^{PI}$. The precalculated transform matrices relate between the projective space and the input images. So, it is possible to merge $\mathbf{T}_i^{WP}$. After the merging process, virtual objects are aligned and posed by $\mathbf{T}^{PI}$.

Zauner proposed another multi-marker registration technique for mixed reality in mobile devices[10]. The method consists of two steps: finding the reference marker and applying the average filter and the linear regression filter. First, a marker is chosen as the reference marker among the detected multiple markers. The center of the reference marker is used as the reference point. Next, the position and the orientation of the camera relative to the marker are computed. The average filter is applied to the positions and the orientations of all the detected markers in order to get the average position vector and the average orientation quaternion. Since the result using only the average filter is unstable, the history of the previous positions and orientations of the camera is considered. The linear regression provides two straight lines representing the correlation between the past time and the tracked placement. The linear regression minimizes the average error of the camera pose estimation.

3   Increasing Camera Pose Accuracy Using Multiple Markers

The transformation between the camera and the marker could be recovered from the marker detection. The transformation consists of the rotation and the translation of the camera, which is represented by:

$$[X_c, Y_c, Z_c, 1_c]^T = \begin{bmatrix} \mathbf{R} & \mathbf{t} \\ \mathbf{0} & 1 \end{bmatrix} [X_m, Y_m, Z_m, 1_m]^T . \tag{1}$$

The equation (1) represents the camera transformation based on the local coordinate system of the marker. The camera position corresponds to the translation vector $\mathbf{t} = [t_x \ t_y \ t_z]^T$ and camera orientation corresponds to the rotation matrix $\mathbf{R}$. We propose an accurate camera pose estimation method that estimates $\mathbf{R}$ and $\mathbf{t}$ from multi-markers. Our method is fast and reliable in most cases. The overall steps of our method are described as following pseudo code.

Step 1 (Initialization):
    1. Detect all visible markers, m_i $(i = 1, \ldots, N)$, where N is the number of detected markers. The four corner points of the ith marker are denoted by $\mathbf{c}_{i,j}$ $(j = 1, \ldots, 4)$.
    2. Calculate the transformation matrix $\mathbf{T}_i$ for the ith detected marker.
Step 2 (Choosing a reference marker):
    1. Compute the marker center $\bar{\mathbf{c}}_i$ using corner points by $\bar{\mathbf{c}}_i = 0.25 \sum_{j=1}^4 \mathbf{c}_{i,j}$.
    2. Calculate the distance d_i between $\bar{\mathbf{c}}_i$ and the image center $\bar{\mathbf{o}}$ by $d_i = \| \bar{\mathbf{c}}_i - \bar{\mathbf{o}} \|$.

   3. Select the reference marker m_k by finding the marker of the minimum $\arg\min_{1 \leq i \leq N} d_i$.

Step 3 (Setting the reference marker):
1. Align the local coordinate system L_i to the reference coordinate system L_k by applying $\mathbf{T}_{i,k}$ where k is the reference marker index and $\mathbf{T}_{i,k}$ is the predefined transformation matrix from the multi-marker setting in the real world.
2. Change the camera transformation matrix in regard to the local coordinate system $\mathbf{T}_i$ to the transformation in regard to the reference coordinate system $\mathbf{T}'_i$ by $\mathbf{T}'_i = \mathbf{T}_i(\mathbf{T}_{i,k})^{-1}$.

Step 4 (Computing error rates):
1. Calculate error rates ρ_i of all detected markers by $\rho_i = w_i / \sum_{i=1}^{N} w_i$ where w_i is the weight of the ith detected marker.

Step 5 (Computing camera pose):
1. Compute the weighted sum of all estimated transformations using ρ_i by $\mathbf{T}'' = \sum_{i=1}^{N}(\rho_i \mathbf{T}'_i)$.
2. Calculate the rotation $\mathbf{R}$ and the translation $\mathbf{t}$ from $\mathbf{T}''$.

3.1   Calculating the Camera Transformation

From each input image, we first find out all visible markers and calculate the transformations for the detected markers. Accurate corner extraction of the marker directly affects the reliability of the recovered marker transformations. Next, we select the reference marker among detected markers. We choose the closest marker to the image center as the reference marker. In the previous step, we found out all visible square areas and the corner points of detected markers. Using the corner points, we calculate the coordinates of the marker center in the image coordinate system. Then, we calculate the distance between the marker center and the image center. We choose the marker that has the minimum distance as the reference marker. The reference marker provides the best confident camera transformation among the markers since the reference marker has the least projective distortion.

   Fig. 1(a) shows the relationship of the local coordinate systems of the markers and the reference coordinate system. We have to calculate the camera pose in terms of the reference coordinate system. Each of the detected markers has its local coordinate system. We need to register the local coordinate systems of the detected markers into the coordinate system of the reference marker. When the local coordinate system L_i is aligned to the reference coordinate system L_k, the aligned local transformation $\mathbf{T}'_i$ of $\mathbf{T}_i$ should be equal to the reference transformation $\mathbf{T}_k$:

$$\mathbf{T}'_i = \mathbf{T}_i(\mathbf{T}_{i,k})^{-1} = \mathbf{T}_i \mathbf{T}_i^{-1} \mathbf{T}_k = \mathbf{T}_k . \tag{2}$$

Due to the estimation error, the transformation $\mathbf{T}_i$ in Eq. (2) is not accurate and the equality does not be satisfied.

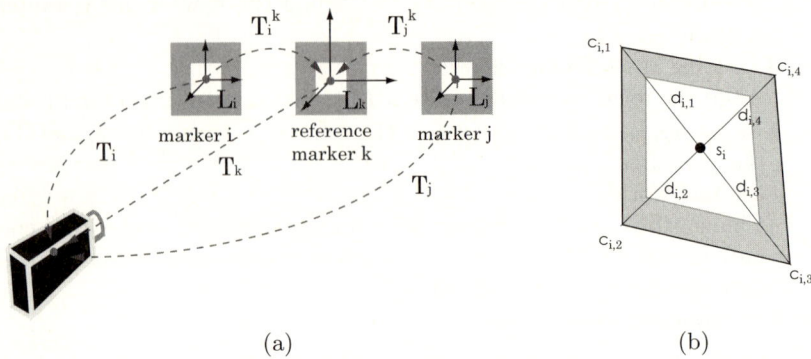

(a)   (b)

Fig. 1. (a) multiple markers and their geometric relationships, (b) the error rate of each detected marker

We suppose the geometric relations of the multiple markers in real world are known. The transformations $\mathbf{T}_{i,k}$ can be computed from the known geometric relation between the ith marker and the kth marker. We denote $\mathbf{p}_i$ as the ith marker center points. Then, the transformation matrix $\mathbf{T}_{i,k}$ is as follows:

$$\mathbf{T}_{i,k} = \begin{bmatrix} \mathbf{I} & \mathbf{p}_k - \mathbf{p}_i \\ 0 & 1 \end{bmatrix} . \tag{3}$$

$\mathbf{T}_i$ is aligned as $\mathbf{T}'_i = \mathbf{T}_i(\mathbf{T}_{i,k})^{-1}$. After the registration, each local coordinate system corresponding to the detected marker is aligned to the reference marker orientation by $\mathbf{T}'_i = \mathbf{T}_i(\mathbf{T}_{i,k})^{-1}$ $(i = 1, \ldots, N)$.

3.2   Camera Motion Reconstruction from the Marker Transformation

The accuracy of the camera pose can be improved using the aligned transformations. For each detected marker, we define the error rate to indicate the confidence rate of the marker. The error rate is related with the camera viewing direction to the target marker. We define the error rate for a marker using the four corner points and the number of pixels inside the marker rectangle. Let $c_{i,1}$, $c_{i,2}$, $c_{i,3}$ and $c_{i,4}$ be the marker corner points as shown in Fig. 1(b). Two diagonal lines intersect at a point s_i. For each marker, we compute v_i using the following equation:

$$v_i = \frac{1}{4} \sum_{n=1}^{4} (d_{i,n} - \bar{d}_i)^2 \text{ where } \bar{d}_i = \frac{1}{4} \sum_{n=1}^{4} d_i^n \text{ and } d_{i,k} = \| s_i - c_{i,k} \| . \tag{4}$$

The projective distortion should be considered for the error rate of the marker. The variance of $d_{i,k}$, the distance from the corner $c_{i,k}$ to the intersection s_i as shown in Fig. 1(b), is proportional to the projective distortion. In the square case,

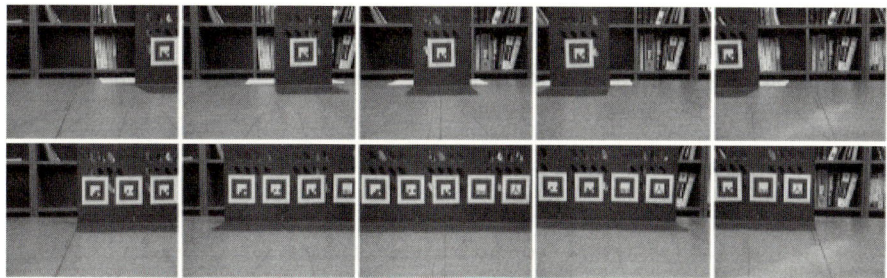

Fig. 2. Experimental setup for the linear camera movement

Fig. 3. Experimental setup for the circular camera movement

all $d_{i,k}$ should have the same distance from the intersection s_i. We calculate the variation v_i of the lengths $d_{i,k}$ $(k = 1, \ldots, 4)$. If v_i goes to zero, the camera orientation approaches to the normal direction of the marker. The image area of the marker should also be considered for the error rate. The area a_i for the ith marker is measured as the number of pixels inside the detected marker.

Using v_i and a_i, we compute the error rate ρ_i as follows:

$$\rho_i = \frac{w_i}{\sum_{i=1}^{N} w_i}, \text{ where } w_i = \frac{a_i'}{v_i'}, \ a_i' = \frac{p_i}{\sum_{i=1}^{N} p_i} \text{ and } v_i' = \frac{v_i}{\sum_{i=1}^{N} v_i}. \quad (5)$$

The weight of the ith marker w_i which is used to compute the error rate ρ is calculated by the pixel area a_i and the degree of variation v_i. The error rate ρ is between zero and one and, if ρ is close to one, the camera orientation closes to the normal direction of the marker. The error rate ρ is used in order to improve the reliability of the camera motion. Multi-markers give more useful information than single marker. The transformations from multi-markers are integrated as follows into the improved camera pose $\mathbf{T}''$:

$$\mathbf{T}'' = \sum_{i=1}^{N} (\rho_i \mathbf{T}_i') \text{ where } \sum_{i=1}^{N} \rho_i = 1. \quad (6)$$

All the camera motions corresponding to the detected markers are integrated in the proportion of the error rates. The estimated camera pose $\mathbf{T}''$ is more reliable than the pose from either the single marker methods or the common multi-marker methods.

4   Experimental Results

We have implemented and tested the proposed camera pose tracking method on a number of real data sets. To measure the accuracy of the proposed method, we estimated the camera pose for each image acquired from a moving camera. Two types of camera movements, a linear movement and a circular movement, were tested and their camera trajectories were recovered. Fig. 2 and Fig. 3 show the images captured while the camera is moving along the two predefined trajectories. In Fig. 2, the camera was moved in a parallel direction with respect to the marker direction. The camera position is 70cm far from the markers and

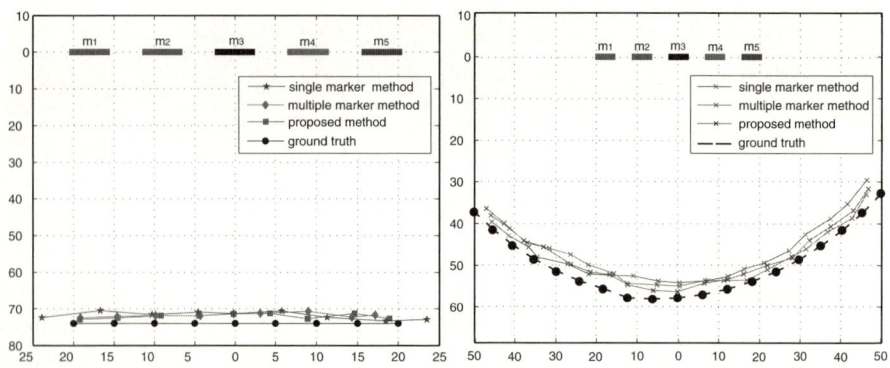

Fig. 4. Comparison of the recovered trajectories

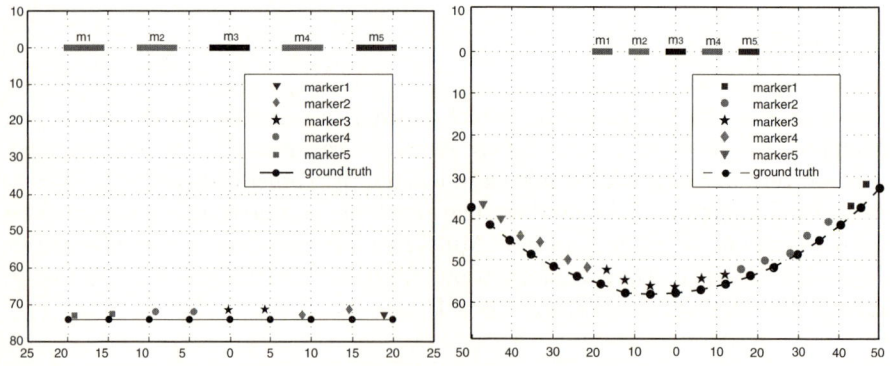

Fig. 5. The selected reference markers

the camera orientation is parallel to the marker normal. In Fig. 3, the camera is moved along a circular path around the markers. Each camera angle for two consecutive images is differed by 5 degrees. The radius of the circular path is 50cm. For the recovery, we use both the ARToolKit markers and the ARTag markers. All the markers have the same size and each marker is a regular square 5cm on a side. Horizontally aligned five markers are used for the multiple marker estimation.

The ground truths of the two camera movement trajectories were measured in advance for the comparison of the recovery accuracy. Fig. 4 shows the recovered trajectories using several different methods together with the ground truth trajectory. The trajectory recovered from our method is compared with the classical single and multiple marker based methods. The left figure is the recovered trajectories for 9 captured frames from the linear camera movement. The right figure is the recovered trajectories for 19 captured frames from the circular camera movement. The comparison of trajectories shows that our method provides the best accurate trajectory toward the ground truth trajectory.

At each frame, a reference marker is selected among the detected markers to align makers into the reference coordinate system. Fig. 5 shows the selected reference markers at the camera positions of the recovered trajectory. The left figure is for the linear camera movement and the right figure is for the circular camera movement.

We measured the errors and compared them with the ground truth for both camera movements. For the linear movement, the single marker method has 2cm error on average, the multiple marker method has 1cm error on average, and the proposed method has 0.5cm error on average. For the circular movement, the single marker method has 3.3cm error on average, the multiple marker method has 2.7cm error on average, and the proposed method has 0.2cm error on average. In all cases, the proposed method shows the best results.

5   Conclusion

This paper has presented a novel method of camera pose estimation using known multiple markers. Our approach is different from previous works in the sense that the proposed method is adaptive to the number of detected markers. If there is at least one accurate detected marker in a frame, reliable camera pose estimation is guaranteed even when there are also erroneous markers in the frame.

We detect all markers shown in each image frame and choose a reference marker among the detected markers. Then, we calculate the transformation from the local coordinate system of each marker to the reference coordinate system of the reference marker. A global optimal camera pose is estimated from the weighted sum of the transformations of multiple markers. Experimental results verified that our method provides more accurate camera poses than those from classical single marker-based methods or multiple marker-based methods.

interactive qualities of major human-robot interaction applications. Our idea and solution is a collaborative board game involving humans and robots played in a shared physical environment. This setup serves as a test bed where various interfaces and robot behaviours can be developed to facilitate game play, and in turn, user evaluations can be performed to test their effectiveness.

Fig. 1. *Sheep and Wolves*: the AIBO robotic wolves closing in on the mixed reality sheep

Following this concept, we developed our test bed, *Sheep and Wolves* (Fig. 1), based on a classic checkerboard game but adapted to allow humans and robots to play together as a team of four wolves hunting a single sheep in an attempt to surround it. The game is played on a large checkerboard where humans, robots, and virtual entities act as game pieces, enabling a large variety of scenarios. Virtual entities were included in the game, using mixed reality, in order to highlight one of the robots' main advantages over humans: their ability to function in both the physical and virtual realms. Humans must rely on the robots' "senses" when it comes to the virtual entities, but for the robots, the virtual entities are as real as the physical components of the task.

Along with designing the test bed, we have also implemented a telepresence and mixed reality interface for playing the game and modeled two robot behaviours that are evaluated using *Sheep and Wolves*. We performed user evaluations asking human participants to play two games using the prototype interface. In one game the robots are always supportive and obedient, and in the other game the robots behave negatively and always ignore input from their human team-mate. The responses from the human participants were found to be sensitive to the contrasting robotic behaviours.

2   Related Work

We first present an overview of research in human-robot interaction (HRI) which serves as a general motivation for the field. Then we provide rationale for the design of *Sheep and Wolves*. Finally we briefly outline two interaction techniques, namely telepresence and mixed reality, which are implemented in our prototype interface for playing the game.

Although the fields of human-computer interaction (HCI) and robotics have generated significant interest and made substantial progress, in the past there has been less attention paid to human-robot interaction (HRI). Certainly, arguments can be made that robots such as mechanical arms used in manufacturing can be operated with similar techniques which have already been explored in human-computer interaction. However, as increasingly intelligent and capable autonomous robots come into existence, traditional human-computer interaction approaches become less applicable, and special attention need to be given to the unique requirements and advantages embodied in intelligent autonomous robots [6]. People intuitively perceive robots to be more anthropomorphic than other computing systems [6]. This hints at the potential for more intimate and natural forms of interaction between humans and robots. Cynthia Breazeal, the head of MIT's Robotic Life Group, designed Kismet [5], an expressive anthropomorphic robot able to convey emotions and provide feedback, allowing humans to engage in natural social interaction. Kismet utilizes facial expression, body posture, gesture, gaze direction, and voice to intuitively communicate with humans. Another unique characteristic of autonomous robots is their ability to learn and make decisions based on information gathered from the physical environment. Many robots designed for entertainment such as Sony's AIBO^{TM} robotic dogs support a cognitive learning model which enables the robot to acknowledge various forms of human and environmental input and mold its behaviour accordingly. The Robotic Life Group's Leonardo [7], a life-like robot designed for social interaction, can interpret gestures and facial expressions from humans as a communication method for learning how to play games. User interaction with such autonomous robots tends to be richer and more intuitive than traditional human-computer interaction paradigms of clicking on icons or opening windows. Furthermore, mobile autonomous robots often bring interaction closer to the physical context of humans, allowing information and subtle social interaction cues to be readily exchanged. NASA's Robotnaut [8], a mobile autonomous humanoid robot, is being developed in an attempt to create future robot astronauts that are able to work alongside human astronauts in space. Efforts such as Kismet, Leonardo, and Robonaut are the prelude to a fascinating future for the field of human-robot interaction. Attitudes for designing robots are already shifting from a "robots as tools" approach to a "robots as partners" outlook.

Simulated computer agents playing games such as chess or checkers with or against humans is a familiar concept (see for example [9]). However, interaction and collaboration between humans and robots within a physical game environment is rare. One example is Carnegie Mellon University's Cognitive Robotics [10], which suggests means of implementing more involved physical interaction between robots and games, presenting a robot-based tic-tac-toe game in which the robot can move game pieces on a physical board. However the potential for human-robot interaction is still limited. Meaningful interaction between humans and robots within a game application can be enhanced by requiring humans and robots to play on the same team within a shared physical environment instead of against each other on a computer. The idea originates from using robots for search and rescue where performing collaborative tasks can be critical. Since human ability, artificial intelligence, and computational ability can be fairly balanced within a controlled game environment, it is conceivable to construct realistic scenarios where humans and robots collaborate as equals.

NASA developed the Web Interface for Telescience (WITS) [11] Software which linked a vehicle for Martian travel to Internet users. This allowed a group of high school students to actively participate in assisting researchers operate the vehicle during a field test. University of Southern California's Telegarden [12] enabled Internet users to operate a remote robotic arm centered in a garden in order to water and care for the plants inside. These projects demonstrate the power of telepresence in encouraging remote collaboration, active and assisted learning, and developing a sense of virtual partnership. With autonomous robots, the benefits of telepresence can be extended further. Arguments can be made that most current telepresence interaction techniques follow the "robots as tools" approach with users having to operate and control many mechanical aspects of the remote robot. Although the direct physical context is missing, previously mentioned interaction techniques based on the "robots as partners" perspective can still be applied by delivering video, sound, and other sensory and communication elements. The experience can be similar to existing interaction between humans online such as chatting using instant messaging programs, collaborating by voice in online games, and participating in video conferences. By exploring these interaction paradigms for telepresence, remote users can collaborate with a team of remote robots as participating members rather than superior operators having to control the entire team.

Mixed reality gives humans the ability to access valuable information processed and stored within digital entities in the immediate context of a physical environment. This is ideal as a human-robot interaction paradigm because many robots operate within the physical world and can also obtain and process digital information. Applications such as the MagicBook [13] or the Human Pacman [14] allow humans to visualize and interact with virtual digital entities by superimposing computer-generated graphics onto physical scenes. In the MagicBook for example users can view a computer-generated animation on how to build a chair as they browse through a physical instruction book using a hand-held display [13]. Naturally the concept of visualizing contextual supplementary information can also be applied to robots, allowing them to directly express implicit information such as thoughts or synthetic emotions.

3   Test Bed Design

Sheep and Wolves (Fig. 1) is a human-robot interaction test bed following the goal of constructing a controlled environment and tasks that will serve as an interaction metaphor for major human-robot interaction applications. The environment and tasks we have devised are based on a classic turn-based game played on a checkerboard. The game involves five game pieces, four of which are the wolves, and one is the sheep. The wolves start on one end of the checkerboard, and the sheep starts on the other. The team of wolves are only allowed to move one wolf forward diagonally by one square during their turn. The wolves' objective is to surround the sheep so it cannot make any legal moves. Meanwhile, the sheep is allowed to move forward or backward diagonally by one square during its turn. Its objective is to move from one end of the checkerboard to the other. Obviously, while the sheep is more flexible in its moves, the wolves' strength is in their numbers and ability to move as a pack.

We chose this game because it is simple yet able to support collaborative game play. The metaphor of the game can be extended to various applications where humans and robots are required to share information, opinions, and resources in order to effectively complete a task. By performing a collaborative task in a controlled physical game environment instead of complex real-world environments, we are able to focus on interaction. Also, since implementing artificial intelligence for checkerboard games is relatively simple, we are able to easily adjust the intelligence of the robots in order to develop varying believable robot behaviours.

In our game we have elected to use Sony's AIBO dogs as our robot participants. These fairly capable commercial robots allow us to rapidly build prototype interfaces for evaluation. For the physical environment of the game, we use a 264 cm (104 in) by 264 cm RolaBoard^{TM} with the standard black and white checkerboard pattern. Each square measures 33 cm (13 in) by 33 cm, providing sufficient room for an AIBO wolf to sit on or humans to stand on. This controlled shared space is ideal for robots to navigate in. The lines and corners of the checkerboard serve as readily available navigation markers for movement on the checkerboard, and camera calibration can also be achieved using corner points to allow for mixed reality interfaces and localization of humans on the checkerboard.

4 Game Implementation

In the setup for our telepresence and mixed reality game, all four wolves are represented by the AIBOs and the sheep is a virtual entity. The AIBOs physically rise, move, and sit down on the checkerboard to indicate position and movement of the wolves in the game. A human player controls a single AIBO wolf at a remote computer using a telepresence interface, personifying the robotic entity within the game. Other uncontrolled AIBO wolves are autonomous robot team-mates which the human player must collaborate with. Live video of the physical game environment from the controlled AIBO's point of view is provided to the remote human player, and mixed reality is utilized for visualizing the virtual sheep's location and moves. Winning the game as wolves requires teamwork: the human player has to provide suggestions to the team and consider propositions made by other team-mates in order to help the team reach intelligent decisions on the moves the team should make.

4.1 Checkerboard Traversal and Augmentations

One of our goals is to introduce physical elements into the board game. By playing the game on a large checkerboard we define a simple environment in which the robotic game entities can easily operate. As a result of the rules of the game, AIBO wolves are only required to traverse the checkerboard moving forward diagonally one square at each turn. This can be achieved using a simple localized vision algorithm without having to map the physical environment of the checkerboard. When an AIBO wolf is about to move, it stands up on all four legs with its snout facing straight down. Since the camera is located in the AIBO's snout, this posture provides a bird's eye view of the board which is also very limited due to the camera's field of view and the relative closeness of the camera to the checkerboard. This limited bird's eye view of the checkerboard is actually ideal for a simple traversal algorithm since there is very little perspective distortion, and for each frame of video obtained by the AIBO in the stand-up posture, we have only several distinct cases to consider for localizing and orientating the AIBO. For our walking algorithm, we decided to use lines and corners as means of localization and determining orientation. Working only with low resolution greyscale image data, we extract lines from the images by first applying a low-pass filter and then performing a binary threshold to generate resulting images similar to the ones shown in Fig. 2 (left). Next, we search for line end points around the perimeters of the images by simply performing exclusive-or operations of the tested pixel with each of its right and bottom neighbours. From the extracted line end points, we derive the line segments present in the image. The case with two line end points is trivial. To correctly match three or four line end points, we simply consider all possible pairings and calculate the resulting angles between the two line segments. Since the bird's eye view of the checkerboard does not suffer from perspective distortion, line segments within the limited view must be orthogonal to each other. Therefore, we can exclude pairings of line segments which are not orthogonal. In frames where two line segments can be extracted, we can also determine the position of a corner point by simply calculating the intersection between the two line segments. Corner points which can be inside or outside of an image are used to localize the AIBO on the checkerboard. The angles between extracted lines and the vertical axis are used to align the AIBO in a proper position.

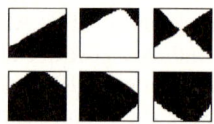 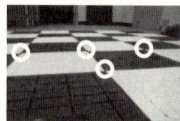

Fig. 2. Images of bird's eye views of the board (left) and extracted corner points (right)

In order to visualize the virtual sheep and demonstrate the application of mixed reality, we enhance the live video provided by the AIBO's camera by superimposing a computer generated 3D sheep onto the scene (Fig. 1). To achieve this, we set up an OpenGL viewing frustum based on the camera's field of view and focal length. In the scene, a rectangle is placed at a distant location from the camera looking down the z-axis. The size and aspect ratio of the rectangle is calculated using the field of view and focal length of the camera to ensure it covers the entire viewing volume when displayed. Frames of video received from the AIBO's camera are then texture mapped onto the distant rectangle to provide a video background for the virtual 3D sheep in the scene. As AIBOs move on the board, the exact positions of the AIBOs' cameras are unknown after each move. To place the virtual sheep within the correct viewing context of the video background, continuous camera calibration is required. We designate the center of the checkerboard as the origin of our world coordinate system. Then, by keeping track of the game entities on the physical board, we know approximately the position of the camera. Next, we fine-tune the calibration using high resolution image data from the camera. First, we extract the checkerboard corner points from the image (Fig. 2 right). This is accomplished using a corner detection algorithm. In most cases, we can extract at least three accurate points close to the camera which we use to perform a simplified camera calibration. After obtaining the corner points we inverse project these 2D points into our 3D world coordinate system. This is possible because we know the y-axis values of these potential 3D points are all supposed to be 0. We then pair the inverse projected 3D corner points together in attempt to find either a potential horizontal or vertical edge of a square. After calculating the angle between the vector resulting from such an edge and the corresponding horizontal or vertical vector, we rotate the virtual scene around the y-axis by the calculated angle to correct misalignments caused by the AIBO not always facing exactly forward. We assume that the AIBO's camera does not require roll adjustment and that its height remains constant. Following this calibration procedure we are able to correctly superimpose the sheep on the live video most of the time. Challenging cases such as the loss of corner points due to occlusions and the introduction of false corner points created by a black AIBO sitting on a white square can result in imprecision.

4.2 Game Play

The game algorithm for both the sheep and the autonomous wolves are implemented based on the concept of searching for paths from the sheep to the other end of the checkerboard. If multiple paths are available, the sheep will move following the shortest path. Otherwise it will make a random move with a preference for moving forward instead of backward and moving toward the center instead of to the side. The non-human controlled members of the wolves will suggest the move which results in the longest available path for the sheep, or which will lead the sheep to a dead-end.

For each turn, the sheep or the wolf pack has sixty seconds to arrive at a decision for the move. As in the classic board game, the wolves win when the sheep can no longer move, and the sheep wins if it gets past the last wolf on its way to the other end of the board. At the end of the sheep's turn, autonomous AIBO wolves assess the game and start to make suggestions to the rest of the team. The human player can also communicate with the team using a text messaging interface, and other autonomous AIBOs provide either positive or negative feedback depending on whether the others' suggestions match their opinion. One advantage of forcing the human player to play the game from a single robot's perspective is the limitation of field of view. Without an overview of the checkerboard, the human player has to deal with vagueness, uncertainties and lack of information. Although we provide the player with the option to pan the head of the AIBO to further explore the checkerboard, situations where the human player is completely clueless as to what the next move should be can occur. This forces the human player to utilize suggestions from the autonomous AIBO wolves, allowing us to explore issues of trust between humans and robots.

To allow a human player to effectively control an AIBO wolf and interact with the rest of the team, we have devised an intuitive graphical user interface (Fig. 3). In the following paragraphs, the various parts of the interface will be outlined, and the motivations behind the design choices will be explained.

In the main area of the screen, live video of the game along with the virtual sheep is displayed. This allows the remote human player to see the physical board from the point of view of the controlled AIBO. The virtual sheep is visible to the player if it is occupying a square in the field of the view of the camera. At the bottom of the main display, game information is provided, indicating what the game entities are doing (thinking or moving), whose turn it is, and the time remaining for making a decision.

On the top right of the interface, a game radar (Fig. 3) indicates the positions of the wolves relative to the edges of the checkerboard. Since our goal is to simulate search and rescue operations, we chose not to provide the human player with the position of the sheep and the grid of the checkerboard. This encourages the human player to actively interact with the physical environment of the checkerboard rather than utilizing the abstract radar to play the game. Each AIBO wolf is represented by a red dot. The AIBO wolf controlled by the human player is indicated with a blue ring around its dot. When an AIBO wolf moves, its dot will flash to indicate the movement. Displayed next to their corresponding dots are the AIBO wolves' nicknames. The nicknames along with their full names, Leonardo, Michelangelo, Donatello, and Raphael, can be used by the player to refer to a particular wolf in the game. For simplicity we designate the direction the wolves are initially facing as north, and therefore the green arrow in the radar always points north.

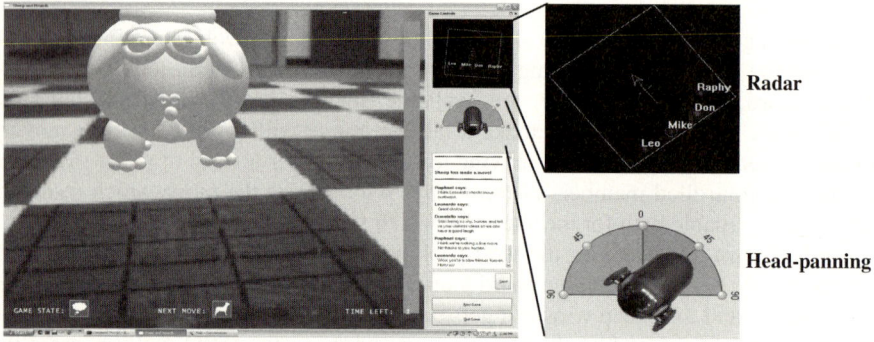

Fig. 3. Telepresence interface with mixed reality and text messaging

Underneath the game radar is the head-panning control (Fig. 3). Since the initial forward-facing view is limited we allow the human player to pan the head of the controlled AIBO 45° or 90° left or right (east or west). This feature can be used to explore the checkerboard, locate the sheep, observe other AIBO team-mates, or watch them move. When the player pans the head of the controlled AIBO, the game radar also rotates to match the orientation of this AIBO's current view and further assists in spatial awareness.

A crucial element of our design is the text messaging interface (Fig. 4). It allows the human player to communicate with the rest of the AIBO wolves following a familiar interaction paradigm. Although currently the richness of the conversation is limited, we believe that this interaction technique has potential in effectively engaging human users in active collaboration with robotic entities especially in telepresence applications because most human users are already familiar with instant messaging programs. In our game, conversation occurs amongst four team-mates. Due to the loss of context or the intended recipient of messages, effective communication can be difficult when the discussion is commencing at a rapid rate. To solve this problem,

we assign four time slots 15 seconds apart within the 60 second decision-making duration. Only one randomly selected autonomous AIBO wolf is to make a suggestion
at each time slot, and a response to a suggestion made by any member of the team is
generated by another randomly selected autonomous AIBO wolf 2.5 seconds after the
suggestion was made. This helps to reduce the number of messages displayed and the
rate at which they must be processed by the human player. Using this interface
(Fig. 4), the human player is able to make a suggestion using the following syntax:
*{AIBO's name or nickname} move {the direction of the target square, either northwest,
northeast, or nw, ne}.* Currently messages not following this syntax cannot be interpreted by the autonomous AIBOs and result in a response indicating incomprehen-
sion, but we found the simple syntax to be sufficient for our present test conditions.

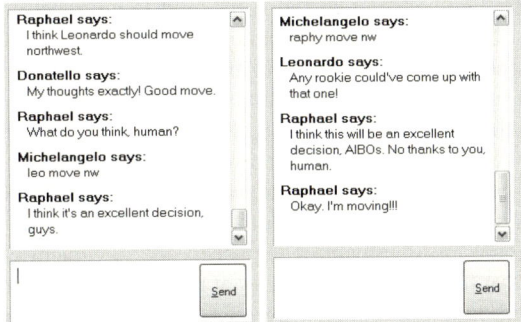

Fig. 4. Conversation samples between the team of wolves (Michelangelo is the human)

5 Two Robot Behaviours

Along with the game-playing interface, we have also designed two simple contrasting
robot behaviours for the autonomous AIBO wolves to test their effect on human-robot
interaction within the game, namely the human-centric condition and the robot-centric
condition. The robot behaviour which humans are most accustomed to is obedience.
The game's human-centric behaviour is designed with that human perception in mind.
When playing the game with human-centric control, the autonomous AIBO wolves
always follow suggestions given by human players. To further invoke a feeling of
superiority, we direct the autonomous AIBO wolves to praise human players for their
input, and all comments provided are communicated in a supportive manner. The opposite of obedience is defiance, and this is reflected in our robot-centric behaviour,
which attempts to agitate human players by placing them in a position of inferiority.
With this behaviour, the game becomes completely controlled by the three autonomous AIBO wolves, thinking alike and neglecting any advice from their human team-
mate. To make the situation worse, we direct the autonomous AIBOs to mock the
human player for any mistakes and suggestions that do not match their own. Even
when human players suggest a move that corresponds with the opinion of the rest of
the team, they are greeted with contempt.

6 User Evaluation

We performed a user evaluation of the two robot behaviours using our telepresence and mixed reality interface to demonstrate the utility of *Sheep and Wolves*. Our goal is to explore interaction issues between humans and robots and see if our test bed is sensitive in discovering possible interaction methods and obstacles. For this evaluation, we want to measure the human response to robot team-mates with different behaviours when immersed in a collaborative task.

The participants played games at a remote computer where the physical checkerboard was not visible. The evaluation was conducted following a written protocol to make sure each participant received the same information and followed the same experimental procedure. We introduced participants to the purpose of our study, showed them the rules and concepts of the game, and familiarized them with the remote user interface. They were told that the game supported a democratic decision-making process for the team of wolves with the decision receiving the majority of votes being selected by the team. Participants were encouraged to actively collaborate with their robot counterparts, either trying to convince the robots to support a decision or trusting the robot's decision when they are unsure about the next move. The robot-centric/human-centric deception underlying the robotic behaviour patterns was not revealed to the participants until the end of the experiment.

To explain occasional misalignment of the sheep due to camera calibration errors, we told participants that the sheep can be tricky at times and may jump from square to square on the checkerboard. Participants were told they may have to trust the advice of their robot team-mates if they are not sure where the virtual sheep is and cannot derive an intelligent move.

Each participant played one game in the human-centric condition and another in the robot-centric condition. Afterward, the participants were given a short questionnaire. Questions such as, "How well do you think you collaborated with your robot team-mates?", "How much trust did you have for your robot team-mates' suggestions?", and "How responsible are the following team-mates for the outcome of the game?" are asked. Participants were instructed to answer these questions by drawing a mark on a line segment to indicate their position between two extremes. Later, the distances denoted by the marks were measured and normalized between 0 and 1.

We started the evaluation with a pilot study involving five computer science graduate students that were not involved with our research. Several interface issues were discovered and corrected during the pilot study, and our questionnaire was refined accordingly. After the revisions we recruited fourteen participants for the main study. The demographic includes University students, professors, staff, as well as members of the general public. They each played two games, one in each condition. We counterbalanced the ordering effect by asking half to play the human-centric condition first and asking the other half to play the robot-centric condition first.

In the pilot study four out of five participants indicated that they collaborated better with their robotic team-mates in the human-centric condition, had a stronger sense of control in the human-centric condition, but had a greater sense of trust for their robotic team-mate's suggestions in the robot-centric condition. For our main study we performed statistical analysis on the data gathered using ANOVA. We found that participants felt they collaborated better in the human-centric condition, and that they had a stronger sense of control in the human-centric condition as well, which is consistent with the pilot study results. However, unlike the pilot study, the effects on trust were inconclusive in the main study. Participants were also asked to evaluate each robotic team-mate's performance during the games, and most of them gave different scores for each team-mate although the autonomous robots ran the same algorithm and always agreed with each other.

7 Discussion and Conclusion

The *Sheep and Wolves* study presented here is an early and limited experiment performed mainly for exploratory purposes and the evaluation of the test bed's capabilities. It is hard to derive solid conclusions from the current measures that, other than the game's final outcome, are mostly qualitative and subjective in nature.

Overall, the *Sheep and Wolves* test bed, hardware and software, performed quite well. Although we had the odd traversal error in games this was fixed quickly and did not affect the game experience. Participants managed to interact with the application and play the two games in full, usually enjoying the experience.

A confirmation from both the pilot study and the main study is that players felt they collaborated better and had more control in the human-centric condition relative to the robot-centric condition. We expected this outcome which indicates that the test bed is not generating arbitrary results. In the pilot study we were surprised to find out that four out of five participants indicated that they trusted suggestions made by the robots in the robot-centric condition more than the human-centric condition. This finding is unexpected since suggestions in the robot-centric condition were forceful, less polite, and even aggressive in tone, and we were expecting them to be generally annoying. The results suggest players translated assertiveness to credibility, and trusted their robotic team-mates more when their suggestions had an added quality of effrontery (or *robotic chutzpah*). However, the follow up results from the main study were inconclusive. This may be due to the fact that participants who played the robot-centric condition in the pilot study won the game most of the time, and in the main study most of them lost the game. We were also surprised to find that most participants believed they were interacting with three autonomous robotic entities with different characteristics and abilities even though the robots ran the same algorithm and always agreed with each other. Most participants gave different scores when asked to evaluate their team-mates' performances, and some even indicated to one of the robots as being seemingly less dependable. This demonstrates the tendency for humans to anthropomorphize life-like computing platforms like the AIBO robotic dogs used in this test bed. Although our autonomous AIBO wolves do not qualify as truly intelligent agents with their own personalities, we are able to produce a convincing collaborative experience by simply using physical life-like robots programmed with limited communication capabilities. Human participants seem to naturally project individual characteristics onto them and perceive them as autonomous team-mates with believable personalities and behaviour patterns.

Is Sheep and Wolves a useful tool for assessment of human-robot interaction paradigms? We believe it is a promising tool. The hardware and software we used and developed are reliable, replicable, and relatively affordable, allowing studies of elaborate human-robot interaction paradigms in laboratory conditions. We think that the use of a mixed reality interface between the robots and humans highlights the unique nature of human-robot interaction tasks and the role and advantages robots will have in future applications, merging the physical and virtual domains and performing actions and accessing information in both realms.

How can we improve Sheep and Wolves? Following the test bed concept, there are many directions in which future research can progress. One is developing novel interaction techniques that will facilitate collaborative game play. We are currently designing a set of more advance mixed reality techniques for interacting with robots, allowing humans to play physically on the game board with a group of autonomous robots (much like the Harry Potter Wizard's Chess). Another interesting area for further experimentation is robot behaviour. Although this can be tested on a PC with agents, we have demonstrated that it is easier to produce a perception of realistic interaction with real robots in a real setting.

What does Sheep and Wolves signify to the domain of human-robot interaction? We are by far not alone in advocating the need to search for effective new interaction paradigms between humans and robots. We believe *Sheep and Wolves* and similar systems will allow high-level human-robot interaction ideas and philosophies to be easily designed, tested, and improved in research laboratory settings.

We presented the idea of constructing an effective test bed for human-robot interaction. With our prototype test bed, *Sheep and Wolves*, we are able to explore and evaluate a telepresence interface using mixed reality and two contrasting robotic behaviours. From our user evaluation, we demonstrated the utility of the test bed and discovered interesting results that may be solidified through further experimentation.

References

1. Licklider, J. C. R.: Man-Computer Symbiosis. IRE Transactions on Human Factors in Electronics, Vol. HFE-1 (1960) 4-11
2. Moravec, H. P.: *Robot Mere Machine to Transcendent Mind.* Oxford University Press Inc. (1998)
3. Dick, P. K.: *Do Androids Dream of Electric Sheep?* (1968)
4. Norman, D. A.: *Emotional Design: Why We Love (Or Hate) Everyday Things.* Basic Books (2003)
5. Breazeal, C. L.: *Designing Sociable Robots (Intelligent Robotics and Autonomous Agents).* The MIT Press (2002)
6. Kiesler, S., Hinds, P.: Introduction to the special issue on Human-Robot Interaction. Human-Computer Interaction. Vol. 19 (2004) 1-8
7. Brooks, A., Gray, J., Hoffman, G., Lockerd, A., Lee, H., Breazeal, C.: Robot's Play: Interactive Games with Sociable Machines. ACM Computers in Entertainment, Vol. 2 (2004)
8. Robonaut, online: http://robonaut.jsc.nasa.gov/
9. Schaeffer, J.: *One Jump Ahead Challenging Human Supremacy in Checkers.* Springer-Verlag, New York (1997)
10. Tira-Thompson, E., Halelamien, N., Wales, J., Touretzky, D., Tekkotsu: Cognitive Robotics on the Sony AIBO. Abstract for poster at International Conference on Cognitive Modeling, Pittsburgh, PA (2004)
11. Web Interface for Telescience (WITS), online: http://www.ia-tech.com/wits/

12. The Telegarden, online: http://www.usc.edu/dept/garden/
13. Billinghurst, M., Kato, H., Poupyrev, I.: The MagicBook: Moving Seamlessly between Reality and Virtuality. IEEE Computer Graphics and Applications (2001) 2-4
14. Cheok, A., Goh, K., Liu, W., Farbiz, F., Fong, S., Teo, S., Li, Y., Yang, X.: Human Pacman: a mobile, wide-area entertainment system based on physical, social, and ubiquitous computing. Personal and Ubiquitous Computing, Vol. 8 (2004) 71-81

Projected Reality – Content Delivery Right onto Objects of Daily Life

Jochen Ehnes and Michitaka Hirose

Hirose, Hirota & Tanikawa Lab, RCAST, The University of Tokyo,
Tokyo, Japan
{ehnes, hirose}@cyber.rcast.u-tokyo.ac.jp
http://www.cyber.rcast.u-tokyo.ac.jp

Abstract. Spatial augmented reality using controllable projector-camera-systems to project onto objects directly, or *Projected Reality* as we call it, offers the possibility to augment objects without requiring their users to wear or carry any devices. In order to provide the freedom of movement to users, we developed an architecture that allows *projected applications* to roam a network of projection units to follow the users. The concept of connecting physical objects with content in form of *projected applications*, although devised for projection based augmented reality systems, can be applied to HMD based or hand held AR systems as well. After a description of our AR projection system and a example application that could be used to provide location specific information to travelers using public transportation systems, we will lay out our vision of a system that may be able to provide content on a global scale.

Keywords: Projected Reality, Projection Based Augmented Reality, Spatial Augmented Reality, Application Roaming, Distributed Augmented Reality, Multi Projection System, Projector Camera System.

1   Introduction

In order to support users without being a hinderance, we developed an Augmented Reality (AR) system based on a combination of a video projector and a video camera mounted on a pan and tilt device. We consider this as an alternative to wearable computers and Head Mounted Displays (HMD). Using this technology, we built a system that can project augmentations on fixed, as well as movable objects around the projection device. However, the nature of the projection introduces some limitations: Objects have to be close enough to the AR-projection system so that the system can detect the markers. Surfaces that shall be augmented have to face the projector since a projection is not possible otherwise. While certain angles between the surface normal and the direction of projection can be compensated by pre-distorting the projected augmentation, the quality of the projection clearly decreases with increasing angles. At 90 degrees a projection becomes impossible. Finally, the line of sight between the AR-projection system and the object to be augmented must not be blocked. Otherwise the augmentation may be partially shadowed or, if an object's marker isn't completely visible, no augmentation would

Z. Pan et al. (Eds.): ICAT 2006, LNCS 4282, pp. 262–271, 2006.

be generated in the first place. In order to overcome these limitations we use several networked AR-projection units. We developed an architecture consisting of an application server and any number of projection units that allows our *projected applications* to roam these units.

While this architecture makes it possible to equip a room or building with projection units that can augment objects within that room or building, it could be extended to reach global scales. Such a system would not only be able to augment the same object in many places, it would open up new ways to deliver dynamic content with otherwise static media, such as newspapers, books and magazines. And that would be just the beginning as we believe. Although we believe that our architecture is a suitable way to provide that functionality, it does not seem to be possible to implement a system based on it with the current technology. Consequently, we will point out where the current (tracking) technology needs to be improved and what additional features would be necessary to implement such a global system.

2   Previous and Related Work

This work builds on our previous work which we published as follows. In [6] we introduced our hardware setup consisting of a video-projector mounted in a controllable pan and tilt device (AV4 from Active Vision) and a video camera mounted on top of the projector (see figure 1(a)). We furthermore described our software that can project augmentations on fixed as well as on movable objects using this hardware. In order to ease the development of applications that augment objects using this projection system, we developed an Application Programming Interface (API), which we introduced in [7]. In [5] we introduced

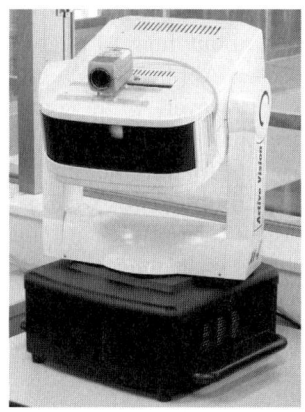

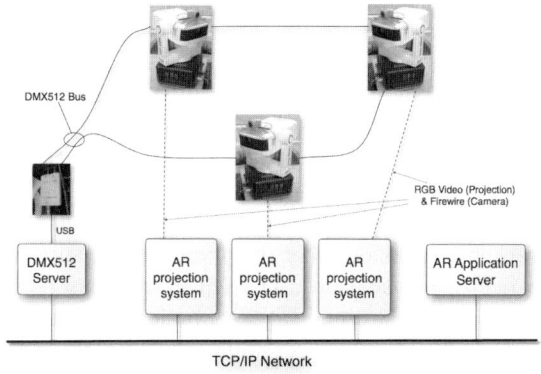

(a) A projection unit.   (b) Our test setup consisting of three projection units.

Fig. 1. A network of projection units can overcome the limitations of a single one

the idea of using several similar AR-projection systems to extent the usable range, as well as to enable augmentations from all sides (figure 1(b)). Finally, in [4] we presented the results of some user tests about how humans perceive projection quality depending on projection distance and projection angle. Other controllable projector camera systems have been presented in [15] (although the application presented here doesn't seem to make use of the possibility to control the system's orientation), [14] and [2]. In [16] the usage of several I/O-Bulbs (projector/camera systems) has been described as well, however they did not provide an application independent architecture and they were not concerned about huge networks of projection units either.

There also have been several works on augmenting books with additional information. [12] describes a the augmentation of a physics text book to provide a more effective learning environment for students. It also describes an interactive Venn Diagram, which is aimed at supporting effective information retrieval. While these applications work on their 'EnhancedDesk' environment (big parts of the augmentation and interaction happens on the desk), we believe it would be much more useful if the augmentation was not restricted to that desk. An other research group worked on the recreation of digital documents on real paper, both using video projection [10] and HMDs [8].

Finally, [3] describes a "Framework for Generic Inter-Application Interaction for 3D AR Environments". A mechanism as the "DataFlows" described therein could be useful to establish communication links between applications that augment physical objects in close proximity in order to let them work together or exchange information. However, this gets more complicated on a system where the applications roam different projection units.

3   Projected Applications and Application Roaming

The basic idea of application roaming in our network of AR-Projection units is as follows. The units themselves have no knowledge about how to augment different objects. This information is coded as 'Projected Applications', which are analogous to applications in a GUI environment. However, while conventional applications interact with the user via windows and widgets on a computer's screen, projected applications use tracked objects for interaction. The AR-Projection systems provide means to identify tracked objects as well as to measure their positions and orientations. They also project the output onto these tracked objects or other fixed and known surfaces, such as walls (encoded in the projected application). The AR-system can be seen as an operating system that loads and executes projected applications and provides an abstraction layer for these applications to communicate with the user and to control the hardware.

The projected applications reside on an *application server*. However, the application server not only serves the applications for the AR-projection systems. More importantly, it also maintains the state of the projected applications and enforces that the state is only modified by one AR-system at the time. Once a projection system detects a marker, it sends its ID to the application server. In reply, the application server sends the application[1] and, if available, the display rights and state of the application back to the projection system. Now the projection system starts the new application. If the system was granted the display rights and sent the last state of the application, it initializes the application with its state and starts to project the augmentations. If the display rights were not available at that moment, the system does nothing but trying to follow the object and waiting to be granted the display rights. If a system that owns the display rights for an application can not detect the corresponding marker any longer, it returns the display rights together with the current state to the application server. It can reapply for the display rights once it detects the marker again. In the mean time, the application server may send the state and display rights to another projection system.

While this simple method of managing the display rights requires only minimal amounts of network bandwidth and is sufficient if the ranges of the projection systems do not overlap, it is not satisfactory if more than one system could perform the augmentation at one time. When two systems compete for the display rights, the system that detected the marker first gets them and keeps them until the marker disappears from its camera's view. However, it would be better if the system with the best view of the object would project the augmentation. Furthermore, the management of the display rights should be more dynamic and find a new projection system that takes over before the active one looses the object and the augmentation disappears completely.

4   Optimizing the Quality of Projection

In order to maximize the visible quality of the projected augmentation, as well as to make the transition between two projection systems as smooth as possible, we had to extend the management of the display rights and make it more dynamic. The application server can actively withdraw display rights (in combination with the applications' states) from a projection system now. This way it can give the display rights (and states) to better suited projection systems at any time, long before the augmentations disappear completely on the systems that held the display rights before. However, in order to decide which system gets the right to augment an object, the application server needs to know which system is suited best to do it. we enumerated the three main points, (1) distance, (2) direction of the surface normal and (3) free line of sight. The quality can be considered to be a weighted combination of these criteria. However, the weighting may be quite task or application specific. In order to keep the task of the application server simple, we introduced a scalar *quality value* (section 4.1). The system with the highest quality value is considered the best and consequently should perform the augmentation. Since the criteria of quality can be very task specific, we decided that the quality value is not something the system can provide. Therefor the projected applications must provide a function that calculates the quality value. The AR projection systems regularly send updates of the quality values of all applications they host to

---

[1] In our prototype it currently only sends the application's name.

the application server. In consequence the application server can easily compare the quality values of the different applications running on the available AR projection systems and in turn can ensure that every application runs on the optimal projection system.

4.1 The "Quality Value"

A crucial point in order to find the optimal projection system to perform the augmentation is the estimation of the projection quality that each system could achieve. In [4] we examined how human test subjects evaluated the projection quality onto tracked objects depending on projection distance and angle, which lead to a formula to estimate the projection quality based on these factors. Furthermore we assume for simplicity that the projection is not shadowed if the camera can 'see' the marker on the object, as projection surface and marker, as well as projector and camera are located closely together and objects in the middle should block both the tracking and the projection.

5   Implementation

5.1 Test Setup

Our test setup consists of three projection systems (AV4 from Active Vision [1] with a Sony DFW-VL500 Firewire camera mounted on it, connected to a dual G5 Power Mac). For more details about the setup, control of the pan and tilt unit and the calibration of various parameters including the offset between camera and projector we would like to refer to [6]. In our current setup, as illustrated by figure 1(b), we control all three projection units with the same DMX512[2] bus. This way we need only one USB-to-DMX512 converter box. In order to be able to send values on the DMX512 bus from all three computers to control their projector, we implemented a server program that runs on the machine with the interface box connected to it. The AR application server runs as an independent application as well. Just as the DMX512 server, it may be running on one of the AR projection systems' computers.

The projected applications are implemented as subclasses of our 'application' class (in Objective-C). We use the dynamic capabilities of the Objective-C runtime system to instantiate objects of these application-subclasses from their class names when needed. Currently we still link the object files implementing the applications (Objective-C classes) to the executable of the projection system, so the instantiation of these objects does not require any more actions. However, in future we plan to pack these application classes in bundles containing the code in form of a dynamically linked library and the necessary additional files like images for textures etc. These could be loaded from the application server before the application objects are instantiated.

---

[2] DMX512 is the most common communications standard used by lighting and related stage equipment.

5.2   Example Application: Guiding Ticket

While developing the AR projection system as well as the architecture to enable applications to roam between several projection systems, we implemented several example applications. The demo application that illustrates the benefit of a large scale network of projection systems best is our *"Guiding Ticket"* example:

We envision the usage of AR projection systems in public spaces. If train stations for example were equipped with a sufficient number of projection systems, it would be possible to guide travelers to their connecting trains. Suppose a person wants to travel from A to B using public transportation and has to change several times on the way. If the traveler does not know the places to change, it can be quite stressful to find the right connection on time. With the system we envision, the traveler could get a special form of ticket that offers room for augmentations. Whenever the travelers have to change trains, they can take out the ticket and wait for an AR projection system to detect it. The system then projects on the ticket the information about the track the train is going to leave from, the wagon where the reserved seat is, how much time there is until the train leaves, as well as an arrow that always points in the direction to walk to. Figure 2 shows the augmented ticket.

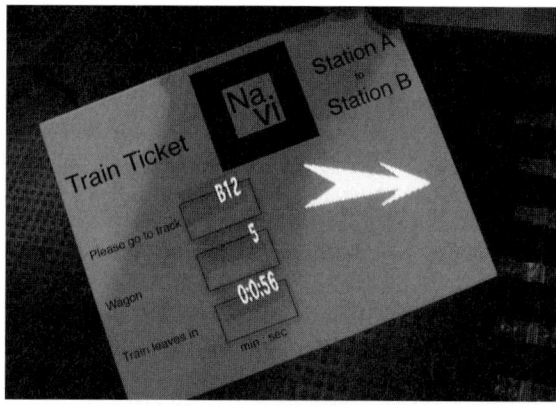

Fig. 2. Future train tickets may guide you to your next train

The text fields in our prototype application just display preset strings and a timer counting down towards a point in the near future. The direction of the arrow is calculated based on the X,Z coordinate of current position and the goal position. The goal position may depend on the current position as well, so that a chain of goal positions can be programmed to direct a user around obstacles. However, there has not been implemented any form of route planning. Since we only have three projection units, it has not been possible to really test the application's usefulness to navigate between several locations. Nevertheless, the application provoked a lot of positive responses at public presentations.

6   Scaling Up the System

For the future, as projectors and cameras get smaller and cheaper, we envision a network of projection units in many (public) places and application servers as common as web servers today. In such an environment information could be obtained by holding the corresponding objects (tickets, magazines, Books etc.) in front of any of those projection units. We already illustrated the possibility to augment special train tickets which could help anyone to find the connecting train fast, which do not require any knowledge about using computers. We believe that there are countless more applications, such as the augmentation of books, magazines or newspapers. While many people feel more comfortable reading printed media than reading from a computer screen, the online media is usually more up to date. This is inevitable, as the production and distribution of the print media requires a certain amount of time. A hybrid form of media could satisfy both. The printed part would be as comfortable to read as any other printed media, while it could be augmented with up to date information when in reach of an AR-projection system. Such a system could furthermore display movies on the paper instead of just images. However, in order to implement such a large distributed AR system, several changes would be necessary.

6.1   Two Level Application Server Architecture

It not only would be unnecessary to use the advanced application roaming algorithm described in section 4 to coordinate projection units far apart, it would also result in a lower quality due to the time lag introduced by connections to distant application servers and would increase the overall network load.   In

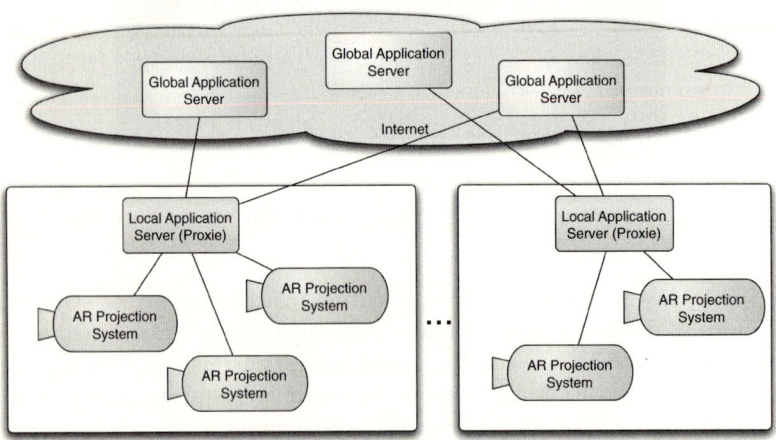

Fig. 3. Hierarchy of AR-Application-Servers for a network of AR Projection Systems on a global scale

order to keep the network load low and the switching of projection units fast, we propose a two level application server architecture. All projection units in a room would be connected to a local application server (a proxy server), that performs the roaming based on quality values (section 4). The local application server connects the room to the rest of the world and communicates with the application servers around the globe using the simpler protocol as described in section 3. Figure 3 illustrates that.

6.2   Enhanced Video Tracking

The majority of possible and necessary improvements lies in the area of the video tracking system. As we have not been developing video tracking systems so far, the following points (at least the first and the third) can be seen as a wish list to the video tracking community.

URLs in Markers. In order to be able to set up a network of application servers and projection units on a global scale, it is necessary that the projection units can decode the application server's address and the ID of the application on that server from the marker. Using ARTag [9] instead of AR-Toolkit [11] would be a step in the right direction in this regard, as it decodes the marker ID from the marker's pattern directly instead of using a pattern matching algorithm to identify the marker. However, with its limitation to 2048 markers, it would not be able to satisfy the needs to distinguish millions of objects. One would have to extend it in order to increase the number of bits encoded in the marker.

On the other hand markers should be as small as possible, which limits the amount of information that can be encoded in them. A standard URL encoded as ASCII text seems to be much to big to be encoded in a marker. However, if a marker could encode six bytes, it would be enough to encode the IP-address with four of them and to use the remaining two bytes to identify the application object on the server. This would allow a server to manage the augmentation of 65535 physical objects[3]. Adding another one or two bytes would allow for an even greater number of managed objects per server.

When books, newspapers or magazines are to be augmented, individual copies of the same book or paper would have to share the same markers. That way the number of individual markers needed, as well as the cost to print these objects can be reduced a lot. However, that means that individual copies can not have their own state and store user dependent data. However, if some user dependent data would have to be stored, one may have something like a virtual wallet, which may be used to store user specific data from other applications. If users bring such a wallet object into close proximity of the printed media, the two corresponding applications could start to communicate with each other. Then

---

[3] That is if every object is identified by one marker only. If multi markers are to be used, the number of physical objects an application server can manage is reduced accordingly.

the information could be stored on the server that manages the virtual wallet. In a similar way the information could be retrieved later.

Invisible Markers. Markers have to be of a certain minimal size, so that the camera of a projection system can recognize them from a certain distance. Furthermore the accuracy of the tracking gets better with increasing marker size, or if several markers are combined into a multi-marker. In practice however that means that a large portion of the object's surface is covered with markers. Space that otherwise could be used to project augmentations on. Furthermore, it is important not to project anything onto the marker, since that results in a different visual appearance and consequently the marker can not be recognized any longer and the augmentation disappears. An approach to improve this situation is to use markers that are invisible to the human eye, but visible in another part of the spectrum, such as IR (in [13] an IR marker is used to visibly hide the marker) or UV. With such a marker it would be no problem to project an augmentation in the visible part of the spectrum over the marker.

Non Planar Markers. For all marker based tracking systems we know of so far, it is a requirement that the markers are planar. However, in order to be able to augment a newspaper or magazine, it would be necessary to track curved markers and measure their curvature as well. While it has been demonstrated before that a grid of AR-Toolkit markers can be used to find 2d coordinates of their corners, and use these 2d coordinates to distort a texture of an image that gets overlaid onto the curved surface that way, it is only possible with video see through AR systems. The offset between projector and camera (as well as the offset between camera and eye in an optical see through HMD) makes it a necessity to have 3D coordinates. While [10] describes a system that projects virtual pages onto a book of empty pages, they require the projection of a lattice pattern to be projected onto the paper in order to calculate the homography necessary to warp the projected image. Since that has to be done every time the paper moves, we cannot consider it as a convenient solution from a user's point of view.

7   Future Work

Although the above section about an enhanced video tracking system could be considered future work as well, we do not plan to work on that for now. We plan to work on the following instead: Currently Projected Applications roam projection systems as a whole. They run on at most one unit at a time and they can also project their augmentations only from that projection unit. That means that the objects they augment have to be flat. Otherwise just one face can be augmented reliably. We are currently looking into possibilities to distribute an application dynamically, such that different surfaces of an object can be augmented by different projection units independently, while keeping the state consistent.

References

1. ActiveVision. Av4 : Computer controlled moving projector. http://www.activevision.jp/english/products/av/index.html.
2. Andreas Butz, Michael Schneider, and Mira Spassova. Searchlight - a lightweight search function for pervasive environments. In *Pervasive*, pages 351–356, 2004.
3. Stephen DiVerdi, Daniel Nurmi, and Tobias Höllerer. A framework for generic inter-application interaction for 3d ar environments, 2003.
4. Jochen Ehnes and Michitaka Hirose. Finding the perfect projection system – human perception of projection quality depending on distance and projection angle. In Edwin Sha et al., editor, *Lecture Notes in Computer Science*, number 4096 in LNCS, pages 1017–1026. Springer, August 2006.
5. Jochen Ehnes and Michitaka Hirose. Projected reality - enhancing projected augmentations by dynamically choosing the best among several projection systems. volume 0, pages 283–284, Los Alamitos, CA, USA, 2006. IEEE Computer Society.
6. Jochen Ehnes, Koichi Hirota, and Michitaka Hirose. Projected augmentation - augmented reality using rotatable video projectors. In *"ISMAR2004 The Third IEEE and ACM International Symposium on Mixed and Augmented Reality"*, pages 26–35. IEEE Computer Society, 2004.
7. Jochen Ehnes, Koichi Hirota, and Michitaka Hirose. Projected applications - taking applications from the desktop onto real world objects. In *HCII2005 Conference Proceedings [CD Rom], Lawrence Erlbaum Associates*, 2005.
8. Mototsugu Emori and Hideo Saito. Texture overlay onto deformable surface using geometric transformation. In *ICAT*, 2003.
9. Mark Fiala. Artag. http://www.cv.iit.nrc.ca/research/ar/artag/.
10. Shinichiro Hirooka and Hideo Saito. Displaying digital documents on real paper surface with arbitrary shape. In *ISMAR*, pages 278–279. IEEE Computer Society, 2003.
11. Hirokazu Kato and Mark Billinghurst. Marker tracking and hmd calibration for a video-based augmented reality conferencing system. In *Proceedings of the 2nd IEEE and ACM International Workshop on Augmented Reality*, page 85. IEEE Computer Society, 1999.
12. Hideki Koike, Yoichi Sato, Yoshinori Kobayashi, Hiroaki Tobita, and Motoki Kobayashi. Interactive textbook and interactive venn diagram: natural and intuitive interfaces on augmented desk system. In *Proceedings of the SIGCHI conference on Human factors in computing systems*, pages 121–128. ACM Press, 2000.
13. Hanhoon Park and Jong-Il Park. Invisible marker tracking for ar. *ismar*, 00:272–273, 2004.
14. Claudio S. Pinhanez. The everywhere displays projector: A device to create ubiquitous graphical interfaces. In *UbiComp '01: Proceedings of the 3rd international conference on Ubiquitous Computing*, pages 315–331, London, UK, 2001. Springer-Verlag.
15. John Underkoffler and Hiroshi Ishii. Illuminating light: An optical design tool with a luminous-tangible interface. In *CHI*, pages 542–549, 1998.
16. John Underkoffler, Brygg Ullmer, and Hiroshi Ishii. Emancipated pixels: real-world graphics in the luminous room. In Alyn Rockwood, editor, *Proceedings of the 26th annual conference on Computer graphics and interactive techniques*, pages 385–392. ACM Press/Addison-Wesley Publishing Co., 1999.

An Evaluation of an Augmented Reality Multimodal Interface Using Speech and Paddle Gestures

Sylvia Irawati [1, 3], Scott Green [2, 4], Mark Billinghurst [2],
Andreas Duenser [2], and Heedong Ko [1]

[1] Imaging Media Research Center, Korea Institute of Science and Technology
[2] Human Interface Technology Laboratory New Zealand, University of Canterbury
[3] Department of HCI and Robotics, University of Science and Technology
[4] Department of Mechanical Engineering, University of Canterbury
{sylvi, ko}@imrc.kist.re.kr,
{scott.green, mark.billinghurst, andreas.duenser}@hitlabnz.org

Abstract. This paper discusses an evaluation of an augmented reality (AR) multimodal interface that uses combined speech and paddle gestures for interaction with virtual objects in the real world. We briefly describe our AR multimodal interface architecture and multimodal fusion strategies that are based on the combination of time-based and domain semantics. Then, we present the results from a user study comparing using multimodal input to using gesture input alone. The results show that a combination of speech and paddle gestures improves the efficiency of user interaction. Finally, we describe some design recommendations for developing other multimodal AR interfaces.

Keywords: Multimodal interaction, paddles gestures, augmented-reality, speech input, gesture input, evaluation.

1 Introduction

Augmented Reality (AR) is an interface technology that allows users to see three-dimensional computer graphics appear to be fixed in space or attached to objects in the real world. AR techniques have been shown to be useful in many application areas such as education [1], entertainment [2] and engineering [3]. In addition to viewing virtual content, a wide variety of interaction methods have been explored by researchers including using mouse input [4], magnetic tracking [5], real objects [6], pen and tablet [7] and even natural gesture input with computer vision [8]. However, further research on finding the best way to interact with AR content still needs to be conducted, and especially usability studies evaluating the interaction techniques.

This paper presents the design and evaluation of an AR multimodal interface that uses speech and paddle gestures for interaction with virtual objects in the real world. The primary goal of our work is to evaluate the effectivenes of multimodal interaction in an AR environment. This work contributes to the collective knowledge of AR interaction methods by providing an example of a combination of speech and paddle gestures to interact with AR content. It also provides results from a rigorous user study that could be used as guidelines for developing other multimodal AR interfaces.

Z. Pan et al. (Eds.): ICAT 2006, LNCS 4282, pp. 272–283, 2006.
© Springer-Verlag Berlin Heidelberg 2006

In this paper, we first review related work and then briefly describe our multimodal architecture. We then discuss our user study and present the results from this study. Finally, we provide design guidelines for the development of multimodal AR interfaces and directions for future research.

2   Related Work

Our work is motivated by earlier research on multimodal interfaces, virtual reality (VR) and AR interfaces. From this research we can learn important lessons that can inform the design of our system.

One of the first multimodal interfaces to combine speech and gesture recognition was the Media Room [9]. Designed by Richard Bolt, the Media Room allowed the user to interact with the computer through voice, gesture and gaze. The user sat in the center of a room with position sensing devices worn on the wrist to measure pointing gestures and glasses with infra-red eye tracking for gaze detection. Computer graphics were projected on the wall of the room and the user could issue speech and gesture commands to interact with the graphics.

Since Bolt's work, there have been many two-dimensional desktop interfaces that show the value of combining speech and gesture input. For example, Boeing's "Talk and Draw" [10] application allowed users to draw with a mouse and use speech input to change interface modes. Similarly Cohen's QuickSet [11] combined speech and pen input for drawing on maps in command and control applications.

Multimodal interfaces can be very intuitive because the strengths of voice input compliment the limitations of gesture interaction and vice versa. Cohen [12, 13] shows how speech interaction is ideally suited for descriptive techniques, while gestural interaction is ideal for direct manipulation of objects. When used together, combined speech and gesture input can create an interface more powerful that either modality alone. Unlike gesture or mouse input, voice is not tied to a spatial metaphor [14], and so can be used to interact with objects regardless of whether they can be seen or not. However, care must be taken to map the appropriate modality to the application input parameters. For example, Kay [15] constructed a speech driven interface for a drawing program in which even simple cursor movements required a time consuming combination of movements in response to vocal commands.

Multimodal interaction has also been used in VR and 3D graphic environments. Early work by Hauptmann [16] employed a Wizard of Oz paradigm and investigated the use of multimodal interaction for a simple 3D cube manipulation task. The study had three conditions; subjects used gestures only, speech only, and gestures and/or speech as they wished. The analysis showed that people strongly preferred using combined gesture and speech for the graphics manipulation.

The QuickSet architecture [11] was integrated into the Naval Research Laboratory's Dragon 3D VR system [17] to create a multimodal system that employs a 3D gesture device to create digital content in a 3D topographical scene. Speech and gesture are recognized in parallel, parsed, and then fused via the Quickset multimodal integration agent. This allowed users to create and position entities by speaking while gesturing in 3D space. Laviola [18] investigated the use of whole-hand and speech input in virtual environments in the interior design. The application allowed a user to create virtual objects using speech commands while object manipulation was achieved using hand gestures. Ciger et al. [19] presented a multimodal user interface that combined a magic wand with spell casting. The user could navigate in the virtual environment, grab and manipulate objects using a combination of speech and the magic wand.

More recent works enhanced the virtual environment by adding semantic models. For example, Latoschik [20] presented a framework for modeling multimodal interactions, which enriched the virtual scene with linguistic and functional knowledge about the objects to allow the interpretation of complex multimodal utterances. Holzapfel et al. [21] presented a multimodal fusion for natural interaction with a humanoid robot. Their multimodal fusion is based on an information-based approach by comparing object types defined in the ontology.

Although AR interfaces are closely related to immersive VR environments, there are relatively few examples of AR applications that use multimodal input. McGee and Cohen [22] created a tangible augmented reality environment that digitally enhanced the existing paper-based command and control capability in a military command post. Heidemann et al. [23] presented an AR system designed for online acquisition of visual knowledge and retrieval of memorized objects. Olwal et al. [24] introduced SenseeShapes, which use volumetric regions of interest that can be attached to the user, providing valuable information about the user interaction with the AR system. Kaiser et al. [25] extended Olwal's SenseShapes work by focusing on mutual disambiguation between input channels (speech and gesture) to improve interpretation robustness.

Our research is different from these AR interfaces in several important ways. We use domain semantics and user input timestamps to support multimodal fusion. Our AR system allows the use of a combination of speech, including deictic references and spatial predicates, and a real paddle to interact with AR content. Most importantly, we present results from a user study evaluating our multimodal AR interface.

3   Multimodal Augmented Reality Interface

The goal of our application is to allow people to effectively arrange AR content using a natural mixture of speech and gesture input. The system is a modified version of the VOMAR application [26] based on the ARToolKit library [27]. Ariadne [28] which uses the Microsoft Speech API 5.1, is utilized as the spoken dialogue system.

In the VOMAR application the paddle is the only interaction device. The paddle, which is a real object with an attached fiducial marker, allows the user to make gestures to interact with the virtual objects. A range of static and dynamic gestures is recognized by tracking the motion of the paddle (Table 1).

Our multimodal application involves the manipulation of virtual furniture in a virtual room. When users look at different menu pages through a video see through head mounted display with a camera attached to it (Figure 1), they see different types of virtual furniture on the pages, such as a set of chairs or tables (Figure 2). Looking at the workspace, users see a virtual room (Figure 3). The user can pick objects from the menu pages and place them in the workspace using paddle and speech commands.

Table 1. The VOMAR Paddle Gestures

Static Gestures	Paddle proximity to object
	Paddle tilt/inclination
Dynamic Gestures	Shaking: side to side motion of paddle
	Hitting: up and down motion of paddle
	Pushing object

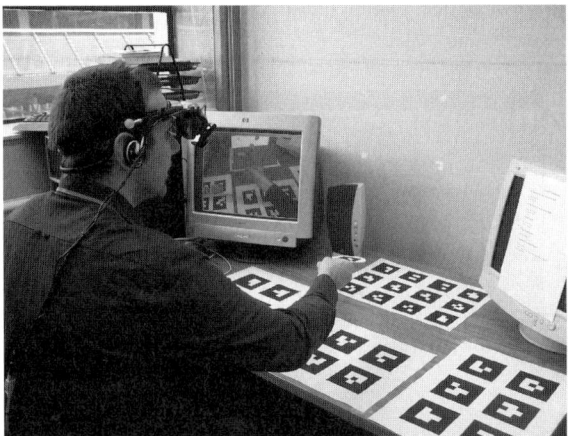

Fig. 1. A participant using the AR system

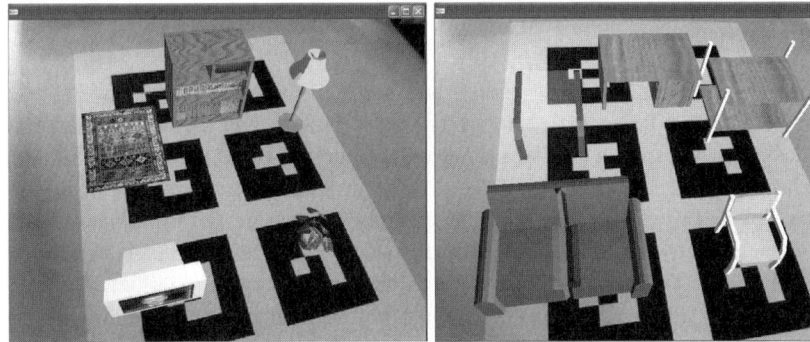

Fig. 2. Virtual menus that contain a set of virtual furniture

The following are some speech commands recognized by the system:

- Create Command "Make a blue chair": to create a virtual object and place it on the paddle.
- Duplicate Command "Copy this": to duplicate a virtual object and place it on the paddle.
- Grab Command "Grab table": to select a virtual object and place it on the paddle.

– Place Command "Place here": to place the attached object in the workspace.
– Move Command "Move the couch": to attach a virtual object in the workspace to the paddle so that it follows the paddle movement.

The system provides visual and audio feedback to the user. It shows the speech interpretation result on the screen and provides audio feedback after the speech and
paddle gesture command, so the user may immediately identify if there was an incorrect result from the speech or gesture recognition system. To improve user interactivity, the system also provides visual feedback by showing the object bounding box
when the paddle touches an object.

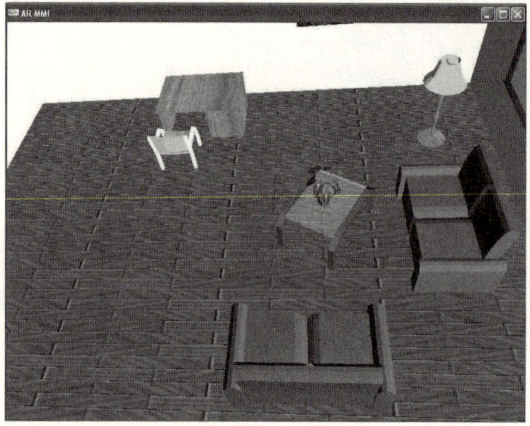

Fig. 3. A virtual room with furniture inside

To understand the combined speech and gesture, the system must fuse inputs from
both input streams into a single understandable command. Our multimodal fusion works
as follows: when a speech interpretation result is received from Ariadne, the AR Application checks whether the paddle is in view. Next, depending on the speech command type
and the paddle pose, a specific action is taken by the system. For example, consider the
case when the user says "grab this" while the paddle is placed over the menu page to grab
a virtual object. The system will test the paddle proximity to the virtual objects. If the
paddle is close enough to an object, the object will be selected and attached to the paddle.
If the paddle is not close enough, the object will not be selected.

When fusing the multimodal input, our system also considers object properties, such
as whether the object can have things placed on it (defined as ISPLACEABLE) or if
there is space under the object (defined as SPACEUNDERNEATH). These properties are
used to resolve deictic references in the speech commands from the user. For example,
if the user says "put here" while touching a virtual couch with the paddle, the possible
locations referred to by 'here' are 'on the couch' or 'under the couch'. By checking the object properties of the couch, e.g. SPACEUNDERNEATH being false and ISPLACEABLE
true, the system understands that 'here' refers to the position 'on top of the couch'. In
case the object properties cannot disambiguate user input, the position of the paddle is

used by the system. For example, the system checks the paddle in the z (up-down) direction. If the z position of the paddle is less than a threshold value (for example the height of the desk), the system understands 'here' as 'under the desk'.

4 User Study

To evaluate our multimodal AR interface, we conducted a user study. The goal was to compare user interaction with the multimodal interface to interaction with a single input mode. Results from this experiment will help identify areas where the interface can be improved and inform future designs of multimodal AR interfaces.

   There were 14 participants (3 female and 11 male) recruited from the staff and students of the HIT Lab NZ. A breakdown of the participants is given in Table 2. The non-native English speakers were foreign-born students who were comfortable speaking English. All male participants used the same male speech recognition profile and all female participants a single female profile. The users did not have to train their own speech recognition profiles. The default profiles proved to be accurate.

Table 2. User breakdown

Criteria	Yes	No
English native speaker	3	11
Familiar with AR	11	3
Familiar with paddle interaction	8	6
Familiar with speech recognition	5	9

   Users were seated at a desktop PC and wore a noise canceling microphone and an e-Magin head mounted display with a Logitech Quickcam USB camera attached. The e-Magin display is a bioccular display running at 800x600 pixel resolution with a 26-degree field of view. The Quickcam was capturing 640x480 resolution video images of the real world that were shown in the head mounted display with virtual graphics overlaid onto this real world view. The application was running at 30 frames per second and is shown in Figures 1, 2 and 3 in Section 3.

4.1 Setup

The user study took about forty-five minutes for each user. In the evaluation phase users had to build three different furniture configurations using three different interface conditions;

   (A) Paddle gestures only
   (B) Speech with static paddle position
   (C) Speech with paddle gestures.

   To minimize order effects, presentation sequences of the three interface conditions and three furniture configurations were systematically varied between users. Before each trial, a brief introduction and demonstration was given so that the users were comfortable with the interface. For each interface condition the subjects completed training by performing object manipulation tasks until they were proficient enough with the system to be able to assemble a sample scene in less than five minutes. A list of speech commands was provided on a piece of paper, so the user could refer to them throughout the experiment.

Before the user started working on the task a virtual model of the final goal was shown and then the furniture was removed from the scene, with only the bounding box frames remaining as guidance for the user (see Figure 4). The user was also given a color printed picture of the final scene to use as a reference. After performing each task, users were asked questions about the interface usability, efficiency and intuitiveness. After completing all three tasks we asked the users to rate the three interaction modes and to provide comments on their experience. Task completion times and object placement accuracy were recorded and served as performance measures.

Fig. 4. Final goal and task guidance for the user

4.2   Results and Discussion

Results for average completion times across the three interface conditions are shown in Table 3. Two subjects did not complete the tasks in the time limit of 5 minutes, so they were excluded from the completion time and accuracy analyses.

Table 3. Average performance times

	A: Paddle Gestures Only	B: Speech and Static Paddle	C: Speech and Paddle Gestures
Time (Sec)	165	106	147

When using speech and static paddle interaction, participants completed the task significantly faster than when using paddle gestures only, an ANOVA test finding ($F(2,22) = 7.254$, $p = .004$). Completion time for the speech with paddle gestures condition did not differ significantly from the other two conditions. The results show that the use of input channels with different modalities leads to an improvement in task completion time. Part of the performance improvement could be due to the extra time required by the system to recognize and respond to paddle gestures. For example, in the paddle gesture only condition, to drop an object the user had to tilt the paddle until the object slid off. In contrast, using speech the user merely had to say "drop that here" and the object was immediately placed in the workspace.

To measure object placement accuracy, we compared the absolute distance and the rotation angle around the vertical z-axis between the target and final object positions; results are shown in Figures 5 and 6. The analyses shows a significant difference for orientation accuracy ($\chi^2 = 6.000$, df = 2, p = .050) but not for position accuracy ($\chi^2 = 2.167$, df = 2, p = .338). Observing the users, we found that users had difficulty translating and rotating objects using paddle gestures alone. This difficulty was because translating and rotating objects often resulted in accidentally moving other objects in the scene.

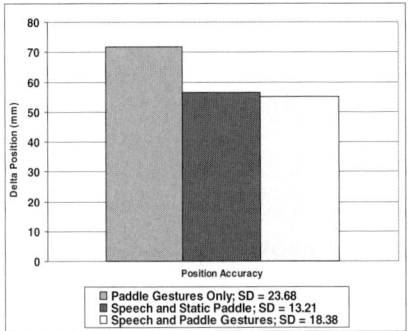

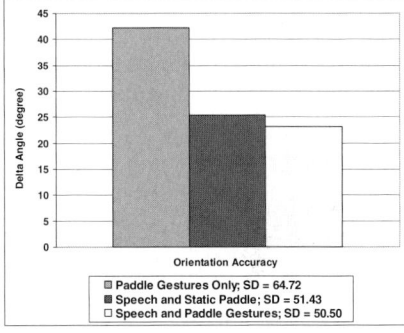

Fig. 5. Result of position accuracy   **Fig. 6.** Result of orientation accuracy

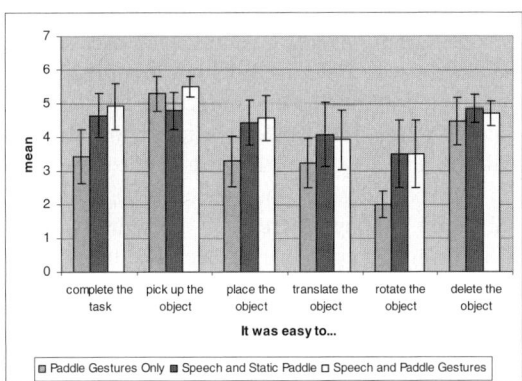

Fig. 7. Result for easiness to do a specific task (95% CI with Bonferroni adjustment)

After each trial, users were given a subjective survey where they were asked on a 6-point Likert scale if they agreed or disagreed with a number of statements (1 = disagree, 6 = agree). Results of this survey are shown in Figure 7. Users felt that completing the task in condition C was easier than condition A (F(2,26) = 5.554, p = .010). They also thought that placing objects was easier in condition C than in condition A (F(2,26) = 4.585, p = .020). Users reported that object rotation was easier

in conditions B and C than with condition A $(F(1.152, 14.971)_{\text{Huynh-Felt}} = 7.800,$
$p = .011)$. Thus, users found it hard to place objects in the target positions and rotate
them using only paddle gestures. Picking in condition A and C had slightly higher
scores than in condition B, although the scores are not significantly different
$(F(1.404, 18.249)_{\text{Huynh-Felt}} = 2.893, p = .095)$. The tendency to prefer picking objects by
using paddle gestures shows that users may find this interaction technique quite easy
and intuitive.

We also asked the users to rank the conditions from 1 to 3 (with 1 as best rating) in
terms of which they liked most (see Table 4). Speech with paddle gestures was ranked
highest (mean rank 1.58), then speech with static paddle (mean rank = 1.91), and at
last paddle gestures only (mean rank = 2.50). These rankings were significantly different $(\chi^2 = 7.000, \text{df} = 2, p = .030)$. This difference could be explained by the observation that users encountered certain difficulties when complementing a specific task.
In condition A, most of the users had difficulties in positioning and orienting the objects precisely while in condition B and C the users had better control of the object
movement.

Table 4. Mean ranks for conditions

	A: Paddle Gestures Only	B: Speech and Static Paddle	C: Speech and Paddle Gestures
Mean rank	2.50	1.91	1.58

After each experiment was finished we asked the users to provide general comments about the system. Most of the users agreed that it was difficult to place and rotate the virtual objects using only paddle gestures. One user said that pushing the object around using the paddle was quite intuitive but less precise than using the verbal
'move' and 'rotate' commands. Some users suggested adding new gestures to make
placement, and especially rotation, of objects easier or to redesign the interaction device (e.g. users should be able to swivel the paddle for easier rotation). Many users
were impressed with the robustness of the speech recognition (the system was not
trained for individual users) although there were a few users who commented on the
difficulties they had in using the speech interface. The users mentioned that accomplishing the task using combined speech and paddle commands was a lot easier once
they had learned and practiced the speech commands.

5 Design Recommendations

Based on the observations of people using our multimodal AR interface and the user
study results there are some informal design recommendations that may be useful for
the design of other multimodal AR interfaces.

Firstly, it's very important to match the speech and gesture input modalities to the
appropriate interaction methods. In our case we were using speech to specify commands and gestures to specify parameters (locations and objects) for the commands. It
is much easier to say "Put that there" rather than "Put the table at coordinates x = 50,

y = 60". The mappings that we used matched the guidelines given by Cohen [13] and others in terms of the strengths and weaknesses of speech and gesture input, and allowed for the use of natural spatial dialogue.

With imprecise recognition based input it is very important to provide feedback to the user about what commands are being sent to the system. In our case we showed the results of the speech recognition on-screen and gave audio feedback after the gesture commands. This enabled the user to immediately recognize when the speech or gesture recognition was producing an error.

It is also important to use a speech and gesture command set that is easy for users to remember. In our case, we only had a limited speech grammar and five paddle gestures. Using combined multimodal input further reduced the amount of commands that users needed to remember; for example it was possible to say "Put that there", rather than "Put the vase on the table".

Finally, the interaction context can be used to disambiguate speech and gesture input. In our case the fusion engine interprets combined speech and gesture input based on the timing of the input events and domain semantics providing two types of contextual cues.

6 Conclusion

In this paper, we describe an augmented reality multimodal interface that uses combined speech and paddle gestures to interact with the system. The system is designed to effectively and easily arrange AR content using a natural mixture of speech and gesture input. We have designed and implemented a test bed application by adding multimodal input to the VOMAR application for the arrangement of virtual furniture. The VOMAR application already had an intuitive tangible AR interface for moving virtual objects using paddle gestures, we enhanced this further by adding speech input.

The results of our user study demonstrate how combining speech and paddle gestures improved performance in arranging virtual objects over using paddle input alone. Using multimodal input, users could orient the objects more precisely in the target position, and finished an assigned task a third faster than using paddle gestures alone. The users also felt that they could complete the task more efficiently. Paddle gestures allowed the users to interact intuitively with the system since they could interact directly with the virtual objects.

Our user study shows that powerful effects can be achieved by combining speech and gesture recognition with simple context recognition. The results also show that combining speech and paddle gestures are preferred over paddle gestures alone. Speech is suitable for control tasks and gestures are suitable for spatial input such as direct interaction with the virtual objects. Contextual knowledge may resolve ambiguous input, in our case, by knowing the object properties, and the position of the paddle, the proper location referred to by the deictic term 'here' can be distinguished.

This is early work and there are several areas of future research that we can explore. The current implementation could be improved by introducing new paddle gestures to optimize the speed, effectiveness and intuitiveness of the interaction, such as gestures for locking/unlocking objects so the user would have more precise control in manipulating the virtual content. The speech grammar could be extended to include more speech commands and dialogue could be added to the system to make the system even more interactive. Finally, this multimodal interface could be extended to other augmented reality application domains to explore if the benefits we have seen in a virtual scene assembly could also be extended to other fields.

Acknowledgments. The first and last authors are funded by the Ubiquitous Autonomic Computing and Network Project, the Ministry of Information and Communication (MIC) 21st Century Frontier R&D Program in Korea.

References

1. Hannes Kaufmann: Collaborative Augmented Reality in Education. Keynote Speech at Imagina Conference (2003)
2. Istvan Barakonyi, Dieter Schmalstieg: Augmented Reality Agents in the Development Pipeline of Computer Entertainment. In Proceedings of the 4th International Conference on Entertainment Compute (2005)
3. Anthony Webster, Steven Feiner, Blair MacIntyre,William Massie, Theodore Krueger: Augmented reality in architectural construction, inspection and renovation. In Proceedings of ASCE Third Congress on Computing in Civil Engineering, Anaheim, CA (1996) 913-919
4. Christian Geiger, Leif Oppermann, Christian Reimann: 3D-Registered Interaction-Surfaces in Augmented Reality Space. In Proceedings of 2nd IEEE International Augmented Reality Toolkit Workshop (2003)
5. Kiyoshi Kiyokawa, Haruo Takemura, Naokazu Yokoya: A Collaboration Support Technique by Integrating a Shared Virtual Reality and a Shared Augmented Reality. In Proceedings of IEEE International Conference on Systems Man and Cybernetics (1999) 48-53
6. H. Kato, M. Billinghurst, I. Poupyrev, N. Tetsutani, K. Tachibana: Tangible Augmented Reality for Human Computer Interaction. In Proceedings of Nicograph, Nagoya, Japan (2001)
7. Zsolt Szalavari, Michael Gervautz: The Personal Interaction Panel – A Two-Handed Interface for Augmented Reality. In Proceedings of EUROGRAPHICS, Computer Graphics Forum, Vol. 16, 3 (1997) 335-346.
8. Buchmann, S. Violich, M. Billinghurst, A. Cockburn: FingARtips. Gesture Based Direct Manipulation in Augmented Reality. In Proceedings of 2nd International Conference on Computer Graphics and Interactive Techniques (2004) 212-221
9. Richard A. Bolt: Put-That-There: Voice and Gesture at the Graphics Interface. In Proceedings of the International conference on Computer graphics and interactive techniques, Vol. 14 (1980) 262-270
10. M. W. Salisbury, J. H. Hendrickson, T. L. Lammers, C. Fu, S. A. Moody: Talk and Draw: Bundling Speech and Graphics. IEEE Computer, Vol. 23, issue 8 (1990) 59-65
11. P.R. Cohen, M. Johnston, D.R. McGee, S.L. Oviatt, J.A. Pittman, I. Smith, L. Chen, J. Clow: Quickset: Multimodal Interaction for Distributed Applications. In Proceedings of the Fifth Annual International Multimodal Conference (1997) 31-40
12. P.R. Cohen, M. Dalrymple, F.C.N. Pereira, J.W. Sullivan, R.A. Gargan Jr., J.L. Schlossberg, S.W. Tyler: Synergistic Use of Direct Manipulation and Natural Language. In Proceedings of ACM Conference on Human Factors in Computing Systems (1989) 227-233
13. P.R. Cohen: The Role of Natural Language in a Multimodal Interface. In Proceedings of the fifth symposium on user interface software and technology (1992) 143-149
14. C. Schmandt, M.S. Ackerman, D. Hndus: Augmenting a Window System with Speech Input. IEEE Computer, Vol. 23, issue 8, (1990) 50-56

15. P. Kay: Speech Driven Graphics: a User Interface. Journal of Microcomputer Applications, Vol. 16 (1993) 223-231
16. Alexander. G. Hauptmann: Speech and Gestures for Graphic Image Manipulation. In Proceedings of ACM Conference on Human Factors in Computing Systems (1989) 241-245
17. P. R. Cohen, D. McGee, S. L. Oviatt, L. Wu, J. Clow, R. King, S. Julier, L. Rosenblum: Multimodal interactions for 2D and 3D environments. IEEE Computer Graphics and Applications (1999) 10-13
18. Joseph J. Laviola Jr.: Whole-Hand and Speech Input in Virtual Environments. Master Thesis, Brown University (1996)
19. Jan Ciger, Mario Gutierrez, Frederic Vexo, Daniel Thalmann: The Magic Wand. In Proceedings of the 19th Spring Conference on Computer Graphics (2003) 119-124
20. M.E. Latoschik, M. Schilling: Incorporating VR Databases into AI Knowledge Representations: A Framework for Intelligent Graphics Applications. In Proceedings of the 6th International Conference on Computer Graphics and Imaging (2003)
21. Hartwig Holzapfel, Kai Nickel, Rainer Stiefelhagen: Implementation and Evaluation of a Constraint-based Multimodal Fusion System for Speech and 3D Pointing Gestures. In Proceedings of the 6th International Conference on Multimodal Interfaces (2004) 175-182
22. David R. McGee, Philip R. Cohen: Creating Tangible Interfaces by Augmenting Physical Objects with Multimodal Language. In Proceedings of the 6th International Conference on Intelligent User Interfaces (2001) 113-119
23. Gunther Heidemann, Ingo Bax, Holger Bekel: Multimodal Interaction in an Augmented Reality Scenario. In Proceedings of the 6th International Conference on Multimodal Interfaces (2004) 53-60
24. Alex Olwal, Hrvoje Benko, Steven Feiner: SenseShapes: Using Statistical Geometry for Object Selection in a Multimodal Augmented Reality System. In Proceedings of the second IEEE and ACM International Symposium on Mixed and Augmented Reality (2003) 300–301
25. Ed Kaiser, Alex Olwal, David McGee, Hrvoje Benko, Andrea Corradini, Li Xiaoguang, Phil Cohen, Steven Feiner: Mutual Disambiguation of 3D Multimodal Interaction in Augmented and Virtual Reality. In Proceedings of the fifth International Conference on Multimodal Interfaces (2003) 12–19
26. H. Kato, M. Billinghurst, I. Poupyrev, K. Imamoto, K. Tachibana: Virtual Object Manipulation on a Table-Top AR Environment. In Proceedings of the International Symposium on Augmented Reality (2000) 111-119
27. ARToolKit, http://www.hitl.washington.edu/artoolkit
28. Matthias Denecke: Rapid Prototyping for Spoken Dialogue Systems. In Proceedings of the 19th international conference on Computational Linguistics, Vol. 1 (2002) 1-7

An Augmented Reality System for Computer Maintenance

Bo Kang, Peng Ren, and Changzhi Ke

School of Automation Engineering & Mobile Computing Center,
University of Electronic and Science Technology of China,
Chengdu, China 610054
kangbo@uestc.edu.cn, raulrp@126.com, kcz1981@163.com

Abstract. Augmented reality (AR) aims to create user interface in which virtual objects are overlaid on the physical environment. Equipment maintenance and training tasks are excellent domains for augmented reality application. In this paper, a prototype of video see-through based AR system for training and supporting to computer maintenance is presented. A vision and inertial based hybrid tracking method is adopted in the prototype and discussed in details. A WIMP-based user interface which is simple, convenient and informative is designed for this system. Experimental results illustrate the effectiveness of the prototype.

Keywords: Augmented reality, Maintenance, Tracking, User interface.

1 Introduction

Augmented reality (AR) is an emerging technology in advanced computing domains. AR aims to amplify a user's sensory perception directly by overlaying computer-generated virtual information on the user's physical environment, so it is a promising technique for human-computer interaction. Unlike virtual reality (VR) which completely immerses a user inside a synthetic environment, AR does not remove the user from their physical environment. The AR system allows the user to see the real world, with computer-generated virtual information, such as images, videos or text, superimposed upon or combined with the real world in real time in such a way that the user cannot tell the difference [1]. There are many potential AR applications in a variety of domains, such as medical visualization, engineering design, maintenance and repair, annotation, entertainment, cultural heritage, military aircraft navigation and targeting, and others[1,2]. Equipment maintenance and training is one of the most important application domains for augmented reality. Though the idea to use AR for manufacturing, maintenance, repair and training dates back to the early 1990's [3,4], up to now it has not been implemented as a real product because of the limitation of current AR crucial techniques, such as tracking, display, and human-computer interaction.

In this paper, a prototype of video see-through based augmented reality system for training and supporting to computer maintenance is presented. The described AR system can assist a user to perform training or maintenance task step by step by giving augmented information on the user's field of view. The system architecture is introduced

Z. Pan et al. (Eds.): ICAT 2006, LNCS 4282, pp. 284–291, 2006.

in section 2. The tracking system, which implements vision and inertial based hybrid tracking, is discussed in section 3. The user interface of this AR system is illustrated in section 4. Some experiments and conclusion are presented in section 5 and 6.

2   System Architecture

Based on the concept of video see-through AR system, the system architecture of the presented AR system in illustrated in Fig. 1. The architecture is divided in five conceptual parts: video capturing, tracking system, user interface, virtual information database, graphics rendering and displaying.

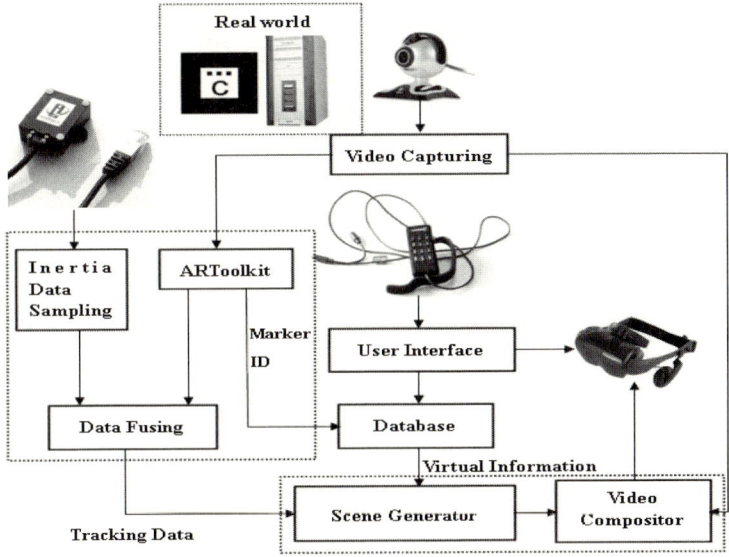

Fig. 1. The system architecture

The video capturing is implemented based on Microsoft's DirectShow with a Logitech QuickCam Pro4000 camera. The captured video images have two uses in this system, one of which is applied to the vision-based tracking; the other is used for substituting the real environment that the user sees.

Tracking the user's viewpoint is crucial for augmented reality. In our AR system, the tracking system combines vision-based and inertial-based tracking techniques, namely vision-inertial hybrid tracking. As mentioned above, the captured image is used for vision-based tracking based on ARToolkit [5]. The inertial sensor in this system is InterSense's InertiaCube3 which integrates 3 inertial gyros and 3 accelerometers. The data fusion is implemented with an Extended Kalman Filter. More details about the tracking system are discussed in section 3.

User interface is one of most important issues for AR applications. Through the user interface, a user can easily interact with the AR system. In this paper, the user interface is designed based on Microsoft's MFC library. At present, the only input device is a handheld keyboard with mouse, namely Twiddler2, and the main output device is a head mounted display (HMD) which is I-glasses SVGA Pro. The design of the user interface is illustrated in detail in section 4.

In the prototype, the camera, inertial sensor, and HMD are integrated in a helmet, as shown in Fig. 2.

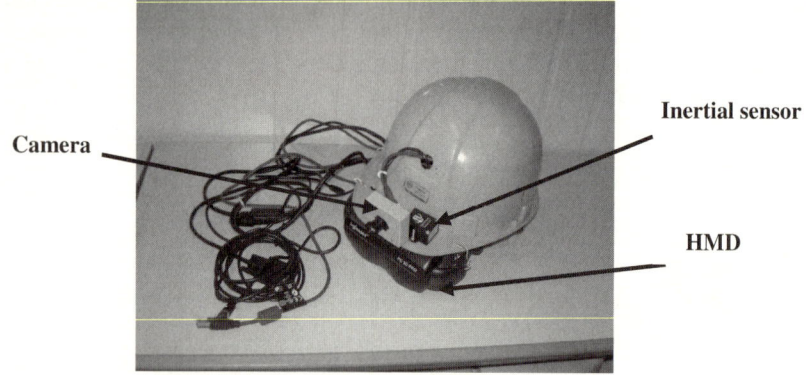

Fig. 2. The helmet which is integrated with a camera, an inertial tracker, and a HMD

In our AR prototype, the virtual information, namely augmented information, includes relevant annotation text, instructions and other useful text, images, and 3D objects. They are stored as XML descriptions in a XML-based database and presented using XSL style sheets.

In video see-through AR system, the graphics rendering is divided in two stages: scene generator and video compositor. The scene generator is responsible for rendering the virtual scene, and the video compositor is responsible for combining the virtual scene and the real world video. In our prototype system, both parts are implemented based on C++ and OpenGL. The augmented video stream, which is the output of the video compositor, will be displayed on the user's HMD by the displaying pipeline.

3   Tracking System

Tracking is very important research subject in the field of augmented reality. In video see-through AR, a vision-based tacking method is usually appropriate. Vision-based tracking method uses cameras that capture real scene as sensing device. Therefore, a video see-through AR system can use a vision-based tacking method without changing its system configuration.

ARToolkit is a well-known open-source software library for building augmented reality applications based on vision-based tracking with markers which are black-white squared cards with different designs. Our previous prototype was built based on ARToolkit [6]. Like other vision-based tracking, the tracking with ARToolkit in our prototype suffers from lack of robustness or stability. A little changing of the environment (such as illumination), and rapid or abrupt camera movement can cause tracking failures or instabilities.

Inertial sensors are widely used for motion tracking. Compare to vision-based tracking, inertial sensor is robustness and can be sampled at high rates. However, inertial sensor measure acceleration or motion rate, so their signal must be integrated to produce position or orientation. Another shortcoming of inertial tracking is the accumulated drift. Hybrid tracking systems attempt to compensate for the shortcomings of each technology by using multiple measurements to produce robust results [7]. In our new prototype presented in this paper, a vision-inertial based hybrid tracking method is introduced.

In the hybrid tracking system for our prototype, vision-based tracking is implemented using ARToolkit, and inertial tracking using InterSense's InertiaCube3 which mainly integrates gyroscopes and linear accelerometers along all three orthogonal axes. An EKF (Extended Kalman Filter), which is similar to [8], is used for the data fusion implementation. As Fig. 3 shows, the fusion filter has a predictor-corrector structure, which computes a tracking prediction from the inertial data (namely angular rate vector ω_i and acceleration vector a_i) , followed by a tracking correction with vision-based tracking data (namely position data p_v and orientation data q_v).

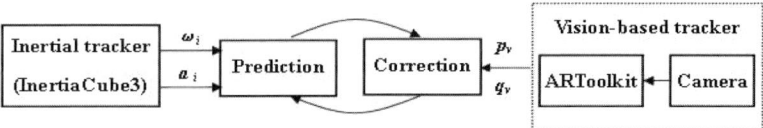

Fig. 3. Fusion of vision-based and inertial tracker with an Extended Kalman Filter

In our method, tracking data for AR scenario is mainly the data from vision-based tracking. When no marker is visible or marker is blur or distortion that causes the vision-based tracking failure, the tracking has to rely on the inertial prediction based on the former correction information and new inertial data. As soon as the vision tracking starts to send normal data, the vision data is directly adopted for AR system again, and the correction terms of the filter are recalculated.

Of course, inertial tracker frame and camera frame coordinate are two different coordinates. Therefore, we need to know the transformation between inertial and camera coordinate before the sensor fusion. Since the inertial sensor and the camera are rigidly mounted to a helmet, the transformation between them can be pre-calibrated and is constant [7,9]. In each circle of the fusion, the transformation will be implemented.

4   User Interface

User interface is very crucial for AR application. In our application, the AR system should present necessary information in proper manner to a user, which assist or guide the user fulfill the maintenance and repair task. In the situation for maintenance, two hands of the user mainly work with the equipment which is being repaired.

Therefore, Interaction with the AR system through the user's hand should be reduced as possible. In a word, the user interface of our prototype should be designed as simple and informative as possible.

Generally, the user interfaces for AR systems differ from the Windows-Icons-Menu-Pointing (WIMP) interface employed in desktop and laptop systems. Up to now, however, a suitable and typical user interface for AR application does not yet exist, and WIMP interface is fairly well studied, understood and accepted. Therefore, in our research, WIMP interface is a suitable choice for quick development of AR user interface at present.

Based on these considerations mentioned above, we have designed a Windows graphical interface based on Microsoft's MFC for our AR application system. The graphical interface which is displayed on the user's HMD is divided into four areas (see Fig. 4): user control area, augmented video area, pure textual information area and marker list area.

Fig. 4. The graphical interface is divided into four areas

In order to keep the user interface as simple as possible, the user control area consist four typical widgets which controlled by the mouse: three buttons and one scroll bar. The only input device is the hand-held keyboard with mouse, namely Twiddler2. Three buttons are used for selecting different type virtual information that is overlaid on the real video stream and displayed in augmented video area. The Threshold scroll bar is used for configuring the threshold parameter of binary image for the vision-based tracking. The functions of the buttons and the scroll bar are shown in Table 1.

Table 1. Functions of the widgets

Widgets Name	Function
Threshold (scroll bar)	Configuring the threshold parameter of binary image
Text (button)	Add text on the video stream
Object (button)	Add 3D object on the video stream
Picture (button)	Add picture on the video stream

The augmented video area is the main area of the AR interface. In this area, the basic and most necessary virtual information, such as the names and annotations of the computer parts, simple instructions, pictures or graphs, and 3D objects for computer maintenance, are superimposed on the real world video stream.

The marker list area is used for displaying marker information in this system, such as marker's ID, position, and state, which is helpful for interaction and debugging. Besides, the marker list is designed as a menu which is used for controlling and selecting the pure textual information in display area.

The pure textual information area, as mentioned above, which is controlled by the marker menu, is used for displaying some complex textual information, such as the troubleshooting guide for the repaired computer.

5 Experiments

To illustrate the performance of our prototype, we tested the system with a laptop in our Lab. For vision-based tracking, four marker cards (3 by 3 centimeters each) are designed and attached on the surfaces of some parts of the computer that need to be repaired. The video capturing rate is 30 frames per second. In our video see-through AR prototype, the sampling rate of the inertial tracker is set at 150Hz. In the experiment process, the user wore the helmet which is connected to the laptop in the user's shoulder bag, as shown in Fig. 5.

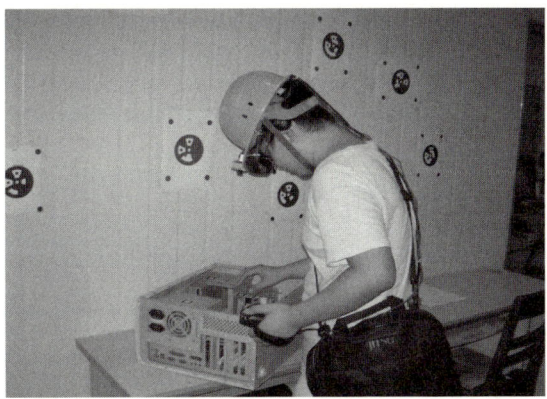

Fig. 5. A user wearing the system in working

When the system begins to work, the default work mode is text-object mode in which the relevant annotations or instructions and 3D objects are properly overlaid on the repaired computer in the real environment video, as Fig. 4 shows in section 4. There are sixteen modes which are controlled by user with three buttons and the Marker menu. Clicking the button Picture using Twiddler2, a picture or a graph which the user requires will be displayed in the user's field of view adaptively. For instance, in Fig.6, an augmented picture for the mainboard of the computer is presented.

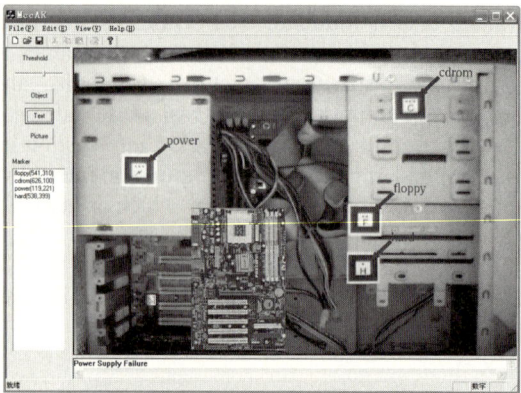

Fig. 6. An augmented picture is presented by clicking button Picture. In the figure, the 3D object is shut off.

When one marker is selected and clicked in the Marker menu, a textual troubleshooting guide which is relative to the selected marker will be shown in the textual information area. As Fig.7 shows, the hard disk failure diagnosis guide is displayed in the textual area.

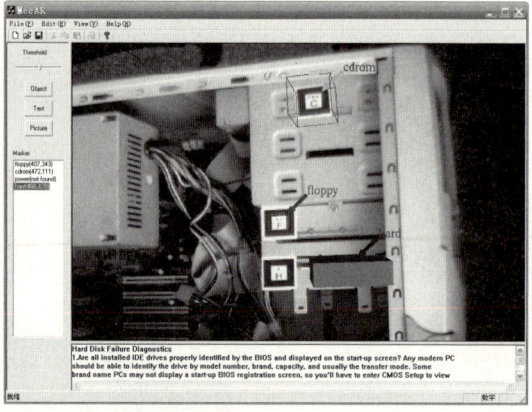

Fig. 7. The guide information is displayed the textual area by selecting and clicking on the Marker menu

To test the performance of the hybrid tracking method, we compared it with a modify system which adopts vision-based tracking only. Experiments show that in a normal scenario of maintenance, tracking failure occurred frequently in the vision-based tracking system, and seldom in the vision-inertial hybrid tracking system. In other word, the vision-inertial hybrid tracking method adopted in our prototype can actually improve the tracking performance.

6 Conclusion and Future Work

In this paper we presented an AR application prototype for computer maintenance, which can assist or guide a user to fulfill training or maintenance task step by step by giving augmented information on the user's field of view. The prototype is a video see-through AR application system with vision-inertial hybrid tracking method which improves its tracking performance. A WIMP-based user interface is designed for this prototype, which is a simple, convenient and informative interaction interface. The architecture and relevant techniques presented in our prototype can be used in diverse equipment maintenance, training, and other AR applications.

Like most of other AR prototypes, the presented system in this paper is far from an end-user product. Much work remains to be done, such as the improvements in tracking, registration, rendering, displaying, and content of augmentation. Considering usability of the system, optical see-through AR system is more suitable for our application. Therefore we will develop an optical see-through version for our prototype. Human computer interaction is also an important issue for AR usability. To our prototype, a new interaction method based on audio or voice is a worthwhile research direction.

References

1. Azuma, R.: A survey of augmented reality. Presense. 6(4), pp355-385, (1997)
2. Azuma, R., Baillot, Y., Behringer, R., Feiner, S., Julier, S. and MacIntyre, B.: Recent Advances in Augmented Reality. IEEE Computer Graphics and Applications, 25(6), pp.34-43, (2001)
3. Caudell, T. P., Mizell, D. W.: Augmented reality: An Application of Head-ups Display Technology to Manual Manufacturing Processes. Proc. of Hawaii International Conference on System Science, Vol. II, pp659-669, (1992)
4. Feiner, S., MacIntyre, B. and Seligmann, D.: Knowledge-based Augmented Reality. Communications of the ACM, 36(7), pp.52-62, (1993)
5. http://www.hitl.washington.edu/artoolkit/
6. Ke Changzhi, Kang Bo, Chen Dongyi, et al, An Augmented Reality Based Application for Equipment Maintenance, Proc. of International Conference Affective Computing and Intelligent Interaction, LNCS 3784, pp.836-841, (2005)
7. You S., Neumann, U. and Azuma, R.: Hybrid Inertial and Vision Tracking for Augmented Reality. Proc. of IEEE VR'99, pp. 260-267, (1999)
8. Ribo, M., Lang, P., and Ganster, H., et. al.: Hybrid Tracking for Outdoor Augmented Reality Applications. IEEE Computer Graphics and Applications, Nov/Dec (2002), pp. 54-63
9. Lang P. and Pinz A.: Calibration of hybrid vision / inertial tracking systems. Proc. of the 2nd InverVis : Workshop on Integration of Vision and Inertial Systems, (2005)

Multi-view Video Composition with Computer Graphics

Artem Ignatov and Manbae Kim

Dept. of Computer, Info. and Telecom, Kangwon National University,
192-1, Hyoja2dong, Chunchon, Kangwondo,
Republic of Korea, 200-701
Tel.: +82-33-250-6395; Fax: +82-33-252-6390
manbae@kangwon.ac.kr, ignatov@kangwon.ac.kr

Abstract. Multi-view video has recently gained much attraction from academic and commercial fields because it can deliver the immersive viewing of natural scenes. This paper presents a composition method of generating composite views combined with graphic objects. First we generate virtual views between multi-view cameras using depth and texture images of the input videos. Then we mix graphic objects to the generated view images. A distinctive feature of our approach is that we use an identical coordinate system for camera, virtual, and graphics views. The reason for using the same system for all types of cameras is the ability of full interactions between real scene and graphic objects. Another merit is that the occlusion between them is handled automatically by a graphics engine because z values of real scene and graphic objects are stored in the same z buffer. We present experimental results that validate our proposed method and show that graphic objects could become the inalienable part of the multi-view video. For the validation of our method we used multi-view sequences where a graphic object is mixed into camera and virtual images.

Keywords: view synthesis, composition, multi-view, image-based rendering.

1 Introduction

Multi-view video has recently gained much attraction from academic and commercial fields [1,2,3]. The multi-view video not only provides the wide viewing of natural scenes, but delivers immersive and realistic contents to users, especially when combined with synthetic contents such as computer graphics. In practice, due to the finite number of cameras and the large inter-camera distance for a wide view, inter-mediate views need to be reconstructed. The virtual view generation requires accurate camera calibration, depth data, and texture image. From the texture image and depth data of camera views, novel views can be reconstructed. One of possible techniques is image-based rendering.

Image based rendering (IBR) has attracted much attention in the past decade [4]. The potential to produce new views of a real scene with the realism impossible to

Z. Pan et al. (Eds.): ICAT 2006, LNCS 4282, pp. 292–301, 2006.

achieve by other means makes it very appealing. IBR aims to capture a real scene using a number of cameras. Any view of the scene can be generated from the camera views.

Previous works for generating virtual images were aimed at generating a novel image at any arbitrary viewpoint using image data acquired from the cameras. An effective way to generate virtual images is the utilization of depth and texture images [5,6]. With depth and image data of all camera views, it is possible to reconstruct any arbitrary views. On the contrary, the research for mixing graphics objects into multi-view video is relatively few. The composition of the multi-view images being composed of camera and virtual views with graphic objects is an important subject, because composite scenes can increase and deliver better immersive perception.

In this paper we present a view composition method that combines a multi-view sequence with synthetic objects. Unlike mono or stereo videos, the view synthesis requires more general camera viewpoint configuration as well as more complex control of graphics camera locations. IBR is used to reconstruct new views and the methodology is also utilized by the generation process of the synthetic objects. The accurate registration of camera and graphics views is also studied. Given input videos, each of which is a combination of a texture image and a depth map, two stages of multi-view composition are to reconstruct a new view (view synthesis) and to mix graphic objects to camera and virtual views (image composition). In the image composition, view geometry used for the view synthesis is utilized. Furthermore, our method allows reconstructing intermediate views as many as an user have selected. From any viewpoint, interaction between real and graphics objects can be observed, that is the advantage of our approach.

Following section describes the overall architecture of our proposed method. Section 3 describes the view synthesis in details. The image composition with graphic objects is presented in Section 4. Finally, Section 5 presents experimental results per-formed on multi-view video followed by the conclusion and future works of Section 6.

2   Overview of the Proposed Method

The basic structure for view synthesis and image composition is given in Fig. 1. Given multiple camera views, camera calibration parameters such as intrinsic and

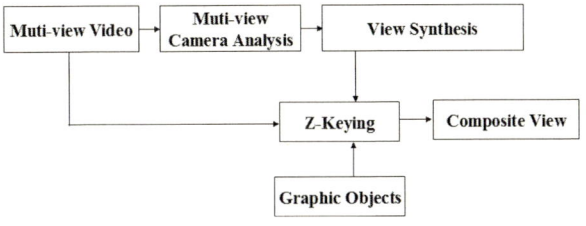

Fig. 1. The basic structure of generating the composite view

extrinsic matrices and depth data can be estimated or given a prior. Based on them, we reconstruct virtual intermediate images. As well, in order to carry out the image composition, the locations of graphic cameras are fixed to be at the identical places of the camera and virtual cameras so that the real scene and graphic objects are correctly registered. The texture image and depth data are obtained for both virtual and graphics views and a final composite image is made using Z-keying.

3   View Synthesis

We use three types of cameras in our method: *base camera*, *virtual camera*, and *graphics camera*. The base camera is a multi-view camera which captures video. With the virtual camera, new intermediate views are generated between two neighboring base cameras. The graphics camera is used to make graphic objects. The three cameras are set to accurately produce synthesized and composite views. For instance, camera parameters of the base cameras are implicitly or explicitly utilized. The position of a graphics camera coincides with that of a corresponding base or virtual camera. The camera setup is illustrated in Fig. 2.

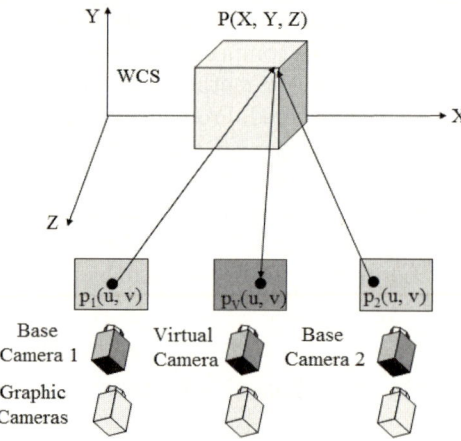

Fig. 2. Camera configuration for generating virtual and graphics views

As shown in Fig. 2, a distinctive feature is that we use an identical world coordinate system (WCS) for all types of cameras. The reason to use the identical WCS is the ability of full interactions between a real scene and graphic objects. Occlusion between them is automatically handled by a graphics engine because their Z-values are stored in the same Z-buffer.

Camera calibration parameters consist of two matrices: an intrinsic matrix $\mathbf{K}$, which describes perspective projection and an extrinsic matrix $[\mathbf{R}|\mathbf{t}]$, which describes camera orientation and position with respect to a world coordinate system [7]. A camera projects a 3-D world point to a 2-D point in an image. If the world and image points are represented by homogeneous vectors, then the mapping between their homogeneous coordinates can be expressed as

$$\mathbf{x} = \mathbf{MX} \tag{1}$$

where $\mathbf{X}$ represents a world point by the homogeneous vector $(X, Y, Z, 1)^T$, and $\mathbf{x}$ represents an image point as a homogeneous vector. The projection matrix $\mathbf{M}$ is expressed by

$$\mathbf{M} = \mathbf{K}[\mathbf{R}|\mathbf{t}] \tag{2}$$

where

$$\mathbf{K} = \begin{pmatrix} \gamma f & sf & x_0 \\ 0 & f & y_0 \\ 0 & 0 & 1 \end{pmatrix}$$

where f is focal length, γ is aspect ratio, s is skew, and (x_0, y_0) is an image center.

A point x in an image, corresponding to the pixel (u, v), can correspond to many 3-D points in the world. The ambiguity in determining the correct 3-D point can be resolved by using depth z of the pixel $\mathbf{x}$, which is the distance along the principal axis from the camera center C to the 3-D point X which projects to x, as shown in Fig. 3. Given depth z for every pixel $\mathbf{x} = (u, v)$ and the calibration matrix $\mathbf{M}$, the corresponding 3-D point $\mathbf{X}$ can be given by the

$$\mathbf{X} = \mathbf{C} + \mathbf{zM}^+\mathbf{x} \tag{3}$$

where $\mathbf{x}$ is pixel homogenous coordinate $(u, v, 1)$, $\mathbf{X}$ represents the 3-D point for the pixel $\mathbf{x} = (u, v)$, z is depth value corresponding to the pixel $\mathbf{x}$, coming from the depth data, $\mathbf{M}^+$ is the pseudo inverse of camera projection matrix $\mathbf{M}$ such that $\mathbf{MM}^+ = \mathbf{I}$ and $\mathbf{C}$ is the camera center coordinate.

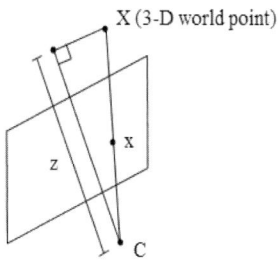

Fig. 3. Reconstruction of 3-D point $\mathbf{X}$ coordinate exploiting depth z of pixel $\mathbf{x}$

Our approach to multi-view video composition with graphic objects includes two main steps. First we generate a virtual texture image between base cameras using depth and texture representation. Second we combine the obtained texture image of a virtual view with a synthetic graphic object. Also during the texture image generation, we generate its depth map. The depth map is stored in graphics Z-buffer and after image composition it is flushed.

Now we present how we determine the virtual camera positions and orientations. To place any virtual camera in a proper position between selected base cameras, we have used information from these base cameras about how they are disposed in the space and in what direction they look. From camera extrinsic matrices of neighboring base cameras, we specify a camera extrinsic matrix $[\mathbf{R}|\mathbf{t}]$ for a virtual camera to set its orientation and position. In case of parallel setup of the base cameras, a rotation matrix for any virtual camera should be identity matrix and we only need to specify a translation vector to set a virtual camera position between two chosen base cameras. For arc setup, we also need to specify a rotation matrix for any virtual camera to aim it in a proper direction, corresponding to viewing directions of the neighboring base cameras. First we compute a translation vector for every virtual camera. We simply compute delta (difference) between x coordinates of neighboring base cameras and do the same for z coordinates. Then we divide the delta into equal intervals according to a specified number of virtual views. Finally we set virtual camera centers at the joints of the intervals. The derivation of a rotation matrix is similarly carried out.

An algorithm to generate a texture image of a virtual camera is carried out as follows:

1) Specify two base cameras; base cameras 1 and 2 (see Fig. 2)
2) Project pixels from the base camera 1 back to 3-D space. For every pixel, its associated 3-D point is estimated by Eq. 3.
3) Project all 3-D points reconstructed in 2) in virtual camera direction and obtain a new image.
4) Repeat 2) and 3) for the base camera 2 and update the new image.

The example in Fig. 4 illustrates the virtual views obtained from the proposed method. Fig. 4(a) shows a virtual image obtained from the base camera 1. The black region contains pixels occluded from the base camera 1. The image in (b) is

(a)   (b)   (c)

Fig. 4. Two virtual images are obtained (a) from the base camera 1 and (b) from the base camera 2. The final image is shown in (c).

a virtual view made from the base camera 2. Also, the black region occluded by the camera 2 is observed. The image in (c) is the final image. Most of occluded pixels are solved. A red synthetic object is mixed according to a method described in the next section.

4   Image Composition

After obtaining texture and depth images of virtual views, we proceed to an image composition. The composition is identically applied to both camera and virtual views. Real-world Z-value is stored in the graphics Z-buffer so that when we insert a graphic object, occlusion between real scene and graphic objects is automatically resolved.

The mixing of the 3-D real image-based scene and graphic objects is performed by Z-keying that compares pixelwise depth information [8]. To maintain the consistency between the real space and the graphics space, we need to use a unified set of camera parameters, that is used as a reference. We first use the camera parameters to set up a multi-view camera. In mixing graphics objects into the real scene, one of the important technical issues is the registration between graphic objects and the real scenes. To provide a natural-looking image, the exact position of the real camera must be known to place the objects correctly in the scene.

To generate a graphic image, we first derive a relationship between base/virtual camera and graphics camera. Then, from the graphics camera corresponding to its associated base or virtual camera, a graphic image is made. For this we need to convert the intrinsic camera matrix $\mathbf{K}$ and the extrinsic camera matrix $[\mathbf{R}|\mathbf{t}]$ of a base camera to the graphics projection matrix $\mathbf{P}$ and the graphics viewing matrix $\mathbf{V}$ accordingly. Remind that the base camera projection matrix $\mathbf{M}$ is $\mathbf{M} = \mathbf{K}[\mathbf{R}|\mathbf{t}]$. This matrix completely determines how a 3-D world point described in the world coordinate system projects to a 2-D point in the image plane.

We derive an analogous projection matrix for the graphics. First we convert $[\mathbf{R}|\mathbf{t}]$ to the viewing matrix $\mathbf{V}$ by adding $[0\ 0\ 0\ 1]$ to the bottom row.

$$\mathbf{V} = \begin{pmatrix} R & t \\ 0\,0\,0 & 1 \end{pmatrix}$$

The next step is to convert $\mathbf{K}$ into a 4×4 projection matrix $\mathbf{P}$ as follows [9].

$$\mathbf{P} = \begin{pmatrix} \frac{2N}{R-L} & 0 & \frac{R+L}{R-L} & 0 \\ 0 & \frac{2N}{T-B} & \frac{T+B}{T-B} & 0 \\ 0 & 0 & \frac{-(F+N)}{F-N} & \frac{-2FN}{F-N} \\ 0 & 0 & -1 & 0 \end{pmatrix}$$

where N is near plane, F is far plane, R is right plane, L is left plane, B is bottom plane, and T is top plane of a view volume.

For consistency, we set N equal to a focal length f. Other parameters are set automatically when we specify a vertical view angle and an aspect ratio.

P puts a view volume (frustum) into the canonical view volume (cube) with all dimensions from -1 to 1. Graphics camera projection matrix **G** is the product of a projection matrix **P** and a viewing matrix **V**, and expressed by

$$\mathbf{G} = \mathbf{P}\mathbf{V} \tag{4}$$

Then, the projection of a 3-D world point **X** in homogeneous coordinate system to 3-D point **Y** in homogeneous camera coordinates is given by

$$\mathbf{Y} = \mathbf{G}\mathbf{X} \tag{5}$$

The base camera projects a 3-D point in the world coordinate system to a 2-D point in the image coordinate system. Essentially, depth information is lost in this process. In homogeneous coordinate system, **M** is a 3 × 4 matrix, which maps a 3-D point to a 2-D point. Graphics camera projection is identical to base camera projection. In addition, the graphics camera projection also stores depth in normalized form, which is used in hidden surface elimination (e.g., z-buffer algorithm). Since a 3-D point is mapped to another 3-D point in the homogeneous coordinates, **G** is a 4 × 4 matrix. Taking into account the features of base and graphics cameras, the reason why we convert the camera matrix from the base camera to the graphics camera is that z-coordinate of 3-D point is stored in the z-buffer, since graphics camera projects a 3-D point to a 3-D point in contrast to base camera that maps a 3-D point to a 2-D point.

Z-keying method implies that on the input we have texture data for real and graphics images, and also we have depth data for them. Merging real and graphics texture images is done on comparing z-values of pixels from depth data of real and graphics images. Fig. 5 shows an example of depth data of real and graphic images, and also presents the combined depth image.

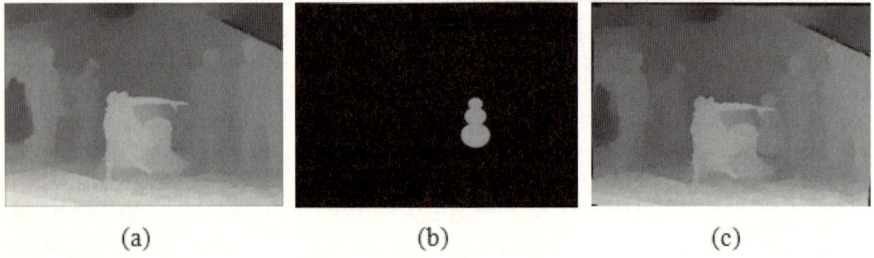

(a)   (b)   (c)

Fig. 5. Depth data of (a) real image, (b) graphic image and (c) combined image

5   Experimental Results

In this section, we present experimental results that prove our proposed method and show that a graphic object becomes the inalienable part of a natural scene. For validation of our method, we have used a *breakdancing* multi-view se-

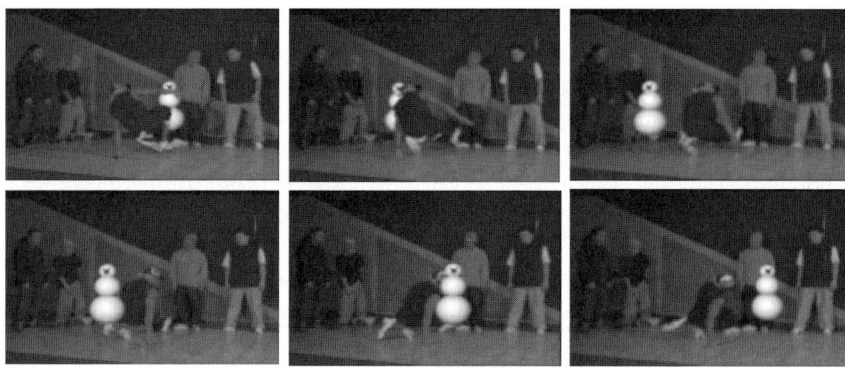

Fig. 6. The six successive images combined with a synthetic graphic object *snowman*

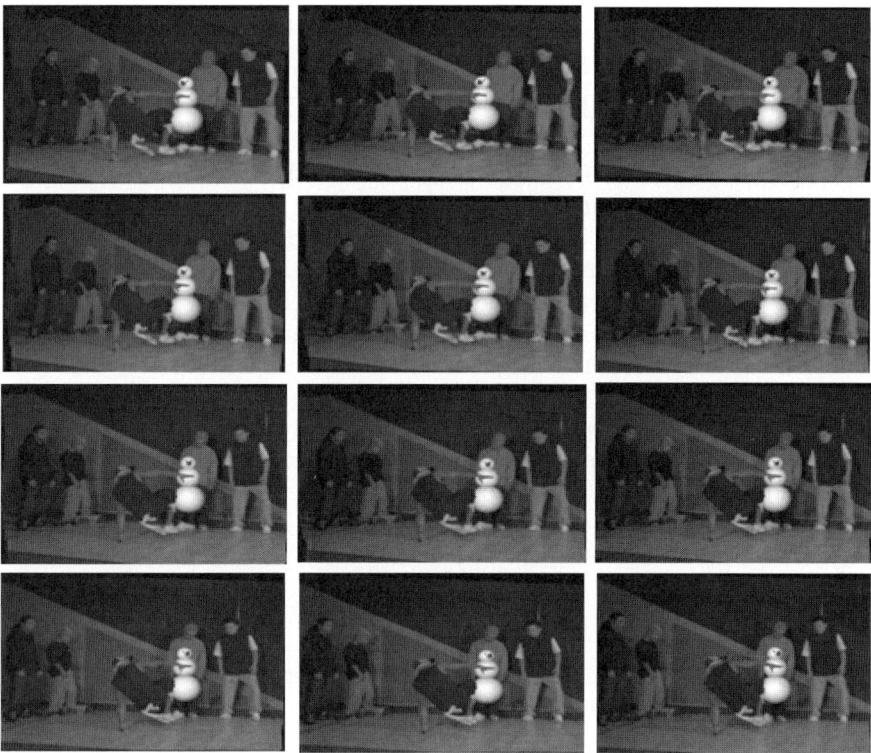

Fig. 7. Four base camera images (left column) and eight virtual images (middle and right columns) combined with a synthetic graphic object "snowman"

quence provided by Microsoft Research (MSR). MSR provides camera calibration parameters of eight base cameras and 100 frames of video along with depth data [9]. The graphics objects are rendered in Open Graphics Library (OpenGL) environment [10]. In OpenGL, the color image and the corresponding depth image are obtained from the front-color and depth buffer.

Fig. 6 shows six composite views captured from a video that was made from camera 4 position. The graphic object *snowman* is designed in a manner that it moves around the dancer in order to show the performance of the proposed method and Z-keying. As we observe, our synthesized graphic object becomes the integral part of the scene, since any occlusion between graphic and real objects are successfully resolved by our algorithm.

Fig. 7 shows four sets of combined images. Each set consist of a base camera image and two virtual images combined with *snowman*. For example, in Fig. 7 the first row shows images from base camera 0 (left) and two virtual images located between cameras 0 and 1. Other sets are organized similarly. Left column presents images from base cameras 2, 4 and 6. It is notable that we can observe the accurate change of the right hand of the dancer and the graphic object when our viewpoint moves from the camera 0 to 7 through the intermediate frames. Also *snowman* is rotating when we change our position in the space.

6   Conclusion and Future Works

In this paper we have presented a method for synthesizing virtual intermediate views and for compositing graphic objects given multi-view sequences. For virtual images, 3-D depth and texture information of base cameras is utilized. As well, for the accurate registration of real scene and 3-D graphics data, the theoretical relationship between them was derived. Experimental results have shown that our method enables to generate high-quality synthesized images using information only from two neighboring base cameras so that graphic objects could become an inalienable part of immersive scenes. Furthermore, the occlusion between real and graphics objects is successfully resolved. Our method is expected to deliver more immersive and realistic multi-view contents, especially when viewed in 3-D multi-view monitors.

Acknowledgment

This research was supported by the MIC(Ministry of Information and Communication), Korea, under the ITRC(Information Technology Research Center) support program supervised by the IITA (Institute of Information Technology Assessment)(RBRC: IITA-2006-(C1090-0502-0022))

References

1. A. Vetro, W. Matusik, H. Pfister, J. Xin, "Coding approaches for end-to-end 3D TV sys-tems," *Picture Coding Symposium* , Dec. 2004.
2. Q. Zhang, W. Zhu and Y-Q Zhang, "Resource allocation for multimedia streaming over the Internet," *IEEE Trans. on Multimedia* , Vol. 3, No. 3, Sep. 2001.

3. C. L. Zitnick, S. B. Kang, M. Uyttendaele, S. Winder, and R. Szeliski, "High-Quality Video View Interpolation Using a Layered Representation," *SIGGRAPH04*, Los Angeles, CA, USA, August 2004.
4. C. Zhang and T. Chen, "A survey on image-based rendering - representation, sampling and compression", *EURASIP Signal processing: image communication*, vol. 19. no. 1, pp. 1-28, 2004.
5. L. McMillan, "An image-based approach in three-dimensional computer graphics", Ph.D thesis, UNC, 1997.
6. P. J. Narayanan, "Visible space models: 2-D representations for large virtual environ-ments," *In ICVC99,* 1999.
7. Hartley, R.I. and Zisserman, A. "Multiple View Geometry in Computer Vision," *Cambridge University Press,* 2nd Edition, 2004.
8. W. Woo, N. Kim, and Y. Iwadate, "Photo-realistic interactive 3D virtual environment generation using multiview video," *In SPIE PW-EI Image and Video Communications and Processing (IVCP),* Bellingham, WA, Jan. 2001, Vol. 4310, pp. 245-254.
9. http://research.microsoft.com/vision/InteractiveVisualMediaGroup/ 3DVideoDownload/, Mircosoft Research
10. F. S. Hill, Jr. "Computer Graphics using OpenGL," *Prentice Hall,* 2nd ed., 2001.

Floating Virtual Mirrors:
Visualization of the Scene Behind a Vehicle

Toru Miyamoto, Itaru Kitahara, Yoshinari Kameda, and Yuichi Ohta

Graduate School of Systems and Information Engineering, University of Tsukuba
1-1-1, Tennoudai, Tsukuba, Ibaraki, Japan
miyamoto@image.esys.tsukuba.ac.jp,
{kitahara, kameda, ohta}@iit.tsukuba.ac.jp
http://www.image.esys.tsukuba.ac.jp

Abstract. In this paper, we propose a visual assistance system that shows the scene behind a vehicle to its driver in the form of a virtual mirror by utilizing a surveillance camera. The virtual mirror will be displayed on a windshield display as if it were floating in the air in front of the vehicle. The driver entering an intersection can confirm the safety around the vehicle by checking the image in the virtual mirror while facing forward, because it shows the image of the scene behind the vehicle in an optically correct manner. We utilize a surveillance camera set up on a signal pole. The image in the virtual mirror was formed by applying geometric its transformation to the image taken by the camera so that it satisfy the optical constraints of a mirror.

1   Introduction

It is very important for drivers to confirm safety around and behind their vehicle when driving a car. To support drivers with new equipment by enhancing their vision, two conditions outlined below are important.

- There should be no or little blind area in images shown to drivers.
- Drivers should be able to instantly understand their spatial relationships relative to other objects by watching the images.

Rearview mirrors and door mirrors are usually used as visual assistance devices to allow the driver to see into blind areas. As people are familiar with such mirrors, they can easily recognize the spatial relationships relative to other vehicles and objects in the blind areas. However, use of these mirrors requires the driver to look aside, and the extent of eye movement can be quite large. In addition, there are some blind areas that the mirrors cannot show. Therefore, drivers require a new visual assistance device capable of showing the scene behind the vehicle without looking aside, so that it is possible to instantly understand the spatial relationships of the vehicle with other objects. In addition, such a visual assistance device should have no or little blind area.

We propose a new method to show the scene around and behind the vehicle in the form of a mirror by utilizing a windshield display device. The image of

Z. Pan et al. (Eds.): ICAT 2006, LNCS 4282, pp. 302–313, 2006.

the scene is shown in a virtual mirror, which is displayed as if it were floating in front of the vehicle. The image on the virtual mirror is formed by applying geometric transformation to the image taken by a surveillance camera installed on a signal pole. The transformed image in the virtual mirror can be considered to be the same as that seen with a real mirror in the same position. Therefore, it is easy for the driver to recognize the spatial relationships of the vehicle to other objects.

In section 2, we discuss related works, section 3 presents an outline of the proposed system, and section 4 presents geometric transformation of an image to realize the virtual mirror. The results obtained with our preliminary imaging system in a real road environment are shown in section 5, along with a discussion of the benefits of the system. In section 6, we conclude the paper with a discussion of future work.

2   Related Works

In this paper, we report the development of a visual assistance system capable to show the driver the images of their vehicle with the surrounding scene. We assume that the image will be presented on a windshield display. The image is made from an image taken by a surveillance camera installed at intersections.

In this paper, we discuss the safety around intersections. There are a number of systems for displaying signs to drivers at intersections[7][8]. However, they present only symbolic information, such as road signs and signal status, without informing drivers of the dynamic status of the intersection. A report described research in which the whole traffic scene is displayed from the viewpoint of the air[11]. However, it is not easy to perceive the locations of objects in map-view relative to objects around the vehicle when driving. It is easy for drivers to recognize the spatial relationships of objects in our method that shows the blind area in the form of a mirror. An HUD (Head up Display) is an ideal display device for visual assistance on a vehicle as it can display information in conjunction with the driver's viewpoint. Among the HUDs available, we feel that a windshield display is a promising device for such a purpose. Such displays have already been used in real vehicle to show vehicle status, such as speedometer and gasoline gage readings. Dynamic visual information can also be displayed on the windshield[10]. An advanced research has been proposed for visualizing the area hidden by other vehicles on a windshield display by making a virtual slope based on images from a surveillance camera[9][12].

There have been a number of studies regarding different forms of virtual mirrors. For example, the blind area can be eliminated by extending side mirrors[5][6], and blind areas can be reduced at blind corners by utilizing a virtual mirror, where there are no real mirrors[1]. In the systems[5][6], an in-vehicle camera must be installed to obtain an image of the virtual mirror. Two cameras are needed to realize the virtual mirrors on both sides. Our method, however, does not require any in-vehicle cameras.

3   System Overview

In this paper, we propose a new visual assistance system that can visualize the whole area around the vehicle near an intersection. The image of the area is shown in the form of a mirror, and is designed to present the virtual mirror on a windshield display. We call this "floating virtual mirror". The mirror image is made by processing images taken by a surveillance camera.

We assume that a surveillance camera is installed at an intersection, looking down on the road, and that it can send images of the area surrounding the drivers vehicle. This system can be realized by installing the surveillance camera on the signal pole at the intersection. The images taken by the surveillance camera are transmitted to the drivers vehicle over a wireless network around the intersection.

The image of the floating virtual mirror is presented on a windshield display, and therefore makes use of the drivers viewpoint for verification. Assessment of the floating virtual mirror is made using the drivers viewpoint camera image. This paper describes a visual assistance system in which the image seen by the drivers viewpoint camera is displayed on the windshield.

An outline of making the floating virtual mirror image is shown in Fig. 1.

Suppose the driver is in a white car and is approaching the intersection. Note that vehicles run on the left side of the road in Japan. The drivers view is as shown in the lower left sub-image in Fig. 1. Let us place a blue vehicle in the blind area around the drivers vehicle. The driver will usually attempt to confirm the safety of the area surrounding and behind the vehicle utilizing side mirrors, but may not be able to see the blue vehicle. A surveillance camera is installed alongside a signal device and looks down on the road as shown in the top right sub-image. Note that both the blue vehicle and the drivers (white)

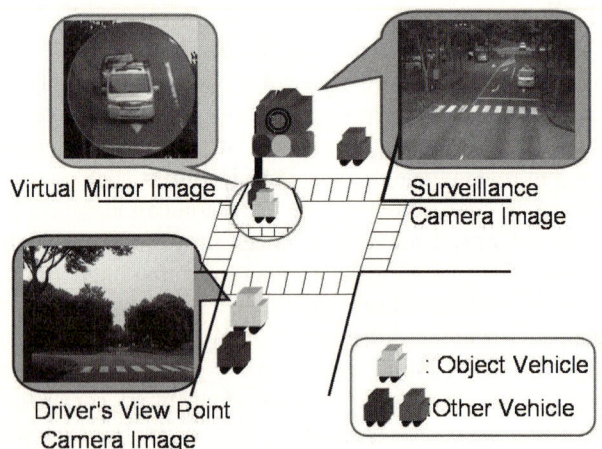

Fig. 1. Virtual mirror implementation

vehicle are captured in the same image taken by the surveillance camera. The image is transmitted, and warped to satisfy the conditions to allow recognition as a mirror. Finally, in the warped image, the corresponding image region that includes both the drivers vehicle and the surrounding area where the blue vehicle is located is trimmed and presented on the drivers viewpoint image. The top left sub-image in figure 1 shows a magnified view of the virtual mirror. The presented region may be perceived as a floating virtual mirror because it is placed in the air overlapping the surveillance camera in the drivers viewpoint image. The size of the virtual mirror can be changed arbitrarily.

If the synthesized image is shown on a windshield display, the driver will not need to move their eyes to see the virtual mirror. This is because the virtual mirror is placed just above the intersection to which the driver pays attention. In addition, the position of the virtual mirror depends on that of the drivers vehicle. For example, the virtual mirror moves upward as the driver approaches the intersection, and is rotated to face the vehicle consistently.

4   Floating Virtual Mirror

The virtual mirror shows the driver the scene around and behind their vehicle. As people are familiar with mirrors, e.g., the curvature of the mirror, they can instantly understand the spatial relationships between their vehicle and other objects in the blind area. A curved mirror cannot show some blind areas, but there are less blind areas that cannot be shown by the virtual mirror.

It is important to make the image of the virtual mirror so that it satisfies the conditions necessary to allow drivers to recognize it as a mirror. In this section, we first discuss the mirror conditions. Then, we describe the image processing to make an image of the virtual mirror and its position for display.

4.1   Mirror Conditions

To visualize the area around the drivers vehicle by the virtual mirror, we transform an image taken by a surveillance camera into an image like that projected

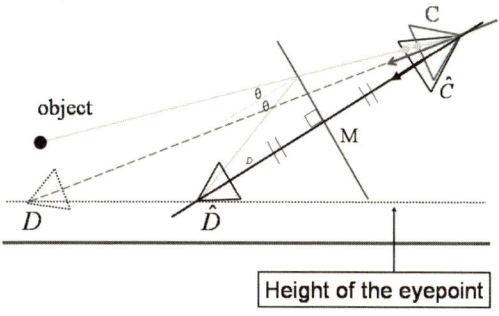

Fig. 2. Satisfying the mirror conditions, and projecting onto the plane

through a mirror. To this end, two conditions should be satisfied between the drivers viewpoint and the surveillance camera. One is that both the drivers line of sight and the optical axis of the surveillance camera should share the same line. The optical axis of the surveillance camera should pass the drivers viewpoint because the eye level is not changed even if the eyes are rotated. The other is that the center of the virtual mirror should be located in the midpoint between the drivers viewpoint and that of the surveillance camera, and the virtual mirror should be orthogonal to this line. We call the two conditions mirror conditions. Fig. 2 shows these two conditions. Here, let C be a surveillance camera, and C' be a surveillance camera that satisfies the mirror conditions for the driver. D indicates the drivers viewpoint and M indicates the virtual mirror. 3D positions of the surveillance cameras are denoted as P_C and $P_{C'}$, respectively, and that of the drivers viewpoint is P_D. The center of the virtual mirror is located at P_M.

According to the mirror conditions, The center position of the virtual mirror P_M depends on both the surveillance camera position P_C and the drivers viewpoint position P_D.

$$P_M = \frac{P_C + P_D}{2} \tag{1}$$

Let us define a point on the virtual mirror P_O. The location of the virtual mirror can be defined as equation (1) and (2). The virtual mirror is displayed in a direction perpendicular to the midpoint of the segment between the drivers viewpoint and the surveillance camera.

$$(P_O - P_M) \cdot (P_C - P_D) = 0 \tag{2}$$

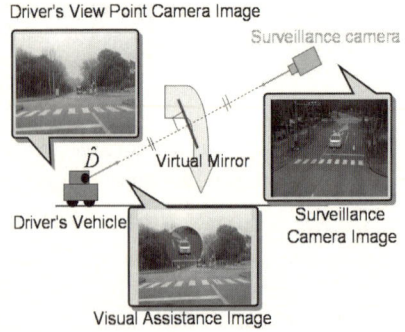

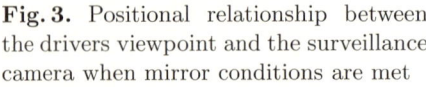

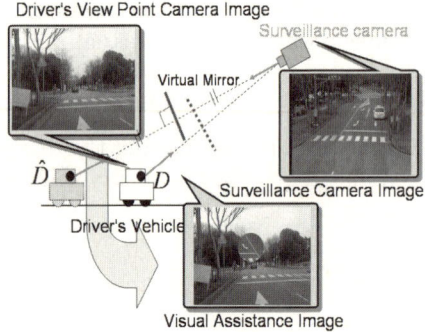

Fig. 3. Positional relationship between the drivers viewpoint and the surveillance camera when mirror conditions are met

Fig. 4. Positional relationship between the drivers viewpoint and the surveillance camera when mirror conditions are not met

Our proposed virtual mirror meets the mirror conditions between the drivers viewpoint and the surveillance camera if we can prepare the camera C' in Fig. 2 and 3. Here, we call the drivers viewpoint that meets the mirror conditions the ideal drivers viewpoint. Let this point be $\hat{D}$. In addition, the drivers viewpoint exists on the optical axis of the surveillance camera. Thus, the driver can visually confirm the safety of the situation around and behind the vehicle while facing forward, as shown in Fig. 3.

As shown in Fig. 3, drivers can see the image as a mirror only if the image from the surveillance camera is inverted appropriately, because it satisfies the mirror conditions. However, as a surveillance camera C is usually fixed and the eye level is fixed, there is only one point $\hat{D}$ where the inverted image of the surveillance camera can be used directly as a mirror image according to the mirror condition-1 (shown in Fig. 3). If the drivers viewpoint is not on $\hat{D}$, the mirror condition-1 cannot be satisfied (shown in Fig. 4). As shown in Fig. 4, the driver cannot instantly understand the spatial relationships between the vehicle and other objects when watching the image of a virtual mirror that does not satisfy the mirror condition.

4.2 Generation of Virtual Mirror Image

To meet the mirror conditions for any viewpoint D at a given height, we transform the surveillance camera image into an image in which the drivers viewpoint is projected in the center. In Fig. 2 as the optical axis of C does not pass P_D, the image cannot be used as the image in the virtual mirror. Hence, we introduce a new camera position, C', which is obtained by rotating C to allow its optical axis to pass D.

It is well known from the literature regarding computer vision that if the camera is modeled by perspective projection, the image warping effect of camera rotation around its focal point can be described by two-dimensional projective transformation[3]. Suppose u is a point on the image plane C, u' represents a point on that of C'. Let us denote their homogeneous coordinates as $\hat{u}$ and $\hat{u}'$, respectively. The two-dimensional projective transformation can project one image plane onto another, and can be described as:

$$\lambda \tilde{u}' = H \tilde{u} \tag{3}$$

where λ is a scale factor and H is the two-dimensional projective transformation matrix.

In this study, we generated an image that satisfies the mirror conditions only by rotating the camera virtually. H is determined if it can compute a rotating angle from C to C', as shown in Fig. 2. That is, H can be computed if the drivers viewpoint D is determined. The 3D position of D is estimated by utilizing RTK-GPS. Standard deviation of measurement by RTK-GPS could be less than 10 cm.

First, we computed the 2D position of D in an image using the 3D position of D estimated by RTK-GPS. Let the position in the image be I_D. Although H has 9 elements, H has 8 degrees of freedom because there is an undetermined scale factor λ in equation (3). Therefore, four pairs of corresponding image points on camera C' are needed to determine the two-dimensional projective transformation.

However, in our approach, only one pair of image points is needed to find a correspondence on the image plane of C and C' because the focal length f of the camera is known. We use the pair I_D on C and the image center of C'.

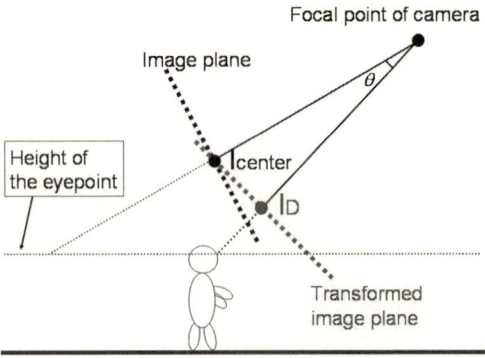

Fig. 5. Outline of calculating the two-dimensional transformation

Fig. 6. Input image

Fig. 7. Output image when the camera is rotated virtually using the two-dimensional projective transformation

Fig. 8. Output image when the camera is actually rotated

Examples of image processed by the two-dimensional projective transformation are shown in Fig. 6 to Fig. 8. In Figs. 7 and 8, the output image is successfully eliminated utilizing the two-dimensional projective transformation.

4.3   Location of Virtual Mirror

As P_C is fixed, P_M is moved in conjunction with the movement of the drivers viewpoint P_D (See Equation (1)). From the drivers viewpoint, P_M is placed to hide the position of the surveillance camera P_C and the mirror is moving back at half speed as the driver approaches the camera. As a result, the virtual mirror appears as if it is floating in the air. Note that the optical features of a mirror are completely preserved on the floating virtual mirror so that the driver does not have any difficulty in recognizing the spatial relationships of the objects in the mirror.

5   Experiment

5.1   Experimental Environment

We set up a surveillance camera C and a wireless Local Area Network in an intersection in the campus of University of Tsukuba. We set the driver's vehicle going into the intersection. The surveillance camera was installed at 5 meter high on the pole, which is almost the same height of traffic signals in Japan. The surveillance camera was directed to look down the lane in which the driver's vehicle was approaching. The 3D position and orientation of the surveillance camera P_C had been calibrated in advance.

Inside the vehicle, we set up a driver's viewpoint camera at driver's eye point for verification.

On conducting the experiment, both the surveillance camera and driver's viewpoint camera are used to record images. In addition, the position of the driver's vehicle P_D is recorded by utilizing RTK-GPS.

5.2   Image Acquisition and Visual Assistance Image

Fig. 9 is an image recorded by the surveillance camera. The white vehicle in Fig. 9 is the driver's vehicle in this experiment. As shown in Fig. 9, the driver's vehicle does not exist on the optical axis (image center) of the surveillance camera C. In other word, it cannot be used as an image in the virtual mirror directly.

Fig. 10 shows the image from driver's viewpoint camera. The driver sees the road in this manner. In the middle of the image, there are the pole and the surveillance camera.

We conducted two-dimensional projective transformation to Fig. 9 to meet the mirror conditions. The warped image is shown in Fig. 11. In Fig. 11, the driver's vehicle is reprojected at the center of the image plane of the camera C'. In other word, it meets the mirror conditions because the driver's vehicle exists on the optical axis of the surveillance camera.

Then, finally, a region around the driver's vehicle is trimmed and it is superimposed in the driver's viewpoint camera image. The result is shown in Fig. 12. A position of the virtual mirror is determined by equation(1)). The size of the

Fig. 9. Surveillance camera image

Fig. 10. Driver's viewpoint camera image

Fig. 11. Source of virtual mirror image

Fig. 12. Virtual mirror imposed to driver's viewpoint camera imae

floating virtual mirror can be changed arbitrary. Note that the driver can easily check the area around his/her vehicle, including both the side area and the rear area simultaneously by watching the floating virtual mirror. In addition, the driver can instantly recognize where the objects are if they exist because it surely works as if it were a normal mirror. Therefore, the driver can confirm the safety of the surrounding area of the driver's vehicle when he/she drives. The other results are shown in Fig. 13. The images are made for the different locations along the lane.

In our current implementation, there might be a possibility of hiding some objects behind the virtual mirror in a traffic scene, which can be seen under normal circumstance (shown in Fig.12). For example, the virtual mirror may hide the traffic signal if it is set close to the signal device. Therefore, we consider showing additional information with the virtual mirror, i.e. a virtual mirror with visual signal sign display.

Fig. 13. Example of the visual assistance system. Driver's viewpoint images (left), and visual assistance images (right). The radius of the mirror was seto to 1.5m. The driver's vehicle was approaching to the intersection.

6   Conclusion

In this paper, we proposed a new visual assistance system that can visualize the whole area surrounding a drivers vehicle in the form of a mirror by utilizing images taken by a surveillance camera. The virtual mirror is very effective for recognizing the scene around the vehicle because the virtual mirror acts as if it were a real mirror.

We clarified the mirror conditions that must be satisfied in making an image in the virtual mirror, and presented an image processing algorithm to realize the virtual mirror. The results of this experiment indicated that our approach is promising as a visual assistance system for drivers.

In future works, it will be necessary to combine the virtual mirror and the information hidden by the virtual mirror. It is also very important to implement this scheme on a vehicle and to conduct on-line tests for subject evaluations.

Acknowledgment. This study was conducted as part of the government project, Situation and Intention Recognition for Risk Finding and Avoidance with the support of the Ministry of Education, Culture, Sports, Science, and Technology of Japan.

References

1. K. Kojima, A. Sato, F. Taya, Y. Kameda, and Y Ohta, "NaviView:Visual Assistance by Virtual Mirrors at Blind Intersection," Proceedings of the 8th International IEEE Conference on Intelligent Transportation Systems, pp. 592-597, 2005.
2. R. Koch and J. M. Frahm, "Visual-Geometric Scene Reconstruction from Image Streams," Proceedings of the Vision Modeling and Visualization Conference, pp. 367-374 2001.
3. R. Szeliski, Microsoft Corporation, "Video Mosaics for Virtual Environments", IEEE Computer Graphics and Applications, Vol. 16, No. 2, pp. 22-30, 1996.
4. S. Gupte, O. Masoud, R. F. K. Martin, and N. P. Papanikolopoulos, "Detection and Classification of Vehicles," IEEE Transcations on Intelligent Transportation Systems, Vol. 3, No. 1, pp. 37-47, 2002.
5. S. Pardhy, C. Shankwitz, and M. Donath, "A Virtual Mirror For Assisting Drivers," Proceedings of the IEEE Inteligent Vehicles Symposium, pp. 255-260, 2000.
6. M. Sergi, C. Shankwitz, and M. Donath, "LIDAR-based Vehicle Tracking for a Virtual Mirror, " Proceedings of IEEE Inteligent Vehicle Symposium, pp. 333-338, 2003.
7. X. Shi, J. Hu, Y. Xu, and J. Song, "A Simulation Study on Agent-network Based Route Guidance System," Proceedings of the 8th International IEEE Conference on Intelligent Transportation Systems, pp. 248-253, 2005.
8. K. C. Fuerstenberg, IBEO Automobile Sensor GmbH, "A New European Approach for Intersection Safety," Proceedings of the 8th International IEEE Conference on Intelligent Transportation Systems, pp. 432-436, 2005.
9. T. Yano, E. Ichihara, and Y. Ohta, "NaviView:Visual Assistance of Drivers by Using Roadside Cameras Visualization of Occluded Cars at an Intersection," World Multiconference on Systemics, Cybernetics and Informatics, X3, Part 2, pp. 175-180, 2001.

10. A. Sato, Y. Kameda, and Y. Ohta, "Adaptive Positioning on Windshield for Information Display," 12th World Congress on Intelligent Transport Systems, 12 pages, 2005.
11. E. Ichihara and Y. Ohta, "NaviView: Visual Assistance Using Roadside Cameras - Evaluation of Virtual Virews -," Proceedings of IEEE Intelligent. Transportation Systems, pp.322-327, 2000.
12. F. Taya, Y. Kameda, and Y. Ohta, "NaviView:Virtual Slope Visualization of Blind Area at an Intersection," 12th World Congress on Intelligent Transport Systems, 8 pages, 2005.

A Scalable Framework for Distributed Virtual Reality Using Heterogeneous Processors

Qishi Wu[1], Jinzhu Gao[2], and Mengxia Zhu[3]

[1] Dept of Computer Science
University of Memphis
Memphis, TN 38152
qishiwu@memphis.edu
[2] Dept of Computer Science
University of Minnesota
Morris, MN 56267
gaoj@morris.umn.edu
[3] Dept of Computer Science
Southern Illinois University
Carbondale, IL 62901
mengxia@cs.siu.edu

Abstract. We propose a scalable framework for virtual reality systems in a distributed environment. As the application scope of and member participation in a virtual environment increase, information sharing among geographically distributed users becomes critical and challenging. In the proposed framework, we partition the virtual environment into a group of cells and upload them to a number of heterogeneous Internet nodes. When a user sends a request to explore the distant virtual environment, visible cells will be identified and processed in parallel to produce a minimal amount of imagery results for remote transmission. To ensure scalability, we extend our scalable occlusion culling scheme using Plenoptic Opacity Function to speed up the identification process of visible cells in a virtual environment. We perform effective occlusion culling in two passes based on a non-binary opacity definition. Our experimental results justify both the efficiency and scalability of our framework in exploring large-scale virtual environments.

Keywords: distributed virtual reality, occlusion culling, logistical networking, plenoptic opacity functions.

1 Introduction

Virtual reality (VR) is acquiring increasing importance due to its extensive use in a wide spectrum of applications including education, medical treatment, vehicle simulation, military training, and digital entertainment. Many of these applications typically consist of a team of collaborators such as instructors, doctors, engineers, scientists, or game players that are geographically distributed across the world. In order to create richer and more lifelike environments, VR system developers need to build and render larger and more complex models at a faster rate, which inevitably produces large

Z. Pan et al. (Eds.): ICAT 2006, LNCS 4282, pp. 314 323, 2006.
© Springer-Verlag Berlin Heidelberg 2006

volumes of simulation datasets over a short period of time. Such large volumes of datasets have posed a significant challenge on issues of data storage, information sharing, network transport, user interactivity, and robustness of the system.

The growing disparity in the proportion of available computational resources and the increasing size of virtual environment (VE) have made it even more challenging to explore distributed VE in a reliable and interactive manner. Interactivity can be achieved by using parallel clusters or supercomputers. However, these high-performance computing facilities are very expensive and usually not deployed at all geographical locations where the participating users reside, hence restricting data sharing among distributed users. Recently, several researchers have launched their efforts on developing distributed virtual reality systems that pool globally distributed and heterogeneous computing resources together to address the issues of large-scale data storage and processing [1, 2]. Since these distributed systems are deployed on Internet nodes with diverse computing capabilities and unpredictable network connections, interactivity, scalability and robustness become the major issues in the development of such systems. Occlusion culling is a common approach to expediting the visual exploration of large-scale virtual environment. When a considerable portion of the scene is occluded by other objects or has very little contribution to the final image, the sooner and more effectively those regions are detected and culled from the rendering pipeline, the better acceleration can be achieved. Unfortunately, applying occlusion culling in large-scale distributed virtual reality systems has remained a challenging problem. Most known occlusion culling algorithms are inherently sequential, primarily due to the strict order of front-to-back data traversal. With conventional methods, it is difficult to obtain a scalable parallel implementation on prevalent parallel computing platforms [6, 8].

In this paper, we present a general, efficient and scalable VR framework that leverages data reduction techniques for rendering acceleration in a distributed environment. We address the scalability challenges in computing occlusion culling by applying *Plenoptic Opacity Functions (POF)*. In [7], we first introduced the concept of POF for volume rendering. Here, we expand our overall framework to support distributed virtual reality using heterogeneous processors.

The remainder of this paper discusses these advances in more detail. In Section 2, we present some background in distributed virtual reality systems and data reduction techniques. The details of the framework and POF assisted occlusion culling are described in Sections 3 and 4, respectively. We present and discuss our preliminary results in Sections 5. Section 6 concludes our work and discusses possible directions for future research in the general area of distributed virtual reality.

2 Background

The need of processing massive volumes of datasets to support large-scale virtual reality has made parallel algorithms indispensable for acceleration. Molnar *et. al.* [14] classified the communication patterns in parallel rendering algorithms into three categories: sort-first, sort-middle and sort-last, based on where in the rendering pipeline the data is redistributed. It is usually useful to employ multiple communication stages in the rendering pipeline to obtain a balanced load. For instance, in [15], a hybrid sort-first and sort-last parallel rendering algorithm was used on PC clusters.

Occlusion culling has been widely used in polygon rendering applications [9-12]. For example, in [11], an occlusion test is performed in image space by comparing the bounding box of each Octree cell with a hierarchically organized z-buffer during front-to-back Octree traversals. Occluder fusion was proposed in [9] using graphics hardware to render the occluders and update the frame buffer accordingly. Occlusion culling can be performed in object space as well, such as Coorg's approach based on shadow volume or shadow frustum of large convex occluders [12]. In [10], an efficient occlusion culling method was implemented to render large-scale polygonal meshes using the metric of potential occluding capability, referred to as "solidity", which is estimated from the number of polygons within each cell. The algorithms discussed above have successfully illustrated that the occlusion culling technique can effectively improve the rendering performance, especially for large-scale polygonal models.

Due to the increasing demand on remote collaborations, the VR community has recently developed several distributed virtual reality systems. A Networked Virtual Environment (NVE) system, called WVLNET, is presented in [1]. This system provides advanced interactivity and supports collaborations among geographically located users. [2] describes a distributed virtual walkthrough system, CyberWalk, which also allows the information sharing among users at different geographical locations. Multiple servers and an adaptive region partitioning technique are utilized to achieve interactivity.

3   The Distributed Framework

Advances in modeling and simulation technologies enable us to produce a virtual environment with a tremendous amount of objects. To support a shared virtual environment with maximum throughput, we propose a scalable framework for distributed virtual reality as shown in Figure 1.

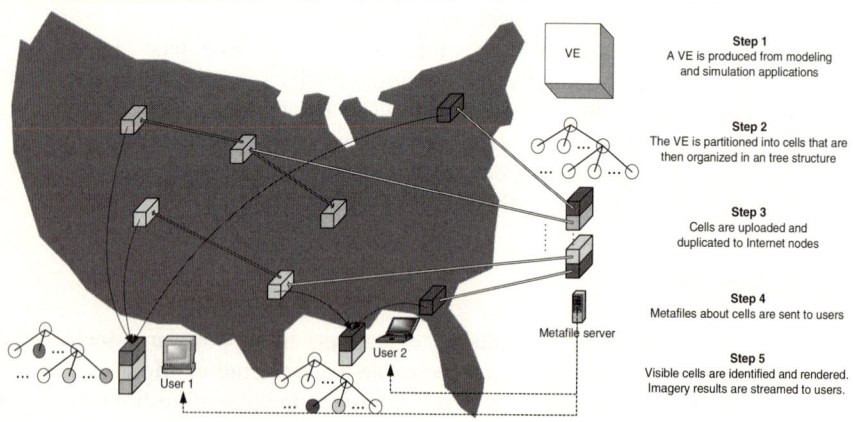

Fig. 1. The scalable framework for distributed virtual reality

This work demonstrated that, by using scalable occlusion culling technique together with a distributed storage system deployed on Logistical networking (LN) [3], a large number of distributed heterogeneous computing nodes, called "depot", can be used to perform multi-user exploration of the VE without the support of dedicated network connections and high-performance computing resources.

Within the system framework, Figure 1 also shows the procedure for data processing and user interactions. After a VE has been generated, preprocessed, uploaded in segments and replicated to LN depots spread across the network, a user is able to explore the VE on 100's of processors. Occlusion culling is performed at the beginning of the run-time pipeline to eliminate the processing cost of invisible regions.

The distributed data storage system in this framework is built on LN, and in particular the Internet Backplane Protocol (IBP), which manages the shared storage and computing resources within a collaborating community. With a highly generic protocol, LN incorporates heterogeneous underlying storage and computational technologies. In terms of storage, IBP is more suitable for being used in a scalable, wide-area community than standard protocols such as iSCSI and the ANSI T10/Object Storage Device standard. IBP has built-in features that allow it to be used by a community that is not tightly bound together by administrative mechanisms, such as a common notion of user identity, or by technical standards, such as file system protocols that enforce a particular style of synchronization between users.

4 POF-Assisted Occlusion Culling

Typically, a large-scale VE consists of thousands of objects and millions of polygons. Since most of these polygons are highly opaque, occlusion culling can be a very effective solution to reducing the processing cost. In this section, we introduce our opacity pre-computation and encoding scheme that is amenable for large-scale polygon models. We follow a coarse-grained approach and first partition the VE into cells. For each cell, similar to the preprocessing described in [7], we compute its opacity, the capability to occlude the objects behind it. Different from the opacity definition in volume rendering, here the opacity depends on the area of the screen footprint of the objects inside each cell, which is still view-dependent. To avoid run-time opacity computation, the opacity variation of each cell from different view angles is encoded in a function, called a Plenoptic Opacity Function (POF). By "plenoptic", we mean that, for any cell, a single opacity function can fully capture its view dependent variation, under all possible external views. The POF is always represented in a space-efficient form to minimize the storage cost. At runtime, the opacity of a cell for any view can then be obtained by a straightforward evaluation of the POFs. Using the POF-based approach, we can perform occlusion culling efficiently without omitting any potentially visible cells; i.e. the algorithm stays conservative. In the following, we introduce: (i) the concept of a POF with regard to a cell in a VE, (ii) calculation of POF for virtual reality applications, and (iii) run-time visibility determination based on POFs.

4.1 POF Basics

Using POF preprocessing, the objects in a given cell can be rendered from all directions, and the opacities of the pixels in various projections can be stored as a function of the viewing angle. POFs therefore encode complete information about the cell's overall occluding capability from different views. At runtime, given a specific viewing direction, the POFs allow quick composition of cells to determine the visible region of the VE. This is done without accessing the individual voxel data or performing detailed rendering, thereby eliminating the need to store all pixels from all potential view angles.

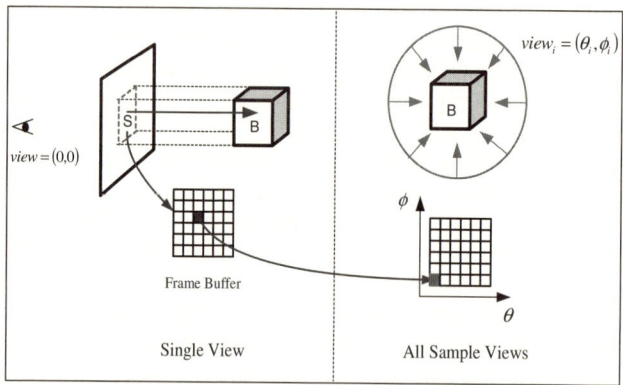

Fig. 2. For each view (left), the opacity channel of a cell B, is rendered into a frame buffer. Suppose that the pixel shaded with blue has the minimal opacity among all non-empty pixels. This minimal opacity value is stored into the entry shaded with green in a 2D table indexed by θ and ϕ (right). The same process is done for all sample views around the cell.

We make two simplifications to obtain a practical form of POF. First, to make sure that our algorithm is conservative, we only capture the minimal occluding capability of a cell from each viewing angle. Hence, we only need to store the lowest opacity among all pixels in the projection of a cell. The POF of a cell is then simplified to be a scalar function of two variables, θ and ϕ, in spherical coordinates, greatly reducing the storage overhead. Second, we estimate the true form of POF for each cell from its discretization, i.e. by taking sample views around the cell. It has been shown that the visibility information under an arbitrary viewing angle can be estimated by interpolating from the visibility information of a limited number of neighboring sample views [16]. Hence, the underlying POF of the cell can be estimated with a reasonable level of accuracy using a manageable number of sample views.

In Figure 2, we illustrate the overall process of POF estimation. We construct a discretized POF by taking samples around the cell, and illustrate a 2-D POF table organized with respect to θ and ϕ in the right portion of Figure 2. For the sample view (0, 0) in the left portion of Figure 2, an opacity image S of the cell B is rendered. We search all non-empty pixels in S for the lowest value. This lowest opacity value, representing the minimal occluding capability of B, is stored at the corresponding location (0, 0) in the POF table. To ensure correctness, we need to choose an appropriate resolution for S such that each cell's projection area is larger than one pixel.

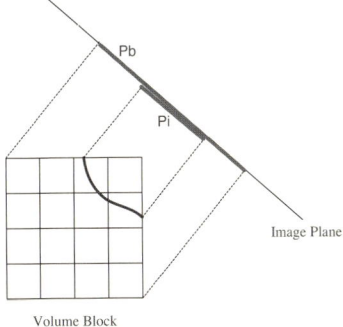

Opacity = Length(Pi)/Length(Pb)

Fig. 3. A 2-D demonstration of the opacity estimation for a cell. *Length(Pi)* is the number of pixels covered by the footprint of the objects. *Length(Pb)* is the number of pixels covered by the footprint of the cell's boundaries.

The discretized POF table is used directly for run-time visibility estimation. We can derive a space-efficient form of POF using function fitting based on a polynomial or spline [17]. In the experiments, we have found that third-order polynomials can provide good approximations with a small set of parameters.

4.2 POF Calculation for Virtual Reality Applications

For polygon models in a VE, we use the term "opacity" to represent the concept of the occluding capability of objects inside the cell. Obviously, opacity here depends on the number and orientation of the polygons. We use the following formula to estimate a cell's opacity from a given view, and opacities from all views are stored in the POF:

$$\text{Opacity} = \frac{\text{proj}(S)}{\text{proj}(B)} \tag{1}$$

where S represents all the objects inside the cell under investigation, and B is the bounding box of the cell. The function "proj" computes the number of pixels covered by the screen space projection of the primitive. Intuitively, the less area the objects covers on the screen, relative to the screen footprint of the cell's bounding box, the more transparent the cell is. Figure 3 shows a 2-D example of Equation 1.

Computing the "proj" function can be accelerated in hardware using the occlusion query capability on current graphics cards. In those queries, the number of pixels that pass the visibility test is returned. S and B must be rendered to frame buffer separately to compute Equation 1. Clearly, the opacity estimation defined by Equation 1 is a view-dependent operation. Computing Equation 1 from a grid of sample views around the cell is necessary to produce a POF.

Although the accuracy of POF depends on the number of sample views, it is impractical to pre-compute and store the opacities from all possible views. Luckily points out that the visibility information from a limited number of sample views can be used to interpolate and estimate the visibility information from any practical sample view [16]. Therefore, pre-computing the opacity information for a manageable set of evenly spaced sample viewpoints is sufficient for us to perform effective occlusion culling.

4.3   Run-Time Occlusion Culling

At runtime, we determine the occluding capability of each cell by evaluating POFs for the current view (θ, ϕ). Then, all cells are traversed in a front-to-back order. As each cell is visited, we first check its opacity and then incorporate its occluding capability (opacity) into an opacity buffer, which is used to indicate the opaqueness of the region in the frame buffer. To test the visibility of each cell, the screen footprint of the cell is first computed. Our visibility test is to check whether all pixels within the cell's screen footprint, in the opacity buffer, have reached a pre-defined threshold of opaqueness, for instance 0.95. If it is false, the cell is considered as visible and its opacity is accumulated into the pixels inside its projection area; otherwise, some additional actions must be taken for cell culling.

Since the exact physical locations of objects inside a cell play an important role in determining occlusion, only using the opacity computed by Equation 1 does not guarantee conservativeness. Therefore, although the above process can identify most visible cells, there is still a chance that some visible cells are culled, resulting in holes in some areas. To address this issue, we perform a second pass that identifies all remaining visible cells. In the second pass, all objects inside the visible cells identified in the first pass form the set of occluders, and the remaining cells need to be tested against this set. Hence, the cells identified as occluded in this pass are truly occluded. The second pass can be implemented in either software or hardware.

The software implementation of the second pass is very similar to the algorithm in the first pass. The pixels in the opacity buffer store a "1" if the corresponding pixels are covered by previously rendered objects, or "0", otherwise. The only caveat is that when a cell is identified as visible in the second pass, the opacity of the cell is not accumulated into the opacity buffer. This is because, in the second pass, only the actual objects determined to be visible from the first pass is used to perform the occlusion culling. The hardware implementation utilizes occlusion query functions. The objects inside visible cells identified in the first pass are rendered into the frame buffer. Before the queries are sent in the second pass, writing into the frame buffers is disabled. Then, the bounding faces of each undecided cell are rendered in the second pass to query for visibility. The visibility status of each cell is determined by the query results.

In sum, as long as the front-to-back order is maintained, POF-assisted visibility discovery is straightforward and carries a low overhead because only the coarse-grained subdivision of the VE is used to perform the culling. The POFs also consume little storage space, which allows us to replicate the POFs of all cells on every node participating in the visibility determination process, which is especially useful if the rendering is done by a PC cluster since it alleviates the inter-process dependency. Parallel execution of the visibility tests could further reduce the absolute time to determine visibility.

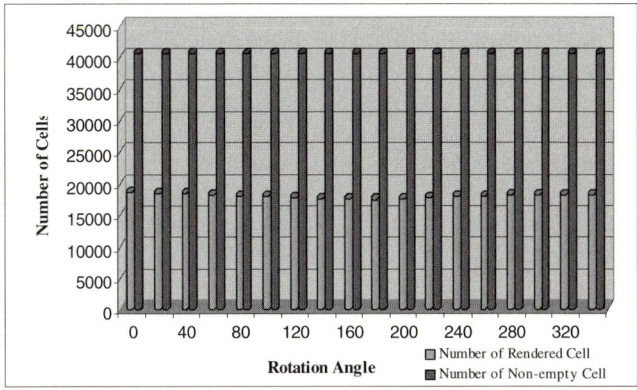

Fig. 4. The occlusion culling effect of our POF-assisted method at 18 test views, rotating the viewpoint around the Y-axis

5   Results and Discussion

To demonstrate the effectiveness of our framework, we tested it on 160 depots from the PlanetLab project [4]. Although these depots are server-class machines, they are shared among a large community. PlanetLab nodes are even virtualized as ``slices'' to enable large-scale sharing. Loads on these nodes differ dramatically and vary over time.   We have also developed a simulation model and partitioned the VE into 110,592 cells. All those cells together with the polygons inside them are uploaded to depots.

Table 1. Culling performance comparison. The table compares the number of visible cells identified at each pass by three different algorithms. All three algorithms finish in 2 passes. Isovalue=700.

Pass No.	Binary opacity (no propagation)	Binary opacity (propagation)	POF assisted
1	2770	4557	6255
2	27585	15775	6805
Total	30355	20332	13060

The performance we achieved with those 160 shared, distributed heterogeneous deports is comparable to that of a dedicated PC cluster of 80 nodes, each of which is equipped with a dedicated 2.2 GHz P4 CPU with 512 KB cache and 2GB of main memory, assuming 90% parallel utilization on the cluster.

The POFs are computed only once in a pre-processing stage and in a straightforward parallel fashion. That is, each depot node only computes POFs for the cells distributed to it and all processors perform this task in parallel. In our experiments, we used 1296 sample views corresponding to a 36×36 spherical coordinate grid. If using 160 processors, it takes about one second to finish the POF computation.

The POFs for each cell can be stored either discretely in a raster table or in a closed form as a third order polynomial. The size of the raster POF table is proportional to the number of sample views. For the model we use, with 1296 sample views, the total storage requires about 55 Mbytes. In the closed form using third order polynomials, we can encode a POF table using ten coefficients, amounting to 40 bytes. Using the polynomial encoding, only about 5 Mbytes is required. However, compression with polynomials may cause the POF encoding to be slightly more conservative. For example, out of 46,037 non-empty cells, 10,862 are determined to be visible when using the discrete POF table, while 12,356 are found to be visible when using the polynomial POF representation. Since both forms of POF encoding cull about 73% of non-empty cells, we believe that the third order polynomial representation is a practical option to improve storage efficiency.

Since our POF-assisted occlusion culling is able to identify most of the visible cells in the first pass, it is not totally necessary to have more than two passes in the actual implementation, which can substantially reduce the synchronization overhead compared to the previous multi-pass algorithm [6]. Traditionally, the occluding capability of a cell is a binary value, either fully opaque or fully transparent, whereas POF uses a non-binary encoding. To show the advantage of using non-binary opacity values in POF, in addition to our new algorithm, we implemented two other algorithms for comparison. The first algorithm uses binary opacity values: if a cell is identified as visible, its opacity is set to 1 (full opacity). The second algorithm optimizes the first algorithm by mimicking the propagation method used in [13]: if a cell is found to be visible, its neighbor cells are also identified as visible. The POF-assisted algorithm and the other two algorithms finish in two passes. In all three cases, the second pass is meant for identifying all the remaining visible cells missed in the first pass. Table 1 gives the number of visible cells identified by the three algorithms during each pass. It shows that the POF-assisted method is able to identify 50% more visible cells in the first pass, and hence is able to acquire a larger occluder to cull more invisible cells in the second pass. Because of this, our new method reduces the number of the passes for visibility query while minimizing the number of invisible cells identified as visible in the second pass.

With the pre-computed POF information, our occlusion culling algorithm can cull away the invisible regions of the VE very effectively, and our algorithm does not need to re-compute opacity information each time the view changes. Figure 4 shows the numbers of rendered cells as we rotate the viewpoint around the Y-axis to demonstrate that the performance of POF-assisted occlusion culling is consistent for varying view angles.

6   Conclusions and Future Work

In this paper, we proposed a scalable framework for distributed virtual reality systems using heterogeneous processors. In this framework, a virtual environment is partitioned into a number of cells that are uploaded to and duplicated on depots in a shared and distributed storage system. To minimize the response time, we modify our previously proposed POF-assisted visibility culling scheme in such a way that invisible regions in the VE can be identified at the beginning of the pipeline and skipped in the later rendering process. To test the efficiency of our framework, we developed a simulation model and test our framework on 160 distributed heterogeneous depots.

In the future, we plan to investigate other major issues in a distributed virtual reality system, such as multi-resolution modeling and rendering, prefetching, and advanced motion tracking. Those acceleration techniques will be further explored and incorporated into our framework.

References

1. C. Joslin, T. Molet, and N. Magnenat-Thalmann, "Distributed Virtual Reality Systems", *citeseer.ist.psu.edu/534042.html*.
2. B. Ng, R. W.H. Lau, A. Si, and F. W.B. Li, "Multi-Server Support for Large Scale Distributed Virtual Environment", *IEEE Transactions on Multimedia*, vol. 7, no. 6, pp. 1054-1065, 2005.
3. M. Beck, T. Moore, and J. S. Plank, "An End-to-end Approach to Globally Scalable Network Storage", *Proc. of ACM SIGCOMM, 2002*.
4. PlanetLab. http://www.planet-lab.org/.
5. E. Lum, K. Ma, and J. Clyne, "A Hardware-Assisted Scalable Solution for Interactive Volume Rendering of Time-varying Data," *IEEE Trans. on Visualization and Computer Graphics*, vol. 8, no. 3, pp. 286-301, 2002.
6. J. Gao and H.-W. Shen, "Parallel View-dependent Isosurface Extraction Using Multi-pass Occlusion Culling," *Proc. IEEE Symposium in Parallel and Large Data Visualization and Graphics*, pp. 67-74, 2001.
7. J. Gao, J. Huang, H.-W. Shen, and J. Kohl, "Visibility Culling Using Plenoptic Opacity Functions for Large Volume Visualization," *Proc. IEEE Visualization'03,* pp. 341-348, 2003.
8. J. Huang, N. Shareef, R. Crawfis, P. Sadayappan, and K. Mueller, "A Parallel Splatting Algorithm with Occlusion Culling," *Proc. 3rd Eurographics Workshop on Parallel Graphics and Visualization*, pp. 125-132, 2000.
9. H. Zhang, D. Manocha, T. Hudson, and K.E. Hoff III, "Visibility Culling Using Hierarchical Occlusion Maps," *Proc. ACM SIGGRAPH'97*, pp. 77-88, 1997.
10. J. Klosowski and C. Silva, "Efficient Conservative Visibility Culling Using the Prioritized-layered Projection Algorithm," *IEEE Trans. on Visualization and Computer Graphics*, vol. 7, no. 4, pp. 365-379, 2001.
11. N. Greene, "Hierarchical Polygon Tiling with Coverage Masks," *Proc. SIGGRAPH'96*, pp. 65-74, 1996.
12. S. Coorg and S. Teller, "Temporally Coherence Conservative Visibility," *Proc. Twelfth Annual Symposium on Computational Geometry*, pp. 78-87, 1996.
13. Z. Liu, A. Finkelstein, and K. Li, "Progressive view-dependent isosurface propagation," *Proc. Vissym'01*, 2001.
14. S. Molnar, M. Cox, D. Ellsworth, and H. Fuchs, "A sorting classification of parallel rendering," *IEEE Computer Graphics and Applications*, vol. 14, no. 4, pp. 23-32, 1994.
15. R. Samanta, T. Funkhouser, K. Li, and J.P. Singh, "Hybrid sort-first and sort-last parallel rendering with a cluster of PCs," *Eurographics Workshop on Graphics Hardware*, 2000.
16. E. Zhang and G. Turk, "Visibility-Guided Simplification," *Proc. IEEE Visualization'02*, pp. 267-274, 2002.
17. W. H. Press, S. A. Teukolsky, W. T. Vetterling, and B. P. Flannery, "Numerical recipes in C: The art of scientific computing," 1992.

A Collaborative Virtual Reality Environment for Molecular Modeling

Sungjun Park[1], Jun Lee[2], and Jee-In Kim[3,*]

[1] Game Engineering, Hoseo University, Cheonan, Korea
sjpark@office.hoseo.ac.kr
[2] Computer Science & Engineering, Konkuk University, Seoul, Korea
junlee@konkuk.ac.kr
[3] CAESIT, Konkuk University, Seoul, Korea
jnkm@konkuk.ac.kr

Abstract. A collaborative molecular modeling environment based on virtual reality techniques is proposed in this paper. The environment consists of a VR based molecular modeling system (VRMMS), a distributed processing system (DPS) and a web service server (WSS). The proposed environment was evaluated in terms of accuracy, performance, and collaboration. The accuracy of the simulation was examined by comparing the simulation results with those produced by the most popular simulation tool, Insight II. The distributed processing system of 4 computers showed good computing performance. The collaborative works of molecular modeling were successfully exercised and the total processing time of the collaboration was 3 times faster than that of a single user's performance.

1 Introduction

Molecular modeling, which is a part of Computational Chemistry, is the science to express molecular structures computationally and simulate their behaviors with the equations of quantum and classical physics. So, scientists are required to have correct three dimensional (3D) structures of molecules and precise results from computer simulation. It can be applied to develop new materials, new drugs, and so on. Many tools of molecular modeling are available not only in the public domain but also in the commercial field. The application areas of the tools include visualization, simulation, web application, etc. So, visualization, simulation, manipulation, real-time rendering, web collaboration, and so on are required technologies. Researchers carefully view and examine 3 D structures of molecules using computer simulation of their behaviors. If multiple researchers could work together, the performance of their researches would be enhanced. The time and energy required for the researches could also be saved.

In this paper, we propose a collaborative VR environment for molecular modeling which consists of a virtual reality based molecular modeling system (VRMMS), a distributed processing system (DPS) and a web service server (WSS). Since biologists

---

* Corresponding author.

Z. Pan et al. (Eds.): ICAT 2006, LNCS 4282, pp. 324 – 333, 2006.

are not necessarily computer experts, they may achieve more productivity with the support of virtual reality technologies such as gesture based interactions, a large display device with a stereoscopic view, a haptic interface, and so on rather than conventional devices such as a mouse and a keyboard. The VR users are expected to have benefits from stereoscopic 3D visualization of molecular models and intuitive interactions with them.

For the simulation of behaviors of molecules, high performance computing is required. A distributed processing system (DPS) is developed to achieve the goal. DPS of the proposed environment consists of 4 computers and its master server controls the computing resources. A job management algorithm is developed to enable the VR users to execute real-time interactions with 3D molecular models.

A web service server (WSS) plays a key role in the collaborative environment. It bridges the VR users and DPS so that simulated behaviors of molecular models can be dynamically and immediately transferred to the VR users. It also delivers the simulated behaviors of molecules to remote users. The inputs from the VR users and the remote users such as gestures are interpreted and delivered to DPS as new parameters for the molecular simulation. The remote users can access WSS through the Internet and their computers do not necessarily have high graphical capability. An adaptive level of detail (LOD) technique is developed for WSS in order to provide precise 3D images with the remote users. The implementation of WSS is based on the Web Service standard. Therefore, the system is flexible and compatible with any application software that satisfies the standard.

2   Related Works

Since information about 3D structures of molecules is essential in molecular modeling, visualization is one of key technologies required for molecular modeling. The 3D structures of proteins are major targets to be visualized [3]. RASMol [4] is the most popular and successful 3D visualization tool. Protein Explorer [5] is a visualization tool running on the web. The project GROPE [6] aims to develop a haptic system of scientific visualization. VMD [7] is another famous molecular visualization system.

In order to study behaviors of molecules, simulation is necessary. The simulation of molecular behaviors is another key technologies required for molecular modeling [8, 9]. Since it requires high computing power, parallel computing and distributed processing are used. Unfortunately, such a high performance computing system is not easily accessible by many researchers. It is also expensive to use.

Like many other scientific fields, collaboration of researchers is indispensable in molecular modeling. Web is an excellent technology for the collaboration. Including experimental results, references and documents, much valuable information can be shared [6, 10]. BioCore [11] supports collaborative works for molecular modeling through the Internet. It consists of Workbench, Notebook, Conferences, and Documents. They perform molecular energy simulation, real-time monitoring, communication among participants and document management, respectively. BioCore can be combined existing tools such as VMD and NAMD.

BioCore uses VMD as its visualization component. Its users complain that the rendering speed becomes slow if they use general PC class computers, notebooks, or PDA's.

This means that real-time collaboration through the Internet with multiple types of computing devices does not seem to become highly active in near future. Also, the network system of BioCore is not open standard. Therefore, their flexibility is not quite high. We could not easily combine BioCore with other application software.

3 System

3.1 Overview

The proposed environment can be described as shown in Fig. 1. VRMMS is a virtual reality system and provides with intuitive interaction methods for a VR user [12]. DPS is a working horse of the environment and performs computations for molecular simulations [13]. WWS is a web service server for distributed processing and collaboration with cooperative clients.

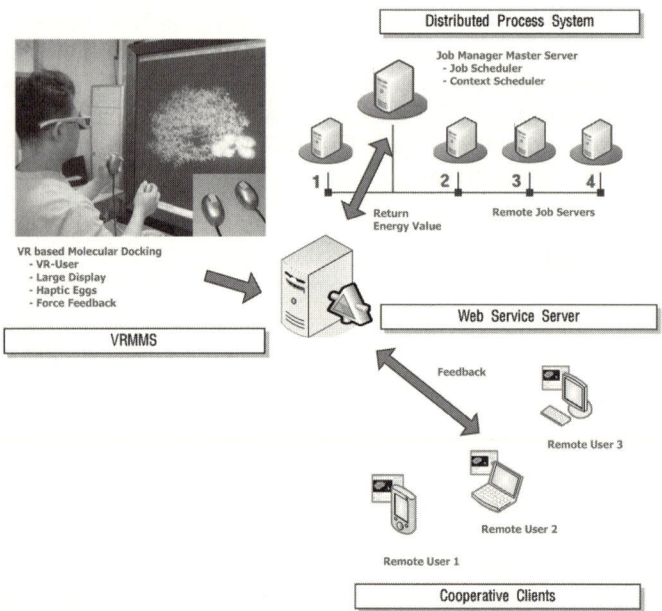

Fig. 1. System Overview

3.2 Virtual Reality Based Molecular Management System

The most critical part of molecular modeling is a docking procedure. The docking procedure aims to find a candidate molecule (a ligand) which can be combined with a receptor at a specific position called an active site (In biochemistry, a receptor is a protein on the cell membrane or within the cytoplasm or cell nucleus that binds to a specific molecule, such as a neurotransmitter, hormone, or other substance, and initiates the cellular response to the ligand. Ligand-induced changes in the behavior of receptor proteins result in physiological changes that constitute the biologicalactions of the ligands[19]). Encrgy between a receptor and a ligand should be calculated in real time, when the receptor and the ligand are combined during the docking simulation. A VR user can view stereoscopic 3D images of molecular models and manipulate the models using intuitive interaction methods such as hand gestures during docking as shown in Fig. 2-(b) [12].

A haptic interface is also developed for gesture-based interactions. It is called Haptic Eggs because it is a pair of devices whose shape and size are quite similar to an egg. Each Haptic Egg has a touch sensor and a motor. The touch sensor behaves like a button of a mouse. The motor generates haptic feedback to VR users, when two molecular models can be combined at active sites. The new interface utilizes direct manipulation and reflects real-time behaviours of users with two hands..

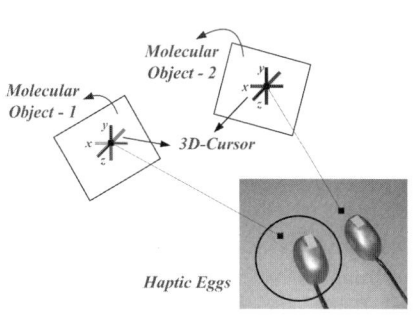 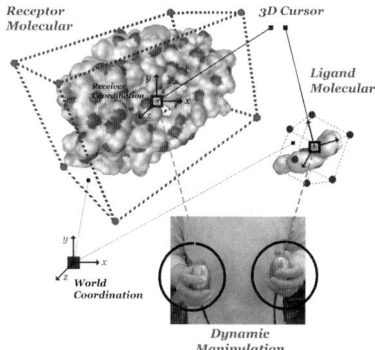

Fig. 2(a). 3D-Cursor and Haptic Eggs   **Fig. 2(b).** Docking simulation with both hands using gestures

3.3 Distributed Processing System

Molecular modeling requires a high performance computing system in order to exercise real-time simulations. We developed a distributed processing system. The system manages multiple jobs from VR users of VRMMS and remote users as follows.

Web Service Server(① in Fig. 3) is a gateway which transfers information from the client (*Web Browser*) to *Remote Job Servers* (⑤ in Fig. 3) and returns the simulation results from the servers to the clients. The information from the clients includes a transformation matrix of molecular models, and information about a receptor and a ligand. SOAP (Simple Object Access Protocol) is used for the communication.

Job Manager Master Server (② in Fig. 3) is a master server and manages the distributed computing resources. It receives information from the Web Service component and searches a proper job from lookup tables (*Job Table Search* in Fig. 3). Then, it partitions the job found in the table into jobs which can be executed by the servers. *Job Manager Master Server* also contextualizes the jobs. The procedure aims to store information of processing resources into each job. That is, the *Job Contextualize* component in Fig. 3 assigns status of processing resources for each job.

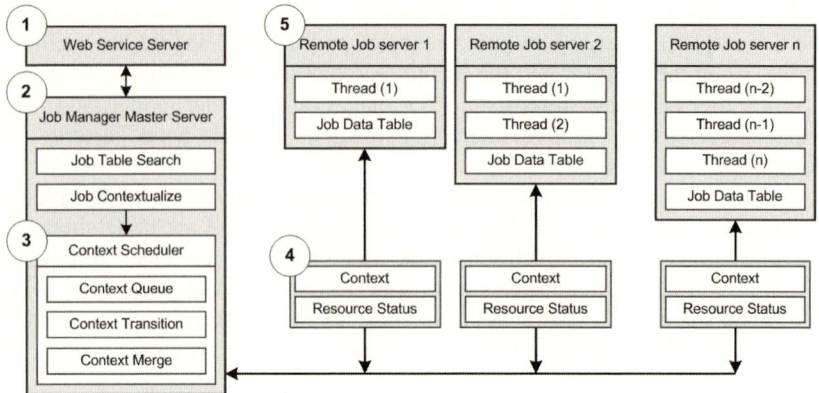

Fig. 3. A distributed processing system

Context Scheduler (③ in Fig. 3) performs job scheduling tasks. There are many jobs from multiple clients. A job of a user is partitioned and contextualized. Then, the contextualized jobs are stored in *Context Queue*. *Context Scheduler* allocates a thread for each job depending on its scheduling policy. The contextualized jobs (④ in Fig. 3) are sent to *Remote Job Servers* (⑤ in Fig. 3). After the computations, the results from the servers are sent back to the client through *Web Service*. *Context Scheduler* (③ in Fig. 3) performs job scheduling tasks. There are many jobs from multiple clients. A job of a user is partitioned and contextualized. Then, the contextualized jobs are stored in *Context Queue*. *Context Scheduler* allocates a thread for each job depending on its scheduling policy. The contextualized jobs (④ in Fig. 3) are sent to *Remote Job Servers* (⑤ in Fig. 3). After the computations, the results from the servers are sent back to the client through *Web Service*.

3.4 Web Service Server

First, we examine how users can collaborate during molecular modeling. A VR user has a large display (an output device) for viewing 3D structures and Haptic Egg (an input and output dedice) for issuing gestures for modeling and receiving haptic feedbacks. As shown in Fig. 4, he manipulates a receptor and a ligand. Energy calculations of simulating molecular behaviors are executed by the DPS. The results are delivered to the VR user and the remote users by the web service server.

The remote users can view the results from the simulation via a web browser in realtime. If they have comments and/or opinions, they can issue them to the VR user. A chatting service is provided. They can send visual makers and messages for manipulating models to the VR user too. Then, the VR user can receive the comments and the messages from the remote users and exercise the docking procedure accordingly.

As presented in Fig. 5, WSS is the key component of the proposed environment. For simulation, WSS sends parameters of energy computation from the VR user to DPS. The simulated values are sent back to the VR user by WSS. During collaboration, WSS is a gateway which distributes the simulation results to the remote users

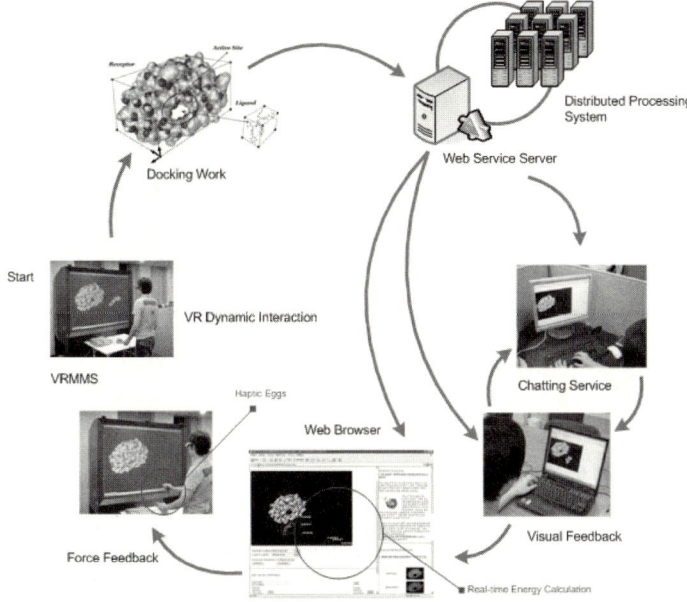

Fig. 4. Workflow in collaboration

and collects feedbacks from the remote users to the VR user and to DPS. The simulation results, the feedback and the parameters are expressed in terms of matrices which are used in rendering molecular models. This approach can reduce sizes of data

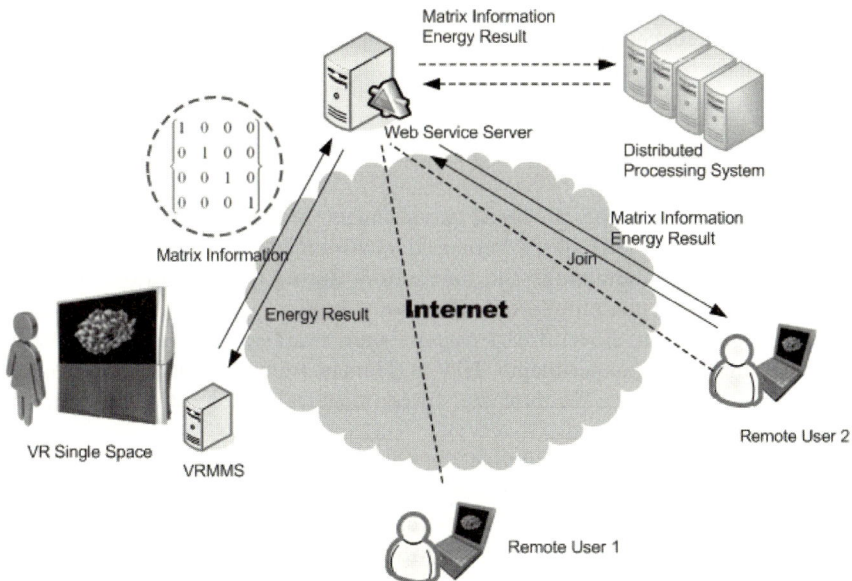

Fig. 5. Information flow during collaboration

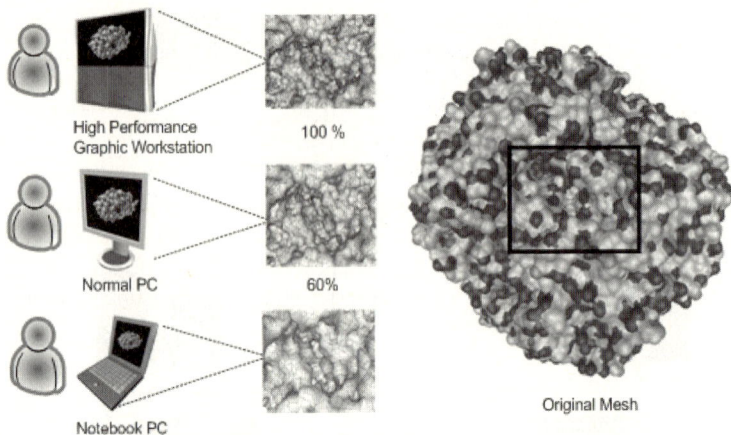

Fig. 6. Adaptive Real-Time Rendering for remote users

transferred via the network. WSS also executes real-time broadcasting services and chatting services using the UDP protocol. This enables a VR user and remote users to collaborate in real-time.

We assume that remote users may not be equipped with high performance graphics workstations. If the size of molecular models becomes large, low-end computers may not be able to display properly. So WSS must provide with various levels of images for remote users depending on graphical capabilities of their computers. For example, as shown in Fig. 6, a user of a high-end computer can view high quality images, while a notebook user may be able to view a 20% reduced version of molecular models. Of course, the shape of the molecular models must be precise and correct, even if the size of the model is reduced. Our adaptive LOD algorithm can generate such images depending on the situation [15].

4 Experiments

We must check (i) if the proposed environment produces reliable values after molecular simulation, (ii) if the proposed environment performs fast enough to exercise real-time computations and interactions during the simulation, (iii) if collaborative molecular modeling processes among multiple can be exercised using the proposed environment. Several experiments were exercised. We executed docking procedures during the experiments. HIV-1 (Human Immunodeficiency Virus) [16, 17, 18] was selected as a receptor and fifteen materials related to reproduction of HIV-1 were chosen as ligands.

First, we checked the reliability of the simulation values. That is, the values of computing energy equations for binding the fifteen ligands with the receptor were calculated. We compared VRMMS with Insight II [19] which is the most popular simulation tool of molecular modeling. RMSD (Root Mean Squared Deviation) was used as a measure for the reliability. The results demonstrated that VRMMS produced reliable values during molecular simulations.

In order to evaluate the quality of computations and interactions of the simulations, we measured processing times of simulations using DPS. We compared processing times with respect to different sized receptors, different number of computers for the distributed system, and different number of threads per computer. We used receptors of 3000 atoms, 6000 atoms and 12000 atoms. The ligand had 100 atoms. The numbers of computers were configured one, two, and four in DPS during the experiment. The numbers of threads were also configured one, two, and four, respectively. For each receptor, a computation of energy equations was executed five times [13]. The results showed that the processing time reduces faster as the number of computer increases when the number of atoms in a molecule is large. Fig. 7 graphically shows the fact.

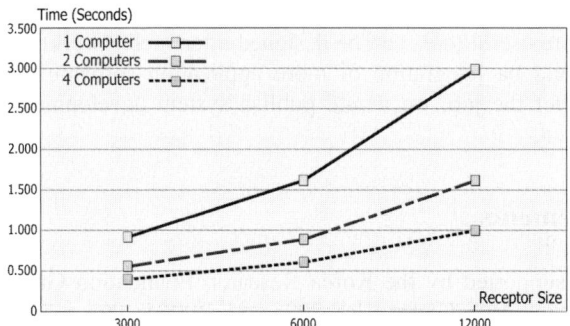

Fig. 7. Average processing times of the distributed system with different numbers of computers and atoms in a molecule [13]

Finally, the collaborative works of molecular modeling were experimented using the proposed environment. The collaborative work was performed by a VR user and two remote users. The VR user manipulated molecular models and two remote users view his performance and recommended ways to find active sites. We measured average times spent to find active sites and combine a ligand and a receptor. The timestamp was used in computing the processing times. As presented in Table 1, the collaborative works among three users showed better performance than that of a single user.

Table 1. Average processing times of docking: a single user's work vs. a collaborative work of multiple users

No. of users	Average processing time
1	336 seconds
3	121 seconds

5 Concluding Remarks

The proposed VR environment is an integrated system for 3D visualization, interactive manipulation, reliable and affordable simulation, and real-time collaboration in the field of molecular modeling. There have been many researches in each area. But no integrated system has been reported to our knowledge. Our experiments demonstrated that the proposed environment performed quite well.

The proposed VR environment can be applied to many application areas. The new drug design field must be the first choice. The drug design experts are not sufficient enough to satisfy all requirements in the world. If they can utilize our proposed environment, their expertise can be efficiently used. Another excellent application area is education. Though there have been many remote education systems and cyber-education systems, their main focuses have been lectures, not experiments and demonstrations. Our proposed environment can be successfully applied to remote and/or cyber education in performing and demonstrating experiments of molecular modeling.

There must be lots of future works to be executed for the proposed VR environment. We will first study more on workflows of new drug design with real-world applications. More useful tools can be designed after such a workflow study. Another future work would be integration of more application software with the proposed environment. After the job, we would publish system development kit for the proposed environment.

Acknowledgements

This work was supported by the Korea Research Foundation Grant Funded by the Korean Government(MOEHRD) KRF-2006-331-D00541 and supported by the Ministry of Information & Communications, Korea, under the Information Technology Research Center(ITRC) Support Program.

References

[1] Pertuz M.F., Rossmann, M.G., Cullis, A.F., Muirhead, H., Will, G. and North, A.C.T., *Structure of myoglobin: A three-dimensional Fourier synthesis at 5.5 Angstrom resolution, obtained by X-ray analysis*, Nature, 185, pp. 416-422, 1960.

[2] Wuethrich, *NMR of Proteins and Nucleic Acids*, John Wiley & Sons, 1986.

[3] F.M Richards, "Areas, volumes, packing and protein structures," in Annual Review of Biophysics and Bioengineering, 6, pp. 151-176, 1977.

[4] RASMOL, http://www.umass.edu/rasmol

[5] Protein Explorer, http://www.umass.edu/micobio/chime/index.html

[6] Frederick P. Brooks, Jr., Ming Ouh-Young, James J. Better, P. Jerome Kilpatrick, *Project GROPE-Haptic Display for Scientific Visualization*, ACM Computer Graphics, Vol 24, pp 177-185, 1990.

[7] William Humphrey, Andrew Dalke and Klasus Schulten, *VMD – Visual Molecul ar Dynamics*, Journal of Molecular Grahpics, 14, pp.33-38, 1996. http://www.ks. uiuc.edu/ Research/vmd/

[8] Brooks, B.R., Bruccoleri, R.E., Olasfson, B.D., States, D.J., Swaminathan, S. and Karplus, M., *CHARMM: A Promgram for Macromolecualr Energy Minimization, and Dynamics Calculations*, J. Comp. Chem, 4, pp 187, 1983.

[9] Kale, L.V., Bhandarkar, M., Brunner, R., Krawetz, N., Phillips, J. and Shinozaki, A., "NAMD: A Case Study in Multilingual Parallel Programming," the 10th International Workshop on Languages and Compilers for Parallel Computing, pp 367-381

[10] Altschul, S.F., Gish, W., Miller, W., Myers, E.W. and Lipman, D.J., *Basic local align-ment search tool*, J. Mol. Bilol., 215, pp403-410, 1990.

[11] Milind Bhandarkar, Gila Budescu, William F. Humphrey, Jesus A. Izaguirre, Sergei Iz-railev, Laxmikant V. Kale, Dorina Kosztin, Ferenc Molnar, James C. Phillips and Klaus Schulten, "BioCoRE: A Collaboratory for Structural Biology", In Agostino G. Bruzzone, Adelinde Uchrmacher, and Ernest H. Page, editors, Proceedings of the SCS International Conference on Web-Based Modeling and Simulation, pp. 242-251, San Francisco, Cali-fornia, 1999.

[12] Sungjun Park, Jun Lee, and Jee-In Kim, "A Molecular Modeling System based on Dy-namic Gesture," ICCSA 2005, LNCS 3480, pp.886-895, 2005

[13] Sungjun Park, Booson Kim, Jee-In Kim, "A Web Service based Molecualr Modeling System using a Distributed Processing System," LNCS 3597, pp208-217, 2005.

[14] Jun Lee, Sungjun Park, Jee-In Kim, "Adaptive Real-Time Rendering for Large-Scale Molecular Models," ISVC 2006.

[15] Earl Rutenber, Eric B.Fauman, Robert J.Keenan, Susan Fong, Paul S.Furth, Paul R.Ortiz de Montellano, Elaine Meng, Irwin D.Kuntz, Dianne L.DeCamp, Rafael Salto, Jason R.Rose, Charles S.Craik, Robert M.Stroud, *Structure of a Non-peptide Inhibitor Com-plexed with HIV-1 Protease*, The Journal of Biological, Chemistry, Vol. 268, No21, pp 15343-15346, 1993

[16] Norio Yasui-Furukori, Yoshimasa Inoue, Misturu Chiba, Tomonori Tateishi, Simultane-ous determination of haloperidol and bromperidol and their reduced metabolites by liq-uid-liquid extraction and automated column-switching high-performance liquid chroma-tography, Journal of Chromatography B, Vol. 805, pp 174-180, 2004

[17] Junmei Wang, Paul Morin, Wei Wang, and Peter A. Kollman, *Use of MM-PBSA in Re-producing the Binding Free Energies to HIV-1 RT of TIBO Derivatives and Predicting the Binding Mode to HIV-1 RT of Efavirenz by Docking and MM-PBSA*, Journal of American Chemical Society, Vol 123, pp 5221-5320, 2001

[18] Insight II, http://www.Accelrys.com

[19] http://en.wikipedia.org/wiki/Receptor_(biochemistry)

An Interest Filtering Mechanism Based on LoI

Sheng Wei, Zhong Zhou, and Wei Wu

School of Computer Science and Technology, Beihang University, Beijing 100083,
P.R. China
{weisheng, zz, wuwei}@vrlab.buaa.edu.cn

Abstract. In large-scale DVE (Distributed Virtual Environment), data filtering is a critical factor to consider in connection with the real-time communications between simulators geographically separated. However, several existing data filtering mechanisms such as region-based, grid-based and hybrid ones result in limitations in computational complexity, filtering accuracy, or scalability. Aiming at providing an extensible filtering approach and reducing the overhead on both host and network, we propose an interest filtering mechanism based on LoI (Layer of Interest). The mechanism performs data filtering by means of multicast region publication, distributed receiver-side matching, and LoI-Based data filtering. We have implemented the mechanism into our RTI (Run-Time Infrastructure) software, and experiments are taken to demonstrate the effectiveness of it.

Keywords: DVE, Interest Filtering, DDM, LoI.

1 Introduction

DVE (Distributed Virtual Environment)[1], based on the technology of virtual reality and network, has become an important field in computer technology. As the continuous increment on the amount of entities, scalability becomes the main issue of the virtual environment. In order to lessen the heavy burden on network and hosts, data filtering mechanism should be taken into consideration.

DDM (Data Distribution Management) services in HLA(High Level Architecture) [2][3] implement data refinement by means of region matching. One critical issue in the data filtering mechanism is the computation of intersections between update and subscription regions. There are three main categories of approaches to perform this filtering process [4]: region-based, grid-based and hybrid method. Some other approaches such as agent-based filtering mechanism [5] and sorted-based matching algorithm [6] are also proposed. No matter how effective these mechanisms would exhibit, all of them have limitations in computational complexity, filtering accuracy, or scalability.

Aiming at reducing the complexity of computation, alleviating the problem of inaccurate matching, and providing an extensible filtering mechanism, we propose an interest filtering mechanism based on LoI. The mechanism performs region matching by means of multicast region publication and distributed receiver-side matching, which is propitious to the extensibility of the applications.

Z. Pan et al. (Eds.): ICAT 2006, LNCS 4282, pp. 334–343, 2006.

2   Related Work

In this section, several existing filtering approaches are listed and summarized and their advantages as well as disadvantages are intensively analyzed. In the end, our previous research made by Zhou is presented for further discussion of our mechanism.

In region-based approach, an update region is checked with all subscription regions, and a connection between publisher and subscriber is established only if their regions overlap. A centralized DDM Coordinator is responsible for collecting all the region information and carrying out the matching process. MAK Technologies [8] has adopted this approach in DDM implementation of the MAK RTI [9]. Despite its simplicity in implementation, the approach brings large amount of computation overhead and cannot avoid recalculating matches when an update region changes. As [11] has announced, the region-based approach only favors a federation that efficiently manages the number of regions and region modifications.

In grid-based mechanism, update and subscription regions are assigned to one or more grid cells according to the region's covering ranges. Data distribution is determined by whether there are common coverage cells between the update region and subscription region. DMSO of DoD [10] implements their RTI Next Generation (RTI-NG) on the basis of grid filtering [11][12], and Azzedine Boukerche also proposes a filtering mechanism based on grid [13]. Grid-based mechanism greatly reduces the computational overhead by means of mapping regions to grid cells, but it has disadvantage in filtering accuracy, for irrelevant data may be received by the subscribers who are not interested in it.

The hybrid approach is proposed in order to reduce the computational complexity in region-based approach as well as irrelevant data transmission in grid-based approach. Pitch Technologies AB has adopted this approach in their pRTI [14]. Gary Tan and Azzedine Boukerche also proposed DDM implementation based on hybrid approach. In Gary Tan's design [15], a centralized DDM Coordinator is assigned to each cell, and all the regions cover this cell is delivered to it by means of point-to-point communication. The coordinator is responsible for matching regions and establishing multicast groups. In Azzedine Boukerche's Grid-Filtered Region-Based DDM [16], instead of a centralized coordinator for each cell, the grid cells are assigned evenly to the joined federates. The hybrid mechanism gets a balance between computation and accuracy. However, centralized coordinator or federate manager limit the scalability and point-to-point region delivery to the centralized node increase the network overload.

In our previous research, Zhou has proposed the concept of LoI to extend HLA and provide a mechanism of DDM implementation [7][17]. LoI is defined as an enumerate value to represent a particular degree for the interest on instance attributes. To perform the data distribution mechanism, five kinds of LoI variables are defined and two theorems based on the definitions are proposed and proved. The definitions and theorems are listed in Table 1 and Table 2. The two theorems give an effective approach in data filtering, which greatly reduce the irrelevant data transmission.

Table 1. Definitions of the LoI

Symbol	Definition
$P_m^{(i)}$	LoI of publisher over object class i with m-size attribute set
$p_m^{(i,o)}$	LoI of local object instance o of object class i with m-size attribute set
$\eta_j^{(i,o)}$	LoI of attribute update/reflect with j-size attribute set of object instance o of object class i
$S_k^{(i)}$	LoI of subscriber over object class i with k-size attribute set
$s_l^{(i,o)}$	LoI of remote object instance o of object class i with l-size attribute set

Table 2. Theorems of the LoI

Theorem	Description
Update Rule	A publisher can only send attribute updates of LoI $\eta_j^{(i,o)} \leq p_m^{(i,o)}$
Reflect Rule	A subscriber can only receive attribute reflects of LoI $\eta_j^{(i,o)} \leq s_l^{(i,o)}$

3 LoI-Based Interest Filtering Mechanism

In this section, we propose a hybrid interest filtering mechanism on the basis of LoI to perform data filtering in large scale DVE. The mechanisms on both grid filtering and region matching are improved comparing to existing hybrid approaches.

3.1 Outline Design

In order to avoid the disadvantage of centralized matching, we make our new mechanism carry out distributed matching on the receiver's side. Accordingly, multicast is adopted as the transmission strategy for the delivery of update region. The multicast groups are allocated in advance for each cell. Once the subscribers express their subscription region, they automatically join the multicast group that their regions cover and will send a request to all the publishers. In the next step, the publishers record related information for the requests and multicast their instances with update regions to multicast groups they cover periodically in the loop "heartbeat" thread. Then, on the subscriber's side, a region matching process based on LoI is made, and the feedbacks are sent back to the publisher. At last, the publisher route update data to multicast groups according to the feedback it receives. During this period, both the publisher and subscriber will perform data filtering in order to abandon irrelevant data packets. Fig. 1 shows an outline view of the mechanism.

At the publisher's side, a local instance list L_{local} is stored and updated in time, which contains all of the object instances that the publisher owns. For each object instance (I_k, $k \in N$, $0 < k \leq$ *size of* L_{local}) in the list, a group of fields are recorded, In which, $g_u^{(i,o)}$ represents the handle of multicast group that instance o of class i is bound to, and $f_u^{(i,o)}$ is a Boolean "dirty flag" identifying whether the update region of

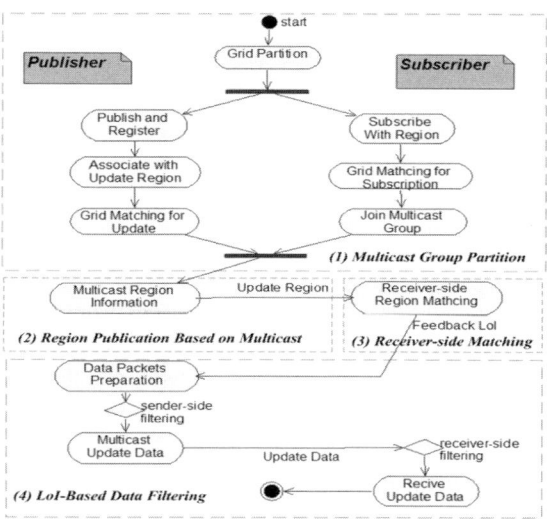

Fig. 1. Outline View of the LoI-Based Interest Filtering Mechanism

instance o has been changed without notifying others. At the subscriber's side, a similar remote instance list L_{remote} is preserved for each object instance the subscriber discovers. The following two definitions are needed for region publication by multicast.

- *Definition 1*: Let T denote an array for each multicast group that at least one of the publisher's local instances has been bound to. Each element in the array denotes the number of joined subscribers in the multicast group.

$$T = \{ T_i | T_i = \text{number of joined subscribers of the group } i, \qquad (1)$$
$$0 < i < \text{total number of multicast groups} \}$$

- *Definition 2*: Let r denote the count of multicast groups that at least one of the publisher's local instances has been bound to and at least one subscriber has joined.

$$r = \text{the size of } \{ T_i | T_i \in T, T_i > 0 \} \qquad (2)$$

3.2 Multicast Group Partition

We assign multicast groups for grid cells before the initialization of simulation process in order to utilize the advantage of multicast to deliver both the region information and data packets. Fig. 2 shows a two-dimension 4×4 grid. For each grid cell C_{ij}, a multicast group M_{ij} as well as a characteristic coordinate (x_i, y_j) is assigned.

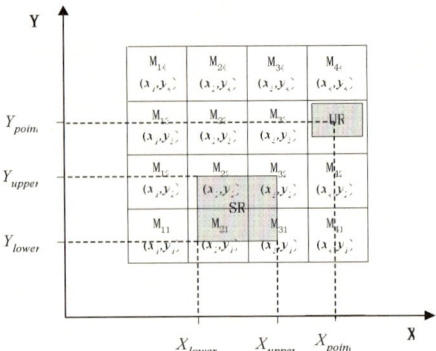

Fig. 2. Pre-assigned Multicast Groups and the Region Covering Mechanism

A subscription region with two dimensions can be denoted by the following two ranges, each on one dimension respectively: $[X_{lower}, X_{upper}]$, $[Y_{lower}, Y_{upper}]$. A binary search is performed for each point in the subscription region to match the region with characteristics of grid cells. By this means, the subscribers can determine their multicast groups to join. After joining the multicast group, the subscriber should send a request with the corresponding multicast groups to all of the publishers, in order to trigger the region publication from the related publishers. When a subscriber cancels its interest on one region, it leaves the multicast group accordingly.

On the publisher's side, since update region is usually assumed small range of areas in real exercises, we consider it as a point when covering with multicast groups, as shown in Fig. 2. The algorithm to determine multicast groups then becomes covering cells with one point. The same binary search method is used as that of the subscription region. After determining the covered multicast group, the publisher then associates it with the related object instance in L_{local} by assigning $g_u^{(i,o)}$ with the group handle. The publisher should also record and update the values of T and r we previously mentioned after receiving requests from the subscribers. The two variables are to be used in the region publication period.

3.3 Region Publication Based on Multicast

The pre-assigned multicast group and determination of covered multicast groups for publishers and subscribers have got prepared for the region matching step. In this step, the publisher multicasts its update region to its covered multicast groups, where the related subscribers has previously joined and prepared to receive the update region information. An instance's information needs to be sent out for notifying others when any of the following situations occur:

- *Situation 1.* (required by subscribers) One or more subscribers have joined the multicast group that the instance is bound to. The variables T and r defined in 3.1 has recorded the situation. The related operation can be described as follows:

```
IF r > 0 THEN
     FOR each object o in L_local
```
$$IF\ T[\ g_u^{(i,o)}\ ] > 0\ THEN\ \text{multicast } o \text{ to } g_u^{(i,o)}$$
```
REPEAT
```

- *Situation 2.* (region changed) The instance's corresponding update region has been changed by region modifying services. The dirty flag variable $f_u^{(i,o)}$ in the local instance record can represent this situation, and operation for the situation is defined as:

```
FOR each object o in L_local that
```
$f_u^{(i,o)}$ ==true
$$\text{multicast } o \text{ to } g_u^{(i,o)}$$
```
REPEAT
```

- *Situation 3.* (object instance verification) A subscriber needs to know whether their discovered remote instances are still existing and valid in the federation execution on account of the consistency issue, so a periodically multicast of all the local instances is necessary even without any changes and requests. We define the operation as follows:

```
FOR each object o in L_local
```
$$\text{multicast } o \text{ to } g_u^{(i,o)}$$
```
REPEAT
```

We design our mechanism by assigning a periodically sending thread called "heartbeat" thread to all the publishers. The thread will multicast local instance information to related subscribers when any of the three situations occur. We choose a fixed time interval variable τ and make the heartbeat thread working as follows:

1. In every τ ms, do operation on *situation 1*.
2. In every 2τ ms, do operation on *situation 2*.
3. In a relatively long period (perhaps *10-15τ*), do operation on *situation 3*.

This approach achieves a balance between simulation requirement and host overload. The accurate value of τ is adjustable according to the actual condition of network.

3.4 Distributed Receiver-Side Matching and Feedback

After receiving update region information from the multicast group, the subscriber will take a receiver-side matching to determine its $s_l^{(i,o)}$ (LoI of remote object instance). The LoI will be used for data filtering in the next step.

For convenience of discussion, we introduce our matching algorithm under the condition of 2 dimension (x,y) and 3 Layers (NO_LAYER, LAYER_VISION, LAYER_ABOUT). Fig. 3 shows the matching rules for the three layers. The auxiliary regions for LAYER_VISION and LAYER_ABOUT is introduced, the former is congruent with the original subscription region, while the latter is achieved by dividing each range of the former region with a constant value *EXTEND*. The two auxiliary regions indicate the rules for region matching. The subscriber performs

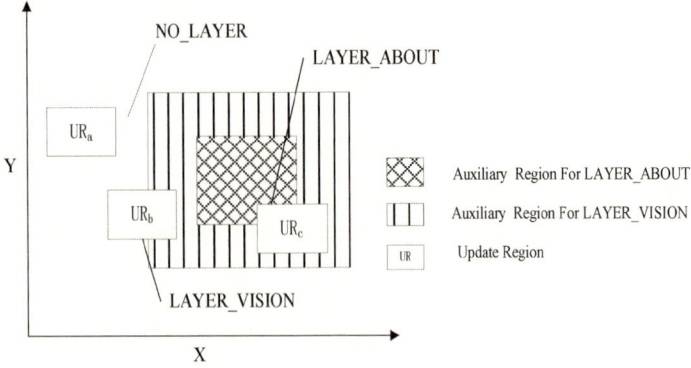

Fig. 3. Matching Rules for Three Layers

accurate matching for each pair of update region and subscription region, and for which the update region intersects with, the corresponding layer is returned. Otherwise, if no intersections occur, NO_LAYER is returned.

At last, the subscriber sends the $s_k^{(i,o)}$ back to the publisher for the sender-side data filtering. Meanwhile, it also preserves one copy of $s_k^{(i,o)}$ for each discovered instance o of class i in its L_{remote} in order to perform the receiver-side filtering.

3.5 Data Filtering Based on LoI

The aim of receiver-side region matching is to reduce the data transmission in data routing. During the data routing period, the publisher and subscriber will both take a filtering operation to discard irrelevant data. The following three steps are taken:

- *Step 1.* sender-side filtering

  As discussed in [7], the publisher calculates $R_u^{(i,o)}$ according to the receiver-side feedbacks and its own $P_m^{(i)}$. Since $P_m^{(i)}$ contains necessary matching result of the subscriber, it becomes the measurement for sender-side filtering. According to the *Update Rule Theorem* mentioned in *Section 2*, the data packets whose $\eta_j^{(i,o)}$ is greater than or equal to $p_m^{(i,o)}$ will be discarded.

- *Step 2.* data routing in the network based on multicast

  After sender-side filtering, the data packets reserved will be sent to the multicast group that the publisher holds. Multicast assures that all of subscribers interested in this data packet will receive it from their previously joined multicast groups.

- *Step 3.* receiver-side filtering

  The sender-side filtering can hardly eliminate all the irrelevant data. Every subscriber checks data packets it receives by comparing $s_k^{(i,o)}$ with the $\eta_j^{(i,o)}$ attached in the update packets. Each instance o whose $s_k^{(i,o)}$ is greater than $\eta_j^{(i,o)}$ will be discarded, as described in the *Reflect Rule Theorem* mentioned in *Section 2*.

4 Experiment and Result Analysis

In order to verify the new mechanism, we have implemented it into our HLA compatible RTI software-BH RTI. Experiments are carried out based on BH RTI within a tank war-game scenario as shown in Fig. 4. The experiment was taken on 2 PCs with 3.0 GHz Intel Pentium 4 CPU and 512 MB RAM on 100M Ethernet.

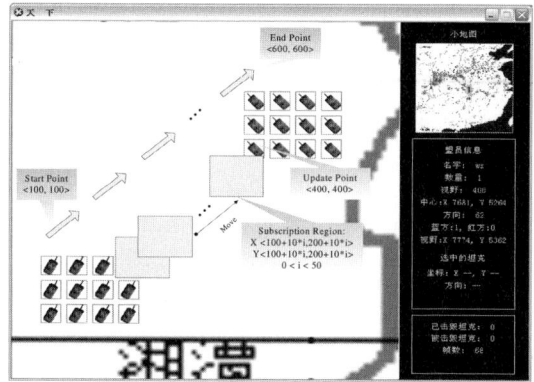

Fig. 4. Scenario of the Experiment

For comparison with the region-based approach, we record the region matching count (indicating load on hosts) at the receiver's side as well as the data transmission amount on the network (indicating load on the network). The results of experiment are based on different number of instances and grid cell divisions, as shown in Fig.5 and Fig.6. The region-based approach is indicated by 1*1 grid cells.

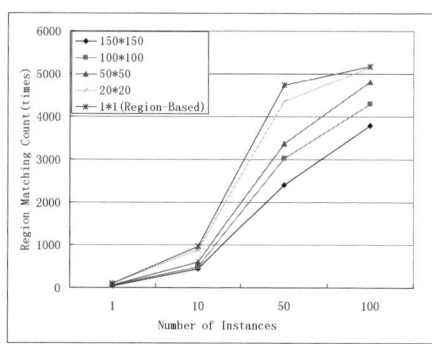
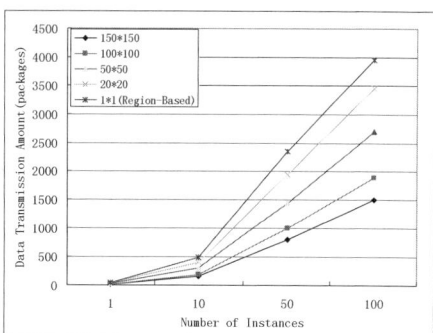

Fig. 5. Region Matching Count   **Fig. 6.** Data Transmission Amount

As expected, the new interest filtering mechanism leads to less region matching count and data transmission amount on the network than the region-based approach. As the number of instances increases, the advantage becomes obvious enough to enhance the performance of both the hosts and network in large-scale DVE. We also conclude from the result that both the region matching count and data transmission amount are improved by the increase of grid cell.

The receiver side filtering is inevitable for accurate data reflection, as we analyzed in *Section 3.5 Step 3*. In large-scale DVE, the amount of data that the receiver filtered is also a factor to influence the load of hosts. We calculate the efficiency on receiving in our mechanism by means of dividing the data packages received by the packages eventually processed at the receiver's side. Results are shown in Fig. 7.

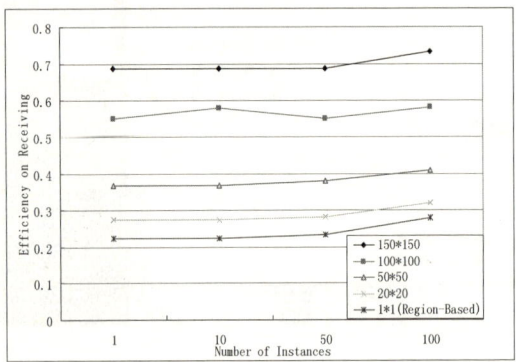

Fig. 7. Efficiency on Receiving

As the resolution of grid division increases, efficiency on receiving increases accordingly. When grid division reaches 150*150, nearly 70% of the packages received by the receivers are effective. That means only 30% of all the packages are to be filtered by the receivers. The resources of computation are greatly saved. The experiment also demonstrates that we may take higher resolution grid division in the scope of specific exercise in order to reduce unnecessary data transmission.

5   Conclusion

Data filtering is of vital importance in contributing a large-scale DVE. In this paper, an interest filtering mechanism based on LoI was proposed to implement data filtering in DDM Services and support for large-scale DVE. The mechanism adopts a distribute receiver-side region matching strategy and carry out data filtering based on LoI. We have implemented the mechanism in our RTI software. Experiment on region matching count, data transmission amount, and efficiency on receiving demonstrate that the mechanism is able to lessen the overhead of both hosts and network in large-scale DVE.

Acknowledgments. The research is supported by the National Grand Fundamental Research 973 Program of China under Grant No.2002CB312105.

References

1. Martin R. Stytz: Distributed Virtual Environments, IEEE Computer Graphics and Applications, Vol.16, No.3 (1996) 19-31
2. IEEE. 2000. IEEE Std 1516-2000: IEEE standard for modeling and simulation (M&S) High Level Architecture (HLA) –Framework and rules.
3. IEEE. 2000. IEEE Std 1516.1-2000: IEEE standard for modeling and simulation (M&S) High Level Architecture (HLA) –Federate interface specification.
4. Morse, Katherine L, Bic, Lubomir, Dillencourt, Michael: Interest management in large-scale virtual environments, Teleoperators and Virtual Environments. Vol. 9, No. 1(2000) 52-68.
5. Tan Gary, Xu Liang, Moradi, Farshad, Zhang Yusong: An Agent-Based DDM Filtering Mechanism, 8th International Symposium on Modeling, Analysis and Simulation of Computer and Telecommunication Systems (2000) 374 - 381
6. Raczy, C,Tan, G.Yu, J: A sort-based DDM matching algorithm for HLA, ACM Transactions on Modeling and Computer Simulation, Vol. 15, No. 1 (2000.) 14-38.
7. Zhou Z, Zhao QP: Extend HLA with layered priority. In: Proceedings of the Spring Simulation Interoperability Workshop .Orlando FL (2003) Paper 03S-SIW-012.
8. MAK Technologies, http://www.mak.com/
9. Wood D.D., Implementation of DDM in the MAK High Performance RTI. Proceedings of the Spring Simulation Interoperability Workshop. Orlando FL (2002) Paper 02S-SIW-056.
10. Defense Modeling and Simulation Office http://www.dmso.mil
11. Mark Hyett, Roger Wuerfel. Implementation of the Data Distribution Management Services in the RTI-NG, Proceedings of the Spring Simulation Interoperability Workshop. Orlando FL (2002) Paper 02S-SIW-044.
12. B. Helfinstine, D. Wilbert, M. Torpey, W. Civinskas, Experiences with data distribution managementin large-scale federations, Proceedings of the Fall Simulation Interoperability Workshop, Orlando FL(2001) Paper 01F-SIW-032.
13. Boukerche, A, Roy, A: Dynamic grid-based approach to data distribution management, Journal of Parallel and Distributed Computing, Vol. 62, No. 3(2002) 366-392.
14. pRTI, Pitch Technologies AB, http:// www.pitch.se
15. Tan, G.,Yusong Zhang, Ayani, R., A hybrid approach to data distribution management, Fourth IEEE International Workshop on Distributed Simulation and Real-Time Applications (2000) 55 – 61.
16. Boukerche, A. Kaiyuan Lu, Optimized Dynamic Grid-Based DDM Protocol for Large-Scale Distributed Simulation Systems, 19th IEEE Internationa Parallel and Distributed Processing Symposium (2005)
17. Zhou Z, Zhao QP: Research on RTI congestion control based on the layer of interest. Journal of Software, Vol. 15, No. 1(2004) 120-130.

Study on Data Collaboration Service for Collaborative Virtual Geographic Environment

Jun Zhu[1,2], Jianhua Gong[1], Hua Qi [3], and Tao Song[4]

[1] State Key Laboratory of Remote Sensing Science, Institute of Remote Sensing Applications,
Chinese Academy of Sciences, Beijing 100101, P.R. China
[2] Key Laboratory of Poyang Lake Ecological Environment and Resource Development,
Ministry of Education
vgezj@163.com
[3] Surveying Engineering Department, Southwest Jiaotong University, 610031, P.R. China
[4] GIS Lab, Department of Geoinformatic Engineering, Inha University, Yonghyundong 253,
Namgu, Inchon, S. Korea, 402-751

Abstract. The use of Collaborative Virtual Geographic Environments (CVGE) is one of the most promising uses of virtual reality in geographic field. Data collaboration can support multi-directional sharing of data and files, allowing ideas and thoughts to be communicated interactively among users. Thus how to integrate diverse and separated data and offer more convenient and intuitive data collaboration service becomes increasingly significant for implementing collaborative work in the CVGE. In this paper, we firstly design a Grid-based CVGE service framework and discuss the data searching mechanism and accessing control. A data collaboration service was built to integrate and share system internal resources and improve collaboration work efficiency. Finally, we built a collaborative virtual environment and implemented data collaboration service in silt dams system planning on a case study area, Jiu-Yuan-Gou watershed of Loess Plateau, China. Experiment results prove that the scheme addressed in the paper is efficient and feasible.

1 Introduction

In recent years, the amount of spatial data is becoming more and more tremendous [1]. However, a lot of data cannot be used efficiently because the rapidly increasing amount of data precludes the presentation of all given data items and the complexity of many datasets surpasses the user's ability to identify the gist or the underlying concepts [2]. Essentially, solving geographic problem is a process of collaborative work among group members, which are often distributed in geographic space [3]. To facilitate the analysis of simulation data, a variety of experts may be needed. As an integrated technology, collaborative virtual geographic environment (CVGE) offers an intuitively and efficiently interactive visualization environment. The CVGE might vary in its representational richness from 3D geographic spaces, 2.5D and 2D environments to text-based environments, which allows geographically separated users to explore complicated spatial information and conduct collaborative work [4,5]. An essential achievement of the CVGE is that it combines the participants and the information it accesses and manipulates in a single virtual geographic space.

Z. Pan et al. (Eds.): ICAT 2006, LNCS 4282, pp. 344 – 353, 2006.

Hence improving the efficiency of data collaboration is very important to keep synchronization in the CVGE collaborative work. In fact, many related works have been implemented to resolve some certain application cases. For example, a visualization environment in a single computer has been developed. So how to integrate data, procedures and algorithms to build and offer more convenient and intuitive data collaboration service in heterogeneous and geographically dispersed environments becomes increasingly significant for collaborative work in the CVGE.

The development of Grid technology endows the CVGE with a promising future. Grid's concept is coordinated at sharing resources and solving problems in dynamic, multi-institutional virtual organizations [6]. The Grid computing system can provide different kinds of services for users [7,8]. Essentially, Grid user sees a large virtual computer despite of the fact that the resources are geographically distributed and connected over the worldwide networks [9]. Based on the concepts and technologies of Grid and Web Service communities, this architecture defines the uniform exposed service semantics (Grid Service). The OGSA (Open Grid Services Architecture) [10] can provide building blocks that can be used to implement a variety of higher-level Grid services such as distributed data management services. This framework is very flexible because services can be implemented and composed in a variety of different ways.

By using Grid computing, the CVGE can integrate and share all internal resources to create a big high-performance computing environment. Since the core of the OGSA is the service idea, the OGSA-based CVGE can integrate services across distributed, heterogeneous and dynamic collaboration environment formed from the disparate resources with a single system and/or from external resources sharing and service provider relationships. In this paper, we pay attention to build up a data collaboration service to high-efficiently support collaborative work in the CVGE.

The rest of this paper is organized as follows. In section 2, we focus on how to build a data collaboration service, some key problems such as Grid-based CVGE service framework, data searching mechanism, data accessing control and service implementing are discussed in detail. A simple prototype system was developed and a data collaboration experiment was implemented as shown in section 3. Finally, some concluding remarks are given in section 4.

2 A Data Collaboration Service

2.1 Grid-Based CVGE Service Framework

In order to integrate and manipulate data across distributed, heterogeneous environments and improve the CVGE service capability, we designed three-layer system architecture: resources layer, service layer, and application layer (Figure 1). In the Grid-based scheme, a series of services are built to collect and integrate resources including data and clients information. By means of Grid platform, the CVGE users can register their resources and publish resources sharing services. Using these basic services, some data manipulating services, such as data searching, monitoring and transmission services, are developed and then turn to be new services for dealing with data collaboration application sceneries.

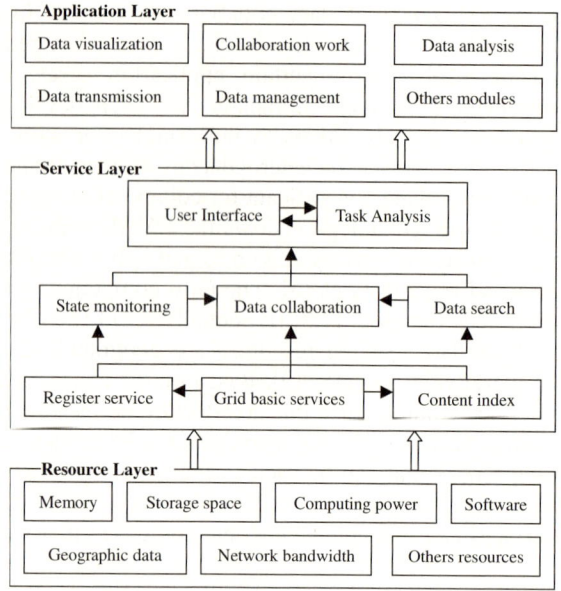

Fig. 1. Grid-based CVGE service framework

The resource layer contains many resources, including geographic data resources and client computer information, which are registered to resource registry center for sharing. All resources can be integrated into a virtual resource environment and used by any user in the CVGE system.

The service layer is built upon the resource layer, and a series of management toolkits and protocol criterions are defined to implement the sharing, integration and interoperation of all the resources in the resource layer. At the same time, the transparent and unified accessing interfaces of resources and services are afforded to support the applications in the application layer. The service layer is the core of the CVGE system, and ensures the whole system running correctly. This layer is comprised of several kinds of functional components. Firstly, we used Grid basic service to support the CVGE system. Secondly, we designed register service and data indexing service to manage data and clients computing information (i.e. network bandwidth). Finally, on the basis of aforementioned services, we designed the data searching mechanism and transmission control model to implement data collaboration tasks.

In the application layer, applications are mainly related to the CVGE functions with the support of the underlying layers. It includes some basic functions such as local data management, data transmission, data visualization, and data analysis, which can be used to support collaboration work. Data management module can deal with local data and files and register them to Grid server. Data transmission module is responsible for accepting request and sending data to other clients. Visualization module can display data in 3D scene for users. According to user's task, analysis module can know which kind of data user requires. If these data cannot be found in local database, we send data request to Grid server.

2.2 Data Searching Mechanism

We designed user management list and data indexing list for all users in system. The user management list includes user name, IP address, bandwidth, CPU frequency and so on. The indexing list is used to manage all shared data, and includes data mark, content, update sign, user attribute and so on. The Grid-based CVGE data searching mechanism is shown in figure 2. By means of uniform accessing interface, user A can submit data request task and get processing results after a series of Grid service operating（the broken line frame in Figure 2）. The whole Grid operation is entirely transparent, and user can get the searching results without knowing where the data resources come from.

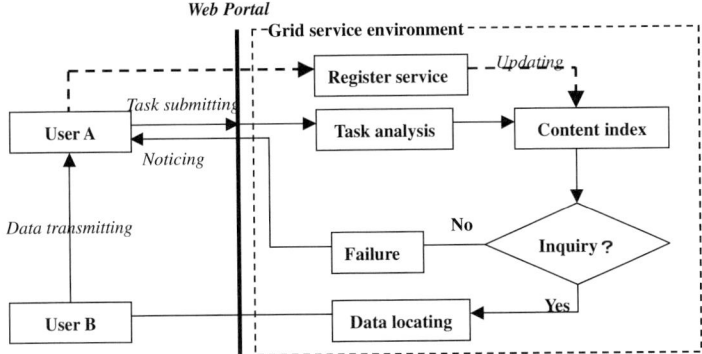

Fig. 2. Data searching mechanism

Figure 2 shows this data searching mechanism, which is described in detail as follows:

1) Through accessing certain Web port, user A submits data request task, then the Grid service environment analyzes the task and carries out the data inquiry by means of content index service.

2) If content index service queries the expected data, the target data will be located (we may suppose user B possesses these target data), then user B will carry on data transmission to user A. Other wise, the data searching will not success.

3) After downloading these required data, user A will notice register service update data content index in Grid server, dashed line arrows in figure 2 shows the whole process.

2.3 Data Access Control

The multi-user participation is one of the most important features in collaborative virtual environment. The traditional data transmission arises only between server and users. This method is very difficult to keep spatial-temporal coherence in a distributed CVGE scene and to resolve synchronization and coherence of a virtual scene. It is mainly caused by the traditional network structures, such as browser/server and client/server, in which the centralized function of the server causes some restrictions of bandwidth, speed and mobility. In order to overcome these restrictions, we can exploit users' resources and data directly exchange among users. Accordingly, based on aforementioned idea and Grid services, we designed data accessing control model shown in figure 3.

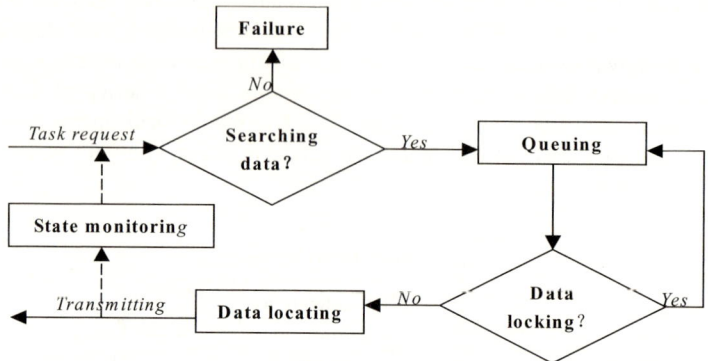

Fig. 3. Flowchart of data accessing control

The basic process could be described in detail as followed:

1) According to request task, sever carries out data inquiry and selects data records in the whole system environment. If the number of records is more than one, they will be queued according to their bandwidth, IP address, and computer performance.

2) In order to prevent the concurrency of data accessing, the accessed data are locked (e.g. 1 means locked, and 0 means unlocked). In order to keep the priority, we should check these data items until there signs are all 0.

3) When one most appropriate data item have been chosen, computer will be asked to send data to destination computer. In the course of the data transmission, the data item is locked till the end of task. Meantime, if the process is broken, the above steps will be restarted.

2.4 Data Collaboration Service

After integrating all data and computing resources in the CVGE system environment, the CVGE users can more rapidly and conveniently query and share data. However, data collaboration is not equal to data sharing. The main difference between data sharing and data collaboration is that data sharing is one-way sharing of data and files, while data collaboration implements multi-directional sharing of data and files, allowing ideas and thoughts to be communicated interactively among CVGE users. For more powerful interactivity and real-time collaboration, we designed a data collaboration model to create a data collaboration group based on our system architecture, which can automatically finish some collaboration tasks. The algorithm of creating a dynamic group is shown in Figure 4 and its basic approach is as follows:

1) Firstly, user sends one request task to Grid server and task analysis service implements data searching and judges if the CVGE system can solve this problem. If the answer is "yes", then continues to the next step; otherwise, stops movement and declares task failure.

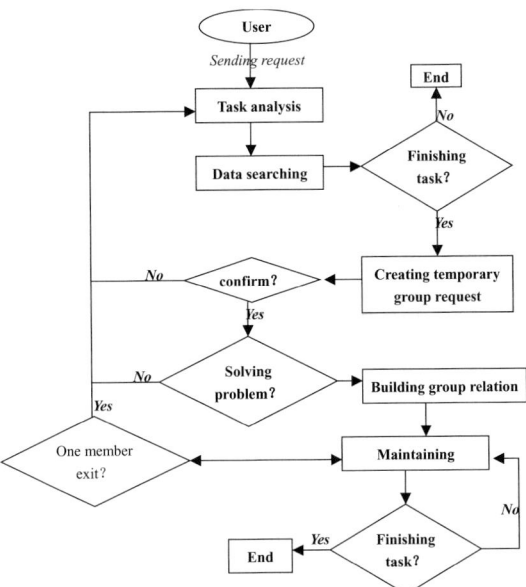

Fig. 4. Flowchart of implementing data collaboration service

2) Secondly, according to the request task and user information list, the data collaboration service chooses some users that can finish the task. These users will receive from cooperative request in turn. If one user agrees, then he joins the data collaboration group; if one user refuses, then returns to judge the first step and repeat these steps until the data collaboration group is created.

3) Finally, the relation of the data collaboration group will be maintained until the request task is finished. One user node may drop out the data collaboration group according to his own situation. Subsequently the data collaboration service will confirm it. If the situation affects the cooperative task implementing, the data accessing control will look for a new node to replace the failure node's position.

3   Application Experiment

3.1   Application Background

In the case study area of Qiu-Yuan-Gou watershed, with a total area of 70.7 km2 and a length of 18 km of the major channel, there are 202 silt dams, of which 17 are the backbone dams (big dams) and 185 are the ordinary dams (middle and small dams). The whole dam system of Qiu-Yuan-Gou watershed is a typical dam system of the massive silt dam construction project on Loess Plateau. Our study aims to build a CVGE for supporting spatial planning of silt dams across the Internet. Of course, we also pay attention to address the data collaboration mechanism in CVGE.

3.2 Geographic Environments Modeling

There are two types of models in terms of virtual geographic scene systems. One is the field-based model, such as the DEM and land use model, and the other is the entity-based model (i.e. the model uses entities), such as dams, trees, and roads. In our case study, we used ArcGIS to process basic scene data including SPOT 5 remote sensing image and 1:10000 DEM. In order to high-efficiently build a three-dimension scene under a web-based distributed environment, we divided the terrain data into different layers and blocks. Each layer of multi-resolutions data layers stands for one kind of resolution. Meantime, a kind of quad-tree structure [11] was adopted to organize the terrain data. Every terrain data block in the quad-tree has the same amount of data. Thus the data package based network transmission would benefit from such a feature. Furthermore, these features are also convenient to design a high-efficiency LOD (Level of Detail) algorithm for simplifying terrain scene. We implemented fast terrain rendering using geometrical MipMapping algorithm [12]. Figure 5-a shows the virtual 3-D watersheds with a sub-regional DEM of Jiu-Yuan-Gou watershed, overlaid by thematic maps of a SPOT 5 remote sensing image. Figure 5-b shows the terrain scene rendered with wireframe when LOD screen projection error is 1. In Figure 5-b, the terrain scene includes 10171 triangles, and its simplification ratio is 1.8%, the rendering speed ratio is 60 frames per second (Celeron 1.7GHZ CPU, 256M memory and 32M integrated graphics card.).

a: Terrain scene after using texture   b: Wireframe terrain scene

Fig. 5. Three-dimension terrain scene

3.3 System Development

Using Java, GT3, C++ and OpenGL technologies, a prototype CVGE system for dam systems planning in watersheds was developed. In order to support different software and hardware environment, it is better to choose a development platform that is descriptive and independent from specific languages. Java is an ideal language to develop Grid services. After the compilation, Java binary code can be executed by any Java interpreter, which is cross-platform. C++ and OpenGL can deal with LOD algorithm for improving terrain scene rendering speed, which can be compiled DLL file to support Java displaying virtual scene by means of JNI (Java Native Interface) methods.

Because the Grid service implementation process is very complicated, we developed and offered some graphical operating interfaces, which can shield physical detail and help users improve working efficiency under the Grid environment. In the CVGE system, video function is also added to help co-workers better understand the intention, improve perceptual knowledge, and enhance working efficiency. Figure 6 shows a snapshot of the user interface of the CVGE prototype system.

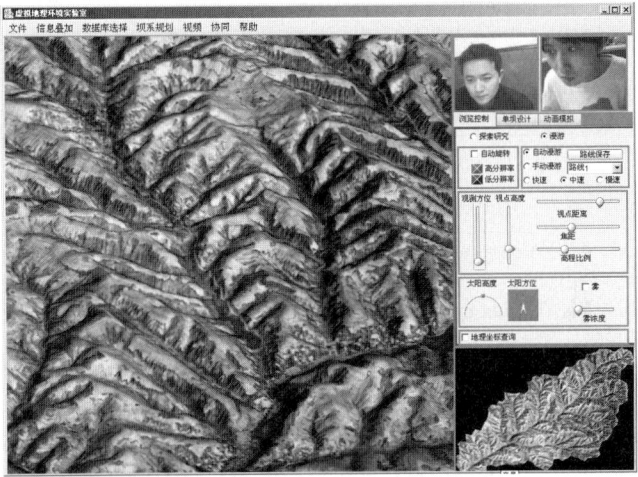

Fig. 6. The user interface of the prototype system

3.4 Data Collaboration Experiment

As mentioned above, all CVGE users register into Grid server and a user management list and user information list are created. Meantime all data in the CVGE system environment are integrated and a data information management list is created. In the collaborative silt dams system planning experiment, we used data collaboration service to create different service instances with a definite lifecycle and deal with different application sceneries (i.e., video and scene visualization collaboration). For example, to implement a request task such as the real-time terrain walkthrough collaboration or video collaboration, some users build a dynamic task group. In this study, one user implemented terrain walkthrough (i.e., checking certain planning result in virtual environment), meantime others can viewed the same terrain scene with the same angles and his (her) video image. By means of collaborative visualization environment, participants can give some revised comments in order to design an ideal distribution of silt dams.

In order to implement high-effective data translation in the CVGE system, the data collaboration service was designed to use full client capacity. This can reduce data server load and provide better data sharing service among users. Figure 7 shows a comparison of data transmission efficiency between our scheme and traditional mode (the experimental network bandwidth is 10 Mbps and the data capacity is 50 MB). The curves in figure 7 indicates that the data transmission efficiency of using data collaboration service is higher if the number of users is added, while the efficiency of using centralized mode is lower.

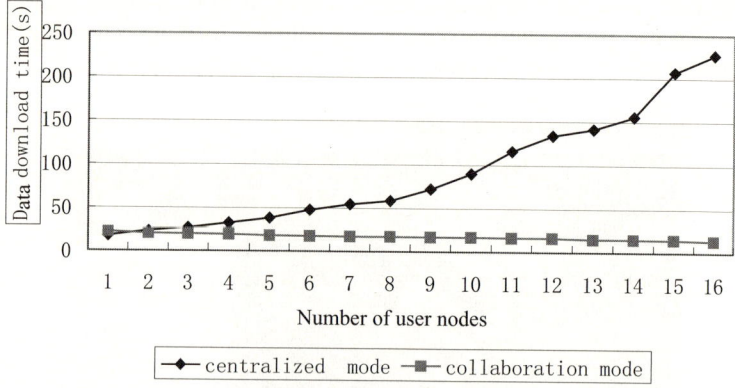

Fig. 7. Data transmission efficiency under different modes

4 Conclusions

The study of geo-collaboration involves diverse aspects ranging from participants and organizations to mediated tools, geo-problem contexts and supportive environments. It is very important to build a collaborative virtual geographic environment for intuitive and efficient interactive visualization, which allow distributed users to explore complicated spatial information and conduct collaborative work. This paper aims to design and develop a data collaboration service. Some key problems, such as Grid-based system service architecture, data searching mechanism, data accessing control and data collaboration service implementing, were discussed in detail. In the case study of dam systems planning in Jiu-Yuan-Gou watershed, a prototype of the CVGE system was developed. The advantages of scheme in this paper are summarized as follows:

Firstly, the traditional collaborative system serves a user by deploying the whole software. However, many users only need part of the software's functions. So we introduced the services idea to resolve this problem because it can serve a user by the means of ''service'' and the user can select the services he need and build ''his software''.

Secondly, the Grid-based CVGE service framework can be not restricted in certain operation platform and system environment. Furthermore, some existent visualization algorithms and programs can be efficiently utilized.

Finally, all users in the CVGE are easy to register their data and computer resources, which can efficiently integrate and share system internal resources. Data collaboration service can make use of users' impacts and improve the data transmission efficiency. Hence the better service capacity and availability are provided to improve collaborative work quality.

Acknowledgement

This research is partially supported by the National Natural Science Foundation Project No. 40471103, the National Key Technologies R&D Program of China No. 2004BA718B06, the Key Project of National Natural Science Foundation No. 30590374, and the Opening Foundation Project No. PK2004018 of the Key Lab of Poyang Lake Ecological Environment and Resource Development, Jiangxi Normal University, China.

References

1. Z.F. Shen, J.C. Luo, C.H. Zhou, Architecture design of grid GIS and its applications on image processing based on LAN, Information Sciences, Volume 166, Issues 1-4, 29 October 2004, Pages 1-17
2. H. Lin, Q. Zhu, Data Visualization: Virtual Geographic Environments combining AEC and GIS. Available from: < http://vrlab.whu.edu.cn/chinese/study/study12.htm>.
3. Q. Wang, Research on Geographic collaborative work and group spatial decision support system, Institute of Geographical Sciences and Natural Resources Research, CAS, PhD Thesis. 2002.
4. Jianhua GONG and Hui LIN. A Collaborative VGE: Design and Development [M], A Chapter to a book entitled "Collaborative Geographic Information Systems"edited by Shivanand Balram and Suzana Dragicevic, Simon Fraser University, Canada, 186-206, 2006
5. C. Bouras, A. Philopoulos, T. Tsiatsos, A networked intelligent distributed virtual training environment: a first approach. In Proceedings of fifth Joint Conference on Information Sciences-JCIS'2000—1st International Workshop on Intelligent Multimedia Computing and Networking, 2000, Vol.2,pp.604–607.
6. I. Foster, C. Kesselman, The Grid: Blueprint for a New Computing Infrastructure, Morgan Kaufmann, 1999.
7. Foster, What is the grid? A three point checklist. Available from:
< http://www.gridtoday.com/02/0722/100136.html >.
8. Foster, C. Kesselman, S. Tuecke, The Anatomy of the Grid: Enabling Scalable Virtual Organizations. Available from: < http://www.globus.org/research/papers.html#anatomy >
9. Foster, C. Kesselman, J. Nick, The physiology of the grid: An open grid services architecture for distributed system integration. Technical report, Available from:
< http://www.globus.org/research/papers/ogsa.pdf>.
10. H.L. Cai, J. Wang, D. Li, S.D. Jitender, A novel state cache scheme in structured P2P systems, Journal of Parallel and Distributed Computing 65(2005) 154-168
11. B. Chen, Z.G. Ma, G.P Wang, et al., Network Based Real-time Fly-through on Massive Terrain Dataset, CAD/Graphics'2001, (2001) 500-505
12. H. Willem, Fast Terrain Rendering Using Geometrical MipMapping. Available from: <http://www.flipcode.com/tutorials/geomipmaps.pdf>.

VCS: A Virtual Collaborative Space Based on Immersive Teleconferencing

Weidong Bao, Maojun Zhang, and Wang Chen

Deptartment of Systems and Engineering, National University of Defense Technology,
Changsha 410073, Hunan, P.R. China

Abstract. The traditional video teleconferencing systems provide a "video in a window" interface paradigm, it's not sufficient for naturally interactive interface for the collaborative work. We design a collaborative space called VCS. In VCS, a virtual collaborative space is built based on immersive teleconferencing. The remote conferees can discuss in the virtual space as similar to do it in the local rooms. VCS can be used to provide a new paradigm for the remote cooperative work. This paper presents the spatial model and video object extraction technique of VCS.

Keywords: teleconferencing, virtual collaborative space, video object extraction, virtual reality.

1 Introduction

Most video teleconferencing applications provide for the users a "video in a window" interface. Though they have been improved significantly over the years, the constraint of field of view still can't address natural interactions in the teleconferencing systems. The field of view of a common TV or window is narrow and below $10°$. The resolution of video from a typical camera is low and below 752*576 pixels. When they are used as the basic interface for a teleconference, it fails to produce a convincing feeling of presence and immersion [3]. Even when the network bandwidth problem is completely solved, one is left with relatively low spatial resolution and a narrow field of view.

In order to construct one more natural and compelling teleconferencing application, we designed and implemented a immersive teleconferencing system called VCS (Virtual Collaborative Space), which combines teleconferencing with virtual reality. The traditional video teleconferencing system is composed of terminals and MCUs (Multi-point Control Unit). MCU receives video and audio from all conferees and switches one-way video and audio for one conferee as he/her demands (Fig 1(a)). In VCS, however, conferees are extracted from the background and form video objects. Video object and audio from all conferees are transmitted to MCS (Multi-point Composing Server) and composed in one virtual conferencing room by MCS. The synthesized virtual conference room is displayed on a scalable environment by tiling a display surface with multiple light projectors (shown in Fig 1(b)). Conferees can navigate in the virtual room and view all other conferees at the same time. They can talk with other conferees and work collaboratively. When conferees move in a real

Z. Pan et al. (Eds.): ICAT 2006, LNCS 4282, pp. 354 – 360, 2006.

place, the actions can be mapped into the virtual conference room in time. The goal of VCS is providing a virtual space contained all conferees and providing a seamless environment that users can immerse in. This paper presents the spatial model and video object extraction technique of VCS.

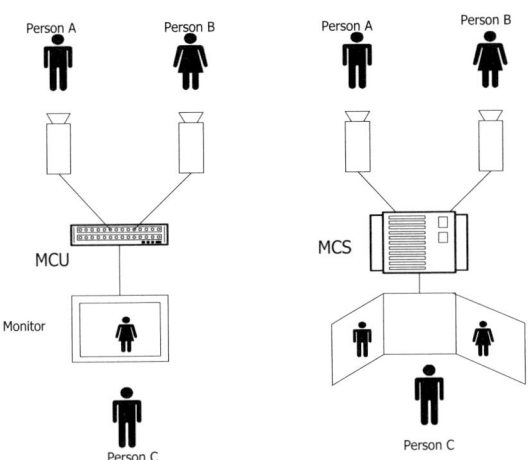

Fig. 1. Difference between traditional teleconferencing and VCS

2 Related Work

There are some researches [1,2,3,4,5,6,7,8] devoted to the research area of immersive teleconferencing. Yun et al[1] and Buyer et al[2] at first proposed the technique of video composing in video teleconferencing, which can composite multi-way video into one-way video. Video composing can reduce the network requirements of video teleconferencing. It can, furthermore, compose conferees from multiple places into one TV or window of a CRT.

Some systems combine elements of both computer graphics and video teleconferencing. CU-SeeMe VR[1] realizes a 3D shared virtual space. In this system, live video streams from conferees are textured onto planar surfaces. These planar surfaces, representing the conferees, are allowed to roam around a shared virtual conference room. This is one approach to use avatars for teleconferencing that conferees see a 3D view of the 2D avatars within the virtual space. Another approach is using 3D avatars for teleconferencing, such as VST[8], Diamond Park[12].

Criminici et al[4] propose a new algorithm for novel view generation in teleconferencing applications. Given the video streams acquired by two cameras placed on either side of a computer monitor, the proposed algorithm synthesis images from a virtual camera in arbitrary position (typically located within the monitor). This algorithm can be used to build a teleconferencing system to facilitate eye contact. Gemmell[5], Yang[8] propose the similar algorithms to rebuild the eye contact.

To allow geographically displaced conferees to experience the full spectrum of manifestation they are use to in real world meetings, 3D images of the conferees are synthesized and positioned consistently around a shared virtual table[10]. Glasenhardt et al [7] propose the concept of "tele-immersion", which enables users at geographically distributed sites to collaborate in the shared, simulated, hybrid environment.

3 Spatial Model

In this paper, we propose a new method to build the virtual collaborative space (VCS). VCS support the following three aspects of context awareness:

- ◆ WHERE, conferees can perceive the virtual environment and obtain the information of the space layout and scene distribution.
- ◆ WHO, conferees should know whom they are working with in the virtual collaborative space.
- ◆ WHAT, conferees should know the status of cooperative work and other participants' work.

In order to verify the above context awareness, we build a prototype system of immersive teleconferencing based on the multiple cameras and multiple projectors. Shown in figure 2, in a teleconferencing system with three conferees, three cameras are placed before each conferee. Three ways of video are transmitted to the remote sites.

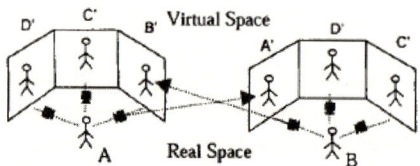

Fig. 2. The displays and cameras in VCS

The received videos and stored 3-D virtual environment are synthesized at a MCS (Multiple Composing Server). The synthesized results are displayed on the large scale display that three light projectors are stitched horizontally (shown in figure 3(a)). The size of each screen is 2m*1.5m and the display resolution of each screen is 1024*768 pixels. The two side screens intersect the central one 160 degree, i.e. $\Phi=160°$ in figure 3(b). The display provides 80 degree FOV(Field of View) if the DOV (Distance of View) is 4 meters. The total resolution is 3072*768.

VCS is consisted of the display projectors, 3-D objects that can be manipulated, virtual scene and so on. Figure 4 shows a snapshot of a VCS.

In order to build a shared, immersive and collaborative space, we need a suitable spatial model of VCS. The spatial model of VCS is built on the GCS (Global Conference Space) and LCS (Local Conference Space).

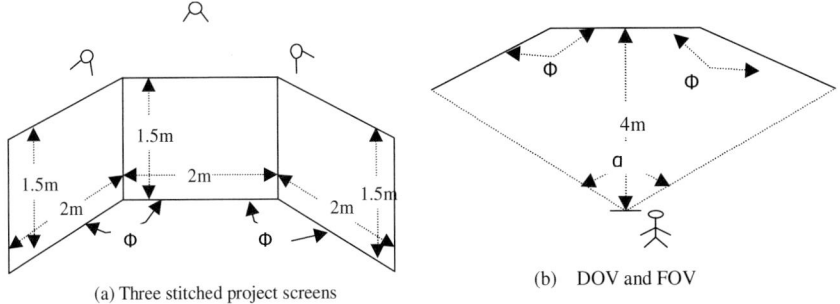

(a) Three stitched project screens

(b) DOV and FOV

Fig. 3. The display system of VCS environment

Fig. 4. A snapshot of VCS

DEF 1 (Global Conference Space: GCS). GCS is a virtual environment that all the conferees share and participate in. It spatially describes all the elements of the immersive teleconferencing in a uniform coordinate system, including virtual scene VS, conferee set CS, object set OS.

GCS ::= <VS,CS,VOS>
<VS> ::= <panoramic image>
<CS> ::= <video object><audio>
<OS> :: = <geometry object><light>...<texture>

CS contains the video objects extracted from the backgrounds and audio. OS contains all the virtual objects that used in the CSCW applications, such as a designing car, virtual whiteboard, virtual pen, etc.

In VCS, VS is constructed from panoramic images. Panoramic image is an image stitching all the views from different directions at one specific site and focal length. The types of panoramic images usually include spherical, cylindrical, polygonal panoramic images. Currently, VCS use cylindrical panoramic images to render the virtual space although cylindrical panoramic images implement less degree of viewing up/down.

In order to insert the conferees into the proper positions in GCS, the mapping relationship between real conference room and GCS must be built. This relationship should be confirmed before each conference and don't be modified during the conference.

As soon as the relationship is built, the movements of each conferee can be also mapped into GCS. When a conferee walks in real conference room, the video object of the conferee will act at similar ways in GCS. We need consider the collision between conferees and OS, such as a virtual table.

DEF 2 (Local Conference Space: LCS). LCS is the projection of GCS with the view position and view direction of the local participant. Each participant corresponds to one LCS.

LCS is displayed on three stitched projectors. Users can change their view direction and location using various input devices to get different LCS views.

4   Video Object Extraction

The spatial model of VCS defines the spatial relationship among the virtual scenes, video objects and virtual objects. In order to synthesize the virtual conference room, we must extract the video objects from the background. To extract the video objects, subtracting the current image from the background model is straightforward. In our application circumstance, considering the background is nearly stationary and there are just tiny changes, our algorithm constructs a simple background model which is a copy of a frame without foreground at the very beginning and then updates the model with the current frame. Unlike other algorithms, our approach is very simple, fast and also works well. The detailed algorithm is given below.

```
(a) Construct the background model
```
Before video extraction, we choose a frame without foreground and grayed it for the background model.
```
(b) Update the background model
```
Let ℓ denote background model and χ present RGB-colored current frame, the new background model $\ell_i = \ell \times (1-\alpha) + \chi \times \alpha$, $0 < \alpha < 1$, α is usually a very small number, in our experimentation, α is 0.003. Then set: $\ell \leftarrow \ell_i$.
```
(c) Video object extraction
```
The video object extraction is finished as the following steps:

• $\chi \leftarrow \mathrm{Gauss}(\chi)$ .Gauss indicates Gaussian filtering.

• $\mathfrak{R} \leftarrow |\ell - \chi|$.

• $\mathfrak{R} \leftarrow \mathrm{Thres}(\mathfrak{R},\beta)$. $\mathrm{Thres}(\mathfrak{R},\beta)$ indicates using threshold β to convert $\mathfrak{R}$ to binary.

• For each pixel in $\mathfrak{R}$, $\mathfrak{R}(i,j) = 1$ indicates this pixel is foreground, else is background.

Fig. 5 shows the examples using our video object extraction algorithms.

(a) The original pictures

(b) The results of video object extraction

Fig. 5. The examples of video object extraction

5 Conclusions

Immersive teleconferencing is a new paradigm for CSCW applications. We have presented the spatial model of virtual collaborative space based on the immersive teleconferencing. This spatial model can bring all the conferees into a virtual conference room. The conferees can immerse in the virtual collaborative space and feel like seating and working together.

To show the initial results, we develop a prototype system. The prototype system supports three terminals and has implemented a large scale display to show the virtual collaborative space. Our future work will focus on improving the effects and speeds of video compositing and freedom of interaction in the virtual conference room.

References

1. Louis C. Y., David G. M., Architectures for Multi-Source Multi-User Video Compositing, Proc. of ACM Multimedia, CA, USA, ACM Press (1993) 215-223
2. Buyer D. G., The Personal Presence System – a Wide Area Network Service Resource for Real Time Compositing Of Multipoint Multimedia Communications, Proc. of ACM Multimedia, USA, ACM Press (1994)
3. Han, J., CU-SeeMe VR Immersive Desktop Teleconferencing, Proc. of ACM Multimedia, Boston, USA, ACM Press (1996) 199-208
4. Criminisi A., Shotton J., Blake A., Torr P.H.S., Gaze Manipulation for One-to-one Teleconferencing, Proc. of the Ninth IEEE International Conference on Computer Vision (2003) 1-8
5. Gemmell J., Zitnick C. L., Kang T., Toyama K., and Seitz S., Gaze Awareness for Videoconferencing: A Software Approach," IEEE Multimedia, vol. 7, no. 4, 2000 (26-35)
6. Schafer R., Image Processing and Coding for an Immersive Teleconferencing System, IEEE Region 8 International Symposium on Video/Image Processing and Multimedia Communications, Zadar, Croatia (2002) 16-19
7. Glasenhardt S., Cicin-Sain M., Capko Z., Tele-Immersion as a Positive Alternative of the Future, International Conf. Information Technology Interfaces, Cavtat, Croatia (2003) 16-19
8. Yang R., Zhang Z. Eye Gaze Correction with Stereovision for Video Teleconferencing, IEEE Transactions on Pattern Analysis and Machine Intelligence, Vol. 26, No. 7 (2004) 956-960
9. Sun L., Zhong Y., Zhong Z., Natural Interaction Synthesizing in Virtual Teleconferencing, IEEE ICIP (2002) 405-408
10. 10.Cooke E., Kauff P., Schreer O., Multiple Narrow-Baseline System for Immersive Teleconferencing, VIPromCom (2002) 367-370
11. Silva L. C. D., Miyasato T., Kishino F., Emotion Enhanced Multimedia Meetings Using the Concept of Virtual Space Teleconferencing, Prof. of IEEE Multimedia (1996) 28-33
12. Waters R. C., Barrus J. W., The Rise of Shared Virtual Environments, *IEEE Spectrum*, Vol. 34, No. 3, 1997 (20-25)

A Scalable HLA-Based Distributed Simulation Framework for VR Application

Zonghui Wang, Jiaoying Shi, and Xiaohong Jiang

State Key Lab of CAD&CG
Zhejiang University, HangZhou, P.R. China, 310058
{zhwang, jyshi, jiangxh}@cad.zju.edu.cn

Abstract. HLA-based Distributed Simulation technology is employed widely in Virtual Reality (VR) applications, such as military simulation, internet games, roaming etc. To support larger number of participants, scalability is becoming a key issue of VR applications. In this paper, we explore the characteristics of distributed simulation, and analyze the scalability of servers and participants, and classify our approach to improve scalability of VR applications into three aspects: a three-tier node management mode to accommodate more participants, an efficient management of servers to manage scalable number of clients and software development interface to achieve reusability and interoperability of VR applications. We present our middleware platform, HIVE, providing a scalable HLA-based distributed simulation framework for VR applications, on which users can develop VR applications easily and quickly. Then we give the method and view of application integration with HIVE. Finally an experimental demo is given.

1 Introduction

With the development of network technology and the increasing requirements of applications in many fields, traditional Virtual Reality (VR) applications which run on only a machine are required to run on network to meet the requirement of large scale participants and scenes. Distributed Simulation technology is employed widely in large scale VR applications.

VR Juggler [1] only provides non-distributed VR application development environment. Existing distributed VR application frameworks include MR Toolkit [2], NPSNET [3], MASSIVE [4], Bamboo [5], DIVE [6], AVOCADO [7], ATLAS [8], etc. Large scale VR applications such as military simulation, internet game, roaming, surgery train etc, have the trends as the following:

(1) They should have a scalable architecture to accommodate more participants.

(2) They should support the collaboration work of large scale distributed nodes to run efficiently to provide services to more participants.

(3) They should be developed quickly and easily with unified specification and development interface.

To fulfill these demands, the scalability of system architecture of VR applications must be improved. There are two parts in network application systems:

Z. Pan et al. (Eds.): ICAT 2006, LNCS 4282, pp. 361–371, 2006.

servers and participants. The key issue to improve scalability, which is related to the design of system architecture, is to improve the capacity of the system and the efficiency of servers group. Most previous systems adopt one or more of the following architectures: peer/peer, client/server, or peer/server. In those systems with servers, resource management and workload balance of servers is very important, which affects the scalability of servers directly. In another side, VR applications should be open, and developers could use the unified interface to develop their own client. In conclusion, there are three factors leading to the architecture scalability of VR applications: node management model, management of servers and software development interface.

Our purpose is to build a general middleware platform, including the APIs and back-ends. On the platform, users can develop VR applications easily and quickly, concentrating more on the logic of application, and spending less time on the infrastructure of application, such as data distribution and management, network architecture [9], etc. In this paper, we propose HIVE, which gives a middleware platform for VR applications development. HIVE has a three-tier node management model: global tier, group tier and client tier. HIVE employs a kind of management of servers to improve the work efficiency of servers. To achieve the reusability and interoperability of VR applications [10], we employ the user interface specification of HLA (Draft 1.3) [11] as reference, which was defined by US DoD, and became IEEE P1516 Standard [12] in 2000.

The remainder of the paper is organized as follows. In section 2, we discuss the key issues on scalability of VR applications. Section 3 depicts the implementation of HIVE in detail. In section 4, we describe VR applications' structure and its integration with HIVE platform. An experimental demo is presented in section 5. Finally we summarize our work in section 6.

2   Key Issues on Scalability of Architecture

Scalability is an attribute of multiprocessor system. What is Scalability? After examining the formal definition of scalability, Mark D.Hill fails to find a useful rigorous definition of it, and thinks that the notion of scalability is intuitive, and use of the term adds more to marketing potential than technical insight [13]. In opinion of Dean Macri, scalability refers to the challenge of making a game that runs acceptably across system configurations that may vary in features, performance, or both [14]. But he only provides his scalability approach in the processor and the graphics subsystem.

In this paper, scalability means the ability to adapt to the system resource changes. In VR applications, high scalability means that it can support large number of users to join in simultaneously and interact with others and objects naturally in virtual world.

Because what we build is a general middleware platform for VR applications development, we don't touch the aspects which are related with applications in practice. We explore the ways to improve scalability of VR application only from system architecture. There are three corresponding factors:

Large number of nodes support. Since distributed simulation contains large number of participants, and also contains many servers to provide the services, how to organize them is one of the main problems of improving scalability.

High efficient servers run. While the number of participants becomes larger, the workload of servers also becomes heavier. If the servers run more efficiently, the simulation could contain more participants. So management of servers is one of key aspect of improving scalability. To make full use of servers, it is very important to deal with participants division and migration to balance the workloads.

Openness of platform. It is important that the simulation platform should have good openness to improve its scalability. It means that the simulation platform should comply with unified specification and be open to the third party, and support developers to develop their own application. More over, the simulation platform should provide the software development kit, on which user could develop the VR application quickly and easily.

According to these three factors, our approach focuses on:

Node management model. Node management model defines the organization structure of nodes, and classify the nodes and give different functions to them. There are three kinds of node management model of network applications. The first is centralization mode, i.e. client/server model. In this mode, the efficiency of mode management is very high because of the coordinating of server. But when the number of the client is large, the server's burden of workload and network interface would be very heavy. The second is distribution mode, i.e. peer to peer model. In this mode, there is no bottleneck of server, and the architecture of system is scalable. But when the number of the client is large, the efficiency of node management is very low without the coordinating of servers. The third is hierarchy mode, i.e. multiple levels of client/server model. In this mode, the efficiency of node management is high, and it supports large number of node. But the implementations of hierarchy applications are very complex.

To get high efficiency of node management and accommodate large number of node, we adopt a three-tier node management model.

Management of servers. The function of servers is to provide services to clients. Management of servers contains server resource management, workload allocation and dispatch. The servers run more efficiently, the system will support more services to more clients, and will be more scalable.

To improve the efficiency of servers run to support large number of participants, we provide two kinds of client distribution.

Software development interface. Software development interface contains the specification of services which the simulation platform provides and the library of them.

To make the VR applications reusable and interoperable, we employ the interface specification of HLA as reference. And to provide more convenience to developers, we provide the software development kit (SDK).

3   HIVE

HIVE is a Middleware Platform, containing the following:

HIVE back-ends. HIVE back-ends consist of three parts, Directory Manager (DM), Group Agent (GA) and Group Manager (GM). Group Manager provides the global services, such as GM/Client resource identity service, monitor and control, workload balance, etc. Group Agent provides GM management to create/manage/destroy GM, following the instructions of DM. GM provides HIVE services to Client.

HIVE library. HIVE library provide the interfaces of HIVE services. Client implements the VR application using the HIVE library.

Figure 1 illustrates the network architecture of HIVE.

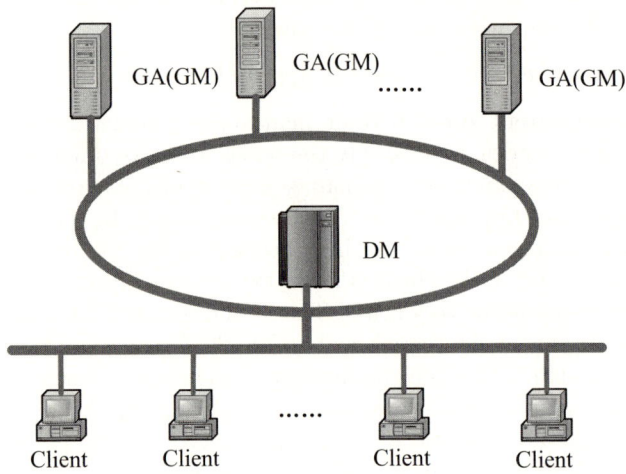

Fig. 1. Network architecture of HIVE. "GM" means Group Manager. "GA" means Group Agent. "DM" means Directory Manager.

3.1   Node Management Model

We present a three-tier mode management model: The first tier, named global tier, contains Directory Manager and Group Agent. Group tier is the second tier, consisting of Group Managers. Client lies in the client tier, which is the third tier.

A critical concept in HIVE architecture is "routing tree". All the nodes in VR applications are organized as a hierarchical tree - routing tree. Routing tree has three levels. The root of it is DM. The children of DM, in the second level, are GMs. The third level contains clients. DM maintains and updates the routing tree dynamically, and each GM has a copy. According to the routing tree, DM and GMs can find any client's owner GM to deliver messages, which is the parent node of the client.

Directory Manager (DM). Directory manager is the process that will be launched first. The architecture of DM is illustrated in Figure 2. It provides the global services: client and GM join / leave, client and GM resource monitor, client migration, workload computation and balance, client distribution, maintaining the "routing tree" and other global service, such as "global time query", "name resolve", etc.

Workload Computing and Balance	Routing Tree Maintenance	Client Distribution
Client and GM Join / Leave Service	Client and GM Resource Monitor	Client Migration Service
Network Communication		

Fig. 2. Architecture of Directory Manager

Group Agent (GA). Group Agent is a daemon process. GA keeps communication with DM, sends the "heartbeat" to the DM to indicate that the GA is working. GA also launches the GM according to the "Create GM" instruction from DM, and destroys the GM according to the "Destroy GM" instruction.

Group Manager (GM). A Group Manager specifies an application. Figure 3 illustrates the architecture of GM. GM maintains the list of the clients which are assigned by the DM. It also communicates with and provides services to the clients, such as time management service, user management service, ownership management service and object distribution management service according to the clients, which will be described later. To provide services, GM keeps all the basic information of the clients, such as "Subscribed List", "Published List", "Update List" and "Discovered List", and updates them. In client message delivery, GM retransmits the messages from source client to destination client. If the destination client is maintained by another GM, the messages are delivered to that GM first, and then retransmitted to the destination by that GM. Message queue is the buffer of messages, which enables processing messages asynchronously.

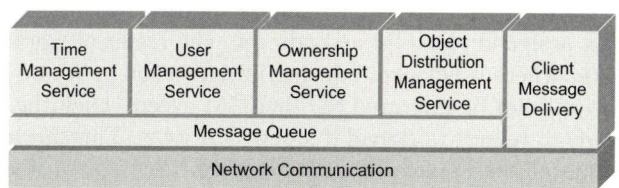

Fig. 3. Architecture of Group Manager

Client. Client can act as various roles in VR, such as the participant, the scene object, or just a passive viewer [15], etc. Figure 4 shows the architecture of client. HIVE Client consists five parts to provide services to VR applications. User management contains the services such as creating / destroying application, joining / leaving application, etc. Object Distribution Management provides the services such as publishing / subscribing object class, registering / discovering object, updating / reflecting object, publishing / subscribing interaction, sending / receiving interaction, etc. Ownership management provides the services such as requesting / divestiture ownership, etc. time management contains the services such as querying Time, advancing Time, etc. Callbacks are the interface of event notification services. When an event comes, the corresponding callback will be called.

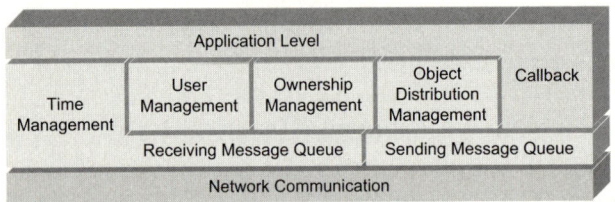

Fig. 4. Architecture of Client

On client side, there are two message queues. One is the sending queue, which is the queue for messages asking for a service. The other is the receiving queue, which buffers the messages and delivers them in proper time with the help of time management.

3.2   Management of Servers

In HIVE, resource management is mainly done by DM. GMs join/leave the DM, and then DM accepts them via GM Join/Leave Service. After GMs join, GM Resource Monitor will monitor and control them. When a client applies for a GM request to get HIVE Service, GM Resource Allocate Service will compute the workload of all GMs, and then select an appropriate GM for the client according to the GM Allocating Strategies. Figure 5 shows the workflow of resource management of HIVE.

We provide two kinds of methods of client distribution: one is that participants are grouped and assigned to a GM according to the result of workload balance of DM, no matter where it is located during initialization or where it goes later. And participant will not be migrated to other GM except when the GM is going to exit or it needs to reduce workload if a new GM joins. This method is helpful when participants of the application move within a wide area and move back and forth quickly, and the states of them don't update frequently. The other is that each GM is in charge of a partition of the virtual world. In this case, when participant joins the DM, the DM will find an appropriate GM according to its original location. When a participant moves to another partition, he will be migrated to the GM that is in charge of that partition. This method is

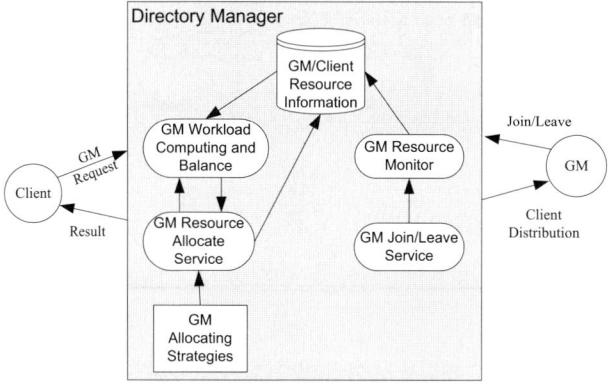

Fig. 5. Resource management of HIVE

useful when participants of the application will not move very frequently, but its frequency of state update can be high.

3.3 Software Development Interface

For convenience of VR applications development, we provide HIVE SDK. HIVE SDK includes APIs specifications and library files to be linked and run. To achieve the reusability and interoperability of VR applications, we employ the interface specification of HLA as reference. The APIs are classified into four parts. We adopt federate management of HLA as our user management, and adopt Declaration Management, Object Management and Data Distribution Management of HLA as our Object Distribution Management, and adopt Ownership Management and Time Management of HLA as our Ownership Management and Time Management.

4   Application Integration

There are two parts in the structure of a VR application. The first part is application logic, which is the content of a VR application. The second part is data presentation, which is the way would be used to show the result of a VR application. The data presentation can be text, 2D graphics or 3D graphics, etc.

Figure 6 illustrates the process flow of HIVE client. First, it selects an avatar from the model database, and loads the scene of the VR application, and then joins in the VR world. Then it goes into the VR application loop. The user interface of the client reflects the changes of dynamic information. Finally it resigns from the VR world.

Figure 7 illustrates the relationship of HIVE back-ends and HIVE applications.

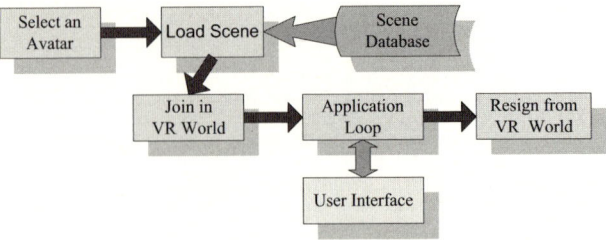

Fig. 6. Process flow of HIVE client

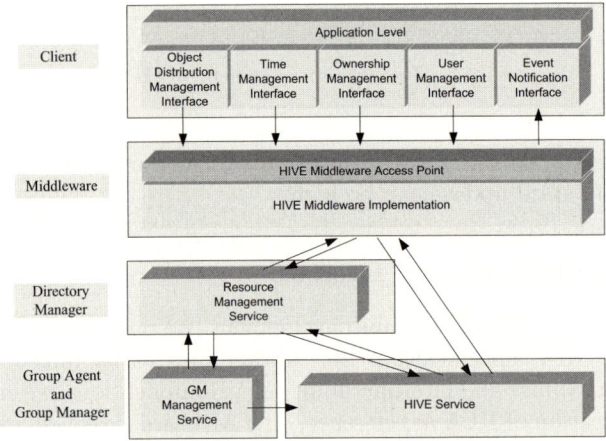

Fig. 7. Relationship of HIVE back-ends and HIVE applications

5   An Experimental Demo

We implement an experimental Demo, Navigator, to demonstrate how a VR application can be developed on HIVE. In Navigator, We use roaming as the application logic, and implement different 3D graphics as data presentations in different clients. Navigator loads the scenes specified by the user, then participants can select 3D models as the avatars of themselves to join in Navigator. After that, the participants can roaming around the scene, and interact with other participants simply. Passive viewer is also supported, who has no avatar of itself in the virtual world but can watch the scene and avatars of other participants.

As the general implementation, Navigator Client use OpenGL to render the scene. Figure 8(a), a snapshot of a running Navigator Client, shows that three avatars (A, B and C) join in it, and A is the avatar of the participant who is viewing the window.

In some cases, large screen display and high resolution of scenes are required. To meet the demands, we employ multi-screen tiled display using MSPR [16] as the data representation. MSPR is a retained-mode based multi-screen parallel rendering system that offers the programmers with a OpenGL-like API. MSPR system could render the scene among multiple computers in parallel.

In Navigator client with MSPR, we use three machines as a client to get a two-screen tiled display. The application logic part is run on one of the machines, and the other two are used as the rendering servers. Figure 8(b) illustrates the result of Navigator Client with MSPR. Avatar A is at the center of the client view, so one half of it is rendered by Server 1 and the other half is rendered by Server 2. Avatar B is flying from the region of Server 1 to the region of Server 2 and at the joint of them, so the image of it is also divided into two screens. But the Avatar C is rendered by Server 2 because it is fully in the region of it.

Navigator is an experimental demo. More advanced and complex applications can be developed on HIVE to meet various demands of users. Currently, we are constructing more experiments and making tests on HIVE to collect results for further performance study and improvement.

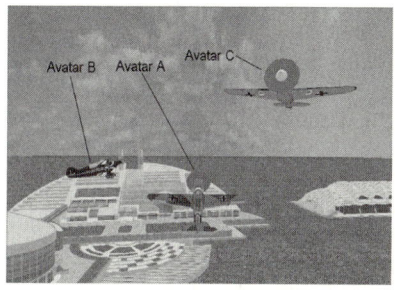

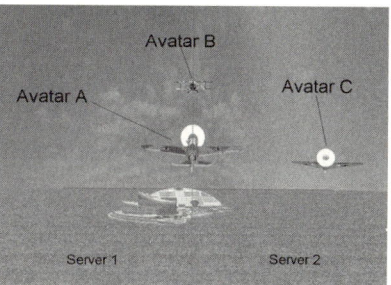

(a) Navigator client   (b) Navigator client with MSPR

Fig. 8. *Navigator client*: three avatars A, B and C join in Navigator simultaneously, roaming and interacting with each other. It is from the view of Avatar A in the third view mode, so it can see avatar A itself which is always in the center of the view. *Navigator client with MSPR*: two-screen Tiled Display. The two images are captured from the two rendering servers respectively from the view of Avatar A.

6   Conclusions and Future Work

As the increasing demands of accommodating larger number of participants in VR, the scalability of participant and scalability of server are becoming the key issue. In this paper, after analyzing the requirements, we draw a conclusion that there are three fundamental factors which affect scalability of VR: node management model, management of servers and software development interface. We present a general middleware platform, HIVE, on which users can develop the scalable VR applications conveniently. HIVE has a three-tier node management model architecture to accommodate more participants, and provide an efficient management of servers to manage scalable number of clients. We employ HLA as the reference to achieve reusability and interoperability of VR applications and provide the software development interface.

To make HIVE more efficient and practical, we will continue to explorer the other aspects of VR application, such as communication model, scene object management and rendering system interface.

Acknowledgments

This work is supported by National Grand Fundamental Research 973 Program of China under Grant No.2002CB312105 and the Key Project of Zhejiang Province under Grant No.2003C21012.

References

1. Bierbaum, A., Just, C., Hartling, P., Meinert, K., Baker, A., Cruz-Neira, C.: VR juggler: A virtual platform for virtual reality application development. Proceedings of IEEE Virtual Reality, Yokohama, Japan, March 2001, 89-96.
2. Shaw, C., Green, M., Liang, J., Sun, Y.: Decouple simulation in Virtual Reality with the MR Toolkit. ACM Transactions on Information Systems 11, 3 (1993), 287-317.
3. Macedonia, M.R., Zyda, M.J., Pratt, D.R., Barham, P.T. Zeswitz, S.: NPSNET: A Network Software Architecture for Large Scale Virtual Environments, Presence, 1994. 3, 4, 265-287
4. Greenhalgh, C. Benford, S.: MASSIVE: A Virtual Reality System for Tele-conferencing, ACM Transactions on Computer Human Interfaces, Volume 2, Number 3 (1995), 239-261.
5. Watson, K.,Zyda, M.: Bamboo - a portable system for dynamically extensible, real time, networked, virtual environments. In 1998 IEEE Virtual Reality Annual International Symposium, 252-260.
6. Frcon, E., Stenius, M.: DIVE: A scaleable network architecture for distributed virtual environments. Distributed Systems Engineering Journal (special issue on Distributed Virtual Environments), 5(3) (1998), 91-100
7. Tramberend, H.: AVOCADO - A distributed Virtual Environment Framework. Proceedings of IEEE Virtual Reality 1999. Houston, Texas. 14-21.
8. Dongman L., Mingyu L., Seunghyun H.: ATLAS - A Scalable Network Framework for Distributed Virtual Environments, proceedings of ACM CVE'2002 , 47-54.
9. Wilson, S., Sayers, H., and McNeill, M.D.J.: Using CORBA Middleware to Support the Development of Distributed Virtual Environment Applications", Proceedings of 9th International Conference in Central Europe on Computer Graphics, Visualization and Computer Vision, Plzen, Czech Republic, 98-105. (2001)
10. U.S. Department of Defense (DMSO): High level architecture run-time infrastructure programmer's guide, Version 1.3 v5, http://www.dmso.mil. (1998)
11. U.S. Department of Defense (DMSO): High level architecture rules, High level architecture federate interface specification, High level architecture object model template specification Version 1.3, http://www.dmso.mil. (1998)
12. Simulation Interoperability Standards Committee (SISC) of the IEEE Computer Society.: IEEE Standard for Modeling and Simulation (M&S) High Level Architecture (HLA)-IEEE Std 1516-2000, 1516.1-2000, 1516.2-2000. New York: Institute of Electrical and Electronics Engineers, Inc., 2000.

13. Mark, D.H.: What is Scalability? ACM SIGARCH Computer Architecture News, 18, 4(1990), 18-21.
14. Dean, M.: The Scalability Problem, ACM Queue: Game Development, 1, 10 (2004), 66-73
15. Steve, B., Chris, G., Tom, R., James, P.: Collaborative Virtual Environment, Communications of the ACM, Vol. 44, No. 7 (2001),79-85.
16. LI, C., Jin, Z. F., Shi, J. Y.: MSPR: A Retained-Mode Based Multi-Screen Parallel Rendering System. In Proceeding of the 4th International Conference on Virtual Reality and its Application in Industry, Tianjin, China, 5444, 173-180 (2003)

Location-Based Device Ensemble Architecture for a Spatial Reality Enhancement of Distributed Multimedia Presentation

Doo-Hyun Kim, Lila Kim, Hwasun Kwon, Dongwoon Jeon, and Songah Chae

Sensor and Embedded S/W Lab.
School of Internet and Multimedia Engineering
Konkuk University, Seoul, Korea
doohyun@konkuk.ac.kr

Abstract. Usual multimedia contents are represented as scenarios with markup language such as SMIL, and then delivered to be played back in terminal machines, e.g., PC or STB(Set-Top Box). However, these multimedia presentations are likely limited within single machine presentation where only the speakers and display devices attached to same computer system are used, so that the spatial reality is necessarily degraded consequently. In order to enhance even audio scenario presentation with such spatial reality, each audio clip for each audio actor, dubbing artist or background music should be assigned a separate speaker mostly close to the location where the author intended. In this paper, we propose a new architecture called L-DEAR(*Location-based Device Ensemble Architecture*) to support the spatial reality using location information of each node in a network environment. The core of the L-DEAR is IBEE(*Immediate-But-Ephemeral device Ensemble*) which is a set of nodes called out for playing back at least one assigned clip at a given time during the whole presentation. We will present the functional modules of L-DEAR and procedures for building IBEE, as well as functional requirements for L-DEAR such as extending the SMIL and using a global clock.

Keywords: Spatial Reality, Location, Distributed Multimedia Presentation, Markup Language, Scenario.

1 Introduction

In this paper, we propose an architecture for a new flavor of distributed multimedia presentation enhanced with the spatial reality. The usual multimedia contents are represented as scenarios with markup language such as SMIL(Synchronized Multimedia Integration Language) [1-3], and then these scenarios are played back in terminal machines, e.g., PC or STB(Set-Top Box). However, these multimedia presentations are likely limited within single machine presentation where only the speakers and display devices attached to same computer system are used. Any visual component of a scenario can not be presented beyond the single display device, and similarly, all the audio components are mixed into one audio signal and then output through a single audio device, i.e., speaker. In such paradigm, the spatial information

Z. Pan et al. (Eds.): ICAT 2006, LNCS 4282, pp. 372–383, 2006.
© Springer-Verlag Berlin Heidelberg 2006

such as *"The audio clip A sounds at upper left of the audio clip B"* is ignored, and the spatial reality is necessarily degraded consequently. In order to enhance even the audio scenario presentation with such spatial reality, each audio clip for each audio actor, dubbing artist or background music should be assigned a separate speaker mostly close to the location where the author intended. This enhancement is not believed to be achieved within single machine presentation paradigm, but possibly within a networked multi-node computing environment.

A node is considered as a networked computing device with H/W and/or S/W for performing proper I/O operations such as decoding MP3 to its speaker. A *device ensemble* is defined as a set of nodes which are called out for playing back at least one assigned clip at a given time during the whole presentation. The device ensemble is definitely logical and ephemeral embodiment immediately brought into the execution of a presentation, thus, is called IBEE, *Immediate-But-Ephemeral device Ensemble*. Figure 1 shows the concept of the spatial reality enhancement where an IBEE is formed and engaged for presenting single scenario with multiple audio clips. The goal of this paper is to derive necessary building-blocks and their integrated architecture, called L-DEAR(Location-based Device Ensemble Architecture), for achieving the spatial reality enhancement by embodying IBEE effectively.

This paper is organized into the following sections. In section 2, we will discuss architectural requirements that should be considered for deriving the L-DEAR. In section 3, we propose three possible approaches for extending the SMIL to incorporate the ability to express spatial reality requirements in the scripts for multimedia presentations. In section 4, we break down the L-DEAR architecture into five modules along with the procedures for assigning devices in an IBEE for a give presentation script. Especially, for the device assignment procedure, we discuss two approaches such as the convergence approach and divergence approach. In section 5, we deals with implementation issues by mainly focusing on the global clock and the session initiation with capability negotiation. We conclude in section 6 with discussions on further research directions.

2   Architectural Requirements

In this paper, L-DEAR and its architectural building blocks are derived by listing the functional requirements covering diverse issues as follows:

– Extending mark-up language for spatial relationship representation: The single machine presentation paradigm seems to have affected the mark-up language, e.g., W3C SMIL 2.0[1-3] not to consider representing spatial relationship among audio clips. It is required to extend this markup language so that authors can specify inter-clip relationships into scripts in the phase of authoring.
– Acquiring location information of devices: There are many research results such as Cricket [4] for localization of mobile devices in indoor environment without using GPS. We may adopt these novel ideas for acquiring the location information of each device. Whichever location systems are used, L-DEAR should gather relatively accurate location information from each device, and use it to form a proper IBEE immediately.

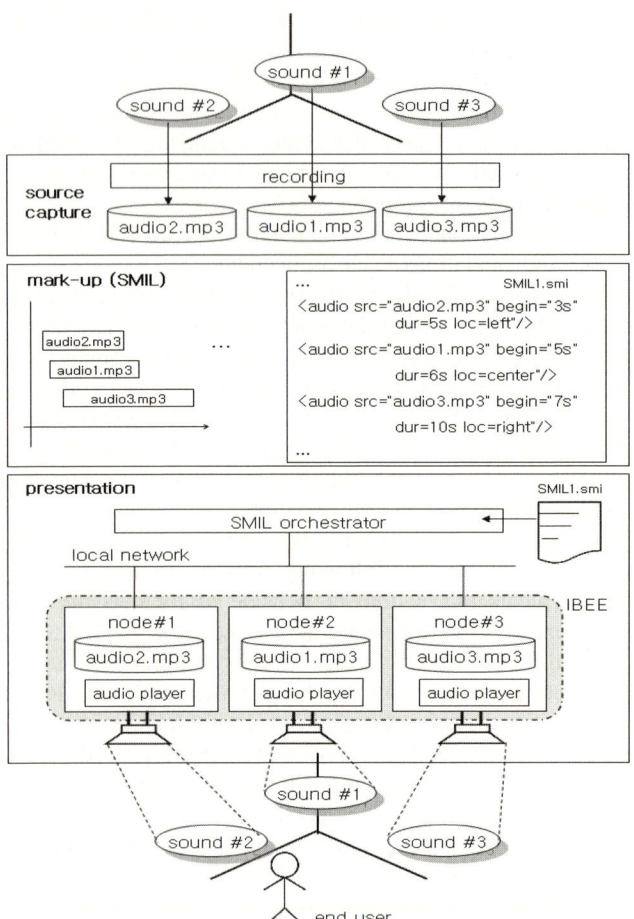

Fig. 1. Location-based spatial reality enhancement

- Forming IBEE: The IBEE is actually to assign each clip to a specific node by seeking a match between the inter-clip spatial relationship specified in the authored script and the location information gathered from each node. This matching procedure is required to pursue an optimal matching between the authored spatial relationship requirement and physical locations of devices.
- Facilitating global time within the IBEE: A device in an IBEE will eventually start playing an assigned audio clip. But if the device does no know the exact time planed to start or stop playing the specific clip, then the synchronized distributed presentation will be disordered. Therefore, we need to make the devices in an IBEE orchestrated on the basis of a global clock. As in case of the device localization, there are many excellent research results such as TMO (Time Triggered and Message Triggered Objects)[5-7] and NTP(Network Time Protocol)[8]. Among those, we may use TMO, since it supports a unified object oriented programming scheme for distributed and time-coordinated actions as well as global clock.

3 Mark-Up Language Extension

3.1 SMIL [1-3]

The Synchronized Multimedia Integration Language (SMIL), recommended by the W3C(World Wide Web Consortium), is a declarative markup language based on the eXtensible Markup Language(XML) for scripting presentations containing multimedia; audio, video, image, and text. The SMIL has unique features supporting the timing and synchronization among heterogeneous types of media.

A SMIL presentation is a structured composition of various media elements over a common timeline by using timing elements: <par>, <seq> and <excl>. The <par> element or parallel time container specifies that its children elements are all rendered in parallel. The <seq> element or sequential time container specifies that its children elements are played in sequence. It means a <seq> element's children are rendered one after the other. The <excl> element or exclusive time container specifies that only one of its children is played at a given time. If any element begins playing while another is already playing, the element in playing is stopped.

In addition to the above the three basic elements, the SMIL provides timing attributes such as <begin>, <dur> and <end> for each element. The <begin> attribute explicitly specifies the start time of children of an element. The <dur> attribute specifies the duration of the children, and the <end> attribute means the end of an element.

The SMIL provides a "test-attribute", e.g. system-Bitrate, system-captions, system-language, system-required, and system-screen-size [3] to process an element only when certain conditions are true, for example, when the language preference specified by the user matches that of a media object. The switch element can express that a set of parts in a document are alternatives each other and that the first one fulfilling certain conditions should be chosen. This is useful to express that different language versions of an audio file are available, and that the client may select one of them. An author can specify a set of alternative elements from which only the first acceptable element is chosen.

```
  . . .
<par>
  <video src="anchor.mpg" ... />
  <switch>
    <audio src="dutchHQ.aiff" systemBitrate="56000" />
    <audio src="dutchMQ.aiff" systemBitrate="28800" />
    <audio src="dutchLQ.aiff" />
  </switch>
</par>
  . . .
```

In the above example, one audio object is selected to accompany the video object. If the system bitrate is 56,000 or higher, the object dutchHQ.aiff is selected. If the system bitrate is at least 28,800 but less than 56,000, the object dutchMQ.aiff is selected. If no other objects are selected, the alternative dutchLQ.aiff is selected, since it has no test attribute and no other test attributes evaluated to *true*. Authors should order the alternatives from the most desirable to the least desirable. Furthermore, authors may wish to place a relatively fail-safe alternative as the last item in the switch so that at least one item within the switch is chosen.

3.2 SMIL Extension for Spatial Reality

In order to enhance the spatial reality of multimedia presentation, it is necessary to extend the mark-up language to embrace the capabilities to allow the authors to express their spatial requests intended for each element or clip. We, in this paper, discuss three approaches to slightly extend the SMIL, including 1) default rule approach, 2) relative position approach, and 3) test-and-switch approach.

3.2.1 Default Rule Approach

Basically, this approach is not to modify any of the current SMIL recommendation. Instead, the author leave SMIL player to assign each media object or clip to a proper device. The only thing that the author should know and follow is the default rule that the media objects shown in an element will be assigned to the devices by the SMIL player from left-to-right one by one at the presentation time. For example, in the following part of SMIL script, the audio2.mp3 clip will be assigned the left most speaker node in the IBEE, audio1.mp3 to the centered speaker, and audio3.mp3 to the right most speaker, respectively.

```
    . . .
    <par>
       <audio src="audio2.mp3" begin="3s" dur="5s" />
       <audio src="audio1.mp3" begin="5s" dur="6s" />
       <audio src="audio3.mp3" begin="7s" dur="10s" />
    </par>
    . . .
```

This default assignment is in case when the IBEE could be organized to contain three speaker nodes. In case when the number of speaker nodes is less than or greater than the number of media objects, a curtain default rule will be applied depending on the implementation of the SMIL player. An example default rule that can be applied to the above case where only two speaker nodes exist in the IBEE is to assign the audio3.mp3 to the right speaker along with the audio1.mp3, that is, to assign all the surplus clips to the right most speaker node.

3.2.2 Relative Position Approach

This approach, as shown in the following example, is differentiated from the default rule approach in that we need to add few attribute symbols so that the authors can express their requests to the SMIL player by specifying relative positions of each media object. The relative positioning attributes are such as posMaster, left, right, leftTo, rightTo, end center. The posMaster attribute is for appointing a clip as a reference point to the others. So the left and right attributes mean that the clips be assigned to the speakers located at left and right to the speaker assigned to the clips with posMaster attribute. The leftTo and rightTo attributes are used to specify more accurate positions. "loc = rightTo audio3.mp3" means this clip should assigned to one of speakers at the right to the speaker assigned for audio3.mp3. But, in case when the number of speaker nodes is less than or greater than the number of media objects, a curtain default rule as in the default rule approach will be applied depending on the implementation of the SMIL player.

```
. . .
  <par>
    <audio src="audio2.mp3" begin="3s" dur="5s" loc="left"/>
    <audio src="audio1.mp3" begin="5s" dur="6s"
                                          loc="posMaster"/>
    <audio src="audio3.mp3" begin="7s" dur="10s"
                                          loc="right" />
  </par>
. . .
```

3.2.3 Test-and-Switch Approach

This approach is to use switch elements to allow the authors separately specify their spatial intensions according to the available number of devices, i.e., speakers in IBEE. For this approach, it is necessary to add a system attributes such as systemAudioDevNum and systemVideoDevNum and etc. The SMIL player organizes IBEE for a given presentation and then counts the available numbers of audio and display device nodes respectively. This counted number is compared with the specified values to systemAudioDevNum, for example, in the switch element to decide the proper part of the given SMIL document to be executed.

```
. . .
  <switch>
   <par systemAudioDevNum=2>
    <audio src="audio2.mp3" begin="3s" dur="5s"
                                          loc="posMaster"/>
    <audio src="audio1.mp3" begin="5s" dur="6s" loc="right"/>
    <audio src="audio3.mp3" begin="7s" dur="10s" loc="right"/>
   </par>
   <par>
    <audio src="audio2.mp3" begin="3s" dur="5s" loc="left"/>
    <audio src="audio1.mp3" begin="5s" dur="6s"
                                          loc="posMaster"/>
    <audio src="audio3.mp3" begin="7s" dur="10s" loc="right"/>
   </par>
  </switch>
. . .
```

4 L-DEAR Architecture

The L-DEAR architecture as shown in Figure 2 consists of five major parts; 1) Extended SMIL Interpreter (ESI), 2) Device Information Base (DIB), 3) Orchestrator, 4) Global Time Base, and 5) Audio Decoding and Player(ADP). The ESI reads and interprets a SMIL script and then produces both of a time schedule for presenting clips and an IBEE. For producing the IBEE, the ESI refers Device Location Information Base(LIB) contained in DIB, and seeks matches between logical locations coded in SMIL script like "loc=left" in Figure 1 and physical locations of nearby devices. The best match is carried to the Orchestrator.

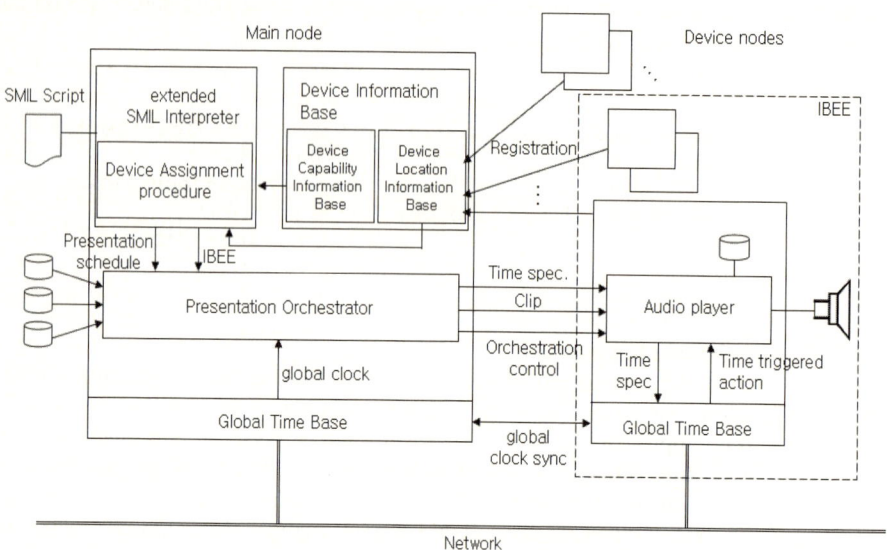

Fig. 2. Block diagram of L-DEAR

```
<par>
  <audio src="a1.mp3" begin="3s" dur="5s" loc="posMaster"/>
  <audio src="a2.mp3" begin="5s" dur="6s" loc="left"/>
  <audio src="a3.mp3" begin="7s" dur="10s" loc="right" />
  <audio src="a4.mp3" begin="3s" dur="5s" loc="leftTo a2"/>
  <audio src="a5.mp3" begin="5s" dur="6s" loc="rightTo a2"/>
  <audio src="a6.mp3" begin="7s" dur="10s" loc="leftTo a3" />
  <audio src="a7.mp3" begin="3s" dur="5s" loc="rightTo a7"/>
</par>
```

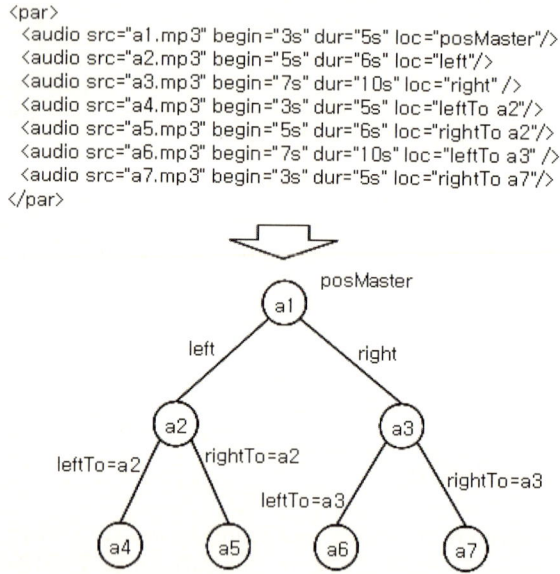

Fig. 3. A Spatial Relationship Tree(SRT)

The DIB is composed of CIB(device Capability Information Base) and LIB. These two information bases are acquired through a series of messages between the main node, i.e., orchestrator node and device nodes. A device node initiates a session with the main node after the boot-up is finished, and then communicates with a series of messages to carry its physical location information and device capability information. The device capabilities may contain the list of audio formats that it supports. The Orchestrator executes presentation schedules over IBEE by feeding clip data files, e.g., audio.mp3, into each corresponding device in the IBEE along with start- and stop-time specifications for the clip. The TMO provides global time basis on which the main node and device nodes in the IBEE should refer for conducting designated actions at a given global time. Once the device node receives time specifications, then ADP of the node registers TMO with time-triggered action requests for executing start and stop functions in the player.

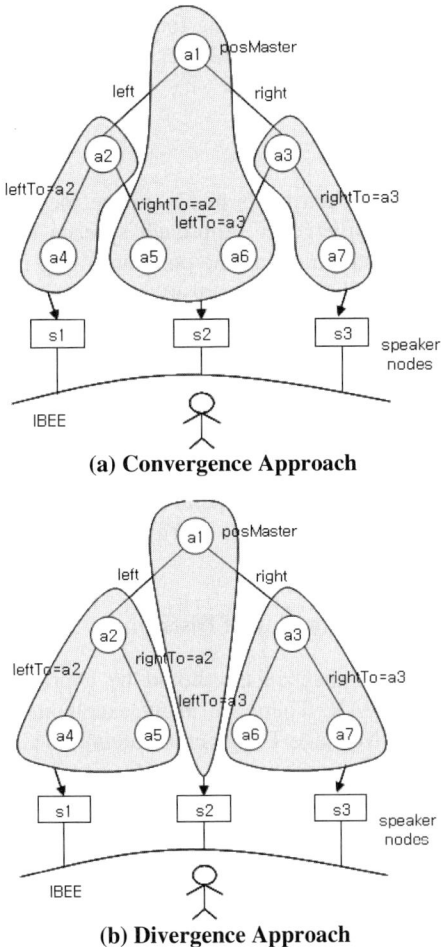

(a) Convergence Approach

(b) Divergence Approach

Fig. 4. A Spatial Relationship Tree(SRT)

4.1 Device Assignment Procedure for IBEE

The core of the L-DEAR is the device assignment procedure for constructing an IBEE. In this section, we discuss two approaches, that is, the convergence approach and divergence approach that can chosen in the implementation of L-DEAR. Ahead of our discussion about these two approaches, we need to explain a data structure, called SRT(Spatial Relationship Tree) for representing the spatial relationships among the clips. The SRT is a binary tree of which node denotes a clip and arc does relative positions, e.g., l, right, leftTo, and rightTo. As show in Figure 3, the given chunk of SMIL document is represented as a SRT with seven nodes assigned to each clip.

4.1.1 Convergence Approach
This approach is to put a focus on assigning the media objects or clips to the device nodes closer to the node to which the posMaster clip is assigned. As shown in Figure 4(a), the a1, a5 and a6 are assigned to the s2 speaker node located at central part of the IBEE.

4.1.2 Divergence Approach
While the Convergence Approach tends to assign the media objects or clips to the central part of IBEE, this Divergence Approach spreads the media objects to the device nodes far from the node to which the posMaster clip is assigned. As shown in Figure 4(b), while only the clip a1 has been assigned to the speaker node s2 at the central part, the clip a5 and a6 are assigned to the s1 and s2 speaker nodes located at left and right part of the IBEE, respectively.

5 Implementation Issues

In this section, we discuss on two topics crucial in embodying the IBEE and executing presentations in the manner of controlling distributed and coordinated actions over a global clock.

5.1 Global Time Based Coordination of Distributed Multimedia Actions

First of all, the global clock mechanism should be a primary basis on which we should implement our L-DEAR. There are many excellent research results such as TMO (Time Triggered and Message Triggered Objects)[5-7] and NTP(Network Time Protocol)[8]. Among those, we propose to use TMO, since it supports a unified object oriented programming scheme for distributed and time-coordinated actions as well as global clock.

The TMO programming and specification scheme was established in early 1990's with a concrete syntactic structure and execution semantics to support economical reliable design and implementation of RT systems [5]. The TMO scheme is a general-style component programming scheme and supports design of all types of components including distributable hard-RT objects and distributable non-RT objects within one general structure [6].

TMOs are devised to contain only high-level intuitive and yet precise expressions of timing requirements. No specification of timing requirements in (indirect) terms other than *start-windows* and *completion deadlines* for program units (e.g., object methods) and *time-windows for output actions* is required. For example, priorities are attributes often attached by the OS to low-level program abstractions such as threads and they are not natural expressions of timing requirements. Once the high-level specification of timeliness requirements is registered, then the middleware does its best to meet the specification by using the CPU scheduler and other resource schedulers in the underlying node OS and network infrastructure. More importantly, the TMO scheme enables the programmer to design *global time based coordination of distributed multimedia actions* very easily. The scheme provides a sound foundation for programming and executing distributed multimedia actions requiring global synchronization among the media units or among the nodes collectively engaged in a multimedia presentation performance.

The use of global time [9] can make it easy to measure QoS (quality-of-service) attributes such as delay jitter and synchronization skew[10]. Conventional approaches to measurement of QoS attributes at execution time were based on RTCP which basically uses QoS monitoring and feedback mechanisms built upon the assumption that the delay is symmetrical across the networks[11]. However, the symmetrical delay assumption is not so realistic and the RTCP based approaches do not produce high-accuracy measurements because of the feedback delay [12]. In contrast, a global time base of good precision, which is nowadays easy to realize due to advances in GPS and clock synchronization protocols [9], facilitates high-accuracy measurement of QoS attributes.

5.2   Session Initiation with Capability and Location Service

In order to organize IBEE, the DIB(Device Information Base) should require nodes registered with their capability and physical locations, which LIB (Location Information Base) CIB(device Capability Information Base). All those actions including connection, capability registration, and location registration can be integrated into one protocol called signaling protocol. Among the various signaling protocol such as H.323 [13] and SIP(Session Initiation Protocol)[14], the SIP likely matches well for our implementation of the DIB.

The SIP is an application layer control protocol for creating, modifying and terminating sessions with one or more participants. Entities in SIP are user agents, proxy servers and redirect servers. The SIP user agent listens for incoming SIP messages, and sends SIP messages upon user actions or incoming messages. The SIP proxy server relays SIP messages and the SIP redirect server returns the location of the host. Both the redirect and proxy server accepts registrations from users, in which the current location of the user is given. The location can be stored either locally at the SIP server, or in a dedicated location server. Deployment of such SIP servers enables L-DEAR to keep track of the locations of device nodes on the network [15].

In addition to the location service, SIP uses the Session Description Protocol (SDP)[16] for carrying out the negotiation for capability identification. Thus, SIP supports session descriptions that allow participants to agree on a set of compatible media types. The information contained in SDP can be used to organize an IBEE proper to decode and play the clip files compressed with certain types of algorithms.

6 Conclusions

We, in this paper, described our main theme, that is, to enhance spatial reality with IBEE(Immediate But Ephemeral device Ensemble). And also, by listing up primary architectural requirements, we derived an architecture called L-DEAR(Location-base Device Ensemble ARchiteture) to embody the IBEE. We proposed the convergence and divergence approaches for assigning networked device nodes to each media clip in the given distributed presentation. In addition, we discussed important issues in implementing L-DEAR, including such as the global clock mechanism and the location registration capability negotiation between main node and device nodes during the session initiation stage.

We also raised the issues for extending the mark-up language, SMIL, for the enhanced ability to express spatial relationships among the clips. Especially, we discussed three approaches for extending SMIL including the default rule approach, relative position approach, and test-and-switch approach. All those approaches are applicable in implementing the extended SMIL interpreter of L-DEAR.

We, however, could not discuss about some advanced topics such as measuring the degree of the spatial reality, and handling 3-D location information of the devices. Especially, the degree of the spatial reality will provide a human-centered objective function that the device assignment procedure should meet for enhancing the spatial reality ultimately. These topics are considered to be tackled later as further research issues.

Acknowledgement. This paper was supported by Konkuk University in 2005.

References

1. W3C, "Synchronized Multimedia Integration Language (SMIL 2.0)", 2001, http://www.w3.org/TR/2005/REC-SMIL2-20050107/
2. Thae-hyun Kim, Kyu-Chul Lee, "SMIL (Synchronized Multimedia Integration Language)-Multimedia Synchronization Language", Journal of Korean Multimedia Society, 2000
3. Sung-hyun Han, "A Study on the Synchronized Multimedia Integration Language: SMIL", Journal of Korean Society for Internet Information, 2001
4. Balakrishnan, H., R. Baliga, D. Curtis, M. Goraczko, A. Miu, N.B. Priyantha, A. Smith, K. Steele, S. Teller, K. Wang, "Lessons from Developing and Deploying the Cricket Indoor Location System," http://nms.lcs.mit.edu/cricket, Nov. 2003.
5. Kim, K.H. et. al, "Distributed computing based streaming and play of music ensemble realized through TMO programming," WORDS 2005, Kyungjoo, Korea, Feb. 2-5, 2005.
6. Kim, K.H., Ishida, M., and Liu, J.Q., "An Efficient Middleware Architecture Supporting Time-Triggered Message-Triggered Objects and an NT-based Implementation", *Proc. ISORC '99 (2nd IEEE CS Int'l Symp. on Object-Oriented Real-time Distributed Computing)*, St. Malo, France, May, 1999, pp.54-63.

7. Kim, D.H., and K H (Kane) Kim , "A TMO-based Software Architecture for Distributed Real-time Multimedia Processing," Proc, WORDS 2003(*IEEE Workshop in Object-oriented Real-time Dependable Systems*), Guadalajara, Mexico, Jan. 2003.

8. http://www.ntp.org

9. Kopetz, H., '*Real-Time Systems: Design Principles for Distributed Embedded Applications*', Kluwer Academic Publishers, ISBN: 0-7923-9894-7, Boston, 1997.

10. Steinmetz, R., "Human Perception of Jitter and Media Synchronization," *IEEE Journal of Selected Areas in Communications, Vol. 14, No. 1, Jan. 1996, pp. 61-72.*

11. 11. IETF, "RTP: A Transport Protocol for Real-Time Application," RFC 1889

12. Kim D.H., K H (Kane) Kim, S Liu, Jin H. Kim, "A TMO-based Approach to Tolerance to Transmission Jitters in Tele-Audio Services," Int'l Journal of Computer Systems Science & Engineering, Vol. 17, No. 6, Nov. 2002, pp. 325-334.

13. ITU-T, "Packet-based multimedia communications systems," Recommendation H.323

14. M. Handly, H. Schulzrinne, E. Schooler, and J. Rosenberg, "SIP: session initiation protocol," Request for Comments 2543, Internet Engineering Task Force, Mar. 1999.

15. Kim, D.H., J.Y. Kwak and K.H. Lee, Using the Session Initiation Protocol for Connected Multimedia Services in a Ubiquitous Home Network Environment, MIPS 2004, Grenoble, France, November 16-19, 2004.

16. Handley, M. and V. Jacobson, "SDP: session description protocol," RFC 2327, April 1998.

Air-Jet Button Effects in AR

Yeongmi Kim[1], Sehun Kim[1], Taejin Ha[2], Ian Oakley[3], Woontack Woo[2],
and Jeha Ryu[1]

[1] Human-Machine-Computer Interface Lab., Dept. of Mechatronics,
Gwangju Institute of Science and Technology,
Oryong-dong, Buk-gu, Gwangju 500-712 Republic of Korea
{kym, kshfire, ryu}@gist.ac.kr
http://dyconlab.gist.ac.kr
[2] U-VR Lab., Dept. of Information and Communication
{tha, wwoo}@gist.ac.kr
http://uvr.gist.ac.kr
[3] Smart Interface Research Team, Electronics and Telecommunications Research Institute,
161 Gaejeong Dong, Yuseong Gu, Daejeon, 300-700, Korea
ian@etri.re.kr
http://etri.re.kr

Abstract. Providing haptic cues can generate increased levels of presence in users as they interact with tangible objects. In this paper, we present button effects delivered by air-jet displays with the aim of providing click-like sensations when virtual buttons in an AR environment are pressed. We derive the profile of the haptic output by measuring the force profile of real physical buttons. To validate our concept, we have built an AR system featuring a cellular phone model which users can tangibly manipulate through a physical AR marker object. When users press a button on the model, they experience a corresponding click-like feeling at their fingertip. In this way, our system enables users to press a button on an AR model and experience a force profile generated by our pneumatic array directly derived from the act of pushing a button in the real world.

Keywords: Air-jet, button effect, AR, fingertip point extraction.

1 Introduction

In order to provide immersive interaction, multisensory feedback composed of visual, auditory and haptic elements needs to be merged together in an appropriate way. Many researchers have shown that performance is substantially improved when haptic sensations are added to visual and auditory environments [5]. We suggest that appropriate haptic cues are an essential component required to support the simple and natural manipulation of widgets and controls such as buttons, sliders and joysticks. Indeed, a haptic button has been a popular mechanism for controlling computer VR applications and the force profile for buttons has been implemented on kinesthetic devices such as the PHANToM™ in several APIs in order to present the realistic feeling virtual buttons. However, these devices are expensive and due to their bulk

Z. Pan et al. (Eds.): ICAT 2006, LNCS 4282, pp. 384–391, 2006.

and desk-based interaction paradigm, unsuitable for many AR scenarios. Tactile devices which present stimuli to the skin may be more suitable in this instance. Of these, pneumatic tactile devices, which feature an array of air jets directed onto the skin, are lightweight, able to provide pressure and to modulate the shape it is displayed in [1]. In addition, they are cost-effective and they have unconstrained workspaces when compared to kinesthetic feedback devices.

As the demand for additional haptic cues in AR increases, applications are being implemented for educational, military, entertainment and medical training purposes. There are several systems that use kinesthetic feedback devices to provide force feedback in AR. Kenneth Fase *et al.* proposed a system that features virtual training for welding tasks using a 3DOF haptic device [6]. Matt Adcock *et al.* have developed medical simulations using the PHANToM™ [8]. Also, Christoph W. Borst *et al.* presented haptic feedback for virtual panels using a force feedback glove [4]. In addition to force feedback, there have been some attempts to combine tactile feedback with augmented reality. Buchmann *et al.* used buzzers mounted in a glove in an urban planning workspace so that users could feel vibration when their hands made contact with an AR model of a city block [12]. Another application is based on an air-jet display consisting of 100 air nozzles and which provides feedback force of objects through an external air receiver [14].

In this paper, we present a button effect delivered by an air-jet display for interaction with a tangible AR object. In order to use appropriate pressure values in our system, we captured real button pressing forces and time plots. Furthermore, we propose a method which extracts the tips of the fingers by finding the convex hull points of the hand object and constraining the radius of palm. We use this in our AR environment, so that users can naturally interact with our haptically enhanced virtual object with their hands.

2 Pneumatic Tactile Interface

In order to produce the sensation of clicking a button, pneumatic tactile system is adopted in this paper since our pneumatic display can deliver appropriately changing stimuli to the surface of the skin as the button moves through the process of being pressed.

2.1 System Configuration

The existing air-jet system is used to presents button effect of the tangible object [13]. Overall configuration of our air-jet system is simple such that a user attaches air-jet display on the fingertip and input commands are coming from PC through an RS232 serial communication to Mexx ATMega 128 microprocessor controlling the state of the valves. As the valves, Yonwoo Pneumatic YSV10s are used to control the flow of air. The overall system configuration is shown in Fig.1. It consists of an air supplier, regulator, interface and control board, and pneumatic tactile display. The air supplier provides pressurized air and the regulator keeps the pressure.

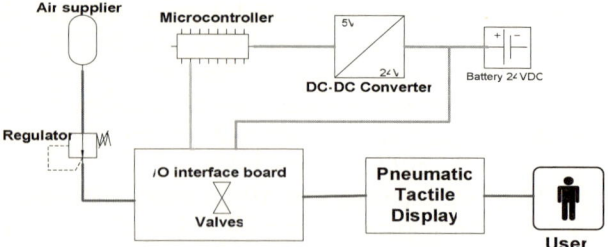

Fig. 1. System configuration of pneumatic tactile interface

The air-jet display forms 5x5 arrays on the finger pad and additional 5 air nozzles which are contacted each side of finger in order to produce the lateral force. The display features air nozzles with an external diameter of 2.4mm and internal diameter of 1.5 mm. Figure 2 illustrates the display design. In order for more natural interaction, the air-jet stimulates the fingertip of index finger which usually used to press buttons. In accordance with our previous psychophysical experiments, it can deliver richer information since air-jet display is mounted on fingertip while feeling of buzzers on the finger nails may be missed for some users as Volkert Buchmann mentioned [12].

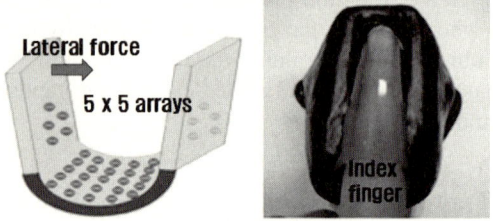

Fig. 2. Display design

3   Experiments on Measuring Force and Time of Buttons

In the previous study on PTI (Pneumatic Tactile Interface) [13], we concluded our experimental data could support that we could deliver cue capability to grow or shrink in magnitude by increasing number of air-jets, and sensory threshold for pneumatic cues are considerably greater than those for vibration cues. Thus, we implemented button effects with pneumatic tactile display by modulating the intensity of air-jet. Therefore, when a button of virtual models is pressed, users are able to feel button clicking feeling. In order to produce button effects, pressing force of the real button is measured and then applied to the pneumatic tactile system. In addition to the force profile, time value is one important factor for producing the button effects. Therefore, experiments have been conducted to figure out the pressing force and time value.

3.1 Experimental Set-Up

Creating the click-like sensation which makes people believe as if they press the physical button is desirable goal of our work. The characteristics of virtual buttons are reported in the literature [11]. In order to produce click-like feeling, we measured the forces while users press the real button. In order to measure the force-profile of physical buttons of the cellular phone [7], Tekscan's FlexiForce® Sensors A201-1(0-1 lb. force range) and a real button panel were used [Fig.3.].

Fig. 3. Measurements on button force

Basically, this sensor is equal to potentiometer; namely, the output of the sensor is proportional to the input force. AD converter in ATmega 128 is used to convert analog input to 10 bit digital data. Also, low-pass filter is adopted in order to avoid the interference of high frequency.

3.2 Force - Displacement Curve Experiment

The total length of a physical button is 0.2 mm. In order to find out the force profile of this button, we measured force data as pressuring down the button with 0.005 mm increment by using micrometer and 3000 samples were acquired at each length. As shown in Fig. 4. the measurement data of real button clicking force is similar to the well known virtual button force model. In other words, at the initial position force is linearly increased, then it suddenly decreasing, and then the force is increased remarkably. Also, it describes the average force of first peak which is about 160(0.7 N) and the average force for dead band is 93(0.4N).

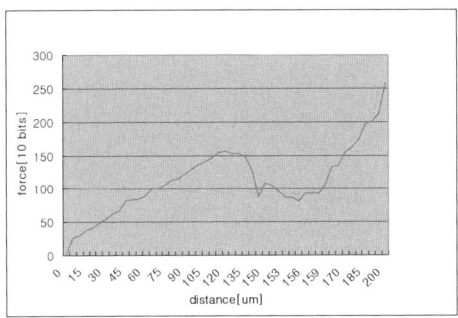

Fig. 4. Result of measurement of button force

3.3 Force - Time Curve Experiment

The timing is also key factor to provide button effects by the air-jet display. We conducted another experiment in order to find out the timing information and the characteristics of force profile related to the time. Eight subjects were participated in this experiment and they pressed the same button 20 times and all data were automatically saved as xls file format. Fig. 5. illustrates the result of experiment.

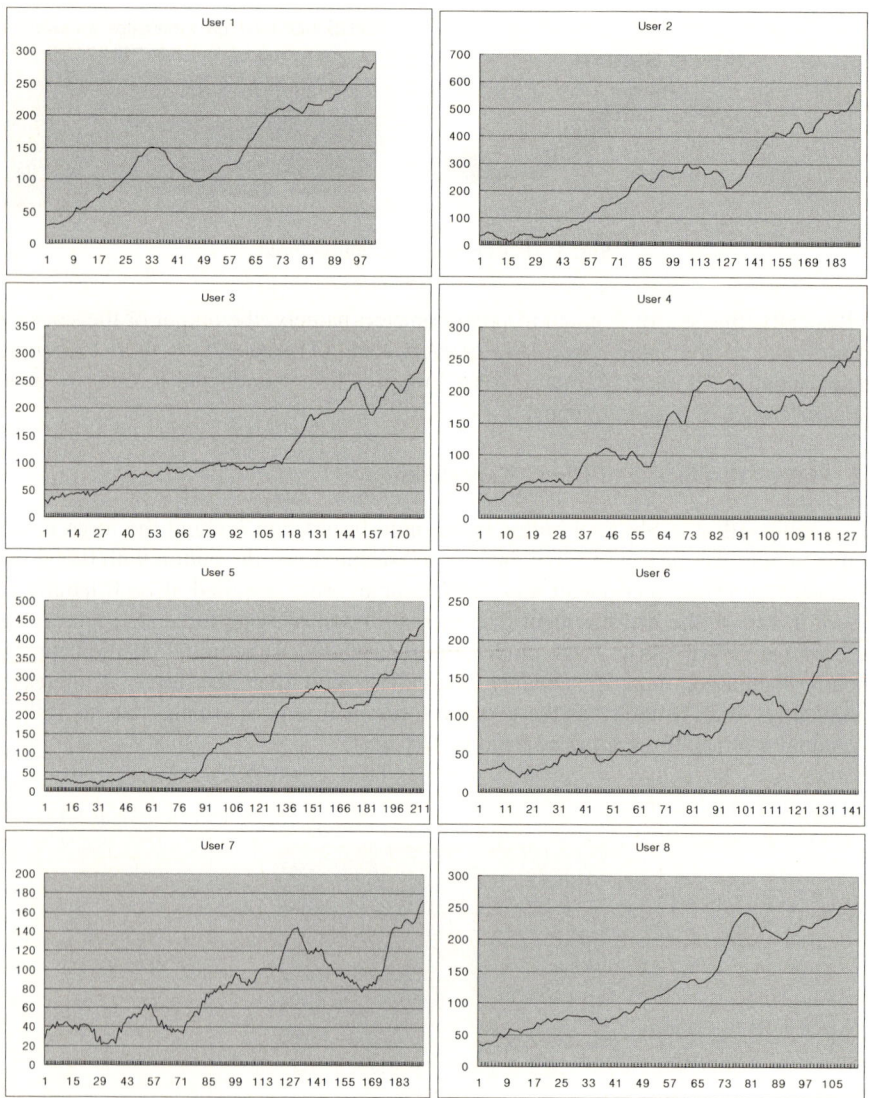

Fig. 5. Result of experiment on measuring force-time curve for a real button

These graphs show slightly different force profile comparing to the results described in section 3.2 since the acceleration while pressing the button may be affected to the results. Also, since the button of cellular phone has short length and the dead band time is too short to sense, the real force profile of button shows small dead band. The average time for initial increasing band is about 200 msec and the average time for dead band is 60 msec [60 msec = (30 samples x 1 sec) /500 samples].

3.4 Mapping Displayed Force to Pressure

Pressure can be obtained by following equation:

$$\text{Pressure [psi]} = \text{Force [pounds-force]} / \text{Area [inch}^2]. \tag{1}$$

That equation refers that if the force and area are known, we can generate the same amount of jet force at the nozzle. As we described the size of tube is known factor and mean of 500 sample force data is given in Fig. 5. Therefore, button effects delivered by air-jet display are provided according to the results of experiments. In order to produce force (0.7 N), the area of tubes should be calculated.

$$\text{Area [inch}^2] = \pi r^2. \tag{2}$$

In our display, the radius of tubes is 0.75 mm (0.0295 inch) so the area of each tube is 0.002734 [inch^2]. Therefore, 58 psi is required to produce the first peak force (0.7 N), when only one air-jet nozzle is used. However, by increasing the number of air-jet nozzles, less pressure is needed since total pressure is distributed into several air-jet nozzles. For example, six air-jets produce the same amount pressure at about 10 psi.

4   Interaction with Tangible Object in AR

The primary goal of our system is to integrate the pneumatic feedback derived from the pressure measurements of the real button with an AR system which allows the user to interact with graphical virtual models. We aim to add touch feedback to this graphical AR environment. To achieve this we focused on a model of a cellular phone and developed an AR system which displays the model and detects the user's fingertip position. When the user's finger touches a button on the phone model, we display the stored button pressure profile on our pneumatic array, in order to create the physical sensation that the button is being clicked. Typical fingertip detection systems rely on fiducial markers [2] attached to various portions of the hands, but this is unsatisfactory as problems of occlusion can occur, and also it can be both unnatural and inconvenient to use. Our system extracts the fingertip points by locating the convex hull points of the hand and using the palm as a constraining radius. Thus we allow the users to naturally interact with the virtual object using their hands. This system is explained in more detail below.

4.1 2D Based Fingertip Point Extraction and Collision Detection

The vision-based fingertip capture interface enables a more natural and intuitive style of interaction. In our system, users are able to interact with virtual objects using their hands and experience the results of their interactions through our pneumatic tactile display. They are able to push buttons on the augmented virtual game-phone, and feel corresponding tactile sensations. This system is enabled by a 2D based fingertip point extraction and simple collision detection.

In order to extract fingertip points, we use the "3 coins algorithm" [3]. However, this leads to the generation of a large number of convex hull points so we filter this data with the constraint that the fingertips must be relatively close to the palm: within 1.5 times its radius. We visually detect and display the hand using a combination of a skin color distribution detection algorithm [9] and a segmentation system designed to reduce visual occlusion [10].

4.2 Implementation

After the 2D finger position has been attained, this data can be easily integrated into the coordinate space of the 3D model. A simple collision detection algorithm then determines if the user is close to or touching a virtual button. When the user's finger is near a button, we display a blue 'cursor' on its tip and if that blue point collides with a button, the air-jet button effect is displayed. Figure 6 shows the user's fingertip approaching a button (left) and when it is on a button (right).

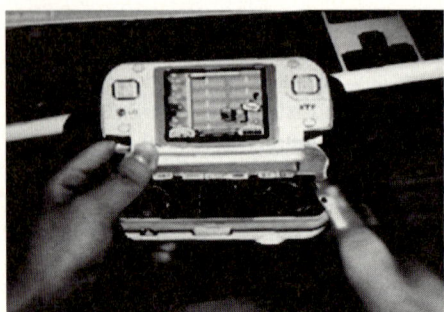

Fig. 6. Fingertip point extraction and providing air-jet button effects

5   Conclusion and Future Work

The proposed system produces button effects whereas most tactile displays have mainly provided weight, shape, meaningful texts and so on. By conducting the experiments on force-distance and force-time curve, it became possible to generate jet force at the nozzle according to the physical clicking force. In AR environment users are usually not perceived any haptic feedback, since augmented objects do not provide physical haptic feedback. In addition, manipulating the widget such as buttons, sliders, and joysticks is related to the performance of the task. Therefore, we provide button effects delivered by air-jet display while interacting with tangible objects for immersive interaction.

From the several fundamental studies, we examined air-jets let users feel the button effects and interact with an augmented object impressively. However, evaluation of this system will be done in the future to see effectiveness of our system. Also, not only button clicking feeing but also the shape of button will be provided.

Acknowledgments

This research was supported by the Republic of Korea's Ministry of Information and Communication (MIC) through the Realistic Broadcasting IT Research Center (RBRC) at the Gwangju Institute of Science and Technology (GIST), ICRC funded by the Ministry of Science and Technology of Korea and the UCN Project, the MIC 21C Frontier R&D Program in Korea and ICRC at GIST.

References

1. Amemiya, K. & Tanaka, Y., "Portable Tactile Display Using Air Jet", In the International Conference on Artificial Reality and Telexistence, 1999.
2. ARToolKit, http://www.hitl.washington.edu/artoolkit/
3. Avis, D. and Toussaint. "An optimal algorithm for determining the visibility of a polygon from an edge", IEEE Trans. Comp. C-30 (1981), 910-914
4. Christoph W.Borst, and Richard A. Volz, "Preliminary Report on a Haptic Feedback Technique for Basic Interactions with a Virtual Control Panel", EuroHaptics 2003 conference, pp. 1-13.
5. Hakan G., Benjamin P., Sankar J., & Uma J., "Design of a Haptic Device for Weight Sensation in Virtual environments", ASME International Mechanical Engineering Congress & Exposition, 2002
6. Kenneth Fase, Timothy Gifford, Robert Yancey, "Virtual Training for Welding", ISMAR, pp. 298-299, Third IEEE and ACM International Symposium on Mixed and Augmented Reality (ISMAR'04), 2004.
7. LG-KV 3600, http://www.cyon.co.kr/good/product/product_view1.jsp?product_id=165
8. Matt Adcock, Matthew Hutchins, Chris Gunn, "Augmented Reality Haptics: Using ARToolKit for Display of Haptic Applications", 2nd Int'l Augmented Reality Toolkit Workshop, Tokyo, Japan, October 7th, 2003.
9. Taejin Ha and Woontack Woo, "Bare Hand Interface for Interaction in the Video see-through HMD based Wearable AR Environment", to appear in ICEC 2006
10. Taejin Ha, Yeongmi Kim, Jeha Ryu and Woontack Woo, "Enhancing Immersiveness in Video see-through HMD based Immersive Model Realization", IEEK 06, pp.685-686
11. Timothy Miller, Bobert Zeleznik, "The Design of 3D Haptic Widget", 1999 Symposium on Interactive 3D Graphics Atlanta GAUSA
12. Volkert Buchmann, S. Violich, M. Billinghurst, A. Cockburn., "FingARtips: gesture based direct manipulation in Augmented Reality", In Proceedings of the 2nd international conference on Computer graphics and interactive techniques in Australasia and SouthEast Asia (Graphite 2004). 15-18th June, Singapore, 2004, ACM Press, New York, New York, pp. 212-221.
13. Yeongmi Kim, Ian Oakley, Jeha Ryu, "Combining Point Force Haptic and Pneumatic Tactile Displays", EuroHaptics 2006, pp.309-316, Paris, France
14. Yuriko Suzuki, Minoru Kobayashi, "Air Jet Driven Force Feedback in Virtual Reality", Computer Graphics and Applications, IEEE, 25(1), 44-77, 2005

Perceptualizing a "Haptic Edge" with Varying Stiffness Based on Force Constancy⋆

Jaeyoung Cheon and Seungmoon Choi

Virtual Reality and Perceptive Media Laboratory
Department of Computer Science and Engineering, POSTECH
Pohang, Republic of Korea
{icejae02, choism}@postech.ac.kr

Abstract. This paper introduces a novel haptic rendering technique devised to perceptualize a "haptic edge" correctly with respect to its stiffness and height models. Our previous study showed that the traditional penalty-based haptic rendering methods are not adequate to the collocated data of surface topography and stiffness since surface topography perceived by the user can be distorted from its model. In order to overcome the problem, we have developed a *topography compensation algorithm* based on the theory of *force constancy* which states that the user maintains a constant contact force when s/he strokes a surface to feel its topography. To the best of our knowledge, our technique is the first of its kind that explicitly considers the effect of user exploratory patterns in haptic rendering. Computationally, the algorithm is adaptive and efficient, not requiring any preprocessing of original data. We also demonstrate the performance and robustness of the proposed algorithm through a psychophysical experiment.

1 Introduction

The most important requirement of haptic rendering is that the properties of a virtual object *perceived by the user* must closely agree to those *modeled in the virtual environment*. However, the requirement can be often prohibited by many causes such as the effect of haptic interface dynamics on the final dynamics that the user feels [1], instability of haptic interaction between the device and the user [2][3], and a haptic rendering technique that fails to adequately account for the governing physics of the target attribute [4]. All of these shortcomings can lead to the user's perception of unintended artifacts in addition to the modeled haptic attributes, or only artifacts in the worst case. A recent survey on the issues and advanced techniques of haptic rendering can be found in [5].

⋆ This work was supported in parts by grant No. 1RE0601701 from POSTECH and grant No. R01-2006-000-10808-0 from the Basic Research Program of the Korea Science and Engineering Foundation (KOSEF). The authors wish to thank Prof. Hong Z. Tan for valuable discussions and Prof. Gerard Jounghyun Kim for carefully proof-reading this paper.

Z. Pan et al. (Eds.): ICAT 2006, LNCS 4282, pp. 392–405, 2006.

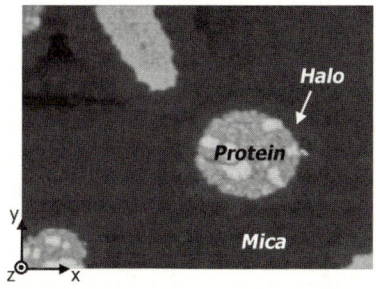

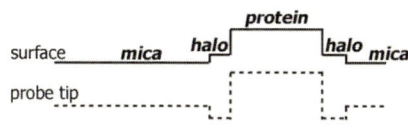

(a) The surface height map. Higher re-   (b) A cross-section of the height map with
gions are coded with lighter colors.   the trajectory of a haptic probe tip.

Fig. 1. "Protein-on-mica" data. See the text for details.

Haptically recreating virtual environment dynamics with high fidelity can be much more difficult in the applications of scientific data perceptualization. Data perceptualization is an emerging interdisciplinary field extended from data visualization so as to utilize other senses such as touch and sound in addition to vision. A pioneering work of data perceptulization was Project GROPE [6] that allowed users to perceptualize the docking of molecules through the use of a force feedback device and a head-mounted visual display. Subsequently, Taylor et al. [7] developed a teleoperation system that interfaced a force feedback display to a scanning tunneling microscope providing both visual and haptic feedback of measured data. Early haptic volume rendering algorithms [8][9] used the local gradient as the surface normal and force transfer functions. Newer systems have incorporated proxy-based haptic rendering techniques for volumetric data rendering [10][11]. Recently, Maciejewski et. al. [12] released a data perceptualization system that included a haptic rendering technique for multiple volumetric data sets. Yano et. al. [13] showed that the perception of stiffness distribution defined on a flat surface may not match to its model and proposed a simple compensation technique that prewarps the stiffness model.

Unlike other virtual reality applications that emulate real environments, the attributes to render are frequently collocated in data perceptualization. One such example that has motivated our work is provided in Fig. 1(a). The figure shows a surface height map of patches of bi-lipid membrane with embedded proteins on a mica substrate with lighter colors corresponding to higher surfaces. The topography map was acquired with a scanning probe microscope that can measure various nanometer-scale collocated features on a flat substrate [14]. The image shows a nearly circular protein membrane patch surrounded by a halo (presumably of lipids that have dissociated from the membrane) resting on an atomically flat mica substrate. Because the membrane patch is filled with a periodic array of the transmembrane protein, it should be considerably stiffer than the halo of dissociated lipids, but not as stiff as the mica substrate. The height profile of the data set is illustrated in Fig. 1(b) with a solid line. For convenience, we will refer to this image as the "protein-on-mica" data set (see [15] for further details about the data set).

In our previous study [15], we attempted to render the "protein-on-mica" data set with the traditional penalty-based haptic rendering techniques (e.g., [16][17]). A user could tap on and stroke the resulting virtual haptic surface to gauge both the local stiffness and topography, respectively. However, it was consistently reported that the halo regions felt lower than the surrounding protein and mica regions in opposite to the model. The observation was confirmed by recording probe-tip trajectories during a user's stroking of the data set. A probe-tip trajectory simplified for clear demonstration is provided in Fig. 1(b). The figure shows that the probe tip was "dipped" in the halo region against the height map. Note that the penalty-based techniques are originally designed to render an object shape with uniform stiffness.

Our follow-up study revealed that the inversion of perceived height difference around the halo region occurs due to a human exploratory behavior named *force constancy* [15]. Force constancy states that a user tends to maintain a constant penetration force while stroking a virtual surface in order to perceive its topography. Applying force constancy to the "protein-on-mica" data set where the mica region had lower stiffness than its surrounding regions, we can confirm that the user maintaining a constant contact force resulted in larger penetration depth in the halo region. If the increase in penetration depth exceeded the modeled height difference between halo and mica, the halo region was incorrectly perceived to be lower than the mica region against their modeled height difference. More detailed analysis using force constancy is provided in Sec. 2.

The "protein-on-mica" data set is an example that substantiates the need of new rendering algorithms for correct perceptualization of data sets with *collocated surface topography and stiffness*. Responding to the need, we have developed a topography compensation algorithm based on force constancy, concentrating on rendering of a haptic edge. By the "haptic edge," we refer to a region where surface height changes abruptly (just as the halo region of the "protein-on-mica" data set), as opposed to a visual edge where color varies quickly. The method adaptively adjusts surface height topography by estimating user-applied force based on force constancy. The algorithm is very computationally efficient, and does not require any preprocessing of the data. The performance of the rendering algorithm was extensively evaluated in terms of both stimulus characterization and human perception. The results showed that our algorithm is very effective and robust at correctly rendering a haptic edge with varying stiffness, without any perceptual distortions. The performance evaluation has also unveiled a few new research issues that need to be resolved to extend our current algorithm to be applicable to a general case of continuously varying surface topography with nonuniform stiffness.

The remainder of this paper proceeds as follows. In Sec. 2, we briefly review the theory of force constancy. The haptic rendering method is proposed in Sec. 3, followed by the results of comprehensive performance evaluation in Sec. 4. We conclude the paper in Sec. 5 with a plan for future work.

2   Force Constancy

The theory of force constancy states that users maintain a constant penetration force when they stroke virtual surfaces in order to perceive the surface topography. Our previous psychophysical study showed that the users indeed maintained a constant contact force when a surface was not too soft (surface stiffness = 0.3 – 1.1 N/mm) [15]. Stiffness less than 0.3 N/mm renders a very soft surface and thus does not provide a clear boundary of the surface. The users tended to use smaller penetration forces in this case.

We can obtain a mathematical expression for perceived height difference subject to nonuniform surface stiffness based on force constancy. Consider a simple case of two vertical virtual planes depicted as P_1 and P_2 in Fig. 2. The heights of the two surfaces are denoted by h_1 and h_2 along the z-axis ($\Delta h = h_2 - h_1 > 0$ in Fig. 2), and the stiffness values are by k_1 and k_2, respectively. The higher plane P_2 is closer to the user than the lower plane P_1. We also assume that force is rendered with the penalty-based method by $f_z = k\,(h - p_z)$ where p_z is the probe-tip position normal to the planes. If the probe tip is under P_1, $h = h_1$ and $k = k_1$, and if under P_2, $h = h_2$ and $k = k_2$.

As the user strokes the virtual surface from P_1 to P_2, the perceived height difference Δp_z traced by the probe tip can be computed as:

$$\Delta p_z = \Delta h + \Delta h_d \ . \tag{1}$$

where

$$\Delta h_d = -f_p \left(\frac{1}{k_2} - \frac{1}{k_1} \right) \ . \tag{2}$$

Here, Δh_d represents the amount of distorted height difference due to the stiffness change and f_p is the constant penetration force applied by the user. The detailed derivation is provided in [15].

Eqn. 1 shows that the perceived surface height difference has two components. The first term (Δh) is the modeled height difference that we intend for the user to feel. The second term (Δh_d), however, introduces a distortion in perceived surface height difference when $k_1 \neq k_2$, i.e., the two planes are not equally stiff. Depending on parameter values, we can think of three possible scenarios:

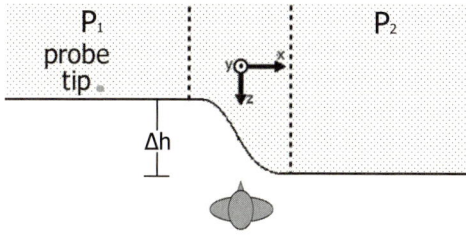

Fig. 2. Top view of the haptic rendering of two vertical planes. The symbol at the bottom represents a user facing the vertical surface.

1. $k_1 = k_2$: $\Delta h_d = 0 \Rightarrow \Delta p_z = \Delta h$. This is the case that most haptic rendering algorithms assume. The probe-tip follows a trajectory that is parallel to the modeled virtual surface topography.

2. $k_1 > k_2$: $\Delta h_d < 0 \Rightarrow \Delta p_z < \Delta h$. This is a case similar to that encountered with the "protein-on-mica" data set if we consider P_1 to be the lower and stiffer mica substrate and P_2 to be the higher and softer halo surface. If $|\Delta h_d| > |\Delta h|$, the higher plane P_2 is perceived to be lower than the lower plane P_1.

3. $k_1 < k_2$: $\Delta h_d > 0 \Rightarrow \Delta p_z > \Delta h$. In this case, the surface-height difference between P_1 and P_2 is perceived to be greater than what it should be.

3   Topography Compensation Algorithm

This section presents the compensation algorithm developed to deliver a haptic edge defined on a surface with nonuniform stiffness in a perceptually correct manner. Our approach is adaptive since proper compensation requires the knowledge of user-applied force (f_p in Eqn. 2) that is unavailable in preprocessing. The basic idea is to cancel out Δh_d (see Eqn. 1) in every haptic update interval. This would make perceived height difference Δp_z equivalent to modeled difference Δh. We thus estimate Δh_d in each haptic update interval and adjust the surface height using the estimated value.

At time instance t, let the probe-tip position of a haptic interface be $\mathbf{p}(t) = (p_x(t), p_y(t), p_z(t))$. Without loss of generality, we assume that a height map $h(\cdot, \cdot)$ and a stiffness map $k(\cdot, \cdot)$ are defined on xy plane, consistently with Sec. 2. We also denote that $h(t) = h(p_x(t), p_y(t))$ and $k(t) = k(p_x(t), p_y(t))$ for simplicity. Consider $t = n$ where n is a discrete time index for haptic update loop. In each loop, we compute $\Delta h_c(n)$ to compensate the height distortion of $\Delta h_d(n)$. Using the compensated height difference $\Delta h + \Delta h_c(n)$ instead of Δh in Eqn. 1 results in

$$\Delta p_z(n) = \Delta h(n) + [\Delta h_c(n) + \Delta h_d(n)] . \tag{3}$$

Therefore, setting $\Delta h_c(n) = -\Delta h_d(n)$ ensures that the modeled height difference will be identical to the perceived difference.

The critical part of the topography compensation algorithm is estimating $\Delta h_d(n)$ in Eqn. 2. When $k(n) = k(n-1)$, it is clear that $\Delta h_d(n) = 0$. When $k(n) \neq k(n-1)$, user-applied force f_p needs to be estimated. In general, a force sensor is required to exactly compute f_p. However, force sensors are not available in many haptic interfaces, especially those of impedance type. Instead, our estimation relies on two fundamental facts on the human motor characteristics. The first one is force constancy. If the user maintains a constant penetration force during stroking a surface, the force that the user is applying to the surface is in equilibrium with the force that the haptic interface is producing. This fact allows to use the force computed by a rendering algorithm for estimating f_p. The other consideration is the human motion bandwidth. A haptic update rate (typically 1 kHz) is much faster than the human motion bandwidth (less than 10 Hz), which implies that user-applied force cannot change abruptly within a few haptic update intervals. Taken the two facts together, we estimate user-applied force $f_p(n)$ as:

$$f_p(n) = f_z(n-1) .\tag{4}$$

where $f_z(n-1)$ is a force command along the z-direction computed in the previous update interval by the haptic rendering algorithm. Then, the estimated height distortion term $\Delta\hat{h}_d(n)$ is

$$\Delta\hat{h}_d(n) = -f_z(n-1)\left(\frac{1}{k(n)} - \frac{1}{k(n-1)}\right) .\tag{5}$$

Finally, our topography compensation algorithm can be summarized as the following three computational steps:

(1) Height Compensation Term

$$\Delta h_c(n) = \begin{cases} 0 & \text{if} \quad k(n) = k(n-1) \\ f_z(n-1)\left(\dfrac{1}{k(n)} - \dfrac{1}{k(n-1)}\right) & \text{if} \quad k(n) \neq k(n-1) \end{cases} .\tag{6}$$

(2) Compensated Height

$$h_c(n) = h(n) + \sum_{i=1}^{n} \Delta h_c(n) .\tag{7}$$

(3) Force Command

$$f_z(n) = k(n)\left(h_c(n) - p_z(n)\right) .\tag{8}$$

Note that in Eqn. 7, the height compensation terms need to be accumulated in order for the previous height distortions to be accounted for.

4   Experiment

We measured the reliability of the topography compensation algorithm for delivering the information of a haptic edge in a psychophysical experiment. The traditional penalty-based method was also tested for performance comparison. During the experiment, we recorded probe-tip trajectories felt by the subjects' hand and used them to judge the similarity of rendered height differences to their models. This section reports the detailed design and the results of the psychophysical experiment.

4.1   Methods

This section describes the design of the psychophysical experiment.

Apparatus: A PHANToM model 1.0A with a stylus shown in Fig. 3(a) is used in the experiment.

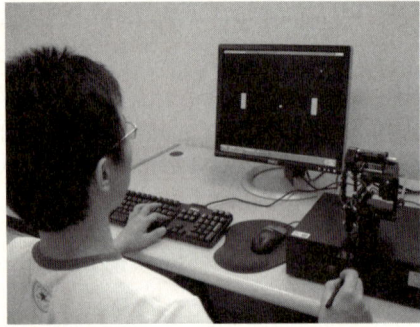
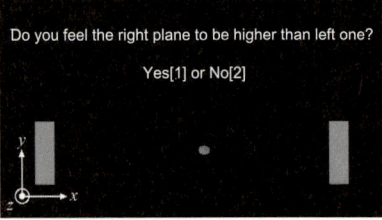

(a) A subject performing the experiment. (b) The visual scene shown on the monitor.

Fig. 3. The setup of the psychophysical experiment

Subjects: Seven subjects (S1–S7) participated in the experiment. S7 was female, and the other subjects were all male. All subjects self-declared to be right-handed, except for S3. S2 and S4 were experienced users of the PHANToM. S1, S5, and S6 were generally familiar with haptic interfaces, but not as experienced as S2 and S4. S3 and S7 had not used any haptic interfaces prior to their participation to this experiment. The age of the subjects ranged from 21 to 32 years with the average of 25.4. No subjects reported any known sensory or motor impairments with their upper extremity.

Stimuli: The haptic stimuli used in the experiment consisted of two vertically adjoined planes facing the user as shown in Fig. 2. A haptic edge between the two planes is modeled using Hanning windows (half-cycle sinusoidal functions) that smoothly connected the two planes in both height and stiffness in order to prevent rendering instability. The equations of the Hanning windows were equivalent to those used in our previous study [15]. The window width was set to 4 mm which resulted in stable transitions across the haptic edges in all experimental conditions. During the experiment, a computer monitor displayed visual information only to provide a spatial reference to the subjects. As shown in Fig. 3(b), the visual scene consisted of two blocks representing the starting and ending regions for stylus stroking, a blue cone showing the stylus-tip position, and texts asking a question to the subjects. Note that the text appeared on the screen only when the subjects were about to enter a response.

Experimental Conditions: Table 1 summarizes the parameter values used in each experimental condition. The height of a haptic edge (Δh) was fixed to 3 mm in all conditions. Three sets of stiffness values were tested, resulting in three conditions (C1–C3 in the table). The table also shows expected perceived height differences (Δp_z) for a range of used-applied forces (0.5 – 3.0 N) when the penalty-based rendering rule was employed. The range covers the distribution (0.87 – 2.23 N) of the preferred contact force levels of the participants measured in our previous study [15]. The conditions were designed so that the penalty-based algorithm would result in different levels of distortion ($\Delta p_z \neq 3.0$ mm). Considering the human detection thresholds of surface height difference ($\simeq 0.66$

Table 1. Parameter values used in the psychophysical experiment

Experimental	k_1	k_2	h_1	h_2	Δh	Δp_z (mm)			
Condition	(N/mm)	(N/mm)	(mm)	(mm)	(mm)	f_p=0.5	f_p=1.0	f_p=2.0	f_p=3.0 (N)
C1	0.6	0.3	-1.5	1.5	3.0	2.17	1.33	-0.33	-2.00
C2	0.9	0.3	-1.5	1.5	3.0	1.89	0.78	-1.44	-3.67
C3	0.9	0.6	-1.5	1.5	3.0	2.72	2.44	1.89	1.33

mm; see [15]), C3 would produce results most consistent with the height model, C2 most inconsistent, and C1 in the middle. We also expect that the topography compensation algorithm would render the height difference between P_1 and P_2 to be modeled, i.e., $\Delta p_z = \Delta h$ regardless the stiffness differences. Throughout the experiment, haptic rendering was updated at 1 kHz.

Procedure: A one-interval two-alternative forced-choice paradigm [18] was used to measure the subjects' sensitivity to height difference between the two planes independent of their response biases. On each trial, P_1 was randomly presented on the left (with P_2 on the right) or on the right (with P_2 on the left) with equal probabilities. We denote these two stimulus alternatives with $P_1 \rightarrow P_2$ and $P_2 \rightarrow P_1$, respectively. The subjects' tasks were to stroke the virtual surface from left to right once and to report whether the plane on the right was perceived to be higher or lower than the one on the left using a keyboard (see Fig. 3). Each subject conducted 60 trials in each experimental condition. The half of the 60 trials was rendered with the topography compensation algorithm, and the other half was with the penalty-based method. The order of trials within each experimental condition was randomized. The order of the three experimental conditions was also randomized for each subject. Once data collection began, no correct-answer feedback was provided to the subject.

In each trial, the subjects were instructed to move the probe tip toward the left block until the color of the block turned from green to red, indicating the beginning of a trial (see Fig. 3(b) again). Once the probe tip entered a ±2 mm band along the y-axis (centered on the line connecting the centers of the two blocks), its motion was constrained to the zx (horizontal) plane. The subjects then stroked the virtual surface from left to right until the probe tip intersected the right block. The color of the right block turned from green to red to indicate the end of the current trial. The two planes were then turned to have the same height until a response was entered. It follows that one trial consisted of one sweep across the vertical planes. The probe-tip position and the force computed from a rendering algorithm were also recorded on a computer file in every trial. The whole experiment took about 20 minutes for each subject excluding training.

Before the subjects started the experiment, they had training sessions each of which was composed of 24 trials. The trials in each session differed in experimental condition and rendering algorithm. Most subjects became familiar with the task with only one training session. Just a few subjects repeated the training session up to two times upon their requests.

Data Analysis: We computed sensitivity index d' from the confusion matrix of each subject and each experimental condition. Sensitivity index is a measure for discriminability and free of response bias [18]. In our setting, a positive d' indicates that a subject judged P_2 to be higher than P_1, a d' close to zero that the subject could not discriminate the relative height difference between P_1 and P_2, and a negative d' that the subject judged P_2 to be lower than P_1.

We also computed the average penetration force of each subject from the recorded data. From the recorded data of a subject in each trial, rendered forces were averaged over the ± 100 ms interval whose center corresponded to the middle point of the haptic edge. These mean forces were averaged again for the average penetration force of the subject.

4.2   Results

The results of the experiment are summarized by bar graphs shown in Fig. 4. Figs. 4(a) – 4(c) represent the sensitivity indices of each subject under conditions C1 – C3, respectively. The d' values averaged across the subjects are plotted in Fig. 4(d). The average d' under each condition was computed from a confusion matrix that pooled the confusion matrices of all subjects under the corresponding condition. In each figure, the left group represents the results of the topography compensation algorithm and the right group those of the penalty-based algorithm. Note that d' values that reached ∞ are truncated to 5 and those reached $-\infty$ to -5 for visibility.

It is apparent from Fig. 4 that our topography compensation algorithm produced large positive d' values under all experimental conditions and for all subjects. This indicates that all subjects perceived P_2 to be higher than P_1 as regardless stiffness differences between P_1 and P_2, which clearly agrees to the height model used in the experiment ($\Delta h_z = 3$ mm). However, the penalty-based algorithm resulted in unreliable perception of height differences. Under C1 and C2, the d' values of the penalty-based algorithms are mostly negative or close to zero. This means that P_2 felt lower than, or equally high to P_1, respectively, which is clearly inconsistent with the height model. Under C3, the d' values of the penalty-based method are all positive. Note that this was expected in our experiment design (see Δp_z in Table 1). However, the d' value of each subject under C3 is mostly smaller than or close to the corresponding d' value of the topography compensation algorithm. This implies that our algorithm was more robust in delivering the height of a haptic edge. All of these results are consistent with our expectations discussed earlier.

The variability of individual discriminability seems to be highly correlated with the average penetration forces of the subjects. Table 2 lists the measured average penetration force of each subject and the corresponding expected perceived height differences under the three experimental conditions computed from the force constancy model when penalty-based rendering is employed. Considering that the detection threshold of surface height change is about 0.66 mm [15], the pairs of subject and experimental condition exhibiting $|\Delta p_z|$ less than 0.66 mm in Table 2 were expected to result in d' close to 0. The values of Δp_z larger

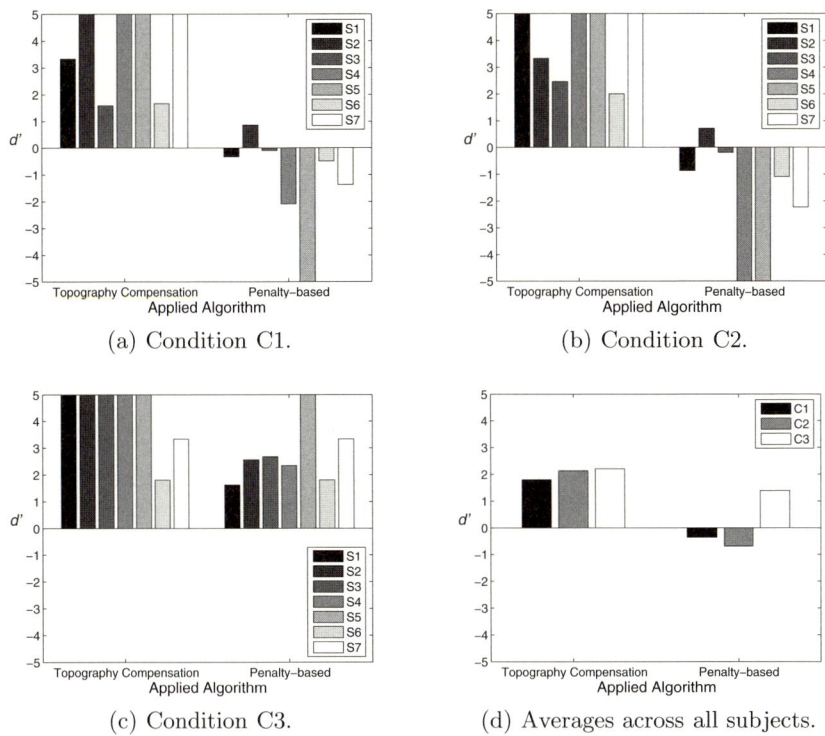

(a) Condition C1.

(b) Condition C2.

(c) Condition C3.

(d) Averages across all subjects.

Fig. 4. Sensitivity indices d' measured in the psychophysical experiment

Table 2. Average penetration forces measured in the experiment and corresponding Δp_z when the penalty-based rendering is used

Subject	S1	S2	S3	S4	S5	S6	S7
f_p (N)	1.41	1.43	1.53	2.57	2.60	2.69	2.72
Δp_z (mm) C1	0.65	0.62	0.45	-1.28	-1.33	-1.48	-1.53
C2	0.13	-0.18	-0.40	-2.71	-2.78	-2.98	-3.04
C3	2.22	2.21	2.15	1.57	1.56	1.51	1.49

than 0.66 mm would make d' larger than 1, and those less than -0.66 mm would d' smaller than -1. These predictions can be well confirmed by comparing the d' values shown in Fig. 4 and the Δp_z values in Table 2, except for the d' of S6 under C1.

We also carefully examined the trajectories of the PHANToM stylus tip recorded during the experiment. Overall, the measured trajectories when the topography compensation algorithm was used were parallel to the surface height model around the haptic edge. However, those of the penalty-based algorithm were often severely distorted from the height model. Four examples of the measured probe-tip trajectories are provided in Fig. 5. Figs. 5(a) and 5(b) show the

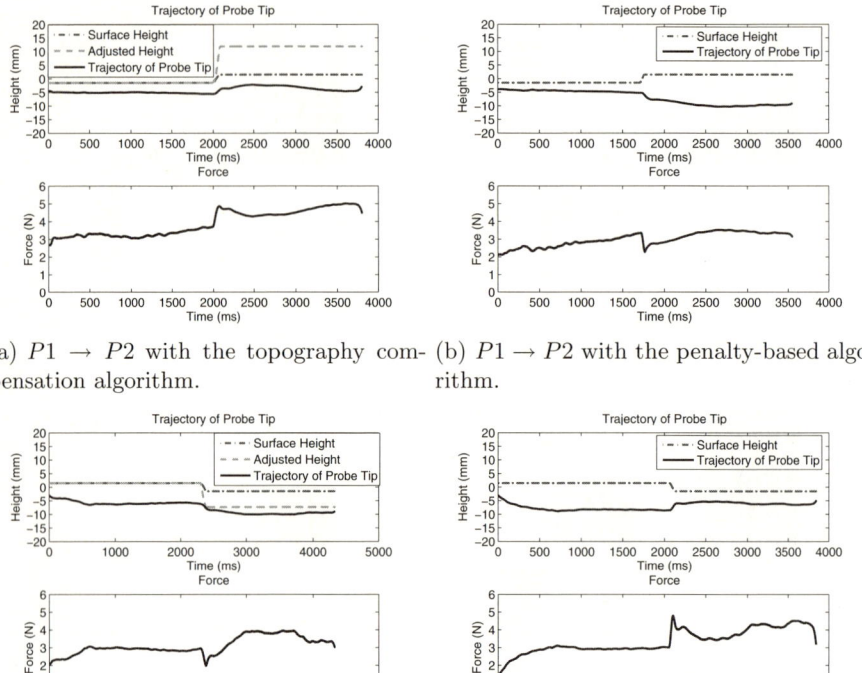

(a) $P1 \to P2$ with the topography compensation algorithm.

(b) $P1 \to P2$ with the penalty-based algorithm.

(c) $P2 \to P1$ with the topography compensation algorithm.

(d) $P2 \to P1$ with the penalty-based algorithm.

Fig. 5. Probe tip trajectories delivered to the hand

data measured in trials where S5 stroked from left to right the surface in the $P_1 \to P_2$ configuration under C2, with and without the compensation algorithm, respectively. In each figure, the trajectory of the probe-tip is represented by a blue solid line in the upper panel along with the surface height model shown in a red dashed-dotted line. Fig. 5(a) also contains the adjusted height model $(h_c(n))$ drawn with a green dashed line. The forces rendered by the corresponding algorithms are shown in the lower panels. One can observe from Fig. 5(a) that the topography compensation algorithm rendered the stylus trajectory to be parallel to the surface model around the haptic edge and thus perceptualized the edge information correctly. However, the penalty-based algorithm in Fig. 5(b) exhibits a probe-tip trajectory inverted from its model around the haptic edge. The same observations can be made in Figs. 5(c) and 5(d) that show the measured data of S5 stroking a surface with P_2 on the left and P_1 on the right. The height differences measured in Figs. 5(a) and 5(c) were approximately 2.6 mm and 3.3 mm, respectively. These values were close to the modeled height difference ($= 3$ mm) and thus well demonstrate the robust performance of the compensation algorithm.

5   General Discussions

In this paper, we have presented a haptic rendering method that correctly delivers the height information of a haptic edge despite its encompassing stiffness change. The algorithm estimates user-applied force based on the human motor characteristics and uses the information in adaptively adjusting surface height. The experimental results have manifested the robust performance of our topography compensation algorithm. To the best of our knowledge, this is among the first attempts to incorporate the effect of human exploratory patterns into computational techniques for haptic rendering, thereby accomplishing more precise perception. We believe that such approaches would lead computer haptics to advance one step further considering the bidirectional nature of haptic interaction.

This work has been our first step towards perceptually correct haptic rendering of collocated surface topography and stiffness. We clarify again that our criterion of "correctness" is whether rendered attributes agree to their models, which is a fundamental requirement in data perceptualization. Investigating what happens on a real object surface with varying stiffness is another research direction that we are pursuing in parallel.

Our future work can be laid out as follows. First, in our experiences, changing force direction according to the geometry of a haptic edge (as opposed to the fixed force direction used in the present study) seems to be beneficial for edge detection. In this case, when a probe tip hits a haptic edge, tactile cues can occur due to the resulting force direction change. These initial tactile cues may help the perception of the haptic edge, in addition to the kinesthetic sensory cues resulted from a position change. We plan to quantify performance enhancement of varying force directions in the near future. Second, we plan to elaborate the way of estimating user-applied force. Inside a haptic edge, it was observed that the force generated by the PHANToM was no longer in equilibrium with the user-applied force (see the bottom panels of Fig. 5). It seems that the user cannot maintain constant contact force when the force exerted by the haptic interface changes abruptly. This would result in errors in the user-applied force estimated using the current algorithm. Although this error was not critical in the present psychophysical experiment (recall that the modeled edge height was 3 mm, which is much higher than the edge detection threshold of 0.66 mm), it may affect the performance of our compensation algorithm for height differences close to the detection threshold. Finally, it was found that surface heights perceived with different exploratory procedures[1] may not be consistent. For example, the perceived height of plane P_2 in Fig. 5(a) by stroking would be one resulted from the adjusted height represented by the green dashed line. However, tapping on P_2 without touching P_1 before would make the current algorithm position the surface at its original height represented by the red dash-dotted line.

---

[1] Exploratory procedure refers to a stereotypical movement pattern that we employ to perceive a certain object attribute by touch [19]. For instances, tapping is an optimal exploratory procedure for stiffness perception, and stroking is for topography change and texture perception.

This inconsistency is because our compensation algorithm was designed solely for the exploratory procedure of stroking. Extending the algorithm to be able to adequately handle all exploratory procedures would be quite a challenging yet interesting assignment for perceptualizing the data of collocated surface topography and stiffness.

References

1. Lawrence, D.A.: Stability and transparency in bilateral teleoperation. IEEE Transactions on Robotics and Automation **9**(5) (1993) 624–637
2. Colgate, J.E., Schenkel, G.G.: Passivity of a class of sampled-data systems: Application to haptic interfaces. Journal of Robotic Systems **14**(1) (1997) 37–47
3. Choi, S., Tan, H.Z.: Perceived instability of virtual haptic texture. I. Experimental studies. Presence: Teleoperators and Virtual Environment **13**(4) (2004) 395 – 415
4. Choi, S., Tan, H.Z.: Perceived instability of haptic virtual texture. II. Effects of collision detection algorithm. Presence: Teleoperators and Virtual Environments **13**(4) (2005) 463–481
5. Otaduy, M.A., Lin, M.C.: Introduction to haptic rendering. In: ACM SIGGRAPH Course Notes on Recent Advances in Haptic Rendering & Applications. (2005) A3–A33
6. Brooks, T.L.: Telerobotic response requirements. In: Proceedings of IEEE Conference on Systems, Man and Cybernetics. (1990) 113–120
7. Taylor II, R.M., Robinett, W., Chi, V.L., Brooks, Jr., F.P., Wright, W.V., Williams, R.S., Snyder, E.J.: The nanomanipulator: A virtual-reality interface for a scanning tunneling microscope. In: Proceedings of the 20th Annual Conference on Computer Graphics and Interactive Techniques. (1993) 127–134
8. Iwata, H., Noma, H.: Volume haptization. In: Proceedings of the IEEE Virtual Reality Annual International Symposium. (1993) 16–23
9. Avila, R.S., Sobierajski, L.M.: A haptic interaction method for volume visualization. In: Proceedings of the ACM Conference on Visualization. (1996) 197–204
10. Lundin, K., Ynnerman, A., Gudmundsson, B.: Proxy-based haptic feedback from volumetric density data. In: Proceedings of Eurohaptics. (2002) 104–109
11. Ikits, M., Brederson, J.D., Hansen, C.D., Johnson, C.R.: A contraint-based technique for haptic volume exploration. In: Proceedings of the IEEE Visualization Conference. (2003) 263–269
12. Maciejewski, R., Choi, S., Ebert, D.S., Tan, H.Z.: Multi-modal perceptualization of volumetric data and its applicatiton to molecular docking. In: Proceedings of the World Haptics Conference. (2005) 511–514
13. Yano, H., Nudejima, M., Iwata, H.: Development of haptic rendering methods of rigidity distribution for tool-handling type haptic interface. In: Proceedings of the World Haptics Conference. (2005) 590–570
14. Sarid, D.: Scanning Force Microscopy. Oxford Unversity Press, New York (1991)
15. Choi, S., Walker, L., Tan, H.Z., Crittenden, S., Reifenberger, R.: Force constancy and its effect on haptic perception of virtual surfaces. ACM Transactions on Applied Perception **2**(2) (2005)
16. Zilles, C.B., Salisbury, J.K.: A constraint-based god-object method for haptic display. In: Proceedings of IEEE International Conference on Intelligent Robots and Systems. (1995) 146–151

17. Ruspini, D., Kolarov, K., Khatib, O.: The haptic display of complex graphical environments. In: Computer Graphics Proceedings (ACM SIGGRAPH Proceedings). (1997) 345–352
18. Macmillan, N.A., Creelman, C.D.: Detection Theory: A User's Guide. Second edn. Lawrence Erlbaum Associates (1994)
19. Lederman, S.J., Klatzky, R.L.: Hand movement: A window into haptic object recognition. Cognitive Psychology **19** (1987) 342–368

Multi-sensory Perception of Roughness: Empirical Study on Effects of Vibrotactile Feedback and Auditory Feedback in Texture Perception

Ki-Uk Kyung[1] and Dong-Soo Kwon[2]

[1] POST-PC Research Group, Digital Home Division, ETRI
161 Gajeong-dong, Yuseong-gu, Daejeon, 305-700, Korea
kyungku@etri.re.kr
[2] Human Robot Interaction Research Center, KAIST
373-1 Guseong-dong, Yuseong-gu, Daejeon, 305-701, Korea
kwonds@kaist.ac.kr

Abstract. This work investigates effects of vibrotactile stimuli and auditory feedback in perceiving roughness. One of objectives in the research is to derive functional correlations between perceived roughness and principal elements of vibrotactile stimuli. A tactile display device having a 5x6 pin array has been developed as the test bed for the quantitative experiment. Sandpapers were used as specimens of perceived roughness. The experimental results show that there is a tight correlation between perceived roughness and vibrotactile stimuli and their functional relations have been derived. The second objective of this research is to analyze the relation between perceived roughness and auditory feedback. Real sound samples recorded during rubbing surface of sandpaper specimens have been adopted as auditory feedback elements. The experimental results showed human could estimate surface roughness from auditory information if and only if he/she recognized the source of sounds. The results in this papers show possibilities to fortify representing roughness by using a tactile-auditory display in a tangible environment beyond conventional approach changing sizes of grits or grooves on a surface.

1 Introduction

In efforts to enhance the efficiency of task performance under a virtual environment or a remotely controlled workspace, numerous studies have been conducted to develop meaning of sharing feelings and creating tactile feelings. However, the existing developed apparatuses only utilize simple contact or the intensity of stimuli. Haptic display in an interactive dynamic environment or texture display still remains challengeable problems[22][9]. Particularly, since perceiving texture is a complex fusion process of multimodal inputs such as vision, sound as well as tactile sensation, the effects of multimodality also has to be investigated.

Since Weber started investigating human tactile sensitivity[20], many researchers have studied the relationship between perceived texture and the physical quantities of stimuli. Katz researched tactile performance quantitatively[7], and the results showed

Z. Pan et al. (Eds.): ICAT 2006, LNCS 4282, pp. 406–415, 2006.
© Springer-Verlag Berlin Heidelberg 2006

that vibrational stimuli are necessary in the perception of surface texture. Lederman and Taylor studied measurements of perceived roughness on various grooved surfaces[13]. Lederman et al. also investigated the role of vibration in tactual perception, [12]. Hollins et al. investigated how, on the basis of texture, tactile surfaces are connected with the perceptual space[6], finding that roughness is one of the essential sensations of touch. Recently, there have been several investigations that sought a relationship between vibrotaction and perceived roughness based on the duplex theory[4][5][6]. More recently, based on neuroscientific approaches, Cascio et al. and Yoshika et al. confirmed that temporal cues contribute to the tactile perception of roughness [1][21], while Smith et al. showed friction and tangential force affect tactile roughness[17]. In addition, recent studies have reported that human tactile sensitivity is a function of frequency of vibration [10]. There has been a research multimodal perception of virtual roughness. McGee et al conducted an experiment to investigate the perceived roughness of audio textures with the hypothesis that the frequency of the audio texture (or number of notes) will affect the perceived roughness of the virtual texture[16][20]. To keep pace with the demands of related research, this paper assesses how the frequency and amplitude changes of vibrational stimuli affect texture perception when using a tactile display system and how the auditory feedback affect roughness perception when using recorded sounds of rubbing real surface.

In section 2, a pin-array based vibrotactile display for quantitative stimuli is described. In section 3, the question of how much roughness, an essential element composing texture, can be represented using a tactile display is assessed experimentally. Therefore, the objective of the section is to derive the functional correlation between dependant variables and the perceived roughness of an arbitrary surface. The dependant variables are the amount of longitudinal movement of pins within an array, that is, the amplitude of vibrotactile stimuli, and the velocity of the pins' up and down movement, that is, the frequency of the tactile display. In section 4, effect of auditory feedback on tactile sensation is described. In this section, we adopt recorded real audio textures instead of using composed digital sounds. The participants' responses to the recorded sound have also been analyzed.

2   Texture Display System

2.1   Planar Distributed Tactile Display

A tactile display which has 5x6 tactors array has been developed as a test-bed for psychophysical experiment[10]. The maximum deflection is greater than 700μm and the bandwidth is about 350Hz. The blocking force of each pin is 0.06N. The specifications of the tactile stimulator with piezoelectric bimorphs were verified to ensure that it deforms the user's skin within 32dBSL (sensation level in decibels above threshold) [3][10][18]. The contact area is 9.7mm×7.9mm- a previous study showed this area is sufficient to discern difference in textures[9]. Since the tactile display unit is small enough to be embedded into a computer mouse, we developed a mouse-type texture display system[11]. The response time of each actuator is a scale of sub-milliseconds. This texture display system has been adopted as a test-bed in this study.

2.2 Performance Evaluation

Static Pattern Display. In order to use the proposed system as a computer interface, the system should provide some kinds of symbols, icons, or texts in a haptic manner. Therefore the performance of the tactile display was evaluated by asking subjects to discriminate between plain and textured polygons, round figures, and gratings. In these experiments, the actuator voltages were adjusted to set the desired shape, which was then held constant. Subjects were allowed to actively stroke the tactile array with their finger pad. The proportion of correct answers (90-99%, depending on the stimulus) far exceeded chance (10%), indicating that the display provides a satisfactory representation of tactile pattern[10].

Vibrotactile Pattern Display. We investigated how vibrotaction affects the identification of forms in which only passive touch, and not rubbing, is used. Craig has already compared the sensitivity of the scanned mode and static mode in discerning tactile patterns[2], but here we compare the sensitivity of the static mode and synchronized vibrating mode. In order to set the other conditions identical to those in the experiment of static pattern display, except for the vibrotaction, the same texture groups used in static pattern display were deployed with three different low frequencies: static, 1Hz, and 3Hz[10]. The frequencies were selected based on identical sensation levels, since the magnitudes of the threshold value in the frequency band of 0~5Hz are almost the same[19]. The experimental showed that the proportion of correct answers generally increases as the frequency rises from static to 1 Hz to 3Hz. From a psychophysical and physiological point of view, it seems likely that a 3Hz vibration can effectively stimulate the Merkel cells and that the associated SA I afferent provides the fine spatial resolution necessary for the subject to make the required discriminations. And we increased vibrational frequency of the patterns up to 250Hz and observed the change of percentage of correct pattern discrimination[10]. This study reported there are several frequency bands that human can easily discern surface's patterns.

From these results, we expect that the texture display, which has been a test-bed, is capable of providing tactile stimuli quantitatively while the user simply grasps and translates the mouse while exploring the virtual environment.

3 Display of Roughness Using Vibrotactile Stimuli

In this section, the question of to what degree roughness, one of the most essential elements composing texture, can be represented using a tactile display is assessed experimentally. Hollins's research verified that vibrotaction could be the necessary and sufficient condition for roughness perception [4]. The objective of this section is to derive a certain functional correlation between vibrotaction and the perceived roughness.

3.1 Subject Training

In this study, the subjects have been trained using pieces of sandpaper before participating in the main experiment. We selected sandpaper grits to be linearized when it is log-scaled. Sandpapers of seven different grits were selected: 24, 32, 60, 100, 220, 600, and 2000. The size of the sandpapers roughly corresponded with that of the contact area of the tactile display. Subjects were asked to respond by giving sensitive strength values of roughness for every specimen on a seven-point scale. Table1 shows averages and standard deviations of the results with changes of the grit sizes during active and passive touches, respectively.

Table 1. Roughness Values of Sandpaper

Grit of Sandpapers	Active Touch		Passive Touch	
	Ave.	Stdev.	Ave.	Stdev.
24	6.7	0.48	5.4	1.63
36	6.6	0.73	5.2	2.07
60	6.4	0.82	4.8	0.75
100	6.1	0.91	3.5	1.21
220	5.5	1.22	2.9	1.33
600	3.0	1.91	1.4	0.84
2000	1.4	0.45	1.2	0.41

3.2 Experimental Method

In this experiment, all pins of the tactile display move simultaneously, and they gives cutaneous stimuli while a user touches the pin array using his/her finger. In order to observe the effects of both the frequency and amplitude of stimuli, the stimuli are composed of the set shown in Table 2. The stimuli are determined to cover the range of perceivable vibrational frequency, which is 0-250Hz, and the range of amplitude satisfies the antinociception area considering pain threshold. A stimulus among the 34 stimuli determined in this section was generated for 8 seconds, and the subject had to answer within 11 seconds, including the stimulation time. The answer was in the form of the sandpaper number with the perceived roughness most similar to that transmitted by the tactile display. In this case, sandpapers should be chosen among the sandpapers that could be discerned through active touch. Since the noisy sound of the tactile display could affect the experimental results, the subject could hear only pink noise via headphones during operation of the pin array. All stimuli were repeated 4 times, and their order was randomized. The entire procedure was repeated under the condition of passive touch.

Table 2. Combinations of Frequency and Amplitude

	0Hz	2 Hz	5 Hz	10 Hz	25 Hz	50 Hz	100 Hz	250Hz
400 μm	O	O	O	O	O	X	X	X
200 μm	O	O	O	O	O	O	X	X
100 μm	O	O	O	O	O	O	O	X
50 μm	O	O	O	O	O	O	O	O
20 μm	O	O	O	O	O	O	O	O

3.3 Experimental Results and Analysis

The experimental results of section 3.2 are analyzed statistically. The objective of this analysis is to find correlation coefficients and functional relations between perceived roughness and the principle variables of vibrotactile stimuli, frequency and amplitude. Figure 1 shows the perceived roughness as a function of log-scaled frequency.

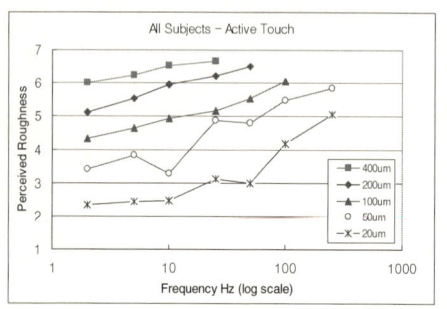
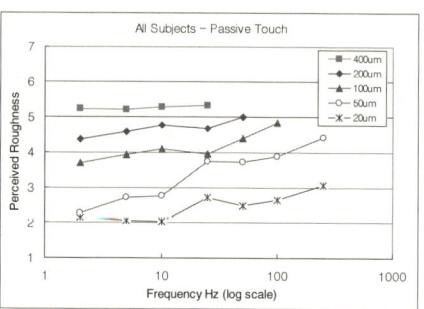

(a) Perceiver roughness for active touch   (b) Perceiver roughness for passive touch

Fig. 1. Perceived roughness as a function of frequency

From the observation of Figure 1, it appears that perceived roughness has certain relations with the following five variables: *frequency, logarithm of frequency, amplitude, logarithm of amplitude, and multiplication of logarithm of frequency and logarithm of amplitude*. From the linear regression of the experimental data, the following functional relation could be derived. In the case of equation (3.1), k1=7.79, k2=3.79, and k3=-0.87 for active touch, and k1=6.68, k2=2.93, and k3=-0.47 for passive touch. The unit of frequency is hertz and that of amplitude is millimeters.

$$R = k_1 + k_2 \cdot log(Amp) + k_3 \cdot log(Freq) \tag{3.1}$$

4 Effect of Auditory Feedback on Tactile Roughness Perception

Tactile perception process is not only a somatosensory response, but also a combination of multimodal sensory fusion such as visual, auditory, and haptic feedback. Lederman et al experimentally assessed the relative contributions of tactual and auditory information to multisensory judgments of surface roughness using a rigid probe, and their results showed auditory feedback contributed to roughness perception[14]. McGee et al conducted an experiment to investigate the perceived roughness of audio textures with the hypothesis that the frequency of the audio texture (or number of notes) will affect the perceived roughness of the virtual texture[15][16]. In this paper, we adopt recorded real audio textures, which occurred between real finger pad and surface, instead of using digitally sound generation methods such as MIDI, PCM etc. The participants' responses to the recorded sound have also been analyzed.

4.1 Stimuli and Apparatus

Sandpaper samples referred to in the previous section have been adopted for the experiment in this section. A trained subject who could maintain gentle pressure and a lateral motion speed of 100-120mm/sec while rubbing the sample surface participated in sound recording. A microphone was located 5 cm away from the sandpaper, and the sound generated by the participant rubbing the sandpaper was transmitted to Microsoft Window's Recorder. Sandpapers are generally sorted by grit number. 7 sandpaper samples having grit numbers of 24, 32, 60, 220, 600, and 2000 were utilized, and the rubbing sound was recorded for every sandpaper sample. Sandpaper sample 1 has a grit number of 24, constituting the roughest surface. As the sandpaper code number increases, the number of grit increases and the roughness decreases. For instance, sample 3 has a grit number of 60. Figure 2 shows the frequency response of recorded audio texture in the band of audio frequency (20-20000 Hz). The back ground and system noise are uniformly distributed in overall frequencies, except the noise has high intensity at a frequency band of 20-40Hz. Compared to the background and system noise, the frequency response of audio texture for sandpaper sample 1 shows very high intensities in the lower frequency band (30-200Hz). In addition, the audio texture for sandpaper sample 1 shows higher intensities in the overall frequency range compared to background noise. The frequency response of audio texture for sandpaper sample 2 shows a similar response to that of sample 1. However, the intensities in the lower frequencies are lower than those of sample 1. For sample 3, the intensities of low frequency sound are lower than previous samples, but the response of sample 3 shows higher intensities at a frequency band of 200-400Hz. For sample 4, intensities of low frequency band (40-80Hz) are higher than the system noise, and the response of sample 4 shows higher intensities at a frequency band of 500-800Hz. For sample 5, intensities of the low frequency band (40-80Hz) are higher than the system noise, and the response of sample 5 shows higher intensities at a frequency band of 500-800Hz. For sample 6, intensities of the low frequency band (40-80Hz) are higher than the system noise. For sample 7, intensities of the low frequency band (40-80Hz) are higher than the system noise, and intensities at higher frequencies are lower than those of sample 6. From an inspection of sounds recorded during rubbing of the sandpaper, it is found that low frequency is related to the physical roughness of the sandpapers. Since the sound during touching is caused by stick slip between the finger pad and the surface's grit, and rough sand papers have bigger grits, we can speculate that low frequency sound could be generated when we larger grit sandpapers are rubbed with the same lateral speed.

4.2 Auditory Feedback and Perceived Roughness

In this section, an experiment to measure the perceived surface roughness from auditory feedback is described. 5 subjects in their twenties participated in this experiment. Through headphones, the subjects heard one of 7 sound samples delineated above, and they were requested to assess how rough the surface would be if they imagined rubbing it. The playing time was 10 seconds followed by 5 seconds of silence. The subjects were not informed that the sound was recorded from rubbing a surface. They responded according to a seven-point bipolar scale. Each of the 7 sound samples was

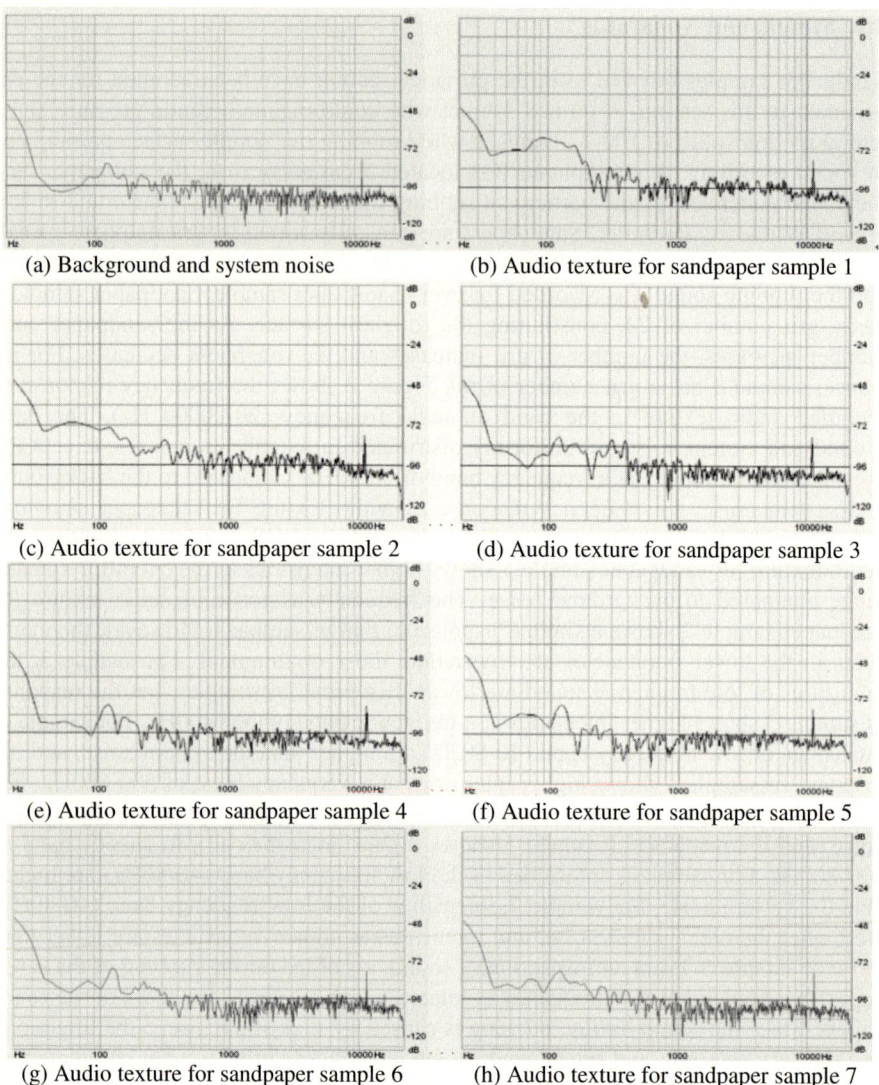

(a) Background and system noise

(b) Audio texture for sandpaper sample 1

(c) Audio texture for sandpaper sample 2

(d) Audio texture for sandpaper sample 3

(e) Audio texture for sandpaper sample 4

(f) Audio texture for sandpaper sample 5

(g) Audio texture for sandpaper sample 6

(h) Audio texture for sandpaper sample 7

Fig. 2. Frequency analysis of recorded audio texture

suggested four times in random order. Table 3 shows the experimental results. The average score of recorded sound for rubbing sandpaper sample 1 shows the highest value, and the score decreases as the sandpaper's roughness decreases. These results indicate that humans may discern surface roughness using only auditory information. Since experimental sound samples were not quantitatively determined, we could not derive functional relations between elements of sound and perceived roughness. However, we can conclude that experience and behavioral learning enable estimation of surface roughness from the rubbing sound.

Table 3. Combinations of Frequency and Amplitude

	Sound Sample 1	Sound Sample 2	Sound Sample 3	Sound Sample 4	Sound Sample 5	Sound Sample 6	Sound Sample 7
Average	6.3	5.4	4.7	3.9	3.8	2.5	1.3
Stdev.	1.79	1.91	1.05	0.96	1.18	1.12	0.46

4.2 Roughness Discrimination from Auditory Information

In section 4.2, the experimental results show that the change of auditory feedback could cause the change of perceived roughness. In order to investigate whether the subjects discern surface roughness using only auditory feedback, an experiment has been conducted using real sandpaper samples and recorded sounds of rubbing these samples. For the experiment in this section, real sandpaper specimens having grit numbers of 24, 36, 60, 220, 600 and 2000 were presented to the subjects. The subjects heard one of the sound samples recorded in section 4.1, and they were guided to match the sound samples with the real specimen. Rubbing and observing real sandpapers were allowed in order to help the subjects estimate their roughness; however, the real sound generated by rubbing the sandpapers was not transmitted to the subjects; this was accomplished by having the subjects wear headphones capable of surround noise cancellation. Each of the 7 sound samples was suggested four times in random order. Figure 3 shows the experimental results in the form of a confusion matrix plot. For sound sample 1, all answers were given as sandpaper of grit number 24, constituting perfect matching. About 65% of the answers were sandpaper of grit number 32 for sound sample 2, and about 30% of the answers were given to neighboring sandpapers. For sample 3 and sample 4, the percentage of correct matches was lower than 50%; however, in the cases of these samples, other answers were concentrated on the neighboring sandpaper samples. Although the total percentage of correct matches is 63.8%, most wrong matches are concentrated on the correct sandpaper's neighboring samples. From these experimental results, we can conclude that auditory feedback alone enables accurate estimation of surface roughness if the subject knows the source of sound.

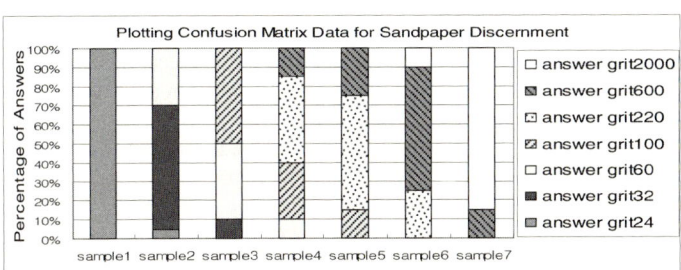

Fig. 3. Confusion rate for sandpaper discrimination

5 Conclusion and Discussion

The first experimental results in section 3 show that there is a tight correlation between perceived roughness and vibrotactile stimuli and their functional relations have been derived. The results of the analyses show that perceived roughness is proportionally intensified as logarithms of frequency or logarithms of amplitude increase and that amplitude and frequency could complement each other. This research suggests a methodology for roughness representation of an arbitrary surface using a pin-arrayed vibrotactile display. In addition, from the experiments described in sections 4.1, 4.2 and 4.3, the following observations could be derived. (1) In the case of sand-papers, intensities of sound in low frequencies are related to physical roughness. (2) The subjects could estimate roughness from the rubbing sound information. (3) If the subject is aware of the source of sound, he/she can discern surface roughness among the various roughness samples. This result means recorded sound can fortify roughness representation in tangible environment. In addition, if the sound samples could be recorded under stricter conditions and analyzed quantitatively, meaningful relations between elements of sound and perceived roughness could be derived. In addition, multimodality combining auditory feedback and tactile feedback will increase human sensitivity of texture perception in a virtual environment.

Acknowledgment

This research has been supported by the Ministry of Information and Communication, Republic of Korea (2006-S-031-01).

References

1. Cascio, C.J. and Sathian, K., Temporal Cues Contributes to Tactile perception of Roughness, The Journal of Neuroscience, Vol. 21(14). (2001) 5289-5296.
2. Craig, J.C., Identification of scanned and static tactile patterns, Perception & Psychophysics, Vol.64(1). (2002) 107-120
3. Diller,T., Schloerb, D. and Srinivasan, M.A., Frequency response of Human Skin in vivo to mechanical stimulation, RLE Technical Report No. 648. MIT. (2001).
4. Hollins, M., Bensmaia, S.J., and Roy, E.A., Vibrotaction and texture perception, Behavioral Brain Research, Vlo.135. (2002) 51-56.
5. Hollins, M., Faldowski, R., Rao, S., and Young, F., Perceptual dimensions of tactile surface texture: a multidimensional scaling analysis, Perception and Psychophysics, Vol. 54. (1993) 697-705
6. Hollins, M. and Risner, S.R., Evidence for the duplex theory of tactile texture perception, Perception & Psychophysics, Vol.62(4). (2000) 695-705
7. Katz, D., The World of Touch, In: Krueger, L.E.(Trans.), Hillsdale, NJ, Erlbaum (1989)
8. Kyung, K.U., Choi, H., Kwon, D.S. and Son, S.W., Interactive Mouse Systems Providing Haptic Feedback During the Exploration in Virtual Environment, Lecture Notes in Computer Science, Vol. 3280. (2004) 136-146.
9. Kyung, K.U, Son, S.W., Yang, G.H. and Kwon, D.S., Design of an Integrated Tactile Display System, Proc. of the IEEE ICRA 2004 (2004) 776-781
10. Kyung, K.U., Ahn, M., Kwon, D.S. and Srinivasan, M.A., A compact planar distributed tactile display and effects of frequency on texture judgment, Advanced Robotics, Vol. 20(5). (2006). 563–580

11. Kyung, K.U., Kwon, D.S. and Yang, G.H., A Novel Interactive Mouse System for Holistic Haptic Display in a Human-Computer Interface, International Journal of Human Computer Interaction, Vol. 20(3). (2006) 247–270

12. Lederman, S.J., Loomis, J.M. and Williams, D.A., The Role of Vibration in the Tactual Perception of Roughness, Perception & Psychophysics, Vol.30. (1982). 82-89.

13. Lederman, S.J. and Taylor, M.M., Fingertip force, surface geometry, and the perception of roughness by active touch, Perception & Psychophysics, Vol.12(5). (1972).401-408

14. Lederman, S.J, Klatzky, R.L., Morgan, T. and Hamilton, C., Integrating Multimodal Information about Surface Texture via a Probe: Relative Contributions of Haptic and Touch-Produced Sound Sources, Proceedings of HAPTICS'02, IEEE. (2002) 97-104

15. McGee, M.R., Gray, P. and Brewster. S., Feeling Rough: Multimodal Perception of Virtual Roughness, Proceedings of Eurohaptics 2001(2001)

16. McGee, M.R., Gray, P. and Brewster. S., Mixed Feelings: Multimodal Perception of Virtual Roughness, Proceedings of Eurohaptics 2002, (2002)

17. Smith, A.M. and Chapman, C.E., Role of friction and tangential force variation in the subjective scaling of tactile roughness, Experimental Brain Research, 144. (2002).211-223

18. Srinivasan, M.A. Surface deflection of primate fingertip under line load, Journal of Biomechanics, Vol.22(4). (1989) 343-349

19. Verrillo, R.T., Fraoli, A.J. and Smith, R.L., Sensation magnitude of vibrotactile stimuli, Perception and Psychophysics, Vol. 7. (1969) 366-372

20. Weber, E.H., E.H. Weber on the Tactile Sense(2nd Edition), In: Ross, H.E. and Murray D.J.,(Edit. and Trans.), Erlbaum(UK) Taylor & Francis (1996)

21. Yoshioka, T., Gibb, B., Dorsch, A.K., Hsiao, S.S. and Johnson, K.O., Neural coding mechanisms underlying perceived roughness of finely textured surface, The Journal of Neuroscience, Vol. 21(17). (2001) 6905-6916

22. Son, W., Kim, K., Jang, B. and Choi, B., Interactive Dynamic Simulation Schemes for Articulated Bodies through Haptic Interface, ETRI Journal, Vol. 25(1). (2003) 25-33

The Research of Spiritual Consolation Object with the Function of Affective Computing

Tang Yiping, Sun Hongjie, Gu Xiaokai, and Deng Tao

Zhejiang University of technology
typ@zjut.edu.cn,
lovenakata@sina.com.cn,
guyaokai@163.com

Abstract. China is running to the aging society. In China, the number of the elder's families of empty nest presents an ascendant trend. It has caused various kinds of demands of the service for spiritual consolation. This article introduces how to distinguish different emotion form the sound sample by affective computing and brings forward the concept of spiritual consolation object. Elder can communicate with this object when they need spiritual consolation. With this, we can set up an interchange environment considering people first, which is intelligent and understandable between children and the elder.

Keywords: Gerontechnology, Affective Computing, Spiritual Consolation Object, Speech Signal Processing.

1 Introduction

China is running to the aging society. The national elder's families of empty nest accounts for 36% of all the families in our country. The experts predict that in the following ten years, the elder's family of empty nest will become the main mode when the elder retire to enjoy the life. Its quantity will be more than 80%. The constant increase of the elder's family of empty nest causes many social problems, such as the elder's healthy guarantee, the personal security, life caring, the spiritual consolation, economy supporting, etc. In the elder's demands of service for life, the spiritual consolation ranks the first. Now the nations of the world treat gerontechnology as the focus of the study[1].

It's better to develop a system, from which the elder can get spiritual consolation instead of their children when the elder feel lonely. The elder can communicate spiritual consolation with the agent first. At the same time the agent can notify their children in the distant place in time. The system can set up an exchange environment, which is people-first, high efficient, automatic, intelligent, fully considering the psychology of the elder.

2 Background

At present, children giving spiritual consolation can only rely on teeter paper, telephone, calling at their parents. Today, the young people face enormous existence

Z. Pan et al. (Eds.): ICAT 2006, LNCS 4282, pp. 416–424, 2006.

pressure and challenge both in life and work. They have not enough time to accompany the elder. This makes the elder have a mental depression. Therefore, there have such problems as the dissymmetry of the opportunity of the communication between solitary elder and their children.

So we develop a spiritual consolation device. The sensors in the device get the elder's emotion parameter, calculate the emotion through these parameters, and then send the result to their children through the wireless network. Children can get the affective state of their parents in time and do something useful to make the elder feel happy.

Affective computing is a computing that relates to emotion, arises from emotion, and deliberately influences emotion. It is a new kind of man-machine exchange. Affective computing mainly includes the expression, the language, the touch and so on. Language, the tool that transmits information and express emotion, is very important to affective computing. So the calculation of the speech emotion is a main content of this research. The research of the speech emotion begins in 1990s. In American, Japan, Britain and other countries, there are many universities and studios that research on affective computing. Speech affective computing has fetched lots of production, and there are many valuable theses. But it has not formed one extensive approved theory and research approach, and it is never used for spiritual consolation to the elder either.

3 Design of the Spiritual Consolation Object

The spiritual consolation object includes the hardware system and the software system.

3.1 Design of the Hardware System

The spiritual consolation object has the touch sensor, speech sensor, microprocessor, the part for sending and accepting information, the information memory, and the

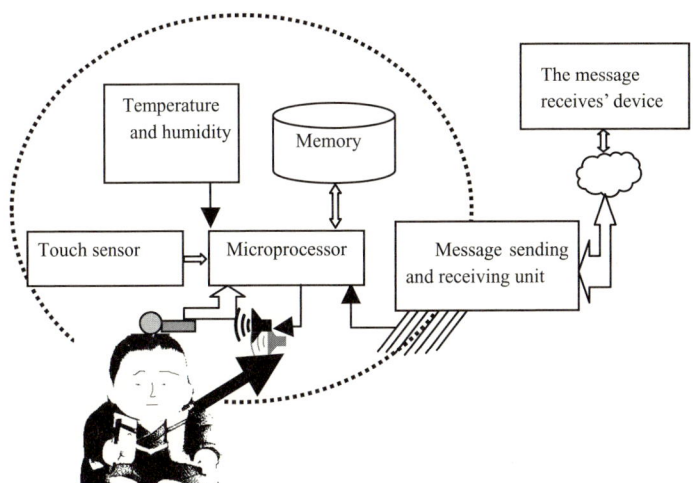

Fig. 1. The hardware structure

information input part, the pronunciation output part, etc. Spiritual consolation object is instead of the children whom the elder expects to communicate with. This research designs the spiritual consolation agent as their children's portrait, as Fig. 1 shows.

3.2 Design of the Software System

This article mainly researches the speech emotion of the elder. Pronunciation sensor is one of the most important instruments to get the elder's emotion information. Microprocessor automatically saves information through interruptive style when the elder speak facing the spiritual consolation device. Emotion information will be read from the information memory; characteristic parameters of the speech signal will be calculated by using affective computing. The device can confirm the emotion classification at the time the elder speaks by pattern search, and then does accordingly spiritual consolation to the elder, as Fig. 2 shows.

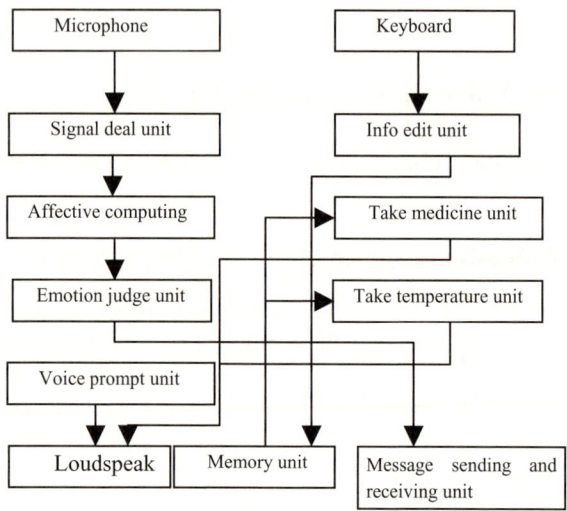

Fig. 2. The software structure

4   Affective Computing of Speech Emotion

It is the key to the system about how to judge the elder's emotion state exactly. The system first gathers the elder's speech signal, secondly gets the characteristic parameter through pretreatment, then calculates the elder's emotion state according to the data from the emotion speech database, and then does accordingly spiritual consolation to the elder. The processing is as Fig 3 shows.

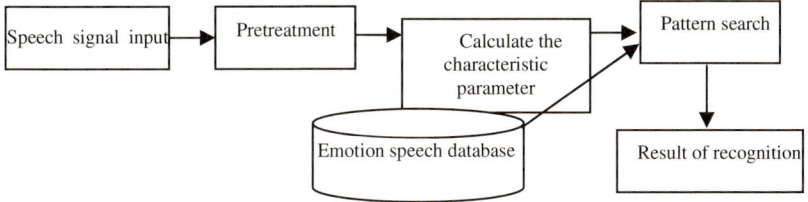

Fig. 3. The process of emotion classifying

4.1   The Pretreatment of Speech Signal

The pretreatment of speech signal is needed before the speech emotion calculating. The goal of endpoint detection is to confirm the endpoint from a speech signal. Effective endpoint detection can reduce the processing time but also can remove the influence of noise, thus makes the judgment result more accurate.

	Judge of surd and sonant	Smoothness	Pass zero rate	Short time energy	Average amplitude	Change of amplitude
Fundamental frequency	The range of frequency	Change rate of fundamental frequency	Affective classify	All the characteristic	Autocorrelation function	

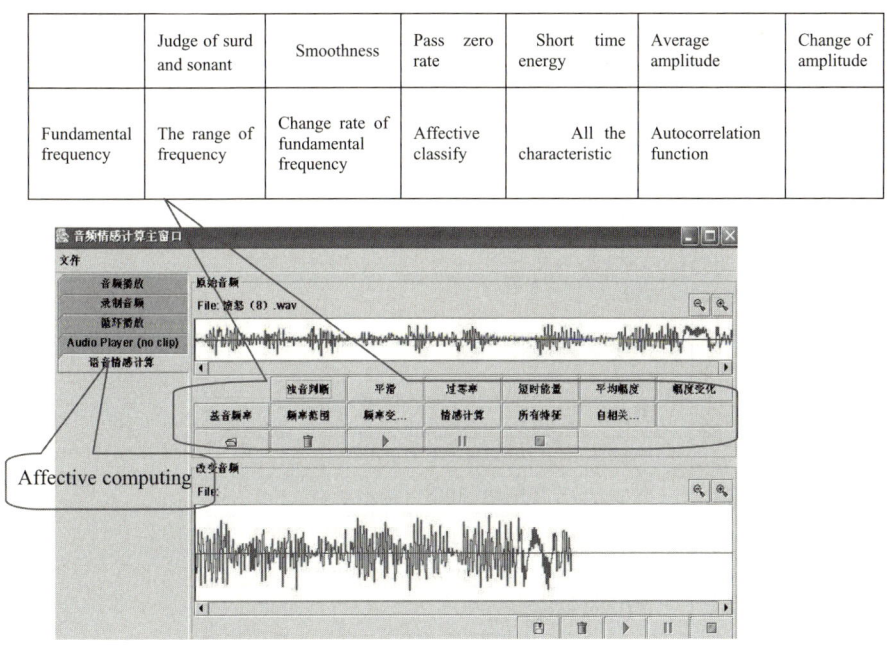

Fig. 4. The speech signal before and after the endpoint detection

Speech is made up of surd and sonant. The experiment results show that sonant includes most of the speaker's emotion characters. The energy of sonant concentrates below 3kHz, nevertheless the energy of surd majority appears in a higher frequency. Short time energy can be used to separate majority sonant from surd. In order to prevent the loss of low energy of sonant, the short time pass zero rate is used as a supplement judgment. The experiment result shows that sonant has a more obvious regularity and much lower pass zero rate than surd. Therefore, by using the two standards to endpoint detection, we can examine the effective speech accurately, as the Fig 4 shows.

4.2   Calculate of the Characteristic Parameter

The fact that the voice can express the emotion due to the voice includes the parameters that can materialize the emotional feature. It is significant to the recognition of speech emotion that gathers these parameters from the speech signal.

Now how to gather these parameters from the speech signal is searched in lots of articles. The main methods include time structure, amplitude structure, fundamental frequency structure, and formant structure.

The speed of speaking is deferent when the speaker is at deferent emotion states. For example, when he is angry his speed of speaking is faster than calmness. Therefore we can judge the speaker's emotion degree by his speed of speaking. The amplitude is correlation with the emotion state also, when the speaker is happy, anger, and fear, the amplitude of his speech is much higher than that he is at the emotion of sad, further more the more discrepancy at amplitude the more discrepancy at emotion state.

The important characteristic parameters, which influence the recognition of emotion, are listed as table 1[2]:

Table 1. The important characteristic parameter

Characteristic parameter
Rate
Average fundamental frequency
Range of fundamental frequency
Intensity
Change of fundamental frequency
FI Average
FI Range

In the research we choose six parameters of the speech as the characteristic parameters of the emotion. They are average short time energy, average change rate of amplitude, average fundamental frequency, average change rate of fundamental frequency, average short time pass zero rate, the time ratio of surd and sonant. Fundamental frequency is the best one that materializes the emotional features among these parameters.

Fundamental frequency is most important parameter of the speech. Fundamental frequency inspection is a rather complicated problem. As the oscillation of vocal cords is not absolute periodically, it is difficult to determine some frames, which mix surd and sonant belong to periodic or nonperiodic.

The method of fundamental frequency inspection may be divided into two parts.（1）Method in time domain, gets the fundamental frequency directly form the wave.（2）Method in frequency domain, first changes the speech signal to the frequency domain, then calculates its fundamental frequency. In this research we use the improvement autocorrelation function to estimate the fundamental frequency of the speech signal.

The short-time autocorrelation function R (x) has a very big peak value in each integral multiple of the fundamental cycle. The principle of autocorrelation algorithm is to estimate the fundamental frequency by seeking a first biggest peak value position, according to short-time autocorrelation function.

$$R_n(k) = \sum_{m=-\infty}^{\infty} [x(m)w(n-m)][x(m+k)w(n-m-k)] \tag{1}$$

The arithmetic uses y0, y1, y2, ……yn to denote a frame of speech signal. From the first sample point of each frame, it uses（y0* y1）+（y1* y2）+……+（yn-1*yn) to denote the value of autocorrelation function when the k equal to zero, then add one to k, calculate until k equal to n-2, save all the values. According to characteristic of the wave, when the k moves to the integral multiple of the fundamental cycle, the value of autocorrelation function is the biggest. Therefore, if we find the max value of autocorrelation function means we find the fundamental cycle. According to the fundamental cycle we can calculate the fundamental frequency easily.

In the research of this article, according to the frequency characteristic of speech and the range of human speech, K needn't start from zero, the calculate length needn't to be as long as one frame either. Because the experiment uses 10kHz sample frequency, and according to the characteristic that human's speech frequency concentrate on the range of 50 to 500Hz, in the experiment the range of k is calculated form 28 to 200.

The computation obtains the K value is not necessarily the fundamental frequency corresponding points, also has the possibility that it is the 2 frequency multiplication or several frequency multiplication point. In order to avoid these mistakes, we take the maximum value method as supplement.

When the point moves to the cyclical integral multiple, the value of autocorrelation function is the maximum, although the true fundamental frequency corresponding value is not necessarily a max value, but definitely is a maximum value, therefore after discovering the max value, establishes a threshold value, then use the threshold value to find the maximum value, then pick up a optimal point as the fundamental frequency corresponding point.

4.3 Emotion Pattern Search

In the experiments, we divide old person's emotion states as calmness, fear, happy, sad and anger. Respecting to 5 different emotion states, 100 samples are collected, which are used as the samples of emotion speech database. We calculate the characteristic parameters of these samples, and then use the method of weighting Euclidean distance to recognize the emotion states[3].

Under the different emotion states, the contribution of various characteristic parameters to the emotion states is different. Therefore we use the contribution analytic method to determine the weight value when we constructer the emotion template. It is defined as:

$$w_j = \frac{1}{n}\sum_{i=1}^{n} \frac{\text{cov}(\hat{\theta}(y_i, \hat{\phi}_j(x_{ij}))}{\text{var}\,\phi(y_i)}$$ (2)

$$t = 1,\cdots,n \qquad j = 1,\cdots,8$$ (3)

$$\theta(y_i) = \sum_{j=1}^{8} \phi_j(x_{ij}) + \varepsilon_i$$ (4)

Here, the $\theta(y_i)$ is the function of t-th emotion speech and template Euclidean distance y, $\phi_j(x_{ij})$ is conic function of x_{ij}, the J-th emotion characteristic parameter of t-th sentence, where ε_i is random error, $\hat{\theta}(y_i)$ and $\hat{\phi}_j(x_{ij})$ is the optimal function determined by iteration of ACE[4] (Ameyded Conditional Expectation).

In the experiments, respecting to 5 different emotion states, 20 samples are collected. 6 emotion characteristic parameters are gathered from 20 emotion sentences for each emotion state. Thus, we turn every emotion sentence to six dimension primitive eigenvector. Each dimension element unit is not unified, therefore they need to be turned to a standard unit by the parameter normalization standard when recognition.

Twenty sentences are used to train according to the function Euclidean, which defined before, therefore n equal to 20. The weight of emotion characteristic parameters are calculated as the table 2 shows:

For each emotion state, the summation of 6 emotion characteristic parameters is 1,

$$\sum_{j=1}^{6} w_j = 1$$

that is . In the table, w_1, w_2, w_3, w_4, w_5, w_6, Separately corresponding to average short time energy, average change rate of amplitude, average fundamental frequency, average change rate of fundamental frequency, average short time pass zero rate, the time ratio of surd and sonant. When recognition, 6 emotion characteristic parameters of the sentence is gathered, then calculate the normalization eigenvector of each emotion template. Match the normalization

Table 2. Emotion state weight starting value assignment

Weight	Emotion state				
	Calmness	**Fear**	**Happy**	**Sad**	**Anger**
w_1	0.21	0.19	0.22	0.20	0.25
w_2	0.16	0.15	0.14	0.11	0.16
w_3	0.23	0.22	0.25	0.24	0.27
w_4	0.11	0.12	0.19	0.18	0.11
w_5	0.14	0.11	0.11	0.16	0.12
w_6	0.15	0.21	0.09	0.11	0.1

eigenvector with five emotion templates. Calculate each Euclidean distance of each emotion state. The emotion state that has the least Euclidean distance is the result of the recognition.

4.4   Result of the Experiment

In the experiments, with respect to 5 different emotion states, 40 samples are collected, which are then recognized and the results are showed as table 3:

Table 3. Result of the speech emotion experiment

Output / Input	Calmness	Fear	Happy	Sad	Anger	Recognition Rate
Calmness	38	0	0	2	0	95%
Fear	0	30	4	0	6	75%
Happy	0	6	27	0	7	67.5%
Sad	0	0	0	40	0	100%
Anger	0	4	3	0	33	82.5%

From the data of the table, we know that the recognition rate of sad and calmness reach 100% and 95%, because the amplitude and the fundamental frequency of this two emotions are much lower than other three emotions. We can differentiate sad and calmness by the average change rate of fundamental frequency easily. But the recognition rate of happy only reaches 67.5%. Sometimes happy would be recognized as fear and anger, because the fundamental frequency and the average short time energy of happy are close to the fear and anger. Similarly fear and anger also have the certain probability to recognize to happy. The recognition rate of fear and anger only 75% and 82 %.

Result of the experiment shows that the recognition of sad and calmness and anger is more exact than the happy and fear. There are 3 reasons for this phenomenon. First of all, since there are significant similarity features of happiness, horror and anger, and thus the Euclidean distance is not good enough to be used to classify these features. Secondly, emotion feature is heavily related with specific context, so the samplings collected in our experiments may be short of emotion feature. Thirdly, the number of our samplings is limited, and thus the training of voice emotion model is far from perfect.

5 Conclusion

This article mainly introduces a design of the spiritual consolation object, and specializes in introduction of the hardware architecture of the system, the principles of pronunciation of signal's emotion. The system realizes how to save speech signal, how to recognize five basic speech emotions and also supplies the service of spiritual consolation. This system can improve the living quality of the elder who live alone; strengthen the connection and communication between solitary elder and their children, relatives and friends. And it offers a kind of new support for establishing harmonious family and harmonious society.

With the quick development of the computer science, computers, which have the function of affective computing, will be used more widely. The future research will pay more attention to affective information got through speech, vision and touch, and improve the precision of emotion recognition, which provides better service for the elder who live alone.

References

1. http://www2.convention.co.jp/5isg/english/
2. Zhao Li,Qian Xiangming, Zhou Cairong, Wu Zhenyang, Pronunciation of signal's Emotion characteristic's analyse and research, Communication journal, 2000, volume(21), page 18-24
3. Zan Yongzhao,Cao Peng, Research and implementation of emotional feature extraction and recognition in speech signal, Jiangsu university,2005,1, volume(26), page 72-75
4. COME Roddy, COTNELIUS Randolph R .Describing the emotional states that are expressed in speech[J] Speech Commurzication,2003, volume(40), page 5-32.
5. Cowie. R. Emotion recognition in human-computer interaction. IEEE Signal Processing Magazine .2001, volume (18), page 32-80.

Real Time Dynamics and Control of a Digital Human Arm for Reaching Motion Simulation

Huijie Yu[1] and Ray P.S. Han[2]

[1] Dept. of Mechanics & Engineering Science, Fudan University 200433 Shanghai, China

[2] College of Automation Engineering, Qingdao University, Qingdao Shandong 266071 China & Dept. of Mechanical & Industrial Engineering, University of Iowa, Iowa City, IA 52242 USA
ray-han@uiowa.edu

Abstract. High-fidelity simulations for dynamics and movement control of the human arm is a complex and challenging problem. To realize such high-quality response in real time using today's computing power is simply not possible. In this paper we have presented a simplified, neural network-based dynamics model of a digital human arm for simulating its reaching movements. The arm is modeled as an assemblage of 2 rigid bodies connected by joints and muscles. A Hill-type model is used to capture the muscle forces. Activation dynamics via a low-pass filtering operation is applied to trigger musculotendon contractions. Since we are interested in real-time macro response, we have replaced the forward dynamics module with a recurrent neural network approach. The results of our simulation show that the model produces fairly realistic reaching motion of the arm and it is able to do so in real-time.

Keywords: Digital human arm modeling, real-time dynamics and control, arm reaching movements, arm musculoskeletal model, neural network.

1 Introduction

The tremendous increase in computing power and modeling technologies has made it viable to develop high-fidelity models of humans or more aptly, "digital humans" for engineering applications. At this point in time, a truly realistic model of the human arm is quite beyond the capabilities of even the most powerful computers. The reason is our knowledge of the interaction between the human brain and the arm is still quite limited. We do not have a good understanding of the brain and how it activates and interacts with specific muscles of the arm. Further, an accurate fatigue-based model of the human muscles is still unavailable. Therefore, in this work, we will present a macro-model of the digital human arm that emphasizes on the gross reaching motions in real time. The reaching motion has the characteristic of fast movement towards a known target via piecewise straight paths and bell-shaped speed profiles.

The movement of the human arm can be analyzed as consisting of the following phases: 1) the brain becomes aware of the target position through the eyes, 2) the central nervous system (CNS) sends appropriate signals to the muscles causing them to contract and produce forces to move the arm, 3) the eyes continue to transmit

Z. Pan et al. (Eds.): ICAT 2006, LNCS 4282, pp. 425–436, 2006.

visual information to the brain as it controls and moves the arm until the target is reached. To simulate the reaching movement of the human arm, 3 key issues should ideally be addressed. First, the arm model should not be just an assemblage of rigid bodies; it must have muscles to mimic the real human arm. So, it is necessary to build a model possessing basic anatomical characters. The second consideration is that the real arm is a redundant system consisting of many muscle types, all of which are prone to fatigue. Third, there are several trajectories that the arm can use to arrive at its target position. The trajectory solution is therefore, not necessarily unique and the model needs to generate a realistic path that consumes the least effort.

Over the past 2 decades, there has been a significant increase in research on the modeling of the human arm. Dornay et al. [1] presented an arm model that employs a controller programmed with a minimum muscle-tension change criterion. Further, by using inverse models of the arm dynamics for controls, their process of simulating the arm reaching movements became fairly complex and computationally intensive. Jordan and Rumelhart [2] created a controller-based forward dynamics model for the supervised learning paradigm. They showed that the algorithm is capable of learning in multi-layer networks. Massone and Myers [3] described the response of a neural network model of an anthropomorphic redundant arm moving in a horizontal plane with gravity loading. They used a 2-joints model with 6-muscle pairs actuators and subjected the system to various patterns of muscle activations. They investigated several control strategies, plant properties and the resulting motion qualities with the objective of developing guidelines for the design of artificial arms. Karniel and Inbar [4] developed a mathematical model for the control of the human arm to simulate reaching movements. Their model consists of a 2-DOF planar manipulator used in conjunction with a Hill-type, 6-muscle unit. Rectangular pulses with varying amplitudes and timings that are set based on the target, are inputted as control signals. By adjusting a handful of parameters in lieu of the entire trajectory, they managed to drastically reduce the dimensionality of the control problem. Fagg et al. [5] developed a cerebellar learning model for controlling arm movement via muscle synergies. In the event that the cerebellum is unable to move the arm to its target, an extra-cerebellar module is activated to carryout low-fidelity corrections and the information is fed back to the cerebellum. Their model employed delayed sensory signals together with the generated motor commands to compute new output signals. Ogihara and Yamazaki [6] built an arm model with neuro-control to generate reaching motion without requiring a trajectory. They used 3-rigid links with 8 principal muscles to construct their musculo-arm model. Further, at each joint they attached a nonlinear viscoelastic element. However, their muscle model uses a constant distance for computing the muscle torque. This method overestimates the torque magnitudes and consequently, produces unrealistic reaching movement. Kashima et al. [7] analyzed a muscle control system in elbow joint movements through theoretical and experimental analyses. They used an EMG-based neural input to control the behavior of individual muscles. In their study, they compared their computed trajectories with experimental observations and showed that their model is capable of capturing the essential responses even in multi-joint motion. Lan [8] provided a stability analysis of a 2-joint limb using muscles that are activated electrically. He constructed a planar arm model with 3 pairs of antagonistic muscles in ADAMS and deployed it for studying the local feedback controller performance. By evaluating the eigenvalues at a current posture of the model he was able to examine the stability behavior for postural control of the motor tasks. Thelen et al. [9] introduced a "computed muscle control" algorithm that employed static optimization with feedforward and feedback controls to guide the trajectory of their musculoskeletal model towards its target. They demonstrated their algorithm by computing muscle excitations for driving a 30-muscle, 3-DOF model to simulate kinematics and kinetics of pedaling. De Sapio et al. [10] presented a task-oriented control strategy for generating feedback controls in their attempt to simulate goal-targeted human motion. They reported a framework to produce musculoskeletal simulations for synthesizing control of human-like motion.

In this paper, we will present a model of a digital human arm that is dynamically operated and controlled in real time for its reaching motions. The arm is constructed as a planar assemblage of 2 rigid links connected by 2 joints and 6 muscles. The neuroexcitations are transmitted to the muscles via a simple arm controller that is trained to generate typical reaching movements. To enhance the computational efficiency, a recurrent neural network is used in lieu of the forward dynamics calculations. In doing so, we are able to simulate in real-time the goal-directed motion of the human arm fairly realistically.

2 The Arm Musculoskeletal Model

As depicted in Fig. 1, the arm musculoskeletal model consists of a rigid multi-body system connected by shoulder and elbow joints, and spanned by a set of musculotendon actuators [3]. Motion in the model is restricted to the vertical plane that takes into consideration the effects of gravity. The 6 muscle-like actuators are located as follows: 2 antagonist actuators that act across the shoulder joint (shoulder muscles), 2 antagonist actuators that act across the elbow joint (elbow muscles) and 2 antagonist actuators that act across both the shoulder joint and the elbow joint (double-joint muscles).

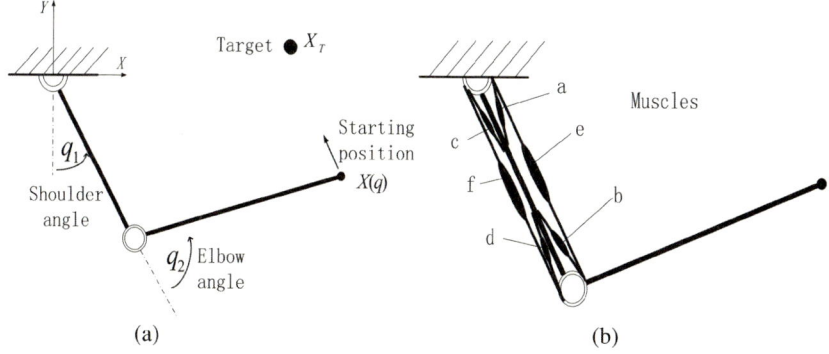

Fig. 1. Arm musculotendon model: (a) arm model with 2 joints (shoulder and elbow); (b) muscle model with the following muscles: a-Pectoralis Major, b-Deltoidus, c-Biceps L-H, d-Triceps S-H, e-Biceps S-H, f-Triceps L-H

2.1 Arm Musculotendon Dynamics

The arm is modeled as a system of constrained 2-DOF mechanical-like manipulator whose configuration is described by a set of generalized coordinates q. The generalized coordinates consist of joint angles defining the orientation of the limb segments. The equation of motion can be written in its standard form as,

$$M(q)\ddot{q} + h(\dot{q},q) + g(q) = T,$$ (1)

where $M(q)$ is a (2×2) inertia matrix, q is a (2×1) vector of joint angles, $h(\dot{q},q)$ is a (2×1) vector of torques arising from Coriolis and centrifugal forces, $g(q)$ is a (2×1) vector of torques due to gravity and T is a (2×1) vector of joint torques computed from the musculo-dynamics forces. To ensure good fidelity of the modeled arm, the inertial and other parameters of each segment are sourced from Atkeson [11]. Their values are listed in Table 1.

Table 1. Inertial parameters of the limb segments

Segment	Mass (kg)	Length (m)	C.G. (m)	Inertia (kg-m^2)
Upper arm	1.82	0.326	0.145	0.0201
Forearm	1.43	0.444	0.302	0.0287

2.2 Neuromuscular Dynamics

The time evolution of muscle states in terms of their length and force magnitudes in response to neural excitation is considered next. As sketched in Fig. 1(b), a system of musculotendon actuators is defined to drive the arm. Each arm segment is driven by a pair of muscles acting in unison. The joint torque is then computed by the net effect of the agonist-antagonist muscle pair as each muscle produces torques that pull the arm in the opposite direction. Further, the torque at each joint is a weighted sum of the torques of the muscles that act on that joint. Following Massone and Myers [3] we can write T_i the torque at joint i as

$$T_1 = T_{sh\_fl} - T_{sh\_ex} + \lambda_1 \cdot (T_{d\_fl} - T_{d-ex}),$$
$$T_2 = T_{el\_fl} - T_{el\_ex} + \lambda_2 \cdot (T_{d\_fl} - T_{d-ex}).$$ (2)

Additionally, T_{sh_fl} and T_{sh_ex} are respectively, the flexor and extensor torques for the shoulder. Similarly, T_{el_fl} and T_{el_ex} are the flexor and extensor torques for the elbow, and T_{d_fl}, T_{d-ex} are the flexor and extensor torques for the muscles that act across both joints. The connection strengths λ_1 and λ_2 can either be arbitrarily set or learned at the time that the arm controller is programmed. In this paper, we adopted the following values: $\lambda_1 = 0.6$, $\lambda_2 = 0.4$ [3].

A Hill-type nonlinear mechanical representation is used to model each muscle [12-13]. As schematically illustrated in Fig. 2, the model consists of a contractile element with a force generator F_0, 2 damper elements of viscosity B and B_p, and 2 spring elements with stiffness K_s and K_p connected together. The force generator is modulated by neural input n_i. Activation dynamics is then applied to bring about musculotendon contractions in the Hill-type model [14-15]. In our model this process is described by a low-pass filtering operation, which can be captured by the following state-form equation written in terms of the activation a

$$\dot{a} = \frac{1}{\tau_{ne}}(n_i - a),\tag{3}$$

where $n_i \in [0,1]$ is the neural input and τ_{ne} refers to the time constant of the filter.

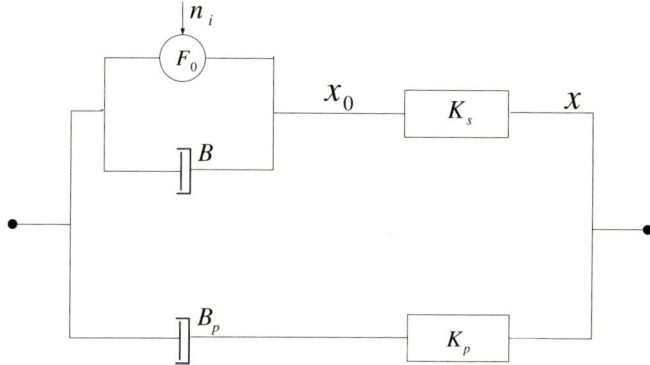

Fig. 2. The general mechanical model of the muscle: n_i : neural input; F_0 : hypothetical tension; B : damper; K_s : series elasticity; B_p : parallel damper; x : muscle length; x_0 : length of contractile element

The activation dynamics result in the following force F_0 given by

$$\dot{F}_0 = \frac{1}{\tau_a}(a - F_0).\tag{4}$$

Note that τ_a is the time constant of the process. The actual force is obtained by calibrating F_0 using the constant F_{max}. Table 2 lists the maximum forces for the six muscles in our arm model [8, 12]. The result is then multiplied by a constant mean moment arm d to yield a theoretical torque T_0.

$$T_0 = F_0 * F_{max} * d\tag{5}$$

Table 2. Maximum force for various muscles

Muscle Type	Function	F_{max} (N)
a: Pectoralis Major	Shoulder Flexor	800
b: Deltoidus	Elbow Flexor	700
c: Biceps L-H	Shoulder Extensor	800
d: Triceps S-H	Elbow Extensor	700
e: Biceps S-H	Double-joint Flexor	1000
f: Triceps L-H	Double-joint Extensor	1000

The relationship between the theoretical torque and the length of the contractile element is described by

$$T_0 + B\dot{x}_0 = K_s(x - x_0) . \tag{6}$$

Finally, the torque produced by the muscle T_m can be determined from

$$T_m = B_p\dot{x} + K_p x + K_s(x - x_0) . \tag{7}$$

The values of various muscle parameters and their corresponding units are tabulated in Table 3 [3].

Table 3. Values of the muscle parameters used

Parameter	Value	Units
B_p	0.2	N.sec/rad
B	4.5	N.sec/rad
K_p	1.5	N/rad
K_s	30	N/rad
τ_{ne}	0.015	sec
τ_a	0.005	sec
d	0.03	m

Further, the relationship between the muscle length x and the joint angle q are listed in Table 4.

Table 4. The relationships between each muscle length and the joint angle (m)

$x_{Shoulder\_Flexor}$	$x_{Shoulder\_Extensor}$	x_{Elbow_Flexor}	$x_{Elbow\_Extensor}$	x_{double_Flexor}	$x_{double\_Extensor}$
$(\frac{3\pi}{2}-q_1)d$	$(\frac{\pi}{2}+q_1)d$	$(\pi-q_2)d$	$(\pi+q_2)d$	$(\frac{3\pi}{2}-q_1-q_2)d$	$(\frac{\pi}{2}+q_1+q_2)d$

3 Dynamics Model

The simulation involves moving the arm from its initial position to a defined target position as depicted in Fig. 1(a). The main characteristics of such a movement are piecewise straight-path with bell-shaped speed profiles. To achieve this, the following potential $U(X)$ is introduced for computing the minimum traversed distance

$$U(X) = (X - X_T)^T K_X (X - X_T) + \dot{X}^T K_V \dot{X} \quad , \qquad (8)$$

where X, X_T are respectively, the initial and target positions of the arm's tip in Cartesian coordinates and $\dot{X}$ is the velocity of the arm tip. Further, K_X, K_V are the gain errors for position and tip velocity. They are (6×2) matrices and their values are chosen to closely reflect the physiological properties of the arm so that the reaching movement appears to be smooth and natural. In Eq. (8) the first term refers to a penalty for not satisfying $X - X_T = 0$ constraint. It decreases as the tip position $X(q)$ approaches the target position X_T. The second term refers to the arm stopping criterion, namely $\dot{X} = 0$ when the arm-tip reaches the target and $U(X)$ approaches zero. Hence the object of the control is to minimize so that $U(X) \to 0$.

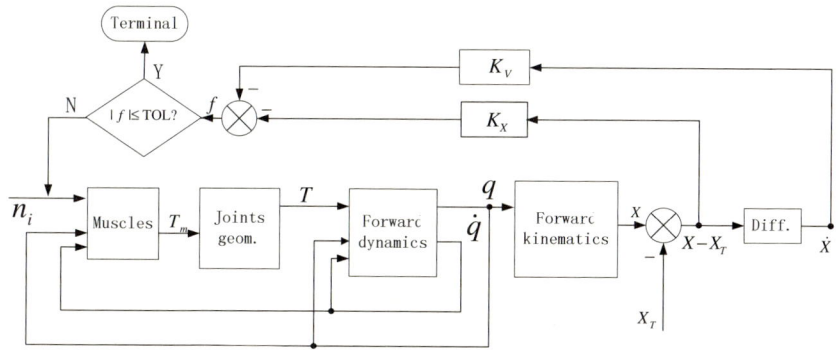

Fig. 3. Controller block diagram for computing the reaching movement of the arm

Modeling the reaching movement of the arm can be a complex operation that requires several steps as schematically illustrated in the block diagram of Fig. 3. The muscles are activated by their neural input n_i and this generates generalized muscle torque $T_m(n_i, q, \dot{q})$. From the arm geometry the muscle torque is then converted into joint torque T. This information is fed into the forward-dynamic block to compute angular acceleration $\ddot{q}$ as a function of the current $T, q, \dot{q}$ values. An integrator is applied to determine new values of the velocity and position $q, \dot{q}$. Upon attaining convergence in the local iteration, the forward-kinematic block is then activated to transform the angular coordinates into Cartesian coordinates of the endpoint X. To guide the iterative process, the error $(X - X_T)$ and $\dot{X}$ are sampled to repeatedly adjust the neural input n_i until a predefined tolerance is achieved at convergence.

3.1 Forward Dynamics

As shown in Fig. 4, the forward dynamics of the arm involves mapping the computed joint torques to angular accelerations and then, applying an integrator to obtain their corresponding angular positions and angular velocities. The process involves repeated local iterations until converged values of the kinematics are attained.

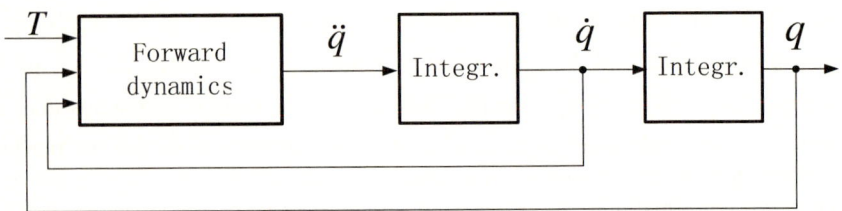

Fig. 4. Forward dynamics integrator for mapping joint torque T to $\ddot{q}, \dot{q}, q$

Eq. (1) can be re-written to compute the angular acceleration $\ddot{q}$

$$\ddot{q} = M(q)^{-1}\left[T(q, \dot{q}, \ddot{q}) - h(q, \dot{q})\right) - g(q)\right]. \tag{9}$$

Since the kinematic quantities on the right-hand-side of Eq. (9) are known only at the previous time-step, Eq. (9) must be solved repeatedly until converged values of $\ddot{q}, \dot{q}, q$ are obtained for computing $M(q)$, $T(q, \dot{q}, \ddot{q})$, $h(q, \dot{q})$, $g(q)$. The forward dynamics simulation can be time consuming as the process requires local iterations at every time-step. To accomplish the simulation for real-time control we have developed a recurrent neural network technique to cope with the computational complexities as well as the inherent nonlinearities in the model.

3.2 Neural Network

Neural network has become a powerful proven tool for controlling complex nonlinear dynamic systems. The basic idea is to employ an appropriate neural network estimator to identify the unknown and/or complex nonlinear dynamics and to compensate for it. To increase the computational efficiency of our model, a recurrent neural network is deployed to replace the forward-dynamics module.

As shown in Fig. 5, the recurrent neural network consists of 3 layers; the first is the input layer, which has 6 units, followed by the second and hidden layer, which has 10 units and the third is the output layer, which has 2 units. The output function of the hidden layer is sigmoid-type, while all others are linear. Training the network is most important, as well as, most time consuming. Thus, for our work it is best to train the network off-line. The weights for learning are from the input layer to the hidden layer, and from the hidden layer to the 2 units that output the angular accelerations. We chose to construct the training set for the forward dynamic simulation of the reaching motion whereby, the endpoint starts out an a predefined initial position of the workspace and moves via a number of straight-line paths towards the given target position.

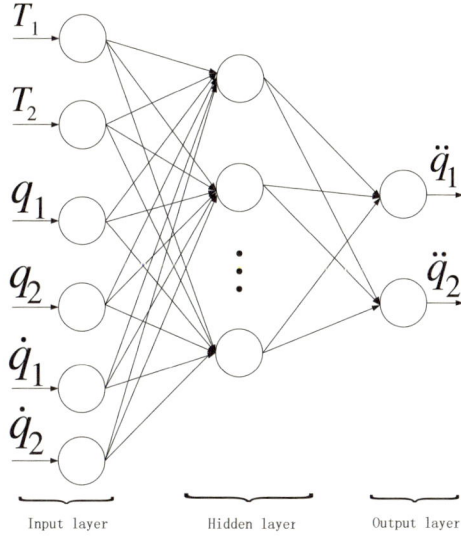

Fig. 5. Structure of the recurrent neural network: the input layer with 6 units is first, followed by a hidden second layer with 10 units and the third layer is the output containing 2 units

There have been many reported cases [16] where the shoulder angle operates in the range of $(-0.817, 2.789)$ while the elbow angle in the range of $(0.000, 2.489)$ in the vertical plane. Our technique involves partitioning the 2 angles into 20 parts and sampling the tip coordinates of each of the 21 movements (that is, inclusive of the start and end points) in an attempt to generate a smoother motion. This is illustrated in

Fig. 6 with 200 samples (with a sample period of 0.005s) in each direction for an assumed bell-shaped velocity profile.

With kinematics solved, that is, $q, \dot{q}, \ddot{q}$ are known, the joint torque T for $21 \times 200 = 4200$ samples can be readily determined via Eq. (1). Prescribing the computed torque values, together with the known angular positions and angular velocities as inputs to the training set, we get as outputs, the angular accelerations. Further, in employing an analytical approach to compute the time derivatives of the angular quantities, our training set should be free of the associated numerical errors. We then trained the 3-layer network using the prescribed training set in conjunction with the standard back-propagation (BP) algorithm [17]. The network was able to learn quite nicely by generating acceptable new values of torques, angular positions and angular velocities that are different from those stored in the training set. We were able to obtain an error less than 10^{-4} during our training of the network 664 epochs. The error curve of the training is plotted in Fig. 7.

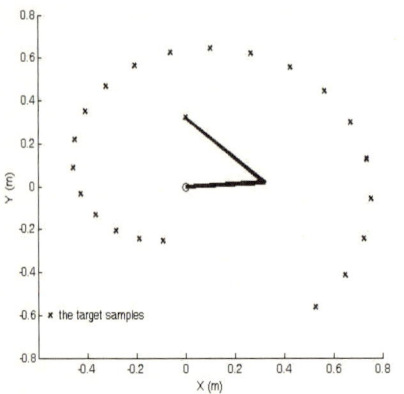
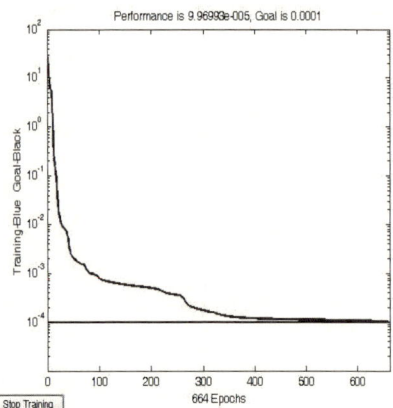

Fig. 6. The reaching movements selected for constructing the training set. Note that the symbol "×" denotes target samples.

Fig. 7. The error curve of the training. The training of the 664 epochs is stopped when an error $\leq 10^{-4}$ is attained.

3.3 Control Method and Simulation

The coordinates of the arm-tip X can be computed via forward kinematics involving the angular position q that in turn, is integrated from angular acceleration $\ddot{q}$ fed by the neural network module. To ensure that the system stays robust even in the presence of disturbances, a feedback control scheme for the model is adopted. The following control response as input to the decoupled system is designed for its use

$$f = -\nabla U = -K_X (X - X_T) - K_V \dot{X} . \tag{10}$$

Simulation experiments are performed to test the model. The arm-tip is initially located at $(0, 0.32)$ and it is required to move to the target position at $(-0.10, 0.67)$.

The simulation results are displayed in Fig. 8. Observe that the arm-tip moves via a series of piecewise straight-line path with a bell-shaped speed profile to the target position. Furthermore, unlike other control models [18], our approach does not make use of the reference trajectory.

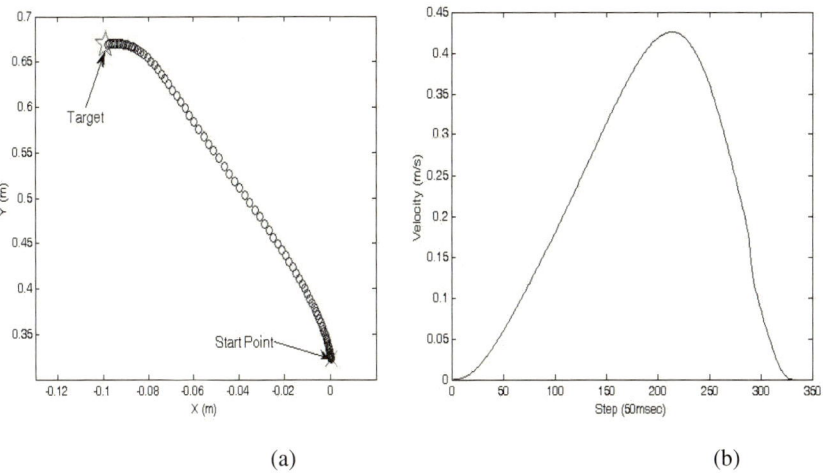

(a)   (b)

Fig. 8. Simulating the reaching movement of the arm: (a) trajectory of the arm-tip as it moves from the initial position to the target position, (b) velocity profile

4   Concluding Remarks

We have developed a 2-DOF planar arm model spanned by 3 antagonist muscle-pairs: shoulder-muscle pair, elbow-muscle pair and double-joint muscle pair to simulate in real-time the reaching movement of a digital human arm. A recurrent neural network approach is used in lieu of the arm forward dynamics module to accomplish the real time movement control. The muscle model used is based on the Hill-type muscle unit. The simulation results show that the digital arm moves in a natural and human-like motion toward a given target position using a series of piecewise straight-line path with a bell-shaped speed profile. Our next step is to incorporate fatigue in the muscle model.

Acknowledgment. Funding for this work from the National Science Foundation of China through Grant No. 50475048 is gratefully acknowledged.

References

1. Dornay, M., Uno, Y., Kawato, M., Suzuki, R.: Simulation of optimal movements using the minimum-muscle-tension-change model. Adv. Neural Info. Processing Syst. 4 (1991) 627-634.
2. Jordan, M.I., Rumelhart, D.E.: Forward models: supervised learning with distal teacher. Cognitive Sci. 16 (1992) 307-354.

3. Massone, L.L.E., Myers, J.D.: The role of plant properties in arm trajectory formation: a neural network study. IEEE Trans. Syst. Man Cybern. B 26 (1996) 719-732.
4. Karniel, A., Inbar, G.F.: A model for learning human reaching movements. Biol. Cybern. 77 (1997) 173-183.
5. Fagg, A.H., Sitkoff, N., Barto, A.G., Houk, J.C.: A model of cerebellar learning for control of arm movements using muscle synergies. 1997 IEEE Int. Symp. Computational Intelligence in Robotics and Automation (CIRA '97) (1997) 6-12.
6. Ogihara, N., Yamazaki, N.: Generation of human reaching movement using a recurrent neural network model. Syst. Man Cybern., IEEE SMC '99 Conf. Proc. 2 (1999) 692-697.
7. Kashima, T., Isurugi, Y., Shima, M.: Analysis of a muscular control system in human movements. Biol. Cybern. 82 (2000) 123-131.
8. Lan, N.: Stability analysis for postural control in a two-joint limb system. IEEE Trans. on Neural Syst. Rehab. Eng. 10 (2001) 249-259.
9. Thelen, D.G., Anderson, F.C., Delp, S.L.: Generating dynamic simulations of movement using computed muscle control. Jour. Biomcch. 36 (2003) 321-328.
10. De Sapio, V., Warren, J., Khatib, O., Delp, S.L.: Simulating the task-level control of human motion: a methodology and framework for implementation. Visual Comp. 21 (2005) 289 – 302.
11. Atkeson, C.G.: Learning arm kinematics and dynamics. Ann. Revw. Neurosci. 12 (1989) 157-183.
12. Winters, J.M., Stark, L.: Analysis of fundamental human movement patterns through the use of in-depth antagonistic muscle models. IEEE Trans. Biomed. Eng. 32 (1985) 826-839.
13. Zangemeister, W.H., Lehman, S., Stark, L: Simulation of head movement trajectories: model and fit to main sequence. Biol. Cybern. 41 (1981) 19-32.
14. Schutte, L.M.: Using musculoskeletal models to explore strategies for improving performance in electrical stimulation-induced leg cycle ergometry. PhD. thesis, Stanford University (1992).
15. Zajac, F.E.: Muscle and tendon: properties, models, scaling, and application to biomechanics and motor control. Critical Reviews Biomed. Eng. 17 (1989) 359–411.
16. Zhang, A.: Motion simulation of the human upper limb based on MATLAB. Master thesis, Tianjin University, Tianjin, China. (2003) (in Chinese).
17. Pineda, F.J.: Dynamics and architecture for neural computation. Jour. Complexity 4 (1988) 216-245.
18. Katayama, M., Kawato, M.: Virtual trajectory and stiffness ellipse during multijoint arm movement predicted by neural inverse. Biol. Cybern. 69 (1993) 353-362.

Emotion Recognition Using Physiological Signals

Lan Li[1] and Ji-hua Chen[2]

[1] School of Electrical and Information Engineering, Jiangsu University,
Zhenjiang, 212013, P.R. China
yaolan_us@ujs.edu.cn
[2] Institute of Biomedical Engineering, JiangSu University, ZhenJiang, 212013, P.R. China

Abstract. The ability to recognize emotion is one of the hallmarks of emotional intelligence. This paper proposed to recognize emotion using physiological signals obtained from multiple subjects without much discomfort from the body surface. Film clips were used to elicit target emotions and an emotion elicitation protocol, verified to be effective in the preliminary study, was provided. Four physiological signals, electrocardiogram (ECG), skin temperature (SKT), skin conductance (SC) and respiration were selected to extract 22 features for recognition. We collected a set of data from 60 female undergraduates when experiencing the target emotion. Canonical correlation analysis was adopted as a pattern classifier, and correct-classification ratio is 85.3%. The research indicated the feasibility of user-independent emotion recognition using physiological signals. But before emotion interpretation can occur at the level of human abilities, there still remains much work to be done.

1 Introduction

Nowadays affective computing has become the hotspot in computer science. Recording and recognizing physiologic signatures of emotion has become an increasingly important field of research in affective computing and human-computer interface [1]. Traditional investigation, which has made considerable achievements, is based on the recording and statistical analysis of physiological signals from Autonomic nervous system [2]. Some researchers have been doing their best to develop wearable devices, while others devoting themselves to implementing a physiological signal-based emotion recognition system [3,4,5].

In 1999, researchers at IBM developed an emotion mouse about 75 percent successful in determining a user's emotional state [3]. In 2001, Picard and colleagues at MIT Media Laboratory developed pattern recognition algorithms which attained 81% classification accuracy [4]. Because of data acquired from only one subject, these emotion recognition methods can only measure one subject's emotion. In 2004, Kim and his group developed a multiple-users emotion recognition system using short-term monitoring of physiological signals. A support vector machine (SVM) was adopted as a pattern classifier, and correct-classification ratio for 50 subjects is 78.4% [5].

This paper discussed how to recognize emotion using four physiological signals obtained from multiple subjects. It is novel and different from previous research. Film clips were used to arouse the inner feelings of the subjects, and an emotion elicitation

Z. Pan et al. (Eds.): ICAT 2006, LNCS 4282, pp. 437–446, 2006.

protocol, verified to be effective in the preliminary study, was provided. 22 features were extracted from 4 physiological signals. Canonical correlation analysis was adopted to find the relationship between three emotions and extracted features. And the recognition accuracy is 85.3%.

2   Method

2.1 Emotion Elicitation Protocol

Compared with other emotion elicitation techniques such as images, sounds, facial and body movement, scripted and unscripted social interactions, music, and so on, films are more reliable and more naturalistic to induce internal feelings of the subjects[6]. In order to evoke specific target emotion statuses effectively, we chose over three film clips (3~8 minutes in length) as stimulus for each target emotion.

89 (male 36; female 53) undergraduate students, aged from 18 to 23, in Jiangsu University took part in the preliminary test. Through completing post-film questionnaire, the subjects were encouraged to report the state of the emotion elicited by the film clips, and to use a five-point scale (0-very low, 1-low, 2-high, 3- median high, 4-very high) to report the intensity of the emotion .

Validity (the percentage of subjects who report that the given stimulus properly induced the intended motion) and the average intensity of the emotion were used to evaluate the quality of the emotion stimulus.

After the preliminary test, we drew conclusions as following:

- The stimulus clips for fear, neutral, and joy were chosen successfully, while others for anger, disgust, sadness, embarrassment, surprise, anguish, contempt, stress, interest, satisfied, were not.
- The most effective stimulus for three emotions was picked out, and showed in Label 1. Validity of fear, neutral and joy is 86.67%, 93.33% and 90.0% respectively; while the average intensity is 2.85, 2.63 and 3.25 respectively.
- Given the same stimulus, female students felt much stronger than male students.
- That three stimulus were shown sequently in a way, 'fear-joy-neutral', was proved to be more effective for the subjects to transition from one emotion state to another emotion state than in the way, 'fear-neutral-joy'.

Table 1. Summary of emotion-elicitation protocol

Target Emotion	Decscription	Film	Clip length
Fear	Frightened	The Doll	5'12''
Joy	Uplifting happiness	Tom and Jerry	6'45''
neutral	Relaxation, vacancy	Noncommercial screen saver	3'26''

2.2 Acquisition of Emotion-Specific Physiological Signals

Subjects. Since target emotion state is easier to be elicited from female students, our target subjects were 60 female undergraduate students aged from 18 to 23. All subjects were healthy volunteers without any history of medical, neurological or psychiatric illness. Before the test, they have not done exercise heavily in four hours and have not taken any medicine in a week. Otherwise, the subjects were chosen randomly, while the order of the subjects is arranged randomly.

Selection of the physiological signals. To develop a practical recognition algorithm, the physiological signals which we can choose are very important as well as very limited at the same time. Although electroencephalogram (EEG), facial electromyo-grams, and blood pressure may be helpful for the research, the attachment of electrodes to the scalp or face seems not to be tolerable for practical use, thus they are left out of consideration. Nowadays almost all wearable devices developed can measure four major physiological signals: skin temperature (SKT), skin conductance (SC), heart rate (HR), and electrocardiogram (ECG).

SKT is an important and effective indicator of emotion states. The variation in SKT due to emotional stimulus was studied by Shusterman, Barnea (1995) and Kataoka(1998) [7]. It reflects autonomic nervous system activity.

Skin conductance (SC), sometimes called the Electrodermal activity (EDA) or Galvanic skin response (GSR), is another important signal to represent the activity of the autonomic nervous system. It characterizes changes in the electrical properties of the skin due to the activity of sweat glands and is physically interpreted as conductance. Sweat glands distributed on the skin only receive output from the sympathetic nervous system, and thus SC is a good indicator of arousal level due to cognitive stimulus.

Heart rate (HR) is dually controlled by the sympathetic (increase) and parasympathetic (decrease) branch of the ANS that may act independently [8]. In addition, time-domain features, such as mean and standard deviation (SD) of the HRV (heart rate variability) time series have also been considered to be significant for the exploration of autonomic nervous system in many previous studies for cardiac function assessment and psychophysiological investigation. They have been frequently used as features [9]. Since ECG signal can be obtained relatively easily, and both time-domain features of HRV and HR can be computed from it, ECG signal seems to be very important in this study.

In addition, respiration is very important in the emotion research. Specific emotion expressions, such as crying, laughing, or shouting, have unique respiratory signatures. A detailed quantification of volume, timing and shape parameters in the respiratory pattern waveform can map into different emotional states along the dimensions of calm-excitement, relaxation-tenseness, and active vs. passive coping [10]. Initial evidence indicates that respiratory parameters also map into the 'affective space' dimensions of valence (aversive vs. appetitive stimulus quality) and arousal (activating vs. calming stimulus quality) [11].

So, in this research, four physical signals--SKT, SC, ECG and Respiration are selected to extract features for emotion recognition.

Experiment devices. Good devices are essential to gather good data. The equipments used in this research are:

World-renowned PowerLab Data Acquisition System with Chart software. It is developed by AD Instruments Company in Australia, including:

ML870   Powerlab 8 channel data acquisition system
MLT409/A SKT probe
ML309   Thermister Pod
ML116F   GSR finger electrodes
ML116   GSR AMP
MLT1132   Piezo respiratory belt transducer
MLA700   Reusable ECG clamp electrodes
ML132   Bio AMP

*A USB camera 800*600 pixels*

Two computers. One is used to show the film clips to elicit the target emotion of the subject; while the other, connecting with PowerLab ML870 and a USB camera in covert, is used to record, analyze, preprocess the physiological data, and monitor the facial or body expression of the subject.

Experimental method
Preparation. Before the experiment, the subject was requested to report the personal information and sign a volunteer grant. By talking, we could make the subject feel relax, not curious and be a calm state. Then, attach the sensors to the subject. The MLT409/A SKT prob was placed on the tip of the thumb of the left hand. The bipolar MLT116F GSR finger electrodes measured SC from the middle of the three segments of the index and middle fingers of the left hand. And based on lead I, three reusable ECG clamp electrodes of the MLA700 were attached to wrists and right ankle. While the MLT1132 piezo respiratory belt transducer was placed around the body at the level of maximum respiratory expansion.

Instructions. The test will begin soon. Please make yourself be as relaxed and comfortable as possible. After 1 minute, film clips will be showed. Please watch the films carefully; don't move casually; let yourself experience whatever emotions you have as fully as you can, and don't try to hold back or hold in your feelings. Thank you for your cooperation!

Data collection. Acquisition of high-quality database of physiological signals is vital for developing successful emotion recognition algorithm.
    The emotion stimulus was showed in a way, 'fear-joy-neutral'. One emotion session took approximately 5~8 minutes. The first 1 min was taken to measure the baseline without any stimulus. Subsequently, emotional stimulus was applied. The physiological signals were recorded, at the sampling rate of 400 HZ for all the channels, by using PowerLab 8−channel physiological Data Acquisition System with Chart software. At the same time, a trained graduate monitored the subject with a hidden PC camera. When there were sudden changes in the facial or body expression, special marks and annotations would be added to the record to provide supplementary information for later data-processing. After one session, the subject was requested to

complete the post-film questionnaire. Then there would be 5 minutes interval for the subject to be calmed down before another emotion session. Two segments of raw data (SC and Respiratory signal) under three different emotion states were shown in Fig. 1.

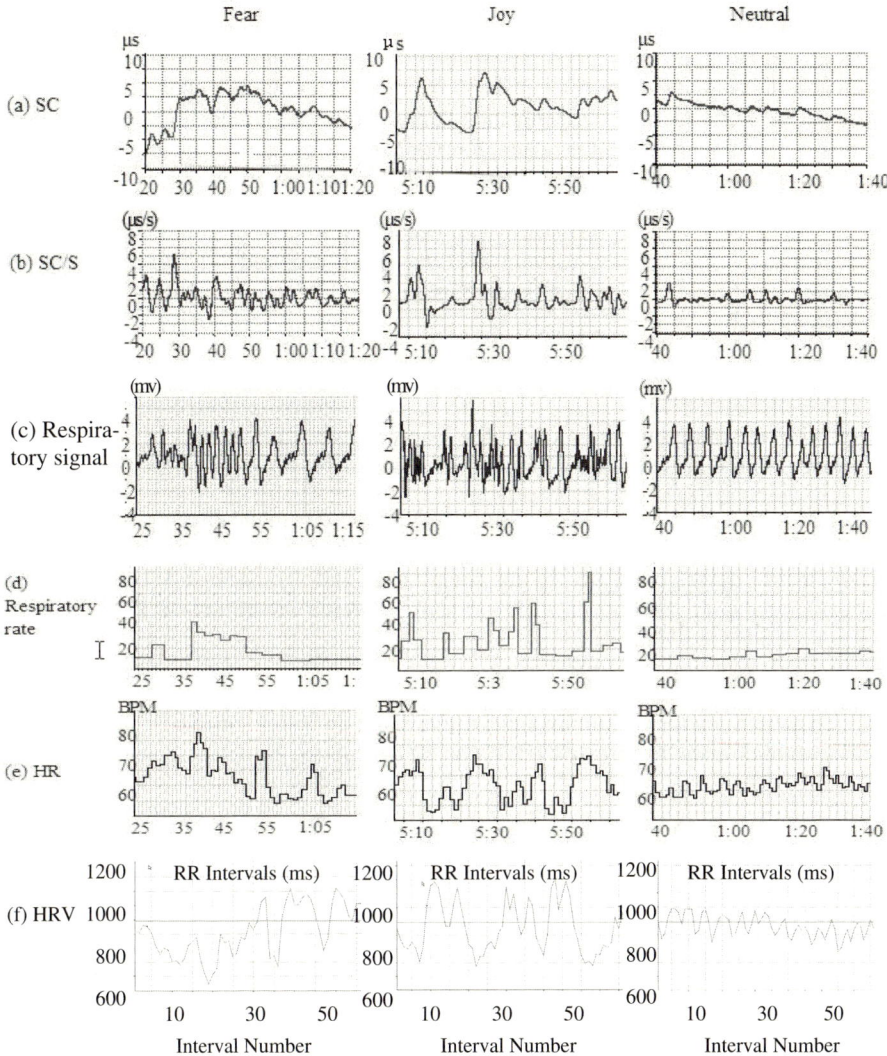

Fig. 1. Examples of physiological signals measured from a user during the period of experiencing the target emotion (Fear, Joy, Neutral). From top to bottom: (a) skin conductivity (MicroSiemens), (b) the difference of skin conductivity, (c) respiratory signal (raw digital signal obtained with the respiratory belt), (d) respiratory rate, (e) Heart rate , (f) HRV time series. The sampling rate is 400/s. The segment shown here are visiblely different for the three emotions, which was not true in general.

2.3 Data Processing

Since each emotion session would last around 5~8 minutes, and signals were sampled at 400Hz, there would be about 120 to 192 thousand samples per physiological signal. It is necessary to extract a short time significant segment of the signals from the raw data. The only criterion of extraction is whether the signals were sampled during the period of experiencing strong feelings of the target emotion. According to the emotion theory, SC is a good indicator of arousal level. Base on the comprehensive consideration of SC differentiation and the marks & annotations made during the period of experiments, data segments (1 min length) were taken for features extraction from the raw pattern waveform of SKT, ECG, Respiration for each of the three emotions.

SKT. No special signal processing was necessary for SKT. Although frequency-domain analysis of the time-varying SKT has been reported [7], here we used the mean and the difference between the maximum and the minimum within 1 min as the features of SKT.

SC. The raw SC signal was shown in Fig. 1a, while differentiation signal, computed by chart software, shown in Fig. 1b. In this research, the SC differentiation signal was used to be one important basis to choose samples from raw waveform. And the first difference of it was used as an important feature [4].

Respiration. Respiration parameters can be computed from the changes in thoracic or abdominal circumference during respiration, which can be measured easily by a piezo-electric device contained by the Respiratory Belt Transducer MLT1132. Here, we took respiratory rate (see Fig. 1d) and peak inspiratory amplitude as features.

ECG. Heart rate can be computed by R-peak detection. Fig. 1e illustrates the heart rate waveform detected from raw ECG signals. Mean of the heart rate and the difference between the maximum and the minimum are taken into account.

The time-domain features of HRV can be calculated by Chart conveniently and accurately. These are :

HF power____high-frequency heart rate variability spectral power [0.15~0.4HZ]
LF power____low-frequency heart rate variability spectral power [0.04~0.15HZ]
LF/HF____ratio of low-to high-frequency power
Mean NN____ the mean of the normal cardiac cycle
SDNN____the standard deviation of the normal cardiac cycle
SD Delta NN____the standard deviation of the delta of the normal cardiac cycles
Mean T____the mean of T-wave amplitude
SDT____the standard deviation of T-amplitude
SD Delta T____the standard deviation of the delta of T-amplitude
Mean R____the mean of R-wave amplitude
SDR____the standard deviation of R-wave amplitude
SD Delta R____the standard deviation of the delta of R-amplitude
PNN50____(NN50 count) / (total NN count), the fraction of consecutive NN intervals that differ by more than 50 ms'
RMSSD____the square root of the cumulate of the square of the delta of the normal cardiac cycles
Ratio____ SDNN/SD Delta NN

The features listed above were adopted in this research. Some of them were considered to correlate with emotion from the literature, and some we supposed to.

2.4 Pattern Classification Using Canonical Correlation Analysis

Feature vectors extracted from multiple subjects under the same emotion state form a distribution in high-dimension space. Duda had projected them onto two-dimension space for visualization by a Fisher project. The research showed that the projected feature vectors from the same emotion state formed a cluster with a large amount of variation, and the clusters of feature vectors from different emotion state significantly overlapped. Kim proposed to solve this difficult high-dimension classification problem with the support vector machine (SVM) classifier[5]. SVM is based on the property that separation by a linear classifier becomes more promising after non-linear mapping onto high-dimensional space. The linear classifier can be obtained with maximum generalization performance derived from the statistical learning theory of Vapnik.

Unlike SVM, CCA, known as multivariate multiple regression analysis, can find two sets of basis vectors in which the correlation matrix between the variables is diagonal and the correlations on the diagonal are maximized. Given two random variables, X and Y, the basic CCA model is:

$$CV_{X1} = a_1X_1 + a_2X_2 + ... + a_pX_p. , \quad CV_{Y1} = b_1Y_1 + b_2 Y_2 + ... + b_m Y_m . \tag{1}$$

The goal is to describe the relationships between the two sets of variables. The canonical weights (coefficients) a_1, a_2, a_3, ... a_p are applied to the p X variables, while b_1, b_2, b_3, ... b_m applied to the m Y variables in such a way that the correlation between CV_{X1} and CV_{Y1} is maximized. It is a combination of predictor and dimension-reducer. More details can be found in [12].

In this research, considering the consistent success in previous evaluations of feature selection algorithms, CCA was adopted as a classifier.

3   Results

The classification results are shown in Table 2. 85.3% of test cases can be correctly classified. The classification rates for fear, neutral, joy were 76%, 94%, 84% respectively. And One combined-group figure was shown in Fig. 2, which can visualize the three emotions' territorial map. In the figure, we can see there is somewhat overlaped between the emotion 'fear' and 'joy', Which may be the reason of low classification rate on 'fear' and 'joy'.

Table 2. Classification rates for three emotions

Initial emotion	Predicted Group Members			Total
	fear	neutral	joy	
fear	38	2	10	50
neutral	1	47	2	50
joy	6	1	43	50

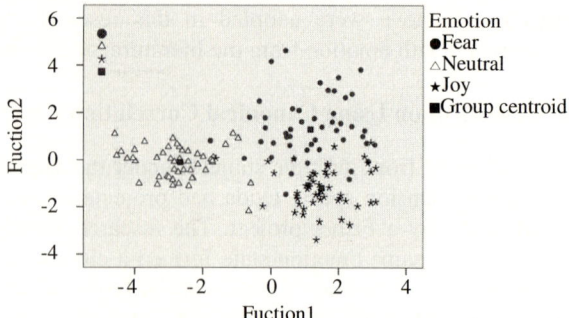

Fig. 2. Combined-group figure

4 Discussion

Like previous research, Our study demonstrated the feasibility of a physiological signal-based emotion recognition again. Although we don't know what emotion is, how it happens and how it reacts, there does lie clues, pehaps facial or body expression, tone of speech, etc., among which the physiological signals are more natural and more belivable ones (see Fig. 1), to estimate the subject's emotion state.

Although there are some clues in physiological signals, no one know exactly which signal will work best, so signals adopted are somewhat different. Furthermore, there is no standard database. All these make the comparitive study of different method impossible. Expecting to share opinion with researchers in this field, I will analyze why the classification accuracy of our method can reach up to 85.3%.

First, data is good and effective. Our data was obtained under emotion states without any external disturbance or interference. To achieve this goal, the subject was left single in a typical room, electrically shielded and soudproof inside. At the same time, the mobile would be turned off. Sequently, carefully sellected film clips were shown to arouse the inner feelings of the subject. In general, target emtion can be elicited, thus our collecting data really corresponding to real emotion states.

Second, emotion category is limited to three kinds, which makes the classification simplified. Since Picard got 88.3% accuracy for three emotion recognition in 2001 [4], it seems that less kinds of emotion, higher accuracy of classification.

Third, all 60 subjects were female undergraduates. Since there have been reports of sex differences in several aspects of emotional responding, and in the preliminary study, we did find the problem, we decided to perform research only for female subjects to avoid the sex differences.

In addition, a good classifier, CCA, was adopted to find the relationship for the high-dimensional classification problem.

The shortcomings of our method is about 3 aspects:

First of all, our database is far from complete. Secondly, only three kinds of emotion are concerned. And thirdly, signal processing is relatively simple for SKT and respiration signal. For pactical application, future work shuld be done according to the three aspects.

5   Conclusion

Emotion recognition is one of the key skills of emotion intelligence for adaptive learning systems. The sheer difficulty in this field is how to gather data corresponding to real emotion states and how to find the relationship between the emotion and the physiological signals in high-dimension space. After 2 years research, we have developed a novel method for a user dependent emotion recognition based on the processing of physiological signals.

In our research, the database used for emotion recognition is obtained from multiple subjects when they were experiencing the specific feelings, so the bio-signal database can represent the nature emotion state. To arouse the inner feelings of the subject, film clips, the more effective technique, were used as stimulus. It is different from most of the previous studies, in which the emotion was intentionally 'tried and felt' [3], or 'acted out'[4]. After the preliminary test, three clips that can successfully elicit the target emotion were selected. A good emotion elicitation protocol for the emotion research on Chinese undergraduates is provided.

For practical application, we selected four significant physiological signals including ECG, SC, SKT, and respiration, which is easy to obtain relatively, to recognize emotion. Based on the data-processing, 22 features were obtained from the raw signals. To overcome the high-dimension classification difficulty, CCA, a combination of predictor and dimension-reducing technique, was adopted. Recognition accuracy is up to 85.3%, which is much higher than previous studies.

The classification results were quite encouraging, and showed the feasibility of a user-independent emotion recognition based on physiological signals.

We expect to develop a simple and accurate affect estimation system for machine to understand the users' feelings. Future work will be aiming at two aspects:

- Build a good database, which is most arduous, difficult, but foundational and significant as well. Since there is no standard database, there is no standard to evaluate the researchers' work. A standard database is a matter of great urgency for the study.
- Featrues extraction. For us, what emotion is, how it happens and how it reacts remain unknown till now, which makes it very difficult to select the most corresponding physiological features for classification. Great foundational work should be done to explore the relationship between emotion and the physiological signals. It is key of the emotion recognition.

In a word, it is feasible to classify emotion with physiological signals. But before emotion interpretation can occur at the level of human abilities, there still remains much work to be done.

Acknowledgement. The work is supported by Academy Natural Science Foundation of Jiangsu Province (04KJB310171), and Advanced Technologist Research Start Foundation of Jiangsu University (05JDG029).

References

1. Picard, R. W.: Affective Computing, MIT press, Cambridge, MA, (1997)
2. Andreassi, J. L.: Psychophysiology: human behavior and physiological response, Lawrence Erlbaum Associates, New Jersey, (2000)
3. Ark, W., Dryer, D. C., and Lu, D. J.: The emotion mouse, 8th Int. Conf. Human-computer Interaction, (1999) 453-458
4. Picard, R. W., Vyzas, E., Healey, J.: Toward machine emotional intelligence: analysis of affective physiological state. IEEE Transactions Pattern Analysis and Machine Intelligence, (2001), 23(10) 1175-1191
5. Kim, K.H., Bang, S.W., and et al.: Emotion recognition system using short-term monitoring of physiological signals, Med. Biol. Comput., (2004) 42: 419-427
6. Gross, J.J., Levenson, R.W.: Emotional suppression: Physiology, self-report, and expressive behavior, Journal of Personality & Social psychology, (1993) 64: 970-986
7. Shusterman, V., Barnea, O.: Analysis of skin-temparature variability compared to variability of blood pressure and heart rate, IEEE Ann. Conf. Engineering Medicine Biology Society, (1995) 1027-1028
8. Berntson, G.G., Cacippo, J.T., et al.: Autonomic determinism: the modes of autonomic control, the doctrine of autonomic space, and the laws of autonomic constraint, Psychological Review, (1991) 98: 459~487
9. Mccraty, R., Atkinson, M., et al.: The effects of emotions on short –term power spectrum analysis of heart rate variability, AM. J. Cardiol., (1995) 76:1089-1093
10. Grossman, P., Wientjes, C. J.: How breathing adjusts to mental and physical demands, Respiration and emotion, spring, New York, (2001) 43-53
11. Ritz, J., Nixon, A., et al.: Airway response of healthy individuals to affective picture series, International Journal of Psychophysiology, (2002) 46(1): 67-75
12. Hotelling H.: Relations between two sets of variates, Biometrika, (1936), 28: 321-377

Animation Preserving Simplification for MPEG Based Scalable Virtual Human

HyungSeok Kim

Department of Internet & Multimedia Engineering, Konkuk University
1, Hwayang-dong, Kwangjin-Ku, Seoul, Korea
hyuskim@konkuk.ac.kr
http://home.konkuk.ac.kr/~hyuskim

Abstract. In this paper, a new method to build an adaptable body shape considering the motion parameters. The proposed method constructs MPEG conforming scalable virtual human by simplifying the body parts which have similar motion parameters while preserving details with characteristic motion parameters. Characteristic motion is classified by its high deformation over time which is extracted from skinning parameter distribution. The proposed method is adaptable with in MPEG framework and is designed to minimize load of adaptation server which keeping compactness as much as possible. It is also targeted to cover devices with small computational power such as PDAs. Example of body simplification is given to show the effectiveness of the proposed method.

Keywords: Multiresolution model, Mesh simplification, Virtual human.

1 Introduction

The virtual human is one of key elements in virtual reality applications including interactive game, virtual fashion, and virtual heritage. The virtual human is applied to give more realism in applications which requires high quality presentation of shape and animation. To give high quality rendering and simulation, the shape of a virtual character is usually too complex to be processed in real-time. For example, laser scanned body has more than millions of polygons, while the model itself need to be animated in conventional PCs or even at light-weight mobile phones. Thus, those complex representation of virtual human should be adapted to the requirements of real-time rendering and simulation. MPEG-21 is a standard for managing multimedia contents including 3D shapes and animations. In this paper, a method to generate MPEG-21 based animatable virtual human is presented.

With respect to regular solid objects in a virtual environment, the most important feature of the virtual character is its animation. The surface of a virtual character is deformed by its facial and body animation. In this paper, both the shape and animation representation of the virtual character is considered to generate real-time renderable representation.

Z. Pan et al. (Eds.): ICAT 2006, LNCS 4282, pp. 447–456, 2006.

There have been many approaches to generate simplified shapes for real-time rendering since the first introduction of multiresolution modeling [2]. Those methods evaluates representations using error metrics with respect to the original models. Most common error metrics are based on geometric and color space distances for the static shape. For the polygon mesh, vertices/edges/faces are removed to generate simplified shape while minimizing errors [6,5,3]. An edge collapsing is a widely adopted simplification operation by merging two vertices into one vertex [7]. In addition to preserve static shape features, dynamic features such as view and light silhouettes are also considered. Hoppe et. al proposed vertex tree which can easily accommodate view silhouettes [7,12,11]. Kim et al. proposed a structure to organize directional relations to be accessed in real-time considering both view and light silhouettes [10].

Although existing simplification methods give good results, applying these methods to animatable object with deformation still has limitations. The animation of the virtual character consists of a *facial animation* and of a *body animation*. The simplification process to generate an LOD model should consider these animation parameters so that the low complexity model can be animated as close as possible to the original model. Kim et. al proposed MPEG-21 based facial animation parameter preserving multiresolution method [8]. In this paper, we extend the method for the body animation.

Body animation can be represented in joint-based movement of solid segment or skinning style deformation. For body animation, it is important to preserve surface detail around deforming parts such as surface parts near joints. For example, a surface part which is close to a joint should have more detail, to preserve overall shapes even when the part is highly deformed by joint rotation [9].

DeCoro et al. proposed a pose-independent simplification method to simplify a shape considering animation parameters [4]. Their method minimizes errors for different body poses in simplification. Importance of each pose can be modeled such that most frequent pose will have less errors. Although the method give high quality simplification, it needs an extension for multiresolution modeling [4]. Also, it does not effectively consider different level-of-articulation mentioned in MPEG-4/21 LOA scheme [9]. In this paper, a multiresolution extension of pose-independent simplification is presented with LOA model.

Ahn et. al proposed a method to simplify skeleton structures based on analysis of pre-recorded motions [1]. Each motion is analyzed by its overall shape and a hierarchy of skeleton structure is generated such that the least number of joint is animated along to its motion complexity and rendering complexity. In this paper, this approach is adopted to create LOA and a link to continuous multiresolution model.

In this paper, a new method to build an adaptable body shape considering the motion parameters. The proposed method simplifies the body parts which have similar motion parameters while preserving details with characteristic motion parameters.

This paper consists of four parts. In the next section, an overview of MPEG-21 based adaptation and discussion on motion consideration is presented. Section 3 presents proposed simplification method and structure. An experimental result is followed in the next section with a few simplification cases.

2   Scalable 3D Model in MPEG Framework

Adaptation within the MPEG framework for the 3D shapes, Kim et al. proposed a generic framework for scalable virtual human [8].

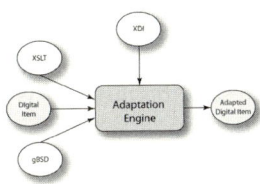

Fig. 1. MPEG-21 Adaptation Engine [8]

The adaptation process of MPEG is basically passing information through the adaptation engine. As illustrated in Figure 1, 3D contents are adapted in the adaptation engine by given description of the binary stream and adaptation information. The structure description should be retained even after the simplification thus the adaptation methods must be inline with the lowest level defined in the schema [8] .

To make a scalable virtual human in MPEG framework, the model should be constructed in multiresolution manner so that arbitrary detail resolutions can be created by MPEG-21 adaptation mechanism. Due to the nature of MPEG-21 based adaptation, the multiresolution model for the MPEG-21 is required to satisfy following requirements.

- Compact representation
  The multiresolution model should be able to be encoded by standard stream formats such as MPEG-4 BIFS or LASER, etc. Also it is desired that the encoded representation is in compact form.
- Binary adaptable
  The standard MPEG-21 adaptation is performed for the binary encoded contents. Instead of letting the adaptation server to decode and re-encode for the process, the binary adaptable data makes the server be free of additional heavy computation.
- Heterogeneous terminal devices
  In common mobile environment, highly heterogeneous devices participate in the network. For the least capable devices, which has very limited memory size, memory access bandwidth and computation power, a simple decoding scheme of the adapted contents should be devised to conform to the limitation of memory and computation power in those devices.

3   Simplification Considering Body Motion

3.1   Clustered Multiresolution Representation

The shape of virtual human is optimized by mesh simplification methods. In this research we adopt a simple decimation method based on quadric error [5]. For a multi-resolution model, we adopt and extended the concept of clustering representation [9]. In this subsection, a summary and extension of Kim et al.'s approach is illustrated.

The multiresolution model is clustered so that a specific complexity can be obtained by simply choosing a set of clusters. From the complex mesh $M_n(V_n, F_n)$ where V_n is a set of vertices and F_n is a set of faces, it is sequentially simplified to $M_{n-1}, , M_1, M_0$. The multiresolution mesh M is presented by V and F which are the set of vertices and faces over all levels [9].

V and F can be partitioned into set of clusters. The first type is a set of vertices and faces that are removed from a mesh of the level i to make a mesh of the level $i-1$, denoted by $C(i)$. The other type is a set of vertices and faces that are newly generated by simplification, denoted by $N(i)$. The simplification operator is sequentially applied to generate multiresolution model. In each simplification step, corresponding $C(i)$ and $N(i)$ can be generated. For more efficient adaptation, $C(i)$ is again clustered into $C(i, j)$ for corresponding $N(j)$ such that $C(i, j)$ is a part of $C(i)$ which is subset of $N(j)$ where $j > i$ and $C(i, i)$ which does not belongs to any $N(j)$. Hence a level i mesh is as follows [9]:

$$M_i = \sum_{j=0}^{i}(C(j, j) + \sum_{k=i+1}^{n} C(j, k))$$

In the previous work, a half-edge collapsing operator is used with modified QEM considering relation to joint animation [9]. To have better result DeCoro's pose-independent quadric can be used [4]. The focus of this work is not in the presenting better error measurement but presenting an integrated method to create efficient clustered representation.

The last process is the concatenation of clusters into a small number of blocks to reduce the number of selection or removal operations during the adaptation process. By ordering vertices of $C(i, i)$ by the order of i, the adaptation process of vertex data for level i is a single selection of continuous block of data, $v_0, v_1, , v_i$. For the indexed face set, each $C(i)$ is ordered by $C(i, j)$ in the ascending order of j. Thus, an adaptation to level i, consists of at most $3i + 1$ selections or at most $2n$ removals of concatenated blocks [9].

3.2   Cluster with Animation Hierarchy

To make real-time presentable human body, it is needed to make plausible simplification over different postures give by motions. The previous work on scalable virtual human in MPEG-21 framework does not effectively consider the differences given by motion [9]. So that, the mesh simplification does not considers effects caused by different LOA by constantly preserving unmoving joint details. Also, LOA architecture presented in their work does not consider the skinning parameter so that only segmented body animation is supported while the skinning based body animation is quite popular for the higher quality animation.

The method presented in this paper is extension of fore-mentioned motion independent simplification. Instead of covering all motions, only the necessary motion part is considered. For example, when a virtual human is placed in distance so that only knee movement is significant for walking motion, it is not necessary to preserve motion parameters for other parts of body.

Ahn et. al. presented an interesting method to construct motion hierarchy so that only necessary joints and motion parameters are used in crowd animation [1]. It is assumed that the motion is created from pre-captured set of motions. It is blended and re-targeted for each virtual human. Following Ahn's method, a generic motion hierarchy is constructed for all motions. In this framework, it is assumed that every motion will be appeared with the same probability but it could be easily extended to put different weight for each clips.

The most simplified motion parameter is given as a static figure considering that no motion is given to all joints. The standard posture is calculated from average position from the given set of motions. Starting from the static figure, it is sequentially refined by adding joints by joints according to given set of motions. Figure 2 shows an example of motion hierarchy used in this paper. In the hierarchy, each bone in coarse level is refined into a set of bones (lines in the figure) by adding corresponding joints (dots in the figure).

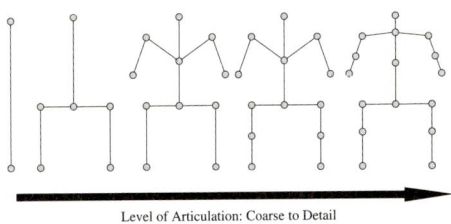

Level of Articulation: Coarse to Detail

Fig. 2. Example of Level of Articulation: Motion Hierarchy

The motion hierarchy is a structure of bones such that the simplest model has only one bone b_0. For each refinement b_i is refined into b_j and b_k such that b_{i+1} is always higher or the same detail level of b_i.

Once the bone hierarchy is constructed, polygon clusters are assigned to the bone structure. At first, each polygon is assigned to the highest level of bones. Polygons around joints which have relations to more than one bones are assigned most relevant one according to skinning weight. Cluster $C(i, j, k)$ is polygons in the cluster $C(i, j)$ related to bone b_k. This process is continued until the shape simplification error exceeds the motion simplification error using maximum QED and maximum positional error estimation of Ahn's work.

By the ith simplification which exceeds the error calculated by motions of bone level l with b_k, the b_k is merged into b_m along with adjacent bones following the pre-constructed hierarchy. From this level, simplified polygons are allocated in $C(i, j, m)$ instead of $C(i, j, k)$ and it is continued until the b_0. Following this procedure, M is again clustered into $C(i, j, k)$ by bones such that part of polygons from M_{s_l} to M_{e_l} where $s_l < e_l$ are assigned to b_k.

The previous equation is extended with bone structures.

$$M_i = \sum_{j=0}^{i} (C(j, j, l) + \sum_{k=i+1}^{n} C(j, k, l))$$

where b_l is the selected bone level.

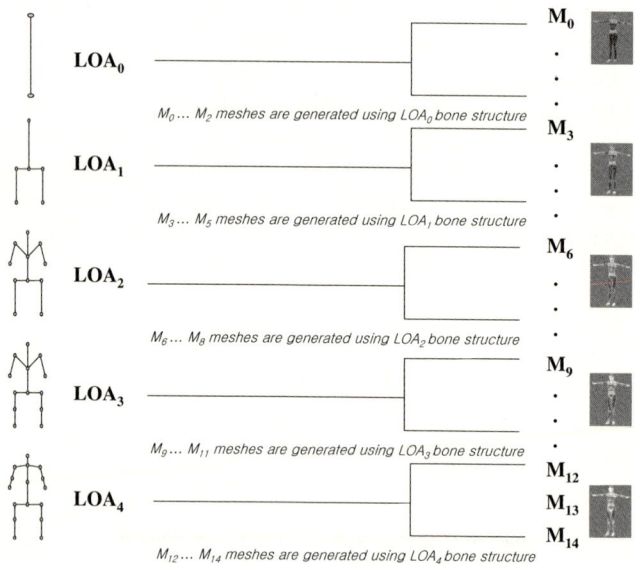

Fig. 3. Example of Level of Articulation: Motion Hierarchy

Figure 3 is an example of combined LOA and shape levels. Each shape levels are constructed with using the corresponding bone structures.

In addition to the vertices and face information, additional vertex properties such as normal, color, and texture coordinates are also clustered by $C(i, j, k)$. The clustering method is basically literal adoption of Kim et al.'s method [9] as those are not related bone levels but only to polygon levels. Only the skinning information need to be reconstructed for different bone levels. As the cluster of skinning parameter resides on each bones, similar method can be applied to the skinning parameter as the vertex. When $C(j, k, l)$ is simplified $C(j-1, k, m)$, newly created skinning parameters belongs to $C(j-1, k, m)$ is just added by the end of previous clusters so that corresponding skinning parameters can be selected. Skinning parameter for the simplified bones are reconstructed by average of previous parameters so that overall motion remain unchanged. For exceptional cases, mapping from the vertex to faces is considered for clusters as for the normal, color or texture coordinates.

3.3   Adaptation Using Clusters

In this work, an extended mechanism for scalable virtual human is presented which considers skinning-based animation and LOA for the shape simplification. The constructed scalable representation contains scalable shape and body animation data. For body animation parts, the shape is mapped onto different LOA such that a single level of articulation representation to have range of shape details. It is processed in the adaptation server which selects the shape complexity by the function of desired level of articulation and shape complexity.

In the adaptation server, at first, the desired shape complexity is selected. The device contexts such as rendering power acts as constraints for the shape representation. The selected representation is the most complex representation within the complexity bound for the desired context. Every representation with less complexity than the selected one conforms to the context constraints.

After the selection of shape complexity bound, LOA complexity bound is selected. LOA complexity bound is selected by constraints on terminal device capability for animation computation along with view parameters.

Following the clusters, each level of shape has unique correspondence to the LOA. If the corresponding LOA of the selected shape complexity is the same or less level than the desired, it makes both animation and shape complexity satisfies the condition of device. If the corresponding LOA is higher than the desired, the most highest complexity shape for the desired LOA is selected.

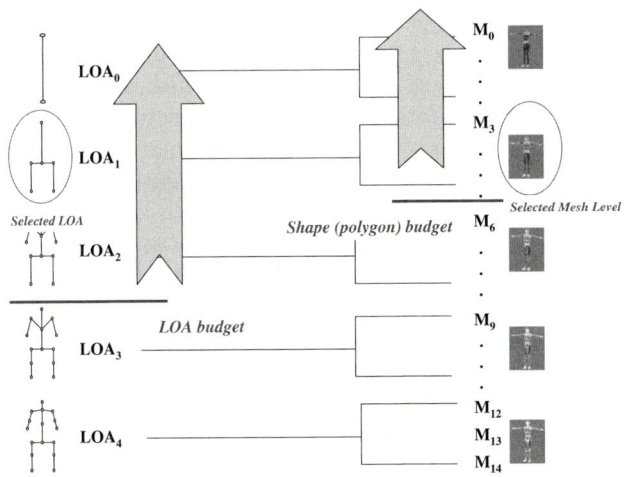

Fig. 4. Adaptation Example with motion and polygon hierarchy

Figure 4 illustrates the selection example. From the given LOA and polygon budget described in device context, the shape and level of articulation is selected by finding the best matching correspondence while keeping everything under the budget.

Selection of level is selection of clusters for the shape level. Each cluster has a set of vertices and vertex properties such as vertex normal, colors, texture coordinates and skinning parameters. Along with vertex information, the cluster has a set of indexed faces, normal faces, color faces and texture faces. Also each cluster can consist of sub-segments with their own material and texture. Each level is selected by choosing blocks of clusters.

4   Experiments

The proposed method constructs different levels of detail to be adapted in MPEG framework. The strong point of propose method lies on its conformity with standard and its compactness.

In terms of compactness, the progressive mesh (PM) approach is known as a method using near an optimal storage for multi-resolution models. In other extreme, the discrete mesh (DM) is a representation of a set of discrete levels of details which is still quite common in most of real-world applications because of its simplicity in adaptation.

Table 1. Size of Multiresolution Model with Different Methods

Number of polygons	Original	Proposed	PM	DM
71k	16.9M / 5.9M	25.8M / 9.7M	18M	132.5M / 29.2M

The table 1 illustrates size of multiresolution model for different methods. The numbers are the size of the VRML and BIFS files respectively. PM stands for progressive mesh representation and DM is for discrete levels of detail. Since the PM cannot currently be encoded in the BIFS format, only the approximated size for the VRML file is noted. As a result of the adaptation, the highest details have a number of polygons of 71K and 7K for each model whilst the lowest details have 1K and 552 polygons each. The models are constructed to have 5 different levels in LOA and 3 shape levels in each LOA. Compared to original or PM model, the proposed model has around 50% more data in both VRML and BIFS representation but it is about 20% of full discrete model.

The number of operations for adaptation is at most selecting 3 clusters for each bones and vertex properties, which is at maximum 270 clusters for 15 bones and 6 properties (position, color, normal, texture coordinate, skinning parameters and polygons). It is quite small when compared to operations for a PM, which requires at least $n/2$ operations, where n is number of vertices (28K for the body model). Furthermore, the method uses a simple selection, whilst PM requires relatively complex substitutions. The proposed method is located in-between of these approaches, and is flexible and simple enough to allow adaptation with relatively small file size and encodable to standard codec and is able to be transmittable via standard MPEG streams. It also utilizes a simpler adaptation mechanism, which is very similar to the simplest discrete level selection.

5   Conclusion

In this paper an extended framework to construct multiresolution 3D virtual human model that can be encoded and adapted using standard MPEG-21 framework. The method is extended from the previous work such that it effectively incorporates body motion hierarchy to preserve more details over animation. It inherits strong points of previous approaches most importantly adaptable with no additional information at the client and can be rendered immediately. In addition, the representation used is suitable for clients with low computational power and provides significant advantages over progressive mesh techniques of devices such as PDAs.

In this work, each mesh representation corresponds to the single LOA in order to make compact representation of skinning parameters. It makes the control of LOA is strongly constrained by the given shape complexity. To make more flexible adaptation for various cases, it is necessary to be able to control both complexities independently. Further more, devising unified error metric for both motion simplification and shape simplification will help to construct more efficient representation of multiresolution model.

Acknowledgements

This work was supported by the faculty research fund of Konkuk University in 2006.

References

1. Junghyun Ahn, Seungwoo Oh, and Kwangyun Wohn. Optimized motion simplification for crowd animation: Research articles. *Comput. Animat. Virtual Worlds*, 17(3‐4):155–165, 2006.
2. James H. Clark. Hierarchical geometric models for visible surface algorithms. *Commun. ACM*, 19(10):547–554, 1976.
3. Jonathan Cohen, Amitabh Varshney, Dinesh Manocha, Greg Turk, Hans Weber, Pankaj Agarwal, Frederick Brooks, and William Wright. Simplification envelopes. In *SIGGRAPH '96 Proc.*, pages 119–128, Aug. 1996.
4. Christopher DeCoro and Szymon Rusinkiewicz. Pose-independent simplification of articulated meshes. In *SI3D '05: Proceedings of the 2005 symposium on Interactive 3D graphics and games*, pages 17–24, New York, NY, USA, 2005. ACM Press.
5. Michael Garland and Paul S. Heckbert. Surface simplification using quadric error metrics. In *Proceedings of the 24th annual conference on Computer graphics and interactive techniques*, pages 209–216. ACM Press/Addison-Wesley Publishing Co., 1997.

6. Hugues Hoppe. Progressive meshes. In *SIGGRAPH '96 Proc.*, pages 99–108, Aug. 1996.

7. Hugues Hoppe. View-dependent refinement of progressive meshes. In *SIGGRAPH '97: Proceedings of the 24th annual conference on Computer graphics and interactive techniques*, pages 189–198, New York, NY, USA, 1997. ACM Press/Addison-Wesley Publishing Co.

8. HyungSeok Kim, Chris Joslin, Thoman Di Giacomo, Stephane Garchery, and Nadia Magnenat-Thalmann. Multi-resolution meshes for multiple target, single content adaptation within the mpeg-21 framework. In *Proceedings of the IEEE ICME Conference*, pages 1699–1702, 2004.

9. HyungSeok Kim, Chris Joslin, Thomas Di Giacomo, Stephane Garchery, and Nadia Magnenat-Thalmann. Device-based decision-making for adaptation of three-dimensional content. *The Visual Computer*, 22(5):332–345, 2006.

10. HyungSeok Kim, Soon Ki Jung, and KwangYun Wohn. A multiresolution control method using view directional feature. In *VRST '98: Proceedings of the ACM symposium on Virtual reality software and technology*, pages 163–169, New York, NY, USA, 1998. ACM Press.

11. David Luebke and Carl Erikson. View-dependent simplification of arbitrary polygonal environments. In *SIGGRAPH '97: Proceedings of the 24th annual conference on Computer graphics and interactive techniques*, pages 199–208, New York, NY, USA, 1997. ACM Press/Addison-Wesley Publishing Co.

12. Julie C. Xia and Amitabh Varshney. Dynamic view-dependent simplification for polygonal models. In *VIS '96: Proceedings of the 7th conference on Visualization '96*, pages 327–ff., Los Alamitos, CA, USA, 1996. IEEE Computer Society Press.

A Virtual Reality Training System for Robot Assisted Neurosurgery

Da Liu and Tianmiao Wang

Robotics Institute, Beijing University of Aeronautics and Astronautics,
100083 Beijing, China
drliuda@buaa.edu.cn

Abstract. Surgical training systems based on virtual reality simulation techniques offer a cost-effective and efficient alternative to traditional training methods. This paper describes a virtual reality system for training robot assisted neurosurgery. The training system undertakes the task of building the 3D environment of the virtual operation room and the surgical robot. The 3D model of the patient's brain is reconstructed based on the 2D images. After the virtual robot move to the entrance pose that is planned by the surgeon, the user can control the virtual needle to insert into the virtual brain to verify his surgical plan. 3-D display device and home-made human-computer interactive devices increase the immersion and telepresence of this system and establish a robot assisted surgical training demo system oriented clinical application.

Keywords: Robot assisted neurosurgery, Training, Virtual Reality, Human-computer interactive device.

1 Introduction

Robot assisted surgery is rapidly becoming an active interdisciplinary field, which has already begun to develop potential practical applications in minimally invasive neurosurgery [1]. Compared to conventional surgery, robot assisted neurosurgery offers less trauma and quicker patient convalescence. However, in robot assisted neurosurgery, the restricted vision and limited mobility of surgical instrument can easily cause unexpected injuries to patients.

Virtual reality training systems provide an elegant solution to these problems. The advantage of using a VR-based simulator stems from the ability to repeat procedures as many times as needed, without hurting the patient. As opposed to cadaver training, the surgeon's actions and outcomes are sampled in real-time and analyzed by the computer running the simulation. At the same time, VR-based simulators allow surgeons to practice new and unusual surgical procedure [6]. So many training systems have been developed [2-5], but these systems are not tailored for robot assisted neurosurgery.

In this paper, a training system for robot assisted neurosurgery is presented. This system can not only greatly improve the training and education quality to doctors but

Z. Pan et al. (Eds.): ICAT 2006, LNCS 4282, pp. 457 – 466, 2006.
© Springer-Verlag Berlin Heidelberg 2006

also increase the understanding for doctors to the robot assisted neurosurgery, which is beneficial to the technique spreading.

2 System Architecture

2.1 Overview of the System

In the real robot assisted neurosurgery, the procedure starts with fixing four markers on the skin in the skull of the patient. When medical images are input to the system, the surgeons identify them in the model of the brain. Then the robot is used to touch the pre-defined four markers on the patient's head, the system get the tip location in the robot local reference system. With the visualization of the brain model, the surgeon can define the route of the incision to avoid puncturing the critical vessel or nerves. Thus we use the robot to locate at the pre-defined incisive site with correct orientation. Surgeons can use the probe installed on the robot to implement the operation.

The training system is established on a PC using WTK software. It provides the surgeon with a virtual brain, virtual robot and virtual operation room. The structure of the system is shown as Fig. 1. A surgical intervention is complicated and requires several activities. The CT/MRI images of the patient's head are input into the system as the original data, and they are segmented to reconstruct the three-dimensional model. The surgeon can make a pre-operative planning to decide the entrance position and direction. The motion of the virtual robot with 5 degree of freedom is controlled by the surgeon. The surgeon can interface with the virtual environment, such as revising the puncture path of surgery (Fig. 2).

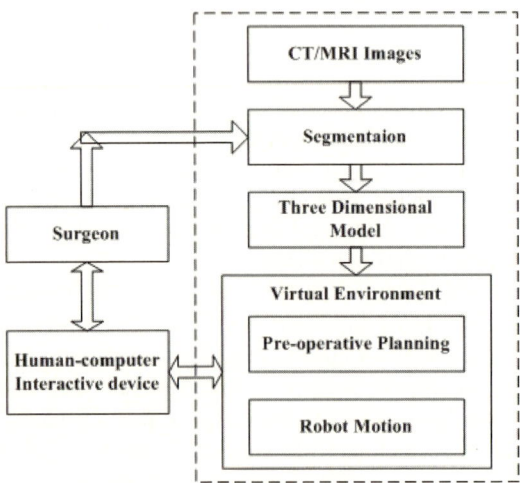

Fig. 1. The structure of the training system

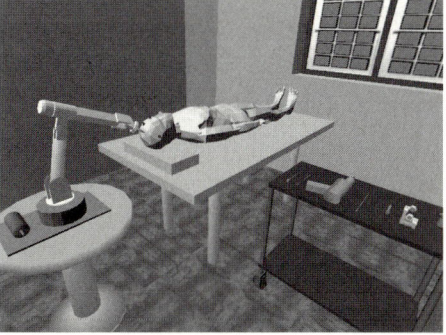

Fig. 2. The virtual training environment

2.2   The Hardware Structure of the System

Considering the practicability of this system, we adopted not the distributed multicomputer system but single computer with human-computer interactive devices. In the meanwhile, in order to improve presence sense, interaction and autonomy, the system integrates many interaction instruments. The main property of this structure is: to add a data processing model between the interaction instrument and the center computer, taking the corresponding algorithm to process the collected data and then send the data to the center computer. In contrary, the output data of the center computer are also sent to the interaction instrument for processing. That can decrease as much as possible the computation of the center computer and increase the simulation plotting speed of the system. The hardware structure of this system is shown in Fig. 3.

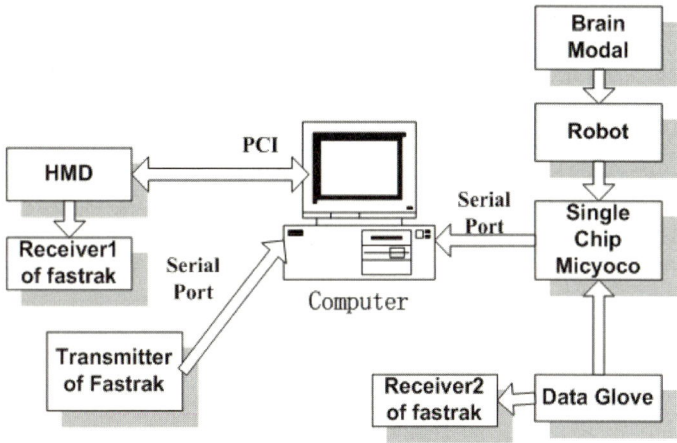

Fig. 3. The hardware structure of the system

This system consists of the several parts: the control model of the robot arm and data glove, HMD（Head Mounted Display）, and transmitter of Fastrak. This system fixes the two receivers to HMD and data glove to implement the visual feedback and bearing tracking.

2.3 The Software Structure of the System

In our system, we use WTK (World Tool Kit) to construct our virtual environment. WTK can be used in WINDOIWS platform, so it provides the possibility of carrying out graphics simulation in the PC with cheap hardware. The software structure consists of database, models of program state setting, sensor data reading, global

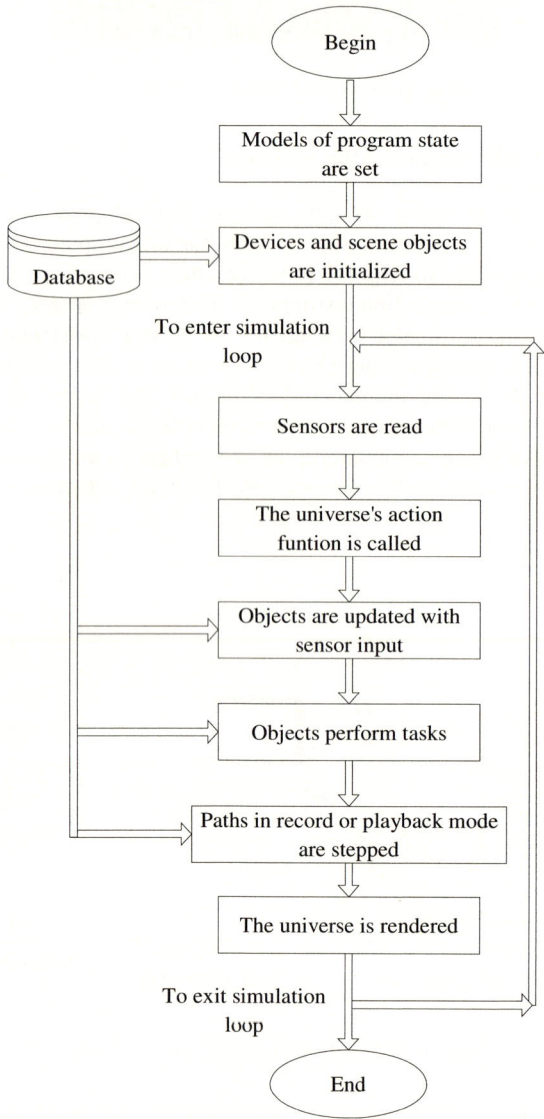

Fig. 4. Flow chart of the system

function performing, simulation object updating, assignment prosecuting and path processing. In all of them, the models of database, object updating (according to the sensor data) and assignment prosecuting are the three parts that affect the program efficiency and simulation effect most. In order to improve the program efficiency, we utilize the scene graph to manage the scene object and introduce switch node to optimize scene tree. The scene display takes the Level of Detail (LOD) technique. Thus can promise the display effect and avoid the waste of system resource. Flow Chart of the system is shown in Fig. 4.

All of the current elements of the scene, such as geometry, lights, fog, and positional information are hold by the scene graph. The scene graph is an ordered collection of nodes, in the form of a directed acyclic graph, which holds hierarchical scene data. The scene graph provides a very powerful scene structure for real-time 3D simulation and enhances performance of the WTK's rendering stage (drawing the scene) because it facilitates spatial culling of the scene.

During model plotting, all new view sub-domains based volume-rendering algorithm are presented. Taking advantage of the separability of the view domain and the equation of color composition, this algorithm separates the whole data set in view domain into several smaller data set in view sub-domains. Thus the rendering task can be implemented by combining the rendering results of all view sub-domains. Because the size and the complexity of the data set in view sub-domain are reduced, the rendering of the data set can be accelerated by the hardware of the normal workstations and desktop machines. This algorithm can also implement the rendering of the hybrid model.

Based on the view sub-domain volume-rendering algorithm, a new fast volume-rendering algorithm for walk through is proposed. This algorithm takes advantage of the correlation of the texture images between two adjacent frames. Some information in the last texture images can be used in the new texture images for rendering. Thus, this algorithm can reduce much calculation time and improve the speed of rendering algorithm.

3   Human-Computer Interactive Device

As the human-computer interactive device, robot arm and data glove are used in our system. So far The Robotics Institute of BUAA has researched a type of robot arm and two types of data glove. They are BH1 robot arm, BHG-I data glove and BHG-II data glove.

To enhance the ability and let operators feel more visual and realistic, we use WTK to produce the visual environment, connecting the system with robot arm and data glove. The arm and the glove can control the training system. In this section, we integrate BH1 robot arm and BHG-II data glove as the VR equipment.

3.1   BH1 6-DOF Robot Arm

BH1 6-DOF robot arm is used as human-computer interaction device, measuring the location of space point (Fig. 5).

We use none-power method to measure the point's location. It looks like human's arm, which is composed of forearm and elbow. The 2-DOF of the hand and the rotating joint of the forearm ensure the arm can get to the target in different status. The maximum error of the arm is 1.83mm, the average error is 1.28mm, covariance is 0.658mm.

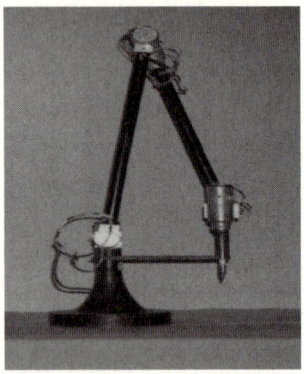

Fig. 5. BH1 robot arm overview

3.2 BHG- Ⅱ 5 Finger 11-DOF Data Glove

BHG-II data glove is designed for VR programming. It is constructed with mechanical main body, A/D data collecting card and simulation software, suiting for different human's hand. It detects the micro movement of five fingers, and use graphics simulation software to realize human-computer interaction at the same time. The range of the joint movement that it can detect is 20°- 90°, the average resolution ratio is 0.49°, the average excursion is $0.045v(4.8^\circ)$. Fig.6 is BHG-II glove sensor distribution.

BHG-II glove is cheap and reliable, which can fit for the requirement of simulation. The connection of arm and glove with the training system depends on RS-232 communication, using SCM to control the data collection and treatment under Windows NT platform.

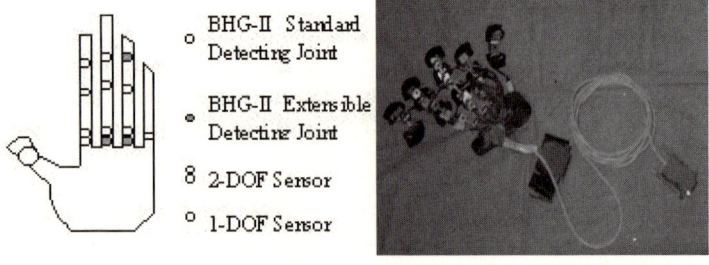

Fig. 6. BHG- Ⅱ data glove

4   The Virtual Three-Dimensional Model Reconstructed

4.1   Segmentation and Surface Mesh Generation

We generate surface meshes to represent organs, such as bone and pathological tissue. When the original image data are input into the system, a semiautomatic seed-based method is used to obtain a two-dimensional (2-D) contour from each slice. From the result of segmentation on a series of CT/MRI images, surface mesh is created from the series of 2-D contours using a three-dimensional (3-D) reconstruction algorithm. The algorithm is to tile the triangles from planar contours [7]. All contours are tiled with their adjacent contours by the triangles. The volumetric model of brain is reconstructed by linear interpolation between CT/MRI image slices.

4.2   The Dissection of 3-D Brain Model

Through the dissection of the brain model, the change of the inner structure of the brain model will shown to surgeons during the needle insertion. When the insertion begins and collision between the needle tip and the model is detected, a judgment about which triangle faces should be hidden will be made automatically.

The origin O of the XYZ coordinate is the needle tip. The dissection planes are designed as XOY plane, XOZ plane and YOZ plane. At each sampling time, the dissection plane intersects with the triangle faces. There are eight dissection directions according the pose of needle. The triangle faces that out of the dissection area are not hidden, otherwise they are hidden.

5   Implementation

The robot arm gives the surgeon a possibility to use surgical instrument to perform a simulation on the virtual environment. For example, the surgeon can plan the surgery path by operating on the robot arm. When the tip of the arm is punctured into the virtual brain model, the model cut automatically according to the depth of puncture. The doctor can observe the adjacent tissues around the tip of the arm in the interior of the brain and analyze if the path is correct.

For detecting collisions of tip and tissues, the model of the Denavit-Hartenberg-matrices needs to be set up. With the help of the Denavit-Hartenberg-matrices, which respect the geometry of the robot arm, the cartesian coordinates are computed. The robot arm is a serial structure. Using the Denavit Hartenberg convention configuration, the joint parameters are indicated in the table below.

Table 1. The joint parameters of our robot arm

Joint	θ_i	α_i	a_i(mm)	d_i (mm)
1	θ_1	$-90°$	0	0
2	θ_2	$0°$	455	-55
3	θ_3	$-90°$	0	55
4	θ_4	$90°$	0	388
5	θ_5	$-90°$	0	55
6	θ_6	$0°$	0	179

Rotate around the x axis by an angle θ_i
Translate along the x axis by a distance a_i
Rotate around the z axis by an angle α_i
Translate along the z axis by a distance d_i

The convert's coordinates from frame i-1 to frame i can be written using the following matrix:

$$^{i-1}A_i = Rot(Z_{i-1}, \theta_i)Trans(0,0,d_i)Trans(a_i,0,0)Rot(X_{i-1}, a_i) \tag{1}$$

The position and orientation of the tip with respect to the base is given by:

$$T_6 = {}^0A_1 {}^1A_2 {}^2A_3 {}^3A_4 {}^4A_5 {}^5A_6 = \begin{bmatrix} n_x & o_x & a_x & p_x \\ n_y & o_y & a_y & p_y \\ n_z & o_z & a_z & p_z \\ 0 & 0 & 0 & 1 \end{bmatrix} \tag{2}$$

The tip coordinate is (P_x, P_y, P_z).

Since the robot arm can be mapped to the model in the computer, when the surgeon moves the robot arm, the correct relative location can also be displayed on the screen. At the same time, because the robot arm has the same structure as the real surgical robot, it can help the surgeon to improve the ability of operating on the surgical robot. Another challenging part is the simulation of tissue behavior caused by the instrument constraint. During neurosurgery operation the surgeon inserts patient brain into probe and absorbs the tumor with injector. To simulate these procedures different approaches are implemented and tested. The tissue specific characteristics should be taken into account, the realism of the simulation should be as high as possible, the real time condition should be as high as possible and the real-time condition doesn't be lost.

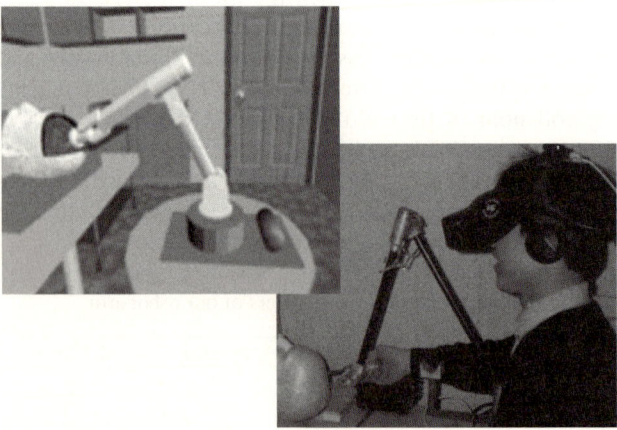

Fig. 7. Operating on the robot arm to simulate the surgery puncturing

For increasing the immersion and telepresence of the system, other virtual reality equipment, such as HMD and data glove is used in our system. The surgeon can wear HMD and data glove, selecting the operation instrument, roaming in and interfacing with the 3-D virtual environment (Fig. 7). We combine the data glove (BHG-2) and Fastrak to implement the puncturing simulation in the neurosurgery. The data glove is used to measure the joint value of the finger and Fastrak is used to measure the position and posture of the hand. The surgeon can wear the data glove, taking the probe to puncture the human brain in virtual environment. The probe in the virtual environment punctures into the brain along with the proceeding of surgeon's hand and the brain is split along with the proceeding of probe. The surgeon can select other instruments to simulate the corresponding operations.

6 Conclusions

In this paper, a structure of a virtual reality training system for robot assisted neurosurgery is proposed, setting up from the concrete practical background of neurosurgery. Combining 3-D display devices and home-made human-computer interactive devices, this system structure can also improve the speed of displaying interaction of 3-D operation model and establish a robot assisted surgical simulation and training demo system oriented clinical application.

The training system represents an advanced training system incorporating VR and multimedia for training in robot assisted neurosurgery. The system not only simulates neurosurgical interventions as realistic as possible, but also tries to train robot assisted surgical skills in several levels. The tasks in level one are established for the training of hand-eye coordination. In the second level some diagnostic tasks with 3D models of the brain have to be performed. Using robot arm the surgeon navigates through the virtual sites identifying landmarks in some exemplary physiologic and pathologic cases. The third level of the system gives surgeons the possibility to use surgical instruments to perform a therapeutic intervention on the virtual model. Therefore not only a model of the surgical instruments has to be generated, but also the interaction of instruments and tissues have to be taken into account. Surgeons are able to practice various techniques without having to advance their learning curve on humans. These medical simulations are on the way to find an educational base that will be perhaps as important to surgery as flight simulators is to aviation.

Acknowledgments. The authors gratefully acknowledge the support of this work by National Natural Science Foundation of China Project under contract 60525314.

The authors also express cordial thanks to Prof. Zengmin Tian and Dr. Hongbo Lv who have also participated in the project.

References

1. Dario P.: Robotics for medical applications. IEEE Robotics & Automation Magazine, Vol.3. (1996) 44-56
2. Downes M., Cavusoglu M. C., Gantert W., at al.: Virtual environment for training critical skills in laparoscopic surgery. In: Medicine Meets Virtual Reality, (1998) 316–322

3. Y. Michiwaki, et al: Simulation training system for undergraduate students of dental school, Journal of Japanese Association for Dental Education, Vol.17, (2002) 311-320
4. C. Basdogan, C. H. Ha, M. A. Srinivasan: Virtual environments for medical training: graphical and haptic simulation of laparoscopic common bile duct exploration. IEEE ASME Transaction on Mechatronics, Vol. 6, No. 3. (2001) 269-285
5. G. Megali, O. Tonet, M. Mazzoni, at al.: A new tool for surgical training in knee arthroscopy. In: Proceedings of the Medical Image Computing and Computer-Assisted Intervention, vol. 2489. Tokyo Japan (2002)170–177
6. R. Satava: Virtual Reality Surgical Simulator-The First Steps. In: Proceedings of VR systems'93, New York, (1993) 41-49
7. D. Meyers, S. Skinner and K. Sloan: Surface from contours, ACM Transaction on Graphics, vol. 11, no.3. (1992) 228-258
8. Wang Z., Tang Z., Wang T.: VR based Computer Assisted Stereotactic Neurosurgery System. Jisuanji Xubao, Vol.23, (2000) 931-936

The Experiment of Improving Students' Spatial Ability by Using VGLS

Ruwei Yun[1], Haixu Xi[2], and Yi Li[1]

[1] Educational Technology Department, College of Educational Science
Nanjing Normal University, Nanjing, 210097, China
yunruwei@njnu.edu.cn
[2] Information Science & Media School, Jinggangshan College, 343009

Abstract. In order to compare the effect of VGLS (Virtual Geometry Learning System) with that of the traditional teaching method in improving students' spatial ability, we selected two classes (total 106 students) in Jingqiao middle school as experimental class and control class, and pre-tested their basic level of spatial ability. The VGLS was applied in the experimental class for four weeks, while the traditional teaching method was applied in the control class. Some conclusions can be drawn from the result of the post-test: Compared with traditional teaching method, VGLS approach is more significant effective in the improving student's mental folding, unfolding as well as rotation ability of students, without obvious superiority in improving student's pattern recognition; VGLS is significant effective in improving females' mental rotating ability and males' mental folding and unfolding ability.

Keywords: spatial ability, Virtual Geometry Learning System (VGLS), Virtual Reality.

1 Introduction

Spatial ability in geometry has been identified as the imagination ability of shapes, structures, size as well as relation of location of objects [1]. Many researchers have used spatial ability to benchmark mathematics [2], science education [3], engineering [4], and so on. Primary education researchers have realized the importance of cultivating students' spatial ability. At present, many teachers use some multimedia software produced by 2D animation tools, such as Flash, with the limitation in presenting three-dimension information. Some teachers would like to use model. With the limitation of time and space, it contributes little to students in grasping the concept geometry and related drawing skills.

In order to compare the effect of Virtual Reality technology with that of traditional teaching method on improving students' spatial ability, we specify six knowledge spots in the learning system, which are "the composition of basic geometry object", "the section shape of basic geometry object", "the motion change of basic geometry object", "the three views maps of basic geometry object" and "the folding and unfolding of basic geometry object". Then we designed the detailed instructional plan, built a VGLS and putted it to practice and experiment.

Z. Pan et al. (Eds.): ICAT 2006, LNCS 4282, pp. 467–473, 2006.

2 Methods

2.1 Participant

Two classes with a total of 106 students from Jingqiao middle school of Nanjing volunteered to participate in this experiment. The experimental class includes 26 girls and 29 boys, while the control class 21 girls and 30 boys.

2.2 Test Material

This paper uses the test material presenting in the dissertation of master (Zhen Zhou 2000) [5].

2.3 Design

Before this instructional experiment, all participant classes took a spatial ability test so that we could obtain a baseline and background information of their prior ability. In order to exclude the disturbance of different teaching experience and teaching plan from different teachers, the same teacher was consistent in teaching schedule in two classes. Some studies have documented that only after students have participated in spatial activity for at least three weeks, their basic spatial ability will significantly be improved [6]. After four consecutive weeks, all participants took a post-test with the same spatial ability test to determine any significant improvement. Internal consistency reliability has been computed for the pre-test and post-test and they revealed coefficient of reliability of .67 and .64, respectively. These values are seemed to be satisfactory since all values are above .60[7].

Since the same spatial ability test was adopted, we had to avoid the influence of pre-test on the post-test. The gap time between pre-test and post-test was about two or three months in order to avoid the influence of memory. In addition, during the pre-test time, we played with students and then tested them with no cue. After the pre-test, we continue the play. In another day, we just told students that they did well in play and yesterday's test. No any more information about the test was mentioned afterward.

2.4 Procedure

In the experiment group, instruction includes teacher's teaching and students' self-studying in the information technology classroom. Teacher explained the basic concepts by using the VGLS courseware. For example, in the explanation of "the composition of basic geometry", teacher controlled the formation animation of column and tapered to summarize the situation of movement forming of point, line and surface. In the information technology classroom, students operated the courseware themselves, did exercises, finished creative activities designed in the VGLS. During the process, teacher tutored for students' learning difficulties.

In the control group, teacher explained the basic concept by using models and other instruction media. Students took part in activities such as designing models to review the knowledge in order to avoiding "extra teaching" in the experiment group.

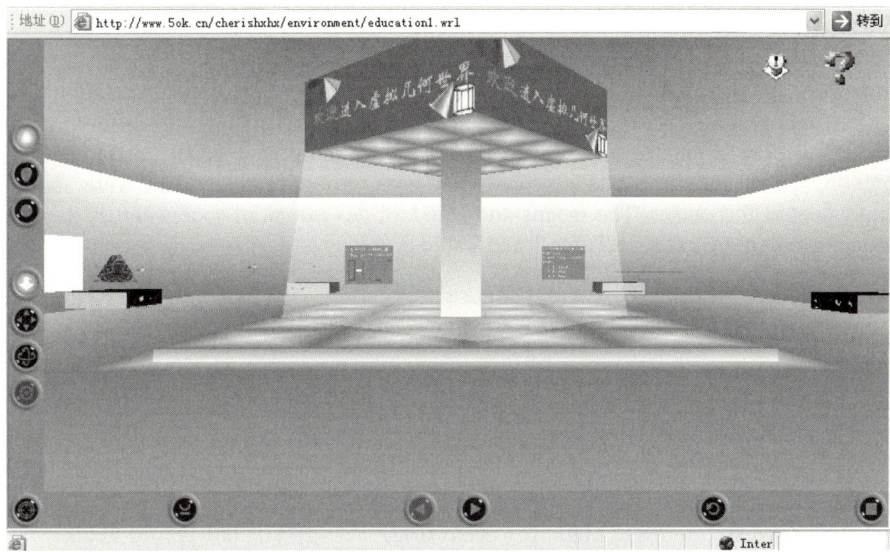

Fig. 1. Main page of VGLS

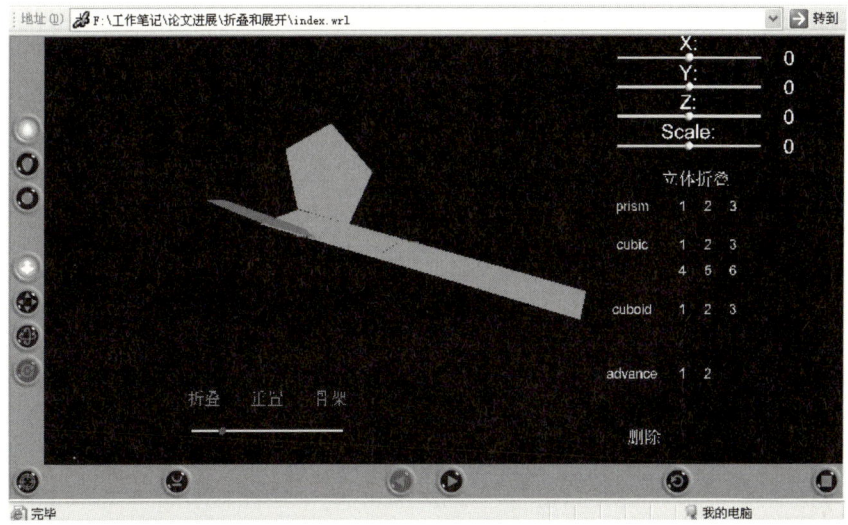

Fig. 2. The control and display of geometry folding and unfolding

Teachers designed some question situations for students' operating exercises, which are analogy to those in VGLS.

VGLS links the six topics in the main page (Fig.1). There are demo, explanations, and exercises in every topic (Fig.2). Students read the introduction of the topic and enter a topic to review or do exercise. After that, they can acquire feedback and suggestion from this system.

3 Data Analysis

Independence-Samples z-tests for mental folding, unfolding, mental rotation and pattern recognition for training groups revealed no significant group differences at p>0.05, t-tests for males and females revealed no significant gender differences at p>0.05. These initial results revealed that both groups and genders were indeed equivalent at the outset. The means and standard deviations of scores across the two groups are demonstrated in Table 1 and Table 2.

Table 1. Mental folding and unfolding accuracy and std. Deviation

Conditions	Mean(M)			
	Mental folding (S)		Mental unfolding (S)	
	Before	After	Before	After
Experimental	2.83 (1.09)	3.65 (0.92)	2.11 (1.00)	2.95 (0.75)
Males	3.03 (0.93)	4.10 (0.84)	2.21 (1.00)	3.28 (0.70)
Females	2.62 (1.21)	3.20 (1.20)	2.00 (1.00)	2.62 (0.90)
Control	2.84 (0.85)	3.00 (0.90)	2.29 (0.94)	2.54 (0.82)
Males	2.86 (0.88)	3.10 (0.95)	2.38 (0.99)	2.61 (1.00)
Females	2.81 (0.79)	2.90 (0.86)	2.19 (0.85)	2.47 (0.66)

Table 2. Mental rotation and pattern recognition accuracy and std. Deviation

Conditions	Mean(M)			
	Mental rotation (S)		Pattern recognition (S)	
	Before	After	Before	After
Experimental	1.71 (0.97)	2.54 (1.01)	3.56 (1.58)	4.40 (1.50)
Males	1.62 (1.00)	2.52 (0.80)	3.48 (1.59)	4.01 (1.65)
Females	1.81 (0.92)	2.56 (1.24)	3.65 (1.57)	4.79 (1.55)
Control	1.66 (0.98)	1.88 (1.24)	4.01 (1.99)	4.26 (1.84)
Males	1.83 (0.97)	2.02 (1.30)	4.07 (2.21)	4.35 (2.10)
Females	1.48 (0.96)	1.74 (1.20)	3.95 (1.62)	4.17 (1.68)

After the training was complete, there were significant group differences for mental folding at $Z=3.68$, $p<0.01$; for mental unfolding at $Z=2.68$, $p<0.01$; for mental rotation at $Z=3.00$, $p<0.01$ and no significant group differences for pattern recognition. These results indicate that the experiment group was more accurate for mental folding, unfolding and mental rotation.

In experiment group, there was no significant difference between females and males prior to treatment and after the training. There were evidences that males outperformed females in mental folding, unfolding at $T=3.18>T_{(52, 0.01)}$, $p<0.01$ and $T=3.00>T_{(52, 0.01)}$, $p<0.01$, respectively. Although the difference of pattern recognition performance between females and males was not significant, the data suggests that the difference was bordering on a significant level.

Further analysis on the performance between females and males in control and experiment groups was also conducted. Both female and male groups (i.e. experiment and control) perform equally prior to treatment and after the training. There were evidences that females in experiment group were better spatial performers in mental rotation tasks. There was a significant difference in mental rotation ability at $T=2.24>T_{(45, 0.05)}$, $p<0.05$ favoring females in the experimental group. For males, there were evidence that males in experimental group were better spatial performers in mental folding and unfolding tasks and the significant differences in mental folding ability is $T=4.20>T_{(57,0.01)}$, $p<0.01$, mental unfolding ability is $T=2.64>T_{(57,0.01)}$, $p<0.01$.

4 Discussion

The data analysis of pre- and post-tests suggests that learning though VGLS was more effective than traditional classroom practices in terms of improving the students' spatial ability. The participants in the experiment group had gained considerable improvement for mental operation ability of their spatial image and analysis ability of objects' interior structure. This can be explained by the fact that students can store abundant mental motion image because they gained more opportunity to look into the detail information and motion process of object in the virtual environment. This finding suggests that exploring, manipulating and interacting with 3D virtual objects play an important role to aid students' understanding spatial shapes, features, relations, and configurations, which is similar to the suggestions of Piaget [8].The improvement of mental rotation ability concurs with some research literacy which confirmed that there was positive relationship between spatial rotation and Virtual Reality technology [9-11]. But there has inconsistent result with the related research, which confirmed that spatial visualization (including mental folding and unfolding) are cognitively more challenging and demanding compared to the mental rotation tasks and may be more reflective of general intelligence[12]. Zhen Zhou's study of the development of figure cognition ability in middle school students confirmed that the first and second year of middle school are the rapid seedtime of mental folding, unfolding and rotation development. There is no doubt great improvement in mental folding and unfolding ability with the effective instruction method.

It also can be concluded that the improvement of students' pattern recognition may require more weeks of training or more hours of exercises within the stipulated duration. Problem solving tasks involving pattern recognition require human to reorganize spatial pattern of two-dimensional and three-dimensional object, which is one kind of creative thought and needs synthetically understanding spatial pattern, image movement and transformation. It needs long time to cultivate because its influence factors are quite complex.

There is different effect on spatial ability improvement between Virtual Reality technology and traditional teaching method and the effect may rely on genders. In VGLS, it is more favorable for males to develop their "visualization" abilities and more suitable for females to develop theirs mental rotation abilities (relatively simple spatial ability). Neither males nor females gained great improvement in pattern recognition because the training time might be too short. In general, males had more spatial problem solving experience in comparison with females as a result of social reason. Hence, males gained more accuracy in spatial rotation. Because of the "ceiling" effect, they are unable to obtain a bigger enhancement in their spatial rotation ability. Simultaneously, because they are accustomed to the "visualization" thought, they may achieve great improvement in the visualized spatial ability.

5 Conclusion

1) Using Virtual Reality technology to cultivate students' spatial ability is more effective than traditional teaching method.
2) VGLS vs. traditional teaching method is more significant effective in improving students' mental folding, unfolding and rotation ability, without more significant effect in the improvement of pattern recognition.
3) VGLS vs. traditional teaching method is more significant effective in improving females' mental rotation ability and males' mental folding and unfolding ability.

6 Future Work

In the process of this instructional experiment, we observed temporal students' behavior, carried on questionnaire after experiment. In the future, we will improve system designing, enrich the content of system, and do experiment again and provide instructional suggestion according to the collected data.

Acknowledgments. The work presented in this paper was funded by Key NSF Project on Digital Olympic Museum (Grant No. 60533080). We would like to thank the staff and students of Jingqiao middle school for supporting this research experiment.

References

1. National Council of Teachers of Mathematics, Curriculum and Evaluation Standards for School Mathematics, NCTM,Reston, VA, 1989.
2. Gallagher, S.A., Predictors of SAT mathematics scores in a causal model of mathematics achievement, Journal for Research in Mathematics Education 15(5)(1989)361-377.

3. Pribyl, J.R., Bodner, G.M., Spatial ability and its role in organic chemistry, a study of four organic courses, Journal of Research in Science Teaching 24(3)(1987)229-240.
4. Gimmestad, B.B., Sorby, S.A., Making connections: spatial skills and engineering drawing, Mathemetics Teachers 89(1996)348-353.
5. Zhou, Z., Research on the development of figure cognition ability of middle school students, dissertation of master,2000,04.
6. Clements, D.H., Battista, M.T., Sarama, J., Swaminathan, S., Development of students' spatial thinking in a unit on geometric motions and area, The Elementary School Journal 98(2)(1997)171-186.
7. Nunnally, J.C., Psychometric Theory, McGraw-Hill, New York,1967.
8. Piaget, J., Inhelder, B., The Child's Conception of Space, W.W. Norton, New York, 1948.
9. Merickel, M., The Creative Technologies Project: A study of the relationship between virtual reality (perceived realism) and the ability of children to create, manipulate, and utilite mental images for spatially related problem solving, 1992 (ERIC Document ED 352 942).
10. Paranandi, M., An Enquiry Into Computer in Design: When Cardboard Met Computers, Proceedings of the 7th international conference on Computer-Aided Architectural Design Research in Asia(CAADRIA), Multimedia University, Malaysia, (2002)329-338.
11. Pantelidis, V.S., Reasons to Use Virtual Reality in Education, VR in the Schools:3rd August, 2003,<http://www.soe.ecu.edu/vr/reas.html>,2000.
12. Shi, J., Zhou, L., The development of mental folding ability in children, Acta Psychological Sinica1997 (2) 160-164.

Sketch Based 3D Animation Copy

Difei Lu[1] and Xiuzi Ye[1,2]

[1] College of Computer Science, Zhejiang University, China
[2] SolidWorks Corporation, USA

Abstract. In this paper, we propose an example-driven approach to transfer deformation from source meshes to a target character based on sketch. Our approach consists of the following steps: (a) a sketch based mapping between parts of the sources and corresponding portions of the target; (b) deforming the portions of the target based on the deformations of the corresponding parts of the sources by means of differential mean value coordinates; (c) stitching the deformed portions of the target together smoothly by minimization to form a key frame of the target animation. We provide new research contributions on all these topics, and integrate them into our newly developed prototype animating system. Our approach is general and does not require the sources and target to share the same number of vertices or triangles, or to have matching connectivity. Our approach is intuitive and is able to produce highly authentic 3D animations. We demonstrate our approach by constructing several animating examples produced from our prototype system.

Keywords: Sketch, Animation, Differential mean value coordinates.

1 Introduction

While many animating systems have been developed and some are in commercial usage, their use has been limited to a set of trained experts, and easy-to-use interactive

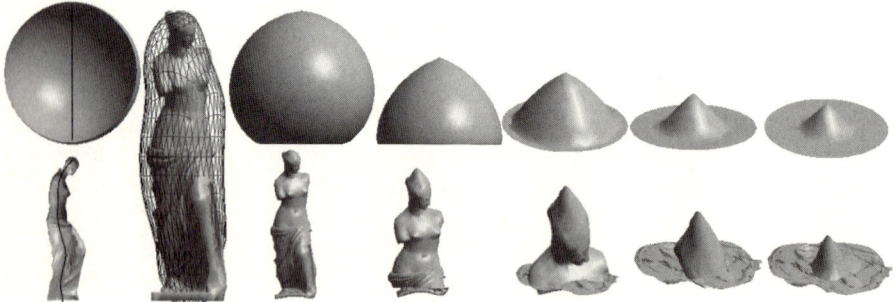

Fig. 1. The first row is an animation that a ball melts like snow. We use this animation to animate the Venus. All we need is a pair of sketches which are in middle of meshes (black curves shown in the pictures in the first column). The picture shows in the second column shows the result that the ball mesh is mapped to the Venus mesh based on sketch. The rest are the results of five key frames produced by our system.

Z. Pan et al. (Eds.): ICAT 2006, LNCS 4282, pp. 474 – 485, 2006.

modeling and animating is still a challenge topic. On the other hand, 3D sketching programs are good for novices, but their functionalities are very limited only for simple meshes or animations practically. At the same time, despite the tremendous amount of artistic, skillful, and time consuming animation crafts existed, there are few techniques to help with their reuses. Our system is to provide a tool with which almost everybody can create authentic 3D animations quickly and easily from existing source animations (Fig.1 shows a brief example).

Our research *Sketch Based 3D Animation Copy* uses a general approach that requires no knowledge of the underlying methods used to create the source animations. Our technique is purely data-driven and does not require the sources and target to share the same number of vertices or triangles, or to have identical connectivity. Users just need to indicate which parts of sources and target should animate similarly by sketch tools.

The major contributions of our work are the following: (1)Introducing a novel sketch based correspondence creating method which bridges source meshes and target mesh; (2)Extending the mean value coordinates for closed meshes to differential mean value coordinates for unclosed meshes; (3)Perhaps the most important impact: By combining of these different algorithms we propose an animating software system based on existing source animations.

2   Related Work

Generating animation largely follows two threads: using examples and using controllers. Many researches have been done based on controllers [1, 2, 3]. All these methods require subtle user inputs and present great challenges to novices. Example based animation synthesis starts from existing animations rather than scratch. The general strategy of example based animation is to acquire a number of examples, break them up into parts, determine the interesting parts, and then assemble them together in interesting ways smoothly [4]. [5] provides a method to compose new models using existing meshes in a database (*Modeling by Examples*). [6] investigates a mesh-based inverse kinematics which relies on example meshes to indicate the class of meaningful deformations. [7] introduces a deformation transfer which transfers the change from one mesh to another. Their technique is limited to meshes which are gross similar. Mean value coordinates for closed triangular mesh is developed in [8] as continuous and smooth interpolants for values defined at vertices of a mesh. We extend it to differential mean value coordinates for unclosed triangular mesh.

We employ and extend the idea in [1], and develop a sketch based interface for correspondence mapping. We use sketches to specify the regions of interest (ROI) and to map the vertices of the source meshes, which serve as control points, to the target. In our approach, we extend mean value coordinates for closed triangular meshes developed in [8] into differential mean value coordinates for unclosed (open) triangular meshes to represent the deformation of meshes. We use the polar decomposition of affine matrix in [9] to control the rigidity of the deformed target.

3   System Overview

The inputs to our system are several animation examples, and the output is a new animation of the target character. The first step of operation involves selecting desired parts of the source meshes to be associated with the corresponding parts of the target by sketch tools. Then each part of target deforms in form of corresponding part of source in each key frames. Next the system stitches all part animations of target together and smooth the stitched mesh.

A brief session with our system is shown in Fig.2. The snake and cat are two example animations and the horse is the target. Let the animation of snake tail be transferred onto the horse tail and animation of cat except tail onto rest parts of the horse. All an user involves are draw twelve sketches: one on tail of snake, one on torso of cat, four on limbs of cat, one on tail of horse, one on torso of horse and four on limbs of horse.

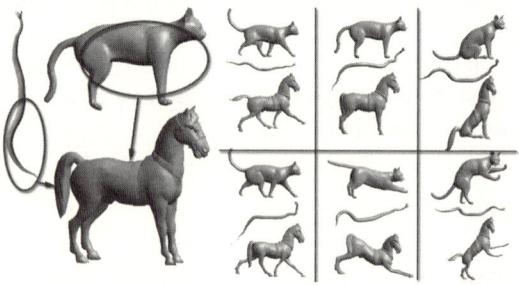

Fig. 2. Brief instance demonstrating the main features of our system being used to compose animations of tail of a snake and torso of a cat to generate a full animation of a horse

In this example, six frames of animation of the horse are produced. The key steps to generate an animation of the horse are: (1) Drawing sketch pairs on part of the sources and the target. To each sketch pair, one is the source sketch which indicates ROI (Region of Interests) in the source mesh; and another is the target sketch which indicates the corresponding ROI in the target mesh. (2) Finding out vertices in the source mesh related to the source sketch and vertices of target mesh related to target sketch based on the closest point approach. (3) Mapping the source sketch to the target sketch. The vertices related to source sketch are also mapped to target sketch along with the source sketch. (4) For each vertex in the target mesh enclosed by the target sketch, the weight of differential mean value coordinates is computed. (5) Using differential mean value coordinates for unclosed triangular mesh to computer new position of the vertices enclosed by the target sketch in each key frame. (6) Stitching all parts of the deformed target mesh together and smoothing the result.

4   Sketch Based Mapping

First and foremost, a bi-jective mapping between the source and the target should be established. We use a pair of sketches to indicate the ROI of the sources as well as

ROI of the target. We begin with a free-form sketch on the surface of mesh. There are two kinds of sketches. (1) Sketch on the surface of a mesh (Fig.3a): the first intersection point (i.e., closest to the view point) between the ray from the view point through the mouse position and the mesh, and take it as a vertex of the sketch. The sketch is represented as a collection of line segments taken directly from mouse events produced by the user's stroke; (2) Sketch in the mesh (Fig.3b): the first two intersection points between the ray from the view point through the mouse position and the mesh are computed, and their middle point is taken as a vertex of the sketch. The raw sketch (Fig.3c) is very likely to be fairly noisy especially when it is drawn with low precise device such as mouse. The raw sketch is then smoothed and regularized as follows: a cubic B-spline curve is generated by interpolating the vertices of the raw sketch; the curve is then smoothed and discretized into a set of new vertices of the sketch (Fig.3d).

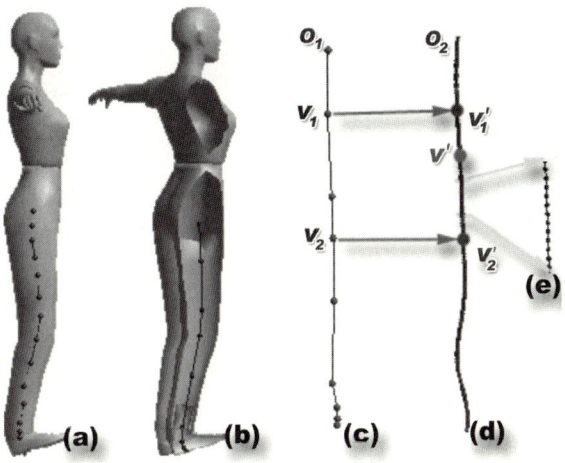

Fig. 3. (a) a sketch drawn on the surface of a leg of the woman; (b) a sketch drawn in the leg of the woman; (c) the raw sketch; (d) the smoothed and regularized sketch; (e) a magnified segment of (d)

The first role of the sketches is to specify the ROI in the sources and the target, i.e., to find the associations between the mesh vertices and the sketch. We use a distance threshold and visibility to a separation plane to compute ROI from the sketch automatically. Any vertex whose shortest distance to the sketch vertices and segments is less than the threshold will be considered as part of the ROI. The sketch shown in Fig.3b induces the ROI shown in red in Fig.4a (called source ROI).

Fig.4 illustrates a pair of sketches used to map a leg of the woman to the corresponding leg of a horse. The source and target sketches are shown in red in Fig.4b and 4c respectively. The red area in Fig.4d is the target ROI.

The next step is to align the source ROI with its corresponding target ROI in size and orientation. We obtain the center Cs of the source ROI, and perform a scaling on the vertices on the source ROI relative to Cs. The default value of the scaling factor is taken as follows: the principal coordinate axes of the source and target ROIs are computed first, and then the volumes of the bounding boxes of the source and target ROIs relative to their principal axes are obtained, and the ratio of the two volumes is computed. The user can adjust the scaling factor from there. The orientation alignment is done by the user in a semantically meaningful way between the source and target ROIs, e.g., the orientation of the horse head points to the same orientation of the cat head.

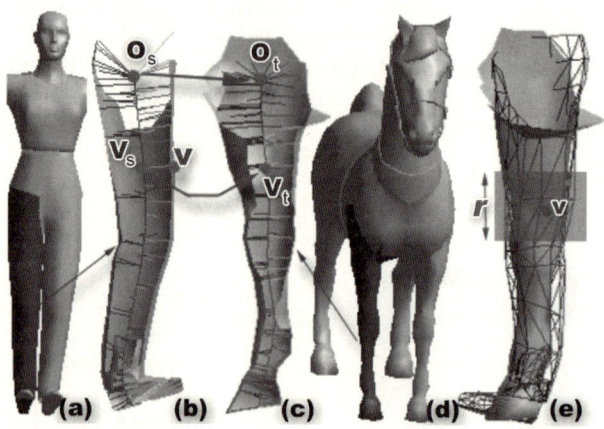

Fig. 4. A pair of sketches used to map a woman leg to a horse leg. O_S and O_t are the start vertices of the source and target sketches respectively. V_s is the point on the source sketch associated to the vertex V in the source ROI, and V_t is the point on the target sketch to which V_s is mapped based on the arc-length parameterization. (a) and (d) show the ROIs of the sketch in (b) and (c), respectively. The yellow lines in (b) and (c) connect vertices of the ROIs with their corresponding points in the sketches. (e) is the result when the source vertices are mapped to the target ROI (the red wire frame).

We then generate the mapping between the vertices in the corresponding source and target ROIs. For each vertex V in the source ROI, we compute the closest point V_s of V in the source sketch. Note that V_s can be a sketch vertex or a point on a sketch segment. Similarly, a closest point on the target sketch can be computed for each vertex in the target ROI. In order to map a vertex in the source ROI to a vertex in the corresponding target ROI, we use a method similar to the one proposed in [1]. We represent each point (e.g., V_s) on the sketch by its normalized arc length l. That is, for a given point we compute the length along the sketch from the start of the sketch to the point. We normalize these values by dividing the total arc length of the sketch so that they range between 0 and 1. Each point V on the sketch has a parameter $l(V)$ to indicate its position on the sketch. For point V_s which has parameter l_s on source sketch we find a point V_t (Fig.4c) whose parameter is also l_s on target sketch. A source vertex V associated to the sketch point V_s can be mapped to a point V′ in the target ROI as follows: $V' = V + (V_t - V_s)$. In this way, we can map all the source vertices to points in the corresponding target ROI. Fig.4e is the result of the mapping.

The target sketch is also used to assign parameters to target mesh vertices. Each vertex of the target mesh is attached with two parameters, *weight* and *scale*. The parameter *weight* will be used to adjust the weights of Equations (9), (10) and (11) in Section 6, and the parameter *scale* will be used to adjust the deformed coordinates in Section 5. The assigning process is shown in Fig.3c and 3d. In the raw target sketch (Fig.3c), we assign parameters t_1 and t_2 to two vertices V_1 and V_2 respectively interactively through the UI. Then we find their corresponding points V'_1 and V'_2 in the smoothed target sketch (Fig.3d) using normalized arc-length: normalized arc-lengths O_1V_1 and O_1V_2 equal to normalized arc-lengths $O_2V'_1$ and $O_2V'_2$, respectively. The parameters of V'_1 and V'_2 will be assigned as t_1 and t_2 respectively. For any point V' between V'_1 and V'_2, we obtain its parameter t' by linear interpolation of t_1 and t_2 based on the arc-length. Vertices that are associated with point V' will be assigned the same parameter t'.

5   Differential Mean Value Coordinates for Mesh Deformation

A common problem in example-based methods is how to induce target deformation in the terms of source deformation. Both mesh parameterization and freeform deformation methods require that a point V be represented as an affine combination of the vertices on an enclosing mesh or shape, i.e.

$$V = \sum_j w_j P_j / \sum_j w_j \,. \tag{1}$$

where $\{P_j\}$ are the vertices on an enclosed mesh, and $\{w_j\}$ are the weight functions relating P_j to V. If $\{P_j\}$ are taken to be the vertices of a closed source mesh and V be the vertex of the target mesh, the target mesh will deform along with the source mesh. The key problem now is how to determine the weight functions $\{w_j\}$.

[8] proposes an extended version of mean value coordinates of 3D closed triangular meshes. Given a triangle T with vertices $\{V', P_0, P_1\}$ and the corresponding projected spherical triangle T_p on the unit sphere S_v centered at V, the weight function w_j in a closed triangular mesh has the form (refer to Fig.5c):

$$w_j = \frac{n_j \cdot m}{n_j \cdot (V'-V)} \,, \ j=1, 2, 3\,. \tag{2}$$

Where n_j is the inward unit normal to the plane defined by the j-th edge of the spherical triangle T_p and the point V, m is the mean vector (Fig.5c) which can be obtained by:

$$m = \sum_{j=1}^{3} L_j \cdot n_j / 2\,, \text{ where } \{L_j\} \text{ are the lengths of the spherical edges.}$$

Note that Equation (2) is just for one triangle related to V'. In our system, to compute the weight for a vertex V related to another vertex V', we need to sum Equation (2) over all the triangles in the mesh connecting V':

$$w_{V'} = \sum_{Tp \in Tsp} n_{V'Tp} \cdot m_{Tp} / \left(n_{V'Tp} \cdot (V'-V) \right)\,. \tag{3}$$

where T_{sp} represents the set of the projected spherical triangles -- the sources of projection is the set of the triangles connecting V' ; and n_{VTp} is the inward unit normal corresponding to V' in the spherical triangle Tp. As shown in Fig.5c, if we move V' along the direction of VV' to V'', the projection of the new triangle (V'', P_0, P_1) onto S_v is also T_p and all the terms in Equation (3) remain unchanged. Note that in Equation (3), when V'' is enough far away from V, we can practically ignore the weight related directly to V''.

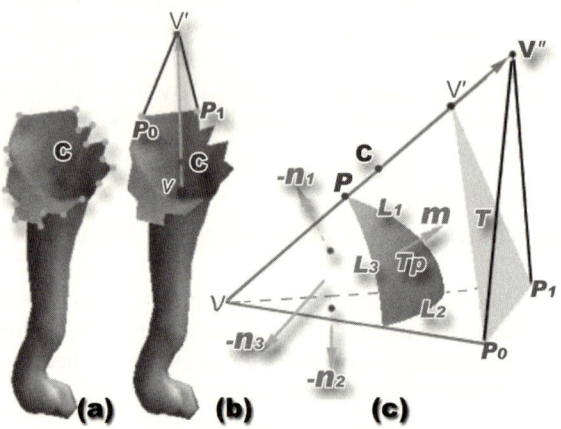

Fig. 5. (a) The unclosed mesh of a dog leg; (b) A point V' is inserted to patch the hole of the part mesh (a); (c) shows the computation of the weight for a single triangle

Note that Equations (2) and (3) are for closed mesh. In our system, we have to extend the above mean value coordinates from closed triangular mesh to unclosed mesh, since we use part of a source mesh (Fig.5a) to control portion of a target mesh. The part of the source mesh and the corresponding portion of the target mesh may not necessarily be closed. We do this by inserting extra vertices to make the mesh closed, and we can compute the weights over the filled mesh. In Fig.5b, for any vertex V in the target mesh, a point V' is inserted to patch the hole of the part mesh (mapped from part of the source mesh by sketching). The point V' is placed on the line between V and the barycenter C of the boundary vertices (Fig.5a), at a far away distance (that can be considered as $+\infty$, Fig.5b). In this way, the direct contributions of V' to the weight computation of V can be ignored. However, V' still effects the computation of the weights of V through boundary vertices. For example, the weight of P_0 in Fig.5b is influenced by V' because the triangle T (Fig.5c) contains vertex V'. When V' is placed on the line VC, V' and C project onto the unit sphere S_V at a same point P (Fig.5c). Therefore, we can replace V' with C in computing the weights of the boundary vertices (e.g., P_0 and P_1), and in constructing the spherical triangle T_P. In this way, the contributions of V' to the weights of V can be completely ignored.

In our system we are interested in the changes of the coordinates of the target vertices induced by the deformation of the example meshes. We can rewrite Equation (1) as follows:

$$\Delta V = \sum_{j=1}^{n} w_j \Delta P_j / \sum_{j=1}^{n} w_j . \tag{4}$$

Where V is a vertex in the portion of the target mesh (Fig.4e), ΔV is the deformation vector of V; P_j is a vertex in the part of the source mesh; ΔP_j is the deformation vector of P_j relative to the first key frame; and n is the number of vertices in the part of the source mesh. In our implementation in order to speed up the performance and to clone the local animating style of the source mesh realistically, we are not using the whole part of the source mesh. Instead, as shown in Fig.4e, we use a region of the mapped source vertices around V. The region is defined by a factor r (masked by the red area in Fig.4e) which is used to specify the width of the range: currently taken as r times the arc length of the target sketch. In our implementation, r = 0.18. From Equation (4) we can get the new position:

$$V_{new} = \Delta V + V_0, \text{ where } V_0 \text{ is the original undeformed vertex of target.}$$

After the new position of V is computed, we adjust it according to the scale parameter s assigned in Section 4 and the arc-length-ratio L_r between the arc-length of the source and target sketches. Let C be the barycenter of all vertices in the corresponding portion of the target sketch, the new position of V after adjustment can be defined as follows

$$V_{new} \leftarrow C + L_r s(V_{new} - C) . \tag{5}$$

For a target ROI, let $\{V_j\}$ and $\{V'_j\}$ be its undeformed and deformed vertex sets respectively. Let C be the barycenter of the vertex set $\{V_j\}$. Let d_1 be the average distance from $\{V_j\}$ to C. We can get a similar average distance d_0 from $\{V'_j\}$. To prevent deformation from shrinking, we perform in addition the following scaling:

$$V_{new} \leftarrow C + d_1/d_0(V_{new} - C) . \tag{6}$$

At this stage, each vertex V in the target mesh falls into the following three categories: (1)V is not covered by any ROIs, and therefore is not involved in any deformation, and hence stays unchanged; (2)V is covered by exact one ROI, and therefore is uniquely deformed; and (3)V is covered by more than one ROIs, and we have overlapped regions in the target mesh after deformation. We perform a weighted averaging of these positions and obtain a new position V_w which will be used in Section 6. The weights in the averaging are determined by the weights of the sketches and the weight assigned to V in Section 4. Fig.6 shows the animation of two legs of a horse according to legs of the woman.

Fig. 6. Animate the two front legs of a horse according to the animation of the two legs of a woman. The deformation is computed based on Equation (4).

6   Stitching and Smoothing

When more than one sources control different parts of the same target, adjacent parts of the target after deformation can be discontinuous and even separated from each other (Fig.7a).We employ a simple strategy to grossly align the different parts of the target mesh. We give the target sketches an order based on the user input, from most important to less important. Alternatively, we can sort the target sketches based on the areas of their ROIs in the target mesh, from biggest area to smallest area. We first find all the boundary vertices $\{V_j\}$ (the blue points in Fig.7c) of the last deformed target part (based on the sorting order), and compute the barycenter of these vertices. For each boundary vertex V_j, we find it's undeformed position, and other deformed positions in other unprocessed deformed target parts and perform a weighted averaging of these positions, and denote this new position as P_j (if V_j is covered by one the last target ROI, P_j is set to V_j). The weights are determined by the weights on the sketches and the weight assigned to each vertex in Section 4. Let C' be the barycenter of $\{P_j\}$. We add the vector (C'-C) to all the vertices in the last deformed part. The process moves forward until the first deformed target part is reached. In this way, overlapped or separated deformed target parts can be grossly stitched (e.g., the tail in Fig.7b).

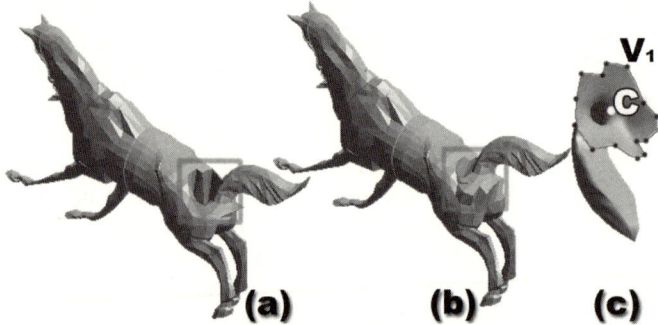

Fig. 7. Deforming the horse using a snake to control the tail of the horse and a cat to control the rest of the horse, as shown in Fig. 2. (a) is the two deformed target parts; (b) is the result after performing the gross alignment.(c) shows the boundary vertices of the deformed tail part (the blue points).

We can see from Fig.7b that the horse is by no means smooth after the gross alignment (actually can have overlaps). In the rest of the section, we will introduce a technique to smooth the result after gross alignment (Fig.7b) based on the following considerations: uniformity of the transform, rigidity of the transform, minimization of the deviation to the gross aligned target, and the flatness consideration.

The smoothing process is similar to another our paper [10] other than that we add some parameters to the constraint functions. Here we briefly introduce these extended constraints functions. For more details please refer to [10].

We define deformation smoothness, E_s, which indicates that the transformations for adjacent tetrahedrons should be as equal as possible:

$$E_s(\overline{V}_1,...,\overline{V}_n)=\sum_{j=1}^{n}\sum_{k=1}^{|a_{V_j}|}\left\|w_j^s\left(M(\overline{V}_j,k)-M(\overline{V}_j,k+1)\right)\right\|_F^2 . \tag{7}$$

Where $\overline{V}$ is the new position of the target vertex V and is the unknown variables need to be solved, $|a_V|$ is the size of the array a_V, and the cyclic rule applies to the index (k+1) (i.e., (k+1) mode $|a_V|$); n is the number of total vertices in the target mesh; and the w^s are the weights.

The second objective function E_r is used to keep the shape being as rigid as possible (w^r are the weights).

$$E_r(\overline{V}_1,...,\overline{V}_n)=\sum_{j=1}^{n}\sum_{k=1}^{|a_{V_j}|}\left\|w_j^r\left(M(\overline{V}_j,k)-Q_w(V_{jw},k)\right)\right\|_F^2 . \tag{8}$$

where Q_w is the orthogonal factor of the intermediate affine transform matrix M_w [9].

The third objective function E_l is used to keep the distance change before after deformation as small as possible:

$$E_l(\overline{V}_1,...,\overline{V}_n)=\sum_{j=1}^{n}\sum_{k=1}^{|a_{V_j}|}\left\|w_j^l\left(\left(\overline{V}_j-\overline{V}_{a[k]}\right)-\left(V_j-V_{a[k]}\right)\right)\right\|^2 . \tag{9}$$

where a[k] represents the k-th element in the array a_{Vj}, and the w^l are the weights.

The last objective function is objective function is E_d, which means the deformed target vertices should be as close as possible to the results of the deformed target parts computed in Section 5:

$$E_d(\overline{V}_1,...,\overline{V}_n)=\sum_{j=1}^{n}\left\|w_j^d\left(\overline{V}_j-V_{j_{new}}\right)\right\|^2 . \tag{10}$$

where V_{new} is the weighted averaging position V_w of V described in Section 5.

Fig. 8. Deformation results before (the upper row) and after (the lower row) smoothing

The global objective function is set to be the sum of the above four objective functions. Therefore, the global minimization problems becomes: finding new positions $\{\bar{V}_1,\bar{V}_2,\cdots\bar{V}_n\}$ of all the vertices $\{V_1,V_2\ldots V_n\}$ in the target mesh, such that the following objective function is minimized:

$$E(\bar{V}_1,\cdots,\bar{V}_n)=E_s+E_r+E_l+E_d=\min .\tag{11}$$

To solve the equation system efficiently, we use a sparse LU solver [11].

7   Conclusion

In this paper, we investigate *Sketch Based 3D Animation Copy*, a new paradigm for creating 3D animation from parts extracted from existing animations. We present algorithms for sketch based interactive mapping; we propose to use differential mean value coordinates to deform the target; we developed methods for aligning and smoothing the deformed parts of the target mesh. Experience with our prototype system indicates that it is easy to learn and useful for creating interesting and complex 3D animation of target character based on example animations.

While our research takes a small step down to a new path, several limits remain as future work. The most conspicuous limitation of our technique is that when the source mesh and target mesh are very dissimilar, the result is not very nature. To solve this problem it requires a method to appropriately adapt the mean value coordinate weights to the target. Another limit of our system is that it can't deal with large scale deformation of source mesh perfectly. In our system, we use differential mean value coordinates to drive target mesh deforming. Other methods such as free-form deformation methods may be employed in the mapping.

References

1. Kho, Y. and Garland, M. 2005. Sketching mesh deformations. In Proceedings of the 2005 Symposium on interactive 3D Graphics and Games (Washington, District of Columbia, April 03 - 06, 2005). SI3D '05. ACM Press, New York, NY, 147-154.
2. Yoshizawa, S., Belyaev, A. G., and Seidel, H. 2003. Free-form skeleton-driven mesh deformations. In Proceedings of the Eighth ACM Symposium on Solid Modeling and Applications (Seattle, Washington, USA, June 16 - 20, 2003). SM '03. ACM Press, New York, NY, 247-253.
3. Yu, Y., Zhou, K., Xu, D., Shi, X., Bao, H., Guo, B., and Shum, H. 2004. Mesh editing with poisson-based gradient field manipulation. ACM Trans. Graph. 23, 3 (Aug. 2004), 644-651.
4. Cohen, M., 2000. Everything by example. Keynote talk at Chinagraphics 2000
5. Funkhouser, T., Kazhdan, M., Shilane, P., Min, P., Kiefer, W., Tal, A., Rusinkiewicz, S., and Dobkin, D. 2004. Modeling by example. ACM Trans. Graph. 23, 3 (Aug. 2004), 652-663.
6. Summer, R. W., Zwicker, M., Gotsman, C., and Popović, J. 2005. Mesh-based inverse kinematics. ACM Trans. Graph. 24, 3 (Jul. 2005), 488-495.
7. Summer, R. W., And Popovi'c, J. 2004. Deformation transfer for triangle meshes. ACM Transactions on Graphics 23, 3 (Aug.), 399-405.

8. Ju, T., Schaefer, S., and Warren, J. 2005. Mean value coordinates for closed triangular meshes. ACM Trans. Graph. 24, 3 (Jul. 2005), 561-566.
9. Shoemake, K. and Duff, T. 1992. Matrix animation and polar decomposition. In Proceedings of the Conference on Graphics interface '92 (Vancouver, British Columbia, Canada). K. S. Booth and A. Fournier, Eds. Morgan Kaufmann Publishers, San Francisco, CA, 258-264.
10. Difei Lu, Ying Zhang, Xiuzi Ye, A New Method of Interactive Marker-Driven Free form Mesh Deformation, gmai, pp. 127-134, Geometric Modeling and Imaging--New Trends (GMAI'06), 2006.
11. Davis, T. A. 2003. Umfpack version 4.1 user guide. Tech. rep., University of Florida. TR-03-008.

Extracting Space Welding Seam for Virtual Teach-In of Robotic Welding System

Wusheng Chou and Tianmiao Wang

Robotics Institute
Beijing University of Aeronautics and Astronautics,
Beijing, 100083, P.R. China
wschou@buaa.edu.cn

Abstract. Extracting the geometric knowledge of space welding seam from virtual models, which representing the real object to be welded, is one of the fundamental issues for virtual teach-in of robotic welding system. An interactive approach to deal with this issue is described in this paper. This interactive approach is based on accurate real-time collision detection and taking advantage of virtual force reflection, and it is particularly suitable for determining complex space welding seam. The proposed approach can be used as a handy and accurate tool to find complex space welding seam for subsequent automatic generation of task planning and path planning of robotic welding system. We demonstrate the effectiveness of this approach with implemented examples.

Keywords: Virtual teach-in, welding robot, virtual contact force.

1 Introduction

Welding is an important process of industrial manufacturing. With the development of robotic technology and due to the demand of improving welding quality and flexibility, robotic welding system is used more and more in industrial community. The welding robot is in fact a kind of automatic welding machine which needs to be programmed a priori. Traditionally, the on-line teach-in method [1] and the off-line programming method [2] are adopted to generate suitable robot program to perform welding task. The on-line teach-in is a process, in which an operator manually manipulates the welding robot along welding seam to make the program of robot. On- line teach-in method can fully utilize the intelligence of human operator, but it is time consuming and not suitable for some kind of space welding seam, due to the limitation of human vision. The more profitable method of building a work program is to use off-line programming, which is a simulation based method and easy to verify the validity of the robot programs through [3],[4].

Some off-line programming and path planning methods for robotic welding system are proposed based on virtual reality and CAD technology[5],[6]. Virtual teach-in is a method similar to on-line teach-in, and the user manipulator the virtual welding robot to move along the welding seam under virtual environment. Virtual teach-in requires the knowledge of welding seam topology and geometry, as characterized by certain set of

Z. Pan et al. (Eds.): ICAT 2006, LNCS 4282, pp. 486–493, 2006.
© Springer-Verlag Berlin Heidelberg 2006

space points. Most methods of off-line programming suppose that the welding seam is known or can be obtained directly from CAD geometric model [7]. For complex geometric model, especially for the model reconstructed by laser measurement, only data cloud can be used as input, and it is difficult to extract the geometric information of welding seam. The position and posture file of welding torch is generated from a three dimension solid model, and the space welding seam is obtained by search the extreme points of geometric model [8], which is only suitable for quadric or regular surface model. Some methods for off-line programming obtain discrete sampling points of the seam on virtual object by using mouse selection. Such methods are often manually extracted and fed into a system as input, which can be extremely tedious, incomplete, and error prone for even tasks of simple geometry and is practically infeasible for complex tasks due to the complex of welding seam.

In this paper, we propose an interactive method to extract welding seam from geometric data set or from complex geometric model taking advantage of virtual force reflection. In this method, the user controls the virtual welding robot to move along the welding seam via a haptic rendering device. If the end of the torch of welding robot contact with the surface of geometric model, then virtual contact force is reflected to the user via the haptic rendering device to keep the trajectory of the end of virtual torch along the welding seam. Thus the space welding seam can be obtained by recording the trajectory of the end of torch. This interactive method enables a user to incorporate naturally human intelligence in identifying the space welding seam.

The rest of this paper is organized as follows. Section 2 describes the contact detection algorithm. The interactive method to extract space welding seam is introduced in Section 3, and Section 4 provides some implemented examples. Section 5 concludes the paper.

2   Contact Detection Between the Tip of Tool and Virtual Object

Conventional collision detection methods, such as bounding volumes, only provide whether two objects interfere or not. It is often needed to obtain the exact contact points when contact occurs. An alterative is to track the minimum distance between two objects.

Since only the information about the contact between the tip of virtual tool and the virtual object Os with welding seam is needed, the tip of virtual tool is simplified to be a point Pt to improve the efficiency of contact detection. The minimum distance d between the tip of tool and the welded object is tracked in real time. When d is zero, contact occurs. We call the closest point SCP (*Surface Contact Point*) on the surface of Os, and SCP is the potential contact point before contact occurs. When penetration occurs, that is to say, the tip of tool Pt is inside the virtual object Os, the SCP is still the closest point of Os.

The object Os is represented by triangular mesh. The minimum distance query between Pt and Os is translated to the problem of calculation of the minimum distance between the point Pt and a triangle. Each triangle has a surface plane, three edges and three vertexes. Firstly, the minimum distance between the point Pt and the plane that the triangle locates in is calculated. If the closest point is inside the triangle, then the calculated distance is the minimum distance. Otherwise, the three edges are checked. If all the closest points between *Pt* and the lines that contain the edges are outside the edges, then the three vertexes are checked. The closest point between *Pt* and a triangle *Ta* must either locate on the surface of *Ta*, or on the edges or is the vertex of *Ta*. The minimum distance between *Pt* and a triangle can then be calculated easily.

Only at the first running circle all the triangles are searched. We exploit the temporal and spatial coherence to track the closest point of *Os*. A special data structure is constructed via pre-processing to establish the relation between vertex and triangular polygon [9]. For each vertex, it has an index that refers to all the triangles that contain this vertex. For each triangle, it has an index that refers to all the three vertexes that this triangle has. Thus, the local area of the previous closest point can be determined via this kind of data structure, and only the local area is searched at the next time step.

3   Interactive Approach to Extracting Space Welding Seam

Given the geometric models of the virtual object *Os*, which contains space welding seam, our approach is to allow a human user to create contact situations between the tip of tool and the model of the object *Os* displayed in a virtual environment, where the user virtually holds the tool via a haptic device to contact the object *Os*. As the user manipulates the tip of tool and creates contacts between *Pt* and *Os* along the space welding seam, a real-time distance computation algorithm continuously runs to provide instant information of the minimum distance and *SCP*. The trajectory of SCP is the extracted space welding seam.

The penetration depth of *Pt* is calculated in the same way described in Section 2, and the vector from *Pt* to SCP changes its direction with respect to the status before penetration occurs. This characteristic can be used to determine when the penetration occurs.

To enable easy creation of contact states between Pt and Os, simple contact normal forces are simulated via the haptic device to provide the user force feedback. Let F denote the magnitude of the contact normal force at SCP. We simply model F based on a spring model as:

$$F = kd \tag{1}$$

Where K is the coefficient and d is the penetration depth. F is not too large with a relatively small K to ensure rendering stability, but it is sufficient to prevent large penetration of Pt and Os as d becomes even smaller. When penetration occurs, if the SCP locates on the edge of a triangle T1, there is another triangle T2 that contains the same edge, then the contact force F is calculated according to the following equation:

$$F = F_1 + F_2 \tag{2}$$

Where F_1 is normal contact force between *Pt* and the plane S_1 that contain triangle T_1, and F_2 is normal contact force between *Pt* and the plane S_2 that contain triangle T_2, as shown in Fig.1.

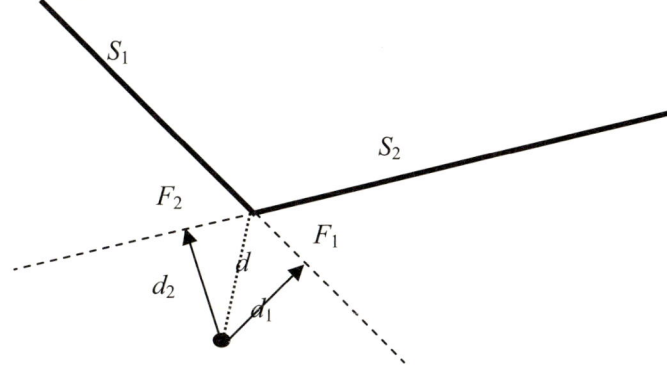

Fig. 1. Contact force when SCP locates on an edge

If the *SCP* is the vertex *V* of a triangle *T*, then the contact force *F* is calculated:

$$F = F_1 + F_2 + F_3 + ... + F_n \tag{3}$$

Where F_i is normal contact force between *Pt* and the plane S_i that contain triangle T_i, and T_i contains the vertex *V*. Fig.2 is an example that the *SCP* is the common vertex of 4 triangles.

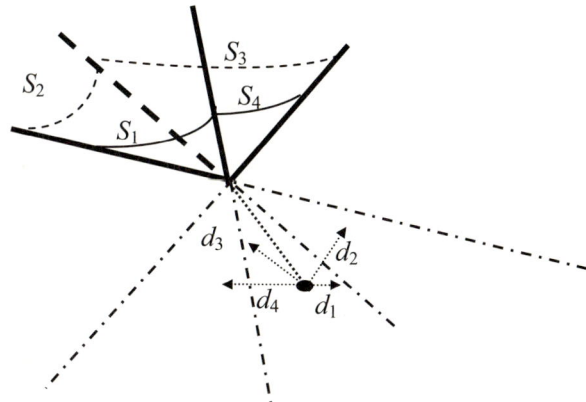

Fig. 2. Contact force when SCP is a vertex of triangular polygonal mesh

With our interactive approach described above, one can obtain complex space welding seam in a virtual environment very intuitively and quickly.

4   Implemented Examples

The proposed method has been implemented in a virtual environment connected to a PHANToM desktop device. A human operator can hold a virtual tool to make contact to virtual object *Os* freely along welding seam via a PHANToM Desktop device. Graphic rendering and the haptic rendering loops are decoupled and communicated via the virtual environment. By doing so, the haptic rendering loop can achieve 1000 Hz update rate to guarantee the stability and fidelity of the force feedback. The values of spring coefficient K is 2.3 (N/mm).

Two kinds of space seams are given then to testify the feasibility of the proposed method. One is a saddle type welding seam generated by the intersection of two cylinders, and the other one is line seam which is the interaction line of three planes, as shown in Fig.3.

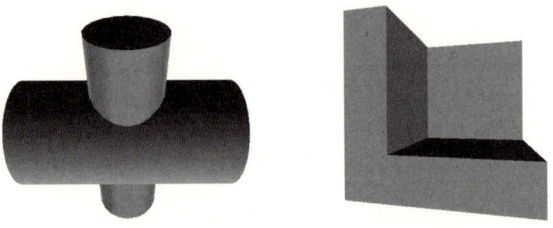

Fig. 3. Space welding seams

Fig.4 shows the positions of the end of the tool controlled by phantom haptic device, the position of SCP and the given saddle type welding seam after interactive extraction. Fig.5 and Fig.6 show the contact force and extraction error of saddle type welding seam, respectively.

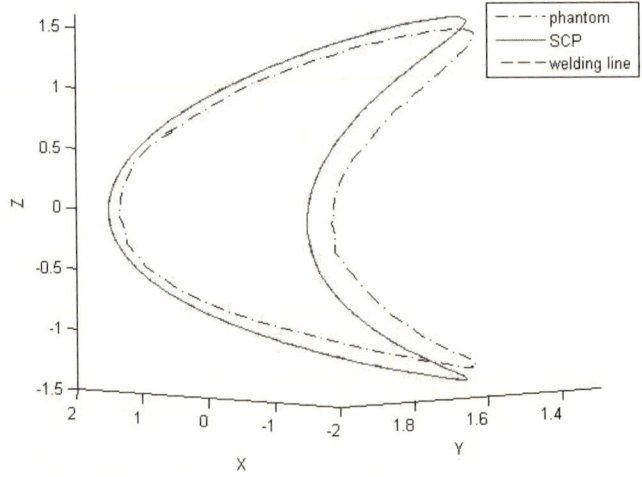

Fig. 4. Position of tool tip, SCP and given saddle type welding seam

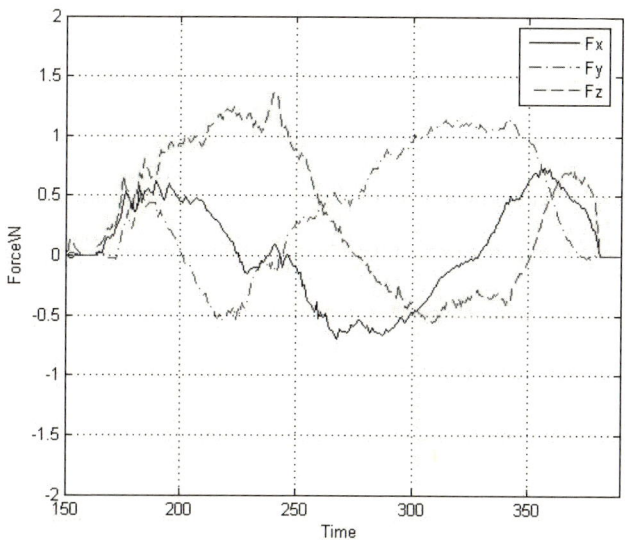

Fig. 5. Contact force when extracting saddle type welding seam

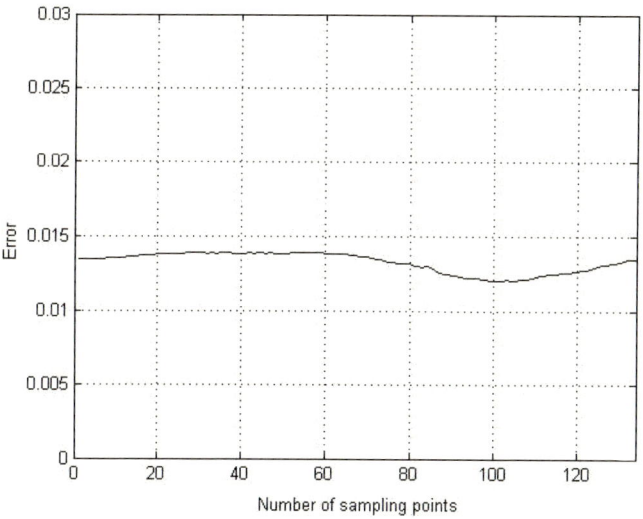

Fig. 6. Error between extracted welding seam and given saddle type seam

From Fig.6, it is obviously that the error is very small. The accuracy can satisfy the requirement of real industrial welding.

For linear space seam generated by three planes, the maximum error is less than 0.005. The trajectories and contact force errors are shown as Fig.7 and Fig.8, respectively.

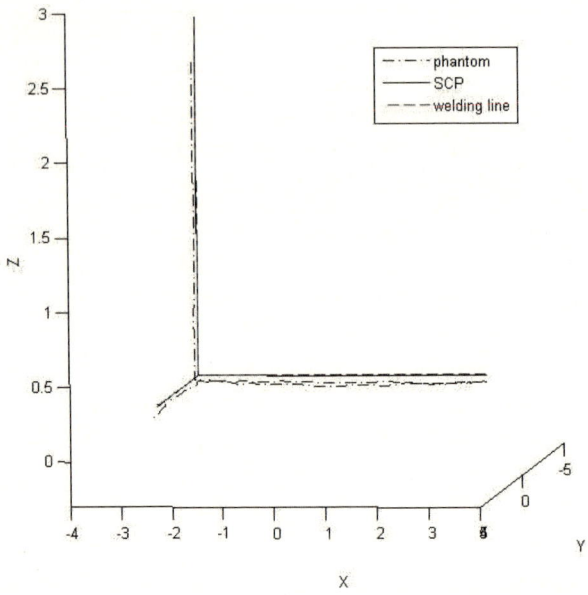

Fig. 7. Position of tool tip, SCP and given linear welding seam

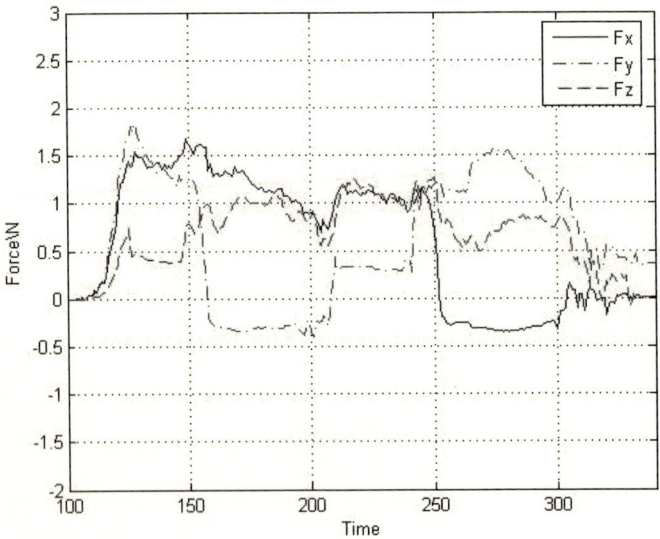

Fig. 8. Contact force when extracting linear welding seam

5 Conclusion

We have introduced an interactive approach to extracting complex space welding seam that takes advantage of real-time distance computation and haptic rendering. Using this approach, the user can naturally and intuitively manipulate virtual tool via a haptic device to make contact to the welding seam and move along the welding seam efficiently and accurately. This interactive approach enables a user to incorporate naturally human intelligence in identifying the complex space welding seam in a virtual environment. The proposed approach makes the virtual teach-in of robotic welding planning more efficient, feasible and accuracy. Our future work is to apply the approach to real robotic welding system.

Acknowledgments. The authors are grateful to the support of National Science Foundation of China under grants 60525314 and the support of the National Key Basic Research Program (973 program) under grant 2002CB312200.

References

1. Ulrich D.: Robot Systems for Arc Welding - Current Position and Future Trends. Welding and Cutting, Vol. 8(1992) 150-152
2. Carvalho G.C., Siqueira M.L., and Absi Alfaro S.C.: Off-line Programming of Flexible Welding Manufacturing Cell. Journal of Materials Processing Technology, Vol.78 (1998).24-28
3. Kim C.S., Hwang H.S., Lee J.H., at el..: Module Based Off-line Programming for Welding Robots of Panel Blocks. Proceeding of the ASCC (2002)783-788
4. Kreuzer B. and Milojevic D.: Simulation Tools Improve Planning and Reliability of Paint Finishing Lines. Industrial Robot, Vol.25, No. 2 (1998) 117-123
5. Breat J. L., Clement F., Jadeau P. , et al.. : ACT WELD - A Unique Off-line Programming Software Tailored for Robotic Welding Applications. Welding in the World, Vol.34, No. 3 (1994) 267-274
6. Hong K.S., Han H.Y., et al.: PC Based Off line Programming using VRML for Welding Robots in Shipbuilding. IEEE International Conference on Robotics, Automation and Mechatronics (2004)949-954
7. Zhu D.L., Xiao S., Hou H., et al . : Automatic Planning of Welding Torch's Gesture of Arc Welding Robot. Journal of Shang Hai Jiao Tong University, Vol.38, No. 9(2004) 1472-1475
8. Yan H., Liu J., Qiu S.H., et al.: Research on the Automatic Planning of Arc Welding Robot Welding Path for Space Weld. Machinery Design and Manufacturing, No.8 (2005)106-106
9. Chou W.S., Xiao J.: A Collision Detection Method for Virtual Manufacturing. Transactions of the North American Manufacturing Research Institute of SME, Vol.32 (2004) 319-326

Primary-Color-Based Spatial Layout Features and New Image Matching Algorithm Based on Dual Features[*]

De-cai Huang, Jia Hu, and Yuan Yuan

College of Information Engineering, Zhejiang University of Technology,
Hangzhou Zhejiang 310014, China
hdc@zjut.edu.cn

Abstract. In the area of Content-Based Image Retrieval (CBIR), feature extraction and matching are the key techniques for image retrieval. In order to overcome the drawbacks of commonly used color features, an approach to extract spatial layout feature is presented which is based on images' primary color, and a new algorithm is also presented for image features matching by combing the spatial layout feature and the color histogram feature. The experimental results show that the new algorithm can achieve much better performance for images with typical spatial layout feature.

Keywords: Image retrieval, primary color, spatial layout feature.

1 Introduction

With the increasing use of digital images, research on content-based image retrieval, which is the foundation of multimedia database and digital library, has been an academic hotspot [1].

Feature extraction and expression is the basis of content-based image retrieval (CBIR). Conventional algorithms are based on mono-feature of the whole image such as color histogram, which is easy to compute and is robust to rotate. However, this kinds of mono-feature are inadequate to express information such as position, shape and texture. In fact, two images might contain very different content, even they have the same color histogram [2].

To overcome the drawbacks of conventional algorithms based on mono-feature of the whole image, some researchers recently use the spatial layout feature of images' color in image retrieval. The most used method is blocking, in which every image was divided into a few regions, and then the color feature of each region is extracted. Stricker and Dimai believe that the center of an image is of significant importance [3]. They divide an image into 5 regions, and the center region is an ellipse. Hsu and Chua retrieve images by combining the color feature and layout feature [4]. The QBIC of IBM extracts the contour of objects in an image, and treats the mean color and color histogram as the features of objects [5]. And there exist some algorithms based on pixel clustering [6] and wavelet transform [7-8].

---

[*] The project supported partially by Zhejiang Provincial Natural Science Foundation of China (Grant No.Y105118 & Y105109).

Z. Pan et al. (Eds.): ICAT 2006, LNCS 4282, pp. 494–501, 2006.

Among the above methods, static blocking is the easiest way. But it does not concern the intrinsic relation of regions and the integration character of the image. Thus its application is limited extremely. To overcome this drawback, we put forward a new method to extract the spatial layout features of images' primary color. Furthermore, we present a new image retrieval algorithm based on both the features of the spatial layout and color histogram. Experiment illustrates that the new algorithm can achieve much better performance in content-based image retrieval system especially for images with typical spatial layout feature.

2   Primary-Color-Based Spatial Layout Feature

As an extension of static blocking method, primary-color-based spatial layout feature extraction includes the following two steps.

Firstly, an image is divided into 16 regions evenly (Fig.1), and then the primary color of each region is extracted, and the feature of the whole image is got by computation of all regions' feature. The so-called "primary color" is the color which appears mostly frequent in an image.

Fig. 1. An image is divided into 16 regions

Before we introduce the details of primary-color-based spatial layout features extraction, we explain the conception of spatial layout features as shown in Fig.2 briefly. The layout of images can be generally divided into 4 types: up-and-down, side-by-side, tilted, and centered (Fig.2). In the images of up-and-down layout (Fig.2a), color varies little on horizontal direction, which varies a lot on vertical direction. In the images of side-by-side layout (Fig.2 b), color varies a lot on horizontal direction, which varies little on vertical direction. And tilted layout is divided into 45 degree tilted and 135 degree tilted (Fig.2 c,d), in this situation, color varies a lot on tilted direction. Centered layout is divided into centered layout and plain layout (Fig.2 e,f). In fact, any kinds of layout can be classified into one of these layouts introduced above. By computing the change of primary color on 0 degree, 45 degree, 90 degree and 135 degree direction, we get the spatial layout feature of images.

Specifically, the primary-color-based layout feature can be expressed in 4 values; each of them reflects the change on one direction. The 4 values combined can express the spatial layout feature of an image. The principle of primary-color-based spatial layout feature extraction is: the content of each region is expressed by the primary color; the layout is expressed as the sum of differences between the primary color of a region and the primary color of the adjacent 4 regions. Specifically, the layout of 0 degree direction is expressed by the difference of the primary color of a region and the nearby region on 0 degree direction, which can be expressed as the Fig.3.

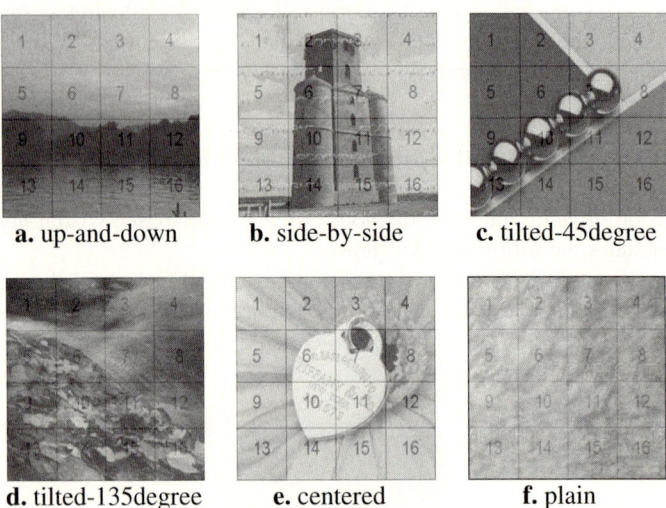

a. up-and-down   **b.** side-by-side   **c.** tilted-45degree

d. tilted-135degree   **e.** centered   **f.** plain

Fig. 2. Samples of layout

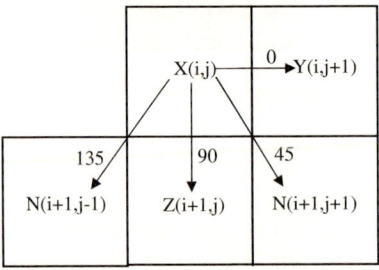

Fig. 3. A region and the adjacent regions

The spatial layout feature of an image can be expressed as following:

$$\text{Spatial\_0} = \sum_{i=1}^{4}\sum_{j=1}^{4}\sqrt{(r_{ij} - r_{i(j+1)})^2 + (g_{ij} - g_{i(j+1)})^2 + (b_{ij} - b_{i(j+1)})^2} \qquad (1)$$

$$\text{Spatial\_45} = \sum_{i=1}^{4}\sum_{j=1}^{4}\sqrt{(r_{ij} - r_{(i+1)(j+1)})^2 + (g_{ij} - g_{(i+1)(j+1)})^2 + (b_{ij} - b_{(i+1)(j+1)})^2} \qquad (2)$$

$$\text{Spatial\_90} = \sum_{i=1}^{4}\sum_{j=1}^{4}\sqrt{(r_{ij}-r_{(i+1)j})^2 + (g_{ij}-g_{(i+1)j})^2 + (b_{ij}-b_{(i+1)j})^2} \tag{3}$$

$$\text{Spatial\_135} = \sum_{i=1}^{4}\sum_{j=1}^{4}\sqrt{(r_{ij}-r_{(i+1)(j-1)})^2 + (g_{ij}-g_{(i+1)(j-1)})^2 + (b_{ij}-b_{(i+1)(j-1)})^2} \tag{4}$$

Where Spatial_0, Spatial_90, Spatial_45, Spatial_135 denote the spatial layout feature on 0,90,45 and 135 degree direction respectively; i,j denote the row number and column number of a region,(r_{ij},g_{ij},b_{ij}) illustrates the primary color of the region on i-th row and j-th column.

The layout can be standardized as the following formulas:

$$average = \begin{cases} 1; & \text{if } \text{Spatial\_0} = \text{Spatial\_45} = \text{Spatial\_90} = \text{Spatial\_135} = 0 \\ Spatial\_0 + Spatial\_45 + Spatial\_90 + Spatial\_135; & others \end{cases} \tag{5}$$

$$\text{Spatial\_0} = \text{Spatial\_0/average} . \tag{6}$$

$$\text{Spatial\_45} = \text{Spatial\_45/average} . \tag{7}$$

$$\text{Spatial\_90} = \text{Spatial\_90/average} . \tag{8}$$

$$\text{Spatial\_135} = \text{Spatial\_135/average} . \tag{9}$$

Where Spatial_0, Spatial_45, Spatial_90,and Spatial_135 illustrate the spatial layout feature of an image repectively. These 4 values can express the spatial layout of an image. If one of the values is much less than other 3 values, we know the image is continuous on this direction. If all the 4 values are small, we know the image is of a plain layout.

Fig. 4. "Up-and-down" layout

For example, the 4 spatial layout values of Fig 4 can be figured out as following:

Spatial_0 = 0.2273829,   Spatial_45=1.1581843.
Spatial_90=1.4700330,   Spatial_135=1.1443998 .

Since Spatial_0 is much less than other 3 values, and Spatial_90 is much larger than other 3 values, we know the color vary little on horizontal direction and vary a lot on vertical direction, and thus its layout is side-by-side.

3 Matching Algorithm Based on Dual Features

Let there be two images I and Q, whose spatial layout values are as following: $Spatial\_0_I, Spatial\_45_I, Spatial\_90_I, Spatial\_135_I$ 和 $Spatial\_0_Q, Spatial\_45_Q, Spatial\_90_Q, Spatial\_135_Q$, then the layout similarity of the two images can be illustrate as following:

$$Spatial\_0 = abs(Spatial\_0_I - Spatial\_0_Q) . \qquad (10)$$

$$Spatial\_45 = abs(Spatial\_45_I - Spatial\_45_Q) \qquad (11)$$

$$Spatial\_90 = abs(Spatial\_90_I - Spatial\_90_Q) \qquad (12)$$

$$Spatial\_135 = abs(Spatial\_135_I - Spatial\_135_Q) \qquad (13)$$

$$SpatialSum(I,Q) = patial\_0 + Spatial\_45 + Spatial\_90 + Spatial\_135 \qquad (14)$$

SpatialSum(I,Q) is the spatial layout similarity between image I and Q. The larger is the SpatialSum, the more similar is the two images.

If using solely spatial layout similarity without out color feature,the performance of a matching algorithm would not be a perfect one. So we combine spatial layout similarity and color feature similarity, devising an image matching algorithm based on both spatial layout feature similarity of primary color and color histogram similarity.

The similarity measure of our algorithm is as following:

$$SimiSum = similar - SpatialSum \times k . \qquad (15)$$

Where *SimiSum* is the total similarity of two images, *similar* is the similarity of the color histogram of two images, *SpatialSum* is the similarity of spatial layout feature of two images, k is layout coefficient, the *SimiSum* varies corresponding to the variation of k

4 Experiments and Analysis

Based on the algorithm put forward in this paper, we realize a content-based image retrieval system with VC.NET and SQL Server2000 which contains 2500 images randomly selected from the 20 classes' image of CorelTM image database. The performance is measured by precision and recall. Fig.5 illustrate the performance varies responding to the variation of k.

From the Fig.5., we know the k (layout coefficient) affects the performance of the retrieval system. When k is small, layout similarity contributes little to the system. When k=0, the algorithm degenerates to the algorithm based on color histogram similarity; when k is too large, the layout similarity dominates the performance of the system, the performance is still not good enough. According to our experience, when k=1000, the system performs best.

The following figures (Fig.6 and Fig.7) are comparisons of performance between image retrieval algorithm of primary-color-based spatial layout feature and color histogram similarity, and image retrieval algorithm based on color histogram similarity.

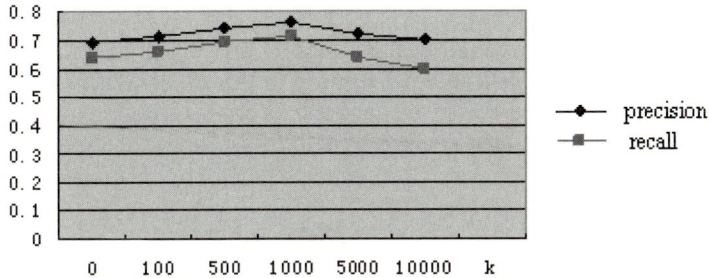

Fig. 5. Precision and recall of the retrieval system respect to different k

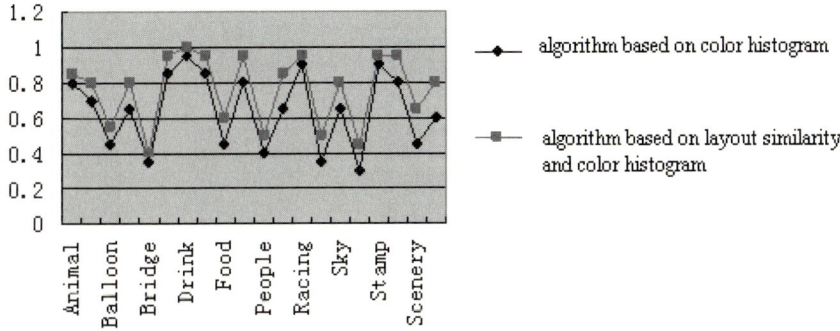

Fig. 6. The comparison on precision

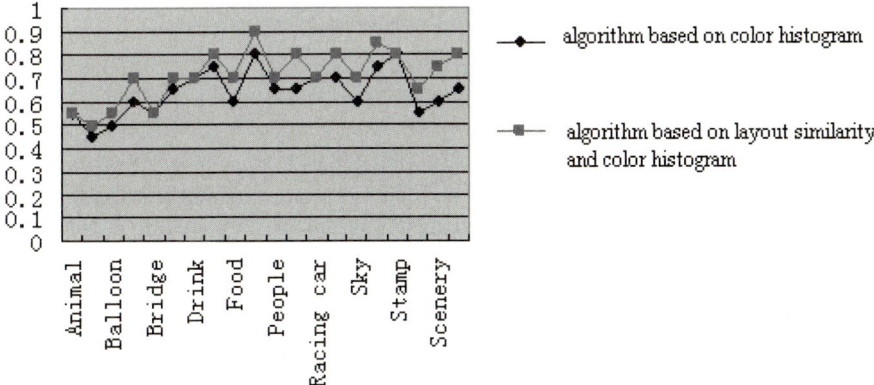

Fig. 7. The comparison on recall

From the experimental results above, we can conclude that image retrieval algorithm based on both of spatial layout feature of primary color and color histogram similarity outperforms algorithm based on color histogram similarity in most circumstances. There is some improvement even the images cannot be classified into a definite spatial layout. And thus the algorithm presented in this paper is better than that one based on mono-feature, and most suitable to retrieve images with obvious spatial layout feature.

The Fig.8. is the result of a retrieval instance by the content-based image retrieval system based on the new algorithm put forward in this paper. Where the first image on the top left corner is the key image, and others are the images similar to the key image and retrieved by the query, ranked from the most similar to less similar.

Fig. 8. A retrieval result by the new matching algorithm

5 Conclusion

Nowadays, Content-Based Image Retrieval (CBIR) technique is the foundation of multimedia database and digital library, and has been an academic research hotspot. In the CBIR area, feature extraction and matching are the key technique for image retrieval. We introduced a spatial layout feature based primary color, and presented a new algorithm based on both of the spatial layout feature and the color histogram feature. The experimental results show that the new algorithm can achieve much better performance in image retrieval system, especially for images with typical spatial layout feature.

References

1. Meng Fanjie,Guo Baolong.Research on content based image retrieval technology[J]. Application Research of Computers 2004, 21(7):21-25
2. Zhuang Yueting, Pan Yunhe, Wu Fei. Multimedia Information Analysis and retrieval in Internet[M]. Beijing: Tsinghua University Press, 2002,09, pp28-66
3. M. Stricker and A. Dimai. Color indexing with weak spatial constraints. IS&T/SPIE Conf. on Storage and Retrieval for Image and Video Databases IV, San Jose,CA:1996 Vol. 2670.pp.29-40
4. W. Hsu, T. Chua, and H. Pung. An integrated color-spatial approach to content-based image retrieval[C]. Proc. Of the ACM MM Conf ,San Francisco, CA: Nov.1995. pp.305-313
5. Q. Huang, B. Dom, M. Gorkani, J. Hafiner. Query by image and video content: The QBIC system[J]. IEEE Computer, 1995,28(9):23-32
6. Xue Jinghao,Zhang Yujin, Lin Xinggang. Pixel clustering Image thresholding 2D histogram SEM algorithm MAP[J]. ACTA ELECTONIC SINICA, 1999,27(7):95-98.
7. He Ning.Image Retrieval Multi-Resolution Partitions Feature Point Extraction[J]. Microcomputer Development, 2003,13(4):61-63.
8. Yuan Yuan, Decai Huang, Duanyang Liu. An Integer Wavelet Based Logo-watermarking Scheme. Proceedings of International Multi-Symposiums on Computer & Computational Science,Hangzhou,China,200-24 June,2006, pp.175-179.

Ridge-Valley Lines Smoothing and Optimizing

Hao Jing, Weixiang Zhang, and Bingfeng Zhou

Institute of Computer Science and Technology, Peking University, P.R. China
jinghao@icst.pku.edu.cn,
zhangweixiang@icst.pku.edu.cn,
cczbf@pku.edu.cn
http://sun1000e.pku.edu.cn/ cczbf/VITA.htm

Abstract. When detecting ridge-valley lines on 3D mesh model, estimation of the curvature and curvature derivatives may often yields to squiggly and noisy result, because the estimation is sensitive against unwanted surface noises. We present two algorithms to obtain smooth and noiseless ridge-valley lines. First, we apply an iterative procedure on ridge and valley vertices and their previous and next neighbors on connected feature lines, which leads to smooth lines. Secondly, we propose an algorithm to distinguish noises from meaningful feature lines based on graph theory model. Each separate feature line is considered as an undirected weighted graph which is called as **Feature Graph**. We can reasonably get rid of most noises and preserve meaningful feature lines through optimizing the minimal spanning tree of each feature graph.

1 Introduction

Lines are powerful shape descriptors which can convey most information on 3D models for designer and artist. Feature lines can be remarkably efficient at conveying shape and meaning while reducing visual clutter, especially in the interactive design of entertainment and engineering system. Feature lines extraction from discrete meshes has become an hot area of intense research in recent decade [1] [2] [3] [4] [5]. In general, feature lines include **Silhouette Edges**, **Boundary Edges** and **Interior Feature Edges** [6]. Boundary edges only exist in non-closed surface meshes. Detection of boundary edges is simple. we just detect edges contained in only one triangle on triangle model. The fast extraction algorithms of silhouette edges have been developed and can achieve good results. [1] [2] [3] [4].

Besides silhouette edges and boundary edges, interior feature edges indicate the internal structure and details on mesh at a finer level. In our method, we mainly deal with interior feature edges as view- and scale- independent ridge-valley lines, which are curves on a surface along which the surface bends sharply. However, it is easy to apply our algorithm to dealing with view-dependent feature lines such as suggestive lines [7] [8].

There have been various existing interior feature edges detection algorithms [9] [10] [11] [12] [7] [8]. All existing feature line extraction methods, however,

Z. Pan et al. (Eds.): ICAT 2006, LNCS 4282, pp. 502–511, 2006.
© Springer-Verlag Berlin Heidelberg 2006

treated the noises and meaningful feature lines of surface as the same role in computing process, the algorithm we present can reasonably separate noises from meaningful lines.

In our study, we first detect ridge and valley vertices via curvature and curvature derivatives analysis, then connect those vertices to generate feature lines. This lead to two problems as the left image of Figure 1 shows. One is squiggly lines result, the other is noises produced because of the computational error of curvature and curvature derivatives estimation. These two problems all come from the curvature-related estimation.

We present two algorithms to resolve these two problems respectively. After obtaining the ridge and valley vertices on mesh surface and connecting them, first we apply an iterative procedure working on local previous and next neighbors of a vertex on connected feature line. This iteration operation which is similar to Laplacian smoothing will achieve smooth feature lines. Secondly, we visit all ridge and valley vertices. Naturally, a separate feature line can be treated as an undirected graph weighted by the length of edges. The extracted feature lines can be viewed as a set of undirected weighted graphs. We call these graph **Feature Graphs** in our paper. For each feature graphs, a root node is chosen by a special condition, then the minimal spanning tree and the longest path of the tree is computed. After optimizing the minimal spanning tree through weight of nodes on graph, we can wipe out noises, and obtain meaningful feature lines as the right image of Figure 1 shows.

The contribution of our paper focus on not only the smoothing procedure of feature lines, but also providing a reasonable and extendable scheme on how to divide noise from meaningful feature lines. In the remaining of this paper, we will introduce previous work in Section 2. In Section 3, the ridge-valley lines smoothing method will be given. Section 4 will describe the optimizing algorithm used to wipe out noises.

2   Previous Work

Various feature detection algorithms have been proposed during the past several years [9] [10] [11] [12] [7] [13] [8]. Earlier papers focus on extraction of view-dependent silhouette edges [2] [3] [4], which separate the visible part from invisible ones of mesh model, i.e. edges shared by front-facing and back-facing polygons, and can be detected fast in real time [1].

However, much more finer details are indicated by interior feature edges. Most of existing algorithms on extracting interior feature edges mainly focused on global feature detection via curvature analysis. DeCarlo [7] define interior feature edges as view-dependent suggestive contour, which is extracted through radial curvature [14] analysis. The authors improved their algorithm in [13] with increasing of detecting speed. Sousa and Prusinkiewicz [8] present another automated algorithm to produce suggestive line drawing using graph theory, but

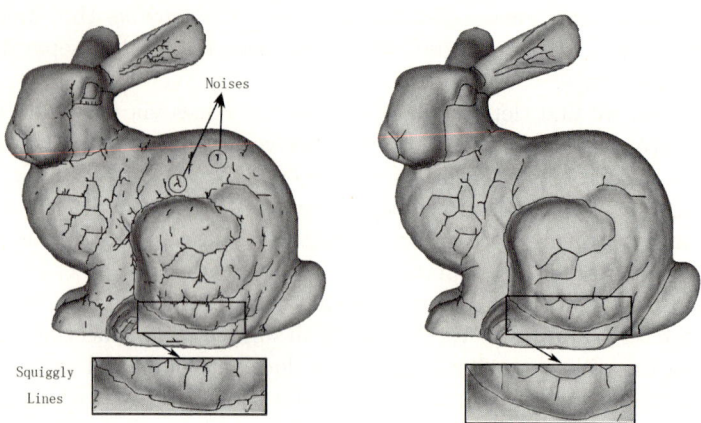

Fig. 1. A feature lines smoothing and optimizing example of bunny model with 69k triangles. The left image is the result before line smoothing and optimizing [10], noises and squiggly lines can be seen. The right image is the result after optimizing, feature lines are smoother and noiseless.

their results are not satisfied when the method is applied on some model, such as the bunny model. Other authors define interior feature edges as view- and scale-independent Ridge-Valley edges [9] [11], and extract feature lines via principle curvature analysis. The benefit of using view- and scale-independent ridge-valley lines is that they only need to be computed once, and are not necessary to be recomputed each time the view point changed. In our study, we focus on ridge-valley lines and mainly follow the definition in [10].

Ohtake [10] proposed simple and effective method for detecting ridge-valley lines defined via first- and second-order curvature derivatives on meshes. The high order surface derivative is achieved by combing multi-level implicit surface fitting. The common drawbacks of these curvature based algorithms are related with the sensitiveness of both curvature and derivative estimations against unwanted surface noise, and they do not make any different from noises and meaningful feature lines.

Those approaches are based on global curvature analysis may yield to squiggly and noisy feature lines. [15] present a modification of Laplacian smoothing algorithm to smooth feature lines, but their scheme works on the entire mesh before tracing feature lines. The algorithm we present in Section 3 is also similar with Laplacian smoothing [16], but works after detecting feature lines. Our algorithm can pay more attention to the local property of extracted feature lines and works well. Isenberg et al. [17] also present image-space algorithm to detect and remove artifact such as zig-zag style. In their study, they use their own visibility determination algorithm not the traditional hardware z-buffer algorithm for the conveniency of generating stroke. The artifact they mentioned in their paper such as zig-zag lines is produced by their own visibility determination algorithm, not from the original model. They didn't mention how to removal the noise like short branches which comes from the original model and curvature estimation error.

Some researchers on image processing focus on the interactive feature detection method. e.g. [18] proposed a method called geometric snakes which is an extension of image snakes [19], [20] proposed an semi-automatic algorithm to obtain smooth lines. But these interactive methods are not fit for automatic 3D applications.

3   Achieving Smooth Feature Lines

In our study, we detect view- and scale- dependent ridge-valley lines as interior feature edges. We estimate the curvature first using [21]. Mainly following the definition in [10], we can get the result of feature lines as the left image in Figure 2 shows.

After feature lines are detected, we apply an iterative procedure on ridge-valley lines as follow to smooth the extracted feature lines. Our approach is similar with laplacian smoothing which is inspired by normal based mesh filtering [22], for each ridge vertex(or valley vertex)v, with its normal vector n_v, we find its two neighbors v_{prev} and v_{next} from the feature line. If a vertex has only one neighbor on the feature line(the start vertex or the end vertex of the line), or a vertex has more than two neighbors on the feature line(the branch vertex), we skip these vertices and don't apply the iteration operation on these vertices.

If the vertex have exactly two neighbors on the line, then let the middle point between v_{prev} and v_{next} be $v_{middle} = (v_{prev} + v_{next})/2$. The vector from v to v_{middle} is $v' = v_{middle} - v$. Define the difference of v on the line as

$$\Delta v = v' - (v' \cdot n_v)n_v \tag{1}$$

the iterative procedure will move v to a new position according to the difference Δv. After each iteration step, the Δv should be updated with the new position of

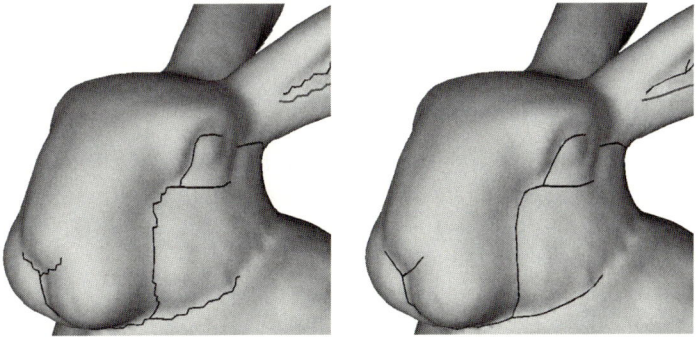

Fig. 2. A feature lines smoothing example of bunny model with 69k triangles. The left image is the result before line smoothing, squiggly lines exists. The right image is the result after smoothing without squiggly lines with $\lambda = 0.4$ after 20 iterations.

v, we use v_0 to represent the original position of vertex v, and v_n to represent the new position of v after the nth iteration. the updated Δv after the nth iteration is represented by $\Delta v_{(n)}$. The new position of the vertex v is calculated by Eq.2

$$v_{(n)} = v_{(n-1)} + \lambda \Delta v_{(n-1)} \tag{2}$$

where λ is a controlling parameter which satisfy $0 \leq \lambda \leq 1$. After applied Eq.2 on ridge and valley vertex, the connected feature line can be more smooth as the right image of Figure 2 shows. For all of our experiments, $\lambda = 0.4$ proves to be a good choice, and the convergence can be achieved after 20 iteration times.

Compared with Laplacian smoothing scheme [15] working on the entire mesh, the proposed smoothing algorithm concentrate more on the local property of feature lines and is more direct and effective.

4   Feature Lines Optimizing

After being smoothed, the results still keep much noises and useless little branch lines which interfere with our observation. The key challenge is to distinguish these noises from meaningful feature lines.

For the feature lines extraction, each separate line can be denoted as $G_i = < V_i, E_i, W_i >$, where V_i is the list of vertices, E_i is the list of edges satisfying $E \subseteq [V]^2$, W_i is the weight function of E_i, in which $w_k \in W_i$ is weight of $e_k \in E_i$. we used the length of edge as weight in our study. Naturally, G_i is an undirected weighted graph. We call G_i a **Feature Graph**. Furthermore, by construction, a Feature Graph is also a connected graph. The extracted feature lines can be represented by a set of Feature Graph $\mathbb{G} = < G_0, G_1, ..., G_m >$, each $G_i \in \mathbb{G}$ correspond a line segment. We develop denoising algorithm through optimizing each $G_i \in \mathbb{G}$.

For each $G_i \in \mathbb{G}$, we computed the longest path P, with length L. Since feature graph G_i is a connected graph, it certainly contains a spanning tree. We build the Minimal Spanning Tree of G_i using the start vertex or the end vertex of the longest path as the root of tree.

Computed the *Longest* Path: Follow the definition of *path* in graph theory [23], a *path* is a non-empty graph $P = < V, E >$ of the form

$$V = x_0, x_1, ..., x_k, E = x_0 x_1, x_2 x_2, ..., x_{k-1} x_k$$

where the x_i are all distinct. Here we refer **the *Longest* Path** as the path $P_j \subseteq G_i$ with the maximal sum of edge weight in P of all path in graph G_i, mathematically, a path P_j is the longest path in the graph G_i if and only if $\sum_{e_k \in E(P_j), P_j \subseteq G_i} w_k$ is the maximum, e.g.

$$max\{ \sum_{e_k \in E(P_0)} w_k, \sum_{e_k \in E(P_1)} w_k, ..., \sum_{e_k \in E(P_n)} w_k \}$$

Since we use the length of edge as weight, **the *Longest* Path** visually is the longest line branch in a separate feature line. Figure 3 shows three different situations during computing, for each branch vertex t in a tree, the length from the root to the vertex t is $L_{t_{root}}$, length of the two longest low level branch of vertex t is L_{t_1} and L_{t_2}, then the longest path $L_{t_{max}}$ crossing the vertex t is $max\{L_{t_{root}} + L_{t_1}, L_{t_{root}} + L_{t_2}, L_{t_1} + L_{t_2}\}$. The longest path of tree T should be $max\{L_{v0}, L_{v1}, ..., L_{vn}\}, (v0, v1, ..., vn \in V(T))$.

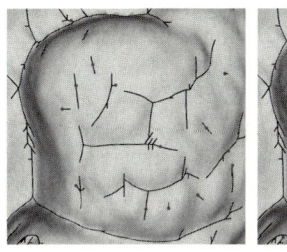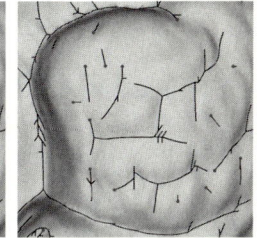

Fig. 3. Example of three situation of the longest path computation. blue vertex is the root node of tree, and red path is the longest path of tree.

Fig. 4. Example of choosing root of Minimal Spanning. The red points are roots of MSTs. In the left image, we choose a vertex randomly as the MST's root to build the first MST T_1. Then we choose root as the start node(or the end node) of the longest path in T_1, rebuild the MST T_2 as the right image shows.

To compute the longest path, we randomly chose a vertex in graph as root, then build the minimal spanning tree of the graph with PRIM [23] algorithm. The left image of Figure 4 shows the random root choosing result. We compute the longest path in the tree, which is also the longest path in graph G_i.

After finding out the longest path in the minimal spanning tree builded first time, we choose the start vertex or the end vertex as root node to rebuild the minimal spanning tree of graph G_i. Figure 4 shows the result of rebuilded minimal spanning tree.

Finishing rebuilding minimal spanning tree of each feature graph, we optimize these trees to wipe out noises. Let P_i be the longest path of feature graph G_i, the length L_i of path P_i can be denoted as

$$L_i = \sum_{e_k \in E(P_i)} w_k$$

A global threshold θ and a local threshold ε are proposed to distinguish noises from meaningful feature, which satisfies

$$min\{L_0, L_1, ..., L_m\} \le \theta \le max\{L_0, L_1, ..., L_m\}$$

and

$$0 \le \varepsilon \le 1$$

We delete noises on extracted lines in the following two cases.

CASE I: If the length L_i of the longest path of feature graph G_i satisfies $L_i < \theta$, the line corresponded feature graph G_i is considered as noise and not rendered.

CASE II: Giving a feature graph G with its minimal spanning tree T. The longest path P with length L has been found. For each node $v_i \in T$, we compute the longest path l_i among all pathes from the node to all leaf nodes. We check each branch node $v_k \in P$ which has more than one child node. With preserving branch belongs to the longest path of tree, if length of one of other branches $l_{branch} < \varepsilon * L$, the branch is considered as noises and deleted. On the contrast, if length of one of other branches $l_{branch} > \varepsilon * L$, we apply same checking step on the subtree T' with the branch node being the root of T'.

Implementation of CASE II: CASE I is easy to implement. Implementation of CASE II is a little difficult. We implement the CASE II through a recursive function.

CHECK-ALL-BRANCH(GraphVertexIndex root)
for all vertex v in the longest path P
    for all branch b of vertex V
        if $l_{v.b} < l_{root} * \varepsilon$
            CUT-BRANCH($v.b$)
        else
            CHECK-ALL-BRANCH($v.b$)
        end if
    end for
end for

Figure 5 shows the optimizing result of Figure 4 with global threshold $\theta = 16$ and local threshold $\varepsilon = 0.05$. Meaningful result is obtained.

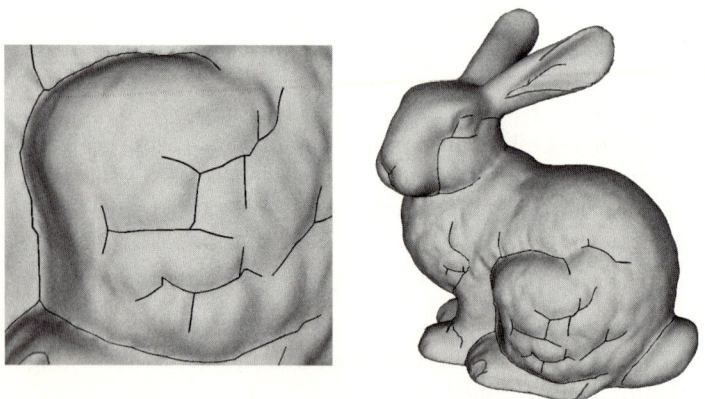

Fig. 5. Example of feature lines optimizing. $\theta = 16$, $\varepsilon = 0.05$

Limitation: In our method, the parameters θ and ϵ in the optimization step are set interactively now, it would be great if the program can compute these two parameters automatically according to different triangle mesh models. For this purpose, more attention should be paid to the relationship between the two parameters and the average of the length of the longest path on all feature graphs of the entire model. This is also one of our future works.

5   Results and Discussion

Feature lines carry essential information about the geometry of a surface. But existing method can not work perfectly because of the computational error during curvature analysis on discrete mesh models, The unwanted noise sometimes annoy the feature detection results very much. The methods we proposed in this paper can not only smooth lines extracted through curvature analysis, but also provide a reasonable scheme to distinguish noise from meaningful feature lines.

Our method works well on various models and can obtain high quality feature line result. Figure 6 and 7 give two examples and the comparison with existing method [13].

Although we mainly focus on the view-independent feature lines, it's also easy to apply our algorithm to deal with view-dependent lines such as suggestive lines [7] [8]. But the computational time may increased. For view-independent lines optimization, we need to build feature graphs only once. But for view-dependent lines, different line-drawing result corresponds to different viewpoint. Each time the viewpoint changed, the feature graphs need to be re-generated and the computational time increases much. In our future work, more efficient algorithm dealing with view-dependent lines should be developed.

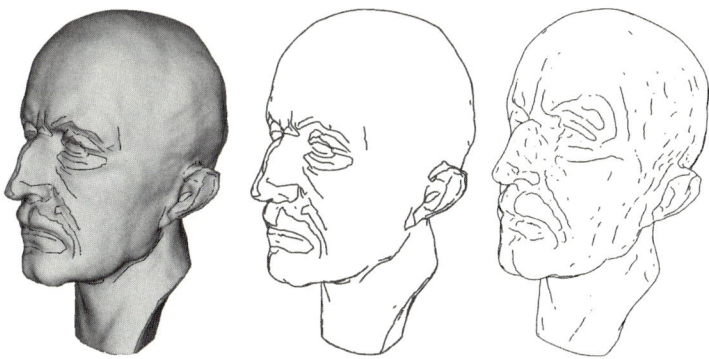

Fig. 6. Example of feature lines optimizing. Left image is the optimizing result with $\theta = 20$, $\varepsilon = 0.3$. Middle image is rendered with ridge-valley lines and silhouette edges. Right image is rendered using the algorithm [13].

Finally, greater precision on distinguish noise and feature line is required. Sometimes, meaningful feature lines would be deleted as noises and noises may be preserved as feature lines. In our future work, we will try to define noise not only by length of line segments, but also by other properties of lines, such as line curvatures.

Fig. 7. Example of feature lines optimizing. Left image is the optimizing result with ridge-valley lines and silhouette edges, $\theta = 0.2$, $\varepsilon = 0.05$. Right image is rendered using the algorithm [13].

References

1. Markosian, L., Kowalski, M.A., Trychin, S.J., Bourdev, L.D.: Real-time nonphotorealistic rendering. In: Proceedings of SIGGRAPH 1997, ACM (1997)
2. Kalnins, R.D., Markosian, L., Meier, B.J., Kowalski, M.A., Lee, J.C.: Wysiwyg npr: Drawing strokes directly on 3d models. In: Proceedings of SIGGRAPH 2002, ACM (2002)
3. Hertzmann, A., Zorin, D.: Illustrating smooth surface. In: Proceedings of SIGGRAPH 2000, ACM (2000)
4. Raskar, R., Cohen, M.: Image precision silhouette edges. In: Symposium on Interactive 3D Graphics 1999, ACM (1999)
5. Winkenbach, G., Salesin, D.H.: Computer-generated pen-and-ink illustration. In: Proceedings of SIGGRAPH 1994, ACM (1994)
6. Strothotte, T., Schlechtweg, S.: Non-Photorealistic Computer Graphics, Modeling, Rendering, and Animation. Morgan Kaufmann Publisher (2002)
7. DeCarlo, D., Finkelstein, A., Rusinkicwicz, S., Santella, A.: Suggestive contours for conveying shape. ACM Transactions on Graphics **22**(3(July)) (2003) 848–855
8. Sousa, M.C., Prusinkiewicz, P.: A few good lines: Suggestive drawing of 3d models. Computer Graphics Forum **22**(3) (2003) 381–390
9. Ohtake, Y., Belyaev, A.: Automatic detection of geodesic ridges and ravines on polygonal surfaces. The Journal of Three Dimensional Images **15**(1) (2001) 127–132
10. Ohtake, Y., Belyaev, A.: Ridge-valley lines on meshes via implicit surface fitting. In: Proceedings of SIGGRAPH 2004, ACM (2004)
11. Belyaev, A., Ohtake, Y., Abe, K.: Detection of ridges and ravines on range images and triangular meshes. In: Proceedings of Vision Geometry IX, SPIE (2000)
12. Watanabe, K., Belyaev, A.: Detection of salient curvature features on polygonal surfaces. Computer & Graphics **20**(3) (2001) 385–392
13. DeCarlo, D., Finkelstein, A., Rusinkiewicz, S.: Interactive rendering of suggestive contours with temporal coherence. In: NPAR 2004, ACM (2004)

14. Koenderink, J.: What does the occluding contour. tell us about solid shape? Perception **13** (1984) 321–330
15. Hildebrandt, K., Polthier, K., Wardetzky, M.: Smooth feature lines on surface meshes. In: Eurographics Symposium on Geometry Processing. (2005)
16. Sorkine, O.: Laplacian mesh processing. In: Proceedings of Eurographics 2005, ACM (2005)
17. Isenberg, T., Halper, N., Strothotte, T.: Stylizing silhouettes at interactive rates: From silhouette edges to silhouette strokes. In: Proceedings of EUROGRAPHICS 2002. (2002)
18. Lee, Y., Lee, S.: Geometric snakes for triangular meshes. In: Proceedings of Eurographics 2002. (2002) 229–238
19. Kass, M., Witkin, A., Terzopoulos, D.: Snakes: Active contour models. IEEE Transactions on Pattern Analysis and Machine Intelligence **20**(11) (1998) 1260–1265
20. Guo, Y., Peng, Q., Hu, G., Wang, J.: Smooth feature line detection for meshes. The Journal of Zhejiang University SCIENCE **6A**(5) (2005) 460–468
21. Rusinkiewicz, S.: Estimating curvatures and their derivatives on triangle meshes. In: Symposium on 3D Data Processing, Visualization, and Transmission. (2004)
22. Chen, C.Y., Cheng, K.Y.: A sharpeness dependent filter for mesh smoothing. Computer Aided Geometric Design **22** (2005) 376–391
23. Diestel, R.: Graph Theory. Springer-Verlag (2000)

Mynews: Personalization of Web Contents Transcoding for Mobile Device Users*

Teuk-Seob Song[1], Jin-Sang Lee[2], Yoon-Chul Choy[2], and Soon-Bum Lim[3]

[1] Department of Computer Engineering, Mokwon University,
Daejeon, 302-729, Korea
teukseob@dreamwiz.com
[2] Department of Computer Science, Yonsei University,
Seoul, 120-749, Korea
{gr20000, ycchoy}@rainbow.yonsei.ac.kr
[3] Department of Multimedia Science, Sookmyung Women's University,
Seoul, 140-742, Korea
sblim@sookmyung.ac.kr

Abstract. Developing wireless internet service and mobile devices, web access mechanism is various. There are various methods for developing wireless internet services, mobile devices, and web access mechanism. However, the existing web infrastructure and content are designed for desktop computers and not well-suited for other types of accesses, e.g, PDA or mobile phone that have less processing power and memory, small screens, limited input facilities, or network bandwidth etc. Thus, there is a growing need for transcoding techniques that provide ability to browse the web through mobile devices. In this paper, we present personalized XML documents transcoding techniques for mobile device users.

1 Introduction

The market of wireless Internet, digital TV, data broadcasting, electronic book, etc. is booming due to the consumer's desire to use digital contents without any limitation of space and time. However, there are some limitations of terminal devices, such as cell phone and PDA (low CPU performance, small output display, simple method of input and output, etc.) in wireless internet, and data broadcasting conditions. Therefore, contents conversion is needed to service contents on these terminal devices to eliminate above limitations. Our solution is transcoding, the conversion of digital contents in accordance with the change of terminal environment.

Other contents with good quality (exception of HTML) have not been offered in wireless Internet environment because previous studies on transcoding were conducted mainly in HTML environment [1,2,3,4,5,6,7]. XML is becoming a de facto standard for exchanging data in Internet data processing environments

---

* This work was supported by the Korea Research Foundation Grant (R01-2004-000-10117-0(2004)).

Z. Pan et al. (Eds.): ICAT 2006, LNCS 4282, pp. 512–521, 2006.

due to the inherent characteristics such as hierarchical self-describing structures, and (please list one more characteristic). Thus, transcoding technique, which utilizes structure information such as XML document environment, is required. Furthermore, a user-centered method in transcoding environment is necessary since the existing transcoding researches are mainly focusing on performance of device.

Mobile devices like PDA or cell phone have smaller display than desktop computer. Hence, more clicks or scrolls are required to get information when viewing web document on a mobile device. To resolve this kind of problem, it is necessary to display information suitable for the users. Consequently, many researches regarding web contents personalization and reorganizing user-centered web contents are being conducted.

The previous research on web contents personalization can be classified into contents-based technology and user context-based technology. The Contents-based technology classifies web contents through keyword matching (or string matching) using frequently used keywords (or strings) by user, while the user context-based technology classifies web contents through web connect pattern of user or log file[8]. However, previous researches on existing web contents personalization are service provider-centric, which makes it difficult to reflect user's continuously changing interest accurately. Therefore, intent of this paper is to recommend interface and technique allowing effective transcoding of standard document like XML as well as HTML document.

2   Related Works

Digital contents transcoding is usually classified into media transcoding and web document transcoding[5]. The web document transcoding covered in this paper has been studied extensively from the advent of small terminal such as PDA to the present. Also, recently researches on web contents conversion with Device Independent Working Group of W3C are being progressed activity. There will be simple introduction to existing transcoding technique and contents personalization technology with mobile environment.

Annotation-Based Web Contents Transcoding (2000)[4], a transcoding system suggested by IBM, is a proxy side conversion technique targeting HTML document. In this paper, the annotation technique reflecting service provider's opinion was applied so as to write page conversion rule. Transcoding is carried out by using outside annotation, created based on RDF and tools allowing to identify the result of transcoding from the writing stage is given. Also it reduces the data amount applying page partition technique through giving priority and shows more important things at higher position of the page. From these reasons, it raises the efficiency of contents usage.

NAC: A Basic Core for the Adaptation and Negotiation of Multimedia Service(2001)[6,7], NAC is a transcoding system developed as a part of the Opera project for development of multimedia electronic document structure and representation model from the France national research, INRIA.(run on sentence)

It defined UPS(Universal Porfile Schema) based on CC/PP(Composite Capabilities/Preferences Profiles) and consisted of server side profile and client side profile. Server side profile covers instance (HTML, WML etc.), resource (jpg, gif, au etc.) and conversion rule(XSLT, Style Sheet etc.) with similar form to annotation, while client side profile describes the delivery context about user device information. Actual contents conversion is carried out at UCM(User Context Module) and ANM(Adaptation and Negotiation Module), and converted to proper form for user's device in consideration of profile information.

WebViews system(2001) [9], a transcoding system developed in Bell Research Institute, was designed for contents personalize in mobile environment. The purpose of system design is to make complicated web page with image, flash, java script etc. to 'simplify' and 'personalize' the content so that it meets the connecting equipment and user's needs.

Web Clip [10] is a transcoding service being used mainly based on PDA recently. It clips the part of web pages such as newspaper articles, stock market situation, bulletin board etc. updated periodically, and provides the information as contents desired by user on PDA using the on line or off line form. Off line service is used for Palm-based PDA, and converts clip selected by user to its own format available on PDA in advance.

3   XML Document Transcoding Using User Annotation

In this chapter, XML document transcoding technique using annotation for personalized contents conversion considering user's interest will be suggested.

3.1   Transcoding Framework

The target of personalized transcoding system is news contents that can be classified into layers by theme in this paper. Because news contents can be classified into different layer groups, it is proper to reflect the user's interest for specific theme.

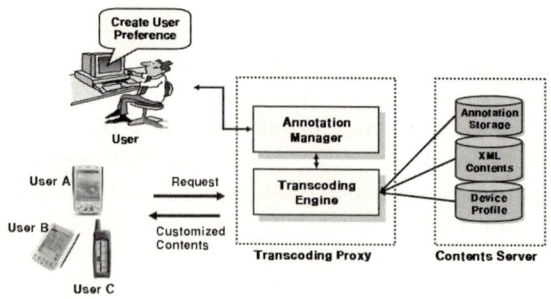

Fig. 1. Transcoding framework using user annotations

It uses annotation as a method to represent the interest of user for the specific theme. The user creates and stores the annotation as target to web document of desktop environment. Since a mobile machine, like PDA, is used to link to a desktop, it can represent the interest of user clearly for specific item on display. Actual contents conversion proper to mobile terminal is processed dynamically at the transcoding engines and provides personalized contents to each user after integrating original XML contents, device profile, and user annotation information. Above Fig. 1 shows the transcoding framework using user annotation.

3.2   The Layer Structure of XML Based News Contents

It defines the layer structure by theme of news for XML-based structural news contents configuration. The layer structure by theme of news follows the normal division system of domestic and abroad news service, and actual report matter is based on NewsML [11] of IPTC (International Press Telecommunication Council) which is standard format for writing and forwarding of news. The whole structure of XML-based web news includes the layer structure by theme and actual report instance group.

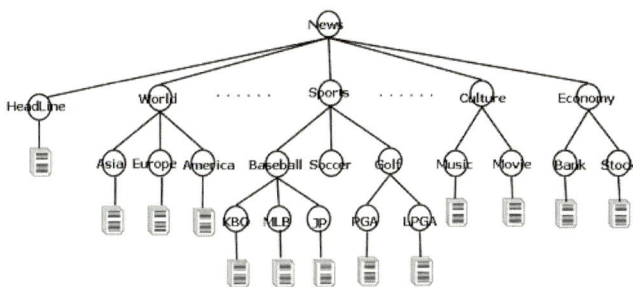

Fig. 2. Example of the DOM tree showing structure of subject hierarchy

3.3   User Annotation Model

Meta information, describing the user's interest information and contents conversion rule about specific theme, is required for meaningful transcoding that reflects user's interest. User-centric annotation model is defined for Meta information technology needing to convert content in this clause. The annotation [9,4], which normally means transcoding, is an additional information required for document conversion. But in this paper, the meaning is extended to interface to represent not only contents conversion rule but also user preference.

The kinds of annotation necessary for personalized transcoding are divided into three; selection, deletion, and grouping. "Selection" and "Deletion" represent the presence of contents conversion, and "Grouping" represents associative relationship of more than themes. Fig. 3 is the annotation layer structure considering selection, deletion, and grouping. User annotation consists of collection of

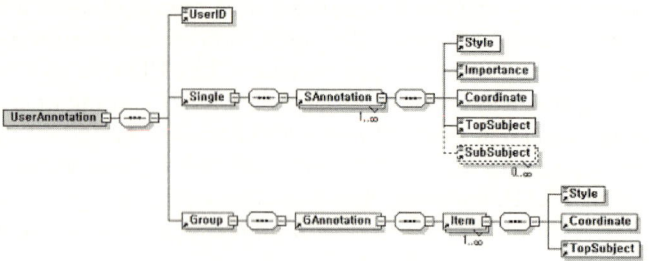

Fig. 3. Hierarchy of user annotation

single annotation and group annotation. Single annotation means selection and deletion regarding one theme, and group annotation means relationship between more than two themes.

3.4   Contents Conversion Using Structural Information and Annotation

The transcoding procedure using structural information and annotation of a document consists of reconfiguration of original document and XSLT [13] conversion in a broad sense. The reforming process of original document covers element filtering, completion of annotation, and determination of priority by theme. Annotation information such as selection, deletion, grouping, importance etc. is reflected to the original documentation through element filtering. The part that is not designated by user is handled by applying the annotation completion rule. The priority by theme is determined using importance value after the importance of every node is determined through completion of annotation. In XSLT conversion process, XSLT conversion script is dynamically created or converted using priority information.

- Element filtering

Element filtering is the first stage for transcoding and reflects the user annotation information to original document tree. Parsed annotation information is converted to data structure of table type and processed from the first line in order. This repeats equal to the user annotation number and gives the annotation type and importance value after finding node on tree that matches the selected theme by user.

- Completion of annotation

The completion of annotation rule using the result of element filtering is needed to give importance of unfixed node without annotation. The completion of annotation rule is determining process for importance of adjacent node with based on the designated node and importance value by user. The followings are annotation completion rules considering selection, deletion, grouping and the depth of corresponding node.

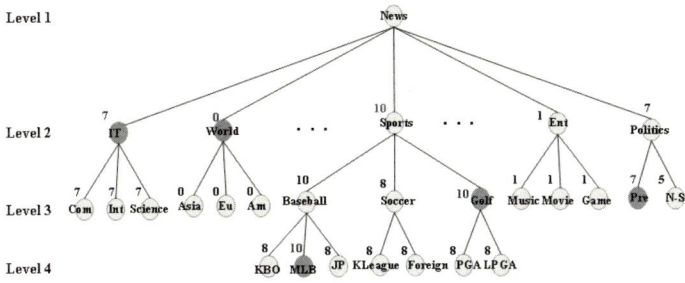

Fig. 4. Example of annotation completion

Rule 1. In case of selecting, deleting and grouping division node (level=2) by theme, the importance of child node succeed to importance of parent node without change.

Rule 2. In case of selected node is the sub node (level=3)to division and has not child node, it delivers importance value to parent node without change and the importance of did not selected brother node is decreased to α ($0 \leq \alpha \leq 10$).

Rule 3. In case of selected node is sub node(level=3) of division and has the child node, the importance value is delivered to parent node and child note without change and the importance of did not selected brother node is decreased with α.

Rule 4. In case of leaf node (level=4), the importance value is delivered to parent and ancestor node without change and the importance of brother node is decreased with α. And rest nodes did not selected within corresponding theme are have the decreased α importance value without exception.

Rule 5. In case there is no node selected in the specific theme, every importance value of child node is 1.

4   Implementation and Evaluation of Proposed System

In this chapter, XML document transcoding system considering user's interest is implemented and its result is analyzed and assessed. The system is implement based on JAVA and configured the detailed module using Swing, JAXP (Java API for XML Processing), Servlet and XSLT.

4.1   System Architecture

Transcoding system consists of annotation interface for creation of user's interest information and transcoding engine processing contents conversion in a broad sense. Fig. 5 shows the whole structure suggesting transcoding system.

User creates annotation(select, delete, group) for specific theme of news targeting web page provided from desktop environment and created annotation information is stored as valid XML document in designated structure. After

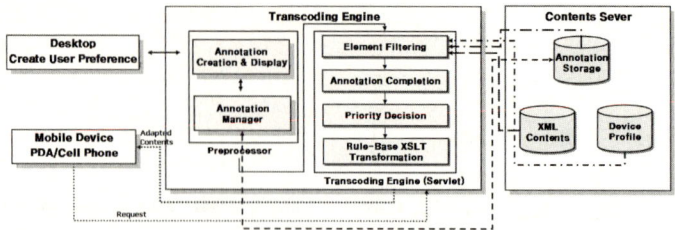

Fig. 5. Overview of proposed Transcoding system

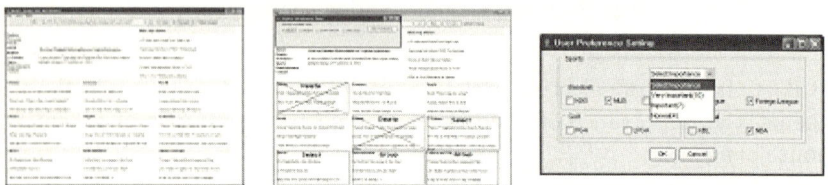

Fig. 6. Screen-Shot of annotation interface. Left: Web document brows- ing mode. Center: Annotation creation mode. Right: Importance and specific subject selection Mode.

that, when requesting corresponding page on mobile machine, it integrates the profile information of connect device, user annotation information and XML contents, and then determines the priority by theme, creates the XSLT script, and transmits the personalized page suitable for each user

Annotation interface was implemented with similar type to normal web browser and provides two modes of 'web document browsing' and 'annotation creation'. Web document browsing mode provides the same function with web browser and creates user's interest information to corresponding document converting to annotation creation mode.

Annotation type is selected using separate popup window and displayed on the monitor in corresponding style by each type. If there is existing annotation created by user, it displays analyzed annotation files stored in server on the monitor. Each annotation is selected by dragging specific theme area, and selection of importance and detailed theme is executed by separate popup menu. Left figure in Fig. 6 is an implemented annotation interface and center figure in Fig. 6 shows the example of popup menu to select importance and detailed theme for selected theme.

In case that it does not reflect user's interest, all contents are converted according to designated rules on system. In case that it reflects user's interest, printing order by theme is determined by considering annotation types and priority information.

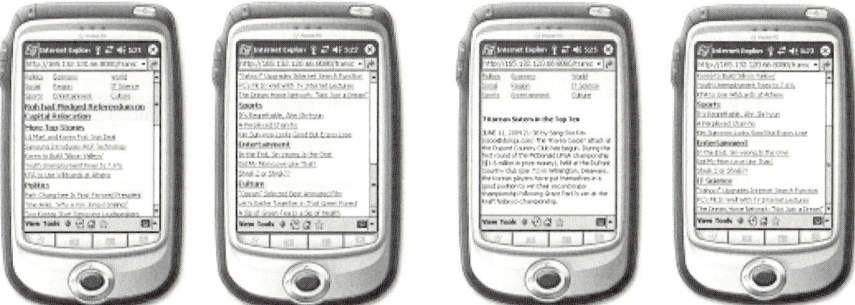

Fig. 7. Screen-Shot of transcoding output using pocket PC 2003 emulator. Left two figures represent that user's interest does not reflect. Right two figures represent that user's interest does reflect.

4.2   Empirical Evaluation

In this clause, the difference is verified by comparison with previous studies and user's assessment to evaluate proposed transcoding system. Proposed transcoding system creates information of user's interest targeting web page of desktop environment and processes personalized transcoding according to information of user's interest. The comparison targets of this system are WebView[9] and Web Clip [10] of NateOn suggested in relative work and their inter comparison is possible from the point of personalized transcoding system considering information of user's interest.

The user assessment was conducted to verify the efficiency of proposed system. In this test, the comparison is processed targeting Web Clip of NateOn to measure satisfaction for information creation interface of user interface and converted transcoding result. 20 subjects (10 subjects who have used PDA + 10 subjects who haven't used) participated in this test, and it was tested in the environment of Microsoft pocket PC 2003 emulator. Assessment was performed from the points of annotation interface for information creation of user's interest and measuring satisfaction about transcoding result. The test result showed similar or higher satisfaction compared with Web Clip as Fig. 8 illustrated.

Two-way ANOVA(analysis of variance) was used to analysis the precision of user according to each system. Fig. 8 shows the average of user assessment and proposed technique could maintain higher satisfaction than existing technique alternatively. And it is identified that the suggested system has higher satisfaction $(F(0.05,5,5)=5.05, F(0.05, 1.5)=6.61)$ than existing system from this paper result.

The assessment items cover 3 items of interface convenience and 3 items of satisfaction with result. The satisfaction assessment has superior result to Web Clip from "Is it possible to represent the interest clearly?" in the questions about interface convenience among assessment items. The reason analyzed is that Web

Clip is convenient to select the specific item but it has more complicated system procedure for giving priority and store process than suggesting system. From the question "Does result of transcoding reflect the interest item clearly?" to assess the satisfaction with transcoding result between two systems, similar satisfaction to Web Clip was obtained. The reason analyzed is that system intending importance value and user judgment importance value do not concord in terms of meaning.

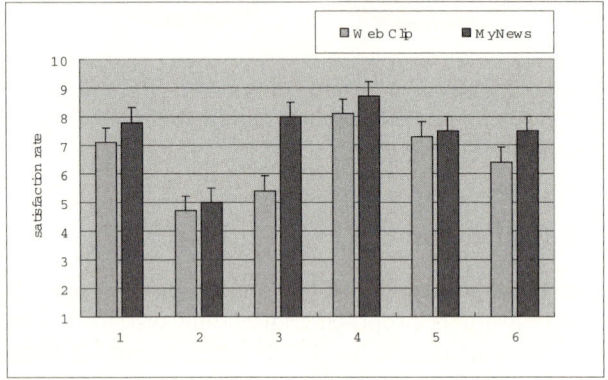

Fig. 8. Result of user test

5   Conclusion

In this paper, we suggested XML document transcoding technique considering user's interest to offer personalized web contents in the mobile environment. The user interface annotation model and interface are designed targeting new contents and XML document conversion technique using annotation information is suggested in this paper. Proposed transcoding techniques in this paper are composed of three modules in a broad sense; creating user annotation for specific theme, reforming original document and priority determination per theme using annotation, and XSLT dynamic conversion considering terminal limitation. The creation of annotation targeting web document in desktop environment selects the theme desired by user and gives the importance value to corresponding theme through described method representing user's interest.

In this paper, service efficiency could be advanced through not by HTML layout-based transcoding or CC/PP-based one-way transcoding[12] but by user-centered personalized contents conversion. And it could have superior satisfaction compared to existing system by user assessment. From the result of this paper, transcoding of various XML document with layer structure by theme not only news contents study seems possible to be applied.

References

1. S. Antonio et. al, InfoStar: An Adaptive Visual Analytics Platform for Mobile Devices, Proceedings of the 2005 ACM/IEEE SC—05 Conference (SC '05), 74-83
2. T.W. Bickmore and B.N. Schilit, Digestor: Device-Independent Access to the World Wide Web, Proc. of the 6th International World Wide Web Conference, Computer Networks and ISDN Systems, **29** (1997) 1075-1082.
3. M. Butler, F. Giannetti, R. Gimson, and T. Wiley, Device Independence and the Web, IEEE Internet Computing, **6** (2002) 81-86.
4. M. Hori, G. Kondoh, K. Ono, S. Hirose, and S. Singhal, "Annotation-Based Web Content Transcoding", 9th World Wide Web Conference, **3** (2000) 197-211.
5. Intel CC/PP Toolkit, http://www.intel.com/pca/developernetwork.
6. T. Lemoluma and N. Layaida, NAC: A Basic Core for the Adaptation and Negotiation of Multimedia Services, OPERA Project, INRIA (2001).
7. T. Lemoluma and N. Layaida, Context-Aware Adaptation for Mobile Devices, 2004 IEEE Inter. Conf. Mobile Data Management, (2004) 19-22.
8. N. Ramakrishan, PIPE: Web Personalization by Partial Evaluation, Internet Computing, IEEE , **4** (2000) 21-31.
9. J Freire, B Kumar, D Lieuwen, WebViews: Accessing Personalized Web Content and Services, 10th international conference on World Wide Web (2001) 576-587.
10. Nate PDA Service, http://pda.nate.com
11. NewsML Homepage, http://www.newsml.org
12. CC/PP Information Page, http://www.w3c.org/Mobile/CCPP/
13. XSL Transformations (XSLT) Version 1.0 W3C Recommendation November 1999, http://www.w3c.org/TR/xslt

Visualization Application in Clothing Biomechanical Design

Ruomei Wang[1], Yi Li[1], Xiaonan Luo[3], and Xin Zhang[2]

[1] Institute of Textile and Clothing Hong Kong Polytechnic University
Hunghom, Kowloon, Hong Kong
[2] Xi'an University of Engineering Science & Technology, Xi'an, 710048, China
[3] Institute of Computer Application, Zhong Shan University
Guang Zhou, 510275, China
Phone: 852-34003361
tcruomei@polyu.edu.hk

Abstract. Visualization in scientific computing and engineering design is receiving wide attention. It can assist engineers, scientists, and technicians to access, analyze, manage, visualize, and present large and diverse quantities of data from the information gained from raw technical data. Clothing engineering design is a complex iterative-decision–making competitive process. Large amount of dynamic data are generated by simulation. The visualization application in clothing biomechanical design is presented is presented in this paper. The simulation results can be described by graph. The subdivision method is used to create the pressure distribute change animation.

Keywords: visualization, simulation, biomechanical, clothing.

1 Introduction

Considerable research is now being done into visualization in scientific computing and engineering design. As a result of the huge increase in computing power, graphic tools are required in many cases for interpreting and presenting the results of various simulations, or for analyzing physical phenomena [1]. The visualization of scientific data has become vital for many researchers. Scientists, engineers, medical personnel, business analysis, and others often need to analyze large amounts of information or to study the behavior of certain processes. Numerical simulations carried out on supercomputers frequently produce data files containing thousands and even millions of data. Similarly, satellite cameras and other sources are amassing large data files faster than they can be interpreted. Scanning these large sets of numbers to determine trends and relationships is a tedious and ineffective process.

The appropriate way to analyze and understand these results is to visualize the data. If the data are converted to a visual form, the trends and patterns are often immediately apparent. Visualization is not just about graphics, but about the power to present large amounts of numerical information in an efficient and effective way so that it is possible to gain insight into the numbers. Visualization is concerned with exploring data and information graphically, as a means of gaining understanding and

Z. Pan et al. (Eds.): ICAT 2006, LNCS 4282, pp. 522 – 529, 2006.

insight into data. Visualization of data is an emerging visual computing technology that uses an intuitionist and innovative graphical user interface and visualization techniques. This technology helps engineers, scientists, and technicians to access, analyze, manage, visualize, and present large and diverse quantities of data from the information gained from the raw technical data. The technology has evolved from the combination of powerful desktop computers with statistical and analysis tools, graphics and visualization, and sophisticated interaction tools. The data visualized enable scientists to explore their research data, to gain new scientific insight, and to communicate their discoveries to others. Visualization allows the conversion of information that cannot be perceived by the human eye into forms most suitable for this highly developed human sense.

The visualization technique is to transform experimental data into graphical primitives. There are many different kinds of data sets, and effective visualization schemes depend on the characteristics of the data. A collection of data can contain scalar values, vectors, high-order tensors, or any combination of these data types. Data sets can also be two or three dimensional. Graphing and visualization techniques can vary from simple charting to volume visualization. Several academic visualization classification schemes have been proposed. Basic techniques include the familiar types of graphs such as scatter, line, and contour, as well as 3D surfaces, and various combinations of these. Advanced visualization methods include 3D geometric rendering, volume visualization, multidimensional visualization, vector fields, and animation.

Clothing engineering design means creating new clothing by enhancing existing designs or by altering existing ones to perform new functions. It is a complex iterative-decision–making competitive process. The clothing engineering design process generates and uses a large volume of dynamic data. The biomechanical engineering design for textile and clothing products is typical of the kind of human-clothing engineering in which the biological human body interacts dynamically with a garment on the large of areas of contact surface. The main simulation results are garment pressure distribution and human body biomechanical performance. The designer needs to quantitative investigate and evaluate the relationship between the mechanical performance of textile and clothing products and human sensory factors, including physiological and psychological aspects. Visualizing and analyzing the results of the mechanical simulation using a broad range of interaction techniques is crucial to the effectiveness of product development in the clothing biomechanical engineering design system. In this paper, the visualization application as the post-processing during clothing biomechanical engineering design is reported. The visualization technology is flexible used to describe the simulation results.

2 Mechanical Performance Visualization of Clothing

2.1 Clothing Deformation

The clothing will become deformed because of a fabric's mechanical property. The clothing deformation can be recorded during a simulation process and it can be visualized by color, form, plot and animation. To ensure that the reproduction of your illustrations is of a reasonable quality, we advise against the use of shading. The contrast should be as pronounced as possible.

To visualize and analyze the results of the mechanical simulation effectively, the following features were used: linear and logarithmic axis scales; axis annotation; a simultaneous display of data and visualization; a diverse range of plotting modes; a diverse range of 3D display modes; the superimposition of mathematical functions; and an intuitive user interface [2]. Most FE packages have their own visualization modules to view the results of the mechanical analysis. Following is an example, using the M-smart software package [3][4] to illustrate the clothing deformation analysis used for a clothing biomechanical engineering design. The simulation scheme is hybrid model (geometric model and particle model).

The visualization process consists three parts: processing simulation results, according to the simulation data to construct the 3D geometric model, graphics process and animation. Fig. 1 shows the outlook of a vest that is fitted to the body with two views: (a) the front view of the vest fitted to the body, and (b) the back view of the vest fitted to the body. The simulation indicates the vest stretch and recovery during the wearing process.

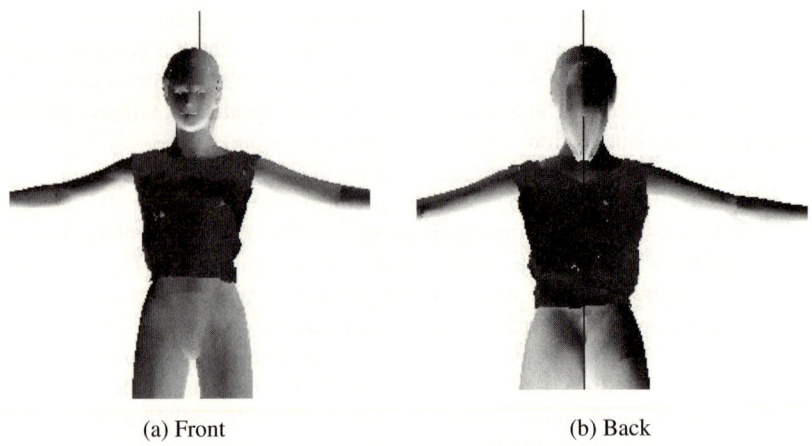

(a) Front   (b) Back

Fig. 1. Deformation of vest in the fitting process

2.2 Clothing Pressure Distributions

With the numerical results of the simulation, various force deformations of garment can be visualized. There are three types forces are generated during simulation process: compression, shearing and bending. Fig. 2 shows the simulation results of forces distributions on the garment.

Fig. 3 illustrates that the forces distribution on the garment are consistent with deformation of garment. The bigger curvature is on the garment, the bigger tensile force is. In Fig. 3(a), the bigger tensile force acted on the garment is the area of breast. In the Fig. 3(e), the bigger bending force acted on the garment is the area of waist. The visualization of garment deformation can help the designer to evaluate the design concept in a virtual platform.

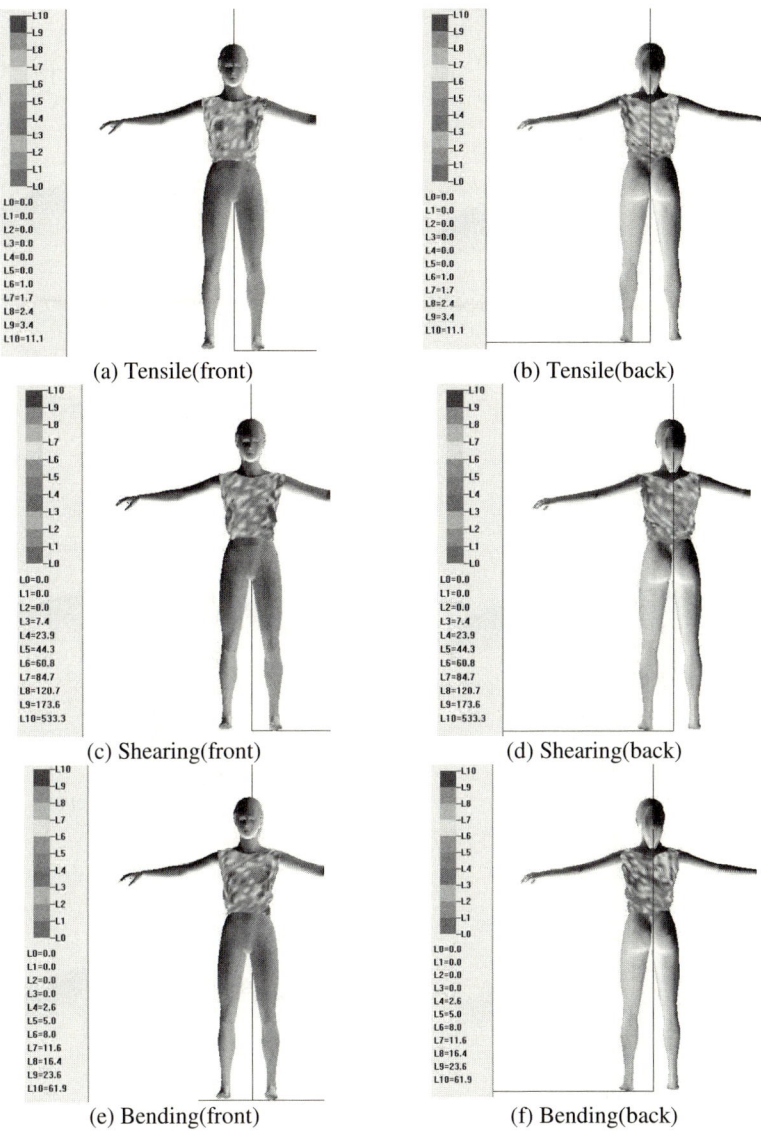

(a) Tensile(front)   (b) Tensile(back)

(c) Shearing(front)   (d) Shearing(back)

(e) Bending(front)   (f) Bending(back)

Fig. 2. Forces distribution

2.3 Clothing Pressure Animation

In order to visualize the change of clothing pressure during the wear, the animation technology can be used. In animation processing, key frame technology often is used to strut all pressure change process. Those key frames have great influence upon the pressure distribution and other in-between frames in animation can be generated from key frames. Linear interpolation and higher order spline interpolation are the regular methods to build in-between frames.

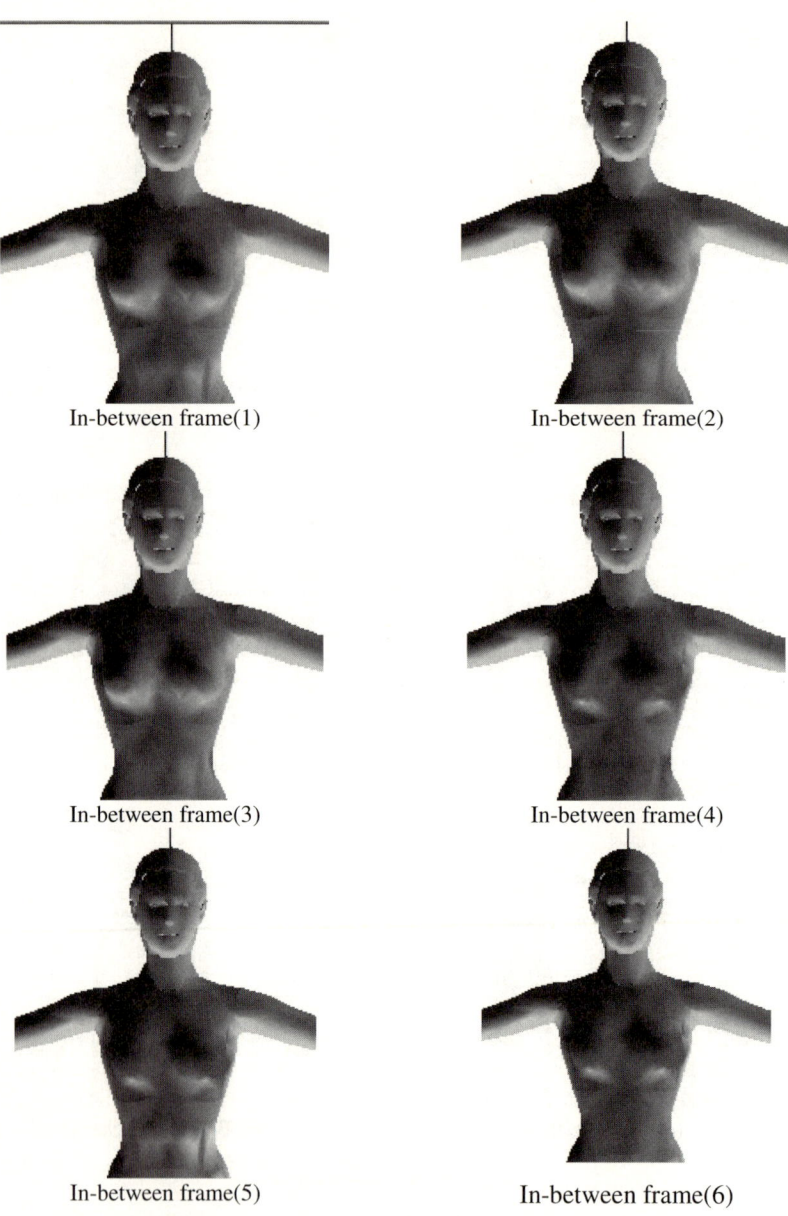

In-between frame(1)   In-between frame(2)

In-between frame(3)   In-between frame(4)

In-between frame(5)   In-between frame(6)

Fig. 3. Frame sequences about Pressure change

Comparing with normal method such as linear interpolation and higher order spline interpolation, 4-Point subdivision scheme has some advantages in building in-between frames. 4-Point subdivision technology can generate blander vision effect than linear interpolation method and gain more efficiency than higher order spline interpolation method.

4-Point subdivision scheme is proposed by N. Dyn, J. Gregory and D. Levin in [5].

$$
\begin{cases}
P_{2i,2j}^{k+1} & -1 \leq i \leq 2^{k} n+1, -1 \leq j \leq 2^{k} m+1 \\
P_{2i+1,2j}^{k+1} = (\frac{1}{2}+\omega)(P_{i,j}^{k} + P_{i+1,j}^{k}) - \omega(P_{i-1,j}^{k} + P_{i-2,j}^{k}) & -1 \leq i \leq 2^{k} n, -1 \leq j \leq 2^{k} m+1 \\
P_{2i,2j+1}^{k+1} (\frac{1}{2}+\omega)(P_{i,2j}^{k+1} + P_{i,2j+2}^{k+1}) - \omega(P_{i,2j-2}^{k+1} + P_{i,2j+4}^{k+1}) & -1 \leq i \leq 2^{k} n+1, -1 \leq j \leq 2^{k} m
\end{cases}
\qquad (1)
$$

In the equation (1), P_i^k is a given control vertex sequence and w is a real number. The choice w = 1/16 is of interest since for this value the scheme coincides with the cubic Lagrange-based scheme proposed in [6].

Here, an adaptive pressure distribution animation algorithm based on 4-Point subdivision scheme is presented to generate in-between frames in the animation for pressure change process.

The algorithm can be described in four steps:

(1) To construct the key frame. The primary variable is the pressure distribution value on the body between the different parts in the body. Given any frame in the state, it contains the pressure dynamic simulation.
(2) Generate boundary frame of the animation. The initial sequence of frames are generated.
(3) Evaluating and checking the space displacement factor in successive frames and using 4-Point subdivision scheme to generate a set of new frames for this in-between frame.
(4) Repeating step 4 until the space displacement factor satisfies the requirement of continuity.

Figure 3 shows the in-between frames according to the key frame result using the 4-point subdivision scheme.

3 Mechanical Behavior of the Human Body

The clothing biomechanical engineering design involves the clothing deformation and human body deformation. Especially, the researcher wants to simulate the clothing biomechanical performances to predict the human body physiology and psychology comfort performance. Here, the software Ansys and M-smart are used to simulate the clothing biomechanical performance and human body biomechanical performances. The core technology includes the programming and the data transfer between software packages. The simulation can be divided into two steps: the first one is to generate the forces acted on the human body by the garment deformation. Then transform these forces data into the Ansys's data format. The second step is to define the human biology parameters and import the forces data to simulate the human body deformation using Ansys software.

Fig. 4 shows the distributions of the skin pressure during the wearing process. The trends of the pressure change correspond to the vest pressure changes. A high skin pressure of 6.8gf/cm2 is observed as wearing vest, and a lower skin pressure of 2.7gf/cm2 is observed, while the garment pressure shows similar values of 61gf/cm2 and 62gf/cm2 for the vest respectively. It suggests that the skin pressure is not only induced by local contact but also by the overall contact situation.

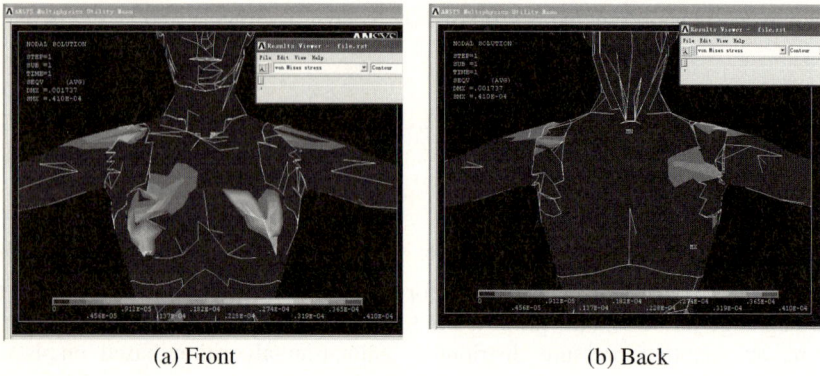

(a) Front   (b) Back

Fig. 4. Skin pressure distribution

4 Conclusions

The computer aided design for clothing biomechanical engineering design is a simulation process to analyze and evaluate the functional performance of clothing. The aim of the biomechanical simulation is the virtual reproduction of the mechanical behavior of a textile object subjected to various geometrical and mechanical conditions, or of the interaction between a clothing object and a human body object. In order to analyze and understand the results of the mechanical simulation effectively, it is necessary to transform simulation numerical data into various graphical expressions to help the engineering designer analysis, evaluate the design process for visually interpreting the data. Graphs and charts, contour plots, surface modeling and rendering, and color-coding are common tools for visualization. In additional, the animation techniques are used to generate the rich virtual description for design process. The subdivision method is used to generate the in-between frames. All these visualization methods have been integrated into a tool set to support the clothing engineering design process as the post-processing.

Acknowledgements

We would like to thank Hong Kong Polytechnic University for funding this research through the projects A188 and G-YD31, also the National Natural Science Foundation of China through project grant 60273063, 60525213.

References

1. Earnshaw, Rae A., Visualization and modeling. c1997: San Diego, Calif. : Academic Press.
2. Judith, R. and Brown, Rae Earnshaw,,Mikael Jern, Visualization : using computer graphics to explore data and present information. c1995: New York : J. Wiley.
3. Ruomei Wang, Yi Li, 3D-Apparel CAD system - M-Smart (Copyright No. 2005SR01691), 2005, China.

4. Ruomei Wang , Yi Li , Xin Zhang ,Xiaonan Luo , Xiaoqun Dai, A CAD system for clothing biomechanical sensory engineering, 17th IMACS World Congress Scientific Computation, Applied Mathematics and Simulation, Paris, France, July, 2005.
5. N.Dyn, J.A.Gregory, and D.Levin. A 4-Point interpolatory subdivision scheme for curve design. Computer-Aided Geometric Design, 4:257-268, 1987.
6. G.Deslauriers and S.Dubuc. Symmetric iterative interpolation. Constructive Approximation, 5:49-68, 1989.

Robot Position Estimation and Tracking Using the Particle Filter and SOM in Robotic Space

TaeSeok Jin[1] and JangMyung Lee[2]

[1] Dept. of Mechatronics Engineering, DongSeo University,
San 69-1 Churye-dong, Sasang-ku, Busan 617-716, Korea
jints@dongseo.ac.kr
[2] Dept. of Elctronics Engineering, Pusan National University,
GeumJeong-ku, Busan 609-735, Korea
jmlee@pusan.ac.kr

Abstract. The Robotic Space is the space where many intelligent sensing and tracking devices, such as computers and multi sensors, are distributed. According to the cooperation of many intelligent devices, the environment, it is very important that the system knows the location information to offer the useful services. In order to achieve these goals, we present a method for representing, tracking and human following by fusing distributed multiple vision systems in Robotic Space, with application to pedestrian tracking in a crowd. And the article presents the integration of color distributions into SOM based particle filtering. Particle filters provide a robust tracking framework under ambiguity conditions. We propose to track the moving objects by generating hypotheses not in the image plan but on the top-view reconstruction of the scene. Comparative results on real video sequences show the advantage of our method for multi-motion tracking. Simulations are carried out to evaluate the proposed performance. Also, the method is applied to the intelligent environment and its performance is verified by the experiments.

1 Introduction

Detection of moving objects has been utilized in industrial robotic systems, for example, in the recognition and monitoring of unmanned systems that also require compression of moving images [1],[2],[3],[4]. Trajectory prediction of moving objects is required for a mobile manipulator that aims at the control and observation of motion information such as object position, velocity, and acceleration. Prediction and estimation algorithms have generally been required for industrial robots. For a simple example, in a pick-and-place operation with a manipulator, the precise motion estimation of the object on the conveyor belt is a critical factor in stable grasping. A well-structured environment, such as the moving-jig that carries the object on the conveyor belt and stops when the manipulator grasps the object, might obviate the motion estimation requirement. However, a well-structured environment limits the flexibility of the production system, requires skillful designers for the jig, and incurs a high maintenance expense; eventually it will disappear from automated production lines.

Z. Pan et al. (Eds.): ICAT 2006, LNCS 4282, pp. 530–539, 2006.
© Springer-Verlag Berlin Heidelberg 2006

To overcome these problems, to tracking a moving object stably without stopping the motion, the trajectory prediction of the moving object on the conveyor belt is necessary [5]. The manipulator control system needs to estimate the most accurate position, velocity, and acceleration at any instance to capture the moving object safely without collision and to pick up the object stably without slippage. When the motion trajectory is not highly random and continuous, it can be modeled analytically to predict the near-future values based on previously measured data [6]. However, this kind of approach requires significant computational time for high-degrees-of-freedom motion, and its computational complexity increases rapidly when there are many modeling errors. In addition, performance is highly sensitive to the change of the environment. Those state-of-the-art techniques perform efficiently to trace the movement of one or two moving objects but the operational efficiency decreases dramatically when tracking the movement of many moving objects because systems implementing multiple hypotheses and multiple targets suffer from a combinatorial explosion, rendering those approaches computationally very expensive for real-time object tracking [7].

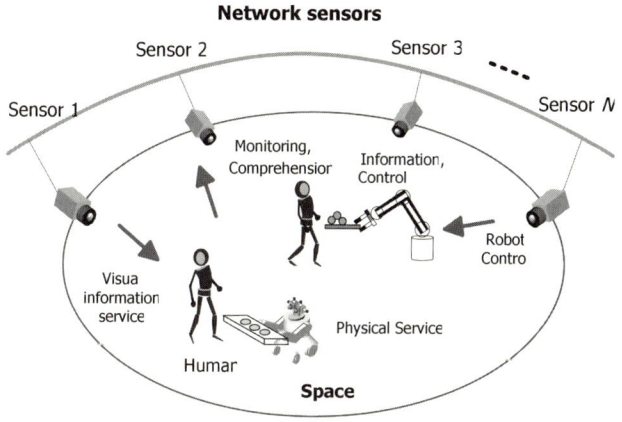

Fig. 1. Intelligent environment by distributed cameras

It is necessary for the intelligent environment to acquire various information about humans and robots in the environment. When the environment does not know where humans and robots are respectively, the environment can not give the enough service to the appropriate user as for the physical service especially. Therefore, it is considered that how to get the location information is the most necessary of all. The system with multiple color CCD cameras is utilized as one of the means to acquire the location information in an intelligent environment. It can achieve the human centered system because the environment acquires the location of human noncontactly and the equipment of the special devices isn't required for human. Moreover, camera has the advantage in wide monitoring area. It also leads to acquisition of details about objects and the behavior recognition according to image processing. Our intelligent environment is achieved by distributing small intelligent devices which don't affect the present living environment greatly.

2 Vision Systems in Robotic Space

2.1 Structure of Robotic Space

Fig. 2 shows the system configuration of distributed cameras in Intelligent Space. Since many autonomous cameras are distributed, this system is autonomous distributed system and has robustness and flexibility. Tracking and position estimation of objects is characterized as the basic function of each camera. Each camera must perform the basic function independently at least because over cooperation in basic level between cameras loses the robustness of autonomous distributed system. On the other hand, cooperation between many cameras is needed for accurate position estimation, control of the human following robot [8], guiding robots beyond the monitoring area of one camera [9], and so on. These are advanced functions of this system. This distributed camera system of Intelligent Space is separated into two parts as shown in Fig. 2. This paper will focus on the tracking of multiple objects in the basic function. Each camera has to perform the basic function independently of condition of other cameras, because of keeping the robustness and the flexibility of the system. On the other hand, cooperation between many cameras is needed for accurate position estimation, control of mobile robots to supporting human [10],[11], guiding robots beyond the monitoring area of one camera[12], and so on. These are advanced functions of this system.

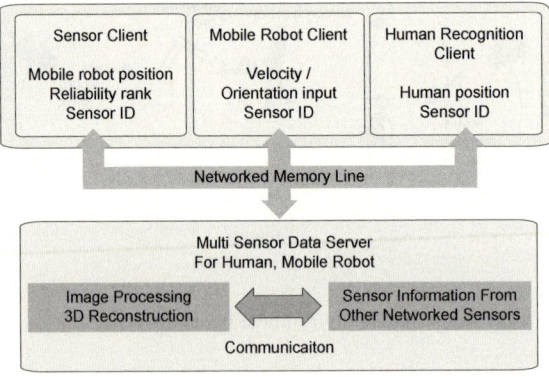

Fig. 2. Configuration of distributed camera system

2.2 Previous Research for Moving Object Tracking

Neural networks can be classified into two categories: supervised learning- and unsupervised learning methods. In most of the previous research, the supervised learning method was adopted to overcome the nonlinear properties [10],[12]. Since the supervised learning method requires the relation between input and output [9] at all times, it is not suitable for real-time trajectory estimation for which the input-output relation cannot be obtained instantaneously in the unstructured environment. Therefore, in this study, SOM (Self Organizing Map), that is, a type of unsupervised learning method, was selected to estimate the highly nonlinear trajectory that cannot be properly

predicted by the Particle filter. Also, SOM is a data-sorting algorithm, which is necessary for real-time image processing since there is so much data to be processed.
Among the most popular data-sorting algorithms, VQ (Vector Quantization), SOM,
and LVQ (Learning Vector Quantization), SOM is selected to sort the data in this
approach since it is capable of unsupervised learning. Since VQ is limited to the very
special case of a zero neighborhood and LVQ requires preliminary information for
classes, neither of them is suitable for the unsupervised learning of the moving trajectory. Fig. 3 shows the estimation and tracking system for this research. The input for
the dynamic model comes from either the Particle filter or SOM according to the
following decision equation:

$$Predicted\ value = k \cdot Particle\ Filter_{out} + (1-k) \cdot SOM_{out} \tag{1}$$

where k=1 for $error \leq threshold$ and k=0 for $error > threshold$.

The threshold value is empirically determined based on the size of the estimated
position error.

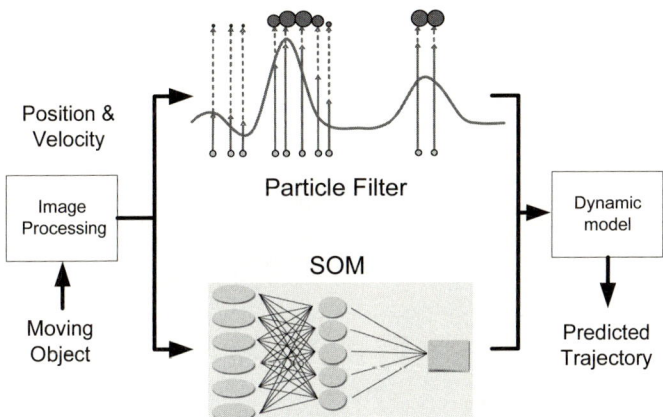

Fig. 3. Estimation and tracking system of robotic space

3 Processing Flow

3.1 Extraction of Object

Classifying the moving-object pattern in the dynamically changing unstructured environment has not yet been tackled successfully [13]. Therefore, in this research, the
camera was fixed on a stable platform in order to capture static environment images.
To estimate the states of the motion characteristics, the trajectory of the moving object was pre-recorded and analyzed. Fig. 4(a) and Fig. (b) represent the object images
at (t-1) instance and (t) instance, respectively.

As recognized in the images, most parts of the CCD image correspond to the background. After eliminating the background, the difference between the two consecutive

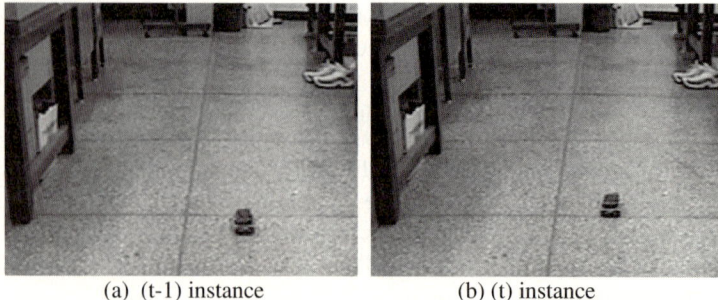

(a) (t-1) instance   (b) (t) instance

Fig. 4. Detected image of moving object at each instance

image frames can be obtained to estimate the moving-object motion. To compute the difference, either the absolute values of the two image frames or the assigned values can be used. The difference method is popular in image pre-processing for extracting desired information from the whole image frame, which can be expressed as

$$\text{Output}(x, y) = \text{Image1}(x, y) - \text{Image2}(x, y) \tag{2}$$

The difference image between Fig. 4(a) and Fig. 4(b) is represented in Fig. 5. When the difference image for the whole time interval can be obtained, the trajectory of the moving object can be calculated precisely.

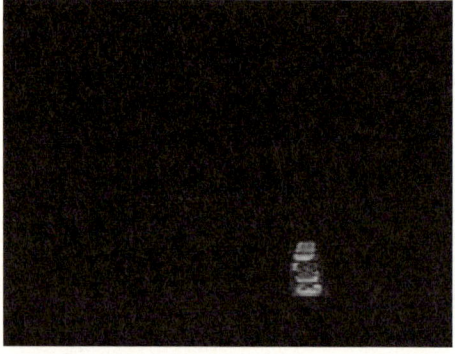

Fig. 5. Difference image between (t) and (t-1) instance images

3.2 Target Regions Encoded in a State Vector Using Particle Filter

Particle filtering provides a robust tracking framework, as it models uncertainty. Particle filters are very flexible in that they not require any assumptions about the probability distributions of data. In order to track moving objects (e.g. pedestrians) in video sequences, a classical particle filter continuously looks throughout the 2D-image space to determine which image regions belong to which moving objects (target regions). For that a moving region can be encoded in a state vector. In the tracking problem the object identity must be maintained throughout the video sequences. The image features used therefore can involve low-level or high-level approaches (such as the colored-based image features, a subspace image decomposition or appearance models) to build a state vector. A target region over the $2D$-image space can be represented for instance as follows:

$$r = \{l,\ s,\ m,\ \gamma\} \tag{3}$$

where l is the location of the region, s is the region size, m is its motion and γ is its direction. In the standard formulation of the particle filter algorithm, the location l, of the hypothesis, is fixed in the prediction stage using only the previous approximation of the state density. Moreover, the importance of using an adaptive-target model to tackle the problems such as the occlusions and large-scale changes has been largely recognized. For example, the update of the target model can be implemented by the equation

$$\overline{r}_t = (1 - \lambda)\overline{r}_{t-1} + \lambda E[r_t] \tag{4}$$

where λ weights the contribution of the mean state to the target region. So, we update the target model during slowly changing image observations.

4   Tracking Moving Objects

4.1   State-Space over the Top-View Plan

In a practical particle filter [5],[6] implementation, the prediction density is obtained by applying a dynamic model to the output of the previous time-step. This is appropriate when the hypothesis set approximation of the state density is accurate. But the random nature of the motion model induces some non-zero probability everywhere in state-space that the object is present at that point. The tracking error can be reduced by increasing the number of hypotheses (particles) with considerable influence on the computational complexity of the algorithm. However in the case of tracking pedestrians we propose to use the top-view information to refine the predictions and reduce the state-space, which permits an efficient discrete representation. In this top-view plan the displacements become Euclidean distances. The prediction can be defined according to the physical limitations of the pedestrians and their kinematics. In this paper we use a simpler dynamic model, where the actions of the pedestrians are modeled by incorporating internal (or personal) factors only. The displacements $M^t_{topview}$ follows the expression

$$M^t_{topview} = A(\gamma_{topview})M^{t-1}_{topview} + N \tag{5}$$

where $A(.)$ is the rotation matrix, $\gamma_{topview}$ is the rotation angle defined over top-view plan and follows a Gaussian function $g(\gamma_{topview}; \sigma_\gamma)$, and N is a stochastic component. This model proposes an anisotropic propagation of M : the highest probability is obtained by preserving the same direction. The evolution of a sample set is calculated by propagating each sample according to the dynamic model. So, that procedure generates the hypotheses.

4.2 Estimation of Region Size

The size of the search region represents a critical point. In our case, we use the *a-priori* information about the target object (the pedestrian) to solve this tedious problem. We assume an averaged height of people equal to 160 cm, ignoring the error introduced by this approximation. That means, we can estimate the region size s of the hypothetical bounding box containing the region of interest $r = \{l, s, m, \gamma\}$ by projecting the hypothetical positions from top-view plan in Fig. 6.

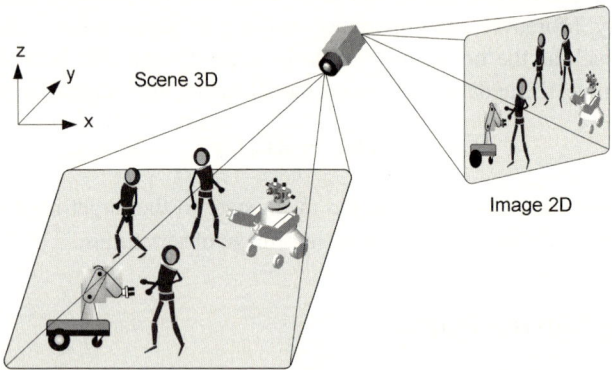

Fig. 6. Approximation of Top-view plan by image plan with a monocular camera

A camera calibration step is necessary to verify the hypotheses by projecting the bounding boxes. So this automatic scale selection is a useful tool to distinguish regions. In this way for each visual tracker we can perform a realistic partitioning (bounding boxes) with consequent reduction in the computational cost. The distortion model of the camera's lenses has not been incorporated in this article. Under this approach, the processing time is dependent on the region size.

4.3 Object Model Update

In multi-motion tracking, the hypotheses are verified at each time step by incorporating the new observations (images). A well known measure of association (strength) of the relationship between two images is the normalized correlation.

$$dc_{i,j} = corr_{nor}(t \arg et_i \; ; \; hypothesis_{i,j}) \qquad (6)$$

where i : target region, and j : an hypothesis of the target region i. The observation of each hypothesis is weighted by a Gaussian function with variance σ.

$$h^{(i;j)} = \frac{1}{\sqrt{2\pi}\sigma_{dc}} e^{\frac{-(1-dc_{i,j})^2}{2\sigma_{dc}^2}} \qquad (7)$$

where $h^{(i;j)}$ is the observation probability of the hypothesis j tracking the target i. The obvious drawback of this technique is the choice of the region size (defined in previous section) that will have a great impact on the results. Larger region sizes are less plagued by noise effects.

5 Experiments

To compare the tracking performance of a mobile robot using the algorithms of the Particle filter and SOM, experiments of capturing a micro mouse with random motion by the mobile robot were performed. As can be recognized from Fig. 7, SOM based

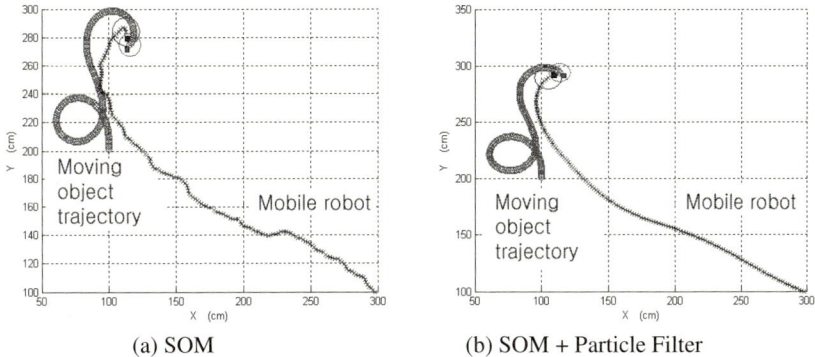

(a) SOM   (b) SOM + Particle Filter

Fig. 7. Tracking trajectory by SOM and SOM based particle filter

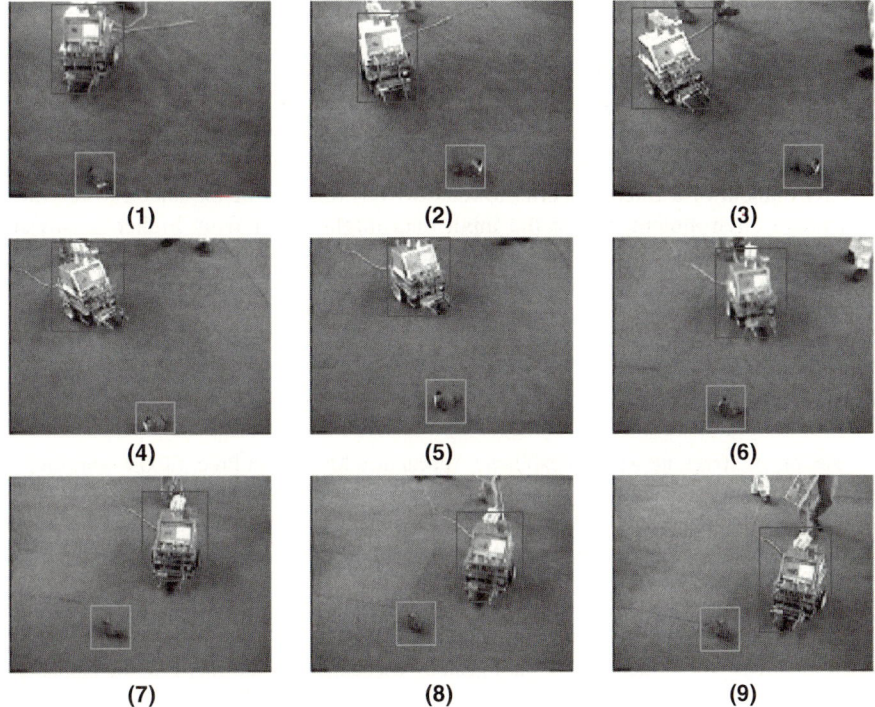

Fig. 8. Experimental results for tracking a moving object

Particle Filter provided better performance to the mobile robot in capturing the random motion object than the other algorithms. As shown in Fig. 7, the mobile robot with SOM based Particle Filter has a smooth curve to capture the moving object. As the result, the capturing time for the moving object is the shortest with SOM based Particle Filter. Finally, as an application experiments were performed to show the tracking and capturing a mobile object in robotic space.

Fig. 8 shows the experimental results for tracking a moving object that is an 8x6[cm] red-colored mouse and has two wheels with random velocities in the range of 25-35[cm/sec]. First, mobile robot detects the moving object using an active camera. When a moving object is detected within view, robot tracks it following the proposed method.

6 Conclusions

In this paper, the proposed tracking method adds an adaptive appearance model based on color distributions to particle filtering. The color-based tracker can efficiently and successfully handle non-rigid and fast moving objects under different appearance changes. Moreover, as multiple hypotheses are processed, objects can be tracked well in cases of occlusion or clutter. This research proposes estimation and tracking scheme for a moving object using images captured by multi cameras. In the scheme, the state estimator has two algorithms: the particle filter that estimates the states for the linear approximated region, and SOM for the nonlinear region. The decision for the switchover is made based on the size of the position estimation error that becomes low enough for the linear region and becomes large enough for the nonlinear region. The effectiveness and superiority of the proposed algorithm was verified through experimental data and comparison. The adaptability of the algorithm was also observed during the experiments. For the sake of simplicity, this research was limited to the environment of a fixed-camera view. However, this can be expanded to the moving camera environment, where the input data might suffer from higher noises and uncertainties. As future research, selection of a precise learning pattern for SOM in order to improve the estimation accuracy and the recognition ratio, and development of an illumination robust image processing algorithm, remain.

References

1. Senior, A.: Tracking with Probabilistic Appearance Models. In Proc. ECCV workshop on Performance Evaluation of Tracking and Surveillance Systems (2002) 48-55.
2. Bierlaire, M., Antonini, G., Weber, M.: Behavioural Dynamics for Pedestrians," in K. Axhausen (Ed.), Moving through nets: the physical and social dimensions of travel, Elsevier (2003) 1-18.
3. Nummiaro, K., Koller-Meier, E., Van Gool, L.J.: Object Tracking with an Adaptive Color-Based Particle Filter. DAGM-Symposium Pattern Recognition (2002) 353-360.
4. P. K. Allen, A. Tmcenko, B. Yoshimi, and P. Michelman, "Trajectory filtering and prediction for automated tracking and grasping of a moving object," *IEEE International Conference on Robotics and Automation* (1992) 1850-1856.

5. Yi Ma, J. Kosecka, and S. S. Sastry, "Vision guided navigation for a nonholonomic mobile robot," *IEEE Transaction on Robotics and Automation*, vol. 15, no. 3, pp. 521-536, 1999.
6. Choo, K., Fleet, D.J.: People tracking using hybrid Monte Carlo filtering. In Proc. Int. Conf. Computer Vision, vol. II (2001) 321-328.
7. Anderson, B., Moore, J.: Optimal Filtering. Prentice-Hall, Englewood Cliffs (1979).
8. Kitagawa, G.: Monte Carlo Filter and Smoother for Non-Gaussian Nonlinear State Space Models. Journal of Computational and Graphical Statistics, Vol. 5 (1996) 1-25.
9. Yi-Yuan Chen and Kuu-young Young, "An intelligent radar predictor for high-speed moving-target tracking," *TENCON '02. Proceedings. IEEE Region 10 Conference on Computers, Communications, Control and Power Engineering*, vol. 3, pp. 1638 -1641, 2002.
10. J. M. Roberts, D. J. Mills, D. Charnley, and C. J. Harris, "Improved Kalman filter initialization using neuro-fuzzy estimation," *Int'l. Conf. on Artificial Neural Networks*, pp. 329-334, 1995.
11. Norlund, P., Eklundh, J.O.: Towards a Seeing Agent. Proc. of First Int. Workshop on Co-operative Distributed Vision (1997) 93-120.
12. Atsushi, N., Hirokazu, K., Shinsaku, H., Seiji, I,: Tracking Multiple People using Distributed Vision Systems. Proc. of the 2002 IEEE Int. Conf. on Robotics & Automation (2002) 2974-2981.
13. Wren, C., Azarbayejani, A., Darrell, T., Pentland, A.: Pfinder: Real-Time Tracking of the Human Body. IEEE Transactions on Pattern Analysis and Machine Intelligence, Vol. 19 (1997) 780-785.
14. Gardner, W.F., Lawton, D.T.: Interactive model based vehicle tracking. IEEE Transaction on Pattern Analysis and Machine Intelligence, Vol.18 (1996) 1115-1121.
15. Swain, M.J., Ballard, D.H.: Color indexing. Int. J. of Computer Vision, Vol.7, No.1, (1991)11-32.

Robust Motion Tracking in Video Sequences Using Particle Filter

Guixi Liu, Chunyu Fan, and Enke Gao

Department of Automation, Xidian University, Xi'an 710071, China
gxliu@xidian.edu.cn, fcy3859@163.com, enkegao@163.com

Abstract. A robust motion tracking algorithm based on color and motion information was presented. Color is an effective feature in visual object tracking because of its robustness against rotation and scale variation. Nevertheless, the color of an object may change with varying illuminations, different image capture devices and different visual positions. Here, the color and motion information were fused in our visual tracking applications. Particle filter was employed as the essential framework because of its capacity of dealing with Non-linear/Non-Gaussian models by randomly sampling in state space. A particle filter can generate several hypotheses simultaneously in state space by randomly sampling and evaluate the states by weighing them respectively. The similarity between prediction data and observation information depends on the integration of Bhattacharyya distance and spacial Euclidean distance. Experimental results show the effectiveness of the proposed approach.

Keywords: motion tracking, particle filter, object detection, color histogram.

1 Introduction

Motion tracking in video sequences has many promising applications in human—computer interface, robot vision, content-based image processing, and so on. Recently, particle filters were often employed in tracking algorithms [1,2,3,4]. N.G. Gordon et al.[1] first introduced bootstrap filter that was an another name of particle filter into bearing-only target tracking. The condensation algorithm [2] proposed by M. Isard and A. Blake first utilized the idea of factored sampling to solve the problem of tracking curves in dense visual clutters. Learned dynamical models and visual observations were used in [2] to propagate the random sample set over time.

Color is an effective feature that can be used in visual object tracking. It is robust against rotation and scale variation. Many color-based tracking algorithm [3,4,5] had been proposed in recent years. D. Comaniciu et al.[3] proposed the mean shift tracker using color distributions of the object. K. Nummiaro et al.[4] incorporated particle filters with color distributions of the object. [5] integrated particle filtering with graphical models and applied it in the color-based tracking.

Z. Pan et al. (Eds.): ICAT 2006, LNCS 4282, pp. 540 – 547, 2006.

But color also has its own limitations in some applications. It may be difficult to distinguish the object from background when they have similar color distributions or the illumination varies. Except color, there are many other kinds of information can be extracted from image sequences. Some of them have been used to calibrate color-based models. For example, the method in [6] integrated color and shape cues in a unique framework.

In this paper, we try to obtain reliable and stable tracking using not only color information but also motion information. We also incorporate multiple cues into particle filter and use resample scheme to deal with degeneracy problem. When occlusion occurs, the particle filter stops updating and the particles are propagated by system model only.

The outline of this paper is as follows. In section II, we describe the idea of particle filters. Section III deals with the utilization of color in object tracking. Section IV discusses the details of our proposed method. Then in next section, we will give some illustration images to testify the effectiveness of our method and make some remarks. In the final section, we will conclude the paper.

2 Particle Filter

Particle filter is a kind of statistical simulation method based on the idea of recursive Bayesian estimation .It uses a set of weighed particles sampled randomly to approximate the posterior possibility density function (pdf) [1,2,4,5]. The problem of tracking can be regarded as the estimation of a state vector which characterizes the object in a state space.

Assume x_k denotes the state of object at time k, and z_k denotes the features in the image at time k. x_k is supposed to evolve according to the system model as follows.

$$x_k = f_k(x_{k-1}, v_{k-1}) \ . \tag{1}$$

where $f_k : R^n \times R^p \Rightarrow R^n$ is the system transition function and $v_k \in R^m$ is a kind of system noise. At discrete times, observation z_k can be obtained from the measurement equation.

$$z_k = h_k(x_k, w_k) \ . \tag{2}$$

where $h_k : R^n \times R^r \Rightarrow R^m$ is the measurement function and w_k is measurement noise.

We make two reasonable assumptions that $\{x_t, t \in N\}$ is a Markov process and all the observations are independent from each other. Our aim is to estimate the posterior pdf $p(x_k \mid z_{1:k})$ with $p(x_k \mid x_{k-1})$ and $p(z_{1:k})$. Suppose that the pdf $p(x_{k-1} \mid z_{1:k-1})$ is available at time k-1 and the initial pdf $p(x_1)$ is known. The pdf $p(x_k \mid z_{1:k})$ at time k can be obtained recursively in two steps: prediction and update.

1) Prediction

$$p(x_k \mid z_{1:k-1}) = \int p(x_k \mid x_{k-1})p(x_{k-1} \mid z_{1:k-1})dx_{k-1} \ . \tag{3}$$

$p(x_k \mid x_{k-1})$ can be obtained from the system transition function (eq.1).

2) Update

$$p(x_k \mid z_{1:k}) = \frac{p(z_k \mid x_k)p(x_k \mid z_{1:k-1})}{p(z_k \mid z_{1:k-1})} \ . \tag{4}$$

where $p(z_k \mid z_{1:k-1})$ is given by

$$p(z_k \mid z_{1:k-1}) = \int p(z_k \mid x_k)p(x_k \mid z_{1:k-1})dx_k \ . \tag{5}$$

The process is shown in Fig.1 below

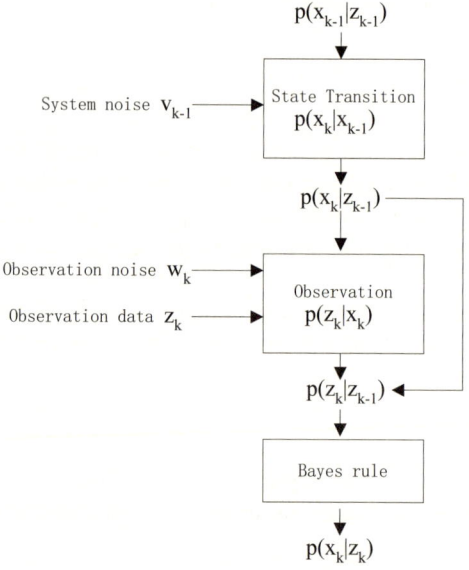

Fig. 1. The main flow of Particle filter

The introduction of particle filter provides a method to implement recursive Bayesian estimation with more general models.

3 Color-Based Tracking

A lot of color-based tracking algorithms have been proposed in recent literatures [3,4,5]. We referred to the color distributions proposed in [4] which focused on color histogram.

It is supposed that the pixels near the center of tracking region should be given larger weighs than those far away from the center. So a color histogram $p(y) = \{p(y)^{(u)}\}_{u=1,...m}$ of a region R at the location y can be calculated as

$$p(y)^{(u)} = k \sum_{x_i \in R} g(\frac{\|y - x_i\|}{a})\delta(h(x_i) - u) . \tag{6}$$

where k is a normalizing parameter, a is a scaling factor, δ is the Kronecker delta function, $h(x_i)$ represents a given color of m bins color histogram at position x_i and $g(\cdot)$ is a weighing function given as

$$g(r) = \begin{cases} 1 - r^2 & ; \quad r < 1 \\ 0 & ; \quad otherwise \end{cases} . \tag{7}$$

To measure the similarity between two color histograms, the Bhattacharyya distance is employed. Assuming that the two color histograms are represented by $p = \{p^{(u)}\}_{u=1,...m}$ and $q = \{q^{(u)}\}_{u=1,...m}$ respectively. The Bhattacharyya distance is calculated by

$$d = \sqrt{1 - \rho(p,q)} . \tag{8}$$

where the Bhattacharyya coefficient is defined as

$$\rho(p,q) = \sum_{u=1}^{m} \sqrt{p(u)q(u)} . \tag{9}$$

So the Bhattacharyya distance is inversely proportional to the Bhattacharyya coefficient.

For the sake of efficient computation, the color histograms here are not calculated in the RGB space which uses $8 \times 8 \times 8$ bins. We convert RGB space to HIS space in which hue and saturation are taken into account because they are independent of illumination. Here an example is given in Fig. 2 about color histogram. The object is located by a red rectangle in the left figure and its color histogram is shown in the right figure.

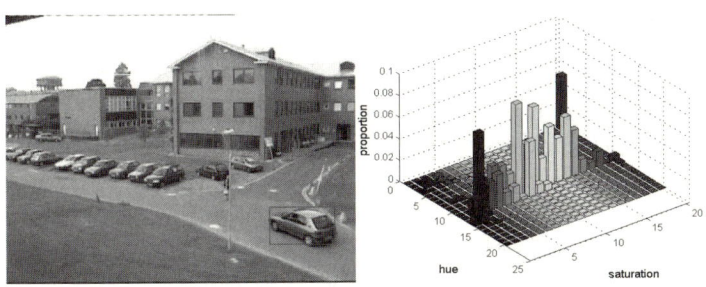

Fig. 2. An example of color histogram

4 Tracking with Multiple Cues

In this section, we will give the details of our proposed tracking algorithm. Before applying particle filter to the tracked video, we should establish a mathematical model for the object. In this model, some essential parameters should be included so that the object we are interested in can be represented by this model. In our experiments, the object is located by a rectangle, so the center coordinates of the rectangle must be involved in the model. To model the dynamic of the object sufficiently and effectively, the velocity of the object is also employed here. So the system model can be defined as follows

$$x_k = Ax_{k-1} + v_{k-1} . \tag{10}$$

where $x_k = \{x, y, \dot{x}, \dot{y}\}$, A is a system matrix used to define the deterministic system model and v_{k-1} is a noise vector. Hence we can propagate particles by this system model.

To verify the multiple hypotheses generated by system models, all the particles will be weighed by observation. We use the formula below to determine the weights..

$$\pi^{(n)} = \frac{1}{\sqrt{2\pi}\sigma} e^{-\frac{\alpha d_1^2 + \beta d_2^2}{2\sigma^2}} . \tag{11}$$

where σ is the variance of a Gaussian distribution. d_1 is the Euclidean distance between observation position and sample position and d_2 is the Bhattacharyya distance between the two histograms. α, β are coefficients used to change the weighs of these two distances.

Our proposed algorithm works as follows

1) Initialize the system model by locating the object in the first two frames, then calculate the coordinates and the velocities of the object in the two axes respectively. Finally, initialize the covariance of the system noise.
2) Draw a sample set $S = \{s^{(n)}, \pi^{(n)} \mid n = 1, ..., N\}$ randomly in the state space. In our algorithm, there are 100 particles. If the number of particles increases, the computational cost will rise sharply. So particle filter is the suboptimal filter because of the limitation of computation cost.
3) Propagate the particles according to the system model we defined using eq.10.
4) Weighing these particles using observation data. In our algorithm, we incorporate color information with motion information. The weights can be calculated by eq.11.
5) Degeneracy is a general problem in particle filter which wastes computation by propagating the useless particles. To cope with it, resample is proposed.

   Suppose μ is a random number over [0,1]. The sample $s^{(i)}$ corresponding to

$$\sum_{j=0}^{i-1} \pi^{(j)} < \mu < \sum_{j=0}^{i} \pi^{(j)} . \tag{12}$$

where $\pi^{(0)} = 0$ is selected as an effective sample. The samples whose weights are too small are discarded. This procedure is repeated for $i = 1,...,N$.

6) Estimate the state vector using the expectation of the sample set as follows

$$\hat{x}_k = E[S] .\tag{13}$$

7) Then it goes to step (3), so the state vector can be estimated iteratively over time.

5 Experimental Results

We made some experiments to confirm effectiveness of our proposed approach (Fig.3 ~ Fig.5). The test videos belong to Performance Evaluation of Tracking and Surveillance 2001 (PETS 2001) database [7].

We tried to track a moving vehicle in dense background clutters. First, the tracking result using our proposed method was shown. Then the approach with color only tracking algorithm was also given below. Finally, an application of our approach in poor illumination conditions is presented in Fig.5.

In Fig.3, the object was a car and the background settings were buildings, grass field, road and some other cars. In some frames, there were a few walking persons who can be

(a) the 550th frame   (b) the 650th frame   (c) the 770th frame

Fig. 3. Test on video 1

(a) the 600th frame   (b) the 640th frame   (c) the 670th frame

Fig. 4. Test on video 1 with color only

regarded as observation noise. Comparing with the 550th frame, the car in the 650th frame changed its pose and its color was also darker than before. In the 770th frame, a white truck occluded the object partially but the tracking program was not distracted. It could be inferred from the figures that with the integration of color and motion information, our tracking approach can resist background clutters effectively.

We made another test on the same video in order to show the importance of the integration of multiple cues. We used color histogram only to weigh the particles in this example. Fig.4 had illustrated the results. As the state vector was estimated iteratively over time, the tracking rectangle gradually drifted. The reason was that color feature can be influenced by illumination, dense background noise and so on. The other information extracted from images could help to calibrate the ambiguity in color distribution. So the proper fusion of multiple cues can give better performance.

(a) the 595th frame   (b) the 620th frame   (c) the 670th frame

Fig. 5. Test on video 2

In Fig.5, the example was tested on a video whose illumination was poor. Under the poor illumination condition, object detection and object tracking were difficult. The integration of all kinds of information (color, shape, motion, corners and so on) may give a better performance. Here we used color and motion information. In the 575th frame, a car was located by a red rectangle and there was a man near the car. Our algorithm still distinguished the car from the walking man who can be regarded as a dense background noise. In the 670th frame, the color of the object was nearly the same as the car beside it because of poor illumination. But the tracker did not miss the object. This was another proof to the effectiveness of our algorithm.

6   Conclusions

We have presented an effective and robust approach to implement visual object tracking. A particle filter, with resample scheme, has been used to estimate the motion parameters. The proposed tracking approach incorporates color distribution with motion information to verify the multiple hypotheses generated by particle filter. Our multiple cues tracker can effectively handle the varying illumination, dense background clutters and partial occlusion. It has been achieved to make reliable and stable visual tracking using not only color information but also motion information.

Our further research will focus on establishing better system and observation models and exploring better proposal distribution for particle filter. Multiple-sensor and information fusion is another region we are interested in.

Reference

1. N.J. Gordon, D.J. Salmond and A.F.M. Smith, Novel approach to nonlinear/non-Gaussian Bayesian state estimation, IEE Proc. Radar and Signal Processing, vol. 140, no. 2, pp. 107-113, April 1993.
2. M. Isard, and A. Blake, Condensation-conditional density propagation for visual tracking, International Journal of Computer Vision, vol. 29, no.1, pp. 5-28,1998
3. D. Comaniciu, V. Ramesh, and P. Meer, Real-time tracking of non-rigid objects using mean shift, in CVPR'00, pp.142-149.
4. K. Nummiaro, E. Koller-Meier and L. Van Gool, An Adaptive Color-Based Particle Filter, Journal of Image and Vision Computing, vol. 21, no. 1, pp.99-110, 2003.
5. P. Perez, C. Hue, J. Vermaak and M. Gangnet, Color-Based Probabilistic Tracking, ECCV, pp.661-675, 2002.
6. Y. Wu and T.S. Huang, A co-inference approach to robust visual tracking, Proc. Int'l Conf. Computer Vision and Pattern Recognition, vol. 2, pp.26-33, 2001.
7. http://www.research.ibm.com/peoplevision/performanceevaluation.html.

Fast Motion Estimation Using Spatio-temporal Correlations

Hyo Sun Yoon, Jae Myeong Yoo, Toan Nguyen Dinh, Hwa Jeong Son,
Mi Seon Park, and Guee Sang Lee*

Department of Computer Science, Chonnam National University,
300 Youngbong-dong, Buk-gu, Kwangju 500-757, Korea
estheryoon@hotmail.com,jmyoo@oracle.chonnam.ac.kr, toanhoian@gmail.com,
sonhj@iip.chonnam.ac.kr, sunnydix@hotmail.com,
gslee@chonnam.chonnam.ac.kr

Abstract. Motion Estimation (ME) is an important part of video encoding systems, since it can significantly affect the output quality of an
encoded sequences. However, ME requires a significant part of the encoding time, because ME is a combination of techniques such as motion
starting point, motion search pattern, etc. For this reason, low complexity motion estimation algorithms are viable solutions. In this paper,
we propose a motion estimation algorithm to find the most accurate
motion vectors(MVs) with the aim to maximize the encoding speed as
well as the image quality. The proposed algorithm takes advantage of
spatio-temporal correlations to decide the search pattern and the search
start point adaptively and to avoid unnecessary motion vector search.
Experiments show that the speedup improvement of the proposed algorithm over Motion Vector Field Adaptive Search Technique (MVFAST)
and Predictive Motion Vector Fiekd Adaptive Search Technique (PMV-
FAST) can be up to $1.5 \sim 8$ times faster while maintaining very similar
image quality.

Keywords: Motion Estimation, Saptial Correlation, Temporal
Correlation.

1 Introduction

Recently, great interest has been devoted to the study of different approaches in
video compressions. The high correlation between successive frames of a video
sequence makes it possible to achieve high coding efficiency by reducing the temporal redundancy. ME and motion compensation techniques are an important
part of most video encoding, since it could significantly affect the compression
ratio and the output quality.

The most popular motion estimation and motion compensation method has
been the block-based motion estimation, which uses a block matching algorithm
(BMA) to find the best matched block from a reference frame. ME based on

---

* Corresponding author.

Z. Pan et al. (Eds.): ICAT 2006, LNCS 4282, pp. 548–556, 2006.

the block matching are adopted in many existing video coding standards such as H.261/H.263 and MPEG-1/2/4. If the performance in terms of prediction error is the only criterion for BMA, full search block matching algorithm (FS) is the simplest BMA, guaranteeing an exact result. FS can achieve optimal performance by examining all possible points in search area of the reference frame. However, FS is very computationally intensive and it can hardly be applied to any real time applications. Hence, it is inevitable to develop fast motion estimation algorithms for real time video coding applications. Many low complexity motion estimation algorithms such as Diamond Search (DS) [1, 2], Three Step Search (TSS)[3], New Three Step Search (NTSS)[4], Four Step Search (FSS)[5], Two Step Search (2SS)[6], Two-dimensional logarithmic search algorithm [7], HEXagon-Based Serch (HEXBS) [8] and MVFAST and PMVFAST [9–13] based on temporal or spatial correlations of motion vectors have been proposed. Most fast block matching algorithms (FBMAs) that use the fixed search pattern and the fixed search start point need high complexity to find a good motion vector (MV). On the other hand, MV prediction (MVP) algorithms such as MVFAST and PMFAST decide the search pattern and the search start point adaptivly by using MVs in temporal or spatial domain. These algorithms shows significant performance improvements.

To accelerate motion vector search, the proposed altorithm takes advantage of the correlations between MVs in both spatial and temporal domains, avoids motion vector search in the Macro Block (MB) when all MVs in spatial and temporal domains are equal and uses the search pattens and the search start point adaptively.

In this paper, three MVs of the above, above-right, left MBs in the current frame (t frame), ,the median motion vector of MVs of these three spatial MBs in the current frame and two temporal MVs of the block with the same coordinate in t-1, t-2 reference frames are used as predictors to avoid the unnessary motion vector search and to decide the search start point and and the search pattern adaptively. The speedup improvement of the proposed algorithm over MVFAST and PMVFAST can be up to 1.5 ∼ 7 times faster while yielding similar image quality.

This paper is organized as follows. Section 2 describes the existing motion estimation algorithms. The proposed algorithm is described in Section 3. Section 4 reports the simulation results and conclusions are given in Section 5.

2   Motion Estimation Algorithms

There are many search algorithms for motion estimation. The full search (FS), the simplest algorithm, examines every point in the search area in the reference frame to find the best match. Clearly, it is optimal in terms of finding the best motion vector, but it is computationally very expense. Hence, several sub-optimal search algorithms such as DS [1,2], TSS [3], NTSS [4], FSS [5], 2SS [6], Two-dimensional logarithmic search algorithm [7], HEXagon-Based Serch (HEXBS) [8], Motion Vector Field Adaptive Search Technique (MVFAST) [11] and Predictive Motion Vector Field Adaptive Search Technique (PMVFAST)

[13] have been developed. The TSS is a coarse-to-fine search algorithm. The starting step size for search is large and the center of the search is moved in the direction of the best match at the stage, and the step size is reduced by half. In contrast, FSS starts with a fine step size (usually 2) and the center of the search is moved in the direction of the best match without changing the step size, until the best match at that stage is the center itself. The step size is then halved to 1 to find the best match. In other words, in FSS the search process is performed mostly around the original search point (0,0), or it is more center-biased. Based on the characteristics of a center-biased motion vector distribution, NTSS enhanced TSS by using additional search points, which are around the search origin (0,0) of the first step of TSS. The DS is also a center-biased algorithm by exploiting the shape of the motion vector distribution. DS shows the best performance compared to these methods in terms of both average number of search points per motion vector and the PSNR (peak signal to noise ratio) of the predicted image. The DS method uses two diamond search patterns, depicted in Fig. 1. the large diamond search pattern (LDSP) is used for the coarse search. When the centered search position of LDSP show the minimum block distortion, the small diamond search pattern (SDSP) is chosen for the fine search. MVFAST [11] uses spatial correlations of MVs to get the search center and to decide the search pattern between LDSP and SDSP. A derivative of MVFAST, called PMVFAST by exploiting spatio-temporal correlations uses a set of thresholds to increase the speed of motion vector at the cost of additional algorithmic complexity. MVFAST and PMVFST among these FBMAs show significant performance improvements.

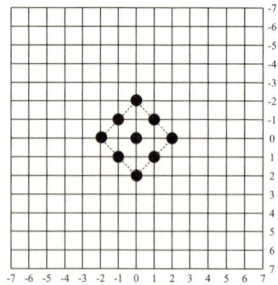

(a) Large Diamond Search Pattern (LDSP)

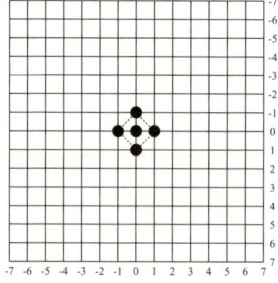

(b) Small Diamond Search Pattern (SDSP)

Fig. 1. Diamond Search Algorithm(DS)

3   The Proposed Algorithm

Since the time interval between successive frames is very short, there are high temporal correlations between successive frames of a video sequence. In other words, the motion of current block is very similar to that of the same coordinate block in the reference frame. And also there are high spatial correlations among the blocks in the same frame. That is to say, the motion of current block is very similar to those of the neighboring blocks in the current frame. Therefore, the proposed algorithm uses the information of spatially and temporally correlated motion vectors to skip unnecessary motion vector search and to decide the search start point and the search pattern.

In this paper, we denote Predictor Lists (PL). PL contains MVs of above, above-right, left MBs in the current frame (t frame), the median motion vector MV_median of these three MVs and the MVs of the same coordinate block in the t-1, t-2 reference frames. The proposed method exploiting MVs in PL depicted in Fig. 2, selects one of two search patterns as illustrated in Fig. 3(a) and Fig. 4(a) adaptively and the search start point and skips unnecessary motion vector search.

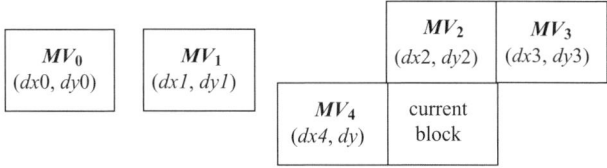

MV_0 : the MV of the same coordinate block in the reference frame (t-2 frame)
MV_1 : the MV of the same coordinate block in the reference frame (t-1 frame)
MV_2 : the MV of above block in the current frame (t frame)
MV_3 : the MV of above-right block
MV_4 : the MV of left block

Fig. 2. Blocks for Spatio-Temporal Correlation Information

$$Px = \lfloor dx1 \times \alpha + median(dx2, dx3, dx4) \times \beta \rfloor \qquad (1)$$

$$Py = \lfloor dy1 \times \alpha + median(dy2, dy3, dy4) \times \beta \rfloor \qquad (2)$$

At first, if all $MV0$, $MV1$, $MV2$, $MV3$, $MV4$ are equal, $MV0$ is selected as the final MV of the current MB and the motion vector search is skipped. Otherwise, if all $MV2$, $MV3$, $MV4$ are equal or one of $MV2$, $MV3$, $MV4$ is unequal to the others or $MV0$ is equal to $MV1$, Mean Square Error (MSE)s of MV_median, $MV0$ are calculated. The MV of the minimum MSE is selected as the predicted MV (Px, Py). Otherwise, (Px, Py) obtained from Eq.(1–2) is used as the the predicted MV (Px, Py). (Px, Py) is the weighted sum of the temporal information and the spatial information.

In this paper, we experimented with $\alpha = 0.5$ and $\beta = 0.5$. If $|Px| < 2$ and $|Py| < 2$, small diamond search pattern (SDSP)[14] as shown in Fig. 3 is selected. In Fig. 3(a), white circles are the initial search points and in Fig. 3(b), black circles are search points added in the second step. Note that the center of black circles is the position which showed the minimum block distortion in the first step. Otherwise, modified diamond search pattern (MDSP) [12], illustrated in Fig. 4 is selected for motion estimation. Based on the fact that about 50%(in large motion case) $\sim$ 98 %(in small motion case) of motion vectors are enclosed in a circular support, as shown in Fig. 4(a), with a radius of 2 pixels around the search origin (0,0)[1,2], the circular support around the search origin becomes the initial search points in MDSP as shown in Fig. 4(a). If one of ⊕ points in Fig. 4(b) shows the minimum block distortion among the search points in the first step of Fig. 4(a), the search procedure terminates. Otherwise, the new search points are set as shown in Fig. 4(c) or Fig. 4(d). If one of ⊕ points in Fig. 4(b) shows the minimum block distortion among the search points in the first step of Fig. 4(a), the search procedure terminates. Otherwise, the new search points are set as shown in Fig. 4(c) or Fig. 4(d).

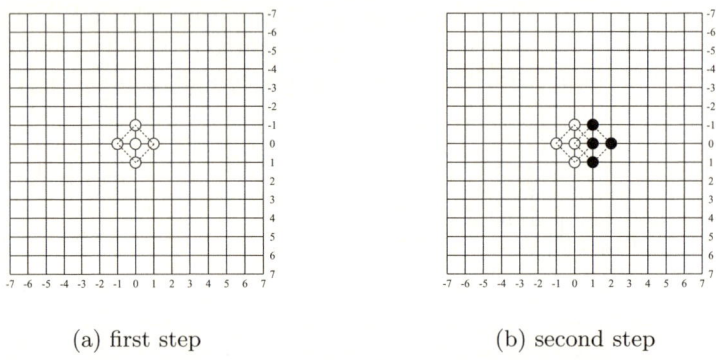

(a) first step   (b) second step

Fig. 3. Small Diamond Search Algorithm(SDSP)

The block diagram of the proposed algorithm appears in Fig. 5. According to the spatio-temporal correlations, the proposed algorithm selects the search start point and the search pattern between SDSP and MDSP adaptively. If $|Px| < 2$ and $|Py| < 2$, SDSP is selected as a search pattern. Otherwise, MDSP is chosen. The proposed method is summarized as follows

Step 1. If all *MV0, MV1, MV2, MV3, MV3* are equal, *MV0* is selected as the final MV of the current MB and the motion vector search is terminated. Otherwise, go to Step 2.

Step 2. If all *MV2, MV3, MV4* are equal or one of *MV2, MV3, MV4* is unequal to the others or *MV0* is equal to *MV1*, MSEs of *MV_median, MV0* are calculated. The MV of the minimum MSE is selected as the predicted MV (Px, Py). Otherwise, (Px, Py) obtained from Eq. (1–2) is used as the the predicted MV (Px, Py) .

Step 3. If $| Px | < 2$ and $| Py | < 2$, go to Step 4; Otherwise, go to Step 5.

Step 4.   I. The search origin in search area is moved to the displacement of (Px,Py). Let's call the moved search origin the search start point.

II. SDSP is disposed at (Px,Py), and the 5 checking points of SDSP as seen in Fig. 3(a) are tested. If the minimum MSE point is located at the center position of SDSP, then it is the final solution of the motion vector. Otherwise go to III.

III. If the minimum MSE pointis not located at the center position of SDSP, three additional checking points as shown in Fig. 3(b) are used. The minimum MSE point founded in the previous search step is repositioned

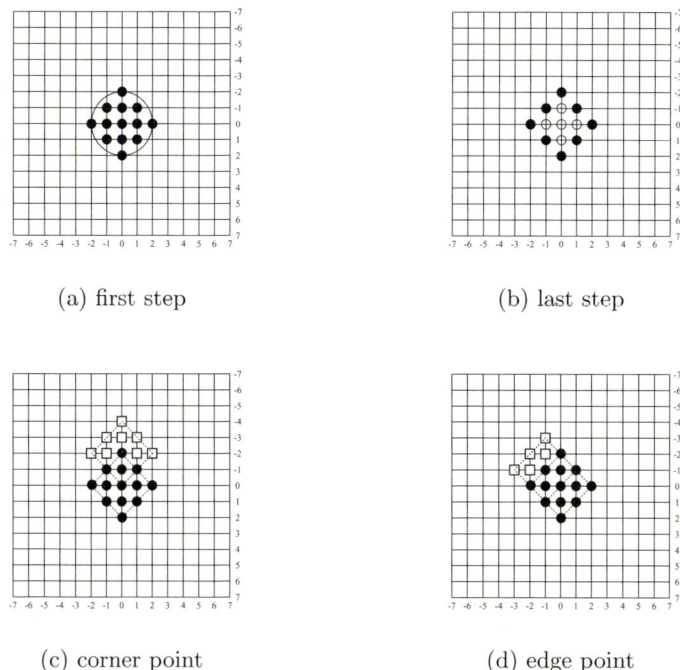

(a) first step   (b) last step

(c) corner point   (d) edge point

Fig. 4. Modify Diamond Search Algorithm(MDSP)

as the center point to form a new SDSP. If the new minimum MSE point
is located at the center position, then it is the final solution of the motion
vector. Otherwise, recursively repeated this step

Step 5.   I. The search origin is moved to the displacement of (Px,Py).

   II. MDSP is disposed at (Px,Py), and the 13 checking points of MDSP as
seen in Fig. 4(a) are tested. If the minimum MSE point is located at the
center position of MDSP or one of $\oplus$ points in Fig. 4 (b), then it is the
final solution of the motion vector. Otherwise go to III.

  III. If the minimum MSE point is located at the corner of MDSP, eight
additional checking points as shown in Fig. 4(c) are used. If the minimum
MSE point is located at the edge of MDSP, five additional checking points
as shown in Fig. 4(d) are used. And then the minimum MSE point found
in the previous search step is repositioned as the center to from a new
MDSP. If the the minimum MSE point is located at the center position
of MDSP or one of $\oplus$ points in Fig. 4(b), then it is the final solution of
the motion vector. Otherwise, recursively repeated this step.

4   Simulation Result

In this section, we show the experiment results for the proposed algorithm.
We compared FS, NTSS, FSS, DS ,HEXBS, MVFAST and PMVFAST to the

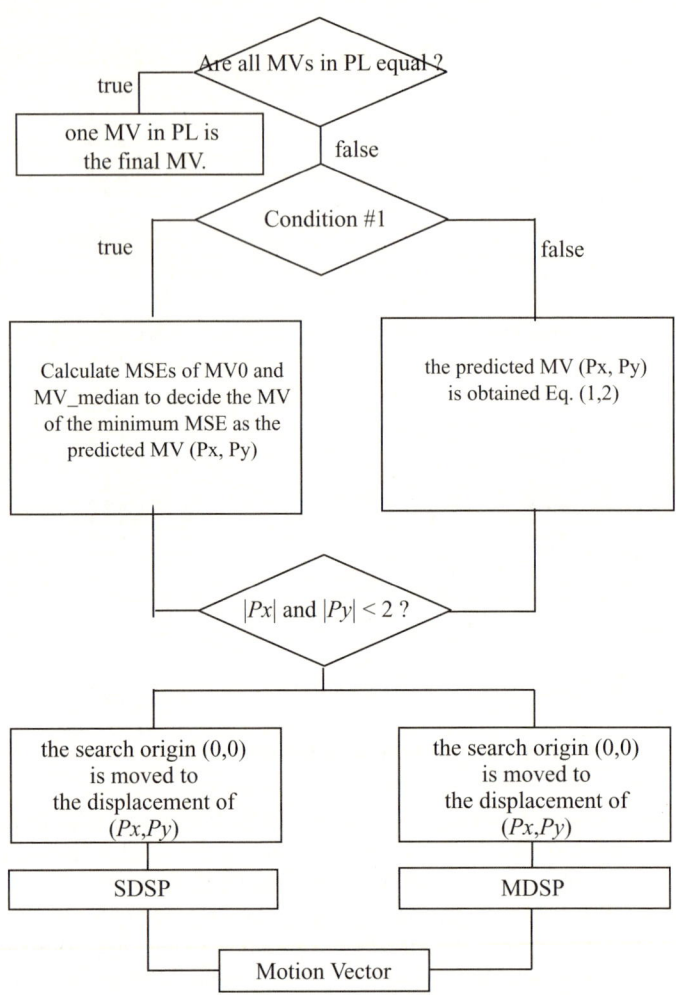

Condiction1: ((MV0 == MV1) || (MV2, MV3, MV4 are equal) ||
          only one MV of MV2, MV3, MV4 is unequal to the others))

Fig. 5. The block diagram of the proposed algorithm

proposed method in both of image quality and search speed. Six QCIF test sequences are used for the experiment: Akiyo, Carphone, Foreman, Mother and
Daughter, Stefan and Table. The mean square error (MSE) distortion function is used as the block distortion measure (BDM). The quality of the predicted image is measured by the peak signal to noise ratio (PSNR), which is
defined by

$$MSE = \left(\frac{1}{MN}\right) \sum_{m=1}^{M} \sum_{n=1}^{N} [x(m,n) - \hat{x}(m,n)]^2 \qquad (3)$$

$$PSNR = 10 \ log_{10} \frac{255^2}{MSE} \qquad (4)$$

In Eq. (3), $x(m,n)$ denotes the original image and $\hat{x}(m,n)$ denotes the motion compensated prediction image. From Table 1 and 2, we can see that proposed method is better than PMVFAST and MVFAST in terms of the computational complexity (as measured by the average number of search points per motion vector) is similar to image quality. In terms of PSNR, the proposed method is similar to MVFAST as well as PMVFST. In stationary sequences such as Akiyo, Mother and Daughter, the proposed algorithm is a little worse than MVFAST and PMVFST. But The speedup improvement of the proposed method over MV-FAST and PMVFAST can be up to 7 times faster. In motioned sequences such as Stefan, Carphone, Table and Foreman, the proposed algorithm is a little better than MVFAST and PMVFAST in Table 1. The speedup improvement of the proposed method over MVFAST and PMVFAST can be up to $1.5 \sim 2$ times faster.

5   Conclusion

Based on the spatio-temporal correlations in the reference and the current frame, a fast motion estimation algorithm is proposed in this paper. The proposed

Table 1. Average PSNR of the test image sequence

	FS	NTSS	FSS	DS	HEXBS	MVFAST	PMVFAST	Proposed
Stefan	23.88	22.24	22.62	22.77	22.59	23.36	23.45	23.63
Foreman	29.54	28.19	28.22	28.66	28.01	29.00	29.00	29.02
Akiyo	34.50	34.48	34.33	34.39	34.30	34.39	34.49	34.31
Table	26.50	26.5	24.81	25.67	24.90	25.49	25.63	25.60
Carphone	30.88	30.14	30.15	30.48	30.07	30.68	30.70	30.65
M&D	31.52	31.37	31.34	31.42	31.37	31.47	31.47	31.11

Table 2. Average number of search points per motion vector estimation

	FS	NTSS	FSS	DS	HEXBS	MVFAST	PMVFAST	Proposed
Stefan	961	20.0	18.9	16.2	12.9	10.8	8.9	4.69
Foreman	961	19.3	18.6	15.4	11.9	8.9	7.8	4.53
Akiyo	961	17.0	17.0	13.0	11.0	5.05	2.9	0.76
Table	961	19.7	18.7	15.5	12.5	10.4	8.5	5.41
Carphone	961	18.6	17.8	14.4	11.7	8.4	7.7	4.61
M&D	961	17.3	17.1	13.2	11.1	5.6	4.7	0.88

method decides the search pattern and the search start and avoids the unnecessary motion vector search based on the spatial-temporal correlations. Experiments show that the speedup improvement of the proposed algorithm over MV-FAST and PMVFAST can be up to 1.5 ~ 7 times faster. And the image quality is similar. The proposed algorithm reduces the computational complexity significantly compared with previously developed fast BMAs, while maintaining similar image quality.

References

1. Tham, J.Y., Ranganath, S., Kassim, A.A.: A Novel Unrestricted Center-Biased Diamond Search Algorithm for Block Motion Estimation. IEEE Transactions on Circuits and Systems for Video Technology. **8(4)** (1998) 369–375
2. Shan, Z., Kai-kuang, M.: A New Diamond Search Algorithm for Fast block Matching Motion Estimation. IEEE Transactions on Image Processing. **9(2)** (2000) 287–290
3. Koga, T., Iinuma, K., Hirano, Y., Iijim, Y., Ishiguro, T.: Motion compensated interframe coding for video conference. In Proc. NTC81. (1981) C9.6.1–9.6.5
4. Renxiang, L., Bing, Z., Liou, M.L.: A New Three Step Search Algorithm for Block Motion Estimation. IEEE Transactions on Circuits and Systems for Video Technology. **4(4)** (1994) 438–442
5. Lai-Man, P., Wing-Chung, M.: A Novel Four-Step Search Algorithm for Fast Block Motion Estimation. IEEE Transactions on Circuits and Systems for Video Technology. **6(3)** (1996) 313–317
6. Yuk-Ying, C., Neil, W.B.: Fast search block-matching motion estimation algorithm using FPGA. Visual Communication and Image Processing 2000. Proc. SPIE. **4067** (2000) 913–922
7. Jain, J., Jain, A.: Dispalcement measurement and its application in interframe image coding. IEEE Transactions on Communications. **COM-29** (1981) 1799–1808
8. Zhu, C., Lin, X., Chau, L.P.: Hexagon based Search Pattern for Fast Block Motion Estimation. IEEE Transactions on Circuits and Systems for Video Technology. **12(5)** (2002) 349–355
9. Deepak, S.T., Tsuhan, C.: Estimation and Mode Decision for Spatialy Correlated Motion Sequences. IEEE Transactions on Circuits and Systems for Video Technology. **11(10)** (2002) 1098–1107
10. Xu, J.B., Po, L.M., Cheung, C.K.: Adaptive Motion Tracking Block Matching for Video Coding. IEEE Transactions on Circuits and Systems for Video Technology. **9(7)** (1999) 1025–1029
11. Ma, K.K., Hosur, P.I.: Report on Performance of Fast Motion using Motion Vector Field Adaptive Search Technique. ISO/IEC/JTC1/SC29/WG11.**M5453** (1999)
12. Yoon, H.S., Lee. G.S.: Motion Estimation based on Temporal Correlations. EurAisa-ICT. LNCS.**2510** (2002) 75–83
13. Tourapis, A.M., Liou. M.L.: Predictive Motion Vector Field Adaptive Search Technique (PMVFAST) SPIE. LNCS.**4310** (2001) 883–891
14. Guy. C. , Michael. G. , Faouzi. K.: Efficient Motion Vector Estimation and Coding for H.263-based very low bit rate video compression. ITU-T SG 16, Q15-A-45. (1997) 18
15. Nam, J.Y., Lee, M.H.: New Block Matching Algorithm for motion estimation based on predicted direction information. Visual Communication and Image Processing 2000. Proc. SPIE. **4067** (2000) 1212–1220

Bi-directional Passenger Counting on Crowded Situation Based on Sequence Color Images*

Ning Liu[1] and Chengying Gao[2, **]

[1] Software School, Sun Yat-sen University Guangzhou,510275, China
[2] Computer Application Institute, Sun Yat-sen University. GuangZhou, 510275, China
{liuning2, mcsgcy}@mail.sysu.edu.cn

Abstract. This paper presents a new method of counting the bi-directional passing people on crowded situations. It deals with an application of image sequence analysis. In particular, it addresses the problem of determining the number of people who get into and out of a surveillance zone when it's crowded, and background and/or illumination changes. The proposed method analyzes image sequences and processes them using an algorithm based on the use of least squares and hausdorff distance. The method's accurate degree will not be influenced by light, sunlight and shade of the passing people. Experimental results show that the new method is robust and more efficient than classic ones.

Keywords: Computer vision, frame differencing method, hausdorff distance, real-time.

1 Introduction

Real-time people flows information is very useful source for security application as well as people management such as pedestrian traffic management, tourist flows estimation. To track and count moving people is considered important in several application areas where the activity of people needs to be analyzed or monitored. Therefore it is necessary to develop the automatic method of counting the passing people. Several attempts have been made to count and track pedestrians in recent years. The early automatic counting approaches, such as turn stiles, rotary bar, and light beams, had suffered one difficulty: they could not count the passing people accurately unless there is only one pedestrian through the gate at one time. To solve this problem, some image-processing based approaches are hence motivated. Tomonoti Yamada et. al. [I] presents an automatic counting method for passing people by analyzing a series of image captured with a video camera, but the method

* Project supported by the Guangdong Province Science Foundation:04300461 and the Scientific Research Start-Up Foundation for Youthful Teachers, College of Information Science & Technology,Sun Yat-Sen University.
** Corresponding author.

Z. Pan et al. (Eds.): ICAT 2006, LNCS 4282, pp. 557–564, 2006.

fails for crowds because one person is hard to be extracted from image data. To increase the count of passing people through a gate at one time, Terada and Yamaguchi [2] utilize a color camera to detect the quantity of pedestrians, but the problem about direction-orienting of passing people is intractable. Later, Kenji Terada et. al. [3] use the stereo images captured by a pair of cameras to cope with both the counting problem of crowds and direction recognition of the passing people. Also, the overlapping problem can be reduced significantly , however, it can't deal with another overlapping problem resulted from the case that a crowd of people walks closely each other. Bartolini et. al. [4] discusses the problem of counting people getting in and out of a bus by image-sequence processing.

These proposed methods use image segmentation could not count the passing people accurately unless there are very few passing people through the surveillance zone at one time. Moreover, they assume that the pedestrian is moving relative to a static background. But some applications being focused on dynamic backgrounds. In this paper, we propose a real-time people counting system with a bi-directional under congestion on dynamic backgrounds. We developed the counting method by using the hausdorff distance [5] and surveillance zone constraint conditions. The moving direction of the pedestrian can be determined by tracking each people pattern through analyzing the HSI histogram. [6-11]

2 The Model of Tracking and Counting System

A scene of the passing people through the gate of the bus is shown in Fig.1-a. There are a lot of the inbound people and the outbound people. In order to avoid overlapping each other, the camera is set on the ceiling of the surveillance zone so that the moving people could be observed from just overhead and the images are obtained in series. Fig1-b indicates the surveillance zone.

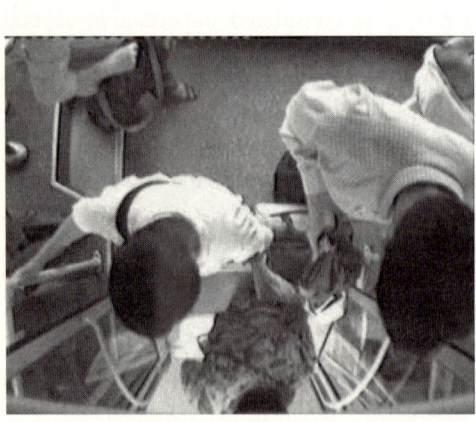

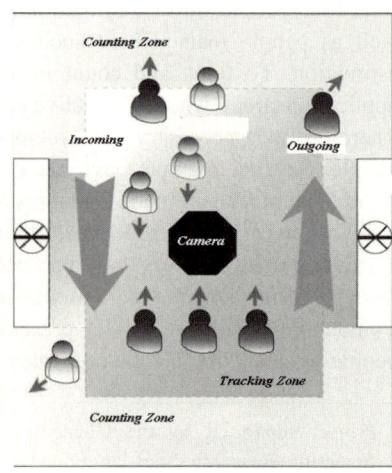

Fig. 1-a Surveillance Zone   **Fig. 1-b** Sketch Map

- **the characteristic of surveillance zone model**
  a) The background is dynamic.
  b) Light, sunlight and shade of the moving people work on rays, so rays vary greatly.
  c) There are many moving objects at one time
- **the characteristic of moving people**
  a) Direction of moving people are two directions (inbound and outbound), the direction changes little.
  b) The density of passing people in Surveillance area often varies, people are not overlapped each other in general. People will overlap under high density which is called congestion.

Moving objects detecting and processing has been described in detail in the other paper. This paper mainly deals with congestion when the monitor with high density. Following we describe the method of counting moving people under congestion based on hausdorff distance.

3   The Prediction Model of Moving People Amount Under Crowded Situation

When a lot of moving people income and outcome into the surveillance area at one time, the high density moving people will cause to a globe congestion. The crowded situation's characters are depicted:

1) The high density moving people in the whole surveillance area, and quite small space between moving people , moreover moving people could come into contact with each other;
2) The pace of moving people is slow and their speeds and directions almost are uniformity;

Owing to the crowded situation's characters, conventional motion detection methods only could detect a small quantity of big blocks of moving objects while

Fig. 2. Congestion situation

could not accurately segment every individual, so the conventional methods could not successful track and count the moving people. Aim at the difficult problem, we proposal a new counting method by using the hausdorff distance and surveillance zone constraint conditions to obtain the interval frame's information of moving people flows. With the obtained information, we construct a predicting model of moving people amount by using the least squares. It could effectively solve counting problem under crowded situation.

3.1 The Detected Model Based on Hausdorff Distance

Hausdorff distance is the maximum and minimum distance, it is mainly used to calculate the matching degree of two points sets, and is little affected by the object's translation, rotation and scaling. Supposed two point sets $A = \{a_1, a_2, \cdots, a_p\}$ and $B = \{b_1, b_2, \cdots, b_q\}$, the definition of Hausdorff distance between point sets A and point sets B is:

$$H(A, B) = \max(h(A, B), h(B, A)) \tag{1}$$

Where $H(A, B) = \max_{a \in A} \min_{b \in B} \|a - b\|$. Hausdorff distance $H(A, B)$ is set to the max value of $h(A, B)$ and $h(B, A)$, thus the matching degree of A and B is obtained.

$\|\cdot\|$ may be arbitrary norm, such as one-norm or two-norm etc, but the above definition can't handle the situation such as that the target has been covered or exterior points exist. So we put forward the conception of Fraction Hausdorff distance:

$$h^K(M, I) = K^{th}_{m \in M} Min\{\|m - i\|\} \tag{2}$$

Where K^{th} returns the kth minimum value. Suppose B is set to mask, A is detected image. Thus $h^k(A, B)$ is employed to denote the matching degree of A and B is obtained.

Highly sampled serial frames possess the strong time relativity, so the adjoining sampled frames of crowded situation also have strong comparability. According to the second character of the prediction model of moving people amount under crowded situation, we could obtain interframe displacement of moving people by calculating the interframe image comparability of the slowly moving passenger in the actual monitor. If the adjoining frames are totally matched, then the moving displacement *of* passing people is zero.

To the given surveillance zone, we use current frame and background frame differencing method to obtain the target area T. While being crowded situation, the person number n of the surveillance zone will vary with the moving object detection area T , and n should satisfy the formula: N_{min}(minimum congestion person number)$<n< N_{max}$(maximum congestion person number). Where the minimum/maximum congestion person number is the minimum/maximum passenger number of the surveillance zone while in crowded situation, and is related to the size of the surveillance zone.

Once obtained the interframe displacement s of moving people and the number n of moving people in the surveillance zone, according to the length of the surveillance zone H, we can get the interframe moving people total number f_{all}. The moving people move in two possibility directions (inbound and outbound), we use the former m frames' passenger flow ratio of inbound and outbound before crowded situation come into being to predict the inbound and outbound of passenger flow's distribution in crowded situation. Suppose current frame is $i, i = 1 \cdots N$, according to the moving object detection area T and the size of the surveillance zone, we can get the total person number of the crowded area $n(i), i = 1 \cdots N$, where $n(i) \in [N_{min}, N_{max}]$. The arithmetic flow is:

a. Do distance transform with the current frame i, get the Hausdorff distance $Hs(i)$ between the current frame i and i-1, according to interframe comparability and the size of the surveillance zone, we can get the interframe displacement s of passing people $s(i)$;

b. According to the length H of the surveillance zone, the total person number moving out of the surveillance zone in the sampling time t is $f_{all} = \dfrac{s \cdot n}{H}$.

3.2 The Predict Model Based on the Least Squares

The adjacency frames under high frames possess strong time correlation, so the amounts of inbound and outbound of moving objects also possess strong time correlation. According to optimization estimate theory, the least minimal squares error is one of the prime predict methods for noise conform to Gauss distribution. With the limitation of real-time processing, we predict the amounts of inbound and outbound of moving people of (i+1) frame by using the least squares with the obtained amounts of inbound and outbound of foregoing m frames.

Suppose $f_{in}(i), f_{out}(i), i = 1 \cdots N$ is respectively the person number moving in and out of the surveillance zone of the ith frame. We predict the variation trend and amounts of inbound and outbound of moving people using polynomial $f'_{in}(i) = \left[\sum_{j=0}^{k} (iT)^j C_j^{in} \right]$ 和 $f'_{out}(i) = \left[\sum_{j=0}^{k} (iT)^j C_j^{out} \right]$ .where k is the degree of polynomial; N is the amounts of sample frames. Their coefficient functions is:

$$
\begin{cases}
f'_{in}(i) = \sum_{i=1}^{N} \left[f_{in}(i) - \sum_{j=0}^{k} (iT)^j C_j^{in} \right]^2 \\
f'_{out}(i) = \sum_{i=1}^{N} \left[f_{out}(i) - \sum_{j=0}^{k} (iT)^j C_j^{out} \right]^2
\end{cases}
\tag{3}
$$

According to the surveillance zone model, the predict function satisfy the following constraint condition:

$$\begin{cases} \alpha_m \cdot f'_{in}(i) + (1-\alpha_m) f'_{out}(i) = f_{all}(i), i = 1 \cdots N \\ N_{min} \leq \alpha_m \cdot f'_{in}(i) + (1-\alpha_m) f'_{out}(i) \leq N_{max}, i = 1 \cdots N \end{cases} \tag{4}$$

Where α_m is the former m frames' moving people flow ratio of inbound and outbound amount:

$$\alpha_m = \frac{\sum\limits_{i=N-m}^{N} f_{in}(i)}{\sum\limits_{i=N-m}^{N} f_{in}(i) + \sum\limits_{i=N-m}^{N} f_{out}(i)} \tag{5}$$

When crowed situation continues, the moving people predicting number of the former adjoining frame will be added to the former m frames to predict the inbound/outbound amount of moving people of current frame, thus it could effectively ensure the arithmetic robust and efficiency.

4 Experiment and Data Analyze

In virtue of VC++, the proposed method has been successfully implemented in an actual system. Comparing with former methods, the method has higher computation efficiency and higher accuracy. Furthermore, it could well avoid the influence of illumination and background changes. The following is experiment results:

Table 1. Experiment Result

№	Time	Actual Amount	Predict Amount	veracity
1	14:40:33	63	60	95.24
2	14:57:14	78	76	97.44
3	15:08:42	116	108	93.10
4	15:46:32	104	100	96.15
5	15:55:59	98	103	94.90
6	16:14:56	96	96	100.00
7	16:36:34	88	92	95.45
8	16:45:02	84	80	95.24
9	16:52:02	82	87	93.90
10	17:00:10	89	86	96.63

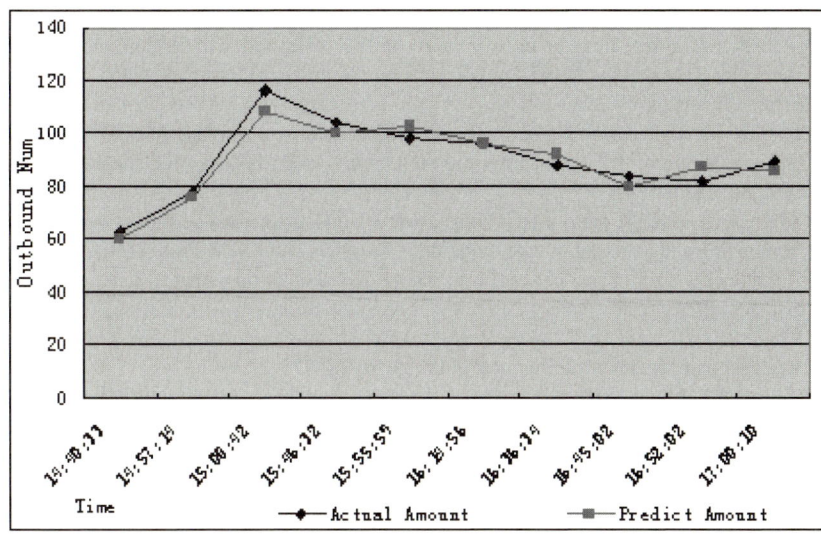

Fig. 3. Experiment Result

5 Conclusions

The paper presents a new method of counting the moving people under congestion. It calculates similar degree of adjacent frames with Hausdorff distance to obtain adjacent frames displacement of moving people. In addition, it well utilizes the former frames to predict the number of inbound and outgoing moving people by using the least squares and the similar degree of adjacent frames. The method overcome the limitation of conventional counting methods could not deal with congestion. Its average error is only 8% in the case of congestion. Consequently, our method is robust and high efficiency. It can deal with 16-channel visual counting area at one time, and it has already obtained prefect result in application.

References

1. Tomonori Yamada, Toshinari Nonaka and Shinji Ozawa, "A Method for Counting Persons Using a Series of Images," proceeding of the 1996 IEICE General Conference., no. D-633, pp. 7-345, 1991.
2. Kenji Terada and Junichi Yamaguchi, "A System for Counting Passing People by Using the Color Camera," The Transactions of The Institute of Electrical Engineers of Japan.. vol.118-C, no. 3, pp. 322-328, 1998.
3. K. Terada, D. Yoshida, S. Oe and J. Yamaguchi, "A Method of Counting the Passing People by
4. Using the Stereo Images," IEEE International Conference on Image Processing (KIP)., vol.2, pp. 338-342, 1999. Bartolini F, Cappellini V and Mecocci A, "Counting People getting in and out of a bus by real time image-sequence processing," Image and Vision Computing., vol. 12, no. 1, Feb, 1994.

5. G. Sexton, X. Zhang, and G Redpath, A novel method for tracking and counting pedestrians in real-time using a single camera , Masoud, O.; Papanikolopoulos, N.P.; Vehicular Technology, IEEE Transactions on , Volume: 50 Issue: 5 , Sept. 2001 Page(s): 1267 -1278

6. Thomas Meier, King N. Ngan. Automatic segmentation of moving objects for video object plane generation. IEEE Transaction on Circuits and Systems for Video Technology. 1998,8(5):525~538

7. XIE shuyu, CHEN qian, ZHU hong , Model and algorithm design of real-time object recognizing and counting in video journal of Tsinghua Univ(Sci&Tech).2001, Vol 41, No. 7

8. Huttenlocher D P, Klanderman G A, Rucklidge. Comparing images using the hausdorff distance. IEEE Trans. Pattern Anal. Machine intell, Sept. 1993,15,:850-863)

9. Komaniciu D, Ramesh V, Meer P. Kernel-Based object tracking. IEEE Trans. On Pattern Analysis and Machine Intelligence, 2003,25(5):564-575

10. Collins RT. Mean-Shift blob tracking through scale space. In: Danielle M, ed. IEEE int'l Conf. on Computer Vision and Pattern Recognition, Vol 2. Baltimore: Victor Graphics, 2003. 234-240.

11. DannyB.YangHectorH.Gonzalez-BanosLeonidasJ.Guibas, Counting People in Crowds with a Real-Time Network of Simple Image Sensors, Ninth IEEE International Conference on Computer Vision (ICCV'03)

Moving Object Detection Based on a New Level Set Algorithm Using Directional Speed Function

Dong-Gyu Sim

Image Processing Systems Laboratory
Dept. of Computer Engineering, Kwangwoon University
447-1, Wolgye-dong, Nowon-gu,
Seoul 139-701 Korea
Tel.: +82-2-940-5470; Fax: +82-2-941-6470
dgsim@kw.ac.kr

Abstract. In this paper, a moving object detection method is proposed based on a level set algorithm of which speed function employs three properties based on human visual characteristics. The speed function is composed of three factors: directional filtered difference, proximity weighted spatial edgeness, and directional intensity consistency. For the directional filtered difference factor, directional filtering of the difference image between background and current images is introduced to utilize temporal edgeness along a detected contour. The edgeness in the current image is also employed for an initial estimation of moving object regions. The last factor, directional intensity consistency, is based on the continuity assumption of gray-level intensities along an estimated contour. The effectiveness of the proposed algorithm is shown with four real image sequences in terms of objective detection accuracies for various experimental conditions.

Keywords: object detection, level set, segmentation.

1 Introduction

Surveillance and monitoring have become key components utilized in protection systems of lives and properties. Security cameras used in various surveillance products can acquire a lot of information about some events or accidents [1]. The main functionality of current camera-based security systems is to capture and compress an input video. The video can be transferred and monitored via wired or wireless channels. However, an intelligent active surveillance system is needed for the detection or alarm of an accident on the spot. Moving object detection is one of the most important parts for the video analysis. Although many detection methods based on mathematical morphology, statistical clustering, and active contour models have been proposed, there is yet no method working perfectly in a real environment.

Our goal is to delineate multiple moving objects in an image sequence without any human interaction. We assume that an image sequence is acquired with a static camera and the first frame of the sequence should not have any moving object to be used as an initial background image. This assumption is reasonable in many real surveillance applications because the most security cameras are fixed at a specific spot. For a

Z. Pan et al. (Eds.): ICAT 2006, LNCS 4282, pp. 565–574, 2006.

moving or rotating camera, the background image can be estimated by using pano-ramic image generation. While the conventional algorithms make use of isotropic local features and curvature information, the proposed algorithm is designed based on directional consistencies. Note that human being recognizes ambiguous regions with neighboring clear clues, especially, like image direction information. Directional filtered difference, proximity weighted spatial edgeness, and directional intensity consistency are introduced based on human visual perception in this paper. The direc-tional filtered difference is computed by using directional gradients of a difference image that is obtained by subtracting an estimated background image from the current intensity image. The proximity weighted spatial edgeness factor is computed by using the initial estimation of moving object region that is based on the probability of mov-ing object regions of a previous frame. The directional intensity consistency factor is based on continuity of the intensity values along the estimated contour. Directional filterings of each property for the speed factors make a detected contour smooth so that the proposed algorithm does not need additional smoothness constraint based on a curvature of the contour. Additionally, we make use of the robust background esti-mation to cope with noise and degradation of input video. The proposed moving de-tection algorithm is expressed as a level set notation and it is implemented with the fast marching algorithm. However, we make use of an initial estimation using dis-tance transform, which reduces the computational complexity dramatically. Most previous literatures have shown their subjective performance with some test data having good contrast. In this paper, we show objective evaluation of the detection accuracy with four real video sequences. Here, ground truths for these sequences are produced by two persons for the objective analysis. For surveillance applications, we could observe noise and degradation in input images. Various numerical results with respect to the noise and degradations will be shown to show the robustness of the proposed algorithm.

The rest of the paper is structured as follows. Fundamental level set algorithm is described in Section 2. The proposed moving object detection algorithm is presented in Section 3. Experimental results are shown and discussed in Section 4. Finally, conclusions are given in Section 5.

2   Curve Evolution and Conventional Level Set Algorithm

The level set algorithm was proposed by Osher and Setian to deal with topological merging and breaking of contours [4]. They introduced a higher-dimensional evolu-tion function $\Phi((x,y),t)$ and set up a time-dependent initial value problem with the front $\Gamma(t)$ that is given as a zero level set of the evolution function, that is, $\{(x,y)|\Phi((x,y),t)=0\}$. The level set evolution function on the front can be expressed at any time as $\Phi(\Gamma(t),t) = 0$.

By the chain rule, this equation can be denoted by

$$\Phi_t + \nabla\Phi((x, y),t) \cdot \Gamma'(t) = 0, \tag{1}$$

where $\Gamma'(t) \cdot n = F$ is the speed of the evolution front in a normal direction and where the normal vector n is defined by $\nabla\Phi/|\nabla\Phi|$. The speed function depends on position, time, geometry of the front, and external physics. This gives the level set PDE equation,

$$\Phi((x, y),t)_t + F(x, y) \,|\, \nabla\Phi((x, y),t) \,|= 0, \tag{2}$$

where an initial solution is given by $\Gamma(0)$ satisfying $\Phi((x,y),0)=0$.

3 Proposed Algorithm

The detection algorithm based on a new speed function for the level-set algorithm is designed for extracting multiple objects simultaneously. It does not need any human intervention. Figure 1 shows the block diagram of the proposed system. It is assumed that an input image is acquired with a pre-installed static camera and that the first frame of the input sequence should be the initial background. Moving objects are detected with the level set algorithm consisting of three factors based on directional spatio-temporal consistency, as shown in Figure 1.

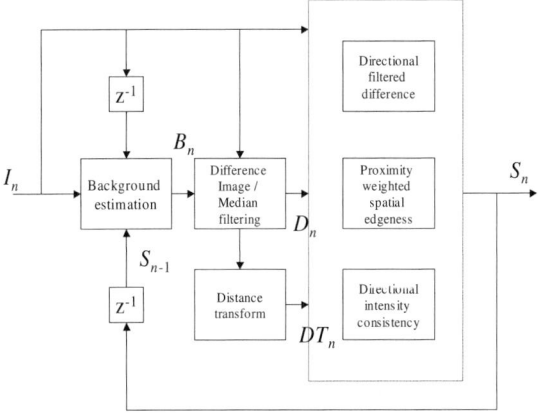

Fig. 1. Block diagram of the proposed system

3.1 Background Estimation

Because illumination can change at any time, background images should be estimated to detect moving object regions in a current image. The accuracy of the background estimation could affect the whole detection system performance. The proposed algorithm estimates the background image with

$$B_n = B_{n-1} - \frac{\max\{\rho_{T1}(B_{n-1} - I_n), \rho_{T2}((1 - S_{n-1})(B_{n-1} - I_{n-1}))\}}{2}, \tag{3}$$

where B_n and B_{n-1} represent the current and previous estimated background images, and I_n and I_{n-1} denote the current and previous input images, respectively. S_{n-1} is the detected moving object mask for the previous image. If a pixel in the mask is in a moving object, S_{n-1} at the pixel is set to 1. Otherwise, it is set to 0. $\rho_T(x)$ is defined by

$$\rho_T(x) = \begin{cases} x, & |x| > T \\ 0, & |x| \leq T \end{cases}. \tag{4}$$

This recursive nonlinear filtering enables to exclude moving objects and noisy regions that are considered as outliers for reliable background estimation.

3.2 Level Set Algorithm with a New Speed Function for Detection of Moving Objects

In applying the level set algorithm to a target application, the performance of the application highly depends on the design of the speed function. The speed function should be designed by using the radical properties of the target application. In image processing and analysis, it is not easy to analyze and interpret obscure objects that do not possess clear boundaries. However, the obscure object and regions can be analyzed by utilizing neighboring distinct information as done by human beings. In particular, directional spatio-temporal edges are important to recognize object contours in ambiguous regions. For the proposed moving object detection, we introduce three properties for the speed function based on these human visual characteristics. Smoothness terms widely used in conventional algorithms are not used in this proposed algorithm because the smoothness based on the curvature of a contour has different units from other external speed terms. Therefore it is hard to harmonize them simultaneously. The proposed speed function is defined by

$$F(x, y) = F_d(x, y) F_e(x, y) F_i(x, y), \tag{5}$$

where $F_d(x,y)$ and $F_e(x,y)$ are the directional filtered difference factor and proximity weighted edgeness factor, respectively, and $F_i(x,y)$ represents the directional intensity consistency.

a. Directional filtered difference factor
The first speed function factor is the directional filtered difference that is computed by filtering difference values along a front contour. At first, the iso-level context set is defined by

$$C(x, y) = \{(x', y') \mid \Phi(x, y) \equiv \Phi(x', y') \text{ and } \| (x, y) - (x', y') \| \leq N \}, \tag{6}$$

where N is the range of the directional effective neighborhood. Normally, N is set to 5. With this support domain, we define the first factor of the speed function as

$$F_d(x, y) = \exp\left(-\alpha \sum_{(x', y') \in C(x, y)} c(x', y')(\| (x', y') - (x, y) \|) \mid \nabla Diff(x', y') \mid \right), \tag{7}$$

where $c(x', y')$ represents the coefficient of the directional filter, which should be all positive as a low-pass filter. The difference image contains moving region clues but it is affected by the background image. Figure 2 (a) shows the direction of the front caused by the directional difference factor. Without considering the directional neighborhood, the contour would be attracted into the dent regions ('a' shown in Fig. 2) because the region has only a small amount of energy in the difference domain. With a continuity assumption of the contour, the contour is likely to be smooth even though the dent region has low difference values. The proposed system can detect a correct contour at the dent regions by the directional filtered difference factor.

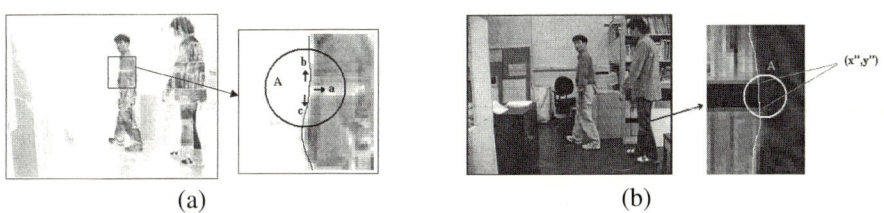

(a)   (b)

Fig. 2. (a) Direction of the front with the directional filtered difference factor. (b) applying the directional intensity consistency.

b. Proximity weighted spatial edgeness factor
The proximity weighted spatial edgeness is computed using the gradient of a current image. Even though the difference-based factor incorporates temporal information from the moving regions, the estimated contour can be corrupted by a background image. However, the current image itself maintains shape information of every object regardless of the background image. The second factor of the proposed speed function is derived based on the edgeness of the current image. The proximity weighted spatial edgeness factor is expressed by

$$F_e(x, y) = \exp(-\beta | \nabla I_n(x, y) | P(x, y)),$$ (8)

where $P(x,y)$ is the proximity from moving objects [5]. Here, $P(x,y)$ is defined by 1-$ND(x,y)$, where $ND(x,y)$ is a normalized distance transform, ranging from 0 to 1. Note that β is a constant.

c. Directional intensity consistency factor
In cases where the color of a moving object is the same with that of the background, hardly any energy is shown in either the difference image or gradient image. In the proposed algorithm, if the brightness at a pixel is continuous along an estimated contour and the difference energy at the pixel is large in its neighborhood, the pixel can be considered to be on the moving object contour. Based on this intuition, the third direction intensity consistency factor is defined by

$$F_i(x, y) = \exp\left(-\gamma p_{ic}\left(\sum_{(x',y')\in C(x,y)} | I_n(x, y) - I_n(x', y') | |Diff(x'', y'')\right)\right),$$ (9)

where (x'',y'') is $\{(x'',y'') | \, \|(x,y)-(x'',y'')\|=N$ and $\Phi(x,y) \equiv \Phi(x'',y'')\}$ and $p_{ic}(x)$ is $1/(1+x)$. Figure 2(b) shows the detected contour by the directional intensity consistency even though the colors between the background and the current image are almost the same. The detection is done by using gray level continuity and neighboring temporal edgeness energy at (x'',y'').

3.3 Fast Implementation Based on the Fast Marching Algorithm

Because the speed function is always positive, the proposed level set equation can be solved by a fast marching algorithm, which is the fastest approach in solving such an initial value problem. Even though the fast algorithm is effective, it still requires computations of the crossing times, $T(x,y)$, of which there are as many as an image's size. Only parts of the whole image have moving objects, so the computation of $T(x,y)$ at the rest of the regions might be unnecessary. Propagation regions of the front can be confined with the distance transform from the initial moving object. The initial front is set to

$$\Gamma(0) = \{(x, y) \mid ND(x, y) \equiv Th_{IC}\},\tag{10}$$

where $ND(x,y)$ is the normalized distance transform of the initial estimation computed from the previous statistics and Th_{IC} is the threshold, which takes values ranging from 0 to 1. In this experiment, Th_{IC} is set to 0.85.

4 Experimental Results and Discussion

The effectiveness of the proposed algorithm is shown with four image sequences, compared with the conventional algorithm [6], in terms of accuracy, robustness against image degradation, and computational complexity. As for the conventional algorithm, Sethian's algorithm [6] was used for the comparison because it is the most popular fundamental method in shape recovery based on the level set algorithm. In this paper, four visible and one near-infrared image sequences are used and the associated ground truths are generated by human inspection. Robustness against noise and degradation of input image is important factor in real surveillance applications because image quality from real surveillance systems may not be good due to many restrictions such as cost, noise, size, and so on. In this paper, we show the objective evaluation in terms of the degradation of input image.

Four visible image sequences (name Corridor, Outdoor, Juggling, and Lab.) are acquired with CCD camera and digitized in 320x240 4:2:0 YUV format. There is one walking person in the Corridor sequence having a good contrast, consisting of 191 frames. Outdoor sequence has two walking persons, consisting of 61 frames. Juggling sequence consists of 126 frames in which a person plays three juggles. Lab sequence has two walking persons indoor consisting of 160 frames. Additionally, near-infrared camera becomes more popular commercially since it is effective in the dark. One near-infrared image sequence consisting of 125 frames is also tested.

For the four visible and one near-infrared image sequences, their ground truths were generated by two people. Outlining of moving objects is subjective and, as such, there is a variation from person to person. The inter-observer variation can be quantified by

$$V = \frac{100}{K} \sum_{k}^{K} \sum_{i,j}^{NM} \frac{\mid S_{p1,k}(i, j) - S_{p2,k}(i, j) \mid}{NM},\tag{11}$$

Table 1. Inter-observer variation

Type	Sequence	Inter-observer variation
Visible	Corridor Outdoor Juggle Lab.	0.24 0.57 0.64 0.42
Near-infrared	Night	0.80

where K, N, and M are number of frames, width, and height, respectively. $S_{p1,k}(i,j)$ and $S_{p2,k}(i,j)$ are segmented masks by different two people. They have 1s or 0s that represent foreground and background pixels, respectively. Table 1 shows the inter-observer variation and the variations are quite small.

In this paper, objective evaluations were performed by counting true foreground (TF), false foreground (FF), true background (TB), and false background (FB) pixels in each frame. For example, TF represents the numbers of pixels that foreground pixels are correctly detected as foreground pixels in a frame. We use three detection error measurements:

$$E_{FF}=FF/(FF+TB), \quad E_{FB}=FB/(FB+TF),$$
$$E_T=(FF+FB)/(TF+FF+TB+FB)=(FF+FB)/NM. \tag{12}$$

Table 2 shows that the errors of the proposed algorithm are significantly smaller than the conventional one, because the proposed algorithm speed function is based on human perception characteristics such as temporal and spatial continuities.

Table 2. Comparison of the conventional and proposed algorithms in terms of detection errors

Sequence	Conventional method (%)			Proposed (%)		
	False background	False foreground	Total error	False background	False foreground	Total error
Corridor	25.91	1.99	3.22	11.99	0.08	0.68
Outdoor	10.66	2.17	2.47	10.32	0.12	0.49
Juggle	8.02	5.82	6.03	6.91	1.09	1.64
Lab.	9.19	3.10	3.53	18.42	0.26	1.55

For the evaluation of the robustness against input image degradation, we generated three image sequences for each original sequence. The first one was generated by applying Gaussian filters to obtain blurred image sequences. Table 3 shows the detection errors of the proposed and conventional algorithms with the blurred sequences. The proposed algorithm is shown to be more robust for smoothed image sequences, as compared with the conventional one.

The performance with respect to dynamic ranges of input images is also evaluated. In real input sequences, the dynamic range could be reduced by low illumination or low SNR characteristics of the CCD sensor. Table 4 shows the detection errors in terms of the dynamic range. Reduction in the dynamic range gives rise to removal of false foreground noise but diminishes gray value resolution at moving object regions.

Table 3. Comparison of detection errors with Gaussian blurred sequences

Se-quence	Standard deviation	Conventional method (%)			Proposed (%)		
		E_{FB}	$E_{\mathbf{FB}}$	E_T	E_{FB}	$E_{\mathbf{FB}}$	E_T
Corri-dor	1.0	39.13	1.95	3.85	13.85	0.10	0.80
	1.5	52.36	1.93	4.51	15.32	0.13	0.90
	2.0	71.94	1.87	5.45	17.46	0.15	1.03
	2.5	86.82	1.78	6.12	20.51	0.15	1.19
Out-door	1.0	26.38	1.89	2.77	22.18	0.08	0.87
	1.5	43.96	1.78	3.29	31.13	0.09	1.20
	2.0	62.75	1.69	3.87	41.83	0.09	1.58
	2.5	81.42	1.60	4.46	53.42	0.08	1.99
Juggle	1.0	19.95	3.64	5.18	8.31	0.56	1.29
	1.5	27.93	3.09	5.44	9.72	0.49	1.36
	2.0	35.38	2.81	5.89	12.10	0.50	1.60
	2.5	44.99	2.58	6.59	16.00	0.53	1.99
Lab	1.0	20.35	2.49	3.76	23.33	0.21	1.85
	1.5	30.96	2.32	4.35	27.10	0.26	2.16
	2.0	43.55	2.22	5.15	31.35	0.28	2.49
	2.5	59.22	2.10	6.16	36.02	0.32	2.86

Table 4. Comparison of detection errors with image sequences having lower dynamic range

Se-quence	Dynamic range	Conventional method (%)			Proposed (%)		
		E_{FB}	$E_{\mathbf{FB}}$	E_T	E_{FB}	$E_{\mathbf{FB}}$	E_T
Corri-dor	90%	30.11	1.95	3.39	14.50	0.07	0.81
	80%	35.69	1.91	3.64	17.33	0.06	0.95
	70%	42.96	1.87	3.97	20.57	0.05	1.10
	60%	53.64	1.83	4.47	25.66	0.04	1.35
Out-door	90%	13.96	2.05	2.48	14.05	0.08	0.58
	80%	18.77	1.94	2.54	18.70	0.06	0.73
	70%	26.67	1.83	2.72	24.33	0.04	0.91
	60%	38.48	1.73	3.04	32.52	0.03	1.19
Juggle	90%	10.41	4.94	5.46	8.42	0.77	1.49
	80%	13.58	4.34	5.21	10.36	0.60	1.52
	70%	17.47	3.80	5.10	13.12	0.46	1.65
	60%	22.10	3.31	5.09	20.46	0.30	2.21
Lab	90%	12.18	2.77	3.44	21.79	0.19	1.72
	80%	16.18	2.48	3.45	26.10	0.12	1.97
	70%	21.70	2.25	3.63	31.60	0.06	2.30
	60%	31.05	2.07	4.13	40.34	0.04	2.90

Zero-mean additive Gaussian noises were added into the four video sequences. Table 5 shows the detection errors of the proposed and conventional algorithm in terms of the Gaussian noisy sequences. The proposed algorithm copes with the large Gaussian noise with median filtered difference image and directional speed function.

Lately, inexpensive near-infrared cameras are commercially available and they have reasonably good image quality in both dark and light situations. False background and foreground rates for the conventional algorithm are 33.98% and 1.57%, respectively, and the total error rate is 1.74%. However, the false background and

Table 5. Comparison of detection errors with image sequences having additive zero mean Gaussian noise

Se-quence	Standard deviation	Conventional method (%)			Proposed (%)		
		E_{FB}	E_{FB}	E_T	E_{FB}	E_{FB}	E_T
Corri-dor	3	21.31	4.17	5.05	11.74	0.08	0.67
	5	13.00	8.71	8.93	10.74	0.09	0.64
	7	5.97	40.31	38.55	9.38	0.10	0.57
	9	2.05	71.01	67.48	8.19	0.11	0.52
Out-door	3	8.33	2.22	2.44	21.38	0.07	0.83
	5	2.44	6.32	6.18	22.75	0.08	0.89
	7	0.43	44.36	42.79	23.05	0.09	0.91
	9	0.15	73.35	70.73	22.83	0.11	0.92
Juggle	3	6.32	6.67	6.64	6.96	1.06	1.62
	5	3.32	16.64	15.38	6.95	1.09	1.64
	7	1.35	49.62	45.06	6.98	0.97	1.54
	9	0.46	73.72	66.79	6.80	1.23	1.76
Lab	3	6.75	3.97	4.17	18.44	0.28	1.57
	5	1.93	17.51	16.41	17.61	1.41	2.56
	7	0.12	54.24	50.40	16.57	2.32	3.33
	9	0.04	77.49	71.99	15.27	2.93	3.80

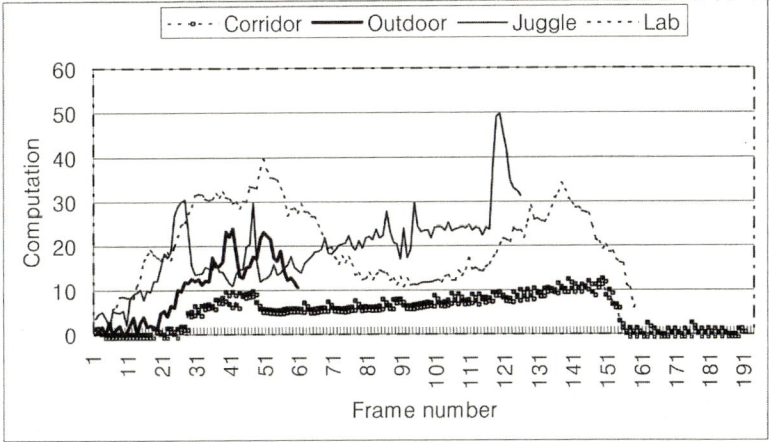

Fig. 3. Computations of the proposed algorithm compared to the conventional algorithm for four visible sequences in terms of the frame number

foreground rates for the proposed algorithm are 21.64% and 1.30%, resulting in 1.41% total error. For the near-infrared image, the proposed algorithm is significantly better in terms of detection error.

The proposed algorithm makes use of distance transform map of the initial detection. The computational complexity depends on size of the moving objects. The percentage of the original computation is shown in Fig. 3. The average computation is

lower than 20% of the conventional algorithm. The computation could be more reduced by adopting hierarchical approach and fast sorting algorithm such as heap sort.

5 Conclusion

This paper proposes a moving object detection algorithm based on the level set
method employing a new speed function according to human visual perception. The
speed function consists of the directional spatio-temporal continuities formed by incorporating neighboring information. Various numerical evaluations were conducted
to objectively show the performance of the proposed detection algorithm with several
image sequences and associated ground truths produced by human observation. Further research should be focused on the development of an active intelligent surveillance system.

Acknowledgement

The present research has been in part conducted by the Research Grant of
Kwangwoon University in 2006.

References

1. Pavlidis, I., Morellas, V., Tsiamyrtzis, P., Harp, S.: Urban surveillance systems: From the
   laboratory to the commercial world. Proceedings of IEEE, vol. 89 (2001) 1478-1497
2. Diehl, N.: Object-oriented motion estimation and segmentation in image sequences. IEEE
   Trans. Image Processing, vol. 3 (1990) 901-904
3. Kompatsiaris, I., Strintzis, M.: Spatiotemporal segmentation and tracking of objects for
   visualization of videoconference image sequences. IEEE Trans. Circuit and Systems for
   Video Technology, vol. 10 (2000) 1388-1402.
4. Osher, S., Sethian, J.: Fronts propagating with curvature dependant speed: Algorithms based
   on Hamilton-Jacobi formulation. J. Computational Physics, vol. 79 (1988) 12-49
5. Sim, D.-G., Park, R.-H.:Two-dimentional object alignment based on the robust Haudorff
   similarity measure. IEEE Trans. Image Processing, vol. 10 (2001) 475-483
6. Sethian, J.: Level Set Methods. Cambridge Univ. Press, Cambridge, U.K. (1996)

An Integrated Robot Vision System for Multiple Human Tracking and Silhouette Extraction

Jung-Ho Ahn, Sooyeong Kwak, Cheolmin Choi, Kilcheon Kim, and Hyeran Byun

Dept. of Computer Science, Yonsei University, Seoul, Korea, 120-749
{jungho, ksy2177, wxman, kimkch, hrbyun}@cs.yonsei.ac.kr

Abstract. In this paper, we propose a new integrated robot vision system designed for multiple human tracking and silhouette extraction using an active stereo camera. The proposed system focuses on robustness to camera movement. Human detection is performed by camera egomotion compensation and disparity segmentation. A fast histogram based tracking algorithm is presented by using the mean shift principle. Color and disparity values are combined by the weighted kernel for the tracking feature. The human silhouette extraction is based on graph cut segmentation. A trimap is estimated in advance and this is effectively incorporated into the graph cut framework.

Keywords: Object Detection, Tracking, Silhouette Extraction, Robot Vision.

1 Introduction

One of the main goals of virtual reality applications is to support natural, efficient, powerful interaction. If interaction is overly obtrusive, awkward, or constraining, the user's experience with synthetic environments can be severely degraded. To support natural communication, we want to not only track human movements, but interpret those movements in order to recognize semantically meaningful gestures. Gestures are used for control and navigation in CAVEs [11, 12] and in other virtual environments such as smart rooms [13] and virtual work environments [14].

This paper addresses a computer vision system which can detect and track multiple people and extract silhouettes with an active stereo camera in real time. This process assists in human gesture, gait and event recognition for virtual reality applications where accurate positions and silhouettes are needed to monitor and extract the features of body configuration. A prime application of this research is Human Robot Interaction (HRI).

Many computer vision systems with same purpose have been developed [4, 7, 8] but most of these were designed only for surveillance purpose, based on the background subtraction method which used fixed cameras. Unlike surveillance systems, the vision systems mounted on mobile robots are required to deal with camera movements so methods such as the background modeling. Therefore totally different approaches are necessary in these applications, and the efficiency requirements of live processing have restricted us to algorithms that are known to be capable of near frame-rate operation. Because of these problems, proper robot vision

Z. Pan et al. (Eds.): ICAT 2006, LNCS 4282, pp. 575–583, 2006.
© Springer-Verlag Berlin Heidelberg 2006

systems for human behavior analysis have not been presented yet. To track people with a moving camera, Nursebot [1] used laser range sensors rather than a vision-based approach. However such hardware-based approaches are too limited to handle implicit communications in HRI such as gesture, gait and event recognition.

1.1 System Overview

The main contribution of the proposed system is the design of an integrated vision system for mobile robots that can perform multiple human tracking and segment silhouettes with an active stereo camera. Our proposed system is composed of three modules such as human detection, tracking and silhouette extraction. These modules work interactively. Their key features and contributions are as follows:

- The detection module detects when new people enter a scene. Their locations and sizes are determined by using egomotion compensation and disparity segmentation by flood fill algorithm. A detected person is called a *track* and the location of this person can be represented by a bounding box.
- The tracking module updates the locations of all tracks in every frame. In this paper we propose a new fast histogram-based tracking algorithm that works with color and disparity values simultaneously. For multiple tracking we present some strategies to handle the occlusion.
- The silhouette extraction module extracts the silhouette of a person of interest. The selected person is determined by the task manger that controls all operations of the robot. In this paper, we present a robust way of object segmentation method in which we estimate a trimap and effectively incorporated it into a graph cut framework.

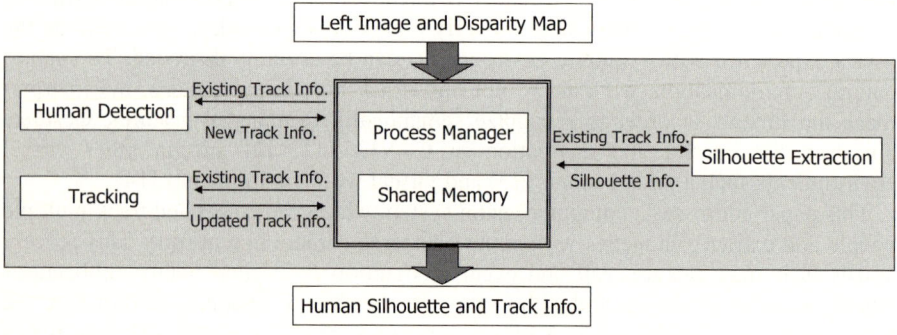

Fig. 1. Overall system flow chart of the proposed vision system

All three modules are robust to camera movements. The input of our system is the left image obtained by the stereo camera and the disparity map that is calculated by the Small Vision System(SVS)[10]. All modules share the track and silhouette information in the shared memory and are controlled by the process manager. Figure 1 shows a flow chart of the proposed vision system.

2 Human Detection and Tracking

The detection and tracking modules exchange the bounding box information obtained from all tracks. In every frame the tracking module updates the track information. Then the detection module observes the outside parts of the bounding boxes of existing tracks. If a new person is detected, a new track is initialized. The process manager associates its bounding box with the track and registers the results in the shared memory.

Human Detection: In general there are two motions that are determined with an active camera; object and background movements. To eliminate the background movements consecutive images can be calibrated by applying the egomotion compensation algorithm [9]. To accomplish this, feature points are generated by the Harris corner detector in every frame. Excluding the outliers, the correspondence between the feature points in the consecutive images can be estimated using the Kande-Lucas-Tomasi(KLT) feature tracking algorithm. Then, the camera egomotion can be estimated using the bilinear transformation model which is defined as:

$$
\begin{pmatrix} f_x^t \\ f_y^t \end{pmatrix} = \begin{pmatrix} a_0 & a_1 & a_2 & a_3 \\ a_4 & a_5 & a_6 & a_7 \end{pmatrix} \begin{pmatrix} f_x^{t-1} \\ f_y^{t-1} \\ 1 \\ f_x^{t-1} f_y^{t-1} \end{pmatrix}
\tag{1}
$$

where (f_x^{t-1}, f_y^{t-1}) and (f_x^t, f_y^t) are corresponding feature points in time t. After compensating for background motion, the frame difference between the compensated previous image and the current image can be obtained. The frame difference can detect only certain parts of the moving objects, for example, the legs and arms. To determine the accurate bounding box of the person, it is necessary to perform the disparity segmentation with the flood fill algorithm. The average of the disparity values in the detected moving area can be computed and the area can be expanded by adding the close pixels with similar disparity values.

Human Tracking: In order to track the detected people, a modified mean shift-based tracking algorithm is used. This algorithm works with color and disparity information. The kernel-based target and candidate models can be defined as in [6],

$$
\hat{q}_u = C_q \sum_{i=1}^{n} k\left(\left\| x_i \right\|^2 \right) \delta[b(x_i) - u], \qquad \hat{p}_u = C_p \sum_{i=1}^{n_h} k\left(\left\| \frac{y - x_i}{h} \right\|^2 \right) \delta[b(x_i) - u]
\tag{2}
$$

When using mean shift-based color tracking it is difficult to separate the objects with similar color distribution. In order to solve this problem, we use a disparity-weighted kernel which combines a disparity value with a spatial kernel. We assume that the disparity of the body shows small variations compared with that of the background. Let M be the histogram bin with a maximum frequency of disparity values in the bounding box of a track. If the bounding box is tight enough, the pixels whose disparity values fall into bin M can be assumed to be target pixels. The weight value W_v of the disparity histogram bin v can be defined as:

$$
W_v = 1 - \frac{|M - v|}{M}
\tag{3}
$$

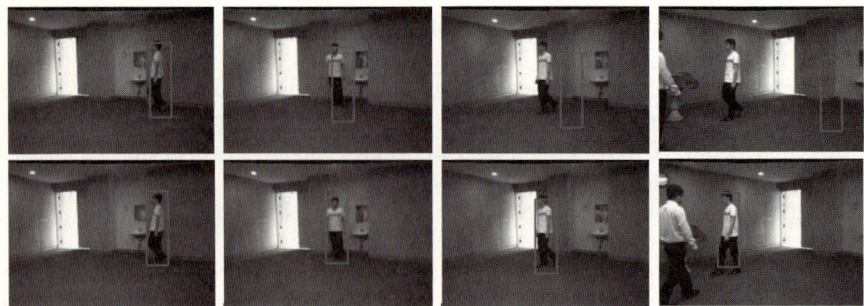

Fig. 2. Comparison of the tracking algorithms. The first row shows the results when using the conventional mean shift-based algorithm [6] and the second row shows the results when using the proposed tracking algorithm.

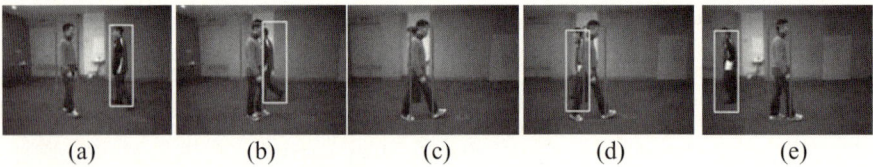

      (a)   (b)   (c)   (d)   (e)

Fig. 3. The process of occlusion handling in human tracking. (a) No occlusion in the 150th frame of the test dataset *CM3*. (b) Before occlusion (checking similarity and distance) in the 163th frame. (c) Occlusion (checking similarity on the both sides of the occluding target) in the 166th frame. (d) Recovered target in the 170th frame (e) No occlusion in the 182nd frame.

for $v = 1, \cdots, k$. The new target and candidate representations with the disparity weighted kernel in (3) can be calculated by

$$\hat{Q}_u = C_{q,w} \sum_{i=1}^{n} W_{i,v}^p k\left(\left\|x_i\right\|^2\right)\delta[b(x_i)-u], \quad \hat{P}_u = C_{p,w} \sum_{i=1}^{n_h} W_{i,v}^q k\left(\left\|\frac{y-x_i}{h}\right\|^2\right)\delta[b(x_i)-u] \quad (4)$$

where $C_{q,w}$, $C_{p,w}$ are the normalization constants, and $W_{i,v}^p$, $W_{i,v}^q$ are the disparity weights for the target and candidate windows, respectively. Figure 2 shows the tracking procedures. For occlusion handling we detected the occluded tracks using the distance among the tracks as well as the histogram similarity after the mean shift tracking. Then, the occluded track was recovered by using the histogram similarities of the both sides of the occluding track. Figure 3 illustrates this procedure. The bounding boxes were accurately obtained by using disparity segmentation as the detection module.

3   Silhouette Extraction Using a Graph Cut with Estimated Trimap

For human silhouette extraction, we used a bounding box surrounding a person. For computational efficiency, this module used the set of pixels $\wp$ within the bounding box only. We define $z = (z_1, z_2, ..., z_{|\wp|})$ as the image where z_n is the RGB color vector for the nth pixel, and $f = (f_1, f_2, ..., f_{|\wp|})$ as a binary vector whose component f_n's specifies the labels of either 1 or 0 where 1 represents an object and 0 represents a background. The vector f defines a segmentation. The segmentation of distant moving objects from the active stereo camera presented problems such as low resolution, shadows, poor stereo matching information and instability of color distributions. To overcome these problems we estimated a trimap in advance that assigned each pixel to one of three labels of 0, 1, and -1 where -1 represented the unknown. The estimated trimap was effectively incorporated in a new graph cut framework, and trimap estimation made the hard object segmentation problem easier.

3.1 Trimap Estimation

Our trimap was motivated by the user-interactive segmentation techniques proposed by Boykov and Jolly[2]. They assumed that a user imposes a hard constraints specifying some object and background pixels (*seeds*). For effective trimap estimation we first segment the input color image by mean shift [5]. The mean shift method segments images into homogeneous small regions and the set of regions is denoted by $\Re^t = \{R^t_i\}$ at the tth frame.

Background Seed Estimation: We assume that the person does not move further than d pixels away in each consecutive frame. Thus we dilate the human silhouette of the previous frame using a $d \times d$ square structuring element. The outside of the dilated silhouette is assumed to be the background area. Also, the regions R^t_i's in $\Re^t$ that are touching the bounding box are assumed to be the background area. The union of the two areas is estimated as the set of background seeds B^t.

Object Seed Estimation: Using the mean m^{t-1}_D and the standard deviation s^{t-1}_D of the object disparity values of the previous $(t-1)$th frame, the set of candidate object pixels O^t_D is defined by

$$O^t_D = \{ p \in \wp \mid m^{t-1}_D - K_D s^{t-1}_D < d_p < m^{t-1}_D + K_D s^{t-1}_D \}$$

where d_p is the disparity value at pixel p. Using the set O^t_D and the previous object silhouette S^{t-1} we define the object region likelihood L_R of pixel p as 1 if $p \in O^t_D$, w_s if $p \in S^{t-1} - O^t_D$, and 0 otherwise. We select the regions $R \in \Re^t$ if

$$\sum_{p \in R} L_R(p) > w_s \tag{5}$$

where n_R is the number of pixels in R. We denote $\Re^t_s$ as the union of the selected regions. Then we remove the background pixels from $\Re^t_s$ by using background spatial-color probability. A five-dimensional histogram is built on the domain that concatenates the pixel locations and the RGB colors using the background seeds in B^t. We define P_B as the background probability induced by the histogram and the set of estimated object seeds $p \in O^t$ is finally determined if

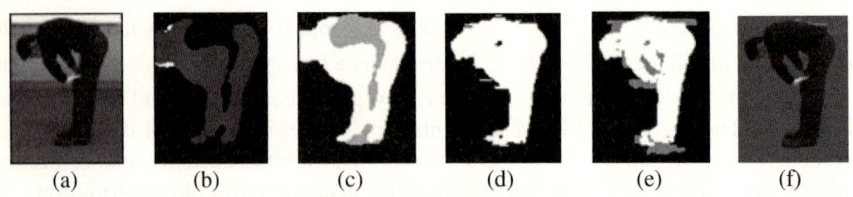

| (a) | (b) | (c) | (d) | (e) | (f) |

Fig. 4. Human silhouette extraction using the estimated trimap. (a) input left image, (b) cropped disparity map (c) object region likelihood L_R, (d) region selection, (e) trimap; white, black, and gray pixels indicate O^t, B^t, U^t, correspondingly, (f) segmented object by the proposed graph cut.

$$-\log P_E(p) > m_C^t + K_C \sigma_C^t \tag{6}$$

and $p \in \Re_s^t$ where m_C^t and σ_C^t are the mean and standard deviation of $-\log P_B(p)$'s of $p \in \Re_s^t$ and the parameter K_C is related to the level of confidence for the estimated object seeds. Figure 4(e) shows the estimated trimap with the input images in Figure 4(a) and Figure 4(b).

3.2 Graph Cut Framework with the Estimated Trimap

Given an image we try to find the labeling f that minimizes the energy[3]

$$E(f) = \Sigma_p \, D_p(f_p) + \Sigma_{\{p,q\} \in N} \, \delta(f_p, f_q) V_{p,q}(f_p, f_q), \tag{7}$$

where N is a standard 4-neighborhood system and $\delta(f_p, f_q)$ denotes the delta function defined by 1 if $f_p \neq f_q$ and 0 otherwise. The smooth term $V_{p,q}$ is defined by

$$V_{p,q} = \exp(- \| z_p - z_q \|^2 / \beta) \tag{8}$$

where β is chosen by the expectation of 2 $\exp(-\|z_p - z_q\|^2/)$ over all $\{p, q\} \in N$. The data term D_p measures how well label f_p fits pixel p given the observed data z_p. We model the object and background color likelihoods of P($\cdot$|1) and P($\cdot$|0) using Gaussian mixtures in the RGB color space, learned from image frames labeled from earlier in the sequence. In every frame we estimate a trimap that consists of O, B, and U. The set $U = \wp - (O \cup B)$. Then D_p is defined as

$$D_p(f_p) = \begin{cases} -\log P(z_p \mid f_p) & \text{if } p \in U^t \\ (K-c)f_p + c & \text{if } p \in O^t \\ (c-K)f_p + K & \text{if } p \in B^t \end{cases} \tag{9}$$

where $K = \max_{\{p,q\} \in N} V_{p,q}(f_p, f_q)$ and c is a small number(usually accepted as 1 or 2). Minimization of the energy (3) is done by using a standard min-cut/max-flow algorithm[7]. The estimated trimap may have been wrong in some pixels. The role of c is to give the min-cut algorithm little chance to assign different labels from their pre-estimated labels of the trimap. This effect is shown in Figure 4. For the pixels in the estimated region, the data term D_p is determined by either of the constant K or c

no matter what the colors or disparities are. This is the reason why trimap estimation improves robustness to changes in illumination and camera movements. Figure 5 shows some human segmentation results for gesture recognition under the camera movements and illumination changes.

4 Experimental Results

The proposed system was implemented in C/C++ and was run on Pentium IV-3.0 GHz PC with 1G RAM. The test videos were acquired with a the pan-tilt stereo camera and multiple people entered an indoor scene. Each video contained 700 frames of 320×240 images. The test video *KC1* and *SS1* were taken by a fixed stereo camera and one person entered the scene. The other five test videos were taken by the pan-tilt stereo cameras. In theses videos two or three people entered the scene, moved around, occluded with each other, and assumed natural poses. Excessive illumination changes occurred in the test video *SY3*. The average running time of the proposed system was about 9 fps.

Performance Evaluation of the Detection and Tracking Algorithm: Performance was evaluated by using the ground-truth bounding boxes. We segmented the silhouettes of moving people manually at every 10th frame and determined their ground-truth bounding boxes. Table 1 shows the results. In the table *Entrance* refers to the total number of people entering the scene. *Detected* refers to the total number of detected objects, and *True+D* and *False+D* represent the number of correct detections and incorrect detections, respectively. If the detected bounding box overlapped by more than 90 percent with the ground-truth bounding box, we counted it as a correct detection. *Tracking rate* shows the average of the ratio of the number of correct tracking instances to that of the correctly detected tracks. If the center point of the tracked bounding box fell in the middle half area of the ground-truth bounding box we counted it as correct tracking. The average detection rate of the seven test video sets ws 98.31 percent.

Table 1. Performance of the detection/tracking and silhouette extraction algorithms

		CM2	CM3	JH3	KC1	KC3	SS1	SY3
Detection/ Tracking	Entrance	4	6	9	1	10	1	7
	Detected	4	8	10	1	10	1	7
	True +D	4	6	9	1	10	1	7
	False +D	0	2	1	0	0	0	0
	Tracking Rate(%)	98.96	99.63	98.83	99.71	99.88	99.91	91.72
Silhouette extraction	Error rate(%)	1.06	2.55	1.25	1.36	1.26	0.61	0.42

Performance Evaluation of the Silhouette Extraction Algorithm: Performance was evaluated with respect to the ground-truth segmentation of every 10th frame in each of seven test stereo sequences. Each pixel of each ground truth image was labeled as object, background or unknown. The unknown label occurred when there were one plus pixel and one minus pixel along the object boundaries to mark the mixed pixels. Ignoring the mixed pixels, the errors were counted. Table 1 shows the averages of the *errors rates* within the bounding boxes. Some results obtained by the proposed vision system are shown in Figure 5.

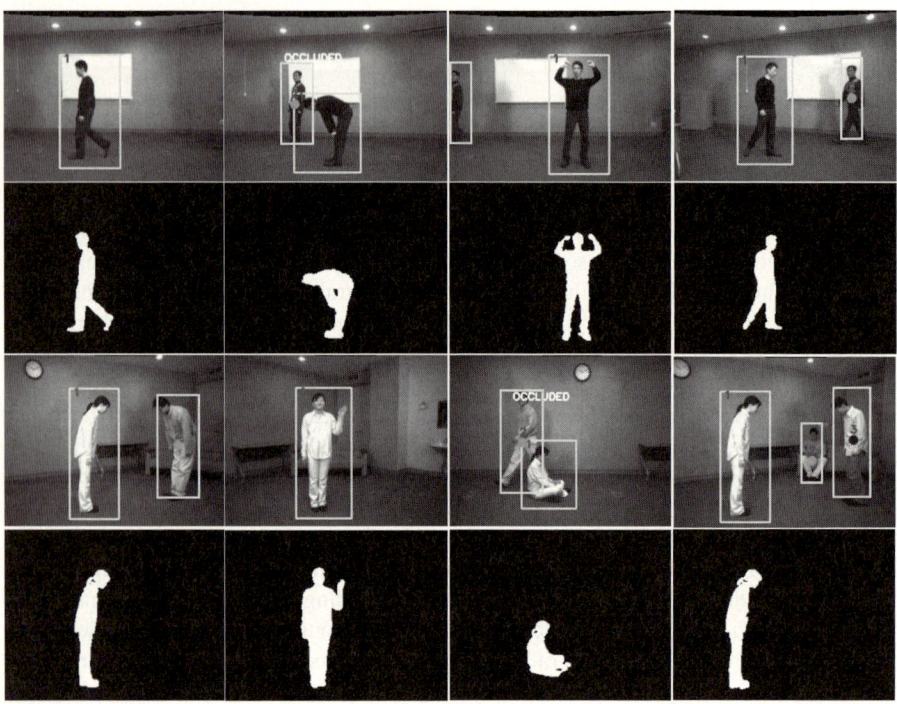

Fig. 5. The results of human tracking and silhouette extraction under an active camera. The images are taken from *CM*2 and *SY*3.

5   Conclusions

In this paper we presented a new integrated robot vision system for multiple human detection, tracking and silhouette extraction when using an active stereo camera. A prime application of this system in gesture, gait and event recognition when working with HRI systems. The background subtraction methods presented easy ways to detect and track people and extract their silhouettes but they were not applicable to mobile robot environments. The proposed system focused on robustness to camera movements and presented several novel vision techniques, such as a fast histogram-based tracking and graph cut segmentation with an estimated trimap, etc. The proposed system showed very good results when working with real sequences at near real-time speed. Further research will involve human identification since the detection module presently only detects moving objects. Mean shift segmentation takes about 60% of the processing time of the human silhouette extraction module so we are also developing faster image segmentation techniques.

Acknowledgement

This work was supported by the Korea Science and Engineering Foundation (KOSEF) through the Biometrics Engineering Research Center (BERC) at Yonsei University.

This research was supported by the Ministry of Information and Communication, Korea under the Information Technology Research Center support program supervised by the Institute of Information Technology Assessment, IITA-2005-(C1090-0501-0019).

References

1. M. Bennewitz, W. Burgard, and S. Thrun: Using EM to learn motion behaviors of persons with mobile robots: Int. Conf. on Intelligent Robots and Systems (2002) 502-507.
2. Y. Boykov and M. Jolly.: Interactive graph cuts for optimal boundary and region segmentation of objects in N-D images. Int. Conf. on Computer Vision, CD-ROM, 2001.
3. Y. Boykov and V. Kolmogorov.: An experimental comparison of min-cut/max-flow algorithms for energy minimization in vision: IEEE PAMI.: 26. No. 9. (2004) 1124-1137.
4. R.T. Collins, A.J.Lipton, T.Kanade, H. Fujiyoshi, D. Duggins, Y. Tsin, D. Tolliver, N. Enomoto, O. Hasegawa, P. Burt and L. Wixson: A system for video surveillance and monitoring: CMU-RI-TR-00-12 (2000)
5. D. Comaniciu and P. Meer. Mean Shift: a robust approach toward feature space analysis. IEEE Trans. on Pattern Analysis and Machine Intelligence: Vol. 24. No. 5. (2002) 603-619.
6. D. Comaniciu, and V. Ramesh.: Kernel-Based Object Tracking. IEEE Trans. Pattern Anal. Mach. Intell. Vol. 25. (2003) 564-577
7. A. Hampapur, L.M. Brown, J. Connell, M. Lu, H. Merkl, S. Pankanti, A.W. Senior, C.F. Shu, and Y.L. Tian.: Multi-scale tracking for smart video surveillance: IEEE Tran. on Signal Processing: Vol. 22. No. 2. (2005) 38-51.
8. I. Haritaoglu, D. Harwood, and L. S. Davis.: W4 :Real-time surveillance of people and their activities: IEEE Trans. Pattern Anal. Mach. Intell..: Vol. 22. No. 8. (2000) 809-830.
9. B.Jung and G.S.Sukhatme.: Detecting Moving Objects using a Single Camera on a Mobile Robot in an Outdoor Environment: Int. Conf. on Intell. Auto. Sys. (2004) 980–987.
10. K. Konolige.: Small Vision Systems: Hardware and Implementation: Eighth International Symposium on Robotics Research, (1997) 111-116.
11. C. Cruz-Neira, D.J. Sandin, and T.A. DeFanti: Surround-screen projection-based virtual Reality: The Design and Implementation of the CAVE: Computer Graphics ACM SIGGRAPH, (1993) 135-142
12. V. Pavlovic, R. Sharma, and T. Huang: Gestural interface to a visual computing environment for molecular biologists: Proc. Int'l Conf. Automatic Face and Gesture Recognition, (1996)
13. S. Shafer, J. Krumm, B. Brumitt, B. Meyers, M. Czewinski and D. Robbins: The new easyLiving project at Microsoft Research: Proc. Joint DARPA/NIST Smart Space Workshop (1998).
14. W. Kruger, C. A. Bohn, B. Frohlich, H. Schuth, W. Strauss and G. Weche: The responsive workbench: A virtual work environment: IEEE Computer, (1995) 28(7) 42- 48.

Disparity Weighted Histogram-Based Object Tracking for Mobile Robot Systems

Cheolmin Choi, Jungho Ahn, Seungwon Lee, and Hyeran Byun

Dept. of Computer Science, Yonsei University
Shinchon-dong, Seodaemun-gu, Seoul 120-749, South Korea
{wxman, jungho, swlee, hrbyun}@cs.yonsei.ac.kr

Abstract. A vision-based real-time human detection and tracking capability is one of the key components of surveillance systems, human computer interfaces and monitoring systems. In this paper, we propose a method which uses color and disparity information obtained with a stereo camera. In order to achieve optimal performance with respect to detection or tracking of objects, it is better to consider multiple features together. We have developed a tracking method in which color and disparity information can be combined in a histogram. We used skin color and disparity distribution information to distinguish between different people. For human tracking, we propose a color histogram that is weighted by the disparity distribution of the target. The proposed method is simple and robust for moving camera environments and overcomes the drawbacks of conventional color histogram-based tracking methods. Experimental results show the robustness of the proposed method in environments with changing backgrounds and the tracking capabilities of targets which have similar color distributions as backgrounds or other targets. The proposed method can be used in real-time mobile robot applications.

Keywords: Real-time, color histogram, mobile robots.

1 Introduction

Recently, there have been remarkable developments in mobile robot systems, which have enabled these robots to provide professional, industrial, and personal services. Personal care services include natural interaction with humans. Visual interpretation of human movements and gestures can be useful in accomplishing natural Human-Robot Interaction (HRI). Vision-based HRI systems have surveillance modules which automatically identify and track people, objects, or events of interest in different kinds of environments. To obtain better performance, it is necessary to consider the robustness and reliability of these surveillance modules. Moreover, intelligent robot systems must be capable of robust object detection and tracking, which are efficient ways of performing real time services. In this paper, we focus on a robust, simple detection and tracking system which can be used with intelligent humanoid robots.

A vision-based human detection and tracking capability is one of the key components of surveillance systems. Generally, these surveillance systems consist of stationary cameras and a background subtraction module, which separates foreground

Z. Pan et al. (Eds.): ICAT 2006, LNCS 4282, pp. 584–593, 2006.

regions from background regions to detect humans. This background subtraction method is robust and simple in static camera environments [5], but it is hard to extract foreground regions when working with moving cameras (such as in mobile robot environments) because there is a large variation of pixels.

There are other approaches which do not perform background subtraction. Typically, these approaches are based on skin color, motion, or disparity models. However, various limitations in robustness and accuracy arise when using only a single approach. For example, the use of skin color alone cannot detect a human body or the back part of a person's head, and the use of motion alone makes it difficult to identify stationary humans with respect to camera motion. Thus, a robust human detection and tracking system must consider multiple approaches simultaneously.

Integration of disparity and color was introduced by Yang *et al.* [1] and Darrell *et al.* [2]. Yang *et al.* built a map from disparity features and subsequently fused it with color and motion information. However, it was difficult to track occluded humans with this method and a static background was required to obtain proper motion information. Darrell *et al.* presented a multi-modal integration system for unknown environments which combined stereo, color, and face detection modules. However, the approach encountered difficulties in recovery when a person was occluded by another person. Also, it was difficult to implement the approach in moving camera environments. This is because the human detection module was highly dependent on foreground disparity segmentation and a sufficiently large face area was required to perform tracking.

Several other approaches have been developed. These approaches include utilizing the statistical information of an object, the learning of scenes, and the evaluation of a hypothesis [3], [4] as well as creating a model of the target and candidates and then solving optimization problems in the feature space [7], [8], [9]. Recently, the mean shift-based object tracking method [9] was proposed, which used a color histogram of the object region and then a mean shift-based optimization method [10], [11], [12] was performed to find a similar local candidate. This method proved to be simple and robust for variations in color and camera environments. However, it often failed to track targets that were of similar color to the background or other targets. In the present study, we introduce a simple, robust detection and tracking method that uses color and disparity information. The proposed method can be used in moving camera environments such as mobile robot systems.

2 Overview

A flowchart of the proposed method is shown in Fig. 1. A face detection module using color images obtained by the left camera operates in the region of interest and then a body detection module operates with the output of the face detection module and the morphologically-smoothed disparity image. After successful detection of the human body, output of the detection module is the target of the tracking module. The human tracking module performs tracking using the optimization method which is based on the disparity-weighted histogram.

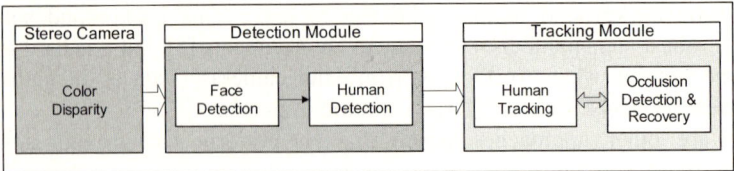

Fig. 1. Flowchart of the proposed method. The detection and tracking modules are classified into two separate sub-modules. The face detection sub-module uses only color information. The body detection and human tracking sub-modules use color and disparity information.

After a successful tracking procedure, an occluding event is checked using the distance between the targets and the similarity measure. The following section describes the detection module. Section 4 describes a module which performs tracking using a disparity-weighted color histogram that is weighted by the probability-based disparity of the target. Experimental results are analyzed in section 5 and section 6 describes the conclusions.

3   Detection Module

One of the most commonly used features for human detection is the color of a human face [5], [6]. In the proposed detection module, we used color information first, and then we used heuristics and a simple geometric model for body detection.

3.1   Face Model

For face detection, we used a face color model which was produced from four differently illuminated scenes of one person. We built a normalized red and green color histogram of the face model and then performed the mean shift algorithm on the region of interest. If a face was present, the position of the face-like area could be found using the mean shift algorithm and the threshold of histogram similarity. Fig. 2 shows the face color model (with its histogram equalized for visualization). Because of the quantization nature of the spatial color histogram, the face model is a sufficient way of finding different faces in a region of interest. The number of mean shift iterations for face detection can be small because the mode position of the face itself is not needed. In the experiment only three iterations were used.

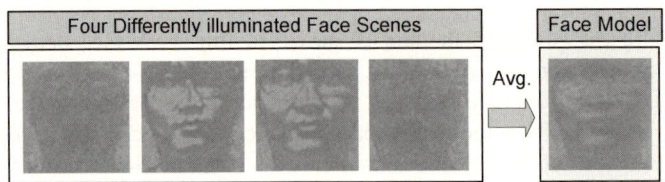

Fig. 2. The face color model

3.2 Human Detection

Using a face-like area coordinate and its disparity value, we can detect the body area by using the following steps.

- **Step 1**: Find a point of the face-like region.
- **Step 2**: Find the horizontal head scale using horizontal edge points.
- **Step 3**: Find the vertical head scale using vertical edge points.
- **Step 4**: Detect a human body using the scale of the head.

In step 4, we can use heuristics which the disparity value of the body part shows a similar value. Fig. 3 shows the result of each detection step. The detected body area is the target for the subsequent frame.

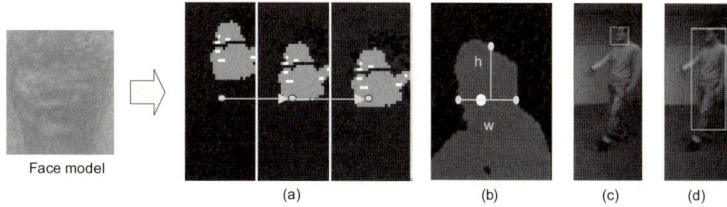

Fig. 3. The human detection module. (a) Find a face-like region (search over the ROI using the face color model and mean shift tracking). (b) Find the scale of the head (the white circle means the detected point of a face-like region). (c) Detect the human head area. (d) Detect the human body area.

4 Tracking Module

In this section, we propose a simple disparity-weighted histogram method which is based on a mean shift tracking algorithm. At each successful tracking procedure we retained the histogram similarity of the candidate target and the distance between targets for occlusion detection and the recovery sub-module. Mean shift based color tracking method is a simple and robust algorithm that climbs the gradient of a probability distribution to find the best local candidate. This method can be divided into three steps: target and candidate representation, similarity measurement, and optimization using the mean shift algorithm. Short descriptions of these steps are presented below.

- **Target and Candidate Representation**

  PDF models of targets and candidates can be defined as in Comaniciu *et al.* [9]

Target :
$$\hat{q}_u = C_q \sum_{i=1}^{n} k\left(\left\|x_i\right\|^2\right) \delta[b(x_i) - u] \tag{1}$$

Candidate :
$$\hat{p}_u = C_p \sum_{i=1}^{n_h} k\left(\left\|\frac{y - x_i}{h}\right\|^2\right) \delta[b(x_i) - u] \tag{2}$$

where k is a profile kernel for spatial weight, h is the kernel bandwidth with respect to the bandwidth of the target model, C_q and C_p are normalization factors, δ is the Kronecker delta function, and u is the index of the histogram bin.

– *Similarity Measurement*
   In order to measure the similarity of two histograms, a metric-based Bhattacharyya coefficient can be utilized as follows:

$$\hat{\rho}(y) = \sum_{u=1}^{m} \sqrt{\hat{p}_u(y)\hat{q}_u} \tag{3}$$

Using Taylor expansion, (3) can be reduced to:

$$\hat{\rho}_u \approx \frac{1}{2}\sum_{u=1}^{m} \sqrt{\hat{p}_u(y_0)\hat{q}_u} + \frac{C_p}{2}\sum_{i=1}^{n_h} w_i k\left(\left\|\frac{y-x_i}{h}\right\|^2\right) \tag{4}$$

$$w_i = \sum_{u=1}^{m} \delta[b(x_i)-u]\sqrt{\frac{\hat{q}_u}{\hat{p}_u(y_0)}} \tag{5}$$

where m is the number of the histogram bins, n_h is the number of pixels that fall in a spatial kernel, and y_0 is the previous target position.

– *Optimization Using the Mean Shift Algorithm*
   The target tracking problem can be reduced so as to maximize similarity, which can be solved by the mean shift algorithm. A new target position, which is based on the previous position, can be calculated according to the following relationship.

New position :
$$\hat{y}_1 = \frac{\sum_{i=1}^{n_h} x_i w_i g\left(\left\|\frac{\hat{y}_0 - x_i}{h}\right\|^2\right)}{\sum_{i=1}^{n_h} w_i g\left(\left\|\frac{\hat{y}_0 - x_i}{h}\right\|^2\right)} \tag{6}$$

where, $g(x) = -k'(x)$.

4.1 Human Tracking Using Disparity-Weighted Histogram

The mean shift based color tracking approach has difficulties when separating objects with similar color distributions. We introduce a disparity-weighted color histogram method to overcome this weakness. The disparity obtained with a stereo camera is an important feature that can be used to separate different objects or foreground regions from background regions.

We assume that the disparity distribution of the detected human body shows small variations with respect to the background regions or other objects. Frame-to-frame differences in disparity values are also small even if the scene is dynamic. In this section, we propose a simple disparity-weighted histogram which combines disparity information and color information. Let $\{\hat{v}_v\}_{v=1...k}$ and v_M be the normalized histogram representation of the target area and its maximum probability. If we choose a target area that is sufficiently restricted in terms of size, it can be assumed that pixels that fall in bin M, which has v_M probability, are the most likely target pixels. Let $\{W_v\}_{v=1...k}$ be the weight value for the disparity histogram bin, which is defined as:

Disparity bin weights :
$$\left\{W_v = 1 - \frac{|M - v|}{M}\right\}_{v=1...k} \tag{7}$$

where v is the bin index of the histogram. A new target and candidate representation with these weights can then be computed as follows:

New Target :
$$\hat{Q}_u = C_{q,w} \sum_{i=1}^{n} W_{i,v} k\left(\left\|x_i\right\|^2\right) \delta[b(x_i) - u] \tag{8}$$

New Candidate :
$$\hat{P}_u = C_{p,w} \sum_{i=1}^{n_h} W_{i,v} k\left(\left\|\frac{y - x_i}{h}\right\|^2\right) \delta[b(x_i) - u] \tag{9}$$

where $C_{q,w}$ and $C_{p,w}$ are the normalization factors for the target and candidate values, respectively, and $W_{i,v}$ is the disparity weight for the pixels which fall in the target region. The Bhattacharyya coefficient of (8) and (9) can be derived as shown in (10). Thus, to maximize the similarity measure, the data being weighted by (11) has to be maximized. A new target position based on the previous target position is derived by the mean shift algorithm.

$$\hat{\rho}_u \approx \frac{1}{2} \sum_{u=1}^{m} \sqrt{\hat{P}_u(y_0)\hat{Q}_u} + \frac{C_{p,w}}{2} \sum_{i=1}^{n_h} W_{i,D} k\left(\left\|\frac{y - x_i}{h}\right\|^2\right) \tag{10}$$

$$w_{i,D} = \sum_{u=1}^{m} W_{i,v} \delta[b(x_i) - u] \sqrt{\frac{\hat{Q}_u}{\hat{P}_u(y_0)}} \tag{11}$$

If the kernel is chosen as the Epanechnikov profile [12], the derivative of the profile, $g(x)$, is constant and a new target position can be reduced to (12). Fig. 4 shows the three steps of the tracking procedure.

$$\hat{y}_1 = \frac{\sum_{i=1}^{n_h} w_{i,D} x_i}{\sum_{i=1}^{n_h} w_{i,D}} \tag{12}$$

4.2 Occlusion Detection and Recovery

Using spatial information of targets and histogram similarities, it is possible to detect occlusion events. If the distance between the targets approached the threshold value, we checked the similarity of each target to find the occluding target with no significant difference in similarity value and the occluded target with a significant difference. To recover the occluded target information, we performed search process on each side of the occluding target. Occlusion detection and recovery is shown in Fig. 5.

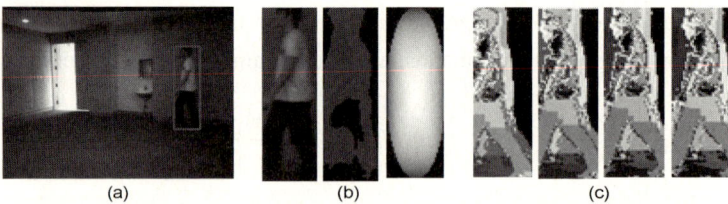

(a)   (b)   (c)

Fig. 4. Three steps of the tracking procedure. (a) Targeting step to obtain the coordinates of the area of interest. (b) Information-combining step wherein color and disparity information are combined with the spatial kernel for mean shift based tracking. (c) Mean shift based tracking step.

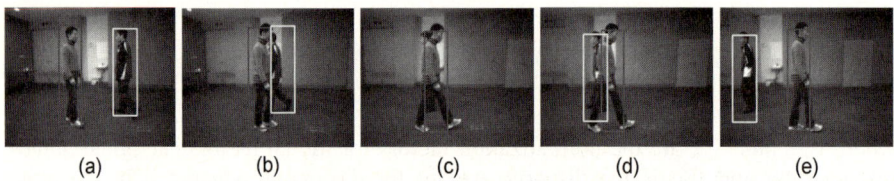

(a)   (b)   (c)   (d)   (e)

Fig. 5. Occlusion detection and recovery. (a) No occlusion in the 150th frame of the test data CM3. (b) Before occlusion (checking similarity and distance) in the 163rd frame. (c) Occlusion (checking similarity on both sides of the occluding target) in the 166th frame. (d) Recovered target in the 170th frame (e) No occlusion in the 182nd frame.

5 Experimental Results

We used well-calibrated stereo cameras (Videre, STH-MDCS2) and the Small Vision System [13] for disparity computation. The computing platform was a Pentium 4, with 3 GHz CPU and 1G RAM. We used a 16×16 histogram in the normalized RG color space for face detection. The targets were represented by a $30 \times 30 \times 30$ histogram in the RGB color space with a 50-disparity histogram.

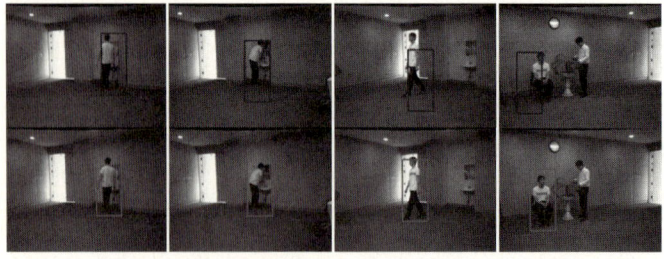

Fig. 6. The Wash sequence. Frames 30, 190, 260, and 460 are shown. The top row (blue rectangles) shows the conventional color histogram method, and the bottom row (red rectangles) shows the proposed tracking method.

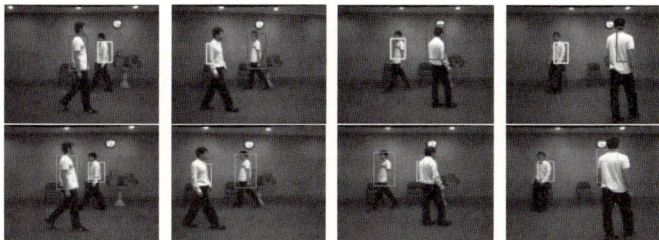

Fig. 7. The Turn sequence. The first row shows the results of the conventional color histogram method. The second row shows the results of the proposed method. The first column shows the target area that was provided manually. Because of color similarities, the labels of the targets changed after each crossing event (see the red and yellow rectangles in the first row).

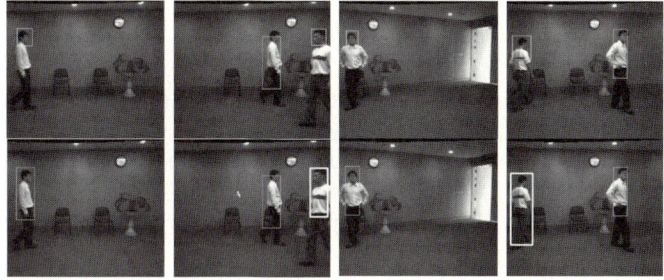

Fig. 8. Output of the detection module in the Two_Man sequence. The yellow rectangles in the top row denote the detected head area, and the blue and white rectangles denote the detected body. Frames 76, 133, 275, and 327 are shown (from left to right). Note that the scenes are dynamic.

Fig. 9. The Two_Man sequences. Frames 0, 76, 133, 149, 153, 183, 275, 327, 387, 408, 426, and 558 are shown (from top left corner to bottom right, left images of stereo camera).

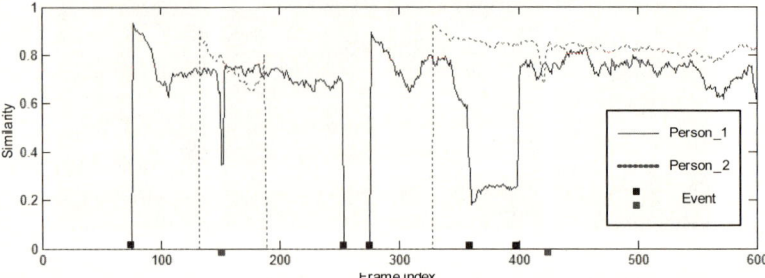

Fig. 10. The value of the similarity function of the frame index for the Two_Man sequence. Every event in The Two_Man sequence was identified. Person_1 appeared in the FOV at the 76th frame, occluded by Person_2 at the 149th frame, and disappeared at the 246th frame. Person_1 reappeared at the 275th frame, disappeared at the 361st frame, and reappeared at the 399th frame (see the blue rectangles and red circles). The occlusion event happened twice.

We used three different video sequences. The first, two sequences, Wash and Turn, where the target area was given manually, were utilized for comparison. Then, the results of the proposed method were compared with a conventional color-based histogram tracking results. The third sequence, Two_Man, was utilized for analysis of the proposed method. In the Wash sequences, the target showed similar color distribution with the background initially, and it changed as the target moved across the room (because of the opened door). This illumination change produced inaccurate tracking results with the conventional color histogram, but the proposed method was able to overcome this drawback (see Fig. 6). In the Turn sequence, two people were walking around each other and they showed a similar color distribution (see Fig. 7). In the Two_Man sequence, there were two people who are walking cross from each other and in and out of the camera FOV independently. There were four different kinds of events in the Two_Man sequence, which included the appearing and disappearing of each person and the occlusion and otherwise of each person. Output of the proposed method is shown in Fig. 8. It can be seen that the detected head and body scale is dependent on the sparseness of disparity distribution. Each detection and tracking module performed well. Also, every occlusion events was detected, and the occluded persons were recovered successfully (see Fig. 9). Fig. 10 shows that each event in the Two_Man sequence can be identified using the histogram similarity function of the frame index.

6   Conclusions

In this paper, we have proposed a real-time human detection and tracking system. The proposed method uses color information to find a face area and then detects a body by using the coordinates of the face area and disparity information. The tracking module uses a disparity-weighted color histogram that combines spatial color and disparity information. The proposed method overcomes the weaknesses of conventional mean shift based color tracking methods and can be applied in applications like mobile robots, where there are moving camera environments. One drawback of the proposed method is a lack of scale adaptation to different scales. In the future, we plan to build a model of the disparity-scale, which will then provide the relationship between the object disparity and the scale. Using this disparity-scale model, we will develop the method into a more flexible system.

Acknowledgement. This work was supported by the Korea Science and Engineering Foundation (KOSEF) through the Biometrics Engineering Research Center (BERC) at Yonsei University. This research was supported by the Ministry of Information and Communication, Korea under the Information Technology Research Center support program supervised by the Institute of Information Technology Assessment, IITA-2005-(C1090-0501-0019).

References

1. M. T. Yang, S. C. Wang, and Y. Y. Lin.: A Multimodal Fusion System for People Detection and Tracking. Int. J. Imaging Systems and Technology, Vol. 15 (2005) 131–142
2. T. Darrell, G. Gordon, M. Harville, and J. Woodfill.: Integrated Person Tracking Using Stereo, Colour, and Pattern Detection. Int. J. Computer Vision, Vol. 15 (2000) 175–185
3. S. Arulampalam, S. Maskell, N. Gordon, and T. Clapp.: A Tutorial on Particle Filters for On-Line Non-Linear/Non-Gaussian Bayesian Tracking. IEEE Trans. Signal Processing, Vol. 50 (2002) 174-189
4. M. Isard, and A. Blake.: Condensation-Conditional Density Propagation for Visual Tracking. Int. J. Computer Vision, Vol. 29 (1998)
5. M. Soriano, B. Martinkauppi, and S. Huovinen.: Skin Detection in Video under Changing Illumination Conditions. IEEE Conf. on Computer Vision and Pattern Recognition, Vol. 1 (2000) 839-842
6. J. Yang and A. Waibel.: A Real-Time Face Tracker. IEEE Work. on Applic. CV. Sarasota. (1996) 108-121
7. P. Viola and W. Wells.: Alignment by Maximization of Mutual Information. Int. J. Computer Vision, Vol. 24 (1997) 137-154
8. C. Olson.: Image Registration by Aligning Entropies. Proc. IEEE Conf. Computer Vision and Pattern Recognition, Vol. 2 (2001) 331-336
9. D. Comaniciu and V. Ramesh.: Kernel-Based Object Tracking. IEEE Trans. Pattern Analysis and Machine Intelligence, Vol. 25 (2003) 564-577
10. K. Fukunaga.: Introduction to Statistical Pattern Recognition. 2nd edition. Academic Press. 1990
11. D. Comaniciu and P. Meer.: Mean Shift: A Robust Approach toward Feature Space Analysis. IEEE Trans. Pattern Analysis and Machine Intelligence, Vol. 24 (2002) 603-619
12. M. P. Wand and M. C. Jones.: Kernel Smoothing. Chapman & Hall. 1995
13. K. Konolige.: Small Vision Systems: Hardware and Implementation: Eighth International Symposium on Robotics Research. (1997) 111-116.

Towards Robust 3D Reconstruction of Human Motion from Monocular Video

Cheng Chen, Yueting Zhuang, and Jun Xiao

College of Computer Science, Zhejiang Univ., China
{happyrobbie, yzhuang, junx}@cs.zju.edu.cn

Abstract. A robust, adaptive system for reconstructing 3D human motion from monocular video is presented. Our system takes a model based approach. To save computation time, we fit the skeleton instead of full body model to the silhouette. End sites positions identified from the silhouettes serve as an extra constraint. The alleviation of computational burden then makes the use of simulated annealing practical to get rid of local minima. The identifiable end sites also serve as the criterion to judge the reconstruction reliability of single frames. According to different reliabilities, the video is segmented into sections, which are reconstructed using different strategies. Our system is robust, getting rid of error accumulation in tracking, and adaptive, being able to tell the user when and where more information is needed.

Keywords: video motion tracking, model based 3D reconstruction.

1 Introduction

3D tracking/reconstruction of human motion is an important subject in fields such as computer animation, virtual reality and so forth. Optical motion capture is widely used nowadays, but there are some applications where the expensive and intrusive optical MoCap systems cannot be employed. Compared to the optical counterpart, video based motion reconstruction is low cost, non intrusive and easy to use and is particularly suitable for a group of applications:

1. In a video teleconferencing environment, 3D poses of the presenter can be reconstructed and shown to the audience to improve the reality and clarity.
2. 3D gestures from video can be used in human-computer interface to allow intuitive control. For example, players can control 3D characters in computer games through gestures instead of keyboards, which greatly improves the experience.
3. Video surveillance systems can benefit from video based motion tracking by automatically tracking and recognizing dangerous actions.
4. There are huge numbers of existing video materials from which motion patterns and styles can be tracked and learned and then used in animation.

However, video based 3D motion reconstruction is also a challenging task. [1]. The difficulty comes from the inherent ambiguity from 2D to 3D, frequent self occlusion of human body, noise in video, and so on.

Z. Pan et al. (Eds.): ICAT 2006, LNCS 4282, pp. 594–603, 2006.
© Springer-Verlag Berlin Heidelberg 2006

Current human motion reconstruction techniques roughly fall into two categories—learning based and model based. In learning based methods, example 3D poses and corresponding images (features extracted from images) are the sources of learning. Then poses for new images are recovered. [2], [3], [4], [5]. For example [2] regresses a function by RVM using the examples silhouettes' local shape context distribution and corresponding poses. [3] uses AdaBoost to select from the enormous amount of possible local features the most discriminative ones and use them to retrieve poses for new silhouettes from database. The main limitation of learning based methods is that they usually enforce a strong model on poses. Most methods only work on specific types of motions (walk, gulf swing [6]…). And they often need a database that is suitable for the problem domain, which also means an enormous training process [3].

Our method falls into the model based approach, which tries to estimate the pose that minimizes some metric that reflects the difference between the pose and the image. [7], [8], [9], [10], [11]. For example [9] precomputes several offline subsidiary databases and then use them to select best match from a captured 3D pose pool using silhouette and edge map. [10] uses genetic algorithm to estimate a pose that best fits the extracted features on images; however, the method heavily relies on successful tracking of feature points, which cannot be robust. Our work is close to [8], where a body is rendered at different poses and compared with silhouette using core-weighted XOR and image features. Our work differs from [8] in that we fit the skeleton instead of full body model to the silhouette to save computation time, that we use discernable end sites (head, hands, feet) as a metric of frame's reconstructing difficulty as well as a constraint for the object function, and that our system has the ability to determine where manual information (key frames) are needed. Model based approaches tend to have two obstacles: high computational burden and spurious local minima.

Some other methods try to reconstruct poses from images taken by multiple cameras. [12] calculates the 3D voxel from 5 synchronized images. These methods are more accurate when the number of cameras increases, but this also enforces severe limitations to the system's application field.

Also, some methods take an optical-hybrid way. [13] puts optical markers (far fewer than normal optical MoCap systems) on the body and recover 3D motions in real time. The markers' locations can be reliably determined and serve as indices into a pre-computed pose database. Then online pose synthesis is conducted locally.

In this paper we present a system reliably generating visually pleasing 3D motions from uncalibrated monocular video. No prior knowledge of the motion pattern (such as database) is used. The system is easy to setup and easy to use. It is free from common problems in motion tracking such as error accumulation/propagation and difficulty in recovering from errors. The system is also adaptive. It can tell the user where it needs more information to complete the task. We'll see that with limited intuitive user interaction, complex motions can be successfully reconstructed.

The novelties and contributions of this paper include:

1. The use of skeleton instead of full body in pose estimation greatly reduces the object function's computational burden and therefore allows the use of simulated annealing, which can solve the local minima problem.
2. We make novel uses of end sites positions as a component of pose estimation object function as well as the criterion of reconstruction reliability.

3. We delicately combine two detectors with different properties in hands detection. The skin color detector learned on the fly adds power to the curvature detector without introducing severe robustness problem.
4. We develop a reconstruction methodology that divides video into sections based on the reconstruction reliability and then uses different strategies for different sections. This eliminates error accumulation and brings the system the ability to automatically decide where and when it needs more information from the user.

Fig. 1 gives an overview of the system workflow. Videos are transformed to silhouettes, from which end sites are identified. Then poses are estimated for frames. Finally, smooth motions from the estimated poses are generated as the final results.

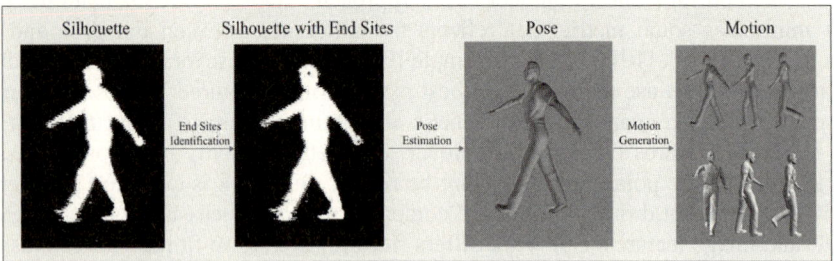

Fig. 1. System workflow

2   Silhouette Extraction and End Sites Identification

The first step of our system is extracting silhouettes from video frames. We choose a silhouette way because it has several advantages:

1. Silhouettes can be relatively robustly extracted, at least when we are in a controlled environment and hence the background model is accessible.
2. Silhouettes are insensitive to irrelevant factors. Many tracking methods based on color or texture can be defeated by variations in clothes texture or even cockle.
3. Simple as they look, silhouettes do reserve much information about the pose.

In this paper the silhouette extraction method presented in [14] is employed. The method models the background in a statistical approach and is robust to global and local illumination changes (shadows). Noises are further removed as described in [15].

After silhouettes are extracted, we try to identify end sites on them. By "end sites" we mean hands, feet and head. By "*identify*" we mean both "*detect*"—finding out the positions of end sites, and "*label*"—distinguish hands from feet and left from right.

The most intuitive detection method might be directly looking at curvatures on the silhouette contour. Fig. 2 shows some results. To be more robust, we employ different strategies for different end sites. Head is the easiest one, because it is almost never occluded by other body parts, it always lies at a local highest position, and its corresponding section on the contour consists of points with not very sharp but steady positive convex curvatures. For feet, they usually lie in the bottom of the silhouette, and since we are not using high resolution cameras, we don't make further distinctions between the ankles and toes. Hands are vital to the pose comprehension, yet they are most difficult to detect, mostly because they are sometimes "shaded" by the body. Also, sometimes the arms bend so heavily that the high curvatures at the elbow can confuse the detector. In light of these, we set the parameters of the curvature detector for hands stricter. We are trading recall for precision here.

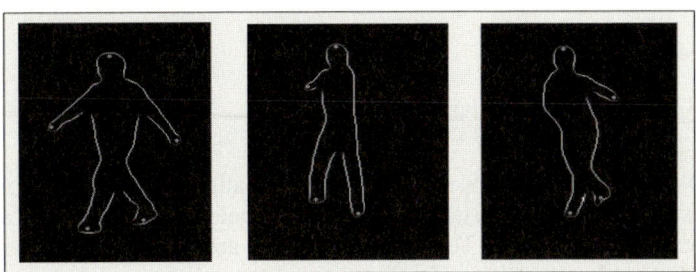

Fig. 2. Sample results for the curvature detector. Red on contour stands for large convex curvatures; blue stands for large concave curvatures. Green dots represent the detected location.

Note in Fig. 2 that only one hand of the 2nd and 3rd silhouettes is detected, respectively. The other one is "shaded" by the body. We have to turn to things beyond silhouettes to deal with this. Since the precision of curvature detector is very high, we build a color model based on the detected hands on the fly and then used the color model to detect remaining hands missed by our high-precision-low-recall curvature detector. In this way we delicately combine the two hand detectors. We use a standard Gaussian color model. Note the hands might be physically occluded by the body and still not discernable.

The use of color might cause robustness problem and might seem contradictory to our initial purpose of using silhouette. However, we constrain our searching area to be only in the corresponding silhouette. This greatly reduces the robustness risk, since we don't search on the background, where most robustness problems come from.

The automatic end sites labeling is based on the temporal smoothness. User is required to label the first frame where all 5 end sites are detected. Then the system uses the temporal information to automatically label successive frames. To be more robust, we predict the end sites positions using Kalman filter before labeling.

3   Pose Estimation

First we formulize the representation for poses. Each joint in the human skeleton model has 3 rotational DOFs. The root joint has 3 additional DOFs representing global translation. In pose estimation step, we consider pose as the vector of all joints' rotations. The root's translation is not included since it reflects the figure's global position. We postpone the consideration of root's translation until motion generation, where feet-ground contact is taken into account.

Videos are essentially 2D projections of the 3D real world. In other words, given sufficient parameters, a projection function projects a pose vector **p** to a 2D silhouette **s**.

Our problem is actually the reverse one: we now have **s**, and we want to recover **p**. This is mathematically ill posed, since the projection function doesn't have a reverse counterpart. But due to constraints such as the anatomy and the temporal smoothness, it's still probable to find a pose **p** that best *explains* silhouette **s**. We take a searching approach—searching for the pose that minimizes some object function E that measures the goodness of the pose according to the silhouette.

3.1   Object Function Design

The object function E is made up of three terms.

1. The core area term $E_{core-area}$.
   The 2D projection of the skeleton at pose **p**, after alignment and scaling, should lie in the core areas of the silhouette, i.e., the limbs should lie in the median axis of the limbs area on the silhouette. To quantify the core area, we do Euclidean distance transformation to the silhouette. (Fig. 3).

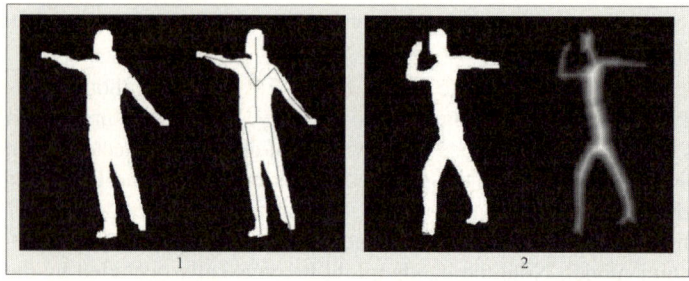

Fig. 3. (*1*) The alignment to core area. (*2*) The Euclidean distance transform.

Stating in detail, we calculate the positions of the 16 joints projected on the 2D silhouette, connect adjacent joints to by straight lines to form the limbs, sample some points on the limbs, and calculate the average value on the distance transformed silhouette at locations of the sampled points.

$$E_{core-area} = -\sum_m \mathbf{s}'(t)(\mathbf{point}(m) \cdot \mathbf{T}(t,\mathbf{p}))/M \cdot \tag{1}$$

In equation (1), $\mathbf{s}'(t)$ is the distance transforms of silhouette at time t, $\mathbf{point}(m)$ is the mth sampled point on the skeleton, $\mathbf{T}(t,\mathbf{p})$ is the t- and **p**- dependent rigid transform that converts the local coordinate vector of $\mathbf{point}(m)$ to 2D location on the silhouette, and M is the total number of sampled points.

Note that if an end site is not identified, equation (1) does not compute the contribution made by the corresponding limb.

2. The coverage term $E_{coverage}$.
   The core-area term alone is not sufficient to determine the pose, because the limbs might be not sufficiently stretched to cover the limbs in the silhouette and still remain a low $E_{core-area}$. To solve this, we make sure that the locations of the end sites projected on the silhouette are close to the locations identified in Sec. 2.

$$E_{coverage} = \sum_{\text{for all identified end sites}} \| \mathbf{loc}_{sil} - \mathbf{loc}_{ske} \|^2 / n \cdot \tag{2}$$

In equation (2), $\mathbf{loc}_{sil}$ is the end site's location identified on the silhouette in Sec. 4, $\mathbf{loc}_{ske}$ is the projected skeleton's end site's location, and n is the total number of end sites identified at the current frame.

3. The smoothness term.

This term comes from the temporal smoothness. The pose should not change abruptly. We use the two previous poses $\mathbf{p}(t\text{-}1)$ and $\mathbf{p}(t\text{-}2)$ to measure the smoothness.

$$E_{smoothness} = \| \mathbf{p}(t) - 2\mathbf{p}(t-1) + \mathbf{p}(t-2) \|^2 . \tag{3}$$

Combining equations (1), (2) and (3), we get the final object function E.

$$E = \alpha E_{core-area} + \beta E_{coverage} + \gamma E_{smoothness} . \tag{4}$$

3.2 Video Optimization Strategy

The determining of the desired pose $\mathbf{p}$ can be formulated as an optimizing problem of minimizing E, by varying $\mathbf{p}$ in the valid range. Note due to biomechanical limitation, the valid range for $\mathbf{p}$ is a closed sub region in the pose vector Euclidean space.

Due to the complexity of E, derive based optimizing methods cannot be used. Worse is that E has many spurious local minima. We use simulated annealing (SA), which helps a lot in avoiding local minima. By setting the parameter such as the initial temperature and annealing rate, it is very easy to control how much ability of getting out of local minima is allowed. That is important, since for most frames we have an initial guess of the pose and we need only conduct partial SA to save time.

In Sec. 1 we have pointed out the two challenges of model based approaches: high computational burden and spurious local minima. Now let's see how we cope with those. To alleviate object function's complexity, we fit the skeleton instead of full body model (such as in [8]) to the silhouette. This significantly reduces complexity since only the 2D projections of joint points need to be calculated. The sampled points on the limbs are interpolated directly from the 2D positions of the joints. Our computationally efficient object function then allows the use of SA to help get rid of local minima. If we fit the full body and still use SA, the object function would be so expensive that the estimation of one pose would possibly takes hundreds of seconds.

It turns out that if we estimate poses based only on single frames, some frames can not be correctly reconstructed, partly because they don't have their end sites completely identified and so information is insufficient. In such cases, temporal information should be made full use of.

First we classify frames as *reliable frames*, if all their end sites are identified, or *unreliable frames* if otherwise. Due to the continuity, reliable and unreliable frames tend to cluster into interleaved *reliable sections* and *unreliable sections*. (Fig. 4).

Clearly, reliable frames have larger chances to be correctly estimated. Also, due to temporal smoothness, unreliable frames near the section boundaries have larger hope than the ones deep inside the unreliable section. Therefore, if an unreliable section is longer than a preset length L, we label it as a *dangerous section*, meaning that frames

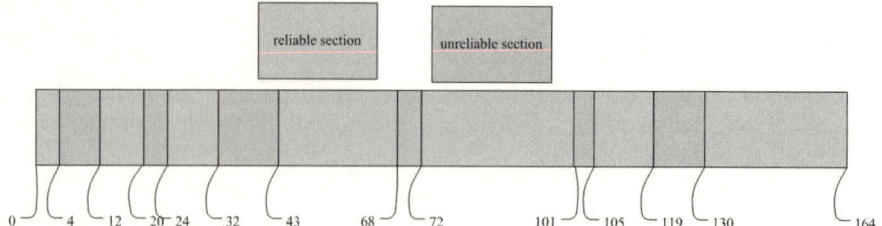

Fig. 4. Segmentation of a real video clip into interleaved reliable and unreliable sections. The number shows the location (in frame sequence) of the section boundaries.

deep inside it are unlikely to be correctly estimated. User is required to specify a key frame in the middle of the dangerous section. Then the key frame splits the long unreliable section into two short ones. This procedure is repeated until no dangerous section is present, and then the following reconstruction algorithm is taken:

1. The algorithm starts at every reliable section. For each reliable section, we choose a base frame and do a full SA to estimate its pose. Full SA means high initial temperature and slow annealing rate. Here the smoothness term of the object function is set to 0. This is the key to getting rid of error accumulation as base frames for each reliable section are estimated independently.

2. For each base frame, we successively estimate frames around it in both directions, until frames in its containing reliable section and two surrounding unreliable sections are covered.

3. Now we have two poses for each unreliable frame from the two surrounding reliable sections. We blend the two poses, using the inverses of the distances to the two surrounding section boundaries as the weights.

Up to now, we have estimated poses for all frames. The next stage is to combine these poses to generate a satisfying motion.

4   Motion Generation

The motion generation stage has two tasks: smoothly combine the poses, and determine the root's translations according to feet-ground contact. We apply a simple Gaussian low pass filter on the poses to get smoothness. To solve the contact problem, we make use of the estimated feet height. For most motions where at any time at least one foot is on the ground and no slide occurs, the feet's height could be used to determine. For motions possible to have two feet flying or where slide exists, such as jumping and skiing, user has to manually adjust the root's translation.

If needed, the generated motion can be further fined by 3D animation tools.

5   Results

We use a skeleton with 16 joints in our experiment. Therefore our pose vector is a 48D. As we discard the root's translation in pose estimation, when calculating the object function, we have to automatically adjust the scaling and alignment of the

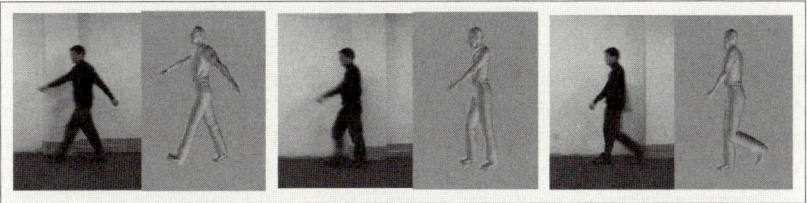

Fig. 5. Representative results for reconstructing walking motions

Fig. 6. Representative results for reconstructing fence motion

Fig. 7. Representative results for reconstructing Latin dance

skeleton according to the silhouette. The alignment is straightforward since we already have head positions detected on the silhouette and calculated on the skeleton by projection. We do the automatic scaling using the method presented in [16].

Most of the computation occurs at pose estimation. It typically takes 5~6 seconds to estimate a base frame and slightly less than 1 second for a non base frame. Usually the proportion of base frame in a video clip is less than 10% (typically around 5%).

We show representative results for walking, fence and Latin dance (Fig. 5~7).

6   Conclusion and Future Work

We've presented and implemented a system that robustly reconstructs 3D motion from monocular video. Instead of tracking features directly on the image, which is sensitive to noise and irrelevant factors, we take a model based approach using silhouettes. In hands detection, we gracefully combine the power of two detectors to achieve excellent results. In pose estimation, we fit the skeleton instead of full body model to the silhouette and it significantly reduces the computational burden and allows the use of SA to cope with the spurious local minima. Our algorithm restarts at every reliable section and avoids error accumulation. Our reconstructing strategy also enables the system to tell when and where more information is needed from the user.

Our system has some limitations. It is difficult to extract silhouettes from videos with highly clustered background and/or unpredictable camera movement. Also, since temporal information is employed, our system might fail on abrupt or very fast motions. Cameras with high sampling rate can be used to solve this problem, but this enforces a serious limitation on the usage. Those are some of the potential future work.

Acknowledgments. This work is supported by National Natural Science Foundation of China (No.60533090, No.60525108), 973 Program (No.2002CB312101), Science and Technology Project of Zhejiang Province (2005C13032, 2005C11001-05), and China-US Million Book Digital Library Project (www.cadal.zju.edu.cn).

References

1. Gleicher M., Ferrier N.: Evaluating Video-Based Motion Capture. Computer animation 2002(CA02). Los Alamitos: IEEE Computer Society Press; 2002. p. 75--81.
2. Ankur Agarwal and Bill Triggs: Recovering 3D Human Pose from Monocular Images. IEEE Transactions on Pattern Analysis and Machine Intelligence, Vol. 28, No. 1, January 2006
3. L. Ren, G. Shakhnarovich, J. Hodgins, H. Pfister, and P. Viola: Learning Silhouette Features for Control of Human Motion. Proceedings of the SIGGRAPH 2004 Conference on Sketches & Applications, August 2004
4. Ahmed Elgammal and Chan-Su Lee: Inferring 3D Body Pose from Silhouettes Using Activity Manifold Learning. 2004 IEEE Computer Society Conference on Computer Vision and Pattern Recognition (CVPR'04) - Volume 2   pp. 681-688
5. V. Athitsos and S. Sclaroff: Estimating 3D Hand Pose from a Cluttered Image. Proc. Int'l Conf. Computer Vision, 2003.

6. R. Urtasun, D. Fleet, and P. Fua: Monocular 3--D Tracking of the Golf Swing. Conference on Computer Vision and Pattern Recognition, San Diego, CA, June 2005.
7. C. Bregler and J. Malik: Tracking people with twists and exponential maps. Proceedings of Computer Vision and Pattern Recognition (CVPR'98), 1998
8. Yisheng Chen, Jinho Lee, Rick Parent, Raghu Machiraju: Markerless Monocular Motion Capture Using Image Features and Physical Constraints. Computer Graphics International 2005, Stony Brook, USA, June 2005.
9. Antonio S. Micilotta, Eng Jon Ong and Richard Bowden: Real-time Upper Body 3D Pose Estimation from a Single Uncalibrated Camera. In Eurographics 2005
10. Jianhui Zhao and Ling Li: Human motion reconstruction from monocular images using genetic algorithms. Computer Animation and Virtual Worlds 2004; 15:407-414
11. D.E. DiFranco, T. Cham, and J.M. Rehg: Reconstruction of 3-D Figure Motion from 2-D Correspondences. Proc. Conf. Computer Vision and Pattern Recognition, pages 307.314, 2001.
12. M. Cheung, T. Kanade, J.-Y. Bouguet, and M. Holler: A real time system for robust 3D voxel reconstruction of human motions. CVPR00, V2, P714--720.
13. Jinxiang Chai and Jessica K. Hodgins: Performance Animation from Low-dimensional Control Signals. ACM Transactions on Graphics (SIGGRAPH 2005)
14. T. Horprasert, D. Harwood, and L. Davis: A statistical approach for real-time robust background subtraction and shadow detection. IEEE ICCV FRAME-RATE Workshop, 1999.
15. Ronald Poppe, Dirk Heylen, Anton Nijholt, Mannes Poel: Towards real-time Body Pose Estimation for Presenters in Meeting Environments. WSCG (Short Papers) 2005: 41-44
16. Jerome Vignola, Jean-François Lalonde and Robert Bergevin: Progressive Human Skeleton Fitting. Conference on Vision Interface, 2003

Wavelet Scalable Video Coding with Minimal Average Temporal Distance for Motion Estimation

Changhoon Yim[1], Hojin Ha[2], Bae-Keun Lee[2], and Woo-Jin Han[2]

[1] Dept. of Internet and Multimedia Eng., Konkuk University, Seoul 143-701, Korea
cyim@konkuk.ac.kr
[2] Digital Media R&D Center, Samsung Electronics, Suwon,
Kyeonggi-Do 442-742, Korea

Abstract. Wavelet scalable video coding (WSVC) can be used efficiently for scalable mesh compression for virtual reality applications over IP networks. This paper proposes efficient methods to improve the coding efficiency of WSVC through the minimization of average temporal distance (ATD) for motion estimation. The ATD is closely related to the peak signal-to-noise ratio (PSNR) performance of WSVC which is based on motion compensated temporal filtering. Simulation results show that the proposed methods with minimum ATD give about 1 to 2dB PSNR improvements compared to the conventional WSVC.

1 Introduction

Three-dimensional (3-D) meshes are used intensively for interactive graphics applications. These applications require 3-D mesh compression algorithm to reduce the transmitted data size [1]. Considerable researches have been performed for 3-D mesh compression [1], [2], [3]. Since single-level compression techniques do not consider network characteristics, the received content cannot be displayed until the whole bitstream is fully downloaded, which introduces additional delay in low-bandwidth networks [2]. Hence scalable mesh compression techniques have been investigated to account for variable bandwidth in networks [1], [3]. The scalable 3-D compression can be used efficiently for virtual reality applications over IP networks with variable bandwidth.

Scalable video coding has received considerable attention for multimedia content applications with variable bandwidth environments [4], [5]. Wavelet scalable video coding (WSVC) inherently provides very flexible scalable bitstream through wavelet transform [6], [7], [8], [9]. Even though scalability is an attractive feature for multimedia content applications in variable bandwidth environments [5], the performance improvement of WSVC is an important issue for its viability in practical applications.

In this paper, we propose efficient methods to improve the coding efficiency of WSVC through the minimization of overall temporal distance for motion estimation. The conventional WSVC method uses only forward direction motion

Z. Pan et al. (Eds.): ICAT 2006, LNCS 4282, pp. 604–613, 2006.
© Springer-Verlag Berlin Heidelberg 2006

estimation. There can be many combinations for the directions of motion estimation. If there are 16 frames in a group-of-pictures (GOP), then there are 15 frame pairs for motion estimation through levels 0, 1, 2, and 3. If forward or backward direction is selected for each frame pair, then 2^{15} cases are possible for the directions of motion estimation in 15 frame pairs. The conventional WSVC, which uses only forward direction motion estimation, is a very special case among the 2^{15} possible cases.

To quantify the overall temporal distance, we define average temporal distance (ATD) for motion estimation, which will be introduced in Section 2. The conventional WSVC method has a large ATD value, which is one of the reasons for quality degradation. This paper proposes two methods which minimize the ATD for motion estimation to improve the coding efficiency of WSVC.

This paper is organized as follows. Section 2 presents the overview of WSVC and the conventional method for the directions of motion estimation in WSVC. In Section 3, we propose methods which minimize the ATD for motion estimation in WSVC. Section 4 shows simulation results for performance comparison with the conventional WSVC. Finally, we present conclusion in Section 5.

2   Wavelet Scalable Video Coding

Fig. 1 represents the encoder block diagram of wavelet scalable video coding (WSVC) [7], [8], [9]. Motion compensated temporal filtering (MCTF) block decomposes image sequences in a GOP using the motion vector information from motion estimation (ME) block. The temporally decomposed images are spatially decomposed in the spatial wavelet decomposition block. This paper presents efficient methods for the directions of motion estimation relating the ME and MCTF blocks in Fig. 1.

Fig. 2 shows the directions of motion estimation in the conventional WSVC [7], [8], [9]. There are 16 frames in a GOP. In Fig. 2, low and high sub-band frames are shown as white and shaded rectangles, respectively. In the motion compensated temporal filtering (MCTF) in Fig. 2, the directions of motion estimation are all

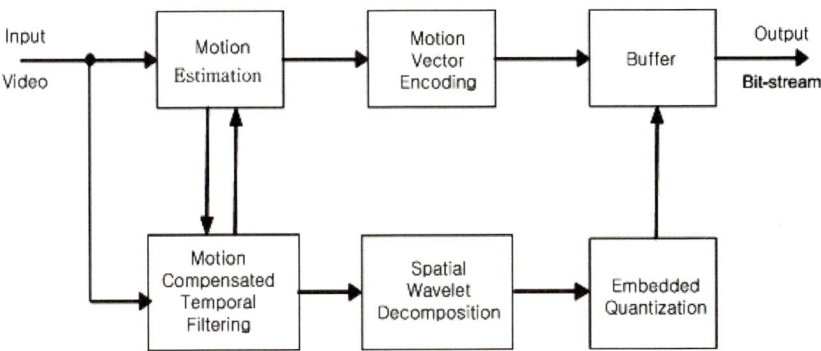

Fig. 1. Encoder block diagram of wavelet scalable video coding

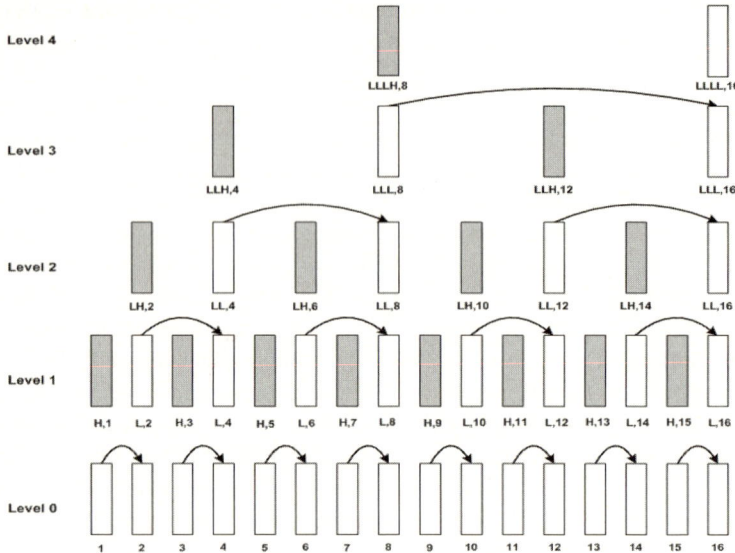

Fig. 2. Directions of motion estimation in the conventional WSVC at each level

forward. For example, the direction for motion estimation between frame 1 and frame 2 at level 0 is from frame 1 to frame 2. Then the temporal high sub-band is located at frame 1 (H,1) and the temporal low sub-band is located at frame 2 (L,2). In this case, the temporal low sub-band L,2 at level 1 is similar to the frame 2 at level 0, and the temporal high sub-band H,1 at level 1 is similar to the edge image of frame 1 at level 0. At level 1, the temporal low sub-band frames are decomposed into low and high sub-bands at level 2. For example, motion estimation is performed from frame L,2 to frame L,4 for temporal decomposition. Then the temporal high sub-band is located at frame location 2 (LH,2) and the temporal low sub-band is located at frame location 4 (LL,4) at level 2. At level 2, the temporal low sub-band frames are decomposed into low and high sub-band at level 3. At level 3, the temporal low sub-band frames (LLL,8 and LLL,16) are decomposed into low sub-band (LLLL,16) and high sub-band (LLLH,8) at level 4.

The temporal distance for motion estimation becomes larger as the level becomes higher in Fig. 2. At level 0, the temporal distance for motion estimation is 1. For example, motion estimation is performed between frame 1 and frame 2, and the temporal distance is 1. At level 1, the temporal distance for motion estimation is 2. For example, motion estimation is performed between frame L,2 and frame L,4, and temporal distance is 2. Similarly, the temporal distance at level 2 and at level 3 is 4 and 8, respectively. In Fig. 2, we can see that there are 8, 4, 2, and 1 frame pairs for motion estimation at level 0, 1, 2, and 3, respectively. Hence there are 15 frame pairs for motion estimation through levels 0, 1, 2, and 3.

Table 1. The number of frame pairs for motion estimation and the temporal distance for motion estimation at each level in the conventional WSVC

	Number of frame pairs for motion estimation	Temporal distance for motion estimation
Level 0	8	1
Level 1	4	2
Level 2	2	4
Level 3	1	8

Table 1 shows the number of frame pairs for motion estimation and the temporal distance for motion estimation at each level in the conventional WSVC. As the temporal distance becomes larger, the magnitude of motion vectors becomes larger, especially in video sequences with high motions. In the conventional WSVC method in Fig. 1, the temporal distance becomes larger as the level becomes higher. The large temporal distance at higher levels is one of the reasons for coding efficiency degradation in the conventional WSVC.

To quantify overall temporal distance for motion estimation, we define average temporal distance (ATD) for motion estimation as the average value of temporal distances in 15 motion estimations. In the conventional WSVC in Fig. 1, the ATD can be calculated as:

$$ATD = \frac{8 \times 1 + 4 \times 2 + 2 \times 4 + 1 \times 8}{15} = 2.13$$

In this paper, we propose methods which minimize the ATD to improve the coding efficiency of WSVC. The proposed methods would give better coding efficiency through smaller ATD values compared to the conventional WSVC.

3   Proposed Methods for Minimizing ATD for Motion Estimation

We propose two methods for the direction of motion estimations as Method 1 and Method 2. We argue that these two methods have minimal ATD values among possible ATD values when there are 16 frames is a GOP.

Fig. 3 and Fig. 4 represent Method 1 and Method 2, respectively. In these figures, the solid arrow represents the forward direction motion estimation and the dotted arrow represents the backward direction motion estimation. At level 0, the directions for motion estimation are forward and backward. The direction for motion estimation between frame 1 and frame 2 is from frame 1 to frame 2, which is forward. The temporal high sub-band is located at frame 1 (H,1) and the temporal low sub-band is located at frame 2 (L,2). However the direction for the next pair of frames is different. The direction for motion estimation between frame 3 and frame 4 is from frame 4 to frame 3, which is backward. The temporal high sub-band is located at frame 4 (H,4) and the temporal low sub-band is located at frame 3 (L,3).

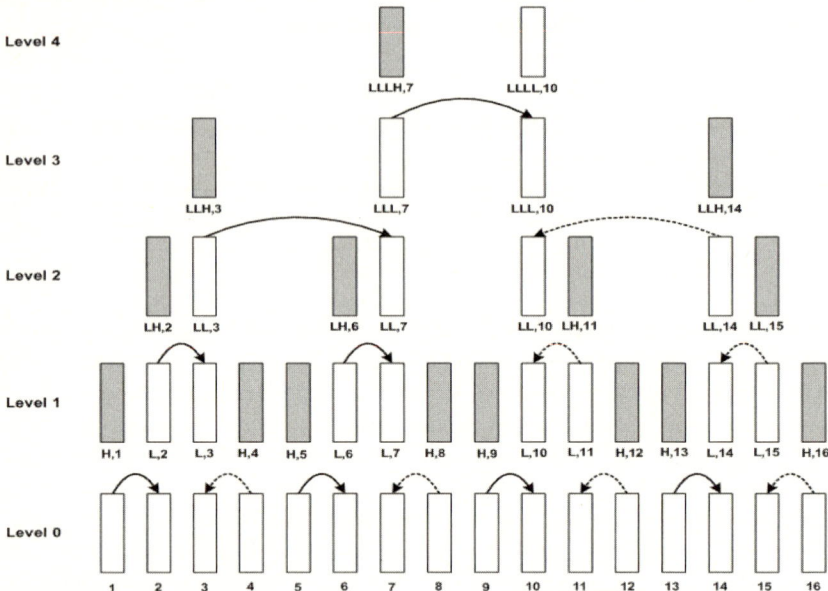

Fig. 3. Method 1 for the directions of motion estimation at each level

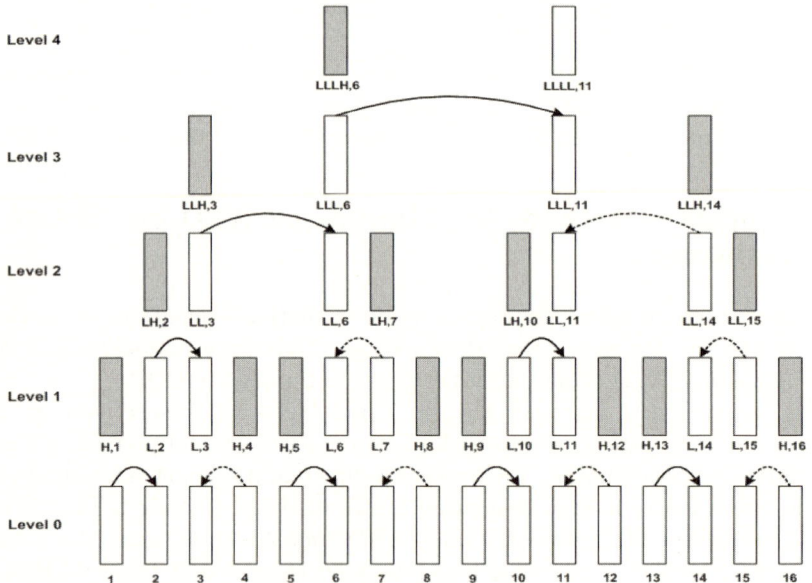

Fig. 4. Method 2 for the directions of motion estimation at each level

At level 1, motion estimation is performed between frame L,2 and frame L,3. Note that the temporal distance for motion estimation is 1 at level 1 in Method 1 (Fig. 3), while the temporal distance for motion estimation is 2 at level 1 in the conventional WSVC method (Fig. 2). By changing the directions for motion estimation to forward and backward at level 0 as in Fig. 3, the temporal distance for motion estimation at level 1 is reduced to 1. There can be two variations in Method 1. The direction for motion estimation at level 3 can be either forward or backward. We call these two variations as Method 1-a and Method 1-b. In Method 1-a and Method 1-b, the LLLL frame is located at 10-th and 7-th frame, respectively. The Method 1-a and Method 1-b have exactly the same number of frame pairs for motion estimation and the same temporal distance for motion estimation as in Table 2.

The directions for motion estimation at level 0 are the same in Method 1 (Fig. 3) and in Method 2 (Fig. 4), while the directions for motion estimation at level 1 are different. The direction for motion estimation between L,6 and L,7 is forward and the direction for motion estimation between L,10 and L,11 is backward in Method 1 (Fig. 3). On the other hand, the direction for motion estimation between L,6 and L,7 is backward and the direction for motion estimation between L,10 and L,11 is forward in Method 2 (Fig. 4). There can be two variations in Method 2. The direction for motion estimation at level 3 can be either forward or backward. We call these two variations as Method 2-a and Method 2-b. In Method 2-a and Method 2-b, the LLLL frame is located at 11-th and 6-th frame, respectively. The Method 2-a and Method 2-b have exactly the same number of frame pairs for motion estimation and the same temporal distance for motion estimation as in Table 3.

Table 2. The number of frame pairs for motion estimation and the temporal distance for motion estimation at each level in Method 1

	Number of frame pairs for motion estimation	Temporal distance for motion estimation
Level 0	8	1
Level 1	4	1
Level 2	2	4
Level 3	1	3

Table 2 shows the number of frame pairs for motion estimation and the temporal distance for motion estimation at each level in Method 1. In Method 1, the average temporal distance (ATD) value can be calculated as

$$ATD = \frac{8 \times 1 + 4 \times 1 + 2 \times 4 + 1 \times 3}{15} = 1.53$$

Table 3 shows the number of frame pairs for motion estimation and the temporal distance for motion estimation at each level in Method 2. In Method 2, the ATD value can be calculated as

$$ATD = \frac{8 \times 1 + 4 \times 1 + 2 \times 3 + 1 \times 5}{15} = 1.53$$

Table 3. The number of frame pairs for motion estimation and the temporal distance for motion estimation at each level in Method 2

	Number of frame pairs for motion estimation	Temporal distance for motion estimation
Level 0	8	1
Level 1	4	1
Level 2	2	3
Level 3	1	5

The ATD value is 1.53 both in Method 1 and in Method 2 while the ATD value is 2.13 in the original WSVC method. We argue that the ATD value 1.53 of the proposed two methods is the minimal ATD value among the possible ATD values with different directions for motion estimation when there are 16 frame pairs in a GOP. The ATD value represents the overall temporal distance for motion estimation. Since the overall temporal distance for motion estimation is minimum, the overall magnitude of motion vectors would be minimum in the proposed methods. This characteristic would give better coding efficiency compared to the conventional WSVC.

4   Simulation Results and Performance Evaluation

In this section, we present simulation results of the proposed methods and the conventional WSVC method. We also simulated another two more methods having different ATD values for comparison. We call these two methods as Method 3 and Method 4. The ATD values of Method 3 and Method 4 are 1.73 and 1.67, respectively.

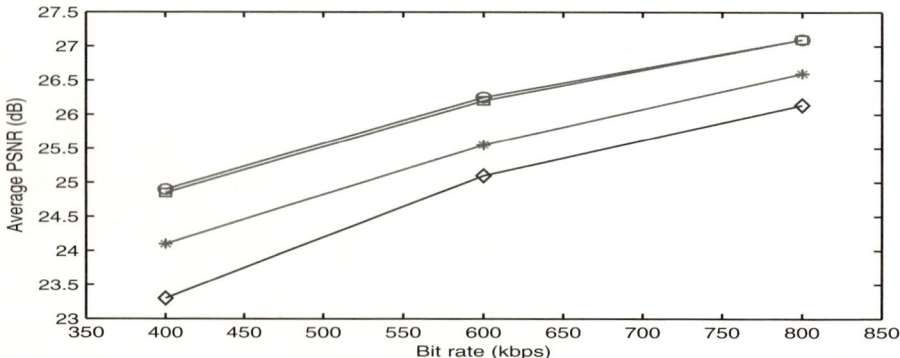

Fig. 5. PSNR comparison between the conventional WSVC method and the proposed methods for the Canoa CIF sequence (diamond: conventional method, circle: Method 1-a, square: Method 2-a, *: Method 3, +: Method 4)

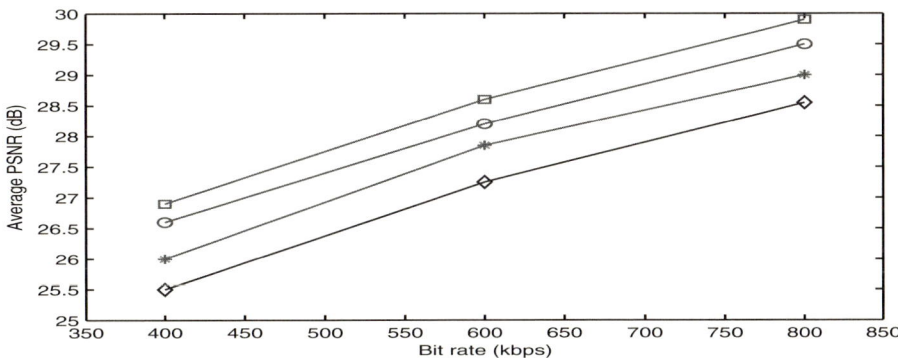

Fig. 6. PSNR comparison between the conventional WSVC method and the proposed methods for the Bus CIF sequence (diamond: conventional method, circle: Method 1-a, square: Method 2-a, *: Method 3, +: Method 4)

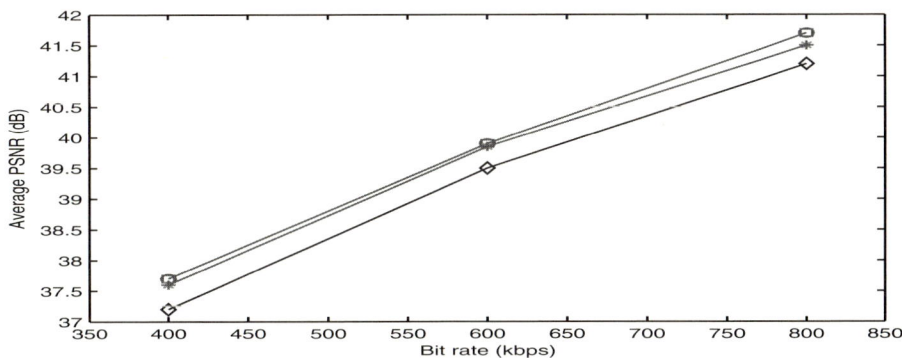

Fig. 7. PSNR comparison between the conventional WSVC method and the proposed methods for the Foreman CIF sequence (diamond: conventional method, circle: Method 1-a, square: Method 2-a, *: Method 3, +: Method 4)

Fig. 5 shows the peak signal-to-noise ratio (PSNR) comparison between the conventional WSVC method and the proposed methods for the Canoa CIF sequence. The performances of Method 1-a and Method 2-a are about the same, and give about 1 to 2 dB higher PSNR compared to the conventional WSVC method.

Fig. 6 shows PSNR comparison between the conventional WSVC method and the proposed methods for the Bus CIF sequence. The Method 1-a and Method 2-a give about 1.0 dB and 1.5 dB PSNR improvements, respectively, compared to the conventional WSVC.

Fig. 7 shows PSNR comparison between the conventional WSVC and the proposed methods for the Foreman QCIF sequence. The performances of Method

1-a and Method 2-a are slightly better than those of Method 3 and Method 4. Method 1-a and Method 2-a give about 0.5 dB improvements compared to the conventional WSVC.

These simulation results show that the performance of WSVC is closely related to the ATD for motion estimation. More specifically, smaller ATD value gives better performance (higher average PSNR). The Method 1 and Method 2 with minimum ATD give best performance. Also, all four methods (Method 1, Method 2, Method 3, and Method 4) give better performance compared to the conventional WSVC.

5   Conclusion

We proposed methods for minimizing the overall temporal distance for motion estimation to improve the coding efficiency of WSVC. To quantify the overall temporal distance for motion estimation, we defined average temporal distance (ATD) as the average value of temporal distance in 15 motion estimations. The ATD value is 1.53 both in the Method 1 and in Method 2, while the ATD value is 2.13 in the conventional WSVC. The proposed methods give minimal ATD when there are 16 frames in a GOP. We also simulated Method 3 and Method 4, which have larger ATD values compared to Method 1 and Method 2, for comparison. Also, all four methods (Method 1, Method 2, Method 3, and Method 4) give better performance compared to the conventional WSVC. Simulation results show that smaller ATD value gives better performance in WSVC. The proposed Method 1 and Method 2 with minimum ATD value give the best performance.

One of the drawbacks of the proposed method is that it leads to non-equidistant temporal position of frames at higher levels of the wavelet tree, which results in more limited temporal scalability compared to the conventional WSVC. Hence there is a trade-off between the PSNR performance and the temporal scalability through the minimization of ATD.

Since the WSVC has good compression capability and very flexible scalability for variable bandwidth environments, it can used efficiently for virtual reality applications over IP networks using scalable 3-D mesh compression.

References

1. Al-Regib, G., Altunbasak, Y., Mersereau, R.M.: Bit allocation for joint source and channel coding of progressively compressed 3-D models. IEEE Trans. Circuits Syst. Video. Technol. **15(2)** (2005) 256–268
2. Taubin, G., Rossignac, G.: Geometric compression through topological surgery. ACM Trans. Graph. **17(2)** (1998) 84–115
3. Compressed progressive meshes. IEEE Trans. Vis. Comput. Graphics, **6(1-3)** (2000) 79–93
4. Sodagar, I., Lee, H.-J., Hatrack, P., Zhang, Y.-Q.: Scalable wavelet coding for synthetic/natural hybrid images. IEEE Trans. Circuits Syst. Video Technol. **9(2)** (1999) 244–254
5. Applications and requirements for scalable video coding. ISO/IEC JTC1/SC29/ WG11 MPEG 65-th Meeting, N5889. (2003)

6. Ohm, J.-R.: Three Dimensional subband coding with motion compensation. IEEE Trans. Image Processing **3(5)** (1994) 559–571
7. Choi, S.-J., Woods, J.W.: Motion-compensated 3D subband coding of video. Proc. IEEE Image Processing, **8(2)** (1999)
8. Hsiang, S.-T., Woods, J.W.: Embedded video coding using invertible motion compensated 3-D subband/wavelet filter bank. Signal Processing: Image Comm., **16** (2001) 705-724
9. Hsiang, S.-T., Woods, J.W.: Highly scalable subband/wavelet image and video coding. Ph.D. Dissertation, Rensselaer Polytechnic Institute, (2002)

Single Camera Remote Eye Gaze Tracking Under Natural Head Movements

Ruian Liu[1,2], Shijiu Jin[1], and Xiaorong Wu[2]

[1] State Key Laboratory of Precision Measuring Technology and Instruments, Tianjin University, Tianjin 300072, China
[2] College of Physics and Electronic Information Science, Tianjin Normal University, Tianjin 300074, China
wdxylra@mail.tjnu.edu.cn

Abstract. Most available gaze tracking systems based on corneal reflection have low tolerance for head movements. In this paper, an eye-gaze tracking method, which can make this system be adaptive to external lighting changes and to the user's head movements, is put forward to alleviate the restriction on the user's head motion. We manage to improve the performance of the algorithm: The thresholds for extraction of the pupil and the corneal reflection are automated; the edge points of the pupil could be obtained by a 1D line search. To improve the resolution and accuracy of the system, the sub-pixel technique is used to locate the feature position accurately in the eye image. We apply a new randomized method of ellipse fitting to the edge points for good results. Our system can work under natural head movements by using only one camera to track eye-gaze. It can run in real time at video rate (25frames/second). A gaze accuracy of 1 degree is observed.

Keywords: Gaze tracking; corneal reflection; threshold; ellipse fitting; calibration.

1 Introduction

The eye is an important organ by which people acquire information from the outside world, and it is also a window, which reflects the activities in one's mind. Eye trackers have been developed for many years and they are used in many fields such as medical research, psychiatry research and human machine interfaces. The eye-gaze interface gives us a more natural way to interact with devices than keyboard and mouse, and is convenient in situations where it is important to use the hands for other tasks.

There are numerous methods which have been developed to track eye-gaze, however many of those methods need special hardware, require the user to wear a device on their head, or place limitations on the user's head movements. Moreover, some eye trackers use more invasive methods, such as ultrasonic or electromagnetic devices to track the head position, which is undesirable for frequent usage. There are still many unresolved problems preventing the use of non-intrusive eye gaze systems in actual applications. The most prevalent of these are: accuracy, restricted head movement, robustness, and ease of calibration.

Z. Pan et al. (Eds.): ICAT 2006, LNCS 4282, pp. 614–623, 2006.

In this paper, a novel corneal-pupil reflection scheme is proposed that using only one camera to track eye-gaze. Combing with the improved algorithms, the system is robust and good results are obtained. The paper is structured as following: Related works are introduced in Section 2. Eye structure and gaze model are described in Section 3. Our proposed eye-gaze estimation system is given in Section 4.The developed algorithms are explained in Section 5. The experiment result is shown in Section 6. Finally, the conclusion and future works are mentioned in Section 7.

2 Related Works

The eye-gaze tracking technique, based on corneal reflection and image processing, has the advantage of unobtrusiveness and has made considerable headway in recent years. Several systems [1-9] have been built based on Pupil Center Corneal Reflection (PCCR) technique. Most of these systems show that high accuracy of the eye-gaze tracking results can be achieved if the user has the ability to keep his head fixed or via the help of a chin rest or bite bar to restrict the head motion. Therefore, the limited head movement is one of the worst issues in the current remote eye-gaze tracking systems. To solve the problem, Sugioka [1] measured the distance between the camera and the eye by using an ultrasonic sensor, however, the accuracy of the system is not good because the distance measured by an ultrasonic sensor is inaccurate. Ebisawa [6] developed an eye-gaze tracking system that used three cameras, and the two stereo cameras measured the 3D position of the pupil of one eye. This increased the complicity of the system and the performance of the system was affected by the accuracy of the stereo camera.

To reduce the dependent on the environment, many systems [2-3], [5-9] employed the bright-pupil technique and the image difference method. But this method increased the pupil-locating error. This paper also uses the bright-pupil and dark-pupil technique, however, different from the traditional method, we only use it to detect the pupil when eye tracking is failed.

Currently many gaze tracking algorithms make use of the technique of thresholding and ellipse-fitting [4], [5], [7], [8], however, owing to the noises in eye images, it is difficult to determine the appropriate threshold values, also the ellipse-fitting algorithm is not robust. In this paper, the algorithms of threshold values extraction, feature detection and ellipse fitting have been improved; also, the sub-pixel technique is used to improve the resolution and accuracy of the system.

3 Eye Structure and Gaze Model

The structure of the eye is shown in Fig.1 [4]. When the head is still, the gaze direction changes following the rotation of the eyeball. Experiments indicate that the rotation of the eyeball is a very complicated process, even only the eye moves horizontally; it is also moving on a trajectory in front and behind, not a simple spherical rotation. The gaze direction is defined as the direction from fovea to the center of the crystalline lens, however, the crystalline lens's changes are very complicated and it is difficult to detect the position of the fovea, so the eye is commonly viewed as a spheroid, which rotates round a fixed point. The rotation center, which is the so-called eyeball center, is defined as the point that is 13.5mm behind the corneal on the gaze direction [10]. Gaze direction is defined as the direction from the eyeball center to the center of the pupil. For simple analyzing and calculating, the paper assumes that the estimated gaze direction can be derived from the center of the corneal curvature and the pupil center. The gaze model is shown in Fig. 2.

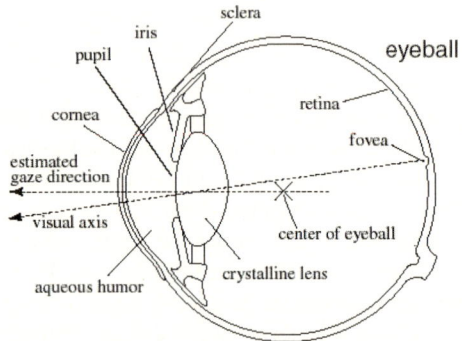

Fig. 1. The structure of the eye

4   System Specifications and Control Model

The system is based on PCCR technique. Our proposed method needs three infrared LEDs and one CCD camera. LED2 and LED3 are used to project corneal reflections onto the eye; LED1 is located at the center of the camera lens to make the bright-pupil effect. A video camera is used to capture the eye movements. The camera is mounted on a pan-tilt unit to scan two-dimensionally, so the user's eye is always in the FOV (field of view) of the camera. A motorized zoom lens is attached to the camera, and an infrared pass filter is used to reduce the amount of ambient visible light reaching the CCD. The system diagram is shown in Fig.2.

   Three glints, formed by the infrared light on the corneal of the eye, are shown in the captured image. The diagram of the captured eye image is shown in Fig.3. The eye images are sent to a computer through the imaging board, and are processed later by the computer to draw the information of the pupil and the glints.

   When the user holds the head still, the positions of the glints are not change, so the glints can be treated as the reference points. The pupil moves while the eye rotates for gazing at different points. The vector of *op* reflects gaze direction's change owing to eye's rotation. The gaze direction is determined by the relationship between the position of the pupil center and the corneal reflections.

   When the head moves in front and behind, the distance between glint2 and glint3 (d=d1+d2) changes; while the head moves horizontally, the ratio of d1 and d2 varies. The pan-tilt unit is controlled according to the central position between glint2 and glint3; the focus of the lens can be adjusted on the basis of the distance d, keeping the magnifying power of the optical system unchanged to overcome the influence of head movements in front and behind. The aperture of the lens and the LED's luminous power can be adjusted according to the intensity value of the glints; lens focusing is based on the gradient value of the pupil boundary points and the size of the glints. While the eye gets out of the FOV of the camera by head movements, making the camera has a large FOV, turn off LED2 and LED3, only turn on LED1. LED1 makes the diffusion of light on the retina to generate the bright-pupil effect; when LED2 and LED3 turn on, a dark pupil image is obtained. The difference image is used to detect the eye. Control signals realize the control through a parallel port of the computer.

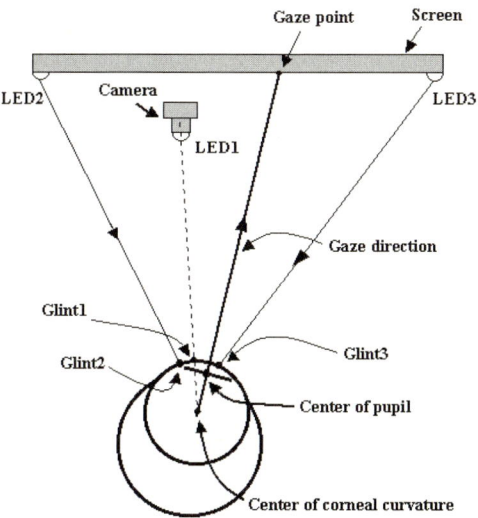

Fig. 2. The diagram of the system and the gaze model

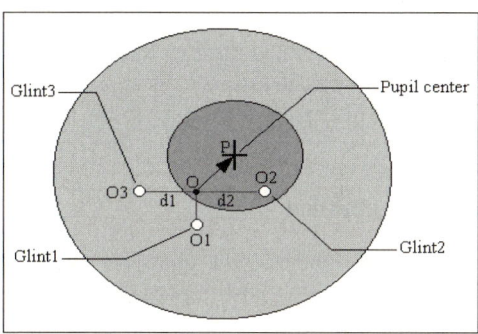

Fig. 3. The diagram of the captured eye image

5   Algorithm Description

The pupil-glint vector is used to determine the gaze direction. This algorithm has the following phases:

5.1 Thresholds Extraction

In order to detect the pupil and the glints accurately, it is crucial and difficult to find the appropriate threshold values owing to the movements of the head and the eye, external lighting changes and noises in the images. Some systems manually determined the thresholds. In this paper, finding the threshold values is automated.

For the captured image a histogram has been calculated in which x-axis indicates intensity value of 0 through 255 and y-axis shows frequency for each intensity value. However, the histogram has small local noises in its envelope, which may result in wrong threshold value. Low pass filtering method is applied to remove this kind of local noises by averaging neighboring three points. The typical histogram of the eye image is shown in Fig.4.

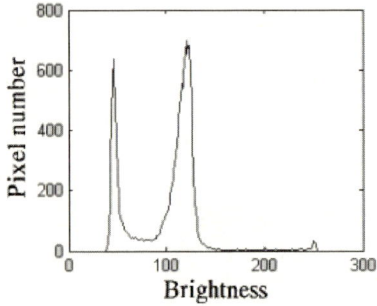

Fig. 4. The typical histogram of the eye image

The histogram shows 3 peaks, which correspond to pupil, the remaining area and corneal reflection respectively. The valley between the first peak and the second peak is selected as the threshold value of the pupil. Glints, which correspond to the brightest regions in the eye image, can be obtained through thresholding. According to the positions of LEDs, camera and eye, we can estimate the approximate pixels of glints in the image, and then we search the histogram from right to the left. When the summarized pixels exceed the estimate pixels, the threshold value for corneal reflection is found.

5.2 Corneal Reflection Localization

Given its small size and high brightness, the glints are approximately circles in the image. After binarizing the image, the positions of the glints are then given by the geometric center (x_c, y_c) of each reflection region in the image. Its size is initialized with $r = \sqrt{area/pi}$.

We assume that the intensity profile of each glint follows a two-dimensional Gaussian distribution. If we find the radius r where the average decline in intensity is maximal and relate it to the radius with maximal decline for a Gaussian distribution, we can take the full extent of the reflection as 2.5r to capture 99% of the reflection profile. We find r through a gradient descent search that minimizes

$$\frac{\int I(r+\delta,x_c,y_c,\theta)d\theta}{\int I(r-\delta,x_c,y_c,\theta)d\theta} \ . \tag{1}$$

Where $\delta = 1$, and $I(r,x,y,\theta)$ is the pixel intensity at angle θ on the contour of a circle defined by the parameters r, x and y. The position of the corneal reflection is computed with sub-pixel accuracy by computing an intensity-weighted centroid from this image. The experiments indicate that this method is robust and the accuracy is within 0.02 pixels for locating the glints even the threshold value changes in a big range.

5.3 Sub-pixel Edge Detection of the Pupil

While other feature-based approaches apply edge detection to the entire eye image or to a region around the estimated pupil location, these approaches can be computationally wasteful as the pupil contour frequently occupies very little part of the image. In this paper, the edge points could be obtained by a 1D line search. This algorithm has the following phases:

Estimation of the Pupil Center
Based on the positions of the glints, a pupil-searching window is determined. All the pixels under the threshold value of the pupil are selected in the original image of the window and its mass center is computed, which is chosen as the estimated pupil center.

$$x_{pupil} = \frac{1}{N}\sum_{n=1}^{N}x_n \ , \quad y_{pupil} = \frac{1}{N}\sum_{n=1}^{N}y_n \ . \tag{2}$$

Searching of the Pupil Contour
Then we detect the edge points along a limited number of rays that extend from this rough center of the pupil. Combining with the intensity value, gradient value of pixels and the smoothness of the boundary, we can find the pupil contour. This is shown in Fig.5.

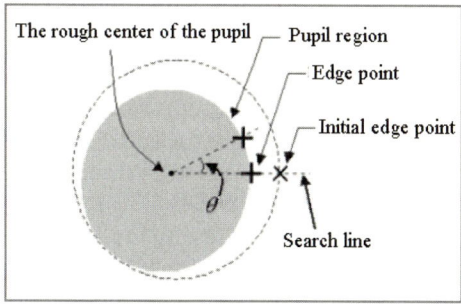

Fig. 5. Edge detection of a pupil region by a 1D search

We search for edge points and find r through a search that maximizes

$$f(r) = k_0 G(r) - k_1 (I(r) - Ip) - k_2 (r - r_{n-1}) \cdot \tag{3}$$

Where, $I(r)$ is the pixel intensity; Ip is the threshold value of the pupil; $G(r)$ is the gradient value of a searching point, it can be calculated through a 1D filter such as [-1 0 1]; r_{n-1} is the obtained radius of the edge point on the near search line, k_0、k_1、k_2 are the weighted parameters decided by experiments.

Noises Elimination
The pupil is always partially occulted by eyelid and eyelashes. When the head or eye moves, corneal reflection sometimes overlaps the pupil's edge region. Affected by these noises in searching of pupil contour, some false edge points may be obtained; these false edge points can strongly influence the performance of the algorithm. Only the noises are eliminated, high accuracy results can be obtained. Ohno [4] used double-ellipse-fitting to eliminate noises, it is time consuming. We, instead, eliminate the overlapped noises from the pupil contour. For noises from eyelid or eyelashes, according to the gradient of the line linking two near points, we can determine if a point is a false edge point or not, those pixels far from the edge are disregarded.

Sub-pixel Edge Detection
Now, the boundary pixels of the pupil have been detected. To obtain the precise location of the pupil center, however, we need edge points at a sub-pixel level. Utilizing the local information of the boundary pixels on search line, the pupil contour can be located in sub-pixel accuracy.

Calculate the gradient value of the adjacent pixels along the search line. Interpolate the gradients at sub-pixel positions with 1-dimentional second order polynomial interpolation. We use y to express the gradient value of a position that is close to the obtained edge point on the search line. The analytic relationship between y and the position's coordinate x can be expressed as:

$$y = ax^2 + bx + c , \tag{4}$$

Find the sub-pixel level edge point located at the sub-pixel position where y gets its maximum (minimum).

$$x = -b/2a . \tag{5}$$

5.4 A Randomized Method of Ellipse Fitting

Given a set of candidate feature points, the next step of the algorithm is to find the best fitting ellipse. While other algorithms commonly used least squares fitting of an ellipse to all the feature points. However, experiments indicate that it is not robust and sensitive to big noises. A few feature points, which are not on the pupil contour, dramatically reduce the quality of the fit and affect the accuracy of the results. So, more robust method needs to be developed. Like Theil-Sen、Repeated Median[11],but these two methods are computationally wasteful and hard to realize.

In this paper, a new method of ellipse fitting is proposed. It is robust and easy-to-implement. Given that discrete data always require 6 points to define an ellipse. So, for an edge point in the detected feature set, five samples are randomly chosen from this point's supplement set. The six different points form a sample sub-set. Then we calculate it. If the result indicates it is not an ellipse or the parameters of an ellipse is not reasonable, we chose samples and calculate it again; if the result is rational, save the parameters. This algorithm makes same processing to every point. Finally, takes the median value of the saved parameters as the estimated ellipse parameters.

5.5 Map to Screen Coordinates

The view vector needs to be mapped to screen coordinates. When a user gazes at a screen point (Xs, Ys), the pupil center's coordinate (x_p, y_p) and the glint 's coordinate (x_g, y_g) in the image are obtained. Then the view vector (shown as op in Fig.3) is given as following:

$$dx = x_p - x_o \; , \; dy = y_p - y_o \; . \tag{6}$$

The transformation from the view vector to screen coordinate is taken to be a pair of simple second order polynomial as:

$$Xs = a0 + a1(dx) + a2(dy) + a3(dx)(dy) + a4(dx)^2 + a5(dy)^2 \; ; \tag{7}$$

$$Ys = b0 + b1(dx) + b2(dy) + b3(dx)(dy) + b4(dx)^2 + b5(dy)^2 \; . \tag{8}$$

Where $ai, bi(i = 0 \sim 5)$ need to be found.

Given several known points on the screen, which serve as the calibration points. We calculate the view vector and draw the transformation coefficients. When the user moves horizontally, we can obtain the parameters in different positions. It can be used to calculate gaze directions in successive frame by interpolation.

6 Experimental Result

Some experiments have been carried out to show the feasibility of the proposed method including the condition of natural head movements. The monitor has a 17''screen; the resolution of the screen is 1280×1024 pixels. There are 6×5 points in the screen of the monitor. The user sat 50~80cm in front of the screen and looked at one of the target points. This system estimated the position where the user looked at, and then calculated the average error. The experimental result is shown in Table1.

The result indicates that the average error is small when the head is still. We find that the average error is about 1-degree visual angle under natural head movements. Also, there is a higher horizontal accuracy in this method is observed.

Table 1. Result of the experiments

User	Average error (pixels)			
	Hold the head still		Natural head movement	
	X	Y	X	Y
1	6.67	11.34	12.05	23.75
2	6.53	10.58	16.26	24.64
3	7.12	15.26	19.97	34.47
4	6.96	17.75	16.64	32.96
5	9.89	16.11	15.52	28.38

Also the system has been tested for dynamic gaze tracking by experiments. In the experiments, there was a moving small ball on the screen, and the user's eyes gazed at and followed the moving ball. In experiment 1, a ball moved from left to right, its y coordinates were measured. The measurement error was between 13.3 pixels and 43.2 pixels, the average was 31.7 pixels; in experiment 2, a ball moved from up to down, its x coordinates were measured. The measurement error was between 12.8 pixels and 35.7 pixels, the average was 26.1 pixels. Then the accuracy of gaze detection was calculated. Assuming that the distance between the user and the screen was 65 cm, this is equivalent to a view angle of 1.0 degree. We also found that the x-coordinate accuracy is better than y coordinate.

7 Conclusion

In this paper, an eye-gaze tracking method, which can make this system be adaptive to external lighting changes and to the user's head movements, is presented to improve the classical PCCR eye-gaze tracking technique. The system can run in real time at video rate (25frames/second) and a gaze accuracy of 1 degree is observed. While enjoying the advantages of high accuracy and robustness, our system uses only one camera to track eye-gaze and can work under natural head movements. Therefore, the user can move his head freely while using our eye tracking system. At the same time, there are still some works should be done to improve the performance of our system; such as the number of calibration procedures should be minimized. In future work we will mainly focus on making the calibration procedure simple. We believe, after further improvement, our system will find many applications, including human computer interaction and assistance of people with disability.

Acknowledgments. The Scientific Research and Development Fund Program of Tianjian Higher Education, China, under Grant No. 20051017, support this work.

References

1. Akira Sugioka, Yoshinobu Ebisawa, Masao Ohtani: Noncontact Video-Based Eye-Gaze Detection Method Allowing Large Head Displacements. In: 18th Annual Internat. Conf.of the IEEE Engineering in Medicine and Biology Society, Amsterdam (1996) 526-528.
2. C.H. Morimoto, D. Koons, A. Amir, M. Flickner: Pupil Detection and Tracking Using Multiple Light Sources. Image and Vision Computing, 18 (2000) 331-335.

3. Wen Gang: Gaze Tracking Using One Fixed Camera. Seventh International Conference on Control, Automation, Robotics And Vision, Singapore(2002)1409-1414.
4. Takehiko Ohno, Naoki Mukawa, Atsushi Yoshikawa: FreeGaze: A Gaze Tracking System for Everyday Gaze Interaction. In Proc. of Eye Tracking Research and Applications Symposium (ETRA), New Orleans (2002) 125-132.
5. Lim Choon Kiat,Surendra Ranganath: One-Time Calibration Eye Gaze Detection System. International Conference on Image Processing (ICIP), Singapore (2004) 873-876.
6. Yoshinobu Ebisawa: Realtime 3D Position Detection of Human Pupil. VECIMS 2004-IEEE International Conference on Virtual Environments, Human-Computer Interfaces, and Measurement Systems, Boston, MA, USA (2004) 8-12.
7. Zhiwei Zhu, Qiang Ji: Eye and Gaze Tracking for Interactive Graphic Display. Machine Vision and Applications 15(2004) 139-148.
8. Dong Hyun Yoo, Myung Jin Chung: A Novel Non-intrusive Eye Gaze Estimation Using Cross-ratio under Large Head Motion. Computer Vision and Image Understanding 98(2005) 25-51.
9. B. Noureddin, P.D. Lawrence, C.F. Man: A non-contact device for tracking gaze in a human computer interface. Computer Vision and Image Understanding 98(2005) 52-82.
10. Zhao Lejun, Wang Chaoying, Chen Huaichen: Research on Calibration and its Algorithm for Head-Mounted Eye Movement Measurement Recorder. Journal of Xidian University, 1998, 25(5): 606-610.
11. Paul L Rosin: Further Five-Point Fit Ellipse Fitting. Graphical Models and Image Processing, 1999, 61(5): 245-259.

High-Quality Shear-Warp Volume Rendering Using Efficient Supersampling and Pre-integration Technique

Heewon Kye[1] and Kyoungsu Oh[2]

[1] School of Electrical Engineering and Computer Science, Seoul National University,
San 56-1 Shinlim-dong Kwanak-gu, Seoul 151-742, Korea
kuei@cglab.snu.ac.kr
[2] Dept. of Media, Soongsil University
156-743 Seoul, Korea
oks@ssu.ac.kr

Abstract. As shear-warp volume rendering is the fastest rendering method, image quality is not good as that of other high-quality rendering methods. In this paper, we propose two methods to improve the image quality of shear-warp volume rendering. First, the supersampling is performed in an intermediate image space. Then is proposed an efficient method to transform between the volume and the image coordinates at the arbitrary ratio. Second, the pre-integrated rendering technique is utilized for shear-warp rendering. To do this, a new data structure called *overlapped min-max block* is used. Using this structure, the empty space leaping can be performed so the rendering speed is maintained even though when the pre-integrated rendering is applied. Consequently, shear-warp rendering can generate on high-quality images comparable to those generated by the ray-casting without degrading the speed.

Keywords: Shear-warp rendering, high-quality volume rendering, pre-integration, supersampling.

1 Introduction

Volume rendering is a technique to visualize information from three-dimensional arrays of digital data, and is mainly used in medical and scientific applications [1]. Earlier volume rendering implementations require a high-performance workstations or special-purpose hardware. After many researches [2-8] to alleviate the weaknesses of rendering algorithms, general-purpose PCs are now capable of presenting quite satisfactory results.

Shear-warp volume rendering [2] is a well-known rendering method. It is faster than others methods except for those which uses graphic hardware [3]. However, it has not been preferable in recent medical applications because it cannot create high-quality image. We propose new methods that improve image quality of shear-warp rendering without noticeable performance loss.

Generally, image-space supersampling and/or object-space supersampling can be used to improve volume rendering image quality. More rays are cast from a pixel in the image-space supersampling and more samples are taken along the ray at smaller

Z. Pan et al. (Eds.): ICAT 2006, LNCS 4282, pp. 624–632, 2006.
© Springer-Verlag Berlin Heidelberg 2006

intervals in the object-space supersampling [4]. However, it is hard to find efficient methods that have been presented for image- and object-space supersampling in shear-warp rendering.

To apply image-space supersampling, Koo et al. generated multiple templates [4] for each ray. Kim et al. proposed one dimensional supersampling method for anisotropic volume data [5]. These methods limit the supersample ratio to positive integer for simplicity while our method is not limited.

Moreover, the object-space supersampling makes the algorithm complicated caused by the tri-linear interpolation. Sweeney et al. tried to supersample in both image-space and object-space [6]. They stored density and the shading information instead of classified color for run-length encoded volume. However, their method duplicates the rendering time while an object-space supersampling is applied. Furthermore, it cannot change classification interactively though it uses post-classification algorithm. The special purpose of the hardware such as VolumePro board [7] enables the supersampling based on shear-warp factorization.

In this study, by the revision of the shear-warp volume rendering, we generate high-quality images compared to using high-quality rendering method such as ray tracing [8]. Fast rendering speed of shear-warp rendering can be conserved. The method applied in this research is composed of two phases. The first is efficient supersampling method on the image space. In this research the volume data in the intermediate scanline order is rendered which could reduce the transform overhead between object and image coordinates. As a result, we can perform efficiently the supersampling with an arbitrary sampling ratio. The second is exploiting pre-integration volume rendering [9] which has same the effect with object-space supersampling. Previously, the pre-integration rendering drops down the shear-warp rendering speed. To solve this problem, a new data structure called *overlapped min-max block* is proposed. By using this data structure the rendering can be accelerated owing to empty-space leaping. As the effects as image and object supersampling respectively of these two methods, high-quality images can be generated with the complementation of both methods.

2 Efficient Image-Space Supersampling for Shear-Warp Volume Rendering

The acceleration techniques for shear-warp rendering are empty-space leaping and early-ray termination [2]. Empty-space leaping is performed in object space and early-ray termination is performed in intermediate image space. For simplicity, traditional shear-warp rendering assumes that the pixel size of the intermediate image is equal to the voxel size of the volume data, so these two acceleration techniques have been performed without transformation overhead between object- and intermediate image-coordinate. While the image-space supersampling is applied, a fast transformation method is needed because the pixel size is not equal to the voxel size.

In order to accelerate the transformation between coordinates, then a volume is rendered on a scanline by scanline basis in intermediate image coordinate. As an intermediate scanline is parallel to an object scanline, the weight value for y-direction becomes a constant for one scanline. In other words, is possible have in consideration only the x-coordinate. It is explained in Fig. 1.

```
Shear-warp rendering

{

for each slice z_v in [0, number of volume slice-1]

(y0_v, y1_v) = Get_Image_Scanline_Range (z_v)

for each scanline y_i in Intermediate_Scanline_Range

        y_v = Inverse Mapping(y_i)

        (x0_v, x1_v) = Get_Voxel_Range (y_v)

        Process_One_Intermediate_Scanline(x0_v, x1_v)

}
```

Fig. 1. Pseudo-code for the image-space supersampling algorithm of shear-warp rendering. For each slice, the range in intermediate image coordinate can be obtained. Then, a rendering scanline by scanline in intermediate image coordinate could be performed.

Each slice of volume data is transformed to intermediate the image coordinate, and is possible to obtain a bounding rectangle for each slice. Each scanline included in bounding rectangle is transformed to an object coordinate and is possible get a weight value for y-direction. After that, each scanline is rendered considering the x-direction of supersampling. The processing of one scanline is illustrated in the Fig. 2. For the simplicity, interpolation between scanlines is ignored without loss of generality.

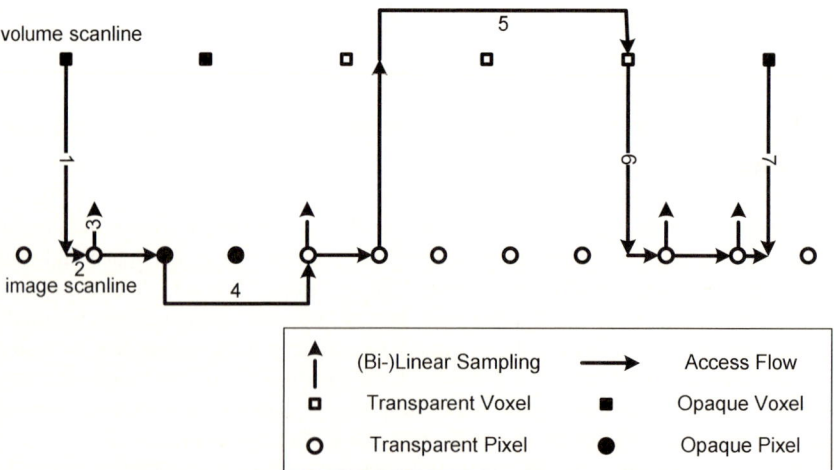

Fig. 2. An example for rendering one scanline. The algorithm is mainly processed in image space except for skipping transparent voxels (step 5), so that transformation between volume- and image- coordinate is only occurred at boundary of transparent voxels.

One scanline is rendered as follows: the first voxel is projected to image scanline (1) and find first transparent pixel is founded (2). To fill the pixel, is sampled to the object coordinate (3) but the opaque pixels are skipped (4). If a sample point is between adjacent transparent voxels, is possible skip transparent voxels (5). The last transparent voxel is projected to image scanline (6). Now is able to finish one scanline at the position that the last voxel of the volume scanline which is projected to (7). To Summarize, pseudo-code is presented in Fig. 3.

```
Process_One_Intermediate_Scanline(x0_v, x1_v)

{

pixel_start = RoundingUp(Mapping(x0_v))

pixel_end = RoundingOff(Mapping(x1_v))

for (x_i = pixel_start; x_i <= pixel_end; x_i = x_i +1)

if(Is Opaque Pixel (x_i) )

          x_i = x_i + opaque_pixel_length

          x_v = Inverse Mapping(x_i)

if(Is Transparent Voxel(x_v))

          x_v = x_v + transparent_voxel_length

          x_i = Mapping(x_v)

Compositing (x_i, Sampling(x_v))

}
```

Fig. 3. An example for rendering one scanline. The algorithm is mainly processsed in image space except for skipping transparent voxels (step 5), so that transformation between volume- and image- coordinate is only occurred at boundary of transparent voxels.

3   Efficient Pre-integrated Technique for Shear-Warp Volume Rendering

Pre-integrated volume rendering is a technique for reconstructing the continuous volume rendering integral [9, 10]. Assuming linearity of the volumetric function along a ray and using a preprocessed lookup table (called pre-integration table), this method eliminates many artifacts in discrete volume sampling and reduces the sampling rate for rendering. The pre-integrated volume rendering defines the color and the opacity of one fragment using two consecutive sample values as an index for the pre-integration table constructed before rendering for a given classification function (Fig. 4).

Engel et al. presented high-quality images with doubled sampling distance than that of traditional method [9]. Pre-integrated technique is a good solution in place of object-space supersampling. However, to exploit this method, pre-classified information for acceleration could not be used such as run-length encoded volume because it is a sort of post-classification technique.

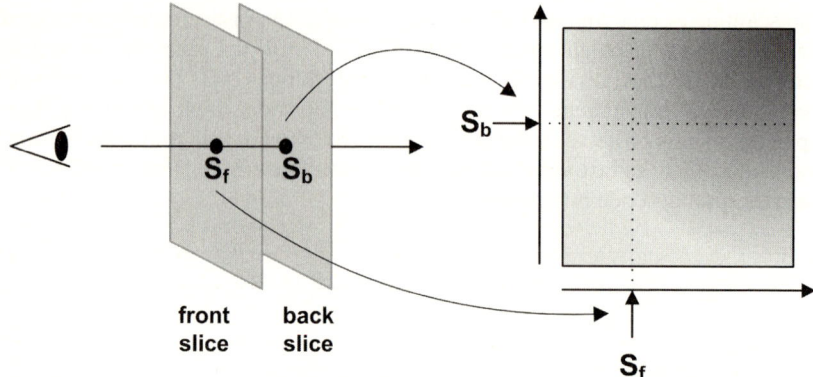

Fig. 4. The pre-integrated volume rendering takes two adjacent samples along the ray. The sample values are used to indices for the pre-integration lookup table. The returned value codes the color and the opacity of the sample segment [1].

As the amount of data becomes huge, the acceleration of the rendering still remains as an important issue even though hardware performance which has been improved. One of the most popular methods to speed up is the empty-space leaping using spatial hierarchy. Because pre-integrated technique samples two consecutive points for one fragment, previously the empty-space leaping methods could not be directly applied. Earlier pre-integrated volume rendering implementation is based on outdated graphics hardware. Little attention has been given to empty-space leaping.

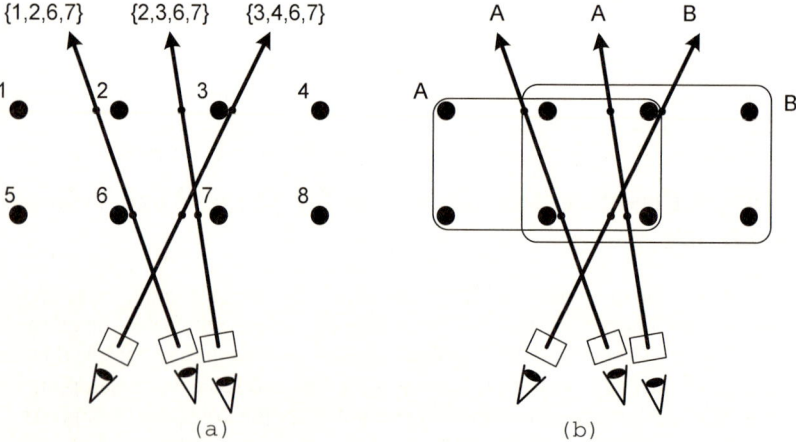

Fig. 5. Because pre-integrated technique requires two adjacent samples, opacity of one segment is determined by four pixel values. For example, there are eight pixels in the left image. Pixel sets that have to be tested are {1,2,6,7} or {2,3,6,7} or {3,4,6,7} according as the viewing direction changes. We generate two min-max block A and B. Each block covers 3×2 pixels and they are overlapped their boundaries. For each viewing direction, just one block is selected and transparency can be obtained from the block.

In fact, Schulze et al. applied pre-integration technique to shear-warp volume rendering and improved image quality. However, they cannot use empty-space leaping and rendering time did not reach to interactive speed [10].

Lacroute et al. [2] presented fast classification algorithm using the min-max octree and the summed-area table. Kim et al. [5] modified the min-max octree into block-scanline min-max table which covers some areas in a scanline such as 16×1×1 voxels, as compared with that of the min-max octree that covers regular hexahedrons, such as those consisting of 2^3, 4^3, and 8^3 voxels.

Kim et al.'s method is revised and adapted to the pre-integrated technique. In this method, each block covers 18×3×2 voxels and adjacent two blocks overlapped their boundaries (I call the block *overlapped min-max block*). Without loss of generality, two-dimensional example illustrates in Fig. 5. To skip empty region, four pixels have to be examined (Fig. 5a). Using *overlapped min-max block*, we can determine whether one block is transparent or not by one test of block (Fig. 5b).

4   Experimental Results

In this section, is demonstrated how this method improves the rendering quality without sacrificing the performance using medical datasets (see Table 1). Experiments have been performed on a PC equipped with Pentirum4 2.4GHz processor, 1GB main memory. AngioS and AngioB datasets are obtained from brain x-ray angiography.

Table 1. Test datasets

Dataset	Resolution	Voxel type	Data size
AngioS	256x256x256	8bit/voxel	16MB
AngioB	512x512x512	8bit/voxel	128MB

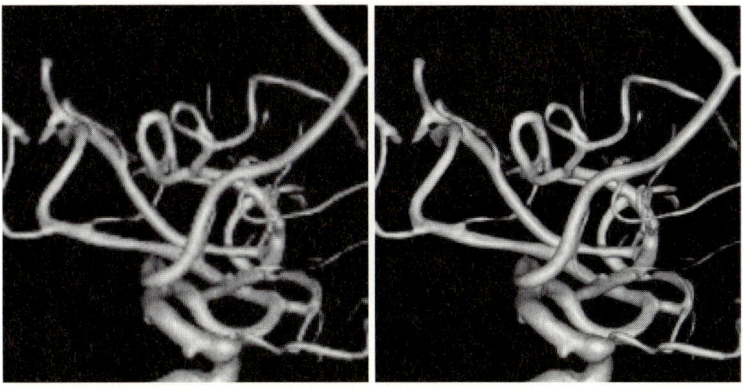

Fig. 6. Comparison between image quality for AngioS dataset without supersampling (left) and using the supersampling (right). Traditional shear-warp rendering produces blurry image while image is magnified. Using image-space supersampling, we can get clear image (pre-integration technique is applied to both images).

Table 2. Time table for supersampling. Time incresed. There is no noticible difference at average time for each area.

Algorithm	Super sampling ratio (A)	Rendering time (B)	Average time for each area (C=B/A)
Ray-casting	1.28	35s	27.3
Shear-warp	1 (no supersampling)	0.989s	0.989
Our method	1.13	1.26s	1.16
Our method	2.26	2.40s	1.06

4.1 Image-Space Supersampling

Fig. 6 shows rendered images of AngioS with the previous method and the presented image-space supersampling method. Image-space supersampling clearly enhances the image quality.

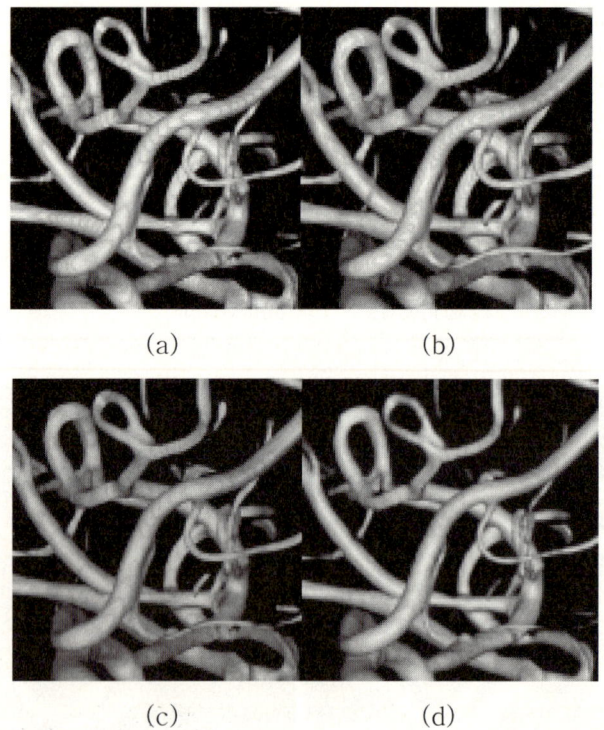

(a)   (b)

(c)   (d)

Fig. 7. Comparison of image quality of ray-casting and our method

Table 2 summarizes the performance of our image-space supersampling method. Previous shear-warp rendering and our method are mush faster than ray-casting method. Although the presented method is slower than shear-warp rendering (see column B), in relative time for pixel, it does not makes a big differences (see column C). Moreover, more supersampling ratio becomes bigger (from 1.13 to 2.26), then the average time is improved (1.16 to 1.06).

4.2 Pre-integrated Volume Rendering

Fig. 7 shows ray-casting images without pre-integration techniques and the presented method with pre-integration technique. Image-space supersampling is used for every image. Fig.7a, 7b, and 7c are ray-casting images with sampling distance 1, 0.5 and 0.2 respectively. Fig. 7d is the shear-warp image using pre-integrated technique presented in this paper. In the Fig. 7a, we can observe wave patterns on the blood vessels. As sampling distance is reduced (Fig. 7b and 7c), wave patterns disappear. There is no wave pattern in Fig 7d without object-space supersampling. Is possible observe that pre-integrated technique (Fig. 7d) has a similar effect to object-space supersampling. (Naturally, pre-integration technique can be applied to ray-casing.)

Table 3. Time comparision for ESL. Our method (d) is noticeably faster than any other methods.

Rendering methods	AngioS	AngioB
(a) shear-warp w/o ESL	16.70s	33.55s
(b) ray-casting w/ ESL	0.98s	1.49s
(c) shear-warp w/ ESL (Fig. 5a)	0.72s	1.72s
(d) shear-warp w/ ESL (Fig. 5b)	0.48s	0.85s

Table 3 summarizes the performance using empty-space leaping (ESL) for pre-integrated technique and the previous pre-integrated technique. Obviously, leaping empty-space gains more performance. Shear-warp rendering time without ESL (a) is too slow to observe the dataset interactively. It can not reach the rendering time using ray-casting (b). The presented method in this paper (d) can exploit ELS, two times faster than ray-casting method. Meanwhile testing every scanline in order to utilize ELS (c) is faster than ray-casting method (b) but slower than (d) using *overlapped min-max block*.

5 Conclusions

This paper proposes a new method to enhance the image quality of shear-warp rendering maintaining the fast speed. Using intermediate scanline order rendering, an efficient image-space supersampling can be performed. As object-space super-sampling is inefficient, then the exploited pre-integrated technique is performed in this research. Contrary to other previous methods, a new data hierarchy called *overlapped min-max* block is generated, so now empty-space leaping for pre-integrated techniques is possible. Experimental results show that this method produces high quality image without sacrificing the performance.

Acknowledgments. This work was supported by the Korea Research Foundation Grant (KRF-2004-005-D00198).

References

1. A. Kaufman, D. Cohen and R. Yagel, Volume Graphics, *IEEE Computer*, 26(7): 51-64, 1993.
2. P. Lacroute and M. Levoy, Fast Volume Rendering Using a Shear-Warp Factorization of the Viewing Transformation, *Proceedings of SIGGRAPH 94*, 451-458, 1994.
3. F. Dachille, K. Kreeger, B. Chen, I. Bitter and A. Kaufman, High-Quality Volume Rendering Using Texture Mapping Hardware, *ACM Siggraph/Eurographics workshop on Graphics Hardware*, 69-76, 1998.
4. Y. Koo, C. Lee and Y. G. Shin, Object-order Template-Based Approach for Steroscopic Volume Rendering, *The Journal of Visualization and Computer Animation*, 10:133–142, 1999.
5. T. Kim and Y. G. Shin, Fast Volume Rendering with Interactive Classification, *Computers & Graphics*, 25(5): 819-831, 2001.
6. J. Sweeney and K. Mueller. Shear-warp deluxe: The shear-warp algorithm revisited, *2002 Symposium on Data Visualization*, 95-104, 2002.
7. H. Pfister, J. Hardenbergh, J. Knittel, H. Lauer and L. Seiler, The volumepro real-time ray-casting system, *Proceedings of SIGGRAPH 99*, 251-260, 1999.
8. M. Levoy, Efficient Ray Tracing of Volume Data, *ACM Transactions on Graphics*, 9(3): 245-261, 1990.
9. K. Engel, M. Kraus, and T. Ertl, High-Quality Pre-Integrated Volume Rendering Using Hardware-Accelerated Pixel Shading, *Eurographics / SIGGRAPH Workshop on Graphics Hardware,* 9-16, 2001.
10. J. P. Schulze, M. Kraus, U. Lang and T. Ertl, Integrating Pre-Integration Into The Shear-Warp Algorithm, *Third International Workshop on Volume Graphics*, 109-118, 2003.

A Simple, Efficient Method for Real-Time Simulation of Smoke Shadow*

Minghao Yang[1], Guangzheng Fei[2], Minyong Shi[2], and Yongsong Zhan[2]

[1] Computer and software School, Communication University of China, Beijing, China
[2] Animation school, Communication University of China, Beijing, China
lingau_doc@163.com, gz_fei@163.com, myshi@cuc.edu.cn,
zhanys227@bbi.edu.cn

Abstract. This paper proposes a simple, efficient method for real-time smoke shadow simulation. In this method, 3D density fields of smoke are directly projected and accumulated into a shadow buffer. Diffusion scheme is creatively taken from fluids dynamics to "soft" shadow texture. These two steps are called Direct-Projection-Diffusion (DPD) which is computationally inexpensive in comparison with traditional methods for participating media volume rendering. For shadow interaction, projective texturing based on the programmable graphics hardware is used to project the shadow texture onto any object's surface in the scene. The test result shows that our method is efficient and is feasible to solve the problem of real-time smoke shadow simulation in 3D computer games and in 3D animation initial production.

Keywords: Smoke Shadow Simulation, Diffusion, Shadow Texture, GPU, Projective Texturing.

1 Introduction

Smoke and shadow simulations play important roles in 3D computer games and in 3D animation production. Their shapes change depending on the position of light and observer. Fluid mechanics is used as the standard mathematical framework on which smoke simulations are based. Currently, realistic and believable animations of smoke are most effectively achieved through physically-based numerical simulations of fluids dynamics [7, 15]. The rendering procedure of smoke and shadow follows the principles of low albedo participating media under global illumination. Volume rendering and Photon mapping are usual methods for participating media rendering. However, these two skills have their own disadvantages. Volume rendering is not fit for smoke shadow rendering especially in multiple objects 3D scene. Photon-Mapping technique makes good results for 3D scene but is time-consuming [7, 11].

There comes the idea that the rendering process for smoke and shadow in 3D space being divided separately will be greatly faster than traditional rendering methods such

---

* The work described in this paper is supported by the Project for National Natural Science Foundation of China under Grant No. 60403037.

Z. Pan et al. (Eds.): ICAT 2006, LNCS 4282, pp. 633–642, 2006.

as Photon-Mapping. Volume rendering based on programmable graphics hardware [12] is already used for real-time rendering for participating media. So, to propose a fast algorithm for smoke shadow and an efficient method for real-time shadow interaction with any object's surface in 3D space is what this paper focus on.

2   Related Works

Many methods for smoke simulation were already presented in computer graphics. Particle system was first introduced by Reeves [25]. Some methods which focus on simulating the random turbulences of smoke were presented [13, 14, 22]. After that, how to solve Navier-Stocks equation more efficiently became a hot topic [20, 21]. An unconditionally stable model for producing complex fluid-like flows was proposed [15] and was widely adopted for fluids simulation [7, 8, 28].

Shadow makes scene more informational especially in 3D space. Ray tracing and attenuation model along ray entry for 3D participating media simulation is efficient but was seldom used for shadow generation [1, 3, 6, 18, 26]. Photon mapping technique made good result for participating media and shadow simulation but rather time-consuming [10, 11, 19, 27]. Splatting method was proposed to display regular volumetric grids [17]. Two phases rendering methods based on accumulated multiple buffers were used to simulate clouds, shafts of light and clouds' shadow projected on ground [4, 5, 12, 24]. C. Zhang and R. Crawfis used splatting volume renderer to model the light attenuation due to low albedo participating media [29, 30].

Inspired by splatting method, a simple, efficient method for real-time smoke shadow simulation is given in this paper. We first propose a computation inexpensive shadow algorithm for low albedo participating media. Unlike splatting, this algorithm consists of two separate phases: direct projection and diffusion. As a result of these two phases, a shadow texture is created. Then this shadow texture is projected onto any object's surface in the 3D scene by projective texturing method based on programmable graphics hardware.

The rest of the paper is organized as follows. First we describe our shadow texture algorithm in section 3. Then in section 4, smoke simulation and the projective texturing method based on programmable graphics hardware is discussed. In section 5, some results will be presented. Section 6 concludes and discusses future work.

3   Shadow Texture

Splatting [17] calculates an image plane footprint for each data sample and uses the footprint to spread the sample's energy onto the image plane. In splatting, each voxel is represented by a 3D kernel weighted by the voxel value. The 3D kernels are integrated into a generic 2D footprint along the traversing ray from the eye. This footprint can be efficiently mapped onto the image plane and the final image is obtained. Splatting with multiple accumulated buffers [4, 5, 12] and shadow-view slices [24] were used to render clouds, shafts of light and cloud shadows. Also, improved splatting method was applied to render soft shadow of participating media [29, 30]. Our method is different from previous methods in following two points: first, each voxel in 3D space and its density value is directly projected to 2D buffer without energy spread and only one shadow buffer exists in our method; second: diffusion method which is taken from fluids dynamics is used to spread the shadow energy since there is no convolution in shadow projection. In a word, the shadow texture algorithm in our method can be divided into two phases: direct projection and diffusion. Now, we discuss these two procedures in details.

3.1 Direct Projection

Direct projection is a simple forward procedure that each voxel in 3D space is directly projected and accumulated into a grid of 2D shadow buffer. Here, projection makes one 3D voxel be projected to a 2D grid directly without energy spread. Fig. 1 shows an overview of this projection.

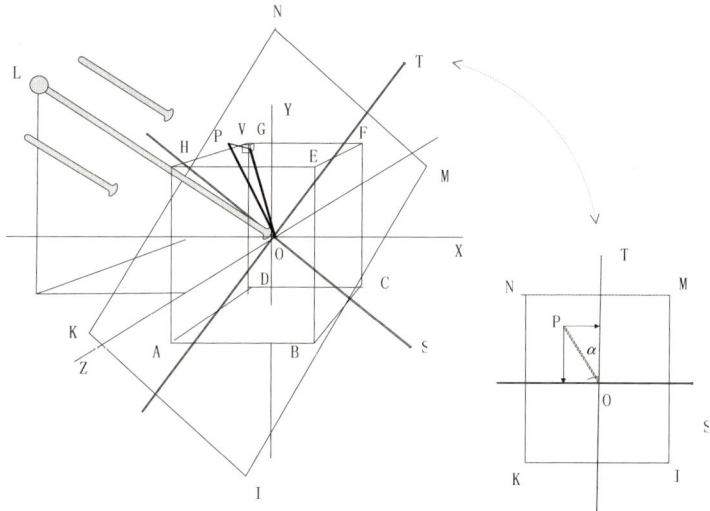

Fig. 1. Overview of direct projection

As shown in fig 1, OX, OY, OZ are positive directions of 3D space. L is the position where light is located. ABCDEFGH is the 3D container for smoke movement. Plane KIMN is the accumulated buffer plane which is perpendicular to LO and passes through the center point O. The right small figure is the shadow buffer in 2D plane. V is current voxel to be projected. P is the position in accumulated buffer which V is projected to. OS, OT are positive directions for 2D shadow buffer.

The projection procedure is as follows: For each voxel V in 3D space, calculate the relative P in accumulated buffer. Here, this buffer is represented by a 2D image plane: buf[][]. Supposing current voxel density is v_den and the x, y coordinate of P in 2D buffer is u, v. Then the accumulated buffer value is calculated by buf[u][v]+=v_den. For there is only one shadow buffer and projection procedure is direct without energy spread, so there's no necessary to project all voxels one by one. For each column of 3D space, if the projected positions of previous two or three voxels are calculated, then the other voxels' projected positions of the same column in buffer can be decided. Therefore, the time-complexity of projection is decided by the column number of 3D space which is 3*m*n (or 3*n*l, 3*l*m). m, n and l are the cell number along one dimension of 3D space. In a word, our projection method has following characters: direct projection without footprints (energy spread); light being viewed as parallel source and only one shadow buffer being presented. Fig 2 (a) shows a shadow texture generated by direct projection for a stochastic 3D density field under the conditions shown as fig 1.

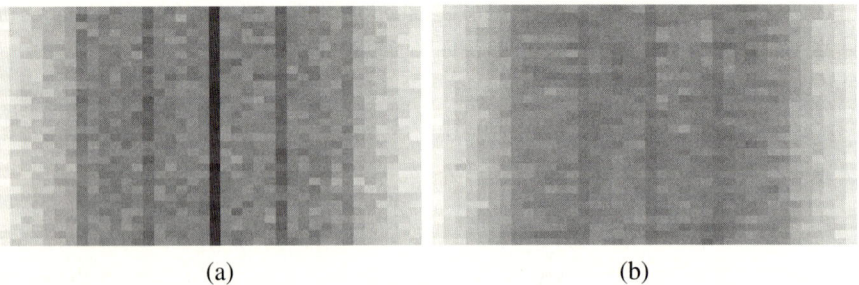

(a)   (b)

Fig. 2. Fig 2(a) is shadow texture for a stochastic density field (the density field size is 32*32*48 and the shadow buffer is 64*48). Fig 2(b) is diffused shadow for fig 2 (a).

3.2 Diffusion

From fig 2(a), it can be seen that some areas or columns of shadow are excessive accumulation since there is no energy spread or footprint in direct projection. Gaussian function (fig 3(a)) was proposed to calculated footprint for splatting [17]. Discrete schema for calculating footprint is shown as fig 3(b). Our method is shown as fig 3(c) from which we can see that some grids is excessively accumulated.

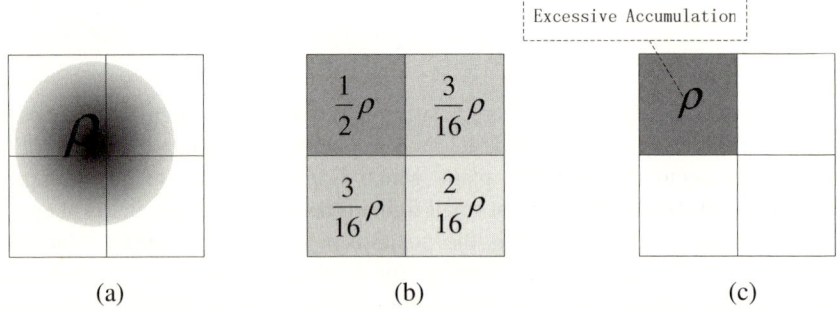

(a)   (b)   (c)

Fig. 3. Fig 3(a) is overview for traditional splatting method which adopts Gaussian function for footprint. Fig 3(b) is splatting method in discrete scheme. Fig 3(c) shows direct projection effect in our method which can be seen clearly that there are some grids being excessively accumulated.

A remedy for the excessive accumulation problem is adopted rightly after direct projection which is taken from fluid dynamics: diffusion. Ray scatter and multiple scatter in participating media is similar to fluid diffusion in following characters: first, they take place mostly between close voxels; second, any voxel will be possibly affected by any other voxel in the long run; third, for low albedo participating media, the higher of scatter and diffuse times happen, the more uniform effect will be gained. Fig 4 show the ray scatter in 2D space and fig 5 show fluid diffusion in 2D plane.

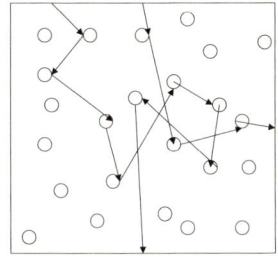

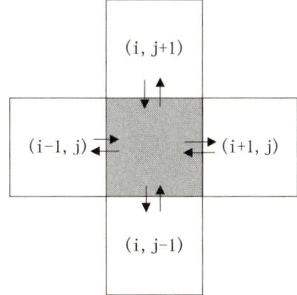

Fig. 4. Ray scatter in 2D space   **Fig. 5.** Fluid diffusion in 2D plane

Formula 1 is diffusion item of Navier-Stocks equation [15]. Where u is velocity, v is the kinematic viscosity of the fluid. In our method, u is viewed as density and v is used to control diffusion speed. Implicit method is preferred to solver this equation (formula 2). As shown in figure 5, we expand the equation 2 following the five-point finite difference scheme (formula 3). Where h is the grid span which can be used control shadow chroma.

$$\frac{\partial u}{\partial t} = v\nabla^2 u .$$
(1)

$$(I - v\Delta t\nabla^2)u_1 = u_0 .$$
(2)

$$u_1(i, j) = \frac{h^2 u_0(i, j) + v\Delta t(u_0(i-1, j) + u_0(i+1, j) + u_0(i, j-1) + u_0(i, j+1))}{h^2 + 4v\Delta t} .$$
(3)

The result of diffusion method used on directly projected accumulation shadow texture (fig 2(a)) is shown as fig 2(b). By comparison of these two figures, it can be seen clearly that the excessive accumulation problem is soften.

4   Smoke Simulation and Projective Texturing

Now, shadow can be created by direct projection and diffusion (DPD) method for smoke density field. In our method, smoke simulation and shadow interaction in 3D scene are separated procedures. This section will discuss these two procedures in details.

4.1 Smoke Simulation

Previous smoke simulation methods focus on describing the visual appearance (shape) of smoke [13, 14, 22, 25]. Foster and Metaxas [20, 21] adopted the full three-dimensional Navier-Stokes equations for creating fluid-like animations. Jos Stam proposed an unconditionally stable model for fluid simulation [15], which made good results for smoke simulation.

Our solver for N-S equation in this paper follows the scheme of Jos Stam, but our method for external forces given is different from his. Fig 6 gives an outline for extern forces generation in our method. In fig 6, $Dist_{Vi}$ is Euler distance of current voxel V_i to center point O. $Dist_{max} = \max\limits_{i=0...n} (Dist_{V0}, Dist_{V1}, ...Dist_{Vi}, ...Dist_{Vn})$. $\lambda \in (0,1]$. φ, θ are stochastic angles. $\varphi \in [0, \dfrac{\pi}{2}]$, $\theta \in [0, \pi]$. Extern force for voxel V_i is given by formula 4.

$$\left\{ \begin{array}{l} f_{Vi\_z} = \| f_{Vi} \| * \cos \varphi \\ f_{Vi\_x} = \| f_{Vi} \| * \sin \varphi * \cos \theta \\ f_{Vi\_y} = \| f_{Vi} \| * \sin \varphi * \sin \theta \end{array} \right. \tag{4}$$

After extern force given, in our method, the same solver as the one proposed in [15] is used to advect and diffuse smoke velocity and density.

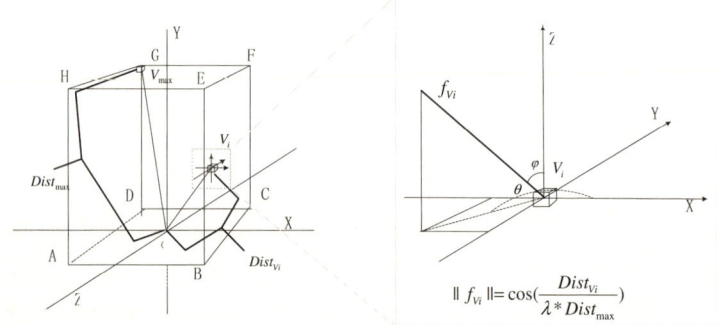

Fig. 6. Extern force for smoke simulation

4.2 Projective Texturing Based on GPU

We use projective texturing [2, 23] based on GPU to project the shadow texture onto any object's surface in 3D scene. Fig 7 gives an outline of projective texturing.

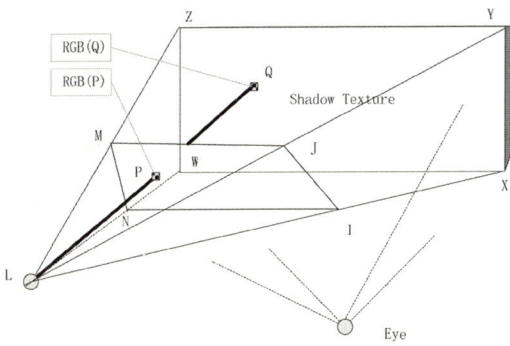

Fig. 7. Overview for projective texturing

Just as fig 7 shown, Plane XYZW is shadow texture which is projected to infinite far away. Plane IJMN is one of projected surfaces of any object in scene. Q is a point on plane XYZW and P is on plane IJMN. Color of point P in eye at last is synthesis of P and Q, which is calculated by formula 5.

$$Color(WC_P) * \alpha + (1 - \alpha) * Color(M_{td} * M_{lfm} * M_{wc->lc} * WC_P) \qquad (5)$$

In formula 5, WC_P is coordinate of point P in word coordinate (WC), $M_{wc->lc}$ is the translation matrix from WC to Light View Coordinate (LC). M_{lfm} is Light Frustum Matrix (LFM) of LC. M_{td} is texture definite matrix and α is sample factor for color synthesis [2]. Using projective texturing, it's convenient to project smoke shadow onto any other objects' surface in scene.

5   Results

We develop a smoke and shadow simulation system with VC, OpenGL and Cg on NVIDIA FX 540 video card. This system runs on Pentium4-2800 or comparable

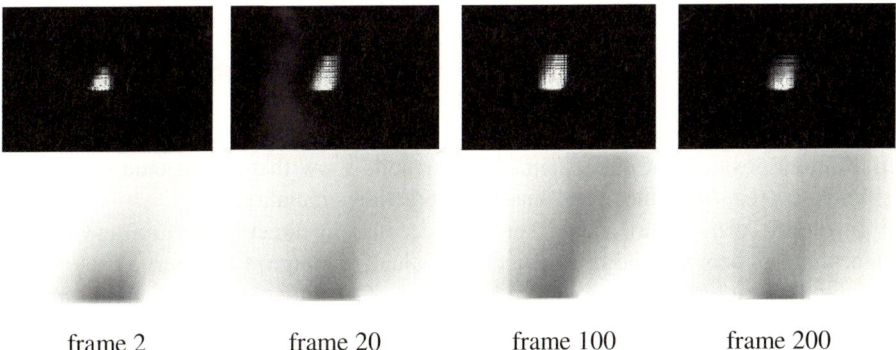

frame 2   frame 20   frame 100   frame 200

Fig. 8. Smoke and shadow at different frame (field: 30*30*30, shadow texture: 64*64)

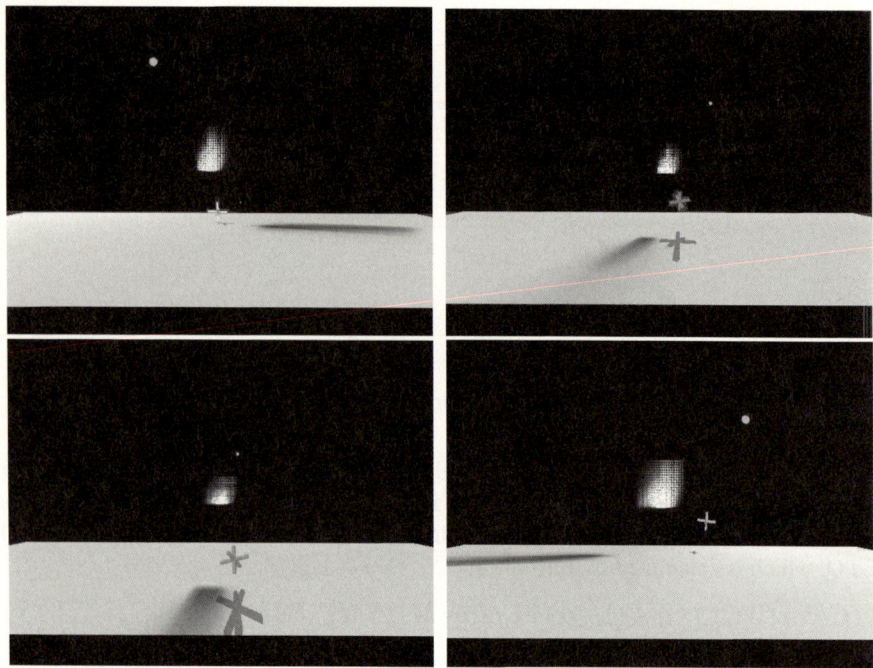

Fig. 9. Real-time smoke and shadow simulation for light and objects in different positions (the density field is 30*30*30 and shadow texture is 64*64)

Table 1. Algorithm consuming-time for different size of field and shadow buffer

3D Field Size	Shadow Texture Size	Algorithm Consuming Time (ms)
32*32*32	64*64	16
64*64*64	64*64	47
100*100*100	128*128	175
256*256*256	256*256	391

machine. Fig 8 shows the smoke density field and relational smoke shadow created by direct projection and diffusion (DPD) method.

Figure 9 shows several examples of real-time simulation results for light and objects in different positions of our system. These results show that our method is fast and efficient for real-time smoke and shadow interaction simulation.

In theory, there is no energy spread procedure in direct projection and diffuse algorithm, so there's no need to project and calculate footprint for every voxel one by one by Gaussian function or discrete scheme. The previous two or three voxels' projection positions of each column can decide other voxels' positions on shadow buffer. So just from the point of view of volume rendering for blur materials, direct projection and diffuse algorithm is faster than splatting method. Table 1 lists algorithm consuming-time for different size of field and shadow buffer on Petuimn4-2800.

6 Conclusions

In this paper, we propose a simple, fast algorithm for low albedo participating media shadow. This algorithm is used in our system for real-time smoke shadow simulation and is proved efficient. The test result shows that our method is efficient and is feasible to solve the problem of real-time smoke shadow simulation in 3D computer games or in 3D animation initial production.

Our method is efficient based on the conditions that smoke is low albedo participating media and smoke shadow is blur. Whether our method is efficient for volume rendering of blur materials and for high albedo participating media is worth further testing. In our system, only shadow for single point light is taken into account. Anyway, shadow for multiple point lights is easily to handle. On the situation of real-time smoke shadow simulation for area light is our future work.

References

1. James F. Blinn,1982:"Light Reflection Functions for Simulation of Clouds and Dusty Surfaces", In Computer Graphics (Proceedings of ACM SIGGRAPH 82),Computer Graphics Proceedings, Annual Conference Series, pages 21–29.ACM, ACM Press / ACM SIGGRAPH, 1982.
2. Randima Fernando, Mark J.Kilgard, "The Cg Tutorial The Definitive Guide to Programmable Real-Time Graphics"
3. T. Nishita, Y. Dobashi and E. Nakamae. "Display of Clouds Taking Into Account Multiple Anisotropic Scattering and Sky Light", Computer Graphics Proceedings(SIGGRAPH'96), Annual Conference Series, 1996, pp. 379-386.
4. Y. Dobashi, K. Kaneda, H. Yamashita, T. Okita, T.Nishita, A Simple, Efficient Method for Realistic Animation of Clouds, Proc. SIGGRAPH2000, 2000, 19-28.
5. R. Miyazaki, Y. Dobashi, and T. Nishita, Simulation of cumuliform clouds based on computational fluid dynamics, Proc. EUROGRAPHICS 2002 Short Presentations, 2002, 405-410.
6. D. Ebert and R. E. Parent. "Rendering and Animation of Gaseous Phenomena by Combining Fast Volume and Scanline A-buffer Techniques". ACM Computer Graphics(SIGGRAPH'90), vol. 24, n. 4, August 1990, pp. 357-366.
7. FEDKIW, R., STAM, J, AND JENSEN, H. W. 2001. "Visual Simulation of Smoke". In Proceedings of SIGGRAPH 2001, ACM Press / ACM SIGGRAPH, E. Fiume, Ed., Computer Graphics Proceedings, Annual Conference Series, ACM, 15–22.
8. FATTAL, R., AND LISCHINSKI, D. 2004. "Target-driven smoke animation". ACM Trans. Graph. (SIGGRAPH Proc.) 23, 441–448.
9. M. N. Gamito, P. F. Lopes and M. R. Gomes. "Two-Dimensional Simulation of Gaseous Phenomena using Vortex Particles". In Proceedings of the 6th Eurographics Workshop on Computer Animation and Simulation. Springer Verlag. 1995. pp. 3-15.
10. Henrik Wann Jensen. "Global illumination using photon maps". Rendering Techniques '96 (Proceedings of the 7th Eurographics Workshop on Rendering), pages 21-30, 1996.

11. Henrik Wann Jensen and Per H. Christensen, "Efficient Simulation of Light Transport in Scenes with Participating Media using Photon Maps", Proceedings of SIGGRAPH'98, pages 311-320, Orlando, July 1998.

12. M. J. Harris, A. Lastra, Real-Time Cloud Rendering,Computer Graphics Forum (Proc. EUROGRAPHICS 2001), 20(3), 2001, 76-84.

13. J. Stam and E. Fiume. "Turbulent Wind Fields for Gaseous Phenomena". ComputerGraphics Proceedings (SIGGRAPH'93), Annual Conference Series, 1993, pp. 369- 376.

14. J. Stam and E. Fiume. "Depicting Fire and Other Gaseous Phenomena Using DiffusionProcesses", Computer Graphics Proceedings (SIGGRAPH'95), Annual Conference Series, 1995, pp.129-136.

15. Jos. Stam. "Stable Fluids". In SIGGRAPH 99 Conference Proceedings,Annual Conference Series, pages 121–128, August 1999.

16. J .T . Kajiya, B .P . Van Herzen, "Ray Tracing Volume Densities", ACM Trans . on Graphics 21, Vol . 9, No . 1 (Juneties", Computer Graphics 18, No . 3 (1984), 165—174 1990), 1—27.

17. L. Westover. Footprint Evaluation for Volume Rendering. In Computer Graphics, Proceedings of SIGGRAPH 90, pages 367--376. August 1990.

18. N. Max, R. Crawfis and D. Williams. "Visualizing Wind Velocities by Advecting Cloud Textures". In Proceedings of Visualization'92, IEEE CS Press, Los Alamitos CA,October 1992, pp. 179-183.

19. Nelson L. Max. "Effcient light propagation for multiple anisotropic volume scattering". Proceedings of the 5th EurographicsWorkshop on Rendering, pages 87-104, 1994.

20. Foster, N., and Metaxas D, "Realistic Animation of Liquids", Graphical Models and Image Proc., 58(5), 1996, pp. 471–483.

21. Foster, N., and Metaxas D, "Controlling Fluid Animation", Proceedings of CGI '97, To appear, 1997.

22. N. Foster and D. Metaxas. "Modeling the Motion of a Hot,Turbulent Gas". In SIGGRAPH 97 Conference Proceedings,Annual Conference Series, pages 181–188, August 1997.

23. M. Segal, C. Korobkin, R. van Widenfelt, J. Foran, and P. Haeberli. Fast Shadows and Lighting Effects Using Texture Mapping. In Computer Graphics (SIGGRAPH 92), pages 249-- 252, July 1992.

24. R. Miyazaki, Y.Dobashi, T. Nishita, "A Fast Rendering Method of Clouds using Shadow-View Slices," Proc. CGIM 2004, pp. 93-98 (2004).

25. W. T. Reeves. "Particle Systems. A Technique for Modeling a Class of Fuzzy Objects". ACM Computer Graphics (SIGGRAPH '83),17(3):359–376, July 1983.

26. Paolo Sabella, "A Rendering Algorithm for Visualizing 3D Scalar Fields", Computer Graphics (Proc. of SIGGRAPH), 22 (4):. 51-58, August 1988.

27. Simon Premo, Michael Ashikhmin, Jerry Tessendorf, Ravi Ramamoorthi, Shree Nayar,"Practical Rendering of Multiple Scattering Effects in Participating Media", Eurographics Symposium on Rendering (2004)

28. TREUILLE, A, MCNAMARA, A., POPOVI 'C, Z., AND STAM, J. 2003. "Keyframe control of smoke simulations". ACM Trans. Graph. (SIGGRAPH Proc.) 22, 3, 716–723.

29. C. Zhang, R. Crawfis, Volumetric Shadows Using Splatting, Proc. Visualization 2002, 2002, 85-92.

30. C. Zhang, R. Crawfis, Shadows and Soft Shadows with Participating Media Using Splatting IEEE, Transactions on Visualization and Computer Graphics,9(2), 2003, 139-149.

Reducing Interrupt Latency at Linux Kernel Level for Real-Time Network

Dae Sung Lee[1], Jeong Seob Kim[2], Jaehyun Park[3], and Ki Chang Kim[3]

[1] School of Computer Science & Engineering, Inha Univ., Korea
Xdilemma@naver.com
[2] Factory Automation Team, Samsung Electronics Co., Ltd., Korea
jeongseob.kim@samsung.com
[3] School of Information and Communication Engineering, Inha Univ., Korea
{jhyun, kchang}@inha.ac.kr

Abstract. Linux is not well suited for real-time environment. Redesigning it for real-time systems, however, is a very complex and challenging task. In this paper, we suggest an approach to convert a large system like Linux into a real-time system with minimal changes. We observe that most of real-time systems demand real-time performance only for a couple of devices they are targeting for. Our approach focuses on this target device and modifies the original system only where this device is involved. This approach is more practical in that it does not unnecessarily change the whole system and in that it still satisfies the demands of most real-time systems. We picked network device as an example. We assumed the device sometimes got a real-time packet which should be processed immediately.

1 Introduction

In many real-time systems, such as distributed control systems, the performance of a real-time network plays an important role. To guarantee the real-time network operation, the latency in manipulating network packets should be maintained as small as possible. In past, there have been numerous researches to design a hard real-time system using a special hardware and software including real-time field buses and sophisticated real-time operating systems, but, nowadays, industry standard Ethernet/TCP/IP are widely used as a communication link between real-time systems. However, they have a large amount of delay and jitter inherently. If they are used with ordinary operating system such as Linux that is one of the most widely used operating systems in embedded real-time systems but designed without considering real-time operation, these uncertainties may increase.

Based on the observation of practical real-time systems, since only a few functions among enormous functions that real-time operating systems provide are frequently used, converting a full Linux into a real-time operating system is an over-killing job. We suggest to tune the Linux code to meet the real-time requirement for the specific function only, in our case, packet processing. By

Z. Pan et al. (Eds.): ICAT 2006, LNCS 4282, pp. 643–650, 2006.

investigating the operation of Linux kernel, we can easily find out the interrupt processing time affects largely on the latency of network performance. Instead of providing real-time capability for all interrupts, we concentrate on the network interrupt, and provide an efficient and painless way tailored to this specific interrupt to handle real-time packets, those that need immediate treatment.

Network interrupt service in Linux is divided into *Top Half* and *Bottom Half* as in other interrupt services. Top Half consists of two steps: copying packets from network device to DMA and analyzing their frame types. Bottom Half transfers packets to the TCP layer. The Bottom Half is where most of the packet handling is processed. Since Bottom Half is not guaranteed to be executed immediately, Linux is not real-time system. The Bottom Halves are serialized in the order they are activated regardless of their relative importance or timing requirements. Our strategy is to identify real-time packets, those that need real-time treatments, and to ensure their handling is done within Top Half. Identifying real-time packets can be done by marking special field in the packet and modify the kernel to recognize such mark. Handling real-time packet inside the Top Half is done by copying and moving kernel code related with this real-time process from Bottom Half to Top Half. We show how they can be done and what effect they have on the remaining code in following sections.

2   Related Researches

Since standard TCP/IP is a best-effort service, it cannot guarantee real-time performance. Many researches seek to reduce the degree of unpredictability by changing the behavior of certain layer in TCP/IP. It could be MAC, network, or transport layer. MAC layer modification focuses on removing the unpredictable delay during packet transmission due to packet collision. BRAM(Broadcast Recognizing Access Method)[1], MBRAM(Modified BRAM)[2] are such modifications. However, they require all network nodes to participate in this new algorithm. ST-II[3] and RSVP[4] cope with the unpredictable delay at network layer. ST-II is developed for multimedia communication in which data transmission rate and delay should be controlled. It provides a useful mechanism for real-time communication but has compatibility problem with the existing protocols. RSVP controls delay by allocating bandwidth at each network node via reservation. It also requires all participating nodes to follow RSVP algorithm which is in most cases impractical. Transport layer can be also modified to cope with the unpredictability problem[5,6]. RTP(Real-time Transport Protocol)[7] is one of the well known algorithms. It provides a mechanism to control the delay time but is not suitable for industrial network where partial data loss is not tolerable.

Another research topic is the real-time operating system. Processing designated jobs within predictable dead-line is not easy, especially in multi-process systems. If a specially designed real-time operating system is used, jitters caused by operating system in communication delay can be removed. However, such operating system is very expensive and not easily portable, Linux is widely used in many soft real-time systems. To give real-time operation to Linux, RT-Linux[8] has been suggested. RT-Linux inserts RT-kernel between the hardware and the original Linux kernel and treats the Linux kernel as a simple RT-task. RT-Linux minimizes code modification and is simple in its concept. However, still the involved code is massive, and requires a full redesign of device drivers if it needs real-time functionality.

3 Real-Time Network Interrupt Processing

3.1 Real-Time Ethernet Frame and IP Message

In this paper, we define a special Ethernet frame, *real-time frame*, to process real-time data, which is identified by *type* of standard Ethernet frame. RFC894 defines that Ethernet use 0x800 in the type field and IEEE 802.3 use a value greater than or equal to 0x0800[9,10]. We propose to use this type field to designate a real-time frame. We put some special value to identify it as a real-time frame and the actual real-time message is transferred in IP header. For compatibility, we use the rarely used fields in IP header: *identification* and *DF flag* field. These two fields are originally provided for packet fragmentation[10]. IP_DF(Don't Fragment) flag is set to prevent this fragmentation. When IP_DF is set, the identification has no meaning. Our algorithm uses these two fields to transmit a real-time packet. It sets the IP_DF flag and uses the identification field as a short real-time message that can be up-to 16bits. However by the nature of the real-time packets, it has to be handled at the fastest speed, and thus should be handled in the Top Half of the network interrupt processing. Messages long enough not to be contained within the IP header are already hard to process in the time-critical Top Half anyway. Figure 1 shows the proposed real-time frame. For our purpose, we used 0xff00 for the type field of real-time frames.

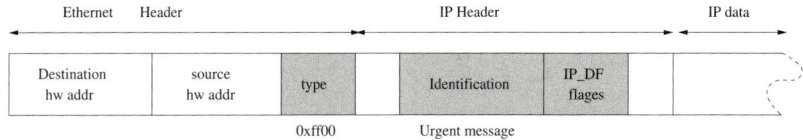

Fig. 1. Format of a real-time frame

3.2 Algorithm of Processing Real-Time Frames/Messages

The algorithm to process real-time packets in receiver side is shown in Figure 2. Basically we analyze the frame header in the Bottom Half. If the packet type is real-time frame, it extracts the message and processes it immediately. After that, it is hoisted to the Top Half to process immediately if necessary. Otherwise, it is enqueued to the system buffer and waits until the network Bottom Half finishes processing.

In sender side, the general socket libraries won't work because we need to modify Ethernet header to insert 0xff00 in the type field so that the real-time

```
while(received frames){
        The allocation of a sk_buff structure
        Copy frame from DMA area to sk_buff structure
        Analyze the Ethernet frame header
        if ( frame type == real-time frame ){
                Extract an urgent message from an IP header
                Process the urgent message
        }
        else {
                En queue the frame in system buffer
                BOTTOM HALF scheduling
        }
}
```

Fig. 2. The pseudo algorithm to detect and process real-time packets

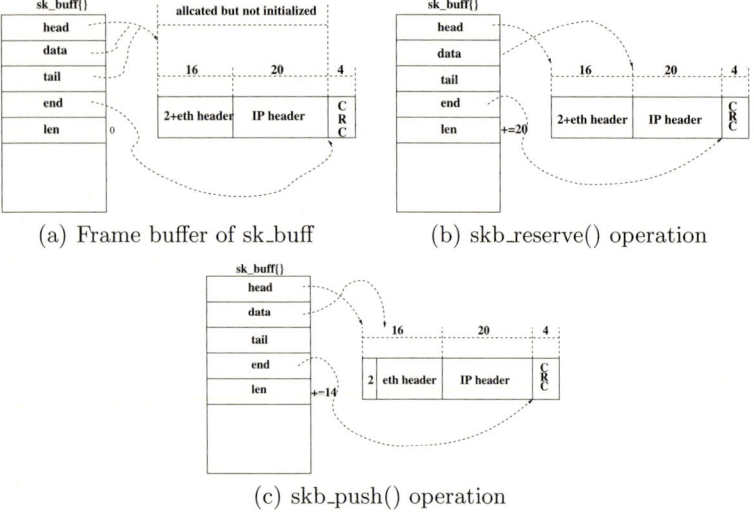

(a) Frame buffer of sk_buff   (b) skb_reserve() operation

(c) skb_push() operation

Fig. 3. Frame Buffer

frame can be differentiated from general Ethernet frames. Generating a packet frame involves two steps: allocating a frame buffer and writing our header onto the frame. Linux manages frame buffers using sk_buff structure. The actual frame buffers are allocated using alloc_skb(). Figure 3(a) shows the allocated frame buffer attached to sk_buff. The filling of the frame buffer can be done using skb_reserve() and skb_push(). skb_reserve() is used to move the *data* pointer to the IP header and fills it as shown in Figure 3(b). The Ethernet header is also filled in with the skb_push() function. This time the *data pointer* reduced by 14 to point to the Ethernet header, which is shown in Figure 3(c).

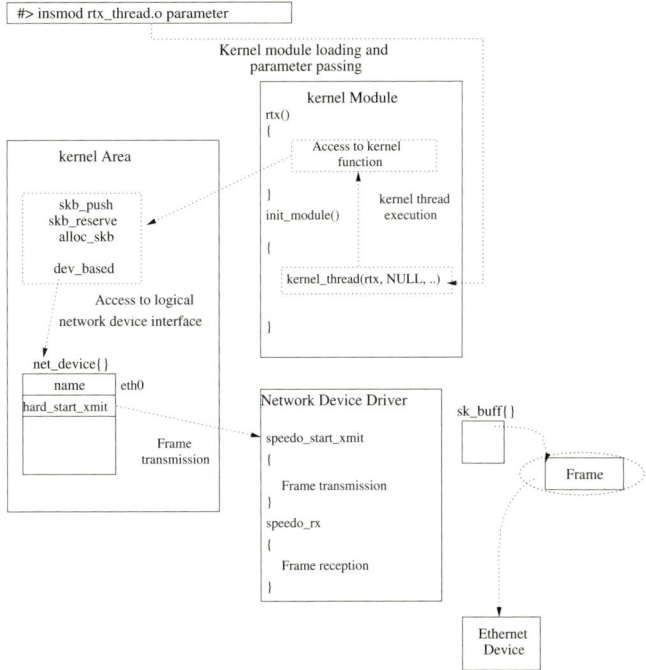

Fig. 4. Overview of our kernel module

To perform a direct I/O for a network device, we need a logical device interface. A global variable *dev_base* is a list of *net_device* structures allocated for all registered logical network devices. Figure 4 shows how we can access to a `net_device` structure using device name from `dev_base` and kernel module, `rtx_thread.o`, operates. Once attached to the kernel, it accesses kernel functions such as `skb_push()`, `skb_reserve()`, `alloc_skb()`, and kernel data structure such as `dev_base`. Using the kernel functions, our module can build a real-time frame, and transmit through `eth0` the interface using `speedo_start_xmit` function pointed to by the `net_device` structure for `eth0` that we extracted from `dev_base`.

4   Experiments

To evaluate the performance of the proposed algorithm, the proposed algorithm is implemented in Linux kernel(ver. 2.4.20) as a external module form. The transmission module forms a real-time frame according to the parameters, the sender IP, receiver IP, receiver Ethernet address, total number of frames to be transmitted, and the ratio of real-time frame against regular frame. Two types of real-time messages are defined: `VAR_UP` and `VAR_DOWN` for increasing and decreasing kernel variables, respectively. The generated real-time frame is inserted into a DMA area via a handler pre-registered by the network device

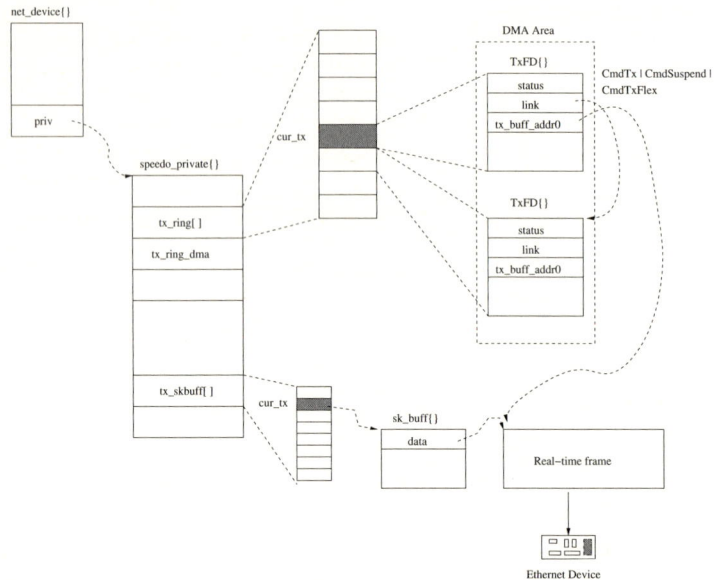

Fig. 5. Data structures for real-time frame transmission

driver. This frame will be transmitted when OUT command is issued to the device. All of the procedure are shown in Figure 5. The packet arriving interrupt makes the corresponding Top Half copy the frames from the DMA area into the system buffer. While the real-time frame, whose type of frame header is 0xff00, is pulled out and processed immediately, other regular frames are queued into a system queue until Bottom Half handles them in ordinary fashion.

For a real experiment, we implemented the Linux kernel module onto two types of platforms; an ordinary Pentium PC and an ARM-based embedded system as shown in Figure 6. Pentium platform has 800 Mhz Pentium III CPU and 256 Mbytes of main memory. Embedded platform consists of ARM 920T processor core running at 180Mhz, 128 Mbytes of main memory, and Ethernet interface. Linux kernel 2.4.20 with the proposed network module is ported onto both experimental platforms.

We have measured the packet processing time and successful processing rate with varying the ratio of real-time frames among the total frames, 1K packets, that are sent every 37 μsec. Figure 7(a) shows that the processing time decreases as the portion of real-time frames grows. However, the processing time saturates if more than 40% of packets are real-time frames because the interrupt handler used in the experiment is so simple that the 37 μsec interval is long enough to handle every packets. With more complex interrupt handler, we expect that the improvement in processing time will continue after 40%.

Figure 7(b) shows another experiment result, ratio of successful processing of real-time frames. Since we don't consider upper level flow control in our experiments, if the number of received frame goes beyond the capacity of receiving

Fig. 6. Experiment Platform

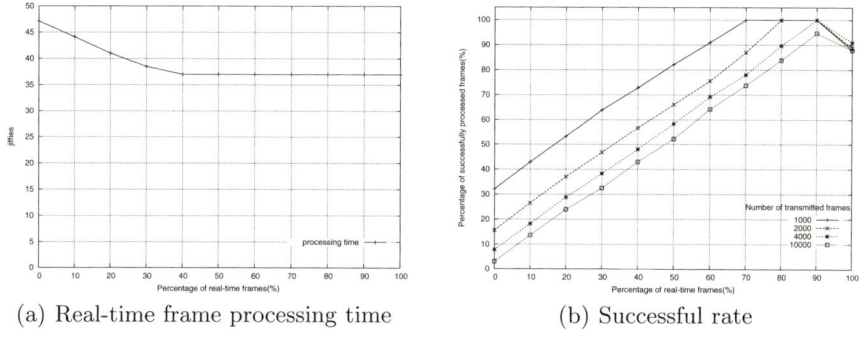

(a) Real-time frame processing time   (b) Successful rate

Fig. 7. Experiment results

side, they are discarded. It is expected that as the percentage of real-time packets increases, the rate of successful processing should improve. With no real-time frames, the rate of success is as low as 3.1% and 32.1% when 10K and 1K packets are transmitted, respectively. With adopting the proposed algorithm, the processing success rate reaches 100% when 70% of packets are real-time frames among 1K packets, The success rate goes down as the packet number increases. However, even with 10K packets, the success rate reaches around 90% when real-time frames comprise over 90% while the success rate was only 3.1% when there was no real-time frame. An interesting point is that the performance with 100% real-time frames is not as good as the one with 90% real-time frames. What happens is with real-time frame we actually spend more time in Top Half where the interrupt is disabled. With 90% real-time frames, the 10% non-real-time frames are not instantly handled and pushed over to the Bottom Half, but at least these frames do not block more important real-time frames of entering the system because they have a shorter interrupt-disable period. With 100% real-time frames, all frames spend most of the time in Top Half once they got into the system, and during this time period, they block other frames entering the system by disabling interrupt.

5   Conclusion

We have implemented a system in which network interrupt processing can be processed immediately. We have observed the major delay in network interrupt processing caused by the postponing of Bottom halves. By moving essential part from the Bottom half to the Top half we can achieve better real-time response. We proposed a technique to ensure this real-time response with a small change in the kernel. The technique is implemented and experimented. The result shows that with 10000 packets poured in, our technique could process 90% of the packets successfully while without real-time handling capacity the inundated system would process successfully only 3.1% of them.

Acknowledgement

This work was supported by Inha University Research Grant.

References

1. Chlamtac, I., Franta, W.R., Levin, K.D.: BRAM: The broadcast recognizing access method. IEEE Transactions on Communications **27** (1979) 1183–1189
2. Signorile, R.P.: MBRAM-A priority protocol for PC based local area networks. IEEE Network **2** (1988) 55–59
3. CIP Working Group: Experimental internet stream protocol, version 2 (ST-II). RFC1190 (1990)
4. Braden, R., Zhang, L., Berson, S., Herzog, S., Jamin, S.: Resource reservation protocol (RSVP). RFC2205 (1997)
5. Park, J., Yoon, Y.: An extended TCP/IP protocol for real-time local area networks. IFAC Control Engineering Practice **6** (1998) 111–118
6. Park, J., Park, J.: A study on RTP/RTCP based real-time protocol over ethernet for distributed control system. In: Procceeding of 16th DCCS 2000, Sydney, Australia (2000)
7. Schulzrinne, H., Casner, S., Frederick, R., Jacobson, V.: RTP: A transport protocol for real-time applications. RFC1889 (1996)
8. Yodaiken, V.: New frontiers for embedded computing. In: Proceedings of 17th International Conference on VLSI Design, India (2004)
9. Postel, J.: A standard for the transmission of IP datagrams over IEEE 802 networks. RFC1042 (1988)
10. Stevens, W.R.: TCP/IP Illustrated, Volume 1. Addison-Wesley Publishing Company, Massachusetts (1994)

Investigation of Surface Integrity in the Case of Chemical Mechanical Polishing Silicon Wafer by Molecular Dynamics Simulation Method

Xuesong Han

State Key Laboratory of Tribology, Tsinghua University, 100084, P.R.China
hanxuesongphd@126.com

Abstract. With the development of semiconductor industry, the chemical mechanical polishing technology has already become the mainstream method of realizing the surface global flatness. In order to understanding physical essence underlying this technology, the author carried out nanometer polishing experiment of silicon wafer using molecular dynamics (MD) simulation method. The simulation result shows that using larger slurry grain can generate much more vacancy, dislocation and larger residual stress than using of small one although using larger slurry grain can acquire better surface quality.

Keywords: Chemical mechanical polishing, molecular dynamics, silicon wafer, vacancy, dislocation.

1 Introduction

Today, the polishing technology has already became main stream technique in acquiring high surface quality in many industry such as semiconductor, optical apparatus, synthesis of nanoscale systems and so on. Polishing involves simultaneous and initiate contact between workpiece surface and pad. The illustration about this technique is shown in Fig. 1. The study of polishing technique is mainly divided into several categories, namely, experimental study and theoretical model study such as materials removal model and pressure distribution model etc. The use of polishing in technology focuses on empirical polishing schemes for specific applications with limited understanding of the fundamental physical essence involved. As the depth of cut in the polishing is always in the range of nanometer or subnanometer, there is a need of powerful toolkit to investigate this micro-mechanism at atomistic level.

Although macroscopic continuum mechanics has been perfectly developed in engineering design and played an important role in the mechanical industry, it can't be applied to solids or liquids which exist in the atomic or molecular state. MD simulation studies, generally proved to be a powerful tool in describing microscopic world , were initiated in the 1950s by Alder and Wainwright in the field of statistical mechanics. Since then, MD simulation has been applied to a wide range of fields including crystal growth, indentation, low-pressure diamond synthesis and so on. However, its application to machining is of only recent origin. In the late 1980s, a

Z. Pan et al. (Eds.): ICAT 2006, LNCS 4282, pp. 651 – 659, 2006.

group at Lawrence Livermore National Laboratory of USA conducted pioneering studies on MD simulation of nanometric cutting of copper with a diamond tool [8]. This work lead other researchers, particular from Japan [9], and in the present author's laboratory in P.R.China [1-3], to explore and extend MD simulation of nanometric manufacturing to many practical machining applications.

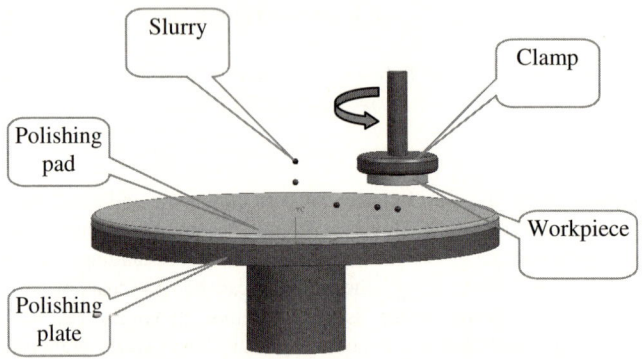

Fig. 1. Scheme of polishing technology

Chi-Wen Liu et al. [4] investigated materials removal mechanism of polishing process on macroscopic level. They proposed a analytic model based on statistical method and elastic theory to describe the materials removal mechanism of silicon wafer surface through polishing process. Their model concerns the effects of applied pressure and relative velocity between the pad and wafer on the removal rate during polishing. The removal rate is dependent on the elastic modulus on the polishing grain. Furthermore, many other scholars such as D.A. Dornfeld [5] etc also studied polishing technology separately.

Presently, most of the polishing model demonstrates limited robustness and predictive power. One basic problem lies in the lacking of fundamental understanding of physical process on microscopic level. In contrast to the many investigations of macroscopic models, a microscopic study of polishing is much more limited. While the generated surface by polishing technology is realized by means of nanometer materials removal process which is different from macroscopic machining process, there is a need to investigate this process at the atomic level. Take the example of single crystal silicon, the author conducted molecular dynamics simulation of polishing process at the atomic level.

2 Molecular Dynamics Method

The problem of molecular dynamics simulating any molecular process, be it chemical reaction, or, physics process, such as machining, involves four essential parts, namely, (a) the choice of molecular model, (b) the development of sufficiently accurate potential energy function for the system, (c) the formulation and integration of classical equations of motion for the atoms comprising the system of interest and (d) the mimics of real experimental conditions.

2.1 Simulation Model

Fig. 2 is the general model used in the MD simulation of polishing. The force acted on the workpiece comes from two sources: namely, the interaction between workpiece atoms themselves and the interaction between workpiece atom and tool atom. The initial configuration of the crystal is arranged according to its lattice model and the initial velocity is arranged by the Maxwell-Boltzman distribution.

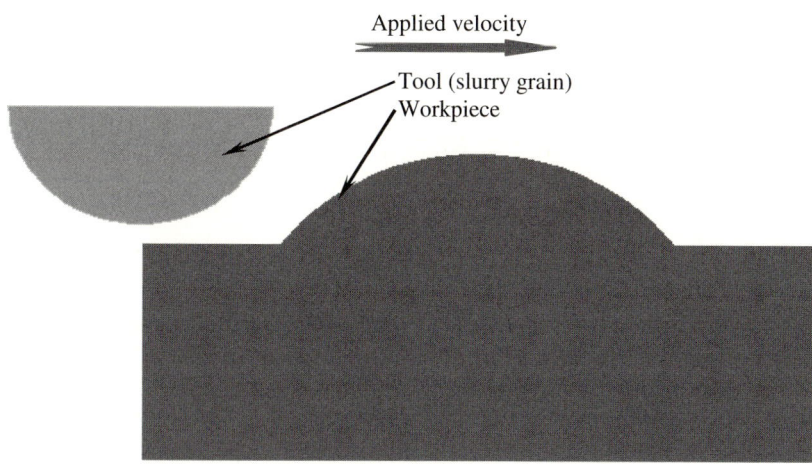

Fig. 2. Scheme of molecular dynamics simulation model

2.2 Numerical Integration Algorithm

The computation of trajectory requires numerical integration of the differential equations of motion from initial to the final state. The classical equations of atom trajectory is listed as follows:

$$m\frac{d^2\vec{r_i}}{dt^2} = \frac{d(m\vec{v_i})}{dt} = \frac{d\vec{p_i}}{dt} = \vec{F_i} \quad . \tag{1}$$

$$\vec{F} = -\nabla_i V(\vec{r_1}, \vec{r_2}, \cdots \vec{r_n}) \quad . \tag{2}$$

$$\nabla_i = \frac{\partial}{\partial x_i}\vec{i} + \frac{\partial}{\partial y_i}\vec{j} + \frac{\partial}{\partial z_i}\vec{k} \quad . \tag{3}$$

where m is the mass of atom and $\vec{r_i}$, $\vec{v_i}$, $\vec{p_i}$ and $\vec{F_i}$ are the position, velocity, momentum, and the force acted on atom i, respectively.

There are variety of methods for performing numerical integration of above ensemble atom trajectory such as fourth-order Runger-Kutta method, Leap-Frog method, Verlet method, Velocity-Verlet method and so on. In the case of MD simulation process, the energy may drift from its nominal value because of the accumulated error which requires the numerical integration method must be convergent and at the same time have the high efficiency. The Velocity-Verlet method is a symplectic algorithm which can prevent the dissipation of energy in the long simulation process and have high computation efficiency, the author adopted this algorithm as follows:

$$r_i^{n+1} = r_i^n + h v_i^n + \frac{h^2}{2m} F_i^n \ . \tag{4}$$

$$v_i^{n+1} = v_i^n + h(F_i^n + F_i^{n+1})/2m \ . \tag{5}$$

where h is the time step adopted by MD simulation.

2.3 Potential Function and Interatomic Force

In the MD simulation process, the accuracy of atom trajectories are highly affected by the choice of potential function. The total energy of system is the sum of the kinetic energy and potential energy. The kinetic energy is simple to compute but the computation of potential energy is rather complex as it depends on the position of all interaction of atoms. There are two kinds of interatomic potentials, namely, the *ab initio* method and the empirical potential. The *ab initio* method is based on quantum mechanics which is difficult to solve except for very simple systems. In reality, the empirical potential function is always adopted for its high computation efficiency and can be executed easily on the computer.

The empirical function can be further classified into two-body, three-body and multibody potentials depend on the kinds of crystal chemical structure. Most of empirical potential comprise an attractive and a repulsive term, the attractive force binds the atoms together while the repulsive force prevent then from coalescing. The empirical potential are based on simple mathematical expression to describe the interaction between two atoms, which contain many parameters to be adjusted to experimental data.

Today, several empirical potential function are used in the MD simulation process including pair potentials, such as Morse potential, Lennard-Jones potential, Born-Meyer potential and complex potential function, such as Embedded atom potential, Bolding-Andersen potential, Brenner potential, Stillinger-Weber potential, and Tersoff potential function. In this study, Morse potential is used to model the interaction between tool and workpiece, while Tersoff potential is used to model single crystal diamond grain and single crystal silicon wafer. This two potential function is listed as follows:

Morse potential [6]:

$$V = D\left(\exp(-2\alpha(r_{ij} - r_0)) - \exp(-\alpha(r_{ij} - r_0))\right) \ . \tag{6}$$

where r_{ij} is the distance between two atoms, r_0 is the distance when the atom lies at its equilibrium position , D and α are parameters adjusted to the measured sublimation and Debye temperature separately.

Tersoff potential [7]:

$$V_{ij} = f_c(r_{ij})[f_R(r_{ij}) + b_{ij}f_A(r_{ij})] \ . \tag{7}$$

where $f_R(r_{ij})$ is the repulsive pair potential, $f_A(r_{ij})$ is the attractive pair potential, $f_c(r_{ij})$ acts as cut off function which determines the number of atoms bonded to atom i.

3   Simulation Results

The simulation system consists of a silicon wafer with a spherical asperity to mimic the surface roughness and a segment of spherical diamond particle moves with a constant velocity. This model corresponds to a slurry particle embedded into a pad. During real polishing process, some slurry particles are partially embedded into the pad for some time and move with it. The polishing speed is 30m/s, the slurry grain is assumed to be rigid without any deformation, the temperature is 293K, the depth of cut is 8Å.

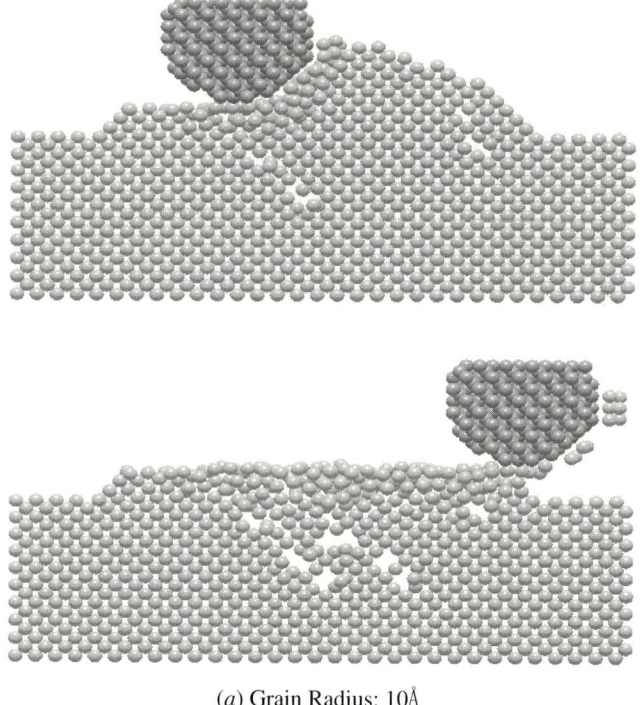

(*a*) Grain Radius: 10Å

Fig. 3. Molecular dynamics simulation results

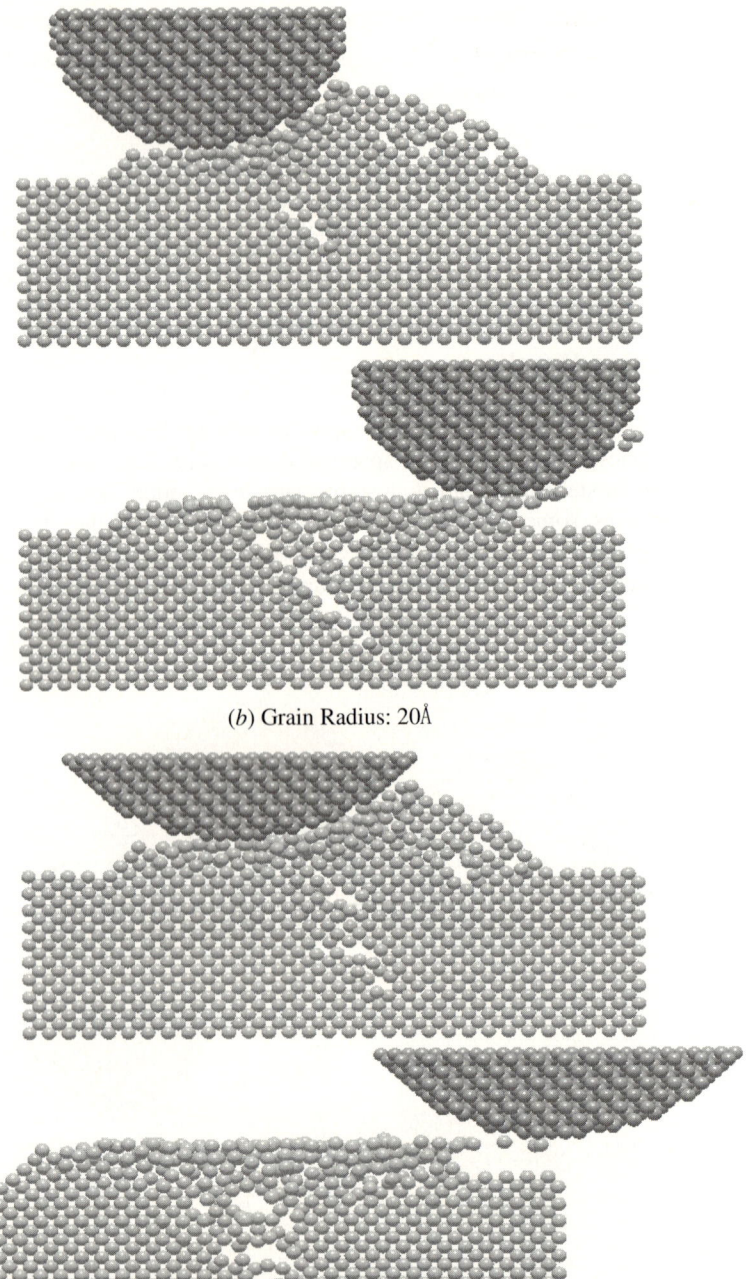

(*b*) Grain Radius: 20Å

(*c*) Grain Radius: 30Å

Fig. 3. *(Continued)*

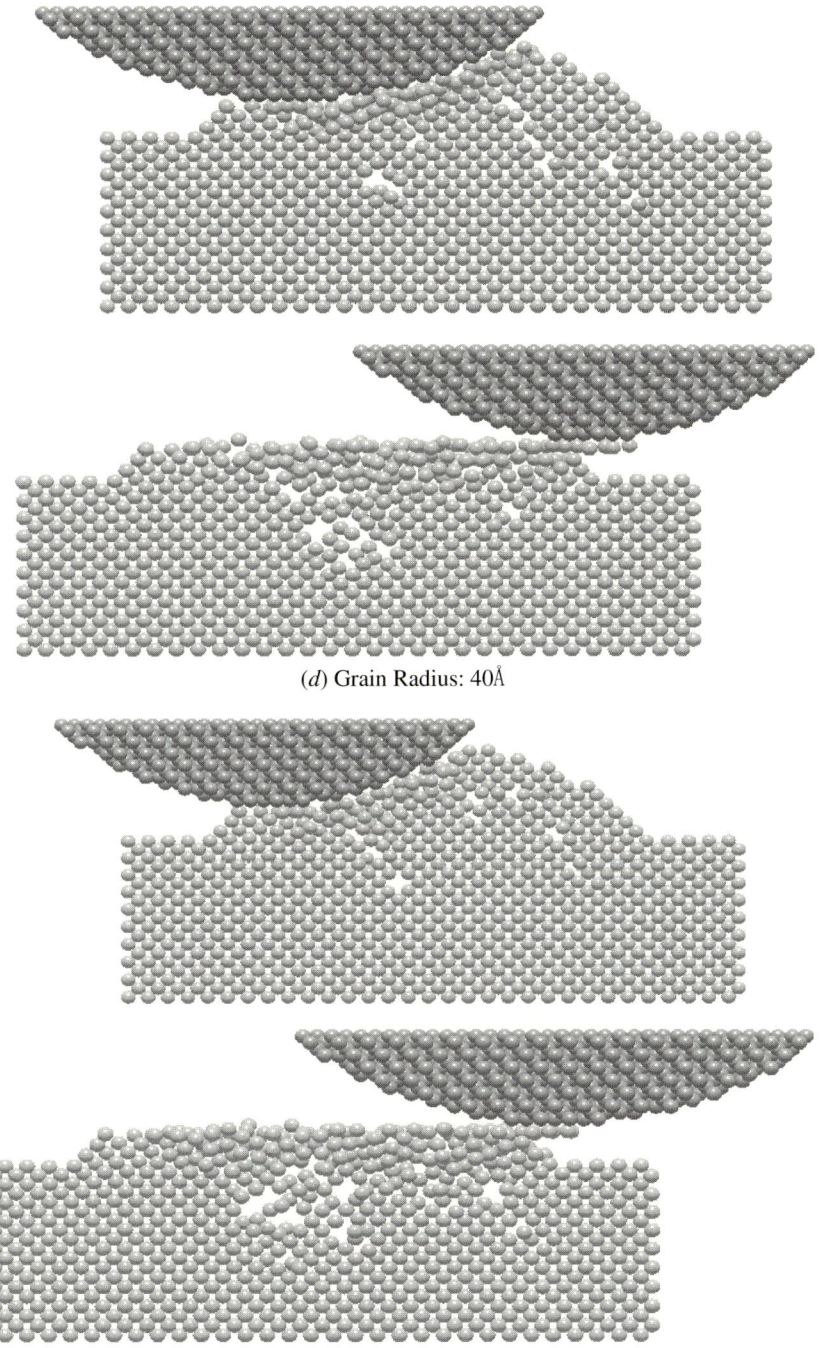

(*d*) Grain Radius: 40Å

(*e*) Grain Radius: 50Å

Fig. 3. (*Continued*)

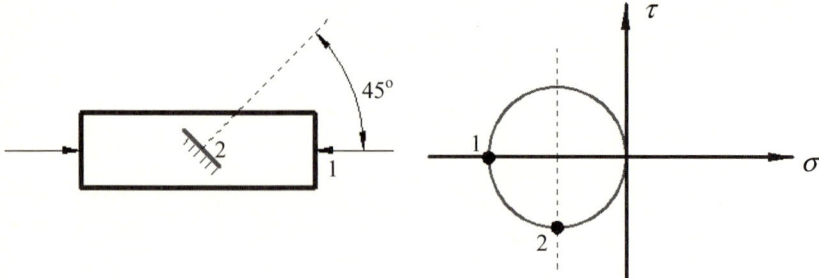

Fig. 4. Stress status

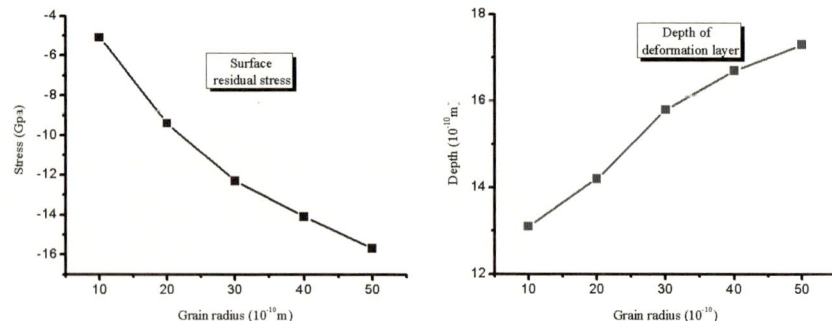

Fig. 5. Surface residual stress   **Fig. 6.** Depth of plastic deformation layer

Fig. 3 shows molecular dynamics simulation of chemical mechanical polishing silicon wafer with different size of slurry grain. The result shows that larger slurry grain generated much more vacancy and thicker deformation layer which indicates the ductile machining process. The animation of the MD simulation of polishing process also indicates elastic deformation in the bulk silicon wafer, the larger grain generate larger deformation. As the grain radius is small, the elastic recovery is obvious and results in bad surface roughness while larger grain generated larger plastic deformation and acquire better surface roughness. The larger grain only plowing the surface while small grain at as cutting tool, all of these effect together generate the polishing surface. There are many vacancy and dislocation generated at ~45° to the cutting direction, where maximal shear stress acted upon this plane 2 which is shown in Fig. 4.

Fig. 5 shows the residual stress of MD simulation machined surface. The larger polishing grain generates larger residual stress although it generates better surface roughness. The larger negative residual stress may induce the structure transformation and lead to ductile machining. Fig. 6 shows the depth of plastic deformation layer of MD simulation process. The larger grain induces larger static hydrodynamic pressure and the thicker amorphous silicon layer which may influence the function of semiconductor chip.

4 Conclusion

In order to understanding physical essence of chemical mechanical polishing technology, the author carried out molecular dynamics simulation of machining silicon wafer. The surface microstructure generated by different size of slurry particle is investigated. The final surface is generated by all of slurry particles, part of which act as cutting tool and remove the protuberant peak while part of them only plowing the surface. The simulation result shows that the cutting effect is decreased while the indent effect is increased accompanying the increasing size of slurry particle. The larger slurry particle may generate much more vacancy and thicker deformation layer comparing with small one. The surface global flatness is mainly realized by cutting effect generated by small slurry particle but too many small particle may accumulate together and form too larger particle then scratch the surface. There may exist a favorable particle size range which can balance between surface flatness and surface roughness.

References

1. Han, X.S., Wang, S.X., Yu,S.Y.: Molecular Dynamics Simulation of Nanometric Grinding - The Effect of Crystal Anisotropy on the Quality of Machined Surface. Key Eng. Mater., 258-259 (2004) 361-365
2. X.S. Han, Yu S.Y.: Investigation of tool geometry in nanometric cutting by molecular dynamics simulation. J Mater Process Technol. 129(1-3) (2002) 105-108
3. S.Y.Yu, X.S. Han: A study on surface quality of ultraprecision grinding for engineering ceramics. Key Eng. Mater. 202-203 (2001) 35-39
4. Liu, Chi-Wen, Dai, Bau-Tong, Tseng, Wei-Tsu: Modeling of the wear mechanism during chemical-mechanical polishing. J Electrochem Soc. 143(2) (1996) 716-721
5. Luo, Jianfeng, Dornfeld, David A.: Effects of abrasive size distribution in chemical mechanical planarization: Modeling and verification. IEEE Trans Semicond Manuf 16(3) (2006) 469-476
6. Morse,P.M.: Diatomic molecules according to the wave mechanics ☐ vibrational levels. Phys.Rev. 34 (1929) 57~65
7. Tersoff, J.: Modeling solid state chemistry: Interatomic potential for multicomponent systems. Phys. Rev. B39 (1989) 5566~5570
8. J. Belak, Boercher, David B.: Molecular dynamics modeling of the mechanical behavior of metallic multilayers. Mater Res Soc Symp Proc 308 (1993) 743-746
9. T. Inamura, S. Shimada: Brittle/ductile transition phenomena observed in computer simulations of machining defect-free monocrystalline silicon. CIRP 46(1) (1997) 31-34

Independent Component Analysis Approach for the Neurobiological Recording Data

Minghai Yao, Jing Hu, and Qinglong Gu

College of Information Engineering, Zhejiang University of Technology,
310032 Hangzhou, China
{Minghai Yao, Jing Hu, Qinglong Gu, ymh}@zjut.edu.cn

Abstract. Electroencephalograms (EEG) can provide a unique window on the human brain. Since contamination of EEG recording with artifacts (e.g., signals caused by muscular activity, eye movements, cardiac rhythm and power noise etc.) can decrease the efficiency of diagnosis procedure, here we apply a kind of fast independent component analysis (ICA) approach to analyze the real multi-variant EEG recorded signals. Besides, the comparison between ICA and a second order statistical algorithm are given in this paper. By the real measured data, our experimental results confirm the validity and usefulness of ICA algorithm.

Keywords: Independent Component Analysis, Neurophysiology, EEG, Artifacts.

1 Introduction

A great challenge in neurophysiology is to asses non-invasively the physiological changes occurring in different parts of the brain [1]. EEG, measuring electric field of signals emerging from neural currents within the brain, is a functional brain imaging technique with millisecond temporal resolution and millimeter spatial sensitivity.

To understand how the brain function works, recent advances statistical signal processing theory has provided new and powerful algorithms for the EEG recording analysis. EEG data generally is contaminated by the artifacts of different origins, such as cardiac activity, head or body movements and muscle contractions. Although there are couples of techniques to deal with that, including adaptive noise canceling and singular value decomposition etc., they cannot provide detailed spatio-temporal information specific to the multiple brain sources that simultaneously contribute to the total signal [2]. Since it can be assumed that most of the artifacts are independent of the brain activity, it is hoped that ICA can find the artifacts.

ICA is a recently developed method in which the goal is to find a linear representation of non-gaussian data so that the components are statistically independent, or as independent as possible [3]. The problem of ICA has received wide attention in various fields such as data mining, wireless communication and biomedical signal processing etc. Here, we present the application of this relatively novel technique to the real EEG recorded data. We focus on the removal of cardiac rhythm from the measured EEG signal in this paper due to the limitation of our

Z. Pan et al. (Eds.): ICAT 2006, LNCS 4282, pp. 660–665, 2006.
© Springer-Verlag Berlin Heidelberg 2006

experimental data. Moreover, comparison between ICA which is based on high order statistic and a second order statistic (SOS) method is also analyzed. Finally, results before and after artifact removal for measured EEG recording are obtained.

2 Methods

As the ICA method interprets the measured data as a linear superposition of statistically independent processes. With this assumption, the data can be written as

$$X = AS \ . \tag{1}$$

Where X is the observed data matrix with m (the number of channels, e.g., electrodes for EEG) by n (sampling time points), A is the so-called mixing matrix. S consists of the original source signals. The goal is to estimate both unknown A and S from X. With appropriate assumptions on the statistical properties of the source distributions, the solution is sought in the form,

$$S_{est} = WX \ . \tag{2}$$

Where W is called the separating or de-mixed matrix. In the ideal case, W should be the inverse matrix of A, thus S_{est} is just the expected source signal S.

The measurements contain signals resulting in the electrical activity of the brain but also signals which can be considered artifacts. The key assumption used to distinguish sources from mixtures is that all the signal components in S, are statistically independent, i.e., the joint probability density is the product of the marginal densities. Meanwhile they should have non Gaussian probability density functions, except at most one which may be a Gaussian.

Solving the ICA problem is to find W iteratively. In our ICA-based method, firstly, the centering and whitening procedure is implemented, in order to get a new measured data $\widetilde{X}$ with zero mean and unit variance. Furthermore, run the following steps, which is a kind of fast ICA algorithm,

Step 1: initialize the de-mixed vector w_i ,
Step 2: the iteration function is:

$$w_i = E\{\widetilde{X}g(w_i^T \widetilde{X})\} - E\{g'(w_i^T \widetilde{X})\}w_i \ . \tag{3}$$

Let

$$g(u) = \tanh(u) \ . \tag{4}$$

Step 3: Decorrelation:

$$w_i = w_i - \sum_{j=1}^{i-1} w_i^T w_j w_j \ . \tag{5}$$

Step 4: Normalization, that is,

$$w_i = w_i / \|w_i\| \ . \tag{6}$$

Go to step 2 if not converged, otherwise, output the vector w.

To prevent different vectors from converging to the same maxima, step 3 is necessary. Thus, we can estimate several independent components with weight matrix W [3].

Additionally, for comparing with ICA algorithm, here we adopt a kind of second order statistics (we call SOS here) algorithm based on eigenvalue decomposition (EVD) to obtain the estimated signals. This SOS method belongs to the decorrelation technique, which ensure only that output pairs are uncorrelated, i.e., $< s_i s_j > = 0, \forall ij$, whereas ICA impose a much stronger criterion, statistical independence, which occurs when the multivariate probability density function factorizes, e.g., $\rho_s(S) = \prod_{i=1}^{N} \rho_{s_i}(s_i)$.

Statistical independence requires that all second-order and higher-order correlations of the s_i are zero, while decorrelation only seeks to minimize second-order statistics (covariance or correlation)[5].

3   Experimental Results

All signals used in our experiments were obtained from online polysomnographic database. There are seven-channel signals recorded synchronously, including one EEG (electrode placement recordings at positions C3), one Electrocardiography(ECG) signal, one electrooculogram(EOG), one electromyography(EMG), the rest signals are caused by abdominal movement, nasal air flow and blood pressure. In consideration of data matrix dimensions, in experiments, we only select 4 signals of 7 signals measured synchronously and meanwhile use a sampled interval of 5.996 seconds recording (a period from 1 to 1500 in the total 15000 sampling length). Therefore, the dimension of the experimental data is 4 by 1500. Fig.1 gives four selected measured signals in our experiments, which are also called the mixed signals, the only data we know before our experiments.

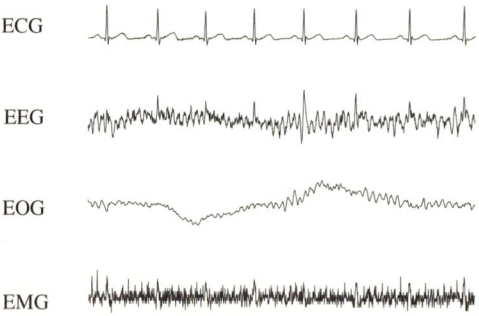

Fig. 1. Recorded signals: EEG (*C3*) with artifacts EOG, ECG and EMG

Then the fast ICA and SOS approaches are performed and then two de-mixed matrixes are computed respectively,

W_{ICA} = [3.4540, 4.5591, -0.7440, 15.3987; 0.6942, -48.5505, 27.9056; 108.8050; 1.3821, -85.4983, -19.3225, 30.1904; 1.7035, -17.0226, 1.8735, -583.3683]

And

W_{SOS} = [0.3603, -4.3362, 33.6008, 17.3818; -1.9786, -60.1187, 0.0019, 66.4222; 3.5488, 79.4060, 5.0823, 103.2395; -0.7451, 2.3277, 1.1076, 333.9881].

The mixture matrix A in Equation(1) is unknown since we cannot know the true original signals, therefore it is impossible to evaluate the separation capabilities of these two approaches quantitatively by two above yielded de-mixed matrixes W_{ICA} and W_{SOS}. We then turn to use the separated results shown in Fig.2 instead to see the result difference between two separation approachs. By comparison, we can know this SOS method is hardly capable of eliminating ECG from EEG signal, the component SOS3 still have the obvious SOS2 interferential effect, whereas by the fast ICA, component IC3 becomes a clean EEG signal.

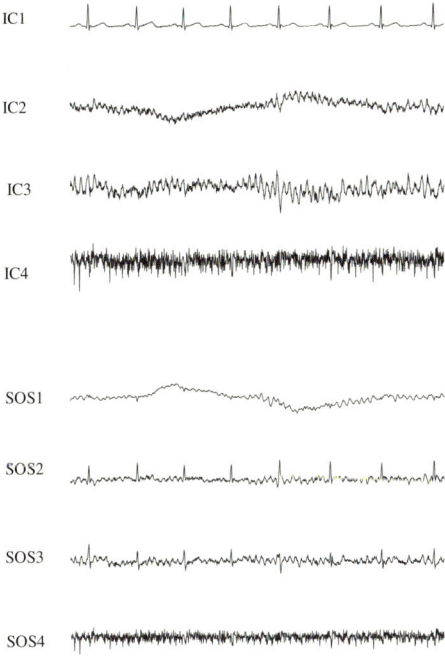

Fig. 2. Comparison of separated results by fast ICA and SOS algorithm: the top one is fast ICA, the bottom is SOS

So, by applying ICA to mixtures of independent sources such as the real biological signals, we can reach the blind separation. We only focus on the removal of cardiac rhythm from the measured EEG signal due to the limitation of the experimental data here. As we know, there is a batch of various ICA algorithm developed so far. Due to the different algorithms suitable to the different applications, hence how to select the right ICA methods to remove affection of artifacts from EOG, EMG or power noise on EEG recording will be in our next work.

Furthermore, the results before and after the artifact removal are illustrated with Fig.3 and Fig.4. It is clear to see EEG is contaminated by ECG before the separation experiment, whereas this phenomena disappears in Fig.4 after running ICA.

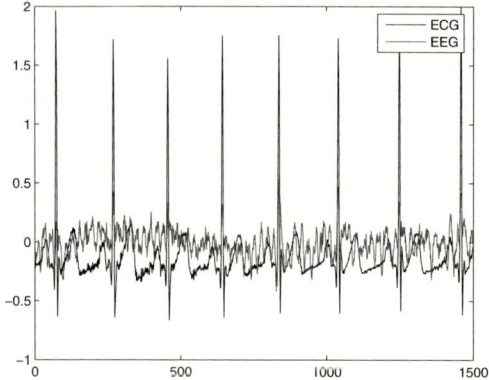

Fig. 3. Comparison between the measured EEG (*red line*) and ECG (*black line*) signals before using fast ICA algorithm

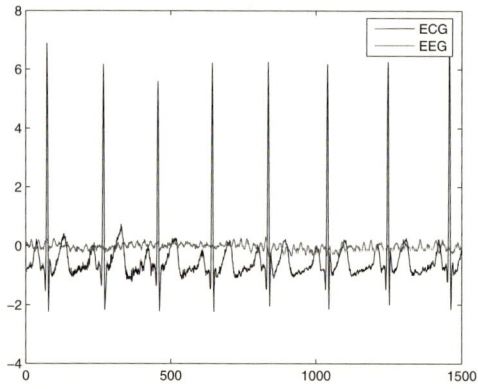

Fig. 4. The clean EEG (*red line*) after artifact removal and ECG signal (*black line*)

4 Conclusions

ICA is a powerful tool that aims to find the independent components from a set of signal. Neurophysiological interpretation of the ICA algorithm sources poses a further research challenge. We will develop this work in the near future. We can project the previously selected components of interest back to the recording space and by doing so we can obtain a set of cleaned measurements, and then we further want to know the relationship between the independent components and brain activities more directly. Meanwhile, we need to combine the prior and clinical neurophysiologic knowledge to analysis these separated components, to tell the true EEG source signals and artifacts among them, to know the information about dipole sources in brain (e.g., the amount of dipoles, and their location, magnitude and direction) which produce the measured electric field around the head and so on. We will try to make a more serious use of ICA into the EEG inverse problem since it can be an additional useful tool in preprocessing EEG data for source analysis

Acknowledgments. This work was supported by Zhejiang Provincial natural science fund(602111), China PostDoctoral science fund(2003033530) and Zhejiang Provincial 14th startup fund for studying abroad and returning personnel.

References

1. Cichiock, A.: Blind Signal Processing Methods for Analyzing Mulitichannel Brain Signals. International Journal of Bioelectronmagnetism. Vol.6, 1 (2004)
2. Salustri, C., Kronberg, E.: Language-related brain activity revealed by independent component analysis. Clinical Neurophysiology, Vol.115,(2004)385-395 Springer-Verlag, Berlin Heidelberg New York (1997) 415–438
3. Hyvarinen, A., Oja, E.: Independent component analysis: algorithms and applications. Neural Networks, Vol.13, (2000)411-430
4. Vigario, R., Sarela, J., Jousmaki, v.: Independent component approach to the analysis of EEG and MEG recordings. IEEE Trans.Biomed.Engi., vol.47, 5(2000)589-593
5. Jung, T.P., Makeig, S., Westerfield, M.: Removal of eye activity artifacts from visual event-related pententials in normal and clinical subjects. Clinical Neurophysiology, Vol.111, (2000)1745-1758
6. Borschbach, M., Schulte, M.: Performance analysis of learning rules for the blind separation of magnetoencephalography signals. Proc.of ICA99, (1999)341-346

Real-Time Virtual Surgery Simulation Employing MM-Model and Adaptive Spatial Hash

Shaoting Zhang[1], Lixu Gu[1], Weiming Liang[2], Jingsi Zhang[1], and Feng Qian[2]

[1] School of Software, Shanghai Jiao Tong University
http://www.se.sjtu.edu.cn/igst/~stzhang.htm
[2] ACM Class, Shanghai Jiao Tong University

Abstract. In this paper, MM-Model is presented for real-time simulation of 3D deformable objects on both global level and local region. This model consists of a deformable centerline and dynamic surface reconstruction mechanism based on Mass Spring and Medial-Representation respectively. When a relatively small force is applied on the object the model works in the same way as the traditional Mass-Spring. Otherwise the force is directly transferred to the centerline and the surface is dynamically recreated according to the position of the centerline. This model works more effectively and efficiently than traditional elastic ones on the global level due to the advantages of the Medial-Representation reflecting the internal information and the Mass-Spring reducing the response time. A novel collision detection algorithm based on adaptive spatial hash, a cutting approach and suture method are also articulated. An artificial blood vessel's deformation effect and surgery processes are presented in our case study.

1 Introduction

Real-time simulation of deformable objects becomes increasingly important in Virtual Reality, especially in the virtual surgery. More and more inexperienced surgeons and students begin to use this technology instead of practicing on cadavers. However, immediately and accurately modeling as well as interaction has still been the bottleneck.

Various models have been proposed to simulate soft tissue and other deformable objects. Finite Element Method (FEM) is famous for accuracy when simulating local deformation [1], but it is time-consuming and difficult to implement. Mass-Spring systems are fast when the number of nodes is relatively small [2], while they are not very accurate and its stability depends on the value of parameters. Chain-Mail satisfies the real-time requirement but it does not reflect the real physical characteristics of these objects [3]. In addition, these models focus on local area deformation, such as cutting, pressing and nipping. All of them might not be suitable for simulating global deformation due to the following problems: (1) the elastic model is inappropriate for simulating global

Z. Pan et al. (Eds.): ICAT 2006, LNCS 4282, pp. 666–675, 2006.

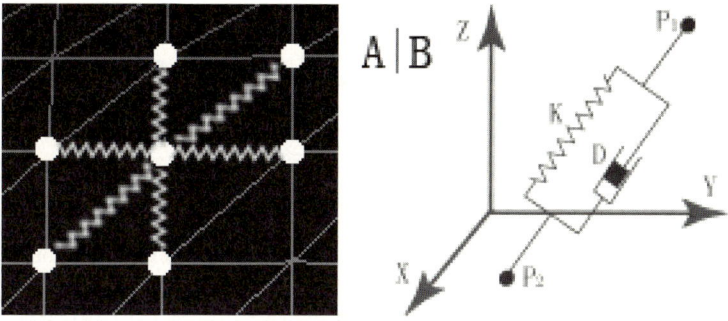

Fig. 1. (A) The topology of mass points and springs; (B) The basic component of Mass-Spring system (D = damper)

deformation because of the unacceptable distortion; (2) global motion requires much more calculation time than local movement [4]; (3) the inner structure is not well presented.

In this paper, we want to solve the problems mentioned above and propose a novel MM-Model. A deformable centerline based on a Mass-Spring system and a Medial Representation model is combined to simulate both large and small scale motion [5]. If external force is applied on a local region, the model works as a pure surface Mass-Spring system; otherwise, the force will be directly applied to the centerline and the surface will be reconstructed according to the position of the moving centerline. Additionally, we advance a multi-resolution hashing algorithm for the real-time collision detection between deformable objects and established a surgery-training system on an artificial blood vessel with cutting and suture simulation.

The following sections describe the hybrid model and collision detection algorithm in detail. In section 2 we introduce the method to model the deformable centerline, Medial Representation modeling and surface-reconstruction mechanism, all of which lead to the MM-Model. In section 3 some virtual reality algorithms such as collision detection, collision response, cutting and suture are presented. Finally, we present the experiment results in section 4.

2   MM-Model

2.1   Deformable Centerline Modeling

Mass-Spring models the non-rigid object as a collection of mass points linked by springs and dampers in a mesh structure. The topology of the mass points and springs on the surface is described in Fig. 1(A), and Fig. 1(B) displays the compositions of the basic unit of the system: the elastic spring and the damper. The former engenders the elasticity force proportional to the springs length change, and the latter generates damping force relative to the velocity of points.

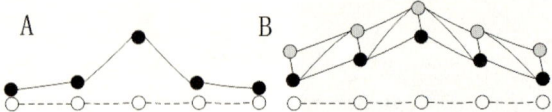

Fig. 2. Apply a force on the middle-point of the centerline. (A) A crest appears on the centerline with the linear topology (The write dots = the initial position of centerline; The black dots = the position after deformation; the black lines = springs); (B) A smooth effect of the centerline with DALs (The grey dots = Virtual atoms).

The Mass-Spring system employs a differential equation to calculate the co-ordinates of mass points:

$$m_i \cdot \frac{\partial^2 \boldsymbol{x}_i}{\partial t^2} + d_i \cdot \frac{\partial \boldsymbol{x}_i}{\partial t} + \sum_{j \in \sigma(i)} k_{i,j} \cdot \delta l_{i,j} = F_i \ . \tag{1}$$

Where m_i, d_i, and F_i are the mass, damping factor and external force of the ith mass respectively. x_i is the $3n$ vector displacement of the ith mass points. σ_i represents the mass points directly linked to the ith mass. $k_{i,j}$ and $\delta l_{i,j}$ denotes the elasticity factor and the length alternation of spring ij respectively. The mass-spring system is employed to model the surface mesh and the deformable centerline.

The Distance Mapping Method is employed to extract the centerline [7], along which media atoms are selected evenly and automatically. The density of the atoms determines the resolution of the surface mesh. After the extraction, the centerline is modeled as a Mass-Spring system: the atoms are considered as mass points and linked with springs.

However, the propagation of the force applied on this linear elastic model is not simultaneous due to the linear layout of the centerline. Therefore, an unreasonable crest will occur in a local area (Fig. 2(A)). To solve the problem, some optimizations are realized. A Dynamic-Assistant-Line (DAL) is created to construct a layered topology (Fig. 2(B)). Virtual atoms and DALs (dash lines) are generated parallel to the centerline and vertical to the external force, and this layered Mass-Spring system can accelerate the propagation of the force, which could ameliorate the crest-problem.

Additionally, an Angular Spring (AS) and Return Spring (RS) are designed to refine the deformation appearance [8][9]. The former is used to simulate the curvature force which controls the bending degree; the latter is utilized to prevent the model from escaping from the initial position.

2.2   Medial Representation Modeling

After the construction of the centerline model, the Medial Representation model used to dynamically obtain the surface information needs to be created.

Stephen M. Pizer presented the M-Rep theory, a type of Medial Representation, based on Blums medial axes [10]. This model uses medial atoms (Fig. 3(A))

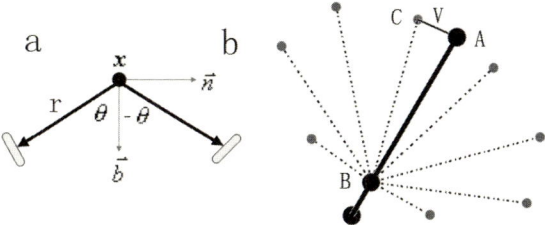

Fig. 3. (A) M-Rep topology in 3D; (B) 3D simplified Medial Representation in stable position (A, B = medial atoms; C = implied boundary; V = Orientation Vector)

to represent the interior section and a particular tuple ($\{x, r, F(\boldsymbol{b}, \boldsymbol{n}), \theta\}$) to imply the boundary position [5]. M-Rep is widely used in the fields of segmentation but it is not suitable for simulation modeling due to the expensive calculation cost. Thus we redefine the topology of medial atoms just like hub-and-spoke (Fig. 3(B)). The corresponding tuple is altered to $\{x, r, F(\boldsymbol{V}, \boldsymbol{AB}), \theta\}$, where x is the 3D coordinates of the medial atom B; r is the length of the spoke $\boldsymbol{BC}$; $F(\boldsymbol{V}, \boldsymbol{AB})$ is the plane determined by $\boldsymbol{V}$ and centerline $\boldsymbol{AB}$; $\boldsymbol{V}$ is the Orientation Vector of boundary C, which links A with C; θ is the angle between $\boldsymbol{AB}$ and $\boldsymbol{BC}$.

The Basic Reconstruction Mechanism. As described in Section2.1 the centerline will move under the global level external force. Here we only simulate the elasticity force and curvature force, but excluding the constraint force, in order to realize the dynamically surface reconstructing. Therefore the movement of the centerline is limited to translation and rotation around the medial atoms but no spin around. Thus the coordinates of boundary C can be dynamically and uniquely determined by the following formula:

$$\underline{C} = x + R_{V, AB}(\theta)\boldsymbol{AB} \cdot r_{BC}/|\boldsymbol{AB}| . \qquad (2)$$

Where $\underline{C}$ and x is the coordinates of boundary C and medial atom B respectively; R denotes the operator to rotate its operand by the argument angle in the plane spanned by $\boldsymbol{V}$ and $\boldsymbol{AB}$; $|\boldsymbol{AB}|$ means the length of the vector $\boldsymbol{AB}$. Other spokes connecting with B can be calculated by rotating $\boldsymbol{BC}$ around $\boldsymbol{BA}$ and scale the r length. Iterating the process can obtain all boundaries [11].

The Advanced Reconstruction Mechanism. The reconstruction mechanism mentioned in the above suffers two drawbacks: (1) If the value of θ is a constant during the deformation, the position of the reconstructed surface points might be inappropriate because the included angle of the centerline's subsections will be changed (Fig. 4(B)); (2) The neighboring spokes might intersect with each other if the centerline bends too much. Both of the problems might deteriorate the appearance of soft tissue (Fig. 4(B)).

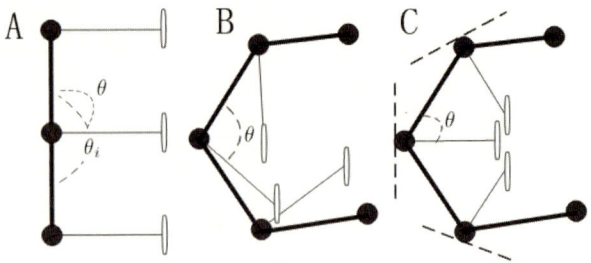

Fig. 4. (A) The initial layout of centerline and spokes (Black dots = medial atoms; blue ellipses = implied boundaries; the bold black line = centerline; thin blue lines = spokes); (B) The irregular topology of spokes according to the basic reconstruction mechanism; (C) The ideal arrangement of spokes according to the advanced reconstruction mechanism (dash lines = tangents)

The first problem is solved by defining a constant degree-ratio λ, which is expressed as the quotient of the initial θ devided by the corresponding initial included angle θ_i. When the centerline is moving, the value of θ is calculated by multiplying the constant λ with the variant θ_i, then tangents are created for spokes to rotate instead of the centerline's subsections. This strategy ensures a reasonable magnitutde for θ during the deformation (Fig. 4(C)).

To conquer the second drawback we rearrange all the intersecting spokes to reasonable positions according to the following algorithm: all of the intersected spokes are discarded except the first one (marked as V_1) until we find the first uncrossed spoke (marked as V_2); then the discarded spokes will be inserted into the the equally divided positions between V_1 and V_2. The two adjustments ensure a reasonable arrangement of all the spokes and polish the appearance of the deformable objects.

The deformation algorithm is switched between the surface mass-spring model and the reconstruction model according to the magnitude of the external force: if the force is larger than the pre-defined threshold, it will be directly transfered to the nearest three media atoms and the position of the surface will be recalculated based on the advanced reconstruction mechanism; otherwise the mass-spring model will be employed to describe the deformation.

3   Virtual Reality

3.1   Collision Detection

Collision detection algorithm is used to determine if and when geometric objects intersect. Physically based modeling simulations depend highly on the physical intersection between objects in a scene. Complex physics engines require fast, accurate, and robust proximity queries to maintain a realistic simulation at interactive rates. Generally, collision-detection algorithms has to deal with two important phases, broad-phase and narrow-phase collision detection. The former one could efficiently determine all potential collision pairs in a scene with n objects, and the latter one checks potentially colliding pairs by applying an primitive intersection test. The problem of collision detection for static environments can be regarded as already solved. Generally, in a preprocessing step, an accelerating data structure is computed, and then, this data structure is used for optimally efficient borad and narrow phase collision detection. if the force is smaller than the threshold. However, the problem is more difficult when dealing with deformable models because such objects might change their shape each simulation step, which means that the accelerating data structure needs to be recomputed at runtime. Moreover, traditional uniform spatial partitioning approach is unsuitable for deformable objects, since the size of primitive (eg: tetrahedrons) will be changed during the deformation, which might make the pre-defined grid-resolution too high or too low. The high resolution means one primitive occupies a lot of grid-cells and the mapping process becomes extremely costly which the check for collisions in the case is very exact and fast, and the low resolution means many primitives are mapped into one single grid-cell, broad-phase collision detection works not very effective which leads to high costs in the narrow-phase since many primitives have to be checked for intersection.

In our approach, we advance an adaptive multi-resolution spatial partitioning algorithm [12] to devide the space and a hash table to store the position information of the deformable objects. Such approach could conquer the uniform-grid problems and achieve an efficient collision detection result.

In the partitioning stage, an optimal cell-size for each tetrahedron needs to be able to find. The assumption is that an optimal cell-size is given when a tetrahedron is mapped into less than eight cells and more than four cells. In the mapping stage, an unique address needs to be found for each possible grid cell. In the hashing stage, the hash function which is efficiently computable and good distribution is chosen to map grid-cells uniformly over the whole hash table.

Thus the previously introduced stages are combined to form the adaptive multi-resolution spatial hashing algorithm. Firstly, assuming a scene consisting of m tetrahedrons. For each tetrahedron the grid-cells that it occupies are computed. A reference to the tetrahedron is hashed into all occupied grid-cells. Secondly, for each vertex in the scene, it is computed which grid-cell it occupies. The vertex has to be tested for intersection with all tetrahedrons that also occupy that grid-cell. Doing those processes in every simulation steps, the collision detection effect is achieved. In the application, the update rate is more than 50 times per second when the collision detection algorithm is employed between two deformable objects each consists of 49848 tetrahedrons, which satisfy the real-time requirement.

3.2   Cutting and Suture

Cutting. A typical approach of cutting is described as the following steps: (1) Constantly collision detecting between the deformable object and the surgery equipment. (2) When the collision is detected, collision response will be invoked

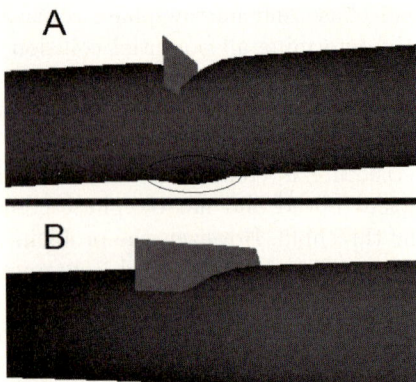

Fig. 5. Comparison between typical cutting method and centerline approach. (A) The force is transferred to the centerline and get a global deformation; (B) The force affects the local region.

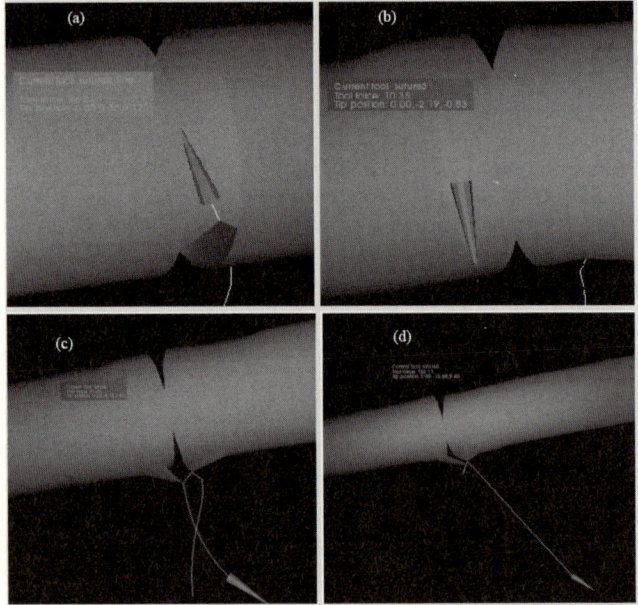

Fig. 6. Simulation of the suture process using FTL algorithm

and the soft object will deformed according to the external force. (3) If the internal force is larger than the pre-defined threshold, the spings will be cut, which means the corresponding triangles or tetrahedrons will be removed, and then the points connected by these springs will move back to the balanced position. (4) A friction force will be appended between the surgery equipment and the deformable object in order to obtain a more realistic simulation effect.

However, this algorithm does not take the global deformation into consideration, which result in the unreasonable effect in the global level. In our approach,
part of the external force will be transferred to the centerline structure through
spokes, and this force could ensure a global deformation result Fig. 5 (A),(B).

Suture. Follow The Leader (FTL) [13] algorithm is employed in the suture
simulation. The algorithm is described here: (1) Define a line to represent the
needle and stitches and evenly select 50 points on the line. Assume that the
needle and the stitch between two neighbouring points are rigid objects, which
means that the length between two points is constant. (2) Add the first point P_0
to the array of Control Points. (3) Move P_0 to a new position P_0'. The moving
vector is $\boldsymbol{P_0 P_0'}$. (4) Move the second point P_1 along the direction $\boldsymbol{P_1 P_0} - \boldsymbol{P_0 P_0'}$
until the distance between P_1 and P_0' is $|\boldsymbol{P_1 P_0}|$, which is the original length of
this stitch. (5) Add the second point P_1' to the array of Control Points and
iterate the above processes until all points are moved to the next position.
Fig. 6 displays the result of suture simulation.

4   Experiments

The tests are performed on a computer with an Intel Pentium IV-2.80 GHz CPU,
1.0 G bytes of DDR2 memory and a GeForce 6800 graphics card. The code is
compiled with Visual C++ 7.0. The model is a part of an artifact blood vessel.
There are 1142 points on the surface and 2280 polygons in the structure.

Fig. 7 compares the global deformation appearance of the hybrid model with
both the surface and volume elastic models. Fig. 7(A) and Fig. 7(B) are the solid
and mesh view of the Hybrid Model under the global-level force based on the
advanced reconstruction mechanism; Fig. 7(C) is the result of the volume Mass-
Spring model under large scale forces (the volume mesh contains 3564 points

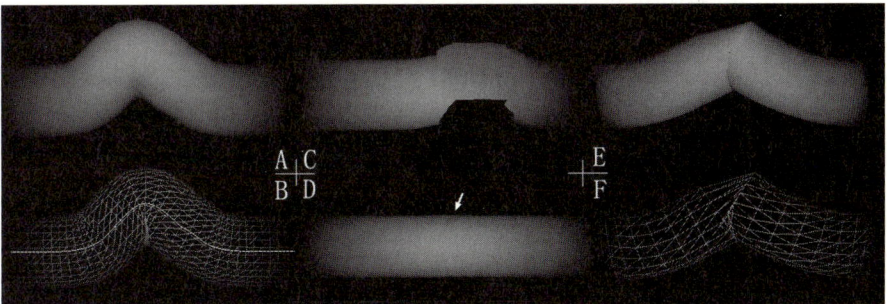

Fig. 7. Deformation effect of the artifact blood vessel (A) Global deformation of the
Hybrid Model based on the advanced reconstruction mechanism; (B) Mesh view of
(A) with the centerline; (C) Global deformation of the volume Mass-Spring model; (D)
Local Deformation of the Hybrid Model (the same as the Surface Mass-Spring model);
(E) Global deformation of the Hybrid Model using the basic reconstruction mechanism;
(F) Mesh view of (E)

(1142 on the surface) and 17887 voxels). Fig. 7(D) is the local deformation effect of the hybrid model, which is the same as the surface mass-spring model. Fig. 7(E) and Fig. 7(F) display the appearance of the hybrid model using the basic reconstruction mechanism.

Table 1. Comparison of the calculation time between different models (milliseconds per update time, the calculation time = the time used for computing the displacements). (LF = local force; GF = global force; 10, 20, 100, 200, 400 = the magnitude of the forces).

	Surface Mass-Spring	Volume Mass-Spring	Mass-Spring + M-Rep
LF(10)	1.281	6.437	1.266
LF(20)	1.265	6.422	1.375
GF(100)	1.406	7.282	0.455
GF(200)	1.657	9.297	0.470
GF(400)	2.093	15.281	0.541

Table. 1 displays the computation time of different models. Here local force means that we apply a relatively small force (less than 50 units) on a surface point, and global force means that a large force (more than 100) is applied on 10 points. The update rate (including the rendering time) of the hybrid model is about 300 times, such rate is more efficient than the volume mass-spring model and meets with the real-time requirement (15-20 times per second). Additionally, the response time of the hybrid model will not be increased with the scale of the external force since the time complexity of the reconstruction mechanism depends on the whole number of spokes, while the mass-spring model does not have the advantadge because the computation time of the elastic formula 1 depends on the springs involved in the calculation.

5   Conclusions and Future Work

In this paper, we proposed a MM-Model based on Mass-Spring systems and Medial Representation to simulate deformable objects and adaptive spatial hash for real-time collision detection between deformable objects. The superior feature of the model is the effective and efficient simulation of global level deformation. Our main contribution is simplifying M-Rep and combining it with Mass-Spring systems. However, this model is unsuitable for bodies with complex surface structure, such as the heart, because the dynamical reconstruction mechanism cannot reasonably deal with lots of centerline branches.

In the future, we want to improve our approach and model more complex soft tissue. Moreover, the topology of the centerline needs to be optimized in order to obtain a more reasonable effect. Our current goal is to establish a clinical training system.

Acknowledgements

This work was partially supported by the Natural Science Foundation of China, grant NO. 70581171, and the Shanghai Municipal Research Fund, grant NO. 045118045. The author would like to thank Prof. Pizer for bringing the concept of M-Rep to our lab and discussing with us patiently. We also thank Shanghai Ren Ji Hospital for the experts' opinion.

References

1. Cotin, S., Delingette, H., and Ayache, N.: Real-time Elastic Deformations of Soft Tissues for Surgery Simulation. IEEE Transactions on Visualization and Computer Graphics. VOL. 5, NO. 1, pp. 72-83, January-March, 1999
2. Frisken, S.: Using Linked Volumes to Model Object Collisions, Deformation, Cutting, Carving, and Joining. IEEE Transactions on Visualization and Computer Graphics. VOL. 5, NO. 4, pp. 333-349, October-December, 1999
3. Sarah, F., Delingette, H., and Ayache, N.: A Fast Algorithm for Deforming Volumetric Objects. 1997 Symposium on Interactive 3D Graphics. pp. 149-154, April 1997
4. Zhuang, Y.: Real-time and Physically Realistic Simulation of Global Deformation. ACM SIGGRAPH 99 Conference. pp. 270, 1999
5. Pizer, S.: Multiscale Medial Loci and Their Properties. IJCV Special UNC-MIDAG issue. VOL. 55(2/3), pp. 155-179, 2003
6. Chen, Y., Zhu, Q., and Kaufman, A.: Physically-based Animation of Volumetric Objects. Computer Animation 1998.
7. Jiang, X., Gu, L.: An Automatic and Fast Centerline Extraction Algorithm for Virtual Colonoscopy. Engineering in Medicine and Biology Conference 2005.
8. Nedel, L., Thalmann, D.: Real Time Muscle Deformations Using Mass-Spring Systems. Proceedings of the Computer Graphics International. pp. 156-166, 1998
9. Zhang, S., Gu, L.: Real-Time Simulation of Deformable Soft Tissue Based on Mass-Spring and Medial Representation. CVBIA, LNCS 3875. pp. 421-428, 2005
10. Blum, Shape Description Using Weighted Symmetric Axis Features. Pattern Recognition. VOL. 10, pp. 167-180, 1978
11. Huang, P., Gu, L., and Zhang, S.: Real-Time Simulation for Global Deformation of Soft-Tissue Using Deformable Centerline and Medial Representation. ISBMS'06, LNCS 4072. pp 67-74, 2006
12. Eitz, M.: Realtime Soft Tissue Simulation employing Constraint Based Particle Systems and Hierarchical Spatial Hashing. Master Thesis of Shanghai Jiao Tong University. 2006
13. Brown, J., Sorkin, S., and Stephanides, M.: Algorithmic Tools for Real-Time Microsurgery simulation. Medical Image Analysis. 2002

Creating Dynamic Panorama
Using Particle Swarm Optimization

Yan Zhang[1], Zhengxing Sun[1,*], and Wenhui Li[2]

[1] State Key Lab for Novel Software Technology, Nanjing University, P R China, 210093
[2] College of Computer Science and Technology, Jilin University, P R China, 130012
szx@nju.edu.cn

Abstract. The dynamic panorama keeps the advantage of providing both full view of scene in static panoramas and the dynamics of the scene, which remarkably strengthens the reality of walkthrough. This paper presents a method to create dynamic panoramas. To gain the static panorama, a multi-resolution mosaic algorithm based on Particle Swarm Optimization (PSO) is first applied to a series of photographs at one fixed point. Moving objects in the scene are then captured periodically or stochastically using a video camera, and the resulted video clips are converted into video texture. Video texture is finally registered with static panorama and combined into a compact representation. A panorama browser is also expanded to play video textures in addition to its original functions.

1 Introduction

Panoramic image is a method of making use of realistic images to get a full view panoramic space. Users can use ordinary cameras to take a serial of images surrounding a scene. When there is overlap in these images, the system can then automatically create a 360 degrees panoramic image. This can provide users with the ability to observe the virtual environment, walkthrough in the virtual environment, and perceive the environment from different viewpoints and directions voluntarily [1][2]. The panorama can be applied to various kinds of fields. For example, in virtual reality, it can be used to replace complicated 3D scene modeling and rendering [1]. It is also applied in the field of video compression, video transmission [3][4] and medical science [5], etc. Although the panorama is simple to construct and can represent static scenes naturally, it is unable to show dynamic scenes. Such monotone scenes make the panorama a very noticeable artifact. In order to overcome this disadvantage, we hope to add the dynamic scene into the panorama. Then an effective method to represent dynamic scenes is needed. Continuous video is a good choice, but the limitation is that it is a very specific embodiment during a very specific period of time. So we need to repeat the video to generate a "timeless" one. However, this method can lead to visual discontinuity between the last frame and the first frame, and bad randomicity may also generate the repeated feeling. Many methods to solve this problem have been proposed. For example, Schodl [6] presented a video texture technique and

---

* Corresponding author.

Z. Pan et al. (Eds.): ICAT 2006, LNCS 4282, pp. 676–685, 2006.
© Springer-Verlag Berlin Heidelberg 2006

Kiran [7] presented flow-based video synthesis and editing technique. But they both cannot provide panorama or large view.

We present a novel method to create dynamic panoramas. We add dynamic scenes to the panorama to implement dynamic panorama. Our system first applies particle swarm optimization (PSO) based multiresolution mosaic algorithm to a series of images taken at one fixed point to get the static panorama, then captures periodically or stochastically moving objects from the scene achieved by video camera, and then implements video texture to synthesize seamless video of arbitrary length, and finally video texture is registered with the static panorama to gain the dynamic panorama. The dynamic panorama preserves both the advantage of full-view walkthrough in static panoramas and the dynamics of the scene, which remarkably strengthens the reality of walkthrough.

2   Algorithm in Creating Panorama

When we synthesize panorama, two adjacent images can be overlapped by each other by approximately 50% because the tripod cannot achieve the absolutely horizontal condition, the camera may slope or turn over in the process of photographing. So one of the main problems for image mosaics is how to compute the accurate position where two images overlap. When we photograph, with the change of viewpoint and the automatic exposal, the light intensity varies greatly in different images for the same scene. So another problem for image mosaics is how to implement natural transition between two registered images, which means without obvious seams or sharp transition. Therefore, how to produce the accurate mosaic view of 360° for the circumstance using an abutting pair of images becomes our main problem [8][9][10].

In this paper, we make use of PSO to find an area, which contains sufficient objective characters in one image and find corresponding area in another image using pattern matching, and then register these images. Registered image might have obvious seam and shade difference at the line of mosaics because of the original explosion difference of images. We apply multiresolution techniques for image mosaics and finally achieve image automated seamless mosaics.

2.1   Optimized Characteristic Block Extraction Based on PSO

In the first image, if we can confirm area A, then we can easily get area B using pattern matching methods in the other image, according to image overlapping theory, taking acceptable range of error into consideration. The more objective characters we are searching in area A, the more difference is required between this area and surrounding areas, and the better. Distance L_2 is the simplest and the most frequently used distance function to compare the degree of similitude of two areas. The value of L_2 is small when two areas are very similar to each other, and vise versa. For a certain area S, we can calculate four values of L_2 by comparing itself with its surrounding up, down, left and right four areas of the same size, denoted as f_1 , f_2, f_3, f_4. The bigger of sum of f_1, f_2, f_3, f_4, the more difference between area S and its surrounding areas.

We denote evaluation function of area S as:

$$F = f_1 + f_2 + f_3 + f_4 \tag{1}$$

The distance L_2 of according areas is:

$$f_i = sqrt\{\sum_{m=1}^{k} \sum_{n=1}^{l} [(R(p_S^{mn}) - R(p_{S_i}^{mn}))^2 + (G(p_S^{mn}) - G(p_{S_i}^{mn}))^2 + (B(p_S^{mn}) - B(p_{S_i}^{mn}))^2]\}$$

(2)

Where, S, S_i are target area and its surrounding areas respectively; k, l are the width and height of the area. $R()$,$G()$,$B()$ are values of three primary colors of pixels. p_S^{mn} is the pixel with the coordinate value (m,n) in area S and $p_{S_i}^{mn}$ is the pixel with the coordinate value (m,n) in area S_i.

For any area S in the right half of the first image, the bigger of value F, the easier we can find an area with sufficient information needed for matching searching. How to find an area S containing sufficient objective characters is a better problem and we just need a satisfied result. Therefore, we can use PSO to searching for area S. PSO is an intelligent optimized method based on iteration and was firstly proposed by Kennedy and Eberhart [11], the basic idea of which originated from the simulation of simplified social systems.

When mosaic two images with overlapping areas, we randomly distribute 10 particles in the right half of the first image. The initial position is the coordinate of several pixels and we define an initial velocity of these particles. Each particle is moving in the solution space. We can find a matching area with certain characters, by adjusting the moving direction and velocity of particles using fitness function. Each particle can decide an area of 20*20, which is used to search for areas with multiobjective characters. Fig. 1 demonstrated how to find area S with sufficient characters in one image using PSO algorithm. The area in the green square is the area S we get.

(a)   (b)

Fig. 1. Optimized characteristic block extraction based on PSO. (a) is characteristic patch we found using PSO algorithm and (b) is the matching patch based on this characteristic patch.

Our PSO-based algorithms to search for characteristic areas can be described as follows:

(i). Randomly distributing 10 particles in the right half of the first area, initializing the original location of each particle and its original velocity;

(ii). Calculation fitness value of areas determined by each particle, using evaluation function F;

(iii). For each particle, comparing its current fitness value and the fitness value of the best location it ever passed and updating;

(iv). For each particle, comparing its current fitness value and the fitness value of the best location the whole particle swarm ever passed and updating;

(v). Adjusting the velocity and location of particles;

(vi). The algorithm ends if termination condition, which is enough good location and biggest number of time of iteration, is met. Current global optimized position is the result. Otherwise, go to (ii).

2.2 Multiresolution Mosaic

If we simply mosaic two images together using PSO algorithm, there might be an obvious seam at the splicing tape, as shown in Fig. 2. It is not permitted. We can apply multiresolution image mosaics to address this problem, in order to smooth the transition of the splicing area and get a high quality seamless image. In order to do so, we expand the original two images and apply multiresolution analysis on them to get a serial of octave like images, and at last we mosaic them at the same resolution and combine the images after image mosaics.

Fig. 2. An obvious seam image

2.2.1 Gaussian Pyramid Generation

We create a region image D, at the size of mosaic image. In the region, the centers found by PSO image mosaics algorithm is used as the boundary line. We fill white in the left side of the line and black in the right. Gaussian Pyramid is applied in the region image D.

The region image is represented initially at the level G_{D0}. This image becomes the bottom or zero level of the Gaussian pyramid. Gaussian Pyramid level 1 contains image G_{D1}, which is a reduced or low-pass filtered version of G_{D0}. Each value within level 1 is computed as a weighted average of values in level 0 within a 5-by-5 window. Each value within level 2, representing G_{D2}, is then obtained from values within level 1 by applying the same pattern of weights.

$$G_{D0}(i, j) = D(i, j)$$

$$G_{Dl}(i, j) = \sum_{m=-2}^{2} \sum_{n=-2}^{2} w(m,n) G_{D(l-1)}(2*i+m, 2*j+n) \tag{3}$$

Where, level l satisfies $0 < l < N$ and nodes i and j satisfy $0 \le i < C_l, 0 \le j < R_l$, C_l and R_l represent the horizontal width and vertical height in level l in the Gaussian Pyramid, and $w(m,n)$ is the generating kernel. In this paper, we set $N=4$. The level-to-level averaging process is called REDUCE. We now define a function EXPAND as the reverse of REDUCE. Its effect is to expand an $(M+1)$-by-$(N+1)$ array into a $(2M+1)$-by-$(2N+1)$ array by interpolating new node values between the given values. Thus, EXPAND applied to array G_{Dl} of the Gaussian pyramid would yield an array G'_{Dl} which is the same size as $G_{D(l-1)}$.

$$G'_{Dl}(i, j) = EXPAND(G_{Dl}(i, j)) = \sum_{m=-2}^{2} \sum_{n=-2}^{2} w(m,n) G_{Dl}((i-m)/2, (j-m)/2) \tag{4}$$

where, $0 < l < N, 0 \le i < C_{l-1}, 0 \le j < R_{l-1}$. When a Gaussian Pyramid is constructed, the Gaussian Pyramid Value of each level in the region image D is recorded and is used to contrast the weight of Laplacian Pyramid for the mosaic image.

2.2.2 Laplacian Pyramid Generation

Two original images $I1$ and $I2$ Expand the size of the region image respectively, the extended part is filled by each original image. For the extended images $I1$ and $I2$, the Laplacian Pyramid of its RGB component chart is a sequence of error images $L_0, L_1...L_N$. Each is the difference between two levels of the Gaussian pyramid. They are Laplacian Pyramid of R channel for the extended images $I1$ and $I2$.

$$L_{IN} = G_{IN}, \quad L_{Il}(i, j) = G_{Il}(i, j) - G_{I(l+1)}(i, j), 0 \le l < N-1 \tag{5}$$

where, N is the total number of levels in Laplacian Pyramid (in this paper $N=4$).

2.2.3 Image Mosaic

If we simply mosaic two images together using PSO algorithm, there might be an obvious seam at the splicing tape, as shown in Fig. 2. We can apply multiresolution image mosaics to address this problem, in order to smooth the transition of the splicing area and get a high quality seamless image. In order to do so, we expand the original two images and apply multi-resolution analysis on them to get a serial of octave like images, and at last we mosaic them at the same resolution and combine the images after image mosaics. As a result, we can get a seamless and smooth image.

The last images in image mosaics can be obtained by calculating the Laplacian Pyramid of its *RGB* system. We set the Laplacian Pyramid image in level *l* in each channel is L_{Ml}. We take the pixel value of G_{Dl} in level *l* in Gaussian Pyramid in the region image as a weight, based on which we can calculate the pixel value of L_{Ml} in its position by:

$$L_{Ml} = G_{Dl}(i, j)LI1(i, j) + (1 - G_{Dl}(i, j))LI2(i, j) \tag{6}$$

Where, *LI1* is the Laplacian Pyramid in the current level of the expanded original image *I1* , *LI2* is the Laplacian Pyramid in the current level of the expanded original image *I2*. *(i,j)* is the position of the pixel. *LI1* and *LI2* can be calculated using formula (5). Each *RGB* channel of the last mosaic image can be rebuilt by decomposed *N*-level multi-resolution image $L_{M0}, L_{M1}, ..., L_{M(N-1)}, L_{MN}$ $(L_{MN} = G_{MN})$ In our paper, *N*=4. i.e.,

$$M = L_{M0} + EXPAND(L_{M1} + EXPAND(...(L_{M(N-1)} + EXPAND(L_{MN}))...) \tag{7}$$

After the rebuilt of each *RGB* channel image, we can calculate the *RGB* value and output the last resulting image, which is a clear and smooth seamless image, as shown in Fig. 3.

Fig. 3. Multiresolution Mosaic image

3   Representation for Dynamic Scenes

Finding a kind of an effective method to represent dynamic scene and joining it into the panorama can make it preserve the advantages of the full-view walkthrough of static panoramas and the reality of static scenes. Besides, it can make the scene preserve the dynamics, which can strengthen the reality of walkthrough. In this paper, we use the video texture technique that first presented by Schodl to represent dynamic scenes [6]. Video texture has qualities somewhere between those of a image and a video, which provides a continuous infinitely varying stream of images. While the individual frames of a video texture may be repeated from time to time, the video sequence as a whole is never repeated exactly. Video textures can be used in place of digital photos to infuse a static image with dynamic qualities and explicit action. Video texture analyzes a video clip to extract its structure, and synthesizes a new, similar looking video for arbitrary length. In the view of the observer, it is like a dynamic endless video, bringing such kind of felling that it keeps on updating and varying. When we use the video camera to capture periodically of stochastically moving objects in the scene, we have to make sure that the viewpoint is as the same as the one when we take the panorama, which means that they have to be taken at the same position. In order to implement the final register, we make the scene, which is taken by the video camera; have great repetition in the background with the panoramic images.

The basic theory of synthesizing the video-camera-taken dynamic scenes according to video texture is: for a given video of dynamic texture, The fist step, we assume that there exist two similar frames of the video sequences, i and j ($j > i$). Because the transition from frame i to frame $i+1$ is the most natural, the transition from frame j to $i+1$ is also viable, which means it will not make a discontinuity in the sense of vision. We call frame j a transition point. After playing frame j, we can continue to play the succeeding ward frame $j+1$, or instead we can continue to play frame $i+1$. As long as we have adequate similar frames in the video, we can continuously transitioning backwards at the transition points and get a video with arbitrary length. The video texture from an input video sequence is to compute some measure of similarity between all pairs of frames in the input sequence. Once the frame-to-frame distances have been computed, it uses L_2 distance:

$$D_{i,j} = \left\| I_i - I_j \right\|^2 \tag{8}$$

which denotes the L_2 distance between each pair of images I_i and I_j. During the new video synthesis, the basic idea will be to create transitions from frame i to frame j anytime the successor of i is similar to j, that is, whenever D_{ij} is small. Then we apply an exponential function to map distance $D_{i+1, j}$ to the probability of transitioning from frame i to frame j:

$$P_{i,j} = \exp(-D_{i+1,j} / \sigma), where : i > j \tag{9}$$

As $\sigma \rightarrow 0$, $P_{i,j}$ will tend to 1 for the best transition, and 0 otherwise. In the processing of synthesizing the video texture, after playing frame i, we find out P_{ik}, the max value in $P_{i,j}$ ($j \neq i+1$), then randomly select one frame from frame k and frame $i+1$ to be the next frame to play.

Once the first stage has identified good transitions for the video texture, it needs to decide in what order to play the video frames. The video texture has two ways of playing: random play and video loops. The first approach uses Monte Carlo technique to decide which frame should be played after a given frame, using the table of frame-to-frame similarities computed by the analysis algorithm. The second approach selects a small number of transitions to take in such a way that the video is guaranteed to loop after a specified number of frames. The resulting video loop can then be played in "loop" mode. For video texture played by traditional media players, loop is necessary. We apply video loops method to implement video texture in this paper.

4 Dynamic Panorama

After getting the static panorama and the video texture, we can organically combine them together to construct the dynamic panorama. In this paper we use particle swarm optimization (PSO) based multiresolution mosaic algorithm to register the video texture and the static panorama. This process is very simple. We have already mentioned that the video texture and the panorama should be taken at the same viewpoint, and the produced sequence of video texture should be deposited into the database. So we take the first frame of the video texture to be registered with the static panorama, then apply particle swarm optimization (PSO) based multiresolution mosaic algorithm to compute the matched position of this frame with the static panorama, and then record it down and deposit it into the database. For each frame of the video, its background overlaps with the others'. In other words, each frame has a fixed matching position. So when we want to play dynamic scenes, we can read the corresponding matching position from the database to implement the matching between frames.

To display the dynamic panorama, there must be an appropriate panorama browser to implement the interactive virtual roaming. We have developed our own panorama browser. In addition to the functions of the original panorama browser, it has all functions of panorama browser and the new functions such as adding, matching, and playing the video texture to our browser.

When the video texture program is finished, the produced video texture has already been deposited into the database by frames. The dynamic panorama browser program first links the database and reads in the video registered data, which means positioning the video texture in the panorama. Then, before displaying the panorama, the browser window will read the video frame which is to be played next into the buffer every 30 milliseconds. Do orthographic projection for the video frame, then mosaic it into the cylinder panorama according to the matching position. Finally, we calculate the anti-projection of the panorama with the video frame on it according the region that will be displayed in the window of the browser and get the color information, so as to finish the whole process of displaying the dynamic panorama.

Fig. 4 gives the static cylinder panorama without video texture and Fig. 5 shows some interfaces of dynamic panorama browser.

Fig. 4. Static cylinder panorama

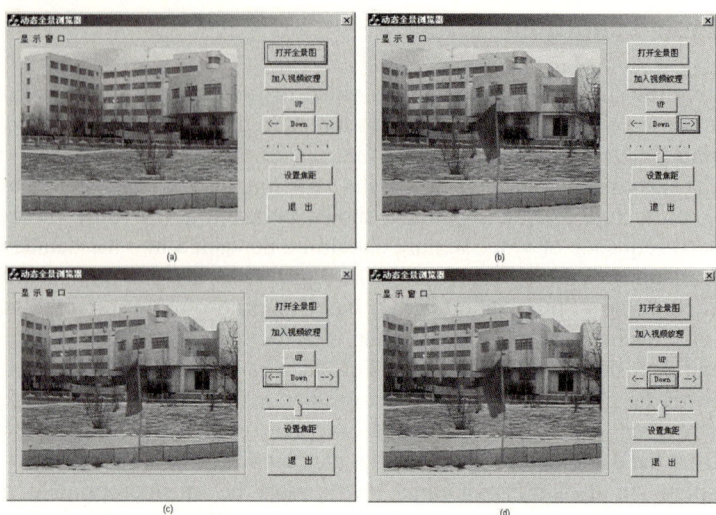

Fig. 5. The dynamic panorama. (a) interface of the browser without dynamic scenes. (b), (c), (d) interface of the browser at different moment with dynamic scenes added.

5   Conclusion

In this paper we present a method to create dynamic panoramas. We construct static panorama and video texture respectively, and add video texture to the static panorama to implement dynamic panorama. The dynamic panorama preserves both the advantage of full-view walkthrough in static panoramas and the dynamics of the scene, which remarkably strengthens the reality of walkthrough. We also proposed a new fast image mosaics algorithm based PSO multiresolution mosaics algorithm. Compared with other image mosaics algorithms, our approach is straightforward and easy to implement. We first use particle swarm optimization (PSO) to find a certain area, which contains sufficient objective characters, then we use pattern matching method to search the matching patch in another image and adjust image; at last, the mosaic image is created by a multi-resolution method. Experimental results testified that this algorithm is able to seamlessly stitch two overlapping images automatically. We have developed our own panorama browser. In addition to the functions of the original panorama browser, we add functions such as adding, matching, and playing the video texture to our browser, which makes the browser perfect.

Acknowledgement

The work described in this paper is supported by the grants from "the National Natural Science Foundation of China" [Grants No. 69903006 and 60373065] and "the Program for New Century Excellent Talents in University of China" [Grant No. NCET-04-04605].

References

1. Szliski R., Shum H. Y., Creating full view panoramic image mosaics and environment maps, In: Computer Graphics Proceedings, Annual Conference Series, ACM SIGGRAPH, Los Angeles, California, 1997, 251-258.
2. Cai Y, Liu X.H., Wu E. H., Image-based rendering a technology for virtual reality system. Journal of Software. Vol 8 No.10, 1997, 721-728.
3. Lee K S., Fung Y. F., Wong K. H, et al., Panoramic video representation using mosaic image, In : Proceedings of CISST'99 , Las Vegas, USA, 1999, 390-396.
4. Hsu S., Anandan P., Hierarchical representations for mosaic based video compression. In : Proceedings of Picture Coding Symposium, San Francisco, 1996, 395-400.
5. Can A.,.Stewart C.V, Roysam B., Robust hierarchical algorithm for constructing a mosaic from images of the curved human retina. In: Proceedings of the IEEE Conference on Computer Vision and Pattern Recognition, Colorado, 1999, 286-292.
6. Schodl A. Szeliski R., video Textures, Proc SIGGRAPH'2000, New Orleans. Louisana. 2000, 489-498.
7. Kiran S. Bhat, S. M. Seitz, J. K. Hodgins, P. K.: Flow-based video synthesis and editing. ACM Trans. Graph., Vol .3, No.3, 2004, 360-363.
8. Feng J.B., Su Z.X., Liu X.P., An similar-curve based automatic mosaic algorithm of panoramic image. Chinese journal of computer, Vol. 26, No.11, 2003, 1604-1608.
9. Fang X. Y., Pan Z. G., Xu D.:. An improved algorithm for image mosaics. Journal of computer-aided design & computer graphics. Vol.15, No.11. (2003) 1362-1365.
10. Peter J. B., Edward H. A.: A Multiresolution spline with application to image mosaics. ACM Transactions on Graphics, Vol. 2 No.4. (1983) 217-236.
11. Kennedy J., Eberhart R C.: Particle swarm optimization. In: Proc. IEEE int'l conf. On neural networks. Vol. IV. IEEE, (1995) 1942-1948.

Real-Time and Realistic Simulation of Large-Scale Deep Ocean Surface

Zhao Xin, Li FengXia, and Zhan ShouYi

School of Computer Science and Technology,
Beijing Institute of Technology, 100081, Beijing, China

Abstract. In this paper, we present a framework for real-time and realistic rendering of large-scale deep ocean surface, which uses LOD scheme and height map to model water surface on CPU and takes full advantage of GPU for vertex and pixel processing. We present multi-resolution nested regular grids, as a LOD scheme, to support free and real-time navigation on large-scale sea area. Previous work neglected the wind changing effect on ocean waves, here we propose a wind model to improve the existing method of ocean wave gen-eration and satisfy the requirement of realistic simulation with wind effect. Experiment results show that our approach is efficient and can achieve interactive rates for the simulation of large-scale deep ocean surface.

1 Introduction

Ocean wave simulation has always been a challenging research in computer graphics. More and more attentions have been given to it as its wide use in military simulation and 3D games.

We present a framework for real-time and realistic rendering of large-scale deep ocean surface, which uses LOD scheme and height map to model water surface on CPU and takes full advantage of GPU for vertex and pixel processing. Compared with traditional methods, which put the whole simulation burden on CPU, our framework makes tradeoff between CPU and GPU, which can meet both visual fidelity and interactive rates.

Perfect ocean wave simulation should consider the wind changing effect on ocean waves, but this was neglected in previous work. In order to implement this, we should model not only waves but also wind. In this paper, we present a wind model to describe the wind speed changing, which improves the existing ocean wave generation method and satisfies the requirement of realistic simulation with wind effect on waves.

LOD serves the purpose of reducing the amount of triangles to be pushed through the rendering pipeline, it is necessary for real-time rendering of large-scale scene. Although LOD algorithms have ripely developed in terrain rendering, there are too many differences between ocean surface and terrain, so that the LOD schemes which are suitable to be used in terrain rendering may not be adapted to ocean surface. In most of Previous work, regular grids were used for ocean surface tessellation, only a few presented LOD schemes (see [1] and

Z. Pan et al. (Eds.): ICAT 2006, LNCS 4282, pp. 686–694, 2006.

[2]), which required a significant amount of calculation on the CPU side. Here we present a LOD scheme for real-time rendering of large-scale ocean surface named multi-resolution nested regular grid, which makes the region of ocean surface can be extended limitlessly and readily adapted to GPU acceleration.

The remainder of this paper develops as follows: Section 2 reviews the existing models for simulating ocean waves. In Section 3, we introduce the wave model based on ocean wave spectrum and subsequently propose our wind model with detailed formulas of parameter calculation for wave state changing. In Section 4, we present an ocean surface LOD schemethat is the multi-resolution nested regular grid. Rendering process based on GPU is detailed in Section 5. We show the implementation results in Section 6, and conclude in Section 7.

2   Previous Work

Previous research pays more attention to ocean wave model. To date, several ocean wave models have been developed in CG, which can be classified into three categories.

2.1   Empirical Models

These models describe explicitly the wave appearance using parametric functions. They are very simple and near real-time, but less realistic. Peachy [3] adopted the linear combination of sine function and quadratic function to simulate the geometrical shape of waves. Fourier and Reves [4] described motion of each water particle as a circle around a fixed point. The resulting profile of the water wave is a trochoid with more or less sharpened crests. Ts'o and Basky [5] represented ocean waves using beta-splines.

These models can simulate wave refraction and reflection effects in shallow ocean, but cannot easily represent agitated waves in deep ocean. So they are only suitable for simulating shallow ocean waves.

2.2   Physical Models

These models are based on physical fluid dynamic equations. Ram [6] used simplified numerical method to solve the Navier-Stokes equation for animation of water waves. Foster [7] proposed a modified semi-Lagrangian equation to simulate viscous liquids around objects. Wang [8] presented a new approach using cellular automata to mimic the motion of ocean waves.

These models are perfectly realistic and can physically represent much water motion, but they are computationally expensive. In fact, many of these models focus on other kinds of water surfaces and are not adapted to the simulation of large-scale ocean surface.

2.3   Spectral Models

These models use the observation and research results of oceanography, such as frequency spectrum and directional spectrum to describe the random agitation of deep ocean surface. Mastin [9] produced a height field having the same spectrum by filtering a white noise with Pierson-Moskowitz's or Hasselmann's filter, and then calculated its Fast Fourier Transform (FFT). Yang [10] presented a method of wave simulation based on ocean wave frequency spectrum and directional spectrum. Tessendorf [11] showed that dispersive propagation can be managed in the frequency domain and the resulting field can be modified to yield trochoid waves.

Although these models have complex mathematic model and computation, they can simulate random agitation very well for deep ocean waves.

Besides the above three categories, Stefan [12] presented a procedural model for breaking ocean waves. Voirel [13] used slice method and 3D Navier-Stokes equations for Animation and Control of Breaking Waves. Recently, some people [2] [14] used GPU to accelerate ocean wave simulation.

3   Ocean Wave Generation Method

3.1   Wave Model

We use the existing ocean wave spectrum method for ocean wave generation. In this method, we use Longuet-Higgins model, which describes the fluctuation of every water particle at fixed point by superimpositions of cosine waves as follows:

$$\eta(x, y, t) = \sum_{i=1}^{\infty} \sum_{j=1}^{\infty} a_{ij} \cos(k_i(x \cos(\theta_p + \theta_j) + y \sin(\theta_p + \theta_j)) - \omega_i t - \varepsilon_{ij}). \quad (1)$$

Where a_{ij}, ω_i, k_i, ε_{ij} respectively denotes the amplitude, frequency, wave numbers and random initial phase of one component cosine wave. θ_p is the angle of wind direction. θ_j is the angle of one component cosine wave direction, we call it direction angle for short. (x, y) is the coordinate of samples on ocean surface and $\eta(x, y, t)$ is the height of the sample at time. In the following, we give methods for calculation of these parameters.

Frequency. We ignore the component waves with low frequency or high frequency, because their wave energy are little. We set $\omega_{min} \sim \omega_{max}$ as the frequency range and segment frequency range with equal interval $\triangle \omega$, then we get frequencies $\omega_1, \omega_2, \ldots, \omega_n$.

$$\triangle \omega = \frac{(\omega_{max} - \omega_{min})}{n}. \quad (2)$$

$$\omega_i = \omega_{min} + (i - 1) \triangle \omega + \frac{\triangle \omega}{2}, (1 \le i \le n). \quad (3)$$

Where n denotes the segment number on frequency range, ω_i denotes the ith frequency, $\triangle \omega$ denotes the frequency interval.

Direction Angle. Ocean wave energy actually distributes on both sides of wind direction from $-\frac{\pi}{2}$ to $\frac{\pi}{2}$. So θ_j should be in the range of $(\theta_p - \frac{\pi}{2}) \sim (\theta_p + \frac{\pi}{2})$.

$$\triangle \theta = \frac{\pi}{m}. \tag{4}$$

$$\theta_j = -\frac{\pi}{2} + (j-1) \triangle \theta, (1 \leq j \leq m). \tag{5}$$

Where $\triangle \theta$ denotes the direction angle interval, m denotes the number of segment in the range of direction angle.

Amplitude. The Calculation formula of amplitude is:

$$a_{ij} = \sqrt{2S(\omega_i)G(\omega_i, \theta_j) \triangle \omega \triangle \theta}. \tag{6}$$

Where $S(\omega_i)$ is the frequency spectrum function of ocean waves. it represents distribution of the wave energy on frequencies. $G(\omega_i, \theta_j)$ is the function of energy distribution on wave frequencies and wave directions.

There are several semi-empirical models for ocean wave spectrum. Here we chose the P-M spectrum (Pierson-Moscowitz frequency spectrum).

$$S(\omega) = \frac{\alpha g^2}{\omega^5} \exp\left[-\beta(\frac{g}{U\omega})^4\right]. \tag{7}$$

Where $\alpha = 8.1 \times 10^{-3}$ and $\beta = 0.74$, g denotes the gravitational constant, U denotes the wind speed at 19.5-meter height above the ocean surface.

According to the proposal of ISSC(International Ship Structure Conference), we chose the directional spectrum function as the following:

$$G(\omega, \theta) = \frac{8}{3\pi} \cos^4(\theta). \tag{8}$$

Wave Number. For ocean waves, there is a well-known dispersion relationship between frequencies and wave number. In deep water, where the bottom may be ignored, that relationship is:

$$\omega^2 = k \cdot g. \tag{9}$$

3.2   Wind Model

We can simulate ocean surface state at a fixed wind speed using aforementioned method. As we know now, when wind speed changes, ocean wave state will change. But how to simulate ocean wave state transformation when wind speed changing? Directly shifting from the beginning state to the end state will bring jumping frame. Here, we propose a wind model to solve this problem. It is a wind speed model defined as the following:

$$U(t) = \begin{cases} u_1 & t_0 \leq t \leq t_1. \\ f(t) & t_1 \leq t \leq t_2. \\ u_2 & t_2 \leq t \leq t_3. \end{cases} \tag{10}$$

Where $U(t)$ denotes the wind speed at 19.5-meter height above sea level at time t. t_0, t_1, t_2, t_3 respectively denotes any time in the simulation with condition $t_0 \leq t_1 \leq t_2 \leq t_3$. The wind speed in time $t_0 \sim t_1$ and $t_2 \sim t_3$ is respectively a constant u_1 and u_2. The wind speed in time $t_1 \sim t_2$ is variable, which is described by function $f(t)$. We simply define $f(t)$ as a single-increasing function when $u_1 \leq u_2$ and a single-decreasing function when $u_1 \geq u_2$, with the conditions $f(t_1) = u_1$ and $f(t_2) = u_2$. A sketch map of the wind speed model is shown in Figure 1.

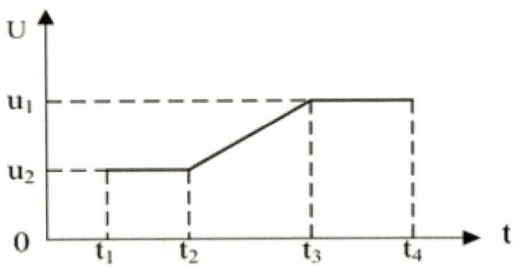

Fig. 1. The sketch map of wind speed model

P-M spectrum represents distribution of wave energy on frequencies at a fixed wind speed. When wind speed changes, wave energy will change. This means different wind speed corresponds to different energy distribution. We should adjust frequency range and wind direction angle using the following formulas as wind changing.

$$\omega_{max} = \omega_{1max} - \frac{f(t)}{u_2 - u_1}|\omega_{2max} - \omega_{1max}|. \tag{11}$$

$$\omega_{min} = \omega_{1min} - \frac{f(t)}{u_2 - u_1}|\omega_{1min} - \omega_{2min}|. \tag{12}$$

$$\theta_p = \theta_{1p} + \frac{t}{t_3 - u_2}(\theta_{2p} - \theta_{1p}). \tag{13}$$

Where $\omega_{1min} \sim \omega_{1max}$ is the frequency range and θ_{1p} is the wind direction angle when wind speed is u_1. $\omega_{2min} \sim \omega_{2max}$ is the frequency range and θ_{2p} is the wind direction angle when wind speed is u_2.

In the above formulas, we proposed a linear changing process to get the interim frequency range $\omega_{min} \sim \omega_{max}$ and interim wind direction θ_p as wind speed changing from u_1 to u_2 at any time $t_1 \sim t_2$. We adjust P-M spectrum formula as following.

$$S(\omega) = \frac{\alpha g^2}{\omega^5} \exp\left[-\beta(\frac{g}{U(t)\omega})^4\right]. \tag{14}$$

4   Ocean Surface LOD Scheme

We define a square region centered at the viewer position in world space, which is partitioned into n levels pyramid regular grids which extending at successive power-of-two resolutions each level. The size of each level grid is $(2^k+1) \times (2^k+1)$ with grid spacing $l = d \cdot 2^j, (j = 1, 2, \ldots, n)$, k is a constant, j is the level number and d is grid spacing on the top level. The area of the square region in world space is $d \cdot 2^{(k+n)} \times d \cdot 2^{(k+n)}$ and it should be large enough to encircle the viewing frustum projection. These grids are nested together and the top level is the finest level. Only the finest level is rendered as a complete grid square and all other levels are rendered as a hollow rings which omit the interior region already rendered at finer resolutions.

The simple LOD scheme described so far suffers from gaps between the render regions at different levels, due to the power-of-two mismatch at the boundaries. We will fill the gaps by zero-area triangles.

During simulation, when the viewer moves along the track, the square region moves synchronously. Figure 2 respectively shows the sketch maps of square region, multi-resolution nested regular grid and free navigation with the LOD scheme on deep ocean surface.

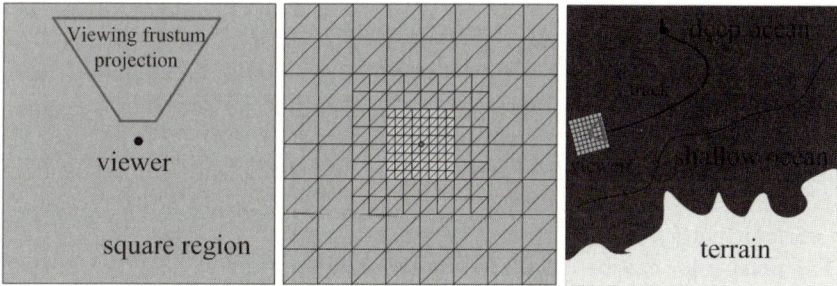

Fig. 2. The left one is the sketch map of square region. The middle one is the sketch map of multi-resolution nested regular grid. The right one is the sketch map of free navigation with the LOD scheme on deep ocean surface.

5   GPU-Based Rendering

Our rendering framework can be classified into two groups: water surface modelling on CPU and processing vertexes and pixels on GPU. Figure 3 shows the whole rendering framework.

The multi-resolution nested regular grid is generated on CPU. We don't calculate every vertex height on the ocean surface mesh but generate the height field data of a $2^k \times 2^k$ grid which is stored as height map. A corresponding normal map can be generated from the height map. Then the height map and normal map are sent to the texture buffer.

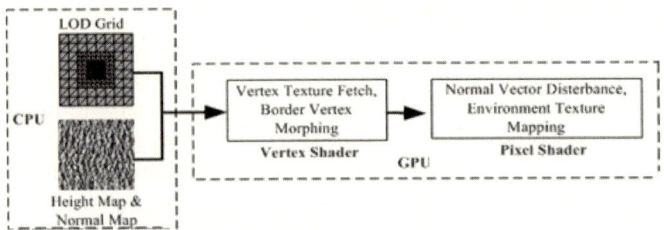

Fig. 3. The rendering framework of large-scale deep ocean surface

5.1   Vertex Processing on Vertex Shader

Using vertex texture fetch of GPU, we sample the height map per vertex on the multi-resolution nested regular grid. Texture filtering is necessary because the vertices are not one-to-one corresponded with the texture samples.

5.2   Illumination on Pixel Shader

We sample normal map per pixel and disturb it for scrappy waves. To get a perfect illumination effect, We calculate each pixel's color. When incident light transmits through ocean surface, some fraction of it reflects at the surface, other fraction refracts, this is called Fresnel phenomenon. We get reflectivity and refractivity by empirical formula 15.

$$R = \max(0, \min(1, bias + scale \times (1 + I \cdot N)^{power})). \qquad (15)$$

Where R is the reflectivity, $bias$ is the Fresnel bias coefficient, $scale$ is the Fresnel scale coefficient, $power$ is the Fresnel exponent, I is the sight line direction, N is the normal vector.

The pixel color can be calculated by formula 16.

$$C = C_{reflect} \cdot R + C_{refract} \cdot (1 - R). \qquad (16)$$

Where $C_{reflect}$ is the color value caused by surrounding environment reflection at ocean surface. $C_{refract}$ is the color value caused by light refraction at ocean surface. We can use environment texture map to calculate $C_{reflect}$ and substitute ambient light and diffuse light for $C_{refract}$.

6   Implementation Results

We set an experimental software environment as Windows XP, Visual C++6.0 and OpenGL running on the Intel Pentium4 3.06G computer with ASUS manager boards, 512M RAM, and NVIDIA GeForce6600 graphics card.

We set the parameters of LOD scheme as $k = 6, n = 6, d = 1$. The size of height map is set to be 128×128. We divide ocean wave state into different levels according to the wind speed as shown in Table 1.

Table 1. Ocean wave state with corresponding wave model parameters

Wave state level	Wind speed	Frequency range	Frequency interval
Gentle wave	≤ 5.0	$1.2 \sim 6.0$	0.4
Small wave	$5.0 \sim 8.0$	$0.6 \sim 3.0$	0.2
Middle wave	$8.0 \sim 11.0$	$0.4 \sim 2.4$	0.2
High wave	$11.0 \sim 14.0$	$0.4 \sim 2.0$	0.2
Large wave	$14.0 \sim 18.0$	$0.3 \sim 1.4$	0.1
Crazy wave	≥ 18.0	$0.2 \sim 1.2$	0.1

Fig. 4. Screen shots of experimental results. The wind speed is 6.5m/s in the left one and 9.0m/s in the right one.

We implement free navigation and wind changing effect with rapid rendering rate. The snapshots of ocean scene can be seen in Figure 4, which respectively represents the deep ocean surface with wind speed 6.5m/s and 9.0m/s.

7 Conclusion and Future Work

We have proposed an efficient method for realistic and real-time simulation of large-scale deep ocean surface. Our LOD scheme and vertex processing efficiently support the real-time simulation. The illumination based on pixel shader brings us a perfect and realistic ocean environment. We propose a wind model and combine it with an existing wave model. Our experiment proves that our wind model is effective for the realistic simulation of wind changing effect on ocean waves. All of these algorithms and models are integrated into our rendering framework.

Considering future work, We should extend the simulation area to sea shore, and farther to terrain, which means we want to find methods to combine deep ocean, shallow ocean and terrain together. Furthermore, the culling and breaking waves, foam, spray and ripple etc, should be paid more attention in our work.

Acknowledgements. This research is supported by National Defence Basic Research of China (No.2220061084).

References

1. Damien Hinsinger, Fabrice Neyret, Marie-Paule Cani: Interactive Animation of Ocean Waves. ACM Symposium on Computer Animation 2002, (2002) 161-166
2. Pi Xuexian, Yang Xudong, Li Sikun, Song Junqiang: High-Performance Navigation and Rendering of Very-Large Scale Landscape and Seascape. Ninth International Conference on Computer Aided Design and Computer Graphics 2005, (CAD/CG 2005)
3. Perchy, D.R.: Modeling wave and surf. In Proc.ACM SIGGraph 1986, (1986) 65-74
4. Fournier, A., Reeves, W. T.: A simple model of ocean waves. In Proc.ACM SIG-Graph 1986, (1986) 75-84.
5. TS'O, P., Barsky, B.: Modeling and rendering waves: Wave-tracing using beta-splines and reflective and refractive texture mapping. ACM Transactions on Graphics, **6** (1987) 191-14
6. Kass.Ram, M G Rapid: Stable fluid dynamics for computer graphics. Computer Graphics, **24** (1990) 49-57.
7. Foster N, Fedkiw R.: Practical animation of liquids. In Proc.ACM SIGGraph 2001, (2001) 15-22
8. Changbo Wang, Zhangye Wang, Jianqiu Jin, Qunsheng Peng: Real-time Simulation of Ocean Wave Based on Cellular Automata. Computer Aided Design and Computer Graph-ics Proceeding 2003, (CAD/CG 2003)
9. Mastin, G. A., Watterberg, P. A., Mareda, J. F.: Fourier synthesis of ocean scenes. IEEE Computer Graphics and Applications, **7** (1987) 16-23
10. Yang HuaiPing, Sun JiaGuang: Wave Simulation Based on Ocean Wave Spectrums. Journal of system simulation, China, **14** (2002) 1175-1179
11. J. Tessendorf : Simulating ocean water, In Proc.ACM SIGGraph Course Notes **47** (1999)
12. Stefan Jeschke, Hermann Birkholz, Heidrun Schmann: A Procedural Model for Interactive Animation of Breaking Ocean Waves. WSCG'2003,(2003)
13. Viorel Mihalef, Dimitris Metaxas, Mark Sussman: Animation and Control of Breaking Waves. Proceedings of the 2004 ACM SIGGRAPH/Eurographics symposium on Computer animation, (2004)
14. Jason L. Mitchell: Real-Time Synthesis and Rendering of Ocean Water. ATI Research Technical Report, April 2005,(2005)

Exploiting Frame-to-Frame Coherence
for Rendering Terrain Using Continuous LOD

Jing Zhang[1] and Guojun Chen[2,3]

[1] College of Resources Environment and Tourism, The Capital Normal University,
Beijing, 100037, P.R. China
zhangjings@mail.cnu.edu.cn
[2] School of Computer Science and Engineering, Beihang University,
Beijing 100083, P.R. China
[3] College of Computer and Communication Engineering, China University of Petroleum,
Dongying, 257061, P.R. China
chengj@upc.edu.cn

Abstract. It is the key issue of the terrain real-time rendering to reduce the time-spending for the level-of-detail. The concept of triangle live frame is introduced in this paper. Using this live frame, the algorithm reuses per-vertex visibility computation from previously displayed frames efficiently during continuous view-dependent level-of-detail visualizations. This algorithm decreases to a certain extent computing the distance from the viewpoint to vertex at each frame. Experimental results show that the algorithm reduces the time effectively to produce the LOD terrain.

Keywords: Multi-resolution, level of details (LOD), frame to frame coherence, rendering terrain.

1 Introduction

The real-time visualization of the terrain plays an important role in computer graphics, three-dimensional geographic information system, virtual reality and simulation. It is impossible to render lots of triangles interactively because of the limit of display hardware. Up to now, the main method adopted is to reduce the complexity of the terrain surface under the situation of acceptant vision. CLOD (the continuous Level of Detail) related to the viewpoint has been the hot topic recently. The quad-tree or bin-tree based on the grids has been proved very effective for the real-time interaction and often be used to built dynamic CLOD[1-4] .

The multi-resolution models of the terrain are built in the location of the viewpoint at rendering each frame. This computation need more time. Now, many optimal computation methods are adopted in order to decrease computing. These methods include view-frustum culling, triangle strips and frame to frame coherence, etc. In order to construct a LOD terrain mesh, the visualization algorithm traverses the data structure looking for all the triangles pertaining to that particular LOD. This process must be done for each frame as quickly as possible. There is a high probability that the required LODs to be displayed in two consecutive frames will be the same or very

Z. Pan et al. (Eds.): ICAT 2006, LNCS 4282, pp. 695 – 704, 2006.

similar. Therefore, instead of searching for all the triangles in each frame, the frame-to-frame coherence can be exploited so that only the set of triangles changed between the two required LODs are searched for, improving the visualization algorithm performance. Ribelles had presented one structure based on MOM (Multi-resolution Ordered Meshes) and this structure accelerated the production of the static LOD by use of the frame-to-frame coherence property[5]. Duchaineau had proposed ROAM(Real-time Optimal Adaptive Meshes) which is bin-tree structure based on the right isoceles triangles[2]. This algorithm adopted a recursive top-bottom traversal of the bin-tree. When dealing with frame-to-frame coherence, it adopted the error to decide the optimal queue to merge and split the triangles. However, more time spent on the maintenance of the queues influenced the rendering efficiency to a certain extent. Bao had proposed the algorithm to forecast the visibility of the vertex by the per-vertex live range in SMART terrain rendering algorithm[6]. ROAM and SMART just supported the static terrain rendering with frame to frame coherence.

We propose to use DAG which adopts the vertex introduced sequence, in order to support the precision of the mesh in this paper. The articles [7-9] did not consider the frame to frame coherence. However the algorithm proposed this paper is based on the production of the LOD supported by the articles [8][9], and deals with the issues of coherence between frames about the terrain rendering. According to the view point range permission of the errors, the algorithm can reduce judging the vertex error each time and decrease the time to compute whether the vertex is active further.

2   Triangle Bin-Tree and DAG of Splitting Vertices

ROAM algorithm adopts the triangle bin-tree to represent the terrain mesh building the terrain CLOD, and represents the mesh precision with splitting and merging queues. In ROAM much time is spent on maintenance of the queues, however this paper adopts the DAG of the introduced vertex to represent the precision of the mesh.

Assume that the dimensions of terrain are constrained 2^n+1 vertices in each direction. Fig. 1 shows the process of constructing a bin-tree of a square terrain when $n = 4$. Dividing the square region along the diagonal into two isosceles right triangles, which are the root triangles T_0, T_1, thus forming the coarsest level of the bin-tree ($L = 0$). At the next-finest level, $L = 1$, the children of the root triangle are defined by splitting a root triangle along an edge formed from its apex vertex to the midpoint of its hypotenuse. Through introducing vertex V_0, the triangle T_0 is divided into T_{00} and T_{01}, thus we define T_0 to be the parent of T_{00} and T_{01} [2]. The rest of the triangle bin-tree is defined by recursively repeating this splitting process. Refinement is implemented by replacing parent triangle with its children triangles; contrariwise, simplification is replacing a pair of triangles with their parent.

The process of constructing a triangle bin-tree implies the order of introduced vertices, which can be described by a directed acyclic graph (DAG)[7]. A directed edge (i, j) from i to one of its children j in the DAG corresponds to a split operation, in which j is inserted on the hypotenuse and connected to the apex vertex i. Thus, all non-leaf vertices not on the boundary of the mesh are connected to four children in the DAG, and have two parent vertices. Boundary vertices have two children and one parent.

It can be seen that triangle bin-tree and DAG can implement refinement and simplification of triangle mesh. Whether vertex i is introduced into triangle mesh will determine whether terrain is to be refined or be simplified locally. For a given refinement M of a mesh, we say that a vertex i is active if it appear in M. It can be concluded that if a vertex i is active, its parents (and by induction all of its ancestors) must be active. This conclusion is the necessary condition on which the mesh forms a continuous surface without crack. The dependency relationship of vertices is included in the refinement criterion implicitly [7,8].

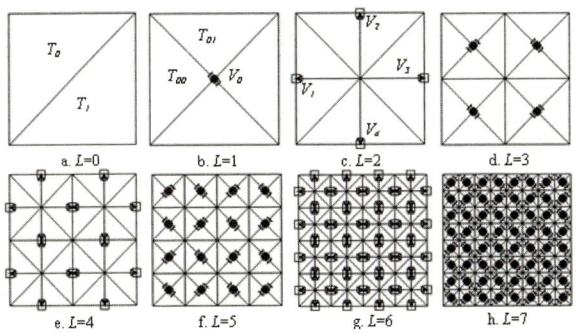

Fig. 1. The bin-tree of the triangle. L is the splitting layer

3   LOD Updates

A new algorithm for optimized view-dependent LOD updates is described in this section. Our goal is to avoid the repetitive cost and only perform LOD for the few vertices that are indeed candidates for updating the LOD for a given viewpoint.

Ideally, when we check a vertex's status, we want to know not only its status at the current moment, we would also like to know when its current status will possibly change, no matter how the view-dependent parameters will vary. This time period is called the live frame of a triangle. To compute a triangle's live frame, we define a splitting-number and merging-number for each triangle. No matter how the view point moves, a vertex status keeps constant if the view point is within some frames. Only if the viewpoint invalidates the safe-distance to a vertex does its visibility status possibly change.

In the following we first introduce a triangle splitting-number and merging-number. Then explain a triangle's live frame and how to use it to reduce calculation for LOD.

3.1   The Nested Errors Sphere

The splitting and merging is related to whether the vertex i is active or not, while the error of the vertex can decide whether the vertex is active or not. The error is classified into object space error and screen space error. The introduction of vertex i, which splits a triangle into two finer triangles, brings a world space error, calculated by the vertical distance (z axis): $\delta_i=|Z_i-(Z_k+Z_l)/2|$, Z_k, Z_l is the altitude of the end points of the hypotenuse.

When rendering the three-dimensional terrain, the projection transformation is necessary. Therefore we need to consider the screen space error. The screen space error based on the distance needs less cost, and the ratio of the terrain simplification decreases very little compared with the error of view-direction [1-3,7]. We adopt formula (1) to compute the screen space error. In order to imply the relationship among the vertexes with error, we adopt the nested errors sphere [7,8], shown in formula (2).

$$\|p_i - e\| = \frac{\delta_i}{\tau} \times d \times \lambda = r_i .\tag{1}$$

$$R_i = \begin{cases} r_i, & \text{if } i \text{ is leaf node} \\ \max\left\{r_i, \max_{j \in C_i}\{\|p_i - p_j\| + R_j\}\right\} & \text{others} \end{cases} .\tag{2}$$

here r_i, δ_i are the screen space error and object space error of the vertex i respectively; p_i, e are the position of the vertex i and viewpoint in space respectively. d is the distance from the viewpoint to the projection plane, λ is the numbers of the pixel on the screen projected by the unit-length in space. d, λ are constant. We can adopt the formula (2) to test whether the vertex is active or not. C_i in the formula (2) is the children of vertex i in DAG. We can conclude the result that the viewpoint move in the error sphere of children, then the viewpoint must be in the error sphere of father. Therefore the nested errors sphere conceals the queues of introducing the vertex.

3.2 Live Frame

When flying over terrain, the viewpoint moves continuously, and the distance between the frame vertex and its viewpoint changes very little. It means that the viewpoint movement in some distance will not influence the splitting and merging of the triangles too much and the set of triangles between consecutive frames will changes very little. It certainly will take more time spent on splitting from the root of bin-tree of the triangle each time. Therefore, instead of searching for all the triangles in each frame, the frame-to-frame coherence can be exploited so that only the set of triangles that changed between the two required LODs are searched for, improving the visualization algorithm performance. It no longer needs to build the LOD of terrain from the bin-tree root, and triangles of current frame can be decided by the triangle mesh of former frame directly. It can take less time to deal with the triangles accordingly.

When the viewpoint V is located between two spheres, it shows that $\triangle ABC$ need not to split or merge as illustrated in Fig. 2. Only when the viewpoint moves into the sphere R_1, the vertex E will become visible and $\triangle ABC$ needs to split. When the viewpoint moves out and is outside of the sphere R_2, the vertex B will become invisible and $\triangle ABC$ need to merge. Thus, the triangles in the former frame will be merged, split or invariable in the current frame. It will take longer time to judge the status of each triangle. The triangle far away from the viewpoint often changes after moving viewpoints many times. Therefore, the status of triangle can keep constant and it need not to test by calculating the distance between the vertex and viewpoint. With the viewpoint moving, $\triangle ABC$ in the former frame will be split into $\triangle ABE$ and $\triangle BEC$ or be merged to $\triangle ACD$. We suppose that the distance from the viewpoint to E is d_1 and to B is d_2 seen in Fig. 2. Suppose that the viewpoint moves with the speed v, witch is the distance of the viewpoint movement. Then when d_1-R_1 is less than or equal to zero, $\triangle ABC$ will be split, and the relationship between the numbers of the frames and d_1-R_1 is shown in formula (3). θ_i is the angle between v and VE. If all θ_i is zero, we will conclude from formula (4) to get the number of frames which is the least value to happen splitting. Similarly, the least number of frame to happen merging into $\triangle ADC$ is computed by the formula (5). So we defined live frame L_f for a triangle as formula (6).

$$d_1 - R_1 = \sum_{i=0}^{n} \|v\| \cos \theta_i .$$ (3)

$$n_1 = (d_1 - R) / \|v\| .$$ (4)

$$n_2 = (R_2 - d_2) / \|v\| .$$ (5)

$$L_f = \min(n_1, n_2) .$$ (6)

here R_1 and R_2 in the formula (3), (4) and (5) is the nested sphere radius of vertex E and Vertex B, while n_1 and n_2 represents the least numbers of the viewpoint change resulting to split and merge the triangles.

When the movement speed of the viewpoint V is constant, n_1 can be computed under the current movement speed, the viewpoint can enter the radius R_1 of the sphere after moving several times. And the delayed splitting numbers n_2 can be computed. Therefore, it is necessary to store the split triangles and merged triangles respectively when organizing the triangles of the frames. We adopt the mechanism of triple-queue to partition the triangles in order to ascertain the unconverted triangles according to the state of the triangles which are split and merged.

3.3 Queues

If the rendered triangles are in one queue, then it needs to judge triangle's n_1 and n_2 value at rendering next frame. When the n_1 or n_2 is zero, the splitting or merging will happen. It takes time to judge the value n_1 or n_2 each frame. In fact, the n_1 and n_2 in some triangles is bigger and thus it is not necessary to judge the n_1 and n_2 of each frame. Therefore, we adopt the splitting queue Q_s to store the split triangles; merging queue Q_m to store the pending merging triangles; and display queue Q_r to store rendering triangles directly. If the vision distance is less than the radius of the error sphere, the triangle happens splitting, meaning that the triangle is put into the splitting queue Q_s; If the vision distance is more than the radius of the error-criterion sphere, the triangle happens merging, meaning that the triangle is put into the merging queue Q_m; Otherwise, the nodes of the triangle are put into the display queue Q_r directly.

When building LOD, it is necessary to deal with the splitting queue Q_s and merging queue Q_m, but it is not necessary to judge the nodes on the display queue, and they need to be rendered directly. If the numbers in the Q_r is larger, the algorithm will save time more obviously. However, doing this needs to compute the distance from the viewpoint to the vertex each time. We adopt the delay numbers to classify the triangles by setting the threshold N and the method is shown in the formula (7).

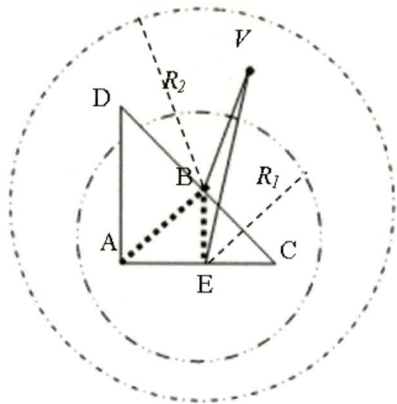

Fig. 2. The status of the triangle splitting and merging

$$\begin{cases} \Delta \in Qs & n_2 < n_1, L_f < N \\ \Delta \in Qm & n_1 < n_2, L_f < N \\ \Delta \in Qr & L_f > N \end{cases} \tag{7}$$

here N in the formula is the threshold to delay the number of disposal. The more the numbers of the triangle in Q_r are, the less time spent on building LOD is. The value N influences the numbers of the triangles in Q_r. N is correlated with the data of the terrain. We need to get the suitable value for terrain by testing in advance.

3.4 The Algorithm and Analysis

When continuously rendering the terrain by the frames, it is necessary to classify the triangles which are not split in the bin-tree according to the viewpoint location at beginning, see the algorithm **Init()** as shown in Fig.3. When building the triangle mesh of the terrain at each frame, the state change of the triangles at each frame is decided by the location of the viewpoint and error sphere. And then the triangle at the current frame will be produced. The algorithm **CaculateLOD()** mainly compute the triangles in three queues. The algorithm **sortQr()** mainly determine the ascription of the triangles in Q_r queue and performs one time after being apart N frames; The algorithm **sortQm()** and **sortQs()** performs at each frame, and the difference between both is that the former performs the merging of the triangles and the latter performs the splitting of the triangles. The triangles in three queues exchange sometimes.

The algorithm to produce LOD

```
Init(viewpoint)
{
  insert(TriQue, root)
  while(!empty(TriQue))
  {
    tri=Get(TriQue);
    if (tri in ViewFrum) and tri need split)
    {
        calculate(tri);//calculate n1,n2
        if(tri.n1>N and tri.n2>N) insert(Qr,tri)
        else if(tri.n1>tri.n2) insert(Qm,tri)
        else insert(Qs,tri);
    }
    else if (tri in ViewFrum) insert(TriQue,tri);
  }
}
CaculateLOD(viewpoint)
{
    frameNum++;
    if (framNum==N)
    {
      frameNum=0;
      sortQr(viewpoint);
    }
    //process triangle in Qm and Qr
    sortQm(viewpoint);
    sortQs(viewpoint);
}
```

Suppose the numbers of the triangle at the former frame is S_1, the numbers of the triangle in the Q_r is S_2, then the formula to compute the complexity S is shown in formula (8). Its complexity of LOD of the triangles is T every time when scanning the root of the bin-tree to produce LOD, we use the formula to represent T, that is

$T=\sum_i^M h_i$, here h_i is the depth of the bin-tree in the triangle and it is more than 1 commonly, namely $T>S$.

$$S = \begin{cases} S_1 & FrameNum\%N = 0 \\ S_1 - S_2 & others \end{cases} \tag{8}$$

4   The Experiment Result and Analysis

We have implemented the algorithm on a Pentium IV 1.7 GHz with nVIDIA GeForce2 MX 400 graphics and 256 MB RAM under Windows XP. The machine is equipped with a single standard 120G IDE hard disk. We use VC6.0 and OpenGL environment. All data sets were rendered to a 1024×768 view port. The source of the data file is the island_1k.zip (terrain1) and southbay_1k.zip (terrain 2) in http://www.vterrain.org/BT/index.html., made up of 1025×1025. The second terrain is more cragged. We test the selection of the threshold N and compare the computing performance with other algorithms.

4.1 The Selection of the Threshold Value

The value of the threshold N decides the numbers of the triangles in Q_r and influences the time to produce LOD. The value range of the terrain is different because of different character of the terrain (for example, the rugged surface). We use two terrain files in the experiment, and test the computing the average-time building the frame of LOD when N is different respectively. The viewpoint during rending different terrains is distributed identically and the experience result is shown in Fig. 3. We can conclude that N increases to some degree before it continues to increase, then the time to produce LOD will increase from the experiment results. The file of the terrain is different and the threshold N is different accordingly. The threshold N will be smaller if the terrain's altitudes change rapidly.

4.2 The Comparison of the Algorithm

We test the time to produce LOD with different methods at the same path: the searching for all triangles in LOD mesh in bin-tree from root [8], the algorithm ROAM and the algorithm proposed by the authors in this paper respectively. We test 50 frames and the location of the viewpoint is the same in different algorithms. The results of these experiments are shown in Fig. 4. The algorithm of searching triangles from bin-tree root costs more computing time; ROAM algorithm adopts self-accommodation method to control the numbers of the triangles, and the time to produce LOD is stable comparatively, it has the characteristic of the real-time strongly; The authors propose the disposal of the consecutive frames algorithm , which basic performance is better than the ROAM algorithm , there is the jump change whose period is N because the triangles in Q_r need to be scanned every other N frames.

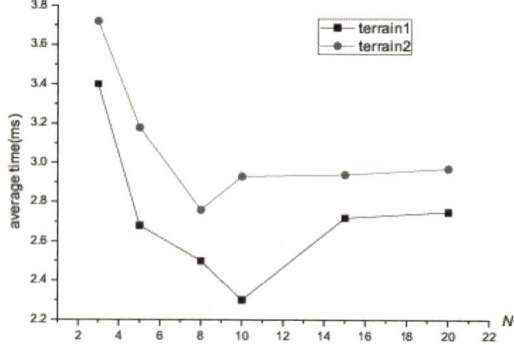

Fig. 3. The threshold N and the time for generation of LOD

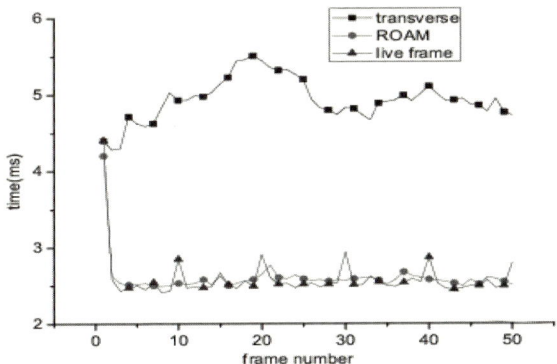

Fig. 4. The performance of both algorithms when LOD updates

Therefore we can conclude from the experiments above that the threshold needs to be decided for each terrain. Due to reducing large amount of distance computation between viewpoint and vertex, and converting floating point calculation to a single integer comparison , great speedup is achieved So, Updating terrain mesh will reduce the time to produce LOD after classifying the triangles to different queue according to the threshold.

5   Conclusion

In this paper we presented a simple and effective algorithm for interactive dynamic terrain rendering. With this technique, the live frame of each triangle is computed and kept when its visibility status is calculated for the first time. Later the costly computation for this triangle is avoided for LOD computation when the live frame of the triangle is not out-of-date. This paper is based on the regular grid data to render the real-time terrain, and adopts the LOD using frame to frame coherence. For given terrain data, we test again and again and then decide the optimal live frame tolerance N. The results of the experiments show that the live frame adopted by us decrease the amount of the computation each frame, and the optimal result to deal with dynamic terrain LOD is obvious relatively. We will continue to do some research including that the technology to perform adding some strips of the triangles further in order to speed the rendering the terrain better.

Acknowledgments. This paper is supported by the National Natural Science Foundation of China under the grant No. 40571126.

References

1. Lindstrom P., Koller D., Ribarsky W., *et al.*: Real-time, Continuous Level of Detail Rendering of Height Fields. In: Computer Graphics Proceedings, Annual Conference Series, ACM SIGGRAPH, New Orleans, LA (1996)109–118
2. Duchaineau M., Wolinsky M., *et al.*: ROAMing Terrain: Real-time Optimally Adapting Meshes. In: Proceedings of IEEE Visualization, Phoenix, Arizona (1997) 81–88

3. Rottger S., Heidrich W., Slusallek P., *et al.*: Real-time Generation of Continuous Levels of Detail for Height Fields. In: Proceedings of the 6th International Conference in Central Europe Computer Graphics and Visualization, Plzen, Czech Republic (1998)315–322

4. Pajarola R.: Large Scale Terrain Visualization Using the Restricted Quadtree Triangulation. In: Proceedings of IEEE Visualization, New Caledonia (1998)19–26

5. Ribelles J., Chover, M., López A., Huerta J.: Frame-to-frame Coherence of Multiresolution Ordered Meshes. Actas del IX Congreso Español de Informática Gráfica (CEIG'99), Jaen (Spain), June (1999)91–104

6. Bao, Xiaohong, Pajarola, R., Shafae, M.: SMART: An Efficient Technique for Massive Terrain Visualization from Out-of-core, Proceedings Vision, Modeling and Visualization (VMV) (2004)413–420

7. Lindstrom P., Pascucci V.: Visualization of large terrain made easy. In: Proceedings of IEEE Visualization, San Diego (2001)363–370

8. Wang Linxu, Li Sikun, Pan Xiaohui: Real Time Visualization of Dynamic Terrain. Chinese Journal of Computers (2003)1524–1531

9. Chen Guojun, Zhang Jing: Dynamic Terrain LOD with Region Preservation in 3D Engine. Proceedings of International Conference on E-Learning and Games. LNCS 3942. Springer-Verlag (2006)711–715

Light Field Modeling and Its Application to Remote Sensing Image Simulation

Mingxiang Huang[1,2], Jianhua Gong[1,2], Zhou Shi[3], and Lihui Zhang[1]

[1] State Key Laboratory of Remote Sensing Science, Institute of Remote Sensing Applications, Chinese Academy of Sciences, Beijing 100101, China
[2] Key Laboratory of Poyang Lake Ecological Environment and Resource Development, Ministry of Education, Jiangxi Normal University, Nanchang 330022, China
[3] Institute of Agricultural Remote Sensing and Information System, Zhejiang University, Hangzhou 310029, China

Abstract. In Virtual Reality (VR) and computer graphic fields, 3-dimension (3D) matter modeling has been developed for many years and successfully applied to many fields. However, researches on 3D energy field modeling are still not enough owing to challenges of full understanding and real-time calculation of invisible energy fields. In the visual information world, energy field modeling is becoming a new research point and should promote relevant research advancement and widen applications. In the paper, after reviewing the 3D object modeling, light field modeling is addressed from three aspects which contain light propagation characteristic, bidirectional reflectance distribution function (BRDF), sunlight transfer process between solar source and observers. Especially the quantitative radiances at ground level and aircraft/space level are presented. According to the sunlight transfer process, a research framework of Remote Sensing Image Simulation (RSIS) is proposed and an experiment is implemented. Our study shows that light field modeling can make invisible energy fields easily understood and demonstrate an example of multi-sciences integration research.

1 Introduction

3D object modeling is to build realistic object scene in cyberspace through editing object surface or material properties and adding textures, bump-maps and other features. There exist a number of modeling techniques, such as constructive solid geometry, NURBS modeling, polygonal modeling, subdivision surfaces, and implicit surfaces [2,4,7,10]. 3D object modeling of real world is an important task in computer graphics, computer vision and many related application areas, such as modeling 3D object for pattern understanding and recognition, representing the real environment for robot programming and visual navigation, and constructing virtual environment for virtual reality system and applications. Most 3D object modeling techniques deal with the matter objects of the real world. However, few are involved in energy fields that are another essential part of the real world, such as heat, acoustic, light and magnetic fields that just can be measured through specific equipments. Moreover how to model energy fields for practical applications is not still enough reliable.

Z. Pan et al. (Eds.): ICAT 2006, LNCS 4282, pp. 705 – 714, 2006.

At present volumes of researches in relation to energy fields can be divided into two categories. One is to understand and clarify the principles of different energy fields. These researches utilize a series of mathematic functions and rules to delineate energy fields [14]. The other is to simulate energy fields through visualization representation based on their own physical principles. Voloboi et al. developed an efficient bidirectional ray tracing method based on the quasi-Monte Carlo integration in the framework of developing a realistic visualization system through physically accurate optical modeling [13]. Montero and Sanín studied modeling of wind field adjustment using finite differences in a terrain conformal coordinate system [9].

Light field modeling is an important part of energy field researches. The known applications of light field modeling are computer graphics and holography [3]. The most successful application of light field is the light rendering of 3D scene in cyberspace, including shadows, specular reflections, and secondary illumination effects [6]. The light rendering of 3D scene just pursues the representation reality for visualization and lacks physical rule concerning. Some researches have involved the interaction between light propagation and matter, which reveals BRDF characteristics of different incoming light and surface [12]. Affected by media in light transfer process, such as atmosphere, cloud and heterogeneous material, precise light transfer models for simulating light propagation are difficult to achieve.

In this paper, the three-folded objectives are to: (i) throughout review the 3D object modeling related to matter and energy modeling; (ii) discuss light field modeling from light propagation characteristics, BRDF characteristic of interaction between light and surface, and sunlight transfer model between solar source and observer; (iii) based on light field model, propose a RSIS research framework and implement an experiment of RSIS.

2 Background of 3D Object Modeling

The physical cosmos is roughly divided into two kinds of stuff. One kind is called Matter, the other Energy. Matter has mass which in the gravity field of Earth are used to thinking of as weight, especially existing with certain shape, geometry and visible to human being. However, Energy with no shape and geometry and invisible to human eyes has no mass, such as heat, magnetic, acoustic and light fields. Modeling both 3D matter object and energy object suitable to visualization has become the important research points in computer science, especially in virtual reality.

The process of creating 3D computer graphics scene can be sequentially divided into three basic phases: Modeling, Scene layout setup and Rendering. A number of approaches to reconstructing models of objects and scenes have been developed. The proposed representations can be categorized as: image-based and model-based. Fig. 1(a) presents an example of 3D matter object modeling for the nature landscape scene.

In accord with Einstein's famous law $E=mc^2$, matter will convert to prodigious amounts of energy under a certain high enough temperature and pressure. This conversion makes shapely matter into invisible energy fields which exist in the form of light, thermal, and magnetic fields etc. Traditional modeling of energy fields mostly focused on mathematic functions or formulas that use numeric values and rules to delineate energy fields. In the support of computer graphics, hardware and VR, 3D or higher dimension modeling of energy fields has become possible and some have been utilized into practical applications. Fig. 1(b) illustrates the thermal field used to facilitate physical design of electronic systems.

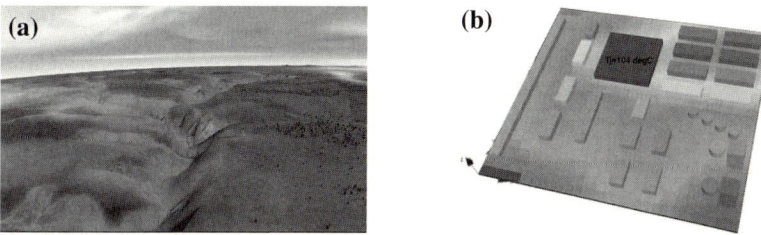

Fig. 1. Demonstrated examples of 3D object modeling

3   Light Field Modeling

3.1   Light Field and Its Propagation

The light field represents the amount of light passing through each point in 3D space along each possible direction. It is modeled by a function of seven variables that gives radiance as a function of time, wavelength, position and direction. For a given wavelength, we can represent a static light field as a 5D scalar function $L(x, y, z, \theta, \varphi)$ that gives radiance as a function of location (x, y, z) in 3D space and the direction (θ, φ) the light is traveling. When light contacts material/surface, there exist three types of interactions including reflection, absorption and transmittance (Fig. 2). In the VR field, most emphases are paid to the reflected right and incoming light. The reflectance of light from a surface is a complex physical problem, dependent on the angle of the incident light on the surface, the spectral distribution of the incident light, the physical properties of the sample, and the observing angle of the reflected light.

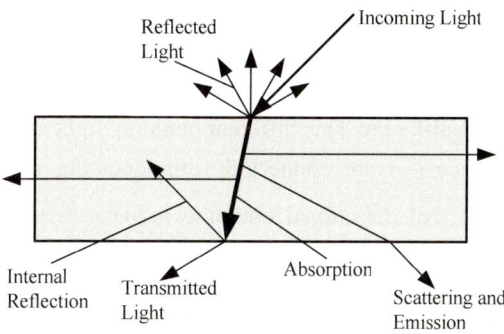

Fig. 2. Illustration of interaction of light and matter

3.2 BRDF

BRDF, one of the crucial parameters extensively needed in light transfer modeling, describes how much light is reflected when light makes contact with a certain material. The degree to which light is reflected depends on the viewer and light position relative to the surface normal and tangent. BRDF is defined by the following equation.

$$BRDF_\lambda \left(\theta_i, \ \phi_i, \ \theta_o, \ \phi_o\right) = \frac{dL(\theta_o, \ \phi_o)}{dE(\theta_i, \ \phi_i)} \tag{1}$$

Where E is the irradiance, and L is the reflected radiance; λ is wavelength; θ_i and ϕ_i represent the incoming light direction in spherical coordinates; θ_o and ϕ_o represent the outgoing reflected direction in spherical coordinates; the units of BRDF are thus inverse steradian (sr^{-1}).

BRDF is a fundamental optical property. It characterizes the energy scattered into the hemisphere above a surface as a result of incident radiation. Schopfer provided a figurative example of BRDF effects by observing the same lawn with different viewing angles [11]. Fig. 3 showed the detail results of the experiment.

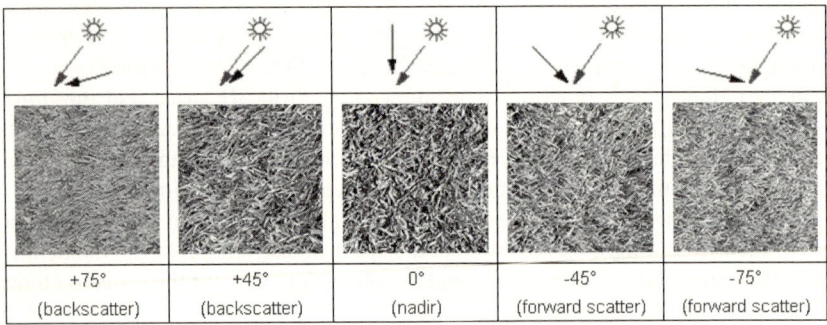

+75°	+45°	0°	-45°	-75°
(backscatter)	(backscatter)	(nadir)	(forward scatter)	(forward scatter)

Fig. 3. Schopfer's experiment for illustrating BRDF effects

Based on the above BRDF characteristics, the outgoing light energies in different observing directions are different. This different outgoing light energies which can be quantified by radiances (L_o) are connected with incoming radiance, BRDF and elevation angle (Eq. 2). All directional outgoing radiances can be calculated only when a certain light source is provided. In a 3D visualization system/application, real time and realistic scenes are indispensable based on physical rules of radiance transferring. In the conjunction, light rendering of 3D scenes for real time visualization can be easily accessible with support of BRDF-based light transfer model. Moreover the introduction of BRDF-based light rendering will surely make the scene more realistic.

$$L_o(\omega_o) = \int_\Omega BRDF(\omega_i, \ \omega_o)L_i(\omega_i)\cos(\theta_i)d\omega_i \tag{2}$$

Where: L_i is the incoming light from direction $\omega_i = (\theta_i, \varphi_i)$;

Ω is the reflectance hemisphere;

L_o is the outgoing light in direction ω_o;

θ is the elevation angle, whereas ϕ stands for the angle in the (local) tangent plane.

3.3 Sunlight Transfer Model

The light transfer process often is described through the quantitative radiances in the different levels including ground level and aircraft/space observing level. The radiance transfer between solar source and observer can qualify the influence of the Earth's atmosphere on the solar irradiance and the reflectance of land surface. A pictorial description of the radiance transfer is presented in Fig. 4. From the illumination of the sun, this incoming radiance passes through the atmosphere before being reflected from the Earth's surface in a manner indicative of the surface material. The reflected light then passes again through the atmosphere before entering the observer [1]. The observer can be cameras or satellite sensors etc.

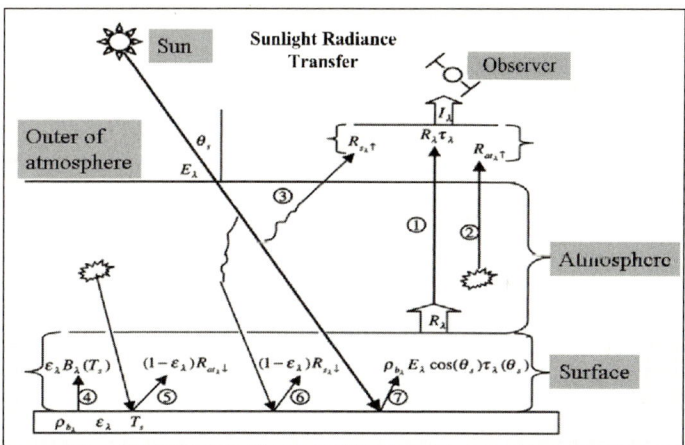

Fig. 4. The quantitative radiance model of sunlight transfer at different levels

In the study, light radiances are qualified at ground level and aircraft/space observer level. In the land surface research of Earth Observing System (EOS), the radiance reflected by ground is the primary concern. This part of radiance leaving the land surface is related with the atmosphere property, solar zenith and azimuth angle, BRDF, land surface property. Equation 3 shows the details of composing parts. The radiance R_i at ground level includes the radiation emitted directly by surface (④ of the Fig. 4), the downward atmospheric thermal radiation and solar diffusion radiation reflected by surface (⑤ and ⑥ of the Fig. 4), and the direct solar radiation reflected by surface (⑦ of the Fig. 4). However, at the aircraft/space observer level, the radiance includes the spectral radiance observed at ground level (① of the Fig. 4), the thermal path atmospheric radiance (② of the Fig. 4) and the path radiance resulting from scattering of solar radiation (③ of the Fig. 4). Equation 4 presents the details at aircraft/space level. In the light transfer model, the bi-directional surface spectral reflectivity is related with BRDF characteristics and land cover types. These above models wholly delineate the sunlight transfer process.

$$R_i(\theta,\ j) = \varepsilon_i(\theta,\ j)B_i(T_s) + (1 - \varepsilon_i(\theta,\ j))\frac{(R_{ati_i} + R_{sl_i-})}{\pi} + \rho_{b_i}(\theta,\ j,\ \theta_s,\ j_s)E_i\cos(\theta_s)\tau_i(\theta_s,\ j_s) \qquad (3)$$

Where: θ, φ is zenith angle and the azimuth angle;

ε, T_s denote surface spectral emissivity and surface temperature;

$R_{ati\downarrow}$ is the downward atmospheric thermal radiance;

$R_{sli\downarrow}$ is the downward solar diffusion radiation;

ρ_{bi} is the bi-directional surface spectral reflectivity;

E_i is the solar irradiance at the top of the atmosphere.

$$I_i(\theta,\ j) = R_i(\theta,\ j)\tau_i(\theta,\ j) + R_{a_i-}(\theta,\ j) + R_{s_i-}(\theta,\ j) \qquad (4)$$

Where: R_i is the spectral radiance observed at ground level;

$R_{ai\uparrow}$ is the thermal path atmospheric radiance;

$R_{si\uparrow}$ is the path radiance resulting from scattering of solar radiation;

τ_i is the total atmospheric transmittance in channel i.

4   RSIS Based on Sunlight Field Model

Remote sensing is a method of visualizing the radiative properties of the Earth's surface using instrumentation mounted in satellites or aircraft. Remote sensing instrumentation measures the radiation reflected and emitted from the earth at different wavelengths, primarily at those wavelengths not absorbed by the atmosphere. For remote sensing science, a new important application of light field model is to simulate the images generated by remote sensing instruments which are mounted in satellite platform. RSIS, a synthesized research involved in many sciences, can accurately and really simulate the images of space sensors receiving the radiance energy reflected by the realistic 3D land surface on the basis of the sunlight transfer model and electro-optical engineering techniques etc [5,8]. In the process of RSIS, light field propagation can delineate the interaction between light field and atmosphere, land surface. BRDF can quantify the hemisphere reflectance of land surface from the solar incoming energy at a given remote sensing sensor's observing angle. Sunlight transfer process can wholly simulate the image generation process of remote sensing sensors. With major effects included, such as BRDF and heterogeneity of land surface, atmospheric adjacency influence, the limited spatial resolution of sensors and the optical-electrical transform and system noise, we can obtain realistically simulated multi-spectral and directional radiance images in different elevation levels.

4.1 Research Framework of RSIS

The Fig. 5 shows the general framework of RSIS. RSIS mainly consists of five parts: (1) ephemeris model for determination of the spatial geometric relationship among the remote sensing sensor, solar source, and the scene; (2) realistic 3D land surface scene with object geometry and property characteristics; (3) sunlight transfer model for simulating the influence of the atmosphere, calculating land surface bi-directional reflectance and emission at the sensor level; (4) modeling satellite platform for determination of sensor position and pose; (5) simulating electro-optical system of space sensor hardware composed of optical and electronic components.

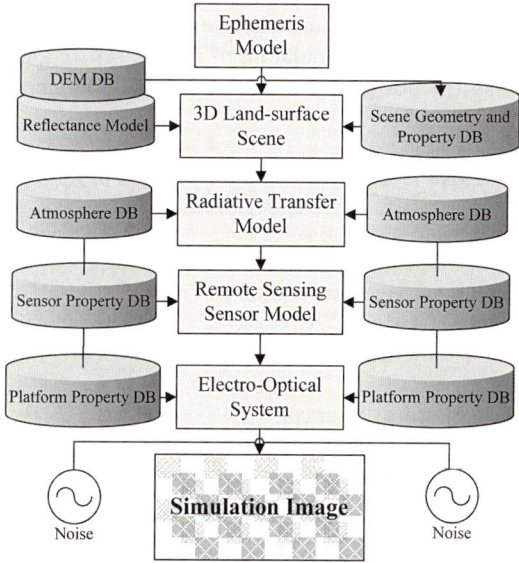

Fig. 5. The research framework of RSIS

4.2 An Experiment of RSIS

According to the research framework of RSIS, an experiment of RSIS was supplied to validate the reliability and accessibility to image simulation base on sunlight field model. The first step for the experiment of RSIS is to model the 3D virtual scene including the nature and art entry. The 3D experimental scene databases include the texture, BRDF and material properties. The modeled 3D scene is showed in the Fig. 6. In the experiment, the above sunlight transfer model is adopted to simulate the light transfer process from solar source to remote sensing sensor. The solar azimuth is 45^0 and the sensor platform elevation is 450km. The subtropical summer mode and 23km of meteorological visibility range are chosen for atmosphere status settings. The main sensor and electro-optical system parameters are presented in table 1. Fig. 7(a) is the simulated radiance intensity image (W/cm^2/sr) including the reflectance and emission energy of 3D land surface land at sensor level. After the introducing of system random temporal noise and sensor platform jitter in the original image, the output image by the addition of realistic sensor effects showed in the Fig. 7b was obviously blurred. Compared with the images in Fig. 7(a) and Fig. 7(b), Fig. 7(a) is the theoretical simulation result that presents smooth characteristic. However, Fig. 7b has the obvious noise in the spoiled image.

From the simulated experiment images of remote sensing, the sunlight transfer model is successfully applied to remote sensing research field. The revolution of the Earth will cause the change of the incoming light which then leads to outgoing light change according the BRDF characteristic. On the other hand, instantaneous field of view (IFOV) change of satellite sensors also will cause the change of radiance received by sensors. All changes surely result in the differences of simulated images. According to the real time changes of above factors in relation to remote sensing, we can obtain the real time simulated images. After analysis of real time RSIS, the designers of remote sensing sensors and satellite platform can obtain the defect of the designed sensors in advance. The simulation of remote sensing image can exert great power on ameliorating the design of remote sensing sensors and reduce expenditure of relevant designing.

Table 1. Parpmeters for the experiment of RSIS

Parameter	unit	value
Spectral band	µm	0.4-0.9
Optical Average Transmittance	-	0.87
IFOV	degree	12
Gain	-	2.97
Bias	-	0.13
Platform Jitter roll	degree	0.1
Platform Jitter pitch	degree	0.1
Platform Jitter yaw	degree	0.1

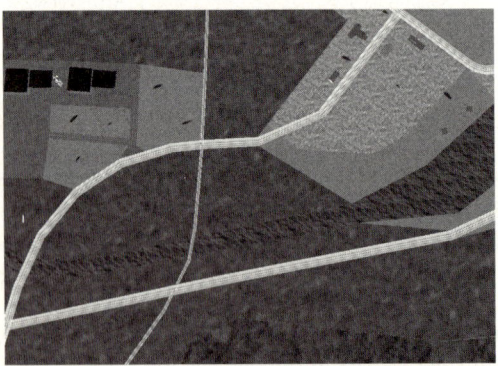

Fig. 6. Realistic 3D scene of land surface for RSIS

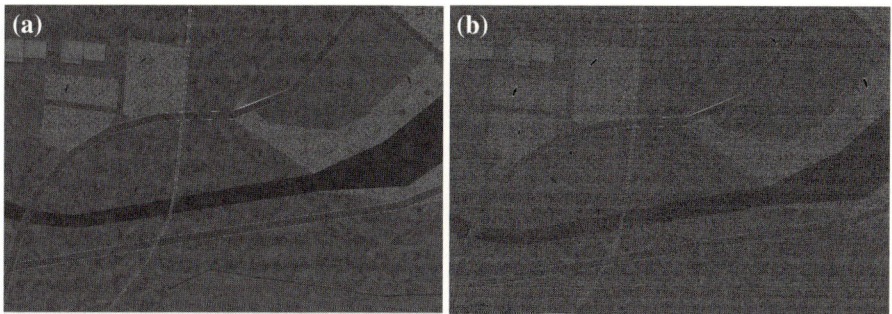

Fig. 7. Simulated radiance images on the sensor level

5   Summary and Prospect

In the VR and computer graphics disciplines, most researches on light field focus on light shadow effect and light rendering for realistic visualization. And these researches are mainly dealt with light rendering of small indoor scenes, and hardly involved in large scale nature light field modeling. Mostly the large-scale nature environment is the geographers' research domain for revealing the nature principles. Energy field modeling has become a new research point, and should exert on great power for many field applications. In the paper, light field modeling is proposed through three aspect illustrations of light field propagation characteristics, BRDF and the quantitative radiance model of sunlight transfer process. Based the light field modeling and remote sensing mechanism, RSIS research framework is put forward and an experiment is implemented. The light field modeling in the paper extends researches of VR/computer graphics and makes the light field application into wider fields. The successful experiment of RSIS demonstrates that energy field modeling can support other science advancement and application.

Although great advancements of computer science have been achieved, energy field modeling in many practical applications still needs more attempts. Especially, the better understanding of their own mechanism of different energy fields is required. Meanwhile, computer graphic and VR development should promote the real time simulation of energy fields. The intersecting researches on energy fields, VR and computer graphic could become a demonstrative example of multi-sciences integration research, and result in profound and far-reaching effects on multi-sciences integration researches.

Acknowledgements

This research is partially supported by the Innovative Project of the Institute of Remote Sensing Applications, Chinese Academy of Sciences No. CX020021, the Opening Foundation Project No. PK2004018 of the Key Lab of Poyang Lake Ecological Environment and Resource Development, Jiangxi Normal University, China, the Key Project of National Natural Science Foundation No. 30590374, and the Opening Foundation Project No. 2005406311 of State Key Laboratory of Hydrology-Water Resources and Hydraulic Engineering, Hohai University, China.

References

1. Berk, A., Anderson, G. P., Acharya, P. K., Chetwynd, J. H., Bernstein, L. S., Shettle, E. P., Matthew, M. W., Adler-Golden, S. M.: MODTRAN4 USER's MANUAL. Hanscom AFB: Air Force Research Laboratory, Space Vehicles Directorate, Air Force Materiel Command, MA 01731-3010 (2000)
2. Bowyer, K. W.: Special issue on directions in CAD-based vision. CVGIP, **55** (1992) 107-108
3. Camahort, E., Lerios, A., Fussell, D.: Uniformly sampled light fields. In Ninth Eurographics Workshop on Rendering, Vienna, Austria (1998) 117-130
4. Hilton A.: Scene modelling from sparse 3D data. Image and Vision Computing. **23** (2005) 900-920
5. Hsu, S. S., Ashton, S., Beltsville, M. D.: Simulation of visible and IR imagery for GOES. Proceedings of IEEE International Geoscience and Remote Sensing Symposium, Pasadena, CA, USA, 8-12 Aug. **3** (1994) 1546-1548
6. Isaksen, A., McMillan, L., Gortler, S. J.: Dynamically reparameterized light fields. In Proceedings of SIGGRAPH 2000, In Computer Graphics Proceedings, Annual Conference Series (2000) 297-306
7. Kang, S.B.: A survey of image-based rendering techniques. SPIE International Symposium on Electronic Imaging: Science and technology, San Jose, CA, **3641** (1999) 2-16
8. Kerekes, J. P. and Landgrebe, D. A.: "RSSIM: A simulation program for optical remote sensing systems," TR-EE 89-48, School of Electrical Engineering, Purdue University, West Lafeyette, IN August (1989)
9. Montero, G., and Sanín, N.: 3-D Modelling of wind field adjustment using finite differences in a terrain conformal coordinate system. Journal of Wind Engineering and Industrial Aerodynamics, **89** (2001) 471-488
10. Pentland, A. P.: Automatic extraction of deformable part models. International Journal of Computer Vision **4** (1990) 107-126
11. Schopfer, J., Dangel, S., Kneubühler, M.: Introduction to BRDF effects. http://www.geo.unizh.ch/rsl/research/SpectroLab/goniometry/brdf_intro.shtml
12. Szymon, R.: A survey of BRDF representation for computer graphics. Paper for CS 348C at Stanford U., Winter (1997)
13. Voloboi, A. G., Galaktionov, V. A., Dmitriev, K. A., Kopylov, E. A.: Bidirectional ray tracing for the integration of illumination by the Quasi-Monte Carlo method. Programming and Computer Software, **30(5)** (2004) 258-265
14. Whitaker, S.: Simultaneous heat, mass and momentum transfers in porous media: a theory of drying. Adv. Heat Transfer **13** (1977) 119-203

Simple and Fast Terrain Rendering
Using Graphics Hardware

Hanli Zhao, Xiaogang Jin, and Jianbing Shen

State Key Lab of CAD&CG, Zhejiang University, Hangzhou 310058, P.R. China
{zhaohanli, jin, shenjianbing}@cad.zju.edu.cn

Abstract. We present a simple and fast LOD rendering technique for terrain visualization, which sufficiently makes use of the GPU capabilities. At load time, we tile the terrain geometry, compute a discrete set of LODs for each tile analog to mipmaps for texture, and cache index buffers for all the levels. At run time, the LOD level is selected on the CPU and the geometrical morphing algorithm is implemented on the GPU. Additionally, we use coherent hierarchical culling (CHC) algorithm to cull away fully occluded tiles to further accelerate the frame rates. Our approach sufficiently exploits both the spatial and temporal coherence of terrain geometry and reduces the bandwidth requirements. Our method can achieve very high frame rates especially when a player wanders through a valley in games or other applications.

Keywords: Real-time rendering, level of detail, occlusion culling, GPU.

1 Introduction

Digital terrain visualization in complex outdoor environment is a challenging problem with applications ranging from interactive games and simulations to cartography at high frame rates.

Today, many games and other real-time applications that render up to millions of triangles per frame have been released. It is still far too many to render interactively on commercial computers by brute force. Furthermore, aliasing artifact arises when triangle in screen space is less than one pixel, just as in texturing without mipmaps. Thus, introducing a level-of-detail (LOD) algorithm to adjust the terrain tessellation is preferable.

Modern GPU enables powerful parallel computation. In addition, recent graphics hardware natively supports an occlusion query to detect visibility an object against the current contents of the z-buffer. In consequence, we sufficiently exploit the GPU capabilities to accelerate the frame rates of rendering terrain.

In this paper, we present a simple and fast terrain geometry rendering method using graphics hardware. We choose uniformly gridded polygonal height fields to represent the terrain geometry, which is simple to implement. The terrain is split into a set of small meshes, which are called tiles. Like the ordinary mipmapping technique for textures [12], we treat the tiles as the highest resolution texture's 3d equivalent. We pre-calculate all the successive lower resolution "mipmaps" at terrain-load time. After view frustum culling, we implement a LOD algorithm for terrain mesh. Then, we use

Z. Pan et al. (Eds.): ICAT 2006, LNCS 4282, pp. 715–723, 2006.

coherent hierarchical hardware occlusion queries to further cull away those tiles that are occluded by other tiles in screen space and thus only render the visible tiles. We use screen space pixel errors to select corresponding geometry LOD level to tremendously reduce the number of triangulations to be actually rendered. Moreover, we replace the sudden change (popping effect) of two successive levels with a smooth transition between both by using tri-linear filtering.

The rest of this paper begins with a review of related work in Section 2. Section 3 describes our simple but fast terrain LOD and culling algorithm in detail. Section 4 presents results obtained by experimental evaluation of our algorithm. Finally, Section 5 concludes the paper and discusses future work.

2 Related Work

With the demand for rendering outdoor scenes of ever increasing size, a large number of researchers have developed algorithms for terrain-like visualization in the last decade. Techniques of partitioning polygonal models into triangle strips presented by Evans *et al* [4] can significantly reduce rendering times over transmitting each triangle individually.

2.1 Visibility Culling

It is one of the major acceleration techniques for the real-time rendering of complex scenes including terrain. Optimized view frustum culling algorithms introduced by U. Assarson and T. Möller [22] efficiently eliminate objects outside of the current view frustum.

The elimination of occluded objects is addressed by occlusion culling. Offline occlusion culling algorithms presented by S. J. Teller and C. H. Séquin [21] compute a potentially visible set (PVS) for cells of a fixed subdivision of the scene as a preprocess, and quickly identify a PVS for arbitrary viewpoint in the scene at runtime. Online occlusion culling algorithms presented by J. Bittner *et al* [8, 10] exploit both the spatial and the temporal coherence of visibility. Online occlusion culling solves most of the drawbacks of offline occlusion culling at the cost of applying extra computations at each frame. Therefore, most online occlusion culling methods rely on a number of assumptions about the scene structure (e.g. presence of large occluders) or occlusion properties (e.g. occlusion by a few closest depth layers).

2.2 Terrain LOD

Terrain LOD algorithms can be classified into four following categories by the structures of hierarchies of mesh refinement operations:

- Triangulated irregular networks (TINs) can approximate a surface at any desired level of accuracy with fewer polygons than other representations, but require the tracking of mesh adjacencies and refinement dependencies. A number of different approaches have been developed to create TINs using Delaunay and other triangulations [2, 6, 7, 19].

- Binary triangle trees that allow polygons to be recursive combined when appropriate have also been researched. Thus, a mesh with fewer polygons can be used to present the terrain height field [9, 15, 16, 17, 18, 20].
- Inspired by texture clipmaps [1], geometry clipmaps [5] caches terrain geometry in a set of nested regular grids, which are incrementally shifted as the viewer moves.
- Tiles based algorithms tessellate each tile at different resolutions, which can sufficiently utilize the GPU accelerated power. D. Wagner [3], L. Bishop *et al* [14] and J. Schneider and R. Westermann [11] choose uniform square tiles as we do.

3   Adaptive Terrain Rendering

In this section we first present an overview of our new algorithm. Then we discuss its steps in more detail, including HLSL (high level shading language) implementation tricks.

3.1   Algorithm Overview

Our new method is inspired by *Terrain geomorphing in the vertex shader* presented by D. Wagner. In particular, it is centered on the following three ideas:

- We reduce the data size transported to video memory. We use vertices' horizontal and vertical index as both x and z components coordinate and corresponding texturing coordinate. Additionally, we avoid re-triangulation when geometry LOD level changes, as index buffer for each level resides in video memory constantly.
- We sufficiently exploit both the spatial and temporal coherence of terrain geometry. We cache per-vertex height values for previous frame, and when some tile's LOD level does not change, the height values it covers need not be re-calculated. At rendering time, we use CHC algorithm to cull away fully occluded tiles in the view frustum.
- We implement the geometrical morphing algorithm of tri-linear interpolation of per-vertex height values simply by using four HLSL instructions natively supported by GPUs.

The terrain is laid out in a grid of vertices with a fixed distance between each other. Because large parts of the terrain will not be visible (i.e. not inside the view-frustum) from a certain viewpoint, they need not be rendered and therefore should be culled away early to prevent unnecessary calculations. Since the terrain layout is essentially 2D, we construct a quadtree instead of octree for fast culling instead. Quadtree nodes consist of 3D bounding boxes which physically contain the node's entire subtrees' bounding boxes, where at the leaf the actual terrain tile's can be found. Thus we use optimized view frustum culling algorithm to cull away the fully invisible tiles, and link up the rest tiles for further processing. Next, we select appropriate LOD levels for all the linked tiles, which will be described in section 3.2. Then, we render the tiles by using CHC algorithm, which will be described in section 3.3. Our geometrical morphing algorithm will be presented in section 3.3.

3.2   Geometry LOD Level Selection

In a preprocessing step, a discrete set of LODs is computed for each tile, and for each level the position of the vertex with the largest error is determined and saved together with the correct position. Before a frame is rendered, we project both max-error vertices and correct vertices into the screen space and calculate the resulting screen error metrics for all coarser levels. Then, each tile level is decided if its largest screen-space error is below a predefined error boundary.

On the other hand, we use a triangles strip to uniformly tessellate the tile geometry, so only a single index buffer is used for all tiles with a given level (see figure 1). As a result, the index buffer for each level can be prestored in video memory constantly. Once the tile level is selected, the corresponding index buffer can be used directly, avoiding tile re-triangulation and index buffer transporting overhead.

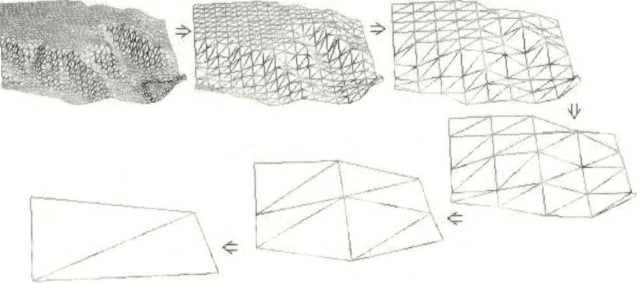

Fig. 1. Tessellation levels from the finest to the coarsest

To avoid gaps between two neighboring tiles with different tessellation levels, we allow the coarser tile to dictate the border vertices' position, and simply add additional zero-area triangles between them. Two arrays are used to wholly cache current and succeeding coarser levels' terrain height values, and only a few parts need be updated for every frame after the level is selected.

3.3   Coherent Hierarchical Culling

Now, the CHC algorithm, which can significantly accelerate the frame rates in many applications, i.e. MMRP (Massive Multi-players Role Playing) games, is used for the terrain rendering to cull away fully occluded tiles (see figure 2). The DirectX 9 takes an IDirect3DQuery9 interface for hardware occlusion queries. An occlusion query returns the number of pixels that pass z-testing. These pixels are for primitives drawn between the issue of D3DISSUE_BEGIN and D3DISSUE_END. This enables an application to check the occlusion result against 0. Zero is fully occluded, which means the pixels are not visible from the current camera position.

Let us briefly describe the CHC algorithm, and you can refer to [10] in more detail. The algorithm performs a traversal of the hierarchy that is terminated either at leaf nodes or invisible nodes that are called *termination nodes*. In the i-th frame, the quad-tree is traversed in a front-to-back order, all interior visible nodes that are called *opened nodes* of the (i-1)-th frame are skipped and only the termination nodes are applied occlusion queries. When reaching a termination node, the algorithm proceeds as follows: for a previously invisible node or a previously visible leaf, we issue the occlusion query and store it in the query queue; additionally for a previously visible leaf, we immediately render the associated tile geometry without waiting for the result of the query. When the query queue is not empty, we check if the result of the oldest query in the query queue is already available. If the query result is not available, we continue by recursively processing other nodes of the quad-tree; otherwise, we fetch the result and remove the node from the query queue. If the node is visible, we process its children in front-to-back order; otherwise, the whole subtree of the node is invisible and is therefore culled. Furthermore, we set the back face culling render state as counter-clockwise, so the back face of the rendered geometry against the view point is culled away automatically.

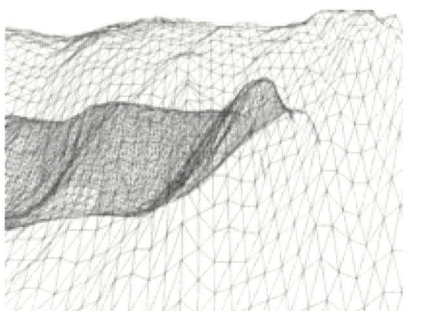 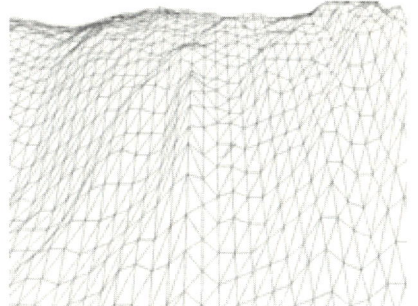

Fig. 2. Terrain without occlusion culling (left) and with occlusion culling (right)

If we use the different GPU rendering passes for the bounding boxes and the actual terrain tiles, it will produce additional pass switching overhead for graphics hardware. It is no need to do geometrical morphing and texture coordinate transforming operations when rendering the bounding boxes. In our method, we add a static conditional branch for the GPU shading program. As a result, the only one pass is used during final rendering while the overhead is almost eliminated.

3.4 Geometrical Morphing

Before the tile is actually rendered, we need update the morphing parameters for vertices to keep triangle-count low without any popping artifact. Note that if the tile is frustum culled or occlusion culled, this step is left out. Then, the geometrical morphing algorithm is implemented on the GPU.

The aim of geometrical morphing is move (morph) vertices softly into their positions in the next level before that next level is activated. Only vertices with odd indices inside a tile have to move and vertices on even position can stay fixed, for they are not removed when switching to the next coarser level (see figure 3). There are three possible cases in which a vertex has to move:

- Case A: The vertex is on an even x- and odd y-position. It would move to the middle position between the next bottom (1) and the top (2) vertices.
- Case B: The vertex is on an odd x- and even y-position. It would move to the middle position between the next left (2) and the right (3) vertices.
- Case C: The vertex is on an odd x- and odd y-position. It would move to the middle position between the next bottom left (1) and the top right (3) vertices.

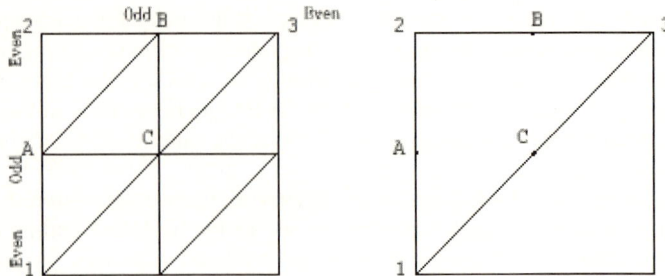

Fig. 3. Fine level with morphing vertices (left) and corresponding coarser level (right) with odd indexed vertex removed

Now we can just use the tri-linear interpolation to implement geometrical morphing. The tessellation selection calculation returns a tessellation factor in the form of a floating-point value, where the integer part means the current level and the fractional part denotes the tweening factor. For *case A* mentioned above, its height value can be calculated as follows:

$$\text{Height} = \text{ActualHeight} + \alpha\text{DiffSelf} + 0.5*(1-\alpha)(\beta\text{DiffBottom} + \gamma\text{DiffTop}) \tag{1}$$

Here, DiffSelf, DiffBottom, and DiffTop are corresponding vertices' height differences between current level λ and next coarser level $(\lambda+1)$. The factor of α, β, and γ are tweening factors respectively. Note that border vertices' positions shared by the neighboring tiles are dictated by the coarser one, so we must take into account four neighbors' tweening factors on the GPU.

The data structure that vertex shader takes as input is defined as: struct *Terrain_VS_Input* {float4 pos: POSITION; float4 alpha: TEXCOORD0; float4 beta: TEXCOORD1;} (which pos.x and pos.z represent horizontal and vertical index respectively, pos.y represents succeeding coarser level height value, while pos.w represents height difference between current level and next coarser one; both alpha.xyzw and beta.xyzw represent lower, upper, left and right neighbor tiles' height differences, but only the needed components would be non-zero), and the data structure that vertex shader takes as output is defined as: struct *Terrain_VS_Output* {float4 pos: POSITION; float4 tex: TEXCOORD0;} (which pos.xyz represents the vertex screen postion; tex.xy represents its overlay texture coordinate, and tex.zw represents its lightmap texture coordinate). Then, the pseudo-code in vertex shader is given as follows. Note that the geometrical morphing operation is done from line 4 to line 7, while the dot and lerp intrinsic functions are natively supported by GPUs.

```
Terrain_VS_Output VS_Program (Terrain_VS_Input Input)
{
  Terrain_VS_Output Output;
  float4        finalPos;
  float         diff;
  diff        = 0.5*dot (Input.beta,neighborFactor);
  diff        = lerp (diff, Input.pos.w,selfFactor);
  diff        += dot (Input.alpha,neighborFactor);
  FinalPos.y  = Input.pos + diff;
  FinalPos.x  = (Input.pos.x+tileWidth*tileIndexX)*
  scale.x/terrainWidth;
```

```
   FinalPos.z    = (Input.pos.z+tileHeight*tileIndexZ)*
scale.z/terrainHeight;
   FinalPos.w    = 1.0;
   Output.tex.zw = float2 (FinalPos.x/scale.x,
FinalPos.z/scale.z);
   Output.tex.xy = Output.tex.zw * textureNumRepeated;
   Output.pos    = mul (FinalPos, matrixWorldViewProj);

   Return        Output;
}
```

4 Results

We have incorporated our method into a DirectX 3D 9.0c based graph library and tested it in order to evaluate its efficiency. All tests were conducted in a PC with an

Table 1. Timings of Tests. ε refers to screen space pixel error.

Data set	Triangle number	Fps (ε = 5)	Fps (ε = 10)
Mountains	2M	93	126
Canyon	500K	125	189
Plane	125K	162	230
Valley	4M	76	108

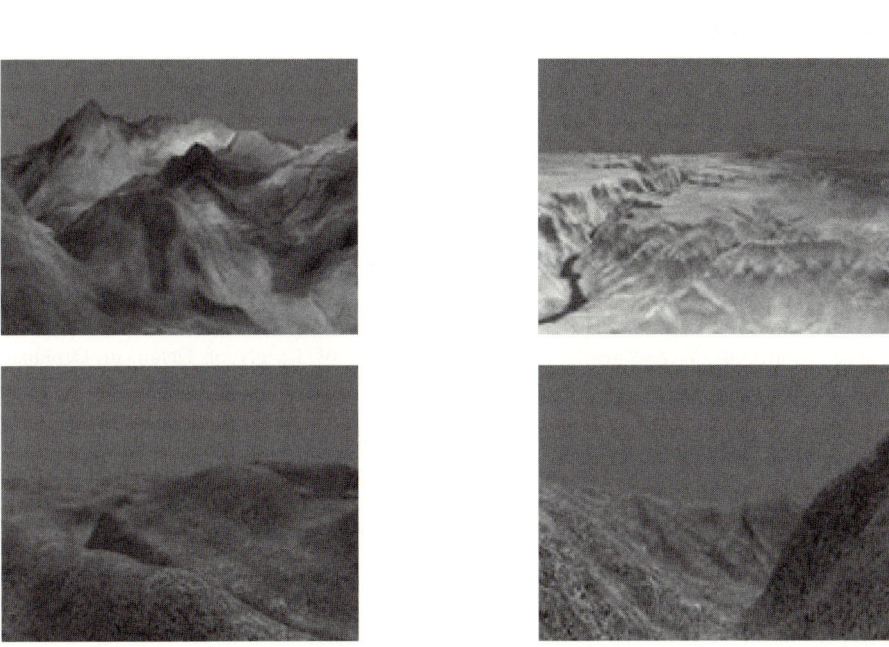

Fig. 4. Tested data sets: Mountains (upper left), Canyon (upper right), Plane (lower left), and Valley (lower right)

Intel Pentium Ⅳ 3.0GHz CPU, 1.0GB of memory and an NVIDIA Geforce 7800 GS graphics card. All data sets were rendered to a view port with 1024×768 resolution.

As our result show, our method can achieve high frame rates for millions of triangulations in common outdoor environments. Also, frame rates can be improved by increasing the screen space pixel error. It still remains visually plausible effect when ε is even greater because of geometrical morphing. Note that the frame rate is high enough when rendering valley, in which many tiles are occluded by others.

5   Conclusion and Future Work

We have presented a method for simple and fast terrain rendering using graphics hardware. The method reduces the data size transported to video memory and sufficiently exploits both the spatial and temporal coherence of terrain geometry. Furthermore, it fully makes use of the GPU capabilities to accelerate the frame rates of rendering terrain. Our method is especially preferable for such applications as MMRP games and urban pedestrian applications.

In the future, we will investigate compression scheme for both terrain hierarchy and texture. Additionally, we will explore to split current vertex stream into two or more streams, and then reduce the data to be updated by further exploiting the coherence between two succeeding frames.

Acknowledgements

This work is supported by the National Natural Science Foundation of China (grant numbers 60533080 and 60573153), and the Program for New Century Excellent Talents in University (grant number NCET-05-0519).

References

1. C. C. Tanner, C. J. Migdal, and M. T. Jones. The Clipmap: A Virtual Mipmap. Proceedings of SIGGRAPH 1998, pp. 151-158.
2. D. Cohen-Or, Y. Levanoni. Temporal Continuity of Levels of Detail in Delaunay Triangulated Terrain. IEEE Visualization 1996, pp. 37-42.
3. D. Wagner. Terrain Geomorphing in the Vertex Shader, Shaderx2 Shader Programming Tips and Tricks With Directx 9. Wardware Publishing House, 2004, pp. 18-32.
4. F. Evans, S. Skiena, and A. Varshney. Optimizing Triangle Strips for Fast Rendering. IEEE Visualization Oct. 1996, pp. 319-326.
5. F. Losasso, H. Hoppe. Geometry Clipmaps: Terrain Rendering Using Nested Regular Grids. ACM Transactions on Graphics (Proceedings of SIGGRAPH 2004) 23(3), pp. 769-776.
6. H. Hoppe. Smooth View-Dependent Level-of-Detail Control and its Application to Terrain Rendering. IEEE Visualization 1998, pp. 35-42.
7. J. El-Sana, A. Varshney. Generalized View-Dependent Simplification. Proceedings of EUROGRAPHICS 1999, pp. 83-94.
8. J. Bittner, V. Havran. Exploiting Temporal and Spatial Conerence in Hierarchical Visibility Algorithms. Journal of Visualization and Computer Animation, 2001, pp. 277-286

9. J. Levenberg. Fast View-Dependent Level-of-Detail Rendering using Cached Geometry. IEEE Visualization 2002, pp. 259-266.
10. J. Bittner, M. Wimmer, H Piringer and W. Purgathofer. Coherent Hierarchical Culling: Hardware Occlusion Queries Made Useful. In Proceedings of EUROGRAPHICS 2005.
11. J. Schneider, R. Westermann. GPU-Friendly High-Quality Terrain Rendering. Journal of WSCG 2006.
12. L. Williams. Pyramidal Parametrics. ACM Computer Graphics, 1983, 17(3) pp. 1--11.
13. L. De Floriani, E. Puppo. Hierarchical Triangulation for Multiresolution Surface Description. ACM Transactions on Graphics 1995, 14(4), pp. 363-411.
14. L. Bishop, D. Eberly, T. Whitted, M. Finch, and M. Shantz. Designing a PC Game Engine. IEEE CG&A 1998, 18(1), 46-53.
15. M. Duchaineau, M. Wolinsky, D. E. Sigeti, et al. ROAMing Terrain: Real-time Optimally Adapting Meshes. IEEE Visualization, Oct. 1997, pp. 81-88.
16. P. Lindstrom, D. Koller, W.Ribasky, et al. Real-Time, Continuous Level of Detail Rendering of Height Fields. ACM SIGGRAPH 1996, pp. 109-118.
17. P. Cignoni, E. Puppo, R. Scopigno. Representation and Visualization of Terrain Surfaces at Variable Resolution. The Visual Computer 1997, 13(5), 199-217.
18. P. Lindstrom, V. Pascucci. Terrain Simplification simplified: A General Framework for View-Dependent Out-of-Core Visualization. IEEE TVCG 2002, 8(3), pp. 239-254.
19. R. J. Fowler, J. J. Little. Automatic Extraction of Irregular Network Digital Terrain Models. Proceedings of SIGGRAPH 79. In Computer Graphics 1979, 13(2), pp. 199-207.
20. R. Pajarola. Large Scale Terrain Visualization using the Restricted Quadtree Triangulation. In Proceedings IEEE Visualization '98, pp. 19-24.
21. S. J. Teller, C. H. Séquin. Visibility Preprocessing for Interactive Walkthroughs. Computer Graphics (Proceedings of SIGGRAPH '91), Jul, 1991, 25(4), pp. 61-69.
22. U. Assarson, T. Möller. Optimized View Frustum Culling Algorithms (technical report 99-3). Chalmers University of Technology, Sweden 1999.

Animating Grass in Real-Time

Linqiang Yao, Liyu Tang, Chongcheng Chen, and Jingjing Sun

Key Lab of Data Mining and Information Sharing of Ministry of Education (Fuzhou University), Spatial Information Research Center of Fujian, Fuzhou 350002, China
{Chencc, Tangly}@fzu.edu.cn, {ylq_82, sun2255}@sina.com.cn

Abstract. Grass occurs frequently in the forest and the high performance grass generation can greatly enhance the reliability and complexity of virtual forest scenes. So the paper presents a simple method to render fields of grass, animated in the wind in real-time. We employ a series of polygons contain several grass blades to construct a basic grass unit. Animation is achieved by translate the grass units according the "wind vector" and we implement the wind effect such as a strong wind. Furthermore, we employ the rendering optimization to acquire faster frames.

Keywords: Virtual forest, grass, animation, real-time rendering.

1 Introduction

People seem to have an insatiable need for the complexity of computer generated images, which immerses oneself in a virtual world. But comparing to the indoor scenes, outdoor, especially for natural scenes, because of their animated details and endless border, it is difficult to render and animate in real-time.

Forest landscape visualization has been widely investigated and a number of methods have been proposed. In our former research, Yu and Chen proposed an approach for dynamically modeling and real-time rendering for a real forest [1]. But in most of forest visualization systems, plants rendering only included trees, grass has been ignored or represented by a static texture. Although the shape of grass blades is not very complex, renderings of countless blades, global illumination computations and effects of waving in the wind, make real-time grass animation become difficult.

We attempt to overcome the problems discussed above, generate wavy realistic-looking grasses in real-time and apply it to our visual forest system finally. Hence, our work has three main objectives: (i) produce realistic-looking grasses at interactive frame rates, (ii) animate the grasses in the wind, and (iii) rendering optimization. We do a short survey of related work in the real-time rendering and animation of grass in section 2 and present an approach to generate the grass model in section 3. We describe how to animate the grass in the wind in section 4. Rendering optimization has been mentioned in section 5. We present our results in section 6 and a short conclusion in section 7.

Z. Pan et al. (Eds.): ICAT 2006, LNCS 4282, pp. 724–731, 2006.

2   Related Work

Animating grass in real-time has been widely investigated. Employing a particle system was one of the first techniques proposed to break free from the barrier of rendering objects with complex geometry. Reeves adopts trajectories of particles to determine the shape of the grass blade [2]. The resulting 2D wind maps are stored, for each animation step. Then, the blades of grass bend proportionally to the intensity stored in the map, according to a given wind direction. Although visual detail is lacking, it is able to approximate grass fairly reasonably when viewed from a distance.

Another technique for generating grass is volumetric texture. Kajiya and Kay proposed using volumetric textures to render furry surfaces [3]. Still using the volumetric texture method, Neyret animated breeze in a meadow by applying a sine wave motion to the control points of ray-traced texels modeling grass [4]. Although it produced excellent results, this work isn't directly applicable to interactive applications. Perbet and Cani do discuss animation of volumetric textures to produce realistic grass in the wind in [5]. Their slices are perpendicular to the ground's surface, and thus their system is better suited to low views, close to the ground. Brook employed vertex shaders to render displacement maps with Russian doll style transparent shells [6].

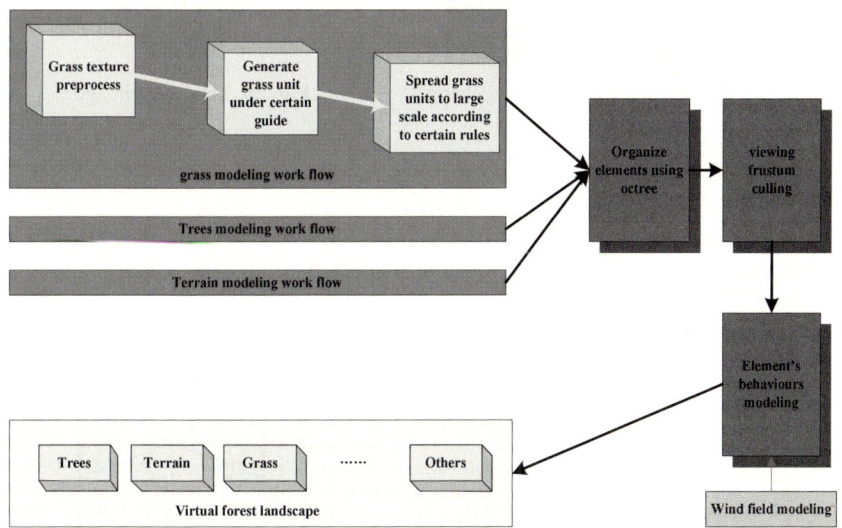

Fig. 1. Dynamically generation of animating grass in our virtual forest system

The transparency in the texture enables it to represent objects with complex shapes such as plants and trees. Pelzer and Bytes present that two perpendicular polygons containing a section of grass are combined to render large fields of grass with wind animation [7]. Wang proposed an approach to dynamic rendering of grasses wagging in wind [8]. Through length preserving free-form deformation of the 3D skeleton lines of each grass blade and using the alpha test to implement transparent texture mapping, this work successfully model grasses of different shapes with rich details.

This paper is inspired by the way of Pelzer [7], the basic grass unit is combined by several polygons in star arrangement. We set up a physical wind field model and compute the affine transformation of grass in this model. Furthermore, based on the octree division, the view frustum culling has been applied to acquire the faster frame rate. Our technique incorporates vertex shaders available on current consumer grade graphics hardware to further increase speed. Figure 1 shows a dynamically generation of animation grass in our virtual forest system.

3 Modeling of Grass

3.1 Grass Texture Preprocess

In order to reduce the rendering number of polygons, we render some different blades in the alpha channel of a texture. Through the alpha blend, we can easily get the grass image. As we see in Figure 2.

Fig. 2a. A grass texture with alpha channel   **Fig. 2b.** The result image

3.2 Generate a Grass Unit

The simple linear arrangement of prepared grass textures makes the grass seem to be very unreal, because it has not any thickness. We can employ a method called "crossed tree" [9]. Pelzer proved that star arrangement is the best choice [7], as shown in Figure 3. The normal direction of all vertexes runs parallel with the perpendicular side of polygon; it assures that all grasses have the correct illumination.

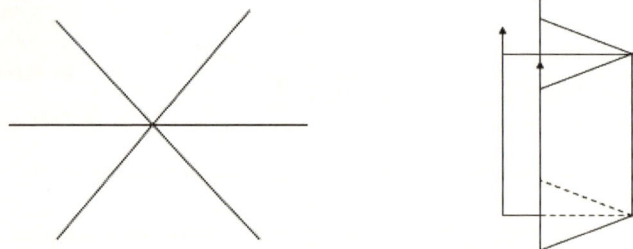

Fig. 3a. A grass unit (Bird's-eye view)   **Fig. 3b.** A grass unit (Front view) [7]

3.3 Distribution of Grass Units

Based on the basic grass unit, we intend to spread it in certain rules to generate fields of grass. The distribution of grass can be obtained by actual data like Remotely

Sensing images. Another approach is the random distribution, such as uniform distribution and normal distribution. In this paper we apply the normal distribution to compute the distribution density of grass, and then through the disturbing effect, the final result is close to the reality, see it in Figure 4.

Fig. 4a. Distribution of grass units. (Bird's-eye view)

Fig. 4b. Distribution of grass units. (Front view)

4   Animation of Grass

The interactive animation of grass is essential in our virtual forest. The effects, such as breeze or strong wind, will have been stochastically generated in aim of increasing realism. We are looking for an appropriate animation algorithm, which is efficient enough to be apply to the whole grassland at interactive rates and can provide the user with an interactive control of wind effects.

4.1   Animation of a Grass Unit

The grass is a gentle object which is very sensitive to the wind. For per grass unit, we use the "wind vector" to represent wind effects. The "wind vector" is a vector stored with each grass unit, and its direction and value respectively means the wind direction and velocity.

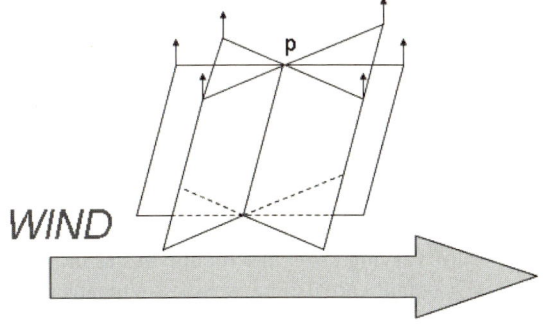

Fig. 5. Animation of a grass unit

Our actual animation algorithm will only consider the contribution of this "wind vector" that is perpendicular to the local surface normal. This restriction would be easy to overcome with additional per-vertex data, which would, however, degrade the performance slightly. Animation is implemented by moving each unit along its "wind vector". See it in Figure 5, we only need consider the change of position of point P according to the "wind vector".

4.2   Examples of Animation

We take a example of strong wind passing over a grassy knoll. For per grass unit, the wind force it has received is oscillating over time, so the value of its "wind vector" dose a shin variety. During the wind passing, the grass should bend according this value. Indeed, as the wind passing over, because of the sequence of receiving wind force, the "wind vector" of each unit has a different value, so their bend direction and degree are different too. The result image is shown in Figure 6.

Fig. 6. A screenshot with a strong wind passing over a grassy knoll

5   Rendering Optimization

5.1   View Frustum Culling Based on Octree

Because of the huge number of polygons, efficiently identifying polygons that are visible from a dynamic synthetic viewpoint is an important problem for animation of grass in real-time. Visibility determination is performed using the z-buffer algorithm, but this algorithm would consume a significant fraction of graphics processing. The view frustum culling can avoid needlessly processing invisible portions of the scene and discard invisible polygons early in the graphics pipeline.

Octree representation is a form of tessellation in which the volume that a 3D scene is subdivided into cubes of varying sizes. Each cube has at most eight neighbors; the relationship between each octant can also be viewed by means of a tree structure (see Figure 7).

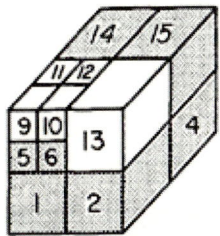 

Fig. 7. The octree data structure

In our virtual forest system, firstly, an Octree organizes all the objects included terrain, trees and grass. Second, view frustum culling can be incorporated into the Octree to check whether the Octree node is inside the current viewing frustum. Lastly, the inside nodes would be rendered. As we see in Figure 8.

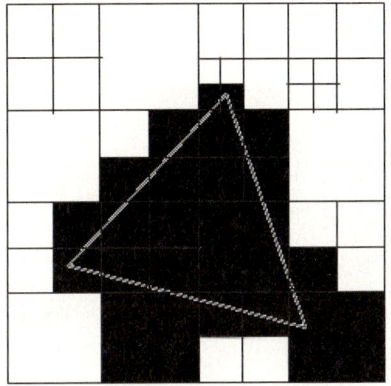

Fig. 8. Octree nodes classified with respect to a view frustum culling. The remain nodes alter the culling are black.

5.2 Texture Compression

Texture compression is also used in this system, which enables a reduction of texture data by one-fourth to one- sixth its original size while maintaining the image quality of the original artwork. Therefore, texture image can be stored with significantly less memory hence improve overall system performance.

6 Results

This section presents some test results that show the efficiency of the algorithms presented in this paper. Our rendering system is written in C++, using OpenGL graph library. We ran our tests on a PC with a 2.8G Intel Pentium 4 processor and 512 Megabytes of memory. The video card is a 64 Megabyte NVIDIA GeForce 4.

Frame rates in our rendering system vary depending on the number of grass units on the screen. In order to increase the frame rates, we do the rendering optimization. The results are presented in table that allows comparison, analysis and discussion of the performance of the rendering system.

Table 1. Results in frames per second

Grass units	Polygons	Non-optimization	Optimization
500	1507	52.6	96.7
2500	7507	20.1	40.3
10000	30007	6.2	18.6

The results are very encouraging that we are achieving real-time frame rates with convincing animation and visual quality. We also apply it to our virtual forest system successfully. It proves that our approach is useful and efficient for the virtual reality, video games and so on. Figure 9 is a screenshot with grass and tree in our virtual forest system.

Fig. 9. A screenshot with grass and trees in our virtual forest system, rendered with 20-25Hz

7   Conclusions

In this paper we have presented a complete solution to the problem of grass animation in real-time. At first, we use three intersecting polygons containing a section of grass to combine a basic grass unit, and then extend them to generate the large scale grassland. Procedural models of wind field are used to animate the grass. After the rendering optimization, our grass animation appears well in quality and efficiency.

Acknowledgement

This research was funded by Preliminary Project of 973 Program (No. 2004CCA07200) in China, Fujian Provincial Natural Science Foundation (D0510010), and Fujian Education Department Project (K04003).

References

1. Yu Qizhi, Chen Chongcheng, Pan Zhigeng, Li Jianwei. 2004. A GIS-based forest visual simulation system. Proceedings of - Third international conference on Image and Graphics, P410-413.
2. Reeves W. T. 1983. Particle systems - a technique for modeling a class of fuzzy objects. ACM Trans. Graph. 2, 2, 91–108.
3. Kajiya J. T. Timothy L. Kay. 1989. "Rendering Fur With Three Dimensional Textures", Computer Graphics 23(3), pp. 271–280.
4. Neyret. Fabrice. 1995. "Animated Texels", Eurographics Workshop on Rendering '96 pp. 97–103.
5. Perbet. F. Cani. M. P. 2001. Animating prairies in real-time. In SI3D '01: Proceedings of the 2001 symposium on Interactive 3D graphics, ACM Press, New York, NY, USA, 103–110.
6. Bakay. B. Lalonde. P. Heidrich. W. 2002. Real-time animated grass. In Eurographics 2002. I. Navazo and P.Slusallek.
7. Pelzer. K. 2004. Rendering countless blades of waving grass. GPU Gems (March), 107–121.
8. Wang Chaobo. Wang Zhangye. Zhou Qi. 2005. Natural Phenomena and Special Effects Dynamic modeling and rendering of grass wagging in wind. Computer Animation and Virtual Worlds. Volume 16 , Issue 3-4 ,377–389.
9. Meyer. Alexandre. Fabrice Neyret. Pierre Poulin. 2001. "Interactive Rendering of Trees with Shading and Shadows,". *12th Eurographics Workshop on Rendering*, pp.182-195.

Gaussian Mixture Model in Improved HLS Color Space for Human Silhouette Extraction

Nurul Arif Setiawan, Hong Seok-Ju, Kim Jang-Woon, and Lee Chil-Woo*

Intelligent Media Lab, Department of Computer Engineering,
Chonnam National University, Gwangju, Korea
Tel.: 82-62-530-1803
arif@image.chonnam.ac.kr, seokju@image.chonnam.ac.kr,
woon418@image.chonnam.ac.kr, leecw@chonnam.ac.kr

Abstract. In this paper, we present an algorithm using Gaussian Mixture Model (GMM) for foreground segmentation which can differentiate shadow region from objects with simple criteria. In the algorithm, we have utilized the Improved HLS (IHLS) color space model as the fundamental description for image, instead of using raw RGB data. IHLS color space has an advantage over the standard RGB space to recognize shadow region from object by utilizing luminance and saturation-weighted hue information directly, without any calculation of chrominance and luminance. By exploiting this feature in GMM, we obtain adaptive background model with good sensitivity to color changes and shadow.

Keywords: Gaussian Mixture Model, Improved HLS, foreground segmentation.

1   Introduction

Foreground segmentation can be defined as the process to mask object of interest in a scene for further process. The idea is to differentiate moving objects as the main focus on the system from the rest "static" background scene. This step is one of the fundamental parts in vision system which includes surveillance, video segmentation, human tracking, and action recognition. For video system, segmentation is used to separate background-foreground object for video encoding. In human body tracking and action recognition, segmentation plays an important role in separating object of interest before extracting motion data and recognition phase. Outdoor surveillances present the most challenging issues for segmentation problem because of highly dynamic and multi modal scene.

In a single modal background such as static indoor scene, segmentation can be handled by using simple background models which assume that background pixels are static and every motion in the scene is caused by foreground object. For such environment, segmentation can be done by calculating the difference between current frame and the background model. Most referred example for

---

* Corresponding author.

Z. Pan et al. (Eds.): ICAT 2006, LNCS 4282, pp. 732–741, 2006.
© Springer-Verlag Berlin Heidelberg 2006

this model is in [15]. The authors modeled pixel intensity values by a single trivariate Gaussian distribution in YUV color space. They use a simple adaptive update algorithm to handle moving background objects and gradual illumination changes. Several limitations in such model are learning phase requirement to model background distribution, limited for single modal background, and adaptability problems for several situation such as sudden illumination changes, slowly moving foreground and lack of sufficient background information in the case of short training time.

To overcome shortcomings found in the simple model, Gaussian Mixture Model (GMM) is proposed by [13]. Every single pixel is modeled as n Gaussian distributions in RGB space. This approach is able to handle adaptation problems mentioned above in a single Gaussian model and it is widely accepted as an adaptive background model. Initial mixture model explained in [13] has limitations that it cannot differentiate shadow from foreground object and its parameters stabilize slowly in initialization step.

Shadow handling for GMM is devised in [9] by using brightness and chrominance statistics derived from RGB space described in [4]. The authors also propose new update algorithms for fast stabilization in GMM initialization. Combination of GMM and color model in [4] using Bayesian theorem is explained in [1]. In [10], luminance change and ratio calculation from RGB statistics is used to detect shadow from scene after GMM background modeling step. A Mixture of three Gaussian distributions is used to model road, shadow and vehicle for traffic surveillance [3]. Fusion of color and depth information obtained from stereo camera in GMM is proposed in [7]. RGB-based GMM and gradient information are used for background-foreground classification in three distinct hierarchy levels i.e pixel level, region level and frame level [8].

In this paper, we propose another variant of Gaussian Mixture Model by exploiting Improved HLS (IHLS) color space as used in [2]. Our work is similar to [9] and [10] as our aim is to combine GMM and IHLS color space to for better foreground segmentation system. But instead of working in RGB space and then calculate chrominance and luminance for shadow detection, we introduce a new approach to model luminance and saturation-weighted hue statistics [2] directly as Gaussian distributions in mixture model. This paper is composed as follows. We will discuss IHLS color space and GMM in section 2. In section 3, we will explain our foreground segmentation model including shadow suppression and frame level background maintenance. The experimental result from this model and comparison to GMM with normalized RGB space will be discussed in section 4. Finally, section 5 concludes this paper and discusses future works.

2   Background Modeling

Chromatic plane in IHLS space is defined by circular statistics while its luminance follows standard linear statistics [2]. In this section, we briefly review circular statistics for IHLS space and one dimensional GMM for a single color channel.

2.1   Improved HLS Color Space

The IHLS color space has been introduced in [5] and applied in [2] for foreground segmentation. Following formulae are used for conversion from RGB to hue θ^H, luminance y and saturation s of the IHLS space [2].

$$
\begin{aligned}
s &= \max(R, G, B) - \min(R, G, B) \\
y &= 0.2125R + 0.7154G + 0.0721B \\
c_{r1} &= R - \frac{G+B}{2}, c_{r2} = \frac{\sqrt{3}}{2}(B - G) \\
c_r &= \sqrt{c_{r1}^2 + c_{r2}^2} \\
\theta^H &= \begin{cases}
\text{undefined} & \text{if } c_r < 0 \\
\arccos(\frac{c_{r1}}{c_r}) & \text{if } c_r \neq 0 \wedge c_{r2} \leq 0 \\
360^o - \arccos(\frac{c_{r1}}{c_r}) & \text{if } c_r \neq 0 \wedge c_{r2} > 0
\end{cases}
\end{aligned}
\tag{1}
$$

Saturation-weighted hue statistic is used as the statistical descriptors. Let $(\theta_i^2, s_i), i = 1, \ldots, n$ be n pairs of observations sampled from a population of hue and associated saturation values. Vector components from hue in Cartesian coordinates is given by $h = (\cos \theta_i^H, \sin \theta_i^H)^T$. Then saturation-weighted resultant of hue components is defined as

$$
C_s = \sum_{i=1}^{n} s_i \cos \theta_i^H, S_s = \sum_{i=1}^{n} s_i \sin \theta_i^H
\tag{2}
$$

The mean of resultant chrominance vector over n samples is

$$
\bar{\mathbf{c}}_n = (C_s/n, S_s/n)^T
\tag{3}
$$

The variation of observed chrominance vector $\mathbf{c} = s\mathbf{h}$ from its mean $\mathbf{c}_n$ is defined as a Euclidean distance in a chromatic plane

$$
D = \sqrt{(\bar{\mathbf{c}}_n - s_o \mathbf{h}_o)^T (\bar{\mathbf{c}}_n - s_o \mathbf{h}_o)}
\tag{4}
$$

where s_o and $\mathbf{h}_o$ are the observed saturation and hue vector respectively.

A simple background subtraction algorithm following [15] has been devised in [2]. A background pixel is modeled as the luminance mean μ_y and its standard deviation σ_y, with mean chrominance vector $\mathbf{c}_n$ and mean Euclidean distance σ_D between $\mathbf{c}_n$ and the observed chrominance vector. Foreground decision is taken if the following conditions are satisfied:

$$
|(y - \mu_y)| > \alpha \sigma_y \wedge \|\bar{\mathbf{c}}_n - \mathbf{c}\| > \alpha \sigma_D
\tag{5}
$$

where α is the foreground decision threshold set between 2 and 3.5.

2.2   Gaussian Mixture Model

Gaussian Mixture Model is pixel-wise segmentation model. Each pixel is modeled as independent random variable from its neighborhood. The value of a pixel over a period of time can be modeled as a random variable $\mathbf{X}$. $\mathbf{X}$ is an n-dimensional space vector (usually 3 for RGB color). This pixel value process $\mathbf{X}$ is assumed to be a mixture of K Gaussian densities (K usually assumed constant between 3 and 7) with parameter sets θ_k for each state density k, such that:

$$f_{\mathbf{X}|k}(X|k,\theta_k) = \frac{1}{(2\pi)^{n/2}|\mathbf{\Sigma}_k|^{1/2}}e^{-\frac{1}{2}(X-\mu_k)^T\mathbf{\Sigma}_k^{-1}(X-\mu_k)} \tag{6}$$

where μ_k and $\mathbf{\Sigma_k}$ are the mean and the covariance matrix of the kth density respectively. Elements of $\mathbf{X}$ are assumed independent so that $\mathbf{\Sigma_k}$ may be represented by n-dimensions diagonal matrix of variance σ_k^2. The density parameter is defined as $\theta_k = \{\mu_k, \sigma_k\}$ for a given k and total parameters for existing K densities become $\Phi = \omega_1, \ldots, \omega_K, \theta_1, \ldots, \theta_K$. The parameter ω_k represents a priory probability of density k to appear in pixel process and $\sum_{k=1}^{K}\omega_k = 1$.

Distribution of $\mathbf{X}$ can be modeled as sum of Gaussian mixture

$$f_{\mathbf{X}}(X|\Phi) = \sum_{k=1}^{K}P(k)f_{\mathbf{X}|k}(X|k,\theta_k) \tag{7}$$

where $P(k) = \omega_k$. All the parameters in Φ are needed to be estimated from observation of $\mathbf{X}$ in parallel with the estimation of hidden state k. Finding maximum likelihood from incomplete data in mixture model could be solved using expectation-minimization (EM) algorithm [13][3][2].

The GMM algorithms that we used for foreground segmentation can be outlined as follows. We will assume single dimension of $\mathbf{X}$ as every channel of color in RGB is assumed to be independent. Initially, for all K Gaussians, variances are set to high values and weights to small values. Current pixel value X_t is compared to K Gaussian distributions. Match is defined if current value is similar to mean value of a distribution within distant threshold $\lambda\sigma_k$, where λ usually between 2 and 3. This can be expressed as

$$(X_t - \mu_{k,t})^2 < \lambda^2\sigma_{k,t}^2 \tag{8}$$

If a match distribution is not found, a new distribution is created with high variance and low weight. Distributions with lowest confidence rank ($\omega_k, t/\sigma_k, t$ sorting criterion) is replaced by a newly created distribution. For a matched Gaussian, its mean and variance are updated with update algorithms from [9]. For initialization where we expected sufficient statistics, update equations are:

$$\begin{aligned}
\hat{\omega}_{k,t} &= \omega_{k,t} + \frac{1}{N+1}(P(k|X_t,\Phi) - \omega_{k,t}) \\
\hat{\mu}_{k,t} &= \mu_{k,t} + \frac{P(k|X_t,\Phi)}{\sum\limits_{i=1}^{N+1}P(k|X_i,\Phi)}(X_t - \mu_{k,t}) \\
\hat{\sigma}_{k,t}^2 &= \sigma_{k,t}^2 + \frac{P(k|X_t,\Phi)}{\sum\limits_{i=1}^{N+1}P(k|X_i,\Phi)}((X_t - \hat{\mu}_{k,t})^T(X_t - \hat{\mu}_{k,t}) - \sigma_{k,t}^2)
\end{aligned} \tag{9}$$

where

$$P(k|X_t,\Phi) = \begin{cases} 1 & \text{match} \\ 0 & \text{otherwise} \end{cases} \tag{10}$$

and $\sum_{k=1}^{K} P(k|X_i, \Phi)$ is the sum of weight K Gaussian distributions. After the initial phase, update equations switches to L recent window update equations

$$\hat{\omega}_{k,t} = \omega_{k,t} + \frac{1}{L}(P(k|X_t,\Phi) - \omega_{k,t})$$
$$\hat{\mu}_{k,t} = \mu_{k,t} + \frac{1}{L}\left(\frac{P(k|X_t,\Phi)X_t}{\hat{\omega}_{k,t}} - \mu_{k,t}\right) \quad (11)$$
$$\hat{\sigma}_{k,t}^2 = \sigma_{k,t}^2 + \frac{1}{L}\left(\frac{P(k|X_t,\Phi)(X_t-\hat{\mu}_{k,t})^2}{\hat{\omega}_{k,t}} - \sigma_{k,t}^2\right)$$

The K distributions are ordered by criterion $\omega_k, t/\sigma_k, t$ and the first B distributions are used as a model of the background

$$B = \arg\min_b \left(\sum_{k=1}^{b} \omega_k > T\right) \quad (12)$$

with T as the threshold for minimum fraction of the background model.

3   Gaussian Mixture Model in IHLS Color Space

Using IHLS statistics in mixture model is straightforward with statistical descriptors luminance and saturated-weighted hue as explained in Sect. 2.1. In this section we explain our background model, shadow detection and background maintenance.

3.1   Implementing IHLS in Mixture Model

Luminance y is one-dimensional GMM with density parameters $\theta_y = \{\mu_y, \sigma_y\}$ which have been explained in Sect. 2.2. While chrominance vector, using circular statistics, has density parameters $\theta_c = \{\bar{c}_n, \sigma_D\}$. Match criteria for chrominance can be expressed in Euclidean distance as in (4).

$$\|\bar{c}_n - c\| < \lambda^2 \sigma_D^2 \quad (13)$$

Using luminance and chrominance statistics, a match is defined if both (8) and (13) condition are true.

$$(y - \mu_y)^2 < \lambda^2 \sigma_y^2 \wedge \|\bar{c}_n - c\| < \lambda^2 \sigma_D^2 \quad (14)$$

The whole of GMM process outlined in Sect. 2.2 applies directly to chrominance vector θ_c with minor modification in update equation (see(9) and (11))

$$\hat{\bar{c}}_{k,t} = \bar{c}_{k,t} + \frac{P(k|X_t,\Phi)}{\sum\limits_{i=1}^{N+1} P(k|X_i,\Phi)}(c - \bar{c}_{k,t})$$
$$\hat{\sigma}_{D(k,t)}^2 = \sigma_{D(k,t)}^2 + \frac{P(k|X_t,\Phi)}{\sum\limits_{i=1}^{N+1} P(k|X_i,\Phi)}(\|\bar{c}_n - c\|^2 - \sigma_{D(k,t)}^2) \quad (15)$$

$$\hat{\bar{c}}_{k,t} = \bar{c}_{k,t} + \frac{1}{L}\left(\frac{P(k|X_t,\Phi)c}{\hat{\omega}_{k,t}} - \bar{c}_{k,t}\right)$$
$$\hat{\sigma}_{D(k,t)}^2 = \sigma_{D(k,t)}^2 + \frac{1}{L}\left(\frac{P(k|X_t,\Phi)\|\bar{c}_n - c\|^2}{\hat{\omega}_{k,t}} - \sigma_{D(k,t)}^2\right) \quad (16)$$

3.2   Shadow Detection

From empirical observation of shadow cast on background objects, it can be concluded that shadows cause a darkening of background pixel or decrease the luminance but they do not affect saturation-weighted hue vector. In IHLS color space, this result can be formulated by the following equation

$$y < \mu_y \wedge |y - \mu_y| < \beta\mu_y,$$
$$||\mathbf{h}s - \bar{\mathbf{c}}_n|| < \tau_{hs}$$

(17)

Equation (17) can be applied directly to suppress shadow after an initial foreground mask has been obtained from GMM with reference values μ_y and $\mathbf{c}_n$ are taken from background model. The threshold constant β is used to take into account the predominant light source [2] while the threshold τ_{hs} is used to differentiate foreground object's hue from shadow because shadow is not affecting hue value of background pixel. Both thresholds are determined empirically. Note that (17) is different from [2] since we do not performing test for saturation. Our empirical observation shows that shadow did not affect saturation as it did not affect hue. To refine segmentation, we apply morphological filter and small area threshold to remove small blobs generated by noise and connected component analysis to fill holes in foreground regions.

3.3   Background Maintenance

In [14], Wallflower utilized frame level maintenance with two states background model to handle sudden changes in global illumination presented as light switch problem. Our approach for background maintenance in frame level is to reinitialize background model using the latest observed pixel value. As in Wallflower, decision is taken by monitoring fraction of foreground pixels in image. If this fraction exceeds a fixed threshold (we used 0.7), background model is reinitialized. Another problems might be occurred in indoor environment is global illumination changes caused by moving foreground objects. During such condition, luminance value changes significantly but chrominance components remains similar under the match criterion (see (13)). Thus, the luminance component will be ignored and only chrominance components are used for match decision.

4   Experimental Result

In practice, there are many challenges for a well performing background segmentation system. Several typical problems found in indoor or outdoor scene during segmentation are discussed in [14]. They also provided several test sequence to represent foreground segmentation problems known as Wallflower datasets. We compare our approach with another two color model in GMM schema: normalized RGB (nRGB) and RGB-only-model available from OpenCV library which did not detect shadow, using Wallflower datasets. However, Wallflower datasets did not test for shadow detection scenario. We used videos from ATON project,

VSSN-Challenge and our own test sequence to compare shadow detection result qualitatively. For normalized RGB model, we used same steps as IHLS model, but we did not change anything for RGB model from OpenCV library. Definition and shadow decision for normalized RGB are taken from [2].

Brief explanation for the Wallflower sequences is as follows: **Moved Object (MO)**: Background object is moved. **Time of Day (TD)**: Gradual illumination changes alter the background. **Light Switch (LS)**: Sudden changes in the global illumination. **Waving Trees (WT)**: dynamic background scene. **Camouflage (C)**: Foreground object's pixel similar with the background model. **Bootstrapping (B)**: Busy scene with no empty scene for background model training. **Foreground Aperture (FA)**: A homogeneously colored object moves thus change in interior may not be detected. Performance of algorithms is evaluated by calculating False Positive (FP), False Negative (FN) and Total Errors (TE). FP is number of background pixel marked wrongly as foreground. FN is number of foreground pixel marked wrongly as background. TE is the sum of total errors (FP+FN) from seven available image sequences.

Table 1 and Fig. 1 show the result obtained by GMM in IHLS color space (GMM-IHLS), GMM in normalized RGB space (GMM-nRGB), GMM in standard RGB space (GMM-RGB) and results from several algorithms reported in [14]. From Table 1 and Fig. 1 we can see that our approach gives better result than normalized RGB and RGB color model when applied in Gaussian mixture model. We obtained better segmentation result for **TD** sequence compared to several algorithms reported in [14].

Table 1. Performance of algorithms on Wallflower test sequences. The first three rows are from our evaluation; the fourth to the seven rows are results reported in [14].

Algorithm	Error Type	MO	TD	LS	WT	C	B	FA	TE
GMM-IHLS	False Neg	0	379	1146	31	188	1647	2327	9739
	False Pos	0	99	2298	270	467	333	554	
GMM-nRGB	False Neg	0	628	1984	1961	170	2105	2157	27736
	False Pos	0	72	15766	83	767	404	1639	
GMM-RGB	False Neg	0	1548	621	593	162	2264	962	41197
	False Pos	217	634	15346	288	5888	192	12482	
GMM [14]	False Neg	0	1008	1633	1323	398	1874	2422	24081
	False Pos	0	20	14169	341	3098	217	530	
Bayesian [14]	False Neg	0	1018	2380	629	1538	2143	2511	26937
	False Pos	0	562	13439	334	2130	2764	1974	
Eigen [14]	False Neg	0	879	962	1027	350	304	2441	14699
	False Pos	1065	16	362	2057	1548	6129	537	
Wallflower [14]	False Neg	0	961	947	877	229	2025	320	10509
	False Pos	0	25	375	1999	2706	365	649	

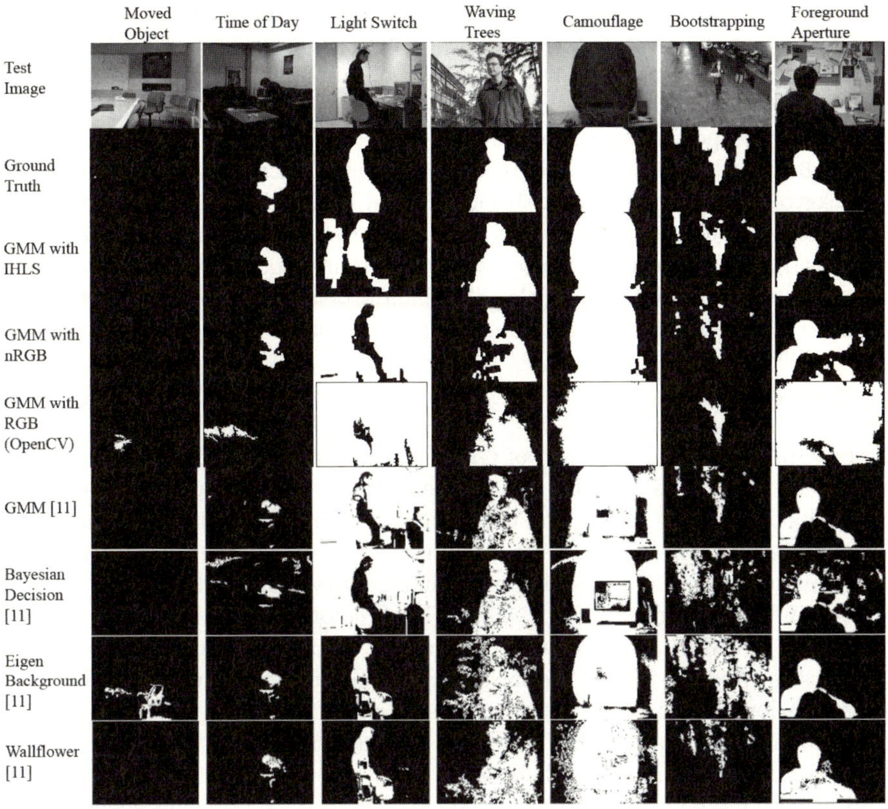

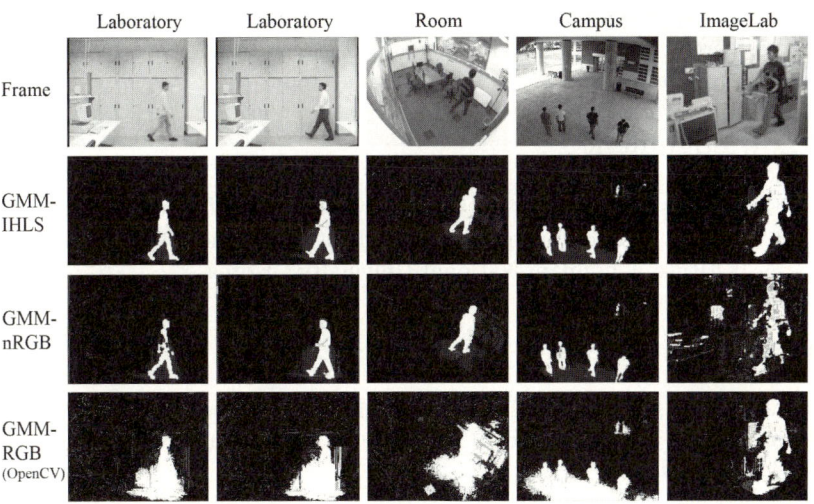

Fig. 1. Wallflower datasets results

Fig. 2. Shadow detection results

Figure 2 shows the results for shadow detection scenario. Red colored pixels are classified as shadow and noise from sequences while cyan pixels are holes area inside foreground contour and will be filled to obtain final foreground mask. Since RGB color space is illumination variant, it cannot not detect shadow directly and gives poor performance compared to improved HLS and normalized RGB space when used in mixture models. Comparison of IHLS with normalized RGB in background segmentation has been reported in [2] with IHLS showed better results and has higher sensitivity to color changes and less sensitivity to noise. We have shown similar result with Gaussian mixture models thus we have added adaptive nature of mixture models with shadow detection capability and better sensitivity for color changes by using IHLS color space.

5   Conclusion

We have proposed a new variant of GMM oriented toward human silhouette extraction by directly using IHLS color space as statistical descriptors. Experimental results on datasets show good foreground segmentation and we have achieved our purpose which is segmentation of human silhouette. Performance evaluation with Wallflower benchmark shows promising results compared to other popular background modeling methods. GMM in IHLS color space has shown better results than in nRGB for shadowed background scenes. By directly using IHLS statistics in Mixture Model, we have avoided additional calculation needed to detect shadowed background at small cost for RGB to IHLS space conversion. By combining GMM and IHLS, we obtain adaptive background model with good sensitivity to color changes and shadow.

Pixel-wise model for segmentation suffers from several problems such as foreground aperture and highly dynamic background scene because it neglects spatial relations between pixels. Current model can be improved by adding spatial correlation using graph-cut method in Bayesian modeling as proposed in [12]. In further research, our foreground segmentation algorithms will be implemented in surveillance and human robot interaction system.

Acknowledgement

This research has been supported by research funding of "Development of humanoid technology based on network, KIST, Korea , and Culture Technology Research Institute, Chonnam National University , Korea .

References

1. Al-Mazeed, A., Nixon, M., Gunn, S.: Classifier combination for improved motion segmentation. In: International Conference on Image Analysis and Recognition, Porto, Portugal. (2004)
2. Blauensteiner, P., Wildenauer, Horst., Hanbury A., Kampel, M.: On colour spaces for change detection and shadow suppression. Computer Vision Winter Workshop 2006, Ond ř ej Chum, Vojt ě ch Franc (eds.) Tel č, Czech Republic. (2006)

3. Friedman, N., Russell, S.: Image segmentation in video sequences: a probabilistic approach. In: Proceedings of UAI97. (1997) 175-181
4. Horprasert, T., Harwood, D., Davis, L.: A statistical approach for real-time robust background subtraction and shadow detection. In: Proceedings of International Conference on Computer Vision (ICCV'99). (1999) 1-19
5. Hanbury, A., Serra, J.: A 3D-polar coordinate colour representation suitable for image analysis. Technical Report PRIP-TR-77, PRIP, T.U. Wien. (2002)
6. Harville, M.: A framework for high-level feedback to adaptive, per-pixel, mixture-of-Gaussian background models. In: Proceedings of the 7th European Conference on Computer Vision, Copenhagen, Denmark. (2002) 543-560
7. Harville, M., Gordon, G., Woodfill, J.: Foreground segmentation using adaptive mixture models in color and depth. In: Proceedings of the IEEE Workshop on Detection and Recognition of Events in Video, Vancouver, Canada. (2001) 3-11
8. Javed, O., Shafique, K., Shah, M.: A Hierarchical approach to robust background subtraction using color and gradient information. In: Proceedings of the IEEE Workshop on Motion and Computing. (2002)
9. KaewTraKulPong, P., Bowden, R.: An improved adaptive background mixture model for real-time tracking with shadow detection. In: 2nd European Workshop on Advanced Video-based Surveillance Systems. (2001)
10. Porikli, F.M., Tuzel, O.: Human body tracking by adaptive background models and Mean-shift analysis. IEEE International Workshop on Performance Evaluation of Tracking and Surveillance. (2003)
11. Power, P.W., Schoones, J.A: Understanding background mixture model for foreground segmentation. In: Proceedings of Image and Vision Computing New Zeland. (2002)
12. Shah, M., Sheikh, Y.: Bayesian Modeling of Dynamic Scenes for Object Detection. IEEE Transactions on Pattern Analysis and Machine Intelligence **27** (2005) 1778-1792
13. Stauffer, C., Grimson, W.E.L.: Adaptive background mixture models for real-time tracking. In: Proceedings IEEE Conference on Computer Vision and Pattern Recognition. (1999) 246-252
14. Toyama, K., Krumm, J., Brummit, B., Meyers, B.: Wallflower: Principles and practice of background maintenance. International Conference on Computer Vision, Corfu, Greece. (1999)
15. Wren, C.R., Azarbayejani, A., Darrell, T., Pentland, A.: Pfinder: Real-time tracking of the human body. IEEE Transactions on Pattern Analysis and Machine Intelligence. **19** (1997) 780-785

Geometry Compression Using Spherical Wavelet

Guojun Peng[1], Jiawan Tan[2,3], Zhigeng Pan[2], and Yicheng Jin[3]

[1] Jimei University, Xiamen, China, 361021
[2] State Key Laboratory of CAD&CG at Zhejiang University, Hangzhou, China, 310027
[3] Navigational Dynamic Simulation & Control Laboratory at Dalian Maritime University,
Dalian, China, 116026
penggj1314@126.com

Abstract. This paper proposed a novel geometry compression method using spherical wavelet. Given a manifold triangle mesh with zero genus and arbitrary topology, it is globally parameterized over the unit sphere S2 in E3 firstly. At the same time, by subdividing an icosahedron and projecting all its vertices onto the unit sphere from the center, we can get a spherical triangle mesh with subdivision topology. Then we re-sampling all signals defined on the surface of the original triangle mesh at the vertices of the spherical subdivision mesh and get a set of discrete geometry signals with subdivision topology which can be compressed by using spherical wavelet.

Keywords: Geometry compression, Spherical wavelet, Subdivision re-meshing, Mesh parameterization.

1 Introduction

Geometry compression has been a hot topic in computer graphics for a decade. Since M. Deering proposed geometry compression firstly in 1995, researchers have made a lot of progress in this field, and various literatures have been reported from then on.

Traditional geometry compression methods mainly focus on the topology of meshes, little attention has been paid to the geometry of meshes itself, such as coordinates of vertices, texture coordinates, BRDF, color and normal of meshes, etc., most of the existing methods overlooked the importance of geometry information compression, or just treat this process as a byproduct of topology coding. Given a triangle mesh with complicated details defined on its surface, effective compression of geometry data seems more important than that of topology, since the geometry data is much more fat than that of topology.

The method described in this paper treats all kind of geometry signals in a unified manner, and there is no need to compress the topology of meshes.

2 Mesh Parameterization

Parameterization is essentially a 1-to-1 map between the parameter domain U and curves L or surface S in E^3, where E^3 stands for the 3D Euclidian space. For parameter curves or surfaces, there is a natural parameterization

Z. Pan et al. (Eds.): ICAT 2006, LNCS 4282, pp. 742–752, 2006.

$$L(u), S(u,v), u \in [a,b], v \in [c,d] \tag{1}$$

Since surfaces are usually presented as a polygonal meshes in computer graphics, especially triangle meshes, we replace symbol S with M hereafter, where M stands for a triangle mesh.

For a given arbitrary triangle mesh, it is a challenge to find a global parameterization for it, but piecewise parameterization are often adopted, then parameterizing a mesh becomes the process of finding this piecewise parameterization.

Let $M = \{V, K\}$ and $M' = \{V', K'\}$ are two triangle meshes and isomorphic to each other, where V and V' are vertex sets of M and M', K and K' are complexes of M and M' respectively, which means that there exists a isomorphic map $\Pi : M \to M'$ that maps $\forall k \in M$ to one and only one element $k' \in M'$, we will show that a homeomorphic map Γ can be deduced from Π and the reverse Γ^{-1} of Γ is just the parameterization of M over M'. Γ can be obtained as follows.

Let triangle $\triangle \Pi(A) \Pi(B) \Pi(C) \in K'$ is the image of $\triangle ABC \in K$ under Π, then for $\forall p \in \triangle ABC$ with barycentric coordinates (α, β, γ) meet $\alpha + \beta + \gamma = 1 (0 \le \partial, \beta, \gamma \le 1)$, we define Γ as $\Gamma(p) = \alpha \Pi(A) + \beta \Pi(B) + \gamma \Pi(C)$, it is clear that $\Gamma : M \to M'$ is a continuous 1-to-1 map, and

$$\Gamma^{-1}(\Gamma(P)) = \alpha \Pi^{-1}(\Pi(A)) + \beta \Pi^{-1}(\Pi(B)) + \gamma \Pi^{-1}(\Pi(C)) \tag{2}$$

From the definition we know that Γ^{-1} is a piecewise linear map, and Γ^{-1} can be regarded as the parameterization of M over M'.

According to the above, parameterizing M comes down to the process of constructing the isomorphic mesh M'. We proposed a simple whereas effective and robust progressive parameterizing method, in which the idea of progressive mesh[20] is adopted, the whole process is accomplished by two steps.

Given a triangle mesh M, it is converted to a progressive representation

$$M = M_n \xrightarrow{eco\ln-1} M_{n-1} \cdots \xrightarrow{ecol1} M_1 \xrightarrow{ecol0} M_0 \tag{3}$$

firstly, then the original mesh can be restored as follows

$$M_0 \xrightarrow{vsplit_0} M_1 \cdots \xrightarrow{vsplit_{n-2}} M_{n-1} \xrightarrow{vsplit_{n-1}} M_n = M \tag{4}$$

where $\{ecol_0, \cdots, ecol_{n-1}\}$ and $\{vsplit_0, \cdots, vsplit_{n-1}\}$ are edge two series of edge collapse operations and vertex split operations respective, and both reverse to each other. As illustrated in figure 1, let two vertices v_1 and v_2 are merged to the new vertex v in some edge collapse operation, what makes different is that it is required to parameterize the merged vertices v_1 and v_2 in the neighborhood of v. Let $Star(v)$ stands for the first ring neighborhood of v, $\triangle v_1$ and $\triangle v_2$ stand for the triangles adjacent to v_1 and v_2 before edge collapse respectively, then v_1 and v_2 can be parameterized by simply project them on to $Star(v)$, the projecting operators are given bellow.

$$p_1 = Pv_1 = \{P|P \in \Delta v_1, \rho(v1, P) = \rho(v1, \Delta v_1)\}$$
$$p_2 = Pv_2 = \{P|P \in \Delta v_2, \rho(v_2, P) = \rho(v_2, \Delta v_2)\}$$

(5)

Where P is Hausdorff distance. When Δv_1 or Δv_2 is empty, we use $Star(v)$ instead.

By applying one edge collapse operation on M, a simplified version of M can be obtained, this process is recursively carried out till we get a convex mesh M_0. Then M_0 is spherical projected onto a sphere from its center, and the merged vertices are added to M_0 using the local parameterizaiton information recorded when edge collapse one by one according to a reverse order that they are deleted, after each vertex is added back, it is spherically projected onto the sphere to ensure that we can get a spherical mesh at any step, this process is carried out till all the vertices have been added back, thus we can get a spherical triangle mesh which is isomorphic to M, and noted as M_p.

To avoid foldovers during the process of restoration, the Laplace operator can be used.

$$L(x_i) = \Delta x_i = \sum_{j \in i^*} w_{ij}(x_j - x_i), i \in \{1, 2, \cdots, n\}, x = \{x_1, x_2, \cdots, x_n\}^T$$
$$V' = V + \Delta V = \{v_i'|v_i' = v_i + \Delta v_i, \Delta v_i = L(v_i)\}$$

(6)

Where i* stands for the vertices that adjacent to vertex i, w_{ij} isconvex combination coefficient that meet $w_{ij} > 0$ and $\sum_{j \in i^*} w_{ij} = 1$, w_{ij} can simply using $w_{ij} = 1/d$, where d is the degree of vertex i.

As a replace of Laplace operator, the relaxation operator can also be used.

$$R(x_i) = \frac{1}{d} \sum_{j \in i^*} x_j, i \in \{1, 2, \cdots, n\},$$

(7)

3 Subdivision Resampling of Geometry Signals

What makes our method different from others is that we tread all geometry data in a same manner, not only shape of meshes, but also normal, colors, texture coordinates, etc.

3.1 Geometry Signal

Geometry signals are defined as all kinds of vector-valued or scalar-valued signals defined on the surfaces of objects in E^3. In computer graphics, geometry signals are always defined as a set of surface attributes defined at the vertices of triangle meshes, noted as A_M. A_M can be spanned to form a vector-valued piecewise linear function space F_M, the element of space F_M is a certain kind of continuous attribute defined all over the surface. For any point $p \in M$, F_M can be defined as following.

$$F_M(p) = Span(A_M)(p) =$$
$$\begin{cases} A_M(p) & p = \{i\} \in K_M \\ \alpha A_M(i) + \beta A_M(j) + \gamma A_M(k), & p \in \{i, j, k\} \in K_M, \\ \text{with barycentric coordinates}(\alpha, \beta, \gamma) \end{cases}$$

(8)

3.2 Resampling

The process of subdivision resampling is straightforward since we have got the spherical parameterization of M. It is started from a regular polyhedron. Given an regular polyhedron, such as icosahedron, it is firstly spherically projected onto the sphere that was used for the parameterization, then recursively 1-to-4 subdivision is applied on it untill the sampling points is dense enough to meet the requirement of Naiquist sampling theorem (see Figure 2). We call this subdivided mesh sampling mesh and note it as M_s.

After each subdivision, the newly inserted vertices are spherically projected to guarantee that the subdivided mesh is a spherical mesh. The re-sampling of geometry signal is just happened on the vertices of sampling mesh M_s thus assuring that the re-sampled signal has a subdivision structure. Let P is a vertex of M_s, and it is within a certain triangle $\triangle ABC$ of M_p with barycentric coordinates (α, β, γ), then its image $p' = \Gamma^{-1}(p)$ under Γ^{-1} must be within a triangle $\triangle A'B'C'$ of M, and $p' = \alpha A' + \beta B' + \gamma C'$. We take $F_M(p')$ as the signal defined at point P, as a result, we get a set of discrete spherical signals F_s defined on the vertices of M_s which has subdivision structure.

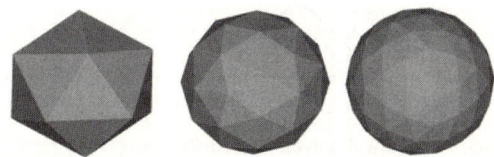

Fig. 1. 1-to-4 subdivision of polyhedron

3.3 Automatic Distribution of Sampling Points

The quality of the parameterization affects the sampling result greatly. A good parameterization should be homogen- eous , since it is very difficult to parameterizing a complex triangle mesh over the sphere, we can only get an approximation of it instead. Caused by distortion of parameterization, the spectrum of F_s has been changed a lot comparing to that of F_M . From the point of energy, the energy of spectrum of F_s will bunch up in the high frequency area while with sparse energy distributed in the low frequency area.

According to Nyquist sampling theorem, to capture all the energy of F_M , the sampling rate must dense enough, that always means the subdivision depth of M_s must be deep enough to meet this requirement at high frequency area. We propose a automatic method to redistribute the vertices of M_s so that less subdivision depth are required without loss of sampling precision.

The vertex distribution density in the neighborhood of vertex $\{i\}$ is defined as

$$D_M(i) = \frac{|N(i)+1| \cdot Area(M)}{|V| \cdot \sum_{\Delta \in T(i)} Area(\Delta)},\qquad(9)$$

where $|V|$ is the number of vertices of M , $N(i)$ is the degree of $\{i\}$, $Area(M)$ is the sum of the area of all triangles of M ,

By this definition, two isomorphic meshes M and M' are considered having the same vertex density if

$$\frac{1}{|V|}\sum_{i=0}^{|V|}\left|D_{M'}\left(\Pi_{M\to M'}(\{i\})\right) - D_M(\{i\})\right| < \varepsilon,\qquad(10)$$

where ε is the specified error threshold.

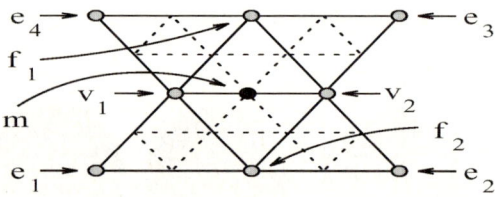

Fig. 2. Neighbors used in spherical wavelet transform $\left(m \in M(j), \{v_1, v_2, f_1, f_2, e_1, e_2, e_3, e_4\} = K_m\right)$

The main task is to redistribute the vertices of M_s to make it has almost the same vertex distribution of M_p . We adopt a progressive and heuristic manner, that is to carry out the distribution operation each time M_s is subdivided, not only on the final mesh, thus improved the performance of the redistribution operator. For a vertex $^{\{i\}}$, we use the following operator to calculate its new position $P'(i)$

$$P'(i) = \frac{1}{W(i)} \left(\sum_{j=0}^{D(i)} w(j) \times P(j) + w(i)P(i) \right), \tag{11}$$

where $P(i)$ and $P'(i)$ are the original position and new position of $^{\{i\}}$ respectively, $D(i)$ is the degree of vertex $^{\{i\}}$, $W(i)$ and $w(i)$ and can be calculated by

$$W(i) = \sum_{j=0}^{N(i)} w(j) + w(i) \quad and$$

$$w(i) = \sum_{T_j \in Star(i)} N(T_j), \tag{12}$$

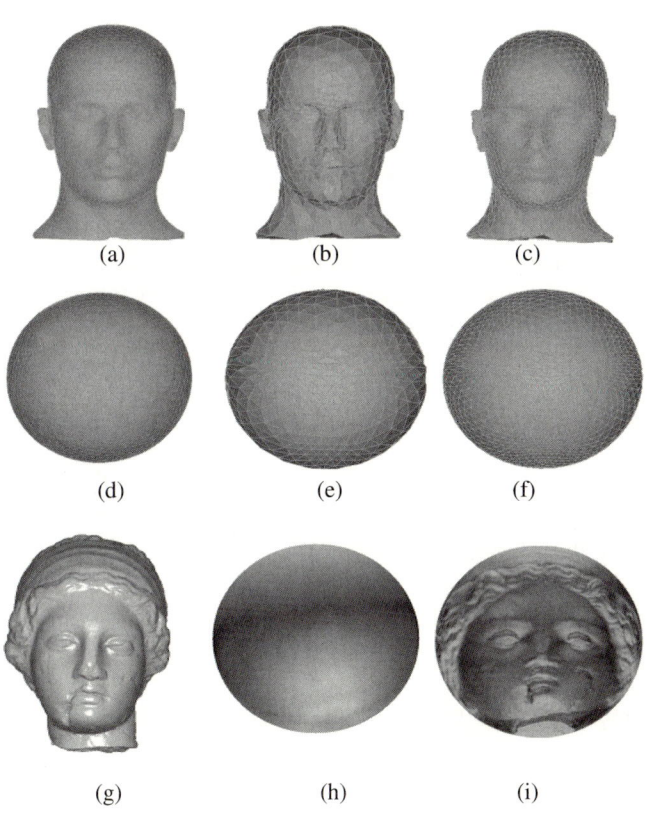

(a)   (b)   (c)

(d)   (e)   (f)

(g)   (h)   (i)

Fig. 3. (a) the original mesh. (b) and (c) are the re-sampling of shape of (a) with a sampling mesh (e) and (f) respectively, (d) is parameterization mesh of (a), (e) and (f) are sampling mesh for (b) and (c). (g), (h) and (i) are venus and its shape and normal signal resamping respectively.

where T_j is the $j-th$ triangle adjacent to vertex $\{i\}$, $N(T_j)$ is the number of vertices of M_p contained in T_j of M_s.

This process is illustrated as in Figure 3, from which we can understand the way that vertex distribution of sampling mesh imitates that of the parameterization mesh.

4 Second and Following Pages

4.1 Geometry Signal Decomposition

In this step, the Re-sampled discrete spherical geometry signal F_s is decomposed using spherical wavelet, the result is a set of wavelet coefficients, which are the input of the succedent coder.

As mentioned above, prediction is an effective method for geometry compression. Wavelet decomposition is somewhat a kind of prediction in essence, the difference is the way that the predictor behaves.

Before dashing into the description of the wavelet analysis, we would like to state the index convention we used hereafter firstly. Let $K(j)$ to be a general index set that $K(j) \subset K(j+1)$ and $M(j) = K(j+1) \setminus K(j)$, indices will be used consistently in the sense that $k \in K(j)$, $l \in K(j+1)$, and $m \in M(j)$. As it comes to subdivision triangle meshes, the index set has a more concrete meaning as illustrated in figure4.

We take the vertex based scheme of spherical wavelet for wavelet analysis and synthesis[42]. As a kind of interpolating wavelet, applying spherical wavelet analysis on signals defined on the sphere is equal to the process of converting $n = 2^{j_1}$ samplings $\left\{ \beta_{j_1, k}, k = 0, \cdots, 2^{j_1} - 1 \right\}$ of the finest level into $n = 2^{j_1}$ coefficients $\left((\beta_{j_0 \cdot}), (\alpha_{j_0 \cdot}), (\alpha_{j_0+1 \cdot}), \cdots, (\alpha_{j_1-1 \cdot}) \right)$, where j_1 is the finest level and j_0 is the coarsest level.

For interpolating scaling functions, the dual scaling functions can be take to be Dirac distributions, this leads to trivial inner products of a function with the duals, namely evaluation of the function at the points $x_{j,k}$, that is

$$\lambda_{j,k} = \left\langle f(x), \tilde{\varphi}_{j,k}(x) \right\rangle = f\left(x_{j,k}\right)$$

So, for unlifted interpolating wavelet transforming, the analysis is accomplished by recursively applying higher pass filter $\tilde{H}$ and lower pass filter $\tilde{G}$ on a set of samplings $(\lambda_{j+1,k \cdot})$ of level $j+1$ into a set of samplings $(\lambda_{j, \cdot})$ of level j and wavelet coefficients $(\gamma_{j,m \cdot})$, and $(\gamma_{j,m \cdot})$ can be considered as the difference of the real value $\lambda_{j+1,m}$ at point $x_{j+1,m}$ and its prediction $\sum_{k \in K_m} \tilde{s}_{j,k,m} \lambda_{j,k}$.

AnalysisI(j):
$$\forall k \in K(j): \quad \lambda_{j,k} := \lambda_{j+1,k}$$
$$\forall m \in M(j): \quad \gamma_{j,m} := \lambda_{j+1,k} - \sum_{k \in K_m} \tilde{s}_{j,k,m} \lambda_{j,k}$$

SynthesisII(j):
$$\hspace{8cm}(13)$$
$$\forall k \in K(j): \quad \lambda_{j+1,k} := \lambda_{j,k}$$
$$\forall m \in M(j): \quad \gamma_{j+1,m} := \lambda_{j,k} + \sum_{k \in K_m} \tilde{s}_{j,k,m} \lambda_{j,k}$$

P. Schröder et al investigated several wavelet transforming schemes in their literature, those are lazy, linear, quadric and butterfly scheme respectively.

Lazy: The Lazy wavelet does nothing but subsampling. The result of the analysis and synthesis steps become

Analysis: $\lambda_{j,k} = j_{j+1,k}$, $\gamma_{j,m} = \lambda_{j+1,m}$ $\hspace{4cm}$ (14)

Synthesis: $\lambda_{j+1,m} = \gamma_{j,m}$, $\lambda_{j+1,k} = \lambda_{j,k}$ $\hspace{4cm}$ (15)

Linear: The scaling coefficients (approximation part) are subsampled and kept unchanged, the coefficients of finer resolution are predicted by linear interpolation:

$$\hspace{10cm}(16)$$
Analysis: $\lambda_{j,k} = j_{j+1,k}$, $\gamma_{j,m} = \lambda_{j+1,m} - \frac{1}{2}\left(\lambda_{j+1,v_1} + \lambda_{j+1,v_2}\right)$

Synthesis: $\lambda_{j+1,k} = \lambda_{j,k}$, $\lambda_{j+1,m} = \gamma_{j,m} + \frac{1}{2}\left(\gamma_{j,v1} + \gamma_{j,v_2}\right)$ $\hspace{2cm}$ (17)

Quadratic: The stencil for this basis is given by $K_m = \{v1, v2, f1, f2\}$ (see Figure 4) and exploits the degrees of freedom implied to kill the functions x^2, y^2 and z^2 (and by implication the constant function [1]). Using the coordinates of the neighbors of the involved sites a small linear system results

$$\begin{pmatrix} 1 & 1 & 1 & 1 \\ x^2_{j,v_1} & x^2_{j,v_2} & x^2_{j,f_1} & x^2_{j,f_2} \\ y^2_{j,v_1} & y^2_{j,v_2} & y^2_{j,f_1} & y^2_{j,f_2} \\ z^2_{j,v_1} & y^2_{j,v_2} & y^2_{j,f_1} & z^2_{j,f_2} \end{pmatrix} \begin{pmatrix} \tilde{s}_{j,v_1,m} \\ \tilde{s}_{j,v_2,m} \\ \tilde{s}_{j,f_1,m} \\ \tilde{s}_{j,f_2,m} \end{pmatrix} = \begin{pmatrix} 1 \\ x^2_{j+1,m} \\ y^2_{j+1,m} \\ z^2_{j+1,m} \end{pmatrix} \hspace{1cm}(18)$$

Since $x^2 + y^2 + z^2 = 1$ this system is singular (but solvable) and the answer is chosen so as to minimize the l2 norm of the resulting filter coefficients. Note that this is an instance of dual lifting with effective filters $\tilde{}$

Butterfly: This is the only basis which uses other than immediate neighbors (all the sites K_m denoted in Figure 4). Here $\tilde{s}_{v1} = \tilde{s}_{v2} = 1/2$, $\tilde{s}_{f1} = \tilde{s}_{f2} = 1/8$, and $\tilde{s}_{e1} = \tilde{s}_{e2} = \tilde{s}_{e3} = \tilde{s}_{e4} = -1/16$. It is inspired by a subdivision scheme of Dyn et al.[11] for the construction of smooth surfaces.

All of the above bases can be lifted to assure that the wavelets have at least on vanishing moment thus results in smaller error when being used for compression. The lifted wavelets take a form of

$$\psi_{j,m} = \varphi_{j+1,m} - s_{j,v_1,m}\varphi_{j,v_1} - s_{j,v_2,m}\varphi_{j,v_2} \tag{19}$$

the weights $s_{j,k,m}$ are chosen so that the resulting wavelet has a vanishing integral

$$s_{j,k,m} = I_{j+1,m}/2I_{j,k} \ , \ \ I_{j,k} = \int_{s^2} \varphi_{j,k} dw \tag{20}$$

Lifting can be regarded as the second step of wavelet transform

AnalysisII(j):

$$\forall m \in M(j): \ \begin{cases} \lambda_{j,v_1} += s_{j,v_1,m}\gamma_{j,m} \\ \lambda_{j,v_2} += s_{j,v_2,m}\gamma_{j,m} \end{cases} \tag{21}$$

SynthesisI(j):

$$\forall m \in M(j): \ \begin{cases} \lambda_{j,v_1} -= s_{j,v_1,m}\gamma_{j,m} \\ \lambda_{j,v_2} -= s_{j,v_2,m}\gamma_{j,m} \end{cases} \tag{22}$$

Since butterfly base is proved to be the most effective ones, we adopted it in our experiment. Figure 4 illustrated the distribution of the shape signals and their wavelet coefficients of venus and rabit models respectively. From which we can see that most wavelets are very small that can be represented by very short bits.

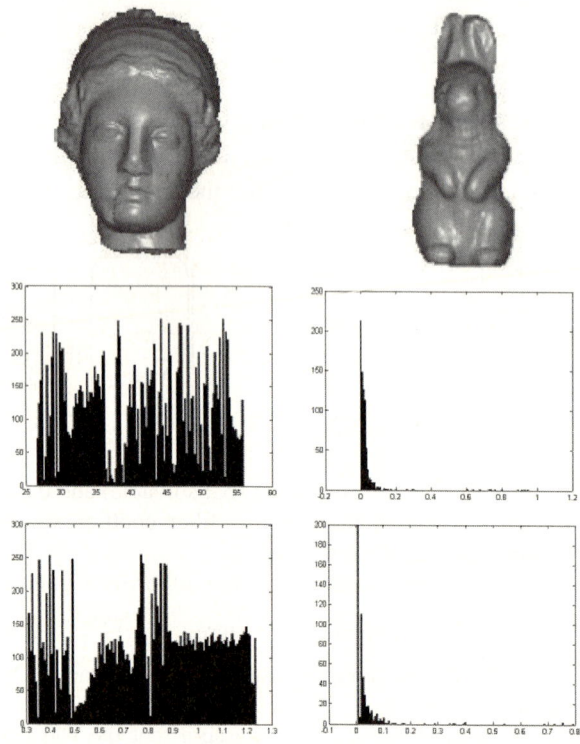

Fig. 4. Distribution of shape signals and their wavelet coefficients of venus and rabit. The middle two are the distribution of shape signal and wavelets of venus model respectively, and the lower two are that of the rabit.model.

4.2 Quantifying and Coding of Wavelet Coefficients

As the result of wavelet transform, we got a series of coefficients $\left\{ \left(\lambda_{j_0,k} \bullet \right), \left(\gamma_{j_0,m} \bullet \right), \cdots, \left(\gamma_{j_1-1,m} \bullet \right) \right\}$, most of them are small enough that have little contribution when restoring the original signal by reverse wavelet transform thus can be ignored or represented by more fewer bits after quantification. By applying reverse wavelet transform on the coefficients the original signal can be restored. Therefore, compression of geometry signal comes down to the problem of compression the wavelet coefficients, this is accomplished by quantification followed by further entropy coding.

Quantification is an effective manner for data compression that is to represent data with smaller number of bits. Wavelet coefficients are commonly represented in computer as single or double precision float number of 32 bits or 64 bits for each, which can represent distances that range from microns to the whole universe known by human at present. In practice, a much coarser precision of representation can meet the requirements of most applications. That is why quantification is called for.

Quantification can be looked as a kind of lossy compression, the error introduced by quantification greatly depends on the levels of it, which are determined by the number of bits used by the quantifier, more levels result in less error. For the sake of simplicity, even quantification is adopted in our scheme. The output bits string is further entropy coded using arithmetic coding to improve coding efficiency.

4.3 Reconstruction of Geometry Signal

The reconstruction process is somewhat straightforward, it is just the reverse process of compression. It begins with a icosahedron as the initial mesh, which is then subdivided to a depth that is the same as that of the sampling mesh, as a result, the sampling mesh is reconstructed. By this means, there is no need to store the sampling mesh for reconstruction of the original signals. This is very important for shape compression, since there is no need to store a base mesh as that of progressive mesh, we can restore the original mesh only with the wavelet coefficients.

Once the sampling mesh is reconstructed, the wavelet coefficients are loaded in a vertex-based manner according to the order when they are stored, depth first or width first are both permitted, then by doing a reverse wavelet transforming, the original signals can be reconstructed.

5   Results and Discussions

To validate our algorithm, we test it with some standard model, the error metric used here is the sum of the errors between the reconstructed signals and the original signals at each vertex. It can be concluded that spherical wavelet is very powerful for geometry compression since most geometry signals are smooth. We can also find that it is more effective for dense meshes, but for sparse meshes, it is of less predominance. Another advantage of our method is that we need not store any other information but the wavelet coefficients, which leads to universal means for different signals, such as shape, normal, color and texture coordinates and any other likely signals.

References

1. M.Eck,   T.DeRose,   T.Duchamp,   H.Hoppe,   M.Loundsbery   and   W.Stuetzle.
   "Multiresolution analysis of arbitrary meshes"[A]. In Proc.of SIGGRAPH'95[C], Los
   Angeles, USA, August 6-11, 1995, pp173-182.
2. M.S.Floater. "Parameterization and Smooth Interpolation in Geometric Modeling"[J].
   ACM Trans.Computer Graphics, 1997, 8(2): 121-144.
3. M.S.Floater, M.Reimers. "Meshless Parameterization and Surface Reconstruction"[J].
   Computer Aided Geometric Design, 2001, 18(2):77-92.
4. M.S.Floater. "Parameterization and Smooth Approximation of Design", 1997, 14(3):231-
   250.
5. K.Hormann, G.Greiner. "MIPS: An Efficient Global Parameterization Method"[C]. In
   Curve and Surface Design: Saint-Malo 1999(2000), P.-J. Laurent, P. Sablonnière, and L.
   L. Schumaker, Eds., Vanderbilt University Press, Tennessee, USA, 2000, pp219-226.
6. U.Labsik, K.Hormann, G.Greiner. "Using Most Isometric Parameterizations for
   Remeshing Polygonal Surfaces"[A]. In Proc. of Geometric modeling and processing,
   Hong Kong, April 10-12, 2000, pp220-228.
7. U.Labsik, K.Hormann, G.Greiner. "Using Most Isometric Parameterizations for
   Remeshing Polygonal Surfaces"[A]. In Proc. of Geometric modeling and processing,
   Hong Kong, April 10-12, 2000, pp220-228.
8. J.R.Kent, W.E.Carlson, R.E.Parent. "Shape Transformation for polyhedral objects"[J].
   Computer Graphics(In Proc.of SIGGRAPH'92[C]), 1992, 26(2):47-54.
9. A.Shapiro, T.Ayellet. Polyhedron realization for shape transformation[J]. The Visual
   Computer, 1998,14(8-9): 429-444.
10. M.Alexa. "Merging polyhedral shapes with scattered features"[J], The Visual
    Computer,2000,16(1): 26-37.
11. C.Grimm.. "Simple manifolds for surface modeling and parametrization Shape Modeling
    International" 2002.
12. HAKER, S., ANGENENT, S., TANNENBAUM, S., KIKINIS, R., SAPIRO, G., AND
    HALLE, M. 2000. "Conformal surface parametrization for texture mapping". IEEE
    TVCG, 6(2), pp. 181-189.
13. SHEFFER, A., GOTSMAN, C., AND DYN, N. 2003. "Robust spherical parameterization
    of triangular meshes". 4th Israel-Korea Bi-National Conf. on Geometric Modeling and
    Computer Graphics, pp. 94-99.
14. GOTSMAN, C., GU, X., AND SHEFFER, A. 2003. "Fundamentals of spherical
    parameterization for 3D meshes". ACM SIGGRAPH 2003.
15. QUICKEN, M., BRECHBÜHLER, C., HUG, J., BLATTMANN, H., SZÉKELY, G. 2000.
    "Parametrization of closed surfaces for parametric surface de scription", CVPR 2000, pp.
    354-360.

Dynamic Radiosity on Multi-resolution Models

Hui Xiao[1], Gary Tam[2], Frederick Li[2], and Rynson W.H. Lau[2]

[1] Department of Computer Science, City University of Hong Kong, Hong Kong
[2] Department of Computer Science, University of Durham, United Kingdom

Abstract. Most existing global illumination methods are computationally very expensive when handling dynamic scenes, in which more than one object is undergoing geometric transformation. Hence, they are not suitable for use in interactive environments. In this paper, we propose a novel approach to address this problem – *dynamic radiosity based on multi-resolution models*. It is based on update prioritization and radiosity redistribution to accelerate illuminate recomputation. Our method is developed to support rendering realistic scenes in dynamic virtual environments, where multiple dynamic objects may be moving around. It can handle occluded dynamic objects that are contributing to the scene illumination.

Keywords: Dynamic global illumination, radiosity, real-time rendering.

1 Introduction

Nowadays, photorealistic rendering techniques become more and more critical for user experience in 3D applications, such as games, VR systems, or e-learning. Among these techniques, radiosity is widely used, and is applicable in the areas of architectural and lighting design, or outdoor scene illuminations. It is a view independent global illumination (GI) solution mainly for diffuse object surfaces. However, due to its expensive computation process, which involves a physically-based light simulation, the majority of existing GI methods could not handle dynamic scenes efficiently. The reason is that when applying such methods in a dynamic scene, all computations have to be re-run from scratch even if it involves only minor changes. Hence, these methods are too expensive to be completed at an interactive rate for dynamic scenes.

To address this problem, we engage multi-resolution modeling into radiosity to accelerate computing the energy interactions among objects. It mainly concerns with how to redistribute the patch radiosities computed at one resolution of the object model to another resolution, while guaranteeing the overall energy conservation. A mathematical approach derived from Harmonic Mapping [9] is proposed.

Based on the above approach, we propose the *Dynamic Radiosity* method to provide an interactive update solution for radiosity, to handle dynamic environments with diverse conditions of dynamic objects. This is typically suitable to support realistic rendering for applications that require interactive rendering frame rate. Meanwhile, dynamic radiosity is the first approach to handle scenes with simultaneous motions of multiple dynamic objects, even with invisible ones. It is

Z. Pan et al. (Eds.): ICAT 2006, LNCS 4282, pp. 753 – 763, 2006.

achieved by the prioritized update decision that we have developed, which concerns with scene geometry and object attributes.

The rest of this paper is organized as follows. Section 2 reviews related work. Section 3 presents the framework of our proposed solution. Section 4 illustrates the novel energy redistribution method. Section 5 discusses our experimental results and Section 6 concludes this paper by summarizing our contributions.

2 Related Works

A few radiosity methods have been proposed to handle dynamic objects. Earlier, incremental radiosity [1] was proposed to explore the change of static scene geometry and arrange to update those parts affected by dynamic objects before those with static objects. Unfortunately, this method is only applicable to simple scenes, as it has to process all affected patches for each update and would take a long time for scene consisting of several objects. Another method is hierarchical radiosity [2], which stores a scene into a hierarchical structure. The method needs to identify the affected links in the structure, which represent the changes of scene, and performs update by following these links. However, the method requires large memory storage and its run-time performance cannot be guaranteed. Later, line-space hierarchy [3] augments a new structure to the hierarchy structure of [2] to accelerate the scene change identification. Although the method is a compromise between time and quality to support interactive update, the resultant quality of radiosity calculation is generally not so good. This is because it starts from the lowest LOD to process all geometry changes within given time interval, and for complicated environment, most details would be lost for dynamic updates.

Non-deterministic methods offer an alternative approach. Typically, these methods extend stochastic particle shooting techniques to support specular reflection and fast dynamic update. For example, instant radiosity [4] implements this idea using graphics hardware to rapidly compute an estimate of illumination, based on a quasi-random walk photon tracing pass. On the other hand, selective photon tracing [5] adopts the same idea by selectively tracing some pilot photons in a scene. Based on the pilot photons, the remaining photons with similar paths to the pilot photons can be identified easily. However, as a good update speed of non-deterministic methods is achieved by limiting the number of particles and the length of path tracing, such arrangement always leads to incomplete illumination.

Another direction is to decouple GI computations from geometric projections and image rendering. Methods adopting this approach do not aim at achieving an accurate illumination result. Instead, such methods provide an interface for the interactive display and fast approximation of global illumination results, when the full computation is too expensive to achieve within the required frame time. Among such methods, shading cache [6] utilizes an object-space caching structure and multi-processing to achieve better performance, while the update parts of objects are computed based on the projected user view. However, this method does not handle occluded objects, which is contributing to the scene illumination.

Hence, we propose a novel approach, called *dynamic radiosity*, to handle scenes with multiple dynamic objects. The method takes into account the scene geometry, scene illumination and motion attributes for dynamic objects to perform radiosity computation. In particular, our method is not confined to visible objects. In addition, we make use of the object-scope priority decision to reduce the computational complexity for updating radiosity results, and a radiosity redistribution method to generate a proper illumination representation to accelerate the rendering process.

3 Our Method

The basic idea of our approach is to decouple the illumination process and rendering process while making sure that the images are properly updated. We construct two separate meshes for each object, called *dual-mesh*, which share the same geometry attributes but may have different resolutions and color representations.

A multi-resolution modeling technique [7] [8] in real-time rendering is adopted for dual-mesh. Originally, this method was developed for selective and progressive transmission of the object details from the server to the client, according to the viewpoint of the client. As the client receives more details, it may progressively refine the model for rendering. Because of the simplicity of this multi-resolution modeling method, it is very efficient. The framework that we propose here helps determine the best resolution for both view and illumination computation, while guarantee the overall update rate in dynamic scenes, by:

- Minimizing the set of elements for radiosity recomputation and timely synchronizing the rendered images with illumination update, and
- Minimizing the number of patches for rendering while keeping an acceptable image quality.

3.1 Method Overview

The dual-mesh structure of our approach can be easily implemented and accelerated with multi-processing techniques. The update of the dual-mesh structure is divided into two main processes, which are executed in order. They are the *pre-process* and *solution process* as shown in Figure 1.

The pre-process is performed before the solution process. It constructs a mesh structure $\{M_0, M_1, ..., M_n\}$ for each object in the form of hierarchical meshes [7], where M_0 is the model at its lowest resolution, i.e., the base mesh, $M_1...M_n$ are subsequent models with increasing resolution, and M_n can be further decomposed into multiple hierarchical meshes. Here, we make use of this incremental resolution changes for fast radiosity calculation.

Solution process is then involved by using the given environment parameters and the definition of dynamic objects. The solution for *static status* is first performed on the base mesh M_0 of each object to compute the basic illumination values and collect necessary shooting information. Given sufficient time, the mesh can be progressively refined and eventually reaches M_n, and the solution will produce a rendered scene with the highest quality at the current resolution level.

When certain movement of a dynamic object is detected, the current solution cycle is then interrupted and turns into *dynamic status* immediately. Such control scheme in dynamic status aims to support real-time update while maintaining an optimal visual quality. To support real-time update, radiosity is first calculated using the base mesh M_0 of the object because such mesh consists of the smallest number of patches. Consequently, *radiosity redistribution* (see Section 4.2) is applied to approximate radiosity for higher resolution meshes of the object progressively.

This solution cycle repeats while the object is moving. As soon as the motion is stopped, our method will start from the static status again to collect information for generating more accurate rendering results.

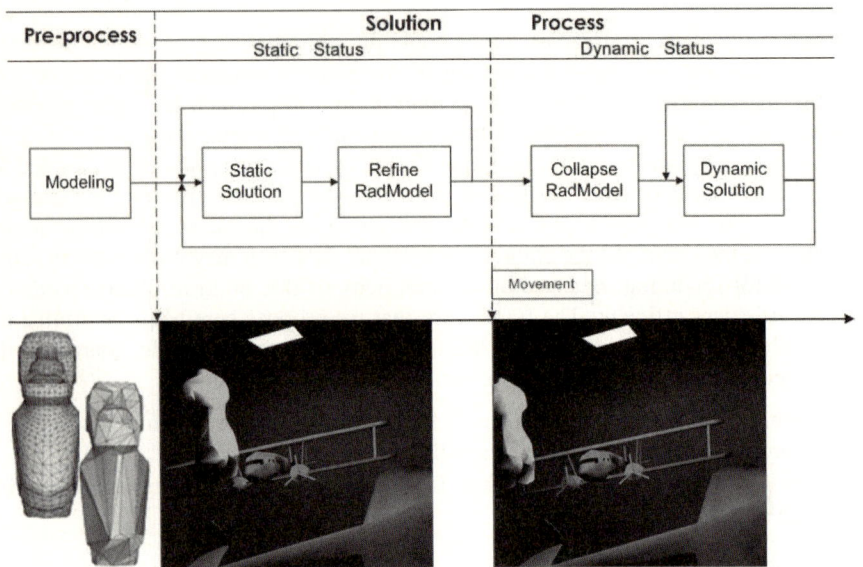

Fig. 1. Overview of dynamic radiosity

3.2 Radiosity Computation

Radiosity, in the literature, is usually calculated based on discrete points and surface areas in a scene. The radiosity equation is defined as:

$$B_i = E_i + \rho_i \sum_{1 \le j \le n} B_j F_{ij}$$

where B_i and B_j are the radiosity values of patches i and j, respectively. E_i is energy per unit area emitted from patch i. ρ_i is the reflectivity of patch i. F_{ij} is the form-factor from patch j to patch i. n is the number of discrete patches.

Our computation originates from a simple progressive method in [1], which evaluates radiosity through matrix equations. Based on this, we solve the matrix of form-factor F_{ij} for one column at a time, by shooting the light from a single patch to all the other patches.

For each cycle with the base mesh, we store the basic information of the shooting patch, the visibility and form-factor of other patches, which is defined as the contribution of the patch, in a data structure called *ShootList* as shown in Figure 2.

Each face p that has shot energy will keep a link to the corresponding ShootList and each ShootList keeps a link to *ReceiverList* to maintain the form-factors from p to other faces, as well as a link to *ShadowList* to maintain a list of faces occluded by the dynamic object. While we iterate during the dynamic status of the solution process, when face p is found to shoot energy again, the other faces are updated directly without recalculating the form-factors.

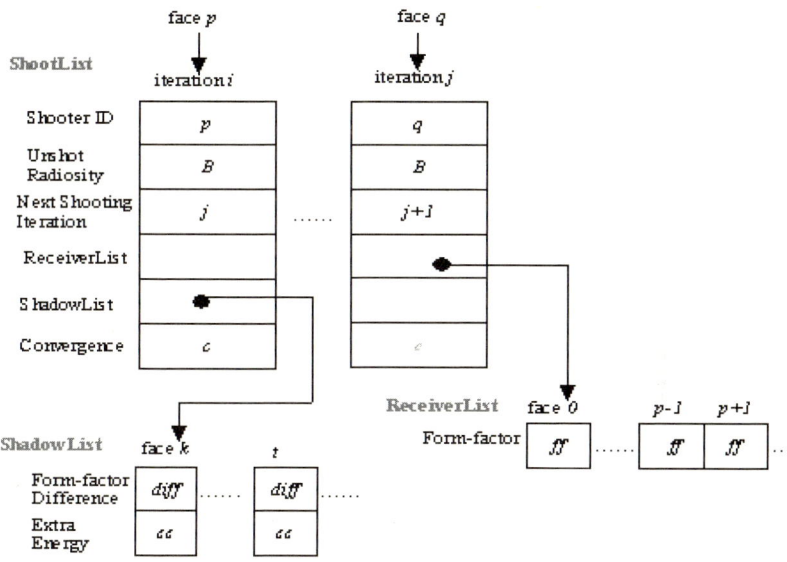

Fig. 2. Illustration of ShootList

Actually, ShootList only maintains information for the faces processed rather than all relevant computation results produced from the completed iterations. Therefore, such minimal set of information is enough to help identify most important shooting faces (key patches) and their contributions to the environment.

3.3 Dynamic Status

Once a dynamic object is found to have moved, the solution process will turn to dynamic status immediately, as shown in Figure 1. The radiosity computation is set to start with a minimal set of objects, which consists of those with higher update priority computed according to their visual importance. This helps minimize the computational cost and provide a real-time feedback to users. Figure 3 illustrates the steps involved in dynamic status. First, it calculates the differences of radiosity. Then, the result is transferred and redistributed to the rendering mesh. Finally, the updated rendering mesh is used for rendering.

To optimize the visual quality with minimal computational cost, we need to focus on the following three issues:

1. *Minimal computational cost*: With limited computational resources during dynamic update, we should first process the objects that have higher update

priority. This priority is determined in a perception-driven approach, with metrics of the object's contribution in static radiosity solution (illumination and occlusion), its motion attributes (direction and speed), and the visual importance (view distance and angle). ShootingList helps store the radiosity information.

2. *Optimized rendering update*: When estimating direct radiosity, the primary changes on the radiosity mesh are updated and then redistributed to the rendering mesh at a higher resolution. We use an *energy hemisphere* to model the radiosity distribution of two corresponding meshes. This method will be described in detail in the next section.

3. *Complete control scheme*: To provide high quality photorealistic renderings, most previous methods will continue refining objects immediately when the motion stops. However, our method will first update the necessary shooting information for future use, and then perform refinement for accurate lighting effects. The update priorities in patch scope are always evaluated to decide whether to reuse the previous results or to recalculate them towards better quality.

With such a scheme, the major changes in view and illumination are updated immediately after object motion. However, it has a few restrictions now: it only supports rigid objects and all the dynamic objects must be marked in advance.

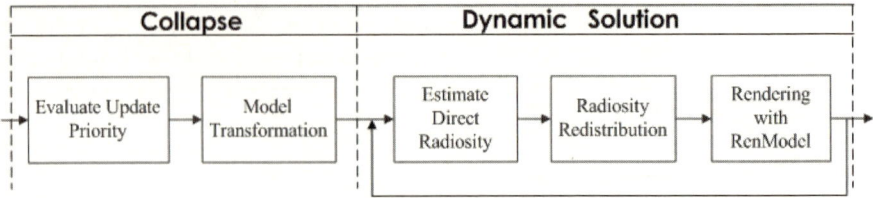

Fig. 3. Solution steps in dynamic status

4   Energy Redistribution

4.1   Energy Hemisphere for Radiosity

The radiosity method describes the equilibrium of energy transfer within an enclosure and the final solution indicates that each object patch i has a balance of incoming and outgoing energy, which is presented by B_iA_i, where B_i and A_i are the radiosity and area of patch, respectively. As radiosity only accounts for diffuse reflection, the emitting energy of a patch is to all directions. Hence, we can model the overall energy of an object patch by a bounding hemisphere that has the same B_iA_i, or so called *Energy Hemisphere (EH)*. To maintain the energy balance within the scene, the radiosity distribution over the hemisphere must follow a rule that the relevant sphere surface should have the same contribution to energy transfer as the underlying object patch does. We assume that an object patch i is mapped to a hemisphere p whose area is A_p, and its radiosity B_p should satisfy:

$$B_pA_p = B_iA_i \tag{1}$$

The energy is emitted to other patches from the centre of p, which corresponds to the centre of i. When receiving energy from other patches, p is projected to the source point. Here, we make an assumption that the distance between the emitting and the receiving surfaces is much greater than the radius of the energy hemispheres so that the error of this approximation can be neglected.

We can further apply the energy hemisphere model to a surface t, which is a group of connected patches. Since the patches may not be co-planar, the center and the radius of the corresponding hemisphere $eh(t)$ are determined from the smallest sphere covering all vertices. The overall energy of $eh(t)$ equals to that of surface t and is evaluated as ΣB_iA_i, which is the sum of energy for each patch i inside surface t. The corresponding sphere area p of i is assigned with the same original energy as in Eq. (1). Hence, we obtain the energy equation for surface t as:

$$\Sigma B_pA_p = \Sigma B_iA_i \qquad (2)$$

When t is refined, the corresponding boundary of $eh(t)$ is preserved and only its subdivisions are refined. Because the surface boundary is always preserved while more patches are introduced inside t, the overall energy of surface t or $eh(t)$ is conserved as ΣB_iA_i. As such, we make an assumption that the overall energy as well as the contribution to energy transfer of surface t remains the same, so that the equilibrium of radiosity is preserved.

The advantage of EH is that it can model the physical path of radiosity transfer on object patch and it provides an abstract view of the patches inside a surface, even though they are non-planar. Hence, we apply it here to redistribute surface radiosity from one LOD to another.

4.2 Radiosity Redistribution

Assume that surface t is at resolution M_k, and the radiosity distribution over t has been computed. The transform function is defined as follows. For a point s within patch i of surface t, it is mapped to a point $eh(s)$ on the surface of $eh(t)$. As s inherits radiosity from i, $B_s=B_i$. Hence, the radiosity of $eh(s)$, $B_{eh(s)}$, is:

$$B_{eh(s)} = B_{eh(i)} = B_iA_i / A_{eh(i)} \qquad (3)$$

where A_i is the area of i and $A_{eh(i)}$ is the area of $eh(i)$.

Therefore, the radiosity redistribution becomes simple. When surface t is refined to a higher resolution M_{k+1}, the transformation function is applied to t and a new partition on $eh(t)$ is also computed. A new patch i' may cover only part of the original patch i, or a combination of a few original patches. With the radiosity values already computed over the energy hemisphere for M_k, the energy of i' on the energy hemisphere, $E_{eh(i')}$, can be computed as an energy sum of each part covered by i' as:

$$E_{eh(i')} = \sum B_{eh(i)}A_{eh(i) \cap eh(i')} \qquad (4)$$

where $A_{eh(i) \cap eh(i')}$ is area of $eh(i)$ covered by $eh(i')$. Finally the radiosity distribution on the refined mesh can be computed as:

$$B_{i'} = \frac{\sum B_{eh(i)}A_{eh(i) \cap eh(i')}}{A_{i'}} \qquad (5)$$

However, it is time consuming to map each of the areas of $eh(i)$ to $eh(i')$. Here, we propose a coarse approximation, approximating the newly inserted vertex to be located at a particular location of one of the original patches within the surface. Then, we can precompute almost all likely configurations in our model database, with three patches to ten patches within a surface. Assuming that we have three patches in our original surface, a single refinement step will introduce 2 more patches into the surface, resulting in 5 patches as shown in Figure 4:

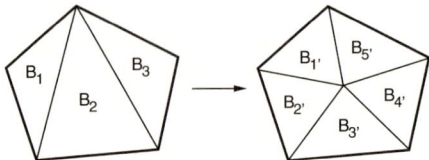

Fig. 4. A single resolution refinement step of a surface

The redistributed radiosity of the refined surface patches, $B_{i'}$, can be calculated as:

$$[B_{1'}\ B_{2'}\ B_{3'}\ B_{4'}\ B_{5'}]^{\mathrm{T}} = R_t\,[B_1\ B_2\ B_3]^{\mathrm{T}} \tag{6}$$

where B_i are the radiosity values of the original surface patches and R_t the radiosity redistribution matrix. For example, if we assume that the inserted vertex is located at the center of one of the three original patches, R_t becomes:

$$R_t = \begin{bmatrix} 1/5 & 0 & 0 \\ 1/5 & 1/3 & 1/2 \\ 1/5 & 0 & 0 \\ 1/5 & 1/3 & 1/2 \\ 1/5 & 1/3 & 0 \end{bmatrix}, \begin{bmatrix} 1/2 & 1/5 & 0 \\ 0 & 1/5 & 1/2 \\ 1/2 & 1/5 & 0 \\ 0 & 1/5 & 1/2 \\ 0 & 1/5 & 0 \end{bmatrix} \text{ or } \begin{bmatrix} 1/2 & 1/3 & 1/5 \\ 0 & 0 & 1/5 \\ 1/2 & 1/3 & 1/5 \\ 0 & 0 & 1/5 \\ 0 & 1/3 & 1/5 \end{bmatrix}$$

depending on whether the inserted vertex is inside B_1, B_2 or B_3 after projecting it onto the energy hemisphere, respectively.

5   Result and Discussion

We have implemented a prototype of our method and performed two sets of experiments on the basic indoor scene as shown in Figure 1 with different object complexities and scene composition. The experiments were conducted on a PC with a P4 2.6GHz CPU, 1GB RAM, and a GeForce FX 5600 graphics card.

5.1   Scene Complexity

This experiment compares the performance of radiosity solution with different accelerations under diverse scene complexities. There is only one dynamic object (consisting of 2,000 patches) moving in a constant direction and speed, while other objects are fixed in their positions. The composition of accelerating methods adopted is shown as in Table 1.

Table 1. Description of test solutions

	DP0	*DP1*	*DP2*
Dynamic Radiosity Estimation	*N/A*	*YES*	*YES*
Prioritized Update	*N/A*	*N/A*	*YES*

Figure 5 shows the update cost of each approach for one dynamic radiosity update, including radiosity recomputation, redistribution and rendering. As described above, the result of DP0 shows the original update cost without any accelerating methods, DP1 shows the acceleration with recomputation and estimation on unrefined models of all objects, and DP2 illustrates the update cost of our method using the lowest resolution of the surfaces.

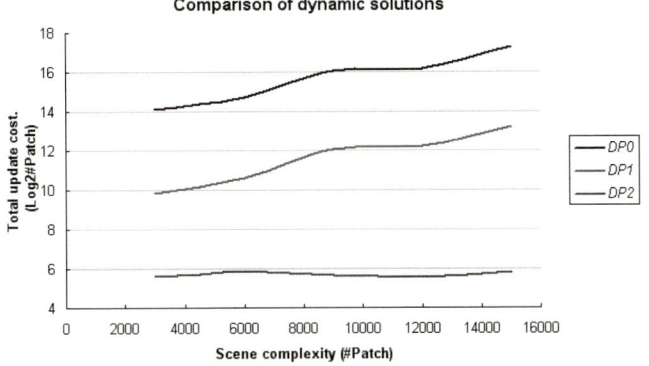

Fig. 5. Experimental result of test 1

We can see the cost of DP2 is quite low and almost constant in spite of the increase in scene complexity; DP1 is much higher since it accounts for all objects in recomputation, and DP0 is increasing greatly as the scene complexity goes on.

5.2 Dynamic Object Complexity

Experiment 2 compares performance of radiosity solution by changing number of dynamic objects. The rendering complexity is constant and the dynamic complexity is increased by allowing more objects to move.

Figure 6 shows the average update of one single dynamic radiosity update, in terms of $\log_2$(number of patches). For DP0 and DP1, the computation costs are always the same as the full complexity of all objects. Hence, they are constant in this experiment. The cost of DP2 is increasing as the number of dynamic and affected objects is growing, however much lower in actual complexity. We must note that the threshold of priority decision is fixed in this experiment. However, it can be controlled by the dynamic object complexity. Hence, its cost will be lowered to save the processing time while the illumination error will increase.

Note that the performance of updating the radiosity as an object moves from one location to another does not really affected by the number of concurrent users if our

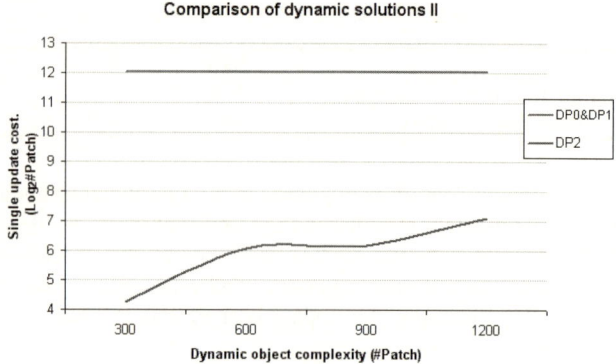

Fig. 6. Experimental result of test 2

method is applied in a multi-user virtual environment, since the update process is performed at the server.

6 Conclusion

In this paper, we have proposed a novel dynamic radiosity method based on multi-resolution models. It focuses on the radiosity solution in dynamic environments. It uses estimation and update priority to accelerate radiosity computation, while at the same time applies radiosity redistribution to improve the rendering process. The main objective is to support user interaction in a virtual environment, where dynamic objects can be moving simultaneously, and in particular, certain occluded objects may still be contributing to the scene illumination.

The experiments show that it efficiently reduces the update cost in dynamic environments, though temporally introduce limited errors during the update stage. When this method is extended to multi-processing, the load of both illumination and rendering update can be shared, so that more details can be solved to provide better visual quality.

References

1. M. Cohen, S. Chen, J. Wallace, and D. Greenberg. "A Progressive Refinement Approach to Fast Radiosity Image Generation." *Proc. of ACM SIGGRAPH'98*, pp.75–84, 1988.
2. P. Hanrahan, D. Salzman, and L. Aupperle. "A Rapid Hierarchical Radiosity Algorithm." *Proc. of ACM SIGGRAPH'91*, pp.197–206, 1991.
3. G. Drettakis and F. Sillion. "Interactive Update of Global Illumination Using A Line-space Hierarchy." *Proc. of ACM SIGGRAPH'97*, pp.57–64, 1997.
4. A. Keller. "Instant radiosity." *Proc. of ACM SIGGRAPH'97*, pp. 49-55, 1997.
5. K. Dmitriev, S. Brabec, K. Myszkowski, and H. Seidel. "Interactive Global Illumination Using Selective Photon Tracing." *Proc. of Eurographics Workshop on Rendering*, pp. 25–36, 2002.

6. P. Tole, F. Pellaccini, B. Walter, and D. Greenberg. "Interactive Global Illumination in Dynamic Scenes." *Proc. of ACM SIGGRAPH'02*, pp.537–546, 2002.
7. R. Lau, D. Kilis, F. Li, and Y. Tsang. "Selective, Progressive Transmission of 3D Geometry Models with the Pre-ordered Hierarchical Meshes." *US Patent Filed*, 2003.
8. F. Li, R. Lau, and D. Kilis. "GameOD: An Internet Based Game-On-Demand Framework." *Proc. of ACM VRST*, pp. 114–121, Nov. 2004.
9. D. Zhang and M. Hebert. "Harmonic Maps and Their Applications in Surface Matching." *Proc. of Computer Vision and Pattern Recognition*, pp. 524-530, 1999.

Mesh Simplification Algorithm Based on N-Edge Mesh Collapse

Hua-hong Chen, Xiao-nan Luo, and Ruo-tian Ling

Computer Application Institute, Zhongshan University, 510275 Guangzhou, P.R. China
{isschh, lnslxn}@mail.sysu.edu.cn,
skymartin@163.com

Abstract. This paper presents a method for dividing the triangle mesh into n-edge mesh and puts forward a new mesh simplification algorithm based on n-edge mesh collapse. An n-edge mesh can be in the form of an edge, a triangle or a quadrangle, it depends on the value of 'n'. The algorithm utilizes iterative collapse of n-edge mesh to simplify meshes and the surface error approximations are maintained using quadric error metrics. There are n-1 vertices and 2(n-1) faces which have to be collapsed during every simplification, so only few collapses are need when n becomes bigger. And this means, the time of the simplification process can be reduced. Our algorithm contains Garland's (n=2) [5] and Pan's (n=3) [11] cases, thus it can be regarded as the summarized algorithm of mesh simplification based on the geometry element collapse. Experimental results demonstrate the different cases, which hold different values of 'n' in the algorithm.

Keywords: Mesh simplification, triangle mesh, Quadric Error Metrics (QEM), n-edge mesh collapse.

1 Introduction

Triangular meshes are widely used in Virtual Reality because meshes can model objects of arbitrary shape and they can be easily constructed from 3D data. However the number of triangles in the mesh is often very high which is troublesome even with fast graphics hardware. Therefore, the mesh simplification is a necessary process which can aid the rendering and the other processes as well.

Geometry removal is one of the significant ways to simplify meshes, and it's operation is to iteratively remove or collapse the basic geometry unit such as the vertex, the edge or the triangle face. In recent years, varieties of surface simplification algorithms in this area have been developed. Those algorithms which are most relevant to our work can be broadly categorized into 3 classes:

Vertex Decimation. A vertex and its surrounding regions are deleted. The resulting hole is re-triangulated (Fig.1(a)). Most of the earlier simplification methods are based on this process [1], [2], [3]. Schroeder [1] utilizes the distance from a vertex to the average plane of its surrounding vertices to order the vertices decimation.

Edge Collapse. An edge is collapsed into a new vertex. Then its two adjacent triangles are deleted (Fig.1(b)). This is the most common process and has been

Z. Pan et al. (Eds.): ICAT 2006, LNCS 4282, pp. 764 – 774, 2006.

studied extensively [4], [5], [6], [7]. Garland [5] introduces the QEM (quadric error metrics) to measure the cost of the vertex pairs collapse process. Under such metrics, an optimal new vertex placement is achievable. Even though QEM is a local error control method, simplified meshes obtained by this algorithm are generally as accurate as the ones which are produced by the other global error control algorithms.

Face (triangle) Collapse. A face is collapsed and its adjacent faces are merged [8],[9],[10],[11] (Fig.1(c)). Hamann [8] and Gieng [10] approximate the underlying surface in the neighborhood of a candidate triangle to obtain the curvature estimation for computing the ordering weight. Pan [11] utilizes Garland's QEM method to evaluate the error in the face collapse process and good results are achieved.

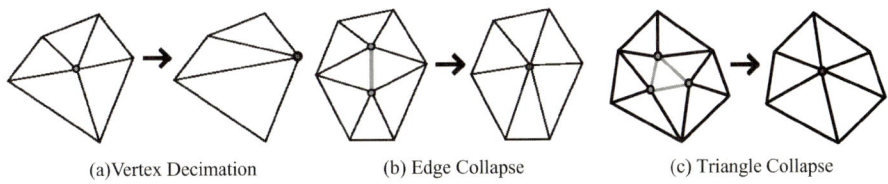

(a)Vertex Decimation   (b) Edge Collapse   (c) Triangle Collapse

Fig. 1. Mesh simplification process based on geometry elements removal

This paper presents a method to define the n-edge mesh in triangle meshes and puts forward a new mesh simplification algorithm based on these new geometry elements collapse. The algorithm utilizes iterative collapse of n-edge mesh to simplify meshes and surface error approximations are maintained using QEM. The proposed algorithm contains Garland's [5] and Pan's cases [11], thus it can be regarded as the summarized algorithm of mesh simplification based on the geometry element collapse.

2   Related Work

Among the above presented methods, Garland's QEM is the most popular one and it can rapidly generate high-quality approximations. A 4x4 symmetric matrix Q_i is allocated for each vertex in the original mesh, so the cost of the vertex pairs collapse can be obtained by the following equations:

$$\varepsilon(E_i) = \Sigma \triangle(v) = v^T (Q(v_a) + Q(v_b)) v = v^T Q v \tag{1}$$

$$= q_{11}x^2 + 2q_{12}xy + 2q_{13}xz + 2q_{14}x + q_{22}y^2 + 2q_{23}yz + 2q_{24}y + q_{33}z^2 + 2q_{34}z + q_{44}.$$

There are several choices to determine the new vertex v_0. The simplest one is to choose it from the vertex pairs. The optimal one is to find a position for v_0 which minimizes $\varepsilon(E_i)$. Since the error Equation (1) is quadratic, to find its minimum is a linear problem. Thus v_0 is found by solving: $\partial\Delta(v)/\partial x = \partial\Delta(v)/\partial y = \partial\Delta(v)/\partial z = 0$, if these equations are solvable, then the optimal position of v_0 is determined by Equation (2). Otherwise choose them from the endpoints or the midpoint of the edge.

$$v = \begin{bmatrix} q_{11} & q_{12} & q_{13} & q_{14} \\ q_{12} & q_{22} & q_{23} & q_{24} \\ q_{13} & q_{23} & q_{33} & q_{34} \\ 0 & 0 & 0 & 1 \end{bmatrix}^{-1} \begin{bmatrix} 0 \\ 0 \\ 0 \\ 1 \end{bmatrix} . \tag{2}$$

Pan [11] utilizes Garland's QEM method to evaluate the error in the triangle collapse process and also achieved good results. Furthermore, Pan brought forward a new question: if the method for dividing the triangle mesh into areas can be found, his algorithm can be extant to simplify the meshes efficiently.

Thus, in this paper, we present a method to define the n-edge mesh in triangle meshes and puts forward a new mesh simplification algorithm based on these geometry elements collapse. The proposed algorithm is containing both Garland's case (n=2) and Pan's case (n=3).

3   Fundamental Concepts

3.1   Combination and Detection of the N-Edge Mesh

The basic simplifying operation in our algorithm is n-edge mesh collapse. In the cases n=2 and n=3, the n-edge mesh mean the edge and the triangle which are the basic units of the meshes. But in the cases n>3, the n-edge mesh are not a simple units in the mesh, so the first problem to solve is to find out and define them from the meshes.

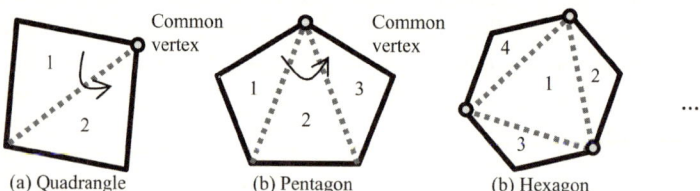

Fig. 2. Combinations of n-edge mesh, real line shows the exterior edge and broken line shows interior edge

As shown in Fig.2, the n-edge mesh can be obtained by combining the adjacent triangles together. For example, two triangles with a common edge can construct a quadrangle (Fig 2(a)), if one more adjacent triangle is joined to it, a pentagon can be obtained (Fig 2(b)). There may be many choices for the combination of a certain kind of n-edge mesh, but two rules must be satisfied during the process.

1) Universality rule: The n-edge mesh which we defined must exist generally in the meshes. Therefore, we can compute and compare the costs of collapse, and then simplify the meshes by iterating the process.

2) Unique rule: Only one choice should be taken for the combination and apply to the whole model. On the other hand, if we apply the combination rule to the basic

geometry units of the mesh, we can obtain only one n-edge mesh. So the n-edge mesh can be expressed or detected by the unit. For instance, in the quadrangle case, a quadrangle can be detected by an edge while a pentagon can be detected by a triangle and a vertex of it in the pentagon case.

3.2 Collapsing Operation

Similar to the collapsing operations of edge collapse and triangle collapse, operation of n-edge mesh collapse is the process which removes the n-edge mesh and the relative triangles and then connects the adjacent vertices to the new vertex (Fig.3).

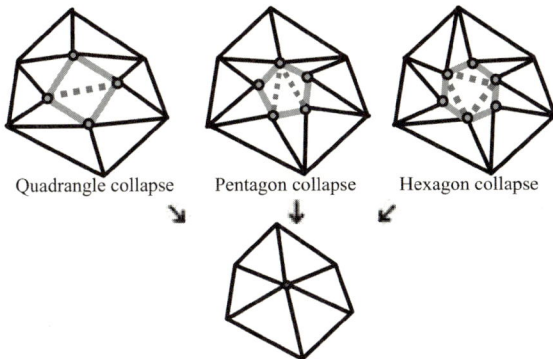

Fig. 3. Operation of n-edge mesh collapse

There are n triangles which have the common edge to the n-edge mesh being removed in every n-edge mesh collapse, and n-2 triangles which construct the n-edge mesh are collapsed simultaneously, so it is summation 2(n-1) triangles are reduced during every process. Table 1 shows the data under the difference n values. It is obvious that the cases when n=2 and n=3 are similar to those of Garland's and Pan's. In fact, left alone the differences in vertex pairs selection or error definitions, their algorithms can be regarded as the n=2 and n=3 cases respectively.

Table 1. Number of geometry elements removed in single n-edge mesh collapse

n-edge mesh in different n cases	Number of geometry elements being removed during single collapse		
	vertex	edge	Triangle
2 (edge collapse)	1	3	2
3 (triangle collapse)	2	6	4
4	3	9	6
5	4	12	8
...			
n	n-1	3 (n-1)	2 (n-1)

4 Proposed Algorithm

4.1 Definitions and Notations

To facilitate the description of the new algorithm, some basic definitions and notations are introduced.

Definition 1. Given a set of triangles, if each triangle has a common edge with every adjacent triangle, then these triangles are called triangle mesh (TM). TM can be expressed by a vertex set V and a triangle set T, where V=(V1, V2,..., Vn), T= (T1, T2,...,Tm).

Definition 2. For an edge in TM, if it is only shared by one triangle, then this edge is called boundary edge. The vertices of boundary edge are called boundary vertices. The triangle containing this edge is called boundary triangle. Analogously, the n-edge mesh containing this edge is called boundary n-edge mesh.

Definition 3. For a triangle in TM, if this triangle and it's n-3 adjacent triangles {n>2 where n is a positive integer} can combine to form a mesh with n edges which only belong to one of these triangles and also the mesh is accorded with the two rules as described in 3.1, then the mesh is called n-edge mesh. An edge in n-edge mesh only shared by one triangle of the n-edge mesh is called exterior edge, or else, it's called interior edge.

Definition 4. The surrounding triangles of n-edge mesh are defined as the set C_i = {T_i | $T_i \neq T$, $T_i \in M$, where T_i shares at least one vertex of n-edge mesh$_i$}. Analogously, the surrounding triangles of a vertex v are defined as the set Pi of triangles containing v.

Definition 5. For triangles in TM, if there is a group of three mutually adjacent triangles, then these three triangles construct a cycle, and the vertex shared by the three triangles at the same time is called cycle vertex.

4.2 Approximating Error with Quadrics

In order to select a collapsing operation to perform during a given iteration, some notions for the cost of a process are needed. This paper introduces QEM to measure the cost in the simplification process. The error of the vertex with respect to the set P_i is the sum of squared distances to its planes is found:

$$\Delta(v) = \Delta([v_x v_y v_z 1]^T) = \sum_{p \in planes(v)} (p^T v)^2 = \sum_{p \in planes(v)} v^T (pp^T)v = v^T \left(\sum_{p \in planes(v)} (K_p) \right)v = v^T Q(v_a)v \cdot \quad (3)$$

where P=[a b c d]^T represents the plane defined by the equation ax+by+cz+d=0 ($a^2+b^2+c^2=1$) and Kp is the matrix:

$$K_P = pp^T = \begin{bmatrix} a^2 & ab & ac & ad \\ ab & b^2 & bc & bd \\ ac & bc & c^2 & cd \\ ad & bd & cd & d^2 \end{bmatrix} \cdot \quad (4)$$

For a given n-edge mesh collapsing n vertices to v_0 , the simple additive rule Q_0= $Q_1+Q_2+...+Q_n$ is utilized which is similar to Garland's method as a new matrix approximates the error at v_0 , so the cost of a n-edge mesh collapsing process is:

$$\varepsilon(E_i) = \Sigma \triangle(v) = v^T (Q(v_1) + Q(v_2) + \ldots + Q(v_n)) v = v^T Q v$$

$$= q_{11}x^2 + 2q_{12}xy + 2q_{13}xz + 2q_{14}x + q_{22}y^2 + 2q_{23}yz + 2q_{24}y + q_{33}z^2 + 2q_{34}z + q_{44}.$$

(5)

4.3 Position of the New Vertex

Several methods exist for defining the position of the new vertex v_0 :

The simplest method is to choose v_0 among the vertices in the n-edge mesh. It depends on which one of these produces the lowest value of $\varepsilon(E_i)$. This method is easy to compute but produces low-quality results.

The optimal method is to find a position for v_0 which minimizes $\varepsilon(E_i)$. Since the error function (5) is quadratic, to find its minimum is a linear problem. Thus v_0 is found by solving: $\partial\triangle(v)/\partial x = \partial\triangle(v)/\partial y = \partial\triangle(v)/\partial z = 0$, if these equations are solvable, then the optimal position of v_0 is determined by (6). Otherwise choose it from the endpoints or the midpoints of the edges of the n-edge mesh.

$$v = \begin{bmatrix} q_{11} & q_{12} & q_{13} & q_{14} \\ q_{12} & q_{22} & q_{23} & q_{24} \\ q_{13} & q_{23} & q_{33} & q_{34} \\ 0 & 0 & 0 & 1 \end{bmatrix}^{-1} \begin{bmatrix} 0 \\ 0 \\ 0 \\ 1 \end{bmatrix}.$$

(6)

4.4 Algorithm Summary

The general framework of the proposed scheme is as follows:

Step 1. Compute the error matrix Q_i for each n-edge mesh$_i$.

Step 2. For each n-edge mesh$_i$, compute the position of new vertex v_0 according to its error matrix Q_i, and compute its corresponding approximation error according to $v^T Q_0 v$, then arrange the n-edge mesh in a heap according to the collapsing cost.

Step 3. Iteratively remove n-edge mesh$_i$ with minimal cost from the heap, collapse it.

Step 4. Update corresponding information.

Step 5. If the heap is empty or the error requirement is met, then go to Step 6, else go to Step 3.

Step 6. End.

5 Additional Details

5.1 Cycle Process

Cycle is a special structure in meshes and sometimes it is considered to be the feature of the meshes. It may cause superposition of the faces if to be collapsed. So cycle process should be processed before the collapse. There are two situations of the cycle process:

a). The n-edge mesh containing the cycle vertex. In this situation the cycle only affects the number of edges and vertices which will be removed during the collapse process. Thus, the n-edge mesh can be collapse in this case (Fig. 4 (a)).

b). The C_i set of the n-edge mesh containing the cycle vertex. In this situation the n-edge mesh can not be collapsed directly, else it will lead to superposition of the remaining two triangles in the cycle (Fig. 4 (b)).

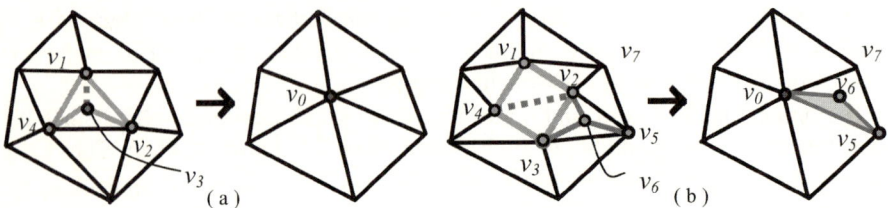

Fig. 4. Two situations of the cycle process

To prevent process from causing superposition, several methods are suitable for the new algorithm. Gieng [10] introduces Edge Swapping to solve the problem. The cycle is removed by swapping the common edge between the triangle and its neighboring triangle that belong to the cycle. Wu [12] considers the cycle as the feature of meshes, so the collapse is identified as illegal while the surrounding triangles contain a cycle. Furthermore, if there is a vertex in C_i with valence 4, then it is said to contain a hidden cycle which would introduce a new cycle. So the collapse must not be processed.

5.2 Preserving Boundaries

Many meshes in practice include boundaries which must be preserved during the simplification process. Boundaries of the mesh will be degenerated in iterative process, if it has not taken any measures to protect them. So it is necessary to preserve boundary curves while simplifying their shapes.

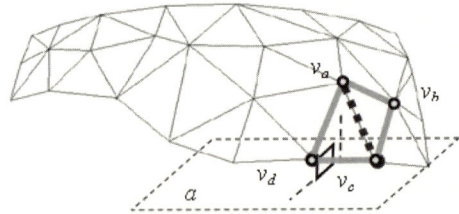

Fig. 5. Generation of a perpendicular plane on running through the edge $v_d v_c$ which belongs to $QUAD\{v_a, v_b, v_c, v_d\}$ (bold)

This research applies a similar method as described earlier [5] to preserve boundary n-edge mesh. For each boundary edge in the n-edge mesh, a perpendicular plane running through the edge is generated. An example of quadrangle collapse is showed in Fig.5. These constraint planes are then converted into quadrics, weighted by a penalty factor, and added into the initial quadrics for the endpoints of the edge. The efficiency of preserving the boundary discontinuity is good with the new method.

5.3 Preventing Mesh Inversion

In this paper, we apply Garland's [5] method which compares the differences between the normal vectors of the encircling triangles before and after the collapse. If the differences are larger than a threshold, then the collapse can be either heavily penalized or disallowed.

6 Results and Discussion

6.1 Quality of the Approximations

The proposed algorithm with n=4 is implemented in C++. Some experimental results are shown in Fig.6 to Fig.7. From these figures, we can see that our algorithm is efficient for models composed of triangles. Fig.6 shows a sequence of approximation generated using quadrangle collapse. The simplified model with 20310 faces is very similar to the original model on the left. The result is acceptable when the triangles are decimated to 98%. And most features are preserved in simplified models.

Fig.7 demonstrates the performance between proposed algorithm (when n=4) , Garland's (n=2) and Pan's (n=3) algorithms. In most case (such as Fig.7(a)(b)(c)) Garland's algorithm performance is a little better than Pan's while Pan's algorithm performance is a little better than the quadrangle collapse case (n=4). This is because when n=2, only an edge or vertex pairs are removed in single iteration, so the algorithm can produce high quality approximations with minimal errors. Therefore, a conclusion of the proposed algorithm can be drawn that the smaller 'n' value, the higher quality of approximation.

6.2 Implementation Time

To present high efficiency of the polygonal simplification algorithm based on n-edge mesh collapses, it's complexities under the various assumptions will be analyzed. The assumptions are: (i) the original model has n' faces, and the target model has m faces; (ii) the number of faces removed in one iteration is bounded by a constant k; (iii) the maximum vertex degree is bounded by a constant g; (iv) 'n' in the n-edge mesh is a constant.

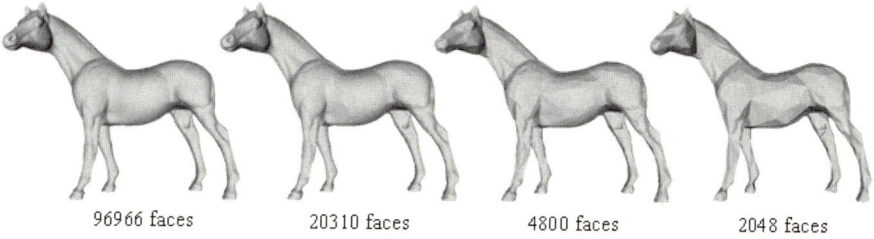

96966 faces   20310 faces   4800 faces   2048 faces

Fig. 6. Simplified model using quadrangle collapse, 0%, 80%, 95%, 98% triangles decimated

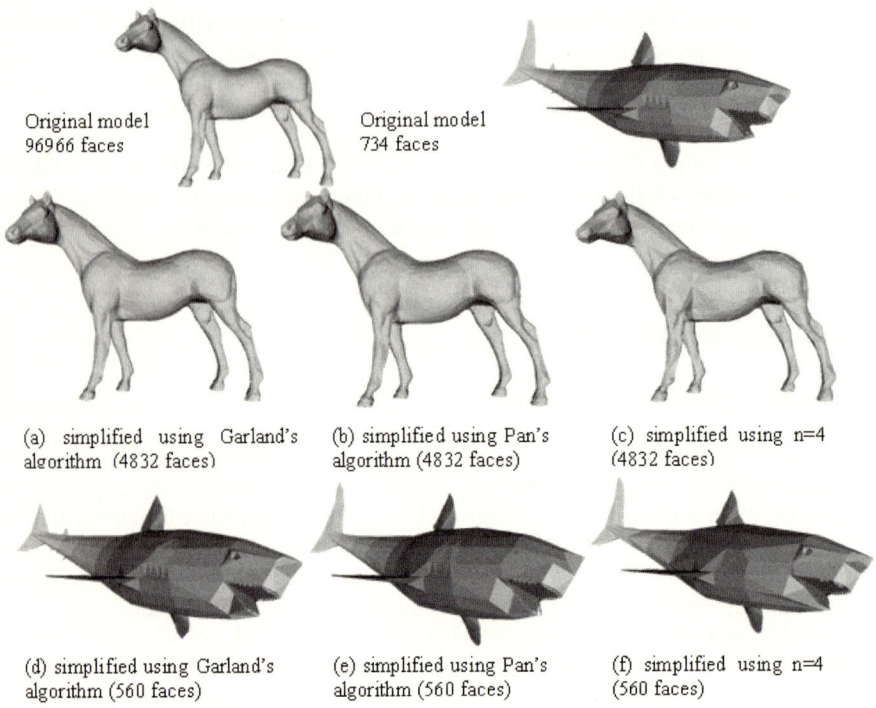

Original model
96966 faces

Original model
734 faces

(a) simplified using Garland's algorithm (4832 faces)

(b) simplified using Pan's algorithm (4832 faces)

(c) simplified using n=4 (4832 faces)

(d) simplified using Garland's algorithm (560 faces)

(e) simplified using Pan's algorithm (560 faces)

(f) simplified using n=4 (560 faces)

Fig. 7. Comparison between approximations generated using Garland's (n=2), Pan's (n=3) and quadrangle collapse (n=4) algorithm

The same as Garland's described, the proposed algorithm begins with initialization phase. Constructing all the initial quadrics takes $O(n)$ times. To place all the resulting candidates in a heap requires $O(n\log n)$ times. Thus, the total complexity of initialization is $O(n\log n)$. A single iteration requires $O(\log(n-ki))$ times while in the simplification phase. So summing over all iterations, the total cost for this phase is:

$$\log n + \log(n-k) + \log(n-2k) + \log(n-3k) + \ldots + \log m = \log n! - \log m! = 0 \quad (7)$$
$$(n\log n - m\log m) .$$

Thus, the overall complexity of the n-edge mesh collapse algorithm is $O(n\log n)$.

Although the complexities are similar, the n-edge mesh collapse with different 'n' cases perform different implementation time in practice. Since Pan has proved his algorithm can be implemented faster than Garland's, so we are more concerned about the comparison between Pan's algorithm and the other 'n' cases such as n=4. As showed in Table 2, the quadrangle case is faster than Pan's algorithm. That means the case n=4 is also fast than Garland's algorithm. Because 6 faces are removed in one iteration, to reach the same simplification target as assumed before. The quadrangle collapse algorithm only needs $(n-m)/6$ times of iteration while the number in Garland's is $(n-m)/2$, and in Pan's is $(n-m)/4$, thus time of correlative process is saved. So another conclusion of the proposed algorithm can be drawn that the bigger 'n' values, reduces the number of iterations, and the algorithm will be more efficient as well.

Table 2. Comparison of implementation time between Pan's and the quadrangle collapse algorithm

Original model (faces)	Simplified model (faces)	Pan's algorithm (s)	Quadrangle collapse (s)
Bunndy (15294)	3062	33.966	30.56
Shark (734)	560	0.293	0.194
Cow (5804)	1448	11.399	9.151
Ball (5000)	508	10.609	8.906
Footbone (4204)	1716	5.428	3.657
Apple (1704)	956	2.115	1.754

However, the maximum vertex degree is bounded by a constant g in most meshes situation, the 'n' of n-edge mesh can not evaluated so big, else there will be few n-edge meshes which can be searched in the whole meshes. On the other hand, if 'n' become too big, the computations to evaluate the error and update the corresponding information will become complex, and then it will restrict the speed of the implementation. Therefore, the 'n' of n-edge mesh should be chosen properly depending on requirements of quality and speed. That is to say to simplify a model with few triangle faces, a smaller 'n' seems to be a good choice while to simplify a model with great deal of triangle faces such as the terrain model, a bigger 'n' will be better.

7   Conclusion

In this paper, we present a method to define the n-edge mesh which is the new geometry element in triangle meshes and put forward a mesh simplification algorithm based on the n-edge mesh collapse. The algorithm utilizes iterative collapse of n-edge mesh to simplify meshes and surface error approximations are maintained using quadric error metrics. The 'n' of n-edge mesh can be assigned by many positive integers such as 2, 3, 4, etc. By assigned a proper value for 'n' of the n-edge mesh, the proposed algorithm is efficient to simplify meshes rapidly or produce a high-quality approximation. Garland's and Pan's algorithms are very similar to the proposed algorithm, that they can be regarded as n=2 and n=3 cases of the new algorithm. Thus, the proposed algorithm can be regarded as the summarized algorithm of mesh simplification based on the geometry elements collapse.

Acknowledgments

This work was supported by the National Science Fund for Distinguished Young Scholars (No.60525213) and the Key Project (No. 60533030) of NSFC, and 973 Program of China (No.206CB303106).

References

1. Schroeder W.J. et al.. Decimation of triangle meshes. Computer Graphics, 1992, 26(2): 65-70.
2. J. Cohen, A. Varshney, D. Manocha, etc, Simplification Envelopes, *Computer Graphics*, 119-128, 1996
3. M. Soucy, D. Laurendeau, Multiresolution Surface Modeling Based on Hierarchical Triangulation, *Computer Vision andImage Understanding*, 63(1), 1-14,1996
4. Hoppe H. Progressive meshes. Computer Graphics, 1996, 30(1):99-108.
5. Michael Garland. Quadric-based polygonal surface simplification [Ph D dissertation]. Carnegie Mellon University,1999.
6. Li Gui-qing, Li Xian-min, Li Hua. Mesh simplification based subdivision. In: Pan, Yun-he, ed. Proceedings of the 2nd International Conference on Computer-Aided Industrial Design and Conceptual Design. Bangkok: International Academic Publishers, 1999. 351-355.
7. Kim Sun-Jeong, Kim Chang-Hun, Levin D.. Surface simplification using a discrete curvature norm. Computer & Graphics, 2002, 26(5): 657-663
8. B. Hamann, A Data Reduction Scheme for Triangulated Surface. Computer Aided Geometric Design ,1994 , 11 (2) :197-214.
9. ISLER V. et al.. Real-Time Multi-resolution Modeling for Complex Virtual Environments. MARK G. Proceedings of the TRST'96. Hong Kong: ACM press, 1996:11-20.
10. Tran Gieng, B. Hamann. et al. Smooth Hierarchical Surface Triangulations. Yagel R, Hagen H. Proceedings of the IEEE Visualization'97. San Francisco: IEEE Computer Society Press ,1997:379-386.
11. PAN Zhigeng, ZHOU Kun, SHI Jiaoying. A New Mesh Simplification Algorithm Based on Triangle Collapses. Journal of Computer Science and Technology, 2001,16(1)
12. Jian-Hua Wu, et al.. An Effective Feature-preserving Mesh Simplification Scheme Based on Face Constriction. Proceedings of Pacific Graphics 2001, 12-21

3-D Personalized Face Reconstruction Based on Multi-layer and Multi-region with RBFs

Yongzhao Zhan, Rongrong Shen, and Jianming Zhang

School of Computer Science and Telecommunication Engineering, Jiangsu University, Zhenjiang 212013, Jiangsu, China
yzzhan@ujs.edu.cn, shenrongrong_2005@yahoo.com.cn, zhjm@ujs.edu.cn

Abstract. Constructing 3-D personalized face model with 2-D face photographs is an active topic in 3-D face modeling research. Presently, almost all methods focus on using a constrained equation to construct 3-D personalized face. Due to the complex structure of human face, these methods can't delicately represent facial organ surfaces, and the computation cost of these methods is greater. In this paper, a method for reconstructing 3-D personalized face based on multi-layer and multi-region with RBFs is presented. First, the generic face model is reconstructed based on multi-layer and multi-region with RBFs, in which two layers are designed and four facial organs are separated. Then, the edges between layers are smoothed with influence factors of the layers. Finally, the facial texture is mapped onto the reconstructed personalized face model. Experiments show that this method is simple and efficient.

Keywords: radial basis functions (RBFs), face model reconstruction, multi-layer, multi-region.

1 Introduction

Many different methods about 3-D face model reconstruction have been proposed in past years, such as laser scanner [1], stereo camera and morphable model [2], etc. In addition, image-based face modeling is an active topic, which extracts feature points from images and then deforms generic face model to generate personalized face model. Compared with the methods above, this approach doesn't need special hardware supporting, but it requires reasonable and effective algorithms to extract feature points and reconstruct the face model. The existing methods of image-based face modeling have their own advantages and disadvantages, but they all need further research before they are widely applied.

Provided with frontal and profile facial images, and a predefined generic 3-D face model, the prevailing construction method is that the feature points from those photos are extracted first, then a constrained equation is used to deform the generic model in order to fit particular facial geometry, finally facial texture is mapped onto a realistic personalized face model. Almost all of existing image-based face modeling methods [3,6] only use one constrained equation to reconstruct the generic face model, which can't delicately represent the face model because of the complex structure of human face. In this paper, we propose a reconstruction method which is based on multi-layer

Z. Pan et al. (Eds.): ICAT 2006, LNCS 4282, pp. 775 – 784, 2006.

and multi-region to generate a 3-D personalized face model. First, we divide the facial organ regions away from the entire face model, and form them as the first facial layer. Then, we organize the remainder facial model as the second facial layer. We apply different constrained equations to reconstruct these two layers, and integrate them with influence factors. Finally, we use a simple texture mapping method to generate the 3-D personalized realistic face model.

2   Generic Face Model and Feature Extraction

Constructing a reasonable generic face model is the first step for reconstruction of 3-D face model. Different faces, however, still have the same structure, like eyebrows, eyes, nose and mouth, etc. Generic face model congregates these characters to represent the universal facial structure. We have developed a generic face model, in which the facial surface is designed in layers and in normal logical lattices. Our generic face model includes 1044 points and the 95 feature points are pre-defined. The generic face model is shown in Figure 1.

Accurately extracting feature points from photos is an important base to reconstruct 3-D personalized face model. Since photos are two-dimensional, the existing methods have limitations and flaws in generating 3-D feature points' coordinates. The traditional methods, such as the method based on complicated computer vision and the method based on image processing, can't get enough feature points. Moreover, if the background against the face is complicated, these methods can't get feature points accurately. At present, the majority of research teams apply a simple system to extract facial feature points by user's interactive manipulation [9]. This method can acquire a large quantity of feature points that are more accurate than other methods. So an easy way is adopted. First, we construct a simple generic model. It only includes the feature points to extract. Then, we deform this model to fit the face in the photos by interacting. Finally, we get the feature points from the adapted model. For simplicity, we apply Candide-3 [7,9] as this simple generic model.

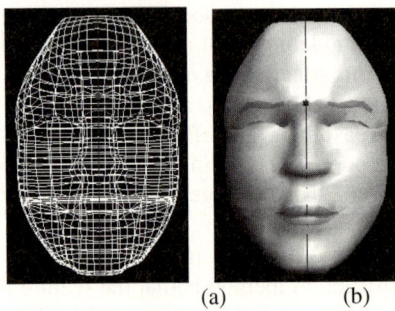

(a)   (b)

Fig. 1. Generic face model, (a) is the wire-frame view, (b) is the rendering view

Before extracting feature points with Candide-3, the images are unified with the same height in front and profile faces. Then, according to the symmetrical characteristics of human face, the left side face photo is mirrored from the right side face photo, which is shown in Figure 2(c). The relationship between the pre-defined 95 facial feature points in the generic model and the key points of Candide-3 is established. In this way, we can acquire all the facial feature points from the orthogonal facial photos by using Candide-3.

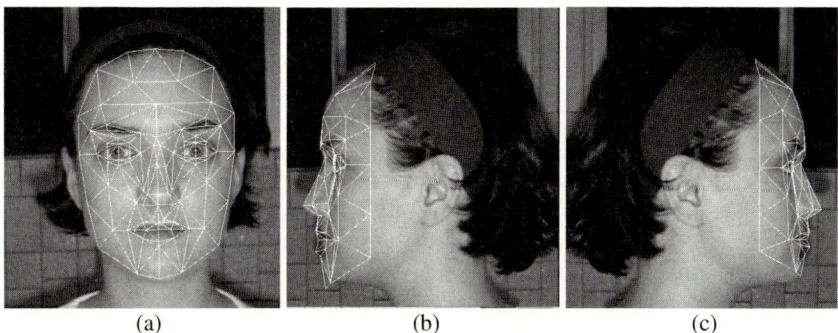

(a)   (b)   (c)

Fig. 2. 3-D Feature points extraction from photos with Candide-3, (a) is the frontal photo, (b) is the right profile photo, and (c) is the left profile photo

3   Personalized Face Model Reconstruction with Multi-layer and Multi-region

The existing methods use one constrained equation to reconstruct personalized face model. By solving the constrained equation with the personalized feature points and generic face model, 3-D personalized face model can be generated. Due to the different distribution of feature point and the characteristics of constrained equation, the influence of each feature point will be distributed to the entire face model. So the methods couldn't accurately express delicate face model. In addition, along with the number of the feature points increase, the cost of model reconstruction increase quickly. In order to solve these problems, we propose a method for 3-D personalized face reconstruction based on multi-layer and multi-region with RBFs. We divide the facial organ regions away from the entire face model, and form them as the first facial layer first. Then, we organize the remainder facial model as the second facial layer. We apply different constrained equations to reconstruct these two layers. Finally, we integrate their boundary points smoothly with their influence factors. Thus we can get a delicate 3-D personalized face model, and noticeably reduce the cost of reconstructing face model.

3.1   3-D Mesh Deformation with RBFs

The family of radial basis functions (RBFs) is well known for its powerful interpolation capability and often used for face model fitting [3,6]. The model deformation is equivalent with multi-variable scattered data interpolation. That is, provided with a generic model and n feature points, when the feature points p_i $(1 \leq i \leq n)$ move to p_i', how can we get the new position of each non-feature point p? We apply RBFs to solve this problem. The formula is as follows:

$$f(p) = \sum_{i=1}^{n} c_i \Phi(\|p - p_i\|) + Mp + t \, , \tag{1}$$

where, the variables n denotes the number of the feature points, c_i the coefficients of the basic function, $p_i(1 \le i \le n)$ the feature points, $\|p-p_i\|$ the Euclidean distance between p and p_i, $\Phi(\|p-p_i\|)$ the basic function, $Mp+t$ the affine basis which represents the global transformation. The affine component M is a 3×3 matrix and t is a 3×1 vector. So the new position of non-feature point p is $p+f(p)$.

The most important step of reconstructing face model with RBFs is the choice of basic functions. Radial basis functions with different basic functions have different characters. The popular choices of basic functions include the Gaussian $\Phi(r)=\exp(-cr^2)$, the thin-plate spline $\Phi(r)=r^2\log(r)$, the multi-quadric and the inverse multi-quadric, etc. After doing experiment with a series of different basic functions, we finally choose $\Phi(r)=e^{-r/R}$ as our basic function, where R is a predefined coefficient that determines the influence range of feature point p_i.

We set $\Delta p_i=p_i'-p_i=f(p_i)(1 \le i \le n)$, where Δp_i is the deformed displacement of feature point, we gain the following formula with n feature points:

$$\Delta p_i = \sum_{j=1}^{n} c_j \Phi(\|p_i - p_j\|) + Mp_i + t, \quad (1 \le i \le n). \tag{2}$$

In order to remove affine contributions from the radial basis functions, we add the following affine constrained transformation:

$$\begin{cases} \sum_{j=1}^{n} c_j = 0 \\ \sum_{j=1}^{n} c_j \cdot p_j = 0 \end{cases} . \tag{3}$$

Then, the equation (2) and (3) may be written in matrix form as follows:

$$\begin{bmatrix} \phi_{11} & \phi_{12} & \cdots & \phi_{1N} & P_{1x} & P_{1y} & P_{1z} & 1 \\ \phi_{21} & \phi_{22} & \cdots & \phi_{2N} & P_{2x} & P_{2y} & P_{2z} & 1 \\ \cdots & \cdots & \cdots & \cdots & \cdots & \cdots & \cdots & \cdots \\ \phi_{n1} & \phi_{n2} & \cdots & \phi_{nn} & P_{nx} & P_{ny} & P_{nz} & 1 \\ P_{1x} & P_{2x} & \cdots & P_{nx} & 0 & 0 & 0 & 0 \\ P_{1y} & P_{2y} & \cdots & P_{ny} & 0 & 0 & 0 & 0 \\ P_{1z} & P_{2z} & \cdots & P_{nz} & 0 & 0 & 0 & 0 \\ 1 & 1 & \cdots & 1 & 0 & 0 & 0 & 0 \end{bmatrix} \begin{bmatrix} c_1 \\ c_2 \\ \vdots \\ c_n \\ M \\ t \end{bmatrix} = \begin{bmatrix} \Delta p_1 \\ \Delta p_2 \\ \vdots \\ \Delta p_n \\ 0 \\ 0 \\ 0 \\ 0 \end{bmatrix}, \tag{4}$$

where $\emptyset_{ij}=\Phi(\|p_i-p_j\|)(1 \le i,j \le n)$, and (P_{ix}, P_{iy}, P_{iz}) is the coordinate of the feature point p_i. The parameter values c_i, M and t in formula (1) can be determined by solving the linear function (4).

3.2 Multi-layer and Multi-region Face Division and Reconstruction

The personalized characters of each face are mainly shown as the shape of the facial organ and the facial contour. So, we use more feature points to describe the facial organs, in order to acquire delicate facial organs.

We separate the organs from the face and set them as the first layer of the model. It includes left eye region, right eye region, nose region and mouth region, in which left eye region (with left eyebrow) includes 17 feature points, right eye region (with right eyebrow) includes 17 feature points, nose region includes 21 feature points and mouth region includes 20 feature points. The remainder face model is formed as the second layer of the face model. It includes 65 feature points, and mainly shows the character of the shape of the facial contour. We reconstruct these two layers of the face model by using radial basis functions with different R respectively.

The feature points of the facial organs in the first layer are dense and their distribution ranges are narrow. We apply small R for their basic function. For example, for the regions of eye, nose and mouth we use 0.6 in our experiments. The feature points of the second layer are sparse and their distribution range is wide. We employ the smooth basic function. The value of R is much greater than the first layer's. In this paper, we use 64. The method of reconstructing face model with multi-layer and multi-region has many advantages. It can avoid the influences of other layer and other facial organ regions for the given layer and organ region. The facial organ regions and the second layer are respectively reconstructed by using their own feature points. In this way, more delicate facial organ regions and smoother facial surface can be gotten.

3.3 Integration of Two Layers with Influence Factors

After reconstructing each layer of face model, we should integrate these layers to form an entire face model. Since the two layers are reconstructed with different basis functions, the feature points in two layers' boundary have the same positions after being reconstructed respectively, while the non-feature points' positions are different. Based on the character of radial basis functions, we employ influence factors to integrate these two layers' boundaries to form an entire face model.

Assume that p is a non-feature point in the organ regions' boundary before reconstruction. Here $face\_region_i$ ($1 \leq i \leq 4$) denotes one of the organ regions in the first layer of face model, and $face\_off\_region$ denotes the second layer of face model. Assume that p_1 is the new position of p in $face\_region_i$ after reconstruction, and p_2 is the new position of p in $face\_off\_region$ after reconstruction. The influence factors of each layer are decided by the feature points' distribution in each layer. We set the influence factors in terms of the feature points' number and the feature points' distribution range. The greater the feature points' number is, the larger influence factor is. While the range of distribution is wider, the influence factor is smaller. So, the entire face model has four groups of influence factors corresponding to the four facial organ regions.

Assume that α_i is the influence factor of the boundary of $face\_region_i$, and α_{0i} is the influence factor of the relative boundary of $face\_off\_region$. $Pface\_region_i = \{p_{ij} | 1 \leq j \leq n_i\}$ ($1 \leq i \leq 4$) denotes the set of feature points of $face\_region_i$, where n_i is the feature points' number of *face_region$_i$*. We set $\bar{P}_i = \frac{1}{n_i}\sum_{j=1}^{n_i} p_{ij} (1 \le i \le 4)$ as the center of all the feature points of *face_region$_i$*. While *Pface_off_region*=$\{p_{0i}|1 \le i \le n_0\}$ denotes the set of the feature points of *face_off_region*, where n_0 is the count of the feature points of second layer surface. Likewise, we set $\bar{P}_0 = \frac{1}{n_0}\sum_{i=1}^{n_0} p_{0i}$ as the center of *face_off_region*. Then the average distance between $\bar{P}_0$ and each feature point of *face_off_region* is calculated as follows:

$$R_0 = \frac{1}{n_0}\sum_{i=1}^{n_0}\left\|\bar{P}_0 - p_{0i}\right\|. \tag{5}$$

The average distance between $\bar{P}_i$ and each feature point of *face_region$_i$* is calculated as follows:

$$R_i = \frac{1}{n_i}\sum_{j=1}^{n_i}\left\|\bar{P}_i - p_{ij}\right\|, \quad (1 \le i \le 4). \tag{6}$$

Considering the relationship of the influence factors between *face_region$_i$* and *face_off_region*, they should have this constraint: $\alpha_i + \alpha_{0i} = 1$. So, we design following formula to calculate α_i and α_{0i},

$$\begin{cases} \alpha_i = n_i R_0 /(n_0 R_i + n_i R_0) \\ \alpha_{0i} = n_0 R_i /(n_0 R_i + n_i R_0) \end{cases}. \tag{7}$$

The position p' of non-feature point p of the boundary of *face_region$_i$* and *face_off_region* can be calculated as follows:

$$p' = \alpha_i * p_1 + \alpha_{0i} * p_2. \tag{8}$$

According to the formula (8), we can calculate all the non-feature points on the boundary of each facial organ. So, the organ regions are integrated into the second layer of face model smoothly. Thus the personalized facial model is reconstructed.

4   Texture Mapping

Now, we mainly consider the feature of frontal face in face modeling, so we use the frontal face photo as facial texture. We extract texture coordinates of the feature points when fitting Candide-3 with face photos. The reconstructed face model fits with face in the photos. Let $P_1(x_1,y_1,z_1)$ and $P_2(x_2,y_2,z_2)$ denote two arbitrary feature points, gain their texture coordinates $T_1(u_1,v_1)$ and $T_2(u_2,v_2)$. $P(x,y,z)$ denotes the point of the frontal face model, its texture coordinate $T(u,v)$ can be calculated as follows:

$$\begin{cases} u = (x - x_1)/(x_2 - x_1) * (u_2 - u_1) + u_1 \\ v = (y - y_1)/(y_2 - y_1) * (v_2 - v_1) + v_1 \end{cases}. \tag{9}$$

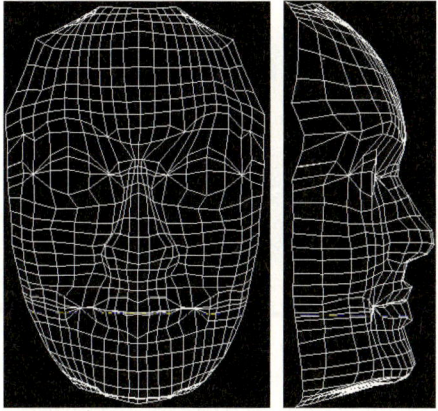

Fig. 3. The frontal and profile facial meshes based on entire reconstruction, (a) is the frontal face mesh, and (b) is the profile face mesh

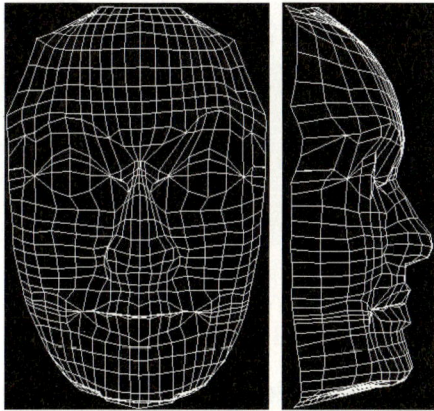

Fig. 4. The frontal and profile facial meshes based on multi-layer and multi-region reconstruction, (a) is the frontal face mesh, and (b) is the profile face mesh

5   Experiment Results and Analysis

On Jeremy's face photos, we respectively accomplish entire reconstruction by using one RBF and multi-layer and multi-region reconstruction by using multiple RBFs. The results are shown in Figure 3 and Figure 4.

We can see clearly that the region between nose and mouth shown in Figure 3 isn't as satisfied as it shown in Figure 4. Moreover, the method of multi-layer and multi-region reconstruction is more delicate and more reasonable for describing the shapes of facial organ regions and the facial contour.

The multi-layer and multi-region reconstruction algorithm has higher efficiency, because it divides one mass set of feature points into some small sets of feature points. On a 1.7G PIV micro-computer with 256MB RAM, we do a number of experiments in

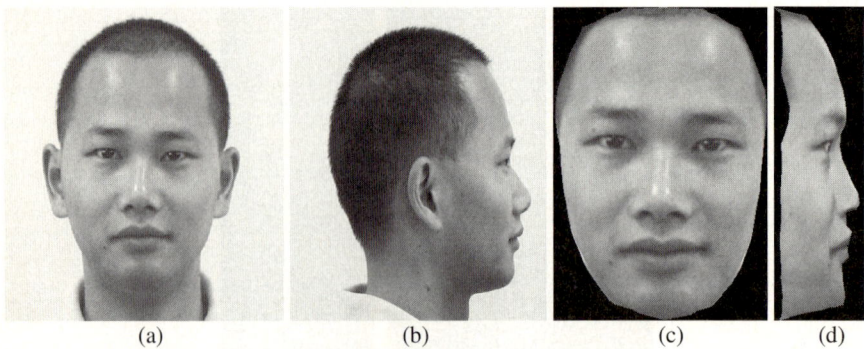

Fig. 5. Personalized face model 1, (a) is the frontal face photo, (b) is the profile face photo, (c) is the frontal personalized face model, and (d) is the profile personalized face model

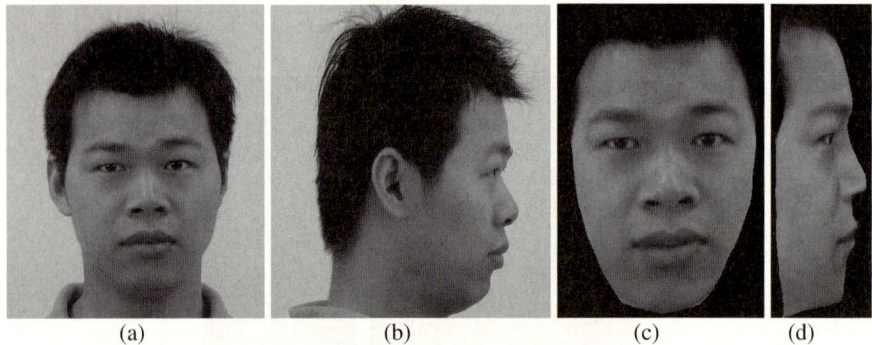

Fig. 6. Personalized face model 2, (a) is the frontal face photo, (b) is the profile face photo, (c) is the frontal personalized face model, and (d) is the profile personalized face model

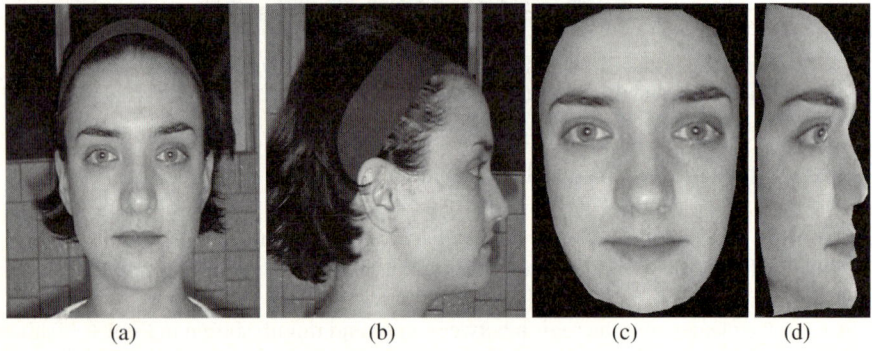

Fig. 7. Personalized face model 3, (a) is the frontal face photo, (b) is the profile face photo, (c) is the frontal personalized face model, and (d) is the profile personalized face model

the same environment for different facial photos by using entire reconstruction and multi-layer and multi-region reconstruction respectively. The average cost of entire reconstruction is 1.2031s, while multi-layer and multi-region reconstruction costs

0.8857s. Comparing with entire reconstruction, the multi-layer and multi-region reconstruction decreases 26.4% on the cost of running time.

We do a series of experiments to reconstruct personalized face model using frontal and profile facial photos of different people. Some reconstructed 3-D face models are shown in Figure 5, Figure 6 and Figure 7. The results are satisfied.

6   Conclusion

Since the structure of human face is complicated, the traditional methods can't describe the delicate facial characters with one constrained equation in reconstruction of personalized face model. Moreover, the computation cost of these methods is greater. This paper presents a method of reconstructing personalized face model based on multi-layer and multi-region with RBFs. First, we separate the facial organs from entire face model and reconstruct them with reasonable basic function. The remainder surface of face model is reconstructed with smooth basic function. Then, we integrate these two layers with their influence factors to form an entire personalized face model. Finally, we map the frontal facial texture onto the personalized face model to generate realistic face model. The experiments show that the reconstructed personalized face model is more delicate and the computational cost of this algorithm is smaller. As a whole, the result is satisfied. In future, we will extract the feature points from face photos automatically and produce view-independent texture from front and profile facial photos.

Acknowledgements. This research has been supported by Qinglan Project Foundation of Jiangsu Province of China under grant No.1191170004, the advanced Professional Talent Research Foundation of Jiangsu University of China under grant No.05JDG020. We would like to thank Jörgen Ahlberg for letting us use the face model (Candide-3) he created. And we would also like to thank Asım Güvendik, Aslı Gülen, Kayhan İnce and Mehmet Özer Metın for their providing manual face interaction software.

References

1. Lee, Y., Terzopulos, D., Waters, K. : Realistic Modeling for Facial Animation. Computer Graphics. In: Proceedings of SIGGRAPH'96, ACM Press, New York , (1996) 55-62
2. Blanz, V., Vetter, T.: A morphable Model for the Synthesis of 3-D Faces. In: Proceedings of SIGGRAPH'99, ACM Press, New York, (1999) 187-194
3. Pighin, F., Hecher, J., Lischinski, D., Szeliski, R., Salesin, D.: Synthesizing Realistic Facial Expressions from Photographs. In: Proceedings of SIGGRAPH'98, ACM Press, New York, (1998) 75-84
4. Takaaki, A., Yasuhito, S., Wallace, R. S.: Automatic Creation of 3-D Facial Models. IEEE Computer Graphics & Applications, 13(5) (1993) 16-22
5. Horace, H.S. Ip, Yin, L.: Constructing a 3-D Individual Head Model from Two Orthogonal Views. The Visual Computer, 12(5) (1996) 254-266

6. Mei, L. Bao, H.J., Zhen, W.T., Peng, Q.S.: Realistic Reconstruction of Human Face Based on Images. Chinese Journal of computers, 23(9) (2000) 996-1002
7. http://www.bk.isy.liu.se/candide/main.html
8. Yin, B.C, Gao, W.: Radial Basis Function Interpolation on Space Mesh. In: Proceedings of ACM SIGGRAPH'97, ACM Press, New York, (1997) 150.
9. http://www.ceng.metu.edu.tr/~e116246/face/

Recognition and Location of Fruit Objects Based on Machine Vision

Hui Gu, Yaya Lu, Jilin Lou, and Weitong Zhang

Information Engineering College, Zhejiang University of Technology,
310014, Hangzhou, China
gh@zjut.edu.cn, {oo327, phonixlou, seasonzwt}@163.com

Abstract. This paper discussed the low level machine vision on fruit and vegetable harvesting robot, introduced the recognition and location of fruit and vegetable objects under nature scenes, put forward a new segmentation method combined with several color models. What's more, it presented a novel conception for the determination of the abscission point, successfully resolved the location of center and abscission point when the fruit were partially occluded. Meanwhile, by the technique of geometry, it settled the locations of the abscission point when the fruit grew askew. It proved good effect under the nature scene.

Keywords: Machine vision, fruit object, recognition, location.

1   Introduction

During the process of human conquering the Nature, rebuilding the Nature and promoting the society, humans are facing the problem of ability limitation. As a result, humans have been seeking for the robots to substitute the man to complete complicated tasks, and the intelligent robot is the best choice.

As we all know, vision is the main way of humans apperceiving the world. About *80%* information is got through vision. So, it is vital to grant vision function for intelligent robots. Here, we can define the machine vision as follows: it is able to produce some description about the content of the image after processing the input image [1].

There are many fields related with machine vision. So, it also has a wide application in various aspects, from medical image to remote sensed image, from industrial inspection to agricultural areas, etc.

The fruit and vegetable harvesting robot which we are going to discuss is one kind of automatic mechanical harvesting systems possessing the perceptive ability, can be programmed to harvest, transfer and pack the crops [2]. During the process of harvesting, the chief problem of the vision system is to recognize and locate the fruit object [3]. Here, recognition means segmentation of the fruit objects from the complicated background [4]. And location includes two aspects: location of the fruit center and abscission point.

Z. Pan et al. (Eds.): ICAT 2006, LNCS 4282, pp. 785 – 795, 2006.

Recently, there're many researches about fruit and vegetable harvesting robot based on machine vision [5][6]. Cai Jian-rong presented the machine vision recognition methods under the nature scene. Using the Otsu algorithm, it got the segmentation threshold automatically and extracted the target [7]. Miyanaga introduced the seeding grafting technique based on machine vision and the robot invented by them has been put into production [8]. Slaughter D.C set up one orange classier model by using the color feature in the chromatic digital image [9].

Among these researches, there have been many methods of extracting the fruits from complicated nature scene. But the basic conception is extracting the fruit object by converting one color model to another one which is easier to process or much more suitable for the case. However, still, there are two problems remain unsettled: 1) How to determine the abscission point when the fruits grow askew; 2) How to determine the center and abscission point when there are so many fruit overlapped each other that it is impossible to detect the whole edge. If both of the problems remain unsettled, it means the harvesting may be a failure.

And, what is more important, there is only about *40%* of the fruit and vegetable is visible in the orchard[10], which means about *60%* objects are partially occluded or completely occluded . Generally, the agricultural robots are fit with fans so as to blow the leaves covering the fruit. So, for the fruit occluded completely, it may be partially resolved in this way.

So, in the paper, we only discussed the problem of the fruit partially occluded, in particular, the case that one fruit overlap another one. As a whole, the problem we are to discuss belongs to the low level machine vision, and is one of the key steps in the machine vision.

2   Methodology Used in the Paper

2.1   Main Idea

From the analysis above, we knew, in order to segment the fruit from leaves and branches, we should use color model suits certain situations. The RGB color model commonly used is not suitable for the orchard images. Because in RGB color space, the tricolor (RGB) not only represent the hue value, but also represent the brightness. So, the change of the outward illumination may add the difficulty of the recognition, so RGB is undependable in the process of the segmentation. In order to make use of the fruit's clustering feature in hue space, we need to separate the hue and brightness information. We can achieve this goal by transferring the RGB to the models which separate hue and brightness.

2.2   Color Models

We use three types of color models in the paper. The first one is *LCD (luminance and color difference)* model. There are four color attributes in this model, including brightness information Y, color difference of red, C_r, color difference of green C_g, color difference of blue C_b. The transform formula is as follows:

$$\begin{cases} Y = 0.299R + 0.587G + 0.114B \\ C_r = R - Y \\ C_g = G - Y \\ C_b = B - Y \end{cases} \cdot \tag{1}$$

During the process of experiment, we found that the color difference of red of fruit is much higher than that of leaves or branches, even the unripe fruit, such as unripe tomato that would be referred later. So we only have to consider about the color difference of red C_r.

The second model we used is Normalized RGB. The diagram was used to represent the color properties of the three portions. The transform formula is defined as follows:

$$\begin{cases} r = R / (R + G + B) \\ g = G / (R + G + B) \\ b = B / (R + G + B) \end{cases} \cdot \tag{2}$$

it is obvious it satisfies: $r + g + b = 1 \cdot$

Combined the advantages of the above two models, we can conclude the third color model called *LHM* in this paper. Choosing Y and C_r from the first color model, r and g from the second model; we can construct the formula as follow:

$$\begin{cases} Y = 0.299R + 0.587G + 0.114B \\ C_r = R - Y \\ r = R/(R + G + B) \\ g = G/(R + G + B) \end{cases} \cdot \tag{3}$$

3 Segmentation

Under the nature scene of the orchard, the factors containing the non-uniform illumination, the occlusion of the leaf and branch all make it more difficult to segment. At present, we can classify the chromatic image segmentation into three classes: (1) Segmentation based on threshold; (2) Segmentation based on edge inspecting and area growing; (3) Segmentation based on color clustering [11].

3.1 Clustering and Classifier

The primary conception of clustering is to distinguish the different objects which include different classes of objects and different parts of the same object [12]. All classification algorithms are based on the assumption that the image in question depicts one or more features and that each of these features belongs to one of several distinct and exclusive classes.

The traditional way of classifier comprises two phases of process: training and testing. In the initial training phase, characteristic properties of typical image features are isolated and, based on these, a unique description of each classification category, *i.e.* training class, is created. In the subsequent testing phase, these feature-space partitions are used to classify image features.

In the experiment, we sampled *60* pixels of leaf, branch, and fruit respectively and constructed a classifier. Adopting two feature patterns m and n, we formed the decision functions: $f(m,n) = am + bn + c$, where a, b, and c are arbitrary constants as long as the points on the line satisfies the condition $f(m,n) = 0$. Here, feature pattern may be color, shape, size, or any properties of the objects. According to the decision functions $f(m,n) > 0$ or $f(m,n) < 0$, we can divide the image into two parts as shown in Fig 1:

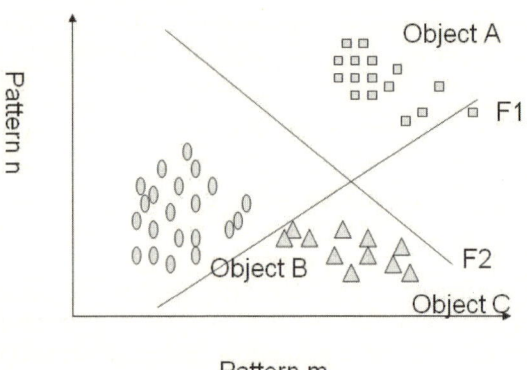

Fig. 1. Model of classifier

3.2 Segmentation of the Fruit Objects

In this study, we adopted the segmentation method of several thresholds. The thresholds are derived from the above three models of the image using the decision functions. According to the above paragraphs, we could get three decision functions: the first function, *F1*, separated the fruit portion and the leaf portion, the second function, *F2*, separated the fruit portion from the branch portion, and the third function *F3*, separated the leaf portion from the branch portion. But, on the basis of the request of the experiment, we only have to segment the fruit from the background, and the leaf and branch portions were regarded as background. So, there was no need to consider *F3*.

3.3 Analyzing the Image Using the LCD Model

It is obvious that the fruit, leaf and branch had the different brightness and color difference of the red. So, sampled *60* pixels of the fruit, leaf and branch to train, from Fig2(a), we knew the distance between the mean values of the fruit object and that of the branch and leaf was rather great, so it was appropriate to use the minimum distance classifier.

From the training set, we could get the decision functions according to the minimum distance classifier as follows:

$$\begin{bmatrix} F_{leaf\,/\,fruit} \\ F_{fruit\,/\,branch} \\ F_{leaf\,/\,branch} \end{bmatrix} = \begin{bmatrix} -17.12 & 104.19 & -15867.4 \\ 41.16 & 80.59 & -8993.86 \\ 24.14 & 184.78 & -24861.26 \end{bmatrix} \begin{bmatrix} Y \\ C_r \\ 1 \end{bmatrix} \quad (4)$$

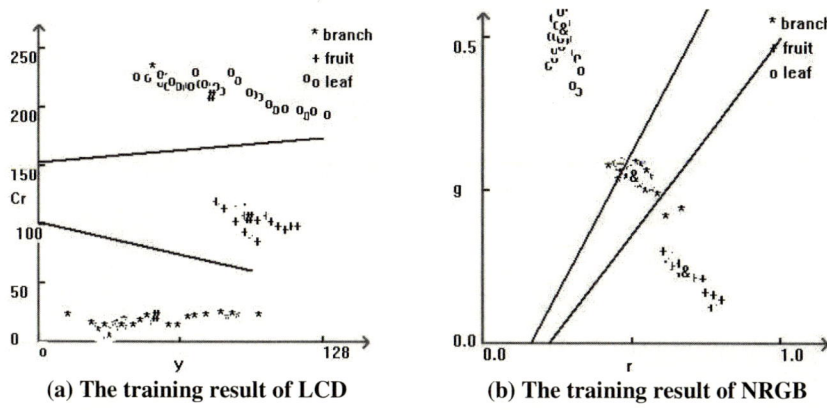

(a) The training result of LCD   (b) The training result of NRGB

Fig. 2. The experimental training result of different color models

3.4 Analyzing the Image Using the Normalized RGB Model

In the same way, we got the training set shown in Fig2 (b) and constructed the decision functions as follows:

$$\begin{bmatrix} F_{leaf\,/\,fruit} \\ F_{fruit\,/\,branch} \\ F_{leaf\,/\,branch} \end{bmatrix} = \begin{bmatrix} -0.358 & 0.33 & 0.101 \\ -0.11 & 0.106 & 0.037 \\ -0.148 & 0.162 & 0.054 \end{bmatrix} \begin{bmatrix} r \\ g \\ 1 \end{bmatrix} \quad (5)$$

3.5 Analyzing the Image Using the LHM Model

Combined the advantages of two models, we could get better result from the intersection of two models. Additionally, the area of blemish points produced in the process of segmentation was rather small and was easy to erase, so the results of intersection did not affect the recognition at all. Results of segmentation by using the three models are as follows:

4 Connected Component Labeling

From Fig3, we can find that the objects obtained from the above steps still have some blemish points, which would disturb the normal recognition. Adopting 8-connected component to label the area, we can get several label values after labeling. So calculated the areas of each label value, we reserved the biggest area, and removed the others. For the further processing, we extracted the edge of the connected component; the result is shown in Fig 4.

Original image	LCD	NRGB	LHM

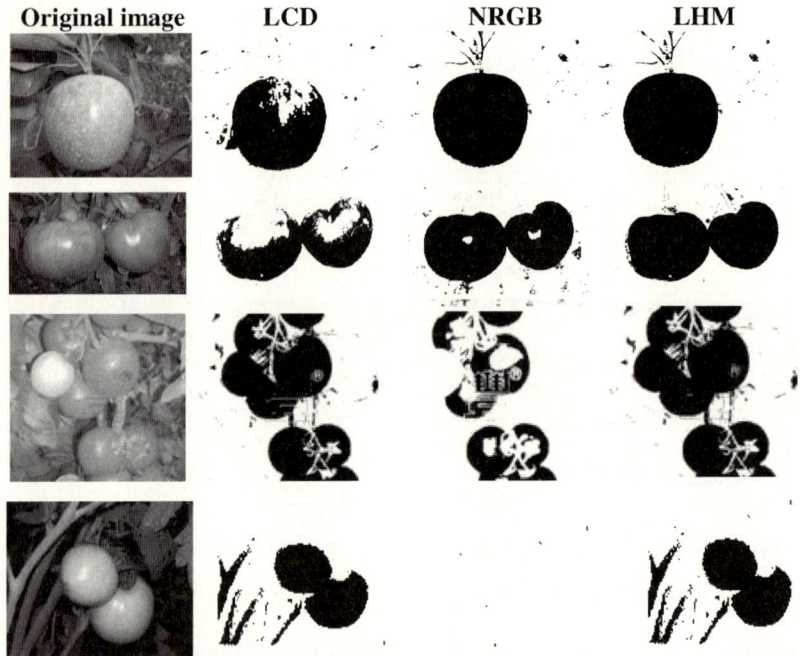

Fig. 3. Results of segmentation using three color models

Fig. 4. Edge of the connected component

5   Location of Center and Abscission Point

For the spherical fruit and vegetable, such as apple, orange and tomato, the two dimension- graphics of these images seem to have a shape of circle because the similarity between them is high to 98% [13]. So, we can simplify the spherical fruits into the problems of the circles.

Unfortunately, most of the paper did not cover the situation when several fruit objects overlapped each other, because the location and picking in such case is difficult. But out of common sense, we could understand the problem as follows: the robot pick the fruit one by one, so it is not necessary to locate the centers of the fruit set obtained from the image acquiring system at the same time. After one fruit was picked, the positions of left fruit objects would be changed accordingly due to the affection of the position and gravity. Under such understanding, we can assurance that locating one center of the fruit in the set is enough. In this way, we can shorten the processing time and simplify the processing step. So, we could claim that the problem lies in which fruit is to pick first. We can give a constraint that the robot always picking the highest fruit at first, which can be easily done by drawing horizontal tangent. And if there are several fruit objects intersect with the horizontal tangent, we can take the first point as the valid point called A from left to right as a rule. Then drew the vertical lines from the left and right at the same time and then got the points of intersection B and C and calculated $|AC|$ and $|AB|$. In the same way, drew a horizontal line from the bottom and got the intersection D, so the exterior rectangle is shown in Fig 5.

Suppose $|AB|>|AC|$, consider all the points in B->A->C->D, give up considering the points in $B \rightarrow D$. Because the points in set $B \rightarrow D$ have the least probability located in the circles passing through point A, so give up considering these points can decrease the computational complexity too. According to the experience, for one kind of the fruit or vegetable, we often can form a model for them. For instance, the tomatoes we experimented can be modeled as Fig6 (a), and apples can be modeled as Fig6 (b). Point O is the center, Point A is the intersection of a horizontal line passing through the center as the leftmost outline of the fruit, and point B is the abscission point. The angle OAB is defined as α. measured the angle of 100 tomatoes and apples; we can get the mean angel value, for example, the tomatoes' $\alpha \approx 48°$, and apples' $\alpha \approx 51°$. So, as long as the fruit nutate naturally, we can get the center and abscission point by the model.

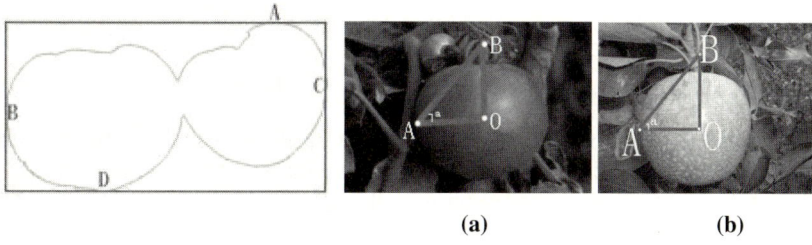

(a)   (b)

Fig. 5. Exterior rectangle   **Fig. 6.** Models of fruit

5.1 Center

We have mentioned above that these fruit and vegetable can be simplified as circles, so the determination of the center of the fruit equals to the determination of the center of the circle. Recently, most researches on center are based on the improvement of the Hough transform [14]; others are based on the geometry methods [15]. Yet, the computational complexity of these methods is rather huge, which result in slow speed of process. As a consequence, it doesn't fit the harvesting machine vision that demands real-time performance.

Consider the points in B->A->C->D of Fig 5, let point A as the starting point, select four points v_1, v_2, v_3, v_4 at random, you can choose A as the constant point that the circle must pass through. According to the theorem that three noncollinear points can determine one circle, we know that four edge points can generally determine four circles: $C_{123}, C_{234}, C_{124}, C_{134}$. And the circle can be written as:

$$2ax + aby + d = x^2 + y^2 . \tag{6}$$

And here it satisfies:

$$d = r^2 - a^2 - b^2 . \tag{7}$$

So, on the condition that three points are noncollinear, we can get one circle. Note this circle as C_{123}, center as (a_{123}, b_{123}) , radius as r_{123}, it can be calculated the center and radius as follows [16]:

$$a_{123} = \frac{\begin{vmatrix} x_2^2 + y_2^2 - (x_1^2 + y_1^2) & 2(y_2 - y_1) \\ x_3^2 + y_3^2 - (x_1^2 + y_1^2) & 2(y_3 - y_1) \end{vmatrix}}{4((x_2 - x_1)(y_3 - y_1) - (x_3 - x_1)(y_2 - y_1))} . \tag{8}$$

$$b_{123} = \frac{\begin{vmatrix} 2(x_2 - x_1) & x_2^2 + y_2^2 - (x_1^2 + y_1^2) \\ 2(x_3 - x_1) & x_3^2 + y_3^2 - (x_1^2 + y_1^2) \end{vmatrix}}{4((x_2 - x_1)(y_3 - y_1) - (x_3 - x_1)(y_2 - y_1))} . \tag{9}$$

$$r_{123} = \sqrt{(x_i - a_{123})^2 + (y_i - b_{123})^2} . \tag{10}$$

Let v_4 $(x_4; y_4)$ be the fourth edge pixel; then the distance between v_4 and the boundary of the circle C_{123} is denoted by:

$$d_{4 \to 123} = \left| \sqrt{(x_4 - a_{123})^2 + (y_4 - b_{123})^2} - r_{123} \right| . \tag{11}$$

If v_4 exactly lies on the circle C_{123}, the equation above equals 0. But due to the images acquired are digital, so it is hard to assure the point lie on the circle exactly. Therefore, the goal of circle detection is to detect a set of edge pixels which lie not exactly but roughly on a digital circle. For convenience, we denote the circle which passes through v_i, v_j, v_k by C_{ijk} and its center and radius are denoted by (a_{ijk}, b_{ijk}) and r_{ijk}, respectively. Let the distance between v_m and C_{ijk} be denoted by:

$$d_{m \to ijk} = \left| \sqrt{(x_m - a_{ijk})^2 + (y_m - b_{ijk})^2} - r_{ijk} \right| . \tag{12}$$

If we find one distance is smaller than given threshold T_d, we claim that this point lie on the circle. Here, we also have to guarantee the distance between any two points of the three points selected randomly should be greater than the given threshold T_a. If two points are too close, the circle may be not a real one. For the example shown in Fig 7, point v_1, v_2, v_3 lie on the boundary of true circle, but undesirable case occurs when v_2 and v_3 are too close, the circle determined by v_1, v_2 and v_3 differs from the true circle. To avoid such case, we should restrict the distances between any two points be greater than a certain threshold T_a.

The following step is to find which circle possesses the most valid points among all true circles. We set a counter $C=0$ for this possible circle how many edge pixels lie on the possible circle. For any pixel in the set V, we can calculate $d_{m->ijk}$ If $d_{m->ijk} <= T_d$, we increment the C by one and remove the pixel v_m from V. Otherwise, we proceed to the next pixel. We continue the above process until all the edge pixels in V have been examined. Note n_p is the number of the pixels lies on the possible circle. If n_p is greater than the global threshold T_g, call this circle a true one, otherwise it is a false one and return all the points to the set V. Then traverse the set n_p, we get the biggest one, and let the corresponding circle as the closest circle.

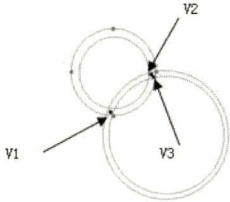

Fig. 7. Example of undesirable Circle

By the way, we should normalize the mentioned global threshold T_g. Because the circles with different radium have different circumferences. Thus, employing some large global threshold T_g is unfair to those circles with small radium. Since any circle in a digital image has a finite radius, the number of pixels on the boundary of a circle is estimated to be $2\prod r$. Hence, when there are n_p edge pixels lying on the possible circle C_{ijk} and the ratio of n_p over the theoretical value $2\prod r_{ijk}$ is larger than the given ratio threshold T_r , we claim that the possible circle is a true circle. Otherwise, the possible circle is a false circle and we return those n_p edge pixels into the set V.

For the original image in Fig 3, the effects are shown in Fig 8.

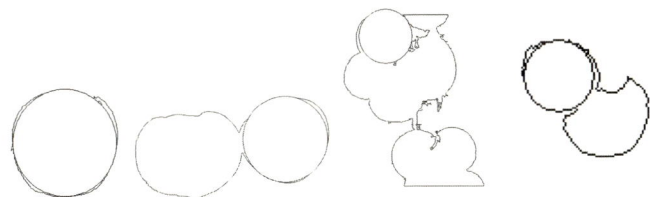

Fig. 8. The closest circle

5.2 Abscission Point

From the analysis, we found the center played an important role in recognition. But due to the randomicity of the development of the fruit, especially when there are several fruit overlap each other. It is common to find that the abscission point deviates from the vertical line passing through center. Take the right tomato in *Fig 3* for example, it is evident the abscission deviates a lot. So, we have to revise the model.

Meanwhile, we could observe the exterior rectangle of the fruit nutate naturally in Fig 9: there is one intersection on each edge, but the top intersection, bottom intersection and the center are collinear nearly. So it is easy to get the abscission point due to the fact that the abscission is on the vertical line passing through the center, and the deviation is too small to ignore.

In addition, we can observe that when the abscission point has a deflection angle, the four intersections in exterior rectangle will be changed correspondingly as shown in Fig 10. Assume point O as center, F as the abscission point, E is the intersection between the vertical line passing through O and the exterior. In true life, we know the length of |OF| almost equals to the radius of the fruit and we have the knowledge that |OA|=r. So, we could easily get $\angle AOE \approx \angle EOF$. Hence, if we can get the coordinates of O and A, we can easily get F. So the correctness of abscission relies on the location of center O. The experimental results are shown in Fig 11 denoted in single lines.

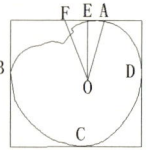

Fig. 9. The exterior rectangle of fruit nutate naturally

Fig. 10. The exterior rectangle of fruit grow askew

Fig. 11. The abscission point of fruit

6 Conclusions

This paper discussed the low level machine vision on fruit and vegetable harvesting robot, introduced the recognition and location of fruit and vegetable objects under nature scenes, put forward a new segmentation method combined with several color models. What's more, it brought forward a novel conception for the determination of the abscission point, resolved the location of center and abscission point when fruit was partially occluded successfully. Meanwhile, by the technique of geometry, it settled the locations of the abscission point when the fruit grew askew. It proved good effect under the nature scene. The accuracy of recognition was high to 94.38 % the location of center was high to 92.6 % and the abscission point was high to 95.65 %

References

1. Milan Sonka, Vaclav Hlavac, Roger Boyle. Image Processing, Analysis and Machine Vision. 2ndVersion. Posts and Telecom press. 2003.
2. Edan Y, Gaines E. Systems engineering of agricultural robot design IEEE Transactions on Systems ,Man , and Cybernetics ,1994 ,24 (8) :1259- 1265.
3. Tang Xiu-ying, Zhang Tie-zhong. Robotics for fruit and vegetable harvesting.Robot, 2005,1(27):90−95.
4. Gu Hui, Cheng Guangyi, Lu Yaya. A curve fitting method based on the direction tracing. Acta Electronica sinica(English Version). 2006 special issue 4.
5. A.R. Jiménez, R. Ceres and J.L. Pons. A survey of computer vision methods for locating fruit on trees. Transaction of ASAE, 2000,43(6):1911-1920.
6. K.F. Sanders. Orange harvesting systems review Biosystem Engineering. 2005,90(2),115-125.
7. Wang Yaqin, Gao Hua. Study on the segmentation and orientation of fruit image under natural environment. Computer Engineering. 2004,30(13):128.
8. Miyanaga T , Fukumo i I, Susaw a K, et al. Technical report of the institute of agricultural machinery. Omiya, Saitama, Japan. 1998.
9. Slaughter D, Harrel R. Discriminating fruit for robotic harvest using color in natural outdoor scenes. Transactions of the ASAE, 1989,32(2):757-763.
10. F. Juste and F. Sevilla, Citrus: A European project to study the robotic harvesting of oranges, in Proceedings, 3rd Int. Symp. Fruit, Nut and Vegetable Harvesting Mechanization, Denmark-Sweden-Norway, 331-338 (1991).
11. Nikhil R ,Pal Sankar K. A Review on image segmentation techniques. Pattern Recognition, 1993,26(9) :1277∼1294.
12. REN Jing. Improved minimum distance classifier-weighted minimum distance classifier. Computer application.2005,25(5):992−994.
13. Zhao Jing. Stem recognition and fruit determination in fruit shape recognition. Journal of Shangdong University of Technology(Sci &Tech).2004,18(5):28.
14. Dimitrios Ioannou, Walter Huda. Circle recognition through a 2D Hough Transform and radius histogramming. Image and vision computing. 1999,17:15-26.
15. Heung-Soo Kim, Jong-Hwan Kim. A two-step circle detection algorithm from the intersecting chords. Pattern recognition letters. 2001,22: 787-798.
16. Teh-Chuan Chen, Kuo-Liang Chung. An Efficient Randomized Algorithm for Detecting Circle. Computer vision and image understanding. 2001,83:172-191.

A New Algorithm of Gray Watermark Embedding

Yong-zeng Shen, Min-jie Zhang, and Feng Liu

The College of Information Engineering, Zhejiang University of Technology,
Hangzhou (310014), China
syz@zjut.edu.cn

Abstract. The problems of the digital information transmission safety, its' copyright protection etc. are seriously increase. Digital watermark is one of the good solutions for many problems mentioned above. Generally the watermark information is a one-dimension random signal. Two-dimension gray watermark is difficult to guarantee the robustness of the information embedding. Put a new kind of discrete wavelet transform (DWT) and the singular value decompose (SVD) on two-dimension gray watermark, the watermark becomes very strong robust to the compression, noise, low pass filter, high pass filter and median filter. It is useful for the safety of digital information transmission and its copyright protection.

Keywords: Watermark; embedding algorithm; discrete wavelet transform (DWT); Singularity value decompose (SVD).

1 Introduction

In recent years, computer multi-media technique is developed very fast. People can conveniently use digital devices to make and handle information media such as image, picture, text, speech sound and video etc.[1]. The developing network technique is making the information transmission easier than any time before. This causes the problems of the safety of digital information transmission and copyright etc. The problems are serious increasingly. So, a kind of new digital encrypts technique, digital watermark, is put forward to provide the good solution for many problems mentioned above[2]. The original thought is that clandestine information is embedded for the purpose of the copyright protection of digital product or for the purpose of enhancing the concealment of embedded information in digital picture, voice frequency and video etc.

Digital watermark needs two important characteristics, one of them is the transparence, and another is the robust. It means that the watermark must be difficult to be punctured of.

The watermark technique of the picture can be divided into two classes, mostly according to the inlaid mode in watermark: the empty field technique and the transform field technique. The empty field technique is that the watermark is brightly embedded in picture value. The transform field technique is that make the picture to a certain mathematics transform, then the watermark is embedded in its' transform coefficient inside. From the current circumstance, transform field method is becoming

Z. Pan et al. (Eds.): ICAT 2006, LNCS 4282, pp. 796–801, 2006.

widespread. Because the transform field method usually has the good robustness, it contains certain resistibility in image compress, picture filtering and noise disturbing. Most majority transform field methods adopt the unitary transformation, discrete cosine transform (DCT)[1], discrete Fourier Transform (DFT) and discrete wavelet transform (DWT)[3,4] etc. One of the most famous methods is the extension spectrum communication method based on discrete cosine transform.

Through several years research, digital watermark technique is developed greatly. Many excellent algorithms appeared. In these algorithms, the watermark information is generally a one-dimension random signal. The research of two-dimension gray watermark is not a lot of. This is primarily because of its data quantity too big and too difficult to guarantee the robust of the embedded information. According to above points, this article put forward a new kind of wavelet transform and the singular value decompose in to two dimension gray watermark. It has very strong robust.

2   The Basic of Theory Analysis

2.1   Discrete Wavelet Transform Analysis Foundation

The wavelet transform theory causes the extensive concern of everyone as soon as it published. Wavelet analysis belongs to a kind of time and frequency analysis. The reason of that it is better than Fourier transform is: it has good local quality with frequency domain and time domain simultaneously. The 2^j flexible rate in wavelet transform is fit in with computer vision and human's vision feature. Mallat used wavelet transform theory to signal transaction in 1988, much put forward the concept of the scale analysis, giving the algorithm to resolve picture as different frequency band and reconstruct it.

The discrete wavelet transform (DWT) [5]of a image signal can be looked upon the lower frequency filter and higher frequency filter on rows and columns of two dimension signal, equal to a four band filtering, get two-dimension signal coefficient on LL1, LH1, HL1 and HH1 sub-bands. According to the demand of analysis, we can then take LL1 sub-band go on the further resolves, until obtain what we need. For the human's vision feature, the eye is sensitive to the change of the smooth region of the picture. But it is not sensitive with the small change of the picture rim and texture region. In wavelet transform, the features of the texture and rim generally concentrate in the higher frequency sub-bands LH1, HL1 and HH1. If we put the watermark information on these coefficients, human's eye do not realizes it easily. We can then put more watermark information on it. But the watermark information on the high frequency will be lost easily by ordinarily picture handling. Its robustness is not enough strong. The more the watermark information on the high frequency, the easier the watermark information is lost. For the sake of enhancing the watermark robustness, the embed watermark amount of information is usually less. If we embed the less watermark information on the larger coefficient of the image's lower frequency sub-bands, the robustness of the watermark will be strengthened consumedly.[6,7]

A method to construct the ranks with different distinguish rate is to relate two passband filters with degrade sample process. Two passband filters must be Quadrature and defined as following:

Higher passband:

$$H(\omega) = \sum_k h_k \exp(-jk\omega) \tag{1}$$

Low passband:

$$G(\omega) = \sum_k g_k \exp(-jk\omega) \tag{2}$$

Here h_k is the filter pulse response and $g_k = (-1)^k h_k$.

The definition of the signal decompose iteration process is:

$$c_{j-1,k} = \sum_n h_{n-2k} c_{j,n} \tag{3}$$

$$d_{j-1,k} = \sum_n g_{n-2k} c_{j,n} \tag{4}$$

The definition of the signal reconstruction iteration process is:

$$c_{j,n} = \sum_k h_{n-2k} c_{j-1,k} + \sum_k g_{n-2k} d_{j-1,k} \tag{5}$$

2.2 The Theory Analysis of Singular Value Decompositions

The singular value decomposition (SVD) in the value analyze is a kind of matrix diagonalizable algorithm. The main reasons applied in images handle are[8,9]:

(1) The stability of the image singular value is very good. When image suffer from small disturbance, the singular value of the image can't have the big change;
(2) The *singular* value express is the inherent characteristic of the image rather than vision characteristic.

2.2.1 Singular Value Decomposition (SVD)

From the view of the linear algebra, a gray image can be looked as a non-negative matrix. If matrix A is used to express the n×n dimension image, then $A \in R^{n \times n}$, the R mean the real number field. The matrix A of the singular value decomposition definition is as follows:

$$A = USV^T \tag{6}$$

The $U \in R^{n \times n}$ and $V \in R^{n \times n}$, they are all of quadrature matrixes. $S \in R^{n \times n}$ is a diagonal matrix. Superscripts T mean that the matrix transpose.

2.2.2 The Embed and Detection of the Watermark

The basic principle of the SVD method is to embed the watermark into the singular value of the primitive image. During the watermark embedding process, first makes the singular value decomposition of the n×n gray image matrix A, get two quadrature matrix U, V and a diagonal matrix S. Watermark matrix $W \in R^{n \times n}$ is added to the matrix S. This generates the matrix $S+\alpha W$. Then we makes the singular value decomposition of the matrix $S+\alpha W$, get matrix U_1, V_1 and S_1. $S+\alpha W = U_1 S_1 V_1^T$. The constant $\alpha>0$, is used to regulate the degree of the watermark intensity. Then multiply the matrix U, S_1 and V^T, get the image $\hat{A}$. $\hat{A}$ include the watermark. Namely if matrix A and W mean the original image and watermark respectively, the three steps passing as follows gets the watermark image:

$$A \Rightarrow USV^T \tag{7}$$

$$S + \alpha W \Rightarrow U_1 S_1 V_1^T \tag{8}$$

$$\hat{A} \Leftarrow US_1V^T \tag{9}$$

During the watermark detection process, if give the matrix U_1, S, V_1 and the watermark image $A*$ that maybe damaged, we can withdraw the distorted watermark $W*$ by the simple inverse process:

$$A^* \Rightarrow U^*S_1^*V^{*T} \tag{10}$$

$$D^* \Leftarrow U_1S_1^*V_1^T \tag{11}$$

$$W^* \Leftarrow (D^* - S)/\alpha \tag{12}$$

3   New Watermark Embedding Algorithm

Using wavelet transform to decompound the primitive gray image I at first layer. Then taking the decomposition low frequency coefficient LL to constitute a matrix A. Using formula (7) to make singular value decomposition. Getting matrixes U, V and S.

Using formula (8) to make the gray watermark matrix W into U1, S1 and V1. Then according to formula (9) to get the LL low frequency coefficient matrix that contains the watermark W.

Reconstructing the wavelet coefficient after changing we can get the gray image I* that containing the embedding watermark.

4   Watermark Detection Algorithm

At first decomposing the gray image $I*$ layer to get the wavelet LL low frequency coefficient. Then constituting the matrix $A*$. According to formula (10), we can get the matrixes $U*$, $S1*$ and $V*$.

Combining matrixes $U1$, $S1*$ and $V1$, getting $D*$ according to formula (11). Then using formula (12) to get the embedded watermark.

5   Experiments

We use MATLAB6.1 as The experiment tool. The experiment image is Lena portrait. The image size is 256×256 pixels. The gray level is 256. The watermark is 32×32 gray image with 256 gray levels.

The experiments using lower passband filter, building out gauss noise, progress median filtering, compression etc. to attack the original image that using new watermark-embedding algorithm. Then examining the watermark using detection algorithm described above. The result is shown as figures following.

Reconstructing the wavelet coefficient after embed watermark, we get the Fig.2.(a). Using watermark detection algorithm on Fig.2.(a), we get the watermark shown as Fig.2.(b). Now we building out gauss noise, add it on the Fig.2.(a). The result shown as Fig.2.(c). From Fig.2.(c)., we detected the watermark like Fig.2.(d). It is almost as same as Fig.2.(b), indicate that the new watermark embedding algorithm has resistibility on gauss noise disturb.

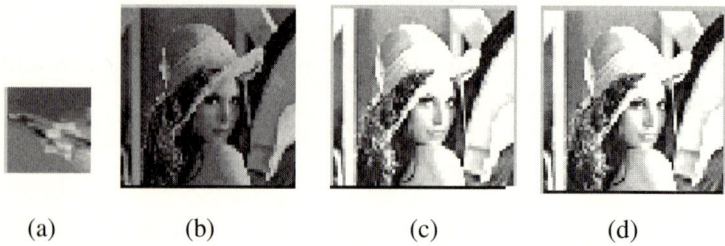

(a)   (b)   (c)   (d)

Fig. 1. (a) is the gray watermark that we would embed into the original image (b). After make DWT on original image (b), we get the LL sub-band image (c). Then embed the gray watermark (a) into the LL sub-band image (c). The result of the LL sub-band image after embed watermark. is (d).

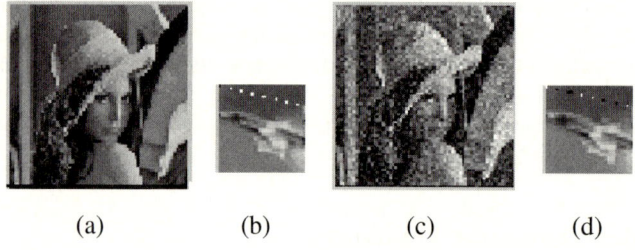

(a)   (b)   (c)   (d)

Fig. 2. (a) is the gray image. (b) is detected watermark. (c) is added gauss noises on the gray image after embed watermark. (d) is detected watermark from (c).

Fig.3. show the resistibility on median filtering and JPEG compression of the new watermark embedding algorithm

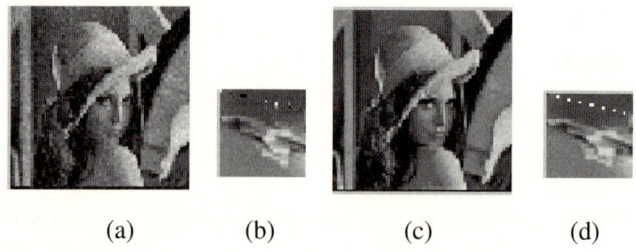

(a)   (b)   (c)   (d)

Fig. 3. (a) is progressing median filtering on the gray image after embed watermark. (b) is the detected watermark from (a). (c) is progressing 10% JPEG compression on the gray image after embed watermark. (d) is detected watermark from (c).

6   Conclusion

This article put forward a kind of new gray watermark embedding algorithm, through the experiments we know the algorithm has some good features that can satisfy the transparency and robustness of the watermark system. The experiments shows it has resistibility in image compress, in picture filtering and noises disturb. It is useful for the safety of digital information transmission and its copyright protection. The new watermark embedding algorithm can resist the attacks of noise, median filtering, compression...etc.. It can still through suffer the high pass filter and low pass filter. The algorithm is especially useful on the watermark embed of the static image.

References

1. Cox.I.J, Killian.J, Leighton.F.T.etal.: Secure spread spectrum watermarking for multimedia. IEEE Trans Image Processing (1997) 6(1 2) :1673-1687
2. Srefan Katzenbeisser, fabien A.P.Petitcolas: Information Hiding Techniques for Ste-ganography and Digital Watermarking. ARTECH HOUSE, INC.
3. Hsu, C.T., Wu, J.L.: Multiresolution watermarking for digital images. IEEE Transactions on Circuits and SystemII: Analog and Digital Signal Processing 45 (8) (1998)
4. Lu, C.S., Huang, S.K., Sze, C.J., Liao, H.Y.: A new watermarking technique for multimedia protection. In: Guan, L., Kung,S.Y., Larsen, J. (Eds.), Multimedia Image and Video Processing. CRC Press, Boca Raton. Available from http://smart.iis.sinica.edu.tw/lcs(2000)
5. Edwards. T.: Discrete Wavelet Transforms: Theory and Implementation. Stanford University (1991)
6. Ohnishi.J, Matsui.K.: Embedding a seal into a picture under orthogonal wavelet transform. Proc ICMCS'96[C] (1996) 514-521
7. Iwata, M., Shiozaki, A.: Watermarking method for embedding index data into images utilizing features of wavelet transform. IEICE Trans. Fundam (2001) E84-A:1772–1778
8. Andrews, H.C., Patterson, C.L.: Singular value decomposition (SVD) image coding. IEEE Trans. Comm. COM-24 (1976) 425–432
9. Jieh-Ming Shieh, Der-Chyuan Lou and Ming-Chang Chang.: A semi-blind digital watermarking scheme based on singular value decomposition. Computer Standards & Interfaces. (2006) 28(4): 428-440

A Semiautomatic Nonrigid Registration in Liver Cancer Treatment with an Open MR System

Songyuan Tang[1,2], Yen-wei Chen[2], Rui Xu[2], Yongtian Wang[1]
Shigehiro Morikawa[3], and Yoshimasa Kurumi[3]

[1] Department of Opto-electronic Engineering, Beijing Institute of Technology, P.R. China
sytang@bit.edu.cn
[2] College of Information Science and Engineering, Ritsumeikan University, Japan
chen@is.ritsumei.ac.jp, gr042049@se.ritsumei.ac.jp
[3] Shiga University of Medical Science, Japan
morikawa@belle.shiga-med.ac.jp

Abstract. A semiautomatic nonrigid registration is proposed to match preoperative CT images and real-time MR images during the ablation of liver tumors. The method includes three parts. Firstly, the livers are extracted from CT and MR images. Since the CT image is acquired a several days before surgery, there is enough time for surgeons to segment the liver from the CT image manually. During the surgery, active contour is used to extract the liver from the MR image. Then, we use affine registration to match the images roughly. Finally, high accuracy registration is reached by free-form deformation registration. The average distance of liver surfaces is within 1.5 mm and the result of visual inspection is very well. The results are far better than Andres'.

1 Introduction

With the development of open configuration MR systems, MR images have been used to guide minimally invasive treatments [1] since MR images have many advantages for image navigation, such as good soft tissue contrast, free from ionizing radiation and multiplanar capabilities. Microwave ablation, an established procedure for the treatment of liver tumors, has been successfully combined with MR image guidance [2]-[4]. During the surgery, when the patient is fixed, the MR image is continuously acquired with gradient echo sequence within 2 seconds. Then the MR images are processed by navigation software on an external computer. The tumor region is manually traced and shown with color on the display. The assistance of this software is quite useful and remarkably expands the indication of this treatment. In some cases with severe chirrhosis, however, visualization of the tumor is still difficult with MR images acquired by the open configuration MR system. In such cases, the combination of preoperative CT images will be greatly helpful, if CT images can be registered to the MR images accurately. An example is shown in Fig.1. In some special case, laparoscopy and MR images are combined to navigate surgery. CO_2 gas is filled into abdomen to enlarge space so as to move the laparoscopy. This causes large deformation of abdomen (fig.1) and makes registration very difficult.

Z. Pan et al. (Eds.): ICAT 2006, LNCS 4282, pp. 802–810, 2006.

Liver image registration goes back to 1983 [5], but most works on liver registration are done in recent years [6]-[10]. Only one paper is found about MR liver image registration with open MR system [10]. In this paper, intensity-based and rigid transform registration is used. There are no previous reports of liver registration using intensity-based nonrigid registration. Actually, nonrigid registration can match image better.

In this paper, we have developed a semiautomatic method to attack the problem. Since CT images are acquired before surgery, the surgeons have enough time to segment them manually and extract liver accurately. During the surgery, a method of active contour is used to extract the liver from MR images after the initial points are selected manually. After segmentation, the segmented images are roughly matched by the intensity-based affine registration, and then free form deformation (FFD) nonrigid registration is used to register the images accuracy. Both registrations use mutual information (MI) as similarity metrics since MI have been proven robust in the multi-model image registration. The registration accuracy is accessed by the visual inspection and the distance of two liver surfaces. Compared with the Andres' method [10], the results are much better.

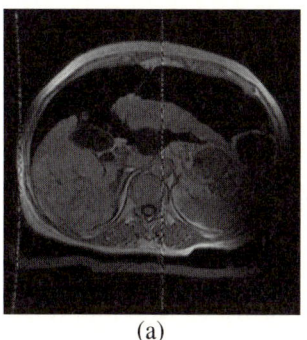
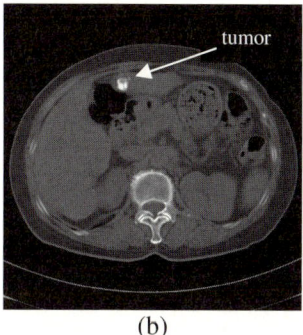

(a)   (b)

Fig. 1.   (a) MR image: the tumor is not clear. CO_2 gas is filled into abdomen and causes abdomen large deformation   (b) CT image: the tumor is very clear.

2   Method

The method includes three parts, preprocessing, registration, and algorithm evaluation as shown in fig.2. The preprocessing includes liver segmentation from CT and MR images, the registration part includes affine and FFD registrations, and algorithm evaluation includes visual inspection, liver surface distance and computing cost.

2.1   Liver Segmentation of MR Images

Since the image of abdomen includes many organs, such as liver, gallbladder, spleen, heart, and soft tissues, and the intensities of them are much closed, it is difficult to segment the liver automatically.   Therefore we adopted a semiautomatic method, active contour, to extract the liver from the MR image.

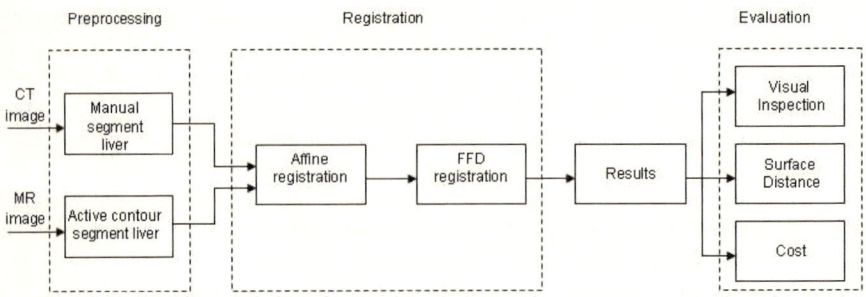

Fig. 2. the diagram of the proposed method

Active contours or snake is curves defined within an image domain. They can move under the action of internal forces coming from the curve and external forces coming from the image data. Both forces drive the snake conform to an object boundary. This property is very suitable to segment the liver from images.

There are two classes of snake models, parametric active contour [11][12] and geometric active contour [13]. We used parametric active contour with the gradient vector flow introduced by [12] to extract the liver since it is robust and can obtain better result.

A snake is a curve $X(s) = [x(s), y(s)]$, $s \in [0,1]$. It moves in an image trending to minimize the energy function

$$E = \int_0^1 \frac{1}{2}\left[\alpha |\mathbf{x}'(s)|^2 + \beta |\mathbf{x}''(s)|^2\right] + E_{ext}(\mathbf{x}(s))ds \tag{1}$$

where α and β are weighting parameters that control the snake's tension and rigidity, and $X'(s)$ and $X''(s)$ are the first and second derivatives of $X(s)$ with respect to s. E_{ext} is derived from the image.

When E is minimized, the snake must satisfy the Euler equation

$$\alpha \mathbf{x}''(s) - \beta \mathbf{x}'''(s) - \nabla E_{ext} = 0 \tag{2}$$

To find a solution of (2), time t is introduced to the snake, that is $\mathbf{x}(s,t)$, and the gradient vector flow field $\mathbf{v}(x, y) = [u(x, y), v(x, y)]$ replaces $-\nabla E_{ext}$. Therefore, (2) is revised as:

$$\frac{\partial \mathbf{x}(s,t)}{\partial t} = \alpha \mathbf{x}''(s) - \beta \mathbf{x}'''(s) + \mathbf{v} \tag{3}$$

When the solution of $\mathbf{x}(s,t)$ is stable, the partial derivative of $\mathbf{x}(s,t)$ is zero, and the solution of (2) is achieved. The solution of (3) can be found in reference [11].

The gradient vector flow field $\mathbf{v}(x, y)$ can be determined by the image. It is acquired when the followed energy function is minimized.

$$\varepsilon = \iint \mu(u_x^2 + u_y^2 + v_x^2 + v_y^2) + |\nabla f|^2 |\mathbf{v} - \nabla f|^2 dxdy \tag{4}$$

where $f(x, y) = -|\nabla[G_\sigma(x, y) * I(x, y)]|^2$, $G_\sigma(x, y)$ is the Gaussian function with standard deviation σ, $I(x, y)$ is the image, and η is regulation parameter.

The initial snake is selected manually firstly, then the gradient vector flow field is achieved by (4), and last the liver is segmented by (3).

2.2 Registration

Affine Registration. After livers are segmented from CT and MR images, Mutual information based affine registration is used to match them roughly. The affine transformation includes three translations, three rotations, three scales and three shears.

The initial translations are determined by the centers of mass of the two segmented livers, the initial scales are set to one, and the initial rotations and shears are set to zero. The Powell optimization is used to obtain these optimal parameters.

FFD Registration. FFD registration is firstly proposed [14] to process breast images, is used to deform the CT image. The shape of image space can be controlled by changing the control grids of the BSpline, and the transform is Cn-1 smooth continuous, where n is the order of BSpline basis function. Usually the C2 continue is enough, therefore, we select three order of BSpline basis function to deform the image space as followed.

$$\begin{aligned}
\theta_0(s) &= (1-s)^3 / 6 \\
\theta_1(s) &= (3s^3 - 6s^2 + 4)/6 \\
\theta_2(s) &= (-3s^3 + 3s^2 + 3s + 1)/6 \\
\theta_3(s) &= s^3 / 6
\end{aligned} \tag{5}$$

The deformation field defined by FFD can be represented as:

$$\vec{u}(x, y, z) = \sum_{l=0}^{3} \sum_{m=0}^{3} \sum_{n=0}^{3} \theta_l(u)\theta_m(v)\theta_n(w)P_{i+l, j+m, k+n} \tag{6}$$

Here P is the control grid.

Usually the cost function includes two parts, one is similarity metrics, which characterizes the similarity of two images, and the other is deformation, which is associated with the particular deformations [15].

$$C = -C_{similarity} + C_{deformation} \tag{7}$$

The positions of control points are optimized so as to deform the CT images. When the cost function reaches minimum, the optimization is stopped.

2.3 Algorithm Evaluation

The proposed method compares with Andres' by visual inspection, liver surface distance and computing cost, which is only report about liver registration of MR images acquired by the open MR system.

The Andres' method selected initial point manually and used mutual information based rigid registration to match images.

3 Data

Six Data sets were acquired from the cooperative hospital. The size of CT images is $512 \times 512 \times 25$, slice thickness is 7.0 mm, and the in-plane dimensions are $0.58mm \times 0.58mm$. CT images were acquired 3 days before the surgery. MR images were acquired by a 0.5 T open configuration MR system. The size is $256 \times 256 \times 28$, slice thickness is 5.0 mm, and the in-plane dimensions are $1.172mm \times 1.172mm$. One of them used both laparoscopic image and MR image to guide surgery. The abdominal cavity was inflated with CO_2 gas for the laparoscopy. MR images were acquired after the inflation during surgical procedure.

4 Experiment Results

4.1 Liver Segmentation

An example of manual segmentation of CT is shown in figure 3(a). It is segmented by experts carefully.

Fig.3 (b)-(d) shows an example of snake segmentation of MR image. The liver includes two separate parts. Therefore, we manually initialized the snake respectively as figure 3 (b) and (c) shown. Then we combined them into a result as figure 3 (d) shown. The liver can be segmented within 20 minutes.

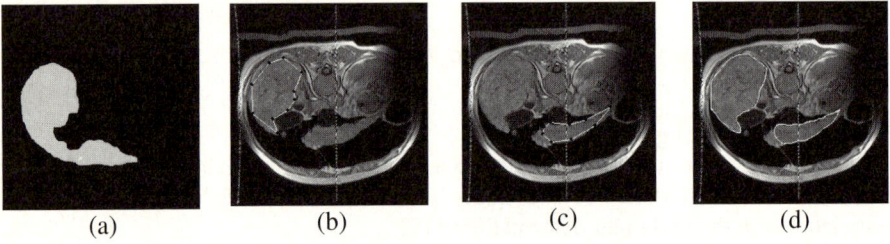

(a)	(b)	(c)	(d)

Fig. 3. (a) liver segmentation of CT image by experts. (b) and (c) manually select initial snakes (d) result of liver segmentation from MR image.

The segmentation accuracy A is evaluated by the result of manual segmentation and uses followed formula:

$$A = 2\frac{R_s \cap R_m}{R_s + R_m} \qquad (8)$$

Where R_s is the result obtained by snake, R_m is the result by manual segmentation.

The value A varies between 0 and 1. When the value is near one, the result obtained by snake is approach the result by manual segmentation. In our experiment, the average value is 0.95. The segmented results are accepted.

4.2 Results of Registration

After segmentation, the segmented livers are used as region of interest (ROI) to match CT and MR images. All data are matched successfully. An example is shown in figure 4 and 5.

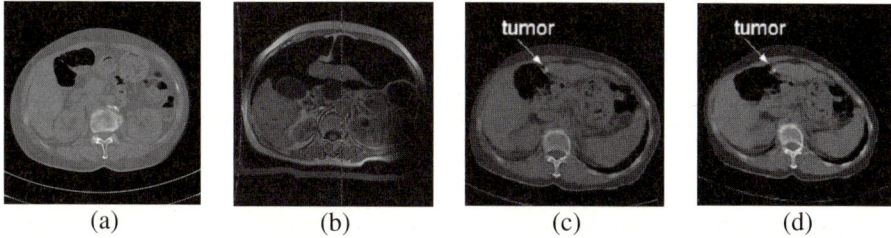

(a)   (b)   (c)   (d)

Fig. 4. (a) a slice of CT image (b) a slice of MRI (c) the slice after rigid registration (d) the slice after FFD registration

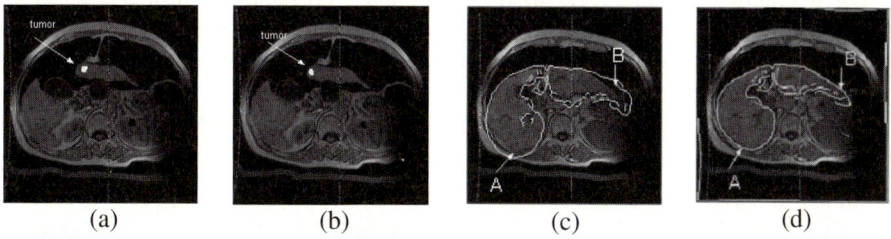

(a)   (b)   (c)   (d)

Fig. 5. Tumors are extracted from CT and overlap on the MR image (a) after rigid registration (b) after FFD registration. Contours of CT overlap on the MR image (c) after rigid registration. (d) after FFD registration.

We use the method mentioned in reference [10] to estimate the distance of two liver surfaces. Detailed can be found in the reference. After FFD registration, the distances of liver surface are calculated and are listed in table 1.

Table 1. The average error of liver surface

	Proposed method (mm)	Andres'(mm)
Error of liver surface	≈ 1.5	≈ 4

The computing cost needed in liver segmentation, affine registration, and FFD registration is listed in table 1.

Table 2. The computing cost

	Proposed method (s)	Andres'(s)
Liver segmentation	≈ 1200	
Affine registration	≈ 300	
FFD registration	≈ 200	
total	≈ 1700	≈ 990

4.3 Algorithm Evaluation

We evaluate our method from visual inspection, distance of liver surfaces, and computing cost, and compare the results of the proposed method with those of Andres', which use rigid registration to match open MR based images.

Visual Inspection. Figure 4 (c) and (d) show the transformed CT images after rigid registration and FFD registration. Both results show that the tumor just beneath the liver surface. We extracted the tumors from the transformed CT images and overlap them on the MR image as shown in Figure 5 (a) and (b). It is easy to find that the position of the tumor is far away from the liver surface after rigid registration, and the tumor position is just beneath the liver surface after FFD registration. Therefore after FFD registration, we can get satisfied result. Figure 5 (c) and (d) show that the liver contours of transformed CT images overlap on the MR image. From the positions pointed by the arrows, we can easily find that FFD registration match liver much better than rigid registration.

From the visual inspection, the accuracy of proposed method is much better than Andres'.

Distance of Liver Surface. From table 1, the distance of the proposed method is about 1.5 mm, while Andre's about 3mm. The proposed method matches liver better.

Computing Cost. Since CT images are acquired before surgery, there is enough time to segment liver from it. We don't include this time in the proposed method when compute the cost. We only consider the time during the surgery. From table 2, snake segmentation needs about 20 minutes, affine registration and FFD registration totally cost about 8 minutes. The total cost is about 28 minutes, while Andres' method only needs 15 minutes. The proposed method needs much time.

5   Discussion and Conclusion

The proposed method can register CT image and MR image acquired from open configuration MR system accuracy even though the abdomen deformation largely. Although the computing time is more than Andres', 28 minutes can be accepted by the surgeons. The high accuracy of the proposed method can be more effective to remove the tumor of patients. In the future, we'll optimize our program and try to reduce the computing time.

Acknowledgement

This work was supported by the Strategic Information and Communications R&D Promotion Program (SCOPE) under the Grand No. 051307017 and Development Program (973) Grant No. 2003CB716105.

Reference

1. Kariniemi, J., Sequeiros, R. B., Ojala, R. , Tervonen O.: MRI-guided abdominal biopsy in a 0.23-T open-configuration MRI system, Eur Radiol, vol. 15, (2005) 1256—1262
2. Morikawa S, Inubushi T, Kurumi Y, Naka S, Sato K, Tani T, Yamamoto I, Fujimura M. MR-Guided microwave thermocoagulation therapy of liver tumors: initial clinical experiences using a 0.5 T open MR system. J Magn Reson Imaging 16: (2002) 576-583.
3. Morikawa S, Inubushi T, Kurumi Y, Naka S, Sato K, Demura K, Tani T, Haque HA, Tokuda J, Hata N. Advanced computer assistance for magnetic resonance-guided microwave thermocoagulation of liver tumors. Acad Radiol 10: (2003) 1442-1449.
4. Sato K, Morikawa S, Inubushi T, Kurumi Y, Naka S, Haque HA, Demura K, Tnai T. Alternate biplanar MR navigation for microwave ablation of liver tumors. Magn Reson Med Sci 4: (2005) 89-94
5. Venot, A. , Golmard, J. L., Lebruchec, J. F., Pronzato, L., Walter, E. , Frij, G., andRoucayrol, J. C.: Digital methods for change detection in medical images. In Deconinck, F. (ed.), Information processing in medical imaging, (1983) 1–16.
6. Hoh, C. K ., Dahlbom, M., Harris, G., Choi, Y., Hawkins, R. A., Phelps, M. E. and Maddahi, J.: Automated iterative three-dimensional registration of positron emission tomography images. Journal of nuclear medicine, 34, (1993) 2009–2018.
7. Scott, A. M., Macapinlac, H. , Divgi, C. R., Zhang, J. J. , Kalaigian, H., Pentlow, K., Hilton, S., Graham, M. C. , Sgouros, G. , Pelizzari, C. , Chen, G., Schlom, J. , Goldsmith, S. J. and Larson, S. M.: Clinical validation of SPECT and CT/MRI image registration in radiolabeled monoclonal antibody studies of colorectal carcinoma. Journal of nuclear medicine, 35, (1994) 1976– 1984.
8. Scott, A. M. , Macapinlac, H., Zhang, J., Daghighian, F., Montemayor, N., Kalaigian, H. , Sgouros, G., Graham, M. C. , Kolbert, K., Yeh, S. D. J. , Lai, E. , Goldsmith, S. J.and Larson, S. M.: Image registration of SPECT and CT images using an external fiduciary band and three-dimensional surface fitting in metastatic thyroid cancer. Journal of nuclear medicine, 36, (1995) 100–103.
9. Mehrdad, S. et al: Automatic CT–SPECT registration of livers treated with radioactive microspheres, Phys. Med. Biol. 49, (2004)
10. Andres, C., Jeffrey, L.D., Jonathan, S.L. and David, L.W.: Semiautomatic 3-D Image Registration as Applied to Interventional MRI Liver Cancer Treatment, IEEE Transaction on Medical Imaging, Vol.19 (2000) 175–185
11. Kass, M., Witkin, A. and Terzopoulos, D.: Snakes: Active contour models. Int. J. Comput. Vis., vol. 1, (1987) 321-331,

12. Xu, C. , Prince, J. L.: Snake, Shape, and Gradient Vector Flow. IEEE Trans. On Image Processing, vol. 7, no. 3, (1998) 359—369
13. Malladi, R., Sethian, J.A. and Vemuri, B.C.: Shape modeling with front propagation: A level set approach. IEEE Trans. Pattern anal. Machine intell.,vol. 17 (1995) 158--175
14. Rueckert, D., Sonoda, L. I., Hayes, C., Hill, D. L. G., Leach, M. O. and Hawkes, D. J.: Nonrigid Registration Using Free-Form Deformations: Application to Breast MR Images, IEEE Transaction on Medical Imaging, Vol. 18, No. 8, (1999) 712–721
15. Hajnal, J. V., Hill, D. L. G., Hawkes, D. J.: Medical Image Registration, CRC Press (2001)

Example-Based Realistic Terrain Generation

Qicheng Li, Guoping Wang, Feng Zhou, Xiaohui Tang, and Kun Yang

Dep. of Computer Science & Technology, Peking University, Beijing, China
{lqc, wgp, zf, txh, yk}@graphics.pku.edu.cn

Abstract. In this paper, a new approach to terrain generation based on terrain examples is proposed. Existing procedural algorithms for generation of terrain have several shortcomings. The most popular approach, fractal-based terrain generation, is efficient, but is difficult for users to control. In this paper, we provide a semiautomatic method of terrain generation that uses a four-process genetic algorithm approach to produce a variety of terrain types using only intuitive user inputs. We allow users to specify a rough sketch of terrain silhouette map, retrieve terrain examples based on support vector machine (SVM) from the terrain dataset, cut a region from the terrain examples and fill in the terrain silhouette map. We also generate a photorealistic texture based on the aerial or satellite images. Consequently, we generate the terrain which has both geometrical data and texture data and provide a balance between user input and real-world data capture unmatched.

1 Introduction

Artificial terrain generation involves the creation of a set of elevation values over a two dimensional grid, such that the resulting model appears to be the surface of a real region of land. While games, movies, and similar forms of entertainment are the most popular applications for terrain generation algorithms, these algorithms also find application in a variety of other contexts, including simulation and training environments. Geographical Information Systems (GIS) are becoming increasingly popular for visualizing spatial data. Most systems layer patterns or colors, which depict data such as soil type, roads, and the like, over a two-dimensional map. As Virtual Reality technology continues to improve, users increasingly expect to view such data in three dimensions. A Digital Elevation Model (DEM) is often used to store three dimensional elevation data via a regular grid. DEMs are often generated from sparse data because they are storage intensive and/or it is difficult to obtain a desired area.

2 Related Work

Existing terrain generation techniques can be grouped into several categories.

The most prevalent class of techniques is fractal. Fractal techniques exploit the self-similarity property exhibited (to a limited extent) by some types of terrain. One can thus use certain forms of fractals to generate height fields that somewhat resemble real terrains [1]. Variability in the resultant terrain can be introduced by incorporating

Z. Pan et al. (Eds.): ICAT 2006, LNCS 4282, pp. 811–818, 2006.
© Springer-Verlag Berlin Heidelberg 2006

randomness into the fractal algorithm. This class of techniques is the current favorite of the computer game industry, largely due to their speed and simplicity of implementation.

Another technique is using surface (such as quadric surface, cubic surface and B-spline surface) to form the terrain. For example Walton [2] adopts B-spline type surfaces on curved knot lines for interpolation of scattered data while preserving desirable terrain breaks or discontinuities which are not necessarily parallel to a given straight line. Many CAD tool (e.g., Maya or 3D Studio) provide the function to generate a terrain model. But it is not easy for users to create a terrain surface by these CAD tools.

A digital terrain surface can also be created from grid-based contour data. Chai [3] use gradient controlled partial differential equation (PDE) surfaces to express terrain surfaces, in which the surface shapes can be globally determined by the contours, their locations, height and gradient values. The surface generated by this method is accurate in the sense of exactly coinciding with the original contours and smooth with C1 continuity everywhere. The method can reveal smooth saddle shapes caused by surface branching of one to more and can make rational interpolated sub-contours between two or more neighboring contours. Gousie [4] computes new, intermediate contours in between existing isolines. These are found by finding the shortest line segment that connects points on two neighboring contours with differing elevations. The midpoint of the line segment becomes a point on the intermediate contour. The contours are completed by connecting individual points. The new contours are then used as data for successive iterations, until an initial- surface is formed.

In this paper, we describe a novel method for terrain generation. Firstly , allowing the human user to simply control over the terrain generation process and using easily understood and predictable parameters. Secondly, the terrain model format should be DEMs, because DEMs are sufficient for most uses and can be highly optimized for rendering and object collision detection [5, 6, 7, 8].Thirdly, our terrain generation is based on real DEM dataset, since it's more authentic and performing well across different terrain types and permitting new terrain types to be added. Fourthly, our terrain generation not only forms the terrain geometrical data but also creates the terrain color data (texture), which generates a whole terrain model.

3   Method

The main idea of our approach is to extract the terrain feature from initial terrain dataset to form the terrain model. And our approach breaks down the terrain generation process into four stages: the terrain silhouette generation phase, terrain feature retrieval based on support vector machine phase, terrain region selection and filling phase and terrain texture generation phase.

3.1 Terrain Silhouette Generation

This phase is to create a 2D "map" of polygonal terrain "regions" specifying the approximate size, shape, and position of different terrain types. One method is to use the linear boundaries of these rough polygonal shapes to represent different terrain

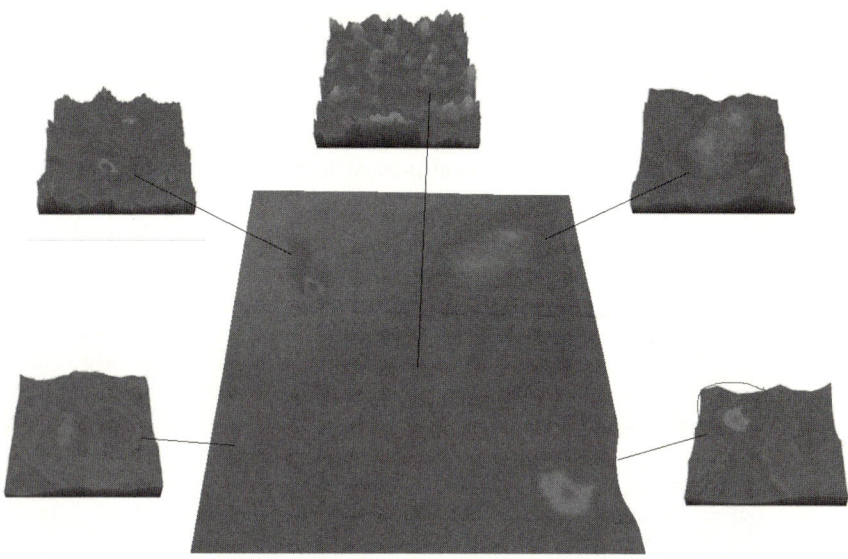

Fig. 1. The terrain generation based on examples

region. For example, Texas A&M University performs an edge modification by subdividing each edge into a sequence of points and applying a GA to produce an acceptable boundary shape [9]. Here we adopt an image to generate the terrain silhouette. We can use an image editing program (e.g., Adobe Photoshop, MS Paint) to draw an image and each colorized region of this image express a terrain type. This terrain silhouette generation method is easy for user to edit and save the terrain silhouette result. And a color of the image is the identification of a terrain type. We can create an image template based on the desired terrain silhouette expediently in this mean.

3.2 Terrain Examples Retrieval Based on Support Vector Machine (SVM)

Each region of the terrain silhouette image is assigned by the user a particular terrain type. In this phase we will prepare the examples of different terrain type. A variety of sources from both the public and private sectors provide DEMs, and these DEMs are specified by a number of parameters. We have to recognize and retrieve the DEMs according to the terrain type. DEM is a well-known 2.5D terrain model implemented as a two dimensional, rectangular grid of height values, and is equivalent to a grayscale image. Thus we can take DEMs recognition and retrieval as image recognition and retrieval. But the DEMs terrain model is not an obvious grey image and we can not make out the terrain type for DEMs even in ocular, so we retrieve the terrain type from the source dataset based on support vector machine (SVM).

SVM is a powerful learning machine. It finds an optimal separating hyper plane that maximizes the margin between two classes in a kernel-induced feature space. SVM-based active learning has been proposed to carefully select samples shown to the users for labeling in order to achieve maximal information gain in decision making [10]. It chooses the unseen images that are closest to the SVM decision hyper plane as the most informative images for feedback. At first we must get the feature vector for the DEMs terrain model. The gurgitation and height is the main feature of a terrain region. These terrain features are then corresponding to the diagrams of the image. We establish a diagram for each terrain type, and these diagrams construct the feature vector of the terrain image. With the research in recent decade image retrieval based SVM has become a ripe technique. Here we adopt the SVM-light [11] to retrieve the terrain models. The retrieval process is divided into two phases: firstly, we use a number of different terrain samples (e.g., plain, hill, mountain, and basin) to train the initial SVM; Secondly, we can use the SVM to retrieve the desired terrain model from the source dataset.

Fig. 2. The terrain retrieval result

3.3   Terrain Region Selection and Filling Phase

In this stage, we will select an area from the terrain examples generated in the section 3.2 to fill in the region of the terrain silhouette map according to the terrain type. Firstly, we need to cut a region from the terrain examples and guarantee that the region is the nicest match for the terrain silhouette. For keeping the continuity of the terrain borderline, we segment the terrain examples based on contour lines. Building a contour map from DEM is very easy [12], Imagine a series of parallel cuts that intersect the profile of the terrain. Starting from a reference elevation H_r, the procedure of building IECM from DEM is as follows:

STEP 1. Create a binary image B_{mn} by assigning:

$$B_{mn} = \begin{cases} 1 & H_{mn} >= H_r \\ 0 & H_{mn} < H_r \end{cases}. \tag{1}$$

Where H_{mn} is the elevation at grid point (m, n) of the elevation map.

STEP 2. Tracking the border of the binary image to extract contours.

STEP 3. Repeat STEP 1 and STEP 2 at a new elevation: Hr=Hr + ΔH.
Next we will compute the similarity between the contour and the bounder line of terrain silhouette. The shape of bounder line can be described quantitatively by using simple statistical moments [13]. For a 2-D continuous function f(x, y), the moment of order (p + q) is defined as:

$$m_{pq} = \int_{-\infty}^{\infty} \int_{-\infty}^{\infty} x^p y^q f(x, y) dx dy \cdot \quad (2)$$

For p, q =0, 1, 2….
The central moment are defined as:

$$\mu_{pq} = \int_{-\infty}^{\infty} \int_{-\infty}^{\infty} (x - \bar{x})^p (y - \bar{y})^q f(x, y) dx dy \cdot \quad (3)$$

In summary, the central moments of order up to 3 are:

$$\mu_{00} = m_{00} \qquad\qquad \mu_{02} = m_{02} - \bar{y} m_{01}$$

$$\mu_{10} = 0 \qquad\qquad \mu_{30} = m_{30} - 3\bar{x} m_{20} + 2\bar{x}^2 m_{10}$$

$$\mu_{20} = 0 \qquad\qquad \mu_{03} = m_{03} - 3\bar{y} m_{02} + 2\bar{y}^2 m_{01} \qquad (4)$$

$$\mu_{11} = m_{11} - \bar{y} m_{10} \qquad \mu_{21} = m_{21} - 2\bar{x} m_{11} - 2\bar{y} m_{20} + 2\bar{x}^2 m_{01}$$

$$\mu_{20} = m_{20} - \bar{x} m_{10} \qquad \mu_{12} = m_{12} - 2\bar{y} m_{11} - 2\bar{x} m_{02} + 2\bar{y}^2 m_{10}$$

The normalized central moments, denoted η_{pq} , are defined as

$$\eta_{pq} = \frac{\mu_{pq}}{\mu_{00}^r} \cdot \quad (5)$$

Where $r = \frac{p+q}{2} + 1$ for p + q = 2, 3…

The central moments are invariant to translation. We select the contour which has the minimal different central moment from the bounder line of terrain silhouette. In succession we cut the region of the terrain example based on the contour and fill in the terrain silhouette map. However, the borderline between the different terrain types is not seamless after the filling process; the final DEM must be found by smoothing the borderline. The elevation value of a point in the borderline is the weighted average of its neighbors in each of the four cardinal directions, where the weight is based on a Gaussian distribution of distance. The smoothing can be done by either interpolation or approximation.

3.4 Terrain Texture Generation

The integrated terrain model not only has the geometrical data but also need the upper information. The realistic upper information is the terrain color (texture) usually from a vertical view angle, such as an aerial or satellite image. Such imagery, scarce just ten years ago, is now widely available from commercial remote sensing agencies, such as Spot and Landsat. The aerial or satellite images are good sources for us to generate terrain texture, and we have found a good way to generate the terrain texture based on the images. "Image Analogies" [14] is a very effective technique. "Image analogies" uses training data A and A^0 in order to learn a filter that can be applied to an unfiltered target image B to produce an analogous image B^0. This means that B^0 relates to B the same way A^0 relates to A. And "texture-by-numbers" as shown in Fig.3 is a typical application of "Image analogies".

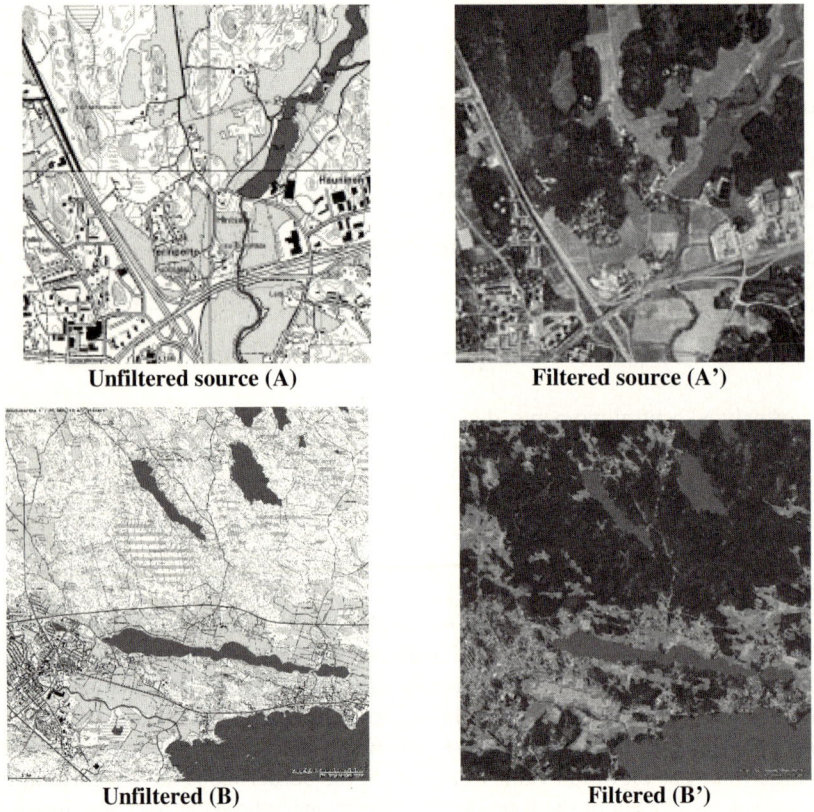

Unfiltered source (A)   **Filtered source (A')**

Unfiltered (B)   **Filtered (B')**

Fig. 3. Texture-by-numbers. Images copyright c° 2001 Jari Kaskelin.

The aerial or satellite image is filtered source A, and we can use an image tool to generate unfiltered source A. The image of the terrain silhouette map described in section3.1 is the unfiltered target B, the output result is filtered target B and the resultant image is the final texture corresponding to the terrain generation.

4 Conclusion and Future Work

We have presented a new approach to terrain generation based on terrain examples. We break terrain generation down into four phases: terrain silhouette generation, terrain examples retrieval based on support vector machine, terrain region selection and filling and terrain texture generation. In contrast to traditional terrain generation such as fractal-based algorithms, our approach provides better control over the shape and layout of the resultant terrain, through the placement of regions of different terrain types. We provide a balance between user input and real-world data capture unmatched by previous approaches. User only needs little interaction to create a desired terrain model .The terrain model has both geometrical data and texture data, which makes it an integrated photorealistic terrain model.   We have used the generated terrain in our flight simulator as **Fig. 4** shown.

Fig. 4. Our flight simulator

There is still much room for improvement. First, although we provide an easy method to create a 2D terrain silhouette map, the borderline is not natural. A smooth transition between different terrain types is a pending problem. Secondly, the terrain examples retrieved based on SVM can do well with the DEMs which have a single terrain type. But that is not so much the case if the DEM has multifarious terrain feature. Thirdly, "Image analogies" is a very time-consuming process, especially when generating a huge terrain texture. Improving the efficiency of "Image analogies" is also the next step of our work.

Acknowledgments

This study was supported by China 973 Program Grant No.2004CB719403.

References

1. Prusinkiewicz, Przemyslaw and Hammel, Mark.,: A Fractal Model of Mountains with Rivers. In proceedings of Graphics Interface '93. (1993)
2. Desmond J. Walton,: Terrain modeling with B-spline type surfaces defined on curved knot lines. Image Vision Comput. 5(1): 37-43. (1987)
3. Jianyun Chai, Takaharu Miyoshi, Eihachiro Nakamae,: Contour interpolation and surface reconstruction of smooth terrain models. Proceedings of the conference on Visualization '98. (1998)
4. Michael B. Gousie, Wm. Randolph Franklin,: Constructing a dem from grid-based data by computing intermediate contours. Proceedings of the 11th ACM international symposium on Advances in geographic information systems. (2003)
5. Duchaineau, Mark et al.: ROAMing Terrain: Real-time Optimally Adapting Meshes. In proceedings of IEEE Visualization '97. IEEE Computer Society Press. (1997)
6. Ulrich, Thatcher. : Rendering Massive Terrains Using Chunked Level of Detail Control. In proceedings of ACM SIGGRAPH. (2001)
7. P. Lindstrom, David Koller, William Ribarsky, Larry Hodges, Nick Faust, and Gregory Turner. : Real-Time, Continuous Level of Detail Rendering of Height Fields. ACM SIGGRAPH 96 Proceedings, pp. 109-118. (1996)
8. P. Lindstrom, Valerio Pascucci.: Terrain Simplification Simplified: A General Framework for View-Dependent Out-of-Core Visualization. IEEE Transactions on Visualization and Computer Graphics 8(3): 239-254. (2002)
9. Teong Joo Ong, Ryan Saunders, John Keyser, John J. Leggett.: Terrain generation using genetic algorithms. Proceedings of the 2005 conference on Genetic and evolutionary computation. (2005)
10. S. Tong and E. Chang: Support vector machine active leaning for image retrieval. Proc. ACM Int. Conf. Multimedia, Ottawa Canada, pp. 107–118. (2001)
11. Thorsten Joachims: Making Large-Scale Support Vector Machine Learning Practical. In Advances in Kernel Methods. MIT Press. (1999)
12. Qiuze Yu, Jinwen Tian, Jian Liu.: a NOVEL contour-based 3D terrain matching algorithm using wavelet transform. Pattern Recognition Letters, Volume 25, Issue 1, Pages 87-99. (2004)
13. Refael C. Gonzalez and Richard E. Woods: Digital Image Processing. Addison-Wesley reading mass. (1995)
14. Aaron Hertzmann, Charles E. Jacobs, Nuria Oliver, Brian Curless, David H. Salesin.: Image analogies. Proceedings of the 28th annual conference on Computer graphics and interactive techniques. (2001)

Bayesian Mesh Reconstruction from Noisy Point Data

Guiping Qian, Ruofeng Tong, Wen Peng, and Jinxing Dong

State Key Laboratory of CAD&CG, Zhejiang University, Hangzhou, 310027, China
qianguiping@163.com, trf@zju.edu.cn, pengwen@zju.edu.cn,
djx@cs.zju.edu.cn

Abstract. This paper presents a new reverse engineering method for creating 3D mesh models, which approximates unorganized noisy point data without orientation information. The main idea of the method is based on statistics Bayesian model. Firstly the feature enhancing prior probabilities over 3D data retrieve the sharp features, such as edges or corners. Then a local polynomial probabilistic model is used to approximate a continuous differentiable manifold. The Bayesian model uses an iterative fitting clustering algorithm to improve the noise tolerance in geometry accuracy. After iteration a density-based estimation function can automatically remove the outliers. Furthermore, the current sphere cover meshing approach is improved to reconstruct the mesh surface from the noisy point data. Experimental results indicate that our approach is robust and efficient. It can be well applied to smoothing noisy data, removing outliers, enhancing features and mesh reconstruction.

Keywords: Mesh reconstruction, Bayesian model, reverse engineering, denoising.

1 Introduction

Surface mesh reconstruction from an unorganized point data has been a very important task and attracted increasing attention in various computer sciences, such as computer vision, virtual reality and CAD/CAM. Many 3D scanning devices can yield rather dense and accurate surface data samples. However, noise, outliers and defective data are inevitable because of the device precision and electronic disturbance. With these point cloud, a number of surface reconstruction techniques have been proposed recently. Despite of the versatility of large amount of algorithms nowadays, however, most of these algorithms are not efficiently enough and make certain strong assumptions on the original surface and its sample points. For example, some approaches become expensive in time and storage, many algorithms [2], [3], [5], [12] need additional knowledge such as surface normal or interior/exterior information, some are not tolerant of noise and defective data.

1.1 Previous Work

Statistical learning techniques, such as Bayesian method, support vector machines and clustering, have begun to be applied to computer graphics during recent years. Statistical learning methods for denoising and retrieving sharp features have attracted

Z. Pan et al. (Eds.): ICAT 2006, LNCS 4282, pp. 819–829, 2006.
© Springer-Verlag Berlin Heidelberg 2006

many researchers' interest. Diebel et al. [1] applied Bayesian model to probable surface reconstruction and decimation from noisy surface meshes. Pauly et al. [4] introduced the clustering method in shaping point cloud. More recently, mean shift method was applied to denoising of noisy point cloud by Schall et al. [7]. However, these two methods cannot retrieve sharp features. Robust statistics [11], such as least median of squares, also has obtained a good experimental effect on reconstructing a piecewise smooth surface, but it is low efficient.

The topic of meshing the scattered point data with sharp features has a long history. Hoppe et al. [13] used a sign distance function to handle different topologies, and they approximate the normal at each sample using principal component analysis, which had been adopted by many researchers. Recently Ohtake et al.[5], Kobbelt et al.[12] extracted the edges or corners by the intersection of two or more piecewise quadratic functions. Both of these methods need the exterior additive accurate normal information. In [6], Ohtake used a local quadric error minimization strategy to get sharp features, but this method may fail to afford a satisfactory reconstruction when the level of noise is very high. Newly a particularly powerful point set surface approach, the moving least squares (MLS), has attracted many researchers' interest [4], [8], [9], [14], [15]. These methods based on MLS and extremal surfaces are very difficult to obtain the sharp feature.

1.2 Contribution

The main contribution of our approach is to provide a very efficient, robust and satisfied mesh reconstruction from noisy point data. Compared to robust filtering of noisy scattered point data [7], our method can retrieve the sharp feature very efficient, and avoid the artificial selection of kernel size. Our approach is also closely related to the Bayesian method of mesh surface reconstruction [1], but our approach is specially designed to work on meshing the noisy scanning point data, and it need automatically remove the outliers.

The main idea of our approach can be stated as followed three steps:

Firstly a nonparametric kernel density function is used to relate the computed qualities to the sample density. It will afford reliable outlier removal and the weight of the point data. We make use of the Shannon entropy to optimize window-width parameter, which avoids the artificial selection of input parameter. The details are described in section 2.

Then a Bayesian probability is introduced to construct the surface model of noisy point data without orientation (explained in section 3). We use an iterative clustering algorithm, which is integrated with Bayesian model, to improve the noise tolerance in geometry accuracy. At the same time, the sharp feature is preserved and enhanced. After iteration, the detached outliers are removed by density function. The iteration process is explained in section 4.

Finally the new point set is generated. We mesh the new point set. The non-manifold mesh is refined by normal comparison between the new vertex and the mesh topology (described in section 5).

The main stages of our approach are described below in detail.

2   Kernel Density Function

Firstly we introduce some basic concepts and definitions. Let R^3 denote the 3D Euclidean space. Considering a set of scattered points $Ps=\{p_k\}_{k\in index(Ps)}$, $p_k\in R^3$, p_k is an arbitrary point in a point set. *index(Ps)* is the index of the point set. $|Ps|$ represents the total element numbers of point set Ps. To describe the local approximation error and weight function, we introduce the support set $SPT(p_k)\subset Ps$ and the support radius R_k of point p_k. Here, $SPT(p_k)=\{p_j\}$, $j\neq k$, p_j satisfies the expression $\|p_k\text{-}p_j\|< R_k$. $\|\bullet\|$ is the Euclidean distance in R^3.

2.1   Density Function

It is often important to attach the computed qualities to sample density for scanned scattered point set. Informally, the kernel density function is a mathematical description of the influence a point data has within its neighborhood. The density function at a point $x\in R^3$ is defined as the sum of the influence functions of all neighboring data at that point. Thus a kernel density function $Ds(x)$ can be given by

$$Ds(x) = \frac{1}{n}\sum_{i=1}^{n} e^{-\frac{\|x-p_i\|^2}{2\sigma^2}} . \tag{1}$$

The Smooth parameter σ is called window-width size. Like the clustering method [16], it is a local density function approximating the overall density function. The density threshold ξ determines our selection to outliers.

2.2   Optimized Parameter

The window-width parameter σ of $Ds(x)$ decides the influence field of each point in its neighborhood. Density-based method is an efficient clustering method, so it can discover outliers and be insensitive to noisy point data. However, this method badly depends on the selection of the parameter. We know that Shannon' entropy can be used to measure the uncertainty of system. In our density function, if function value distributes unevenly, the uncertainty will be small. To obtain an optimized density function, we introduce the density entropy:

$$En(Ps) = -\sum_{k=1}^{N} \frac{Ds(p_k)}{\sum_k Ds(p_k)} \log \frac{Ds(p_k)}{\sum_k Ds(p_k)} . \tag{2}$$

When $\sigma\to 0$, the density function value of each point approximate $1/n$ and the density entropy arrives at maximum $\log(n)$. When σ varys from zero to infinity, density entropy gradually decreases to some optimized value, whereafter increases to maximum again. Simply minimizing the density entropy $En(Ps)$ we obtain the optimized window-width σ. This method helps us to avoid the artificial repetitious selection of input parameter.

After shrinking iteration of our reconstruction model (in section 4), some outliers cannot move to the Bayesian probability surface. We found out that setting density threshold $\xi = 0.4\overline{D}s(x)$ is appropriate. $\overline{D}s(x)$ is the mean density function value when point data even distributes. When $Ds(p_k) > \xi$, the point p_k is preserved for further process. Otherwise, we will regard it as outlier and remove it from point set Ps (see Fig. 1).

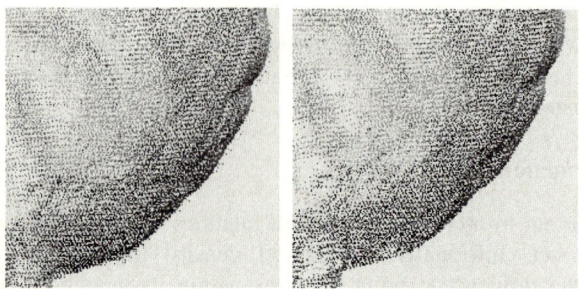

Fig. 1. Density function filtering. Left is the bosom of the raw Stanford bunny. Right is the result of density function filter the noisy point data. The outliers have been removed well.

2.3 Curvature Penalty

Weight is frequently used to give the different feature point a special influence. In this part, we will consider assigning an optimized weight to each noisy point data. Firstly we assess the normals through the correlation matrix M_k of neighboring points.

$$M_k = \sum_{p_i \in SPT(q_k)} (p_i - q_k)(p_i - q_k)' .$$

(3)

Here q_k is the center of the neighborhood p_i. Its three eigenvalues are $\{\lambda_1, \lambda_2, \lambda_3\}$, $\lambda_1 < \lambda_2 < \lambda_3$. Their corresponding eigenvectors $\{v_1, v_2, v_3\}$ form an orthogonal basis and v_1 approximates the surface normal at q_k. We note the normal n_k of each point q_k. From [17], we know the relations of the eigenvalues and shape of correlation ellipsoid. We give each point a curvature penalty weight:

$$Cur(p_k) = (\lambda_2 - \lambda_1)/\lambda_3 .$$

(4)

In the presence of noise or near a discontinuity, the curvature penalty weight will be very small. Finally in our reconstruction model, we attach a weight w_k to each point p_k:

$$w_k = Ds(p_k) \cdot Cur(p_k).$$

(5)

w_k will be large when the small neighborhood of a point is dense and flat (or local smooth). When the small neighborhood is noisy or local discontinuous, w_k is very small even approximating zero.

3   Reconstruction Model

We define a surface approximating the noisy point data as a differentiable manifold $S(x,y)$. Let x be the real surface sample point of the object being scanned. Instead of x, the sensor detects noisy measurements $\{y_i\}_{i=1,2,...,N}$ of the surface of the object. The measurements are the noisy point data for our analysis. Intuitively, if we know some hints about the most probable location of the differentiable manifold in the 3D space, we can see this idea results from the probability density $P(x|\{y_i\})$. So we give the higher probability to the measurements which close to the most probable proximity of the manifold in space. Bayesian formula enables us to realize this probability.

3.1   Bayesian Probability

Given the measurements $\{y_i\}_{i=1,2,...,N}$, with Bayesian rule we construct followed model

$$P(x|\{y_i\}) = \frac{P(\{y_i\}|x)P(x)}{P(\{y_i\})}. \tag{6}$$

Here $P(\{y_i\}|x)$ is the probability of the measurements in the hypothesis that y_i approximates x, and $P(x)$ is a prior probability distribution on surface of the object. From the maximum principle, the process of most probable surface reconstruction is to find the surface x that maximizes the posterior probability $P(x|\{y_i\})$ in (6). Because $P(\{y_i\})$ is a constant which is independent of x, maximizing $P(x|\{y_i\})$ just is maximizing $P(x)$ and $P(\{y_i\}|x)$ respectively. These two different parts need us to construct corresponding models. In the followed two paragraphs, we will present how to construct the prior probability $P(x)$ and measurements probability $P(\{y_i\}|x)$.

3.2   Prior Probable Surface

Without a prior, the most probable surface should be the measurement $\{y_i\}$ itself. The prior probable surface is quite important to our surface mesh reconstruction. Applying the prior probability distribution can help us to preserve or enhance the shape features.

We define the prior probable function

$$\varphi_k = \sum_{i\in SPT(p_k)} (w_i n_i \cdot (p_i - p_k))^2. \tag{7}$$

where weight w_i has been explained at paragraph 2. Thus each φ_k is a field potential and nonnegative. If all p_i and p_k are on the plane $C \subset R^3$, then $\varphi_k=0$. This field distance function is essential used to enhance the shape features, like edges or corners. It is developed firstly by Hoppe et al. [13]. From equation (7), we can see the prior probable function φ_k is linear piecewise, but the general fit functions, like piecewise quadratic polynomial, are wholly differential manifold, i.e. smooth and continuous.

When x locates on the prior surface function, φ_k reaches minimum. Then we think that surface prior probability has been maximized. The surface prior probability has followed formula

$$P(x) = -\ln(\varphi_x).$$
(8)

Negative natural logarithm is made the most of to obtain positive $P(x)$.

3.3 Manifold Surface

$P(\{y_i\}|x)$ has been defined for the probability of the measurements ahead. Here x is the true surface point of the scanned object. Subjected to sensor noise and merged error, the original scattered point cloud in hand are often very difficult to model directly. We can't assume that the preprocessing points follow the Gaussian probability distribution, because the point cloud is commonly merged by several layers. Thus such distribution probability is very difficult to formulate. Approximating the intrinsic surface of unorganized space points is still a quite young topic.

In defining point-set surfaces [14], [15], we know that the extremal surfaces, include MLS surface, are defined by an energy function and a vector field. The extremal surface is essential a smooth continuous manifold reconstruction. When multiple surfaces intersect, forming sharp feature, the vector field singularities will cause non-manifold singularities in the extremal surface. The non-manifold singularities just can be extracted by the prior probable function φ_k.

Inspired by point-set surface [15], we define an implicit function:

$$\phi(x) = n(x) \cdot \nabla f(x).$$
(9)

where $n(x)$ is vector field, and $\nabla f(x)$ is gradient potential field of iso-surface $f(x)$. $\phi(x)$ is a extremal manifold surface. The effect of $\nabla f(x)$ in our approach is that we can let the scattered point iteratively shrink towards the zero iso-surface along the vector field. Transforming equation (9) adapted to scattered points, we can obtain a more computable formation:

$$\phi(x) = \varepsilon \cdot n(x) \cdot (x - \frac{\sum_k w_k p_k}{\sum_k w_k}).$$
(10)

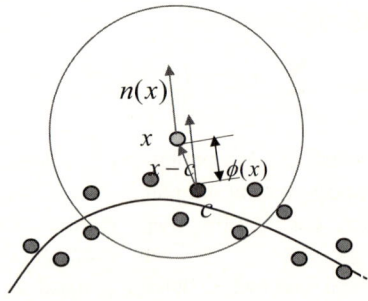

Fig. 2. The manifold surface function (a 2D example). Red vector x-c is used to approximate $\nabla f(x)$, when x locates on the blue line(manifold surface), $\phi(x)=0$. $\phi(x)$ is the approximative estimation of the distance between point x and manifold surface.

$x - \sum_k w_k p_k / \sum_k w_k$ is used to approximate $\nabla f(x)$. ε is a ratio coefficient and set 0.4~0.6 (see Fig. 2). If ε is too large, it will cause shape shrinking at high curvature regions. $\phi(x)$ might be negative, it isn't suitable for probabilistic measurement function. Easily we square $\phi(x)$ and use negative nature logarithm to generate probabilistic measurements function:

$$P(\{y_i\} \mid x) = -\ln(\phi(x)^2). \tag{11}$$

4 Shrinking Iteration

With equation (6) constructed, maximizing the posterior probability can obtain the optimized surface reconstruction. We invert equation (6) into:

$$\frac{\partial P(x \mid \{y_i\})}{\partial x} = \frac{1}{P(\{y_i\})} \cdot (P(x) \frac{\partial P(\{y_i\} \mid x)}{\partial x} + P(\{y_i\} \mid x) \frac{\partial P(x)}{\partial x}). \tag{12}$$

When equation (12) approximates zero, the posterior probability arrives at the maximum. Equation (12) can be decomposed into two key parts:

$$\frac{\partial P(\{y_i\} \mid x)}{\partial x} = 2\varepsilon^2 [n(x) \cdot (x - \frac{\sum_k w_k p_k}{\sum_k w_k})] n(x) \cdot \frac{1}{\phi(x)^2}, \tag{13}$$

$$\frac{\partial P(x)}{\partial x} = \sum_{i \in SPT(p_k)} 2w_i^2 [n_i \cdot (p_i - p_k)] n_i \cdot \frac{1}{\varphi_x}. \tag{14}$$

This means to move all measurements to positions of high probability. The iterative moving process alters the sample positions along the gradient ascent maximization. When equation (12) iteratively converges approximately to zero, we stop the iteration. To control the total computation time, In fact, we also need to decide reasonable steps. We use followed practical point-iteration equation:

$$p_i^{k+1} = p_i^k - \frac{\partial P(\{y_i\} \mid x)}{\partial x} \cdot \phi(x)^2 - \frac{\partial P(x)}{\partial x} \cdot \frac{1}{\sum_i w_i^2} \cdot \varphi_x. \tag{15}$$

When $\parallel p_i^{k+1} - p_i^k \parallel < 10^{-2} \sigma$, the iterations stop.

5 Meshing and Visualization

In the section 4, we have finished the shrinking iteration, and then we remove the detached outliers to acquire new point set. We need to connect them to generate mesh data struct Ω. The traditional meshing method is to compute the Delaunay triangulation. Computing the Delaunay triangulation can be slow and susceptible to numerical errors. Our meshing approach is based on spherical cover method [6].

We use equation (7) as an error function instead of Ohtake' local quadric error function. Then we generate the adaptive spherical cover. By this means, the resulting triangle mesh may have non-manifold parts and hole boundary. Each vertex with 1-ring neighborhood is classified: simple, non-manifold and hole boundary. We need to refine the original mesh further.

The optimal mesh should satisfied two conditions: the triangles are approximate to the surface of the object; the mesh is fair. Ohtake's mesh cleaning method takes the disk-shaped 1-ring neighborhood that has minimal curvature, which cannot satisfy the two conditions. By comparing the normal deviation of the neighboring triangles with the vertex, we remove disk-shaped 1-ring neighborhoods which have large normal deviation. From equation (3) we get the normal of the vertex $n(i)$. We define the normal of the kth disk-shaped 1-ring neighborhood of vertex **i**

$$N(k) = \sum \theta_j \xi_j \Big/ \sum \theta_j . \tag{16}$$

Where θ_j is the area of the triangle T_j, ξ_j is the normal of the triangle T_j. The deviation of the two normals is

$$D = | n(i) \cdot N(k) |. \tag{17}$$

If $D < 0.8$, the kth 1-ring neighborhood of vertex **i** is recognized as false and eliminated. If $D \geq 0.8$, then we compare the fairness of the triangle mesh. We define the fair parameter

$$\varepsilon(k) = \sum \ell_j / \theta_j \Big/ \sum 1 / \theta_j . \tag{18}$$

Where ℓ_j is the length ratio of the longest edge and the shortest edge in triangle T_j. To fair the mesh we take the minimal $\varepsilon(k)$. So we get the optimal disk-shaped 1-ring neighborhood.

By above process, the hole boundary of the mesh is remained. We remove the isolated vertices and check the hole boundary loops to fill the holes. If the holes are too big, The subdivision can be adopted to increase the hole mesh density.

6 Results and Discussion

The goal of our work is to design an efficient and robust algorithm for meshing noisy point data. Our method can be applied to unorganized point set consisting of millions of points without orient information on standard PCs. We will show several representative experimental results for the Bayesian mesh model reconstruction. All examples presented in this paper are computed on a P4 2.0 GHz PC with 512Mb RAM running on WINDOWS 2000.

Next we will compare our mesh reconstruction method to the other method in existing literature. Fig. 3 compares Bayesian mesh reconstruction to the quadric-error function iteration method of Ohtake et al. [6]. Here we don't use the density function to filter the outliers. Obviously our method is very robust to smooth noise and recover the shape of the object. Fig. 4 shows the different mesh reconstruction results from the Bimba model. The triangle faces numbers of two different Bimba mesh models are both 147K. These comparisons show our Bayesian probable surface mesh method performs well.

Table 1 shows the computational time comparison of Bayesian probable surface mesh reconstruction process for different models. However, dragon scans model with fewer points than Bimba scans consumes more time, because the point data of dragon scans is noisier and distributes unevenly. From the results we notice that out method is very fast. The memory usage of our method is very low. The peak RAM is 350Mb in processing AIM@SHAPE Bimba model with 1.8M scanning points.

Table 1. The experimental results on computational time and the size of the point set for different models

Point Set	Points N	Triangle F	Time
Bunny	361K	74.1K	17.5sec
scans	361K	185K	24.7sec
Dragon	1406K	21K	114.3sec
scans	1406K	243K	227.6sec
Bimba	1873K	149K	75.6sec
scans	1873K	255K	84.7sec

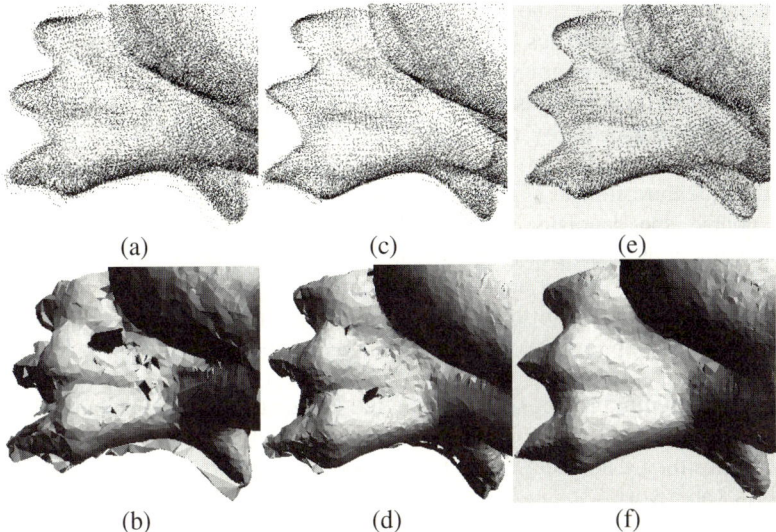

Fig. 3. A comparison to the public results of Ohtake et. al [6]. (a) (b) are raw scanned point data of Stanford dragon nail consists of 47 scans and mesh reconstruction [6]. (c) shows Ohtake's quadric-error iteration which is used to smooth noisy data in (a). (d) is mesh reconstruction. (e) shows the results of shrinking iteration of Bayesian probable surface in (a) and we don't remove the outliers. (f) is the mesh reconstruction of point data in (e).

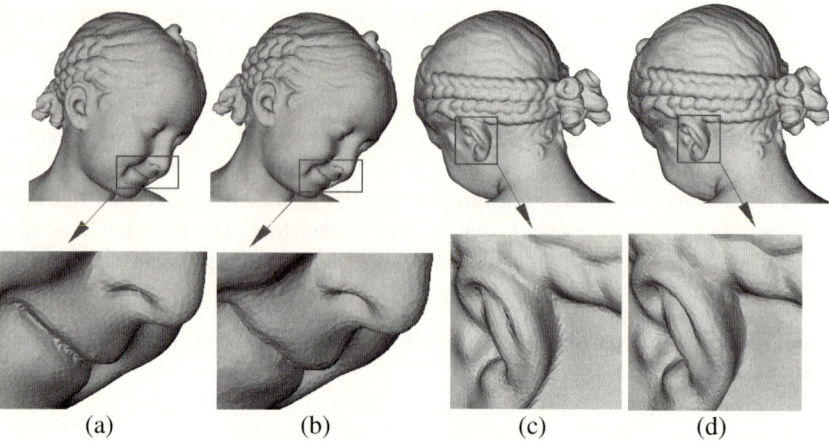

(a)	(b)	(c)	(d)

Fig. 4. A comparison to the public results of ReMESH [18]. (a) and (c) shows Simplification of scanned Bimba model with PlyDeci. Cleaning, hole-filling and smoothing with ReMESH [19]. (b) and (d) shows our results of Bayesian probable surface method. From the comparison our method can preserve and enhance the features.

7   Conclusion and Future Research

In this paper we present a novel noise-tolerable surface mesh reconstruction method, which is based on a statistics Bayesian model. Compared to other mesh reconstruction approach for processing noisy point data, our algorithm is very robust, efficient and easily to realized. Our method also consumes low memory with large point data set. The feature is enhanced by our prior probable surface model. We believe that our method can be applied to many surface reconstructions, such as multi-level smoothing, feature enhancing, noise filtering, and decimation.

Of course, the denoising procedure and automatic outliers removal remain an intensive research topic. Our method is an important step to the robust smooth, but so far no algorithms is perfect and satisfied to any noisy point data set. Many scanning model need new algorithm to apply. Our holes repair region may not look optimal when there are complex holes with highly curved shapes.

Acknowledgments. Project supported by the National Grand Fundamental Research 973 (No.2002CB312106) of China. The Bimba model is courtesy of AIM@SHAPE Shape Repository. The Bunny and Dragon models are courtesy of Stanford Computer Graphics Laboratory.

References

1. Diebel, J., Thrun, S., Bruning, M.: A Bayesian Method for Probable Surface Reconstruction and Decimation. ACM Transactions on Graphics, Vol. V, No. N, September, (2005) 1–20
2. Steinke, F., Schölkopf, B., Blanz,V.: Support Vector Machines for 3D Shape Processing. Computer Graphics Forum (Proc. EUROGRAPHICS) 24(3), (2005) 285 – 294

3. Schölkopf, B., Steinke, F., Blanz, V.: Object Correspondence as A Machine Learning Problem. Proceedings of the 22nd International Conference on Machine Learning,(2005) 777 - 784

4. Pauly, M., Gross, M., Kobbelt, L. P.: Efficient Simplification of Point-sampled Surfaces. IEEE Visualization, (2002) 163– 170

5. Ohtake, Y., Belyaev, A., Alexa, M., Turk, G., Seidel, H.-P.: Multi-level Partition of Unity Implicits. ACM Transactions on Graphics 22, 3 (July), page 463-470, Proceedings of SIGGRAPH 2003

6. Ohtake, Y., Belyaev, A., Seidel, H.-P.: An Integrating Approach to Meshing Scattered Point Data. ACM Symposium on Solid and Physical Modeling, (2005)

7. Schall, O., Belyaev, A., Seidel, H.-P.: Robust Filtering of Noisy Scattered Point Data. Eurographics symposium on point-based graphics, (2005)

8. Adamson, A., Alexa, M.: Approximating and Intersecting Surfaces from Points. In Proceedings of EG Symposium on Geometry Processing, (2003) 245–254

9. Amenta, N., Kil, Y. J.: Defining Point Set Surfaces. In Proceedings of SIGGRAPH, (2004) 264-270

10. Ju, T., Losasso, F., Schaefer, S., Warren, J.: Dual Contouring of Hermite Data. ACM Transactions on Graphics, 21, 3, (2002) page 339-346

11. Fleishman, S., Cohen-or, D., Silva, C.T.: Robust Moving Least-squares Fitting with Sharp Features. In Proceedings of ACM SIGGRAPH, (2005)

12. Kobbelt, L.P., Botsch, M., Schwanecke, U., Seidel, H.-P.: Feature Sensitive Surface Extraction from Volume Data, In Proceedings of ACM SIGGRAPH, (2001) 57–66.

13. Hoppe, H., Derose, T., Duchamp, T., Mcdonald, J., Stuetzle, W.: Surface Reconstruction from Unorganized Points. In Proceedings of ACM SIGGRAPH, (1992) 71-78

14. Amenta, N., Kil, Y.J.: The Domain of A Point-set Surface. Eurographics Workshop on Point-based Graphics, (2004) 139-147

15. Amenta, N., Kil, Y.J.: Defining Point Set Surfaces. In Proceedings of SIGGRAPH, (2004) 264-270

16. Hinneburg, A., Keim, D. A.: An Efficient Approach to Clustering in Large Multimedia Databases with Noise, In Proceedings of the 4th International Conference on Knowledge Discovery and Data mining, (1998) 58-65

17. Gumhold, S., Wang, X., Mcleod, R.: Feature Extraction from Point Clouds. In Proceedings of 10th International Meshing Roundtable, Sandia National Laboratories, (2001) 293-305

18. Attene, M., and Falcidieno, B.: ReMESH: An Interactive Environment to Edit An Repair Triangle Meshes, SMI 2006

19. http:// shapes.aim-at-shape.net/viewmodels.php?page=2

Efficient Retrieval of 3D Models Based on Integer Medial Axis Skeleton

Yong Tang and Xuefan Zhang

College of Information Science and Engineering, Yanshan University,
Qinhuangdao, 066004, China
tangyong@ysu.edu.cn

Abstract. In this paper, we describe a novel algorithm for searching and comparing 3D models, called the Integer Medial Axis Skeleton (IMAS), in which the geometric and topological information is encoded in the form of an IMAS and uses skeletal binary tree matching techniques to match the skeletons and to compare them. The skeletal binary tree is constructed based on the IMAS that was constructed using a modification of an IMA transforms algorithm. The similarity calculation between 3D models is processed using a coarse-to-fine strategy. A feature of skeletal binary tree matching is the ability to perform part-matching and provide a fast estimation of similarity between models. The performance of the proposed algorithm is compared to some previous approaches by means of precision/recall tests. Generally, results show that the new algorithm introduces improvements in the 3D-model retrieval process.

Keywords: 3D model retrieval, feature transform, Integer Medial Axis Skeleton.

1 Introduction

Recent developments in modeling and digitizing techniques have made the construction of 3D computer models much easier. This has led to an increasing accumulation of 3D models, both on the Internet and otherwise. There is an increasing need for tools supporting the automatic search for 3D models. A 3D model could be searched by its textual annotation by using a conventional text-based search engine. However, this approach wouldn't work in many of the application scenarios for the 3D shape model. The annotations added by human beings depend on culture, language, age, and other factors. It is also extremely difficult to describe by words a shape that is not in a well-known shape or semantic category. Therefore, since recently, concentrated research efforts are being spent on content-based retrieval techniques for efficient retrieval of 3D models.

One of the major challenges in the content-based retrieval is to elaborate a suitable canonical characterization of the 3D models to be indexed. Up to now there are only few methods to the specific problem of retrieval of 3D models. However, an extensive amount of literature can be found in the related fields of computer vision, object recognition and geometric modeling. For a broad introduction to this literature, please consult the survey paper by Tangelder and Veltkamp [1].

In this paper, we propose an Integer Medial Axis Skeleton (IMAS) approach to 3D model comparison and retrieval, which is constructed based on the Integer Medial Axis Transform (IMAT) algorithm [2]. We established a skeletal binary tree, which is

Z. Pan et al. (Eds.): ICAT 2006, LNCS 4282, pp. 830–838, 2006.

constructed based on the IMAS, as a search key. The skeletal binary tree allows a similarity between 3D models to be calculated using a coarse-to-fine strategy. During the matching, we introduce a threshold variable that provides a fast estimation of similarity between 3D models.

The outline of the paper is as follows. The next section contains a summary of related work. Section 3 describes how we extract the IMAS and how we compute the similarity between tow models. Experimental results are presented in the Section 4. Finally, we present our conclusions in Section 5.

2 Related Work

Shape matching is one of the fundamental problems in retrieval of 3D models. In [3], Novotni and Klein described a geometric similarity method to 3D models retrieval based on calculating a volumetric error between one model and a sequence of offset hulls of the other model. However, this method is not symmetric and dose not obey the triangle inequality. In [4], a 3D shape matching algorithm and system is presented which computes a shape signature for each object and then matches an object into a database of signatures. The shape functions are computed stochastically by randomly sampling over the shape and then creating a continuous probability distribution as a signature for the 3D shape. However, such distributions do not capture where features are located and can't deal with partial queries, missing feature, or part articulation.

In [5] used a global histogram as a search key for a database of 3D model. This method is computationally stable and suitable for representing rough feature of 3D models, but can't estimate local features.

To obtain an intuitive description of the shapes, the use of a skeletal or graph representation is very attractive. These approaches permit us to keep the topology of the objects that have rich information for matching purpose.

In [6], Hilaga et al. presented a 3D matching algorithm based upon a multi-resolution Reeb graph (MRG). The MRG is computed for each 3D shape and then a graph matching technique is used to match the MRG's. Their algorithm uses Reeb graphs based on a quotient function defined by an integer geodesic distance. However, the nodes in the graph have no intuitive interpretation with respect to parts of the model. Therefore, geometric distortions of the parts relative to each other could have significant impact on the graph structure. In [7], Tung proposed to augment the MRG with geometrical attributes and provided a new topological coherence condition to improve the graph matching. Moreover 2D appearance attributes and 3D features are extracted and merged to improve the estimation of the similarity between models. Bespalov et al. [8] presented preliminary research on a modification of Hilaga's algorithm, which computes a scale-space decomposition of a model, represented as a rooted undirected tree instead of a Reeb graph. This reduced the problem of comparing two 3D models to computing a matching among the corresponding rooted trees.

In [9, 10, 11], proposed using a skeletal structure of a 3D model as a search key. Those algorithms were used in various applications such as shape deformation, modeling, and path planning. The medial axis skeleton is a well-known skeletal structure [9, 10, 12, 13, 14]. However, this method is inappropriate as a search key for 3D models because calculating the medial axis has a high computational cost and is sensitive to noise and small undulations.

After examining various options, we have chosen a skeletal structure called the integer medial axis skeleton as the basis for our search key. The integer medial axis skeleton was defined by Hessellink [2]. The algorithm is based upon the computation of 3D feature transforms, using a modification of an algorithm for Euclidean distance transforms. The skeletonization algorithm has a time complexity which is linear in the amount of grid points, and can be easily parallelized.

3 Overview of Skeleton Matching

Our approach is to use a matching methodology based upon an "IMAS" of a 3D model. The IMAS used in this context is a graph-like representation of a 3D model. This IMAS is computed directly from the 3D model and contains the topological and geometric information about the 3D model, which are held at each node in the IMAS. This information includes the radius, degrees of freedom about the node (for topological matching).

In the preprocessing step, to compare two models independently of orientation, position and scaling, we first apply a classical spatial alignment technique such as the Principal Components Analysis to bring the models in a standard pose [15].

3.1 3D Skeletonization

The skeleton is computed at the first step in the skeleton-based 3D matching. The method we utilize here is an Integer Medial Axis Transform (IMAT) algorithm described in [2]. The advantage of using the method is that an IMAS can be computed very quickly for large 3D datasets.

We briefly describe the extension of the IMAT algorithm to the computation of IMAS, closely adhering to the notation and approach given in [2].

Definition 1. The length of a vector $r \in R^3$ is denoted by $\|r\| = \sqrt{\sum_i r_i^2}$. We regard Z^3 as a grid embedded in R^3 . The elements of Z^3 are called grid points.

Let B be the surface of 3D model, which is a given nonempty set of grid points. The feature transform FT is defined as the set-valued function that assigns to r the set of closest surface points. So we have $FT(r,B) = \left\{ y \in B \middle| \min\{\|r - y\|\} \right\}$. An IMAS of surface B is a set of points denoted as $IMAS(B)$.

Definition 2. Let $E = \left\{ e \in Z^3 \middle| \|e\| = 1 \right\}$. The IMAS consists of the points $p \in Z^3$ such that   for   some $e \in E$ we   have $\|FT(p+e) - FT(p)\| > 1$ and $\|m - FT(p+e)\| = \|m - FT(p)\|$ where $m = p + \frac{1}{2}e$ is the midpoint of the line segment from p to $p + e$.

Let $\varpi(p) = \|m - FT(p)\|$, $\varpi(p)$ is the radius of the inscribed sphere of the point p, $\gamma(p)$ is defined as the degree of freedom of the point p, which represents a sum of the point that is linked with the point p in the IMAS.

A well-defined skeleton of surface B should satisfy three properties (neighborhood, uniformity and compactness) [16]. We want to find major IMAS points to preserve the primary shape structure. For each point q on the surface B we can find a point p which belongs to IMAS. So we have $p = IMAS(q)$. For each p on IMAS, we can also find an inverse of the IMAS point denoted as $IMAS^{-1}(p)$ that is a set of points on the surface B .Let $q \in B$ and $p = IMAS(q)$. The distance between q and p is denoted as $dis(q)$. The auxiliary function $Average(dis(q))$ is the average value of $dis(q)$ $(q \in IMAS^{-1}(p))$. The IMAS point p should satisfy the following function:

$$\min\left(\sum_{q \in IMAS^{-1}(p)} \|dis(q) - Average(dis(q))\| \right). \tag{1}$$

An example for the extracting IMAS is given in Fig. 1.

Fig. 1. Extracting IMAS

3.2 Construction of the Skeletal Binary Tree

In models matching, the skeletal binary tree is used as a search key that represents the features of a 3D model. The basic idea of the skeletal binary tree is to partition the

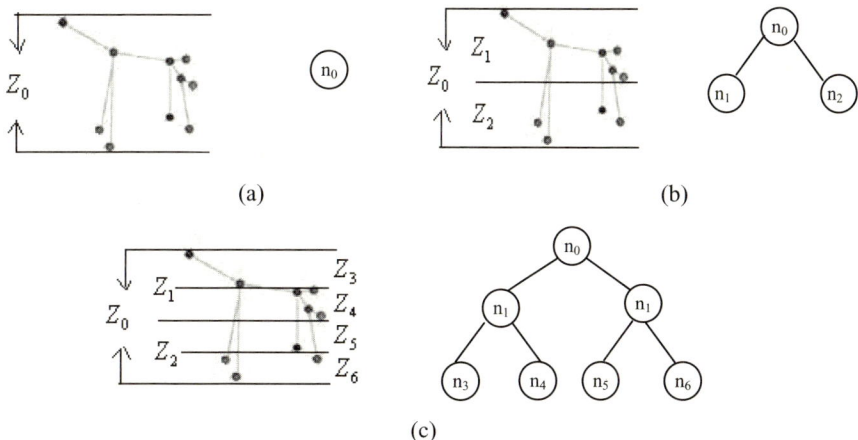

Fig. 2. The construction of the skeletal binary tree

IMAS into different regions at various levels of detail. A node of the skeletal binary tree represents a particular region. Fig. 2 shows the distribution of the IMAS and the corresponding nodes of the skeletal binary tree.

The re-partitioning is done in a binary manner for simplicity. In Fig. 2(a), there is only one region Z_0, the corresponding node is n_0, which is the rooted node of the skeletal binary tree. In Fig. 2(b), the region Z_0 is re-partitioned to Z_1 and Z_2, the corresponding nodes are n_1 and n_2 respectively. Finer levels of the skeletal binary tree are constructed in the same way as show in Fig. 2(c).

The skeletal binary tree has the following properties:

Property 1: There are parent-child relationships between nodes of adjacent levels. n_{2i+1} is the left child node of n_i, $n_{2(i+1)}$ is the right child node of n_i. In Fig. 2(c), the node n_0 is the parent of n_1 and n_2, and n_1 is the parent of n_3 and n_4, etc.

Property 2: By repeating the re-partitioning, the skeletal binary tree is constructed. That is, finer levels approximate the original model more exactly.

Property 3: The corresponding region of the parent node is partitioned equally with the child nodes on the Z-coordinate. Let $\delta\max(n_i)$ be the maximum value of the Z-coordinate of the corresponding region of the node n_i • $\delta\min(n_i)$ be the minimum value of the Z-coordinate of the corresponding region of the node n_i. We construct the functions $\delta\max$ and $\delta\min$ as follows:

$$\delta\max(n_{2i+1}) = \delta\max(n_i) \ . \tag{2}$$

$$\delta\min(n_{2i+1}) = \frac{\delta\max(n_i) + \delta\min(n_i)}{2} \ . \tag{3}$$

$$\delta\max(n_{2(i+1)}) = \frac{\delta\max(n_i) + \delta\min(n_i)}{2} \ . \tag{4}$$

$$\delta\min(n_{2(i+1)}) = \delta\min(n_i) \ . \tag{5}$$

Use these properties, the skeletal binary tree is easily constructed and a similarity between models can then be calculated using a coarse-to-fine strategy of different resolution levels as described below.

3.3 Matching the Skeletal Binary Tree

Definition 3. Let n_i be a node of skeletal binary tree, the corresponding region is Z_i, $\alpha(n_i)$ be the weight of n_i, the function $\alpha(n_i)$ is calculated as follows:

$$\alpha(n_i) = \sum_{p \in Z_i} \varpi(p) \ . \tag{6}$$

During matching, we must take the topological information into account. Let the function $\mu(n_i)$ be the sum of the degree of freedom in the corresponding region of the node n_i. It is define as follows:

$$\mu(n_i) = \sum_{p \in Z_i} \gamma(p) \ . \tag{7}$$

Let S and T are 3D models. The corresponding skeletal binary trees are s and t, m_i is a node of s, n_i is a node of t. The similarity of S and T is computed by matching their skeletal binary tree.

Definition 4. The similarity $sim(m_i, n_i)$ between m_i and n_i be defined as follows:

$$sim(m_i, n_i) = 1 - \frac{\|\alpha(m_i) - \alpha(n_i)\|}{\alpha(m_i)} \times \frac{\|\mu(m_i) - \mu(n_i)\|}{\mu(m_i)} \ . \tag{8}$$

Then, the similarity $SIM(s,t)$ between s and t be defined as follows:

$$SIM(s,t) = \sum_{m_i \in s, n_i \in t} sim(m_i, n_i) \ . \tag{9}$$

In order to improve the efficient of the matching between s and t, we define a threshold variable ψ. Calculate the similarity using a coarse-to-fine strategy. The matching algorithm is described as follows:

Step 1: Calculate the similarity of rooted nodes m_0 and n_0 of the skeletal binary trees s and t, if $sim(m_0, n_0) \le \psi$, then do step2; else $SIM(s,t) = -\infty$ and do step 3.

Step 2: if $sim(m_i, n_i) \le \psi$, then $i = i+1$, repeat step 2; else $SIM(s,t) = -\infty$.

Step 3: Calculate $SIM(s,t)$ and stop matching.

A larger $SIM(s,t)$ means a larger similarity.

4   Experimental Results

In order to test the IMAS algorithm, experiments were conducted to test the efficiency and accuracy of this new search key. A database of 140 different models was used. Those models were selected from the Princeton Shape Benchmark Database. Those models were grouped into 6 classes: 8 horses, 14 dogs, 41 cars, 11 humans, 20 birds, 46 airplanes. The computer used was an Intel Pentium IV 2.8GHz processor with 1024 Mb internal memory. Throughout the experiments, the layer-count of the skeletal binary tree was 6; the threshold variable used was $\psi = 0.5$ in the $sim(m_i, n_i)$ calculation.

The time required for the calculate of similarity between a model and other models in the same class varied from 0.5 sec. to 3.5 sec., on average, it took only 0.07 sec. to calculate one similarity. The computation time depends on the layer-count of the skeletal binary tree and the threshold variable ψ. The experimental results for the query time are reported in Table 1.

The retrieval performance can be expressed in so-called precision-recall diagrams. Briefly, precision is the proportion of retrieved models that are relevant (i.e., in the correct class) and recall is the proportion of the relevant models actually retrieved. By

Table 1. The query time for each class use the IMAS algorithm and the skeletal graphs algorithm [13]

Models class	query time (sec.)
cars	3.2
dogs	0.8
airplanes	3.5
birds	1.2
humans	0.6
horses	0.5

Models class	query time (sec.)
cars	3.9
dogs	1.2
airplanes	4.0
birds	1.6
humans	0.9
horses	0.7

(a) The IMAS   (b) The skeletal graph

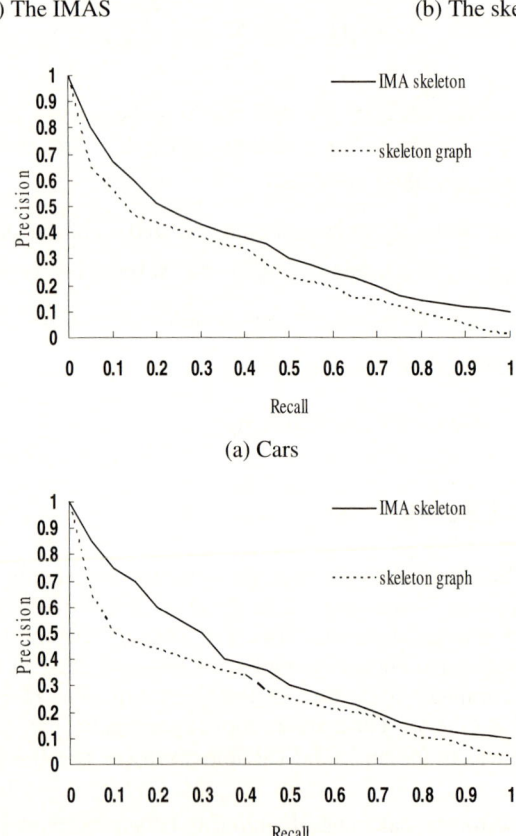

(a) Cars

(b) Airplanes

Fig. 3. Precision vs. recall results for tow classes (cars, airplanes) using two algorithms, the IMAS algorithm and the skeletal graphs algorithm [13]

examining the precision-recall diagrams for different queries we obtained a measure of the retrieval performance. For our tests we selected one class of models and used each of the models in the class as a query model. The precision-recall values for these experiments were averaged and yielded one curve in the corresponding diagram, as show in the Fig. 3.

Some example results of the experiment are showed in Fig. 4, Each row illustrates a query, the top row shows the query models, the second row the nearest model, the third, fourth and fifth row show the second, third and forth nearest model, respectively.

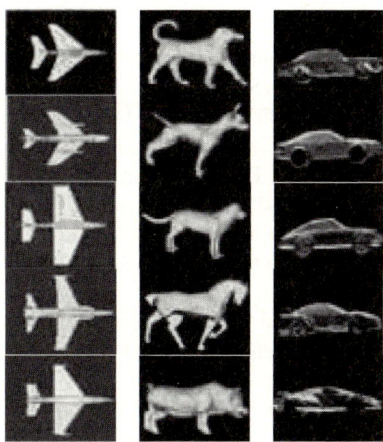

Fig. 4. Results of the search experiment

5 Conclusions

The skeleton approach has a number of advantages over the global and local shape descriptor methods. It is an intuitive representation of 3D objects that can be easily used to understand the similarities present in the matched models. In this paper, we presented a new algorithm called the Integer Medial Axis Skeleton (IMAS) for the accurate, efficient and automatic of similarity between 3D models.

Our first contribution is the proposal of IMAS based on the IMA transforms algorithm. In this approach, we extracted both topological and geometrical information, which was held at each node in the IMAS. The time complexity required for skeletonization is linear in the amount of grid points, and can be easily parallelized. Secondly, the similarity is calculated with a coarse-to-fine strategy. We established a skeletal binary tree constructed based on the IMAS that was beneficial for improving retrieval effectiveness in a 3D search system. During the matching, we proposed a threshold variable that provided a fast estimation of similarity between models. Our experiments indicate that IMAS matching provides a fast and efficient computation of the similarity between models and provides results that agree well with human intuition.

Currently, the IMAS algorithm uses the radius, degrees of freedom about the skeletal point in calculation similarity. However, additional information, such as the curvature, color, texture est. can be introduced if necessary, to provide a more accurate match.

References

1. Johan W.H. Tangelder and Remco C. Veltkamp. A survey of content based 3D shape retrieval methods. In International Conference on Shape Modeling and Applications 2004, (Genova, Italy), 2004, 12 (7):145-156
2. Wim H. Hessellink, Menno Visser, Jos B.T.M. Roerdink. Euclidean skeletons of 3D data sets in linear time by the integer medial axis transform[A]. ISMM'2005[C], Paris, France, (2005) 259-268
3. M. Novotni, and R. Klein. A Geometric Approach to 3D Object Comparison. Int. Conf. on Shape Modeling and Application (SMI 2001), (2001) 167-175
4. R. Osada, T. Funkhouser, B. Chazelle, and D. Dobkin. Matching 3D Models with Shape Distributions. In Shape Modeling International, Genova, Italy, May 2001. (2001) 154-166
5. P.J. Besl. Triangles as a Primary Representation Object Recognition in computer Vision. LNCS 994, Splinger-Verlag, (1995) 191-206
6. M. Hilaga, Y. Shinagawa, T. Kohmura, and T. Kunii. Topology Matching for Fully Automatic Similarity Estimation of 3D Shapes. ACMSIGGRAPH 2001 Proceedings, Aug. 2001,(2001) 203-212
7. Tung, T., Schmitt, F.: Augmented Reeb Graphs for Content-Based Retrieval of 3D Mesh Models. In: International COnference on Shape Modeling and Applications 2004, Genova, Italy (2004) 157-166
8. D. Bespalov, A. shokoufangeh, W. C. Regli and W. Sun. Scale-space representation of 3D models and topological matching. In Solid Modeling'03, (2003) 208-215
9. J.-H. Chuang, C.-H. Tsai, M. –C. Ko. Skeletonization of Three-Dimensional Object Using Generalized Potential Field. IEEE Trans. PAMI, 2000, 22:1241-1251
10. T. Culver, J. Keyser, D. Manocha. Accurate Computation of the Medial Axis of a Polyhedron. Proc. Symp. Solid Modeling, (1999) 179-190
11. Y. Zhou, A. Kaufman, A.W. Toga. Three-dimensional skeleton and centerline generation based on an approximate minimum distance field. The Visual Computer, 1998, 14(7):303-314
12. E.C. Sherbrooke, N.M. Patrikalakis, E. Brisson. An Algorithm for the Medial Axis Transform of 3D Polyhedral Solids. IEEE Trans. Visualization and Computer Graphics, 1996, 2(1):44-61
13. K. Siddiqi, A. Shokoufandeh, S. J. Dickinson, et al. Shock graphs and shape matching. Int'L J. Computer Vision (1998) 222-229
14. H. Blum. A Transformation for Extracting New Descriptors of Shape. Proc. Symp. Models for the Perception of Speech and Visual Form, MIT Press, (1967) 362-380
15. D.V.Vranic, D. Saupe and J.Richter. Tools for 3D-object retrieval: Kahrune-Loeve Transform and spherical harmonics, IEEE Workshop Multimedia Signal Processing, Cannes, France, Oct. (2001) 293-298
16. Wan-Cun Ma, Fu-Che Wu, Ming Ouhyoung. Skeleton Extraction of 3D Objects with Radial Basis Functions. Proceedings of the Shape Modeling International (SMI'03), (2003) 295-302

Implicit Surface Boolean Operations Based Cut-and-Paste Algorithm for Mesh Models

Xujia Qin[1,2], Xinhua Yang[3], and Hongbo Zheng[4]

[1] College of Software, Zhejiang University of Technology, Hangzhou, 310032, China
qxj@zjut.edu.cn
[2] State Key Lab of CAD&CG, Zhejiang University, Hangzhou, 310027, China
[3] School of Mechanical Engineering, Dalian Jiaotong University, Dalian 116028, China
yangxh@djtu.edu.cn
[4] College of Information Engineering, Zhejiang University of Technology,
Hangzhou, 310032, China
zhb@zjut.edu.cn

Abstract. Cut-and-paste operation for 3D models is a new geometry modelling method by examples. The method constructs a new model from two or more existed models by cutting some useful parts from source models and pasting to target model. A novel cut-and-paste algorithm for mesh models based on implicit surface Boolean operations is proposed. The algorithm composes of following steps: Firstly, cut part of mesh from source model and align it with the target model. Secondly, convert the two mesh models into point models and convert the point models into implicit surfaces with RBF interpolation. Thirdly, merge the two implicit surfaces by union operation. And finally, polygonize the implicit surface. Then the final new mesh model is obtained. Because the two elements of Boolean operation are not mesh models, it can avoid complex and time consume intersection calculations of facets and edges. The experiments show that good results can be obtained with the algorithm. The approach can be used to create special and exaggerated models for computer animation.

Keywords: Cut-and-paste, mesh models, Boolean operations, implicit surface, point models.

1 Introduction

In 3D animation, movie special effects, 3D graphic arts and CAD applications, to construct a complex model is a time-consuming, tedious and complicated work. 3D scan technology can quickly get the point-cloud data of an object's surface, and the data can be used to construct geometric models. However, this method still can't meet the need of modeling and editing of computer animation, because operations such as denoising, hole repairing, and polygonizing are needed during the process. Most geometric modeling systems expect the user to manipulate control points of NURBS, individual mesh vertices and polygons, or use conventional, higher-level operations such as volume deformations, but it is

Z. Pan et al. (Eds.): ICAT 2006, LNCS 4282, pp. 839–848, 2006.

inconvenient to manipulate. Cut-and-paste is a convenient operation in text and image editing; now they are also used in 3D model editing.

2   Related Works

The development of graphic technology and the necessity of various applications require more convenient editing methods. In recent years, many methods were presented to perform cut-and-paste on 3D models [1-16]. These methods can be categorized into two main types. The main idea of first type is to extract a basis surface as an intermediate from the source model or target model, then transfer the features (details) of the basis surface to the surface of target model [3,5-9]. In order to fit the shape of the pasting region on target model, this kind of method needs a whole transformation from the cutting source surface to target surface, then pastes the region on the surface of the target model. During the editing process, most of the work concentrates on B-Spline surface. What's more, both of the source model and the target model are tensor product B-Spline surfaces, so polygonal mesh model could not be processed in this way. In order to solve the problem of feature construction in CAD product design. Ranta et al. presented a cut-and-paste operation between solids [11], but his method didn't deal with the smooth of conjunction region. Biermann et al. presented a semi-regular multi-resolution subdivision surfaces based method which can cut the features to target region. But his method doesn't suit the case of fusion of complex objects because it requires both the source and the target feature region to be isomorphic to a disk shape. Furukawa and Masuda presented a constrained B-spline surface/solid approximate based cut-and-paste method [5]. Although it can deal with the situation where the cutting region is non-zero genus, it is not interactive, what's more, in some cases the conjunction region would not be smooth naturally. The second type of method uses mesh fusion to cut the surface from source model and then to paste it on target model [4,10-14]. The advantage of this type of method is that instead of performing a global deformation on the source surface, it transits smoothly from the source surface to target surface along the conjunction region. For example, Signh et al. [12] presented a method to connect polygons with processing implicit function surface, but it requires the fusion region to be star like in shape. Pedersen [13] presented an implicit surface method. Using this method the smooth fusion feature of implicit surface can make the smooth transition very easy after cut-and-paste, but it is only suitable for source objects represented as balls (or other implicit surface). Kanai et al. presented a mesh fusion method based on global harmonic mapping [4,14,15]. This method requires the cutting feature region and the pasting target region to be isomorphic with disk like mesh in topology. G. Liu et al. presented a improved version of Kanai's method [16]. It uses a local harmonic mapping instead of global harmonic mapping to speed up the cut-and-paste process and to improve its stability at the same time. Museth et al. used a surface editing operator based on level set to implement the local and global editing of closed surface [10]. This method converts mesh into complex volumetric data at first, and then performs volumetric data fusion, converts the volumetric data into polygonal meshes at last, so it needs complex and time consuming computing. In this paper, we presented a cut-and-paste algorithm for mesh models based on implicit surface Boolean operations to overcome some of the shortcoming of algorithms mentioned above. The basic idea of our method is as following: First, we represent the mesh model as point-sampled model. If the source mesh model is sparse, we can subdivide the meshes. Then convert the point model into implicit surface by using variational interpolation, and use implicit surface Boolean operation to perform the union operation at last. The final mesh model is derived by polygonizing the result of union operation. The advantages of the algorithm we presented are as following: (1) it can realize the smooth transition of fusion region. (2) It doesn't need to construct a harmonic mapping for the cutting source region or pasting target region or parameterize them, and self-intersected facets in fusion region will not occur. (3) It can be applied to cases where the acting source region is non-zero genus. (4) It can be applied to arbitrary models.

3   Boolean Operations on Implicit Surface

In Euclid space R^3, point set defined by inequation $f(x, y, z) \geq 0$ is a function representation of geometry object. Surface (boundary of the object) defined by equation $f(x, y, z) = 0$ is an implicit surface. In solid which defined by implicit function, let $p = (x, y, z)^T$, if $f(p) > 0$, and then p is inside the solid. If $f(p) = 0$, then p is on the boundary of the solid. And if $f(p) < 0$, then p is outside the solid.

Let $f_1 = 0$ and $f_2 = 0$ to define two implicit surface, f_3 is the result implicit surface by Boolean operation of f_1 and f_2. Wyvill [17] presented a definition of implicit surface Boolean operation by means of limit form of functions fusion.

$$f_3 = (f_1^n + f_2^n)^{\frac{1}{n}} . \tag{1}$$

Pasko proposed a general form of Boolean operations by functions fusion [18].

$$f_3 = (f_1 + f_2 + \alpha(f_1^2 + f_2^2)^{\frac{1}{2}})(f_1^2 + f_2^2)^{\frac{1}{2}} . \tag{2}$$

In Eq. (2), $\alpha \in [-1, 1]$, when $\alpha = -1$, the equation indicates intersection of f_1 and f_2, and when $\alpha = 1$, indicates the union of f_1 and f_2. Although the Eq. (2) presents a uniform mode of Boolean operations and functions fusion for implicit surfaces, but it is inconvenient to implement. In order to decrease the computation cost and convenient to implement, we present following Boolean operations for implicit surfaces.

Union:

$$f_3 = f_1 \cup f_2 = max(f_1, f_2) . \tag{3}$$

Intersection:

$$f_3 = f_1 \cap f_2 = min(f_1, f_2) . \tag{4}$$

Subtraction:
$$f_3 = f_1 - f_2 = min(f_1, -f_2) . \tag{5}$$

Fig. 1 shows Boolean operation results from two spheres defined by implicit function.

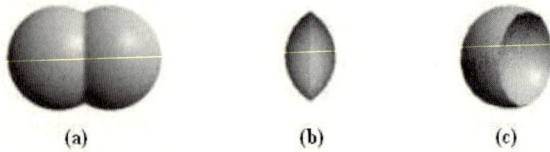

(a)   (b)   (c)

Fig. 1. Boolean operation results from two spheres defined by implicit function. (a)Union; (b)Intersection; and (c)Subtraction.

4   Interactively Cutting and Alignment for Mesh Models

In order to implement the cut-and-paste operation of meshes, part of the meshes of source model should be cut down and then be pasted to the target model. So a convenient and quick interactive method is necessary. Since the mesh model will be converted to point model, on which Boolean operations will be performed, the cutting does not need to be accurate. What's more, the cutting edge does not need to be plain. Here, we use simple polyhedron such as plains, cubes and balls to cut the mesh model. During the cutting process, inside-and-outside test is done for vertexes and triangle facets of the mesh model, vertexes and facets inside the cutting cube are saved, thus complicated, time-consuming of facet-to-facet and facet-to-line segment intersection testing are unnecessary. For example, in Fig. 2, balls are used to cut the rabbit model interactively, Fig. 2(b) is part of the meshes cut down from Fig. 2(a).

The part of meshes cut from source model should be pasted on target mesh. We designed interactive tools such as moving, rotation, zooming and so on, with manual interaction, it is convenient to aligning the mesh. Fig. 2(c) is the result of alignment meshes.

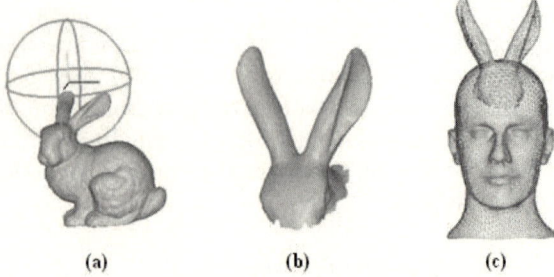

(a)   (b)   (c)

Fig. 2. Cutting and aligning for mesh models. (a)Interactively cutting for mesh model; (b)Result model after cutting; (c)aligning the two models.

5 RBF Implicit Surface Converting and Boolean Operation for Mesh Models

5.1 Converting Mesh Model to Point Model

In order to convert mesh model into point model, we can just use vertexes of mesh model as sample points of point model. The accuracy of point model is related to the density of sample points. For dense mesh model, it can be converted to point model directly, for sparse mesh model, we can improve its density by subdividing the mesh, then converted the subdivided mesh into dot model. Hence, we use Loop method [19] to subdivide the mesh. Fig. 3 is an example of subdivision of sparse mesh and its convention into point model. Fig. 3(a) is a source model. Fig. 3(b) is the result of mesh after twice Loop subdivision. Fig. 3(c) is the corresponding point model of Fig. 3(b).

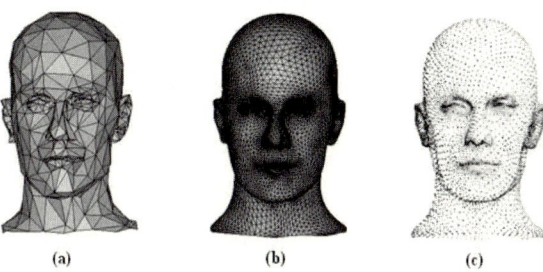

(a)   (b)   (c)

Fig. 3. Subdividing spare mesh model and converting it to point model. (a)Original model; (b) subdivided twice with Loop subdivision method; (c) convert into point model.

5.2 Implicit Surface Transforming and Boolean Operations on Point-Sampled Models

Transforming point model to implicit function representation, obviously it is a multi-variant scatter data interpolation problem. We use variational interpolation to obtain the implicit surface of the point model, the form is $f(p) = 0$. Considering that the interpolated surface is smooth, in CAGD, smooth property of surface can evaluate by thin-plate energy function [20].

$$E = \int_{\Omega} [f_{xx}^2(x,y) + f_{xy}^2(x,y) + f_{yy}^2(x,y)]dxdy . \tag{6}$$

Where f_{xx}, f_{xy}, f_{yy} are second partial derivatives of f, Ω is region of interpolate points. Because the energy E essentially is a square curvature evaluate of function f in region Ω. When f is rumpled, the energy E is increase. So, minimize the energy can make the surface f smooth .

The above energy function can easily to extend to high dimension case. The equation's general solution form is linear combination of radial basis functions $\phi(p)$ and a linear term $Q(p)$. Its general expression is:

$$f(p) = \sum_{j=1}^{n} \lambda_j \phi(|p - p_j|) + Q(p) \ . \tag{7}$$

where $Q(p)$ is a polynomial of degree at most a specified number, λ_j is a real-valued weight, $\phi(\bullet)$ is a radial basis, and $|\bullet|$ is a Euclid norm. In order to solve the weights , we can convert to solve the following linear system:

$$\begin{pmatrix} \phi_{11} & \phi_{12} & \cdots & \phi_{1n} & x_1 & y_1 & z_1 & 1 \\ \phi_{21} & \phi_{22} & \cdots & \phi_{2n} & x_2 & y_2 & z_2 & 1 \\ \vdots & \vdots & \ddots & \vdots & \vdots & \vdots & \vdots & \vdots \\ \phi_{n1} & \phi_{n2} & \cdots & \phi_{nn} & x_n & y_n & z_n & 1 \\ x_1 & x_2 & \cdots & x_n & 0 & 0 & 0 & 0 \\ y_1 & y_2 & \cdots & y_n & 0 & 0 & 0 & 0 \\ z_1 & z_2 & \cdots & z_n & 0 & 0 & 0 & 0 \\ 1 & 1 & \cdots & 1 & 0 & 0 & 0 & 0 \end{pmatrix} \begin{pmatrix} \lambda_1 \\ \lambda_2 \\ \vdots \\ \lambda_n \\ c_0 \\ c_1 \\ c_2 \\ c_3 \end{pmatrix} = \begin{pmatrix} h_1 \\ h_2 \\ \vdots \\ h_n \\ 0 \\ 0 \\ 0 \\ 0 \end{pmatrix} \ . \tag{8}$$

where denoting $h_j = f(p_j)$, $\phi_{ij} = \phi(|p_i - p_j|)$, $Q(p) = c_0 x + c_1 y + c_2 z + c_3$.

In Eq. (8), the coefficient matrix is obviously real symmetric, and with proper selection of basis functions it can be made positive-definite. Thus, a solution always exists to the linear system [21].

Use the variational interpolation described above, we can construct a scalar distance field $f(p) = r$ from point-sampled model. This is a typical implicit surface form. When $r = 0$, $f(p) = r$ is the interpolated surface of the point model.

After obtaining the implicit surface of the point model, we can realize Boolean operations for point models by using the implicit surface Boolean operation method described in section 3. Those points in two point models that satisfy the equation $f_3(p) = 0$ are the points of Boolean operations result model. Fig. 2 indicates the Boolean operation of two point models.

5.3   Polygonization for Boolean Operation

Because after the point model is converted into implicit function, the result of Boolean operation is an implicit surface, we can get the mesh after Boolean operation by polygonizing the implicit surface. For the polygonization of implicit

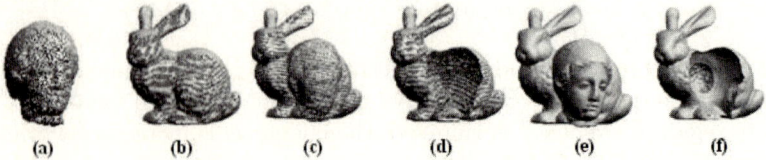

(a)   (b)   (c)   (d)   (e)   (f)

Fig. 4. Boolean operation on point models. (a) Venus head model;(b) Bunny model; (c) Union of (a) and (b); (d) Subtraction of (a) and (b); (e) Polygonization result of (c); (f) Polygonization result of (d).

surface, Marching cubes [22] and Bloomenthal [23] are two well known and classical algorithms. In this paper, we choose the latter. Fig. 4(c) and 4(d) is the result of Boolean operation on point models, Fig. 4(e) and 4(f) is the result of polygonization.

6   Experiment Results

We develop a prototype system to test our algorithm on PC with CPU of 2.4 GHZ, RAM of 512M, and using the platform of Microsoft Visual C++ 6.0. Fig. 5 shows that the wings of felines model are cut down and pasted on horse model. Fig. 5(b) is the model after trimming. Fig. 5(c) is the mesh model after aligned. Fig. 5(d) is the point models convert from the two mesh models. Fig. 5(e) is the point model after union operation. Fig. 5(f) is the result of polygonization after union.

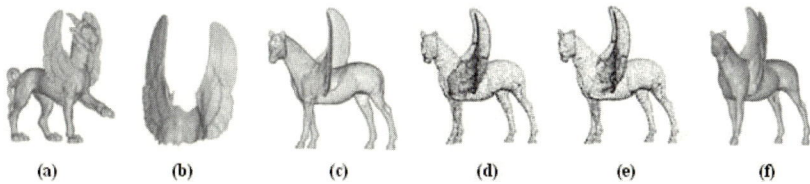

Fig. 5. Cut-and-paste operation on felines and horse models. (a) felines model; (b) model after cutting;(c) mesh model alignment; (d) Convert into point model; (e) point model after Boolean operation; (f) Polygonization result.

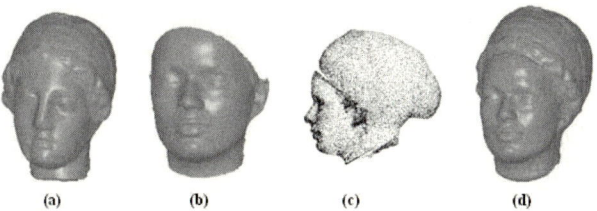

Fig. 6. Cut-and-paste operation on mesh models. (a) Venus head model; (b) Face model; (c) Result of Boolean operation; (d) Surface model after polygonization.

Fig. 6, Fig. 7 and Fig. 8 are results of Boolean operations on mesh models. Fig. 6(a) and 6(b) are original models. Fig. 6(c) is the point model after union operation. Figure 6(d) is the polygonizing surface model from Fig. 6(c). In this way, we can cut part of mesh from one model and paste it on another model. Fig. 7 shows an ox head fusion with horse head. Fig. 8 shows fusing Venus head and body. Table 1 shows the running time of Boolean operations on point models in Fig. 4 to Fig. 8, including RBF distance fields constructing time and polygonizing time for Boolean operation result represented by implicit surface.

From Table 1 we can easily see that the time efficiency of the algorithm can acceptable.

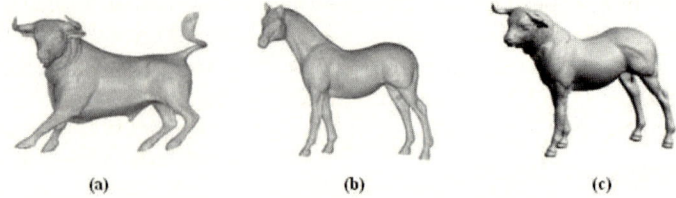

Fig. 7. Fusing the ox head with horse body. (a) ox model; (b) horse model; and (c) result model of fusion.

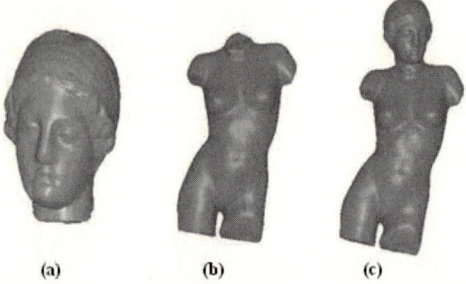

Fig. 8. Fusing the Venus head and body. (a) Venus head model; (b) Venus body model; and (c) result model of fusion.

Table 1. Running time of Boolean operation on point models

Figure	Points of model A	Points of model B	RBF constructing time(model A)	RBF constructing time(model B)	Polygonizing time
Fig. 4	35947	8266	6.141s	1.203s	12.172s
Fig. 5	7251	7689	0.813s	1.125s	3.031s
Fig. 6	8268	6461	1.219s	0.841s	3.422s
Fig. 7	6668	6195	0.843s	0.817s	2.859s
Fig. 8	8268	4509	0.819s	0.704s	3.121s

7   Conclusions

A novel cut-and-paste algorithm for mesh models is presented. The algorithm use Boolean operation for implicit surface to fusion two mesh models. Using the approach, the fusion region is smooth, complex harmonic map and local parameterization for fusion region is not necessary. The algorithm can used in the case of genus is not zero of the models. Because the Boolean operation is not directly with the mesh models, so mass of time consuming intersection test for facet-to-facet, and facet-to-line segment is avoid. The experiments show that good results can be obtained with the algorithm.

This approach belongs to the part of novel method of geometry modeling by examples with cut-and-paste editing. The method constructs a new mesh model from two or more existed mesh models by cutting some useful parts from source models and pasting to target model. The new approach can be used to create lots of special exaggerated modeling effects for computer animation.

Acknowledgments. This research is supported by Zhejiang provincial Nature Science Foundation of China (Grant No. Y104341 and Y105303), and Opening Research Fund of State Key Laboratory of CAD&CG, Zhejiang University.

References

1. Barghiel H., Bartels R., Forsey D.: Pasting spline surfaces. In: Mathematical Methods for Curves and Surfaces, Vanderbilt Univ. Press,(1994)31-40
2. Biermann H., Martin I., Bernardini F., et al.: Cutand-paste editing of multiresolution surfaces. In: Proc.of ACM SIGGRAPH'02,(2002)312-321
3. Conrad B., Mann S.: Better pasting via quasiinterpolation. Curve and Surface Design: Saint-Malo 1999, Vanderbilt Univ. Press, (2000)27-36
4. Kanai T., Suzuki H., Mitani J., et al.: Interactive mesh fusion based on local 3D metamorphosis. In: Proc. of Graphics Interface'99, June, (1999)148-156
5. Furukawa Y., Masuda H., Miura KT., et al.: Cut-and-Paste Editing Based on Constrained B-spline Volume Fitting. In: Proc. of Computer Graphics International, (2003)222-225
6. Bartels R. and Forsey D.: Spline overlay surfaces. In: Technical Report CS-92-08, University of Waterloo, waterloo, Ontario, Canada N2L 3G1, (1991)
7. Chan L., Mann S., and Bartels R.: World space surface pasting. In: Proc. of Graphics Interface, May ,(1997)146-154
8. Ohtake Y., Belyaev A., Alexa M., et al.: Multi-level partition of unity implicits. ACM Trans. Graph. Vol.22(3):(2003)463-470.
9. Mann S. and Yeung T.:Cylindrical surface pasting. In: Geometric Modeling'99, (1999)233-248
10. Museth K., Breen D. E., Whitaker R.T., et al.: Level set surface editing operators. ACM Transactions on Graphics, Vol.21(3):(2002)330-338
11. Ranta M., Inui M., Kimura F., Mäntylä M.: Cut and paste based modeling with boundary features. In: Rossignac J., Turner J., Allen G.,(eds.): Proc. of the 2nd ACM Solid Modeling. ACM Press, (1993)303-312
12. Singh K., Parent R.: Joining polyhedral objects using implicitly defined surfaces. The Visual Computer, Vol.17(7):(2001)415-428
13. Pedersen   HK.:   Decorating   implicit   surfaces.   Computer   Graphics, Vol.29(3):(1995)291-300
14. Kanai T., Suzuki H., Kimura F.: Three-Dimensional geometric metamorphosis based on harmonic maps. The Visual Computer, Vol.14(4):(1998)166-176
15. Kanai T., Suzuki H., Kimura F.: Metamorphosis of arbitrary triangular meshes. IEEE Computer Graphics and Applications, Vol.20(2):(2000)62-75
16. Liu G., Jin XG., Feng JQ.,et al.: Montage mesh musion. Journal of Software, Vol.14(8):(2003)1425-1432
17. Wyvill B., Gallin E., and Guy A.: Extending the CSG tree. warping,blending and Boolean operations in an implicit surface modeling system. Computer Graphics Forum, Vol.18(2): (1999)149-158
18. Pasko A., Adzhiev V., Sourin A.,et al.: Function Representation in Geometric Modeling: Concepts, Implementation and Applications . The Visual Computer, Vol.11(8): (1995)429-446.

19. Loop C.: Smooth subdivision surfaces based on triangles. USA: Department of Mathematics, University of Utah, (1987)
20. Zhu XX.: Free form Curve/Surface Modeling. Beijing: Science Press, (2001)
21. Morse BS., Yoo TS., Rheingans P., et al.: Interpolating Implicit Surfaces From Scattered Surface Data Using Compactly Supported Radial Basis Functions. In: Proc. of Shape Modeling Conference, Genova, Italy, May, (2001) 89-98
22. Lorensen WE., Cline HE.: Marching Cubes:A high resolution 3D surface construction algorithm. Conputer Graphics, Vol.21(4):(1987)163-169
23. Bloomenthal J.: An implicit surface polygonizer. In: Graphics Gems IV, New York: Academic Press, (1994) 324-350

Meshes Simplification Based on Reverse Subdivision

Jian-ping Ma, Xiao-nan Luo, Shi-jia Ma, and Guifeng Zheng

Institute of Computer Application, Sun Yat-sen University, Guangzhou 510275, China
lnslxn@mail.sysu.edu.cn

Abstract. In Virtual Reality, 3D graphics is generally illustrated by meshes of 3D geometric model. This paper provides a novel algorithm to construct progressive meshes based on the reverse subdivision. The dense mesh is simplified into coarse one by decimating the redundant information level by level. Loop subdivision scheme, which is an approximating scheme, is adopted as interpolatory one in the simplification process. The implementation of our algorithm consists of three key steps, splitting, predicting and updating. The progressive mesh can be reconstructed lossless. The experiments have shown that the new algorithm is efficient and more faster than previous related techniques.

1 Introduction

3D Graphics is a very important technology in Virtual Reality, wherein the 3D graphics is usually illustrated by meshes of 3D geometric models[1], and often it needs real-time rendering with Level Of Detail(LOD)[2].

Two methods are often used to construct the geometric meshes. One is through 3D laser scanner, in which the meshes of the model are dense and arbitrary. Another is from subdivision scheme, in which the mesh is a Remesh[3]. A Remesh is of subdivision connectivity and provides a user-friendly environment for mesh editing and splitting. Subdivision scheme is an efficient method, which generates geometry meshes from initial coarse ones. According to a regular rule, a coarse mesh is split into the dense mesh and a smooth surface with subdivision connectivity is obtained after a limited process. The meshes from 3D scanner are highly detailed and expensive to represent, store, transmit and manipulate. So it is mandatory to simplify the dense meshes. The key problem in Virtual Reality application is what kind of meshes can represent graphics and can they be reconstructed efficiently in short time.

Many researchers have considered the problem of the geometry surface model simplification[4][5]. In the mesh simplification, frequently used algorithms are vertex decimation[6], iterative edge contraction[7], and triangle decimation[8]. The aim of most approaches is to simplify arbitrary triangle meshes into the Remesh[4][9]. Among these methods, Mongkolnam[5] has used the Quadric Error Metrics (QEM)[10] to compress the arbitrary meshes. Then the meshes are fitted to the original mesh by adjusting to the subdivision limit positions[11]. Finally a remesh is obtained by performing a displacement operation[9].

Z. Pan et al. (Eds.): ICAT 2006, LNCS 4282, pp. 849–860, 2006.

The concept of progressive mesh was first introduced by Hoppe[12]. Khodakovsky proposed a progressive geometry compression methods based on smooth semi-regular meshes and wavelet transforms[13]. Luo applied the progressive meshes on mobile device based on reverse butterfly subdivision scheme[14]. This has partly solved the rendering speed in graphics. But the vertex affine combination of butterfly scheme is relatively complex. Thereby, it reduces the speed of mesh simplification and reconstruction.

This paper presents an algorithm for constructing progressive meshes based on the reverse subdivision. Loop subdivision scheme[15], which is approximating scheme, is adopted as interpolatory one in the simplification process, without adjusting the vertex points position. Three key steps: splitting, predicting and updating are implemented in our simplification algorithm. The algorithm which is based on reverse subdivision can be used in many stationary subdivision schemes, such as butterfly and Loop. Practically, the algorithm using Loop scheme is faster and more efficient than using butterfly scheme.

The rest of this paper is organized as follows. Section 2 introduces Loop subdivision scheme and fundamental idea of new algorithm which is acquired from this scheme. Section 3 reviews the principle and algorithm to generate the progressive meshes based on the reverse subdivision. Section 4 describes the progressive meshes reconstruction process. In the last two sections, some examples are provided followed by further analysis and conclusion.

2   Loop Subdivision Scheme and Basic Idea

Subdivision surface produces a finer mesh from a given mesh according to a refinement rules. Most known refinement schemes are based on triangle or square tilings. The well-known triangle refinement schemes are butterfly subdivision[16], $\sqrt{3}$ subdivision[17] and Loop subdivision[15]. Loop subdivision is an approximating scheme. A vertex is inserted at each edge, the original vertices are allocated to new positions accordingly. Then the new vertices form a new topology, as a consequence, each triangle face is split into four faces.

In a subdivision level, see Fig.1, the triangle with light lines is a mesh, v^j is vertex set of level j. e^{j+1} denotes edge point and v^{j+1} represents vertex point. The sets of both edge points e^{j+1} and vertex points v^{j+1} are the new vertices generated by affine combination[18] of v^j. As a result, one triangle face is split into four faces, denoted with the darker lines. By repeating the above steps, a smooth surface modeling could be achieved.

Both the coordinates of edge point e^{j+1} and vertex point v^{j+1} can be calculated from subdivision mask[15]. It can be expressed by following formula.

$$v_e = \frac{3}{8}(v1 + v2) + \frac{1}{8}(v3 + v4) . \tag{1}$$

$$v_v = (1 - n\beta_n)v + \beta_n \sum_{i=0}^{n-1} v_i \quad (n \geq 3) . \tag{2}$$

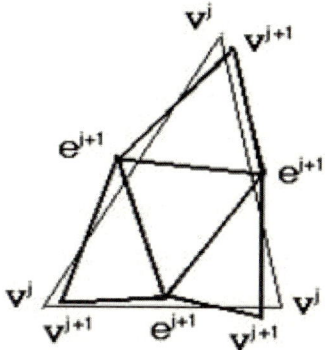

Fig. 1. Loop subdivision

where $v1$ and $v2$ are the positions of the vertices incident to the split edge, $v3$ and $v4$ are other two vertices of the triangle sharing this edge, $\beta_n = \frac{1}{n}(\frac{5}{8} - (\frac{3}{8} + \frac{1}{4}\cos\frac{2\pi}{n})^2)$, where n is valence of the vertex.

The vertex position of Loop subdivision can be expressed in the form of matrix equation:

$$\begin{bmatrix} V^{j+1} \\ E^{j+1} \end{bmatrix}_{(n+m)\times 1} = M_{(n+m)\times n} \begin{bmatrix} V^j \end{bmatrix}_{n\times 1}. \tag{3}$$

where V is the set of vertex points, E represents the set of edge points, j denotes the subdivision level, and M stands for the subdivision matrix. The new set of edge points is obtained from one lower level vertices. The set of edge points E^{j+1} does not contribute any new information in solving the Eq.(3), so it can be ignored. Thereby Eq.(3) is rewritten as:

$$\begin{bmatrix} V^{j+1} \end{bmatrix}_{n\times 1} = M_{n\times n} \begin{bmatrix} V^j \end{bmatrix}_{n\times 1}. \tag{4}$$

Subdivision surface converts the coarse mesh into the dense one, whereas a coarse mesh can be obtained by reversing this process. That is, in the matrix Eq.(4), the V^{j+1} is given, thereby V^j can be determined. To solve the Eq.(4) is complex and difficult, so alternate algorithm is opted in this paper.

By carefully analyzing the generation of edge and vertex points in Loop subdivision scheme gives rise to the following ideas which are used in the proposed mesh simplification.

- Subdivision scheme can generate dense meshes from coarse ones. Certainly, the coarse meshes can be obtained by reversing this process. We denote this process as reverse subdivision.
- The edge points generated by subdivision are only affine combination from the vertices of fore-level, and these vertices are vertex points in this level. That is, in the reverse Loop subdivision, the edge points do not contribute any new information of next-level vertices. They are redundant and can be deleted.

- The new vertex points obtained by Loop subdivision are derived from the vertices of previous level with adjacent vertices affine combination. The aim of adjusting vertex points is to generate a smooth surface. Whereas in the reverse process, the surface is supposed to be smooth, so there is no need to adjust the vertex points.

3   Methodology of Mesh Simplification

3.1   The Principle of Mesh Simplification

We assume that input triangle mesh has 2-manifold topology and no boundaries. We further assume that the input mesh is a Remesh. Any arbitrary mesh should be preprocessed to a Remesh. A mesh that every vertex has valance six is a regular mesh and most of vertices have valance six is a semi-regular mesh.

For a regular case, see Fig.2, according to the Loop subdivision, circle vertices are the edge points and the others are vertex points. By reversing this subdivision process, the mesh can be simplified. During each level of simplification, the edge points are decimated and the vertex points are preserved for the next level.

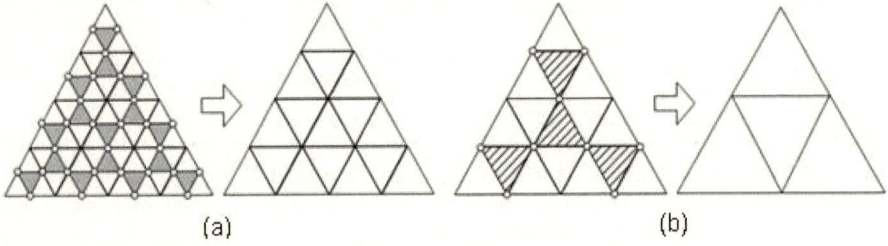

Fig. 2. Regular mesh simplification,the dark triangles are decimated. (a)Simplification time one, (b)Simplification times two.

From the close examination of Fig. 2(a), the edge points and vertex points are dotted regularly in the triangle mesh and each vertex point is encircled by six edge points.

For a semi-regular case, see Fig.3, since the extraordinary vertices generally express the sharp features such as creases and corners of the models, they should be preserved for the next level. So the extraordinary vertex is assigned as the vertex point. The vertices around this vertex point are edge points. Fig.3 shows the irregular mesh simplification.

The analysis results from regular and irregular meshes are that each vertex point is encircled by the edge points. The number of edge points around a vertex point is the valence of that vertex point.

3.2   The Algorithm for Mesh Simplification

Firstly, we introduce some notations which are adapted in [19][20]. We denote a triangle mesh as a pair (P, K),where P is a set of n point positions $p_i = (x_i, y_j, z_i)$

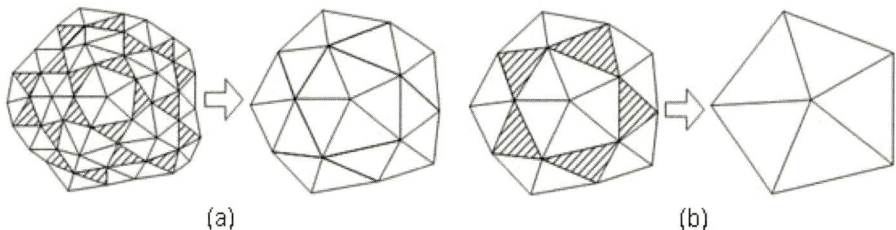

Fig. 3. Irregular mesh simplification, the dark triangles are decimated. (a) Simplification time one, (b) Simplification times two.

with $1 \leq i \leq n$, and K is an abstract simplicial complex which contains all the topologies.

The significant part of our algorithm is to construct a mesh hierarchy. The original mesh $M^n=(P^n, k^n)$ is simplified into a series of homeomorphic meshes $M^j=(P^j, k^j)$ with $0 \leq j \leq n$, where $M^0=(P^0, k^0)$ is a base mesh.

Consider M^n is the initial mesh. M^{n-1} is obtained after first simplification level. For a level M^j simplifying process, it contains the following three steps.

(1) Splitting: Split all the vertices P^j of the mesh M^j into two sets: $EVEN^j$ and ODD^j, which contain vertex points and edge points, respectively. The set of ODD^j is the candidates to decimate. For a regular mesh, firstly any vertex

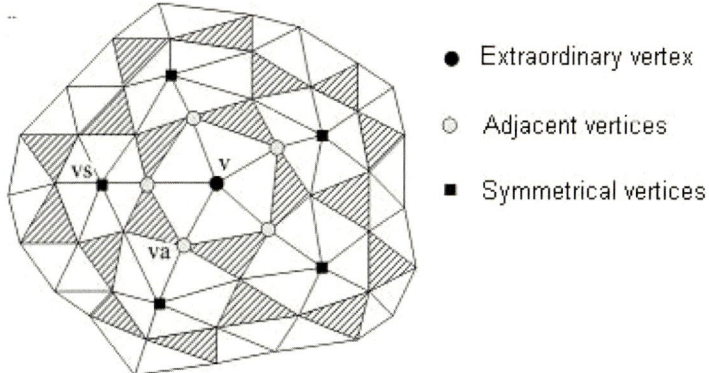

Fig. 4. Vertices relationship. v is an extraordinary vertex, va is adjacent to v, vs is in the symmetrical position of v and va.

is assigned as vertex point. Then the six adjacent vertices are assigned as edge points. The vertices which are in the symmetrical position of these six edge points are assigned as vertex points. By repeating this process, the mesh can be split.

For a semi-regular case(see Fig.4), firstly, an extraordinary vertex v should be determined and assigned as vertex point. Then the adjacent vertices va are assigned as edge points. The vertices **vs** which are in the symmetrical position of these edge points are assigned as vertex points.

Generally, all surface models have at least one extraordinary vertex, so the algorithm of assigning even points could be described as following.

Procedure *Set_Even_Vertex(v)*

   begin

      if $v \in EVEN$, return true;

      if $v \in ODD$, return fault;

      Set_Even_Vertex(v);

      For each adjacent *va* of *v*

      begin

         if *va* is an extraordinary vertex or $va \in EVEN$, return fault;

         Set_Odd_Vertex(va);

         Find *vs*;

         Set_Even_Vertex(vs);

      end

      return true;

   end

The *Set_Even_Vertex(v)* is recursively called until all the vertices are split. The split mesh must be a Remesh which is of subdivision connectivity. That is the Eq.(5) must be satisfied.

$$Distance(P_i, P_j) = 2^k, \quad k = 1, 2, 3.... . \tag{5}$$

where P_i and P_j are any extraordinary points in the dense mesh, $Distance(P_i, P_j)$ denotes the number of edges between P_i and P_j.

(2)Predicting: In order to reconstruct the mesh, for a level j, displacement value d_i^j of each edge point odd_i^j must be calculated before they are decimated. The vertex points are utilized to predict the position of edge points odd_i' by using Eq.(1), thereby the displacement value d_i^j can be obtained by Eq.(6).

$$d_i^j = odd_i^j - odd_i' \quad (i = 1, 2, ...n) . \tag{6}$$

Fig.5(b) illustrates the predicting process, O is an edge point and O' is the predicted edge point, displacement values are the distances from the edge points to the corresponding predicted edge points. Now, the displacement values d_i^j are obtained and persevered for reconstruction.

(3)Updating: After decimating the redundant edge points, the remaining vertex points form a new point set P^{n-1}. They are re-triangled and a new topological structure K^{n-1} is updated. Thereby the new level mesh $M^{j-1}=(P^{n-1},K^{n-1})$ is obtained.

By repeating the above three steps, the dense mesh M^n can be simplified into a base mesh M^0 with a series of displacement values $(M^0 d^0 d^1...d^{n-1})$. During each level of simplification, there is no need to adjust the coordinates of vertex points and each of the edge points has its displacement value. These groups of data could be packed by the several packets and form a set of progressive meshes.

$$M^0 \to (M^0 d^0) \to (M^0 d^0 d^1) \to ... \to (M^0 d^0 d^1...d^{n-1})$$

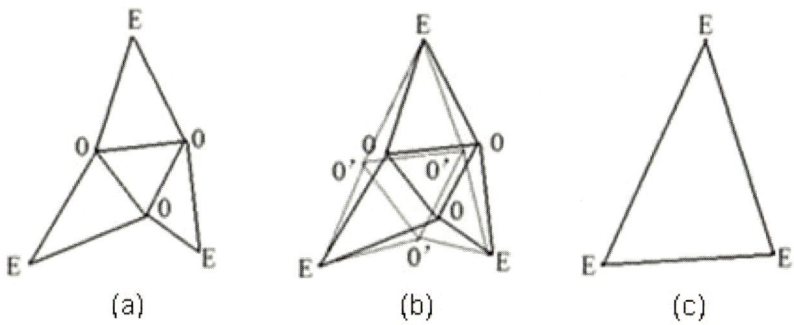

Fig. 5. Predict and update process. (a) Before simplification. (b) Predicted edge points. (c) After simplification.

Table 1. Progressive Meshes with a base mesh and a series of displacement values

Progressive Mesh	M^n	M^{n-1}	...	M^j	...	M^1	M^0
Displacement Value		d^{n-1}	...	d^j	...	d^1	d^0

That is, M^1 is determined by $(M^0 d^0)$, M^2 is determined by $(M^0 d^0 d^1)$, ... , and M^n, $(M^0 d^0 d^1 ... d^{n-1})$. It is shown in Table 1 .

4   Progressive Meshes Reconstruction

Progressive meshes which is a base mesh and a series of displacement values have been obtained. The progressive meshes are easy to manipulate and store. It can be packed into several small packets and transmit through wire/wireless network. The key aim of constructed progressive mesh is to supply a good mesh structure to represent the 3D graphics and the mesh could be reconstructed in a short time. A progressive mesh reconstruction method is given as follows.

The progressive mesh reconstruction is a reverse process of the mesh simplification. To reconstruction the mesh from $M^j=(P^j,K^j)$ to $M^{j+1}=(P^{j+1},K^{j+1})$, the following step should be done.

(1) set P^j as the vertex points $EVEN^{j+1}$ of level j+1

(2) use P^j to predict the edge points ODD' at level j+1;

(3) use d^j and ODD' to calculate the predicted position of edge points by use Eq. (6), and the set of ODD^{j+1} is obtained.

$$odd_i^{j+1} = odd_i' + d_i^j \quad (i = 1, 2, ...n) . \tag{7}$$

(4) $EVEN^{j+1}, ODD^{j+1}$ constitute the vertices P^{j+1}. Re-triangling the meshe form a new topology K^{j+1}, thereby the mesh M^{j+1} is achieved.

That is, when the base mesh M^0 is achieved, by adding predicted positions of edge points odd_i' to d_i^0 , the real position of edge points odd_i^1 are achieved.

By updating the topology, M^1 can be obtained. By repeating this process, the mesh M^n could be reconstructed. At this situation, the mesh is the same as the original one. So the mesh reconstruction from the progressive meshes is lossless.

In application, a mesh is reconstructed on-demand according to resolution of device. If the resolution of the user device is low, it is not necessary to reconstruct the whole data, just a base mesh and few levels of displacement values are sufficient to represent, that is M^i (i=0,1,2,...,n-1) will satisfy the resolution request of user. Because M^i is the middle level comparing with the original mesh M^n. It is noted that the new mesh is very close to M^n but not the same. At this situation, progressive meshes reconstruction is not seamless.

From above analysis, using any reverse subdivision either the Interpolatory or approximating schemes such as butterfly subdivision or Loop subdivision, the meshes can be simplified efficiently. According to their subdivision mask, the vertex affine combination of Loop is four[15] and Butterfly is eight[16]. Obviously, the algorithm utilized Loop subdivision could accelerate the simplification and reconstruction speed.

5   Results and Discussion

This algorithm is implemented by using VC++. The models such as head, e-sphere and venus are tested. The progressive meshes can be seen in Fig.6-8. Fig.7-8. show the rendering effect of the e-Sphere and venus model.

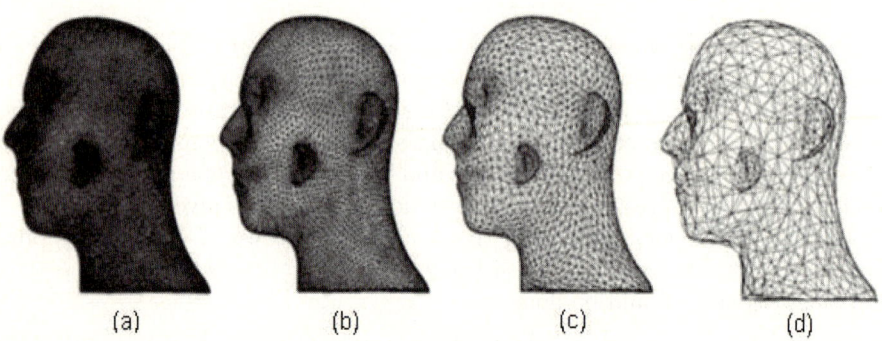

Fig. 6. Four levels of head model (Vertices/faces). (a) Original Mesh(45442/90880) (b)After simplification times one(11362/22720). (c) After simplification times two(2824/5680) (d) Base mesh(712vertices/1420faces).

Both reverse Loop approximating and reverse Butterfly interpolatory subdivision schemes are utilized in the new algorithm. The base meshes obtained from two schemes are the same, but their displacement values are different. Table 2. shows the runtime statistics of both schemes. Times are in seconds, measured on a PC(AMD 1800Mhz,256MB RAM). The experiments have indicted the speed

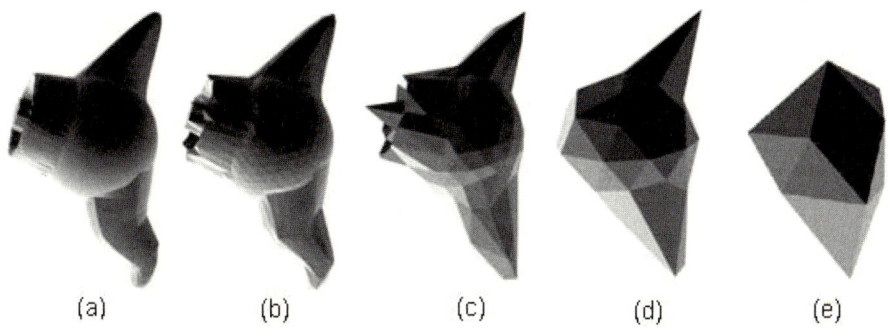

Fig. 7. e-Sphere simplification preserving vertices/faces from left to right (a) 2562/5120 (b) 642/1280 (c) 162/320 (d) 42/80 (e) 12/20 respectively

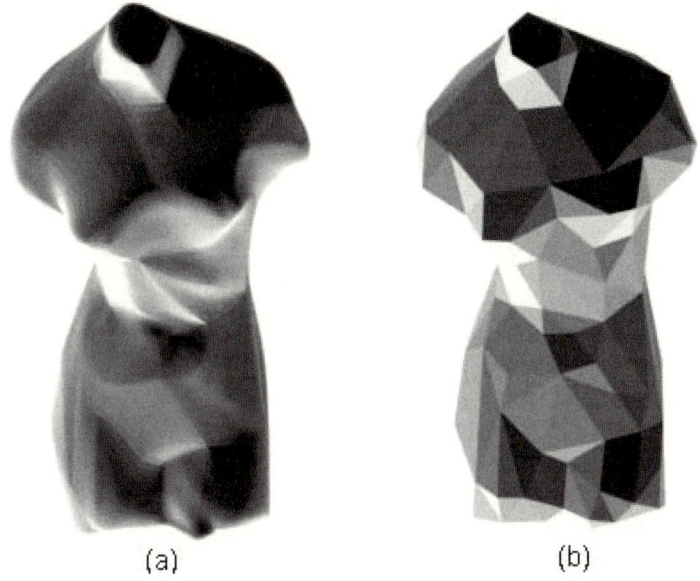

Fig. 8. Venus simplification(Vertices/faces). (a) Original(9603/19200). (b) Base mesh(153/300).

of simplification and reconstruction by the new algorithm are more faster than by butterfly scheme.

The meshes can be progressively represented. It is lossless if the entire meshes are reconstructed. Otherwise, the reconstruction is not seamless. To measure the distortion between the reconstructed mesh and the original mesh, we use the Metro error measurement software [21](Metro v4.06) to compute the Maximal error and Mean error.

Table 2. Runtime Statistics for simplification and reconstruction

Data	Vertices no./ Faces no. (In)	Vertices no./ Faces no. (Out)	Simplified times	Runtimes			
				simplification		reconstruction	
				Loop	Butterfly	Loop	Butterfly
Head	45442/90880	712/1420	3	101.1	152.232	17.744	23.314
e-Sphere	2562/5120	12/20	4	3.164	4.005	0.512	0.646
Venus	9603/19200	153/300	3	14.617	21.124	2.406	3.152

Table 3. Error Statistics for e-Sphere Model

Progressive Meshes	Vertex no.	Face no.	Box Diagonal	Maximal Error	Mean Error	RMS	Hausdorff Distance
M^4	2562	5120	20.963922	0	0	0	0
M^3	642	1280	20.987868	0.197355	0.020310	0.032450	0.225822
M^2	162	320	21.227575	0.949826	0.078561	0.111246	0.949826
M^1	42	80	19.838592	0.932492	0.152490	0.195484	1.626944
M^0	12	20	15.714804	1.506523	0.374888	0.449767	3.836133

See table 3, where M^4 is the original mesh, M^0 are base mesh, others are middle level of the progressive meshes. All the errors and hausdorff distance are compared with the original mesh M^4.

Actually, natural and efficient 3D interactions play one of key role in the development of Virtual Reality applications. It is always a tradeoff between the runtime and details of graphics. In some cases, such as on mobile device, there is no need to reconstruct the entire mesh. Only a base mesh M^0 and parts of displacement values($d^0, d^1, ..., d^i$) are sufficient to represent the 3D graphics for visibility. In other cases, M^i(for all i) can be allocated as the base mesh according to screen resolution, processor speed and memory capacity of the user device. Adopting fewer levels of the progressive meshes can increase the speed of the mesh reconstruction, and choosing denser mesh as a base mesh can achieved the good detail of graphics in shorter time but need good performance of computing devices.

6   Conclusion and Future Work

Our goal is successfully fulfilled by simplifying the dense mesh into progressive meshes which is a base mesh with a set of displacement values. Three key steps of our simplification process are illustrated based on the reverse subdivision. The original mesh can be reconstructed lossless. It can be reconstructed with loss by using the middle level of progressive meshes when it is used in the low resolution systems. Errors analysis is given using Metro software. The main contributions of this work are:

- Loop subdivision scheme, which is a approximation scheme, is adopted as interpolatory one in simplification process, without adjusting the coordinate of vertex points. It greatly improves both the simplification and reconstruction speed.
- A novel algorithm to simplify the dense mesh by splitting, predicting and updating steps is presented, which is easily represented and reconstructed in application, without solving the Eq.(4) or calculating the complex vertex affine combination of butterfly scheme as in literature[14].

The experiments have shown that the new algorithm is efficient and more faster than previous related techniques. The progressive meshes obtained by our method can represent 3D graphics efficiently and the original can be reconstructed quickly. It certainly can represent object movement through a virtual 3D workspace rapidly. On the other hand, our work still has limitation that the input mesh must be a Remesh. So more work need be done on surface fitting. In addition, improvement on the data structure could greatly accelerate the computational speed of our algorithm.

Acknowledgements. The work described in this article is supported by the National Science Fund for Distinguished Young Scholars(N0.60525213) and the Key project(No.60533030) of the National Natural Science Foundation of China, and 973 Program of China (No.206CB303106).

References

1. Sequeira V., K.N., Wolfart E.,Goncalves J.G.M.,Hogg D., Automated reconstruction of 3D models from real environments. Journal of Photogrammetry and Remote Sensing, 54(1999)1-22.
2. Ridha Hambli, A.C., Hedi BEl Hadj Salah, Real-time deformation of structure using finite element and neural networks in virtual reality applications. Finite Elements in Analysis and Design,42(2006)985-991.
3. Eck M, DeRose T, Duchamp T, Hoppe H, Lounsbery M, Stuetzle W. Multiresolution Analysis of Arbitrary Meshes. ACM SIGGRAPH 1995 Conference Proceedings (1995)173-182.
4. Weiyin Ma, Xiaohu Ma, Shiu-kit Tso and Zhigeng Pan, A direct approach for subdivision surface fitting from a dense triangle mesh,Computer-Aided Design, 36(2004)525-536.
5. Mongkolnam P.,Raidan A. and Farin G., Loop Progressive Geometry Compression for Triangle Meshes, Computer Aided Geometric Design, 16(1999)837-840.
6. William J. Schroeder, Jonathan A. Zarge and William E. Lorensen, Decimation of triangle meshes, In:Computer Graphics(SIGGRAPH'92 Proc.),26(1992)65-70.
7. Gueziec A. Surface simplification inside a tolerance volume. Technical Report RC 20440,IBM T.J. Watson Research Center,1996.
8. Hamann B., A data reduction scheme for triangulated surfaces, Computer Aided Geometric Design,11(1994)197-214.

9. Lee.A, Moreton.H and Hoppe.H, Displaced Subdivision Surfaces, in:Proceedings of the 27th annual conference on computer graphics(SIGGRAPH 2000),(2000)85-94.

10. Garland M. and Heckbert P.S., Surface Simplification Using Quadric Error Metrics, In:Proceedings of the 24th annual conference on Computer graphics and interactive techniques(SIGGRAPH 1997),(1997)209-216.

11. Suzuki H.,Takeuchi S. and Kanai T., Subdivision Surface Fitting to a Range of Points, in:The 7th Pacific Conference on Computer Graphics and Application,IEEE Proceedings,(1999)158-167.

12. Hoppe H., Progressive meshes. In:Proceedings of the 23rd annual conference on Computer graphics and interactive techniques(SIGGRAPH 1997),(1996)99-108.

13. Khodakovsky A.,Schroder P. and Sweldens W., Progressive Geometry Compression, in:Proceedings of the 27th Annual Conference on Computer Graphics and interactive Techniques(SIGGRAPH 2000),(2000)271-278.

14. Xiaonan Luo and Guifeng Zheng, Progressive Meshes Transmission over a Wired-to-wireless Network, ACM Journal of Wireless Networks(WINET),2005, (In press).

15. Loop C., Smooth subdivision surface based on triangles,[Master's thesis], University of Utah, Department of Mathematics,1987.

16. Dyn N.,Levin D. and Gregory J.A., A butterfly subdivision scheme for surface interpolatory with tension control, ACM transactions on Graphics(TOG), 9(1990)160-169.

17. Labsik U. and Greiner G., Interpolatory $\sqrt{3}$ subdivision, in:Computer Graphics Forum (EUROGRAPHICS 2000), (2000)131-138.

18. Farin G.E. Curves and Surfaces for Computer Aided Geometric Design: A Practical Guide. 5th Edition. Morgan Kaufmann,2001.

19. Aaron WF Lee, Wim Sweldens, Peter Schroder, Lawrence Cowsar, and David Dobkin. MAPS: Multiresolution Adaptive Parameterization of Surfaces. In:Proceedings of the 25th annual conference on Computer graphics and interactive techniques(SIGGRAPH 98),(1998)95-104.

20. Hoppe H., Efficient Implementation of Progressive Meshes. Technical Report MSR-TR-98-02, Microsoft Research, 1998.

21. Cignoni P., Rocchini C. and Scopigno R., Metro:Measuring Error on Simplified Surfaces. Computer Graphics Form,17(1998)167-174.

Kd-Tree Based OLS in Implicit Surface Reconstruction with Radial Basis Function

Peizhi Wen[1,4], Xiaojun Wu[2], Tao Gao[3], and Chengke Wu[4]

[1] Guilin University of Electronic Technology, Guilin, 541004, China
[2] HIT Shenzhen Graduate School, Shenzhen, 518055, China
[3] Xi'an Jiaotong University, Xi'an, 710071, China
[4] Xidian University, Xi'an, 710071, China

Abstract. In this paper, we propose a new method for surface reconstruction from scattered point set based on least square radial basis function (LSRBF) and orthogonal least square forward selection procedure. Firstly, the traditional RBF formulation is rewritten into least square formula. A implicit surface can be represented with fewer centers. Then, the orthogonal least square procedure is utilized to select significant centers from original point data set. The RBF coefficients can be solved from the triangular matrix from OLS selection through backward substitution method. So, this scheme can offer a fast surface reconstruction tool and can overcome the numerical ill-conditioning of coefficient matrix and over-fitting problem. Some examples are presented to show the effectiveness of our algorithm in 2D and 3D cases.

1   Introduction

The problem of surface reconstruction from scattered cloud points has been studied extensively in computer graphics and engineering, in particular, the use of a range scanner or laser scanners produces large amount of unorganized point sets in industry, entertainment and archeology, etc. It is desirable to quickly and robustly reconstruct a continuous surface with attributes from the unorganized points. Researchers in computer graphics and computational geometry offer some useful tools and method to tackle this problem, for example, Hoppe's [7]signed distance function based method, Amenta's [1,2] Voronoi and crust based method, Bernardini's [3] α_shape based algorithm, Dey's [4] concone based approach, Level-set based method of Zhao [5], Moving least square(MLS) of Shen [10] and MPU of Ohtake [9], etc.

Radial Basis Function (RBF) has been used in several fields because of its accurate and stable interpolation properties. It is proved that any continuous function can be modeled up to a certain precision by RBF [6]. In this paper, we use the least square radial basis functions to solve the problem of surface reconstruction with fewer interpolation centers. Implicit surface models are popular since they can describe complex shapes with capabilities for surface and volume modeling and complex editing operations are easy to perform on such

Z. Pan et al. (Eds.): ICAT 2006, LNCS 4282, pp. 861–870, 2006.

models. Radial basis functions attract more attentions recently in data interpolation in multi-dimensions [8,11,12,13,14]. Though traditional RBF can offer
efficient reconstruction algorithms, some significant problems still remains un-
solved. Since the collocation method uses the scattered points as both data and
centers, numerical ill-conditioning often occurs due to too small distance between some centers, which will cause linear dependency of coefficients matrix.
Moreover, when the number of centers used in interpolation is too large, it will
cause the so-called over-fitting problem, which means that the interpolant is too
flexible so that it not only fits the surface but also fits the noise that was introduced into the data. Lastly, in order to further reduce the computational cost,
greedy algorithm or so-called "thinning" algorithm was introduced into RBF reconstruction methods by using only a small portion of given points. Least square
RBF, fortunately, lends us powerful tools to solve all the problems mentioned
above.

In this paper we describe an algorithm to the problem of surface reconstruction
from large unorganized point sets. We adapt the methodology of least square
RBF to surface reconstruction and deduce a set of corresponding formulations.
Then the orthogonal least square method is used to select significant centers
from the large data set, from which a upper triangular matrix is produced and
the RBF coefficients can be solved via backward substitution directly rather
than using LU, SVD or preconditioned conjugate gradient method (PCG) [18].
Paper is organized as follows. The radial basis functions networks are introduced
in section 2, and in section 3 the LSRBF scheme is described. The OLS selection
procedure is presented in section 4. Some reconstructed examples are presented
in section 5. Part 6 is the conclusion section.

2   Radial Basis Function

RBF has traditionally been considered as single-layer networks with symmetrical
radial functions. Samples $\{x_i\}_{i=1}^N$ are inputs of this network and $\{\alpha_i\}_{i=1}^N$ are the
coefficients. The problem of scattered data interpolation can be stated as given a
set of fixed points $\mathbf{x}_1, \mathbf{x}_2, ..., \mathbf{x}_N \in \mathcal{R}^d$ on a surfaces S in $\mathcal{R}^d$ (in three dimensions
$d = 3$) and a set of function values $f_1, f_2, ..., f_N \in \mathcal{R}$, find an interpolant ϕ :
$\mathcal{R}^3 \to \mathcal{R}$ such that

$$\phi(\mathbf{x}_i) = f_i, \quad i = 1, 2, ..., N \tag{1}$$

The traditional RBF has the following form

$$\phi(\mathbf{x}) = \sum_{j=1}^N \alpha_j g_j(\|\mathbf{x} - \mathbf{x}_j\|) + p(\mathbf{x}) \tag{2}$$

where $p(\mathbf{x})$ is a polynomial, α_j are coefficients corresponding to each basis and
$\|\cdot\|$ is the Euclidean norm on $\mathcal{R}^3$. The basis function g is a real valued function
on $[0, \infty)$, usually unbounded and of a global support. There are several popular
basis functions used in literature [8], therein. The polynomial $p(\mathbf{x})$ is appended

for achieving polynomial precision according to the basis functions used. Additional so-called natural constraints are needed. For example, if $p(\boldsymbol{x})$ is a linear polynomial, the coefficients α must satisfy the following side conditions.

$$\sum_{j=1}^{N} \alpha_j = \sum_{j=1}^{N} \alpha_j \boldsymbol{x}_j = \sum_{j=1}^{N} \alpha_j \boldsymbol{y}_j = \sum_{j=1}^{N} \alpha_j \boldsymbol{z}_j = 0 \tag{3}$$

Combining equation (1) and (2) and using collocation technique, we can give rise to compute the RBF coefficients.

$$\phi(\boldsymbol{x}_i) = \sum_{j=1}^{N} \alpha_j g_j(\|\boldsymbol{x}_i - \boldsymbol{x}_j\|) + p(\boldsymbol{x}_i) \tag{4}$$

The coefficients can be found by solving the linear system 4. The solutions of the system compose of the weighting coefficients and the polynomial coefficients for the interpolation function $\phi(\boldsymbol{x})$.

However, it is unpractical to solve the linear system (4) directly for large scale point dataset and with complexity of $O(N^3)$ interpolant computing and $O(N)$ evaluation. The concept of partition of unity (POU) is rooted in applied mathematics [15,16]. The main idea of the partition of unity method is to divide the global domain of interest into smaller overlapping subdomains where the problem can be solved locally on a small scale. The local solutions are combined together by using blending functions to obtain the global solution. The smoothness of the global solution in the overlap regions of two subdomians can be guaranteed by a polynomial blending function. The POU method for RBF based surface reconstruction has been applied by Tobor et al. [17] where all the points in each subdomain are offset along the normal to avoid the RBF trivial solutions.

3   Least Square Surfaces

Only a portion of points are used to interpolate the implicit surface. We rewrite the RBF formulation (2) into

$$\phi(\boldsymbol{x}) = \sum_{j=1}^{M} \alpha_j g(\boldsymbol{x} - \boldsymbol{x_j}) = \boldsymbol{g}^T \alpha \tag{5}$$

where $\boldsymbol{g} = [\boldsymbol{g}_1, \boldsymbol{g}_2, \cdots, \boldsymbol{g}_M]^T$, $\boldsymbol{\alpha} = [\alpha_1, \alpha_2, \cdots, \alpha_M]^T$, $M$is the number of points used to estimate the coefficients ($M \ll N$), and T is the transpose operator. Function values on the data h and $\hat{h}$ indicating the funciton value with noisy data. Let $G = [\boldsymbol{g}_1^T, \boldsymbol{g}_2^T, \cdots, \boldsymbol{g}_N^T]_{N \times M}^T$, we have

$$\phi(\boldsymbol{x}) = \boldsymbol{G}\boldsymbol{\alpha} \tag{6}$$

We write equation 6 into matrix form

$$[\boldsymbol{G}_{x,\bar{x}}][\alpha_{\bar{x}}] = [\boldsymbol{f}_x] \tag{7}$$

where $\boldsymbol{x} = x_1, x_2, \cdots, x_N$ stands for the the input points in a processing unit, and $\bar{\boldsymbol{x}} = \bar{x}_1, \bar{x}_2, \cdots, \bar{x}_n$ is the selected centers. $(\boldsymbol{G})_{i,j} = \phi(\|\boldsymbol{x}_i - \bar{\boldsymbol{x}}_j\|), i = 1, 2, \cdots, N, j = 1, 2, \cdots, M$. $\boldsymbol{\alpha} = [\alpha_1, \alpha_2, \cdots, \alpha_M]^T$. $\boldsymbol{f} = [f_1, f_2, \cdots, f_N]$.

In these equations the low degree of polynomial is not considered. It can be appended in accordance with specific basis functions. When coefficients $\boldsymbol{\alpha}$ are solved, the implicit surface can be reconstructed with fewer centers, M, much less than the total of whole set of samples N. Some significant centers can be used to compute the RBF coefficients from which the implicit surfaces can be achieved. As a illustration, a 2D example is displayed in Fig.1. In this example, the interpolation centers are selected uniformly instead of using significant centers. From Fig.1, we can find when the interpolation centers are not fewer enough, the reconstructed curve has almost no visual distinctions.

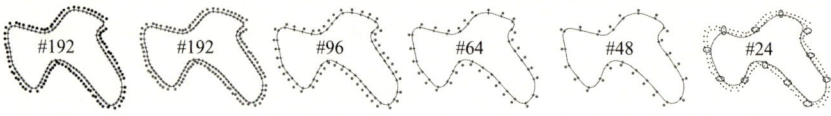

Fig. 1. Curve interpolation using fewer RBF centers

4   Orthogonal Least Square Procedure

The orthogonal least square method often used to select a suitable set of centers from large scale point sets and a fixed RBF center corresponds to a given regressor in a linear regression model [19]. We utilize the Gram-Schmidt orthonolization process [18] to ensure the new added column of RBF matrix is orthogonal to all previous columns, and then the corresponding approximation error is reduced. Other non-orthogonal column vectors can be regarded as the linear combination of the orthogonal basis, which can eliminate the problem of ill-conditioning.

In our another method, we use Chen's OLS method as a forward regression procedure [20]. But in that scheme, we just used OLS method to select significant centers and reconstruct implicit surfaces from these selected set using conventional RBF interpolation technique. We also employed a octree structure to organize the large point set, and we took each octree cell as a unit to carry out the selection procedure individually. Though the point in each octree cell can be resampled according to OLS selection criterion, the points in the area of

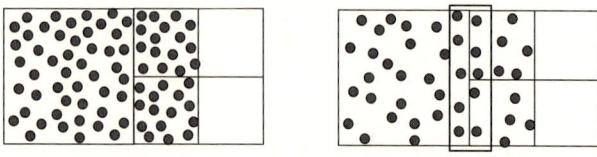

Fig. 2. The drawback of octree based OLS method

the two neighbor cells can not be handled correctly, as illustrated in Fig. 2. We call this a neighboring cell problem. The left figure in Fig.2 is octree cells and the corresponding point data. The afterward result is shown in the right figure from which we can find that the points near the wall of two neighbor octree cells remain the same.

4.1   OLS Selection Criterion

For completeness, we write out the pseudo code for OLS selection in a subdomain with the input point set C with the amount of points N and approximation tolerance ρ, $0 < \rho < 1$, which is a user defined tolerence controlling the amount of crucial centers.

- The first selected center
  for $1 \leqslant i \leqslant N$
  $$w_1^{(i)} = \boldsymbol{p}_i;$$
  $$q_1^{(i)} = (\boldsymbol{w}_1^{(i)})^T \boldsymbol{h}/((\boldsymbol{w}_1^{(i)})^T \boldsymbol{w}_1^{(i)})$$
  $$[err]_1^{(i)} = (q_1^{(i)})^2 (\boldsymbol{w}_1^{(i)})^T \boldsymbol{w}_1^{(i)}/(\boldsymbol{h}^T \boldsymbol{h})$$
  end for
  Find $[err]_1^{(i_1)} = \max [err]_1^{(i)}, 1 \leqslant i \leqslant N$
  And select $\boldsymbol{w}_1 = \boldsymbol{w}_1^{(i_1)} = \boldsymbol{g}_{i_1}$
- At the kth step, where $k \geqslant 2$,
  for $1 \leqslant i \leqslant N, (i \neq i_1, \cdots, i \neq i_{k-1})$
    for $1 \leqslant j < k$
    $$\alpha_{jk}^{(i)} = \boldsymbol{w}_j^T \boldsymbol{p}_i/(\boldsymbol{w}_j^T \boldsymbol{w}_j)$$
    $$\boldsymbol{w}_k^{(i)} = \boldsymbol{p}_i - \sum_{j=1}^{k-1} \alpha_{jk}^{(i)} \boldsymbol{w}_j$$
    $$q_k^{(i)} = (\boldsymbol{w}_k^{(i)})^T \boldsymbol{h}/((\boldsymbol{w}_k^{(i)})^T \boldsymbol{w}_k^{(i)})$$
    end for
    $$[err]_k^{(i)} = ((\boldsymbol{w}_k^{(i)})^T \boldsymbol{h})^2/(((\boldsymbol{w}_k^{(i)})^T \boldsymbol{w}_k^{(i)})(\boldsymbol{h}^T \boldsymbol{h}))$$
  Find $[err]_k^{i_k} = \max [err]_k^{(i)}, 1 \leqslant i \leqslant N, i \neq i_1, \cdots, i \neq i_{k-1}$
  Select $\boldsymbol{w}_k = \boldsymbol{w}_k^{i_k} = \boldsymbol{p}_{i_k} - \sum_{j-1}^{k-1} \alpha_{jk}^{i_k} \boldsymbol{w}_j$
- The procedure is stopped at the Mth step when the error ration satisfies
  $1 - \sum_{j=1}^{M} [err]_j < \rho$

In above procedures, $\boldsymbol{p}_i, i = 1, 2, \cdots, N$ is the column vector of Matrix $\boldsymbol{G}$.

In the OLS selection, we can get a upper triangular matrix $\boldsymbol{Q}$ and a vector $\boldsymbol{q}$ from which the coefficients can be solved by backward substitution unlike the traditional RBF reconstruction method by using LU decomposition or SVD. So this method can avoid the ill-conditioning problem.

$$[\boldsymbol{Q}][\boldsymbol{\alpha}] = [\boldsymbol{q}] \tag{8}$$

4.2   Kd-Tree Based OLS

In the above subsection, we have obtained a criterion for significant center selection. We will describe the new scheme specifically. Firstly, the point data is divided via a octree into some local subdomains. Here, and we use the idea of partition of unity [15,9] to blend the local surface into global solution. Readers can refer the technique of partition of unity in [15,9,11]. Then, we substitute the processing unit from octree cell to a ball centered at the the octree cell and using a Kd-tree to collect points in this spherical subdomian that can avoid the neighboring cell problem, shown in Fig. 3.

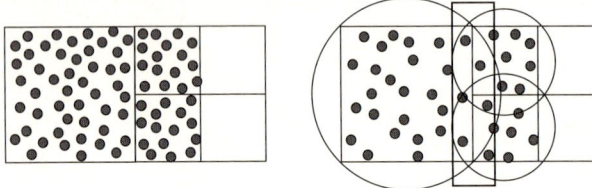

Fig. 3. New processing units are used for OLS selection

By comparing the Fig. 2 and Fig. 3, we can find that our new scheme can get more optimal data set than the previous method. Thus, the final reconstructed surface will achieve good quality.

5   Experimental Results

All results revealed in this section were performed on the hardware configurations of Intel PIV 3GHz with 513M RAM running Windows XP.

Table 1 shows the results of three examples reconstructed with conventional RBF method, where LU decomposition is employed to solve the linear system and the triharmonic basis function is used. And Table 2 gives the reconstruction time and OLS parameters. In table 1, N_points stands for the the number of points, and T_rec is the time of reconstruction including octree setup and linear system solving. T_isosurf means the iso-surface extraction cost, and T_total is the total time consumption of surface reconstruction. In table 2, P_ration refers to the ration of selected point set and the whole point set. T_rec includes the time of

Table 1. Traditional RBF surface reconstruction

Model	N_points	T_rec	T_isosurf	T_total
Sculpture	25,382	12.41	197.65	210.06
Bunny	34,834	18.05	218.25	236.3
Igea	72,545	51.77	291.72	343.43
Sk_hand	327,323	365.64	1261.04	1,626.68

Table 2. Surface reconstruction with Orthogonal least square

Model	ρ	P_ration	T_rec	T_isosurf	T_totl	Max_error	Mean_error	RMS
Sculpture	0.01	63%	20.81	123.86	144.67	0.0942	0.0084	0.0127
	0.05	21%	4.08	118.96	123.04	0.1029	0.0098	0.0133
	0.1	20%	3.56	115.83	119.39	0.1731	0.0096	0.0129
Bunny	0.01	59%	32.92	168.63	201.55	0.1079	0.0060	0.01
	0.05	20%	5.64	149.48	155.12	0.0848	0.0079	0.0108
	0.1	19%	5.07	145.95	151.02	0.1335	0.008	0.0116
Igea	0.01	67%	53.34	243.86	297.2	0.1614	0.0078	0.0117
	0.05	21%	9.65	167.31	176.96	0.1674	0.0112	0.0161
	0.1	16%	8.76	112.47	121.23	0.2821	0.0174	0.0287
Sk_hand	0.1	15%	156.23	827.66	983.89	0.0699	0.0049	0.0061

(a)   (b)   (c)   (d)

Fig. 4. Meshes from different point sets, (a) is resulted from the original point set, (b) is reconstructed from 64% point set, (c) and (d) are from 21% and 20% point data sets

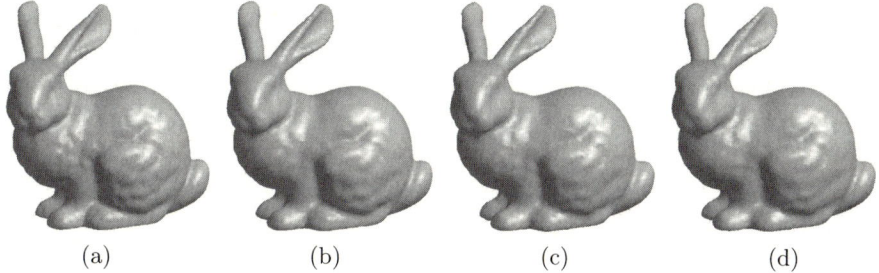

(a)   (b)   (c)   (d)

Fig. 5. Meshes from different point sets, (a) is reconstructed from the whole data set, (b) is from 59%, (c) is got from 20%, and (d) is from 19%

octree setup, OLS selection and backward substitution. Max_error, Mean_error and RMS represent maximal error and mean error between the results from OLS and the the surface reconstructed from original points, and root-mean-square,

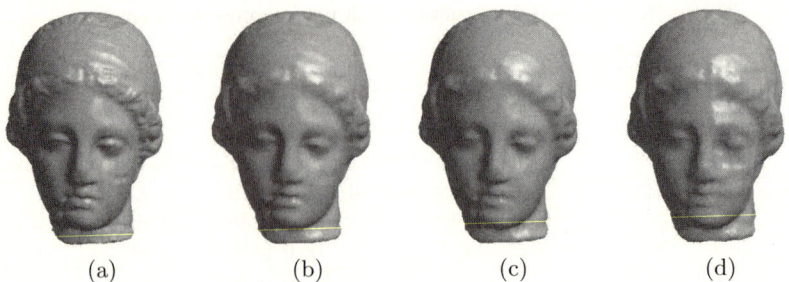

Fig. 6. Igea model reconstructed from different point sets, (a) is from 100%, (b) is reconstructed with 67%, (c) is from point set of 21%, (d) is obtained from 16%

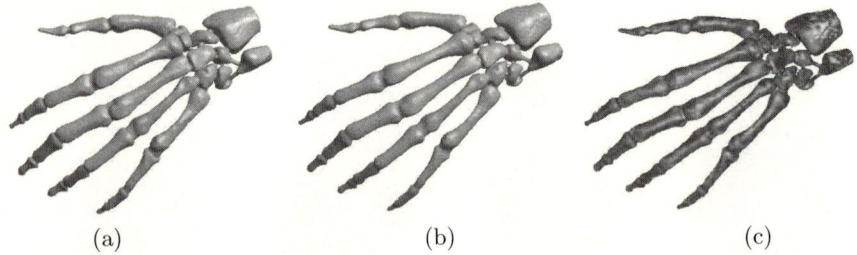

Fig. 7. Skeleton hand reconstructed from original point set(a) and 15% point set (b), (c) is error map of mesh (a) and (b)

respectively. Fig.4, Fig.5, Fig.6 and Fig.7 are reconstructed surface models. There are almost no visual artifacts on these series of experimental results.

By comparing the two tables, we can find that the computation time is reduced greatly but the quality of the surface does not affected severely. We use the a free available tool–Metro, to measure the error differences between two meshes[21]. As indicated by the last three columns of Table2, the mean-error and RMS are relatively small. Taking Stanford bunny as an instance, the mean_errors and the RMS are 0.006, 0.0079, 0.008 and 0.01, 0.0108, 0.0129 in case of ρ=0.01, 0.05 and 0.1, respectively. However, when ρ=0.1, the Max_error is obviously standing out, for example, maximal error equals to 0.1731 of sculpture model and igea is 0.2821. Fig.7 (c) also shows a error color map of surface (a) and (b). As a matter of fact, most of the computational time is consumed by the iso-surface extraction procedure, which also can be found from Table 1 and Table 2. Actually, the time cost of solving RBF linear system in the example of skeleton hand is only 13.3 second. Most of the time spends on the preprocessing and iso-surface extraction. So a fast implicit surface polygonization algorithm is necessary in our approach.

6   Conclusions

In this paper, we presented a RBF implicit surface reconstruction method on the basis of modified orthogonal least square subset selection through which the interpolation centers can be reduced and the reconstruction speed can be improved significantly but not severely affect the quality of the surface. In this scheme, unlike the traditional RBF method, the LU, SVD or PCG method will needed to solve the linear system, instead we use the triangular matrix obtained in the OLS selection and backward substitution to resolve the coefficient. The experiments show that our method are very efficient to deal with the large point set and can also be utilized in many fields, such as virtual reality, archeology, video game development, etc.

References

1. Amenta, N., Bern, M. and Kamvysselis, M.: A new Voronoi-based surface reconstruction algorithm. In Proceedings of SIGGRAPH'98, (1998), 415-421.
2. Amenta, N., Choi, S. and Kolluri, R.: The power crust. In Proceedings of 6th ACM Symposium on Solid Modeling, (2001), 249-260.
3. Bernardini, F. and Bajaj, C.L.: Sampling and reconstructing manifolds using alpha-shapes. In proceedings of 9th Canada Conference on Computational Geometry. (1997), 193-198.
4. Dey, T. K. and Goswami, S.: Tight cocone: A watertight surface reconstructor. In Proc. 8th ACM Sympos. Solid Modeling Applications, (2003), 127-134.
5. Zhao, H., Osher, S. and Fedkiw, R.: Fast surface reconstruction using the Level Set method, 1st IEEE Workshop on Variational and Level Set Methods, in conjunction with the 8th International Conference on Computer Vision (ICCV), Vancouver, Canada, (2001), 194-202.
6. Park, J. and Sandberg, J.W. Universal approximation using radial basis functions network. Neural Computation, (1991), Vol.3, 246-257.
7. Hoppe, H, DeRose, T., Duchamp, T., McDonald, J. and Stuetzle, W. Surface ronstruction from unorganized points. In Proceedings of ACM SIGGRAPH 1992, (1992), 71-78.
8. Carr, J. C., Beatson, R. K., Cherrie, J. B., Mitchell, T. J., Fright, W. R., McCallum, B. C. and Evans, T. R. Reconstruction and representation of 3D objects with radial basis functions. In Proceedings of ACM SIGGRAPH 2001, (2001), 67-76.
9. Ohtake, Y., Belyaev, A., Alexa, M., Turk, G. and Seidel, H. P. Multi-level partition of unity implicits. ACM Transactions on Graphics, Proceedings of SIGGRAPH 2003. (2003), Vol. 22, No. 3, 463-470.
10. Shen, C., O'Brien, J.F., and Shewchuk, J.R.: Interpolating and approximating implicit surfaces from polygon soup. In Proceedings of ACM SIGGRAPH (2004), 896-904.
11. Tobor, P., Reuter, and Schilck, C. Efficient reconstruction of large scattered geometric datasets using the partition of unity and radial basis functions. Journal of WSCG 2004, (2004), Vol. 12, 467-474.
12. Turk, G. and O'Brien, J.: Variational implicit surfaces. Technical Report GIT-GVU-99-15, Georgia Institute of Technology, (1998).
13. Turk, G. and O'brien, J., Modelling with implicit surfaces that interpolate. ACM Transactions on Graphics, (2002), 21(4), 855-873.
14. Morse, B., Yoo, T.S. Rheingans, P. et al. Interpolating implicit surfaces from scattered surfaces data using compactly supported radial basis functions. In Proceedings of Shape Modeling International (SMI2001), (2001), 89-98.

15. Babuška, I. and Melenk, J.M.: The partition of unity method. International Journal of Numerical Methods in Engineering, (1997) 727-758.
16. Wu J. and Kobbelt, L. P., A stream algorithm for the decimation of massive meshes. In Graphics Interface 2003 Proceedings, Halifax, Canada, 2003, 185-192.
17. Tobor, I., Reuter, P. and Schlick, C. Multiresolution reconstruction of implicit surfaces with attributes from large unorganized point sets. In Proceedings of Shape Modeling International (SMI 2004), (2004), 19-30.
18. Horn, A.E., Johnson, C.R.: Matrix analysis. Cambridge University Press, Cambridge, UK (1985).
19. Chen, S., Billings, S.A., and Luo, W.: Orthogonal least square methods and their application to nonlinear system identification. International Journal of Control, (1989), 50(5), 1873-1896.
20. Chen, S., Cowan, C.F.N., and Grant, P.M.: Orthogonal least square learning algorithm for radial basis function networks. IEEE Transactions on Neural Network, (1991), 2(2), 302-309.
21. Cignoni, P., Rocchini, C. and Scopigno, R.: Metro: measuring error on simplified surfaces. Computer Graphics Forum, (1998), 17(2), 283-390.

Retrieving 3D CAD Model with Regional Entropy Distributions

Liu Wei and He Yuanjun

Department of Computer Science and Engineering, Shanghai Jiaotong University,
Shanghai, 200240, P.R. China

Abstract. In this paper, we present a novel method to match and retrieve 3D CAD models. Firstly the CAD model is voxelized. Then the voxelized model is divided into several regions, and the entropy of each region is calculated. All the entropies constitute the feature vector representing the models when compared with other models using Euclidean distance. A system based on this idea is implemented and its feasibility is validated.

Keywords: Voxelization, 3D model retrieval, entropy, feature extraction.

1 Introduction

Now 3D models play an important role in many applications and become the forth multimedia type after sound, image and video. Recently, the development of 3D modeling and digitizing technologies has made the model generating process much easier. Also, through the Internet, users can download a large number of free 3D models from all over the world. In the field of mechanical engineering, various kinds of 3D CAD design tools such as Pro/Engineering, CATIA, SolidWorks, etc, have replaced the status of the 2D ones. As a result many manufacture enterprises commonly have a 3D parts library which contains tens of thousands of CAD models. These models are used to communicate the exact shape and dimensions of components to both customers and sub-contracting manufacturers. Consequently these models are of great value and importance to the companies. Since even the simplest components have significant production costs, designers should make use of existing parts whenever practicable, which gives rise to a following problem of rapidly finding the parts needed in large parts library. However, obtaining and surveying catalogues of existing parts, even within a single enterprise, is still a costly, time-consuming task.

Traditionally CAD models are indexed by alpha-numeric part numbers with syntax specific to each company and in the area of group-technology, various "part coding" schemes have been proposed[1]. But in despite of their wide use, such manual shape classification schemes are subjective and limited to standard or general mechanical parts, so they can't wok automatically only with computers. To enable the savings of time and money that are associated with design reuse, which will greatly reduce the cost of part design in manufacture enterprises, it is necessary to develop a 3D CAD automatic retrieval system based on content with its goal being to find the similar

Z. Pan et al. (Eds.): ICAT 2006, LNCS 4282, pp. 871 – 879, 2006.

parts for a given query mainly according to their shape. One of the main challenges in this context is the mapping of 3D model into compact canonical representations referred to as descriptor or feature vector, which serve as search keys during the retrieval process. The descriptor decisively influences the performance of the search engine in terms of computational efficiency and relevance of the results. In this paper, we put forward to a regional distributions based method with entropy which proves to be effective in CAD model retrieval. The motivation behind our work is to enhance the performance of 3D mechanical models retrieval and to develop a fast, simple, and robust system acted on CAD model library.

The outline of the rest of this paper is as following: in the next section we review the previous work. In Section 3 we describe our method for descriptor extraction based on voxelization and entropy. In Section 4 experiments and results are presented in detail. Finally we give the conclusions and future work in Section 5.

2 Previous Work

Last several years have seen increasing academic research into 3D shape retrieval methods for various kinds of applications including mechanical components. Paquet[2-3] made the initial research in 1990s and got remarkable achievements. From then on, a lot of researches have been carried on. Now many approaches have been proposed. In general, they can be divided into four types: shape-based retrieval, topology-based retrieval, image-based retrieval and surface-attributes-based retrieval. Anderst[4] directly syncopated 3D model with some mode, then calculated the proportions of points number of each unit in that of the whole model, thus a shape histograms was formed to compare different models. Suzuki[5] put forward to a different method to syncopate 3D models which was called point density. This method did not form feature vector simply by the syncopated units but classified the syncopated units, so the dimension of feature vector and computational quantity decreased greatly. Osada[6] investigated a 3D model retrieval system based on shape distributions. The main idea was to calculate and get large numbers of statistical dates which could be served as shape distributions to describe the features of models. The key step was to define the functions which could describe the models. He defined five simple and easy-to-compute shape functions: A3, D1, D2, D3 and D4. Because this method was based on large number of statistical dates, it was robust to noise, resampling and predigestion. Vranic's[7] method firstly voxelized the 3D model, then applied 3D Fourier Transform on these voxelizations to decompose the model into different frequencies, finally chose certain amount of coefficients of frequency as this model's feature vector. Another approach[8-9] investigated by Vranic and Saupe was spherical harmonics analysis, which was also called 2D Fourier Transform on unitary sphere. This method needed sampling and harmonics transform, so the process of feature extraction was slow. Chen[10] had developed a web-based 3D model retrieval system in which a topology method using Reeb graph[11] was introduced. Reeb graph could be constructed by different precisions, thus in this way multi-resolution retrieval was available. There are also many researches on image-based retrieval[12-14] of which Chen at Taiwan University made outstanding productions. Surface-attributes-based retrieval is not mature as the above three types and only few researches were carried on[15].

Different from common 3D models, structures or semantic information is often used to differentiate mechanical ones. Elinson[16] described a domain-specific approach to assessing similarity of mechanical parts. He developed design signatures for mechanical parts which was a graph structure containing nodes that represented various attributes of the design, and edges that were labeled to represent relationships among those attributes. He used graph isomorphism theoryto to compare objects and subgraphs. Sun[17] reported a system for assessing the shape similarity of polyhedra by matching subgraphs extracted from their boundary models. However the system required input of two types of solid models. A prototype implementation successfully identified similarities between various mechanical parts with intersecting features. McWherter[18] described a system for partitioning a collection of models into clusters of similar shapes. Models were characterized by a MSG(Model Signature Graph) generated from the model's face-edge graphs. Various semantic and structural properties of the MSG were used to place each in a multidimensional vector space. The approach had been used to cluster the contents of the Design Repository and the results appeared to group approximately similar parts into the same clusters.

3   Our Method

In this paper, we don't intent to use any structural or semantic information to extract the feature of 3D models as described in Section 2 to retrieve mechanical models. Our method also mainly depends on the shape character of 3D CAD models.

Comparing with other medium such as image, sound and video, the structure of 3D model is correspondingly complicated. It is well known that 3D models are in an arbitrarily curving space which can't be continuously parameterized, and generally they are composed of various spatial polygons and haven't been sampled, so they can be viewed as irregularly signal. As a result, many classical analysis methods such as moment invariant, Fourier and wavelet transform can't be applied on 3D models directly, which not only makes the process of feature extraction difficult but also depresses the distinguishing power of the features extracted. A common way to convert irregularly signal to regularly signal is sampling. But for common 3D model, sampling will lost many details unless using enormous sampling points because of the complexity of 3D model. Instead, we notice that the 3D CAD models have particular characteristic which are obviously different from other types of models. Generally speaking, CAD models are comparatively simpler than other ones, especially models of animals, plants, natural scenes, etc, and have stronger trend of symmetry. At the same time, they are usually composed of several finite planes or curves and the normal of their surfaces vary drastically at certain places thus often they have distinct contours. So we can suppose that CAD models can be sampled by a set of small cubes which are called voxels in the later depiction without biggish distortion. Then we can get an approximation of the original 3D part by means of voxelization which proves to approach the original model with considerable precision. The following entropy-based arithmetic for feature extraction is entirely based on this supposition. In this paper, we assume that the CAD models are not solid ones and their surfaces are composed of polygons.

3.1 Voxelization of 3D CAD Models

Let the continuous 3D space $(R \times R \times R)$ be marked as R^3, while the discrete 3D voxelized space $(Z \times Z \times Z)$, which is a 3D array of grid points, shall be referred to as Z^3. We term a voxel or the region contained by a 3D discrete point (x, y, z), as the continuous region (u, v, w) such that:

$$
\begin{aligned}
x - 05 \prec u \le x + 0.5, \\
y - 0.5 \prec v \le y + 0.5, \\
z - 0.5 \prec w \le z + 0.5.
\end{aligned}
\tag{1}
$$

This assumes that the voxel occupies a unit cube centered at the grid point (x, y, z), and the array of voxels tessellates Z^3. The aggregate of all voxels is a tessellation of 3D Euclidean space. A voxel's value is mapped into the set $\{0, 1\}$: voxels assigned the value "1" are called "black" or "non-empty" voxels, while those assigned the value "0" are called "white" or "empty" voxels.

A straightforward algorithm is to compute the intersection of the surface of 3D model and the voxel grids. But this method leads to contain more voxels than necessary. Various improved voxelization algorithms for spatial polygons have been proposed[19-20]. Kaufman proposed a 3D scan-conversion for polyhedra in Reference [19] which is a variation of 2D scan-line filling algorithm and uses only simple operations like additions and testy inside the inner loops. This method is a most effective one. Fig.1 shows the voxelization of a hammer using this algorithm and from this figure we can observe that the original model and the voxelized one are very similar, so we can use the feature of the latter to replace that of the former. Through this step, we convert an irregular polygonal model to a regular voxelized model, which bring great convenience for analysis.

Fig. 1. An example of voxelization

3.2 Feature Extraction

Shannon's Theory of Information defines information as a transcendentally bushtailed factor and information's loader is called "message"[21]. Suppose that there is a limited message set $A = \{a_1, a_2, \cdots, a_n\}$ in which the emergence of each message is unattached to each other and the probability is respectively:

$$P = \{p_1, p_2, \cdots, p_n\}, (\sum_{i=1}^{n} p_i = 1, p_i \geq 0).$$ (2)

Then the entropy of this message set can be defined as:

$$H(x) = -\sum_{i=1}^{n} p_i \log_2 p_i .$$ (3)

The value of this entropy embodies the average bushtailed factor of emergences of the messages in the set A.

As for the voxelized 3D models, since different voxels with different probability distribution in different spatial regions, they exhibit multifarious shape features. There are only two kinds of voxels: "non-empty" voxels(Valued 1) and "empty" voxels(Valued 0), then its entropy is

$$H_2 = -p_1 \log_2 p_1 - p_2 \log_2 p_2, \ p_1 + p_2 = 1.$$ (4)

And p_1 and p_2 are the proportions of the two kinds of voxels in the total $L \times L \times L$ space(L is the resolution for voxelization). Since the entropy is only related to the numbers but not the locations of the two kinds of voxels, two completely different models may have the same value of entropy, as illustrated in Fig.2 using 2D case with its resolution being 2×2. They have obvious difference in vision while having the same entropy.

a)   b)

Fig. 2. Different objects have the same entropy

So using global entropy as feature of the 3D model is inapposite. Since partial entropy also reflects the distributing of the region it covers, so if we divide the voxelized model into several regions and compute their entropies, the union of them will represent the feature of the model in a more elaborate manner.

We divide the total $L \times L \times L$ voxels containing the voxelized original model into $K \times K \times K (K \in N)$ regions, and to ensure that the voxel be the minimal unit, we presume that $d = L/K \in N$. Let V be the $L \times L \times L$ voxels and V_i be the i-th region. If the entropy of V_i is f_i, then the feature vector of the model can be constructed as:

$$f = \{f_1, f_2, \cdots, f_{d^3}\} .$$ (5)

Through this method, we solve the problem that different models have the same value of entropy. The feature vector not only describes the global characteristic but also reflects the spatial distributing of the 3D model. Fig.3 shows a model and its feature vector in one situation.

Fig. 3. A model and its feature vector in one situation

3.3 Models Comparison

Let f_A and f_B be the feature vectors of two 3D CAD models, then the difference between them can be defined using a certain Distance Metric such as L_1, L_2 and Mahalanobis distance, etc. Throughout our experiments the common Euclidean distance(L_2) is used, that is to say:

$$D(A,B) = L_2(f_A, f_B) = \sqrt{\sum_{i=1}^{d^3}(f_{Ai} - f_{Bi})^2} \, . \tag{6}$$

But direct computation doesn't work since 3D CAD models have arbitrary placements when they are created. 3D CAD models have different position, orientation and scaling in 3D space and an entropy component in the feature vector represents the distribution of a certain region at the 3D model, so an important work we must do firstly is to find the correspondence between two models and make the comparison valid. Since a majority of CAD models are created in a comparatively standardized place as mechanical parts generally have obvious orientations and usually have at least a symmetry axis, we can easily find the correspondences. We needn't search for all possible placements, and later experiments showed that finite postures will be enough to get a good correspondence. There are 6 orientations from the center of the cube to the center of its faces, called as main orientations superposed by the primary symmetry axis of the CAD model. For each main orientation, we rotate the model around it per 90 degrees and get 4 postures. And if we take reflection into account, we can get total $6 \times 4 \times 2 = 48$ postures.

As each orientation's symmetrical situation is also within the 48 cases, when matching two 3D CAD models, we can assume that one remains fixed while the other adjusts its pose to the 48 cases, if D_1, D_2, $\cdots$, D_{48} be the matching distances, then the actual difference between the two 3D models can thus be denoted as:

$$D = \min(D_1, D_2, \cdots, D_{48}) \, . \tag{7}$$

4   Experiments Result

According to the method described in Section 3, we have developed a 3D CAD models retrieval system using Visual C++ on a PC with Pentium IV 1.8G CPU and Windows 2000 Server Operation System. The system consists of two parts: offline process module and online retrieval process module, as showed in Fig.4. In the offline process, features of 3D models are extracted and stored in database. To efficiently search a large collection online, an indexing data structure and searching algorithm is available with B+ Tree. In the online process, users select a 3D model as the query mode, then the system engine compares the distances between the query and the models in model library, finally several models most similar to the input one are returned.

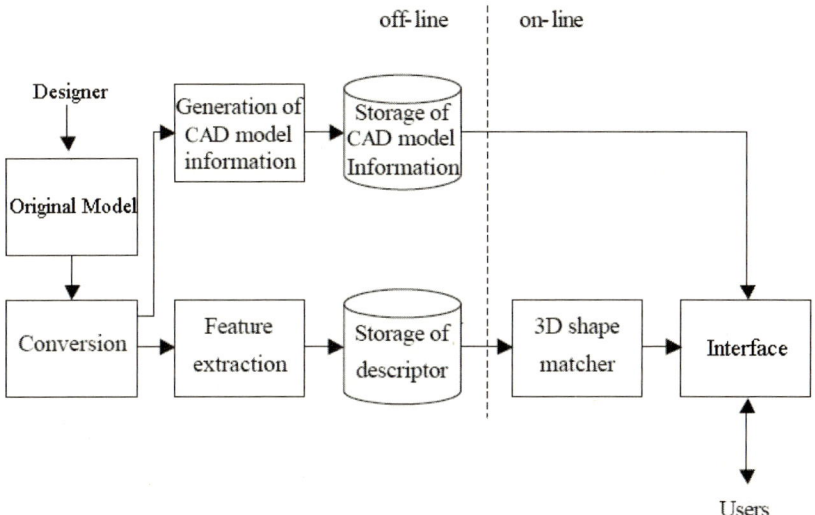

Fig. 4. Architecture of our system

In this method, we need choose two appropriate parameters: L and K where $L/K \in Z$. As for L, the larger L is, the better the voxelized model approaches the original one, but the computation is accordingly increasing. The same discussion to K, the larger K is, the subtlier the entropy information is expressed, but the pertinence among voxels decreases. In our experiments, we tested several combinations of L and K, in which we find that when $L = 100$ and $K = 5$ the arithmetic obtains optimal performance(perhaps related to model library), and in this case the dimension of the feature vector is $K^3 = 125$. Fig.5 shows a series of 3D CAD models of plane and the distributions of their feature vectors.

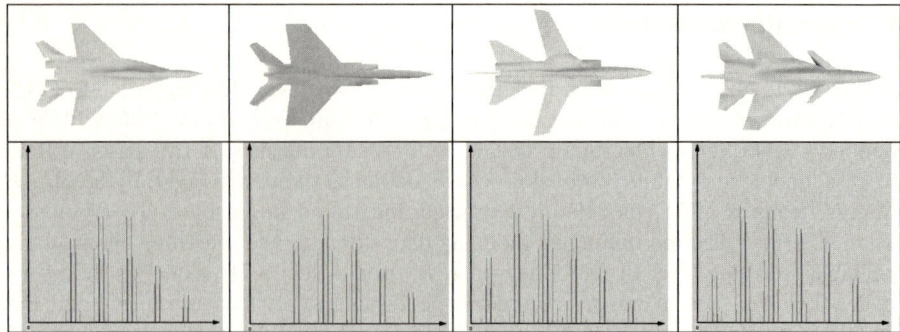

Fig. 5. 3D CAD models and corresponding feature vectors

5   Conclusions and Feature Work

Retrieval and reuse of 3D CAD models in part library is an effective way that can significantly reduce development costs and time. For this reason, the paper has presented a novel method for retrieval of 3D models, extraordinarily for CAD models. We use voxelizaion to representation the original 3D model, then calculate the entropies of all sunspaces as feature vector, and experiments preliminarily validate our method.

As for the further work, we plan to orderly organize and delaminate the models library according to the PLIB standard[22] to make the similar models stored in the same categories, so the system can quickly eliminates the obvious dissimilar models. The future aim of our system is that each input model can automatically find its category and be stored in corresponding position to quicken and optimize the retrieval performance in online retrieval.

Acknowledgements. This research has been funded by The National Natural Science Foundation of China (60573146).

References

1. Burbridge, J. Group Technology in the Engineering Industry. London: Mechanical Engineering Publications, 1979.
2. Paquet E, Rioux M. A query by content software for three dimensions database management. Proceeding of International Conference on Recent Advances in 3D Digital Imaging and Modeling, Ottawa, Canada, 1997, 345-352
3. Paquet E, Rioux M. A content-based search for VRML database. Proceeding of the 1998 Computer Society Conference on Computer Vision and Pattern Recognition, Santa Barbara, CA, 1998, 541-546
4. Ankerst Mihael, Kastenmller Gabi, Kriegel Hans. 3D Shape Histograms for Similarity Search and Classification in Spatial database. Proceeding of the 6th International Symposium on Large Spatial Database, Hong Kong, 1999, 207-226
5. Suzuki T, Kato Toshikazu, Otsu Nobuyuki. A Similarity Retrieval of 3D Polygonal Model Using Rotation Invariant Shape Descriptors. Proceeding of IEEE International on Systems, Man, and Cybernetics, Nashville, Tennessee, 2000, 2946-2952

6. Osada Robert, Funkhouser Thomas, Chazelle Bernard. Shape Distributions. ACM Transactions on Graphics, 2002, 21(4): 807-832

7. Vranic D V, Saupe D. 3D Shape Descriptor Based on 3D Fourier Transform. Proceeding of the EURASIP Conference on Digital Signal Processing of Multimedia Communications and Services, Budapest, Hungary, 2001, 271-274

8. Vranic D V, Saupe D. Description of 3D Shape Using a Complex Function on Sphere. Proceeding of the IEEE International Conference on Multimedia and Expo, Lausanne, Switzerland, 2002, 177-180

9. Vranic D V , Saupe D. Tools for 3D object retrieval: Karhunen-Loeve Transform and spherical harmonics [A]. In : IEEE Workshop on Multimedia Signal Processing , Cannes, 2001.1 293-298

10. Chen Dingyun, Ouhyoung Ming. A 3D Object Retrieval System Based on Multi-Resolution Reeb Graph. Proceedings of Computer Graphics Workshop, Taiwan, China, 2002, 16-20

11. Hilaga Masaki, Shinagawa Yoshihisa, Kohmura Taku. Topology matching for fully automatic similarity estimation of 3D shapes [A]. In : Computer Graphics Proceedings , Annual Conference Series, ACM SIGGRAPH, Los Angeles, CA ,2001.1, 203-212

12. Min Patrick, Chen Joyce, Funkhouser Thomas. A 2D Sketch Interface for a 3D Model Search Engine. Computer Graphics Proceedings, Annual Conference Series, ACM SIGGRAPH 2002 Technical Sketch, San Autonio, Texas, 2002

13. Chen Dingyun, Tian Xiaopei, Shen Yute. On Visual Similarity Based 3D Model Retrieval. Computer Graphics Forum, 2003, 22 (3): 223-232

14. Jobst Loffler. Content-Based Retrieval of 3D Models in Distributed Web Databases by Visual Shape Information. IEEE International Conference on Information Visualization, London ,UK, 2000.1, 82-87

15. Suzuki M. A web-based retrieval system for 3D polygonal models. In : Proceedings of Joint 9th IFSA World Congress and 20th NAFIPS International Conference , Vancouver , Canada , 2001 , 2271-2276

16. Elinson A., Nau D. S, Regli, W. C. Feature-based Similarity Assessment of Solid Models. Proc ACM Solid Modelling Conference, 1997, May

17. Sun T. L, Su C. J, Mayer R. J. Shape similarity assessment of mechanical parts based on solid models. Proc of the 1995, ASME DETC, Vol.83, No.2 Pt 2, pp. 953-962, Boston, MA, USA, Sep 17-20

18. McWherter D, Peabody M, Shokoufandeh, A. Database techniques for archival of solid models. Proc Solid Modeling 01, pp. 78-87, Ann Arbor, Michigan, ACM Press

19. Kaufman A, Shimony, E. 3D Scan-Conversion Algorithms for Voxel-Based Graphics'. Proc. ACM Workshop on Interactive 3D Graphics, Chapel Hill, NC, October 1986, 45-76

20. Jian Huang, Roni Yagel, Vassily Filippov. An accurate method for voxelizing polygon meshes. IEEE Symposium on Volume Visualization, 119-126

21. Qingsheng Meng. Theory of Information. Press of Beijing University of Technology, 1991

22. Cao Yunfu, Li Feng, Han Yongsheng. Information Model of Parts Library and Its Representation Based on PLIB. Journal of Computer-Aided Design and Computer Graphics, 2002, 14(6): 598-602

Virtual Tang-Style Timber-Frame Building Complex*

Deren Li[1], Yixuan Zhu[2], Zhiqiang Du[1,**], and Tao Hong[1]

[1] State Key Lab of Information Engineering in Surveying Mapping and Remote Sensing,
Wuhan University, 129 LuoYu Road, Wuhan, Hubei, 430079, China
lideren@www.whu.edu.cn, duzhiqiang@lmars.whu.edu.cn,
goodfeeling_hc@yahoo.com.cn
[2] School of Remote Sensing Information Engineering, Wuhan University, 129 LuoYu Road,
Wuhan, Hubei, 430079, China
Pw67@yahoo.com

Abstract. Timber-frame building is one of gems of Chinese ancient buildings. Protecting and researching historic buildings by using computer technologies has become a hot topic and urgent task in the field of digital cultural heritage, with increasingly disappearing the timber-frame buildings and their architectural arts and crafts. This paper introduces constructing an information system based on virtual reality technology of timber-frame buildings, and addresses important technologies involved in reconstructing ancient buildings, such as data collection, 3D reconstruction, data organization and management, virtual assembly, and virtual roaming. An integrated solution is proposed and provides a brand-new method for 3D reconstruction, documentation, repair, research and protection of timber-frame buildings.

Keywords: digital cultural heritage, timber-frame building, 3D construction, virtual assembly, 3D roaming.

1 Introduction

Digital Cultural Heritage (DCH) is to research and protect the world history, cultures, and natural heritages by utilizing computer technologies. DCII emphasize that it should link people in the virtual environment with human culture tradition, who will realize function and orientation of current culture in the human history, and make a experience from furthest foretime, recently to future in the historical corridor.

Multi-dimensional information is expressed by DCH, which realizes the truth of history, has the cultural art, and possesses the fidelity of real environment. The process of the multi-dimensional information not only is supported by high-performance hardware, but also involved in the developed computer technologies, which include Virtual Reality (VR) as one of the key technologies. It is an important measure to apply and synthesize photogrammetry, architecture and archeology for collecting the multi-information.

---

* This research is funded by the project titled the Digital Architectural Information System of Tang-Style Temple Complex for Chi Lin Nunnery.
** Corresponding author.

As a new technology, VR is extensively concerned in science and engineering in the last decades. It produces one kind of simulation environment using the computer, and realizes the interactive action between the users and the virtual environment in which the user immersing through many kinds of sensory equipment. Using 3D digital reconstruction of ancient buildings or places within VR, it is possible to simulate, discuss, and evaluate diverse solutions to archaeological, cultural, or restoration-related problems without touching the original. A novel research platform and an enjoying approach are provided to kinds of users by applying several techniques, such as virtual preservation, information demonstration and 3D visualization.

2   Chinese Ancient Timber-Frame Building

Sui and Tang Dynasty are the mature period during the development course of Chinese ancient architectural system and scale the peak of ancient architecture in the Chinese feudal age. The ruins of an ancient city, palaces, tombs, grottoes, pagodas, and bridges which leave over from Sui and Tang Dynasty have very high level of architectural art and technology no matter distribution and shaping, especially the sculptures and frescoes.

The distribution of Chinese ancient palaces and temples employs the manner symmetrical. The main buildings are centering and have longitudinal axis; a courtyard is composed through covered corridors connecting some buildings which are constituted by rooms; and the courtyards as unit elements spread along the axis to form a depth arrangement. The feature of Tang timber-frame architecture takes the timber frame as structure system, in which the columns, TouKung and beams as the essential elements compose the weight-bearing system and mortise and tenon in the timber components are fit each other to grouping a frame full of elasticity [1]. The architecture, especially timber-frame building, is characterized by magnificent, unpretentious and religious architectural style. It has broad and curved roof, unadorned and practicable doors and windows, and concise and bright color.

(a)   (b)   (c)

Fig. 1. (a) The timber-frame building complex. (b) A hall in the complex. (c) A set of Toukung.

The wood, as the basic material of buildings in Tang Dynasty, is easier to be perishable and the construction of timber structure can be easily razed by wars or religious struggles; many crafts have seldom survived to this day due to the manual skills and crafts of timber-frame building are orally passed; and a few literatures record the arts and crafts about them hardly exist, so that the research and protection about timber-frame buildings in Tang style become a critical task, which includes how to represent the vanished or destroyed historic buildings and sites and how to preserve cultural information about the ruins of ancient buildings. This also is the main object of historic building research using computer technologies in DCH.

3 Virtual Tang-Style Timber-Frame Buildings

Chi Lin Nunnery, which is a famous Tang-style timber building complex, is on a grand scale; is great and momentous; and is magnificent but not stiff. Virtual architectural information system of Tang-style timber-frame building complex for Chi Lin Nunnery can bring forth a new technology for documentation, research and protection of Chinese ancient buildings.

3.1 Data Collection

Collecting real 3D data is the essential prerequisite for reconstructing 3D model of virtual building complex. It is important that different modeling method is corresponding different data resource, for example, the modeling method based on remote-sensing image and LIght Detection And Ranging (LIDAR) is suitable for modeling large-range 3D city; vehicle-carried photogrammetry can apply to modeling 3D landscape beside of street; a single building or buildings are usually modeled by engineering survey, close-range photogrammetry, or laser scan on ground [2].

3D block models based image modeling methods can not particularly describe the all details or features of buildings although they can be used in rapid modeling urban scene. Computer Aided Design (CAD) technology has a unique advantage in graphic process and real 3D modeling. A 3D CAD model is composed of one or more polyhedral models and can represent detailed geometric characteristics of a building. These models demonstrate not only the detailed appearance but also inner complicated structure of objects comparing with the models established by imaged-based modeling method. But the modeling process is involved in sophisticated man-machine interaction, overload manual work, and higher cost.

In the practical modeling for virtual Tang-style building complex, several data collecting methods are utilized: engineering survey, close-range photogrammetry, ground laser scan, and architectural design blueprint.

For the regular timber components, the traditional survey can satisfy the requisition of data precision and obtain the effective featured point. But the data received by this method usually have the problem that the 2 adjacent surfaces have not a shared line. It is required to think carefully about sample frequency of featured point [3].

For the irregular timber components, like *Chiwen* on the roof, laser scan is the best method for data collection although the degree of the automatic processing point cloud is not in high level yet. The textures are mapped onto the 3D model is another effective method for obtaining photorealistic effect. But the textures collected by digital camera are usually processed by color or geometric correction. This method is usually suitable for collecting data of the architectural decoration [2].

The architectural design blueprint has become another important data resource. 2D CAD data provided in blueprints can help survey sampling and quality checking, and moreover, it can be converted to 3D model through giving special reference data.

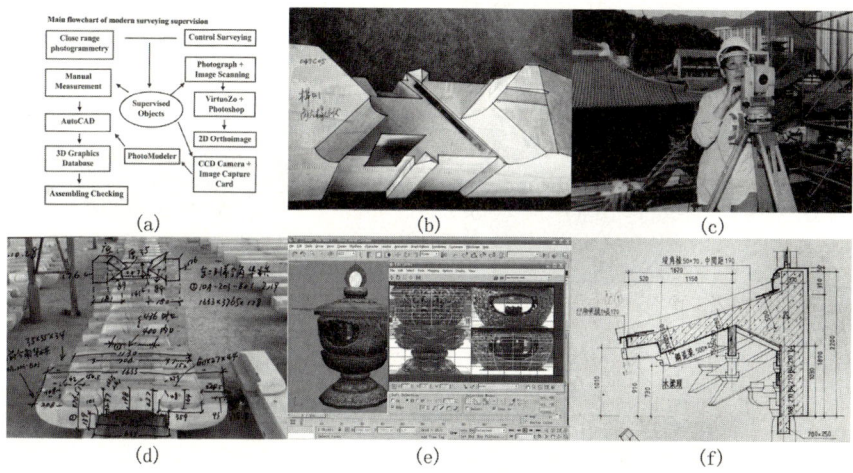

Fig. 2. (a) The workflow of supervision for a timber-frame building. (b) Model Normalization. (c) Surveying. (d) Data sampling. (e) Texture mapping. (f) Blueprint.

3.2 3D Modeling

3D modeling based on CAD is the best choice to reproduce the structural characteristics of timber-frame building and make possible virtual assembling, dynamic browsing, interior and exterior data management and component information inquire. Volume-based model in CAD can build complicate forms by composing simple volumes, and architectural component can be digitalized quickly on the base of second developing [4].

Timber-frame buildings are composed of thousands or even millions wooden components, so 3D models are highly complicate and have a huge data volume. Even high performance graphic computer can't render scene with fluent frame rate. Modeling reductionism basing on CAD 3D data is the important method in the process of 3D reconstruction.

The usual solution is to reduce the amount of triangles and vertexes for simplifying the scene. But LOD is the method to describe less important visual subjects with simple geometry forms, which includes discrete and continuous LOD. Continuous LOD model's generation algorithm is applicable to regular modern architecture and macro-scale urban model. Discrete LOD can improve the efficiency of rendering greatly by taking measures to reduce visual mutation phenomenon. At the same time it can find a balance between rendering efficiency and representing effect to meet the demands of representing historic Timber-frame architecture.

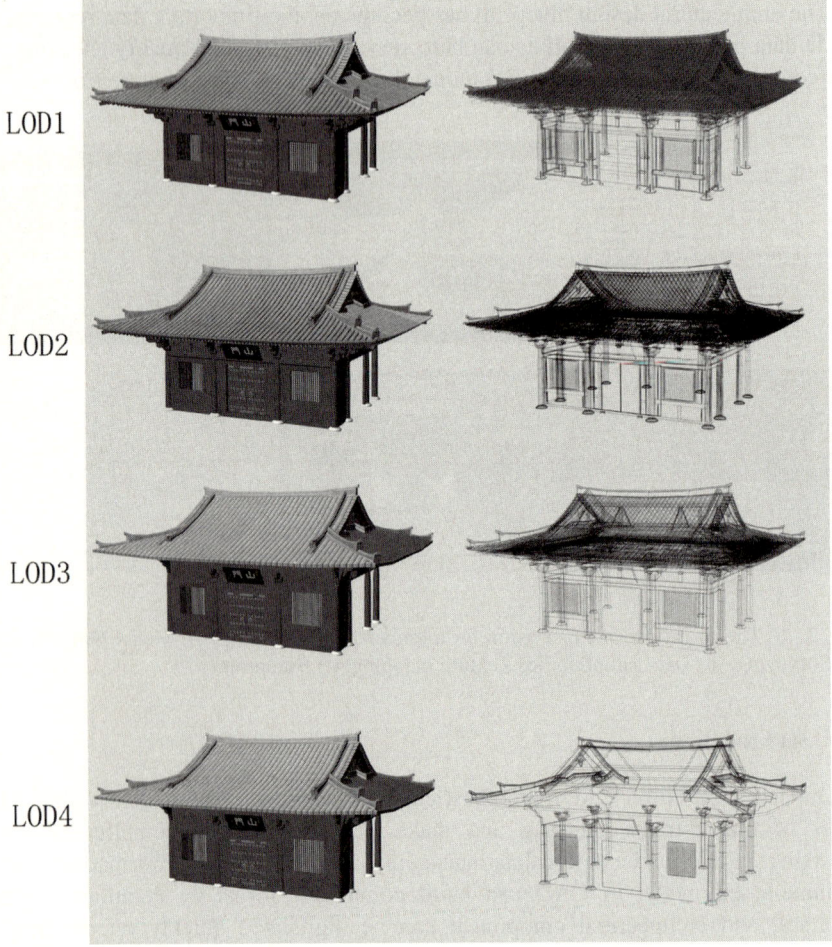

LOD1

LOD2

LOD3

LOD4

Fig. 3. 3D models of a hall with different levels of details

The method based on LOD and CAD incarnates fully the idea from complexity to simplicity during 3D modeling, filling the requirements of acquiring the possible best quality of rendering images and achieving virtual roam at smooth frame rates [5]. Furthermore, it is important to determine how many levels of discrete LOD models to establish. The limited system resource would be used in over-frequently locating and loading huge volumes of data from storage so that real-time rendering is not smooth enough considering too many levels of a model are plotted out, obviously it conflicts with the principle of LOD. But the "popping effect" caused by models switching would be notable if plotting out over-less levels, especially when outline of model needs to be kept consistent. In fact, 4-5 levels discrete 3D models with different detailed degrees would be a feasible scheme for real-time rendering of virtual tang-style timber-frame building complex [5].

3.3 Data Organization and Management

For virtual Tang-style building complex, more fine degree of 3D CAD model is, much more data of model will be. It is important to establish an appropriate spatial index to accelerate calling and invoking 3D vector model data [6]. LOD-R-trees, which is perfectly suited to organize and manage large amounts of 3D data, as shown as Figure 5, the majority of models in the scene are subdivided into several parts according the different detailed representation, and they can become integrated effectively by R-trees index. The disassembled models can also serve for 3D space partitioning. Moreover, the 3D models based on LOD-R-trees are contributed in smoothly real-time rendering and meet the goal of multi-scale spatial query and spatial analysis by integrated applications of database management techniques [7].

In fact, an independent-developed 3D model database management engine (DBME) that is based on the integration of Oracle 8i/9i database and file management system, allows for efficient management and manipulation of 3D data and other data within the visualization environment.

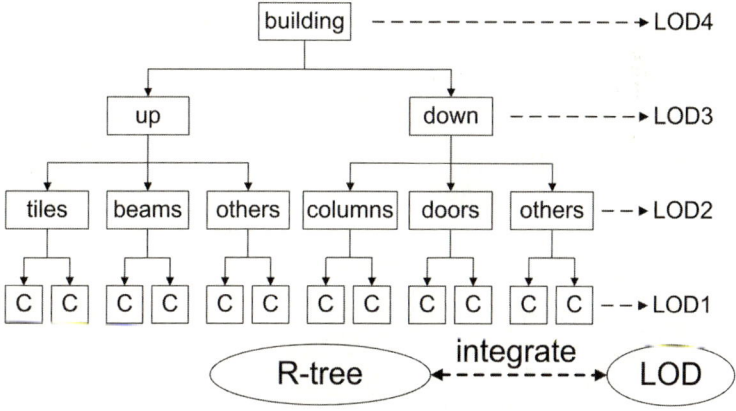

Fig. 4. Data organization based on LOD-R-tree [5]

3.4 Virtual Assembly

Virtual assembly not only can be utilized in engineer quality check, but also is helpful for structure and craft research of ancient timber-frame building [8]. It is possible to face with dismantlement and reworks for constructing or repairing an ancient building because there are errors in the process of design or machining and the timber-frame building is made up of components through mortise and tenon accurately. So the mistakes and errors will be found in time by virtual assembly, which provides a solid foundation for design and construction. The process of virtual assembly can entirely show the whole structure of building, can analyze structural relationship among components in important nodes, and also can make the finite element analysis combining with the theory of architectural mechanics.

Planning the process of the virtual assembly is the first step, which includes recording the order of assembly and path information and considering the physical attribution of models. And then the 3D component model is imported into the virtual assembly system from CAD platform. The original position of every component is valued by practical survey data. The viewpoint and watching direction can be adjusted freely and the operation including pan, rotation, scale, can be finished conveniently. The system can achieve real-time collision detection and constraint discernment and generate the assembly animation according to the movement path of components.

Collision detection, a key technology for virtual assembly and dynamic roaming, can avoid the penetration between the viewpoint and objects in order to promote the fidelity in the navigation. The combination of collision detection algorithm based on object space and based on image space can enhance the capability of detection, that is, firstly to analyze intersection of scene objects based on 2D projection and depth information in reference frame, then to compute intersection of points, lines and faces of the "intersecting" objects.

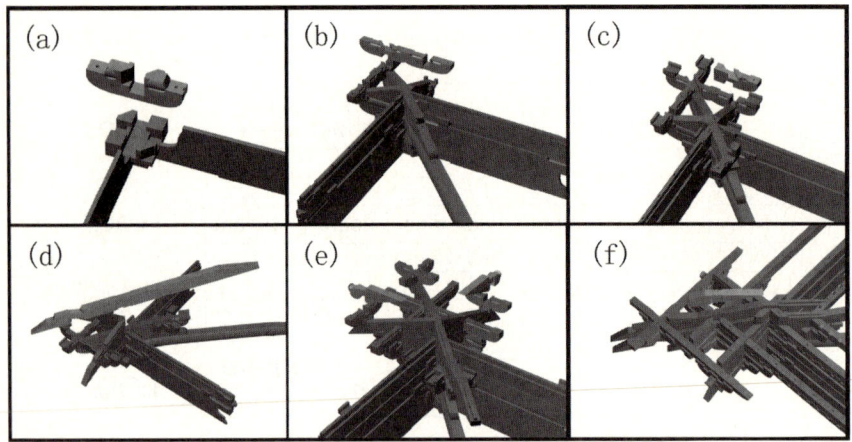

Fig. 5. A sample of assembling process from image (a) to (f)

3.5 Virtual Roaming

Verisimilitude of display and real-time response are two important guidelines to evaluate visual function [9]. While roaming in the dummy wood-frame buildings scene, image quality is the same important as response time. Data needed to render always exceed them though the capacities of graphic hardware have been advanced, so it is necessary to use software techniques to resolve the problem. Some acceleration techniques, such as occlusion culling, LOD, and programmable rendering, are adopted for balancing between the highest rendering quality and smooth animation.

Occlusion culling is designed to cull the invisible objects during rendering. When a dummy visitor is walking through the scene, because of being occluded by other buildings closed the viewpoint, many buildings and decorations are not visible although they are within the view frustum. The most culling algorithms are based on partitioning the view position space or finding out the set of potential visible objects. The real-time culling algorithm used in the system is sufficient to utilize the spatial and temporal consistency. The algorithm is sufficient to cull the majority of invisible objects if the user is walking through the scene, though it is not efficient for the height of viewpoint above the roofs. Fortunately, the navigation of users is mainly used in simulating human activities in the virtual scene, and the system will automatically call LOD4 models for a complement of display speed depressed by occlusion culling invalidation when the height of viewpoint above the roofs.

It is difficult to achieve the satisfied display speed although the multi-levels data management and occlusion culling technique are adopted in rendering process. Programmable rendering technique is one of the most effective approaches for obtaining a balance between image realism and smooth display, whenever flying over or walking through the scene, it can optimize the refreshing frequency and graphic quality of rendering by batch program of vertex and illumination computing of segment render, and improve evidently verisimilitude of virtual roaming.

Fig. 6. The image on the left is a snap of 3D virtual scene and the image on the right is a photo of Chi Lin Nunnery

4   Conclusion and Future Works

An architectural information system based on virtual reality technology of Tang-style timber-frame building complex is introduced particularly. The experiment suggests that survey, 3D laser scan and close-range photogrammetry are the effective way for obtaining multi-resource spatial information, especially the 3D laser scan promote the efficiency and quality of collecting data. The modeling method integrated LOD with CAD is suitable for 3D reconstruction of timber-frame building. This method not only really represents the detailed appearance features, but also makes possible for smooth roaming. LOD-R-tree, a spatial index, provides a solid foundation for multiple levels query and dynamic visualization combining database management engine. Virtual assembly supplies a new method for craft research of timber-frame buildings. Finally, interactive virtual roaming shows the architectural art of Tang-style timber-frame building complex sufficiently.

It is an important for utilizing the computer technologies to protect and research historic building in digital heritage. The technologies, such as fast collecting data, automatic 3D reconstruction, multi-resolution rendering will become the important development for 3D modeling and dynamic visualization.

References

1. Liang, S.: A Pictorial History of Chinese Architecture. Baihua Literature & Art Publishing House, Tianjing (2001)
2. Li, D., Yang, J., Zhu, Y.: Application of Computer Technique in the Reconstruction of Chinese Ancient Buildings. Proceedings of the ISPRS commission V symposium, Corfu, Greece, Intern Archives of P&RS Volume XXXIV, Part 5 Comm. V. (2002) 404 406
3. Li, D., Hong, T., Zhu, Y., Yang, J.: 3D Reconstruction and Simulating Assembly of Ancient Chinese Timber-frame Building. In the proceedings of CIPA 2005 XX International Sympsium, Torino, Italy (2005) 906-911
4. Xu, M., Zhu, Y.: Computer-Based Simulation and Quality Control for Building. Working Group V/5, ISPRS, (1998) 252-258
5. Du, Z., Li, D., Zhu, Y., Zhu, Q.: 3DGIS-Based Reconstruction and Visualization of Timber-frame Building Cluster. Xitong Fangzhen Xuebao/Journal of System Simulation. Vol.18, No.7 (2006) 1184-1189
6. Zhu, Q., Lin, H.: Digital City Geographic Information System. Wuhan University Press, Wuhan (2004)
7. Berndt, E., Carlos, J.: Cultural Heritage in the Mature Era of Computer Graphics. Computer Graphics and Applications, IEEE, Vol. 20, No.1 (2000) 36-37
8. Zisserman, A., Fitzgibbon, A., Baillard, C., Cross, G.: From Images to Virtual and Augmented Reality. In: Confluence of Computer Vision and Computer Graphics, NATO Science Series. Kluwer Academic Publishers (2000) 1–23
9. Gruber, M.: Managing Large 3D Urban Databases. 47th Photogrammetric Week (Dieter Fritsch and Rudi Spiller, editor). Wichmann, Germany (1999) 341-349

An Accelerating Rendering Method of Hybrid Point and Polygon for Complex Three-Dimensional Models*

Aimin Hao, Guifen Tian, Qinping Zhao, and Zhide Li

Ministry of Education Key Laboratory of Virtual Reality Technology,
Beihang University, Beijing, China
ham@buaa.edu.cn

Abstract. This paper presents an accelerating hybrid rendering method for complex three-dimensional models using both points and polygons. In circumstance of current PC hardware, our rendering method that integrates advantages of both GBMR (Graphics -Based Modeling and Rendering) and PBMR (Point-Based Modeling and Rendering) works well with complex geometric models which consist of millions of small triangles. In the pre-processing phase, model faces are segmented into regions, triangles and vertex point clouds of each region are stored, and all vertices are sorted in an ascending order according to their importance degree and serialized into a linear structure. In the real-time rendering phase, view-dependent frustum culling and backface clipping are performed; different regions are rendered using triangles or points according to their distance from the viewpoint. These two phases fully utilize the parallelism nature of GPU (Graphic Process Unit) and efficiently implement a continuous multi-resolution rendering for HPPO (Hybrid Point and Polygon Object).

Keywords: Virtual reality, Modeling and rendering, Real-time property, Point clouds, Continuous multi-resolution models.

1 Introduction

Recently, the number of complex geometric models get by 3D scanning technique has increased a lot. Usually these models contain high surface details and dense vertices. As a result, these models contain huge data information and hence the real-time processing is tough. In order to resolve such problem, researchers have tried various techniques, such as LOD (Levels of Detail)[1], view-frustum culling [2], image transformation [3], and Light Field Rendering [4]. These techniques all help to improve performance, but pity that limitations go with them at the same time.

Point-Based Rendering (PBR) is a new accelerating rendering technique recently developed. It takes the geometric point as its rendering primitive and

* Supported by Opening Foundation of Beijing Key Laboratory of Multimedia and Intelligent Software in Beijing University of Technology.

Z. Pan et al. (Eds.): ICAT 2006, LNCS 4282, pp. 889–900, 2006.

works well with the rendering of large-scale complex models with rich, organic shapes or high surface details. In contrast to the polygon-based technique, this method does not need to store topologic information between vertices, which does a lot of good for efficiency. However, it has some disadvantages as follows: It requires a lot of projection, clipping and transmission of large numbers of geometric points and has a high requirement in hardware pixel filling. Another disadvantage is that holes and alias usually appear during this rendering technique. To avoid these holes and alias, many Point-Based Rendering methods (such as Far Voxels [5] in SIGGRAPH 2005) request that point sampling on object surfaces should meet sufficient sampling conditions and that the viewpoint should not be too close to the target object. Obviously, the latter request makes arbitrary interactivity impossible.

Hybrid rendering can solve partial problems mentioned above and currently it has become the prevailing method of modeling and rendering. Hybrid of point and polygon [6,7], one of such hybrid rendering methods, uses triangles, points and images together to present the same model. To go into detail, this method uses points with textures to render objects far away from the viewpoint and uses texture-mapping triangles to render objects close to the viewpoint. It has been proved that this hybrid method can successfully avoid holes, which may appear when purely applying point-based method to render close or middle-positional objects. At the same time, rendering speed is notably improved.

Here, referring to the nomenclature for IBO [8](Image-based object) , BVO [9] (Volume-based object), V_Object[10] (Object in virtual environment) defined by former researchers, our paper defines HPPO (Hybrid Point and Polygon Object). HPPO is especially applicable to present two-dimensional continuous manifold models in virtual environment, which may contain dense and complex geometric information, and this presentation itself is continuous and multi-resolution. Further more, our paper presents a new accelerating technique of hybrid of points and polygons, which is competent for the rendering of large-scale, dense geometric models. By choosing polygons or points as rendering primitives, our method gets a good balance between rendering speed and image quality.

2   Related Work

There are two disadvantages [6] inherent to pure point representation. First, once objects are represented in point representation, their resolution is fixed. When the resolution of the destination image is larger than the maximal resolution that can be presented by points, interpolation between adjacent points must be done to ensure smooth shading. Second, for large, flat surfaces, point rendering becomes less efficient than polygon rendering. To resolve this problem, Chen et al. put forward an algorithm called POP [6], which in nature is an extension of pure point rendering systems such as Qsplat [10]. For POP algorithm starts from triangles as leaf nodes in its hierarchical tree structure: when the screen contribution of the node is larger than one pixel, the node is presented by a polygon rather pure points In this way, POP can accelerate the rendering of large models, compromising little in image quality. Improvement made by POP lies in that QSplat only works well with models consisting of triangles of approximately equal sizes, while POP works well for any triangular model.

Wimmer [11] substitutes point-based impostors for distant geometric models.This approach relies on object-space sampled representation similar to point clouds or layered depth images; therefore the appearance of holes is successfully prevented at sampling phase. For large, complex models, as sample points are not enough to make a complete surface of an object, Wimmer computes the contribution of these points to the image using Monte Carlo integration. The resulting representation is compact, and by using existing graphic hardware, renders can produce a high quality image with little aliasing, and no missing or disappearing objects as the viewpoint moves.

Another rendering system PMR presented by Dey et al. [12] builds an octree of points and triangles similar to POP. However, unlike POP, the hierarchy in PMR is built on input point clouds, and then the Voronoi diagram is used to estimate local features of the point clouds and simplify them in the object space. Continuously, the simplified result is transformed into multi-resolution triangles. Similar to other mentioned rendering methods, PMR chooses points to render distant objects and triangles to render close objects. A simple user-defined parameter can be used to control the balance of points and triangles, thus achieving the speed/quality tradeoff. However, simplification of point clouds is consumptive and inefficient. Similar work researched by Liviu Coconu [13] is Hardware-Oriented hybrid Rendering with the layered depth octree as its basic data structure. As regard to domestic work on hybrid point-polygon rendering, P-Quadtrees algorithm presented by Junfeng Ji [15], could be a representative. Another researcher, Yanci Zhang, also makes some contributions.

3   Hybrid of Point and Polygon Rendering

3.1   Basic Definitions

Point cloud: A set of dense discrete points. Mathematically, it can be represented as $P = \{P_i\}_{i \in index(P)}, P_i \in IR^3$. IR^3 represents Euclid space, $index(P)$ represents the index set of sample points, usually in $[1, n]$. Here, suppose $n = |P|$ represents the number of points in a point cloud.

Surfels: A sort of rendering and presentation primitive, defined by the local geometric attributes of a small surface that the sample point is on. Typically, sample points are acquired by 3D scanning.

Dense geometric model: A sort of triangle mesh. If more than 30% of the triangles' screen width is less or equal to 1 pixel, we can call it a dense triangle mesh or a dense geometric model. Typically, high dense meshes acquired by 3D scanning belong to this sort.

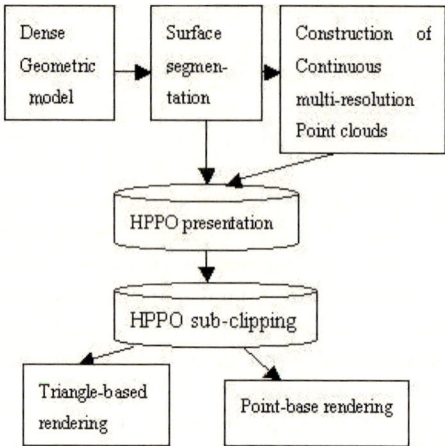

Fig. 1. Procedure of the accelerating hybrid rendering

3.2   Operating Principle of Our Hybrid Rendering Method

The accelerating rendering method of hybrid point and polygon introduced in our paper takes the complex, dense manifold triangle model as its processing object. There are two main steps: pre-processing and real-time rendering as shown in Fig 1. Pre-processing sees to data re-organization of the input geometric model. Concretely, it performs region segmentation on model mesh faces, so the input model is segmented into sub-models. Meanwhile, the importance degree of each vertex is estimated. According to their importance degree, vertices are re-sorted in an ascending order and stored in a linear structure. After this, we get a new model and we call it HPPO (Hybrid Point and Polygon Object) in our paper. Through the pre-processing phase, the number of triangles of the input model remains the same, but the number of vertices increases a little bit because vertices on the verge are stored more than once. Then comes to the real-time rendering. During this phase, we can fully utilize the parallelism nature of GPU (Graphic Process Unit) and its vertex shader. In detail, triangles or point clouds of sub-models are chosen as the rendering primitive according to the distance from the viewpoint to the center of each sub-model, that is, triangles are chosen to render close targets and point clouds to render distant targets. As the distance becomes larger, the number of points needed becomes continuously smaller, and thus we can achieve a continuous multi-resolution point-based rendering.

3.3   Region Segmentation Algorithm for the Geometric Model Mesh

In the pre-processing phase, our paper presents a region segmentation algorithm directed by the frame rate feedback. And it is based on dynamic normal clustering. Its aim is to segment the input model into normal related sub-models, so that in the rendering phase we can accelerate backface clipping and continuous point cloud rendering for each sub-model.

In our algorithm, segmentation depends on the divergence of each triangle's normal vector. Concretely, normals in the same sub-model or group should be as adjacent as possible, while those in different sub-models or groups should be as disjunct as possible. With segmentation completed, the original model is separated into sub-models, and each sub-model has a normal cone. In addition, region connectivity is considered to ensure that sub-models are topologically continuous. Pay attention that the number of triangles produced by segmentation is limited within an appropriate range, neither larger than the maximal value allowed nor smaller than the minimal value controlled. In this way, sub-models are properly controlled in scale. The following steps show how our segmentation algorithm works.

1. Initialize the controlling parameter, and use the neighbor extension method to implement neighbor clustering on the input model.
2. Re-compute the average normal of all clusters. Take the results of step 1 as the initial segmentation. Conduct the second clustering using ISODATA algorithm.
3. Unite the small clusters that may appear in some special cases.
4. Test the current rendering frame rate according to clustering results.
5. Adjust the controlling parameter according to the frame rate tested in step 4. Then go back to step 1 to iterate the controlling parameter until the maximal frame rate is reached. Then end clustering.

Specifying the three parameters by hand is too arbitrary. Besides, the result of clustering is also uncertain. Therefore, step 4 tests the current frame rate and uses it as the feedback to iterate AngleofNormal. As a peak point does exist on the curve of the frame rate and the clustering result, iteration is convergent and thus we can get an optimal value for AngleofNormal. The round-looking test function is adopted in our algorithm to test the frame rate, that is, to suppose that the viewpoint locates on a circle with the target object as its center. As the viewpoint changes its position but remains on the circle, we compute the average frame rate and take it as the rendering frame rate of mesh segmentation.

After region segmentation on the model surface, the input model is separated into a group of sub-models with the maximal rendering frame rate.

3.4   Importance Degree Sorting Based Continuous Multi-resolution Point Cloud Presentation

Taking vertices of each sub-model acquired in 3.3 as a point cloud, this section will talk about a new continuous multi-resolution presentation of point clouds. By this kind of presentation, we can utilize GPU to accelerate rendering. See Fig. 2 to get a clear understanding.

The rectangle above represents a linear vertex data pool. Pay attention to the color of the rectangle: the heavier it becomes, the more important the vertex is. Variable t, which varies from 0 to 1, represents the importance degree of vertices.

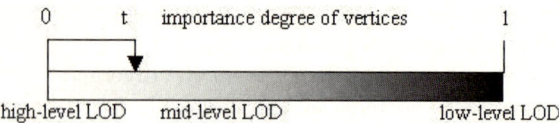

Fig. 2. Control the production of continuous LOD according to importance degree of vertices

Obviously, when t becomes closer to 1, fewer vertices are needed to form a point cloud and the current point cloud is in a low-resolution state; whereas, when t becomes closer to 0, the point cloud is in a high-resolution state. Remarkably, in a low-resolution state, vertices hold a high importance degree and our rendering algorithm can preserve the appearance of models.

How to define the importance degree of each vertex is a key issue. Through comparison with PM [14](Progressive Meshes), we try to give a new definition. For all triangles adjacent to the current vertex, we compute dihedrals between every two triangles that share the same edge, and then average them; for all edges adjacent to the current vertex, we compute their average length. Then we use these two averages to define the importance degree of the current vertex.

Import $\bar{L}$ to represent the average length of all edges. Thus

$$\bar{L} = \frac{1}{n_b} \sum_{i=1}^{n_b} Length(L_i),\tag{1}$$

n_b shows the number of edges that are adjacent to the current vertex, namely the degree of the current vertex. Function $Length()$ computes the length of each edge. $L_1, L_2......L_{n_b}$ represent all adjacent edges.

Import $\bar{\Psi}$ to represent the average dihedral. By mathematic deduction, we have following results: (1) if current vertex is an inner vertex, then

$$\bar{\Psi} = \frac{1}{n_t} \sum_{j-1}^{n_t} Angle(T_j, T_{mod((j+1),t)}),\tag{2}$$

(2) if current vertex is an border vertex and $n_t \neq 1$, then

$$\bar{\Psi} = \frac{1}{(n_t - 1)} \sum_{j=1}^{(n_t-1)} Angle(T_j, T_{(j+1)}),\tag{3}$$

(3) if there is only one adjacent vertex for current vertex and $n_t = 1$, then $\bar{\Psi} = \pi$.

n_t shows the number of adjacent triangles of the current vertex. Function $Angle()$ computes the dihedrals between every two triangles. $T_j, T_{j+1}, j = 1, 2....$ represents triangles which are adjacent to the current vertex and share the same edge. Pay attention that T_{n_t} and T_1 share the same edge. We can see that vertices are divided into three types: the inner vertex, the border vertex and the isolated vertex (with only one triangle adjacent to it). For each type, we can get the average dihedral from the above mathematic expression easily.

Now, using the linear combination of the average dihedral and the average length, we can define the importance degree of a given vertex:

$$Important(p) = \alpha \langle \bar{L} \rangle + (1 - \alpha) \langle \bar{\Psi} \rangle, \tag{4}$$

$\langle \rangle$ denotes normalization of numeric values. Here,

$$\langle \bar{\Psi}_i \rangle = \frac{\bar{\Psi}_i}{max(\bar{\Psi})}, \tag{5}$$

$$\langle \bar{L}_i \rangle = \frac{\bar{L}_i}{max(\bar{L})}, \tag{6}$$

i varies from 1 to the number of vertices. Function $max()$ computes the maximal average dihedral or average length. By normalization, we ensure $|\bar{\Psi}| \leq 1$, $|\bar{L}| \leq 1$.

α is the coefficient of linear combination. By appointing different values of α, we can control the contribution of the two parameters $\bar{L}$ and $\bar{\Psi}$ to the importance degree of the current vertex.

In conclusion, our presentation of the importance degree of vertices has several advantages: (1) Using the average dihedral and the average length together to define the importance degree of vertices can avoid many problems that may appear in quadric error measuring (QEM). And it also can improve the presentation of high curvature positions. (2) Compared with quadric error measuring (QEM), importance degree computing in our algorithm requires shorter time and less space. (3) By appointing different α, we can adjust the contribution of $\bar{L}$ and $\bar{\Psi}$ to the importance degree of the target vertex.

3.5   Real-Time Rendering of HPPO

The real-time rendering phase implements normal cone based backface clipping of sub-models first, and then it carries out a continuous multi-resolution rendering using point clouds. In this rendering, view-dependent LOD selection is also performed.

Combine viewpoint parameters and point clouds that are stored as a linear structure in section 3.4. When given the viewpoint, we can compute levels of details of each sub-model in HPPO. Main data structures in LOD selecting algorithm include the object-level attribute definition of HPPO and the sub-model-level attribute definition of HPPO. Four parameters related to LOD selection are listed below:

Object-level parameter defined in LOD selection consist of the following three: (1)$m\_fNearClip$, represents the near control point distance of point clouds; (2)$m\_fFarClip$, represents the distant control point distance of point clouds; (3)$m\_fPercent$, the percentage of points used for point clouds. Sub-model-level parameter defined is "center",which is the center coordinate of sub-models.

LOD selecting algorithm for HPPO is described below in detail.

Step 1: for each sub-model, compute the distance from its center to the current viewpoint.

Step2: If $distance < m\_fNearClip$, select triangles to render the current sub-model. And it represents as the highest level of details. If $m\_fNearClip \leq distance \leq m\_fFarClip$, select the point-based rendering method to render the current sub-model. Levels of details of the sub-model linearly change with distance. At this point, the sub-model represents as a serial of mid-level continuous LOD. The percentage of surfels involved in rendering is computed as below:

$$percent = \frac{(1 - m\_fPercent)(m\_fFarClip - distance)}{(m\_fFarClip - m\_fNearClip)} + m\_fPercent, \quad (7)$$

If $distance > m\_fFarClip$, we also choose point-based rendering. However, let $percent = m\_fPercent$. The number of surfels involved in rendering no longer decreases so as to preserve visual attributes of HPPO. And at this time, the sub-model represents as the lowest level of details.

Step3: For each sub-model of HPPO, implement LOD selecting rendering in turn.

As a sort of GROUP node, HPPO can be easily added to synthetic scenes. The instance of HPPO, which also can be viewed as a GROUP node, provides a container for the appointed object to display and update. So an object in a synthetic scene like Buddha can be represented in many nodes, namely, it can be instantiated as objects in many scenes. HPPO nodes contain specific three-dimensional coordinate information. Besides, they define implicative and subordinate relationships between objects. HPPO in our algorithm doesn't contain other rendering information, and the rendering is completed by the transformation matrix and the objects subordinate to low layer nodes. Notice that the matrix is acted on the current HPPO node.

The object layer of the HPPO node provides the detailed rendering method, including:

(1)DWORD IPointCloudObject::OnCreate ObjectInit * pParams),this function initializes the point cloud object and perform the matrix transformation (including scaling, rotation, translation and etc.) with parameters provided by the controlling node.

(2)DWORD IPointCloudObject: Release (void),this function echoes with the function "OnCreate" defined abovewhich releases all applications and memory-then deletes the current point cloud object.

(3)void IPointCloudObject::Update(void)

(4)void IPointCloudObject::Render(DWORD dwRenderFlags)

These two functions are the key procedure in the emulation loop. "Update" is a must in every loop but "Render" is not, for the display may need to be optimized.

(5)PROCESSRESULT   IPointCloudObject::OnInputMessage   (DWORD dwMSG, WPARAM wParam, LPARAM lParam), this function is responsible for message processing and parameter updating. It enables the current object to react to specific controls and thus achieve interactive effects in time.

4   Experiments and Results

Our hybrid of point and polygon algorithm is implemented and verified by using C++ and DirectX 9.0 SDK, on an ordinary PC with the PIV3.0G CPU, the 256M memory, and the Nvidia6200 128M display card. Tested models come from the standard model base of Stanford University, including Happy, Dragon, Bunny and Armadillo. Related data are described in Table 1.

Table 1. Tested model data

model name	number of triangles	number of vertices	storage
Happy	1087474	553898	41621K
Dragon	871306	447600	33039K
Bunny	69451	34834	2963K
Armadillo	345944	174840	6757K

4.1   Verification of Region Segmentation for the Geometric Model Mesh

Fig. 3 shows the relational curve of the normal threshold parameter and the rendering frame rate. It reflects two important facts. First, region segmentation on the model mesh surface is significant for efficiency. Without segmentation, the rendering frame rate of Happy is 17 fps or so. However, using our rendering algorithm with AngleofNumber set to 18 (4518 clusters), the frame rate increases to 49.44 fps, nearly triples the former. Second, it is not always the case that more sub-models lead to higher rendering efficiency. On the contrary, when the number of sub-models comes to a point that the cost of employing rendering API surpasses the processing ability of the hardware, the rendering efficiency will be greatly damaged. From Fig.3 we can also see that the curve is single-peaked. so our segmentation algorithm can be fast converged.

4.2   Verification of Importance Degree Definition

Given different α , we verify the contribution of $\bar{L}$ and $\bar{\Psi}$ (defined in section 3.4) in the importance degree formula (4). When $\alpha = 1$, the importance degree only depends on $\bar{L}$. When $\alpha = 0$, the importance degree only depends on $\bar{\Psi}$. Fig 4. shows the rendered image when $\alpha = 1$ and $\alpha = 0$ respectively. In order to observe the distributing effect of point clouds, our verification chooses Bunny rendering object, for its point cloud density is comparatively low. And we make some special limitations to LOD controlling parameters and the point size. Consequently, when viewpoint is very close to the object, we use only 20 percent of points to render Bunny.

Pay attention to the top edge of Bunny's right ear. Obviously, we can see that using the same percentage of points, $\bar{\Psi}$ gives better representation for edge characteristics and parts with big changes in curvature. Through repeated verifications, we find that when $\alpha = 0.2$, we get a better visual effect.

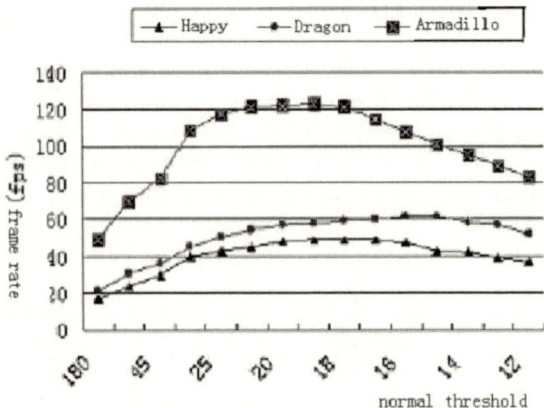

Fig. 3. Relationship between the normal threshold and the rendering frame rate

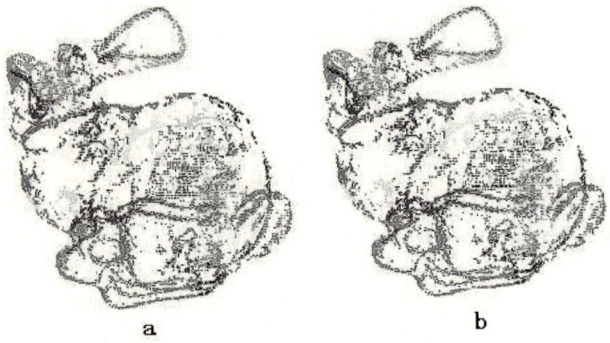

a   b

Fig. 4. (a) $\alpha = 1$, vertex distribution of 20% points rendered (b) $\alpha = 0$, vertex distribution of 20% points rendered

4.3 Rendering Effect of HPPO

Fig.5 (a)-(d) shows the continuous LOD rendering effect of Happy, which consists of 1080,000 triangles. In our experiment, Happy is put into a synthetic scene and viewed from different positions, so the rendering is at different levels of details. Fig.5(d) shows the real-time rendering effect that 10 Happy are added to a synthetic scene and located in the view field. On a PC with the PIV3.0G CPUthe 256M memory and the Nvidia7800 display cardour real-time rendering frame rate is 20 fps. In all, from Fig.5 we can see that when HPPO gets farther, fewer points are needed for rendering. The image quality is acceptable and rendering speed is apparently increased.

Fig. 5. (a)Happy is rendered using triangles and the current frame rate is 29.94 fps (b) Happy is rendered using 50.86% of points and the frame rate is 43.83 fps (c)Happy is rendered with 20% of points and the frame rate is 62.88 fps (d)Rendering of multi-HPPO with tens of millions of triangles and the frame rate is 21.3 fps

5   Conclusion

In order to render large-scale, dense geometric models effectively, this paper introduces a hybrid point and polygon rendering method that integrates the advantages of both point-based rendering and polygon-based rendering. Region segmentation on the model surface and vertex data linearization are performed at the pre-processing phase. And the real-time rendering is implemented on GPU to improve efficiency. For example, when rendering a model consisted of 30,0000 point clouds on a PC with PIV2.4G CPU, 1GRAM, NV5900 graphics card, sequential point tree method put forward by Miguelsainz [15] in 2004 , achievces a frame rate of about 30 fps. At the same time , when rendering a model consisted of 50,0000 point clouds on a PC with PIV3.0G CPU, 256MRAM, NV6200 graphics card, our HPPO method achieves a frame rate of 51.6 fps. So our rendering speed nearly doubles that of the sequential point tree. There are two reasons: firstly, data organization of HPPO is more effective; secondly, the implementation of HPPO method on GPU only uses Vertex Shader. In all, HPPO uses both points and triangles as rendering primitives, with the point-based rendering used to render middle or distant objects. In this way, there's no need to use Pixel Shader to fill holes that may appear in pure point-based rendering. Thus, our algorithm gets good efficiency.

Even though the point-based rendering in our algorithm has some damages in image quality, it can satisfy general simulation applications. In future work, we will explore ways to improve image quality and further enhance realistic features.

References

1. Scopigno R. Puppo E.: Simplification LOD and Multiresolution - Principles and Applications. In Eurographics'97 Tutorial Notes PS97 TN4, (1997)31-42
2. Levoy M. and Hanrahan P.:Light Field Rendering. In Computer Graphics, Proceedings of SIGGRAPH 1996,(1996)31-42
3. Gobbetti Enrico, Fabio Marton.Far Voxels: A Multiresolution Framework for Interactive Rendering of Huge Complex 3D Models on Commodity Graphics Platforms ACM Trans. Graph. 2005,24(3): 878-885
4. Chen B.and Nguyen M.X. POP: A Hybrid Point and Polygon Rendering System for Large Data. In Proceedings of IEEE Visualization, (2001)45-52
5. Cohen J.D., Aliaga D.G., Zhang W.: Hybrid Simplification: Combining Multiresolution Polygon and Point Rendering. Proceedings of IEEE Visualization 2001.(2001)37-44
6. Oliveira M., Bishop G.: Image-Based Objects. Proceedings of 1999 ACM Symposium on Interactive 3D Graphics. Atlanta, Ga, April 6-28, (1999)191-198
7. Zhirkov A.: Binary Volumetric Octree Representation for Image Based Rendering. Proc.of GRAPHICON'01,(2001)
8. Rusinkiewicz S. and Levoy M. Qsplat: A Multiresolution Point Rendering System for Large Meshes. In Computer Graphics, Proceedings of SIGGRAPH 2000,(2000)343-352
9. Wimmer Michael, Wonka Peter, Sillion Francois X.: Point-Based Impostors for Real-Time Visualization. Proceedings of the 12th Eurographics Workshop on Rendering Techniques. (2001)163-176
10. Coconu L., Hege H.C.: Hardware-Oriented Point-Based Rendering of Complex Scenes. In Proceedings Eurographics Workshop on Rendering. (2002) 43-52
11. Guthe M., Borodin P., et al.: Real-Time Appearance Preserving Out-of-Core Rendering with Shadows. In Proceedings of Eurographics Symposium on Rendering (2004)69-79
12. Junfeng Ji, Sheng Li, Xuehui Liu, Enhua Wu.: Parameter Space Based Multiresolution Structure for Hybrid Rendering Software Jurnal.(2004) 15(10): 1515-1521
13. Yanci ZhangEnhua Wu.: Research On Image Based Real-time Wandering .Doctor paper of Institute of Software, The Chinese Academy of Sciences,2003.6
14. Hoppe H.: Progressive Meshes.Proc.SIGGRAPH 1996,Perth,Australia.(1996)99-108
15. Sainz M., Pajarola R. and Lario R.: Points Reloaded: Point-Based Rendering Revisited. In Proceedings of the EG Symposium on Point-Based Graphics, pp. (2004)121-128

User Mediated Hypermedia Presentation Generation on the Semantic Web Framework

Jayan C Kurian, Payam M. Barnaghi, and Michael Ian Hartley

School of Computer Science and Information Technology, University of Nottingham
(Malaysia Campus), Jalan Broga, 43500 Semenyih,
Selangor Darul Ehsan, Malaysia
{cyx5jkc, payam.barnaghi, michael.hartley}@nottingham.edu.my

Abstract. The art of authoring digital multimedia involves collecting and organizing different sorts of media items and transforming them into a coherent presentation. Existing authoring tools for multimedia presentations provide functional support for the authoring process that requires domain knowledge or presentation skills. The authoring process can be enhanced if the authors are supported with decision making, material collection, selection, and presentation composition in generating web presentations. We apply the semantic web technology to generate hypermedia presentations based on media resources retrieved from the web. A discourse model represents the discussion of a subject with a theme supported by a discourse structure that represents the arrangement of contents in a discourse. In this paper we define a discourse model (i.e. Neural Network Architecture) that specifies the knowledge of composing various discourse entities (e.g. Feed-Forward Neural Networks) which enables the building of discourse structures for various themes (e.g. Lecture Notes).

Keywords: Multimedia Applications, Hypermedia Presentation Generation, Semantic Web.

1 Introduction

Multimedia authoring is the process of creating multimedia applications. The main phases in the authoring process are the data selection phase (i.e. searching the binary media objects), the presentation structuring phase (i.e. organizing the collected data in sequence), and the presentation generation phase (i.e. constructing the presentation based on the organized data).

For existing authoring systems, authors must have knowledge about what contents they want to author and how they want to author these contents. Three general classes of support systems exists: systems that support strict manual presentation authoring (e.g. Microsoft PowerPoint) [1], systems that support mainly automatic presentation generation with limited user influence (e.g. Topia) [2], and semi-automatic authoring environments (e.g. SampLe) [3] that provide semantic-based support during at least one of the authoring phases. With respect to content collection and meaningful integration of content into a discourse structure the manually crafted authoring tools

Z. Pan et al. (Eds.): ICAT 2006, LNCS 4282, pp. 901–907, 2006.

do not offer any support. In automatic authoring approach, the author involvement is only at the beginning of the authoring process. The approach towards semi-automatic authoring will support the different types of authors in getting through the presentation generation process starting from the initial exploration of the domain to the final presentation.

The semantic web, which is an extension to the current web, enables the access and retrieval of machine-processable web contents and can support information interoperability at various phases in an authoring process. In a semantic environment, Resource Description Framework (RDF) [4] models the knowledge representation structure. Relations between conceptual structures are explicitly defined by an ontology that facilitates knowledge sharing and reuse in a discourse domain. To make the content of the multimedia objects accessible, a data model with rich metadata structure that can annotate the diversity of the media, the subject matter, and the context are required. In this paper we investigate semantic based semi-automatic authoring methods to support the authors during the presentation generation process.

The remainder of this ongoing research paper is structured as follows. The next section describes the related work. Section 3 describes the knowledge representation and the data model. Section 4 describes the system architecture and section 5 concludes the paper.

2   Related Work

In this section we investigate and describe a number of authoring systems that use semantic web technology as means for generating presentation contents.

Topia [2] uses RDF multimedia repository of the Rijksmuseum collection [5] and creates hypermedia presentations as a result of a query. In Topia, clustering is done on pre-selected concepts in the domain semantics and the users can indicate their preferences of the topic using a web interface. This supports the users with useful information while exploring a repository. Topia uses a domain specific clustering mechanism for generating the presentations.

The SemInf [6] system semi-automatically generates multimedia presentations by combining semantic inferencing with multimedia presentation tools. The system applies an iterative sequence of searches across the Dublin Core (DC) [7] metadata to infer semantic relationships between mixed media objects which are retrieved from a repository. These semantic relationships are mapped to spatial and temporal relationships between the objects using predefined mapping rules and are expressed within SMIL [8] format to generate multimedia presentations.

The Artequakt [9] project applies semantic associations between different entities which are representing an artist's personal and professional life to generate biographies. The domain ontology is used to provide a common understanding on concepts in the discourse domain. The web resources are associated to these ontology concepts. The inferring process refers to these concepts and attempts to realize implicit relationships between these resources. Interpreting the relationships enables the system to create a coherent presentation structure that demonstrates an artist's biography using objects retrieved from heterogeneous resources.

The domain ontology and the annotated multimedia repository of the Rijksmuseum are used by DISC [10] to create multimedia presentations. The aim of the system is to build a multimedia presentation about a certain topic by traversing a semantic graph. A semantic graph consists of domain ontology of classes, instances and relations between them together with the media material related to the instances. The semantic graph is transformed into structured progression and this data structure supported by the domain, discourse, and design knowledge is used for generating the multimedia presentation.

A hypermedia presentation generation system in a multi-facet environment is described in SampLe [3]. The system employs semantic web technologies and supports authors during a hypermedia presentation generation process. The process is divided in to four phases: topic identification, discourse structure building, media material collection, and production of the final-form presentation. SampLe supports authors during every phase of the process independent of the particular workflow using ontology-based and context oriented information as well as semantic interrelationships between different types of meta-data.

3   Knowledge Representation and Data Model

For knowledge representation, we employ an ontology that defines a common vocabulary for machine-interpretable definitions of common concepts in the domain and relations among them. The ontology gives information related to media objects (e.g. media type), content of the image (e.g. subject) and semantic relationship between media objects (e.g. relation identity). Protégé [11], an ontology editor tool is used to develop the knowledge-base for the domain ontology. This is represented in RDF(S) [12]. A simplified version of the domain ontology for a Neural Network instance domain is illustrated in Fig. 1.

A data model represents the basic guidelines for annotating the media items for data selection. The data model adopted from [13] has the components content schema, semantic schema, and media schema that describes the multimedia objects. The content schema is represented by Dublin Core attributes (e.g. title, identifier), the semantic schema is represented by Learning Objective Metadata (LOM) [14] attributes (e.g. language, level), and the media schema is represented by MPEG-7 [15] attributes (e.g. media type, media URI).

The ontology and the data model make the knowledge representation structure independent from the data representation structure. MPEG-7 Multimedia Description Schemes can effectively describe the multimedia entities. MPEG-7 Visual Description Tools describes the visual features (e.g. color, motion). MPEG-7 Audio provides the standard for describing the audio contents (e.g. sound recognition). MPEG-7 standard is chosen since Dublin Core is not specifically designed for representing spatial and temporal aspects of multimedia data. The above data model has been adopted since the schema components can effectively represent the media objects used in generating the presentation.

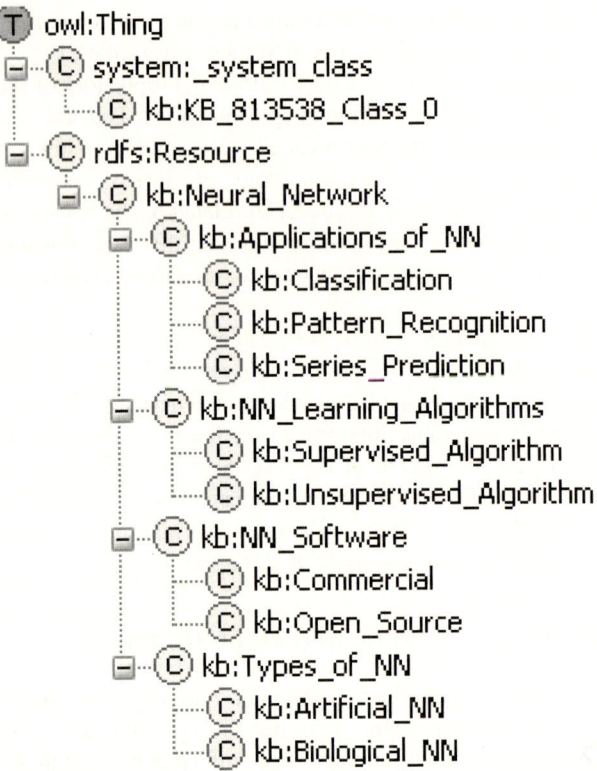

Fig. 1. A simplified version of Neural Network domain ontology

4   The System Architecture

In the proposed system the domain ontology is represented in RDF/XML and the media objects are stored in a relational database or are coming from heterogeneous resources. The Jena [16] application API will be used to query the RDF/XML knowledge-base. Using the author interaction interface the author can browse the domain ontology and select a particular concept.

The methodology involves Selection, Assembling, Transforming and Presenting. In the selection phase, the author selects the theme of the presentation (e.g. Lecture Notes). Next the title (e.g. Neural Network Architecture) of the presentation is selected and the contents are assembled in the presentation. In the media addition phase, the relevant media items are added to the presentation. The presentation style (e.g. style sheets) is selected in the next phase. In the transformation phase of this ongoing research, the hypermedia presentation will be generated in the form of SMIL. The system architecture is illustrated in Fig. 2.

The user interface of the proposed system shows the summarized information of all the selections the author has made (author activities) in creating the presentation.

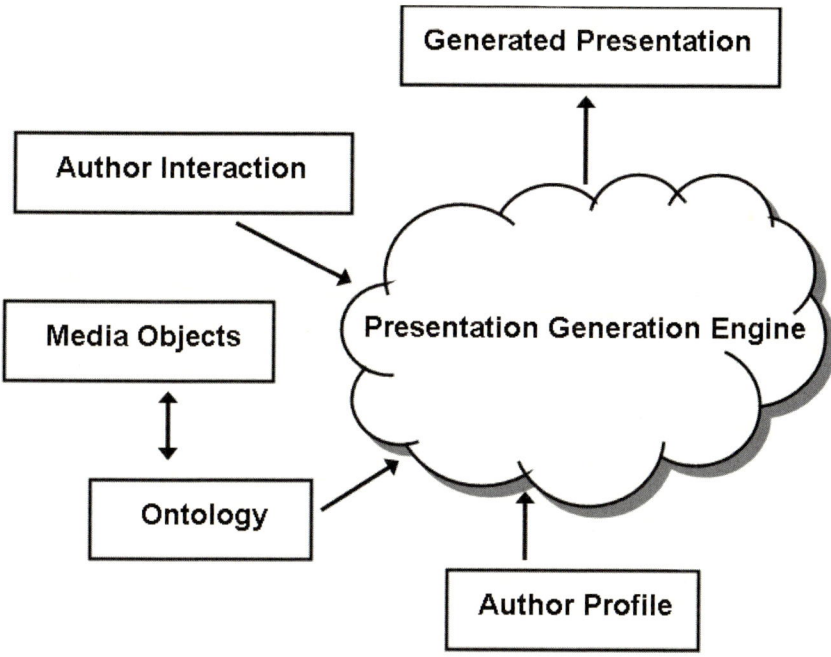

Fig. 2. Logical diagram of the system architecture

This includes the duration or size of the presentation as well as which phase the user is currently active and with which task within that phase. The presentation will be generated in the form of a time-based mode (slide-show) or static modes (interactive and thumbnail views) based on the user choice.

Successful hypermedia presentations will be stored in the system repository based on the concept searched so that these built-in presentations can be suggested when a new user browses for a related concept. These suggestions can be done by using the a priori algorithm [17] for generating association rules. On a generated presentation, the user can click on a particular media object of his/her interest to trigger a new presentation of related concepts. This process is called the tangent [2] and will be done by dynamically grouping media objects using agglomerative clustering algorithm [18]. The algorithm provides groups depending on the level in the hierarchy and provides structures for simple interactive selection and rapid non-linear expansion of a selection. In this way, new presentations, focusing on a related concept can be generated dynamically.

5   Conclusion

This paper describes an ongoing research to develop a semi-automatic interaction of author within the different stages of hypermedia presentation generation. A context aware guidance for authors is provided in the authoring process by defining a discourse model that specifies the knowledge of composing various discourse entities which enables the building of discourse structures for various themes. The domain ontology for Neural Network is designed for representing the domain concepts and relations. Dublin Core, MPEG – 7 and IEEE LOM are used for representing the meta-data structure in a data model. Protégé is used to develop the knowledge base and shared web resources are described using RDF. Jena, a Java API is used to query the RDF/XML knowledge-base.

Future work will concentrate on the automatic classification of new annotated media items to different user levels (e.g. novice, beginner, and expert) based on the Bayesian model [19] and how to make inferences for calculating the system's determination on a user's knowledge for generating customized presentations.

References

1. Microsoft PowerPoint, the Microsoft Office presentation program, available at: <http:// office.microsoft.com>
2. Rutledge, L., Alberink, M., Brussee, R., Pokraev, S., Van Dieten, W., Veenstra, M.: Finding the Story —Broader Applicability of Semantics and Discourse for Hypermedia Generation, In Proceedings of the 14th ACM Conference on Hypertext and Hypermedia, (2003) 67–76
3. Falkovych, K., Bocconi, S.: Creating a Semantic-based Discourse Model for Hypermedia Presentations: (Un)discovered Problems, In Workshop on Narrative, Musical, Cinematic and Gaming Hyperstructure, 2005
4. The Resource Description Framework (RDF), available at: <http://www.w3.org/RDF>
5. Rijksmuseum Amsterdam, a museum of Dutch art and history, available at: <http:// www. rijksmuseum.nl>
6. Little, S., Geurts, J., Hunter, J.: Dynamic Generation of Intelligent Multimedia Presentations through Semantic Inferencing, In 6th European Conference on Research and Advanced Technology for Digital Libraries, (2002) 158–189
7. Dublin Core Metadata Element Set Version1.1 (DC), Reference Description, Dublin Core Metadata Initiative (1999), available at: <http://dublincore.org/documents/ 1999/07/02/dces>
8. Synchronized Multimedia Integration Language (SMIL), available at: <http://www.w3. org /TR/REC-smil>
9. Kim, S., Alani, H., Hall, W., Lewis, P.H., Millard, D.E., Shadbolt, N., Weal, M.J.: Artequakt: Generating Tailored Biographies with Automatically Annotated Fragments from the Web, Workshop on Semantic Authoring, Annotation & Knowledge Markup, 15 European Conf. on Artificial Intelligence (ECAI), (2002) 1-6
10. Geurts, J., Bocconi, S., van Ossenbruggen, J., Hardman, L.: Towards Ontology-driven Discourse: From Semantic Graphs to Multimedia Presentations, In Second International Semantic Web Conference, (2003) 597–612
11. Protégé, an ontology editor and knowledge-base framework, available at: <http://protege. stanford.edu>
12. Resource Description Framework (RDF) Schema, available at: <http://www.w3.org/ TR/ rdf-schema>
13. Barnaghi, P.M., Kareem, S.A.: Ontology-Based Multimedia Presentation Generation, IEEE TENCON Conference, (2005)

14. Learning Object Mctadata (LOM), available at: <http://ltsc.ieee.org/wg12/20020612-Final- LOM-Draft.html>
15. Manjunath, B.S., Salembier, P., Sikora, T.: Introduction to MPEG-7: Multimedia Content Description Interface. John Wiley (2002)
16. Jena, a semantic web framework for Java, available at: <http://jena.sourceforge.net>
17. Larose, T.D.: Discovering Knowledge in Data: An Introduction to Data Mining. Wiley-Interscience (2004)
18. Chiu, P., Wilcox, L.: A Dynamic Grouping Technique for Ink and Audio Notes, In the Proc. ACM UIST (1998) 195-202
19. Han, J., Kamber, M.: Data Mining: Concepts and Techniques. 1st edn. Morgan Kaufmann (2000)

Progressive Transmission of Vector Map Data Based on Polygonal Chain Simplification

Haisheng Zhan and Guangxin Li

School of Network Education, Xidian University, Xi'an 710071, China
{Zhan_haisheng, Li_guangxin}@vip.163.com

Abstract. In distributed Geographic Information Systems (GIS) and Web-GIS, remote access to geospatial database is recognized as a time-consuming task. Progressive transmission, a technology dealing with massive amounts of data and slow communication links, can be used to solve this kind of problem because it allows users to start work with a partially delivered dataset. In this paper, we particularly discussed this problem and propose a method, by which we can progressively transmit the sequence of levels of detail of map representation while preserving topological consistency between different levels. We employ the algorithm of minimum number of safe sets to simplify the polyline. In addition, we propose a structure based on Simplicial Multi-Complex and Reactive-tree to avoid data redundancy as well as reduce the space complexity of geospatial database. We show that the volume of coarsest level data can generally be reduced to one tenth of that of the finest level.

Keywords: progressive transmission, vector map, polyline simplification, Simplicial Multi-Complex, geospatial database.

1 Introduction

Following communication technology and Internet development, distributed GIS and Web-GIS arise. In these systems, large geospatial datasets reside in some computers called server. Users can make remote access to these datasets with a computer called client through communication links. It also generates new problems such as the availability of vast amounts of data stored in huge unstructured that need to be downloaded. Therefore, users need better tools to search and download the datasets they required, be it through improved spatial metadata or spatial summaries.

Metadata in the form of textual summaries is only used to convey the idea of what is contained in the database but to manipulate the datasets. For example, during remote access, overview of the fully detailed dataset may be used to perform some preliminary manipulations or analysis. For this purpose, spatial summaries can be generated by means of subsetting techniques in which a meaningful sample of the data is provided instead of the whole dataset in [1].

Progressive transmission of raster images over the WWW has been successfully applied to provide the user with temporary versions of the data before downloading a complete image. While implementations have focused on progressive transmission of

Z. Pan et al. (Eds.): ICAT 2006, LNCS 4282, pp. 908–917, 2006.

raster data through the Web, the transmission of vector data, with the exception of the particular case of data in form of triangular meshes, is generally done by means of a one-step long process. The user attempting to download a vector file needs to wait for the complete version without having the possibility to start working with a coarser version of the data in a smaller file in [2], [3].

2   Background and Requirement of Progressive Transmission

In this section, some essential preliminaries, include vector map representation, polygonal chain simplification, and SMC, are declared first.

2.1   Polygonal Chain Simplification

Let S be a subdivision that models a map. A subdivision is a geometric structure that represents an embedded planar graph. We adopt the terminology standard in computational geometry and say that the subdivision S consists of vertices, edges and faces. The degree of a vertex is the number of edges incident to it. A vertex of degree one is a leaf, a vertex of degree two is an interior vertex, and a vertex of degree at least three is a junction. Generally the number of leafs and junctions is small compared to the number of interior vertices. Any sequence of vertices and edges starting and ending at a leaf or junction, and with only interior vertices in between, is called a polygonal chain, or simply a chain. For convenience we also consider a cycle of interior vertices (which occur for islands) as a chain, where we choose one of the vertices as the junction. It is the start and the end vertex of the chain.

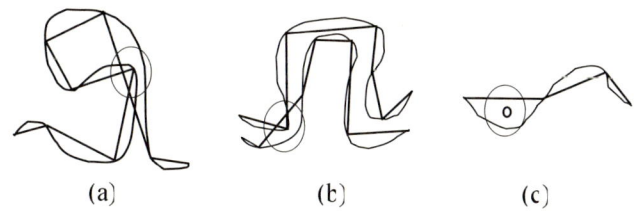

(a)   (b)   (c)

Fig. 1. Incompatible topological relationships accruing in polygonal chain simplification

Let P be a set of points that model special positions inside the regions of the map. Subdivision simplification can now be performed as follows. Keep the positions of all leaf and junctions fixed, and also the positions of the points in P. Replace every chain between a start and end vertex by a new chain with the same start and end vertex but with fewer interior vertices. For a polygonal chain $C=\{v_1, v_2, \ldots, v_m\}$ of size $size(C)=m$, we require of its simplification $C' = \{v_1= v_{j1}, v_{j2}, \ldots, v_{jm} = v_m \}$, which is a chain whose vertices are a subsequence of the vertices of C:

(1)   No point on the chain C has distance more than a specified error tolerance to its simplification C'.

(2)   The simplification C' is a chain with no self-intersections. See Fig.1(a).

(3) The simplification *C'* may not intersect other chains of the subdivision. See Fig.1(b).
(4) Each point of *P* lies to the same side of *C'* as of *C*. See Fig.1(c).

In the simplification *C'*, a line segment $v_{jk}v_{jk+1}$ is a shortcut for the subchain $\{v_i, v_{i+1}, \ldots, v_j\}$ ($i = j_k, j = j_k+1$) in chain C, The error of a shortcut $v_{jk}v_{jk+1}$ is the maximum distance from $v_{jk}v_{jk+1}$ to a point v_k, where $i \le k \le j$. A shortcut is allowed if and only if the error it induces is at most some prespecified positive real value ε. We wish to replace *C* by a chain consisting of allowed shortcuts. This chain should have as few shortcuts as possible. In this paper we don't consider simplifications that use vertices other than those of the input chain.

2.2 Simplicial Multi-complex

The concept of simplicial complex derives from algebraic topology. An abstract simplicial complex *K* consists of a set of vertices $\{1, \ldots, m\}$ together with a set of non-empty subsets of the vertices, called the simplices of *K*, such that any set consisting of exactly one vertex is a simplex in *K*, and every non-empty subset of a simplex in *K* is also a simplex in *K*. In geometry, an abstract simplicial complex *K* is a combinational structure specifying the adjacency of vertices, edges, triangles, and tetrahedron.

Definition 1. A *k*-dimensional cell (or *k*-cell, for brevity) in IE^d is a subset of IE^d homeomorphism to a closed *k*-dimensional ball, $k \le d$. Let Γ be a connected finite set of *n*-cells of heterogeneous dimension embedded in the Euclidean space IE^d, where n is the maximum of the dimensions of the cells of Γ, and the boundary of each cell in Γ is a collection of cells of lower dimensions, called facets, belonging to Γ. Then, Γ is an *n*-dimensional mesh if and only if it satisfies the following properties:

(1) The interiors of any pair of *n*-dimensional cells of Γ are disjoint;
(2) Any *k*-dimensional cell of Γ, with $k < n$, bounds at least one *n*-dimensional cell of Γ.   □

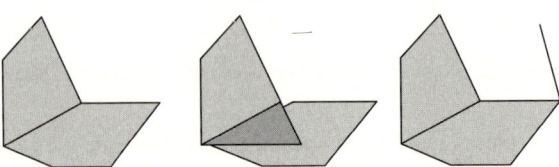

Fig. 2. A two-dimensional mesh (left) and two sets of cells that are not meshes: (central) violates condition 1 and (right) violates condition 2 in the definition of a mesh

Fig.2 shows an example of a two-dimensional mesh, and two connected sets of cells in IE^2 that are not meshes in [4].

Definition 2. A simplicial multi-complex (or *k*-simplex, for brevity) in IE^d is the locus of the points in IE^d that can be expressed as the convex combination of *k*+1 affinely independent points.   □

Definition 3. A mesh is called conforming if and only if, for each pair of n-dimensional cells Y_1, Y_2, the intersection of the boundaries of Y_1 and Y_2 is either empty, or it consists of a k-facet belonging to the boundary of both Y_1 and Y_2, for some $k < n$.

Definition 4. A modification is the basic operation for changing a mesh locally. For simplicity, we define modifications in the case of meshes without boundary. We define an n-dimensional modification as a pair of n-dimensional meshes $M = (\Gamma_1, \Gamma_2)$, such that the boundaries of Γ_1 and Γ_2 are coincident. The intuitive idea is that modification M can be applied to a mesh Γ, such that $\Gamma_1 \subseteq \Gamma$, and its application modifies Γ by replacing Γ_1 with Γ_2. The condition on the boundaries ensures that Γ_2 fits the hole left in Γ by the removal of Γ_1.

Definition 5. A modification $M = (\Gamma_1, \Gamma_2)$ is conforming if meshes Γ_1 and Γ_2 are conforming meshes, and Γ_1 and Γ_2 have the same combinatorial boundary. Examples of a conforming and of a non-conforming modification are shown in Fig. 3. The result of applying a conforming modification to a conforming mesh (if it gives a mesh) is a conforming mesh.

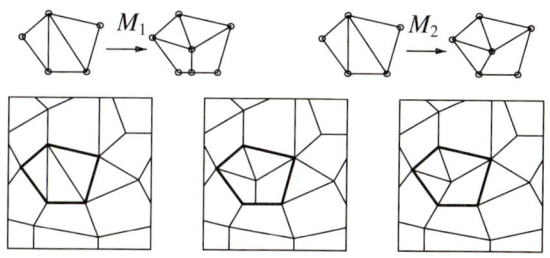

Fig. 3. Modification M_1 is not conforming, while M_2 is conforming. (left) shows a mesh Γ, (central) the results of applying M_1 , and (right) the results of applying M_2.

Definition 6. A modification $M = (\Gamma_1, \Gamma_2)$ is said to be non-redundant if no n-cell belongs to both Γ_1 and Γ_2, i.e., M does not delete and re-create the same cell. From now on, we will implicitly assume that all modifications we consider are non-redundant.

A modification can be reversed. The inverse of a modification $M = (\Gamma_1, \Gamma_2)$ is $M\text{-}1 = (\Gamma_2, \Gamma_1)$. We say that a modification $M = (\Gamma_1, \Gamma_2)$ is a refinement modification if $\#\Gamma_2 > \#\Gamma_1$. M is a coarsening modification if $\#\Gamma_2 < \#\Gamma_1$. M is a neutral modification if $\#\Gamma_2 = \#\Gamma_1$. In what follows, we will always assume non-neutral modification, and we will use the alternative notation M^- and M^+ to denote the two meshes forming a modification M, according to the intuition that M^- has fewer n-cells than M^+.

As described in subsection 2.2, a polygonal chain modeling the boundaries of subdivisions is the most important geometric entity in planar map. A chain is a collection of line segments which are 1-simplex while a line segment is bounded by

0-simplex (vertex). So a planar map can be treated as a very big collection of 1-simplexes and 0-simplexes. To manipulate the collection and modification applied to it, we design a correspondent data structure and algorithms in Section 5.

3 Related Work

We briefly survey previous work in the domain of progressive transmission of vector map as well as of map simplification and multi-display of geometric objects related to it. A straightforward way to transferring vector map over WWW progressively is storing multiple map representation from coarse level to fine level in the server. Because some entities are preserved throughout the levels they should be stored once in the sequence instead of redundantly encoding them at cach level. Bertolotto and Egenhofer [2], [4] proposed a strategy for progressive vector transmission in which a model generating multiple map representation [5], [6] is used for progressive transmission. The model is built by applying a set of generalization operators that perform topological changes on vector maps. In their method polyline simplification is not employed because it is time-consuming and may cause topological error as we describe later. But polyline simplification can reduce the number of vertices of map object greatly while preserving visual similarity (see Fig. 4). We introduce polygonal chain simplification to reduce the volume of the geospatial database in our method. To encoding levels of detail efficiently, Reactive-tree [7] and SMC [8] based data structure are both used.

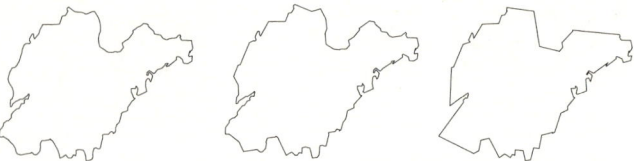

Fig. 4. Polylines with 378 vertices (left), 186 vertices (central) and with 95 vertices (right)

There are many algorithms for polyline simplification in the literature of GIS, Computer Vision, and Computational Geometry. The practical literature tends toward heuristic that run in linear or near linear time, while the Computational Geometry literature tends toward optimal simplification under various criteria (e.g. minimum error for a given number of segments, or minimum number of segments for a given error) using algorithms that run in quadratic to cubic time.

Most algorithms consider each linear feature in isolation, and run risk of introducing intersections and topological changes in data. The cartographer's favorite algorithm, reported in Douglas and Peucker [9], can even introduce self-intersections within a single line.

There has been some work in computational geometry on algorithms that guarantee to preserve map topology. De Berg et al. [10] give a simplification method that simplifies a polyline without passing over specified points in near quadratic time. Recent work [11] has shown that the map simplification is NP-hard. Moreover, Estkowski [12] has also shown that it is hard to obtain a solution to this problem that approximates the optimal answer to within a polynomial factor. Mustafa et al. [13] propose a Voronoi diagram based algorithm with the goals of avoiding intersections. However, none of the methods for chain simplification guarantees that the output chain will not intersect itself. A. Mantler et al. [14] also propose a Voronoi diagram based algorithm by which user can identify safe sets in a linear time. A safe set is an ordered set of consecutive points defining a fragment of a single polyline that is monotone in some direction and whose convex hull contains no other points. A complex polyline can be divided into a collection of safe sets in which each safe set can be simplified using either a single line or a standard polyline simplification algorithm such as [9], without introducing intersections or topological changes in the collection of safe sets. We generalize Mantler's algorithm to calculate the minimum number of safe sets to obtain base polyline as described in the next section.

4 Map Representations for Progressive Transmission

Popovic and Hoppe [15] first detailed the progressive transmission of triangulated model represented with simplicial complex. Floriani and Magillo [8] generalize this method to multiresolution representation of general vector data such as tetrahedron. In this paper, we apply the concept of simplicial complex to representation of vector map datasets, and show that it is appropriative for progressive transmission of this type of datasets.

In simplification of a polygonal chain, a sub-chain is replaced by a new chain with the same start and end vertex but with fewer interior vertices. This procedure can be treated as a modification on original 1-dimensional mesh. We can reverse the modification and use it to generate original polygonal chain from its simplification. The modification is conforming and non-redundant. A polygonal chain can be represented by its simplification with few vertices as possible, namely base polyline, and a sequence of refinement modification $\{M_1, M_2, ..., M_h\}$, such that, for each 1-simplex $\gamma \in M_i^-$, $i = 1,...,h$,exactly one of the following two conditions holds: either $\gamma \in \Gamma_0$, or $\gamma \in M_i^+$ for exactly one $i \neq j$. Intuitively, the previous condition means that each line segment must either appear in the base polyline Γ_0, or be created by some modification.

Definition 7. A modification M_j directly depends on a modification M_i if M_j removes some line segments inserted by M_i. More formally, M_j depended M_i if there exists some line segments which belongs to both M_j^- and M_j^+. □

If the transitive closure $\prec$ of the direct dependency relation is a partial order, then we say that the triplet $M = (\Gamma_0, \{M_1, \cdots M_h\}, \prec)$ is a multiresolution polygonal chain. We call Γ_0 the base polyline, since it is the polygonal chain with the fewest vertices, and modifications in set $\{M_1, M_2, ..., M_h\}$ tend to refine it. The collection of all cells γ contained in $\Gamma_0 \cup \{M_i^+ \mid i=1,\cdots h\}$ and not contained in $\cup \{M_i^- \mid i=1,\cdots h\}$ exactly is original polygonal chain, and its cells are not further refined by any other modification.

The Hesse diagram of the partial order defining a multiresolution mesh is a Directed Acyclic Graph (DAG) in which the nodes describe modifications, and the arcs describe links of direct dependency between modifications. By convention, arcs are directed from M_i to M_j if M_j directly depends on M_i. This choice reflects the intuitive idea that Mi should be performed before M_j.

Consider starting from the base polyline $\Gamma 0$ and applying all modifications of set $\{M_1, M_2, \ldots, M_h\}$ to it in a sequence corresponding to a total order extending $\prec$. Regardless of the specific order, all such sequences produce the original polygonal chain. The intermediate collections of cells generated in the process correspond to representations at intermediate LODs, and they depend on the specific sequence used. All possible sorted sequences extending $\prec$ give all possible intermediate LODs.

We can truncate the refinement process described above by selecting a proper subset of the modifications in $\{M_1, M_2, \ldots, M_h\}$, which is closed with respect to the partial order. A subset S of the modifications in a multiresolution polygonal chain is called closed if, for each modifications $M_i \in S$, all modifications M_j, such that M_i depends on M_j, are in S.

A closed subset of modifications can be applied to the base polyline Γ_0 in any total order extending $\prec$. Each closed subset S provides a set of cells Γ_S, which is the result of applying its modifications to Γ_0. If Γ_S defines a chain, then we call it an extracted chain.

Data structures for multiresolution chains must represent, either explicitly or implicitly, the modifications and the partial order. The encoding of the base polyline Γ_0 is not treated here because we assume that Γ_0 is small, and that it can be encoded through standard data structures for polygonal chain such as array. In what follows, we will demonstrate the details about how to obtain the base polyline Γ_0, encoding modification, and encoding dependencies.

(1)   In order to evaluate the space complexity of the data structures and the computational cost of the query primitives operating on them, we consider the following parameters for a multiresolution chain $M = (\Gamma_0, \{M_1, \cdots M_h\}, \prec)$:

(2)   the number h of modifications;

(3)   the total number c of line segments appearing in all modifications, i.e., the cardinality of the set of 1-simplexes $\bigcup_{i=1}^h (M_i^- \cup M_i^+)$;

(4)   the number a of links of direct dependency among modifications (i.e., the number of arcs in the DAG or tree).

The main task of this step is to find the simplification with the fewest vertices of original polygonal chain while preserving topological consistency, described in subsection 2.2, between them. We generalize the Safe-Sets algorithm to compute the minimum number of safe set of polygonal chain, i.e., the algorithm of min-SSs.

In algorithm of Safe-Sets, Voronoi diagram of all input points and its dual Delaunay triangulation are used to identify a collection of safe sets. If a Delaunay edge e_d connects two consecutive points v_i and v_{i+1} on the polyline, then the Voronoi edge e_v dual to e_d is the window from v_i to v_{i+1}. If there is no Delaunay edge connecting v_i and v_{i+1}, then there is no window. Each window is oriented. You can only look through it from v_i to v_{i+1}. See figure 5.

A cone is a region of the plane bounded by two rays anchored at a point. The outer cone from v_i to v_j is defined as the largest cone anchored at v_i that will pass through all the windows between v_i and v_j. The inner cone from v_i to v_j is defined as the smallest cone anchored at v_i that contains all of the points from v_i to v_j. See figure 5.

The first step of this algorithm is to compute the Voronoi diagram of points. Once we have got the Voronoi diagram, we start at one end of some polyline and add consecutive points until the inner cone is no longer contained with the outer cone. This can be done in linear time. So we get the first safe set of original polyline. By same step we can get all safe sets. Any simplification of the points contained in each safe set produces polyline that are homotopic to the input polylines in the region of the plane minus all input points [14].

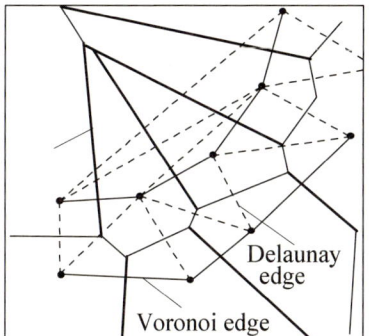 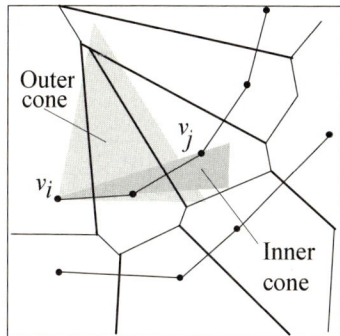

Fig. 5. Definition of window (left), Inner and outer cone(right)

Subsets of safe sets are also safe sets because the convex hull of a safe set constructed by the algorithm will not contain any points that are not in the safe set. We can find the minimum number of safe sets by a greedy approach after we obtain all safe sets of a polygonal chain. We start at one end of first safe set and add consecutive points while the set is monotone and there are no extra in the convex hull. For computing the minimum number of safe set efficiently, we incorporate this process into the procedure of computing safe sets. The whole procedure is shown as follows:

(1) Compute the Voronoi diagram of input points, including vertexes of all polygonal chain in a map and points that model special positions inside the regions of the map;
(2) Select one end of some polygonal chain and add consecutive points until the inner cone is no longer contained with the outer cone;
(3) Add consecutive points while the set is monotone and there are no extra points in the convex hull;
(4) Select next consecutive points, repeat step (2) and step (3) until reach the other end of the polygonal chain;
(5) Select one end of another polygonal chain, repeat step (2) to step (4) until have worked with the last chain in the map.

A complex polyline is divided into a collection of safe sets in which each safe set can be simplified using a single line. In principle all the single lines in a collection compose the base polyline, but for the purpose of visual consistency, a standard polyline simplification algorithm such as Douglas-Peucker is further used to compute the base polyline within an error ε. The refinement modification of the base polyline can be computed by the standard polyline simplification algorithm with an error ε', where $\varepsilon' < \varepsilon$. The original polygonal chain may be reached when the error $\varepsilon = 0$.

5 An Example

In this section, we describe an example of a multiple representation sequence with three levels of detail, and each level with three different importance value (Fig.6). The coarsest level (Fig.6(a)), namely level 3, only contains the map object which importance is 3. The map object, which importance is 2, is added in Fig.6 in the same level, and the object with importance of 1 in Fig.6(c).

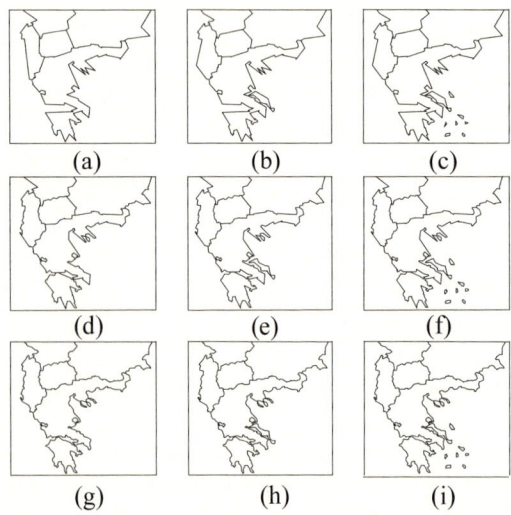

Fig. 6. An example for progressive transmission of vector map

Level 2 corresponds to a refinement modification of all map objects in level 3. More details (i.e., vertices) of map object are added in this level. Finally, the fully detailed map at level 1 refines the shape of all objects.

The representation with the coarsest level and the highest importance is processed first in progressive transmission and the client can efficiently receive an overview of whole map because the data quantity of the coarsest level is much smaller than the full detailed level. See Table 1. We can conclude that the data quantity of the coarsest level is about one tenth of that of the finest level. So the simplification of polygonal chain can speed up the progressive transmission of vector map greatly.

Table 1. The number of vertices in different level and importance

	Importance 3	Importance 2	Importance 1
Level 3	167(9.7%)	220(9.7%)	270(12.8%)
Level 2	430(25.0%)	470(27.3%)	582(33.8%)
Level 1	1498(87%)	1588(92.3%)	1721(100%)

6   Conclusions

Our contribution is a solution to vector map data transmission, based on a distribute architecture. By means of Reactive-tree and SMC, we design a model generating multiple map representations that can be used for progressive transmission. The model is built by applying a sequence of operators, such as simplification of polygonal chain, organizing the map data in SMC-based data structure and Reactive-tree, and so on. These defined operators guarantee the preservation of topological and visual consistency.

References

1. D.Flewelling, Comparing Subsets from Digital Spatial Archives: Point Set Similarity, Ph.D. Thesis, University of Maine, Orono, ME, 1997.
2. M.Bertolotto, M. Egenhofer, Progressive Transmission of Vector Map Data over the World Wide Web, GeoInformatica, 2001, 5(4):345-373.
3. E. Puppo and G. Dettori. Towards a formal model for multiresolution spatial maps, In 4th International Symposium on Large Spatial Databases, pp. 152–169, 1995.
4. L. De Floriani, P. Magillo, Multiresolution Meshes, Principles of Multiresolution in Geometric Modeling - PRIMUS01 summer school, pp. 193-234, 2001.
5. M. Bertolotto, Geometric Modeling of Spatial Entities at Multiple Levels of Resolution, Ph. D. Thesis, Department of Computer and Information Sciences, University of Genova, Italy, 1998.
6. E. Puppo and G. Dettori. Towards a formal model for multiresolution spatial maps, In 4th International Symposium on Large Spatial Databases, pp. 152–169, 1995.
7. Oosterom, P. V., The Reactive-tree: A Storage Structure for a Seamless Scaleless Geographic Database, Proceedings of Auto-Carto 10, pp. 393-407, 1991.
8. L. De Floriani, P. Magillo, Multiresolution Meshes, Principles of Multiresolution in Geometric Modeling - PRIMUS01 summer school, pp. 193-234, 2001.
9. D. H. Douglas and T. K. Peucker. Algorithms for the reduction of number of points required to represent a digital line or its caricature. Canadian Cartographer, 10(2):112-122, 1973.
10. M. de Berg, M. van Kreveld, and S. Schirra. A new approach to subdivision simplification. In ACMS/ASPRS Annual Convention and Exposition, volume 4, pp. 79–88, 1995.
11. R. Estkowski. No Steiner point subdivision simplification is NP-Complete. In Proc. 10th Canadian Conf. Computational Geometry, 1998.
12. R. Estkowski and J. S. B. Mitchell, Simplifying a Polygonal Subdivision While Keeping it Simple, SCG'01, Medford, Massachusetts, USA, 2001.
13. N. Mustafa, E. Koutsofias, S. Krishnan, S. Venkatasubramanian, Hardware assisted view-dependent map simplification, Manuscript, 2000.
14. A.Mantler,J.Snoeyink,Safe sets for line simplification, In 10th Annual workshop on Computational Geometry, 2000.
15. J. Popovic and H. Hoppe, Progressive simplicial complexes, SIGGRAPH'97, ACM Press, pp. 217-224, 1997.

Image-Based Fast Small Triangle Rasterization

Jim X. Chen, Harry Wechsler, and Jian Cui

Computer Science Department
George Mason University
Fairfax, VA 22030
jchen@cs.gmu.edu

Abstract. Many graphics and visualization applications require fast rendering and animation of fine detailed objects, which are named atomic primitives here. A primitive is a basic graphics shape such as a line or triangle that is directly rasterized into the framebuffer. An atomic primitive is a primitive that is small in size. A large and complex geometric model can be divided into lines, rectangles, and atomic triangles. Here we introduce a new method in the graphics pipeline hardware design to speed up rendering atomic primitives. Specifically, we present a new image-based atomic triangle rasterization algorithm. The algorithm stores the bitmaps of small triangles in memory and quickly retrieves a triangle bitmap when required. Our simulation experiments show that the image-based approach leads to faster rendering in primitive rasterization without sacrificing accuracy. At the same time, clipping, shading, hidden-surface removal, texture mapping, antialiasing, and other basic graphics functions and components are studied with suggested solutions as well. We believe our work is a novel approach that has potential of value and impact in graphics.

Keywords: Atomic primitives, bitmaps, pixmaps, triangles, image-based, rasterization.

1 Introduction

In our previous work on line statistics research [Chen, Wang, and Bresenham 02], we also analyzed triangles statistics. Specifically, we collected 600 application programs in OpenGL randomly from the web. Then, our modified graphics library (using the source code of Mesa) captured all triangle fillings in these programs and found that 416 of the 600 programs draw totally 1,414,858 triangles. The following tables list the statistical results. First, these 1,414,858 triangles have totally 4,244,574 edges. The length distribution of the edges is listed in Table 1. Here the number of pixels includes the two end points of each edge. We can see that 91% edges are shorter than or equal to 17 pixels. Furthermore, more than 95% edges are shorter than and equal to 33 pixels.

From the statistics, we learned that most triangles in computer graphics applications are *atomic* (very small). If we can speed up atomic triangle or polygon filling, we can significantly improve the efficiency of graphics drawing. In graphics, many 3D graphics models are tessellated as filled triangle meshes. Therefore, most

Z. Pan et al. (Eds.): ICAT 2006, LNCS 4282, pp. 918–927, 2006.
© Springer-Verlag Berlin Heidelberg 2006

polygons are really rendered as triangles. Besides, any large geometric object can be subdivided into lines, rectangles, and atomic triangles [Akeley and Jermoluk 88; Estkowski, Mitchell, and Xiang 02].

Table 1. Statistics on the length of all edges

# of pixels	# of edges	percent
0 < # ≤17	3879974	91.410%
17 < # ≤33	182028	4.288%
33 < # ≤65	93756	2.209%
65 < # ≤129	49709	1.171%
129 < # ≤257	30157	0.710%
257 < # ≤385	6465	0.152%
385 < # ≤513	2390	0.056%
513 < #	95	0.002%
Total	**4244574**	**100.00%**

We propose to consider *atomic primitives* as *bitmaps* that can be retrieved from memory directly, so to save setup overhead and pixel by pixel coordinates calculations. Here we focus our attention on atomic triangles. In the related work, we presented speeding up line rasterization and antialiasing through pattern look-up and coping [Chen and Wang 99]. Greene presented a novel polygon tiling algorithm with recursive subdivision of image space and other related work in hidden surface removal and sub-pixel antialiasing [Greene, Kass, and Miller 93; Greene and Kass 94; Greene 96; 99]. Here our image-based approach is different in that we have small triangles as primitive entities for rasterization, while Greene's method is a BSP tree regular space subdivision. Greene's method is very creative and important in space subdivision related methods, but it is not based on a primitive entity. We are taking a different approach to the similar problem. There are various approaches to triangle rasterization algorithms as well. Edge-walking [Deering, et al. 88; 93] and edge-equation [Fuchs et al. 85; Pineda 88; Olano and Greer 97; McCormack and McNamara 00; McCool, Wales, and Moule 01] are the two most popular algorithms that we will use as our comparison. Compared to edge-walking and edge-equation algorithms, our image based approach avoids overhead setup time and calculations of the edge-equations. Compared to Greene's method, our method will likely save on time required in space subdivision.

In summary, due to the overwhelming large portion of short lines and small polygons, we save atomic primitives in a bitmap library as a font library. Rasterization is then a process of indexing and copying. The new data structure and implementation are totally different from traditional methods. Many graphics functions including rasterization, shading, hidden-surface removal, texture mapping, antialiasing, and clipping can be redesigned according to the imaged-based approach, which will be addressed in this paper. We believe our work is a novel approach that has potential of value and impact in graphics. There can be quite different implementations to this approach. In the rest of the paper, we present our specific implementation examples with some statistics and comparisons to justify this work.

2   The Image-Based Rasterization Algorithm

We use a *w×h bitmap* (rectangular binary array) to save a triangle, and therefore a *bitmap library* is used to save all possible small triangles. Our original design uses a *(8×5)* bitmap library to save all triangles with edge lengths up to 8 pixels, which needs about 26.4K Byte space to store all possible small triangles in the bitmap library. To allow *memory-aligned access*, we redesigned using *(8×8)* bitmap library for efficiency. The rest *(8×3)* is used to save the lengths of the three edges (in terms of numbers of pixels) for vertex value interpolations. When a program draws a small triangle, our algorithm calculates an index to the triangle in the bitmap library and retrieves the bitmap. Then, according to the bitmap and edge lengths, color and depth values are retrieved for rasterization with optional antialiasing, texture mapping, or other advanced calculations. After that, clipping pattern is retrieved and the final pixmap is copied into the framebuffer. To certain extend, most of these operations are image-based operations, which we will discuss in detail.

2.1   The Index Scheme

First, let's assume that we have a *(2w-1)×(2h-1) imaginary area*. In our example, its size is *(15×9)*. We use the center pixel to divide the imaginary area into four quadrants. Pixels lying on the dividing lines will be included in a specific quadrant, as shown in Fig. 1.

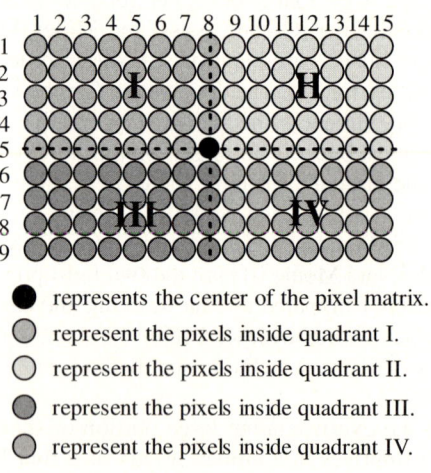

● represents the center of the pixel matrix.
◯ represent the pixels inside quadrant I.
◯ represent the pixels inside quadrant II.
◯ represent the pixels inside quadrant III.
◯ represent the pixels inside quadrant IV.

Fig. 1. An example of the imaginary area

Second, we will enumerate all possible triangles as our index scheme for later retrieving a triangle bitmap from the bitmap library. We fix a vertex at the center of the imaginary area and walk through all pixels as the second vertex of a triangle. Fig. 2 shows how we determine the bounding box (corresponding to a bitmap) when the second vertex falls into a different quadrant. As in the figure, when the second vertex falls into quadrant I, II, III or IV, we will use it as the upper-left, upper-right, lower-left or lower-right pixel of the bounding box, respectively. Since the size of a bounding box is fixed, which is the same as the size of a bitmap or (8×5) in this example, the bounding box is determined. After we have determined the bounding box, we walk through all the pixels in the bounding box as the third vertex of the triangle. So the index of the bitmap library is a two level index. The high-level index will be determined by the location of the second vertex. The low-level index will be determined by the location of the third vertex.

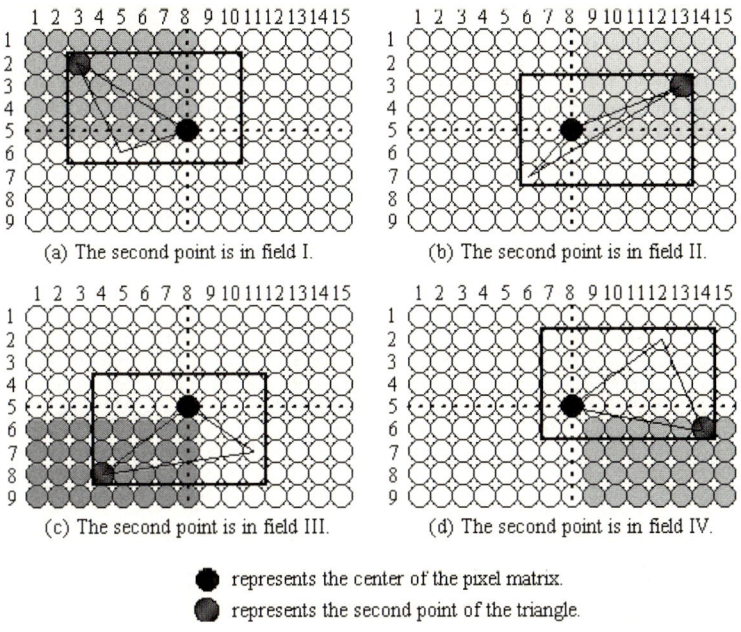

(a) The second point is in field I.   (b) The second point is in field II.

(c) The second point is in field III.   (d) The second point is in field IV.

● represents the center of the pixel matrix.
● represents the second point of the triangle.

Fig. 2. Determine if a triangle is inside a bitmap

We save all possible triangles according to the following order, which corresponds to our index scheme. The second vertex will move from left-to-right and top-to-bottom inside the (15×9) imaginary area. For each second vertex, the third vertex will move from left-to-right and top-to-bottom inside the (8×5) bounding box. This scheme saves duplicates of some triangles, which is a disadvantage. However, it significantly improves the efficiency of indexing and retrieving. We have designed and tested several different schemes [Cui, Chen, and Zhou 03] including one that saves no duplicates. Compared to the alternative indexing schemes, the current method is the fastest in retrieving. It is a matter of trade-off in time and space efficiency.

2.2   Retrieving a Triangle

When a program calls to draw a triangle, we will calculate its width and height and see if it is within the bitmap. If it is, we will retrieve its bitmap directly from the bitmap library. As the statistics report [Cui, Chen, and Zhou 02] points out, 69% of the triangles will be within the (*8×5*) bitmap. If the triangle doesn't fit into the bitmap, we can draw them through traditional method, or divide it into rectangles and triangles, and draw them separately. This subdivision of large primitives requires further consideration and work, which will be studied in the future.

Fig. 3 shows an example of retrieving the bitmap of triangle ABC. In the example, we first choose a vertex as the *center point* and put it at the center of the imaginary area. Then, we use one remaining vertex as the *corner point* together with the center point to determine the bounding box. The corner point is the vertex at the corner of the bounding box. Finally, the last vertex is used to locate the bitmap. However, we cannot choose the first and second vertices randomly. As in Fig. 3 (b, c, d, and f), some choices fail to find the bitmap. For example, if we choose B as the center point, the algorithm may fail or succeed depending on whether we use A or C as the corner point. It is even worse when we choose C as the center point, which will never lead us to a success.

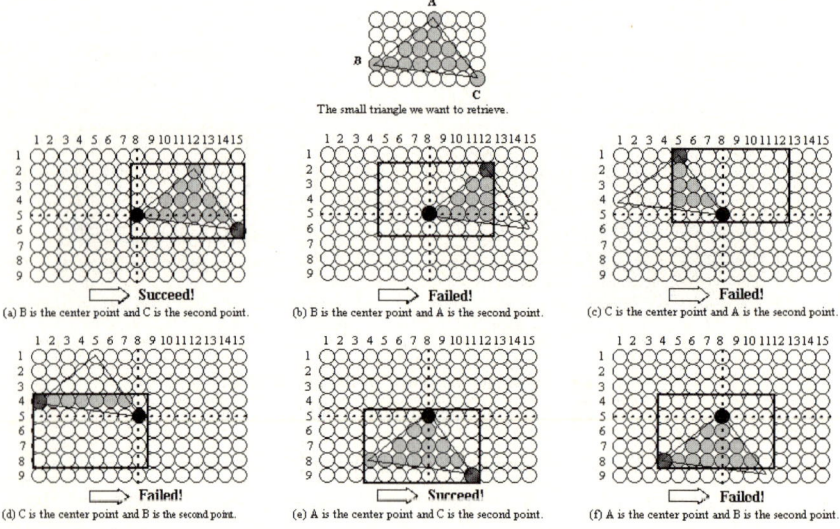

Fig. 3. Retrieve a triangle from the bitmap library

In order to succeed in the first try, we make some rules. The procedure to find the center point and the corner point is as follows. Because we will always calculate the width and height of the triangle to determine if it is inside a bitmap area, we can determine the center point and the corner point at the same time. First we determine the farthest two points along *x* axis. The remaining point is used as the center point. Then we calculate the *y* distance from these two farthest points (in *x* direction) to the center point respectively. The one with the larger *y* is the corner point. According to these rules, as in Fig. 3, we will always choose situation (e), which will find the triangle bitmap at the first try. Incidentally, some other situations may work/exist as well, as in Fig. 3 (a).

2.3   Interpolating Vertex Values

The above retrieved triangle bitmap provides the shape. The colors, depths, texture coordinates, and other values, which we call vertex values here, are needed to be interpolated into every pixel in the triangle. Let's first consider interpolating values along an edge (line).

For a line with *GL_SMOOTH*, the vertex colors (specified or calculated by lighting) are linearly interpolated along the pixels between the two end vertices. The intensity of each RGB component is interpolated separately. Here we use I_λ to represent the brightness level *i* of an RGB component. In general, given the end point intensities ($I_{\lambda 1}$ and $I_{\lambda 2}$) and the number of pixels along the line (*N*), the intensity increment of the linear interpolation is:

$$\Delta I_\lambda = \left(I_{\lambda 2} - I_{\lambda 1} \right) / \left(N - 1 \right). \tag{1}$$

That is, for each pixel from the starting pixel to the end pixel, the color component changes ΔI_λ [Chen 02]. Given a triangle primitive, the number of pixels along each edge is defined. In our specific implementation, the lengths of triangle edges are saved along with the triangle primitive. Therefore, the interpolation of vertex values can be pre-calculated in parallel and there is no need to calculate edge equations and pixel coordinates.

In addition to color components, the parallel pre-calculations can be applied to vertex depth values for hidden-surface removal and texture coordinates for texture mapping. For example, as shown in Fig. 4, N_1, N_2, and N_3 are edge lengths in numbers of pixels saved with the triangle. Given the depth values of the three vertices Z_1, Z_2, and Z_3, according to Eq. 1, the interpolation increments along the three edges are:

$$\Delta Z_{12} = \left(Z_2 - Z_1 \right) / \left(N_3 - 1 \right), \quad \Delta Z_{23} = \left(Z_3 - Z_2 \right) / \left(N_1 - 1 \right),$$
$$\text{and } \Delta Z_{31} = \left(Z_3 - Z_1 \right) / \left(N_2 - 1 \right).$$

Therefore, we can interpolate along three edges and then along horizontal pixels to have all pixels' depth values saved in a *pixmap*, which means an array of values other than binary in contrast to a bitmap. This interpolation process does not require calculating pixel coordinates, and therefore it does not require vertex coordinates and edge equations.

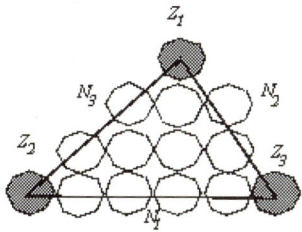

Fig. 4. Z-value interpolation pre-calculation

The depth value of a pixel is to decide hidden-surface removal as well as near/far clippings during copying a pixmap into the framebuffer. If two of the three vertex depth values go astride a near or far clipping plane, each pixel in the triangle will be tested for clipping as well. Clipping will be discussed in detail later in this section.

The interpolation of different vertex values can be calculated in parallel and saved in different pixmaps corresponding to the bitmap. The bitmap provides the shape, and the pixmaps provide the attribute and other values for rasterization.

2.4 Imaged-Based Pixmap Library

Instead of calculating and interpolating vertex values into pixmaps as above in real time, as an alternative we can actually pre-calculate and save all these value patterns in pixmap libraries for retrieval directly. Specifically, the normalized vertex values (such as depths, color components, texture coordinates, etc.) are really represented in 8 bits to 24 bits. Due to the small bitmap size, the pixel values are represented with limited combinations.

Because these images require multiple times of the amount of current memory size, it remains for future research when memory is nominal before we spend too much effort on details that are not very practical at present.

2.5 Antialiasing

Line antialiasing methods are important techniques to handle the "jagged" triangle edges [Crow 77]. In Gupta and Sproull's antialiasing method [Gupta and Sproull 81], the distance from each pixel (to be intensified) to the center of the mathematically specified line is used to determine the intensity of the pixel. Given a pair of end points, the pixel patterns as well as each pixel's distance to the center of the line are defined [Chen and Wang 99]. We propose saving the distance from each pixel on the edge of the atomic triangle to the line along with the bitmap library, and use the distance to calculate and decide antialiasing. Given a pixel's distance to the line is D, as shown in Fig. 5, all surrounding pixels' distances to the line can be derived quickly so to facilitate antialiasing on variable width of a line (edge).

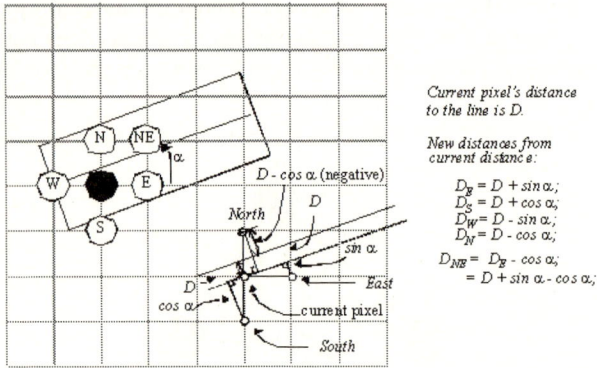

Fig. 5. Distances from the pixels to the line

As discussed in [Chen and Wang 99], a discrete line has multiple segments, and the identical pixel positions in different segments always have the same distance to the line. So these pixels must have the same intensity in antialiasing, and we only need to save the first segment's pixel distances. If texture mapping is applied, this method can be integrated to modify the textured pixels (*texels*). At least the texels can be intensified by the distances which are repeating in multiple segments.

An alternative approach is to save sub-pixel bitmaps for over-sampling [Barkans 91; Schilling 91; Greene 96]. This needs extra memory space and image-based operations as well. We have not studied further in this direction.

2.6 Clipping

In 2D viewing (Fig. 6a), instead of transforming a model in the modeling window to a model in the display device coordinates (viewport) directly, traditional OpenGL implementation first transforms the modeling window into a square. The coordinates of the square are called the *normalized* coordinates. Clipping of the primitives is then calculated in the normalized coordinates against the square. 2D viewing is a special case of 3D viewing. In 3D viewing, as shown in Fig. 6b, we need to specify a viewing volume, which determines a projection method (*parallel* or *perspective*). For example, in OpenGL *glOrtho()* actually specifies a matrix that transforms the orthographic viewing volume into a *normalized* viewing volume, which is a cube. Similarly, *glFrustum()* also specifies a matrix that transforms the perspective viewing volume into a normalized viewing volume. Therefore, normalization transformation is carried out first to simplify clipping.

In summary, all primitives are first transformed into the normalized viewing coordinates, clipped against the planes of the normalized viewing volume, and then transformed and projected into the viewport device coordinates for rasterization. As we know, although we usually consider the device coordinates are in 2D, they are actually in 3D with normalized z values for hidden-surface removal.

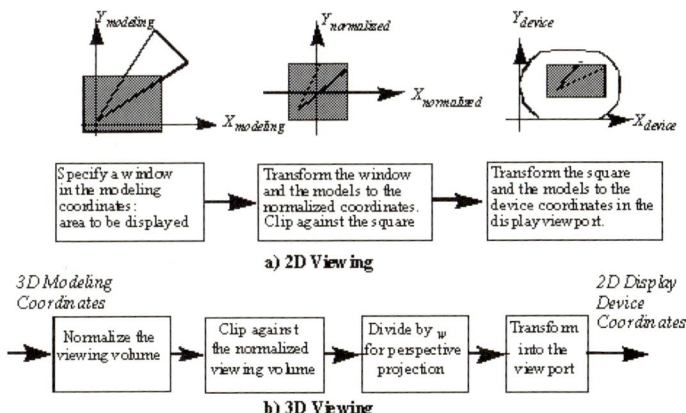

Fig. 6. OpenGL Graphics Pipeline

If we know that a primitive is atomic, we would rather defer the clipping into after transforming into the device coordinates. This will allow us to take advantage the primitive bitmaps and clipping will not require calculating boundary and edge equations. There can be many different implementations for this idea. Since transforming into the viewport is really a simple scaling operation, it can be applied to those atomic primitives for deferred clipping and allow other primitives that are big in size to be clipped against the normalized viewing volume. Alternatively, we can deal with all clipping in device coordinates. Also, we can first divide a large primitive into lines, rectangles, and atomic triangles for clipping and rasterization.

3   Conclusion and Future Work

We have presented an imaged-based rendering system based on triangle bitmaps. Obviously, the work is far from complete and more future work will follow. We hope our work is a valuable contribution to computer graphics system.

References

1. K. Akeley, and T. Jermoluk, "High-performance Polygon Rendering," *Proceedings of ACM SIGGRAPH*, Vol. 22, No. 4, 1988, pp. 239-246,.
2. C. Barkans, "Hardware-Assisted Polygon Antialiasing," IEEE *Computer Graphics and Applications*, vol. 11, no. 1, January/February 1991, pp. 80-88.
3. J. X. Chen, "Color Interpolation," *Guide to Graphics Software Tools*, Springer Verlag, 2002, pp. 58-59.
4. J. X. Chen and X. Wang, "Approximate Method and Analysis of the Multiple Segment Line Scan-Conversion," *Computer Graphics Forum*, vol. 18, no. 1, March 1999, pp. 69-78.
5. J. X. Chen, X. Wang, and J. E. Bresenham, "The Analysis and Statistics of Line Distribution," *IEEE Computer Graphics & Applications*, vol. 22, no. 6, November/December 2002, pp. 100-107.
6. F. C. Crow, "The Aliasing Problem in Computer-Generated Shaded Images," *Communications of the ACM*, vol. 20, no. 11, 1977, pp. 799-805.
7. J. Cui, J. X. Chen, and X. Zhou, "Triangle Statistics Report," *Technical Report (TR7)*, http:// www.cs.gmu.edu/~jchen/report/, GMU Graphics Group, 2002.
8. J. Cui, J. X. Chen, and X. Zhou, "Triangle Fast Scan-Conversion Algorithm Report," *Technical Report (TR8)*, http://www.cs.gmu.edu/~jchen/report/, GMU Graphics Group, 2003.
9. M. Deering, S. Winner, B. Schediwy, C. Duffy, and N. Hunt, "The Triangle Processor and Normal Vector Shader: a VLSI System for High Performance Graphics," *Proceedings of ACM SIGGRAPH*, vol. 22, no. 4, 1988, pp. 21-30.
10. M. F. Deering and S. R. Nelson, "Leo: A System for Cost Effective 3D Shaded Graphics," *Proceedings of ACM SIGGRAPH*, 1993, pp. 101-108.
11. R. Estkowski, J. S. B. Mitchell, and X. Xiang, "Optimal Decomposition of Polygonal Models into Triangle Strips," *Proceedings of the eighteenth annual symposium on Computational geometry*, 2002, pp. 254-263.

12. H. Fuchs, J. Goldfeather, J. Hultquist, S. Spach, J. Austin, F. Brooks, Jr., J. Eyles, and J. Poulton, "Fast Spheres, shadows, Textures, Transparencies, and Image Enhancements in Pixel-Planes," *Proceedings of ACM SIGGRAPH,* vol. 19, no. 13, 1985, pp. 111-120.
13. N. Greene, M. Kass, and G. Miller, "Hierarchical Z-Buffer Visibility," *Proceedings of ACM SIGGRAPH*, 1993, pp. 231-238.
14. N. Greene and M. Kass, "Error-Bounded Antialiased Rendering of Complex Environments," *Proceedings of ACM SIGGRAPH*, 1994, pp. 59-66.
15. N. Greene, "Hierarchical Polygon Filing with Coverage Masks," *Proceedings of ACM SIGGRAPH*, 1996, pp. 65-74.
16. N. Greene, "Efficient Occlusion Culling for z-Buffer System," *Proceedings of Computer Graphics International*, 1999, pp. 78-78.
17. S. R. Gupta and R. Sproull "Filtering Edges for Gray-Scale Displays," *Proceedings of ACM SIGGRAPH,* vol. 15, no. 3, 1981, pp. 1-5.
18. Intel Corporation, IA-32 Intel Architecture Optimization Reference Manual, 1999.
19. M. D. McCool, C. Wales, and K. Moule, "Incremental and Hierarchical Hilbert Order Edge Equation Polygon Rasterization," *Proceedings of the ACM SIGGRAPH/EUROGRAPHICS Workshop on Graphics Hardware*, 2001, pp. 65- 92.
20. J. McCormack and R. McNamara, "Tiled Polygon Traversal Using Half-plane Edge Functions," *Proceedings 2000 SIGGRAPH/EUROGRAPHICS Workshop on Graphics Hardware,* 2000, pp. 15-21.
21. M. Olano and T. Greer, "Triangle Scan Conversion Using 2D Homogeneous Coordinates," *Proceedings of the ACM SIGGRAPH/EUROGRAPHICS Workshop on Graphics Hardware,* 1997, pp. 89-95.
22. J. Pineda, "A Parallel Algorithm for Polygon Rasterization," *Proceedings of ACM SIGGRAPH,* vol. 22, no. 4, 1988, pp. 17-20.
23. Schilling, "A New Simple and Efficient Antialiasing with Subpixel Masks," *Proceedings of ACM SIGGRAPH,* vol 25, no. 4, July 1991, pp. 133-141.

On Volume Distribution Features Based 3D Model Retrieval

Mingyong Pang[1,2], Wenjun Dai[2], Gangshan Wu[2], and Fuyan Zhang[2]

[1] Dep. of Educational Tech., Nanjing Normal Uninversity, Nanjing 210097, China
[2] Dep. of Computer Sci. & Tech., Nanjing University, Nanjing 210093, China
{panion, czdwj}@graphics.nju.edu.cn, {gswu, fyzhang}@nju.edu.cn

Abstract. In this paper, a 3D mesh retrieval method is proposed based on extracting geometric features of models. The method first finds three principal directions for a model by employing the principal component analysis method, and rotates the model to align it in a reference frame. Then, three sets of planes are used to slice the model along to the directions respectively. Subsequently, three character curves of the model can be obtained and be used as descriptor to key the model in 3D mesh model library. By comparing descriptors of two models, our method can compute similarity of models. Experiences show that our method is rapid, stable and robust to deal with various mesh models with arbitrary geometric and topological complexity.

1 Introduction

Prevailing in the communities of CAD, virtual reality and gaming environment, 3D mesh models become more and more a common feature of nowadays multimedia. Efficiently accessing such rich and complex 3D data turns into an essential issue and motivated numerous and extensive research work within the area of content based indexing and retrieval. A key aspect of the issue is how to extract features from models to describe their geometric shapes or topologies.

At present, there are approximately two types of methods for extracting features: geometric or topological. The former describes shape characters according to the distributions of geometric properties, e.g, area, curvature, normal and volume, of models. In general, a normalizing preprocessing is needed to ensure that the extracted features satisfy invariance properties with respect to geometric transforms such as isometries and isotropic scaling[1]. In [2],[3], histograms of volume distributions of models concerning their bounding spheres were used to describe the features of the models. A systematic comparison and analysis about various histogram methods can be found in [2]. In [4], a set of parallel planes were employed to slice a model, and then profile on each cross section of the model is extracted and resampled uniformly to calculate the feature of the cross section. All the features were collected and gave a total description of the model. Results show that expensive cost are involved in the method. In [5], a visual similarity based method was developed on the idea that if two 3D models are similar, they also look similar from all viewing angles. According to

Z. Pan et al. (Eds.): ICAT 2006, LNCS 4282, pp. 928–937, 2006.

the idea, a camera system defined on regular dodecahedron were introduced. The cameras located at vertices of the dodecahedron first took "photographs", i.e. silhouettes, for a model from 20 different directions, and then translated the silhouettes into feature curves. The set of the curves forms a *descriptor* of the model. On the other hand, the topological methods characterize the features of models by analyzing branchedness, connectivity and skeleton. In [6] and [7], the Morse theory and Reeb graph were used to describe the topological characters of models, respectively. Hilaga et al [8] further present a multiresolution Reeb graph algorithm. The algorithm represented the skeletal and topological structure of a 3D shape at various levels of resolution. The similarity calculation between 3D shapes was processed using a coarse-to-fine strategy while preserving the consistency of the graph structures.

Besides the methods mentioned above, there some other analytic methods extracting and indexing models, for example, Fourier analysis [9] and spherical harmonic [10]. In spherical harmonic method, the features of every model were represented by rotation invariant descriptors instead of rotation dependent descriptors that were aligned into a canonical coordinate system defined by the model. For a thorough summary of shape matching and a comparison of techniques, see [11] and [12].

In this paper, we present a volume distribution features based method that is capable of retrieving similar models from mesh model library for a given model. The method consists of two phases: building and retrieving. The building phase extracts feature curves along three principal axes of each model. The curves form a descriptor of the model and be used to organize database of feature data for the model. In the retrieving phase, descriptor of a given key-model is first extracted and then is used to search similar models in the library by comparing the dissimilarity between key descriptor and the descriptors in the database.

The rest of the paper is organized as follows: Section 2 introduces the concept of solid mesh model and the data structure used for representation of models in memory. Section 3 discusses how to extract volume distribution features from a model and Section 4 shows how to compute the similarity of two models from their descriptors. Section 5 gives some experimental results produced with our method followed by conclusions of our work in Section 6.

2   Solid Mesh Model and Basic Data Structure

In this paper, the model, called *solid mesh model*, prefers to the closed 3D manifold mesh, which satisfies following conditions: a) each face of model is a simple planar convex polygon; b) each edge in the model must be exactly shared by two faces; c) topology around every vertex of the model is homeomorphous to a disc, i.e. manifold property.

In order to conveniently extract cross section of a model sliced by a plane, it is very important to select an appropriate and versatile data structure to represent model in computer. We use halfedge-based data structure [13] to store model

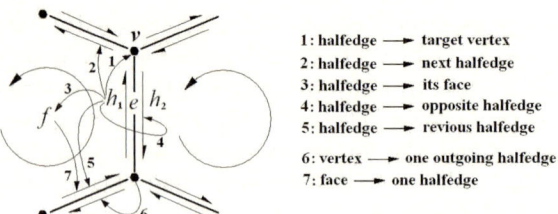

Fig. 1. Halfedge data structure

data in computer memory. One of advantages of the halfedge structure is that it provides fast, constant-time access to the one-ring neighbors of each vertex.

The connectivity information stored in the halfedge structure in this paper is illustrated in Fig.1, where 1 to 5 are pointers pointing to the vertex, next halfedge, face, previous halfedge and opposite halfedge of the halfedge respectively, and 6 and 7 are the pointers pointing the first halfedge of a vertex or a face, respectively.

3   Extracting Volume Distribution Features

3.1   Aligning Model on Principal Directions

In order to compute the simularity between two models by comparing their volume distribution features, our approach must first seek the three orthogonal principal axes for the model. In the paper, we use the well-known Principal Component Analysis (PCA) method to find the principal axes of the model. PCA is a common method in the area of signal analysis, which translates an initial data set into the space of principal components by performing an orthogonal transformation on coordinates of the vertices of the model and then evaluates the principal axes directions by minimizing the correlativity of a single sample of data, see reference [14] for details .

Once the principal directions are worked out, the model can be rotated such as its principal directions align to the axes of fixed frame system.

3.2   Slicing Model and Picking Up Section Polygons

Without loss of generality, we only discuss the case that a set of equidistant and horizontal planes, i.e. parallel to xy-plane of the frame system, is used to slice the model. Obviously, the position of each plane can uniquely be described by a pure scalar z_k, the intercept of the plane on z-axis. Here, we name z-axis *slicing axis* and denote the plane or *slicing plane* by $P(z_k)$. According to the difference of topological complexity of the model, the cross section of the sliced model on slicing plane may consist of a series of nested and nonintersect planar simple polygons, called *section polygon group* or SPG, in the paper (Fig.3).

For a set of slicing planes, our approach maintains a list for each plane $P(z_k)$ recording all the edges intersected with the plane, and denotes set of the edges by $E(z_k)$. A single-pass visiting over the edges of the model can finish the construction of the lists. As an example, we give a process of computing SPG from $E(z_k)$. We first get an arbitrary edge, h_0^k, from $E(z_k)$. Following the definition of $E(z_k)$, h_0^k must intersect with $P(z_k)$. According to the relations between the ends, v_i and v_j, of h_0^k and z_k, we can simply work out the intersection, s_0, of $P(z_k)$ and h_0^k. Generally, let us suppose that v_i is on the upper side of $P(z_k)$ and v_j under $P(z_k)$, so the halfedge h_0^k points downwards v_j from v_i. In Fig.2(a), the halfedge h_1 is just an example for h_0^k. Further, let us denote by h_{next}^k the next halfedge of h_0^k. If both ends of h_{next}^k are under $P(z_k)$, we replace h_0^k by h_{next}^k and repeat the process above until the target end of h_{next}^k is above the plane. At the moment, we denote the opposite halfedge of h_{next}^k by h_1^k, and h_1^k is the second halfedge pointing downwards and intersected with the slicing plane. So the second intersection, s_1, can be evaluated. Next, see h_1^k as h_0^k above, and repeat the aforesaid process, and a series of intersections, $s_0, s_1, \ldots$, can be obtained. Once a intersection point is repeated in the series, the process is stopped and a section polygon is formed.

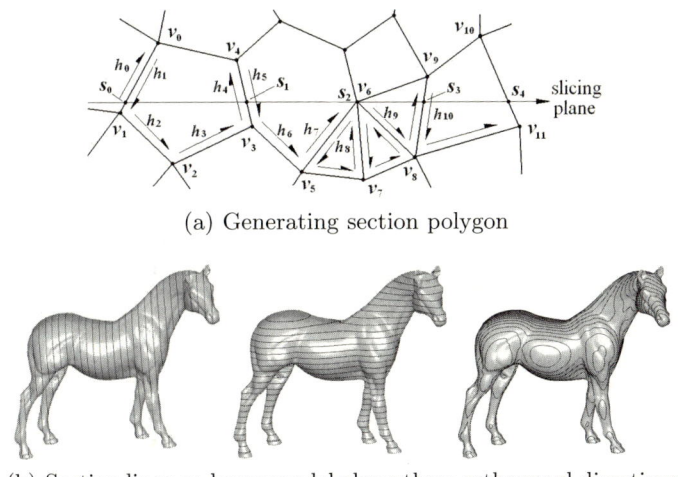

(a) Generating section polygon

(b) Section lines on horse model along three orthogonal directions

Fig. 2. Extracting section polygons from polygonal model

During the process above, once a halfedge intersected with the slicing plane is visited, its corresponding edge is immediately removed from $E(z_k)$. If the $E(z_k)$ is not empty when a section polygon is created, one can repeat the process to find another section polygon until $E(z_k)$ becomes empty. Collecting the created polygons, SPG for the $P(z_k)$ can be obtained on the fly.

A special case needs to be seriously dealt with is that one end or both ends of a halfedge are on the plane, e.g, the halfedges taking v_6 as their one end in

Fig.2(a). A recommended method as following: if the beginning end of halfedge is on $P(z_k)$, treat it as under the plane and oppositely, see the target end of halfedge as above the plane. Fig.2(b) shows an example of horse sliced by three sets of slicing planes from three orthogonal directions.

3.3   Evaluating Areas of SPGs

Since edges belong to each face in the model is arranged counter-clockwise viewed from outer of the model, the polygons of each SPG have directions themselves, which are defined by the order of the series of the intersections (Fig.2(a)). When looking down the SPGs from the positive direction of the reference system, one can find that when one "walks" along the boundary of the polygon, the inner of polygon is always on his left(Fig.3).

For an arbitrary planar polygon $s_0, s_1, \ldots, s_n$ and $s_i = (x_i, y_i)(i = 0, 1, \ldots, n)$, the signed area of the polygon can be calculated by following formula

$$S = \frac{1}{2}\left\{ \begin{vmatrix} x_0 & y_0 \\ x_1 & y_1 \end{vmatrix} + \begin{vmatrix} x_1 & y_1 \\ x_2 & y_2 \end{vmatrix} + \cdots + \begin{vmatrix} x_n & y_n \\ x_0 & y_0 \end{vmatrix} \right\}. \tag{1}$$

When direction of polygon is counter-clockwise, the sign of the area of the polygon is positive, otherwise negative. Thus, the area of a SPG equals to the absolute value of algebraic area sum of its section polygons.

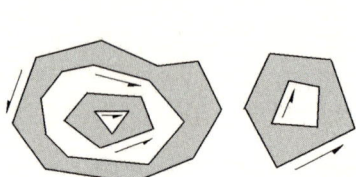

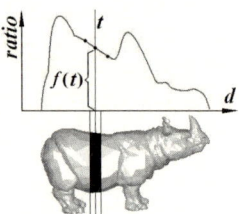

Fig. 3. Section polygon group   **Fig. 4.** Defining volume distribution curve

3.4   Building Features Curves of Volume Distributions

The geometric features of a model can be described by three curves of volume distributions defined on its principal axes, where each curve is defined as $ratio = f(d)$, here, d is discretely defined on the principal axes. In Fig.4, the value $ratio = f(d)$ at $d = t$ is the ratio of volume of shading area in the whole volume of the model. Here, the width of the shading part is the distance between two adjacent slicing planes.

Suppose the number of slicing planes is $N+1$, and the most upper and lower planes are $P(z_{max})$ and $P(z_{min})$ respectively. Obviously, the distance between two adjacent planes is $(z_{max} - z_{min})/N$. So, the slicing planes from bottom to top can be decided as

$$P(z_i) = P\left(z_{min} + i \times \frac{z_{max} - z_{min}}{N}\right), (i = 0, 1, \ldots, N). \tag{2}$$

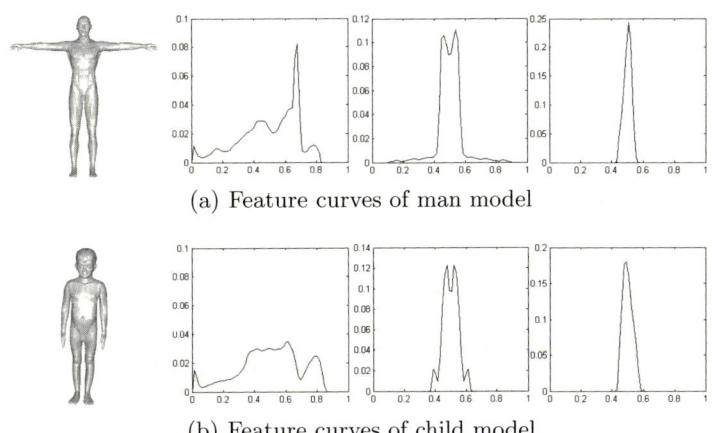

(a) Feature curves of man model

(b) Feature curves of child model

Fig. 5. Two character models and corresponding feature curves

According to Section 3.3, suppose the areas of SPGs on the planes are S_0, $S_1, \ldots, S_N$, respectively, the volume of the model can be approximately evaluated by

$$V \approx \frac{z_{max} - z_{min}}{N} \sum_{i=0}^{N-1} \frac{S_i + \sqrt{S_i S_{i+1}} + S_{i+1}}{3} . \tag{3}$$

When N is big enough, the areas of two adjacent SPGs is close to identical. In this case, we use $(S_i + S_{i+1})/2$ to replace S_i and S_{i+1} in formula (3). So (3) can be simplified as

$$V \approx \frac{z_{max} - z_{min}}{N} \sum_{i=0}^{N-1} \frac{S_i + S_{i+1}}{2} . \tag{4}$$

where, volume of the model between the ith and $(i+1)$th slicing planes is about

$$V_i \approx \frac{z_{max} - z_{min}}{N} \frac{S_i + S_{i+1}}{2} . \tag{5}$$

Notice that (4) and (5) avoid the expensive square-root operator in (3). Let $d_i = (z_i + z_{i+1})/2$, then

$$ratio_i = f(d_i) = \frac{V_i}{V} = \frac{S_i + S_{i+1}}{\sum_{t=0}^{N-1}(S_t + S_{t+1})} . \tag{6}$$

From the discrete feature points $(d_i, f(d_i))$, we can obtain the volume distribution curves by interpolating or fitting methods. Here, the set $\{f(d_0), f(d_1), \ldots, f(d_{N-1})\}$ is named a *feature* of the model. Fig.5 illustrates an example of volume distribution feature curves of two character models.

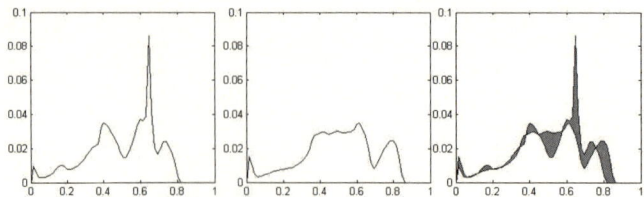

Fig. 6. Evaluating dissimilarity of two feature curves

4   Evaluating Similarity

Suppose that feature sets of two models M^0 and M^1 are $R^0 = \{f_X^0, f_Y^0, f_Z^0\}$ and $R^1 = \{f_X^1, f_Y^1, f_Z^1\}$ respectively, where $f_i^k = \{g_{i0}^k, g_{i1}^k, \dots, g_{iN-1}^k\}, (k = 0, 1; i = X, Y, Z)$ are features. Here, we use the dissimilarity between M^0 and M^1 to measure the similarity of them. The dissimilarity is specialization of Minkovski distance in the discrete case, which is defined as

$$Diff^{init}(M^0, M^1) = \left(\sum_{i=X,Y,Z} \sum_{j=0}^{N-1} \left(g_{ij}^0 - g_{ij}^1\right)^2 \Delta_i \right)^{\frac{1}{2}}. \tag{7}$$

where, $\Delta_i (i = X, Y, Z)$ is the distance between two adjacent slicing planes. To simplify computing, we normalize the model on each direction of slicing axes. Consequently, we have simplified version of the dissimilarity

$$Diff(M^0, M^1) = \sum_{i=X,Y,Z} \sum_{j=0}^{N-1} \left(g_{ij}^0 - g_{ij}^1\right)^2. \tag{8}$$

Since the principal directions of M^0 and M^1 may be exactly reverse when PCA method is used, we have to consider the two possible cases and take the best matching as the similarity of the two models. This is, in (8), let

$$\sum_{j=0}^{N-1} (g_{ij}^0 - g_{ij}^1)^2 = min \left(\sum_{j=0}^{N-1} (g_{ij}^0 - g_{ij}^1)^2, \sum_{j=0}^{N-1} (g_{ij}^0 - g_{i,N-j-1}^1)^2 \right). \tag{9}$$

5   Results

We have implemented a prototype retrieval system using C++ on 2.8GHz P4 PC with 512M memory. The system consists of two modules. The building module extracts features from model library and organizes them into a feature database. At same time, it also provides user a way of selecting the number of slicing planes used to extract features. The matching module has capability of offering some key models complying with keywords input by user and searches similar models by matching the features of a selected key model.

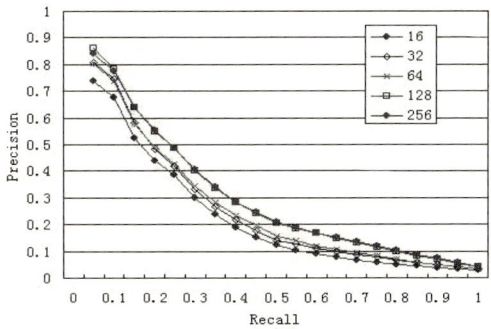

Fig. 7. Evaluation diagram of "precision vs recall" of our method

Table 1. Time costs of extracting and comparing descriptors

Levels of slicing	Extracting(ms)	Comparing(ms)	descriptor size(k)
16	0.143	0.0083	1.05
32	0.156	0.0110	1.94
64	0.192	0.0159	3.72
128	0.258	0.0322	7.28
256	0.393	0.0893	14.4

In our experiences, we use the same mesh model set as used in [16]. The set includes 1834 different models manually categorized into 90 subclasses. Since more the number of slicing planes more accuracy of the retrieval will be obtained, and at same time more the calculating costs will be involved, we have to compromise the aspects. We use 16, 32, 64, 128 and 256 planes to slice the models respectively and the related time costs and sizes of feature data are illustrated in Tab.1 and Fig.7. In the table, the *extracting time* is the average time of extracting 1834 descriptors, including the time of reading models and writing key data. the *comparing time* is average time of matching a key descriptor with the descriptors of 1834 models. Fig.7 shows the relation between precision and recall of our method when different number of slicing planes is used. Traditionally, the diagram of "precision vs recall" is a common way of evaluating performance in text and visual information retrieval. Recall measures the ability of the system to retrieve all models that are relevant and precision measures that the ability of the system to retrieve only models that are relevant. The figure illustrates that our method has near performances when 128 and 256 slicing planes are used. So, 128 planes is the better selection than 256 planes with represent to the tradeoff.

Fig. 8. Retrieval results of our method from an unorganized library consisted of 10991 models, where leftmost column are key models and top 4 matchings are placed on their right

Fig.8 shows some retrieval results of our method from an unorganized model library consisted of 10991 models of size 3.2G. The leftmost column are key models and their top 4 matchings are placed on the right.

6   Conclusion

In the paper, we present a solution of retrieving models from 3D data library based on extracting volume distribution features and implement a prototype system of the solution. Experiential results shows that our method is well of precision-recall diagram and both the aspects of constructing key database and matching similar models are rapid and efficient. Our method can deal with various solid mesh models with arbitrary geometry and topologies. Especially, it can identify the cases that the traditional methods are difficult to handle, e.g, silhouette based method can't distinguish the hollow sphere from solid sphere.

References

1. Zaharia T, Preteux F. Shape-based retrieval of 3D mesh models. IEEE International Conference of Multimedia and Expo'2002 (ICME '02), 1: 437–440.
2. Ankerst M, Kastenmuller G, Kriegel H. 3D shape histograms for similarity search and classification in spatial databases. Proc. of 6th International Symposium on Large Spatial Databases, Hong Kong, China, 1999, 207–226.
3. Osada R, Funkhouser T, Chazelle B, et al. Shape distributions. ACM Transactions on Graphics, 2002, 21(4): 807–832.

4. Pu J, Liu Y, Gu Y, et al. 3D model retrieval based on 2D slice similarity measurements, Proc. of the 2nd International Symposium on 3D Data Processing, Visualization and Transmission, Thessaloniki, Greece, 2004, 95–101.

5. Chen D, Tian X, Shen Y, et al. On visual similarity based 3D model retrieval, Computer Graphics Forum, 2003, 22(3): 223–232.

6. Shinagawa Y, Kunii T. Constructing a Reeb graph automatically from cross section. IEEE Computer Graphics & Applications, 1991, 11(6): 44–51.

7. Xiao Y, Werghi N, Siebert P. A topological approach for segmenting human body shape. 12th International Conference on Image Analysis and Processing, Mantova, Italy, 2003, 82–93.

8. Hilaga M, Shinagawa Y, Kohmura T, et al. Topology matching for fully automaticSimilarity estimation of 3D shapes, ACM SIGGRAPH'2001, 2001, 203–212.

9. Kazhdan M, Funkhouser T, Rusinkiewicz S. Rotation invariant spherical harmonic repressentation of 3D shape descriptors. ACM SIGGRAPH'2003, 2003, 156–164.

10. Vranic D V, Saupe D. Description of 3D-shape using a complex function on the sphere. Proc. Of the IEEE International Conferece on Multimedia and Expo(ICME2002), Lausanne, Switzerland, 2002, 177–180.

11. Iyer N, Jayanti S, Lou K, Kalyanaraman Y, and Ramani K. Three dimensional shape searching: State-of-the-art review and future trends. Computer-Aided Design, April 2005, 37: 509–530.

12. Tangelder J, Veltkamp R. A survey of content based 3D shape retrieval methods. in International Conference on Shape Modeling and Applications 2004, pp145–156

13. Weiler K. Edge-based data structure for solid modeling in curved- surface environments, IEEE Computer Graphics & Application, 1985, 5(1): 21–40.

14. Jolliffe I T. Principal component analysis. New York, Springer, 2002.

15. Puzicha J, Rubner Y, Tomasi C, et al. Empirical evaluation of dissimilarity measures for color and texture. IEEE International Conference on Computer Vision, 1999, 1165–1173.

16. Min P, Kazhdan M, Funkhouser T. A comparison of text and shape matching for retrieval of online 3D models. Proc. European Conference on Digital Libraries, Bath, UK, 2004, 209–220.

Personalized Model Deformation Based on Slice Space Representation

Lifeng Ren[1], Mingmin Zhang[1], Yunlong Xu[2], and Zhigeng Pan[1]

[1] State Key Laboratory of CAD&CG, Zhejiang University, Hangzhou, P.R.C.
[2] School of Computer Science, Soochow University, Suzhou, P.R.C.
{lfren, zmm, zgpan}@cad.zju.edu.cn

Abstract. Human body modeling is essential for virtual environment, sports simulation and digital entertainment. In this paper, we present an improved slice-space deforming algorithm and use it to add shape details extracted from pictures to a reference model in order to get a personalized and structured model. Our method begins with sample image collection and reference image generation followed by silhouette extraction and segmentation. Then it builds a mapping between pixels inside every pair of silhouette segments in the reference image and in the sample image. This novel mapping algorithm is based on a slice space representation that conforms to the intrinsic structure of human body. Finally, based on this mapping, the position of every point in the reference model will be changed. Our deforming algorithm can extract shape details from pictures more precisely and preserve shape connectivity of the reference model in more situations.

1 Introduction

Recently, there are increasing interests in modeling articulated human body for researchers in virtual environment, sports simulation, and digital entertainment. However, building an animatable human model is not an easy process. Difficulties lie in many aspects. The shape of a human body is rather complex but the vision system is highly developed to distinguish small error in bodies. Furthermore, the body is an elastic organ. Thus a good model must deform according to the surface inflection of the human bodies when people move.

Moreover because of the rapid progress of virtual environments, games and entertainments, the demand for human body keeps on increasing steadily. Existing modeling method can not fulfill this demand. They are either too expensive to deploy or too complicated to learn, and thus can not be applied in large scale. All these factors call for easy and low-cost modeling methods.

We propose an easy, cheep, and efficient method for building articulated human body. Neither expensive hardware nor hard-to-learn software is required. And the modeling process is intuitive. Taken a generic model and two pictures of an individual as input, the method extracts shape features shown in pictures and embeds them into the generic model.

Z. Pan et al. (Eds.): ICAT 2006, LNCS 4282, pp. 938–947, 2006.

1.1   Classification of Human Body Modeling Methods

A variety of body modeling methods exist [1]. They fall into 4 major categories: authoring, capturing, interpolating, and modeling fitting.

For authoring methods, authors create a model from scratch by interacting with low-level building primitives such as vertices and edges. They often resort to complicated commercial modeling software such as Maya[1] for this purpose. Recently capturing methods became more popular. They use special equipments ranged from stereos [2] to 3D scanners[2]. The resulting model often has holes in it and is over complex. More importantly, it must go through a hard and tedious rigging procedure to be animated. Then there are data-driven methods, which generate new model by interpolating [3] or segmenting then re-compositing [4] existing sets of example models.

The last category is model-fitting methods [5, 6, 7, 8], which derive a new model by using information extracted from pictures to modify the generic one. The resulting model is visually appealing and animatable.

1.2   Related Work on Model Fitting Methods

The methods in the last category best suit to our need. There are two representatives. The first one is presented by Hilton et al [5] uses four orthogonal pictures to capture shape details of an individual. The core of the method was to project the generic model to the image space, make modification in 2D, then project back to 3D.

Lee et al. [7] argue that Hilton's method can cause visible seam in the result model and propose an enhanced method to solve this problem. Their method first computed the 3D position of a set of manually specified feature points. Main processing is composed of three steps: skeleton modification, rough skin modification based on feature points, and fine skin modification based on silhouette. The second step addressed the connection problems. But her method required that the generic model have strict grid topology linkage not found in almost all existing model.

1.3   Related Work on Mesh Deformation

Model fitting methods have three key points: identifying and extracting personal shape feature, deforming the generic model accordingly, preserving connectivity in the generic model. These issues have close relation to mesh deformation. Magnenat-Thalmann et al. use joint-local deformation [9] to deform the shape of animated hand. Others [10, 11, 12] use similar mechanism to deform animated human body. All these algorithms made use of the cross-section structures of human body parts.

In this paper, we devise a slice space representation which better conforms to the intrinsic structure of human body. With this representation every body

---

[1]   http://www.alias.com/
[2]   http://www.cyberware.com/

part can be thought as a set of slices, and every point lies on a single slice. So all points in the body part is re-parameterized with two variables: the relative position of the slice it lies in, and its relative position in the slice. With this novel representation, our method can achieve better deformation of the generic model. More details in captured picture are extracted and more connectivity in the generic model is preserved.

Details of our method are provided in Section 2. Section 3 presents experimental results and discussions. Section 4 concludes this paper and gives possible future research directions.

2   Slice Space Representation Based Deformation

Our method expects two inputs: a) the pictures (referred as captured image in the context) of an individual taken from front and side view, and b) a generic human model. The method first calculates the camera setting for capturing those images, then renders two images (referred as model image in the context) with this setting. Next, body silhouette in all images are extracted and segmented into correspondent parts.

The core of our method is an improved two-dimensional mapping algorithm based on slice space representation, which builds correspondence between points inside every pair of correspondent parts. After building this two-dimensional mapping, the method projects every point in the generic model to image space, computes its corresponding pixel in captured image by applying the above 2D mapping, and finally inversely projects the new pixel to 3D space to get the new 3D position of that point in the generic model. Images from front view modify the width and height of model whereas those from left view modify the depth and height. The final result model is a combination of these two modifications, Fig. 1 shows the flowchart.

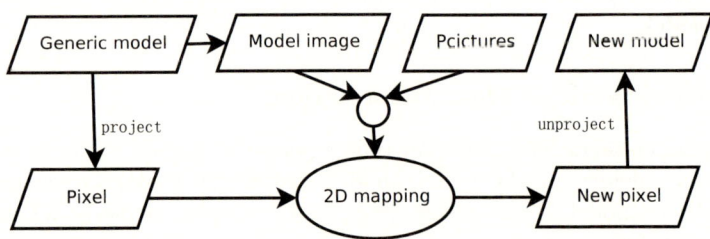

Fig. 1. System flowchart

2.1   Generic Model Building

Our method use a generic model composed of two parts. The first part provides a joint tree structure which describes the skeleton of the human body and defines how to manipulate this tree to generate animation. Joints also divide the whole human body into a set of segments detached to it. If the location and orientation of a joint are changed, related segment will move accordingly.

Segment is the second part. It provides shape information of the surface such as geometric coordinate, normal, color and texture, etc. Adjacent segment have a common subset of points lying exactly on the same position in 3D space to ensure C1 connection of the surface.

Our generic model conforms to H-Anim[3] LOA1 joint hierarchy (as in Fig. 2(b)). It is better than the one (as in Fig. 2(a)) in Hilton's method [5]. Hilton use an over simplified segmentation scheme demanded by his mapping algorithm. The difference is shown in Fig. 2. Notably, in his scheme the upper torso and a large part of upper arm are in a single segment, which is problematic and can cause breaks and/or overlaps when the model is animated.

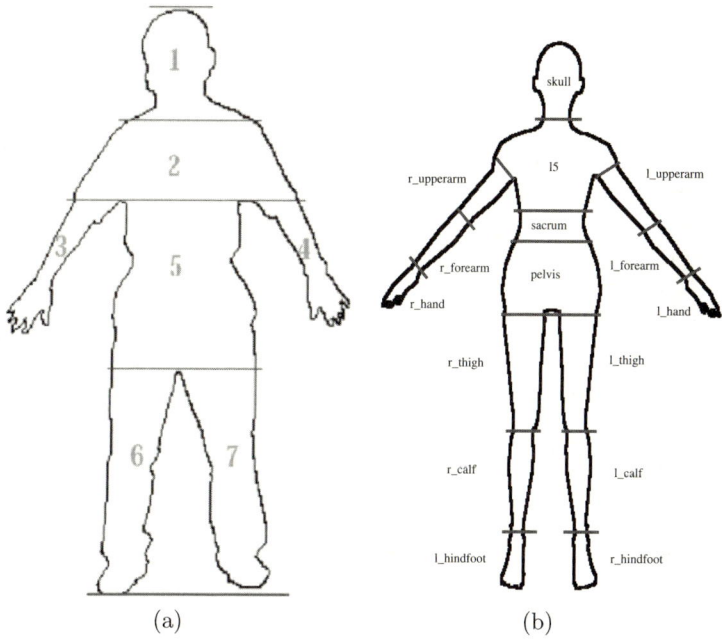

(a)   (b)

Fig. 2. Model segmentation: (a)Hilton's scheme [6]: upper torso and large part of upper arm are mixed into a single segment. (b) our scheme: the border between torso and arm is slant, which is more natural.

2.2   Image Generating and Segmenting

In the second part of preparation stage, camera settings of captured images were calculated. Since these pictures are known to be taken from exact front and side view, only the focus length and the distance between the camera and the person need to be calculated. Then simulated pictures (model images) are generated

---

[3] http://www.h-anim.org/

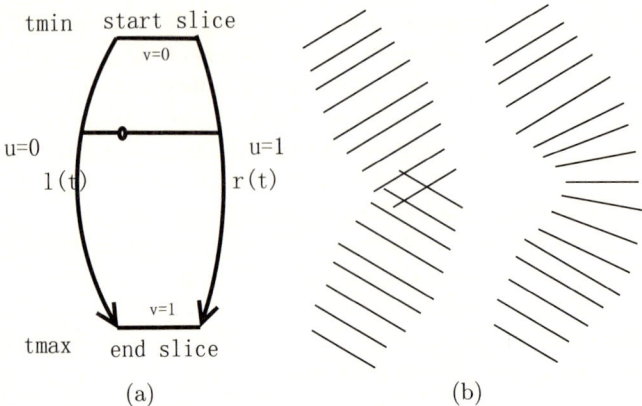

Fig. 3. 2D mapping: (a) coordinates system mapping. (b) slice re-orientating.

under the same camera settings. With all these images, silhouettes are extracted and segmented into parts. Output of this stage is four sets of borders of all body parts: front model borders, side model borders, front-captured borders, and side-captured borders.

2.3   2D-Mapping

This section describes our new 2D-mapping algorithm based on slice space deformation. Given the model border and captured border produced in the previous section, the 2D-mapping algorithm will map every point inside the model border to a point inside the captured border. Mapping algorithm under basic condition will be introduced first, followed by further enhancements necessary to tackle practical conditions.

Coordinate System Mapping. The simplest case is shown in Fig. 3(a). Every border is composed of left and right halves. The line (referred as start slice) from the start point of left side to the start point of the right side is parallel to the line (referred as end slice) from the end point of left side to the end point of right side. For every point inside the border, there exists a line which passes through it and is parallel to the top line. The union of these lines will cover the whole space inside the border. Such line are referred as slice. Therefore, a point inside the border can be defined by two parameters, u, which describes the relative position of the underlining slice in the set of slices, and v, which describes the relative position of the point on the slice.

Let border $\mathbf{B}$ be a union of two sides $\mathbf{L}$ and $\mathbf{R}$, both of which are point sets, and let point be $(s,\ t)$, two auxiliary function $l(t)$ and $r(t)$ computing the s coordinate of a point on left/right border will be:

$$\begin{cases} l(t) = s, & \text{if} (s,t) \in \mathbf{L} \\ r(t) = s, & \text{if} (s,t) \in \mathbf{R} \end{cases} . \tag{1}$$

Let point in Cartesian Coordinates be (s, t), and point in slice space be (u, v), the mapping between them will be:

$$\begin{cases} v = \frac{t - t_{\min}}{t_{\max} - t_{\min}} \\ u = \frac{s - l(t)}{r(t) - l(t)} \end{cases} \tag{2}$$

and

$$\begin{cases} t = t_{\min} + v \cdot (t_{\max} - t_{\min}) \\ s = l(t) + u \cdot (r(t) - l(t)) \ . \end{cases} \tag{3}$$

Slant Segment Handling. In practice, not all segments are vertical. For example, the arms and legs are often slanting. A certain rotation around the middle point of the start slice will transform the border to condition described in the previous section. Let the rotation angle be θ and the coordinates corresponding to the slant and vertical axis be defined as (x, y) and (s, t), the transformation between them will be:

$$\begin{cases} s = \cos(\theta) \cdot (x - c_x) + \sin(\theta) \cdot (y - c_y) \\ t = -\sin(\theta) \cdot (x - c_x) + \cos(\theta) \cdot (y - c_y) \end{cases} \tag{4}$$

and

$$\begin{cases} x = s \cdot \cos(\theta) - t \cdot \sin(\theta) + c_x \\ y = s \cdot \sin(\theta) + t \cdot \cos(\theta) + c_y \ . \end{cases} \tag{5}$$

Pose Difference Handling. Generic models are usually at relaxing pose with corresponding points in adjacent parts lie in the same position. If neighboring segments are transformed independently, the result model will exhibit seams and/or overlaps. Like Babski's method [11] in 3D, our method operates in 2D by re-orientating the slices. All points in the body part will rotate around the center of the slice it lies on according to distance from the underlining slice to start slice. The angle of rotating decreases as the distance increases. After this re-orientating, adjacent segments will stay connected, neither seam nor overlap will occur. Fig. 3(b) is the schematic diagram. Let the point with and without deformation be (a, b) and (x, y), the transformation between them will be:

$$\begin{cases} b = y \\ a = u \cdot \cos(w(y)) \end{cases} \tag{6}$$

and

$$\begin{cases} y = b \\ x = \frac{a}{\cos(w(y))} \ , \end{cases} \tag{7}$$

in which $w(y)$ is the weight function,

$$w(y) = \begin{cases} \frac{1}{y-1}, & y > 1 - \varepsilon \\ 0, & \text{othterwise} \\ \frac{1}{\varepsilon - y}, & y < \varepsilon \ . \end{cases} \tag{8}$$

2.4   3D Location Modifying

In this section, we will first introduce the mapping between 2D points and 3D points, then combine this mapping and the 2D mapping in Section 3.3 to modify all points in the generic model. Points in 2D and those in 3D can be related to each other by projection matrix, model-view matrix and viewport matrix [13]. Let R be a rotation matrix and $t = [t_x \ t_y \ t_z]^T$ a translation vector, the mapping will be [14]:

$$
\begin{bmatrix} x \\ y \\ 1 \end{bmatrix} = \begin{bmatrix} f & 0 & 0 \\ 0 & f & 0 \\ 0 & 0 & 1 \end{bmatrix} \begin{bmatrix} 1 & 0 & 0 & 0 \\ 0 & 1 & 0 & 0 \\ 0 & 0 & 1 & 0 \end{bmatrix} \begin{bmatrix} R^T & -R_t^T \\ 0_3^T & 1 \end{bmatrix} \begin{bmatrix} X \\ Y \\ Z \\ 1 \end{bmatrix} . \tag{9}
$$

Both of these matrices can be computed from the extracted camera setting. Furthermore there are two utility function called gluProject and gluUnproject to help us do this task.

Every 3D point (X, Y, Z) in the generic model is projected to a 2D point (x, y) with a depth value z. The 2D mapping algorithm will then find the corresponding 2D point (x', y') in the captured image. Combining this new 2D location with the depth value got before, forms a triad, which can be inversely projected to a 3D point. After changing the position of all 3D point, the model will exhibit similar shape to that in the captured image. As in Hilton's method, our method also employs the depth value in the generic model as an approximation of that in the new model. But since the distance between the camera and person, about three meters, is large relative to the difference of corresponding points in the two models, this is a reasonable approximation.

Modification based on pictures of a single view only changes the shape orthogonal to the viewing direction and is incomplete. Full adjustment is the combination of the modifications obtained from two views. Repeating this procedure for every point in the generic model will give us the new model.

3   Experimental Results

We implemented the above algorithm in a PC with 512M memory and 1.2G CPU. Low level algorithms are implemented in C whereas the GUI part is written in Python. The generic model is captured by 3D whole body scanners. We filled the holes in it with Blender[4], and cut it into segments with a script. When capturing reference pictures, we fixed the distance from the camera to the center of the person being photographed at 3m. As head, feet, and hands were too small in the pictures, there was not enough information to apply the above algorithm to it. They were simply scaled and translated. The results is shown in Fig. 4.

Besides the obvious resemblance of height and weight between the result model and the picture, local features such as delicate contour details in arms and legs

---

[4]   http://blender.org/

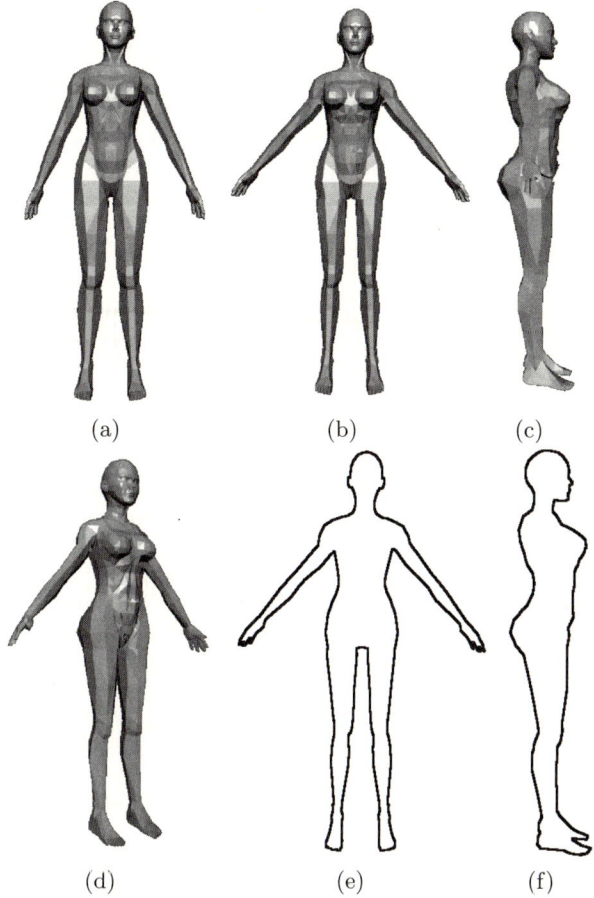

Fig. 4. Results. (a) generic model. (b), (c), and (d) result model from front, side, and new view. (e) and (f) silhouettes extracted from front and side pictures.

are also captured. Neither seams nor overlaps exist. And because of the structure inherited from the generic model, the result is ready to be animated. Our method does not require the strict topological restriction in [8]. Neither does it require the pose in the picture to be similar to that in the generic model, which helps the potentially wide use of our method.

4   Conclusion and Future Work

This paper presents an improved method for building articulated human body, which deforms the generic model with features extracted in individual pictures. Our contribution is the novel slice space representation conforming to the natural feature of human body, which captures more details in individual pictures and preserves the connectivity of surface in more cases.

Although it gives satisfactory result in most case, sometimes it cannot handle the shoulder joint very well. Solving this problem completely will require incorporation of other specialized deformation techniques such as pose space deformation [15] or difference coordinates [16], which is our future work. Integrating our modeling method with path-planning techniques [17,18,19] generate realistic human animation of individuals in pictures is also a promising direction.

Acknowledgements

This project is co-supported by 973 project (grant no: 2002CB312100) and Key NSFC project on Digital Olympic Museum(grant no: 60533080).

References

1. Magnenat-Thalmann, N., Seo, H., Cordier, F.: Automatic modeling of virtual humans and body clothing. Journal of Computer Science and Technology **19** (2004) pp.575–584
2. Devernay, F., Faugeras, O.D.: Computing differential properties of 3-d shapes from stereoscopic images without 3-d models. In: Proc. of Computer Vision and Pattern Recognition. (1994) 208–213
3. Sloan, P.P., Rose, C., Cohen, M.: Shape by example. In: Symposium on Interactive 3D Graphics. (2001)
4. Funkhouser, T., Kazhdan, M., Shilane, P., Min, P., Kiefer, W., Tal, A., Rusinkiewicz, S., Dobkin, D.: Modeling by example. In: ACM SIGGRAPH 2004. (2004)
5. Hilton, A., Gentils, T.: Capturing human models to populate virtual worlds. Technical report, CVSSP, University of Surrey, UK (1998)
6. Hilton, A., Beresford, D., Gentils, T., Smith, R., Sun, W.: Virtual people: Capturing human models to populate virtual worlds. In: IEEE Computer Animation. (1999)
7. Lee, W., Goto, T., Magnenat-Thalmann, N.: Making h-anim bodies. In: Avatars2000. (2000) pp.37–44
8. Lee, W., Gu, J., Magnenat-Thalmann, N.: Generating animatable 3d virtual humans from photographs. In: Computer Graphics Forum. Volume 10 of 3. (2000) pp.1–10
9. Magnenat-Thalmann, N., Laperrière, R., Thalmann, D.: Joint-dependent local deformations fo hand animation and object grasping. In: Proc. Graphics Interface. (1988) 26–33
10. Jianhua, S., Magnenat-Thalmann, N., Thalmann, D.: Human skin deformation from cross sections. In: Proc. Computer Graphics International '94. (1994)
11. Babski, C., Thalmann, D.: A seamless shape for hanim compliant bodies. In: VRML 99: Fourth Symposium on the Virtual Reality Modeling Language. (1999) 21–28
12. Thalmann, D., Shen, J., Chauvineau, E.: Fast human body deformations for animation and applications. In: Proceedings of Computer Graphics International 1996. (1996) 166–174
13. Neider, J., Davis, T., Woo, M.: OpenGL Programming Guide: The Official Guide to Learning OpenGL. first edn. Addison-Wesley, Reading Mass. (1993)

14. Pollefeys, M.: Visual 3d modeling from images. Tutorial Notes (2002)
15. Lewis, J.P., Cordner, M., , Fong, N.: Pose space deformations: A unified approach to shape interpolation and skeleton-driven deformation. In: ACM SIGGRAPH 2000. (2000)
16. Alexa, M.: Differential coordinates for local mesh morphing and deformation. The Visual Computer **19** (2003) 105–114
17. Xu, W., Pan, Z.: A novel method for generating curved path human walking animation. In: Proceedings of 2nd Internatinoal Conference on Image and Graphics. (2002) 993–998
18. Zheng, L., Zhang, M., Tang, B.: Using motion graph for motion editing in path synthesis. In: 9th International Conference on Computer Graphics and Artificial Intelligence. (2006)
19. Ge, Y., Pan, Z., Xu, W.: Vision-based path planning in intelligent virtual environment. In: 6th International Conference on Computer Graphics and Artificial Intelligence. (2003) 25–34

Flexible Camera Setup for Visual Based Registration on 2D Interaction Surface with Undefined Geometry Using Neural Network

Ary Setijadi Prihatmanto[1], Michael Haller[2], and Roland Wagner[1]

[1] Kepler University of Linz, Institute of FAW, Altenbergerstrasse 69,
A-4040 Linz, Austria
{asetijadi, rrwagner}@faw.uni-linz.ac.at
[2] Upper Austria University of Applied Science and Digital Media,
Hagenberg, Austria
haller@fh-hagenberg.at

Abstract. Camera setup, calibration and visual based registration of Augmented Reality (AR) based tabletop setups can be a really complicated and time-intensive task. Homography is often used liberally despite its assumption for planar surfaces, where the mapping from the camera to the table can be expressed by a simple projective homography. However, this approach often fails in curved and non-planar surface setups. In this paper, we propose a technique that approximates the values and reduces the tracking error-values by the usage of a neural network function. The final result gives a uniform representation of the camera against combinations of camera parameters that will help in the multi-camera setup. We present the advantages with demonstration applications, where a laser pointer spot and a light from the lamp will be tracked in non planar surface.

Keywords: camera calibration, visual based registration, tabletop application, function approximation, neural network.

1 Introduction

Tabletop augmented reality (AR) applications with multiple cameras and projector systems are becoming more and more popular. The current generation of projectors allows a fast combination of multiple projectors that can be used simultaneously. Molyneaux and Kortuem demonstrate in [1], how the future environment can be more accommodative to the ubiquitous display paradigm rather than conventional collection of displays.

Bimber and Raskar describe in [2] a novel approach to create an application that has taken augmented reality beyond traditional eye-worn or hand-held displays. They call this technology Spatial Augmented Reality (SAR). Its popularity is also boosted by the fall in cost and availability of projectors, high-resolution cameras, personal computers and 3D graphics cards. Moreover, new generation of projection such as a Dome projector [3] gives new opportunities to create new interaction metaphors.

Despite the availability of other tracking technology, it has been shown in the recent years that vision-based tracking systems have a tremendous potential. The most

Z. Pan et al. (Eds.): ICAT 2006, LNCS 4282, pp. 948–959, 2006.
© Springer-Verlag Berlin Heidelberg 2006

common method for visual-based pose registration is the use of a homography matrix along with quadratic lens distortion model. Despite its success in the past, it suffers from inherent limitations. Hence, a more efficient and flexible solution that gives the possibilities for automation and adaptability is required to support the display ubiquity paradigm and the trend to utilize non-planar surface such as dome projection surface[3].

This paper describes the technique to use a vision-based system for visual based registration on 2D interaction surface with undefined geometry in the tabletop application. Our technique utilizes the fact that tabletop application can control what information that can be perceived by camera to create a more adaptable and easy to configure vision-based *sensor*. It also utilizes the universal approximation nature of multi-layer perceptron so the system can adapt to as wide as possible geometry of the interaction surface.

Furthermore, by maximizing the above utilization, the technique is designed so that the system can be configured without the knowledge of the internal camera parameters. Moreover, the result gives a uniform camera representation despite the various possible camera parameter combination. This feature makes fusion policy among cameras in multi-camera setup can be managed in more tangible manner. Although this paper emphasizes on tracking purposes, it will be shown that the extension to more general purposes is also possible.

In the next section, we review the related work on general camera calibration and related work on the application of neural network in connection to camera usage. Next, we describe the proposed framework starting by explaining the general overview of the problem. It is then followed by a description on the proposed method. In section 4, we demonstrate our results. Next, we illustrate various possibilities of extension and finally, we discuss the future work.

2   Related Work

Good and efficient camera calibration and visual registration have become more and more important over the last decade. As described by Baratoff et al., the calibration of an AR system can be very complex and has to be done with care [4]. A good calibration is important when we need to reconstruct a world model and interact with the world based on information that comes from a vision system tracked by a camera. Tsai's techniques can be seen as one of most influential papers in the last decade [5] [6]. The goal of the camera calibration in a conventional sense is to find the internal quantities of the camera that affect the imaging process.

In contrast, we do not model the geometry of the camera. Neither do we have to know the camera parameters nor do we have to know the relationship between the camera and the projected image. We only generate an approximation of the function that is triggered by the camera existence according to the application context by using the neural network's universal approximation feature to coup the non-linear dynamic of the imaging process due to distortions and/or non-planar geometric shape.

There are only few reported publication regarding the use of neural networks in camera calibration [7, 8, 9, 10, 11, 12]. These techniques used neural-networks either to learn the mapping from 3D world to 2D image without specifying the camera models[12] [7], as an additional stage to improve the performance of other existing techniques [9, 8], or to approximate an imaging process of camera i.e. camera representation. In [11], carefully design neural network structure is developed so each weight has its own physical meaning and different role during the training. The physical meaning of the weight of neural network is correlated to camera parameters value. It has more robust approach than the previous work, but still it gives no considerable advantage over the standard camera calibration procedure.

In the next section, we proposed a method to use neural network to create a camera representation that is used to solve visual registration problem. The MLP is used only to deal for what is intended to do which is to approximation a non-linear function. The function is carefully chosen so the universal approximation capability of MLP can be maximally utilized over all possible data region. The proposed method also addresses issues of scalability, reliability and robustness. This gives considerably advantage over the standard camera setup.

3   Proposed Framework

Fig. 1 (a) illustrates the typical setup of a tabletop application. It consists of one (or more) projector(s) and one (or more) camera(s) for tracking users' interactions (e.g. for tracking a laser pointer interaction). The interaction range and space of the application is usually limited due to the resolution of the projectors. Furthermore, most applications limit the interaction to a 2D interaction. Fig. 1 (b) shows the transformations between the spaces in a typical tabletop application. Let $C \subset \mathbb{Z} \times \mathbb{Z}$ to be the camera image space, $M \subset \mathbb{Z} \times \mathbb{Z}$ to be the application image space, $W \subset \mathbb{R}^3$ to be the world space, and $S \subset \mathbb{R}^2$ to be the 2D virtual interaction surface.

Let $f : C \to M$ denotes the mapping that map a pixel in the virtual interaction surface to the corresponding pixels in the camera image; $f^{-1} : M \to C$ denotes the mapping that map a pixel in the camera image to the corresponding pixels in the virtual interaction surface.   Mapping $\{g, h, i\}$ and its inverse are the usual transformation between respective spaces.

One of the promising features of a tabletop application is, however, that the interaction surface usually comprises an overlapping of the input and the output interaction space. Thus in this case, the interaction can be defined directly inside M and be detected visually by the camera in C. Consequently, what we need to implement the interaction is only to develop the mappings $\{f, f^{-1}\}$ (cf. Fig. 1(b)).

Before we have a discussion over the main algorithm of our approach, it is common in general practice of computer vision system, especially in tabletop application to have an indication whether a pixel in camera is part of interaction surfaces. This indication is called Screenmask.   Additionally, when we deal with multi camera setup, we also need quantities that can be compared from one camera to the other for the same interaction surfaces. This quantity is in the form of some kind of camera confidence function. A camera confidence function is a function that gives indication on how good camera sees a point in the considered surface in compare to other camera.

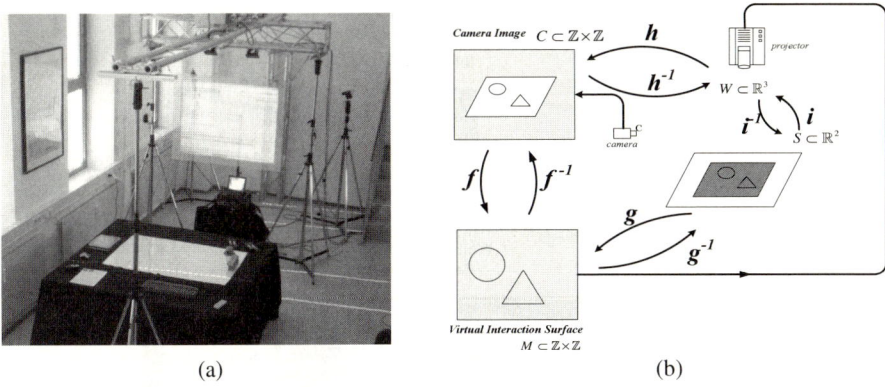

(a)   (b)

Fig. 1. The setup of the Office of Tomorrow project[1]; (a) Usually the tabletop setup consists of multiple projectors and multiple cameras; (b) Transformation between spaces in tabletop application

Hence, we have noticed that the proposed camera calibration method needs to compute: (1) a function $s(x)$ to specify whether the points in camera image space is part of interaction surface image; (2) mappings $\{f, f^{-1}\}$; and (3) a function $\delta(x)$ to specify a degree of confidence of mappings in specific points in camera setup relatives to other camera.

3.1   Screenmask Generation

Often we want to limit the processing only to the region that is really needed. For this reason, we need an indicator on whether a pixel is part of the region. In tabletop application with a 2D interaction space, it is useful to limit only to the region under consideration since it will preserve computing power and limit possible interference from the surrounding environment.

Let $s(\overline{x}): \mathbb{Z} \times \mathbb{Z} \rightarrow [0,1] \in \mathbb{Z}$ indicate whether the point $\overline{x}$ is in the region which defines an interaction surface, $J \subset C$. It is defined as

$$s(\overline{x}) = \begin{cases} \mathbf{0}, & \overline{x} \notin J \\ \mathbf{1}, & \overline{x} \in J \end{cases} \tag{1}$$

We generate the $s(\overline{x})$ function by using the ability to control what is projected onto the surface. As depicted in Fig. 2, we firstly project a black image and capture it as a background image for the reference image. Secondly, we reduce the noise and increase the contrast. Next, we project a white image onto the surface and capture it again (a), followed by a conversion to a grey colored image and a threshold operation which is applied to the image (b). The next operation is the segmentation operation based on white color (c). Since we usually place manually the camera, the surface can be seen as dominant as possible in the camera image space.

---

[1] www.coeno.org

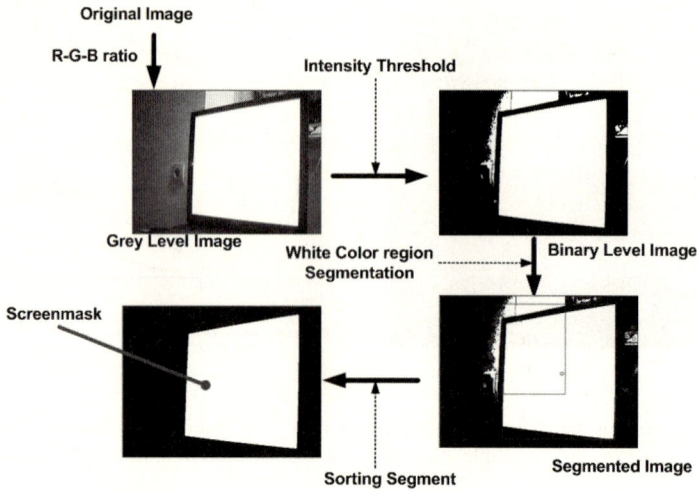

Fig. 2. The automation of the Screenmask generation

The result represents the Screenmask. The corresponding matrix representation is a popular representation due to its simplicity although it takes a huge chunk of memory and there are other possibilities to be used, e.g. a neural network classifying function. The availability of Screenmask will also help in generating data sample for calibration of mapping $\{f, f^{-1}\}$ by minimizing interference from environment, especially in automatic setup.

3.2 Neural Network Based Function Approximation

Universal approximation is a nice property of multilayer perceptron (MLP) neural networks that has unique feature to the universality of approximation using standard fixed mathematical model such as polynomial approximation. The most important difference of the approximation function using neural network is that they are better able to cope with the curse of dimensionality in the sense that the approximation error becomes independent of the dimension of the input space (under certain conditions), which is not the case for polynomial expansions. The approximation error for MLPs with one hidden layer is of order of magnitude $O(1/n_h)$, compare to $O(1/n_p^{2/n})$ for polynomial expansions where n_h denotes the number of hidden units, n the dimension of the input space and n_p the number of terms in the expansion. Models that are based on MLPs will be able to better handle larger dimensional input spaces than polynomial expansions, which is an interesting property towards many real life problems where one has to model dependencies between several variables.

One of the problems of using MLPs is the problem to decide the number of units in hidden layer. Although it has been proven that neural network with one hidden layer is in fact a universal approximator, the number of neuron unit in hidden layer that is needed is dependent on the smoothness properties of the function approximated and the desired error of approximation. Maiorov et al. show in [13] that any continuous function on the unit cube in $\mathbb{R}^d$ can be uniformly approximated to within any error by two hidden layer MLP with $3d$ units in the first hidden layer and $6d + 3$ units in the second hidden layer. Hence, we are using a four-layer with a six neurons unit in the first hidden layer, and fifteen units in the second hidden layer with the hope that it will maximize the use of sigmoid activation function.

Hence, having calibration data, the mapping f can be generated by applying backpropagation algorithm to the neural-network. Moreover, with the same calibration data only with different order, the invese mapping f^{-1} also can be generated with the same function structure as the neural network for mapping f.

3.3 System Calibration

Sample data that is needed to be generated is a set of pair interaction surface image point (x_s, y_s) and its corresponding camera image point (x_c, y_c). Since we can control which image has to be projected, we can generate the calibration image by putting a special designed calibration image to the interaction surface, detect it by the camera and calculate the corresponding camera image points.

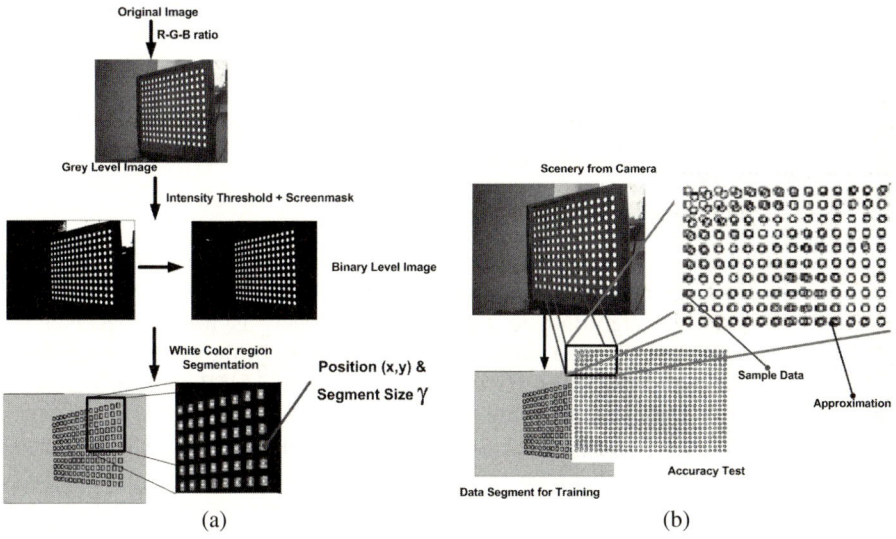

(a)   (b)

Fig. 3. (a) Vision algorithm for sample data gathering; (b) Example of a calibration scene and the accuracy of the neural network approximation

Moreover, by using the above techniques, the sample data density will change according to the degree of importance. The near region, since it has more accurate reading, only needs more sparse data. The far region of the interaction surface will generate more sample data. A region with more spatial dynamic will generate data according to the bumpiness of the region.

For calibration, we use the usual dot pattern as depicted in Fig. 3(a). We use the same algorithm as it has been used for creating the Screenmask to detect the dots (cf. Fig 2). After the dots are detected, we simply calculate the center of each dot by

$$\begin{pmatrix} x_{sc} \\ y_{sc} \end{pmatrix} = \frac{1}{\gamma} \sum_{i=1}^{\gamma} \begin{pmatrix} x_{si} \\ y_{si} \end{pmatrix}, \tag{2}$$

where (x_{sc}, y_{sc}) is the center point of each dot segment, γ is the size of the segment in pixel values and (x_{si}, y_{si}) pixel position of ith segment member.

4   Implementation and Experimental Result

We implemented the neural network by using open source FANN neural network library [14]. In the experiment, we are using a desktop PC with 3 GHz, Pentium IV, for the projection we used a single-projector setup with a resolution of 1024 x 768 pixels. The typical learning time for a calibration image with 20 pixels radius dot was computed in around 117 seconds. In this case, we used the MPL network with 21 neurons in hidden layers.

Fig. 3(b) illustrates the accuracy of the MLP-based mappings implementation. The red dots represent sample data generated for learning, and the blue dots represent an approximation achieved by the neural network. Notice that the right part of the camera space is naturally a region with better accuracy, and left part considered lower. It is shown that the region with lowest accuracy expectation i.e. image region of far top of the computer screen can be well approximated despite the limited amount of camera image pixels represents the area.

4.1   Automatic Calibration Algorithm

We automate the calibration process by using the same algorithm as the manual calibration model. In contrast, we project the individual dots one-by-one to the surface and apply the algorithm to each image. A delay is needed between the projection of a single dot on the surface and the capturing of the camera to grab the dot image. In our setup using a 3 GHz Pentium IV PC with a USB camera, we used a frequency of 0.5 seconds to project one dot image after the other.

Notice that in our system, we use various number of dots based on its size. Smaller dot give more sample data with the expense of processing time. The typical setup is 20 pixels radius dot so for an interaction surface with 1024 x 768 resolutions will gives 540 dots, thus it took about 270 seconds for the automatic projection of the entire dot pattern. Unfortunately, we cannot put more than one dot images at a time, since we cannot differentiate which dot in the camera image surface corresponds to the dot in the calibration image. This feature gives the system high flexibilities that the camera does not need to see any additional cue with special feature.

4.2   Experimental Result

We developed a demo-application that tracks the movements of a laser pointer [15]. Thus, the users can manipulate the cursor by moving the red laser pointer. We used two different combinations of camera-interaction surfaces, a planar (cf. Fig. 4(a)) and non-planar (cf. Fig. 4(b)), and two different cameras with different properties, i.e. a low-end USB webcam (640x480 pixels) and a firewire Imaging Source camera with a resolution of 1024x768 pixels and a Fujinon fisheye lens with 180° field of view. The non-planar surface is basically beyond the intended design which is a smooth and continuous surface. It contains a discontinuity and sharp edges. These direct usages of mapping f showed interesting mapping accuracy of the approach.

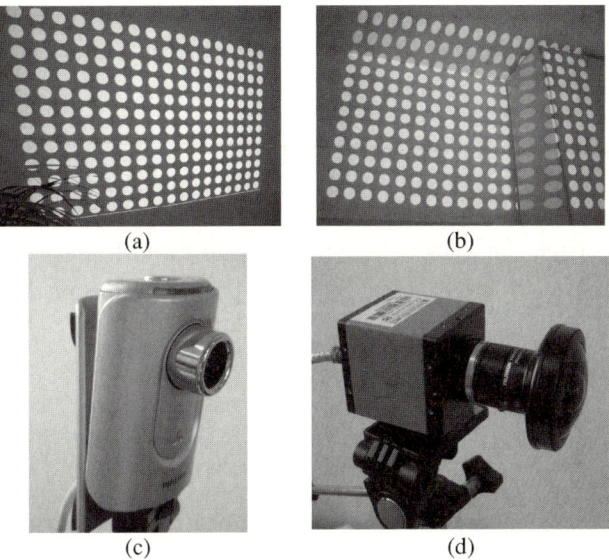

(a)   (b)

(c)   (d)

Fig. 4. In the demo-application, we used a planar wall surface (a), a distorted environment (b), a non-expensive USB webcam (c), and a firewire camera with fisheye-lens with 180° (d)

Fig. 5 depicts the accuracy results. Blue dots represent a calibration dot in application image space. Red dots represent approximation accuracy. The image (a) presents the accuracy by using a USB camera with no special lens and the planar surface of Figure 5 (a). Notice that the red dots are neatly overlapped by the blue dots. Figure (b) depicts the accuracy of the USB camera on the non-planar surface of Figure 5 (b). Notice that the approximation is practically similar. It is only a little bit off in the far left region of the surface, which is a normal since we stretch the application surface to such a distortion.

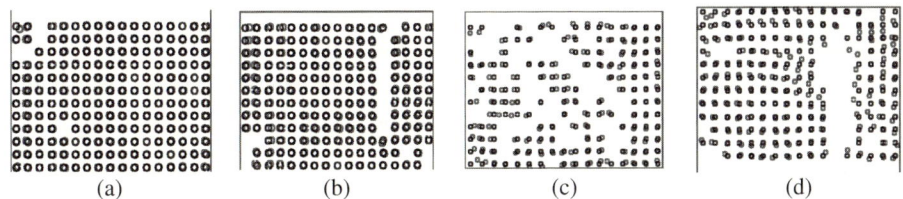

(a)   (b)   (c)   (d)

Fig. 5. Approximation accuracy for planar & distorted environment on wall surface with normal camera (a) and (b), fisheye lens (c) and (d)

6   Multi Camera Setup in 2D Interaction Surface

One of the main problems in the setup of the system with more than one camera is on how to manage the information come from more than one camera with various combinations of camera parameters. Considering Equation 2 which shows the quantity γ, i.e. the size of a dot segment. In our approach, this quantity can be a good basis to develop the third estimate, $\partial(\overline{x})$. The apparent size of dot by the camera consistently indicates how good the estimation by mapping f will be. Bigger dot sizes, which are related to closer distance between the points to the camera, give more degree of confidence to the estimation result. This γ value for each of the camera that is looking at the same point in the system gives a kind of probability function of estimate of that point for each camera.

Let $\partial_i(p_i)$ denote for camera-i degree of confidence γ for a calculated point $p_i = f_i(\overline{x})$ with $\overline{x}$ is a detected camera image pixel by camera-i. A probability for point $\overline{n}$ is given as

$$\rho(\overline{n}) = \begin{cases} \dfrac{\partial_i(p_i)}{\sum \partial_i(p_i)}, & \overline{n} = p_i \\ 0, & elsewhere \end{cases} \tag{3}$$

Hence, like the mapping f for each camera, the degree of confident function $\partial(\overline{x})$ is also being presented by the neural network based approximation function, which results in a smooth representation function over C. Notice that the neural network has the same structure of mapping f.

Given the probability function $\partial_i(p_i)$ denotes for camera-i degree of confidence γ for a calculated point $p_i = f_i(\overline{x})$ with $\overline{x}$ is a detected camera image pixel by camera-i. The best estimates for $\overline{x}$ is $\hat{x}$ will be

$$\hat{x} = E[\rho(\overline{n})] = \frac{\sum \partial_i(p_i) \cdot p_i}{\sum \partial_i(p_i)} \tag{4}$$

Additionally, to coup with various possible camera resolutions, we can start with the idea by considering the fact that the camera with lower resolution has a lower degree of confidence than the camera with higher resolution with the factor as the ratio of the size of each camera image area. Let resolution for camera-i is specified by parameter $\zeta_i = width \times height / k$ where k is a scaling factor. Given probability function $\partial_i(p_i)$ denotes for camera-i degree of confidence γ for a calculated point $p_i = f_i(\overline{x})$ with $\overline{x}$ is a detected camera image pixel by camera-i. Thus, the best estimates for $\overline{x}$ is $\hat{x}$ can be given by

$$\hat{x} = E[\rho(\overline{n})] = \frac{\sum \zeta_i \cdot \partial_i(p_i) \cdot p_i}{\sum \zeta_i \cdot \sum \partial_i(p_i)} \tag{5}$$

7   Discussion

Although the above technique is designed specifically to solve the registration problem on the 2D interaction surface, it has been found that it can directly be used for solving 2D object augmentation problem. Furthermore, having the knowledge the geometry of the interaction surface and the pose of the camera relative to the interaction surface are known by a simple additional step, another kind of visual based registration problem can also being solved. Even the development of stereo camera pair can be done with the degree of complexity as simple as the complexity of the setup for one camera.

Suppose we have a 2D object, such as 2D image, texture or video images etc., is defined in virtual interaction surface M, by using directly inverse mapping f^{-1}, we can simulate the imaging process of the camera which put the 2D object inside camera image space C as seems as the 2D object is lied in physical surface S. Fig. 6(a) illustrates the augmentation achieved for 2D texture into environment scenes. It is illustrated in that the original scene can be altered by augmentation of 2D object into the image of original scene with correct perspective. Notice that the screen monitor is not a planar surface and the augmentation also shows such quality. The ability to be

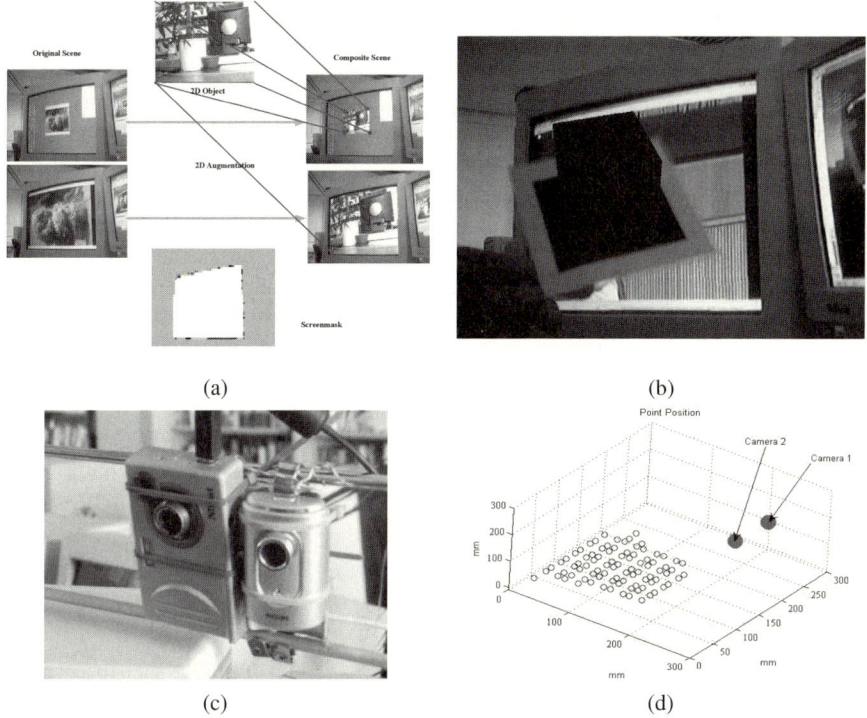

Fig. 6. The example of extensions of the proposed method; (a) 2D object augmentation problem; (b) 3D object augmentation problem; (c) The camera pair for stereo camera experimentation; (d) Experimental data from points of a plane are seen by the stereo camera pair

used for tracking accurately and augmenting 2D object for more wide class physical surface is one of the strength of the proposed method over the standard method.

A fiducial marker based applications is a popular augmented reality application. To be useful, the proposed framework should be able to do the same. Knowing the knowledge the geometry of the interaction surface and the pose of the camera relative to the interaction surface means that we have a knowledge of set of mapping $\{f, g, i\}$. Hence, we can use that knowledge to implement 3D object augmentation like *Magic Book*. Fig. 6(b) illustrates the implementation of the proposed method for solving a 3D object augmentation problem.

Having similar setup like the 3D object augmentation problem above for two cameras with fixed position to each other, the stereo camera pair equation can be generated instantly. Fig. 6(c) shows the stereo camera pair that we have used and Fig. 6(d) illustrates experiment range data of a plane for the stereo camera pair.

8   Conclusion and Future Work

For a 2D interaction surface with unknown geometry, the framework gives a straight-forward solution to generate mapping between camera image space and interaction surface and still able to capture the spatial dynamic of the surfaces. Moreover, the technique gives a basis to create simple setup to manage system with multi-camera setup, especially for the future tabletop application where more than one projectors and cameras are needed. However, implementation of the technique into various applications is still needed to understand the complete behavior of the proposed method.

In theory, the neural network approximation error can be minimized as small as possible. This allows developers to focus more on computer vision algorithm which can produce good visual cue detection with small error detection, rather than fighting with calibration errors. Nevertheless, more thorough analysis and experimentation need to be made to gain complete understanding the comparative advantage in the accuracy gain by the proposed technique over the standard method for various scenarios.

Acknowledgments. This research is partly funded by the Austrian FFG consortium (FHplus framework, project no. 811407) and Voestalpine Informationstechnologie.

References

1. D. Molyneaux and G. Kortuem, *Ubiquitous displays in dynamic environments: Issues and opportunities*, Ubiquitous Computing 2004, 2004.
2. O. Bimber and R. Raskar, *Modern approaches to augmented reality*, SIGGRAPH 2005, 2005.
3. R. Raskar, "http://www.Mpcnet.Co.Jp/prodct/proj/index.html," 2006.
4. G. Baratoff, A. Neubeck and H. Regenbrecht, *Interactive multi-marker calibration for augmented reality application*, International Symposium on Mixed and Augmented Reality (ISMAR'02), 2002, 107.

5. R. Y. Tsai, *An efficient and accurate camera calibration technique for 3d machine vision*, IEEE Conference on Computer Vision and Pattern Recognition, 1986, 364-374.
6. R. Y. Tsai, *A versatile camera calibration technique for high-accuracy 3d machine vision metrology using off-the-shelf tv cameras and lenses*, IEEE Journal of Robotics and Automation **RA-3** (1987), no. 4, 323-344.
7. M. Lynch and C. Dagli, *Backpropagation neural network for stereoscopic vision calibration*, SPIE Internationa Society of Optical Engineering, 1991.
8. J. Wen and G. Schweitzer, *Hybrid calibration of ccd camera using artificial neural network*, International Join Conference on Neural Network **1** (1991).
9. D. Choi, S. Oh, H. Chang and K. Kim, *Nonlinear camera calibration using neural network*, Neural, Parallel and Scientific Calibration **2** (1994), no. 1, 29-41.
10. M. Ahmed, E. Hemayed and A. Farag, *Neurocalibration: A neural network that can tell camera calibration parameters*, IEEE International Conference on Computer Vision (ICCV'99), 1999.
11. M. Ahmed and A. Farag, *Locked, unlocked and semi-locked network weights for four different camera calibration problems*, IEEE International Joint Conference on Neural Networks (IJCNN'2001), 2001.
12. Q. Memon and S. Khan, *Camera calibration and three dimensional world reconstruction of stereo vision using neural networks*, International Journal of Systems Science **32** (2001), no. 9, 1155-1159.
13. V. Maiorov and A. Pinkus, *Lower bounds for approximation by mlp neural networks*, Neurocomputing **25** (1999), 81-91.
14. S. Nissen, A. Spilca, A. Zabot, D. Morelli, E. Nemerson, Freegoldbar, G. Megidish, Joshwah, M. Pereira, M. Vogt, S. Hauberg, T. Leibovici and V. D. Massa, *Fast Artificial Neural Network Library*, http://leenissen.dk/fann/, 2006.
15. J.-Y. Oh and W. Stuerzlinger (Editors), *Laser pointers as collaborative pointing devices*, 2002.

Painterly Rendering with Vector Field Based Feature Extraction

Chen Pang, Mingli Song, Jiajun Bu, Chun Chen, and Dong Wang

Zhejiang University - Microsoft Joint Lab of Visual Perception,
Key Lab of Ministry of Education
Zhejiang University, Hangzhou, P.R. China*
{pangc, brooksong, bjj, chenc}@zju.edu.cn

Abstract. In this paper, a novel technique is presented to incorporate vector field based feature extraction schemes into painterly rendering. This approach takes a raster photograph as input and automatically creates a hand-painting style picture. Via techniques formerly used in image segmentation, a vector field representation are generated, identifying color and texture variations at each pixel location, and a series of brush strokes are created with sizes and alignments controlled by the vector field and color matched from the original picture. Moreover, different scale parameters could be utilized to produce several vector fields depicting images features of the original photograph from rough outline to detail. The final output could be rendered first by brushstrokes in the coarsest scale and refined progressively. Unlike conventional techniques that used taking account only of local color gradients, this approach employs multi-scale feature extraction scheme to guide stroke generation with image structure on larger scale.

1 Introduction

The automatic creation of artistic paintings from photographs has long been a favored topic of non-photorealistic rendering. Artists create representations of their view of the real world with expressive paintbrushes, usually with some level of abstraction. Researchers have made efforts to simulate this process and automatically produce images bearing visual resemblance to artistic works. Most methods in this class create a set of brush strokes from the source image and render them on a simulated canvas. The two steps address two major issues concerned: brush stroke generation and rendering.

Some earlier systems created brush strokes randomly[1], later ones used local color variations[2], but a better representation of structural features in the source image usually leads to finer results. Computer vision techniques provide plenty of methods to extract useful information from raster images, ranging from color variations to object structures. When these features are employed as guidance of generating strokes, the resulting stroke set could be seen as an abstraction of

---

* This paper is supported by the National Science Foundation of China (60573176).

Z. Pan et al. (Eds.): ICAT 2006, LNCS 4282, pp. 960–968, 2006.

the source image. The stroke rendering process varies from simply flood filling the area the stroke covers, to mapping real paintbrush texture, and further to sophisticated physical simulations of specific paint media.

With the aims of utilizing image features on various scales in the stroke generation process, we incorporated into painterly rendering a recently proposed vector field based edge detection and image segmentation scheme[3][4]. These systems create 2D vector field representations of the source image as a preprocessing step for finding object boundaries. The vector fields contain quantitative information of image boundaries at each pixel location, which is essential in simulating many painting styles because the orientations of strokes in real paintings are also generally affected by adjacent edges. The quantitative representations of image features as vector fields therefore provide a superior basis for stroke alignment.

In this paper, we take a raster photograph as input, and automatically generate a painting like image consist of several layers of brush strokes. The system starts by constructing multiple Edgeflow vector fields [3][4] from coarse to fine scales. At each scale and at each pixel location, a flow direction pointing to the closest boundary are obtained. Therefore by following the perpendicular direction of the vectors, strokes can be aligned to their adjacent edges. The overall painting process runs afterwards, first generating and rendering the strokes created from the vector field of the coarsest level, and update the canvas progressively on each finer scale, where minor edges cause inconsistencies with those of the previous layer.

The next section introduces some techniques related to our work. Section 3 presents the multi-scale edge flow vector generation scheme. Section 4 discusses the overall painting process, followed by a detailed description of the brush stroke generation and rendering mechanism in Sect. 5, where image features represented in vector fields are mapped to characteristics of composed strokes. We provide some sample results in Sect. 6 and then conclude this paper.

2   Related Work

This paper follows a long line of works on stroke-based non-photorealistic rendering that began with Haelberi[1], who have shown that abstract paintings could be simulated using an ordered collection of brush strokes. Meier[5] created painterly rendered animations with a particle system. Litwinowicz[6] used clipped strokes with a given center, length, radius and orientation to produce impressionist-style video. Gooch et al.[7] pointed out image features obtained from segmentation could guide stroke generation. Kovács[8] applied multi-scale edge and ridge detection[9] to control stroke sizes and painting directions. This approach bears some resemblance with the one in this paper, but in [8] strokes are modeled simply as rectangles and their orientation correspond only to the local color gradient of its nearest edge.

Much of the inspiration of this paper comes from Hertzmann[2], who produced images with long curved brush strokes built up by several layers. Brush strokes are modeled as a series of B-splines positioned to a grid mapped on the image, and created with guidance of local color gradients. He also introduced rendering an image with multiple layers, starting from the coarsest level containing large strokes depicting the sketches of the image, to progressively finer scales of smaller strokes.

Some other works focus on simulating artistic media, including brush, ink and the canvas. Curtis et al.[10] did some very successful simulations of western watercolor painting using a fluid model. Chu and Tai built a brush dynamics model[11] and a ink flow model[12] that provide a remarkable resemblance of eastern calligraphy and ink paintings.

Improvements in image feature extraction techniques are also concerned. We focus our interest especially in boundary detection and image segmentation, because object edges require special consideration in various art forms. Plenty of methods on edge detection worked by convolving the image with predefined filters[13]. Detection of boundaries in these approaches is equivalent to finding the local maxima in gradient magnitude. Detecting and analyzing edges in multiple scales as well as resolutions is another widely studied technique, both from fine to coarse[13] and coarse to fine scales[14]. Lindeberg[9] introduced scale-space edge and proposed techniques on estimating optimum scales. Tabb[15] suggested an interesting idea of building a vector field for edge detection, and later in [3], Ma designed a Edgeflow vector field such that the direction of vectors at each pixel location points to the adjacent edge, and leaving scale as the only significant user parameter. Sumengen[4] augmented this approach by constructing multi-scale Edgeflow vector fields to reinforce major edges of an image, and to suppress insignificant boundaries.

3   Creating Multi-scale Vector Fields

As a preprocessing step, vector field representations of the source image is created for painterly rendering. Ma proposed in [3] the Edgeflow vector field scheme as an indirect method for boundary detection. It utilizes a predictive coding model to identify and integrate the direction of changes in image attributes. The result is a flow direction that points to closest boundary at each pixel location, with magnitude suggesting the possibility of finding an edge nearby. By propagating the flow following its direction, edges can be found at where two opposite directions of flow encounters. After boundary detection, image segmentation are completed by edge connection and region merging. The only user defined parameter significantly influencing the result is the scale value, which relates to standard deviation of the Gaussian. We are especially interested in the part of the work that a vector field representation of the original image is created that contains detailed edge information. By following the perpendicular directions of edge flow vectors strokes can be aligned to their nearby edges.

Sumengen[4] extended Ma's vector field design to multi-scale edge detection. The edge flow vector field is generated from finest scale and selectively updated with values of coarser ones. At each step, edge flow vectors whose magnitude are below certain level directly take the value from coarser scale, meaning empty areas are filled with vectors from larger scales. This way it can handle better some boundaries that cannot be detected in fine scales, such as shades and blurred edges, yet can be captured at coarser levels. In addition, edge flow vectors with coherent directions are summed up to represent major edges. The result is a vector field that expresses image feature from multiple scales.

To generate multiple vector fields, we takes much of the essence of Sumengen's approach[4] but explicitly process oppositely, from coarse to fine scales, so that the painting process can proceed starting with larger strokes of more general level and refining by progressively smaller strokes. Begin on the coarsest scale, an Edgeflow vector field is generated as described in [3], and utilized to paint the first layer of the output image. The algorithm for generating vector fields on subsequent scales in this paper is almost identical to the one proposed by Sumengen[4], except that at each step the vector field is updated with the previous one on a coarser scale. This scheme suppresses edges that are detected only in fine scales because of noise or clutters, and favors those exist at a range of levels. The resulting stroke set thus correspond to salient image structures. Every intermediate result after one update are utilized to create a layer of the output image.

4   Overall Painting Process

A painting is built up by rendering multiple layers, based on the idea proposed in [2]. Artists often draw on a blank canvas with rough sketches first, creating the outlines by following the main contours of the objects, and then continues by adding smaller strokes to refine the details. Computer algorithms[2] based on the same motivation can also yield desirable effects. We start with a blank single color canvas, renders the stroke set generated from one vector field as a layer, and repeat the process to paint all layers from coarsest to finest scales with progressively smaller strokes. On each scale, only at places where the vector field suggests inconsistency with previous scale new strokes are created and the canvas is updated. The algorithm is adapted from the one presented in [6] to work with vector fields. Starting points of strokes are positioned with a jittered grid.

```
program PlaceStrokes
    {Place stroke for one layer};
    const
        GridSize;
    var
        I, J, ImageWidth, ImageHeight : Integer;
        S, T:VectorField;
        R:Real;
    begin
        for I:=0 to ImageWidth step GridSize
            for J:=0 to ImageHeight step GridSize
            begin
                Jitter [I,J] randomly within the grid;
                Let S be the vector field at the current
                scale;
```

```
                    Let T be the vector field at the previous
                    scale;
                    if S(I,J) does not equal T(I,J) then
                         Generate the stroke at [I,J] with radius R;
          end
end.
```

In the vector field generation process, vectors with very small magnitudes are directly replaced by their equivalents in coarser scale[4]. At these image locations, little color variations can be found in local areas. Therefore strokes of coarser scales covering these area already provided enough detail of the original image, eliminating the need of further updates. In the algorithm, such vector $\overrightarrow{S(x,y)}$ on scale s is obtained by taking the value from the next coarser scale, $\overrightarrow{T(x,y)}$. Hence the condition test to generating a new stroke is checking whether their values equal. The radius of generated strokes is consistent in the same layer, and provided as an user parameter. Radius R associated with each layer should correspond to the scale of that layer. Coarse scales have larger radius values.

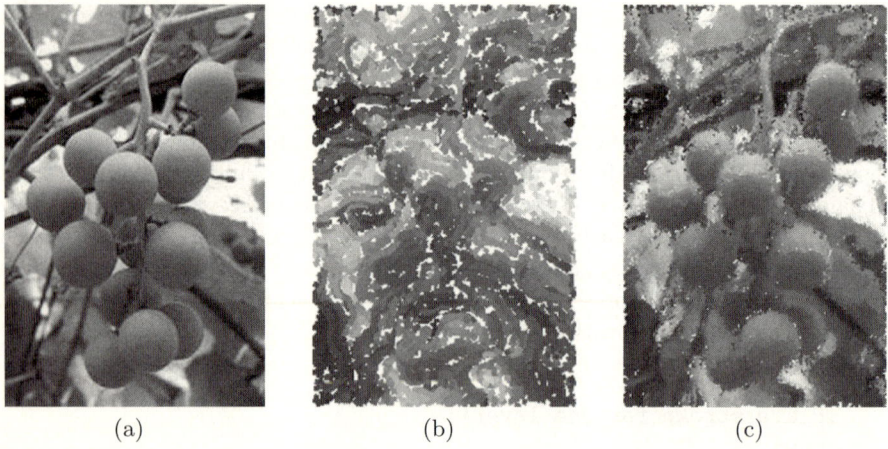

| (a) | (b) | (c) |

Fig. 1. Example of painting multiple layers with progressively smaller strokes. (a) A source image. (b) Output image after rendering the first layer. Large strokes follows the edges of grapes. (c) Output image after successively rendering three layers.

5   Generating and Rendering Strokes

With the vector field on each scale, we generate a set of B-spline strokes and renders them on a layer of the result image. Each individual stroke is a weighted curve that follows the direction perpendicular to edge flow vectors, and tends to be parallel to its adjacent edges in the original image. Each stroke takes a constant color. To obtain this color, a *reference image* is created by convoluting

Fig. 2. Example image demonstrating placement of strokes. The two images on the right are the first and second layers of rendering result. Rectangle region on the original photo is magnified to show that brush strokes on the grassland are aligned parallel to major edges and shadows, while the ones above the grassland apparently carries more curves.

the original image with a Gaussian kernel of standard deviation corresponding to the scale used in creating vector fields, e.g. by multiplying the scale value by a constant factor. Then a stroke take the color at its starting point in the *reference image*, same as the method described in [2].

The stroke generation algorithm creates a list of control points from a given location $[x_0, y_0]$ in the image. With the vector field $\vec{S}$, from any pixel location $[x, y]$, the location of the next control point is obtained by adding to the location coordinates a vector with the perpendicular direction of $\overrightarrow{S(x, y)}$, and length of R. If $\overrightarrow{S(x, y)}$ has the value of $[S(x), S(y)]$, the vector $\vec{s'}$ with value $[-S(y), S(x)]$ is perpendicular to $\overrightarrow{S(x, y)}$. Thus the location of the next control point is given by:

$$[x', y'] = [x, y] + R \times \frac{\vec{s'}}{\|\vec{s'}\|} . \tag{1}$$

where R is a user parameter that has larger values on coarser scales. We repeat propagating control points this way until any one of the following conditions is meet:

- The stroke length reaches its maximin value.
- Color difference between the reference image at $[x, y]$ and the stroke color is greater than that between the reference image at $[x, y]$ and canvas at $[x, y]$.
- The vector at $[x, y]$ is zero.
- The angle between the vectors at $[x, y]$ and at the start location of the stroke is larger than a predefined value A_1.

(a) (b)

Fig. 3. Example of a photograph rendered with three layers. Brush strokes curving to the edges and color variations on the flowers are still perceptible.

Fig. 4. More examples of results

- The angle between the vectors at $[x, y]$ and at the previous location is larger than a predefined value A_2.

The first two conditions is suggested and explained in [2], where color difference is defined as $((r_1 - r_2)^2 + (g_1 - g_2)^2 + (b_1 - b_2)^2)^{1/2}$. The other three are specifically suitable for vector fields. When the propagation stops, a brush stroke is determined by the list of control points. Limiting the angle between the vector at the two ending of a stroke is optional. Without it, circular brush strokes are allowed in the result. The throttle parameter A_2 mentioned in the last condition also leads to different visual effects. A small value will cause the resulting strokes be shorter and straighter, while a relatively larger value, e.g. π, only prevents the stroke from crossing image boundaries and restricting its curvature to a reasonable degree. Figure 2 demonstrates stroke alignments controlled by vector fields.

6   Results

In this section, we demonstrate some of the results from our implementation. Experiments shows that three to four layers with the final scale and grid size both set to 1 pixel provide satisfactory results. Over rendering usually leads to realistic appearance that bears too little artistic effects. Results are presented in Fig. 2 and Fig. 3.

Both intermediate outputs and final results shows that brush strokes are aligned in the presence of multi-level image features.

7   Conclusion

This paper presents a painterly rendering technique that incorporated image feature extraction methods based on multi-scale vector field into the stroke generation process. Several layers of B-spline strokes are created according to quantitative edge information presented in multi-scale vector fields, and represent salient boundaries better than methods that takes into account only local color variations.

References

1. Haeberli, P.: Paint by numbers: abstract image representations. In: SIGGRAPH '90: Proceedings of the 17th annual conference on Computer graphics and interactive techniques, New York, NY, USA, ACM Press (1990) 207–214
2. Hertzmann, A.: Painterly rendering with curved brush strokes of multiple sizes. In: SIGGRAPH '98: Proceedings of the 25th annual conference on Computer graphics and interactive techniques, New York, NY, USA, ACM Press (1998) 453–460
3. Ma, W.Y., Manjunath, B.S.: Edgeflow: a technique for boundary detection and image segmentation. IEEE Transactions on Image Processing **9**(8) (2000) 1375–1388
4. Sumengen, B., Manjunath, B.S.: Multi-scale edge detection and image segmentation. In: EUSIPCO '05: Proceedings of the 13th European signal processing conference. (2005)
5. Meier, B.J.: Painterly rendering for animation. In: SIGGRAPH '96: Proceedings of the 23rd annual conference on Computer graphics and interactive techniques, New York, NY, USA, ACM Press (1996) 477–484

6. Litwinowicz, P.: Processing images and video for an impressionist effect. In: SIG-GRAPH '97: Proceedings of the 24th annual conference on Computer graphics and interactive techniques, New York, NY, USA, ACM Press/Addison-Wesley Publishing Co. (1997) 407–414

7. Gooch, B., Coombe, G., Shirley, P.: Artistic vision: painterly rendering using computer vision techniques. In: NPAR '02: Proceedings of the 2nd international symposium on Non-photorealistic animation and rendering, New York, NY, USA, ACM Press (2002) 83–ff

8. Kovács, L., Szirányi, T.: Painterly rendering controlled by multiscale image features. In: SCCG '04: Proceedings of the 20th spring conference on Computer graphics, New York, NY, USA, ACM Press (2004) 177–184

9. Lindeberg, T.: Edge detection and ridge detection with automatic scale selection. Int. J. Comput. Vision **30**(2) (1998) 117–156

10. Curtis, C.J., Anderson, S.E., Seims, J.E., Fleischer, K.W., Salesin, D.H.: Computer-generated watercolor. In: SIGGRAPH '97: Proceedings of the 24th annual conference on Computer graphics and interactive techniques, New York, NY, USA, ACM Press/Addison-Wesley Publishing Co. (1997) 421–430

11. Chu., N.S.H., Tai, C.L.: Real-time painting with an expressive virtual chinese brush. Computer Graphics and Applications, IEEE **24**(5) (2004) 76–85 0272-1716.

12. Chu, N.S.H., Tai, C.L.: Moxi: real-time ink dispersion in absorbent paper. ACM Trans. Graph. **24**(3) (2005) 504–511

13. Canny, J.: A computational approach to edge detection. IEEE Trans. Pattern Anal. Mach. Intell. **8**(6) (1986) 679–698

14. Bergholm, F.: Edge focusing. IEEE Trans. Pattern Anal. Mach. Intell. **9**(6) (1987) 726–741

15. Tabb, M., Ahuja, N.: Multiscale image segmentation by integrated edge and region detection. IEEE Transactions on Image Processing **6**(5) (1997) 642–655

Reducing Time Cost of Distributed Run-Time Infrastructure[*]

Zhong Zhou and Qinping Zhao

School of Computer Science and Engineering, BeiHang University,
Beijing 100083, P.R. China
zz@vrlab.buaa.edu.cn

Abstract. RTI(Run-Time Infrastructure) provides services for HLA-based distributed simulation, and decides to a great extent the simulation scalability and efficiency. Distributed RTI has good scalability, but its time cost is always higher because of the architecture complexity. BH RTI is based on a distributed RTI architecture. Some techniques are used to overcome the problem of time cost. LoI-based data delivery algorithms are presented to speed up data delivery. PDU(protocol data unit)-function registry and RTI process model are designed to promote the efficiency of data packet processing. Experiment results illustrated that distributed BH RTI depressed the negative influence of architecture complexity and achieved a relatively lower time cost.

1 Introduction

High Level Architecture (HLA) is the prevailing standard of distributed simulation. It consists of three parts, framework and rules, object model template (OMT) and interface specification[1]. Run-Time Infrastructure (RTI) is prescribed to implement the interface specification. It provides services for HLA-based simulation, and decides to a large extent the simulation scalability and efficiency. The standard of HLA 1.3 has been widely used in military fields[1]. However, when HLA was approved as IEEE 1516 standard in September 2001, a lot of changes were made[2,3,4].

Some RTIs have been developed such as DMSO RTI NG[5,6], pRTI[7], MÄK RTI[8], BH RTI[9], KD-RTI[10] and starlink[11] etc.. Because HLA doesn't specify RTI implementation and interoperability, RTI design differs much. Different RTI cannot interoperate without the participation of each producers[12]. RTI architecture and performance are one of the main concerns in HLA/RTI applications.

This paper presents a distributed RTI architecture implemented in BH RTI. It supports multiple HLA standards by shielding interface differences in Local RTI Component(LRC). Then some techniques to overcome the problem of time cost in distributed RTI are presented. In the end experiment and result analysis are given.

---

[*] This paper is supported by the National Grand Fundamental Research 973 Program of China under Grant No. 2002CB312105.

Z. Pan et al. (Eds.): ICAT 2006, LNCS 4282, pp. 969–979, 2006.
© Springer-Verlag Berlin Heidelberg 2006

2 Problem Initiation

There are many changes in HLA interface specification transition. Messages from SISO CFI workgroup said that next evolution of HLA standard would possibly be made in 2006 or 2007. Some means have been put forward to interoperate HLA 1.3 and IEEE 1516 federates. The Pitch AB inc. developed 1516 adapter [13]. It provides HLA 1.3 APIs based on 1516 RTI implementation. Then HLA 1.3 federates can run on pRTI 1516. The MÄK Technologies Inc. said that MÄK RTI 1.3 and MÄK RTI 1516 were built from the same code base. The two can retain compatibility between 1.3 and 1516 federates[14]. We developed RTIBridge [16] based on bridge federate[15] to link 1.3 and 1516 federates. RTIBridge can link federates between HLA 1.3-based BH RTI, DMSO RTI NG and IEEE 1516-based starlink. RTIBridge covers only part interfaces, and is only suitable for small scale simulations because of the bottleneck of bridge federate.

Unpredicted revision may be made to HLA standard in future. There exist several versions of HLA standard. These problems bring much work for interoperation, other than transplant or modification. The trouble also exists in code preservation and tedious test procedure. In this background, the interoperation problem should be taken into consideration in further RTI development.

3 Distributed RTI Architecture

RTI implementation has no fixed architecture. Current RTI architectures mainly have three types: central, distributed and hierarchical, according to the relationship of CRC (Central RTI Component) and LRC. DMSO RTI is the first RTI, and had been published for several years. It has a great influence on the field. A large portion of current RTIs are based on a traditional DMSO RTI like architecture as Figure 1. Considering the interoperation of heterogeneous systems, we made an effort in distributed RTI architecture and developed BH RTI.

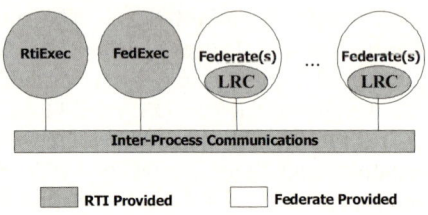

Fig. 1. Traditional DMSO RTI like architecture

The distributed RTI architecture owns several RTI nodes in peer to peer. Each RTI maintains only the required data to serve connected federates. BH RTI is divided into two processes, LRC and rtiexec (Figure 2). LRC provides a programming library following the standard. It is responsible for interface implementation based on the rtiexec. Process rtiexec is designed to provide common services of distributed simulation for LRC. The standard differences are shielded in RTI-LRC services. Then minor modification is required when the standard changes. New LRC can be developed based on RTI-LRC service for a revised HLA standard or even another standard. With this distributed RTI architecture, much work on the standard transition can be cut off, and federates of different standard are easier to interoperate.

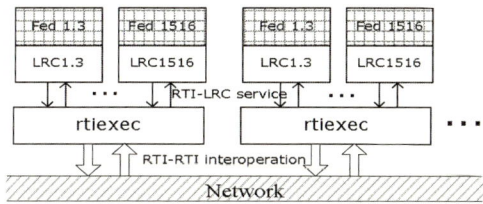

Fig. 2. Software Architecture of Distributed RTI

Although distributed architecture is good at scalability, time cost is a main negative problem for more layers and architecture complexity. Liu compared time cost of three RTI architectures[11] in which the time cost of distributed RTI is narrated as

$$T(distributed)=T(sender\_localLRC)+T(globalComputing)+T(localLRC\_remoteLRC)$$
$$+ T(remoteLRC\_receiver)$$

The time cost of distributed RTI is higher than the other two with the comparisons. To be more precise, the time cost of this distributed RTI architecture should be

$$T(distributed)=T(sender\_localLRC)+T(globalComputing)+T(localLRC\_RTI)+T(sender\_rti)+T(RTI\_RTI)+T(remote\_RTI)+T(remoteRTI\_LRC)+T(remoteLRC\_receiver)$$

The constitution of total time cost is rather complicated, including three network cost factors, $T(localLRC\_RTI)$, $T(RTI\_RTI)$, $T(remoteRTI\_LRC)$, together with four process cost factors. However, this is just analysis in theory. Each part of the cost may vary much in different implementations. The following parts present techniques applied in BH RTI to overcome the problem of time cost.

4   LoI-Based Data Delivery Algorithms

Data delivery in HLA requires attribute set matching for publish/subscribe. Sometimes region overlap is also required when DDM is used. Existing publish-subscribe mechanisms can only judge whether a message is relevant to a subscriber or not. Aiming to solve the relevance evaluation problem, a new relevance evaluation mechanism Layer of Interest (LoI) was proposed in our previous work [17][18]. LoI defines a relevance classifier based on the influence of spatial distance on receiving attributes and attribute values. Some related LoI variables are listed in Table 1. Based on LoI, new data delivery algorithms are presented in this section.

In our recent research, we drew two important deductions about the LoI relationship among the three parts, LoIs of the publisher, the subscriber and messages.

Table 1. Symbols in the LoI Mechanism

Symbol	Definition
$P_m^{(i)}$	LoI of publisher over object class i with m-size attribute set
$p_m^{(i,o)}$	LoI of local object instance o of object class i with m-size attribute set
$\eta_j^{(i,o)}$	LoI of attribute update/reflect with j-size attribute set of object instance o of object class i
$S_k^{(i)}$	LoI of subscriber over object class i with k-size attribute set
$s_l^{(i,o)}$	LoI of remote object instance o of object class i with l-size attribute set

Deduction 1. A publisher can only send attribute updates of LoI $\eta_j^{(i,o)} \leq p_m^{(i,o)}$.

Deduction 2. A subscriber can only receive attribute reflects of LoI $\eta_j^{(i,o)} \leq s_l^{(i,o)}$.

In the new publish-subscribe environment, the publisher works with $P_m^{(i)}$ of object class i and $p_m^{(i,o)}$ of local object instance o. And a subscriber works with $S_k^{(i)}$ of object class i and $s_l^{(i,o)}$ of remote object instance o. The four LoIs denote the dynamic detail relevance in publish-subscribe sides. Messages will be tagged with LoI $\eta_j^{(i,o)}$. $\eta_j^{(i,o)}$ represents the fundamental relevance of messages. Then new data delivery algorithms below can be obtained, according to Deduction 1 and 2.

Algorithm 1. (Algorithm for sending data) LoI_UAV

```
FOR each attribute update of local object instance o

    int 1 = η_j^(i,o), compute according to the Definition.

  IF (1 ≤ p_m^(i,o))

      //attach 1 to the update packet;
      update.loi = 1;
    multicast the update packet to the subscriber group;
END FOR
```

Algorithm 2. (Algorithm for receiving data) LoI_RAV

```
FOR each attribute reflect of remote object instance o

    int 1 = reflect.loi; //get η_j^(i,o)

  IF (1 ≤ s_l^(i,o))

      //the reflect packet is wanted by the subscriber
      accept the reflect packet;
    callback the corresponding user function;
END FOR
```

Complex and costly attribute set matching is simplified, and the data sending and receiving become more efficient. Receivers can also perform precise attribute set matching as Algorithm 3.

Algorithm 3. (enhanced receiving data) PreciseLoI_RAV

```
FOR each attribute reflect {HVPⱼ{<attrᵢ, valueᵢ>}, loi} of
remote object instance o

    int l = reflect.loi;

    IF (l ≤ sₗ⁽ⁱ'ᵒ⁾)

    WHILE(int h = 1; h <= j; h++){

        IF attrₕ ∉ subscription attribute set {cᵢ, <attrᵢ>}

            remove <attrₕ, valueₕ> from HVPⱼ{<attrᵢ, valueᵢ>}; }

    IF (sizeof HVPⱼ{<attrᵢ, valueᵢ>} = = 0)  break;

    accept the reflect's remaining data HVPⱼ{<attrᵢ, valueᵢ>};

    callback the corresponding user function;

END FOR
```

LoI-based data delivery algorithms were applied into BH RTI. Figure 3(a) is the sending process. Figure 3(b) is the receiving process. Four processes are included, HLA application (federate), LRC, RTI and other RTIs. Here RTI means rtiexec of BH RTI. BH RTI provides services for federates by LRCs, each LRC for one federate.

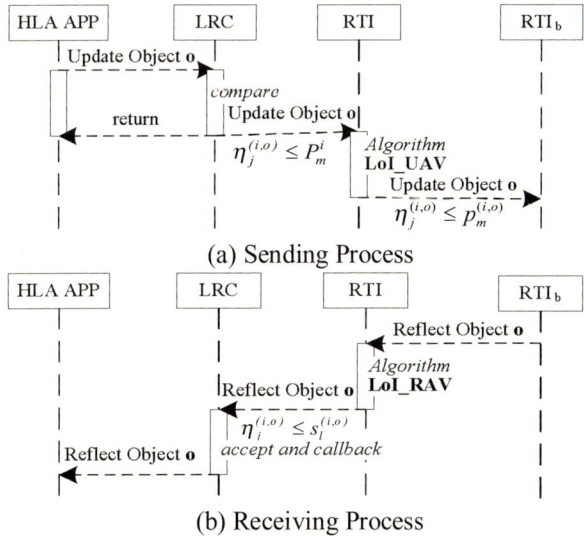

(a) Sending Process

(b) Receiving Process

Fig. 3. LoI-based Data Delivery Process in BH RTI

5   PDU-Function Registry

BH RTI involves two types of inter-process communications (IPC), RTI-LRC service and RTI-RTI interoperation. RTI-LRC service communication is using TCP. RTI-RTI interoperation is based on multicast UDP, using multicast to filter irrelative messages. We define a set of protocol data units (PDUs) for each communication, inter-PDU for RTI-LRC service and outer-PDU for RTI-RTI interoperation.

PDU is made up of PDUheader and PDUdata, illustrated in Figure 4. The PDU-header comprises PDU version, type, length, time stamp etc.. The PDUdata uses union data structure, which stores data of each PDU. The length in PDUheader is calculated by adding up the actually used size of PDUdata to the size of PDUheader. That is, it indicates the actual space requirement of a PDU (Figure 4). In this way only the useful data of PDU is communicated to save the bandwidth and transportation time. When a PDU is arrived, RTI will extract the PDU type from the header and pick up data from PDUdata according to the PDU type.

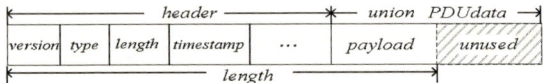

Fig. 4. PDU Structure

Distributed architecture has more layers and complicated structure. The PDU design can only simplify the coupling of IPC. Some methods should be taken to simplify the modules' coupling and invoking. BH RTI uses multiple threading to enhance the efficiency of services, but too many critical sections may induce efficiency decrease or dead lock. Aiming to speed up data packet processing, a mechanism of PDU-Function registry for data process is designed on the thought of callback.

PDU has fixed format to parse, so the declaration of process functions can be fixed. First, we bind a PDU type to the memory address of corresponding functions. Second, when the process thread picks up a PDU of this type, it looks up in the registry for function addresses. Then the process functions can be invoked directly(Figure 6). There may be access to other services or data in the body of function. So a pointer to the services or data is attached to the registry while binding. Then addresses requiring critical sections in the functions can be easier to check.

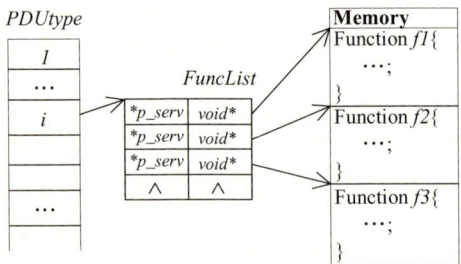

Fig. 5. PDU-Function Registry

The pseudo code of processing an interPDU is as the following. The relationship between adjacent layers of distributed architecture is simplified with this method.

```
interPDU pdu = receiveNextPDU();

int type = pdu.header.type;

KernelService* p_service = getServicePTR();

IF( funcList(type)==NULL || funcList(type).totalcount==0)

   RETURN;

func* p_func = funcList(type).first();

LOOP{

(*p_func)(&pdu, p_service);

p_func = funcList(type).next(p_func);

} UNTIL(p_func == NULL);
```

7 RTI Process Model

The time to callback user code is an important issue. HLA standard doesn't specify exactly how RTI process model should work. Three types of RTI process model are used in current RTIs: single-threaded, asynchronous and multi-threaded[19].

BH RTI implements single-threaded and multi-threaded process model. User can select either by configuration. BH RTI processes PDU queue of LRC according to the configurations in Figure 6. (a) When the single-threaded model is used, LRC puts received PDUs into queue and the federate executes the callbacks to the queue in tick(). (b) In the multi-threaded model, tick() is unnecessary and the process PDU thread will execute the callbacks after an arrived PDU is valid to be processed.

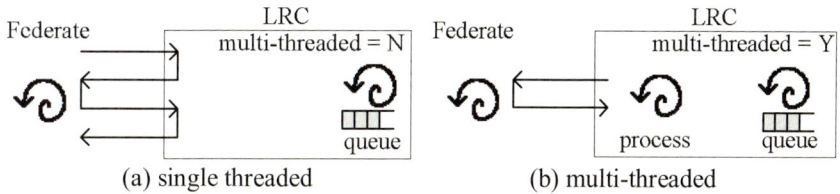

(a) single threaded   (b) multi-threaded

Fig. 6. Implementation of BH RTI Process Model

There are advantages and disadvantages for each process model. Single-threaded model has no thread switching, but the frequency and occasion of invoking tick() are often puzzles. It's easy to use an asynchronous model because developers needn't think about occasion for tick(). But the specific time is required to be waited no matter whether there is a callback. It's efficient to use multi-threaded model, but developers are required to treat with the threading safety.

8 Experiment Evaluation

Two experiment results are presented in this section, after introduction to the experiment of pure TCP/UDP time cost. First, we investigate the time cost constitution of BH RTI to analysis the factors. Second, the delay comparison of some commonly used RTIs is performed. The experiments are conducted in network using Huawei Switch Quidway S3050. The detailed setup is shown in Table 2.

Table 2. Host Setup for Experiment

Host Id	CPU	RAM	OS	NetworkCard
A1	P4 2.8G	512M	winXP	10/100M
A2	P4 3.0G	512M	winXP	10/100M
A3	P4 2.4G	768M	winXP	10/100M

The setup for experiments is shown in Figure 7 for traditional DMSO RTI like RTI experiments and Figure 8 for distributed RTI experiments.

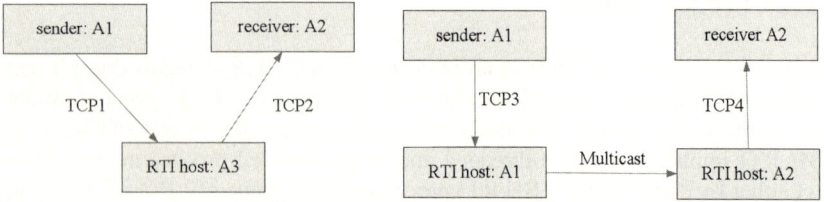

Fig. 7. Setup for Central RTI Experiment   **Fig. 8.** Setup for Distributed RTI Experiment

Before the two experiments, the variation of data delivery in pure TCP/UDP links is measured for reference. We have measured the time cost of all the links including the TCP of A1 to A3, TCP of A3 to A2, A1's multicast, localhost TCP of A1, localhost TCP of A2 used in Figure 12 and 13. Figure 9 is the results of time cost in pure TCP/UDP links with different payload.

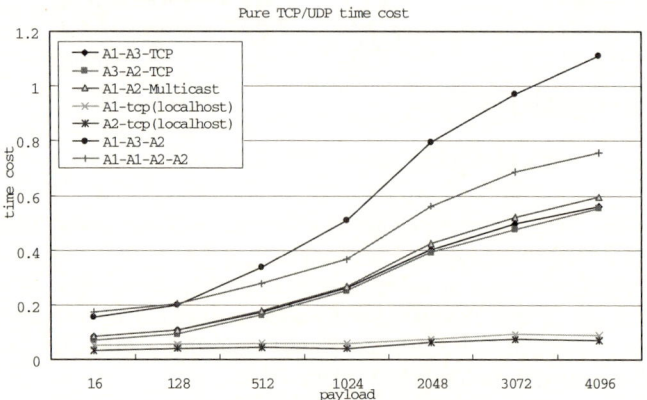

Fig. 9. Pure TCP/UDP time cost

To better study the time cost constitution, we divide the time cost of BH RTI into 4 parts as Figure 10. T(BH RTI) = t1 + t2 + t3 + t4. We test the 4 factors carefully by setting check points in code. Figure 11 presents the time cost constitution of BH RTI 2.2 using the setup in Figure10. We can see that time cost of A1's localhost TCP subtracted from t1 is below 0.05ms. And t2 or t3's subtracting corresponding delivery time cost is below 0.1ms. Factor t4 is nearly 0.03ms. This comparison denotes that each factor in BH RTI's time cost is rather small.

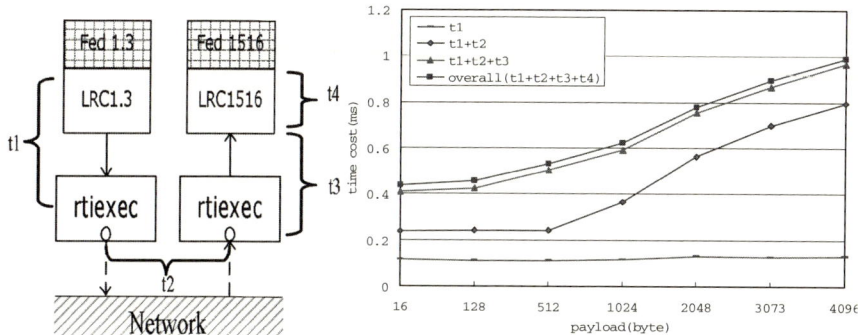

Fig. 10. Time cost experiment of BH RTI   **Fig. 11.** Time Cost Constitution of BH RTI 2.2

The RTI delay experiment results is as Figure 12, in which BH RTI 2.2(Central mode), DMSO RTI 1.3NGv6, pRTI 1516v2.3 is using the setup of Figure 7 and BH RTI 2.2 is using the setup of Figure 8. The central mode of BH RTI refers to that several federates connect to a unique BH RTI for RTI services. From the experiments results, we can see that BH RTI 2.2 has comparatively smaller time cost. The distributed mode of BH RTI 2.2 is premier in the time cost in the experiments. The central model of BH RTI 2.2 is relatively smaller in small payload, and there's an increase when the payload adds because of the increase of time cost in heavy payload.

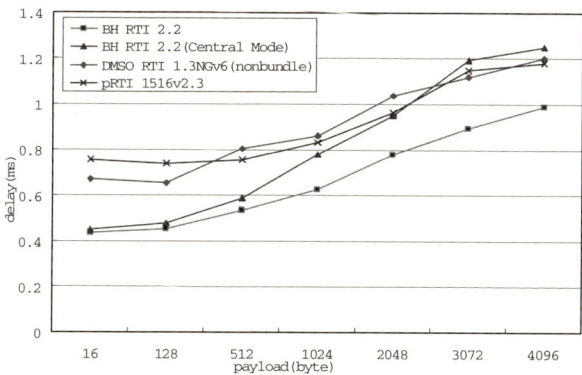

Fig. 12. Delay Comparison of RTIs

The results of both experiments give us an idea that different factor of time cost may have different weight. The time cost of different architecture cannot be compared by simple adding up. The weight of factors should be taken into consideration. And the architecture is not the only dominating factor in time cost. The concrete design and techniques also contribute much to the time cost.

9 Conclusion

Distributed RTI architecture has good scalability and comparatively higher time cost in theory. A distributed RTI architecture used in BH RTI is presented in this paper. Some key techniques to overcome the problem of time cost are introduced, including data delivery, data packet process and RTI process model. Experiment results illustrated that the distributed BH RTI overcame the negative influence of architecture complexity and had a relatively lower time cost. Techniques narrated in this paper have been evaluated in practical applications, some of which may be useful to the development of other distributed systems.

References

1. Defense Modeling and Simulation Office, High Level Architecture interface specification version 1.3, April 1998.
2. IEEE standard for modeling and simulation (M&S) High Level Architecture (HLA) – Framework and rules. (IEEE Std 1516-2000). New York:The Institute of Electrical and Electronics Engineers Inc., 2000.
3. IEEE standard for modeling and simulation (M&S) High Level Architecture (HLA) – Federate interface specification (IEEE Std 1516.1-2000). New York:The Institute of Electrical and Electronics Engineers Inc., 2000.
4. IEEE standard for modeling and simulation (M&S) High Level Architecture (HLA) – Object Model Template (OMT) Specification (IEEE Std 1516.2-2000). New York:The Institute of Electrical and Electronics Engineers Inc., 2000.
5. S.Bachinsky, J.Noseworthy, F.Hodum, Implementation of the Next Generation RTI, Spring Simulation Interoperability Workshop, Orlando, FL., USA, 1999.
6. Defense Modeling and Simulation Office, Department of Defense. 2002. RTI 1.3 – Next generation programmer's guide version 6. http://www.dmso.mil/.
7. Mikael Karlsson, Lennart Olsson, pRTI 1516- Rationale and Design. Fall Simulation Interoperability Workshop, Orlando, FL., USA, 2001.
8. Douglas D Wood, Len Granowetter. Rationale and Design of the Mak Real-Time RTI. Spring Simulation Interoperability Workshop, Orlando, FL., USA, 2001.
9. BH RTI 2.3 User Guide. http://www.hlarti.com/
10. Hao JG, Huang H. Implementation architecture of KD-RTI. System Modeling & Simulation, 2002,1(1):48-52.
11. Liu Buquan, Wang Huaimin, Yao Yiping. Key techniques of a hierarchical simulation run-time infrastructure—StarLink. Journal of Software(in Chinese), 2004, 15(01): 9-16
12. Michael D Myjak, Duncan Clark, Tom Lake, RTI interoperability study group final report. Fall Simulation Interoperability Workshop, Orlando, FL., USA, 1999.
13. 1516 adapter for HLA 1.3 federates, http://www.pitch.se/1516adapter/default.asp
14. Mak high performance RTI, http://www.mak.com/products/rti.php

15. Juergen Dingel, David Garlan, Craig Damon. Bridging the HLA: problems and solutions. Sixth IEEE International Workshop on Distributed Simulation and Real Time Applications Fort Worth, Texas, USA, 2002
16. Cai Nan, Zhou Zhong, Wu Wei. Research on the interconnection of heterogeneous RTIs and multi-federations based on Bridge Federate. Journal of Computer Research and Development. to be appeared in vol.43, 2006
17. Zhou Z, Zhao QP. Extend HLA with layered priority. In: Proceedings of the Spring Simulation Interoperability Workshop. Orlando FL, 2003. Paper 03S-SIW-012.
18. Zhou Z, Zhao QP. Research on RTI congestion control based on the layer of interest. Journal of Software, 2004,15(1):120~130.
19. Mikael Karlsson, Peter Karlsson, An in-depth look at RTI process model, Spring Simulation Interoperability Workshop, Orlando, FL., USA, 2003.

Wearable Multimodal Interface
for Helping Visually Handicapped Persons

Byeong-Seok Shin[1], Honam Ahn[1], and Gye Young Kim[2]

[1] Department of Computer Science and Information Engineering, Inha University
253 Yonghyeon-Dong, Nam-Gu, Inchon, 402-751, Korea
[2] School of Computing, Soongsil University, 511 Sangdo-Dong, Dongjak-Gu, Seoul, Korea
bsshin@inha.ac.kr, honami82@inhaian.net, gykim11@ssu.ac.kr

Abstract. Handicapped Persons who partially or entirely lose their sensory for external stimuli struggle to lead on daily life due to lack of the ability of sensors. We propose a system to provide alternative sensory for visually handicapped persons with wearable multimodal interface. It acquires visual information with a variety of sensors, converts them to high-level information, and represents the information with alternative sensory such as sound or vibration. The system is mainly composed of two sub-systems. The first is obstacle detection and avoidance module with multiple ultrasound sensors and a tracker. It helps handicapped person to access to target place easily and safely. The second is stereo vision system to provide ability to track some target objects, to recognize persons around a user, and to understand color and gray-level of a specific object. Since our system is designed for wearable computers, visually handicapped persons carry and operate it very easily.

1 Introduction

A handicapped person is someone who has a physical or mental disability that prevents them living a totally normal life. Especially, Sensory handicapped persons struggle to lead on daily life due to lack of visual or auditory ability. As computer technologies advance, several researches have been done to devise a variety of methods and systems helping visually or auditory handicapped persons [1], [2], [3].

However, most of them have some problems to obstruct wide-spreading. The first one is that they only depend on single modality such as a CCD camera or a microphone. Their output is also limited to conventional representation including texts, symbols and sound. This restricts the range of application of each system and its performance. Another problem is that it is difficult to carry and operate them because they are not considered as portable systems. This impels user to stay in front of computer system and makes it difficult to assist daily life of handicapped persons.

In order to achieve high applicability and accuracy, multimodal interface is important since it provides multiple sensing and output for single situation. We propose a wearable multimodal interface for helping visually handicapped person. It acquires visual (or spatial) information of environment with a specially-designed ultrasound sensor array, an orientation tracker, and stereoscopic cameras. Each of them acquires range data, orientation of sensors, and a stream of stereoscopic images, respectively.

Z. Pan et al. (Eds.): ICAT 2006, LNCS 4282, pp. 980–988, 2006.

A portable computer gathers all information, interprets the meaning of them, and supports user to make a decision. Finally, it converts processed data to auditory and tactile information that can be understandable to visually handicapped persons. Multimodal information from a variety of sensors collaborates to perform the specific function more precisely.

The system is designed for wearable computer, which is not just portable but makes user feel comfort as putting on a dress. We consider the shape, size, and weight of each component (sensors and processing module) as well as the performance of them. Small number of sensors limits the field-of-view and brings inaccuracy of acquired data. On the other hand, larger number of heavy weight sensors and computers decrease the portability and sense of comfort. So we designed and implemented optimal system to assist visual ability of handicapped person.

In Sect. 2, we explain our system in detail. A prototype system and its experimental results are presented in Sect. 3. Finally we conclude our method.

2   Multimodal Interface for Visually Handicapped Persons

In this section, we briefly explain our system. As depicted in Fig. 1, our system is composed of two modules, obstacle detection and avoidance module and stereo vision module. The obstacle avoidance system contains a sensor array equipped with eight ultrasound sensors, a controller with USB interface, an orientation tracker and a portable station. Stereo vision system consists of pre-calibrated stereo camera, a controller with PCMCIA interface, and a portable station. Output data are provided to user as audio command and vibration jacket with eight vibrators.

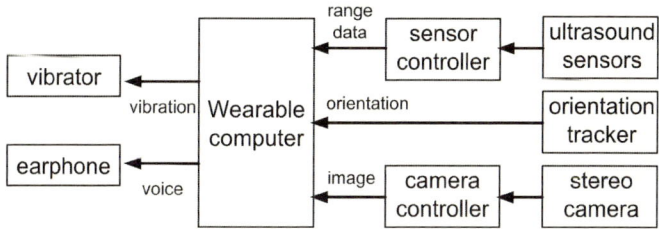

Fig. 1. Block diagram of our handicapped person support system. It is composed of an obstacle detection and avoidance module and stereo vision module.

2.1   Obstacle Detection and Avoidance System

In order to access to a target point, a user has to identify the obstacles located on the way to the point. Because a handicapped person cannot see the objects, we have to devise alternative method that does not require visual ability.

An ultrasound sensor acquires distance to an object by estimating the time-of-fly of ultrasound signal. When the range value decreases while walking, we conclude that a suspicious object is located on the path and we have to change the direction. Since a handicapped person moves around continuously, we have to obtain the range data in front of user within short time (at least 2~3 times per second). Therefore we use a set of ultrasound sensors called sensor array. Each one has its own direction and coverage of conic shape that does not overlap with those of neighboring sensors and acquires range data for its own direction. Fig. 2. shows the layout of sensors in our system. Assume that the maximum horizontal and vertical angles of target region are φ_h and φ_v, a valid angle of a sensor is θ ($\theta < \pi$). Then the number of sensors in a row is $\lfloor \varphi_h / \theta \rfloor$ and the number of rows is $\lfloor \varphi_v / \theta \rfloor$. Although the sensor array takes considerably large space, it guarantees high-speed range sensing since it scans a scene at once. Range data are gathered and sent to wearable computer through USB interface.

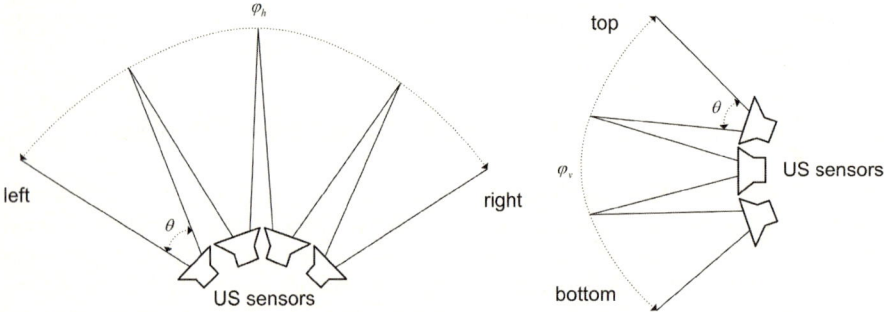

Fig. 2. Horizontal (left) and vertical (right) layout of ultrasound sensors in our system. To cover the entire region in front of a user, each sensor is located on the semi-sphere coordinates.

Unlike mobile robots, human body is trembled while walking. Therefore, three axes as well as origin of reference coordinates are changed simultaneously. In the case of mobile robots, when it moves from a point $p_1(x,y,z)$ to $p_2(x',y',z')$, z-coordinates of two point and z-components of sensor direction vectors do not changes. However, in the case of human walking, those values are also changed. For accurate scanning of environment, we have to check the validity of range data by considering the relative direction of sensor array. We use the orientation tracker estimating roll, pitch, and yaw angle of sensor array. Whenever the range data are transferred from sensors, portable station verifies the range data by using the orientation data transferred from the tracker. Fig. 3 shows how to check the validity of the range data with orientation information. When the value of pitch angle from the tracker is stiffly changed in a moment, the value is regarded as "not available" and it does not considered in decision making.

Previous methods for path generation have some problems to demand a lot of computation to generate a local/global map of environment in preprocessing step and to require extra storage for spatial information [4], [5], [6]. In order to assist user's walk-through on a low-performance mobile computer, navigation method should be simple to make a decision in real-time with small amount of computation. Also it should not require a lot of storage.

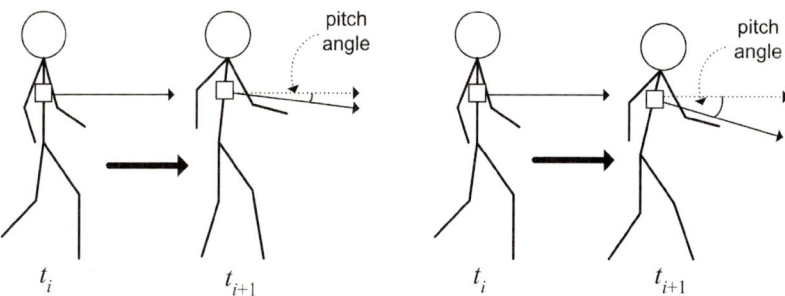

Fig. 3. Verifying the range data by considering the orientation of sensor array. When the pitch angle between a direction of i-th scanning and that of $i+1$-th scanning is small, the range value is regarded as valid one (left), otherwise, it is ignored (right).

While single sensor can only acquire the distance to an obstacle, multiple sensors can select a specific direction to avoid collision to objects. We apply the following heuristics to find a safe path.

- If a user orients the direction of sensor that have the maximum distance in comparison to distance values of its neighboring sensors, the user can avoid the collision to objects.
- A user has to change the direction drastically when the distance to object toward current orientation is too small. On the other hand, the user may alter the direction slowly if the distance value is considerably large.

According to the above heuristics, we can minimize the collision possibility by chaging the user's orientation to the direction of sensor that has the maximum distance. Assume that current orientation is D_{curr}, direction of sensor having the maximum value is D_{max} and the minimum distance value is d_{min}. Then the direction of rotation (r_i) and the angle of rotation (ψ) can be defined as Eq. (1) where C is a maximum sensing range (constant) larger than d_{min}. All the vectors are normalized.

$$\mathbf{r}_i = \mathbf{D}_{max} - \mathbf{D}_{curr}$$
$$\psi = \arctan\left(\frac{C - d_{min}}{C}\right) \tag{1}$$

However, it is very hard to represent a vector $\mathbf{r}_i$ and a scalar value ψ with vocal command or tactile feedback since they produce a limited number of output. So we have to quantize the value into several discrete values and map those values to a set of voice command or vibration patterns.

Since our method computes the user's orientation in every scanning, unnecessary change might occur in open area, that is, all sensors acquire sufficiently large distance values. This causes trembling of user's orientation. To solve this instability, we define the threshold distance value d_{th}, and we do not change the orientation when d_{min} is larger than d_{th}. Consequently, Eq. (1) can be rewritten as Eq. (2).

$$\psi = \begin{cases} 0 & \text{if } d_{min} > d_{th} \\ \arctan(\dfrac{d_{th} - d_{min}}{d_{th}}) & \text{otherwise} \end{cases} \tag{2}$$

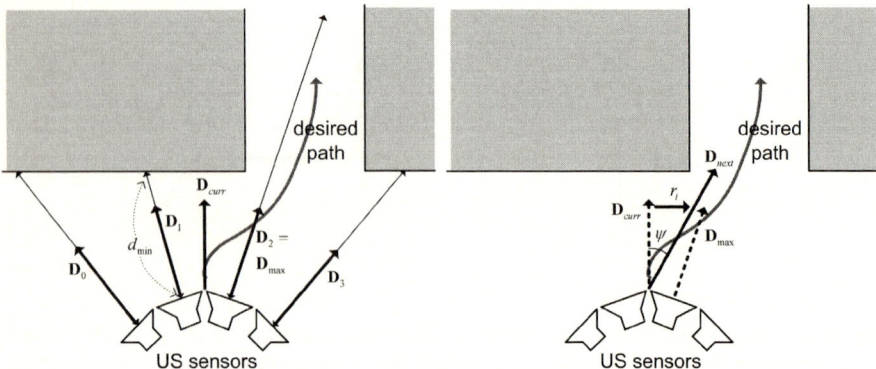

Fig. 4. Determining the direction of walk-through using the range data from ultrasound sensors. The next direction $\mathbf{D}_{next}$ can be decided with $\mathbf{D}_{curr}$, $\mathbf{D}_{max}$ and d_{min}.

2.2 Stereoscopic Vision System

We develop a stereo vision system for helping a visual handicapped person. The system is composed of a hardware device and several software components. The two stereoscopic cameras are connected to the portable station. Software components include Color Detector, Face Recognizer and Object Finder/Tracker.

The Color Detector analyses an input image from a camera and outputs a voice message. For the purpose of learning color values, we make 16 color plates, capture the images and extract the average color values, $A_{1..16}$, of each image. In the color detection step, we use eigencolor normalization [7] for compensating the adverse effect due to shape distortion for 2D planar image. And we extract the major color value, C, from a histogram of the image and find a color code using Eq. (3).

$$C_{code} = \arg \min_{i=1..16} | A_i - C |. \tag{3}$$

The Object Finder/Tracker is used to guide handicapped persons toward an object that they want to take. The scenario is as follows: (1) it manually captures an image and points an object, (2) automatically finds and tracks the object using Snake [8], and (3) computes the object's position and orientation from stereo matching. In learning step, it performs SIFT (scale invariant feature transformation) to extract some descriptors from training set. It performs SIFT on a target image and compares the stored descriptors and newly extracted ones in recognition step.

The Face Recognizer is used to identify persons around the user. The Face Recognizer is composed of face detection module and recognition module. We apply an efficient and robust face detection algorithm to extract facial regions in a sequence of images when persons are moving in front of the camera. Popular techniques to detect faces in an image often involve skin-color segmentation [9]. Skin-color segmentation is fast, however, it can only be done in well defined surroundings. We want our detection algorithm to be robust even under totally different lighting conditions. So, instead of using skin-color, we implemented the Haar face detection algorithm [10]. Fig. 5. shows an example of detected faces using Haar face detection algorithm.

Fig. 5. An example of applying Haar face detection algorithm. Rectangles represent facial region on images.

To recognize the detected facial regions robustly, we applied embedded HMM-based face recognition algorithm [11]. This algorithm is known to be more efficient and robust to scale changes than the classical eigenface methods and the previous HMM-based algorithms.

3   Experimental Results

Fig. 6 shows the configuration of our system for visually handicapped person. Main processing is performed on ARM9-based embedded system equipped with RS-232C/USB interface and 1GB memory. Operating system is embedded Linux. Output of this system is represented as a series of voice message or vibration pattern with earphone and vibration jacket.

Eight ultrasound sensors are arranged with three rows, top row has two sensors to detect objects hazardous to user's head, middle row has four sensors to compute safe path to target point, and bottom row has two sensors to recognize small obstacles on the floor, staircases, or cliffs. The number of sensors is trade-off manufacturing cost and the size of sensor array for accuracy. Eight sensors are sufficient for this application. The sensor array scans a scene 2.5 times per second. For safe work-through, computed direction vectors are quantized into four directions and mapped to voice messages or vibration patterns representing "rotate-left", "turn-left", "turn-right", and "rotate-right", respectively. It produces additional commands such "start", "stop", "watch your step" (in staircase or cliff), and "take care of your head" according to some situation.

Fig. 7 depicts an example of performing our obstacle detection and avoidance feature. A user recognizes a wall in front of him and changes his direction to avoid collision to the wall.

Fig. 8 shows an example of a detected face and the recognized face retrieved from the facial DB. For evaluation of the recognition algorithm, we learned 50 persons from a public facial database provided by AT&T. 50% of the facial images of each person were used for learning and the remaining 50% were used for the evaluation. From our evaluation the recognition rate was 99% for the public database. Experimental results show that detecting the facial regions takes 40ms~120ms while using 320×240 images and face recognition requires about 100ms for sample data. Fig. 9 shows an example of finding and tracking an object with our method. Tracking time is about 1 second.

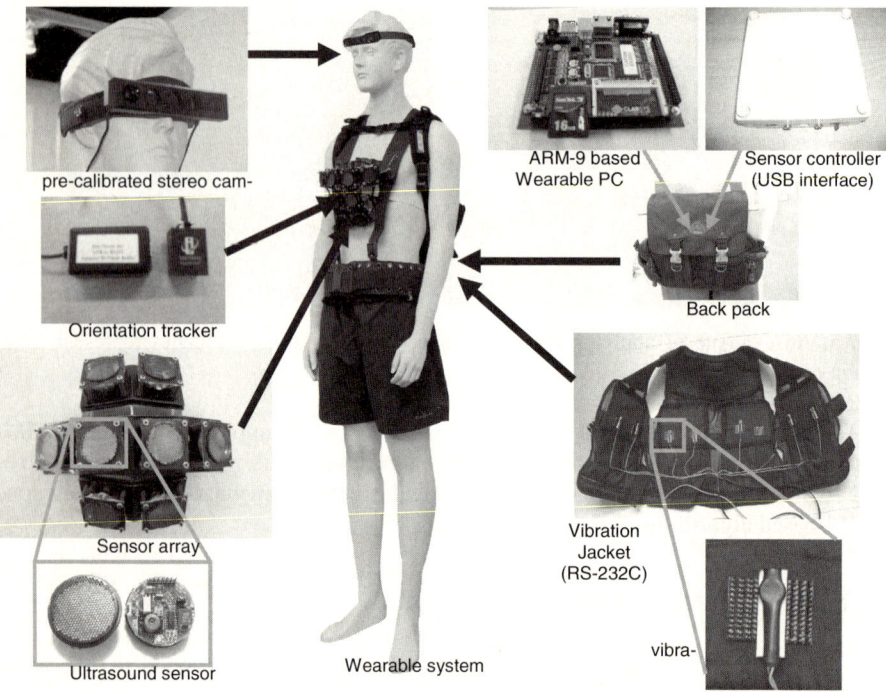

Fig. 6. Configuration of prototype system

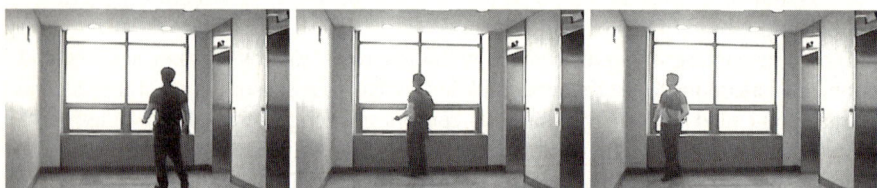

Fig. 7. An example of using obstacle avoidance system

Fig. 8. Face recognition using an embedded HMM. It can detect a facial region (left) and recognize the face using face database. Actual output is converted to voice message and offered to the user.

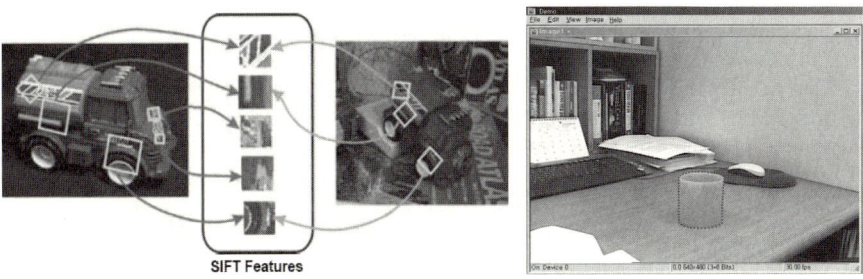

Fig. 9. An example of finding target objects using SIFT features (left) and tracking and object using Snake

4   Conclusion

We designed and implemented a system to provide alternative sensory for visually handicapped persons with wearable multimodal interface. It acquires visual and spatial information with a variety of sensors, converts them to high-level information, and represents the information with voice command or vibration patterns. The system is mainly composed of two sub-systems, obstacle detection and avoidance module and stereo vision module. The first is formed with multiple ultrasound sensors and a tracker and it helps handicapped person to access to target place easily and safely. The second is stereo vision system to provide ability to track some target objects, to recognize persons around a user, and to understand color and gray-level of a specific object. Since our system is designed for wearable computers, it is very easy for visually handicapped persons to operate the system.

Acknowledgements

This work was supported by IITA through IT Leading R&D Support Project.

References

1. Borenstein, J., Ulrich, I. : The GuideCane : A Computerized Travel Aid for the Active Guidance of Blind Pedestrians, Proceedings of the IEEE International Conference on Robotics and Automation (1997) 1283-1288
2. Mori, H., Kotani, S. : Robotic Travel Aid for the Blind: HARUNOBU-6, Proceedings of the 2nd European Conference Disability, Virtual Reality & Assoc. Tech. (1998) 193-202
3. Borenstein, J : The NavBelt - A Computerized Multi-Sensor Travel Aid for Active Guidance of the Blind, Proceedings of the CSUN's Fifth Annual Conference on Technology and Persons with Disabilities (1990) 107-116
4. Jiang, K., Seveviratine, L. D., Earles, S. W. E. : A Shortest Path Based Path Planning Algorithm for Nonholonomic Mobile Robots, Journal of Intelligent and Robotic Systems (1999) 347-366
5. Divelbiss, A. W., Wen, J. T. : A Path Space Approach to Nonholonomic Motion Planning in the Presence of Obstacles, IEEE Transactions on Robotics and Automation, VOL. 13, No. 3(1997) 443-451

6. Hu, H., Gu, D., Brady, M. : Navigation and Guidance of An Intelligent Mobile Robot, Second Euromicro Workshop on Advanced Mobile Robots (EUROBOT '97) (1997) 104-111
7. Lin, Z., Wang, J., Ma, K. : Using Eigencolor Normalization for Illumination-Invariant Color Object Recognition, Pattern Recognition, Vol. 35 (2002) 2629-2642
8. Kass, M.m Witkin, A., Terzopoulos, D. : Sankes: Active Contour Models," Internation Journal of Computer Vision, Vol. 2 (1988) 321-331
9. Majoor, T. : Face Detection using Color-based Region of Interest Selection,. Technical report, University of Amsterdam, Amsterdam, NL, 2000
10. Lienhart, R., Maydt, J. : An Extended Set of Haar-like Features for Rapid Object Detection, IEEE ICIP, Vol. 1 (2002) 900-903
11. Nefian, A.V. and Hayes, M.H. : An embedded HMM-based approach for face detection and recognition, Proc. IEEE International Conference on Acoustics, Speech, and Signal Processing, Vol. 6 (1999)

Personalized Primary Port: Analysis of User View for the Smart Environment

Wei-jin Park[1], Junhwan Kim[1], and Doo-Hwan Bae[2]

[1] WRG, 22th Floor, Parkview Office Tower, Jeongja-Dong 6, Bundang-Gu
Seongnam-Si, Gyeonggi-Do, 463-863, South Korea
{jin.park, james.kim}@wrg.co.kr
[2] Dept. of Computer Science, Korea Advanced Institute of Science and Technology
373-1, Kusong-dong, Yusong-gu, Taejon 305-701, Korea
bae@salmosa.kaist.ac.kr

Abstract. In this paper, the user side view of smart space based on a hand-held device was proposed. We gave precedence to the personalized primary port (PPP) —currently the cell phone—which is the most popular personal belonging with a powerful functionality among the ubiquitous computing environment. It can be used as the gateway to ubiquitous computing for the smart environment. The implementation focus is a combination of short-term-based sensing using an accelerometer and long-term-based user preference sensing through a software robot.

Keywords: Smart space, personalized hand-held device, software robot, sensor.

1 Introduction

Since the concept of ubiquitous computing (ubicomp) was presented by Weiser [1], many different kinds of approaches and domain applications have been provided. One of the application views is the smart environment technology. Smart environments integrate technologies in pervasive computing, artificial intelligence, interfaces, mobile communications, sensor networks, and wireless networking into our everyday setting, including homes, classrooms, offices, laboratories, shops, cars, etc. [2]. The phrase "smart space" has also been used in some research projects such as the NIST Smart Space Project [3] and the CSIRO Smart Space [4]. The words 'space' and 'environment, are often used interchangeably and are relatively abstract concepts of general sites or places [2].

There are various reasons for developing a prototype that involves hand-held devices, which are sensed and activated in the user context:

(1) There are different levels of priority among multiple computers per user in the ubiquitous computing environment. Some computers play more significant roles than others or a specific computer can be the primary.

(2) Currently, hand-held devices, especially cell phones, can be regarded the nearest computing, communicating, content-creating devices available to users anywhere. Ubiquitous computing should give a more concrete form to involving hand-held devices at this time.

Z. Pan et al. (Eds.): ICAT 2006, LNCS 4282, pp. 989–997, 2006.
© Springer-Verlag Berlin Heidelberg 2006

(3) Even though many context-aware frameworks have been presented in the last few years, what is usually missing is the notion of characteristic features of contexts that are accumulated during long time intervals.

(4) It is necessary to extend the concept of limited space of smart environment to every general space where we live..

If a user in a ubiquitous environment has more than one computer, there should be priorities or precedence set among computers. We define the concept of primary computer among many computers and deal with the role, interaction, and coordination of the primary computer. This research aims to develop a smart space application with short-term sensing and long-term preference capture from a personal point of view. The implementation of smart space can provide popularized personalization, which can resolve the conflict between personality and popularity. This paper provides insights on the current and future role of hand-held device systems for the smart environment. The technical goal is preservation and transmission of user preference during context transfer so that the user's intention can be recognized in the personalized primary port (PPP) as though it had originally appeared there.

The structure of the paper is as follows. Section 2 presents the current research status and a review of the smart environment-related research. Section 3 describes our concept of the hand-held centric smart space and PPP. Section 4 introduces the prototype implementation, including personalized user interface using software robot (sobot) and sensor interface embedded into the hand-held device. Section 5 gives a summary of the paper.

2 Related Research

It is generally difficult to specify the smart space because every researcher has his/her own focus of interest and, in some sense, we already have been living in certain level of smart space. We can find lamps with sensors; ovens capable of cooking automatically following instructions from the Internet; and smart functions using embedded computers in a car, furniture, and so on. Related research regarding personalized smart environment based on hand-held device is presented in three categories: (1) smart environment, (2) personalization in ubicomp, and (3) hand-held application in ubicomp. In a broad sense, smart space means ubiquitous computing environment. In a narrow sense, smart space refers to specific spaces of intelligent interplay to maximize the convenience of people without limitations of time and space among every object that is part of a future ubiquitous environment. It is also a new space created by computing for intelligence, communication for access, and service for delivery of information and knowledge.

To specify a more meaningful ubicomp environment or smart space, it is necessary to specify or define a degree/level value attached to the definitions describing the terms ubicomp and smart environment technology. It is a fact that some objects already have a certain level of smartness and we have already been surrounded by these. A smart space is an environment with numerous elements that "(1) sense + (2) think + (3) act + (4) communicate + (5) interact with people" in a way that is robust, self-managing, and scaleable [CSIRO]. In research projects such as Boulder's Adaptive House and Buxton's Reactive Environment, their smart space is only focused on a single specific space, and the different spaces developed are isolated, looking like small islands in an ocean. However, a person's daily activities often cover multiple spaces or environments. [MA 21]. The smart space of NIST ITL and DARPA focused on 'smart' than on other elements. For example, for the phrase semantic web, pervasive computing is widely used. A set of associated and integrated smart spaces as a unity can be regarded a higher level space—i.e., a smart hyperspace or a hyperenvironment. And the smart "hyperspace" can be seen as a subset of the "hyperworld." FLAME2008 described an approach, focusing on ontology design, user model, contexts and situations, and how all these are used to provide a user with personalized situation-dependent services. Shahi's personal operating space is an entity formed for the personalization of space-specific services—i.e., by treating a user's personal mobile device as an identity for personalization. One of the personalized applications, mPERSONA, is a flexible personalization system for the wireless user that takes into consideration user mobility, the local environment, and the user and device profile. Ozen described the architecture for mobile network operators to deliver highly personalized information from XML resources to mobile clients. The smart card-based personalization approach shows that the use of a smart card to host the personal profile engine answers both privacy and ubiquity requirements.

Until recently, research regarding smart environments or ubiquitous space has been limited to describing a specific space and has been incapable of handling general spaces in our everyday lives. This work provides ubiquitous computing with particular emphasis on the role of primary hand-held device, which can be used as the gateway to smart space. Other related research differs from ours in the following sense:

(1) Experience vs perception: In the smart space of NIST, a perceptual interface was set up in a limited space and personality was recognized. If the results of perception could be transmitted through the mobile device to the service in space by the mobile device as medium for perception, experience could take the place of perception. The implementation of smart space had centered around the cell phone to recognize personality.

(2) Our hand-held centered smart space (HHCSS) differs from the previous one in the following aspects:
- Primary reasoning engine to protect the user in the smart flow
- HHCSS have interaction modes with objects based on user experience
- Position and orientation of the user can be used by some service through the hand-held device but not restricted to the certain bounded space like a room or house.

3   PPP in the Hand-Held Centric Smart Space

The Jansen formalized the smart space consisting of three entities–user, sensor, actuator–that are relevant to creating a programming model for pervasive space. Based on context, a user has a different set of desires about the behavior of space. Actuators, whose invocation has an intended effect on a particular domain observed by a sensor, influence the state of the space [14]. A user interacts with the space and has a set of long-term preferences and short-term intentions. The sensor senses the

user's current status and any status brought by any other behavior in the smart environment and provides information to the system about the current state of space.
It is a fact that computers are becoming smaller and smaller and can be attached and embedded into almost all things—from man-made devices to natural ones in the world. The design modeling of smart-space is divided into the four levels: 1) framework (e.g., smart classroom framework, NIST smart space framework); 2) device (e.g., smart furniture of Hosei University); 3) component (e.g., springs); and 4) elements (e,g., rectangular cells on the mask). The Smart_Space, Smart_Flow, and Smart_Component classes are subclasses of the Smart_Artifact class. The sensor, actuator, and user are the subclass of Smart_Feature. The sensor is specialized into an HW_Sensor and an SW_Sensor.

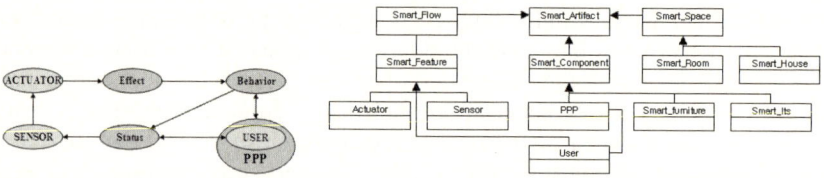

Fig. 1. (a) User is encapsulated by the PPP in the loop of Smart flow. (b) Object relations in smart space for describing PPP.

PPP is the generalized concept of current hand-held device—the cell phone is the 2006 version of PPP. It may disappear into our clothes or embedded in other belongings, all through the wearable computer paradigm with functionality as follows.

(1) Identifier: To identify a person, an identification (ID) card, such as a driver's license, is mainly used. However, this may be cloned illegally and has no other functionality beyond the ID. Nowadays, diverse ways, with pros and cons from the points of view of security or cost, are being used, including other parts of the body such as the fingerprint. Future electronic purse including ID may converge into an invisible pervasive wearable device.

(2) Preference management: If PPP can sense the user's action and store it for future use, an analysis may be done to capture user preferences.

(3) Convergence of digital belongings: Recently, the functions of personal devices and belongings are becoming more integrated—for example, the digital camera and MP3 player or the portable memory stick may be the default function of cell phones. The cell phone will have more functionality, including devices whose life cycles are not long and are easily out of fashion.

(4) Security: In the ubiquitous computing environment, the user may be exposed to unauthorized computing device anywhere.

(5) Basic actuation: This function can be covered by the PPP. Examples are emitting flavor, automatic scheduling in diary, etc.

(6) Controlling other devices: For example, a noncontact car key using smart card may be developed. It can be used instead of a 3-D wireless mouse or joystick or keyboard because some small device has no input device.

4 Personalized Primary Port (PPP) Prototype

The PPP can be used to capture not only short-term-based user context but also long-term-based preference. This section describes the PPP prototype from the user point of view.

4.1 Short-Term User Action Sensing on PPP by Sensor

Application with an accelerometer in the PPP has two main features. One is static application of measuring the tilting angle to the ground and applying it to a UI manipulation. The other is dynamic application of measuring the signal on a specific bandwidth and applying it to calculate human step and kinetic energy. The acceleration, speed, and displacement of the object can be measured through the accelerometer, making it possible to calculate the motion of the object.

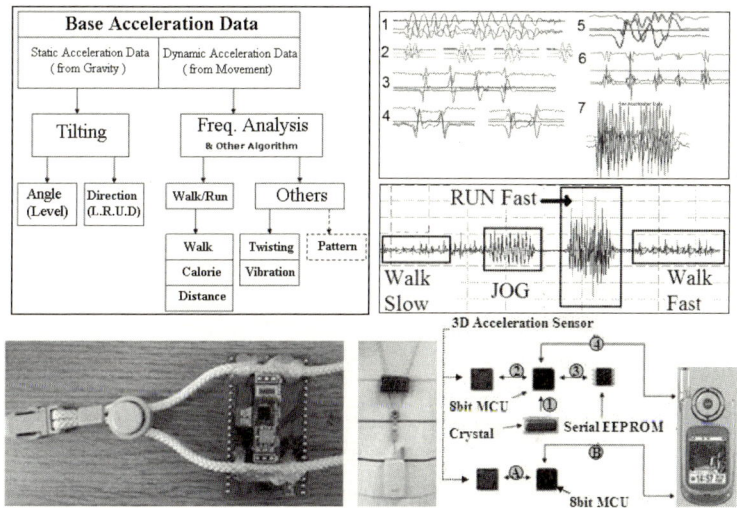

Fig. 2. Short-term sensing framework by hardware sensor: (a) acceleration sensor-based application, (b) wave from user gesture using an accelerometer, (c) wave and relevant action of user, (d) prototype implementation, and (e) process of sensor attachment into the cell

The PPP can recognize some user gestures. Waves in the figure show some examples of user gestures: (1) 9 clock direction to the 3 clock direction; (2) heart shape; (3) up, down, left, or right; (4) diagonal direction; (5) drawing a rectangle; (6) two-time shacking for the manner mode; and (7) sample emergency call.

The PPP can recognize user movements such as stopping, walking, and running and how much they have moved. The figure shows capture of acceleration signal at different speeds. There are several attachment methods at this stage: pocket in pants, pocket in shirts, necklace type, and attachment to belt. In this prototype, the necklace type was used because it does not depend on the mobile phone type as shown in the figure. Fig.17 (?) shows the embedding sensor into the cell. The external attachment consists of main chip sets. A precise periodic clock should be provided to the MCU of the solution as (1) the MCU captures acceleration data and (2) stores data to the serial EEPROM. After opening the folder of the phone and executing the application, data from (3) stage can be transferred to the sobot application. The internal attachment needs a smaller number of main chip set and space. Flash memory in the cell-phone is used to store captured data and communication between sensor and phone performed through the I2C. Data on sensed and measured movement can be accessed by the sobot application.

4.2 Long-Time-Based User Experience Sensing

The user context manager, which aims to process long-term user experience, has the sensor (accelerometer) for user status, especially gesture and movement sensing. It has several pattern managers for the user's long-term preference analyses. For instance, a device configuration may ask "whether it has DVB-H functionality or not;" the browsing pattern is similar to a cookie in the Web browser. The calling pattern is "who does the user like or do not like to call" or "when and how much time does the user like to call in a specific context." Another pattern may mean "when does the user go to bed at night". When an event occurs that is matched with the case in the event database, the proper UI is shown for the user. The gray box is the PPP which has the user context manager and sobot processing module.

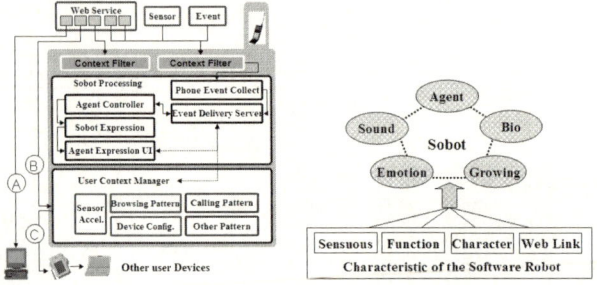

Fig. 3. Processing framework of the PPP

All ubiquitous services should be through the PPP as it has control over other devices so that user preferences are directly reflected and services and events are selected and customized. There are two cases of coupling—tight and loose. In the loosely coupled case, the other device can refer to the user preference in the PPP but it is the device's

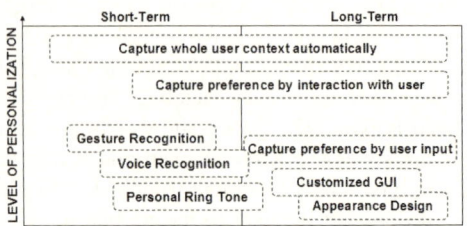

Fig. 4. Kinds and levels of personalization

choice how much context information in the PPP to take or not to take. The figure shows the GUI of the sobot (software robot) interacting with the user. The sobot interface consists of five parts: icon, background, speech balloon, button list, and sobot.

Figure 4 shows the user profile consisting of short-term sensing context and long-term preferences for managing personalization through the PPP. The Y axis is the level of personalization and the X axis is the term duration of the personalization. The simplest example of widespread personalization is "personal ring tone" and "appearance" of the cell.

Figure 5 shows the composition structure of the sobot, illustrating its character-istics and functionality.. The PPP provides users with sensuous interface using sobot which can be the virtual identity of the user for the smart space. The sobot character can be used by linking with the web or from a game character, which has several parameters compatible with those of the game character. This sobot upgraded automatically has intelligence and user's preference. Besides the basic function like spam mail and message filtering, schedule management, and help for the cell phone menu item, sobot plays the role of an agent, which recognizes and expresses the current context. As a biological model, it is an electronic pet with intimate interaction with the user; as a motion model, it has its own characteristic response to the user, considering his/her preference; and as a growing model, by user manipulation, it can be growing. Thus, appearance, intelligence, preference, and game character parameters can vary, depending on the interaction with the user.

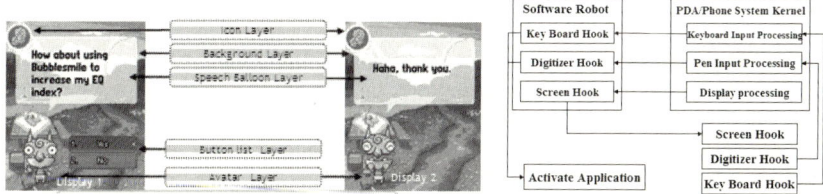

Fig. 5. Display and structure of lifelike character in the sobot architecture

As a sample response, sobot notifies the user when a message is received from someone and opens it when the user gets to open the message. The response depends on the sender. If a male user gets the message from a female sender, the sobot may ask, "Is she your girl friend?". The sobot thread is executed as a subprogram, but the programming environment for a hand-held device is so limited. The over-ray function for displaying outputs of two programs simultaneously may not be available. Three kinds of Avatar system implement the hook in the PDA/phone system kernel. The kinds of hook are the keyboard hook, the digitizer hook, and the screen hook. The keyboard hook is for receiving keyboard input; the digitizer is for receiving pen input in the phone OS, and the screen hook is for getting a memory buffer value before displaying it in memory buffer. The calling hook makes it possible to display the output of more than one program. The PPP prototype presents a framework of integration of sensing from the hardware and the software. Not only can current short-term context but also long-term user experience be captured by the PPP. Since the PPP is not yet part of a user's identity but rather just a kind of mobile device, the benefits of interaction based on PPP may not be easily seen.. However, the concept of

PPP is still feasible because the cell phone is the most common belonging that has the communication and computing capabilities and that uses other recent technologies such as multimedia content viewing. Sensor attachment is possible only with the small variation of the existing model because, in MEMS manufacturing technology, size does not matter. Currently, the sensing interface is limited to only the area of sensing of the project. User reaction to the sobot is restricted to the push button that the sobot displays or to gestures with the phone. Several kinds of extension are in progress such as the diverse interaction method that includes voice interaction.

5 Conclusion

The perceptual interface through a mobile device, especially a person's PPP (currently the cell phone), can be the most likely gateway to smart space. In this research, the concept of user side view of the hand-held centric smart space and PPP was introduced. For the implementation prototype of the PPP, the capture of user preference (through an investigation of long-term user experience) and user context (through the hardware sensor in the PPP) was presented. Future research includes exploring advanced combination technology between mobile device experience and numerous services in smart space.

References

1. Weiser M. 1993. Hot topics: ubiquitous computing. IEEE Computer.
2. Jianhua Ma. 2005. Ubiquitous intelligence: the Intelligence Revolution. Wise Media, http://cis.k.hosei.ac.jp/~jianhua
3. Abowd GD., Atkeson C, and Essa I.. 1998. Ubiquitous smart spaces. A white paper submitted to DARPA (in response to RFI).
4. http://www.smartspaces.csiro.au/
5. Abowd GD, Iftode L, Mitchel H. 2005. The smart phone: a first platform for pervasive computing. Pervasive computing. p 18-19..
6. Gellersen HW, Schmidt A, Beig M. 2002. Multi-sensor context-awareness in mobile devices and smart artifacts. Mobile Networks Appl. 7 (5).
7. Benbasat AY, Paradiso JA. 2001. An inertial measurement framework for gesture recognition and applications. Paper presented at the International Gesture Workshop, GW 2001, London, UK.
8. Hansen TR, Eriksson E, Lykke-Olesen A. 2005. Mixed interaction space–designing for camera-based interaction with mobile devices. CHI (ACM Computer-Human Interaction) 2005 Apr 2-7, Portland, Oregon, USA.
9. Dannenberg RB, Amon D. 1989. A gesture-based user interface prototyping system. In: Proceedings of the 2nd ACM SIGGRAPH, User Interface Software and Technology.
10. Hinckley K, Pierce J, Horvitz E, Sinclair M. 2005. Foreground and background interaction with sensor-enhanced mobile devices. ACM TOCHI 12 (1).
11. Mantyjarvi J, Kela J, Korpipaa P, Kallio S. 2004. Enabling fast and effortless customization in accelerometer-based gesture interaction. Paper presented at the Third International Conference on MUM.

12. Jianhua MA, Yang LT. 2005. Towards a smart world and ubiquitous intelligence: a walkthrough from smart things to smart hyperspaces and bicKids. J. Pervasive Comput. Comm.1(1).

13. Shahi A, Callaghan V, Gardner M. 2005. Introducing personal operating spaces for ubiquitous computing environments. Paper presented at the Third Inernational Conference, PERMID, 8-13 May 2005.

14. Jansen E, Abdulrazak B, Yang H, King J, Helal A. 2005. A programming model for pervasive spaces. Paper presented at the Third International Conference on Service-oriented Computing, The Netherlands, December 2005.

15. Van der Meer S, Jennings B, Barrett K, Carroll ,R. 2003 Design principles for smart space management. Paper presented at the First International Workshop, MUCS, Waterford, Ireland, 11 December 2003.

16. Tokuda H. 2003. A prospect of ubiquitous computing environment: new applications and issues. Paper presented at the IEEE International Workshop on Networked Appliances, Tokyo.

17. Potonniée O. 2002. Ubiquitous personalization: a smart card-based approach. Paper presented at the 4th Gemplus Developer Conference, Singapore, 12-14 November 2002.

18. Panayiotou C, Samaras G. 2004. mPERSONA: personalized portals for the wireless user: an agent approach. Mobile Networks Appl. 9: 663–677.

Mobile Information Presentation Schemes for Supra-adaptive Logistics Applications

Björn Schwerdtfeger, Troels Frimor, Daniel Pustka, and Gudrun Klinker

Fachgebiet Augmented Reality, Department of Informatics,
TU München, Germany
{schwerdt, troels, pustka, klinker}@in.tum.de
http://campar.in.tum.de

Abstract. In supra-adaptive logistics systems, operative workers must be able to quickly and precisely retrieve objects from large storage areas with minimal training. We explore concepts toward providing workers with location-based wayfinding and picking information on mobile and spatial displays, varying both visualization schemes (1D: textual descriptions, 2D: map-based overviews and 3D: AR-based arrows) and display devices (head-attached, hand-held and spatial displays). In this paper we describe the system and report on first user evaluations.

Keywords: Augmented reality, order picking, commissioning, mobile information presentation, user interface evaluations.

1 Introduction

With markets becoming increasingly global and supply and demand chains undergoing rapid changes in quality and quantity, today's logistics systems need to become *supra-adaptive*, i.e., they have to be able to adapt with minimal effort to global dynamic changes [1]. As one consequence, logistics companies need flexible workers who can adapt to new working conditions and environments quickly and with minimal training – e.g. for order picking. Mobile and flexible information presentation is a key issue toward reaching this goal.

1.1 Item Picking in Logistics Applications

In order picking tasks, workers collect sets of items from an assortment in a warehouse according to a work order and deliver them to the next station in a precisely designed material flow process [2]. The efficiency of such picking processes is divided into time measurements of four interleaved tasks: the *base time* for getting the next order information, the *dead time* during which a worker interprets and understands the order as a 3D navigation and picking task, the *way time* during which the user physically moves to the selected item and the *picking time* to actually grab the item. While the base, way and picking times have been the subject to many optimizations, we focus providing schemes to reduce the dead time.

Z. Pan et al. (Eds.): ICAT 2006, LNCS 4282, pp. 998–1007, 2006.

Traditionally, order picking is accomplished by providing workers with printed-out pick lists of articles, stating their position in the warehouse, the amount to be collected, and short descriptions. To increase efficiency and reduce the number of picking errors, current industrial setups start using two techniques [2]. *Pick-by-Light* approaches use lamps (LEDs) that are installed with each lot of items on the warehouse shelves. When a new order is processed, lamps corresponding to each item on the list are turned on to show the lot and the amount to pick. A drawback of Pick-by-Light solutions is the chance of errors when lamps fail. Furthermore, the system cannot simultaneously support multiple workers picking items in the same shelf area. In *Pick-by-Voice systems*, workers wear headsets and receive auditory information about the next item to collect. The advantage is that workers do not need their hands to operate the system. Yet, the system requires considerable mental efforts since workers have to remember what has been said.

1.2   Related Work

To overcome problems with large and complex warehouses or with inexperienced workers, different systems have been developed with the focus of easing the work burden.

Several researchers have investigated approaches supporting navigation in large environments. Raskar et al. [3] focus on building context aware systems with a variant of RFID tags that are attached to the items in warehouses and transmit geometric data of the items. This is used together with hand-held projectors to highlight the boxes and items or show other information for the worker. Butz et al. [4] attach visible markers on the points of interest and combine the projector with a camera. Mück et al. [5,6] use ARToolkit markers attached to the shelves. They then use HMDs with attached cameras to register and augment the points of interest in the shelves. This approach is also explored by Reitmayr and Schmalstieg where they augment sign posts into the environment [7]. Föckler et al. [8] use camera-equipped mobile phones as a guide for museum visitors where the devices themselves perform the object recognition.

Measuring human performance has become an important consideration in the VR community [9,10]. Smith and Hart have conducted experiments to evaluate the cognitive load of a user with different wayfinding aids [11]. Kopper et al. [12] have evaluated how users can navigate in multiscale virtual environments. Also for virtual environments, Swan et al [13] have evaluated how users performed with different map based techniques on four different virtual environment setups. With respect to augmented reality, Tönnis et al. [14] have evaluated different visualizations for directing a user's attention in a car.

2   Mobile Information Presentation Schemes

We have conceived several approaches to support two phases of the picking scenario: *wayfinding* (going to the correct shelf) and *picking* (finding the correct item on the shelf). The approaches systematically vary along two orthogonal axes: *display devices* and various *visualization schemes*.

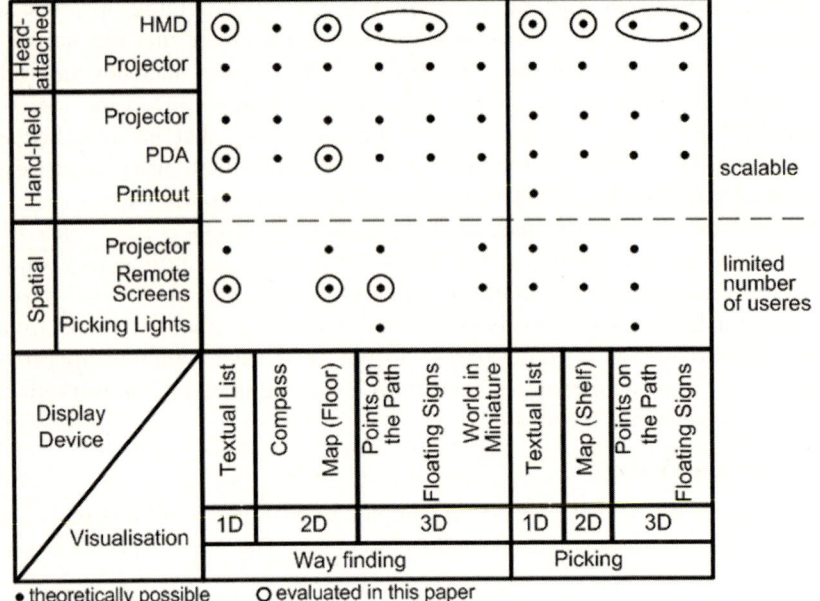

Fig. 1. Displays and their possibilities to show a visualisation

Extending the classification by Bimber and Raskar [15], we distinguish between the following *display devices*:

Spatial Ubiquitous Displays are all those which are placed in the environment, such as remote screens, projectors or pick-by-light lamps.

Hand-Held Displays refer to mobile devices which are held in the hand, attached to the user's wrist or mounted on a trolley. Such displays include classical print-outs, tablet-PCs, PDAs or hand-held projectors.

Head-Attached Displays most commonly refer to head-mounted displays which present information directly in front of users' eyes.

Several taxonomies of *visualization schemes* exist [16]. They classify visualizations with respect to criteria such as dimension, functionality, intention of use, etc. For logistics applications, we have developed schemes that show information in different numbers of dimensions.

One-dimensional information presentation arranges data items along one axis. In our case, this scheme corresponds to the printed-out lists.

Two-dimensional information presentation arranges items in a plane. The plane can be positioned vertically in front of a shelf or horizontally on the floor. Information on the plane can be oriented ego-centrically with the user (compass) or with respect to an exo-centric viewpoint (2D map).

Three-dimensional information presentation schemes [10] use three axes. Metaphors vary from *World in Miniature* (3D map) to the AR-based presentation of symbolic icons. Such icons can be placed as *Points on a Path* in world-fixed locations (traffic signs and 3D arrow at the position of the next item) or as *Floating Signs* in a user-related coordinate frame (3d compass with rubber band - connecting the compass to the next item location).

Putting it all together, the aforementioned information presentation options span a spectrum of 3 visualization schemes × 3 types of display devices = 9 options each for presenting wayfinding and picking information to mobile workers in logistics applications. Figure 1 gives an overview of all schemes and indicates which visualization can be displayed on which device. We have implemented and evaluated 11 of these schemes, as indicated by circles in Figure 1 and discussed in section 3.

3   Experimental Environment/System Design

This section gives a short overview of the hardware and software wayfinding and the picking setups for our usability experiments. Options for visualizing information were developed and discussed in an interdisciplinary team of usability and augmented reality experts, psychology students, and logisticians.

3.1   Hardware Setup

Tracking. To provide real-time optical see-through augmented reality and to track user's locations for evaluation, we used an ART DTrack system with 5 infra-red cameras. The system tracks up to 10 users or objects with sub-millimeter precision in a tracking area of about 6 × 4 meters.

Head-Mounted Display. To evaluate the use of head-attached devices we used a Sony Glasstron HMD connected to a light-weight laptop computer in a backpack. The display provides only monoscopic presentations. In order to avoid wrong depth perceptions, we presented information only to one of the user's eyes.

PDA. We used a Dell Axim X51v PDA for the hand-held presentations. It was attached with a wristband to the participants' arm.

Remote Screens. For the evaluations of spatial displays, we placed 5 monitors next to our shelves. The monitors were connected to stationary computers.

3.2   Software Components

The software system is based on our distributed DWARF middleware [17]. It allowed us to focus system development on components that are central to the underlying research questions while providing only very simple temporary solutions (shortcuts) for other systems components – to be easily replaced with more mature versions when more elaborate industrial setups are considered. Using DWARF, we have implemented the following main services:

Visualizations. A different rendering component exists for each display device, configurable for 1D, 2D and 3D visualization schemes via XML descriptions.

User Input. System notification after a user has picked an item is currently provided interactively by the supervisor (*Wizard of Oz* method).

Warehouse Management. A warehouse management system is simulated using pre-defined order lists from XML files.

Logging. A logging service writes time stamps to a log file, indicating when a
test person starts and completes a task (wayfinding, picking).

3.3 Wayfinding Setup

For the wayfinding experiments, the warehouse consisted of 4 double-sided
shelves with 5 × 5 boxes on each side, resulting in a total of 200 boxes (see
Fig. 2a). The shelves were numbered sequentially.

Fig. 2. Warehouse setup for the *Wayfinding* test with a) spatial b) hand-held and c)
head-attached displays

Spatial Displays. (Fig. 2a): We implemented one-, two-, and three-dimensional
visualizations for spatial displays (Fig. 3). The 1D visualization showed item locations as a textual list on the closest monitor (Fig. 3a). For the 2D visualization,
we used an ego-centric *you-are-here strip-map* (Fig. 3b). As 3D visualization, we
implemented the *Points on the Path* metaphor. We displayed 2D arrows on the
screen, yielding a 3D meaning according to the monitor's position and orientation. The visualization is shown on Fig. 3c.

Hand-Held Displays. (Fig. 2b): As for head-attached displays, the 1D visualization showed a text-based list, and the 2D visualization used the *you-are-
here strip-map* metaphor. We decided not to implement and test 3D AR-based
visualizations because hand-held displays could not be tracked by our system
inbetween the shelves.

Head-Attached Displays. (Fig. 2c): The 1D visualization shows a textual
list, and the 2D visualization uses the *you-are-here strip-map* metaphor. This
was favored over the compass, as [6] showed good results using the strip-map for
picking applications. For the 3D visualization we used the ego-centric *Points on
the Path* metaphor and set up a virtual traffic sign in front of the next shelf (see
Fig. 4a+b), using occlusion relationships between the shelves and the sign as
an additional depth cue. Since users had trouble finding augmentations within

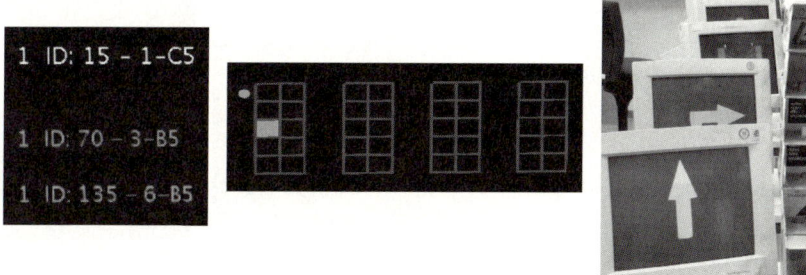

Fig. 3. Visualization schemes on spatial displays. a) Text-based list (1D): amount, id, shelf, box number (letter = column, digit = row), b) You-are-here strip-map (2D), dot: user position, square: position of the next item, c) Points on a Path (3D).

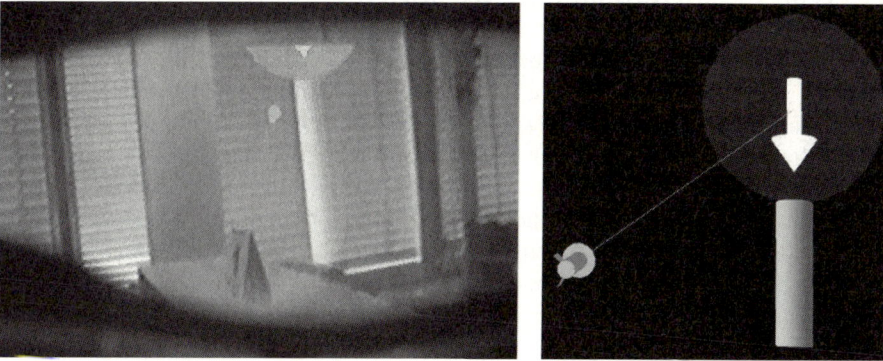

Fig. 4. Wayfinding scenario. Virtual traffic sign to indicate the next position. a) Seen through a HMD occluded by s real shelf. b) Just the augmentation.

the small field-of-view of our HMD, we added a rubber-band visualization. It consists of a compass-like arrow about one meter in front of the user. It points to the next relevant augmentation and is extended with a rubber band of flexible length.

3.4   Picking Setup

The warehouse for the picking test uses a shelf, 5 boxes wide and 10 boxes high. The subjects stood in front of this shelf during the entire test. We did not expect seeing considerable variations across mobile device types and thus tested this scenario only for the *Head-Attached Device*. As 1D visualization we again chose the textual list. For the 2D visualization we implemented a map for a vertically oriented shelf, similar to the strip-map. To highlight the box in 3D we implemented a 3D arrow slightly immersing into the box (Fig. 5b). This reinforced the effect of depth perception provoked by the occlusion. As recommended by pre-testers, we added a ball in front of each box (Fig. 5b).

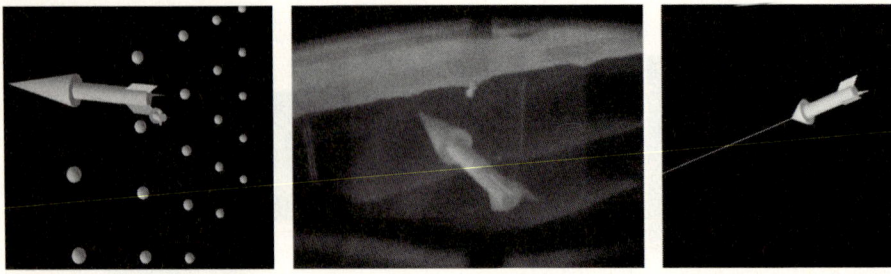

Fig. 5. Picking scenario. a) Arrow indicating the box to pick from and a ball in front of each box. b) The arrow seen through an HMD. c) Arrow with rubber band point at target.

4   Test Performance and Results

We designed two separate experiments for the *wayfinding* and *picking* tasks, allowing for a summative evaluation [18]. To obtain significant results from a moderately-sized group of subjects, we then separated the dimension of display devices from the dimension of visualization schemes. We thus made three individual evaluations, one for each display device, using a single independent variable in each test: the visualization scheme. The disadvantage of this procedure is that we did not get a unifying conclusion that compared all concepts. We used 18 subjects (age 23-48) in a *Within-Subject Design*.

As the primary dependent variable, we used the time subjects needed to find a target or to pick an object, respectively. More precisely, we measured *Way Time + Dead Time* for the wayfinding evaluations and *Picking Time + Dead Time* for picking evaluations. Additionally, we investigated the number of picking errors the participants made. During the experiments an observer watched the test persons and the displayed information. Furthermore, the subjects were interviewed and had to fill out questionnaires. Our hypothesis in each experiment was that the execution speed of the *Wayfinding/Picking* tasks increases with the dimension of the visualization, i.e.: users are faster when they are provided with 3D information than with 2D and 1D information.

4.1   Wayfinding

For wayfinding, the participants had to go to specified shelves, always starting from an initial position in the lab. Each basic batch of tests consisted of 3 wayfinding orders listing 6 positions, i.e. 18 operations. Subjects had to run a batch for each display device for each implemented visualization scheme (i.e., $3 + 2 + 3 = 8$ batches). Subjects thus were requested to perform $8 \times 18 = 144$ wayfinding operations. To compensate for learning effects all subjects ran the tests in the same sequence: *Head-attached*, *Hand-held* and *Spatial Display*.

We could not measure significant time differences between the 1D list and the 2D you-are-here strip-map, independently of the used display device (top row of

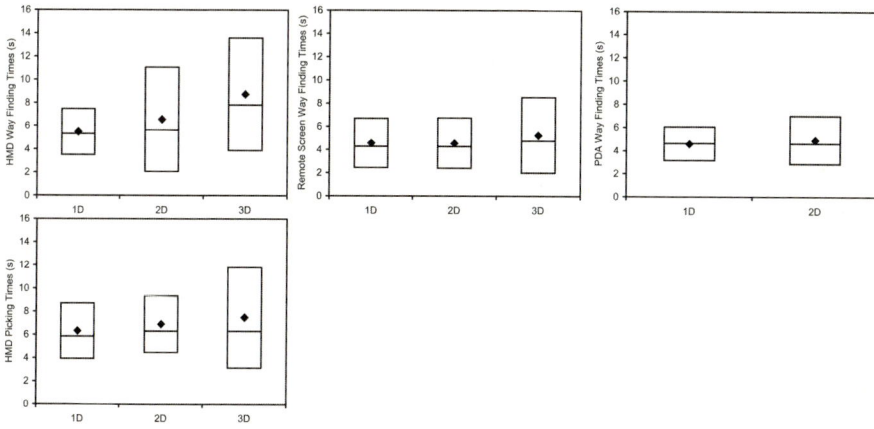

Fig. 6. Measured times in the experiment. Diamond: average, line: median, box: standard deviation.

Fig. 6). However, most subjects said that they preferred the list because a single look sufficed for understanding and remembering the task whereas, with the strip-map, they had to check continuously. Interestingly, they found the map to be confusing on the *Head-Attached* and on the *Hand-Held Display*, but not on the *Spatial Display*. We attributed this to the fact that the map uses an exo-centric reference scheme and our presentation did not provide enough unsymmetric information to help users disambiguate between different principal orientations on mobile displays. On the *Spatial Displays*, this effect was compensated by the fact that the map could be aligned with orientation of the (permanently fixed) display. But even for the visualization on the *Spatial Displays*, we could not measure significant differences compared to the list.

The 3D visualizations were significantly slower than the 1D and 2D visualizations. Especially the AR visualization on the *Head-Attached Display* was several seconds slower (Fig. 6). Yet, we observed two interesting effects: Firstly, the subjects were almost 50% faster in the third cycle than in the first. This was not only a learning effect, but also a increasing fascination people felt when experiencing Augmented Reality for the first time. Secondly, subjects clustered into two distinct groups of fast and slow users. There were no average users. These sub-clusters correlated with subjects who already prior exposure to computer games or AR/VR applications and those who did not.

4.2 Picking

The picking task required subjects to pick a specified number of items from the correct box on a shelf. Each basic batch of tests consisted of 3 picking orders listing 10 items. Subjects had to run a batch on the HMD for each visualization. Subjects thus were requested to perform $3 \times 30 = 90$ picks.

We could not measure significant speed differences between the 1D, 2D and 3D visualizations (lower row in Fig. 6). However, failure rate showed clear differences. Subjects made up to 10 times more mistakes with the AR-based visualizations than with the lists and maps. In most cases, subjects picked items one row too high or too low. This indicates a problem with depth perception using current HMDs. For 2D maps, most subjects noted that they took mental efforts to explicitly count the row and column of the visualization and then read the tags on the real shelves. This means that they transferred the information back from the 2D visualization scheme to the 1D list. Something similar happened with the 3D visualization (see Fig. 5a)). In the interview we found out that subjects divided into two camps: One group used the arrow, while the other group counted the balls (as they already did with the 2D visualization) and then used the tags on the shelf.

5 Discussion and Future Work

This paper presents on first results on comparing visualization schemes for order picking across several types of displays. Thus far, we did not find the perfect mobile visualization to provide robust and fast general guidance for the picking process. We measured that neither the 2D strip map nor the 3D visualization is on average faster for *Wayfinding* or *Picking* than the 1D textual list. But separating the subjects into AR/VR experienced and unexperienced users showed that there is a group of users, at least in one of our scenarios, which is faster with an AR system. In future evaluations the subjects will have to execute different task in parallel, such as examining the quality of the picked items while picking/wayfinding. Aside from this, we are looking for a suitable classification for users concerning their amenability to spatial concepts, as needed in AR/VR applications and games.

Acknowledgments. We would like to thank D. Walch, R. Reif and J. Boppert for their help in understanding the picking process. Thanks go also to all members of the Fachgebiet Augmented Reality for the feedback towards choosing the visualizations, as well as participants of the experiment. Finally, we thank ART GmbH for providing us with supplementary tracking hardware. This work was supported by the Bayerische Forschungsstiftung within the ForLog project.

References

1. Günthner, W.: Bayerischer Forschungsverbund Supra-adaptive Logistiksysteme (ForLog) (2004) Förderantrag an die Bayerische Forschungsstiftung, München.
2. Gudehus, T.: Logistik: Grundlagen, Strategien, Anwendungen. Springer-Verlag, Berlin, Heidelberg, New York (2005)
3. Raskar, R., Beardsley, P., van Baar, J., Wang, Y., Dietz, P., Lee, J., Leigh, D., Willwacher, T.: RFID lamps: interacting with a self-describing world via photosensing wireless tags and projectors. ACM Trans. Graph. **23**(3) (2004) 406–415

4. Butz, A., Schneider, M., Spassova, M.: SearchLight - a lightweight search function for pervasive environments. In: Pervasive 2004. (2004) 351–356
5. Mück, B., Höwer, M., Franke, W., Dangelmaier, W.: Augmented reality applications for warehouse logistics. In Abraham, A., Yasuhiko, D., Furuhashi, T., Köppen, M., Azuma, O., Ohsawa, Y., eds.: Soft Computing as Transdisciplinary Sience and Technology - Proceedings of the fourth IEEE International Workshop WSTST'05. Advances in Soft Computing, Springer-Verlag (2005) 1053–1062
6. Dangelmaier, W., Mück, B., Höwer, M., Franke, W.: AR support for picking. In: Simulation und Visualisierung 2005, SCS European Publishing House (2005)
7. Reitmayr, G., Schmalstieg, D.: Location based applications for mobile augmented reality. In: Proc. of the fourth Australasian user interface conference. (2003) 65–73
8. Föckler, P., Zeidler, T., Brombach, B., Bruns, E., Bimber, O.: PhoneGuide: Museum guidance supported by on-device object recognition on mobile phones. In: Proc. International Conference on Mobile and Ubiquitous Computing (MUM'05). (2005) 3–10
9. Swan, J., Ellis, S., Adelstein, B.: Conducting human-subject experiments with virtual and augmented reality. In: Proc. IEEE Virtual Reality. (2006)
10. Boman, D., Kruijff, E., Joseph, J., LaViola, J., Poupyrev, I.: 3D User Interfaces, Theory and Practice. Addison-Wesley (2005)
11. Smith, S., Hart, J.: Evaluating distributed cognitive resources for wayfinding in a desktop virtual environment. In: Proc. IEEE Symposium on 3D user interfaces. (2006) 3–10
12. Kopper, R., Ni, T., Bowman, D., Pinho, M.: Design and evaluation of navigation techniques for multiscale virtual environments. In: Proc. IEEE Virtual Reality. (2006)
13. Swan, J., Gabbard, J., Hix, D., Shulman, R., Kim, K.: A comparative study of user performance in a map-based virtual environment. In: Proc. IEEE Virtual Reality. (2003) 259–266
14. Tönnis, M., Sandor, C., Lange, C., Klinker, G., Bubb, H.: Experimental evaluation of an augmented reality visualization for directing a car driver's attention. In: Proc. IEEE International Symposium on Mixed and Augmented Reality (ISMAR). (2005)
15. Bimber, O., Raskar, R.: Spatial Augmented Reality: Merging Real and Virtual Worlds. A. K. Peters Ltd. (2005)
16. Ellis, S.: A taxonomy of visualization techniques for simulation in production and logistics. Proceedings of the 2003 Winter Simulation Conference (2003)
17. Bauer, M., Brügge, B., Klinker, G., MacWilliams, A., Reicher, T., Riß, S., Sandor, C., Wagner, M.: Design of a componentbased augmented reality framework. In: International Symposium on Augmented Reality ISAR. (2001)
18. Hix, D., Hartson, H.: Developing User Interfaces: Ensuring Usability through Product & Process. John Wiley and Sons (1993)

Interactive Collaborative Scene Assembly Using AR on Mobile Phones

Miroslav Andel, Alexander Petrovski, Anders Henrysson, and Mark Ollila

VITA, Linköping University, Sweden
miroslav.andel@cmar.se, alexander.petrovski@cmar.se,
andhe@itn.liu.se, marol@itn.liu.se

Abstract. In this paper we present and evaluate a platform for interactive collaborative face-to-face Augmented Reality using a distributed scene graph on mobile phones. The results of individual actions are viewed on the screen in real-time on every connected phone. We show how multiple collaborators can use consumer mobile camera phones to furnish a room together in an Augmented Reality environment. We have also presented a user case study to investigate how untrained users adopt this novel technology and to study the collaboration between multiple users. The platform is totally independent of a PC server though it is possible to connect a PC client to be used for high quality visualization on a big screen device such as a projector or a plasma display.

1 Introduction

Recently, mobile phones have developed into an ideal tool for interaction with virtual objects in Augmented Reality (AR) environments. One particularly interesting area of research is collaboration and manipulation with a shared scene on mobile phones.

The small size of a handheld device such as a mobile phone naturally provides tangible interaction possibilities. Tangible interaction means that the user can interact with virtual objects in an AR environment by simply moving the phone. By physically moving the phone, a selected object can be translated in the same direction as the physical movement. Tangible rotation can be used as well, by simply rotating the phone. Tangible interaction provides a grab and move metaphor, which feels natural and is easy to adopt for most users.

The Bluetooth technology makes it possible to create a wireless close range network between connected mobile phones. The sufficient transmission speed allows users to share data in real time and thus Bluetooth is feasible for AR collaboration. Today's AR collaboration systems uses special made equipment such as tracked head mounted see-trough displays connected to a computer. Instead of using expensive laboratory systems easy accessible mobile phones can be utilized.

The problems arise when a complex scene is shared between all connected devices. Every user's action is to be viewed simultaneously on all devices' screens in real time. The issue is to distribute the data at a sufficient rate of speed. Another issue to be solved is when different users want to manipulate with the same object in the scene. Furthermore the computing capabilities of a mobile phone are limited and floating point operations are emulated and therefore slow.

Z. Pan et al. (Eds.): ICAT 2006, LNCS 4282, pp. 1008–1017, 2006.

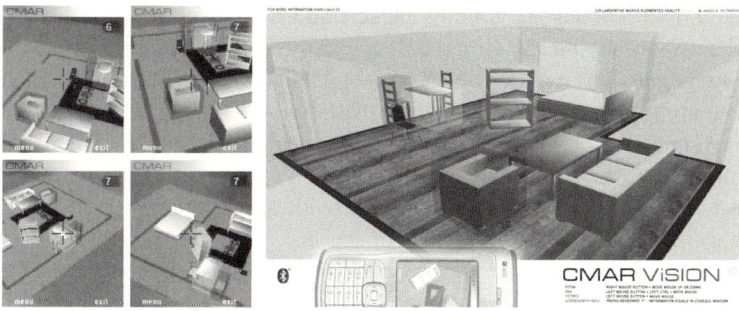

Fig. 1. Screenshots from a four people collaboration session and an overall view

In this paper we present and evaluate our platform for interactive collaborative face-to-face AR using a distributed scene graph on mobile phones and an example application showing the features of our platform called Collaborative Mobile Augmented Reality (CMAR). We believe that CMAR is the first platform to support multi-user collaborative AR scene assembly on mobile phones. In the next section we review related work. We then describe the CMAR platform and its' implementations, and a user study of our demo application. Finally we present the results, conclusions and future work.

2   Related Work

Rekimoto has shown how several users can interact with the same shared scene with his system called TransVision [8]. The system consisted of two sub parts connected by cables, a display and a computer for graphics computations. The display consists of a LCD TV, a CCD camera, a 3D sensor, and two buttons for interaction. D. Mogilev et al. have extended TransVision into AR Pad [5], which allows users to both view and interact with AR content using a combination of camera, button and trackball input.

The first light weight handheld multi collaborative AR system for the general public was the "the invisible train" [9]. Wagner et al. have created a mobile collaborative multi-user augmented reality PDA game where players control virtual trains on a real wooden miniature railroad track. The players maneuver the trains by using the stylus on the PDA as interaction tool. The goal of the game is to prevent collision between the virtual trains.

Nowadays, a decade after TransVision mobile phones are very similar to Rekimoto's system but are more compact and with Bluetooth short range wireless connectivity standard, cables are unnecessary. Mobile phones have their own CPU with sufficient computing power, which makes external computers needless. This increases the portability and by using optical tracking the mobile phone transforms into an ideal handheld AR device.

Several AR applications for camera based phones have been developed but very few collaborative ones. The best known application of this kind is "AR Tennis" [2]. AR Tennis is a face to face collaborative AR game where two players plays tennis against each other. The players can see a virtual tennis court overlaid on the real marker between them. The mobile phones are used as rackets and the players interact by physically moving their phones to hit the virtual ball across the net. This application is limited to only two users and does not involve any object manipulation except hitting the ball.

Palke et. al. implies in their work "Foot-based mobile Interaction with Games" [7] that interaction with mobile applications is often awkward due to the limited and miniaturized input modalities available. Their approach exploits the video capabilities of camera equipped smart-phones and PDAs to provide a fun solution for interaction tasks in simple games like "Pong", "Breakout" or soccer.

To be able to distribute the data between the devices in a smart manner the following distributed scene graph architectures has been examined. Hesina et al. presents Distributed Open Inventor, an extension to the Open Inventor toolkit [4]. The toolkit is extended with the concept of a distributed shared scene graph, which means that multiple devices can modify or use scene graph data. Distributed Open Inventor is a layer on the original Open Inventor and the programmer is not being forced to change the usual work style because of distribution. Similar ideas have been introduced by Martin Naef et al. with The blue-c Distributed Scene Graph [6] which is an extension to OpenGL Performer.

3   CMAR

CMAR is a platform for collaborative mobile augmented reality, which allows several users to interact and manipulate with a shared scene. The platform also contains a PC program called CMAR ViSION (figure 1) to visualize the shared scene in high-quality on a big screen device like a plasma screen or a projector. CMAR is implemented in C++ and OpenGL ES 1.1 based on Henrysson's ported version of ARToolKit to Symbian Series 60 [2]. The coordinate system convention is the same as in ARToolKit[1] and the platform is totally independent of a PC server.

3.1   Scene Graph

To be able to manage an advanced scene assembly the scene must by represented in an efficient data structure. The narrow bandwidth of the Bluetooth network makes it unsuitable to resend a whole scene representation to all connected devices in every frame. Therefore we are using a tree representation of the scene, a scene graph. This solution where each node is inheriting properties from its parent reduces the traffic over the network radically. Scene graphs are also simple, familiar and an intuitive environment to use for application developers. The few existing non-commercial distributed scene graph libraries are far too complex to port to the Symbian OS. For that reason, we have created our own simple distributed scene graph which provides easy management of large numbers of objects in the scene. This data structure also makes it easier to interact with and modify the scene. Our scene graph uses OpenGL ES which provides a low-level API between software applications and hardware or software graphics engines. When 3D hardware in mobile phones becomes a standard feature, this solution will automatically result in increased rendering speed and rendering quality. Our implementation of the scene graph is simple, compact, extendable and optimized for mobile AR

---

[1] ARToolKit, http://www.hitl.washington.edu/artoolkit

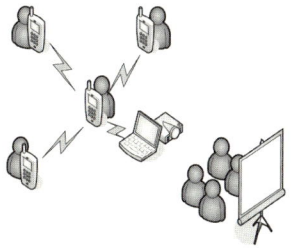

Fig. 2. Example of a CMAR network

Table 1. CMAR Bluetooth protocol

Id Package	Parameters
0 Send client id (server)	package id, client id
1 Update color	package id, node id, RGB color
2 Update rotation	package id, node id, XYZ rotation
3 Update translation	package id, node id, XYZ translation
4 Select/deselect object	package id, node id, client id, current selection id
5 Delete object	package id, node id
6 Insert object	package id, object id, XY position
7 Print screen	package id

purposes. It consists of following node types; group node, root node, transform node, geometry node, camera node, light node and material node. To be able to modify or edit an arbitrary node, every one has it's own identification number and can be accessed through an access list. This list constitute the base of how the protocol will access the scene graph data structure and perform updates.

3.2   Bluetooth Network and Protocol

The network is a Bluetooth multi point based on BoomslangBT[2], where at least one client is connected to a mobile phone server. In CMAR there are two kinds of clients; mobile phones for interaction with the shared scene and PC clients for a high resolution overall view (figure 2). Every device attached to the network has its own copy of the scene graph and is synchronized by updates from the server through a protocol. To keep the scene graph synchronized during interaction, following steps are performed.

1. The unit(s) who wants to modify the scene graph sends a request to the server
2. If the server approves the modifications it broadcasts the update information to all attached devices including itself
3. All units receive and commit the modifications

To achieve this, a protocol must be designed. Our simple binary protocol contains a number of packages that can be sent over the network (table 1). When the server connects to a client *package 0* is sent, telling the unit which id it has and in that way its'

---

[2] BoomslangBT, http://www.boomslangstudios.com

selection color. The coordinates in the protocol corresponds to the coordinate system center on the marker. A user can only select one object at a time and this is assured by the protocol. If the user selects an object that is already selected by the same user, the object will become deselected. If the user has an object selected and selects another the first object will become deselected and the second selected. If no object is selected the *current selection id* is equal to -1. The last package in the protocol makes it possible to simultaneously capture screenshots on all attached mobile phones to the network.

3.3   Selection and Interaction

To select an object, instead of calculating distances from the camera vector and check for object intersections, it is possible to store object id in the alpha channel. By backtracking the alpha channel value of the pixel in the crosshair's center of the framebuffer, it is possible to immediately obtain the selected object which is fast and requires no calculations. It is possible to have an alpha value on an object without having any transparency. Figure 3 illustrates one frame with three opaque objects and corresponding alpha channel. When an object is selected a transparent bounding box appears around the selected object with a predefined user dependent color. For interaction, based on Henryssons et al. user case study [3] we have chosen tangible interaction for the translation, joypad input for the rotation and key based interaction for all other functions. Tangible translation means in practice that a selected object can be moved by physically moving the phone in any direction.

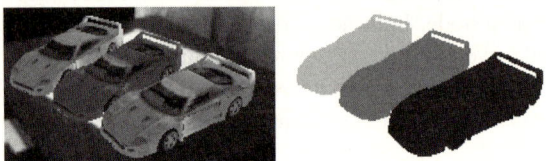

Fig. 3. Picking in the alpha channel, the RGB frame to the left and the corresponding alpha channel to the right

3.4   PC Client - CMAR ViSION

The purpose of the PC client CMAR ViSION[3] is to be used as a group display for visualization, giving an overall view of the scene on a big screen device. The only form of interaction is that the user can change the view of the real-time high-quality rendering. Therefore no camera is connected and thus the rendering contains no AR, only pure computer graphics. CMAR ViSION uses an almost unchanged version of the mobile phone scene graph except for minor changes which regards only data type substitutions and that it uses standard OpenGL instead of OpenGL ES. The functionality and syntax of the scene graph is still the same as for the mobile phone version. To achieve different quality on the renderings of the two types of clients while using the same scene graph,

---

[3] It is possible to connect several PC clients to the network. The total number of clients including mobile phone clients should not exceed eight though.

two different levels of detail of the objects are created. For the mobile phone client rendering speed is important and having objects with high amount of triangles, will lead to a significant decrease in rendering speed. To best preserve appearance of the 3D objects, a mesh simplification algorithm called "Surface simplification using quadric error metrics" [1] is utilized by CMAR ModConverter[4].

4   User Study

The evaluation was carried out in a standard conference room where the participants could communicate without disturbance during the session. The usability and experience of the user collaboration and the CMAR platform were assessed with an individual user evaluation. The purpose with this study was to elucidate characteristics of the platform limitations and advantages and to receive an insight of how this kind of interactive collaboration is adopted.

4.1   Demo Application

Our demo application that we based our user study on consists of nine pieces of furniture that can be moved freely. The virtual crosshair in the center of the screen on each mobile phone is used for selection. Selection (or deselection) is done by pressing the keypad button '5' when the object is in the crosshair. As indication that the object is selected, a transparent box around the object is visible with each of the collaborators specific and individual color. After selection, moving the selected object is performed by holding down the keypad button '2' and moving the phone physically (tangible translation) in the desired direction. The selected object is then fixed to the crosshair until the button is released. It is also possible to rotate the objects around their z-axis by pressing right or left on the joypad.

4.2   Subjects

Twenty students from Linköping University, eight males and twelve females, took part in the evaluation. Their age ranged from 22 to 28, averaging at 25. The group sizes vary from two to four collaborators and the test users had technical as well as non-technical background. To test how much experience our test users have of interaction combined with graphics the following question was asked: "How often do you play games on your mobile phone?" The majority of the test users played games more then once a year and no one played more then once a month. This was good since we wanted to focus our user study based on mobile phone users with basic knowledge.

4.3   Hardware and Setup

The hardware consisted of three Nokia 6630 and two Nokia 6680 running Symbian OS v8.0 (Series 60 Feature Pack 2) that ships with a software implementation of OpenGL ES. They have a 220 MHz ARM processor and an integrated 1.3 megapixel camera.

---

[4] This tool is a part of our platform and simplifies OBJ and PLY models to our own compact binary format supported by the scene graph.

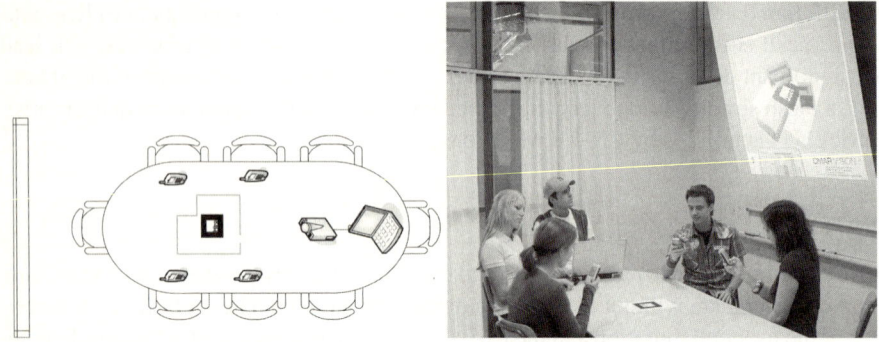

Fig. 4. The test setup and a group of four persons collaboration session with the group display to the right

The screen size is 178 x 208 pixels and the video capture resolution is 160x120 pixels. The notebook is an Acer TravelMate 8102wlmi running Windows Xp Pro Service Pack 2 with an ATI Radeon X700 graphics card and integrated Bluetooth. As group display a standard DLP projector was connected to the notebook to visualize the overall view. The test users sat at a table with the projector screen to the left of the table (figure 4).

4.4 Design and Procedure

The test users were given instructions over the functionality of the application. By letting them play around, we could actually listen and make records of their very first experience with the furnishing program. As the test users got familiar with the application (usually after a few minutes) a task was given with no time limitations. The task was to furnish their virtual apartment from a random state to a predefined state. A paper printout with the predefined state of the furniture was placed next to the marker. After completing the task the test users completed a questionnaire addressing various aspects of the perceived usability and user experience. The questions in the questionnaire (table 2) had all graded answers ranging from one to five.

4.5 User Comments

The test user's experienced the furnishing application to be fun to use and to collaborate. Some thought that it was a bit tricky to get the furniture to the exact position (as the predefined design planning) by only watching the mobile phone screen, since the tracking is not completely accurate. One test user said: "With conventional design tools as paper and pen it would not be possible to obtain the 3D effects". People in the test group liked the idea to use the mobile phone as a collaborative tool, where they could see other users moving pieces of furniture in real-time. All test persons found the tool intuitive and very easy to use. Almost all of the users found the big screen to be very useful to get better overall view and the virtual walk through (by pan, zoom and rotate the scene) provided them very good visual feedback. Some users found it frustrating when they moved the phone too far and lost their tracking. When the phone is far away from the marker, the whole scene starts to wobble due to inaccurate tracking. One user actually experienced slightly cyber sickness.

Table 2. Question protocol

Q1 How easy was it to move the furniture to the desired position?
A1 1: Very difficult, 5: Very easy
Q2 How did the cooperation worked between the collaborators?
A2 1: Very bad, 5: Very good
Q3 How important is the oral communication in the collaboration?
A3 1: Not important, 5: Very important
Q4 How would more users affect the effectivity?
A4 1: Not at all, 5: Very much
Q5 How much did the projector help to place the furniture?
A5 1: No help at all, 5: A lot of help

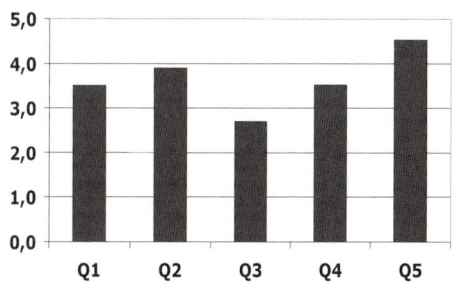

Fig. 5. The compilation of the test users answers to the questionnaire. The mean value corresponding to each question is displayed.

4.6   Results

For brevity we just summarize some of the main results: all groups were able to complete the task successfully. Almost all of the users thought it was easy to move the furniture to desired position and more than 60% thought that the projector with CMAR ViSION gave a lot of help when positioning. The collaboration between the users worked out well even though the oral communication was not found to be important. Most of the test users agreed that it would be possible to accomplish the task without speaking, but it would probably take more time. The test users also concluded that the effectiveness would be better if their group size was bigger. The main advantage with CMAR ViSION is the help in positioning that the group display gives. The main limitation of the platform is the inaccurate tracking. For a more quantitative summary of the survey see figure 5. The tracking accuracy of CMAR could be improved and applications where quick movements are used may create irritation or work bad. Good tracking is a very good start and more markers will increase the working area. The limited screen resolution is in this case helped out by the group display, which provides high quality graphics in real-time. It would be smart to make use of the vibrator to notify collisions between objects. Sound notifications could also be for the same purpose. The physical manipulation of the phone as an interaction tool is very natural and provides an intuitive approach.

5   Conclusions and Future Work

We present a novel implementation of a distributed scene graph structure for interactive collaborative Augmented Reality on mobile phones. In our work we consider the phone to be a tangible interaction tool and use the motion of the phone to translate objects. The platform gives the possibility to create a collaborative Bluetooth network containing up to eight mobile devices. If high quality real time rendering is needed, it is also possible to connect one or more PC applications to the Bluetooth network of phones for pure visualization. This platform is totally independent of a PC server and makes it therefore portable. We also presented a user study of a furnishing application that is based on our platform for group interaction on mobile phones which includes Augmented Reality, 3D graphics and tangible 3D translation. The target group of this platform are the general public with no special training. The essential equipment to run CMAR is existing consumer camera mobile phones and a marker. This makes the technology accessible and cheap. The conclusion of this user study is that untrained users adopt the technology fast and in an intuitive way. They quickly took on the task and the collaboration worked out well and the test users thought that more collaborators will lead to a faster accomplishment of their task. It was easy to move the furniture but sometimes difficult to get the furniture on exact position. The big screen visualisation was found to be helpful in many situations and could be used to walk around in the apartment.

For future work it would be interesting to compare CMAR to similar collaborative scene assembly systems on the PC platform. We would also investigate how the tracking could be improved for accuracy. Furthermore, the possibilities to save a scene to file for later collaboration sessions should be explored. How to use collision handling and physics with tangible translation needs to be investigated. In this case haptic feedback through the phone vibrator would be a nice feature to add as collision indicator. Implementing a snap function that aligns the furniture to walls and corners would help users to place the furniture faster and more accurate. Obviously we would also improve the platform according to the comments of the user study to elucidate platform drawbacks. At this moment, the platform does not allow late joining, which could be implemented by requesting a complete scene graph update from the server, and have a buffer to guarantee no pending updates are missed. This feature would also require an Ad Hoc Bluetooth network which could be solved by not letting the phone to stop searching for new CMAR running devices. Later on we have discovered that it can be a bit confusing for users to find out which selection color they have. This can be solved with a legend in the GUI. We should also consider the color choices, the server selection color is white and it can be hard to se a white selected object on white background. It would also be neat to continuously broadcast all camera positions in the local coordinate system to CMAR ViSION, where a grid of all users' camera views could be viewed.

References

1. M. Garland and P. S. Heckbert. Surface simplification using quadric error metrics. In *SIGGRAPH*, pages 209–216, 1997.
2. A. Henrysson, M. Billinghurst, and M. Ollila. Face to face collaborative ar on mobile phones. In *ISMAR*, pages 80–89, 2005.

3. A. Henrysson, M. Billinghurst, and M. Ollila. Virtual object manipulation using a mobile phone. In *ICAT 2005: of the 15th International Conference on Artificial Reality and Telexistence*, pages 164–171, 2005.

4. G. Hesina, D. Schmalstieg, A. Furhmann, and W. Purgathofer. Distributed open inventor: a practical approach to distributed 3d graphics. In *VRST '99: Proceedings of the ACM symposium on Virtual reality software and technology*, pages 74–81, New York, NY, USA, 1999. ACM Press.

5. D. Mogilev, K. Kiyokawa, M. Billinghurst, and J. Pair. Ar pad: An interface for face-to-face ar collaboration, 2002.

6. M. Naef, E. Lamboray, O. Staadt, and M. Gross. The blue-c distributed scene graph. In *EGVE '03: Proceedings of the workshop on Virtual environments 2003*, pages 125–133, New York, NY, USA, 2003. ACM Press.

7. V. Paelke, C. Reimann, and D. Stichling. Foot-based mobile interaction with games. In *ACE '04: Proceedings of the 2004 ACM SIGCHI International Conference on Advances in computer entertainment technology*, pages 321–324, New York, NY, USA, 2004. ACM Press.

8. J. Rekimoto. Transvision: A hand-held augmented reality system for collaborative design. In *Proceedings of Virtual Systems and Multimedia (VSMM) '96*, 1996.

9. D. Wagner, T. Pintaric, F. Ledermann, and D. Schmalstieg. Towards massively multi-user augmented reality on handheld devices. In *Third International Conference on Pervasive Computing (Pervasive 2005)*, Munich, Germany, may 2005.

Design of the Multimedia Communication Protocol and System for Wireless LAN

Qingzhang Chen[1,2], Jianghong Han[1], and Keji Mao[2]

[1] College of Computer and Information, Hefei University of Technology
Hefei ,Anhui, China
qzchen@zjut.edu.cn
[2] College of Information Engineering, Zhejiang University of Technology
Hangzhou, Zhejiang, China

Abstract. The protocol of wireless LAN —IEEE 802.11 put forward DCF/PCF to offer the real time transmission, but it did not meet the need of multimedia transmission, so a new MAC protocol is developed to solve this problem. In this paper we discuss the way of implementing and processing the multimedia data streams in WLAN. We regard the transmission of multimedia as multi-channel accessing with synchronization to study it. We start from the parameter QoS and mapped the multimedia transmission data streams to the different priorities, and use negotiation approach to allocate the resource.

1 Introduction

1.1 Wireless LAN

Now we are in the age of communication revolution. In the recent decades, traditional wireless network system developed very quickly, and many kinds new technology appeared, just like wireless LAN. In order to give users a better wireless communication service, IEEE draft out the protocol of 802.11.

The 802.11 MAC protocol supports two kinds of operation modes, PCF and DCF. PCF provides an entering mode that can avoid the competition, and DCF adopts a kind of CSMA that also can avoid conflicting based on entering competition. These two modes can trade off, that means a DCF competitive period follows a PCF non-competitive period.

1.2 Multimedia Communication

IEEE 802.11 use RTS/CTS to avoid collision, but the duration of RTS and CTS are same in length, so only the problem of base-to-peer hidden terminal can be solved, but to the transmission shape of multipeer, it can not solve the problem of hidden terminal and collision. Besides, IEEE 802.11 thought that PCF/DCF could provide the real transmission in some degree, but it didn't equal to the character of multimedia transmission, so a new kind of MAC protocol is also needed.

Z. Pan et al. (Eds.): ICAT 2006, LNCS 4282, pp. 1018–1025, 2006.

1.3 Project Aim

1.3.1 Putting Forward a Kind of Multimedia Transmission Protocol to Apply the MAC in the Wireless LAN

In this paper we regard the transmission of multimedia as multi-channel accessing with synchronization to study it, and in every contention period one multimedia transmission competition by one group that maybe formed by many members. The so-called multi-channel access with synchronization means that a sender needs one or more contention free transmission authority for channel before transmitting, and transmitting different streams by these channels synchronously, every stream need a different transmission time.

1.3.2 The Design of QoS

The way of TDMA, FDMA and CDMA are all belong to static allocation methods. They should be improved to meet the need of multimedia transmission of QoS. We start from the parameter QoS and mapped the multimedia transmission data streams to the different priorities. As soon as priority model come into existence, we will use negotiation in the admission and resource management of streams handover. When high priority requests enter the system, and there is not enough resource to meet the need of new requests, we will give some new resource to the high priority requests by lowing low priority users' service quality.

2 The Design of System

2.1 Overview

Actually we also need driver and firmware. Drivers offer service to the system to control the wireless LAN adapter. Firmware takes change to the practice process of the wireless LAN adapter, including the carrier wave and sense in physics and receiving and transmitting data, and also provides service to drivers.

2.2 Firmware

In firmware, after initialization we should wait a new event, for the convenience of implementing, we use an endless circulation to poll every queue, check the happen of event and call for processing it.

2.3 Drivers

In drivers, we use windows operating system as platform, and program the drivers of wireless network according to NDIS (Network Driver Interface Specification).

2.4 Multimedia Service

2.4.1 The IEEE 802.11 Standard of Real Time Service

Besides using the technology of CDMA/CA offer the basic visiting control, IEEE 802.11 also supports the Point coordination function (PCF for short).

The main principle of the PCF is establishing a polling mechanism, PC (Point Co-ordinator) will poll by a polling list on which recorded all the workstation that need to transmit real time data, and the workstation which have been polled can transport frame.

According to the standard of IEEE 802.11, the polling list that PCF maintained are not compelled, and the polling list only know which workstation can be polled, it doesn't give the information of that how many real time data that the workstation needed to be transmitted. Workstation also cannot dynamically request the time and length for polling, every workstation have one frame time. Allotting the resource on average so side by side cannot reflect the real request.

2.4.2 Processing the Multimedia Data

According to the character of multimedia data, we divide the emergency of the data into three types in the rough, there are real time data, harmonizing data and random data. According different request, every workstation can put forward specific request to the three types.

In order to describe the parameter QoS in quantity, we use smooth model to de-scribe the problem, to the general situation that there may be several workstations, we put forward the following expression.

$U=\{u_i|\ i\in N\}$ u_i means the workstation I.

U means the all workstations that in the same infrastructure. Every workstation should obey the smooth model, and according this put forward the parameter of the data streams. The four parameter of the smooth model are

$\{n_i, T_i, P_i, W_i\}$

n_i means when the workstation I wants to establish a multimedia transmission, the quantity of the multimedia transmission data streams that it needs.

T_i means the data streams n_i of workstation I belongs to which type of data. $\{t_i^j|\ j=1, 2, 3, ..., n_i ,\ t_i^j\in$ stream type$\}$

P_i means the data transmission jitter n_i of the workstation I. $\{p_i^j|\ j=1, 2, 3, ..., n_i, p_i^j\in N\}$。

W_i means the max. and the allowed min. that the bit rate of the data stream needed of the workstation I. $\{(x_i^j, y_i^j)|\ j=1, 2, 3, ..., n_i \}$.

According to the smooth model, $\{n_i, T_i, P_i, W_i\}$ means the demand of one work-station that wants to establish realtime multimedia. For example, the basic demands of online movie are video, sound and letter. So you must put forward the request pa-rameter when you are establishing the online service, the smooth model maybe ex-pressed like this $\{3, \{1, 2, 3\}, \{1, 3, 7\}, \{\{150\}, \{20, 13\}, \{NULL\}\}\}$.

2.4.3 Analysis

Before the establishing of every online multimedia, the workstation will put forward the requested parameter that depend on the fore-mentioned model, then checked and affirmed by IBSS PC. Because of the hardware limit of the physics, we must use a fair and dynamic allot principle to the parameter request of users. The principle of allocating is adopting a kind of admission control testing model. So we have to ana-lyze the behavior of three different kinds of streams in PCF.

2.4.3.1   Real Time Data. If we observe the whole transmission program IEEE 802.11 from the transmission period, and add the time of DCF to PCF regarded as one period of transmission, we call it super-frame (DCF time + PCF time= K, K∈ constant). If we look one super-frame as QoS transmission unit, on the base of period, we also can quantify the parameter of jitter as period parameter in order to translate the request of jitter into synchronic mechanism. If we can look jitter as bit rate guaranteed, lingering reference variable; if we look the period as the basic unit of transmission, jitter means the allowed period parameter that can meet the requirement. That is to say, if the period counted by jitter, and the finish of period also is the synchronic point of the stream.

Through the period transition, the real time data stream can be quantified to the number of frames that must be transmitted in every period. And in every period must be a PCF period in order to insure the certain number of frames should be transmitted. Admission test should fetch the smallest common factor from the quantified period of all period parameter, and then looks the min. common multiply as the longest period. All the allowed bandwidth limited streams in the longest period and also accord with their jitter request can get reservation. A simple math expression like this,

Order $L = \text{LCM}(\{P_i^j\})$

$\sum_{j=0}^{ni}(W_i^j/L) + \text{DCF time} < 1$

Get $\sum_{j=0}^{ni}(W_i^j/L) < 1 - \text{DCF time}(= \text{max of PCF period time})$.

After meeting the need of bandwidth, the PRI of transmission adopts pre-scheduling on demand. In advance, we maintain the PCF polling list by jitter to decide every time unit save to which stream to transmit a frame. On every time point we directly appoint the use attach of channel, and it doesn't have to be counted again. The keystone of scheduling mechanism is maintaining the polling list, and polling list must record the transmission order, destination and data and so on of every stream in every big period in detail. Every time there is a new request of online, it must find a transmission time from the polling list and does not affect all the online quality.

2.4.3.2   Harmonizing Data. Unlike the real time data, this is a data stream that the requirement of the bandwidth are variable depends on the network under allowed range. Without prejudice to the basic requirement, adjusting the use of bandwidth, but it also need PCF time, so admission control model like the real time data streams model, only at the time of scheduling, can consider the limit of bandwidth, to seek the time point and allowed transmission quantity accord with the parameter jitter.

2.4.3.3   Random op Data. Random data has no time emergency, so there is no jitter as period parameter, and also it dose not need admission control and scheduling. The CDMA/CA mechanism which operating in DCF period offers the request of random data. Here we do not offer the efficiency evaluation, only suppose under the request of plentiful bandwidth remained, PCF can engross the longest time, and the time of DCF must meet the need of transmitting the longest frame, such shortest DCF time including DIFS、RTS/CTS、SIFS、max frame length and ACK time.

3 Implement

3.1 Implement the Simple PCF Mechanism

In general wireless LAN adapter, only the DCF transmission mechanism realized, to the PCF are mostly not. In order to implementing the multimedia corresponding mechanism we must add PCF model by ourselves, especially, about the usage of beacon frame, probe response frame in CF-parameter, and also the minuteness of polling list and the running mechanism of poll must be finished.

Another keystone is the design of point coordinator, for the sake of convenience, we adopt Ad-hoc network frame, and use one IBSS Creator as point coordinator to imitate the centralized control model of access point. Under such a principle and subordinate frame, point coordinator shoulders the work of admission control, schedule and poll.

Element ID	Length	CFP Count	CFP Period	CFP MaxDuration	CFP DurRemaining
Byte: 1	1	1	1	2	2

Fig. 1. CF Parameter Set element format

From figure 1 we can observe the every parameter of CF Parameter, and the fixation of CFP Period and CFP Max. Duration separately express how many beacon period as one CFP period and the maximums allowable duration of one CFP period.

Deciding the two number properly can help to the efficiency of the whole mechanism to the bandwidth. Beacon use CFP Count to declare the beginning of PCF after several beacon periods, CFP DurRemaining descended timely the parameter of beacon frame transmitted by DCF period to zero.

The above CFP parameters mentioned are all decided by point coordinator. And use beacon timer to timing transport beacon frame. On one hand, all the mobile stations timing synchronization, also can harmonize the subrogation of DCF and PCF.

Before the beginning of PCF period, we must decide the polling list. If it involves admission control and scheduling, it will wastes more time to count time and memory size, so it is dealt with by drivers and not realized by the firmware on the network adapter. The firmware process of point coordinator only charge to affirm the object that drivers wanted to be transmitted or the object of polled transmission data to transmit in time. Common workstations are in passive situation, only when they received the frame of poll, they can transmit the data, or when they received data frame, they can response ack frame. In the whole period of PCF, it use piggyback to transmit the messages of poll and ack to save the bandwidth. Besides the transmission of frame, CFP also have to cooperate null-function frame to use in the condition of that there is no data frame to be transmitted, and the messages of piggyback should be transported.

3.2   Offering QoS Service

3.2.1   Admission Control

The quality of the service is very important to the high quality video, sound and the multimedia applied in WLAN. IEEE 802.11 standard has no criterion to the request of the avoid-competition bandwidth, that is to say, how to let point coordinator know which user should what time to transmit the data?

If there is only have a bandwidth remained non-competition mechanism, and there is no chance to use it. It is also useless. In order make good use of PCF period, we should have a seeking way to the bandwidth, and let every bandwidth user who want to the bandwidth take part in the competition fairly, it will not lose the bandwidth remained mechanism because of the competition. Obviously, we remain enough bandwidth to the PCF period, and the use the remainder DCF period to deal with the reservation request.

But IEEE 802.11 standard did not define such request/response frame. Fortunately, the frame type that management frame defined did not use up, and the remainder used to enlarge the type. We can dauntlessly use these two to define the offered frame type, and we call QoS request frame and QoS response frame, permeating the information exchange of these two groups to obtain the remained bandwidth mechanism.

The frame type of QoS request frame / response frame is also management frame, but sub-type (4 bit) separately use 1110 and 1111, that is the whole field of frame control separately add 0x00E0 and 0x00F0, and the results as these two type of frame type.

The information of the body of QoS request frame are the QoS parameter of the data streams, and at most n data streams can be allowed.

The information of the body of QoS request frame is very easy, response to the request whether allowed of not, when it is allowed it can be allocated several data streams' ID.

3.2.2   The Maintenance of Admission Test and Polling Test

According to the traditional IEEE 802.11 standard, the speed of wireless LAN adapter has two types, 1Mbps and 2Mbps. But on the implement of the network adapter, 1Mbps is used and 2Mbps is not for insurance and the validity of the data. Millions of bits can be transmitted in one second, and the longest frame is 2304 bits, every five beacon periods as one new start of PCF period, every beacon period transmitted in 100 microsecond. So the period of PCF is $5 \times 10^5 \mu s$, if every second transmit 10^6 bits, every period of PCF can hold 217 longest frames, except the DCF period time, and the time of the IFS and back-off. The efficiency of 200 frames/PCF period is prospective.

$$100 \text{kbps} = 10^5 \text{ bits}/10^6 \text{ }\mu s$$
$$= 5 \times 10^4 \text{ bits}/5 \times 10^5 \text{ }\mu s$$
$$= 21 \text{ MPDU}/1 \text{ PCF}$$

To the request of users' bit rate, we can change it into the number of frame that every non-competition period should be transmitted. This the fact speed contrast to the request of the users.

The change of time parameter according to the PCF period, every PCF period less than one second, so we suppose every time parameter as one, means every PCF period as one synchronization, if the point of synchronization can meet the number of transmitted frame means QoS is satisfied. For example, bit rate= 100kps, jitter= 2 come into being in the MAC, the time that the first frame begin to transmit to the 42th frame finished transmitting must be in the two period of PCF.

Implementing the QoS on the wireless LAN adapter to maintain the link list of array of polling list, PollingListTab[1], PollingListTab[2]…to PollingListTab[n] means the time synchronization period of 1,2,to n data streams, and clustered by the way of link –list. In every node's information, there are the number of frames to be transmitted and the total number to be transmitted and destination address and data stream model and synchronous remained time. Every time deal with the request of the bandwidth should according to this table to count.

3.2.3 Sequence
Every time IBSS PC transmit the beacon frame, it will check the polling list table according to the remained CFP duration. The frame has smaller period has higher priority, one by one in the same period and the workstation that has more frames need to be transmitted has higher priority.

4 Conclusions

About the development of the wireless LAN adapter, firmware and drivers are the closed two parts, if you want to develop the wireless LAN multimedia communication, you must firmly grasp these two parts, and experience be sufficient. On the implement of multimedia, the core of a new operating system has been support in some degree, such as Windows 2000 /XP, I believe that it will bring great help to the development of the wireless multimedia communication.

Acknowledgements

The Project Supported by Zhejiang Provincial Science Foundation of China (Y105388).

References

1. Sunghyun Choi and King G. Shin, A cellular wireless local area network with Qos guarntees for heterogeneous traffic, Mobile Networks and Applications 3 (1998)89-100 .
2. Andrew Muir and J.J. Garcia-Luna-Aceves, An efficient packet sensing MAC protocol for wireless networks, Mobile Networks and Applications 3 (1998) 221-234 .
3. Andrew Muir and J.J Garcia-Luna-Aceves, Group Allocation Multiple Access with Collision Detection, Computer Engineering Department University of California Santa Crus, CA 95064 .
4. Macro Conti, Claudio Demaria and Lorenzo Donatiello, Design and performance evaluation of a MAC protocol for wireless local area networks, Mobile Networks and Applications 2 (1997) 69-87 .

5. Paramvir Bahl, Imrich Chlamtac and Andras Farago, Optimizing Resource Utilization in Wireless Multimedia Networks, 1997 IEEE .

6. Cheng-Shang Chang, Member, IEEE, Kwang-Cheng Chen, Member, IEEE, Ming-Young You, and Jin-Fu Chang, Fellow, IEEE, Guaranteed Quality-of-Service Wireless Access to ATM Networks, IEEE JOURNALON SELECTED AREAS IN COMMUNICATIONS . VOL. 15. NO. 1. JANUARY 1997 .

7. Chane L. Fullmer and J.J. Garcia-Luna-Aceves, Complete Single-Channel Solutions to Hidden Terminal Problems in Wireless LANs, Computer Engineering Department Unitersity of California, Santa Crus, California 95064

8. Brocha Epstein and Mischa Schwartz, Reservation Strategies for Multi-Media Traffic in a Wireless Environment, 1995 IEEE .

9. Part11 : Wireless Lan Medium Access Control(MAC) and Physical Layer(PHY) specifications, LAN MAN Standards Committee of the IEEE computer Society .

10. AMD, Wireless LAN DSSS PC Card Reference Design Application Note, application note .

11. Microsoft Driver Develop Kit. Microsoft, 1999 .

Representation of Color in Ancient Noh Masks

Xin Yin[1], Yasuo Miichi[2], and Hiromi T.Tanaka[1]

[1] Ritsumeikan University,
Nojihigashi 1-1-1, Kusatsu, Shiga, 5258577 Japan
[2] Noh Mask Maker

Abstract. Noh is a traditional Japanese dramatic art. The color of the Noh mask constantly changes in appearance, because of natural factors. In this paper, a digital technique for representing the original color of Noh masks is introduced. At first, an image which shows the normal on surface is generated from the constructed 3D Noh mask mesh. And then, the color of the Noh mask is updated by reference to the color of the surrounding points. As the result, the original color is obtained. Finally, the implementation is carried out using a current Noh mask and an ancient Noh mask. The technique introduced in this paper can also be used to represent the original color in other 3D objects.

Keywords: Representation, 3D object, Noh mask, Color, Retinex algorithm.

1 Introduction

Objects of cultural assets which are exposed to the natural environment can undergo changes in appearance. The original colors may fade and some parts of the object may be lost. For this reason, much research has been undertaken into the preservation of cultural assets. Various digital representation techniques have been developed for preservation of cultural assets.

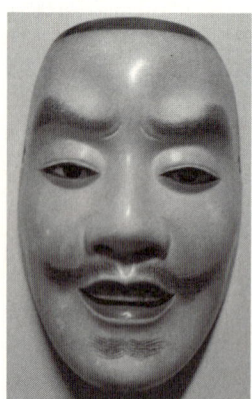

Fig. 1. Noh masks

Z. Pan et al. (Eds.): ICAT 2006, LNCS 4282, pp. 1026–1034, 2006.
© Springer-Verlag Berlin Heidelberg 2006

Noh is a famous Japanese traditional drama in which the faces of the players are covered with masks. Noh masks are vulnerable to environmental weathering which can result in fading and loss of the surface pigments. Two Noh masks are shown in the Fig. 1. The left mask is made about thirty years ago and the right one is made about three hundreds years ago. The representation of original color in Noh masks is a challenging area of research.

2 Previous Work

Long ago, the restoration of cultural objects was based on the rich knowledge and experience of craftsmen. More recently, digital techniques using image processing software have been developed, but like the craftsman of former times, the operator applies his or her knowledge and experience in restoration the color of the object. One example of this type of technique is [3], by which the color of an ancient "hell scroll" was represented perfectly. In addition, some color representation techniques based on computer graphics (CG), such as [2], have been developed. In this technique, the three-dimensional (3D) shape of the object is measured by a machine. Next, the artist draws pictures based on the historical record, which are then mapped onto the surface of the 3D model by computer. The color of an ancient statue was reproduced using this technique. This technique allows manual adjustment of detail based on the experience of the operator. But these techniques pain the color on the surface of object and lost some real information of color on the surface.

Automatic or semi-automatic color-representation techniques have also been developed. Reference [8] used a technique which makes use of color information remaining on the object. A color that is lost may be reproduced by reference to the color information surrounding the missing section. Reference [7] developed a system for representing the color base on the experience of the exporters. Reference [1] introduced some digital techniques which can clean the surface and repair the crack pattern on the objects. And [4] developed an algorithm, based on the ability of human eyes to adjust to environmental lighting conditions, for removing the influence of dirt on computer simulations of ancient drawings. This technique has mainly been used in the color representation of oil paintings. These techniques mainly represent the color on 2D images. We propose a technique for representing the color on 3D objects in this paper.

Usually, for representing the color in the culture assets, the investigation of the pigment on the surface and segmenting the pigment field is needed. But there are some problems are not solved well. The same pigment can show different color if the pain method is different. As this reason, it is very difficult to understand original color in the culture assets even we know what type pigment is used. By another hand, segmenting the pigment field well is not easy. The segment technique is developing now. To avoid these problems, we develop a technique to represent the color based on the information of pigment on the 3D surface directly.

The color variation process is different, the craftsmen always represent the color by referencing the color where is look new on the surface. This means that the different color on the surface implies the some rules of color variation process. If these color information on the surface is used well, the original color can be represented. The

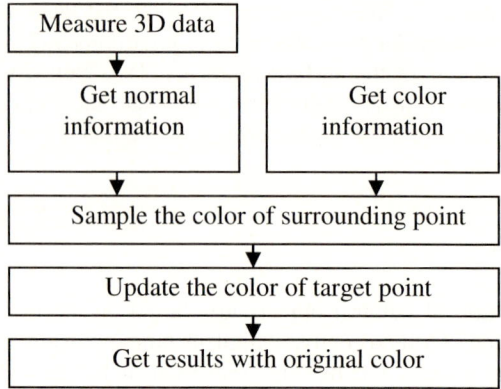

Fig. 2. Computer process

technique represented in this paper needs not segmenting the pigment field detail. The point where the color need updated is called target point, and the surrounding points are called sample points. Shown as Fig. 2, the first step was measurement of the 3D data and color of the Noh mask. Next, we sample the variation in color over the 3D surface based on the surface normal variation, then, the color of the Noh mask is represented using a digital algorithm. Finally we show some implementing results and discuss this technique.

3   Background Knowledge on Noh Masks

Noh masks are made from wood on which a design is painted ([5]). In creating a Noh mask, the first step is to carve and polish the wood to provide detail, so that a shape similar to that of the human face is obtained. Next, pigments are painted onto the wooden mask. As shown in Fig. 3a, the Noh mask has two surfaces, the back and the front. The back surface is nearest to the face of the player, and is painted uniformly because it cannot be seen. The front surface is painted with various types of pigments. There are two types of coating: the undercoat and the topcoat. The undercoat is painted in a uniform color and represents the color of the skin. The topcoat is painted in different colors to show the hair, eyes, mouth and so on. Finally, certain other pigments are applied to the surface so that the Noh mask can be seen well on the stage.

A glue is used to cause the pigments to adhere to the wood. Light passes through the glue and is reflected outward by pigment particles. As shown in Fig. 3b, when the glue deteriorates, some of the pigment particles are lost, with the result that the formerly smooth surface of the mask becomes rough and decreases in brightness. If the deterioration extends deep into the mask, some areas of pigment are lost completely, and the color of the mask cannot be seen. The pigment particles are mixed slowly and the surface become dark. One subject of representing the color is taking off this dark efficiency.

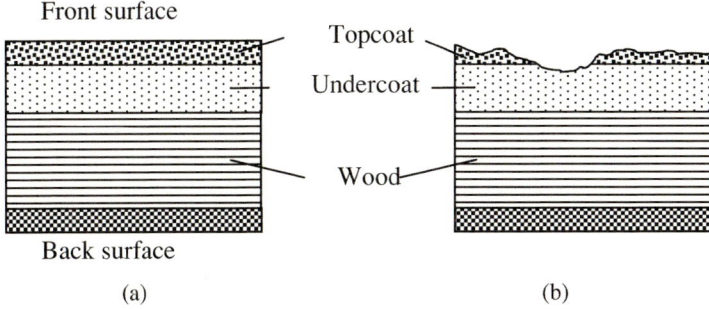

Front surface

Topcoat

Undercoat

Wood

Back surface

(a)   (b)

Fig. 3. Pigments of Noh mask

4   Representation of Noh Mask Original Color

The techniques used in ancient times for fashioning and painting Noh masks are not well understood. In addition, the variation of pigments is a complex process. For these reasons, it is very difficult to represent color completely. The key idea for representing the color in this paper comes from [4] which use Retinex (come from "retina" and "cortex") algorithm ([6]) to represent the color on 2D image. To update the color of a target point, the Retinex algorithm uses the color information found in the vicinity of the point. The influence of one pixel on another varies according to the distance between them. Similar to the Retinex algorithm, we also use the color information found in the vicinity. Then compute the original color based on this information. The detail will be introduced as follow.

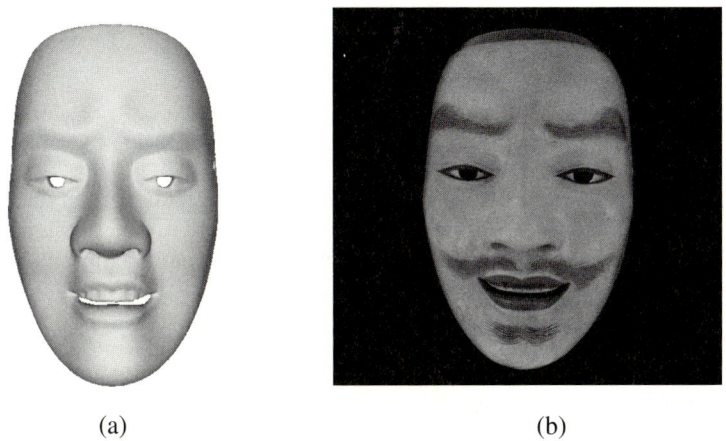

(a)   (b)

Fig. 4. Measure 3D mesh and color

4.1 Measure 3D Mesh and Color

Because there are some techniques can measure and construct 3D mesh of object well, we use these techniques directly. The 3D surface data were obtained using a 3D object measurement machine (Vivid 910). The data got by the Vivid 910 are about thirty patches. Then use exist software to compose these patches together and fill the hole on surface. Fig. 4a shows the final 3D mesh surface. We will use the 3D mesh surface to calculate the image which shows the normal information on 3D surface in the section 4.2.

Because the Noh mask is a 3D object, the normal of the 3D object can cause color variations when the color of the mask is measured; the same color may show a different value if the view point is different. For example, there are some highlight and shadow when take photo of a mask shown as Fig. 1. To avoid the highlight effect, the mask is put into a white dome. In this white dome, the light is diffused and there is not highlight on the mask when take the mask photo. One photo taken in this dome is shown in Fig. 4b.

Since the mesh is 3D and the color image is 2D, the registration process between the 3D mesh and the 2D image is needed. Three reference points are used. Two points

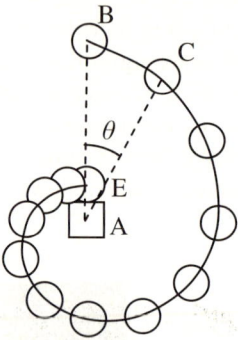

Fig. 5. Sample route

are the center of the eyes. One point is the center of the mouth. Then the 3D mesh is rotated and scaled until these three points are match between the mesh and the color image. The result is shown in Fig. 4a and 4b. The mesh and the image are seen from same view point.

4.2 Sample on 3D Surface

As mentioned before, when update a point (called target point) color, the around point (called sample point) color information is used. To get uniform samples, a sample rout shown as Fig.5 is used. The color of point A is updated based on the colors of the surrounding points (circle points). Reference [9] has introduced the concept of aesthetic curves. We assume that these curves are beautiful because color information obtained as along with these curves are uniform. To decrease the compute cost, the expression of the curves is simplify and is represented in polar coordinates as follow:

$$\begin{cases} R_2 = a \bullet R_1 \\ \quad \theta = b \end{cases} . \tag{1}$$

Where R is the length between the point A and sampled points. For example, R_1 is the length of AB and the R_2 is the length of AC. Shown as Fig. 5, θ is the variation in angle. a and b are constants. In this paper, a is 0.9 and b is $\pi/6$. As shown in Fig. 5, the surrounding points (circle points) are distributed according to this curve, and the color of point A is calculated from the color of the surrounding points (B, C etc.).

But the surface of the object is 3D. It is need adjust the sample method on the surface according to the normal of the surface. Shown as in Fig. 6a, A1 is the point which needs updating the color. B1 is the sample point which is computed by the expression (1). B2 is the projection of B1 on the surface according to the vector to the camera. As the result, the sample point on the 3D surface is the B2. In Fig. 6b, three

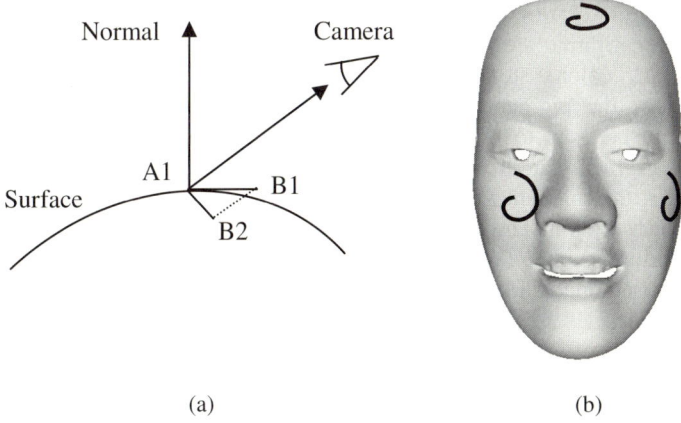

(a)   (b)

Fig. 6. Sample on 3D surface

states of the route on the different position of the surface are shown. Then according to these adjusted routs, the color of the target points is updated.

For generating the route, the information of the normal on surface and the vector to the camera are need. These are draw into normal image shown as Fig.7a and the camera-vector image shown as Fig. 7b. The values of the RGB color show the xyz values of the vectors. By this translation, the 3D problem is translated to the 2D problem. As the result, the process of representing the original color becomes simple. The sample rout can be adjusted from these vector images.

4.3 Update the Color

This color updating is calculated in the logarithmic field using the LMS color system. RGB color values are converted into LMS values in the logarithmic field, and the color of each point is then updated along the sample route. Finally, the LMS color

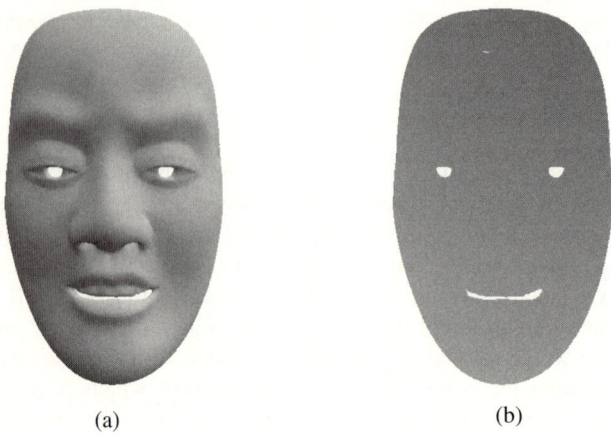

(a)   (b)

Fig. 7. Vector images

values in the logarithmic are converted back to the RGB system. The discussion at next is in the LMS color system.

The speed of the pigment variation on surface is different, so this different information can be used to represent the original color of the mask. Usually, the process of the pigment variation is similar on the different superficial position. If the position is near, the pigment variation is more similar. As this reason, when update the color of a target point. The color of the sample points along with the rout will give some contribution to the color of the target point. The near points give more contribution. Based on this idea, the next expression is constructed:

$$NP(x, y) = OP(x, y) + \sum_{i=0}^{N} \frac{OP_i(x', y') - OP(x, y)}{k^{N-i+1}} . \tag{2}$$

Here, $NP(x,y)$ is the new color of the target point (point A in Fig. 5); $OP(x,y)$ is the old color of the target point; $OPi(x',y')$ is the old color of the sample points (points B and C in Fig. 5). i is the index of the sample points along with the sample route. N is the total number of the sample points and is 12 in this paper. If the index i is small, the distance between the sample point and the target point is large. k is a constant and is the parameter that control the amount of influence one point has on another. In this paper, k is 2.0.

Expression (2) sums the influence of all the sample points. The influence is big if the sample point is near to the target point. Using this expression, the color of target point is updated based on the color of sample points. This compute process is done by some times. If the same pigment shows the same color, it is mean that the original color is got and the compute process is finished.

Despite the pigment variation process is not understood well, the difference of the color on surface can help us to know something about the pigment variation. The compute process that mentioned above can infer the original color of the pigment automatically.

5 Implementation and Discussion

Implementation is carried out using two Noh masks. One is the mask that is made about thirty years ago. The other mask is famous one that is made about three hundreds years ago.

Shown as in Fig. 8a, the current mask color is a little dark. After the cleaning process, the color becomes new and is bright shown as Fig. 8b. This mask is made thirty years ago. The maker of the mask says that the color is similar to the original one. When this mask is cleaned, the photo of the mask is used directly as mentioned above.

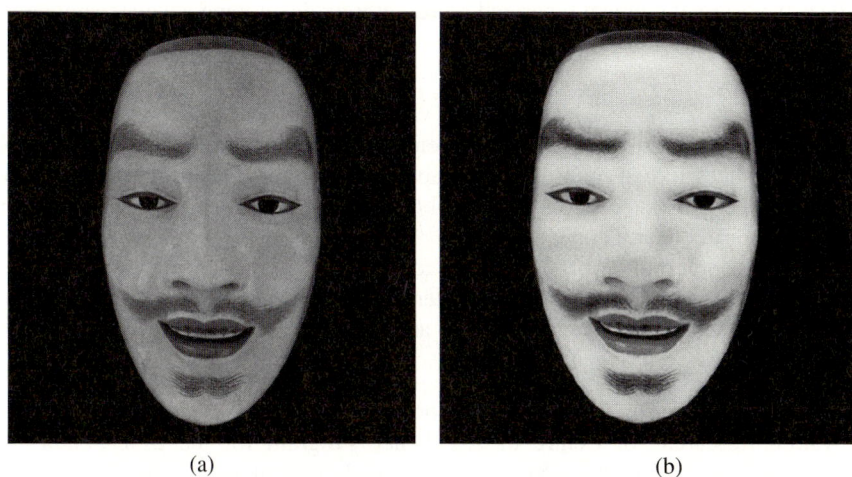

(a)   (b)

Fig. 8. Implement of a current Noh mask

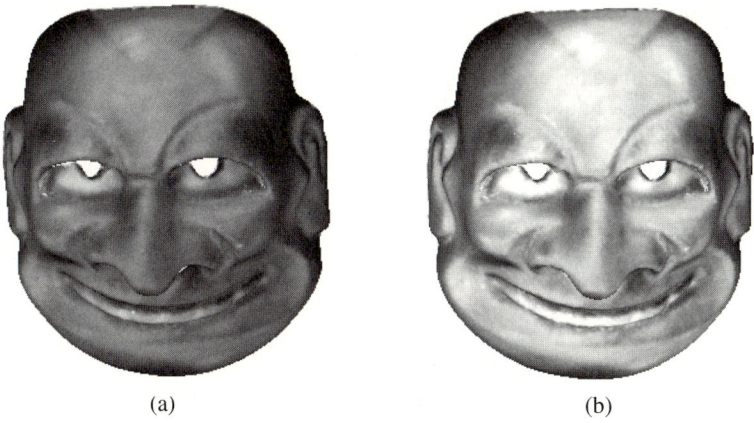

(a)   (b)

Fig. 9. Implementation of a famous ancient Noh mask

Another mask is made about three hundreds years ago and nobody know the original color. At this case, the photo is projected to a column surface and a texture is got. The sample algorithm and cleaning process is carried out same as above. And then the result texture is mapped on the 3D mesh surface. Fig. 9a show the current

Noh mask with color texture and Fig. 9b show the color restored one. All of the color is bright and look like a new one. Especially, the color of the skin and the red color of the lip is look well.

The key idea of the technique proposed in this paper is using the different color information on the surface which is similar to the weathering process of pigment. By this method, the original color of the Noh mask can be got. This technique need not segment the pigment field and can be applied on the 3D object easily. These are the main advantages of this technique.

In some cases, the pigment of Noh mask is lost. The technique presented in this paper can not represent the original color of Noh mask in this case. So it is need to analysis the original pigment types and represent it by developing a new technique.

6 Summary

In this paper, we describe the color representation of a Noh mask by use of a sample route which takes into account the 3D shape of the object. The effectiveness of this technique is demonstrated by the results obtained. The technique can also be used to represent color in other 3D objects.

To further develop this work, we intend to calculate the influence of weathering on the pigment colors in order to obtain a better result. We will also attempt to develop a new rendering technique which takes into account the pigment microstructure of the Noh mask.

Acknowledgments. This work was supported partly by "Kyoto Art Entertainment Innovation Research" of Centre of Excellence Program for the 21st Century by Ministry of Education, Culture, Sports, Science and Technology of Japan.

References

1. M. Barni, F. Bartolini, and V. Cappellini: Image Processing for Virtual Representation of Artworks. IEEE MultiMedia, Vol. 7, No. 2, pp.34-37, (2000)
2. CAD CENTER CORPORATION: http://www.cad-ceter.co.jp/casestudy/detail.php?ID= cg0067. (in Japanese)
3. DNP DIGITALCOM CO. LTD, and NHK. Representation the color of "Hell Scroll", http://www.dnp.co.jp /nenshi/nenrin/lab/syufuku.html (in Japanese).
4. F.Drago and N.Chiba: Locally Adaptive Chromatic Representation of Digitally Acquired Paintings. The International Journal of Image & Graphics, Vol.5, No.3, pp.617-637, (2005)
5. S. Ihara: Seigen Ihara and Noh mask. http://www5.ocn.ne.jp/~seigen/ (in Japanese)
6. E. H. Land and J. J. McCann: Lightness and the Retinex Theory. Journal of the Optical Society of America, Vol. 61, No. 1, (1971)
7. X. Li, D. Lu, and Y. Pan: Color Representation and Image Retrieval for Dunhuang Fresco Preservation. IEEE MultiMedia, Vol. 7, No. 2, pp.38-42. (2000)
8. S. Schar, H. Bieri, X. Jiang: Digital Representation of Medieval Tapestries. In the 6th International Symposium on Virtual Reality, Archaeology and Cultural Heritage, VAST 2005, pp.235-240, (2005)
9. N.Yoshida, T.Saito: Aesthetic curve segment. IPSJ SIG technical report, Vol.2005, 2005-CG-121, (2005) (in Japanese)

Modeling and Immersive Display of Cultural Heritage[*]

Lei Zhao, Duan-qing Xu[**], Yi Li, and Yi-min Yu

College of Computer Science, Zhejiang University, Hangzhou, China
xdq@zju.edu.cn

Abstract. In order to display virtual cultural heritage environment in CAVE based on multiple cheap PC, we implement a collaborative display platform called Multipro. The application developer doesn't need to know anything about stereo display principles and the platform architecture. We reconstruct the model of No285 cavern of Dunhuang and Hemudu virtual environments by a variety of software and techniques. The paper also addresses the issues of the modeling and display of immersive virtual heritage environments (VHEs).We in detail describe the methods we use to model the heritages and how we fill the holes in the raw heritage models and remove noise of the models. This work is being developed in the context of the National Grand Fundamental Research 973 Program of china.

Keywords: CAVE, Virtual Reality, Hybrid Rendering, Cultural Heritage, Rendering System.

1 Introduction

In conventional computer graphics, the computer-generated scene is viewed through a window, thus, users have an outside-looking-in experience. VR offers the means to leap through that window, allowing users to participate in the computer-generated scene with an inside-looking-out experience [1]. Many control tasks can be intuitively accomplished by walking or flying through the environment; and, manipulation of objects is done by hand and finger gestures. Users can also receive feedback from the virtual environment as audio, tactile or force cues. So the VR has been applied to various areas, this paper is to utilize the VR device to display the cultural heritages in order to protect them. With the development of computer software and hardware, the personal computer is very cheap according to graphic workstation. In these circumstances, constructing a hardware system consisting of cheap personal computer can reach a high performance. In order to display virtual heritage environment based on multiple cheap PC, we implement a display platform called *Multipro*, which provide a platform to display immersive application, which can be extended to be used in the areas of urban planning/architecture and cultural heritage education. *Multipro* is a PC cluster based system developed by C++ and Qt library, *Multipro* is responsible for communication among multiple machines. Benefiting from modular design, the application developer doesn't need to know anything about stereo display

---

[*] This work is supported by the National Grand Fundamental Research 973 Program of China (2002CB312106).

[**] Corresponding author.

principles and the platform architecture. Besides, different applications can be switched at run-time of the platform, without the inconvenient switch of application processes.

In this paper, we build a CAVE virtual environment using multiple personal computers. The model of these objects can be acquired by different methods such as photograph, scanner. The unearthed relic model can be from the 3d scanner, which generates a huge volume of point samples with complex details and texture. Rendering or manipulating this mass of data is a main challenge for the community. In order to render this point cloud, a common way is to reconstruct triangle meshes from the samples using mesh reduction [2]. Although the capabilities of computer graphics hardware have dramatically increased in the past decade, the handling of scene complexity is still one of the most fundamental problems in computer graphics. Although sophisticated hardware implementations are available, these algorithms are not capable of displaying highly complex scenes in real-time. So we introduce a new efficient screen space approach for highly complex models real-time rendering, this method can render large complex model acquired by scanner with high detail texture.

The creation of realistic 3D models has, typically, been a time-consuming labor-intensive manual process, requiring well-trained artists. Recent advances in computer graphics and vision allow the creation of realistic models based on photographs that are of very high quality. Many methods [3] have been developed to perfect and display such models. We take a lot of time to scan the frescoes and figures of Buddha of *Dunhuang*, also take photos of this frescoes and figures of Buddha. We reconstruct the model of No 285 cavern of *Dunhuang* and *Hemudu* virtual environments by a variety of software and techniques.

In this paper we focus our attention on two areas, realism and speed. For realism, we introduce a hybrid rendering method for realistic display of existing heritage model based on triangle-based, and a point-based (PBR) method to render a relic. By introducing view-dependent display techniques we achieve unprecedented realism for *VHEs*. The software could potentially be used for some of the applications we examine; each approach has different tradeoffs.

The following sections will in detail describe the methods we use to model the heritage and how we fill the holes in the raw heritage models and remove noise of the model. *Multipro* system is also discussed .The whole work is being developed in the context of the National Grand Fundamental Research 973 Program of china. The aim of the project is to protect the cultural heritage by realistically recreating archaeological site that can be displayed in a range of immersive VR systems using a high-quality, view-dependent algorithm, the observer can observe the heritage in near distance in virtual environment. Finally, *Dunhuang* No 285 cavern and *Hemudu* are as examples demonstrated in the virtual environment.

2   Reconstruction of a Realistic Virtual Heritage Environment

The model of cultural heritage is acquired by scanner, the texture of the model can be from photograph, and then the photograph as texture is mapped onto model. The raw data provided by a 3D scanner may contain several artefacts, including noise, difference in resolution between near and far surfaces, and distortions due to intensity bias. The following sections in detail describe data acquisition and how to remove noise and fill the holes in the raw models.

2.1 Data Acquisition

The selected cultural heritage is, *Duhuang*, located in *Gansu* province in northeast china. This cultural heritage site was chosen due to its cultural, educational, and symbolic significance, since ultimately our goal is to use this VE reconstruction as an educational and presentation tool in a museum. This site now exists, but in order to protect them, we need reconstruct them so that the people can observe the cultural heritage through virtual display environment, so we reconstruct it by scanning the real heritage. A single scan usually contains holes due to occlusion, and samples near and far objects at different resolutions. Thus, to get a more complete model, or to obtain a more uniform resolution, we need to scan the cavern from multiple locations. Automatically determining the best set of locations for scanning is a hard problem [4]. The simplest approach is to select the scanning locations annually, trying to minimize the number of scans necessary for a good coverage of the environment, and making sure that there is some overlap between the scans [5]. Other low-end systems [5] rely on a human operator, who uses an interactive tool to select matching features on each scan. From the matching features, a rigid transformation is computed that aligns the two scans [7]. Automatic feature detection, although desirable, is a hard problem, and is currently an active area of research [6]. Optical methods may be passive or active. Passive methods do not interact with the object being scanned, and include computer vision techniques such as shape-from-shading for single images, stereo triangulation for pairs of images, and optical flow and factorization methods for video streams. Passive methods require little special purpose hardware, they rarely construct accurate models, and their main application is object recognition, so we use active method to scan the heritage model.

2.2 Data Filtering

The raw data provided by a 3D scanner may contain several artefacts, including noise, difference in resolution between near and far surfaces, and distortions due to intensity bias. Many researchers have studied the artefacts related to triangulation scanners [8]. Here we focus on artefacts related to optical time-of-light scanners [5]. One artefact related to optical time-of-flight scanners is intensity bias: points with too low or too high intensity tend to have unreliable radius. One approach to minimize the intensity bias of the scanner is to scan a calibration pattern, and build a correction table. Correa et al. [5] use a calibration image that changes linearly from black to white, and is surrounded by a white background. The image is placed on a flat surface, and then scanned. From the scan, a bias correction table that is used for correcting subsequent scans is built. One approach to deal with noise is to average samples from overlapping scans. Another approach is to resample the points based on a local estimate of the underlying surface. We adopt the latter to filter the heritage models from scanner.

2.3 Filling Small Holes

In locally smooth surfaces, holes can be filled using surface interpolation methods. Wang and Oliveira [9] describe a procedure for automatic identification and filling of holes in point clouds. The method consists of first creating a triangle mesh using a surface construction algorithm. Holes are then automatically identified by analyzing the resulting mesh searching for cycles of non-shared edges. Note that since it is not possible to distinguish between an under-sampled region and a real hole in the surface, user interaction is required to guarantee proper reconstruction. Once a hole has been identified, the missing region can be interpolated from its neighborhood. Whereas several surface fitting techniques can be used to reconstruct missing regions, for most of them, the resulting surfaces do not pass through the original samples, which tend to introduce discontinuities. Avoiding discontinuities between the original and filled areas is important in order to guarantee the quality of the reconstructed models. The hole filling strategy proposed by Wang and Oliveira [9] consists of adding new samples to under-sampled regions by re-sampling an interpolated surface reconstructed using moving least squares [11], a variation of the original least squares method that guarantees the interpolation of the original samples. An important requirement during the introduction of new samples is to enforce that the sampling density inside the hole matches the sample density of the interpolation context. This is necessary to guarantee that the surface reconstruction algorithm used will not just leave even smaller holes. The next one is perpendicular to the plane. Once the plane has been computed, the samples belonging to the corresponding interpolation context are projected onto it. The problem of deciding the re-sampling positions inside the hole is then reduced to the 2D problem of finding a set of (x; y) positions inside the projection of the hole that preserves the sampling density of the projection of the interpolation context. These positions are computed, and the new samples are obtained by re-sampling the interpolated surface at these points. Once these samples have been added, a new triangle mesh is created for the object using the surface reconstruction algorithm described in [10].

In addition to reconstructing geometry, it is also necessary to reconstruct color and texture. The moving-least-squares procedure can also be used for the reconstruction of smoothly varying colors.

2.4 Texture Acquisition

The texture can reduce the amount of triangles of heritage model, and can increase the sense of realism. How a surface point reflects light depending on its normal, the incident light direction.

The emerging light direction, and the light's wavelength is known as the bi-directional reflectance distribution function (BRDF) of a surface. Measuring BRDFs accurately is a hard problem [12]. The simplest approach for acquiring the texture of an environment is to take pictures of it, and then map these photographs onto the previously acquired geometry. To map a photograph to the geometry, we need to know the camera projection parameters (intrinsic parameters), and the position and orientation of the camera when the photograph was taken (extrinsic parameters). Real cameras do not perform a perfect perspective projection as a pinhole camera does, and present many kinds of distortions, e.g., radial distortion. One solution to this problem is to model the action of the distortions, and to find an inverse mapping. A widely used model was proposed by Tsai [13]. Tsai's camera model has five intrinsic parameters, namely the focal length, the first-order coefficient of radial distortion, the coordinates of the image center, and a scale factor. One way to calibrate these intrinsic parameters is to take a photograph of a planar checkerboard pattern with known geometry, and then find the image location of the checkerboard corners with sub-pixel accuracy. Implementing these algorithms, which require full non-linear optimization, is fairly complex. Luckily, high quality implementations are available from Willson [14]. After calibrating the intrinsic camera parameters, the process of acquiring the images goes as follows. First, we take photographs of the heritage and cavern, keeping the same camera settings for all photographs to avoid having to recalibrate the intrinsic parameters. Then, for each photograph, we first remove its radial distortion, using a warp based on the coefficient found above, and then find the position (translation) and orientation (rotation) of the camera when we took the photograph relative to an arbitrary global coordinate system It is hard to automatically solve the image-geometry registration problem. By specifying pairs of corresponding points between the images and the geometry, it is possible to find the extrinsic camera parameters [14]. The approach taken by McAllister et al. [15] is to keep the center of projection (COP) of the camera coincident with the COP of the 3D scanner, while acquiring panoramic images. This simplifies the registration problem by only requiring the computation of a rotation. Furthermore, this enforces that no occlusion artifacts arise. Correa et al. [5] uses an interactive program to specify corresponding points, typically requiring only 7 to 10 correspondences to obtain a good calibration of the camera. One advantage of this approach is that it allows the user to take pictures from any position. Once all the parameters have been found, it is straightforward to map the colors from the photograph to the scan (or scans) that it covers. For each 3D point in a scan covered by the photograph, we find its 2D projection on the camera plane, and assign the corresponding pixel color to it (Figure 2). To support view-dependent effects (such as highlights), we can store multiple color samples per point, and at runtime find the color of a point by interpolating the closest color samples.

The texture can reduce the amount of triangles of heritage model, and can increase the sense of realism. How a surface point reflects light depending on its normal, the incident light direction, the emerging light direction, and the light's wavelength is known as the bi-directional reflectance distribution function (BRDF) of a surface. Measuring BRDFs accurately is a hard problem [12]. The simplest approach for acquiring the texture of an environment is to take pictures of it, and then map these photographs onto the previously acquired geometry. To map a photograph to the geometry, we need to know the camera projection parameters (intrinsic parameters), and the position and orientation of the camera when the photograph was taken (extrinsic parameters). First, we take photographs of the heritage and cavern, keeping the same camera settings for all photographs to avoid having to recalibrate the intrinsic parameters. Then, for each photograph, we first remove its radial distortion, using a warp based on the coefficient found above, and then find the position (translation) and orientation (rotation) of the camera when we took the photograph relative to an arbitrary global coordinate system It is hard to automatically solve the image-geometry registration problem. By specifying pairs of corresponding points between the images and the geometry, it is possible to find the extrinsic camera parameters [14]. The approach taken by McAllister et al. [15] is to keep the center of projection (COP) of the camera coincident with the COP of the 3D scanner, while acquiring panoramic images.

3 System Overview

The software engineering aspects of this work are excellent. The whole system is based on dynamic link library. The display platform provides an interface definition which can be derived by developers of the application to implement their own code, the code of special application is compiled into a file of DLL. The display platform will let user to load a given DLL to run, and DLL as a call-back module is invoked by the display platform. This platform is based on Microsoft OpenGL library. *Multipro* can be run on multiple PC, so this system can make full use of the power of cheap pc since now the price of single pc has decreased so much. Every PC generates two view images, one for each eye, switched by electronic glasses. Existing stereo development libraries, e.g. *CAVELib, Avocano*, require fully or partially understanding, at least caring of stereo display principles. Furthermore, most of existing libraries are used to develop a full application with all stereo display functions, e.g. multi-tasking, shared memory, stereo displaying, and so on. *Multipro* is a PC cluster based system developed by C++ and Qt library. *Multipro* is composed of following modules of controller, renderer, *Multipro* Library, communication layer and application module. Benefiting from modular design, the application developer doesn't need to know anything about stereo display principles and the platform architecture. Besides, different applications can be switched at run-time of the platform, without the inconvenient switch of application processes. But *Multipro* is not responsible for rendering the scenes, just responsible for network communication and collaboration of multiple PC, so we have to do extra things in order to display immersive interactive scenes. *Multipro* is not responsible for rendering, so the developer need to customize a specified rendering code to render scenes according to different application. Figure 1 is the framework of a collaborative system platform *Multipro*.

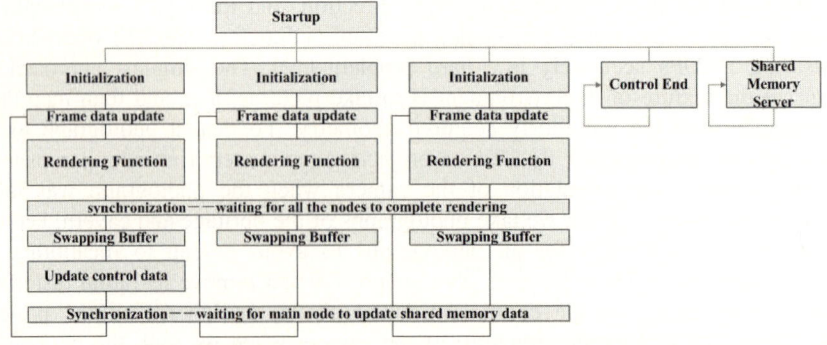

Fig. 1. The framework of a collaborative system platform (*Multipro*)

4 Rendering

As VR technology becomes commonplace, there has been a proliferation of VR in fields such as design, education, and entertainment or, in other words, areas where VR applications are more easily available to and accessible by the general public. In the field of education, *VE*s have been developed to help teach concepts that are hard to learn or difficult to visualize otherwise. In design, VR has been used where conventional media are ill-suited to represent the work processes in ways that make them easy to visualize. In both cases, VR, with its immersive and interactive properties, can offer possibilities and solutions that are otherwise very difficult to obtain. For these reasons, we have chosen two application domains that relate to learning and working in VR, an archaeological reconstruction and automobile appearance display project, in this paper we will focus on the archaeological site reconstruction. In the first case, the Society of *Dunhuang* Studies has been involved for years in display frescos and the cavern on which the frescos are drawn, reconstructing the archaeological site in order to make it more accessible to visitors (Fig. 2). We use cubic display environments called CAVE to display the frescos of *Dunhuang*. These frescos are scanned form real wall of *Dunhuang*, which consists of huge points data and high detail texture. For the second application, we display an outdoor complex scene which consists of lot of objects, and these objects can be from scanner or photograph or triangle model.

For scanned model we adopt PBR-based rendering method, in order to speed up the rendering we introduce a new efficient screen-space rendering algorithm to render point-based objects. Our algorithm refers to the randomized z-buffer algorithm. The main idea of the algorithm is utilize hierarchical data structure to represent the models. (Every model is presented by uniform spatial data structure which is multi-resolution hierarchy based on bounding spheres, see [13]). Before the scenes are rendered, the visibility test is conducted using the bounding sphere of every object in the scenes. Our algorithm only renders all visible object nodes, we adopt conservative visibility test, so the rendering quality of the scenes is not damaged .we will adopt different rendering policy for different object nodes. Our algorithm conducts hierarchical visibility culling and multi-resolution rendering for every object nodes. We render object nodes from scanner data represented by triangle primitive using the method similar to QSpat. The object nodes represented by triangle primitive are reconstructed in pre-process phase using Octree, we utilize back-face culling, occlusion culling, frustum culling to reduce the number of triangles according to the position of viewpoint dynamically. Finally we utilize screen space approach to generate a set of point-sample, and construct an image of this object from a dynamically chosen set of surface sample points.

All the set of sample points of object nodes represent the complex model, hence not every single triangle must be handled separately during rendering. First, given number of point-samples are chosen so that they cover the projections of visible objects in the image plane. This can be done in highly output-sensitive time. Here, the sample point selection is the key to avoid expensive geometric queries. Thus, for choosing sample points, a probability density proportional to the projected area of the surfaces of the objects has to be used. However, a sample selection using this viewpoint-dependent probability density does not seem to be possible in sub-linear time. Therefore, we use a multi-resolution hierarchy based on bounding spheres. In a preprocessing step, we construct hierarchical data structure based on bounding spheres. For each viewpoint, a suitable set of visible object is chosen dynamically from the hierarchy. The projected area of object bounding box to be used to determine the number of sample points to be chosen from each object: The set of point sample of the whole scenes consists of all visible objects set of point sample. In most cases, it is sufficient to consider only the distance between an object and the viewer in order to estimate the projection area. The sample points are then chosen within a specific object according to the number of point sample our sample algorithm traverses the hierarchical data structure, records the number of inner node plus leaf node in every layer, if the number is more than the object's expected set of point sample, this layer's nodes including inner node is the set of point sample we want. Using pre-computed search structures, we can show that this multi-resolution data structure does not harm the image quality. In a second step, the algorithm conduct occlusion test with z-buffer between the chosen sample points and renders the resulting image using the visible points.

5   Interaction and Animation

Interaction is the key element of the virtual environment. If there is no interaction with virtual environment, the environment will lack no sense of realism. So we introduce interaction into the *Hemudu* scene, the observer can interact with the virtual environments through a data gloves, the user can take a harpoon to fish. We use FOB(The Flock of Birds) to track the position of eyes and hand. FOB is a six degrees-of-freedom measuring device that can be configured to simultaneously track the position and orientation of multiple sensors by a transmitter. Each sensor is capable of making from 20 to 144 measurements per second of its position and orientation when the sensor is located within ± 4 feet of its transmitter. We use Cybe-Grasp to track the action of the finger, and the user can get force feedback form the objects of scenes by wearing the Cybe-Force device. By introducing viewpoint dependent texture mapping technique the user also observe the relic in near distance.

We use Motion Capture to capture the animation. Motion Capture is the process of capturing the movement of a real object and mapping it onto a computer generated object. Motion Capture creates synthetic actors by capturing the motions of real humans. In this case, special markers are placed over the joints of actors. Then, a special hardware samples the position and/or orientation of those markers in time, generating a set of motion data, also known as motion curves. Our prototype system renders the key-frame animation generated by Motion Capture.

6   Results

For the *Dunhuang* 285 cavern, the overall photography, calibration, modelling and texturing required about 8 person-months. The total number of triangles is about 3M. Figure.2. A) the fresco and figure of Buddha of *Dunhuang* displayed on the single PC, C) The female ancient about 7000years ago is pounding rice with a pestle (animation) in *Hemudu* virtual scenes in CAVE virtual environments, D) virtual display of the No 285 cavern of *Dunhuang* in CAVE virtual environments.

7   Conclusions and Futureworks

We reconstruct the model of No285 cavern of Dunhuang by a variety of software and techniques, we implement a collaborative display platform called Multipro, which provide a platform to display immersive application which can be extended to be used in the areas of urban planning/architecture and cultural heritage education. Multipro is a PC cluster based system developed by C++ and Qt library.

As mentioned above, Multipro is not responsible for rendering the scenes, just responsible for network communication and collaboration of multiple PC, so we have to do other things in order to render special application data, we plan to implement the rendering engine which provide the developer a interface. Rendering engine should has the following features:

It is Simple, easy to use, and Supports vertex and fragment programs (shaders), provides automatic support for many commonly bound constant parameters like worldview matrices, light state information, object space eye position etc; It Supports the complete range of fixed function operations such as multi-texture and multi-pass blending, texture coordinate generation and modification, independent color and alpha operations for non-programmable hardware or for lower cost materials.

Fig. 2. A) The acquisition of photographs, B) Calibration of the photograph, C) The female ancient about 7000years ago is pounding rice with a pestle (animation) in *Hemudu* virtual scenes in CAVE virtual environments, D) virtual display of the No 285 cavern of *Dunhuang* in CAVE virtual environments, E) The model of Buddha

References

[1] Bishop, G., Fuchs, H., et al. Research Directions in Virtual Environments. *Computer Graphics*, Vol. 26, 3,Aug. 1992, pp. 153--177.

[2] Chamberlain, B., DeRose, T., Lischinski, D., Salesin, D., Snyder, J.: Fast Rendering of Complex environments Using a Spatial Hierarchy.In: *Proc. Graphics Interface '96*, 132-141, 1996.

[3] Gorther, S. J., Grzeszczuk, R., Szeliski, R., Cohen,M. F.: The Lumigraph.In: *SIGGRAPH 96 Proceedings,*

[4] S. Fleishman, D. Cohen-Or, and D.Lischinski. Automatic camera placement for image-based modeling. *Computer Graphics Forum*, 19(2):100–110, 2000

[5] W. T. Corr^ea, S. Fleishman, and C. T. Silva. Towards point-based acquisition and rendering of large real-world environments. In *Proceedings of the 15th Brazilian Symposium on Computer Graphics and Image Processing*, 2002. To appear.

[6] G. M. Cortelazzo, C. Doretto, and L. Lucchese. Free-form textured surfaces registration by a frequency domain technique. In *Proceedings of the International Conference on Image Processing*, pages 813–817, 1998.

[7] B. K. P. Horn. Closed form solution of absolute orientation using unit quaternion. *Journal of the Optical Society A*, 4(4):629–642, Apr. 1987.

[8] P. H´ebert, D. Laurendeau, and D. Poussart. Scene reconstruction and description: Geometric primitive extraction from multiple view scattered data. In *Proceedings of IEEE Computer Vision and Pattern Recognition*, pages 286–292, 1993.

[9] J. Wang and M. M. Oliveira. A hole filling strategy for surface reconstruction from range images. Technical Report TR02.07.18, SUNY at Stony Brook, 2002.

[10] M. Gopi and S. Krishnan. A fast and efficient projection-based approach for surface reconstruction. High Performance Computer Graphics, Multimedia and Visualization,1(1):1–12, 2000.

[11] P. Lancaster and K. Salkauskas. Curve and Surface Fitting. Academic Press, London, 1986.

[12] H. Lensch, M. Goesele, J. Kautz,W. Heidrich, and H. Seidel. Image-based reconstruction of spatially varying materials. In Rendering Techniques 2001, pages 103–114,2001

[13] Szymon Rusinkiewicz and Marc Levoy. Qsplat: A multiresolution point rendering system for large meshes. In Proceedings SIGGRAPH 2000, pages 343–352. ACM SIGGRAPH, 2000.

Personalized Content Presentation for Virtual Gallery[*]

Wonil Kim[1], Hanku Lee[2,**], Kyoungro Yoon[3], Hyungseok Kim[2], and Changduk Jung[4]

[1] College of Electronics and Information at Sejong University, Seoul, Korea
wikim@sejong.ac.kr
[2] School of Internet Multimedia Engineering at Konkuk University, Seoul, Korea
hlee@konkuk.ac.kr, hyuskim@konkuk.ac.kr
[3] School of Computer Engineering at Konkuk University, Seoul, Korea
yoonk@konkuk.ac.kr
[4] School of Information and Communication at Korea University, Korea
jcd1234@korea.ac.kr

Abstract. Utilizing Virtual Reality technologies for virtual museum brings new ways of interactive presentation of the contents. In addition to interactivity, personalization is an important emerging issue in digital content management especially with virtual reality. For the virtual museum or gallery, selection and presentation of personalized content will improve user experience in navigating through huge collections like Musée du Louvre or British Museum. In this paper, we present a personalization method of massive multimedia content in virtual galleries. The proposed method is targeted for the pictures that could be characterized by its large amount of source in galleries. The method is based on classified image features which are extracted using standard MPEG-7 visual descriptors. Using Neural Networks, the best matching pictures are selected and presented in the virtual gallery by choosing similar styles from the extracted preference features. The simulation results show that the proposed system successfully classifies images into correct classes with the rate of over 75% depending on the employed features. We employ the result into a virtual gallery application which gives opportunities of automatically personalized gallery browsing.

1 Introduction

As the era of information flood begins, everyday we encounter much more digital data than the traditional textual data on the Internet and TV. The attention and focus of information shift from textual forms to digital multimedia forms. Digital multimedia brings a new perspective on information presentation accompanied by technological advances including virtual reality. Interactivity has been a quite popular issues in multimedia content management. It has enabled a range of new multimedia applications such as interactive TV, virtual museum and virtual heritage [18]. With this digital form of the media, conventional museum, gallery or cultural sites could be extended from current forms enriched by additional objects which could not be presentable in physical

---

[*] This paper is supported by Seoul R&BD program.
[**] Author for correspondence: +82-2-2049-6082.

location due to limitation on space and security issues. With these new services the quantity of digital media being presented to user is drastically gained. In this paper, we deal with a method to manage massive amount of multimedia contents for easy access by the user. Among many media types, we focus on the picture which typically shows the problem of efficient presentation in virtual gallery due to its massiveness in quantity.

In addition to interactivity, personalization is an important emerging issue in digital content management. For the virtual gallery, selection and presentation of personalized content will improve user experience in navigating through huge collections like Musée du Louvre or British Museum. The virtual gallery presents personalized contents among millions of pictures according to user preference. A preference of user can be given to the virtual gallery in a form of visiting history and evaluation on different types of pictures. In this paper, we present a personalization method of massive multimedia content in virtual galleries. We adopt MPEG framework as current MPEG standard incorporates issues of personalization within MPEG-7 and MPEG-21 [19].

Personal preference is a complex and difficult aspect to be measured. In this paper, we propose a method to measure preference by its styles. Digital contents are automatically classified by their styles. By specifying preferred styles, users can choose and watch their favorites from the sea of digital contents.

The main purpose of this paper is to apply MPEG-7 standard to digital multimedia images by utilizing MPEG-7 descriptors. By analyzing MPEG-7 descriptors, we create a prototype system that can be used to categorize digital picture styles under visual environments, and introduce effective methodology of image classification via experiments. For example, it will tell that a given image belongs to scenery pictures, peoples, animals, and vehicles image with confidence rate from 0.0 to 1.0. The system uses MPEG-7 visual descriptors for image features and the classification module employs neural network. The usage of this system is enormous. It can be properly fit into the image classification engine for search system.

We discuss related works for the image genre classification in section 2. In section 3, we propose our Neural Network based image genre classification system. The simulation results are presented in section 4. We conclude in section 5.

2 Related Works

2.1 MPEG-7 Descriptors and Image Classification Systems

MPEG-7 is a recent emerging standard used in image classification systems. It is not a standard dealing with the actual encoding and decoding of video and audio, but it is a standard for describing media content. It uses a XML to store metadata and solves the problem of lacking standard to describe visual image content. The aim, scope, and details of MPEG-7 standard are nicely overviewed by Sikora of Technical University Berlin in his paper [1].

There are a series of researches that use various MPEG-7 descriptors. Ro et al. [2] shows a study of texture based image description and retrieval method using an adapted version of homogeneous texture descriptor of MPEG-7. Other studies of image classification use descriptors like a contour-based shape descriptor [3], a histogram descriptor [4], and a combination of color structure and homogeneous descriptors [5]. As a part of the EU aceMedia project research, Spyrou et al. propose three image classification techniques based on fusing various low-level MPEG-7 visual descriptors [6]. Since the direct inclusion of descriptors would be inappropriate and incompatible, fusion is required to bridge the semantic gap between the target semantic classes and the low-level visual descriptors.

There is a CBIRS that combines neural network and MPEG-7 standard: researchers of Helsinki University of Technology developed a neural, self-organizing system to retrieve images based on their content, the PicSOM (the Picture + self-organizing map, SOM) [7]. The technique is based on pictorial examples and relevance feedback (RF). The PicSOM system is implemented by using tree structured SOM. The MPEG-7 content descriptor is provided for the system. In the paper, they compare the Pic-SOM indexing technique with a reference system based on vector quantization (VQ). Their results show the MPEG-7 content descriptor can be used in the PicSOM system despite the fact that Euclidean distance calculation is not optimal for all of them.

Kim et al. [8, 9] proposed a neural network based classification module using MPEG-7. In this model, inputs for the neural network are fed from the feature values of MPEG-7 descriptors that are extracted from images. Since the various descriptors can represent the specific features of a given image, the proper evaluation process should be required to choose the best one for the given image classification. In their adult image classification, it is found that color related descriptors, such as Color Layout and Color Structure are very effective in performance. In fact, classifying adult image is closely related with skin color detection.

2.2 Image Classification

Image classification is a core process of digital image analysis. It is used in many areas, such as remote sensing and image retrieval. Remote sensing is an acquisition of meaningful information from an object by a recording device, which is not in physical or intimate contact with the object. For example, image classification is applied to a data interpretation process of remotely acquired digital image by a Geographic Information System (GIS). Image retrieval is another research area using image classification. A user requests an image by query. It returns an image (or a set of ordered images) from its image database by matching features of a query image, such as color histogram and textual measures, with those of database images. Image classification is also used to create image databases and adding images into for the image retrieval system. The system extracts semantic descriptions from images and putting them into semantically meaningful categories.

The automatic classification of WWW images as photographs or graphics including cartoons is a well-known contents image classification. Examples are the Web-Seek search engine [10] and the systems described in [11]. Unfortunately, their features take advantage of some characteristics of web images that do not exist in cartoon images, notably the aspect ratio and the word occurrence in the image URLs. In the same fashion of [10, 11], [12] emphasizes the basic characteristics of cartoons and implemented nine color descriptors in order to distinguish photos and graphics on a database of 1200 samples.

The photo/graphics classifier of [12] had been previously implemented as part of the Acoi system [13]. A decision rule classifier [14] has been trained on the features given in [12] on varying quantities of training data. The implementation has a classification score of 0:9 on a data set of 14,040 photos and 9,512 graphics harvested from the WWW.

One of the classic classification problems in content-based image retrieval systems is city images vs. landscapes. [15] separates urban images and rural images using a multiscale steerable pyramid to find a dominant orientation in four by four subblocks of image. They classify the image as a city scene if enough subblocks have vertical orientation tendency.

A texture orientation used in [15] is one of popular low-level features of images, which is used for pattern retrieval. [16] proposes to use the Gabor wavelet features for texture analysis. In their paper, they provide a comprehensive experimental evaluation and they indicate an analysis using Gabor wavelet features are more accurate in pattern retrieval than analyses using three other multiscale texture features: pyramid-structured wavelet transform (PWT), tree-structured wavelet transform (TWT), and multiresolution simultaneous autoregressive model (MR-SAR) features by comparing them.

Another popular feature used to retrieve images from digital image libraries or multimedia databases is a color histogram. It is the efficient and insensitive method, but it has coarse characteristics as well. So images of totally different appearance can have similar histograms. [17] proposes a *Histogram refinement* technique to compare images using additional constraints. The technique includes of splitting the pixels in a given bucket into several classes, based upon local property. Pixels in the same class can be compared with others in the same bucket.

3   The Proposed Image Genre Classification System

3.1   The Proposed Architecture

The sample photos of animal, car, people portrait, and scenery are illustrated in Figure 1. The proposed system classifies these images as one of four categories. The categories are predefined like (a) animal photos, (b) car photos, (c) people portrait photos and (d) scenery photos.

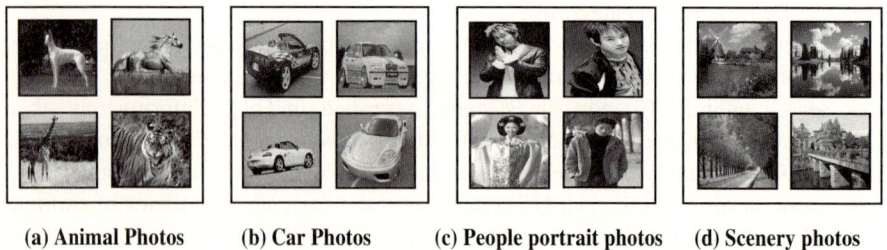

(a) Animal Photos   (b) Car Photos   (c) People portrait photos   (d) Scenery photos

Fig. 1. Example images from the four categories used for simulation

Figure 2 represents the overall architecture of the proposed image gallery classification system. The proposed architecture consists of two modules; feature extraction module and classification module. Features defined in the MPEG-7 descriptors for the given query images are extracted, and then used as inputs for the following classifier module.

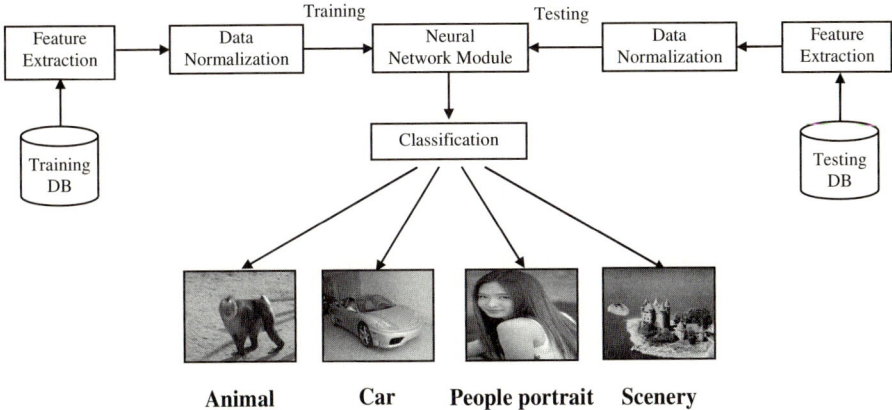

Fig. 2. The overview of the proposed Image Gallery Classification System

3.2 Feature Extraction Module

By running the MPEG-7 XM program, features of training images are extracted in XML format. This feature information in XML format is parsed in the next step and is normalized into values between 0 and 1 with respect to values generated by each descriptor. These normalized values are used as inputs for the neural network classifier. An illustration of extracting input values for Edge Histogram is shown below. The original values,

```
0 1 1 0 0 6 2 2 4 2 5 2 6 4 4 1 1 0 4 0 4 0 4 0 1 4 1 6 7 4 5 0 6 4
4 5 0 1 5 3 2 3 4 6 3 2 4 6 6 5 4 2 5 6 3 5 4 4 4 2 3 3 3 5 4 2 4 2
5 4 2 4 5 4 4 2 4 6 5 2
```

are converted into normal values,

```
0.0 0.1 0.1 0.0 0.0 0.6 0.2 0.2 0.4 0.2 0.5 0.2 0.6 0.4 0.4 0.1 0.1 0.0 0.4 0.0 0.4 0.0
0.4 0.0 0.1 0.4 0.1 0.6 0.7 0.4 0.5 0.0 0.6 0.4 0.4 0.5 0.0 0.1 0.5 0.3 0.2 0.3 0.4 0.6
0.3 0.2 0.4 0.6 0.6 0.5 0.4 0.2 0.5 0.6 0.3 0.5 0.4 0.4 0.4 0.2 0.3 0.3 0.3 0.5 0.4 0.2
0.4 0.2 0.5 0.4 0.2 0.4 0.5 0.4 0.4 0.2 0.4 0.6 0.5 0.2
```

and followed by the class information. The class information, which is attached to the feature value, is the orthogonal vector value. For example, an Animal image is represented as (1 0 0 0), whereas a Car image would be as (0 1 0 0).

3.3 Classification Module

Using the data set of the normalized input features and classes of sports, we can model an NNC in the classification module. According to different MPEG-7 descriptors, the number of the input features can be various. Let us denote the input feature vector obtained from the first MPEG-7 descriptor as $X_{D_1} = (x_{D_{1,1}}, x_{D_{1,2}}, \cdots, x_{D_{1,i}}, \cdots, x_{D_{1,n_1}})$, here $x_{D_{1,i}}$ is the ith input feature extracted from MPGE-7 descriptor 1 and the subscript n_1 is the dimension of the input features from the first MPEG-7 descriptor. With the same way, the input feature vector obtained from the last MPEG-7 descriptor k can be expressed as $X_{D_k} = (x_{D_{k,1}}, x_{D_{k,2}}, \cdots, x_{D_{k,i}}, \cdots, x_{D_{k,n_k}})$. Also, the output vector can be expressed as $Y = (y_1, y_2, \cdots, y_i, \cdots, y_s)$, here y_i is the output from the ith output node and the subscript s is the number of classes. By utilizing the *hard limit* function in the output layer, we can have binary value, 0 or 1, for each output node y_i as Equation (1).

$$y_i = f_o(netinput_o) = \begin{pmatrix} 1, & netinput_o \geq 0 \\ 0, & otherwise \end{pmatrix} \tag{1}$$

where f_o is the hard limit function at the output node and $netinput_o$ is the net input of f_o. As shown in Equation (2), the net input is can be expressed as the product of the output vector in the hidden layer, denoted as Y_h, and the weight vector W_o at the output layer.

$$netinput_o = W_o^{\ T} Y_h \tag{2}$$

With the same way, the hidden layer output vector, Y_h, can also be computed by functioning the product of the input weight vector and the input vector. Thus, the accuracy of the NNC depends on the values of whole weight vectors. To obtain the optimal weight vectors, the NNC is trained using the back-propagation algorithm which is commonly utilized for training neural networks. The training is done after coding each class of sports into s dimension orthogonal vector. For example, since we have four classes, the classes are coded to (1 0 0 0), (0 1 0 0), (0 0 1 0) and (0 0 0 1). Once obtaining an optimal weight vector, we evaluate the performance of NNC using the test data which is unseen during training phase.

4 Simulation

4.1 Environments

The simulation uses a total of 800 images for training (200 for each photo class images), and 400 for testing (100 for each photo class images). It employs five descriptors for image description features, Color Layout, Color Structure, Region Shape, Homogeneous Texture, and Edge Histogram. The inputs consist of MPEG-7 normalized descriptor values. Several classification modules were evaluated; five modules for each descriptor and the others for performance evaluation of selected two descriptors; Edge Histogram and Color Structure. The number of hidden layers and nodes used in the modules as well as the number of iterations are illustrated in each result Table descriptions. The output layer consists of 4 nodes, one for each photo image class.

4.2 Result

The simulation results of five descriptors for the photo image are shown in Table 1. The overall successful classification rate of the five descriptors is 61.25%, which is a disappointed result. On the other hand, the proposed photo image classification system performs better result in Color Structure and Edge Histogram descriptors; 65.00% and 77.50% respectively.

Moreover, in Table 2 and Table 3, we simulated the selected two descriptors in detail. Both the Color Structure and Edge Histogram descriptors did not improve much with the various combinations of tests.

Table 1. Test Results of Five descriptors after 100,000 iterations with 2 hidden layers with 30 nodes each (%)

		Animal	Car	People	Scene
Animal	CL	**42.50**	26.25	13.75	17.50
	EH	**70.00**	3.75	0.00	26.25
	HT	**55.00**	7.50	15.00	22.50
	RS	**45.00**	20.00	15.00	20.00
	CS	**60.00**	13.75	16.25	10.00
	average	**54.50**	14.25	12.00	19.25
Car	CL	22.25	**60.00**	12.50	5.00
	EH	1,25	**85.00**	0.00	13.75
	HT	16,25	**40.00**	13.75	30.00
	RS	21.25	**43.75**	16.25	18.75
	CS	12.50	**68.75**	7.50	11.25
	average	14.70	**59.50**	10.00	15.75
People	CL	5.00	21.25	**73.75**	0.00
	EH	6.25	0.00	**93.75**	0.00
	HT	8.75	7.50	**71.25**	12.50
	RS	16.25	12.50	**55.00**	16.25
	CS	17.50	10.00	**68.75**	3.75
	average	10.75	10.25	**72.50**	6.50
Scene	CL	8.75	18.75	7.50	**65.00**
	EH	27.50	8.75	2.50	**61.25**
	HT	13.75	10.00	1.25	**75.00**
	RS	26.25	22.50	20.00	**31.25**
	CS	13.75	17.50	6.25	**62.50**
	average	18.00	15.50	7.50	**59.00**

Table 2. Test Results of Edge Histogram descriptor after 500,000 iterations with 2 hidden layers with 50 nodes and 100 nodes (%)

	nodes	Animal	Car	People	Scene
Animal	50	**67.50**	3.75	0.00	28.75
	100	**67.50**	3.75	0.00	28.75
Car	50	6.25	**83.75**	0.00	10.00
	100	6.25	**82.50**	0.00	11.25
People	50	6.25	0.00	**93.75**	0.00
	100	5.00	0.00	**95.00**	0.00
Scene	50	25.00	11.25	1.25	**62.50**
	100	25.00	10.00	1.25	**63.75**

Table 3. Test Results of Color Structure descriptor after 500,000 iterations with 2 hidden layers with 50 nodes and 100 nodes (%)

	nodes	Animal	Car	People	Scene
Animal	50	**62.50**	13.75	11.25	12.50
	100	**61.25**	13.75	16.25	8.75
Car	50	10.00	**68.75**	8,75	12.50
	100	10.00	**65.00**	7.50	17.50
People	50	17.50	12.50	**67.50**	2.50
	100	12.50	10.00	**68.75**	8.75
Scene	50	12.50	16.25	5.00	**66.25**
	100	12.50	15.00	1.25	**71.25**

Overall, the proposed photo image classification system performs better result in Color Structure and Edge histogram than other three descriptors. The results seem very promising and can be applied to various image processing domains. It can be easily extended to medical image processing, in which identifying a particular image belongs to a certain symptom is very critical. Also it can be implemented as the main part of image search engine or image collection engine. For a large image data base, it is very useful tool for image retrieval system.

5 Conclusion

In this paper, we proposed a method to classify pictures for personalized virtual gallery navigation. The proposed system categorizes images into different styles, such as animals, vehicles, peoples and scenery images. The classification module of the system learns corresponding classification task according to feature values, which is extracted from MPEG-7 descriptors. The simulation results show that the proposed system successfully classifies images into correct classes with the rate of over 80% depending in the employed features.

Utilizing the proposed method, users of virtual gallery can store their preferences by recording the visiting history with their personal devices. Recorded history can be evaluated by its duration and, if given, user's explicit preferences on each pictures. Using this evaluated measure, for the next visit the virtual gallery proposes newly added or not yet visited items to user for their new experience.

This approach can be applied not only for the virtual gallery, but into generic picture management by tagging each picture automatically. The MPEG-7 descriptors can be enriched by this classification along with pre-existing features. By extending proposed preference measurement method, multimedia content querying can be enhanced in more user friendly, context describing ways.

References

1. Sikora, T.: The MPEG-7 visual standard for content description – an overview. IEEE Transactions on Circuit and Systems for Video Technology, Vol. 11, No. 6 (2001) 696-702
2. Ro, Y., Kim, M., Kang, H., Manjunath, B., Kim, J.: MPEG-7 homogeneous texture descriptor. ETRI Journal, Vol. 23, No. 2 (2001) 41-51
3. Bober, M.: The MPEG-7 visual shape descriptors. IEEE Transactions on Circuit and Systems for Video Technology, Vol. 11, No. 6 (2001) 716-719
4. Won, C., Park, D., Park, S.: Efficient use of MPEG-7 edge histogram descriptor. ETRI Journal, Vol. 24, No. 1 (2002) 23-30
5. Pakkanen, J., Ilvesmaki, A., Iivarinen, J.: Defect image classification and retrieval with MPEG-7 descriptors. Lecture Notes in Computer Science, Vol. 2749. Springer-Verlag, Berlin Heidelberg, New York (2003) 349-355
6. Spyrou, E., Borgne, H., Mailis, T., Cooke, E., Arvrithis, Y., O'Connor H.: Fusing MPEG-7 visual descriptors for image classification. Lecture Notes in Computer Science, Vol. 3697. Springer-Verlag, Berlin Heidelberg, New York (2005) 847-852
7. Laaksonen, J., Koskela, M., Oja, E.: PicSOM – Self-organizing image retrieval with MPEG-7 content descriptor. IEEE Transactions on Neural Networks: Special Issue on Intelligent Multimedia Processing, Vol. 13, No. 4 (2002) 841-853
8. Kim, K., Lee, H., Yoo, S., Baik, S.: Neural Network Based Adult Image Classification. Lecture Notes in Computer Science, Vol. 3696, pp 481-486, Springer-Verlag, Berlin Heidelberg, New York in 2005
9. Kim, W., Lee, H., Park, J., Yoon, K.: Multi Class Adult Image Classification using Neural Networks. Lecture Notes in Computer Science, Vol. 3501, pp 222-226, Springer-Verlag, Berlin Heidelberg, New York in 2005
10. Smith, R., Chang, S-F.: Searching for images and videos on the world wide web, Tech. Rep. 459-96-25, Center for Communications Research, Columbia University, 1996.
11. Rowe, C., Frew, B.: Automatic caption localization for photographs on word wide web pages, Tech. Rep., Department of Computer Science, Naval Postgraduate School, 1997.
12. Athitsos, V., Swain, J., Frankel, C.: Distinguishing photographs and graphics on the world wide web, in IEEE Workshop on Content-Based Access of Image and Video Libraries, Puerto Rico, June 1997.
13. Windhouwer, A., Schmidt, R., Kersten, L.: Acoi: A System for Indexing Multimedia Objects, in International Workshop on Information Integration and Web-based Applications & Services, Yogyakarta, Indonesia, November 1999.
14. Quinlan, R: Programs for Machine Learning, Morgan Kaufmann, 1993.

15. Wang, J., Li, J., Wiederhold, G.: SIMPLIcity: Semantics-sensitive Integrated Matching for Picture LIbraries, *IEEE Transactions on Pattern Analysis and Machine Intelligence*, vol 23, pp. 947-963, 2001

16. Manjunath, S., Ma, Y.: Texture features for browsing and retrieval of image data, *IEEE Transactions on Pattern Analysis and Machine Intelligence,*" vol. 18, no. 8, August 1996.

17. Pass, G., Zabih, R.: Histogram refinement for content-based image retrieval, In *Proceedings of the 3rd IEEE Workshop on Applications of Computer Vision,* Sarasota, Florida, USA, December 1996.

18. Papagiannakis, G., Schertenleib, S., O'Kennedy, B., Arevalo-Poizat, M., Magnenat-Thalmann, N., Stoddart, A., Thalmann, D.: Mixing Virtual and Real scenes in the site of ancient Pompeii, *Computer Animation and Virtual Worlds, p 11-24, Volume 16, Issue 1.* February 2005.

19. Kim, H., Joslin, C., Di Giacomo, T., Garchery, S., Magnenat-Thalmann, N.,: Device-based Decision-making for Adaptation of Three-Dimensional Content. *The Visual Computer.* 22(5) May 2006.

Accessible Information from Radiated Sound of Extracorporeal Shock Wave Lithotriptor for Improving Fragmentation Efficiency

Yun Seok Jang[1] and Jin Ho Choi[2]

[1] Dept. of Electrical Engineering, Pukyong National University, San 100, Yongdang-Dong, Nam-Gu, Busan, 608-739, Korea
jangys@pknu.ac.kr
[2] Dept. of Computer Engineering, Pusan University of Foreign Studies, 55-1, Uam-Dong, Nam-Gu, Busan, 608-738, Korea

Abstract. This paper investigates the information related to the radiated sounds during treatment using the extracorporeal shock wave lithotriptor(ESWL). First, we observe the vibration of the objects from the radiated sounds and extract the information about the change of the peak frequency from the relation between the vibration and the radiated sounds. Next, we observe the change of the peak frequency according to the position of the focus and demonstrate that it is more difficult to vibrate objects exactly at the focal point than above or below the focus of the ESWL device. Lastly, we analyze the relation between the cavitation and the radiated sounds and examine the benefiting condition for the object fragmentation.

Keywords: ESWL, radiated sound, bending vibration, peak frequency, cavitation bubble.

1 Introduction

The effectiveness of piezoelectric extracorporeal shock wave lithotriptor(ESWL) for the therapy of calculus has been well known in the field of urology. The piezoelectric ESWL is machinery that can generate underwater shock wave using piezoelectric elements [1-3]. The piezoelectric ESWL has an effective feature to treat calculus. The calculus after treatment is well-eliminated out of body, because it can break the calculus into fragments.

In this paper, we measure and analyze the radiated sounds induced by the piezoelectric ESWL. We observe the vibration of objects, the change of peak frequency in the power spectra of the radiated sounds and the cavitation related to the use of the ESWL. From the results of the observations, it is found that the benefiting information for the therapy of calculus can be extract from the radiated sounds during the breaking process.

2 Information Related to Vibration of Object

To begin with, the sounds radiated from objects induced by the piezoelectric ESWL are measured and analyzed in order to observe the proper vibration by underwater

Z. Pan et al. (Eds.): ICAT 2006, LNCS 4282, pp. 1055 – 1061, 2006.

shock wave. A bronze bar is employed as a phantom in this experiment. The length and radius of cross section of the metal bar are $6.2\,cm$ and $0.5\,cm$, respectively. Figure 1 shows the waveform and its power spectrum of the radiated sound measured by a microphone when the bronze bar is struck by the shock wave of the ESWL. The range to observe the power spectrum is restricted to the audio frequency range of 0-$20\,kHz$, because a skilled operator can distinguish whether the calculus is hit by the shock wave or not.

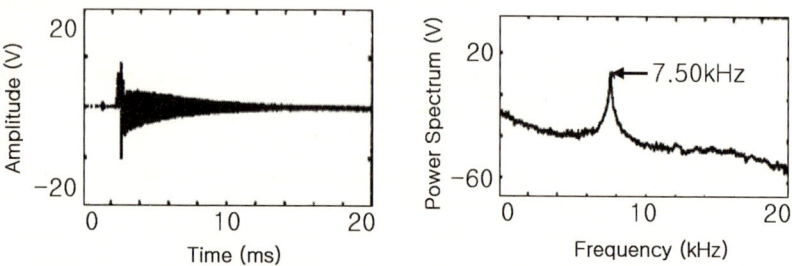

Fig. 1. The waveform and the power spectrum of the metal bar struck by the shock wave of the ESWL

In the power spectrum of Fig. 1, clear peak is observed at $7.50\,kHz$. It is found that this peak frequency coincides with the resonance frequency of the bending vibration, which is theoretically given by

$$f_n = \frac{a\lambda_n^2}{4\pi l^2}v_l \;.$$

$$(1)$$

where $\lambda_1 = 4.73$, $\lambda_2 = 7.85$, $\lambda_3 = 10.99$, ... l is the length, a is the radius of cross section, and v_l is the velocity of the longitudinal wave in the bar. The velocity of the longitudinal wave in bronze is $3300\,m/s$ when it is calculated theoretically. The theoretical frequency calculated by above equation is $7.64\,kHz$ in the case of this metal bar. This value almost coincides with the experimental value.

Next, we observe the phenomena associated with the fragmentation of the object due to the piezoelectric ESWL and investigate why the radiated sound changes during the breaking process. A piece of chalk is employed as the object in this experiment because the acoustic impedance of chalk is almost equal to that of a urethral calculus. The vibrations are measured by a laser Doppler velocimetry, the results of which are analyzed by a FFT analyzer.

Figure 2 (a) shows the waveforms and the spectra for the object vibrations measured by a laser Doppler velocimetry. Each waveform and power spectrum in Fig. 2 is analyzed from the 100th, 300th, 500th, 700th, 900th and 1,500th shock wave shot. It is found that the peak frequency in the spectrum vary with the number of shock wave shot, or the degree of fragmentation of the object. Figure 2 (b) shows that the peak frequency varies to the lower frequency as the number of shots increase.

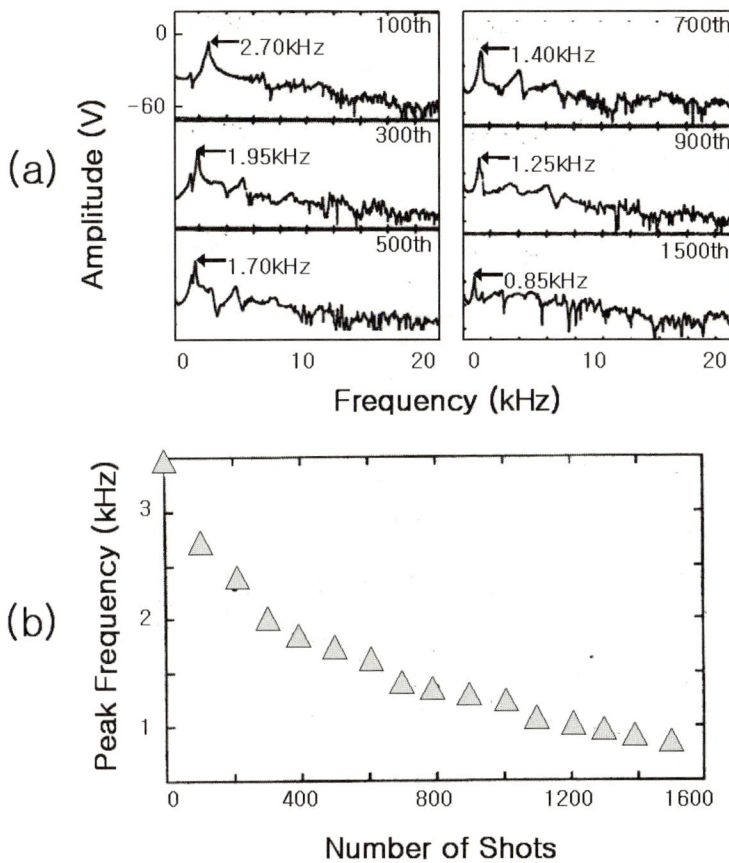

Fig. 2. (a) The power spectra of the vibrations detected when the shock wave is applied to the object, (b) Variations in the peak frequency with the number of shots during the breaking process

3 Information Related to Focal Position on Objects

The parameter d_r is defined as the relative position between the focal point and the position of the object. The value $d_r = 0$ indicates that the center of the object exactly coincides with the focal point of the ESWL. When the center of the object is laid to the direction of the ESWL from the focal point, d_r has a negative value. When it is laid to the opposite direction, d_r has a positive value. Figure 3 shows the relative positions of the object and the focal point of the ESWL using the parameter d_r.

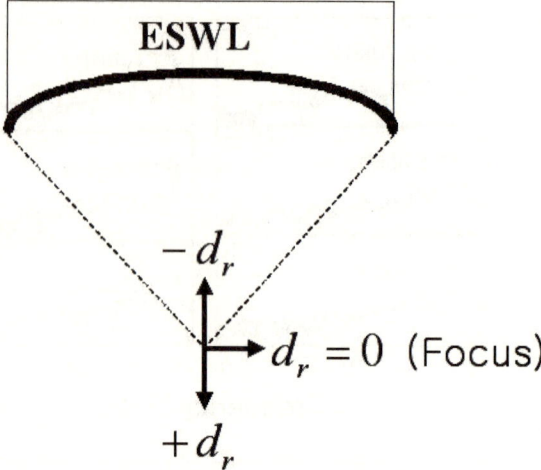

Fig. 3. The relative positions of the model and the focal point of piezoelectric ESWL

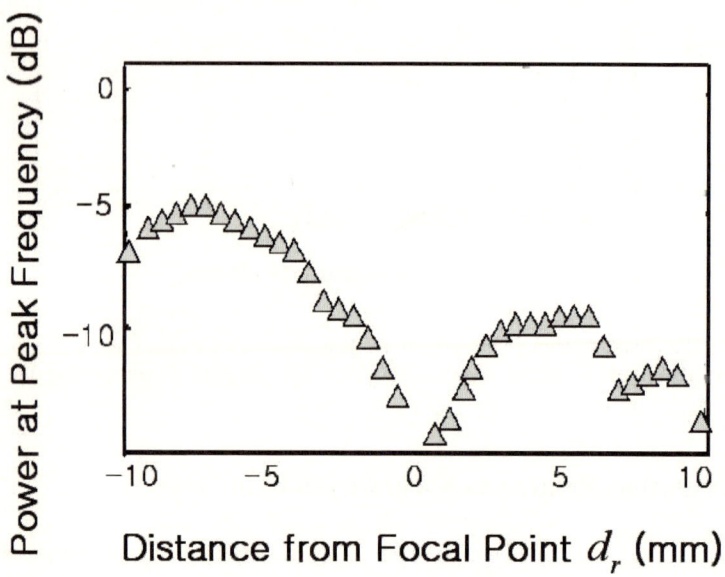

Fig. 4. The power at the peak frequency when the value of d_r is changed

We observe the variation in the amplitude at the peak frequency by changing the value of d_r from $-10\,mm$ to $+10\,mm$. The result is shown in Fig. 4. The amplitude at the peak frequency decreases near the value $d_r = 0$. The vibration mode of the bar considered in order to analyze this phenomenon. When a bar is free to move at its ends, the center of the bar is a node of the mode 2 in the bending vibration. For this reason, it is difficult to make the center of the bar-shaped object vibrate. From these experimental results the amplitude of the peak frequency at the position $d_r = 0$ is smaller than that at the position $d_r > 0$ or $d_r < 0$ in the focal region. This result demonstrates that it is more difficult to vibrate a bar-shaped object exactly at the focal point than above or below the focal point.

Thus, we can estimate that the effective method to break the object is to focus above and below the focal point because it is easier to make the object vibrate exactly at the focal point.

4 Information Related Cavitation Bubble

There are many studies about the performance of the ESWL and the influence into human body by the shock wave from the ESWL [1-4]. It is an important issue that cavitation is always considered together with shock wave [5-7]. A medium of the shock wave is related to the cavitation phenomenon. Therefore, we investigate the break efficiency and the power of the shock wave on focal region due to the medium of the shock wave.

First, we observe the break efficiency by changing d_r as above mentioned. Chalk is employed as the object of this experiment. We compare the number of the shock wave to shot until the time the chalk is broken to two pieces with d_r change. Undegassed water and degassed water is used as the medium of the shock wave.

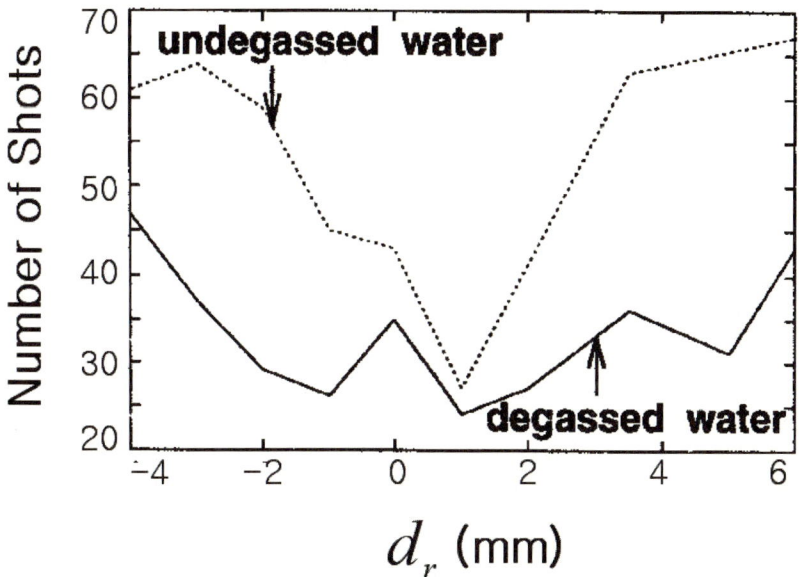

Fig. 5. The number of shots to break due to the positions of the focal point on the object

The result of this experiment is represented as shown in Fig. 5. From this result, we observe that there is a difference of the shot number until the break by nature of the medium. This result demonstrates that the cavitation bubble affects on the break efficiency of the ESWL.

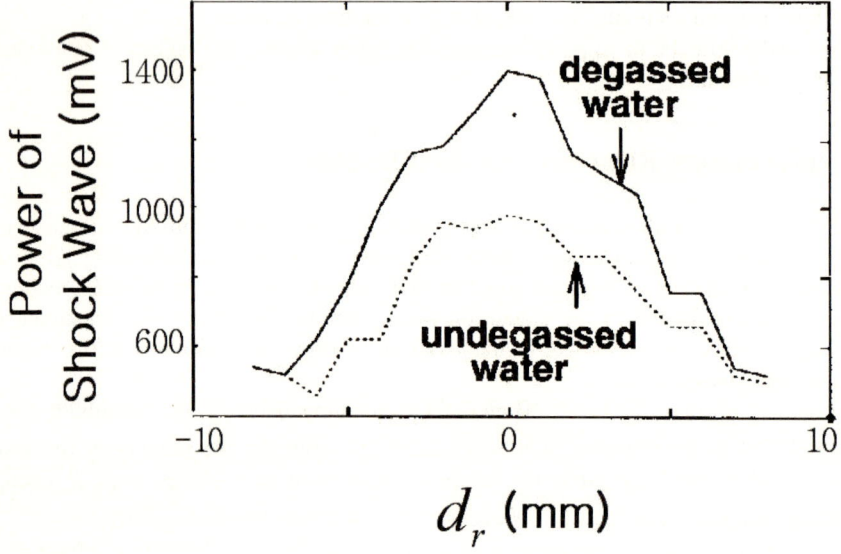

Fig. 6. The comparison of the ESWL power in the focal region due to the medium

The case of degassed water is better medium than that of undegassed water when the ESWL is used on the therapy of calculus.

Next, the power of the shock wave is examined in the focal region by changing a kind of the medium for examining closely the influence of the cavitation bubble. The power of the shock wave is measured on the focal region using a special hydrophone.

Figure 6 shows the result to observe the power of the shock wave in both media. Clearly, the power in the degassed water is stronger than that in the undegassed water on the focal region. These experimental results related the cavitation demonstrate that the shock wave of the ESWL in degassed water is more powerful.

5 Conclusions

This paper report the information related to the radiated sounds from the ESWL. It contains the vibration of the object, the focal position on the object and the relation between the break efficiency and the cavitation.

In the experiment related to the vibration, the peak frequency of the bending vibration varies with the number of shock wave shots. Accordingly, it is possible to hear sounds of lower frequency as the object is gradually fragmented.

We can obtain the information related to the position of the focal point in the next experiments. The amplitude of the peak frequency at $d_r > 0$ and $d_r < 0$ is greater than that at $d_r = 0$ on the focal region. It can be shown that it is easier to make the object vibrate above and below the focal point than at the exact focal point.

Lastly, we investigate the information related to the cavitation bubble. It is found that the case of degassed water might be better medium than that of undegassed water when the ESWL is used on the therapy of calculus because the shock wave of the ESWL in degassed water is more powerful. The information obtained in this paper will be applied to using the piezoelectric ESWL for treatments.

Acknowledgements. This work was supported by Pukyong National University Research Fund in 2003.

References

1. E. Heusler and W. Kiefer, Destruction of kidney stones by means of autofocused guide shock waves, In 2nd European Cong. On Ultrasonics and Medicine, Munich (1975)
2. Ch. Chaussy and E. Schmidt, Shock wave treatment for stones in the upper urinary tract, The Urologic Clinics of North America, Vol. 10, no. 4 (1983) 743-750
3. H. Kanai, Y. S. Jang, N. Chubachi and Y. Tanahashi, Power difference in spectrum of sound radiation before and after break of phantom by piezoelectric shock wave lithotritor, JJAP, Vol. 33-1, no. 5B (1994) 3159-3161
4. Y. S. Jang, Effect of focusing position on the relation between vibration of phantom and break efficiency of piezoelectric extracorporeal shock wave lithotripter, J. Acoust. Soc. Korea, Vol. 19, no. 5 (2000) 35-40
5. A. J. Coleman, J. E. Saunders, L.A. Crum and M. Dyson, Acoustic Cavitation Generated by an Extracorporeal shock wave lithotripter, Ultrasound Med. & Biol., Vol. 13, no. 2, (1978)
6. C. C. Church, A theoretical study of cavitation generated by an extracorporeal shock wave lithotripter, J. Acoust. Soc. America, Vol. 86, no. 1 (1989) 215-227
7. N. Samada, J. Ikeuchi, K. Takayama and O. Onodera, Interaction of an air bubble with a shock wave generated by a microexplosion in water, Proc. Int. Symp. on Cavitation (1986) 67-72

Visualization of Segmented Color Volume Data Using GPU

Koo-Joo Kwon and Byeong-Seok Shin

Department of Computer Science and Information Engineering, Inha University
253 Yonghyeon-Dong, Nam-Gu, Inchon, 402-751, Korea
`kjkwon@inhaian.net, bsshin@inha.ac.kr`

Abstract. Recently, several color volume data such as Visible Human became available for generating a realistic image. These dataset are commonly operated on CPU, however, the rendering time is time-consuming task on CPU. GPU-based volume rendering method can visualize color volume data more easily and quickly because it provides 3D texture including RGB channel. In this paper, we present the GPU-based visualization method of segmented color volume data. During the rendering stage, we need two volume datasets, color and segmented volume. However, the segmented volume requires additional memory. In our method, we use only one 3D texture in GPU. We encode three kinds of values in the 3D texture, color, segmented index and tagged values. Segmented index means the index value of internal organ. And the tagged values are the information of region of interest. We can visualize fast the color image of real human body without additional memory.

Keywords: Color Volume, Photographic Volume, VKH, GPU.

1 Introduction

To visualize a realistic color image using volume rendering method is difficult since the volume dataset is composed of scalar values such as density and temperature of material. If we want to distinguish special material from entire object, we use the pseudo color that is mapped into the scalar value using color transfer function. The gray-scale volume dataset composed of density value from CT, MR and ultrasound, are used in medical imaging area. However, the requirement of visualizing original color of human organ is on the increase. The Visible Human [1], [2], Visible Korean Human [3] and Visible Chinese Human [4] dataset are made for this requirement and these dataset are serially sectioned photographs of cadaver. These dataset are useful for generating realistic image of human organ since they contain real color. The detection of object boundary is very difficult in the color volume data in comparison to gray-scale volume data that contains a kind of scalar value. Therefore, we segment the organs using the color value or shape in pre-processing stage. In order to segment organs area from the color image, we may apply some segmentation algorithm after converting the color image to gray-scale image or separating it into several color channels. However, a skillful anatomist is required for accurate segmentation because the human anatomical structure is very complicate. We get the segmented volume dataset after stacking segmented images made by manual segmentation method. Then,

Z. Pan et al. (Eds.): ICAT 2006, LNCS 4282, pp. 1062–1069, 2006.

we calculate and composite the color value during ray casting stage using both color and segmented volume dataset (see Fig. 1). A recent technique to accelerate rendering uses programmable hardware. These SIMD processors called graphic processing unit (GPU), are useful to perform general volume visualization such as volume ray casting since the GPU presents parallel processing and tri-linear interpolation on board. The size of volume dataset is important factor in rendering since the storage of GPU is limited unlikely that of CPU and the transmission time between the main memory and GPU is considerably long. In case of visualizing segmented color volume data, the efficient memory management is essential because the segmented volume data is used for rendering besides the color volume data. In this paper, we present a visualization method of segmented color volume data on GPU. Our method reduces the memory usage in GPU by using only one 3D texture. This 3D texture contains three kinds of information, color, segmented value and the tag value of region of interest.

In section 2, we explain some related work. Color volume visualization method on GPU will be described in detail in section 3. Some experimental result and discussion will be shown in section 4. Lastly, we summarize and conclude our work.

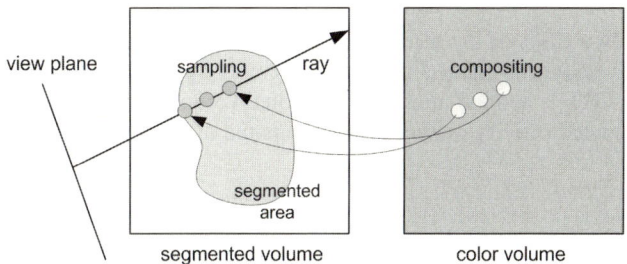

Fig. 1. Color volume data visualization method using segmented volume data

2 Related Work

Color volume data called photographic volume or multi-channel color volume, can generate a realistic image since it uses real color value. Contrary to representing one material using one scalar value (e.g. density and temperature), it is difficult to decide the opacity of material in color value because one material consists of several colors. That is, color value needs an opacity transfer function (OTF) from color data to scalar opacity data (3D to 1D) for volume visualization [5].

Ebert et al. proposes the color transfer function using the CIE $L^*u^*v^*$ color space [6]. However, it contains some problems such as color calibration and internal registration.

A GPU basically presents a 3D texture (volume texture) composed of RGBα channel. It is suitable for visualize color volume data. GPU-based volume ray-casting method is proposed by J. Krüger and R. Westermann [7]. The basic idea of hardware ray casting is simple. The dataset is stored in a 3D texture and a bounding box for this dataset is generated on a position inside the dataset encoded in the color channel. The viewing vector at any given pixel can be easily computed by subtracting the color of the front faces of the color cube from the color of the back faces. Normalizing and storing this vector in a 2D-texture of the exact size of the current viewport for every screen pixel. Then, Render the front faces again and step along the viewing vector for this pixel until the ray has left the bounding box again. Compositing the final color can be done in a separate texture, which is blended onto the screen at the end.

3   Color Volume Rendering on GPU

We present the efficient volume rendering method using auxiliary dataset which classify the region of internal organ, and we propose a method that saves the capacity of texture memory. In order to reduce the memory consumption, we use just one 3D texture for color and segmented value. RGB channels are filled with color values and the alpha cannel is filled with opacity values determined by segmented value. And our method provides diverse cropping image using volume of interest (VOI). These VOI tag values are also stored in the alpha channel of 3D texture.

3.1   Opacity Transfer Function

Fig. 2 shows two cases of the usage of segmented texture. Firstly, the OTF is applied before the 3D texture is loaded in texture memory (pre-computed opacity method). Secondly, the OTF is applied after the segmented volume data loaded in texture memory (post-computed opacity method). Pre-computed opacity method is shown in Fig. 2

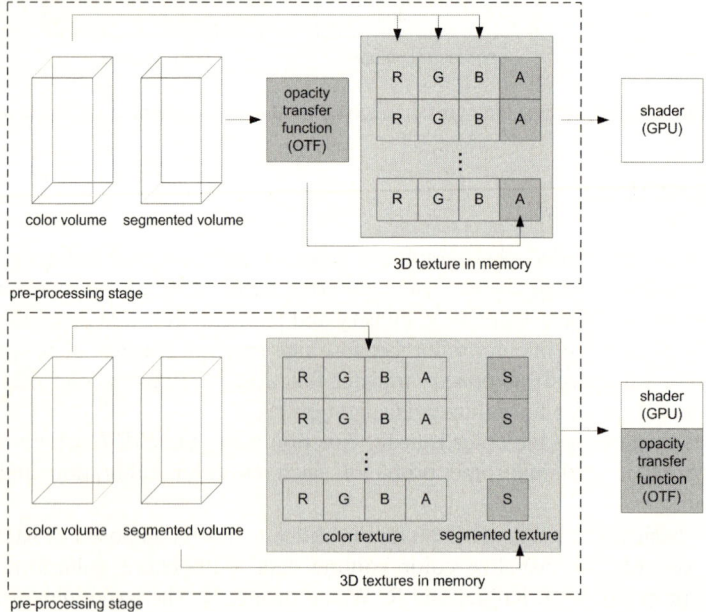

Fig. 2. Usage of 3D texture in GPU. The case of applying the OTF before the 3D texture has loaded in memory (top), the case of applying the OTF in rendering stage (bottom).

(top). The rendering speed of this method is improved slightly than post-computed opacity method since the shader reduces the number of addressing instruction for referring segmented texture. And the memory efficiency is better than post-computed opacity method since the segmented volume data is not loaded in texture memory. However, when user wants to change the OTF, it requires more pre-processing time since the 3D texture was changed and reloaded to GPU. The other case, as shown Fig. 2 (bottom), post-computed opacity method is possible for user to manipulate the OTF in rendering stage interactively. However the rendering speed becomes slower since the fragment shader has to process more instructions per pixel for OTF calculation (see Fig. 3). And GPU needs more space of the texture memory for storing segmented texture. We use the first method for the memory efficiency.

```
// pre-computed opacity method (with VOItag)    // post-computed opacity method (without VOItag)
Voxel = tex3D(Volume);                          Voxel.color = tex3D(Volume);
If(Voxel.VOItag)  composite(Voxel);             Voxel.svalue = tex3D(segVolume);
                                                Voxel.opacity = OTF(Voxel.svalue);
                                                Voxel.VOItag = checkVOI(Voxel.position);
                                                If(Voxel.VOItag)  composite(Voxel);
```

Fig. 3. Pseudo code of our method. The case of the pre-computed opacity method (left) and the post-computed opacity method (right).

3.2 Value of Alpha Channel in 3D Texture

The VOI tag volume is composed of the tag values represented as 1bit binary value. However, it is inadequate for GPU-based method since the GPU does not provide 1bit texture and can not execute bit operation. So, we include the VOI tag value to the alpha channel in 3D texture. Each RGB channels in 3D texture are filled with color values and the alpha channel is filled with an E-value. E-value is a value that encoded using both segmented value and VOI tag value.

$$S_i = \{I_0, I_1, I_2, ..., I_n\}$$
$$T_i = \{V_{in}, V_{out}\} \qquad (1)$$
$$E_i = S_i + T_i$$

$$S_i = \mathrm{mod}(E_i, V_{in}) \qquad (2)$$
$$T_i = E_i - S_i$$

Where, S_i is an i-th value in segmented volume data (I_n representing organ index) and T_i is an i-th value in VOI tag volume data. V_{in} and V_{out} are tag values, it represent that the voxel lie on VOR or not. E_i is the E-value. We encode the E-value in pre-processing stage using equation (1) and decode in rendering stage using equation (2). As shown the pseudo code in Fig. 3, we composite the color of pixel in fragment shader after we decide the pixel lie on VOI or not using T_i. This method preserve the rendering speed fast since the color and opacity value at sampling position are acquired using one 3D texture addressing and one comparison operation. And it also

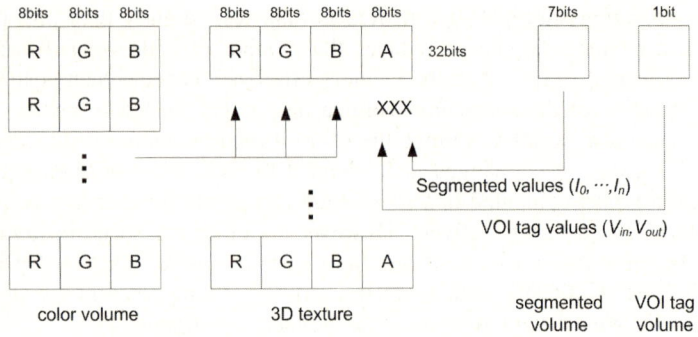

Fig. 4. The red, green and blue values are loaded by each color channel, and the segmented and tag of VOI value are loaded by alpha channel in 3D texture

detects the position lie on the VOI or not. This method can reduce the texture memory space because it requires just one 3D texture during rendering stage. Fig. 4 shows the procedure of making 3D texture.

4   Experimental Result

Our method is implemented on a PC equipped with AMD Athlon™ 64×2 Dual Core Processor 4200 (2.21GHz), 2GB main memory and NVIDIA 7800 GTX graphics card with 256MB video memory. Our method is implemented using C++ and fragment programs are implemented using HLSL shader version 3.0. The volume dataset is VKH head dataset of which the resolution is 256×256×256 and the view plane size is 512×512.

Table 1 shows the rendering speed of proposed method. The rendering time of software-based method on CPU is 2.09 seconds per frame. In our method, the average rendering speed is 21 fps when we use the pre-computed opacity method. When we change the VOI value, the rendering speed is 9 fps. It means that the uploading time is needed since the 3D texture in GPU was changed and uploaded in CPU. In the case of using the post-computed opacity method, the rendering speed is 5 to 12 fps. It means that the shader has to process more instructions for applying the OTF as shown Fig. 3 and the changed VOI data loaded from main memory to texture memory.

Table 1. Rendering speed between pre-computed opacity and post-computed opacity methods

	CPU-based	pre-computed opacity method	post-computed opacity method
no changing VOI	2.09 sec/frame	21 frame/sec	12 frame/sec
with changing VOI		9 frame/sec	5 frame/sec

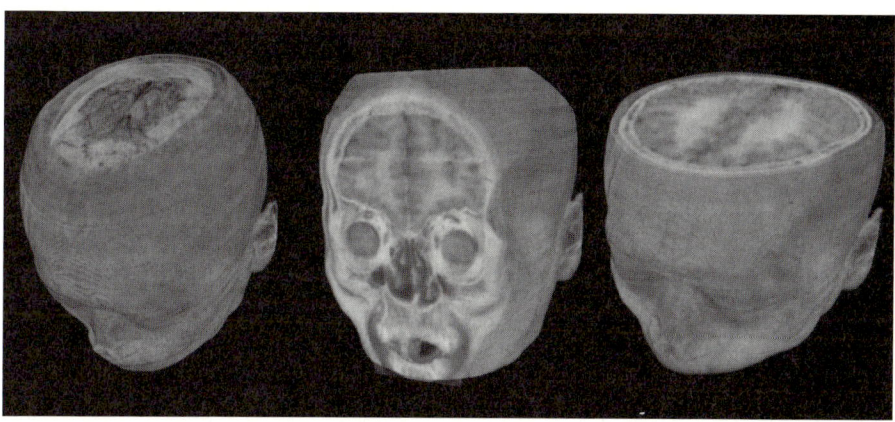

Fig. 5. Result images of our method. The skin image of VKH head dataset on different view and the cross-sectional images (middle and right).

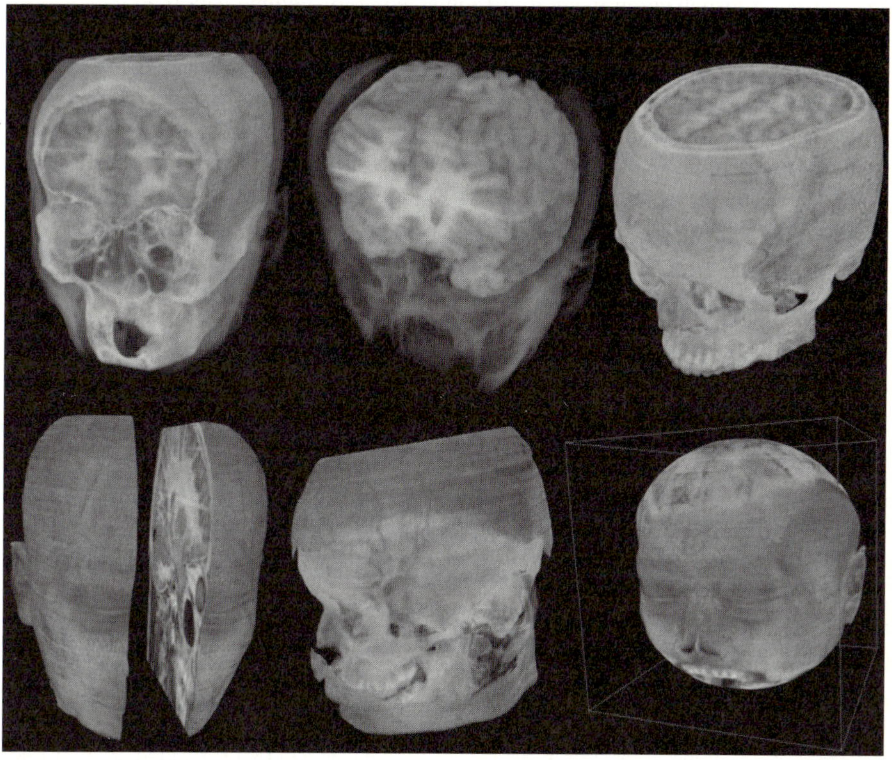

Fig. 6. Skull and brain with semi-transparent skin. Some cross-sectioned image (top row) and various 3D models (bottom row).

Fig. 5 depicts the result images of our method using Visible Korean Human head data. The middle and right images are cross-sectioned head image against by y and z axis. As you see, we verify the original color and shape of internal region using both 3D shape and cross-sectional plane (called axial, sagittal and coronal). Some semi-transparent images and others are shown in Fig. 6. It presents also real color and inner structure semi-transparently. And our method produces a various 3D images when we manipulate the VOI tagged region (shrink, stretch, cut and extract). Bottom left image shows the 3D head with extraction of the vertical area. The middle of bottom shows the skull model torn away skin some area around the head. And the right of bottom is the environment mapped model with sphere. Using this sphere model, we find the structure which lie on the same distance from center. These images are helpful in medical imaging area since user can confirm clearly the internal and external color and shape.

5 Conclusion

We present a visualization method of segmented color volume data in graphics hardware. In our method, only one 3D texture composed RGB color and alpha channel is used. We combine three kinds of value into 3D texture, color, segmented and VOI tag value. We can visualize fast the color image of real human body since we reduce the addressing instruction of texture in shader program. And our method reduces the memory usage in GPU. It is possible that user can verify the various 3D images with real color, semi-transparent, cross-sectioned and mapped into other shapes when we use the various VOI.

Acknowledgement

This work was supported by grant No.R01-2005-000-10197-0 from the Basic Research Program of the Korea Science & Engineering Foundation.

References

1. Spitzer, V. M., Ackerman, M. J., Scherizinger, A. L., Whitlock, D. G.: The Visible Human Male: a Technical report. J. Am. Med. Inform. Assoc. Vol. 3 (1996) 118-130
2. Ackerman, M. J., : The Visible Human Project. A resource for education. Acad. Med., Vol. 74 (1999) 667-670
3. Park, J. S., Chung, M. S., Hwang, S. B., Lee, Y. S., Har, D and Park, H. S.: Visible Korean Human: Improved Serially Sectioned Images of the Entire Body. IEEE Transactions on Medical Imaging, Vol. 24, No. 3 (2005) 352-360
4. Zhang, S. X., Heng, P. A., Liu, Z. J., Tan, L. W., Qiu, M. G., Li, Q. Y., Liao, R. X., Li, K., Cui, G. Y., Guo, Y. L., Yang, X. P., Liu, G. J., Shan, J. L., Liu, J. J., Zhang, W. G., Chen, X. H., Chen, J. H., Wang, J., Chen, W., Lu, M., You, J., Pang, X. L., Xiao, H., Xie, Y. M. : Creation of the Chinese Visible Human data set. Anat. Rec., Vol. 275B (2003) 190–195

5. Pfister, H., Lorensen, B., Bajaj, C., Kindlmann, G., Shroeder, W., Avila, L., Martin, K., Machiraju, R., Lee, J.: The transfer function bake-off. IEEE Computer Graphics and Applications, Vol. 21, No. 3 (2001) 16-22
6. Ebert, D., Morris, C., Rheingans, P., Yoo, T.: Designing effective transfer functions for volume rendering from photographics volumes. IEEE Trans. On Visualization and Computer Graphics, Vol. 8, NO. 2 (2002) 183-197
7. Krueger, J., Westermann, R.: Acceleration techniques for GPU-based volume rendering. Proceedings of IEEE Visualization'03 (2003) 38-46
8. Hong, W., Qiu, F., Kaufman, A.: GPU-based Object-Order Ray-Casting for Large Datasets. Fourth International Workshop on Volume Graphics (2005) 177-240
9. Scharsach, H.: Advanced GPU Raycasting. Proceedings of CESCG (2005) 69-76

Research on Segmentation Algorithm of 3d Medical Data[*]

Yanjun Peng[1,2], Dandan Zhang[1], Weidong Zhao[1], Jiaoying Shi[2], and Yongguo Zheng[1]

[1] Dept. of Computer Science, Shandong University of Science & Technology Qingdao,
266510, China
[2] State Key Laboratory of CAD&CG, Zhejiang University, Hang Zhou, 310027, China
yjpeng@cad.zju.edu.cn

Abstract. A segmentation algorithm in 3d medical data is proposed based on boundary model and local character structure in this paper. We found out inner voexls and outer voexls by pre-appointed voxel based on boundary model. And then, boundary voexls are correctly classified into different tissues by their eigenvalues of Hessian matrix based on the local character structure. Only eigenvalues of the boundary voxels are computed, so little time is used compared with other algorithms based on local character structure. It can quickly and effectively realize the segmentation of single tissue.

Keywords: segmentation, boundary model, local character structure, voxel.

1 Introduction

Drebin R A implemented tissue segmentation by use of Bayes probability in 1988[1]. In this method, the prior conditional probability distribution function of every kind of substance must be estimated from the input messages by one of the two methods of parameterization[2] and non-parameterization[3, 4]. Accurate model and long-playing calculation are absolutely necessary in this method. In addition, boundary voxels could not be classified correctly, especially for slice data of low resolution.

There are fuzzy clustering, fuzzy rule based, fuzzy geometry, fuzzy threshold and fuzzy integer in fuzzy segmentation method[5]. Fuzzy c-means extended from fuzzy clustering is the common method[6~8]. In this method, the object was classified into C kinds, and a member matrix based on the probability of every voxel belongs to a certain substance was established. However, time-consuming iterative computations are necessary to realize each element's convergence of this matrix.

The density of voxel is used simply to implement the tissue segmentation in above two methods, and their segmentation functions are only one-dimensional. In fact, some important information is not considered in the two technologies, such as the location of voxel, density gradient, local character structure, and so on. So the segmentation effect is not satisfying. Levoy designed a two-dimensional segmentation

---

[*] This work is supported by Shandong Province Education Department Foundation of China under Grant No. J05C10 and State key Lab. CAD&CG of Zhejiang University Opening Foundation.

Z. Pan et al. (Eds.): ICAT 2006, LNCS 4282, pp. 1070–1077, 2006.

function firstly[9]. He implemented the medical slice data tissue segmentation applying the density and the gradient of each voxel. In recent years, Gordon K and James W D put forward transfer functions including the density gradient and the two-order derivative along the gradient direction after analyzing a 3D graph, which corresponded separately to the density of a voxel[10]. Voxels are classified correctly by the eigenvalues of Hessian matrix based on the two-order derivative of the voxel's density considered the local character structure of 3D volume data, such as the linear structure (vessel, trachea, nerve), sheet structure (organ, pallium), punctate structure (never cell) in Sato Y and Nakajima S's articles[11~12]. We name it LCA (Local Character Algorithm) method.

In this article, we begin with a pre-appointed voxel belong to a certain tissue. On the basis of LCA algorithm and boundary model, all voxels approximately belong to the tissue in the appointed box are found out. The number of these voxels is more than that of the actual. Then the misclassified voxels in the appointed box but out of the boundary voxels are deleted. At last, the boundary voxels are correctly classified based on the local character structure. In order to accelerate data processing, linked storage structure indexed by voxels' densities is used to delete all the same density voxels not belong to the tissue at a time in this paper. We called this method BMLCA (Boundary Model and Local Character Algorithm) method.

2 Boundary Model and Computing

Define 1 Boundary voxel set B: Given a data set and an object O defined in the inner of the 3D data set, there is a segmentation function Q. Q can divide the data set into two subsets, one is a subset of the inner of O and the other is a subset of the outer of O. A voxel is called boundary voxel, if some of its contiguous six voxels are in the inner of O and others are in the outer of O.

Define 2 Special tissue voxels set T: T is defined as all voxels belong to the inner of the certain tissue, including all boundary voxels and inner voxels.

What we are interested in are the tissues having local character structures, such as linear structure, punctate structure and sheet structure. Assumed the maximum and the minimum density of the inner of the certain tissue are separately I_{max}, I_{min}, and the density of voxel is I, the coordination of the voxel is $X(x,\ y,\ z)$, moreover $I = f(X)$.

Because the voxels at the two sides of different tissues' boundary have almost the same gradient changes of voxels' densities, we express the symmetric changes using Gaussian function. The boundary model can be defined as follow function I

$$I \ = g(d) = I_{min} + (I_{max} - I_{min}) \frac{1 + h(\dfrac{d}{\sigma\sqrt{2\pi}})}{2}$$

d stands for the distance along the gradient direction of the voxel's density. For different voxel and different density, d is different. If $d=0$, the voxel is boundary voxel, that is, its one-order derivative has one maximum at least, $h(x) \in [-1,1]$.

$$g'(d) = \frac{I_{max} - I_{min}}{\sigma\sqrt{2\pi}} \exp(-\frac{d^2}{2\sigma^2}) \tag{1}$$

$\exp(-\dfrac{d^2}{2\sigma^2})$ is Gaussian function. σ is standard deviation, deciding the width of the boundary.

From the above equation, we know that $g'(0)$ is the maximum of $g'(d)$. Meanwhile, $g'(d)$ expresses the one-order directional derivative along the gradient direction. According to the definition of directional derivative, we can deduce the following equation

$$g'(d) = f'_{\nabla f(X)}(X) = \nabla f(X) \bullet \frac{\nabla f(X)}{\|\nabla f(X)\|} = \|\nabla f(X)\| \tag{2}$$

$\nabla f(X)$ stands for the gradient of voxel's density, $\|\nabla f(X)\|$ stands for the value of the gradient, and the sign " $\bullet$ " stands for the dot product of vectors.

From Equ. (1) and Equ. (2), if $d=\pm\sigma$, then $g'(d)$ is an inflection point. Hence, $g''(d)$ is the maximum, when $d=\pm\sigma$.

$$g''(d) = -\frac{d(I_{max} - I_{min})}{\sigma^3\sqrt{2\pi}} \exp(-\frac{d^2}{2\sigma^2}) \tag{3}$$

We can also conclude the following equation from Equ. (2)

$$f''_{\nabla f(X)}(X) = \nabla(f'_{\nabla f(X)}(X)) \bullet \frac{\nabla f(X)}{\|\nabla f(X)\|} = \nabla(\|\nabla f(X)\|) \bullet \frac{\nabla f(X)}{\|\nabla f(X)\|}$$

By Taylor expansion, it can be written as a matrix

$$g''(d) = f''_{\nabla f(X)}(X) = \frac{1}{\|\nabla f(X)\|^2}(\nabla f(X))^T Hf(X)\nabla f(X)$$

$Hf(X)$ is the Hessian matrix of voxel X. By Laplace expansion, we can get the approximation of $g''(d)$, as follows

$$g''(d) = f''_{\nabla f(X)}(X) \approx \frac{\partial^2 f(X)}{\partial x^2} + \frac{\partial^2 f(X)}{\partial y^2} + \frac{\partial^2 f(X)}{\partial z^2} \tag{4}$$

From Equ. (1) and Equ. (3), we get the results

$$\sigma = \frac{g'(0)}{\sqrt{e}\, g''(-\sigma)} \tag{5}$$

$$d = \frac{-\sigma^2 g''(d)}{g'(d)} \tag{6}$$

That is, if we can find out the extremal values of $g''(d)$ and $g'(d)$, the width of boundary σ will be decided. If given the values of $g''(d)$ and $g'(d)$, the value of d can be computed.

Because $\|\nabla f(X)\|$ maybe get 0 in the inner of tissues, we transform Equ. (4) into the following equation

$$d \approx \frac{-\sigma^2 g''(d)}{g'(d) + 1} \qquad (7)$$

Let

$$m(I) = \frac{1}{n} \sum g''(d) \qquad (8)$$

$$l(I) = \frac{1}{n} \sum g'(d) \qquad (9)$$

$m(I)$ and $l(I)$ correspond separately to the centers of mass of $g''(d)$ and $g'(d)$. n is the number of voxels whose densities are I. Replace $g''(d)$ and $g'(d)$ in Equ. (7) with Equ. (8) and Equ. (9), and then the following equation is deduced.

$$d_I \approx \frac{-\sigma^2 m(I)}{l(I) + 1} \qquad (10)$$

d_I means that the value d of all voxels whose densities are I is equal to d_I.

3   Delete Extra Voxels Not Belong to the Given Tissue Voxels Set T

In the method of above, it is inevitable to add some voxels not belong to this certain tissue into set **T**. Notice that these voxels have two characteristics: their locations are between the pre-appointed box and this tissue; their densities are equal to densities of the inner voxels of this tissue. Hence, we regard the pre-appointed voxel A in the inner of this tissue as a seed point. Beginning with the voxel A, those voxels having the same densities and not belong to this tissue are deleted. Then the same operation is done to the contiguous voxels of A and all voxels extended to boundary voxels. The boundary voxels defined as Define 2 are strict. Here we haven't completed the tissue segmentation, so we put forward an undemanding definition.

Define 1′ Boundary voxels set **B**: According to the gradient value $\|\nabla f(B)\|$ of the pre-appointed boundary voxel B, we can initialize a domain [-v, v]. For the voxels generated according to Define 2, if their gradients are in the domain [$\|\nabla f(B)\|$-v, $\|\nabla f(B)\|$+v], these voxels are belong to the boundary voxels set **B**, moreover **B**⊂**T**.

Define 3 Greatest-span voxel: Among these voxels, the fastest voxel away from C is called the Greatest-span Voxel of C that along the path of from Z axis to X axis, then to Y, travel voxels which have the same densities with C. In the linked storage structure indexed by densities, the location of D is only at the start of the link or at the end of the link.

We begin with a voxel C in the inner of a certain tissue and find out the Greatest-span voxel D of C. Then travel voxels from C to D in order of first slices (Z) and then rows (X) and last volumes (Y). At the same time, the locations of those voxels must be marked, which are belonging to the boundary voxels set **B**. In this way, these voxels areas among the marked boundary voxels are deleted. According to the above process, it is easy to delete the voxels not belong to the certain tissue **T** at the beginning of the pre-appointed voxel A. In succession, we find out the contiguous voxels of A and deal with these voxels by the same method in order of $Z-X-Y$. If some voxel's density hasn't been dealt with, we repeat this process. Otherwise, turn to the next contiguous voxel and go on until all the volume data of **T** have been dealt with. Obviously, there only are the operations of search and delete, and no calculations in the whole course.

4   Local Character Structure

By Taylor expansion, Sato Y and Nakajima S expanded $f(X)$ at its one-order derivation and two-order derivation, as follows

$$f(X)=f(X_0)+(X-X_0)^T \nabla f(X_0)+\frac{1}{2}(X-X_0)^T \nabla^2 f(X_0)(X-X_0)$$

$$\nabla^2 f(X)=\begin{bmatrix} f_{xx}(X) & f_{xy}(X) & f_{xz}(X) \\ f_{yx}(X) & f_{yy}(X) & f_{yz}(X) \\ f_{zx}(X) & f_{zy}(X) & f_{zz}(X) \end{bmatrix} \tag{11}$$

$\nabla^2 f(X)$ denotes the two-order derivation of voxel's density, that is, Hessian matrix. Therefore, we describe the original densities of voxels by Hessian matrix. According to the analysis of the voxels' local character structures (linear, sheet, punctate), they draw a conclusion: If there are a special connection between the voxels' densities and its eigenvalues of Hessian matrix, like Table 1, the voxels will have the corresponding character structure. Provided the eigenvalues of the matrix separately are λ_1, λ_2 and λ_3.

Table 1. Basic conditions of local different character structures

Local character structures	Conditions of eigenvalues	Conditions of decomposition	Examples
sheet structure	$\lambda_3 \langle\langle \lambda_2 \approx \lambda_1 \approx 0$	$\lambda_3 \langle\langle 0 \& \lambda_3 \langle\langle \lambda_2 \approx 0 \& \lambda_3 \langle\langle \lambda_1 \approx 0$	Organ, pallium
linear structure	$\lambda_3 \approx \lambda_2 \langle\langle \lambda_1 \approx 0$	$\lambda_3 \langle\langle 0 \& \lambda_3 \approx \lambda_2 \& \lambda_2 \langle\langle \lambda_1 \approx 0$	Vessel, trachea, nerve
Punctuate structure	$\lambda_3 \approx \lambda_2 \approx \lambda_1 \langle\langle 0$	$\lambda_3 \langle\langle 0 \& \lambda_3 \approx \lambda_2 \& \lambda_2 \approx \lambda_1$	nerve cell, node

In order to filter to the given local character structure, we use Gauss function and its two-order derivation to deal with the 3D data. The response filter of one-dimension function can be expressed an $R(x)= -\dfrac{d^2 G(x,\sigma)}{dx^2} * f(x)$. The symbol " $*$ " stands for the operation of convolution and σ stands for the standard deviation, controlling the width of the boundary. Correspondingly, the Hessian matrix changes into as following:

$$\nabla^2 R(X) = \begin{bmatrix} R_{xx}(X) & R_{xy}(X) & R_{xz}(X) \\ R_{yx}(X) & R_{yy}(X) & R_{yz}(X) \\ R_{zx}(X) & R_{zy}(X) & R_{zz}(X) \end{bmatrix} \tag{12}$$

5   Results

We experimented with the lunge CT date sets (102×256×256) provided by Visible-Human, and have implemented the above algorithm (BMLCA) using Intel 2.8G CPU, 256M memory. The time to accomplish this algorithm is 200 seconds. The resulting images are shown as Figure 1 to Figure 7 Figure 1 is a slice with lunge data sets. Figure 2 is the resulting image of linear structure (trachea, bronchia) drawing from this slice as Figure 1 using the above algorithm. Figure 3 is the resulting image of linear structure (trachea, bronchia) of volume rendering using by BMLCA algorithm.

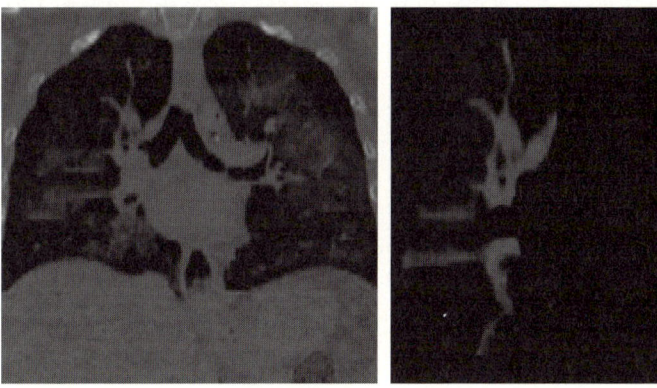

Fig. 1. A slice image of lung data sets   **Fig. 2.** Line structure image of Fig 1

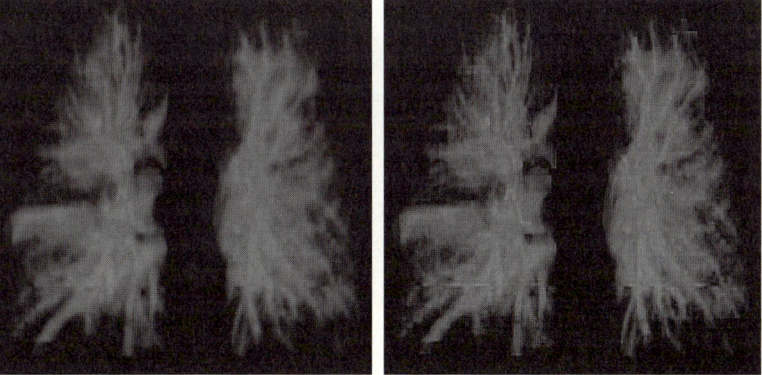

Fig. 3. Result image using by BMLCA   **Fig. 4.** Result image using by LCA

Figure 5 is a slice with abdomen data sets. Figure 6 is the resulting image of sheet structure drawing from this slice as Figure 5 using the above algorithm. According to the data provided by Sato Y and Nakajima S , for the medical images data (102×256×256), on Sparc server (8×168MHz   CPU, 1G Memory), using the technology of multi-threading, the time of implementation is about 10 minutes. The time to accomplish this algorithm is about 20 minutes using the LCA algorithm on our machine. Figure 4 is the linear structure image of volume rendering using by LCA algorithm. Compared with the resulting image by the two algorithms, there is almost no difference. However, the time to implement the tissue segmentation is reduce to 300 seconds from 20 minutes. Figure 7 is the sheet structure image of volume rendering using by BMLCA algorithm.

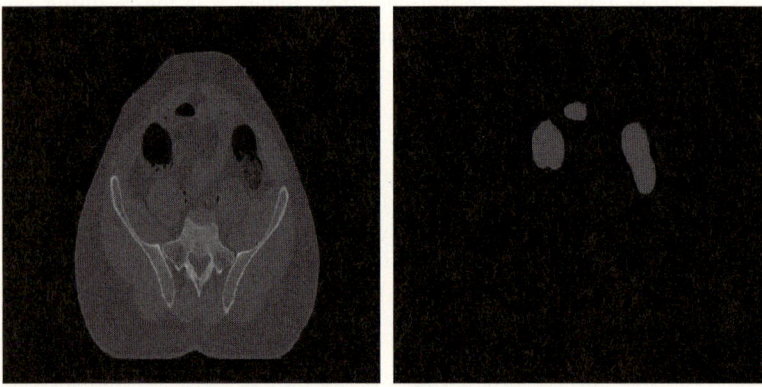

Fig. 5. A slice image of abdomen   **Fig. 6.** Sheet structure image of Fig 1

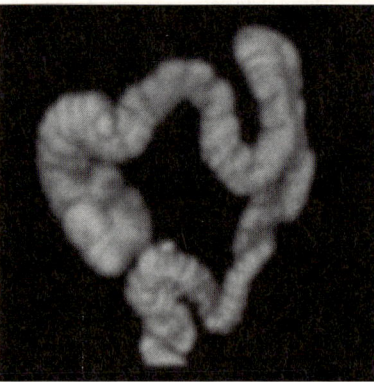

Fig. 7. Result image using by BMLCA

References

1. Rosenblum L J. "Research issues in scientific visualization". *IEEE Computer Graphics and Application*, 14 (2): 61~63 (1994).
2. Derbin R A, Carponter L, et al. "Volume rendering". *Computer Graphics*, 22 (4): 65~74 (1988).
3. Gorte B, Stein A. "Bayesian classification and class area estimation of satellite images using stratification". *IEEE Transaction on Geoscience and Remote Sensing*, 36 (3): 803~812 (1998).
4. Ma F, Wang W, et al. "Probabilistic segmentation of volume data for visualization using SOM—PNN classifier". *IEEE proceedings of visualization symposium*, 71~78, North Carolina, USA (1998).
5. TizhooshHR."Fuzzyimageprocessing".http://pmt05.et.uniagdeburg.de/~damid/segmnt.htm l, (1998).
6. Dzung L P, Jerry L P. "Adaptive fuzzy segmentation of magnetic resonance images". *IEEE Transaction on Medical Imaging*, 18 (9): 737~752 (1998).
7. He S J, Wang X. "MRI brain images segmentation". *Asia Pacific Conference on Circuits and Systems*, 113~116, Tianjin, China (1998).
8. Albert K W, Zhu H. "Semi-automatic tumor boundary detection in MR image sequences". *Proceeding of 2001 international symposium on intelligent multimedia, Video and Speech*, 28~31, New York, USA (2001).
9. Levoy M. "Volume rendering: Display of surface from volume data". *IEEE Computer Graphics and Application*, 8 (3): 29~36 (1988).
10. Gordon K, James W D. "Semi-automatic generation of transfer functions for direct volume rendering". *IEEE Symposium on Volume Rendering Processing*, 79~86, Washington, USA (1998).
11. Sato Y, Nakajima S, et al. "Three-dimensional multi-scale line filter for segmentation and visualization of curvilinear structures in medical images". *Medical Image Analysis*, 2 (2): 43~167 (1998).
12. Sato Y, Nakajima S, et al. "Tissue classification based on 3D local intensity structures for volume rendering". *IEEE Transaction on Visualization and Computer Graphics*, 6 (2): 160~168 (2000).

Kidney Diseases Diagnosis System for Sensation Type Using Physiological Signal Analysis

Bong-hyun Kim[1], Se-hwan Lee[1], and Dong-uk Cho[2]

[1] Department of Computer Engineering
Hanbat National University, Daejeon, Korea
{bhkim, sian}@hanbat.ac.kr
[2] Department of Information & Communication Engineering
Chungbuk Provincial University of Science & Technology, Chungbuk, Korea
ducho@ctech.ac.kr

Abstract. In the opening on the ripe aging society, in an effort to maintain their healths are improving through with their prevention. The internal organs of human body have good relationship with each other. Being the kidney keeps with best relationship in the internal organs, that the kidney function filtering the wastes to pick out into the urine on the processing to replace the old with the new blood. In this paper among the great four diagnosis, using the way of Ocular inspection & Auscultation, we would like to propose in the way of the kidney trouble shooting. To do these, through the assistance of the input image, extract the value of the color with optimization output, analizing the color of the face with related to the kidney.

Keywords: Kidney Diseases Diagnosis, Physiological Signal Analysis, Ocular Inspection, Auscultation, Chin, Formant.

1 Introduction

The most important thing is health to live in this world. The interest for the health is growing and also the interest for the span of human life time is growing here after. Being the interest for the health is highiering, the probability of the human life time have been increased. Today, All of the man kind want to live and so they would like to prolong not only the average span of life for ever but also the healthy span of life[1][2]. When we think of comparing with our economic circumstances, it is very low level to any other advanced country. This is good evidence to the contrary that there is no much way to do to keep our health. Clearly, we have been improved our life time, but we can find out that many person take his sickbed before their dying for a long time almost ten years. To prevention to this symptom, we need continual health care but much more important things is the early stage diagnosis enough to not changing for the worse in malady. Medical science is being exist to maintain the human desirable health pattern, the existing our medical science can be said as a dualized system, so to speak, western medical science and oriental medical science[3]. These two medical science have something difference in its come into existence of its processing and development. The western medical science would like to heal on their patient, but the oriental medical science would like to weight to reinforce patient inner power to heal one's main factor[4].

Z. Pan et al. (Eds.): ICAT 2006, LNCS 4282, pp. 1078–1087, 2006.

In oriental medical science, if they become weak enough to change their own condition, sickness can act in their body freely. Owing to this principal, we are living with great interest in oriental medical science in this ripe age society. But in spite of this great excellent merit in oriental medical diagnosis and remedy this field of medical science could not have great activity by the shadow of the western medical science. The reason why is that the western medical science can show the visuality and objectivity to the patients. It can be generalized if the oriental medical diagnosis theory can be grafted with image and voice processing technology in the field of IT, the remedy benefit can be true in the future. And also, through this, we can have a great efficiency to make the way for the patients as a base data offer to network service. In this paper, we would like to design the diagnosis system using this theory that can diagnosis and remedy of kidney problem in advance. For this, from the front part of the patient face, we can verification of kidney problem from the analizing the voice signal using from above two facts and comparing with the normal human we would like to propose to proof its usefulness.

2   The Method of Oriental Diagnosis and Kidney

The way of medical diagnosis for patient have four methods of diagnosis of the pulse for diagnosis. In the first rate, we can catch with the patients observation of appearance and inspection of the color we call his as a ocular inspection[5][6]. In the second rate, using auscultation who can catch out patients voice and smell. In the third rate, we can catch the disease with Inquiring which can be diagnosis by the asking the symptom of patients condition. In the fourth rate, we can catch out some one's disease touching his pulsation. We call this diagnosis as a Pulse feeling. As you know, in the oriental medical diagnosis they took ocular inspection and auscultation as a best way to catch out diagnosis of disease. Therefore, to do more accurate the most important thing that diagnosis we must operate all of this diagnosis under the hybrid form. But, the most great problem of the oriental medical diagnosis can not solve with a visualization to patients only to intuition. And so, the most great problem to the oriental medical doctor is to objectively and visualization for their intuition on the same problem. We would like to realize this problem using IT technology.

In the oriental medical science of ocular inspection, it is the way of decision for patient using the power of doctor's sense of vision from the patient, for example, the doctor can check the patient body, the effected part, etc. After this check, the doctor can decide the patient enough to diagnosis. The ocular inspection is very important field for improving on the science of diagnosis. Our predecessors have been too much weight this point. The important contents of the ocular inspection is to observe the variation of color, power of vital energy and form of body. In the state of human body, the expression of its color, form and power o.k. but unhealth human body express itself infirmity from his face[7]. Specially observation of appearance and inspection of the color is the most important part among the ocular inspection, observation of appearance is to observe that appearance of body is fat or not, wonderful power or not, and also, inspection of the color is to observe the related intestines color[8]. In case of inspection of the color, five kinds of color related to the fire viscere is very important factor, as you know from the table 1. we would like to follow this table. That is the blue color express the liver, the red color express the heart and the yellow color express the spleen, the white color express the lungs and the black express the kidney. And also, among the method of oriental medical science with the ocular inspection, the auscultation is the most important field in these area. All of this flow(state) can be decision by the following level.

① the breathing of the patient and his voice.
② the clean voice of stomach.
③ the voice of the belly.
④ the smell and color of the evacuations.

In the oriental medical science, the kidney express water and fire of the internal organs.(water means making peaceful joy, fire means making anger) If the kidney goes to weak, the color of skin goes to black, the body of patient goes to thin and dry, and goes to black around his eye side. And also, if the kidney is small, the internal organs are comfort and would not be hurt easily. If the kidney is large, the patient become uneasy enough to making feel pain and hurt with injustice easily. And also, each part of face and its five element attachment can function by the Dong-Ui bogam(The Precious mirror of oriental medicine). If we observe the principle of 5 element attachment and look upon as a round plate, what you call. wood(木 one of the five phases) means the liver on the left side part of the round plate, fire(火 one of the five phases) is the heart on the upper side of the round plate, soil(土 one of the five phases) is the spleen on the middle part of the round plate, gold(金 one of the five phases) is the heart on the right part of the round plate, the down side part express the kidney of the face. So, the part of the chin express the kidney. If the color of chin shows black, the kidney goes to damage limit. Finally, as we can see table 1, through the symptom of each ear, neck, mouth and nose, we can catch the symptom of kidney. From this table, the kidney is related with black color.

Table 1. Relation of Color and Kidney

position	color	symptom
hair	yellow, Non-luster	Patient with serious illness or infirmity patient, Being paralysis, bundle of hair picked out with easy to the youth. The hair style is loose and no healthy symptom with fall off the hair often.
	white	The kidney is infirmity. Owing to taking over pains with nerve hot blood shade out. The child who has entangled hair must be abnormal on the part of the spleen and the stomach.
eye	white	The eye goes to dim. The block pupil and pupil of the eye become with white mote. The eye is swelling up.
tongue	blue	In case of covered with white mote the tongue expresses blue color. The margin of tongue is blue if it be dry tongue, don't like to drink anymore.
	black	Emergency patient.
mouth	black purple	In case of salty taste, smell rotten smell. Around the mouth shows block color in case of drying lips and shows popular this case is very serious illness. In case of following symptom.
Tooth	yellow	Narrow crack of tooth goes to tooth. The root of tooth appear out. The tooth's color goes to yellow.

3   Optimization of Input Image

3.1   White Balance

We know the ray has a color temperature. If we have taken a picture, the color tone of its picture come to vary in course of illumination. The color of ray which ideal black body emits color temperature, it is decided by temperature. When object is shining the emanating visible ray, in case of the sack sees with color that black body of some temperature copies. See and speak that temperature is color temperature of object, that temperature of the black body and temperature of object are same. That is, color temperature of the object is marked by temperature of same colored light's black body. We speak this temperature as a color temperature with modificate these color temperature, to express the source color, we call this white balance to adjust white balance means to show the white color as a white color[9]. To adjust this color, we must decide the limits of white color. It is the most important fact to get the input image far getting accurate color.

If we observe with our own maked eye, it is very difficult to find out its difference. But it can be find out from photographing. Therefore, when we would like to get face image in the room, the best way is to adjust white balance under the right illumination color. This is the best way to get original color for face image.

3.2   The Assistance by the QP Card

In case of white balance, it is the color assistant technical on processing or before. The method of QP card correspond to after job, that is the finishing touches[10]. As you see fig1, QP card is composed with white color, gray color and black color. In this case, as the limits of setup point, the value of RGB is (0,0,0),(255,255,255). In case of gray, the base color as a gray spot is the rate of 18% reflection. Before photographing, under the same illuminating circumstance, do the photographing job and after this job using graphic tool, in case of adjusting the basis of original color to QP card color itself with filtering. The color of photographic object comes to revive.

Fig. 1. QP Card

3.3   Reflection Assistance Using Polarized Light Filter

Generally, to experiment this, if we photographing under the direct rays or any other under the scattered lights. Because of the surface of photographing object, we need to remove this part. To do this normaly, we can use the polarized light filter (PL), this time, the ray process by the vibration toward uniform. If it be the reflection on surface

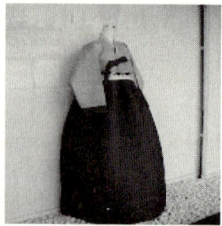

Fig. 2. Before PL   **Fig. 3.** After PL

of nometal as the water or glass. That's the vibration is one direction. The polarized light means the light of one sided. On this place, the filter of polarized light have the function enough to protection this PL[11].

4   System Organization and Design

On the basis of the oriental medical science diagnosis theory, using the It tech, to design the diagnosis system of the kidney disease. This thesis has studied two kinds of field, one is ocular inspection, the other is Auscultation. From this study, designing the basic clinical DB, to proof the effectiveness of its accurate results, being connected with the ocular inspection & auscultation system. First of all, the system construction for ocular inspection for input image setup to optimal creation from the transferred input image, the method of infra partition, After this the color system for RGB transferred to CMYK color system. From this transferred input image applying the method of infra partition, using the erosion job, we must doing job to remove the small object of total image, or doing job to reduce the expanded object as so.

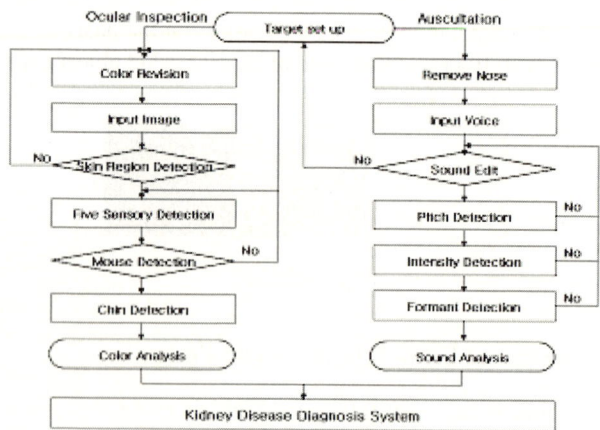

Fig. 4. Integration System of Ocular Inspection & Auscultation for the Kidney Diseases Diagnosis

After this, apply median filtering sliding the optional size of window for the picture element from sorting from ascending order, the value of median should come to the center of window enough to correspond to output image. And so, assigning the pixel as a median value, we can enforce the existing edge. From this removed image, using vertical and horizontal scanning we can extract out the area of eye, nose, mouth and eyebrow. Finally the extension line to extracted area (eye, nose, mouth, eyebrow etc) with expanded line, we extracted necessity part to the kidney diagnosis, that is around the chin. And also, the system construction for Auscultation classified the group of kidney disease and normal person. We have recorded on tape the same sentence composed from lip voice related the kidney disease. Among from this input voice, analying the infra structure for phonetic character istic factor. We extracted the similerity between the experiment group for the kidney diagnosis.

4.1 Face Image Analysis for Ocular Inspection

Today, we use the RGB system mode to produce the color of monitor. Here, we can get the R0.G0.B0 information for black color. But using this combination with 3 color tone, it is very difficult to extract black color. And so, we would like to use the CMYK formation. Using this CMYK color model, we can transform the RGB color tone to CMYK color tone in this experiment. You can see the following equation[12].

$$C = 1.0 - R$$
$$M = 1.0 - G \tag{1}$$
$$Y = 1.0 - B$$

$$K = \min(C,M,Y)$$
$$C = C - K$$
$$M = M - K \tag{2}$$
$$Y = Y - K$$

In case of RGB color system for adding the color tone to produce color, we can make the white color with the multiple color tone, this method can use for computer monitor. On the other hand, CMYK model system is produced black color from mixing multiple color tone. First time we used CMYK model system, but we would like to use CMYK model system to produce complete black color adding numeric factor. Being express the degree of the black color in the system of CMYK model. We would like to use on measuring the degree of black color in the face which correspond to the K area. And also, this thesis would like to extract the skin area of face mean while, to extract the skin area of face enough to process the color tone. In results, we will extract the area of best place which is correspond to the kidney. Here after, removed the small object of total image or scale-down the object from the total image in proportion of enlargemention background. After this, removed all of noise through median filter. Now, the filtering results for color image as following equations[13].

$$\sum_{i=1}^{N} \left| x_{med} - x_i \right| \leq \sum_{i=1}^{N} \left| y - x_i \right| \tag{3}$$

This thesis would like to use the part of best position nose or apex nasi enough to diagnosis the kidney disease without fail.

① Namely Detect the five sensory organs(ear, neck, mouth and nose)
② After this we can exact the mouth from image of the result.

Using the extracted mouth, the width of mouth : x, the length of mouth : y, the spot to down side as far as right and left the position of y is determined chin enough to get right or left of 2y[14].

4.2 Voice Signal Analysis for Auscultation

We would like to proof the following point. What is the difference between the kidney patient and normal person? if it be, what part are think? we would like to check from voice analysis. This thesis used the Praat[15] in order to sound signal analysis. We measured voice signal through the Praat the value of Pitch, Intensity and the value Formant we can measured voice signal. Pitch means the number of vibrations per second.

For example, for normal people :

male : 120Hz
female : 330Hz
child : 300Hz

Intensity is very important measure to express the volume of voice. The amplitude value of vibration on a certain time classified as a "minus, plus,". Formant means the power of the distributed frequency, in case of vocal sound, if we hang the vocal sound up to the machine of frequency gauge. we can get the frequency distribution diagram. If it be vowel sound, it is composed as follow.

① Basic frequency and must of high frequency of the fixed number times.
② The number of vibration per second of the vocal cord.

There are emphasis point in these high frequency. We call these with ascending order. For example, Fist Formant, second Formant... According to the size of oral cavity, peculiar tone color(quality) There are so many personal difference(gap), This point goes to make peculiar tone color for person, and enough to be the main voice controller. With this thesis, we would like to diagnosis the kidney disease by the recorded the source of sound. on oriental medical science we call the following sign as a lip sound "ㅁ : Mi Eum", "ㅂ : Bi Eup", "ㅍ : Pi Eup". Namely the labial sound is correspond to water(水 one of the five phases) under the five elements Consequently, Through the basis of labial sound between non-patient and kidney patient we must observe the result of that test.

5 Experimental Results

In this paper, for experiment of ocular inspection has finished on the IBM-PC using Visual C++ and C# program included with Photoshop 7.0. And also used Praat which is the voice analysis program for auscultation system. The process of experiment for the kidney disease classified as follows table 2.

① the kidney disease patient : experiment group.

② non-patient : Comparison group.

We have compared and analized the difference of ① and ②. Check A up with B comparison group as you see, fig 5 is the input image for the kidney disease, fig 6 is the binary image by the face area partition, fig 7 is the extracted image for the five sensory organs. Using fig 7, we have got the extracted image fig 8 which is the best position nose or apex nasi around the part of chin. Fig 9 shows the value of Total CMYK color tone in the system of CMYK color Model. As the out come of the experiments form the part of chin, we have detected 39% for the value of K which come out black color. As same, fig 10 is the management process & the image of results for the Ocular inspection of kidney disease : Fig 11 is the handling process & the image of results for the experiment of normal group. From this, we could a great out come enough to get. We have the very good results from this experiments enough to extract black color through computing analysis from any other method (: observing naked eye)

Table 2. Test Group and Comparison Group's Data

Classification	Sex	Age	Name of Disease	Degree of Disease
Test group (kidney patient)	female	65	renal failure	serious
	female	72	renal failure	serious
Comparison group (normal person)	male	26	none	none
	female	23	none	none

 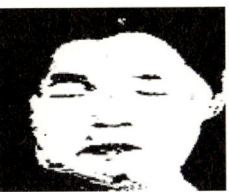 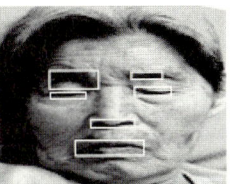

Fig. 5. Input Image   **Fig. 6.** Binary Image   **Fig. 7.** Sensory Extract Image

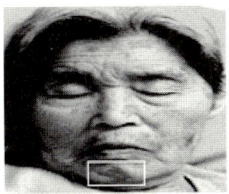

C : 47%   C : 47%
M : 58%   M : 58%
Y : 99%   Y : 99%
K : 39%   K : 39%

X : 7.90   W :
Y : 8.11   H :

Fig. 8. Image of Extract Chin Part   **Fig. 9.** Value of Color Analysis

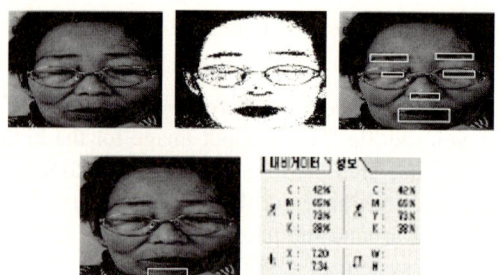

Fig. 10. Ocular Inspection System Process & Image for the Kidney Disease

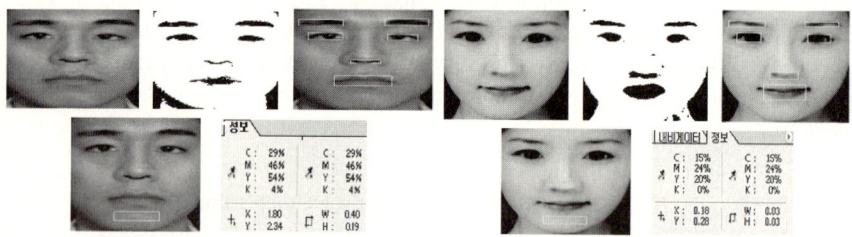

Fig. 11. Ocular Inspection System Process & Image for the Normal A / B

And also, on the experiment for the Auscultation & on the basis of the oriental medical science theory. We have recorded 『pyung min bakmi pung eui mang bal gwa mimi eui balpyo』 and analized the following sentence. On the voice analysis which is related to lip sound, we used the method of Formant, which is the element of voice analysis. You can see the voice analysis results in fig12, fig13 and for normal person in fig14, fig15. According to the degree of weight for the kidney disease. We could check out the definite difference(gap) with the normal person group from the value of first Formant.

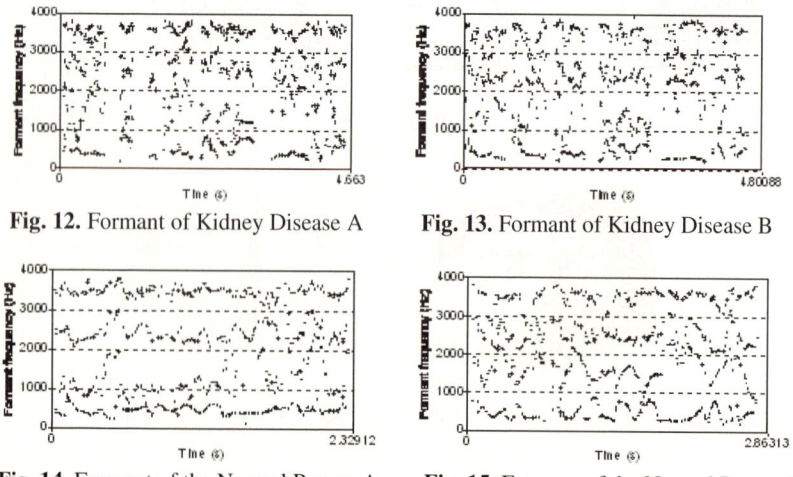

Fig. 12. Formant of Kidney Disease A   **Fig. 13.** Formant of Kidney Disease B

Fig. 14. Formant of the Normal Person A   **Fig. 15.** Formant of the Normal Person B

6 Conclusion

Today, most of us stretch our best effort for our health enough to live forever. In this ripe age society, it is too much important job to extension our span of healthy life. To accomplishment this aim, in this thesis we designed the diagnosis system enough to check out kidney disease using Bio signal processing. From this, proposed the check method what's the status of the kidney disease with this experiments, on the basis of ocular inspection and auscultation, we realized scientific engineering tech. Finally we would like to design the unification system with these two diagnosis systems. In case of using the method of Ocular inspection, extraction the best position of related with the kidney, we could recognized the disease of yes or no for the kidney through this color analysis. In the course of doing experiment, we could lots of many patient. And also, we could proof the basis of oriental medical science theory. Specially, if we take a good look at the face of patient carefully, we could find out black color staying on their face without exception. Seeing this on the basis of the Oriental medical science theory, if any one has the kidney disease, the best part of position (:nose or apex nasi) looked more strong of course, this is nothing but only the subjective out look theory. Through clinical experiment and using objective method, this theory could be got the infra structured Home network. And also, in case of using auscultation on the oriental medical science, we could verified the accuray which we have set up the relation ship between the kidney and voice. Finally, we could proofed with experiment, which the kidney have close relationship with lip voice to the patient in the 1 Formant. On the basis of this results, if we design for the kidney diagnosis system, the universalization of medical treatment could be realize without fail.

References

1. http://100.naver.com/100.php?id=744082/
2. http://www.genomelife.com/
3. http://kin.naver.com/db/detail.php?d1id=6&dir_id=60
4. Dong won Sin, Nam il Kim, In suk Yeo, with reading one volume Dong-Ui bogam(The Precious mirror of oriental medicine), Deul Nyuk Publishing Co., (1999)
5. Hun young Cho, Great Book of Oriental Medical Science with Easy and Funny, Hakwon Publishing Co., (2003)
6. Yang geun Lim, Diagnosis Atlas 1 Ocular Inspection , Jung Darn Publishing Co., (2003)
7. http://www.isom.or.kr/
8. http://www.hyunsang.or.kr/
9. http://www.dcinside.com/
10. Hyun jun Pyo, DSLR Applications Technique for Smart Photo, YoungJin.com, (2005)
11. Chang ho Choi, Teaching for Photos Time Space, (2004)
12. Randy crane, Image Processing Theory & reality, Hong Reung Publishing Co., (1999)
13. Jun sik Kwon 7, Digital Image Processing Theory & Applications, Hong Reung Publishing Co., (2002)
14. Dictionary edit committee, Oriental Medical Science, Korea-English Dictionary, Ji Moon Dang Publishing Co., (2004)
15. Byong gon Yang, Voice Analysis Theory and Reality using Praat, Man Su Publishing Co., (2003)

A Computer-Aided Driving Posture Prediction System Based on Driver Comfort

Qun Wu[1], Shiwu Luo[2], and Shouqian Sun[1,3]

[1] Institute of Modern Industrial Design,Zhejiang University,Hangzhou, P.R. China
[2] Industrial Design Department, Jiangxi University of Finance & Economics, Nanchang, P.R. China
[3] Center of Digital Art and Design, Hubei University of Technology, Wuhan, P.R. China
`wuqun2001@tom.com, luoshiwu@163.com, ssqq@mail.hz.zj.cn`

Abstract. The objective of this study was the application of driving comfort for the prediction of the driver's posture. At the first, triangular type membership function was introduced to depict the driver's feeling of comfort for the uncertain meaning of "comfort", and then a model was built to assess the relation between design parameters and comfort assessment based on Fuzzy SVM. To get an appropriate driving posture, the comfort result was feed back to the design phase and some design parameter changing rules were built. At the last, a computer-aided driving posture prediction system was formed. This method can also be used to solve other relative problems.

Keywords: Driving posture, Driver Comfort, Fuzzy SVM.

1 Introduction

The automotive industry strongly encourages research in the field of objective comfort assessment, especially dedicated to the seat and the related postures[1], Driver posture is one of the most important issues to be considered in the vehicle design process[2] ,regarding not only the design factors of car, but also the comfort feeling of driver[3,4]. This paper discusses a methodology applied in static experimentation for the investigation of the relationship between driver comfort and design factors, and develops a computer-aided system toward the driving postural prediction in the design process.

Generally, the analysis of driving posture could be dealt with by considering many parameters. Such as the EMG activity of the dorsal and para-spinal muscles, which is more frequently used not to maximize or minimize muscular activities, but to find the proper balance [5,6]; the postural angles, obtained by photographic techniques or by opto-electronic systems, which are helpful for evaluation of the joint ranges of comfort [7];the pressure maps at the body–seat interface, which describe how forces are exchanged between man and seat[8,9]; and the morphological description of the interfacing surfaces of seat and body, useful to verify the proper "anthropometric" sizing of the seat [10].

Our study about the analysis of seated posture is base on the driving comfort. Traditional driving comfort assessment only built models from auto driving space to comfort result, and for the uncertain meaning of "comfort", Fuzzy set theory and

Z. Pan et al. (Eds.): ICAT 2006, LNCS 4282, pp. 1088–1097, 2006.

Fuzzy logic were taken to emulate the comfort assessment to deal with this problem, [11,12,13]. In this study, we proposed a method base on Fuzzy SVM to build a model to assess the relation between design parameters and comfort assessment. Using this model, we develop a computer-aided driving posture prediction system prototype.

2 Fuzzy SVM

SVMs are primarily two-class classifiers that have been shown to be an attractive and more systematic approach to learn linear or non-linear decision boundaries[14,15]. Their key characteristic is their mathematical tractability and geometric interpretation. Suppose we are given a set of n training samples $S = \{(x_i, y_i)\}_{i=1}^{n}$, where $x_i \in R^m$ an m-dimensional sample in the input space is, and $y_i \in \{-1, 1\}$ is the class label of x_i. In most cases, the searching of a suitable hyperplane in an input space is too restrictive to be of practical use. A solution to this situation is mapping the input space into a higher dimension feature space and searching the optimal hyperplane in this feature space. SVM first maps the input data into a high-dimensional feature space through a mapping function $z \in \varphi(x)$ and finds the optimal separating hyperplane with the minimal classification errors. The hyperplane can be represented as:

$$w \cdot z + b = 0 \tag{1}$$

where w is the normal vector of the hyperplane, and b is the bias that is a scalar. The optimal hyperplane can be obtained by solving the following optimization problem [25]:

$$\text{Minimize } \frac{1}{2}\|W\|^2 + C\sum_{i=1}^{n}\xi_i \tag{2}$$

$$\text{Subject to } y_i(w \cdot z_i + b) \geq 1 - \xi_i, \ \xi_i \geq 0, i = 1,2,...,n$$

where C is the regularization parameter controlling the trade-off between margin maximization and classification error. ξ_i is called the slack variable that is related to classification errors in SVM. The optimization problem can be transformed into the following equivalent dual problem:

$$\text{Maximize } \sum_{i=1}^{n}\alpha_i - \frac{1}{2}\sum_{i=1}^{n}\sum_{j=1}^{n}\alpha_i\alpha_j\gamma_i\gamma_j z_i \cdot z_j \tag{3}$$

$$\text{Subject to } \sum_{i=1}^{n}\gamma_i\alpha_i = 0, \ 0 \leq \xi_i \leq C, i = 1,2,...,n$$

where α_i is the Lagrange multiplier. The decision function of the SVM can be represented as:

$$f(x) = w \cdot z + b = \sum_{i=1}^{n}\alpha_i\gamma_i\varphi(x_i) \cdot \varphi(x) + b = \sum_{i=1}^{n}\alpha_i\gamma_i K(x_i, x) + b \tag{4}$$

where $K(x_i, x)$ is the kernel function in the input space that computes the inner product of two data points in the feature space. Using the kernel trick, we can construct the optimal hyperplane in the feature space without knowing the mapping φ.

In many real-world applications, the effects of the training points are different. It is often that some training points are more important than others in the classification problem. We would require that the meaningful training points must be classified correctly and would not care about some training points like noises whether or not they are misclassified.

So we introduce a fuzzy membership $\{\mu_i\}_{i=1}^n \in [0,1]$ associated with each training point x_i. The membership value μ_i reflects the fidelity of the data; in other words, how confident we are about the actual class information of the data. The higher its value, the more confident we are about its class label. The optimization problem of the FSVM is formulated as follows [16].

$$\text{Minimize } \frac{1}{2}\|w\|^2 + C\sum_{i=1}^n \mu_i \xi_i$$
$$\text{Subject to } \quad y_i(w \cdot z_i + b) \geq 1 - \xi_i, \ \xi_i \geq 0, i = 1,2,...,n \tag{5}$$

It is noted that the error term ξ_i is scaled by the membership value μ_i. The fuzzy membership values are used to weigh the soft penalty term in the cost function of SVM. The weighted soft penalty term reflects the relative fidelity of the training samples during training. Important samples with larger membership values will have more impact in the FSVM training than those with smaller values.

Similar to the conventional SVM, the optimization problem of FSVM can be transformed into its dual problem as follows:

$$\text{Maximize } \sum_{i=1}^n \alpha_i - \frac{1}{2}\sum_{i=1}^n\sum_{j=1}^n \alpha_i\alpha_j\gamma_i\gamma_j K(xi,xj)$$
$$\text{Subject to } \quad \sum_{i=1}^n \gamma_i\alpha_i = 0, \ 0 \leq \xi_i \leq \mu_i C, i = 1,2,...,n \tag{6}$$

Solving equation (6) will lead to a decision function similar to (4), but with different support vectors and corresponding weights α_i.

The only free parameter C in SVM controls the tradeoff between the maximization of margin and the amount of misclassifications. A larger C makes the training of SVM less misclassifications and narrower margin. The decrease of C makes SVM ignore more training points and get wider margin.

In FSVM, we can set C to be a sufficient large value. With different value of μ_i, we can control the tradeoff of the respective training point x_i in the system. A smaller value of μ_i makes the corresponding point xi less important in the training. There is only one free parameter in SVM while the number of free parameters in FSVM is equivalent to the number of training points.

For applying SVMs to multiclass classifications, the approach is to reduce the multiclass problem to a set of binary problems, enabling the basic SVM approach to be used. [17,18].

3   Driving Posture Prediction Model Based on FSVM

3.1   Independent Variables and Dependent Variables

Independent variables in this model are steering wheel height (SW Height), seat cushion angle (SCA) and the distance between steering wheel to ball of foot (SW to BOFX) [19], which are the design factors in this study and shown in the figure 1. Moreover, the proportion of drier's height to weight (H/W), which has been proved a key point to driving comfort parameter selecting, was take into account.

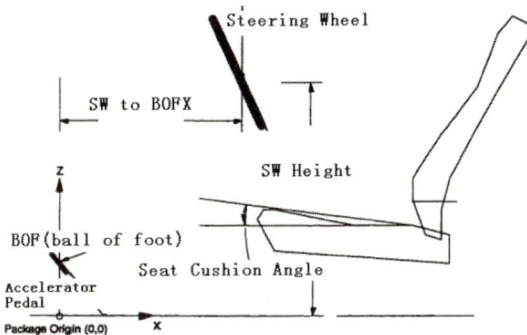

Fig. 1. Design factors

Postural angle is important indication of driving comfort, in this study, cervical flexion, elbow angle, hip angle and knee angle, are selected as dependent variables based on the result of experiment [20], which is showed in figure 2:

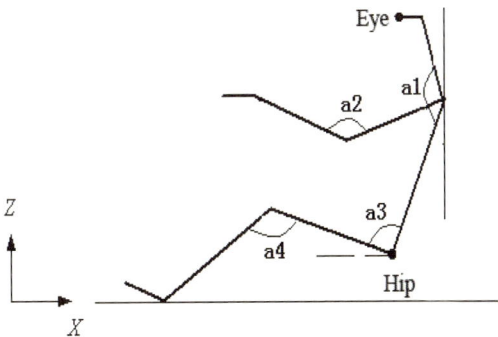

Fig. 2. Postural angle, where a1: Cervical flexion, a2: elbow angle, a3: Hip angle, a4: knee angle

For getting the data of postural angle and relative design factors, a simulation platform was established.

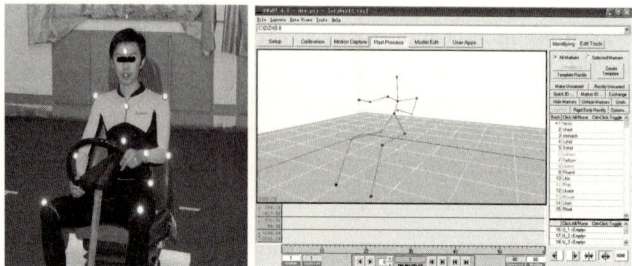

Fig. 3. A simulation platform for getting the data

3.2 Form Fuzzy Membership

Based on [21], we can get the relation of postural angle and driving comfort.

Table 1. Range of comfort and movement for the postural angle

Postural Angle	Range of movement (°)	Range of comfort (°)	Preferred (°)
Cervical Flexion	110-225	130-160	150
Left Elbow Angle	60-180	92-153	117.3
Left Hip Angle	65-120	99-115	105.9
Left Knee Angle	75-180	112-139	126

For the uncertain meaning of "comfort", triangular type membership function was introduced to depict the driver's feeling of comfort.

$$\mu(u) = \begin{cases} \dfrac{1}{b-a}(u-a), a \leq u \leq b \\ \dfrac{1}{b-c}(u-c), b \leq u \leq c \\ 0, \text{other} \end{cases} \qquad (7)$$

Form the table1 and Eq.7, we can get the Fuzzy membership function of comfort of each postural angle.

Table 2. Fuzzy membership function of comfort of postural angle

Postural Angle	Fuzzy membership function of comfort
Cervical Flexion	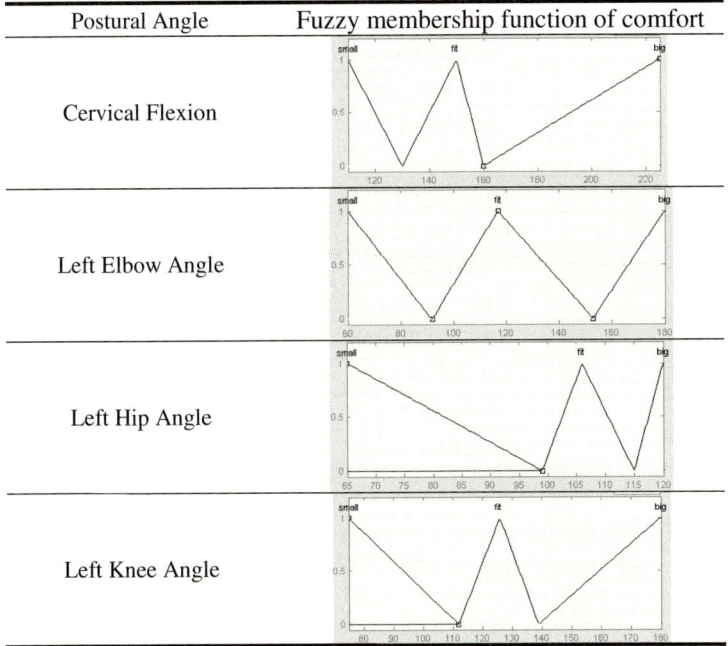
Left Elbow Angle	
Left Hip Angle	
Left Knee Angle	

3.3 The Relation Between Design Factors and Driver Comfort

Design factors selected and H/W affect each postural angle and then comfort. To get the relationship between design factors, H/M and the degree of each comfort for postural angle, thirty subjects participated in experiments [24], which measure the postural angle on different design parameter. The data acquired from these experiments was used for training set.

To apply Fuzzy SVM to get the relation between the driving posture parameters and relative design factor, at the first, we define driver comfort as three classes:

$$f[\phi(x)] = \text{sign}(w \cdot z_i + b) = \begin{cases} +1, & \text{if postural angle over the range of comfort} \\ 0, & \text{if postural angle between the range of comfort.} \\ -1, & \text{if postural angle below the range of comfort} \end{cases} \quad (8)$$

Where +1 indicates the postural angle should be decrease, 0 indicate the postural angle is fit and needn't change and -1 indicate the postural angle should be increase.

Base on Eq.7 and Table 2, we assign outputs of, say, +1, 0 and -1 to encode these three possible values for four categories, which were shown in table 3,

Table 3. Outputs of comfort about each postural angle

Class	Postural Angle	Definition
+1	Cervical Flexion	160<y≤225
	Left Elbow Angle	153<y≤180
	Left Hip Angle	115<y≤120
	Left Knee Angle	139<y≤180
0	Cervical Flexion	130≤y≤160
	Left Elbow Angle	92≤y≤153
	Left Hip Angle	99≤y≤115
	Left Knee Angle	112≤y≤139
-1	Cervical Flexion	110≤y<130
	Left Elbow Angle	60≤y<92
	Left Hip Angle	65≤y<99
	Left Knee Angle	75≤y<112

In this study, penalty parameter C was set as 10. From the range of classifications undertaken, a high overall accuracy (90.75%) was obtained from the SVM trained. And the degree of comfort/discomfort about each postural angle can be assessed by the distance between the xi and the hyperplane, which can be shown in:

$$g[\phi(x)] = w \cdot z_i + b \qquad (9)$$

3.4 Design Factors Changing Rule

From the SVM trained, the degree of comfort/discomfort about each postural angle can be get expediently. But in some instance, to get an appropriate driving posture, the comfort result should feed back to the design phase, and some design parameter changing rules should be built to ensure an appropriate driving posture.

- If more than one postural angle is out of the range of comfort, the changing sequence of postural angel was decided by numerical value of discomfort degree. The priority of postural angel with higher discomfit degree is over other factors.
- The design factors have no coupling relation, and so we can deal with single design factor each time. The changing sequence of design factors was decided by correlation coefficients for design factors and relative postural angle [24].

4 A Computer-Aided System Prototype Toward the Driving Postural Prediction

Based on above model, we formed a computer-aided driving posture prediction system, take a driver model as example, whose height is 1760mm and weight 62kg, and the H/C is calculated as 28.387, which is shown as figure 5:

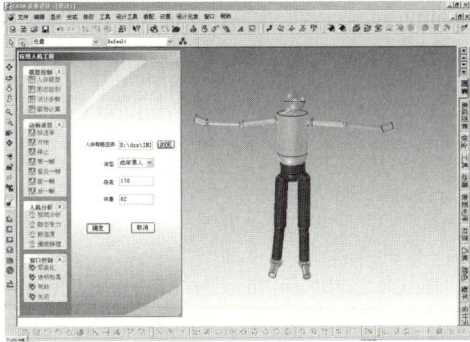

Fig. 5. Driver parameter enactment

Then a car model has been imported, its initial parameters are: SW Height=613mm, SCA=20°, SW to BOFX=300mm, which is shown as figure 6:

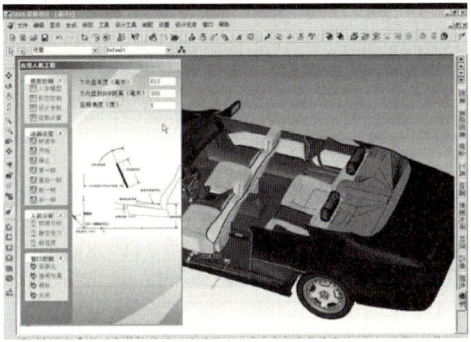

Fig. 6. Import car model

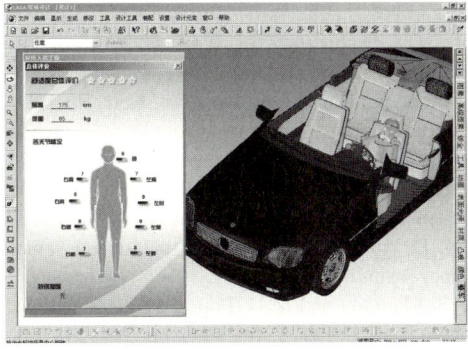

Fig. 7. Driver comfort emulation

From the classifications undertaken, we can get the class of each postural angle, and the degree of discomfort can be calculated by Eq.9.After three times computation base on design factors changing rule, an appropriate driving posture was gotten, and the relative design parameters are: SW Height=613mm, SCA=20°, SW to BOFX=300mm

5 Conclusion

The objective of this study was the application of driving comfort for the prediction of the driver's posture. At the first, triangular type membership function was introduced to depict the driver's feeling of comfort for the uncertain meaning of "comfort", and then a model was built to assess the relation between design parameters and comfort assessment based on Fuzzy SVM. To get an appropriate driving posture, the comfort result was feed back to the design phase and some design parameter changing rules were built. At the last, a computer-aided driving posture prediction system was formed. This method can also be used to solve other relative problems.

Acknowledgments. This work is supported by the National Natural Science Foundation of China (Grant No. 60475025), and Hubei Province Young Elitist Project (Grant No. 2002AC001).

References

1. D.E. Gyi, J.M. Porter and N.K.B. Robertson , Seat pressure measurement technologies: consideration for their evaluation. Appl. Ergon. 27 2 (1998), pp. 85–91.
2. J.M. Porter and D.E. Gyi , Interface pressure and the prediction of car seat discomfort. Int. J. Vehicle Des. 19 3 (1998), pp. 255–266.
3. L. Zhang, M.G. Helander and C.G. Drury , Indentifying factors of comfort and discomfort in sitting. Hum. Factors 38 3 (1996), pp. 377–389.
4. K. Ebe and M.J. Griffin , Factors affecting static seat cushion comfort. Ergonomics 44 10 (2001), pp. 901–921.
5. G.B.J. Andersson , Loads on the spine during sitting. In: N. Corlett, J. Wilson and I. Manenica, Editors, The Ergonomics of Working Postures, Taylor & Francis, London (1986), pp. 309–318.
6. Reynolds, H.M., Rayes, K., Eppler, M., Neal, D., Kerr, R., 1996. Development of vehicle laboratory to investigate driver comfort from physical measurements. SAE Technical Paper Series 960480.
7. Tilley, A.R., 1994. Le misure dell'uomo e della donna: dati di riferimento per il progetto. Henry Dreyfuss Associates - New York - Be-ma ed. Milan, Italy.
8. Ward, E., Southall, D., 1993. A technique for measuring vehicle seat interface pressure. SAE Technical Paper Series 930116
9. M.L. Magnusson, T. Hansson and M.H. Pope , The effect of seat back inclination on the spine height changes. Appl. Ergon. 25 5 (1994), pp. 294–298.
10. Z. Jianghong and T. Long , An evaluation of comfort of a bus seat. Appl. Ergon. 25 6 (1994), pp. 386–392.

11. Zhanxun Dong, Chunlei Chai, Yongchuan Tang, Driving Comfort Assessment Model Construction Based on Fuzzy Inference, The 6th World Congress on Intelligent Control and Automation, (2006)

12. Luo Shijian, Study of Driving Comfort Based on Biological Response, Zhejiang University, (2005).

13. Hanson, L., Wienholt, W., Sperling, L., A control handling comfort model based on fuzzy logics, International Journal of Industrial Ergonomics 31 (2), pp. 87-100

14. V. Vapnik. The Nature of Statistical Learning Theory, Springer, Berlin (1995).

15. C. Burges, Tutorial on support vector machines for pattern recognition. Data Mining Knowledge Discovery 2 2 (1998), pp. 955–974.

16. Chun-Fu Lin; Sheng-De Wang; Fuzzy support vector machines, Neural Networks, IEEE Transactions on Volume 13, Issue 2, March 2002 Page(s):464 - 471

17. M. L. Zhu, Y.Wang, S. F. Chen, and X. D. Liu, "Sphere-structured support vector machines for multi-class pattern recognition," Lecture Notes in Artificial Intelligence, vol. 2639, pp. 589–593, 2003.

18. C.-W. Hsu and C.-J. Lin, "A comparison of methods for multiclass support vector machines," IEEE Trans. Neural Networks, vol. 13, pp. 415–425, Mar. 2002.

19. Chai Chunlei, Research on Technology of Ergonomics Design based on Driving Posture Prediction Model, Zhejiang University, (2005).

20. Zhou Yiming, Mao Enrong, Ergonomics of Vehicle, Peking: Beijig Institute of Technology Press, (1999).

21. Se Jin Park, Chae-Bogk Kim, Chul Jung Kim and Jeong Woo Lee, Comfortable driving postures for Koreans, International Journal of Industrial Ergonomics Volume 26, Issue 4 , October 2000, Pages 489-497

Height-Based Deformation and Ray Supersampling for Colon Unfolding

Honam Ahn and Byeong-Seok Shin

[1] Department of Computer Science and Information Engineering, Inha University
253 Yonghyeon-Dong, Nam-Gu, Inchon, 402-751, Rep. of Korea
honami82@inhaian.net, bsshin@inha.ac.kr

Abstract. Virtual colon unfolding is a method to produce an unfold image from volume data. The previous method generates only 2D images casting rays from a central path toward the colon surface and maps the color value into 2D regular grid. However, since rays cannot be reached behind folds, some regions are not represented on the final image. In order to represent those areas adequately, we exploit a height field derived from ray casting. Since the problematic areas have high gradient in comparison to neighboring regions, the differences of height value in those areas are relatively large. Therefore, we can find problematic areas using the height field. To visualize those areas, we exploit supersampling method that casts additional rays toward perpendicular direction of the original rays. Experimental results show that our method represents colon folds accurately.

1   Introduction

Virtual endoscopy deals with the inspection of organ and anatomical cavities using computer graphics technology [1], [2], [3]. Virtual endoscopy has the potential of becoming a substitute of optical endoscopy for diagnostic procedures. Optical endo-scopy is invasive and, furthermore, involves a certain degree of risk for the patient. Most of the virtual endoscopy techniques concentrate on simulating the view of an optical endoscope. However, in order to examine entire colon, the virtual endoscopy requires frequent changes of a camera direction and position because it has a small field of view. Therefore, it takes a long time to find pathologies and it may lose im-portant features.

Unfolding is a noble method to compromise the problems of virtual endoscopy [4], [5], [6], [7], [8]. Unfolding method takes not much time as well as represents entire colon at a glance. Previous unfolding method generates 2D images casting rays on a central path toward the colon surface [6], [7], [8]. However, since the rays cannot reach behind folds, some regions are not represented adequately. We call it as *ray-shaded region*. One of the methods to avoid the possibility of producing erroneous areas is surface reconstruction methods [9]. However, they need complicated geomet-ric deformation after geometry reconstruction since the deformation step that changes the pipe-like colon mesh into the unfolded mesh takes a long time.

Z. Pan et al. (Eds.): ICAT 2006, LNCS 4282, pp. 1098 – 1107, 2006.

Our method solves problems of the conventional unfolding and surface reconstruction methods, simultaneously. Firstly, we perform the volume ray casting to get the distance values between a central path and the colon surface. We make a height field from the distance values. We can achieve better performance than surface reconstruction because it does not require complicated deformation. Then, we perform additional sampling on the problematic areas. Therefore, we can easily inspect the entire area of colon at a glance.

In Section 2, we briefly review the related work, and we illustrate our algorithm in detail in Section 3. Experimental results are presented in Section 4. Lastly, we conclude our work.

2   Related Work

The shape of colon cross-section dominates a performance of unfolding method. The simplest is oblique planes that are planar and orthogonal to the central path. However, it encounters a major problem in high-curvature areas of the central path, i.e., in some position where the radius of curvature is larger than the organ diameter. Because orthogonal cross-sections may intersect each other, it produces the double appearance of polyps or loss of significant features.

Wang et al. used electrical field lines generated by a locally charged path to govern curved cross-sections instead of the planar cross-sections [5]. The cross-sections tend to diverge avoiding conflicts. If the complete path is charged then the curved cross-sections will not intersect. However, for each point of the field lines the contribution of each charge in the path must be calculated. This operation is so computationally expensive that the authors proposed to just locally charge the path.

Vilanova et al. presented a non-linear ray casting method using a distance map [7]. A distance map is a volume data set whose voxels contain the distance to the nearest boundary point on the central path. Non-linear rays follow the negative gradient direction of the precalculated distance map. To compute a correct gradient direction, a trilinear interpolation must be performed. However, the access time to the distance map in a trilinear interpolation process is too long.

Another method is to cast straight rays, called radial ray casting [8]. It requires less computations and a little memory. It uses control points that are the part of sample points on a central path, and planar sections (ray-plane) are generated from the control points. The intersection test is performed in between ray planes, and ray directions are adjusted when intersections occur. The ray directions for remaining sample points are determined by interpolation according to the distance of neighboring control points. Although the method reduces the rendering time, it cannot perfectly solve intersection problems because intersection tests are performed only on control points not entire sample points.

The previous unfolding methods may produce the *ray-shaded regions* [4], [5], [6], [7], [8]. A ray-shaded region is an area where the rays cannot be reached. Especially, since the colon surface is composed of lots of folds, this problem occurs frequently.

Surface reconstruction methods do not generate the ray-shaded regions [9], because they convert volume data into an intermediate surface representation. The representative algorithm for surface reconstruction is Marching Cubes. However, this method takes a long time to perform the complicated geometric deformation procedure.

3   Colon Unfolding Method

Our method is composed of two parts: height-field generation process and height-based deformation process. Fig. 1 shows the block diagram of our method. Since the height-field generation process is similar to the previous work proposed by Lee et al. [8] except for generation of height field from the distance value between a central path and the colon surface. Therefore, we explain the height-based deformation process in detail.

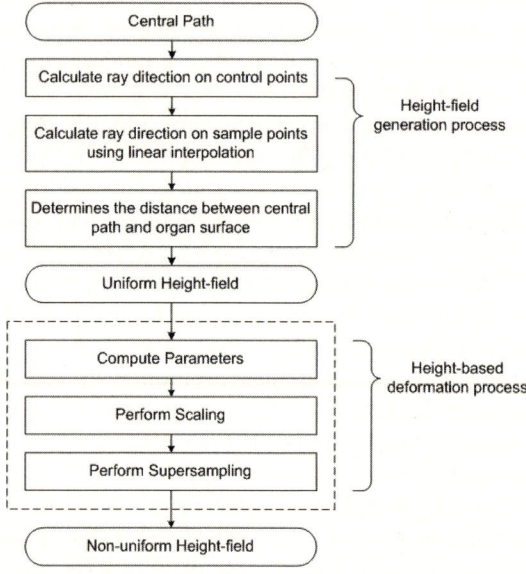

Fig. 1. Overview of our method. Our method is composed of two main parts; height-field generation process and height-based deformation process.

Firstly, we calculate a distance between boundary points for consecutive rays. In the scaling step, we adjust the length of the edges on the grid in the uniform height field by considering the distances between boundary points. Ray-shaded regions are identified in this step. In order to get the geometric information on those areas adequately, we determine new starting points and directions for additional rays. Then, we perform additional volume ray casting.

3.1 Computing Distance Between Boundary Points

A ray $R_{i,j}$ is fired from a point c_i on the central path toward the colon surface. $s_{i,j}$ is the boundary point of colon surface hit by $R_{i,j}$. The first index i corresponds to the order of points along the central path and the second index j is the order of ray fired from c_i. The parameter space is sampled uniformly in the i and j direction, but this does not

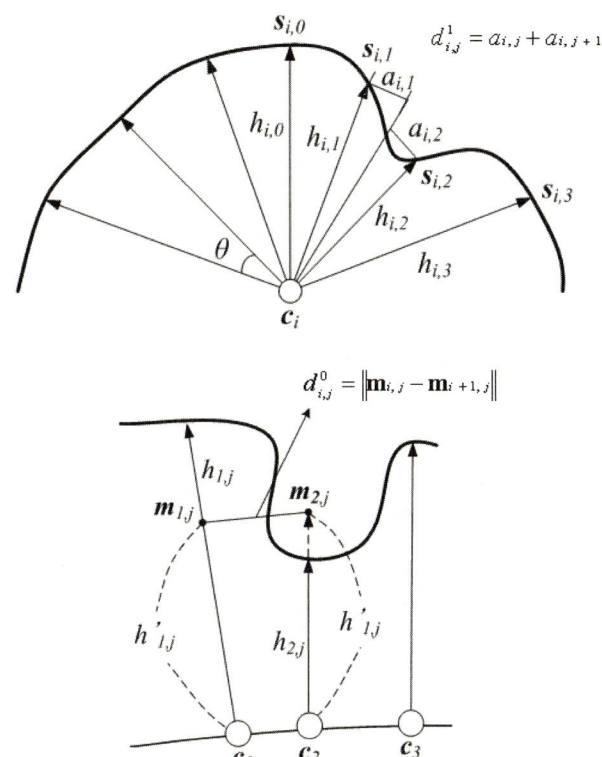

Fig. 2. Computing parameter d. it illustrates computation in the j direction (top), and computation in the i direction (bottom)

correspond to a uniform sampling of $s_{i,j}$. We desire that the unfolded height field preserves the length of the edges of $s_{i,j}$ in i and j direction and, therefore, we also preserve the area [7].

To calculate the edge lengths, we use different approximations for the i and j direction. In the j direction (see Fig. 2), each sample represents a length approximated by

$$a_{i,j} = \tan\left(\frac{\theta}{2}\right) * h_{i,j}. \tag{1}$$

Where θ is the angle between the straight rays from the path to $s_{i,j}$ and $s_{i,j+1}$. The edge distance between two consecutive samples in the j direction is approximated by

$$d^1_{i,j} = a_{i,j} + a_{i,j+1}. \tag{2}$$

This equation cannot be used for the i direction since angle θ is not defined. Therefore, in the i direction the following expression is used.

$$h'_{i,j} = \frac{h_{i,j} + h_{i+1,j}}{2}.$$

$$\mathbf{m}_{i,j} = \mathbf{c}_i + \frac{\mathbf{s}_{i,j} - \mathbf{c}_i}{h_{i,j}} * h'_{i,j}. \tag{3}$$

$$d^0_{i,j} = \left\| \mathbf{m}_{i,j} - \mathbf{m}_{i+1,j} \right\|.$$

Using Eq. (2) and Eq. (3), we have defined the length of the edges of the grid such that the unfolded height field preserves the length of the edges of $s_{i,j}$.

3.2 Scaling

In this step, we generate a non-uniform height field using the parameters $d^k_{i,j}$. We used a method proposed by Vilanova et al [7] for scaling. The scaling algorithm starts from a uniform height field. Assuming that $D^k_{i,j}$ is the length of edge between consecutive grid points of the height field. $e^k_{i,j}$ is a difference between $D^k_{i,j}$ and $d^k_{i,j}$. The edge of grid is adjusted by the difference of $D^k_{i,j}$ and $d^k_{i,j}$.

The convergence factor σ is measured by Eq. (4). The iteration stops, when σ becomes smaller than the predefined threshold value or no considerable improvement occurs anymore. Given a grid of size M×N, the convergence factor σ is defined as follows.

$$\sigma = \sqrt{\frac{\sum_{j=0}^{M-1}\sum_{i=0}^{N-2} e^0_{i,j} + \sum_{j=0}^{M-2}\sum_{i=0}^{N-1} e^1_{i,j}}{2MN - M - N}}. \tag{4}$$

3.3 Supersampling

The ray-shaded regions are easily identifiable from the scaled height fields since those areas have high gradient values. In order to present the ray-shaded regions correctly in the final image, we perform supersampling for those areas.

When the difference of height value in a grid is larger than the predefined interval t, we regard the region as a ray-shaded region. We set the predefined interval t as size of a voxel. When the difference of height value is smaller than one voxel, it means that any significant features are not missed.

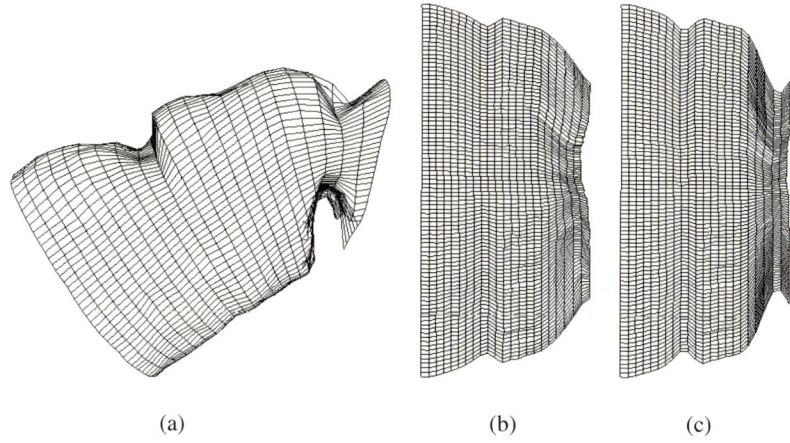

(a)   (b)   (c)

Fig. 3. Illustration of result of applying the scaling algorithm. (a) a 3D mesh before unfolding. (b) after 50 iterations. (c) after 222 iterations.

(a)   (b)

Fig. 4. Identifying a ray-shaded region. (a) non-uniform height field obtained by scaling. (b) blank regions indicate the ray-shaded areas. The difference of height value in those areas is bigger than one voxel. In the gray region, the difference of height value is smaller than one voxel.

For supersampling, the number of additional rays is approximated by Eq. (5), where $0 < t <= 1$.

$$count = \frac{\left|h_{i,\,j} - h_{i+1,\,j}\right|}{t}.$$ (5)

When the computed *count* value is greater than 1, this area is regarded as a ray-shaded region, and our method cast additional rays. So, the additional rays are cast toward i direction. If $h_{i,j}$ is greater than $h_{i+1,j}$, the position of additional ray is approximated by Eq. (7), otherwise Eq. (8) , where $k \in [1, count]$, sp_k is starting points of additional rays. Additional rays are cast toward tp_k.

$$q = h_{i+1,j} + \frac{|h_{i,j} - h_{i+1,j}|}{count} \times k .$$

(6)

$$\mathbf{sp}_k = \mathbf{c}_i + (\mathbf{s}_{i,j} - \mathbf{c}_i) \times \frac{q}{h_{i,j}} .$$

$$\mathbf{tp}_k = \mathbf{c}_{i+1} + (\mathbf{s}_{i+1,j} - \mathbf{c}_{i+1}) \times \frac{q}{h_{i,j}} .$$

(7)

$$\mathbf{sp}_k = \mathbf{c}_{i+1} + (\mathbf{s}_{i+1,j} - \mathbf{c}_{i+1}) \times \frac{q}{h_{i+1,j}} .$$

$$\mathbf{tp}_k = \mathbf{c}_i + (\mathbf{s}_{i,j} - \mathbf{c}_i) \times \frac{q}{h_{i+1,j}} .$$

(8)

Subsequently, we compute the direction of additional rays. The direction of the rays is approximated by Eq. (9).

$$\mathbf{dir}_k = \mathbf{tp}_k - \mathbf{sp}_k .$$

(9)

Then, we perform the volume ray casting, and add the new points in height field. After supersampling, we can construct the height field that contains the shapes of the shaded-regions.

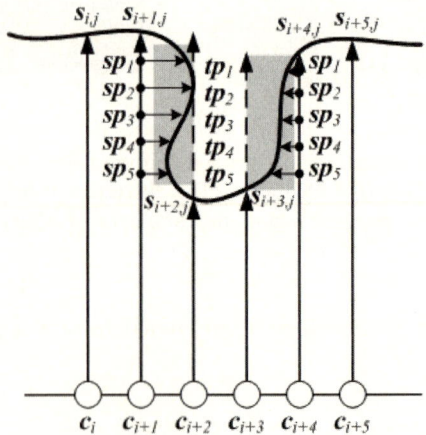

Fig. 5. An example of ray supersampling. Gray regions indicate ray-shaded areas.

4 Experimental Results

Our method is implemented on a PC equipped with Intel Pentium 4 2.6GHz and 1 GB main memory. The volume dataset of which the resolution is $512 \times 512 \times 271$ is used.

We randomly set the number of sample points as 352, 1108 and 2004. We exploit 360 rays per sample point. Table 1 shows the comparison of time to perform scaling and supersampling. To generate uniform height field does not need additional costs because the height values are already computed in volume ray casting step. The time for supersampling is shorter than ray casting time because the supersampling is performed on the small part of height field. In addition, since a result of our method is an unfolded height field, to render it can be performed on GPU. Fig. 6 shows the ray-shaded regions and the results by applying supersampling

Table 1. The time to perform scaling and supersampling

sample points	ray casting (sec)	iterations	scaling (sec)	supersampling (sec)
352	1.203	167	8.654	0.234
1108	3.235	203	28.347	1.281
2004	5.469	178	44.251	2.625

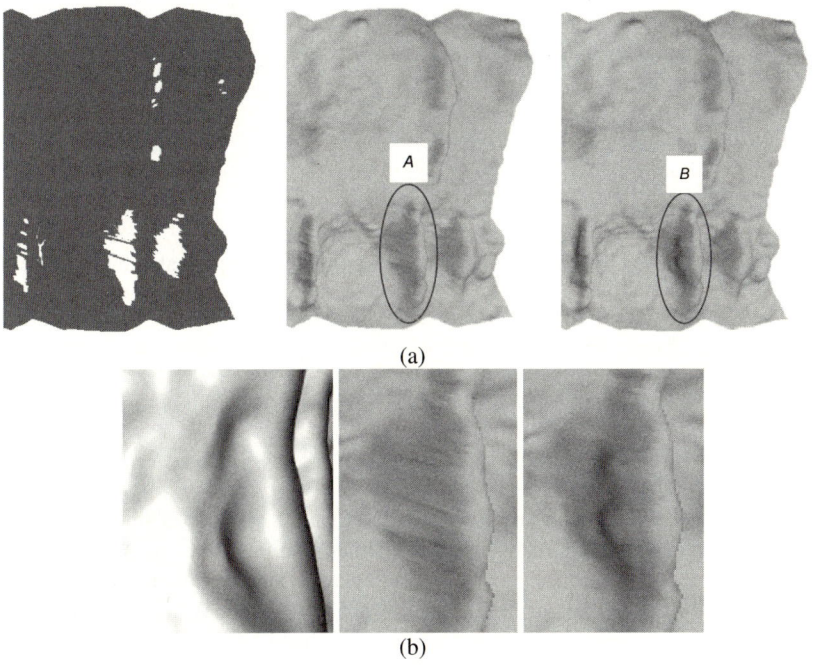

(a)

(b)

Fig. 6. A result produced by our method. A ray-shaded region is represented by supersampling adequately. (a) blank regions indicate the ray-shaded regions (left). A non-uniform height field obtained by scaling (center). A non-uniform height field obtained by supersampling (right). (b) Virtual endoscopy image (left). An image magnifying a region A (center). An image magnifying a region B (right).

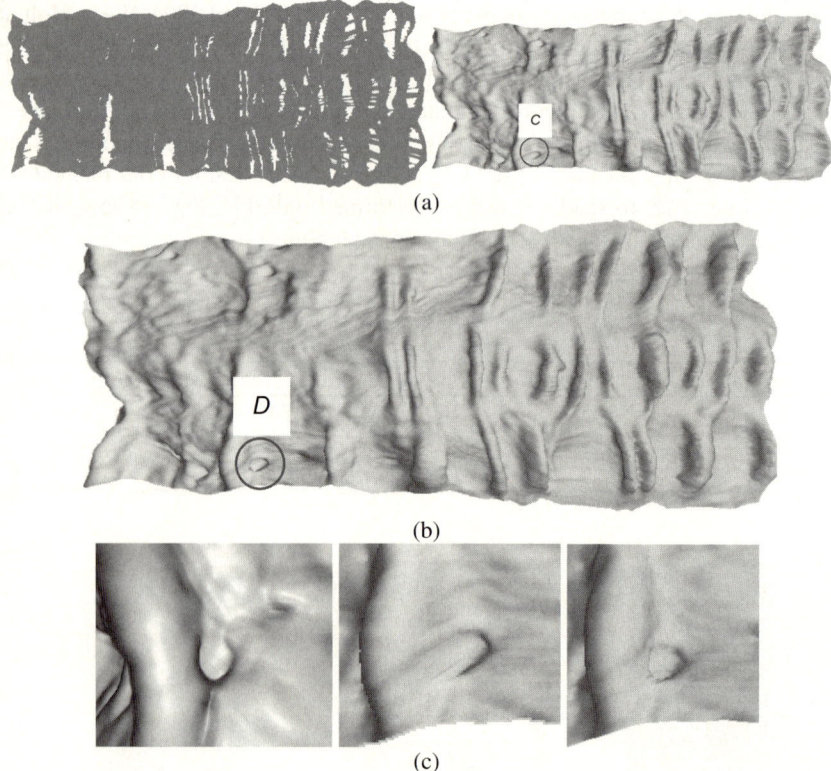

Fig. 7. A result produced by our method. A ray-shaded region is represented by supersampling adequately. (a) blank regions indicate the ray-shaded regions (left). A non-uniform height field obtained by scaling (right). (b) A non-uniform height field obtained by supersampling. (c) Virtual endoscopy image (left). An image magnifying a region C (center). An image magnifying a region D (right).

5   Conclusion

We proposed an efficient colon unfolding method that can solves problems both conventional unfolding and surface reconstruction methods simultaneously. We can achieve better performance than surface reconstruction because it does not require complicated deformation. We exploit a height field derived from ray casting. We can find problematic areas using the height field, and those areas are visualized by supersampling method. In addition, we can easily diagnose pathologies because our method requires simple camera operation. Therefore, our method is useful for a fast and accurate diagnosis.

Acknowledgment

This work was supported by grant No. RTI05-03-01 from the Regional Technology Innovation Program of the Ministry of Commerce, Industry and Energy(MOCIE).

References

1. Levoy, M.: Display of surface from volume data. IEEE Computer Graphics and Applications, Vol. 8. No. 3. (1988) 29-37
2. Hong, L., Kaufman, A., Wei, Y., Viswambharan, A., Wax, M., Liang, Z.: 3D Virtual Colonoscopy. IEEE Symposium on Biomedical Visualization (1995) 26-32
3. Sabella, A.: A rendering algorithm or visualizing 3D scalar fields. Computer Graphics, Vol. 22, No. 4. (1988) 51-58
4. Wang, G., Vannier, M. W.: GI tract unraveling by spiral CT. In Proceedings SPIE, Vol. 2423. (1995) 307-315
5. Wang, G., Dave, S.B., Brown, B.P., Zhang, Z., McFarland, E.G., Haller, J.W., Vannier, M.W.: Colon unraveling based on electrical field: Recent progress and further work. In proceedings SPIE, Vol. 3660. (1999) 125-132
6. Vilanova, A., Wegenkittl, R., Kőnig, A., Gröller, E., Sorantin, E.: Virtual colon flattening. Proc. VisSym '01 Joint Eurographics – IEEE TCVG Symposium on Visualization (2001) 127-136
7. Vilanova, A., Wegenkittl, R., Kőnig, A., Gröller, E.: Nonlinear Virual Colon Unfolding. IEEE Visualization (VIS) (2001) 411-579
8. Lee, H.J., Lim, S.H., Shin, B.S.: Unfolding of Virtual Endoscopy Using Ray-Template. In Proceedings ISBMDA, Vol. 3745. (2005) 69-77
9. Lorensen, W.E., Cline, H.E.: Marching Cubes: A high resolution 3D surface construction algorithm. In Proceedings SIGGRAPH (1987) 163-169

Content-Based Retrieval of Cultural Relic Images in Digital Museum[*]

Tongwei Ren[1,2] and Gangshan Wu[1,2]

[1] State Key Laboratory for Novel Software Technology, Nanjing University,
Nanjing, 210093
[2] Department of Computer Science and Technology, Nanjing University, Nanjing, 210093
rentw@graphics.nju.edu.cn

Abstract. With the popularization of digital museum, effective retrieval in huge image databases of special domain has attracted much research attention. As an effect approach, corresponding semantic information is adopted in many retrieval systems. However, most cultural relic retrieval systems only supply the explicit use of semantic information. It requires the user to be professional in this domain. In this paper, we propose a novel relevance feedback method which combines semantic annotation to visual feature implicitly. With this method, the user can unknowingly use professional semantic information to retrieve images. We also do some improvement in feature extraction and similarity measurement methods to fit the retrieval basis of unprofessional user better. The experiment results show that our approach is effective and efficient.

Keywords: Content-Based Image Retrieval, cultural relic image, relevance feedback, implicit combination.

1 Introduction

With the popularization, digital museum becomes more and more important in knowledge acquiring for commonalty. Effective retrieval in the huge image databases has been an active research area in the past few years. Differing from general image sources, the image databases in digital museum focus on special domains, and the corresponding semantic information plays an important role in retrieval. So the combination of visual feature and semantic information is accepted as an effective approach. In cultural relic image retrieval, several approaches have been proposed.

Li et al. presented an approach for Dunhuang fresco in [1], which selected color, element shape and layout as the visual features and supplied semantic-based retrieval by keywords. Wei et al. presented a retrieval approach for cultural relic image database in [2], which extracted 19 features from preprocessed images and supplied retrieval based on example image and keywords. However, the above approaches only make the explicit use of the semantic information, which may be invalid when the user does not have enough professional knowledge in this domain.

---

[*] Supported by the National Natural Science Foundation of China under Grant No.60533080.

Z. Pan et al. (Eds.): ICAT 2006, LNCS 4282, pp. 1108–1117, 2006.

To conquer the weakness, we proposed a relevance feedback method which combines the semantic annotation to visual feature implicitly. In this method, semantic annotation is not presented but automatically analyzed based on feedback during the whole retrieval procedure. Considering visual feeling is the most important basis in requirement description and feedback operation for unprofessional user, we analyze the visual related characters of cultural relic images in digital museum, and do some improvements in feature extraction and similarity measurement to fit human-vision characters better. Finally, we implement a prototype system, and evaluate it according to the analysis of the retrieval model classification in digital museum. The experiment results show our system is efficient in all application conditions.

The rest of paper is organized as follows. Section 2 analyzes the characters of cultural relic images and the retrieval models in digital museum. Section 3 describes the preprocessing, feature extraction and similarity measurement approaches. Section 4 proposes a novel relevance feedback method combining semantic annotation to visual feature implicitly. Section 5 evaluates the retrieval approach, and presents the experiment results. Finally, Section 6 concludes the paper and provides future research directions.

2   Analysis

For visual feeling usually plays the most important role in requirement description and feedback operation for unprofessional user, we analyze the visual-related characters of cultural relic images in digital museum. Based on the analysis, we improve the feature extraction and similarity measurement methods to fit human vision characters better. We also analysis the classification of retrieval models in digital museum and design our experiment based on it.

2.1   Visual-Related Image Characters

For the characters of cultural relic and strict capture criterion, the cultural relic images in digital museums are normative and have the following visual-related characters:

- Centered object region and simplex background. To emphasize the exhibit, the exhibit usually lies near the center position and the background has simplex visual characters. The large proportion of background provides the requirement to eliminate background before feature extraction.
- Transform relations between object regions. To display the exhibit fully, several images are usually captured for the same exhibit from different directions or positions. The object regions in these images have translation, rotation, scaling or reflection relations. The relations require the visual feature descriptors to be invariable in the above aspects.
- Complex visual characters of object region. Various properties of cultural relic bring the great varieties in color, texture or shape between different exhibits. The complexities in visual characters require the features descriptors should be particular and adaptive to human vision characters.

Based on the analysis, the visual features should be extracted from object region and the descriptors should fit human vision characters and have good invariance.

2.2 Retrieval Models for Digital Museum

Base on the conclusion in [3], we classify the retrieval models in digital museum into three classes:

- ◆ Certain exhibit searching. The aim may be a certain cultural relic in user impression. Just the images of the exhibit fit the user's requirements.
- ◆ Category retrieval. The aim is searching for a special category of cultural relics which are close in appearance, material or function. And each exhibit in this category belongs to the result set.
- ◆ Browsing. The user starts his search without specific aim and modifies the aim by operating on result set.

In actual retrievals of each model, the unprofessional users usually describe their requirements by approximate image or sketch than professional keywords, and the visual feeling is always emphasized more than professional characters in object characters' description.

3 Content-Based Retrieval

Based on the analysis in 2.1, we preprocess the images by a background-forecast method and extracted visual features from object region by the improved descriptors. Then we normalize the feature vectors by Guassian model and measure the similarities by Quadratic distance and Euclidean distance.

3.1 Preprocessing

The purpose of preprocessing is eliminating the infection of background to feature extraction. Based on the background and layout characters of cultural relic images in digital museum, we propose a background-forecast method as follows:

Input: original gray image
Output: segmented matrix, in which the open-pixel set denotes the object region and the close-pixel set denotes the background region
Procedure:

1. Divide the original image into 8×8 blocks.
2. Assume the blocks on board as "background block", and compute the mean gray level of each background block as "block value".
3. Assume threshold d_G, select a block with 3 neighboring background blocks, and compute $\overline{bValue}$ as the mean value of their block values. Select the pixels whose gray level g satisfies $|g - \overline{bValue}| < d_G$, and assign the mean value of these pixels' gray levels to block value of this block. If no such pixels, assign $\overline{bValue}$ to the block value.
4. Repeat step 3 to compute the block value of each block.

5. Create the forecasted background in the same size of original image, and the gray level of each pixel equals the block value of the block which it lies in. Smooth the forecasted background by linear smooth filter.
6. Do minus operation on the original image by the forecasted background, and smooth the result by linear smoother filter.
7. Binarize the smoothed result, and get the segmented matrix. Finish.

The experiments show that the obvious difference between background and object is not always represented in gray level. It may be represented in any component of HSV model. So the above algorithm is carried out on each component of HSV model, and the best segmented matrix is automatically selected by evaluating the following aspects:

♦ The inner-aggregation property of object region and background region. It is measured by the standard deviations of object region and background region.
♦ The difference between object region and background region. It is measured by the difference between the mean values of object region and background region.
♦ The area proportion and location of object region. The area proportion is computed and measured whether larger than a pre-assumed threshold p_{area}.
And location is measured by the distance between the centroid position of object region and the center position of image.

The proposed method can deal with the cultural relic with holes and get a good effect in experiment. Fig. 1 shows a sample of preprocessing consequence.

Fig. 1. Preprocessing Consequence

3.2 Feature Extraction

In this paper, we describe the visual feature of cultural relics by color, texture and shape. Based on the analysis in 0, we select the descriptors with good invariance and improve them to fit human-vision characters better.

In order to describe color feature, we select HSV model as color space and quantize it based on human-vision characters. We divide the color space into four parts as black, white, gray and bright color [4], and quantize the gray part and bright color part [5] further. In this way, the color space is quantized uniformly into 21 levels. Then we select color histogram as the primary descriptor and dominant color as the assistant descriptor of color feature. The experiment results show the combined color feature can emphasize the major factors in color comparison by human.

We select Co-occurrence Matrix to represent the texture feature of object region, and test the 14 descriptors [6] on rotation invariance, scaling invariance, clustering ability and partition ability. We carry out the test on 1536 images of 24 classes, which belong to Brodatz Album image library. The result show that F_{con}, F_{cor}, F_{ssv}, F_{sv}, F_{se}, F_{dv} and F_{de} have good performance in the above four aspects. We prove that F_{cor} and F_{ssv} are identical. So we compute four co-occurrence matrixes of each image on direction (0,1), (-1,1), (1,0) and (-1,-1), and calculate the rest six descriptors of each matrix. Then we compute the mean value and the standard deviation of the four values by each descriptor. Finally, we use the 12 values as the texture feature descriptor.

We select Hu Invariant Moment to represent the shape feature. We test the variances of translation, rotation, scaling and reflection of Hu Invariant Moment on the above image library. The results show ϕ_1 to ϕ_6 have good performance in the above four aspects, and ϕ_7 is invariable in the previous three aspects but not invariable in reflection. We prove the shortage of ϕ_7 in reflection is caused by its definition, and use the absolute value of ϕ_7 instead of it. Finally, we use the values of ϕ_1 to ϕ_7 as the shape feature descriptor.

3.3 Similarity Measurement

According to the relativities between the components, we use different similarity measurement methods.

To color feature, it is obvious that the relativities among each color are not the same, i.e. red is more similar to orange than purple. So we use Quadratic distance to measure the similarity of colors:

$$d^2 = (c_i - c_j) A (c_i - c_j)^T .$$

(1)

where $A(i, j)$ denotes the similarity between color i and color j. In order to compute the color similarity matrix, we divide the color space into bright colors and un-bright colors (black, gray and white). To bright colors, we only consider the hue component, and compute the similarity between color i and color j as follows:

$$A(i, j) = \frac{\int_{iStart}^{iEnd} \int_{jStart}^{jEnd} \Delta\phi(x,y)\, dx\, dy}{\int_{iStart}^{iEnd} x\, dx \int_{jStart}^{jEnd} y\, dy} .$$

(2)

where x is an arbitrary legal hue value of color i and y is the same to color j, and $\Delta\phi(x, y)$ is defined as follows:

$$\Delta\phi(x,y) = \begin{cases} 2 \times |x-y|, & |x-y| \leq 0.5 \\ 2 \times (1-|x-y|), & |x-y| > 0.5 \end{cases} .$$

(3)

We compute the similarity between un-bright colors on their value component, and assume the similarity between any bright color and un-bright color is zero.

We compute the dominant color distance d' using the same expression, and modify the previous distance in proportion to the value of d'. If the modified value overflows, we intercept it and let it in the range [0,1].

It is consented that the components of texture feature vector extracting from co-occurrence matrix are independent. So we use Euclidean distance to measure texture similarity. However, the experiment results show that the magnitudes of each component are obvious different. In order to exactly control the contribution to similarity measurement of each component, we use Guassian model [7] to normalize each component as follows:

$$t_i' = \frac{t_i - m}{6\sigma} + 0.5 \;. \tag{4}$$

where m denotes the mean value of the values of the component, and σ denotes the standard deviation. After the processing, 99% of texture vector component values will fall in the range [0,1], and the rest will be intercepted. In order to get available values of m and σ for changing retrieval circumstance, we make a training set with enough size and complexity, and compute the distances on each component of any image couple. Based on this, we compute m and σ values of each component.

For the component of shape feature vector extracting by Hu invariant moment is also consented independent, we use the same method to process shape feature vector and measure the similarity.

For the numbers of vector components of each feature are not the same, color, texture and shape similarities make different contributions in the integrated similarity measurement. We solve the problem by the above method. After the processing, each feature makes the same contribution to similarity measurement in default condition. In actual retrieval, the user can modify the priority of each feature to satisfy the retrieval requirements.

4 Relevance Feedback

Based on the normalization of annotation in digital museum, we extract the cultural relic property descriptions from image annotation automatically. Then we combine extracted semantic information to visual feature in relevance feedback implicitly and use clustering method to refine user requirements iteratively.

4.1 Visual Feature Clustering

To simplify the problem, we assume the user choose all related images. So the chosen images compose the positive example set, and the rest compose the negative example set. We use a 63×10 vector to present the modified requirement vector (the dimension of original feature vector is 63), which is composed of the value range and mean value of both positive example set and negative example set, positive weight, negative weight, and overlapping value region of each component. The algorithm is as follows:

Input: the visual feature vector sets of positive examples and negative examples
Output: modified requirement vector
Procedure:
1. Count the positive example number N_{pos} and the negative example number N_{neg}.
2. Select a component as the processing component, and order the value sequences on this component in positive examples and negative examples respectively.
3. To positive value sequence, process as follows:
   ♦ Assume threshold p_{num}, select the closest $N_{pos} \times p_{num}$ values, and compute the average distance $\bar{d}_{pos}$ of the selected range.
   ♦ Assume threshold α, for each left value, if distance between it and any boundary value of the selected range is less than $\alpha \times \bar{d}_{pos}$, add it into the range. And repeat the step till no available values left.
   ♦ Modify the range by the value in original requirement vector and history retrieval data, and the result is the positive value range on the component.
   ♦ Compute the mean value of positive value range m_{pos}.
4. Compute the negative value range and m_{neg} as the above steps.
5. Compute the overlapping range.
6. If the overlapping range is null, assign 1 to positive weight w_{pos} and -1 to negative weight w_{neg}. Otherwise, compute the proportions of overlapping range in positive value range and negative value range. Assume threshold p_{over}, assign 0 to the weight if the corresponding proportion is lager than p_{over}, or compute the weight according to the proportion.
7. Repeat step 2 to step 6, compute the values on each component. Finish.

Since the modified retrieval vector becomes a set of weight and value range, a new similarity measurement is required. After modification, each component affects the similarity independently. So we compute the effect of each component and compute the similarity as follows:

$$d = \sum_{i=1}^{63} e_i. \tag{5}$$

where e_i denotes the effect of component i, which is computed as follows:
   ♦ If the retrieval value falls in the positive range (not including overlapping range), assign w_{pos} to e_i.
   ♦ If the retrieval value falls in the negative range (not including overlapping range), assign w_{neg} to e_i.
   ♦ If the retrieval value falls in the overlapping range, compute e_i according to the distances from the retrieval value to m_{pos} and m_{neg}.

4.2 Implicit Combination with Semantic Annotation

Considering the annotations of culture relic images are normal in format and description, we extract some properties of exhibit as the feature. We select the properties which are described by normative and finite word sets, i.e. the material of cultural relics are described by the word set {Jade, Stone, Copper, …}. We describe such property by a vector which is composed of the candidate values, and describe any value of the property by assigning 1 to the corresponding component value (the default value of each component is 0).

The annotation feature vector is also modified during relevance feedback. Unlike visual feature vector, each component of the annotation feature vector is only two candidate values: 0 or 1. That means the value range and mean value are worthless here. So we use the positive weight w_{pos} and negative weight w_{neg} to present the modified annotation feature vector. The algorithm is as follows:

Input: the visual feature vector sets of positive examples and negative examples
Output: modified requirement vector
Procedure:
1. Assume threshold N_0, count the "1" value numbers N_i on each component in the return set.
2. If only one component is hit, let its $w_{pos}=1$ and $w_{neg}=1$. Process the rest components as follows: if $N_i<N_0$, treat the component as low- probability component, and let $w_{pos}=w_{neg}=0$; if $N_i \geq N_0$, let $w_{pos}=0$ and $w_{neg}=-1$. Finish. Otherwise, go to step 3.
3. Compute the current precision P. To each component, if $N_i<N_0$, let $w_{pos}=w_{neg}=0$; otherwise, process it as follows: compute its hit rates h_i on each component, if $h_i \geq P$, let $w_{pos}=(h_i-P)/(1-P)$ and $w_{neg}=0$; if $h_i<P$, let $w_{neg}=(h_i-P)/P$ and $w_{pos}=0$. Finish.

In similarity measurement, the effect of a component equals the nonzero one of w_{pos} and w_{neg}. If both of them are zero, then assign 0 to the effect value.

5 Experiment

We evaluate the performance of proposed approach based on the analysis in 0. We select 1680 high quality cultural relic images from the archeology digital museum of Northwest University, which contain the cultural relics of different classes. We obtain 50 nonstandard cultural relic images from internet and draw 50 sketches by hand, and combine them to be the test set. Fig. 2 shows a sample of retrieving roof tile by sketch, in which the left part shows the sketch and corresponding segmented image and the right part shows the retrieval result. Fig. 3 shows the relation between average retrieval precision and relevance feedback times. The experiment results show that our approach is effective and efficient in each retrieval model.

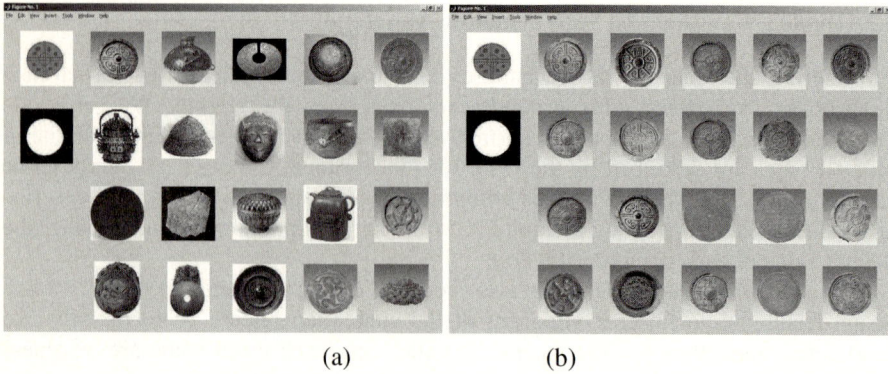

(a)   (b)

Fig. 2. A Sample of Retrieving by Sketch. (a) shows retrieval result before relevance feedback, and (b) shows retrieval result after 3 times relevance feedback.

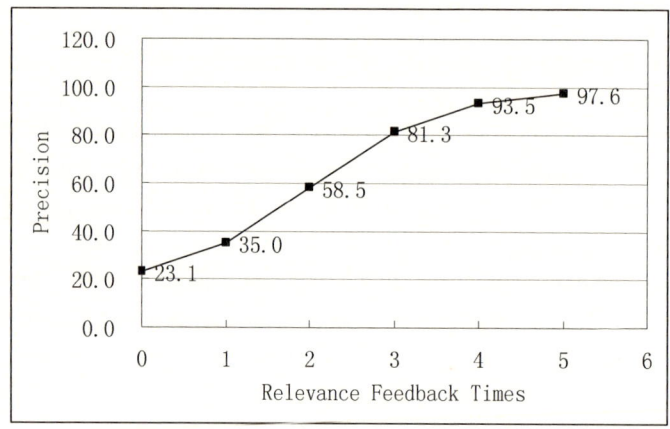

Fig. 3. Consequence Broken line diagram

6   Conclusion and Future Work

In this paper, we present a solution of making implicit use of semantic information in cultural relic image retrieval in digital museum. We propose a relevance feedback method which combines semantic annotation to visual feature implicitly. We also do some improvement in visual feature extraction and similarity measurement to fit unprofessional users' retrieval basis better. The experiment results show our approach is effective and efficient.

Our research will continue to improve the performance of relevance feedback method in part-feedback condition and to implement the auto-partition of user's retrieval model.

Acknowledgments. Our research is funded by Digital Museum of Chinese Universities and China Digital Science and Technology Museum.

References

1. X.Y. Li, D.M. Lu, Y.H. Pan, "Color Restoration and Image Retrieval for Dunhuang Fresco Preservation", Multimedia, IEEE, 7(2):38-42, 2000.
2. N. Wei, M.E. Celebi, G.H. Geng, "Content Based Retrieval and Classification of Cultural Relic Images", Proceedings of the Second International Symposium on Neural Network, Chongqing, 2005.
3. I.J. Cox, M.L. Miller, T.P. Minka, T.V. Papathomas, "The Bayesian Image Retrieval System, PicHunter: Theory, Implementation, and Psychophysical Experiments", IEEE Transactions on Image Processing, 9(1):20-37, 2000.
4. D. Androutsos, K.N. Plataniotis, A.N. Venetsanopoulos, "Image Retrieval Using the Directional Detail Histogram", Proceeding of SPIE, 3312:129-137, 1997.
5. Y.M. Tian, G.S. Lin, "Retrieval Technique of Color Image Based on Color Features", Journal of XiDian University, 29(1):43-46, 2002.
6. R.M. Haralick, K. Shanmugam, I. Dinstein, "Textural Features for Image Classification", IEEE Transactions on Systems, Man, and Cybernetics, SMC3:610-621, 1973.
7. H.Y. Lee, H.K. Lee, Y.H. Ha, "Spatial Color Descriptor for Image Retrieval and Video Segmentation", IEEE Transactions on Multimedia, 5(3):358-367, 2003.

Virtual Biology Modeling Method Based on Validity Confirmation Mechanism

Ying Liang, Wen-Yong Wang, Shao-Chun Zhong,Qing-Rong Zhang, Yao Wang,
Xiao-Lin Quan, and Qian Xu

Institute of Ideal Information Technology, Northeast Normal University,
JiLin, ChangChun 130024
sczhong@sina.com, gaoren1998@163.com

Abstract. The problem of the existing constructing process for virtual biology model is that it is not analyzed whether the enacted initial condition of the judgment model is reasonable or satisfying with the natural biological rule. Based on this, we propose an idea to construct the virtual biology model using validity confirmation mechanism method. The novel mothod considers both the complexity of the system model, and the characteristics of alternation and cooperation between various essential factors. The feasibility of the new mechanism is confirmed in the biology teaching.

Keywords: virtual biology model; valid confirmation; model match; similarity appraisal; teaching confirmation.

1 Introduction

In recent years, along with the overlapping and rapid development between many kinds of subjects and computer graphics, visually describing other subjects by means of graphics has become hot spot. Along with the unceasing consummation of 3-D data gain equipment function, as well as the development of modeling technology, the virtual biology model auxiliary applied in the class has achieved a more ideal effect. But the problem is that the initial condition hypothesis in the model structured by students and teacher may not satisfy the natural structure rule. In order to avoid this, this paper proposes a new modeling mechanism.

2 Concept of Virtual Biology Model

2.1 Concept of Model

The "model", is refers to a simulation form of prototype, i.e., system structure shape or movement shape which the virtual prototype needs to study). The model is the prototype substitute created by people in order to study some object (prototype). The model has double status: One, it is a tool or a method by which the main body studies the object; The other, it is also a substitute of studying the object. Therefore, the model is a special intermediary between the main body and the object.

Z. Pan et al. (Eds.): ICAT 2006, LNCS 4282, pp. 1118–1127, 2006.

2.2 Concept of Virtual Biology

Since 1980's, the European and American countries have started to surge up the simulation of natural biology with the computer medium. This new artificial system is so-called "virtual biology". The virtual biology research is refers to the artificial system research taking the computer as a medium and computer program as biology. Therefore, the virtual biology research is an important domain of artificial life research.

So far, the virtual biology research can be divided into three stages:

First stage: Express the behavior and phenomenon of nature biology type with some marks, such examples as characteristics of reproduction, evolution, death and so on. An instance is Neoterics procedure created by Kevin Coble.

Second stage: In the interactive real-time environment, the visitor and the virtual biology carry on alternation, which affects the behavior of virtual biological, even its evolvement. An example is the interactive computer installation, "A—Volve"[1] , which created by Chrism Sommerer and Laurent Mignormeau.

Third stage: Combine the artificial life method and the computer animation, which can construct the lifelike virtual biology. For example, the Chinese mistress scholar Tu xiao yuan constructs a "the artificial fish" system.

2.3 Concept of Virtual Biology Model

"The virtual biology model" is the simulation of third dimension (3-D) object truly according to the nature biology structure shape and the movement shape through the computer simulation. It has the shape and structure characteristic of simulated life. And it may reflect the life's substantive characteristics to the people according to the biological intrinsic structure. It is divided into: virtual animal model and virtual plant model.

The virtual animal model is divided into: individual level virtual animal model and community level animal model. In the individual level virtual animal model, attention is paid to establishing the natural form structure of single virtual biology, and how its behavior carries on alternation with the environmental condition; In community level virtual animal model, group behavior is emphasized, besides all characteristics of the individual animal are structured.

The virtual plant model is divided into: structural model and growth model. The structural model is a computation visualization model established based on mensurating the plant shape structure data, which is used to study the nature related to the plant spatial structure. The growth model is established based on growth rule abstracted from the research of the topology evolution and geometry shape change rule in the plant growth process, which is used to reflect the rule of plant growth process.

3 Modeling Method

The modeling method is a scientific method to open out the shape, characteristic and essential of the prototype by the research of model (simulated object). The virtual animal modeling method and the virtual plant modeling method are classified to construct the virtual biology model.

3.1 Virtual Animal Modeling Method

A. Virtual Physique Modeling Method
We regard the animal's trunk as a defined function with four parameters, i.e., the mass (m), the length (l), the cross section area (s), the diameter (d), as shown in fig 1. The cylindrical trunk is regarded as an elastic girder supporting four limbs. Under the action of the animal body weight f, its biggest droop δ, i.e., elasticity coefficient, is

girder's most great curve, according to the theory of elasticity research, $\delta \propto \dfrac{fl^3}{Sd^2}$,

where $\propto$ expresses direct ratio)

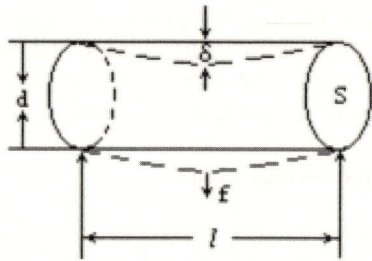

Fig. 1. Defined function with four parameters to describe animal's trunk

Because $f \propto m$, and $m \propto Sl$, so $\delta \propto \dfrac{l^4}{d^2}$ or $\dfrac{\delta}{l} \propto \dfrac{l^3}{d^2}$. In order to make it more reasonable, the assumption that $l^3 \propto d^2$ is given. Because $f \propto Sl$ and $S \propto d^2$, we can conclude that $f \propto l^4$, from which we can obtain the animal physique based on the result that its body weight is proportional to the power 4 of its trunk length

B. Sensation Behavior Modeling Mothod
The sensation behavior modeling method is dynamic, obtaining tradeoff among the mutually conflicting goals in order to choose the appropriate behavior movement for hypothesized animal according to the environment.

$$V_B = V_B - I_{AB} \times V_A , \qquad (1)$$

V_A and V_B are two arbitrary continual behaviors, I_{AB} is a suppression parameter of behavior A and the behavior B。 By (a) limiting the suppression coefficient more than 1;(b) causing a behavior no less than 0; (c) making behaviors be suppressed each other, we guarantee that the current system is stable and only one of behavior systems is not 0.

From this, the behavior system group is constructed, i.e.,

$$V_{it} = Max\left[li_{it} \times Combine(\sum_{k} rm_{ki}, \sum_{j} iV_{jt}) - \sum_{m} n_{mi} \times V_{mi}, 0 \right],$$ (2)

where V_{it} is the weight of behavior i in the t instance, li_{it} is fatigue parameter of i in the t instance, rm_{ki} is the internal variable of external part iV_{jt} which system senses. k and j are the interior and exterior scopes in the filter mechanism, respectively. n_{mi} is suppression coefficient of behavior m to behavior i. So we have defined the sensation behavior model by limiting the overall system.

3.2 Virtual Plant Modeling Method

A. Rinden Meyer's L- System
In 1960's, empirically generalizing and abstracting the growth process of plant object, Dutch biologist Rinden Meyer [2] structured the axiom and the resuling equation collection, constructed the character development sequence to display the plant topology The L system first defines an element collection, each element of which represents different functional node or the paragraph in the tree; Then according to its growth process, initial elements and growth rule P are defined, these three essential factors (H,G,P) constitute a three-dimensional L system.
     For instance:
     H={F, +, -, [,]};   G =F,   G ∈ H ;
     P={F⟶ F[+F] F[-F],+   +,- ⟶ -, [⟶ [,]⟶]}

B. Reference Axis Technique
The reference axis technology is a typical stochastic process method proposed by DE Reffye [3.4], which is based on the simulation of plant morphogenesis with the finite automation. Based on this, Godin[5] proposed the plant model of topology geometry (MTG) under the significance of multi-scale. Zhao Xing[6] further developed dual-scale automation model, this method began with the botany, proposed the micro condition and the great condition based dual-scale concept, and considered plant's growth mechanism. Its structure is orderly and succinctly, its image is direct-viewing, easily understanding and programming realization.

C. Fractal Method
The fractal theory is a new scientific method and theory to exploration complex structure, proposed by Benoit B.Mandelbrot, whivh describes the similar natural fragments or irregular structures. Fractal method[7] is to show the topology structure of plant growth according to the fractal theory.

D. 3-D Reconstruction Method
The method is to gather the plant spatial data using the instrument, compile the procedure on the computer to transfer the obtained data, thus realize plant's three-dimensional simulation. This is a simulation method for realistic plants. Its simulation

effect has the close relationship with the precision of instrument to measure plant spatial data.

4 A New Virtual Biology Modeling Mechanism

To meet the needs of simulating natural biological teaching, a good virtual biology model must have following request:

1) The virtual biology model should have the unique characteristic of natural biological itself.

2) The virtual biology model should satisfy the principles of biology, the zoology and the physiology.

3) The virtual biology model should be dynamic, non-static.

4) The virtual biology model is "transparent", teachers and students may see the required biology structure.

5) The virtual biology model is controllable, teachers and students may choose different biological growth stage to observe and analyze according to different need.

Based on above strategy, we apply the multi-model match detection mechanism to construct the dynamic virtual biology model, using the form of U+D+C+3M, which is as shown in fig 2.

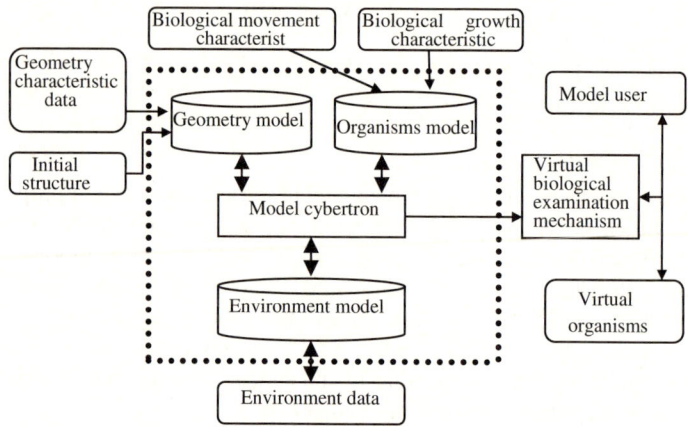

Fig. 2. Dynamic virtual biology model

4.1 Explanation of Constructed Model

U is user, refers to the instructional teacher and his (her) students. They must propose the concrete demand for the virtual biology model.

D is the detect mechanism of virtual biology model. We define a virtual biology model as data struture M, and M is a matrix, which is automatically produced in produces of the model construction at a time. The number of its row is biology model M, and the number of its volume is geometry model N, and all the elements of matrix are zero at the beginning. After the students complete the enactments of model request and submit them, the data collection begins. A stipulation is formulated that the position of matrix element be 1 when the geometry model and the biology model are both influenced by environment model; and the position of matrix element be -1 when either of the two models are not influenced by environment model; the position of matrix element be 0 when neither the geometry model nor the biology model are influenced by environment model.

After this, the model construction is completed to obtain a recorded matrix, such the matrix as the following:

$$M(m*n) = \begin{pmatrix} 1 & 0 & 1 & 1 & -1 \\ 1 & -1 & 1 & 0 & 0 \\ -1 & 0 & 0 & 1 & 0 \end{pmatrix} \quad (m=3, n=5) \tag{3}$$

That is to say, a virtual biology model uses five geometry models. For example, the first biology model relates to four geometry models, i.e., 1,3,4,5. Among the applied 5 geometry models, one is not influenced by environment model, another itself is influenced by environment model, and the other 3 models are all influenced by geometry model. Suppose a new matrix M', b_{ij} is an item of M', a_{ij} is an item of M.

Let $b_{ij} = a_{ij} * w_{ij}$, w_{ij} is the weight about ith virtual model uses and jth geometry model.

C is the model cybertron, including: (a) a group of exchanging rule among geometry model, biology model, and environment model, by which the sequence of virtual biological dynamic geometry structure is infered; (b) a flow of biology growth and development process and its simulation computation on computer; (c) the modality structure description of the output biology at a certain time.

$3M$ is represented as geometry model, biology model, and environment model, respectively.

The geometry model, gives the static geometry description of the biological shape structure. To each living body, decides its basic shape structure and establishes the initial geometry model according to its gene or the priori knowledge.

The biology model, divides the animal and the plant according to the biology. According to the front narration, the plant model is established by protracting plant growth process based on the different plant characteristics using the L system or the alternative method. On the basis of animal characteristic, the animals model is established by constructing the basic physique through the physique structure modeling method and the sensation behavior model to form the life feeling model.

The environment model, according to the need, may join the light model, the water model, the temperature model, the wind model, the soil model, and so on. Thus three-dimensional models are formed to constitute the hypothesized biology model together.

4.1.1 Model Matching Rate

Using the record matrix M_{m*n}, we can calculate the matching rate $r(k_i)$ between the virtual biology model k_j (j=1,2,3, ... n) and the user required model :

$$r(k_i) = (\sum b_{ij}') / (\sum |b_{ij}|) \tag{4}$$

$$i = 1,2,3,\Lambda \ m \quad j = 1,2,3,\Lambda \ n .$$

Note: $b_{ij}' = b_{ij}$ (when $b_{ij} > 0$), and $b_{ij}' = 0$ (when $b_{ij} \leq 0$).

From this, the matching rate vector $R = (r_1, r_2, r_3 \cdots, r_n)$ is obtained.
where $r_j = r(k_j)$.

4.1.2 Similarity Appraisal

The similarity appraisal is the key of detection. In the multi-model matching, the importance of each attribute in the similarity appraisal is different, therefore, various attributes need virtual different weight value. The model attribute similarity can be expressed as:

$$Sim(a,b) = \frac{\sum_{i=1}^{m}(f_i^a \cdot f_i^b \cdot w_i^2)}{\sqrt{\sum_{i=1}^{m}(f_i^a \cdot w_i)^2}\sqrt{\sum_{i=1}^{m}(f_i^b \cdot w_i)^2}} \tag{5}$$

where w_i expresses the weight of ith attribute vector, and $\sum_{i=1}^{m} w_i = 1$.

The matching rate has considered external factor of the biology model, but the similarity considered intrinsic connection of the biology model.

4.2 Principle of the Model

The model receiver firstly submits the concrete environment data to establishe the environment model; Submits the biological characteristic data and the initial structure data to establish the biological initial geometry model; Submits the biology growth characteristic data and the biology motion state data to establish the living model. Afterwards, under the actuation of time series, the simulation cybertron calculates the change of shape structure, and controls the geometry model to complete the calculation of these changes, thus obtains the three dimensional structure for biological growth process at a certain time. Afterwards, virtual biology detection mechanism is executed, if in the scope of matching degree and similarity degree, the virtual model is produced, and according to the specific request, the next step simulation is carried on. Otherwise, return to tell it.

5 Experiment and Result Analysis

In order to confirm the validity of the model, we introduce the model to the biology class of senior high school in a section of 'human and biosphere '. We construct the process of a seed germinates, in which the seed is affected together by the model of soil, moisture, illumination, and earthworm. The overall system is realized through PC programming utilizing VC++6.0 and OpenGL.

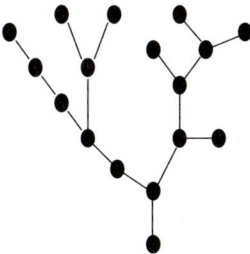

Fig. 3. A branching model

Fig. 4. Protract the final state of seed germination

Fig. 5. The entire state change driven by one kind of model (e.g. light model)

Table 1 describes the required model parameters and their value in the entire simulation process.

Table 1.

Parameter	Value	Note
Water (w)	3	Water model of the system
Soil (S)	2	Soil model of the system
Biology(B)	4	Animal model of the system
Light (L)	3	Light model of the system
Geometry(G)	28	Geometry model of the sysytem
K	20	Parameter

In Table 2, NDM indicates the constructed virtual living model without using the multi-model matching detection method. In Table 3, DM indicates to use this method. WS indicates that the initial condition only applies the light model and the geometry model in this plan. According to the model parameter given in Table 1, WOS,WLOS and WSOLG can in turn indicate which concrete condition they use,respectively.

The protracking time is the sum of establishment initial condition and finally obtaining the model result. Average protracking time is the mean of protracking model time under the same initial condition.

Fidelity is used to scale protracking similarity. If there are bracket and plus sign behind, they indicate that the protrack accords with the actual need.

Table 2.

NDM (Testing sequence)	6/32	8/32	8/32	10/32
Condition	WS	WOS	WLOS	WSOLG
Average control time	30s	68s	119s	125s
Fidelity ( )	0.92(+)	0.81(+)	0.5	0.37

Table 3.

DM (Testing sequence)	6/32	8/32	8/32	10/32
Condition	WS	WOS	WLOS	WSOLG
Average control time	38s	66s	90s	112s
Fidelity ( )	0.951(+)	0.914(+)	0.921(+)	0.918(+)

Through test and contrast for many times, we know that, if there is no detection mechanism, the more we use model in protract, the longer the protrack time is. With this mechanism, we can avoid forgotting the individual condition in the experiment, or avoid producing the model in the situation that the condition hypothesis and the nature rule do not match, which may reduce the meaningless time consumption caused by the wrong model based further research, and enhance the efficiency of the model in the teaching application.

6   Application Significance in Teaching

On the one hand, this kind of model enables student to understand scientific knowledge, and change student's cognition level to abstraction. By abstracting the substantive characteristics of prototype and simplifying complex prototype object, they can construct the model which reflects the prototype essence relationship. On the other hand, the model constructing process is also a process of science exploration. In this process, the students need to determine the research object, establish parameter, choice the research method, and finally validate whether the experiment result is consistent with the actual,which fully display the student's independent learning capability and innovation ability.

7 Summary

The paper proposes a new method of virtual biology model construction based on valid confirmation mechanism. According to the model system structural, we design the model cybertron, the model detector and the multi-model of geometry, environment and biology. It verifies the rationality and authenticity of biological model through the condition enactment combined with the natural biological logic relations. And its celerity and accuracy have been confirmed in the biological experiment class. However, along with the scientific development, as well as more and more people pay attention to the model match, our research needs to ceaselessly deepen, which is the work we will have to do from now on.

References

1. Laurent MIGNONNEAU and Chrism SOMMERER, Designing Interfaces for   Interactive Artwo~s[EB∕OL].
2. Lindenmayer, A Developmental systems without Cellular Interactions. their languages and Grammars, [J]InJournal of theoretical Biology, (1971)30: 455—484
3. deReffye P,Edelin C, Francon Jetal. Plant models faithful to botanical structure and development[J]. Computer Graphics, 1988, 22(4):151-158.
4. Bouchon J, de Reffye P, Barthelemy D. Model is ationet Simulation del' Architecture des Vegetaux [M]. Paris, INRA, 1997.23 : 441-487
5. Godin C, Carglio Y. A multiscale model of plant topological structures [J]. theor Bio, 1998, 84(3): 1-46.
6. Zhao xing, de Reffye Philippe, xiong fanlun. virtual plant growth double criterion automaton model [J], 2001, 24(6): 608-615.
7. Mandelbrot.B.B. The fractal geometry of nature [M], Free man,San Fransisco, 1982. 64(2):6-34
8. M˘ech, R., and Prusinkiewicz, P. Visual models of plants interacting with theirenvironment. Computer Graphics (SIGGRAPH '96 Conference Proceedings) (August 1996), 397–410.
9. Prusinkiewicz, P., James, M., and M˘ech, R. Synthetic topiary. Computer Graphics (SIGGRAPH '94 Conference Proceedings) 38 (July 1994), 351–358.

Virtual Reconstruction of Two Types of Traffic Accident by the Tire Marks

Xiaoyun Zhang, Xianlong Jin, and Jie Shen

Shanghai Jiaotong University
{Jxlong, Shenjieihn, General_zhang}@sjtu.edu.cn

Abstract. With the development of simulation technology, the numerical methods can help to reconstruct the traffic accidents. Based on the dynamic models of collisions, a Momentum/Energy method to predict the pre-impact motion was introduced through the optimization of the rest positions of the vehicles. With the help of Pc-Crash, the method of traffic accident reconstruction can be achieved, and several simulation runs will be performed, to find a solution, where post impact trajectories and rest positions correspond with the real accidents. In the paper, two kinds of collision accidents, the car crash to the wall and the car crash to another car, are analyzed based on the method. The simulation results show that applying the tire marks in the accident scene and the Momentum/Energy method can provide the scientific and numerical references for the analysis and judgment of the traffic accidents.

Keywords: Vehicle; Traffic accident; Virtual reconstruction; Skid marks.

1 Introduction

With economy developing in China, more and more family own their private cars as the necessary living tools. Compared with the years of 2001 and 2002, the number of traffic accidents, deaths, injury and direct economic loss increased 2.14%, 3.26%, 2.85% and 7.66%. Compared with the years of 2002 and 2003, these numbers decreased 13.7%, 4.6%, 12.1% and increased 1.4%, respectively, in 2004, they increased 14.9%, 4.9%, 8.6% and 17.6%. According to the statistical data, the drivers breaking the traffic rulers are the main reasons in these traffic accidents. The reasons include over speed, wrong way, driving without licence, drunk driving and tired driving, etc. More and more traffic accidents increase the pressure of the relative department. On the other hand, with the developing and opening, stricter requirements for the appraisal of traffic accidents are needed: international conventions; more rapidly responding; standard operation routines.

One complete traffic accident disposal includes three parts: survey at the accident scene, accident analysis and responsibility ascertaining. The main tasks of the accident scene survey are: measuring, drawing the accident scene draft and taking photos at the accident scene, etc. Accident analysis will take the survey as the basis and analyze the accident reasons. Based on the accident analysis and according to the relative codes, the accident responsibility can be decided at last.

Z. Pan et al. (Eds.): ICAT 2006, LNCS 4282, pp. 1128–1135, 2006.

The skid marks are the main research objects in accident reconstruction. In the paper, the dynamic models were studied. And the method to predict the pre-impact motion of the vehicle is introduced. Then two typical accidents are reconstructed by the methods.

2   The Optimization Method

Before the optimization process can be done, a quality function has to be found. And before defining a quality function for the simulation results, the parameters, which can be used to describe the real accident, have to be defined. [1-3]

2.1   The Collision Model

The impact center is determined by a fundamental principle, the equation of linear and angular impulse-momentum. An x-y vehicle coordinate system is selected such that the origin is located at the center of gravity. The dynamic impact model uses numerical integration of Newton's second law in the form of differential equations whereas the analytical impact model uses the law of conservation of momentum and is presented by a set of algebraic simultaneous equations without reference to forces.

As defined the impact can be divided into two phases: the "compression" phase and the "restitution" phase. At the end of the compression phase the velocities for both vehicles at the "impulse point" are identical in case of a full impact. Due to a certain elasticity of the vehicle structures, the two vehicles will separate again. Linear momentum and angular momentum are conserved, and energy loss is accounted for with a coefficient of restitution.

The "coefficient of restitution" is defined as ratio between restitution momentum and compression momentum, and the range of the coefficient lies between 0~0.3. [1]

2.2   Definition of Post Crash Movement

Depending on the available data from the accident scene, some of these parameters may be uncertain. In many accident situations the approximate location where the vehicles collided can be found due to the tire or scratch marks, the shatter fields or the dust marks. If the vehicles have not been moved from their rest positions when the scene investigations were made, these positions and the car directions are well defined. If skid marks were found on the accident scene, intermediate vehicle positions can be defined on the post impact trajectories. Therefore, from the trajectories, the impact position, rest positions and intermediate positions can be used to define the accident situation. [2]

2.3   Optimization Strategies

As for the optimization strategies, several different algorithms like the Coordinate Approach by Gauss-Seidel, the Simplex method, the Gradient and Newton approach, Monte Carlo and Evolutionary methods deal with the problem of multidimensional optimization. Not all these methods are applicable, because some of these methods need derivatives of the target function to the input parameters. Thinking of the factors of robustness, numerical stability and high progress rates, the Evolutionary method, that is, the genetic algorithm is chosen. [2, 4]

3 Application Cases

Using the optimization methods and the Pc-Crash software, two kinds of traffic accident, car crash to the wall and one car crash to another car, are reconstructed with the information of the tire marks in the scene.

3.1 The Case of One Car Crash to the Wall

The accident happened in Hainan Province in 2001 and the photo of the accident scene as shown in Fig. 1. The weather of the day was sunny and the road surface was blacktop.

Fig. 1. The photo of the accident scene

In the accident, the high-speed test of the vehicle in the design process was just finished, and the car was driving to the park. The driver operated error lead the car crash to the wall. Because the seat belt was used, the driver was not injured seriously.

With the help of photogrammetry programs, the three dimensional model of the accident scene (as shown in Fig. 2) can be obtained from the photographs. Then the

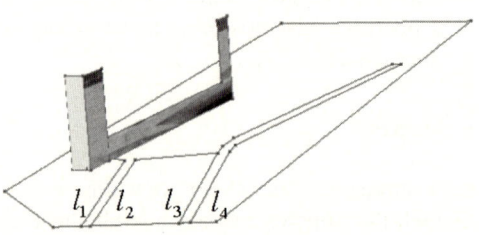

Fig. 2. 3D model of the accident scene

three-dimensional model of the scene can be used as an input of the software Pc-Crash, and the parameters that defining post-impact movement of the accident are available in the model data. In the accident, the degree of the angle between the tire mark and the wall is 17 and the position of the car at the state of stop can be decided.

After trajectories optimization for this accident, the pre-impact velocity can be calculated to be 50km/h, and the simulation error is 1.0%. As shown in Fig. 3, this result is quite coincident with the accident scene.

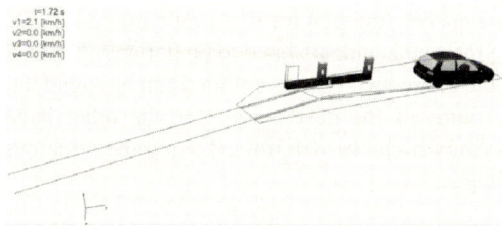

Fig. 3. Reconstruction of the accident

The researcher also can view at the position of the driver by the Open GL technique, just as shown in Fig. 4.

Fig. 4. At the view of the driver

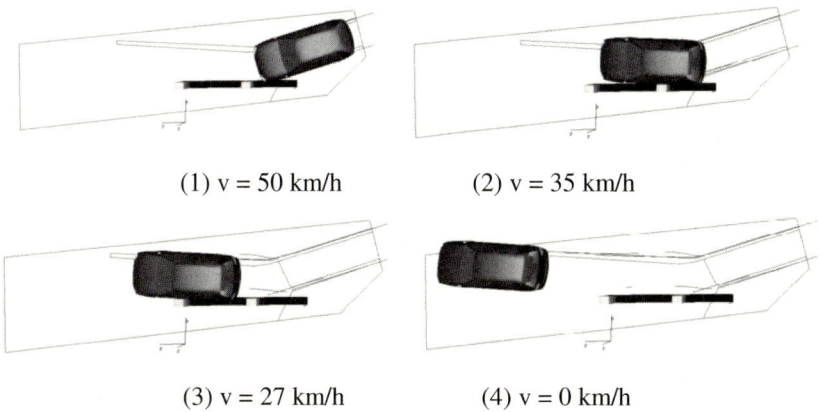

    (1) v = 50 km/h   (2) v = 35 km/h

    (3) v = 27 km/h   (4) v = 0 km/h

Fig. 5. The course of the car crash to the wall

The movement process of the car crash to the wall was shown in Fig. 5, and the velocity of the car at the different stage was also shown in the figure.

3.2   The Case of the Car Crash to Another Car

One vehicle-to-vehicle collision traffic accident that happened in Shanghai in 2004 was reconstructed on computer. The weather of the night is rainy and the road surface is blacktop. The photo of the accident scene was show as the Fig. 6.

Before defining a quality function for the simulation results, the parameters that can be used to describe the real accidents have to be defined. In the accident situations the approximate location where the vehicles collided can be found due to the tire or scratch marks, the shatter fields or the dust marks. On the other hand, the overlap of the vehicles during the impact can be determined using the remaining deformation of the vehicles after the impact.

(a) The photo of the vehicle (No.1)   (b) The photo of the vehicle (No.2)

Fig. 6. Photos of the accident scene

In the accident, the stop position should be gotten from the drawing of the accident scene, and from the photos of the accident vehicles, it is known that the left side tires of the vehicle No.1 all exploded due to the collision, so it can be concluded that the tractor of the vehicle No.2 slide and collided continuously with the left side of the carriage of the vehicle No.1, and causing the tractor and the trailer of the vehicle No.2 to form a

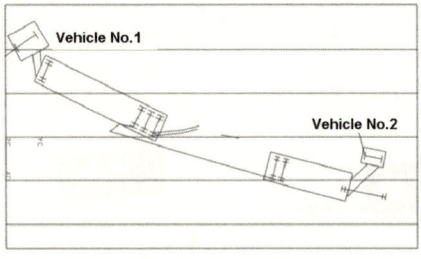

Fig. 7. The CAD model of the accident scene

larger angle at the stop position. The vehicle No.1 turned right after the collision and knocked down the tree in the roadside finally. In the accident, the driver of the vehicle No.2 died, and the driver of the vehicle No.1 was injured seriously. The CAD model of the accident scene is shown in the Fig. 7.

The information of the two vehicles is show in the table 1.

Table 1. The information of the two vehicles

Vehicle	NO.1	No.2 tractor	No.2 trailer
Overall length/mm	16500	5750	7196
Overall width/mm	2480	2490	2480
Overall height/mm	3020	2780	1500
Wheelbase/mm	13410	3410	5550
Total mass/mm	41000	6500	23520

According to the theory of vehicle dynamic models and the method of trajectories optimization, the results of the accident reconstruction were shown as the Fig. 8. On the other hand, the velocity of the vehicles at the moment of contact can be calculated in the simulation result.

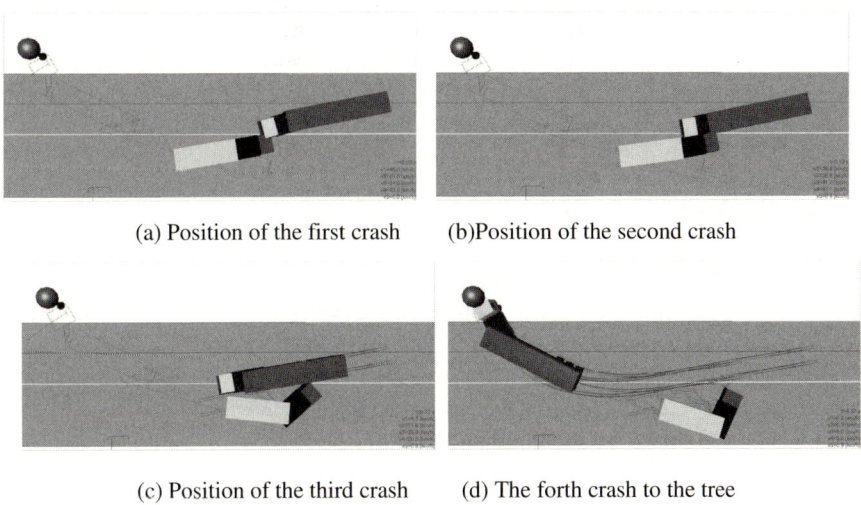

(a) Position of the first crash   (b)Position of the second crash

(c) Position of the third crash   (d) The forth crash to the tree

Fig. 8. The result of the accident reconstruction

In the figure 8(a), crash happened between the tractor of the vehicle No. 1 and the tractor of the vehicle No.2, at the moment of contact, the velocity of the tractor of vehicle No.1 is 44.0km/h, and the velocity of the tractor of vehicle No.2 is 45.0km/h. In the figure 8(b), crash happened between the trailer of the No.1 vehicle and the tractor of the No.2 vehicle, the velocity of the trailer of vehicle No.1 is 41.1km/h, and the velocity of the tractor of vehicle No.2 is 36.6km/h. In the figure 8(c), crash happened between the trailer of the No.1 vehicle and the trailer of the No.2 vehicle, the velocity of the trailer of vehicle No.1 is 32.0km/h, and the velocity of the tractor of vehicle No.2 is 9.2km/h. In the figure 8(d), crash happened between the tractor of the No.1 vehicle and one tree, the velocity of the tractor of vehicle No.1 is 18.8km/h.

The optimization error of the simulation result is 9.0%, usually optimization error below than 10% is allowed. In this case, the reason of a big optimization error is that the rest positions of the two vehicles are known, but only litter tire marks were kept well.

3.3 The Range of Application

Based on the information of the skid marks, collision accidents analysis can be finished quickly, however these methods have strict requirements on the accidents scene. Now most advanced vehicles have equipped with ABS, so the skid marks are much fainter or non-existent. On the other hand, in collision accident the driver maybe damage the accident scene because of unconsciousness or being nervous. For example, the driver may move the vehicle to the roadside, or moves on slowly to stop, or back slowly to stop, without following "The law of road traffic security, People's Republic of China". All these will badly damage skid marks and other key factors in accidents, then the spot survey and justice appraisal will be influenced. Moreover, the weather (for example rain) and other vehicles (pedestrians), even conscious action will damage the spot. So accident analysis with skid marks has its limitations.

To reconstruct the accident without skid marks, the new methods: vehicle body deformation, event data recorders etc, and new devices will be applied in accidents to resolve the problem mentioned above. [5-7]

4 Conclusions

This paper studies the dynamic models of collision accidents, based on the study, a method to predict the pre-impact motion of the vehicle is introduced through the optimization of the post impact trajectories and rest positions correspond with the real accident. Then one typical collision accident case was simulated based on the method, it is proved to be effective on analysis of this kind of accidents, and so can provide a scientific foundation for accident judgments.

References

1. Steffan H, Moser A. The Trailer Simulation Model of PC-CRASH. SAE paper 980372, USA
2. Moser A, Steffan H. Automatic Optimization of Pre-Impact Parameters Using Post Impact Trajectories and Rest Positions. SAE paper 980373, USA
3. Steffan H, Moser A. The Collision and Trajectory Models of PC-CRASH. SAE paper 960886, USA

4. William E C, Moser A. Reconstruction of Twenty Staged Collisions with PC-Crash's Optimizer. SAE paper 2001-01-0507, USA
5. Zhang X Y, Jin X L, Sun Y, et al. Vehicle Crashworthiness Simulation Based on Virtual Design of Auto-body, Journal of Dong Hua University, 2004, 21(2): 63~68
6. Zhang X Y, Jin X L, Qi W G, et al. Virtual Reconstruction of Vehicle Crash Accident Based on Elastic-plastic Deformation of Auto-body, Key Engineering Materials, 2004, 274-276: 1017~1022
7. Zhang X Y, Jin X L, Qi W G, et al. Crashworthiness Simulation and Structure Optimization Design of Auto-body Based on Finite Element Method, Journal of Systems Engineering and Electronics, 2004,15(4): 112~116

A Seamless Visualizaton Model of the Global Terrain Based on the QTM

Xuesheng Zhao[1,2], Jianjun Bai[1], Jun Chen[2], and Zhilin Li[3]

[1] Department of Surveying and Land Science
China University of Mining and Technology (Beijing), Beijing, China, 100083
zxs@cumtb.edu.cn
[2] National Geometrics Center of China,
No.1 Baishengcun, Zizhuyuan, Beijing, China, 10004
chenjun@nsdi.gov.cn
[3] Department of Land Surveying and Geo-Informatics
The Hong Kong Polytechnic University, Kowloon, Hong Kong
Tel.: (+852) 2766 5960; Fax: (+852) 2330 2994
lsllz@polyu.edu.hk

Abstract. A seamless & adaptive visualization model of global DEM based on the QTM (Quaternary Triangular Mesh) is made to approximate to the Earth terrain in this paper. The approaches start with an Octahedron QTM partition based on the spherical surface. In order to improve the operation efficiency, the global DEM array points are organized as a hierarchy of *Diamond*s and the corresponding algorithms on indexing mechanism, coding scheme, and neighbor finding based on linear quadtree are given in details. Then, a dynamic operation method of the multi-resolution *Diamond* datasets in visualization is approached. Furthermore, an adaptive simplification rule of hierarchical triangles in *Diamond* data blocks is presented, in which an idea of the *Binary Triangle Tree* is introduced to form a continuous DEM mesh on the edges between different resolutions. In the end, the experiment and analysis are done with the GTOPO30 dada. The results is smoothly and receivable.

Keywords: Visualization model, DEM, QTM, Diamond, Adjacent index.

1 Introduction

Real-time and realistic visualization model of the Earth terrain is the significant component in Digital Earth and has been one of the research hotspots in geography and spatial information science for many years. The regular or irregular grid Digital Elevation Models (DEM) based on the idea of map projections are effective traditional methods to modeling the terrain on the local spherical surfaces as a flat, and many corresponding algorithms are presented over the last decade [Lindstrom *et al.* 1996; 2002; Duchaineau *et al.* 1997; Hoppe 1996]. However, the spherical surface is not as topologically equivalent as planar Euclidean space in geometry. Although the traditional DEM grid may support an individual project or small-scale terrain visualization modeling, they do have some significant drawbacks for modeling the large-scale or the whole Earth surface, such as unacceptable geometric distortions,

Z. Pan et al. (Eds.): ICAT 2006, LNCS 4282, pp. 1136–1145, 2006.

data broken or overlap, space inefficiency, and difficulty with data sharing between different map projections [Gold and Mustafavi 2000; Kolar 2004].

To overcome these deficiencies, a number of approaches to subdividing the surface of the earth in a continuous and hierarchical way for the global terrain visualization have been suggested in recent years, such as latitude & longitude grids [Gerstner 2003; NIMA 2003; Bjroke *et al.* 2004] and the adaptive subdivision grids [Lukatela 2000; Kolar 2004], *etc.* These global discrete grids tessellate the Earth's surface directly with non-overlapping (or broken) cells. They can be simulated the earth terrain when they are recursive partitioned to a certain degree and can resolve those problems caused by map projections [Dutton 1999]. However, latitude/longitude grids do not have equal area cells, which is important for many applications and a lot of redundancy data is occurred near the pole areas [Sahr and White 1998]. The shape and area of those adaptive subdivision grids are irregular and ununiformity in a same subdivision. Both of them are difficult to manage large volume of global DEM data and to manipulate multi-resolution data visualization efficiently. It is desirable to have grids consisting of highly regular regions with evenly distributed elevation points.

This paper aims to present a QTM (Quaternary Triangular Mesh)-based method for the construction of a visualization model of the earth terrain seamlessly and adaptively. The reason is that the QTM grid structure is uniformity, hierarchical, and numerically stable everywhere on the spherical surface. Its hierarchical grid structure can be used to efficiently manage multi-resolution global data, and it allows spatial phenomena to be studied at different levels of detail in a consistent fashion across extensive regions of the sphere [Sahr *et al.* 2003; Chen *et al.* 2003]. Another reason is that the QTM grids would not only allow the same structure to be used over a wide range of spatial resolutions and efficiently load only needed segments [Faust *et al.* 2000], but also allow the presentation of data at multiple levels and offer several major advantages, such as being unique and domain-independent, appropriately indexed or linearized grids express spherical surface location in a single string, preserving geometrical integrity both locally and globally, and making resolution explicit in the length of the string [Goodchild & Yang 1992], *etc.*

Following this introduction is a modeling principle of the global DEM grids based on QTM is then presented in briefly. This is followed by the presentation of a hierarchical data organizing and adjacent indexing algorithm of the *Diamond*-based structure in details. Then, the dynamic paging method of *Diamond* blocks is given. An adaptive simplification rule of hierarchical triangles in *Diamond* data blocks is presented by recursive edge bisection. Following that, GTOPO30 data (which are from Courtesy of US Geological Survey) of the whole Earth are used to test these methods and algorithms presented in this paper. Finally, the conclusions and recommendation for future work will be presented.

2   Modeling Principle of the Global DEM Grids Based on QTM

The QTM structure used in Fekete [1990], Dutton [1989; 1999], and Goodchild and Yang [1992], are all based on inscribed octahedron. The reason is that its vertices occupy cardinal points and its edges assume cardinal directions, following the equator, the prime meridian, and the 90th, 180th and 270th meridians, making it simple to determine which facet a point on the planet occupied [Dutton 1989]. When a triangle is subdivided, the latitudes/longitudes pairs of any two of its three vertices are averaged to yield edge midpoint locations. Clearly after each level of subdivision, the triangles become smaller, and at the 21st level of subdivision, their size is approximately 1*m*, going down to 1 *cm* at 28th level. Fig.1 illustrates subdivisions at levels 1, 2 and 3.

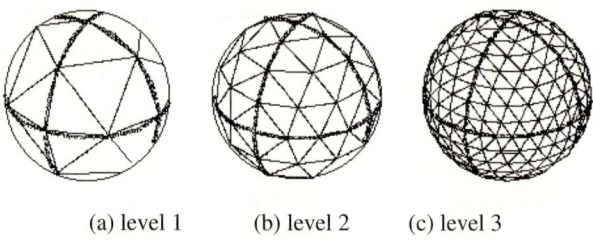

(a) level 1   (b) level 2   (c) level 3

Fig. 1. QTM partition of spherical facet based on octahedron [Dutton 1989]

This partition scheme preserves the properties of uniformity, hierarchical, and numerically stable everywhere on the spherical surface. The vertices, which make up QTM, are called *QTM vertices* whose position can be identified by latitude/longitude coordinate. Thus, the global terrain can be represented by the array of elevation values of the vertices.

3   Hierarchical Organizing Method Based on the *"Diamond"s*

It is well known that the QTM grids are hierarchical triangles and do not have uniform orientation (some triangles point up while others point down). Many algorithms defined on triangle grids are more complex because of taking into account triangle orientation. White [2000] notes that pairs of adjacent triangle faces may be combined to form a *Diamond*, and this *Diamond* may be recursively sub-divided in a fashion analogous to the square quadtree subdivision.

3.1   Indexing and Coding of *Diamond* Based on Linear Quadtree

According to this idea, the whole earth surface can be represented as a quadtree that the root has four children node (four base-*Diamond*s as shown in Fig.2), and the interior node has four children node (four child-*Diamond*s). The global DEM data is organized based on levels of *Diamond* as basic storage unit, which correspond to different resolution traditional map. In the file system, they are the binary terrain data files in which the height values of the *QTM vertices* are stored in Binary Large Object (BLOB).

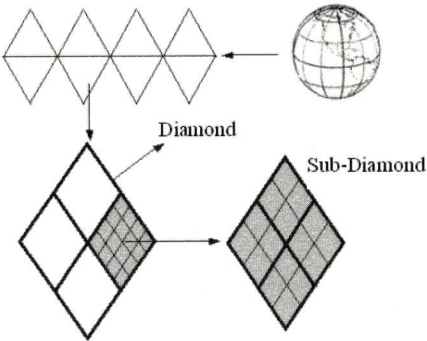

Fig. 2. The DEM data organizing based on the levels of *Diamond*s

The surface of the earth can be found an expression in a linear quadtree and only the locations of leaves need to be registered in the storage process. The leaves can be labeled by its *Diamond* code and indexed according to the Z space-filling curve (shown as Fig.3). Each *Diamond* be assigned a Morton code $M_Q = q_0 q_1 q_2 .... q_k$, in which q_0 is the quadcode of the base *Diamond* assigned a numerical label 0,1,2 or 3 according its location on the surface of the earth. It is illustrated as: $q_0 = 0$ $(90° > \lambda \geq 0°)$, $q_0 = 1$ $(180° > \lambda \geq 90°)$, $q_0 = 2$ $(270° > \lambda \geq 180°)$, and $q_0 = 3$ $(360° > \lambda \geq 270°)$. Each *Diamond* will be substituted by four smaller *Diamond*s when performs subdivision and can be labeled respectively through adding an additional digit 0, 1, 2 and 3 according to their location (left, down, up and right) in the parent *Diamond*.

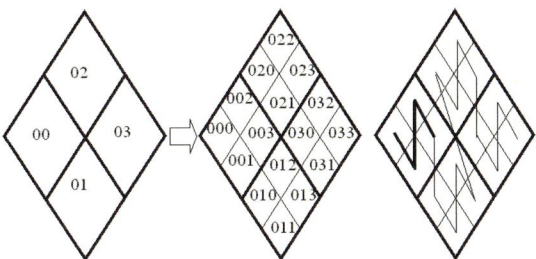

Fig. 3. The Morton code and Z space filling curve of *Diamond*s

3.2   The Neighbor Finding of the *Diamond*

It is easy to determine the Morton codes of either the sons or the parent of a *Diamond*s according to the properties of the Morton codes. The sons of a *Diamond* are determined by appending the digits 0,1,2 and 3 at the end of the Morton codes, and the address of the parent of a *Diamond* is obtained by simply discarding the trailing quaternary digit. In order to determine adjacent neighbors of the *Diamond*, firstly the conversion process between the Morton codes and row/column number of the *Diamond* must be done by formula (1), which is introduced in details in paper [Lee and Samet 2000]. The correlation between them is shown as following as Fig. 4:

$$M_Q = 2I_b + J_b \qquad (1)$$

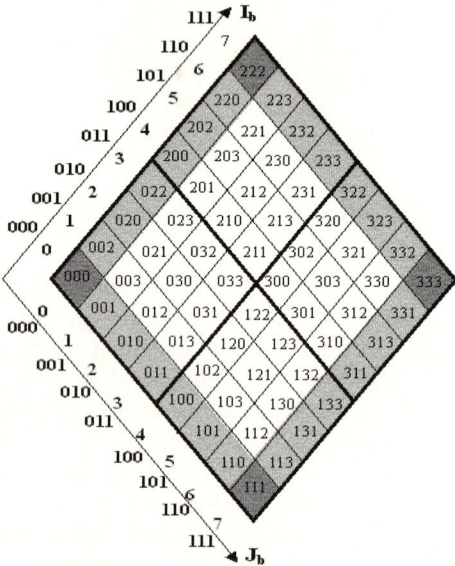

Fig. 4. The correlation between quaternary Morton code and row/column number

There are three cases in the neighbor-finding of the *Diamonds*: the *Diamond* located in the inside of the base *Diamond* (quadrant), the *Diamond* located in the boundary of the base *Diamond*, and the *Diamond* located in the corner of the base *Diamond*. As the Morton codes of adjacent *Diamond* inside the same base *Diamond* can be calculated easily. To the briefly, only the row/column numbers of adjacent *Diamond*s in the different base *Diamond* is presented as table 1.

Similarity, the row/column numbers of neighbor *Diamonds* in Right boundary, South corner and East corner can be figured out. Moreover, the Morton codes of these neighbors can be calculated by formula (1).

Table 1. Row/column numbers of adjacent *Diamond*s in the different base *Diamond*

Diamond location	Row/column numbers	Row/column numbers of Edge-neighbor Diamond	Row/column numbers of Vertex-neighbor Diamond
Left(up) boundary	*(i, 0)*	*(I, I-i)*	*(I, I-i-1), (I, I-i+1)*
Left(down) boundary	*(0, j)*	*(I-j, J)*	*(I-j-1, J), (I-j+1, J)*
North corner	*(I, 0)*	*(I, 0), (I, 0),*	*(I, 1), (I-1, 0), (I, 0)*
East corner	*(I, J)*	*(0, 0)*	*(I 0), (0, 1)*

3.3   The Dynamic Operation Algorithm of *Diamond* Blocks

As the amount of dataset is too much to be stored in main memory at one time, in the visualized operations of terrain data, only several *Diamond*s in a given level of data are added in according to proportion between the screen space distance and its corresponding object space distance. Usually the screen resolution is a constant. With the changing of the viewpoint and angle of view, the object space distance corresponding to the adjacent pixel in the screen is changed. The object space distance D corresponding to the adjacent pixels can be calculated by:

$$D = \frac{2 \times d \times tg \dfrac{\alpha}{2}}{l \times \lambda} \tag{2}$$

In which λ is number of the pixels per distance unit in the projection plane; d is the distance between the view and the object plane; α is angle of view; and l is the length of the projection plane.

For all *Diamond*s located in the same level, only the *Diamond*s inside the view-frame are selected to add, and the *Diamond*s located outside are not considered for the efficient rendering. *Diamond*s are chosen as the active areas based on considerations for memory size of available PC and desired range of view. This amount of terrain data is in the main memory at any given time and available for operation. When the operation algorithm is initialized, the viewpoint is centered on the 4 *Diamond*s. A bounding box is established around the screen center. When the user reaches the bounding box in any direction, memory space is freed in the direction opposite of travel, *Diamond*s terrain is added in the direction of travel (shown as Fig. 5).

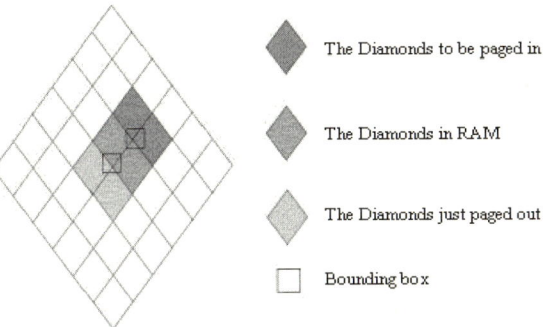

Fig. 5. The dynamic adding or removing of *Diamonds*

4   An Adapting Simplification Method of DEM Data Block

In order to improve the efficiency in visualization, the *Diamonds* data blocks located in the memory need to be simplified to multi-resolution triangle grids base on the terrain propertied. In this model, it cannot preserve the continuity of the terrain surface along the edges between the different subdivision levels (shown as Fig.6). Traditionally, the continuity of the terrain can be kept by tessellating the triangles in the higher level.

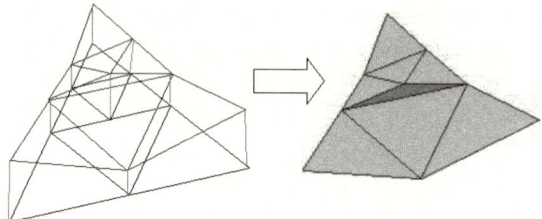

Fig. 6. Hierarchical QTM and the crack caused by different subdivisions

However, the traditional method exists some deficiencies. Firstly, the subdivisions need to be controlled by people and the operation can be done only when the difference between the adjacent levels are no larger than one. Secondly, the regularity of tessellation grids can not be preserved, in which some grids are QTM and others are irregular. In order to overcome this problem, an adaptive idea of *Binary Triangle Tree* [Lindstrom & Pascucci 2002] is introduced.

Firstly, it is supposed that the edge that wants to be subdivided is called *base edge* in one triangle, the two triangle that share the same *base edge* is made up a pair of triangles (shown as triangle *a* and *b* in Fig.7a). The simplification principle of the adapting grid is as following (shown as Fig.7):

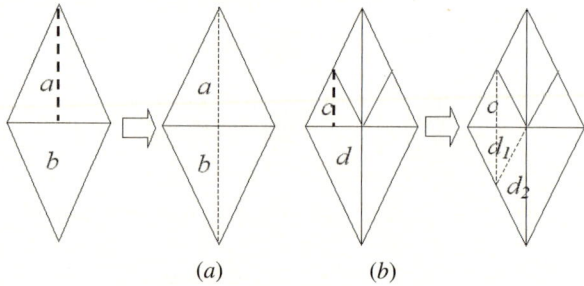

(a)   (b)

Fig. 7. Bisecting partition of triangles

Step 1, the triangle is part of a *Diamond*---the triangle and its *Base Neighbor* is split simultaneously, such as triangle *a* and *b* in Fig.7a.

Step 2, the triangle is not part of a *Diamond*--- Firstly, its *Base Neighbor* is split and then do step 1. For example in Fig.7b, if triangle *c* is to be split, its *base neighbor d* must be split into d_1, d_2 and then the triangle *c* and d_2 are split simultaneously.

Step 3, the process is to be done recursively until its error exceeds the tolerance value.

By recursively subdivision based on *Binary Triangle Tree*, an adapting, continuous, and hierarchical triangular mesh is formed in the data blocks and their vertices coincide with the vertices of QTM completely. The problem of discontinuity in different subdivision levels is overcome and the number of triangles of paged *Diamond* in visualization is reduced greatly.

5 Experiments and Analysis

The experiment results of the hierarchical algorithm of the global terrain visualization are analyzed in this section. In order to be organized into *Diamond* based file, the GTOPO30 dataset (from Courtesy of US Geological Survey) should be translated into a QTM data structure before visualized operation. In this section, it

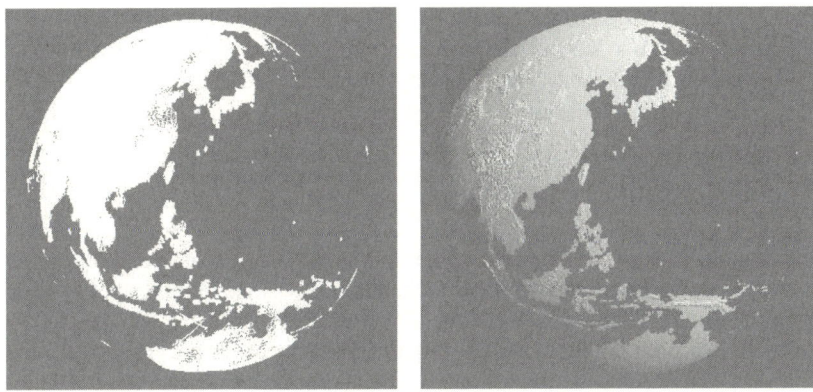

(a) $\tau-1$; $N=70912$

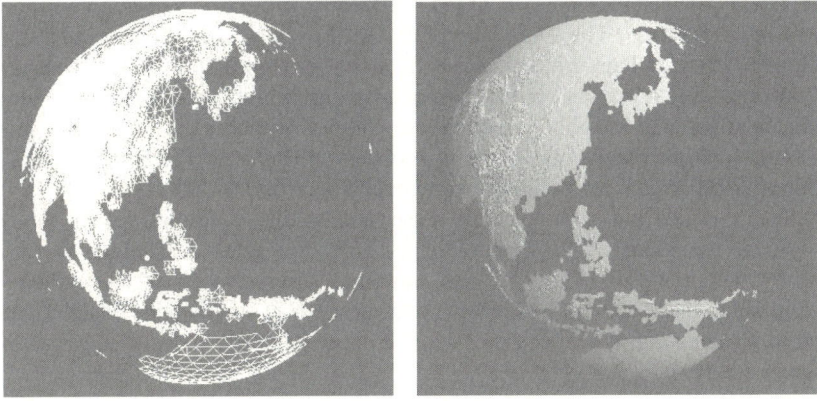

(b) $\tau=2$; $N=33786$

Fig. 8. The visualization of global DEM at four different error tolerances (left: triangulation grid map, right: shaded map)

is interpolated onto 4 *Diamond*s, and then 16 *Diamond*s, 64 *Diamond*s and 256 *Diamond*s dataset respectively; each includes 2049*2049 grid vertices. Each elevation value in the *Diamond* file represents the height value in meters above sea level and is stored using 2 bytes as a signed integer. Ocean areas are marked by *nodata* values. Compare with the GTOPO30 Data, the volume of the QTM based DEM data is reduced about a half of its initial. It can be illuminated by formula (3) (*Q* is the volume of the QTM based DEM data, while *G* is the volume of the GTOPO30 DEM data):

$$Q\!\!\Big/\!\!G = \frac{4n^2 - 4(2n-1)}{(2n-1) \times (n-1) \times 4} = \frac{(n-1)^2}{2n^2 - 3n + 1} \approx \frac{1}{2} \tag{3}$$

The number of the triangles on the Earth is N =33445532 before simplification and it decreases greatly by using different error tolerances, such as τ=1, 2 respectively. The correspondent visualized results are shown as Fig.8 (All ocean area are not display). Number of triangle is decreased greatly (left figures of Fig.8a and 8b) with their error tolerances increase, but the visualized results among them have no obvious change (right figures of Fig.8a and 8b). That is to say, in order to improve visualized efficiency, a simplified model can be applied by selecting a suitable error tolerance τ.

6   Conclusions and Future Work

A global multi-resolution Digital Elevation Model and a feasible solution for its visualization and management remains a challenging vision. In this paper, a seamless & adaptive visualization model of the global terrain based on Modified-QTM is approached. Not only the deficiencies of data broken or overlap caused by traditional DEM are overcome, but the distortion in area and/or shape and a lot of redundancy data occurred in the latitude/longitude grids are avoided as well.

One contribution in this paper is developing a quadtree structure of *Diamond*s to organize the global DEM data on QTM vertices, which can be storied and indexed using linear quadtree. The *Diamond* is as topologically equivalent to the square, which has some excellent properties, such as radial symmetry, translation congruence, and uniform orientation, and the corresponding algorithms on indexing mechanism, coding scheme, and neighbor finding are simple and effective. In visualization operation, when the viewpoint move at a change distance to the Earth surface, the neighboring *Diamond*s can be indexed and paged in or out dynamically.

Another contribution in this paper is presenting an adaptive simplification model of hierarchical triangles in DEM data blocks based on *Binary Triangle Tree*. This adaptive triangle mesh is regular and uniform. The problem of discontinuity in different subdivision levels is overcome and the number of triangles of the diamond added in visualization is reduced greatly. The experiment illustrates that the results is smoothly and receivable.

Acknowledgement. The works described in this paper was substantially supported by an award from the Natural Science Foundation of China (under grant No.40471108) and by a project from the Hong Kong Polytechnic University (Project No. G-U045).

References

1. Bjørke J., Grytten J., Morten H. and Stein N., Examination of a Constant-Area Quadrilateral Grid in Representation of Global Digital Elevation Models. International journal of geographic information science, 18 (7): 653-664, 2004.
2. Chen J., Zhao X.S., and Li Z.L., An Algorithm for the Generation of Voronoi Diagram on the Sphere Based on QTM. *Photogrammetric Engineering & Remote Sensing*. 69(1):79-90, 2003.
3. Clarke K., Dana P. and Hastings J., A New World Geographic Reference System, *Cartography and Geographic Information Science*, 29(4): 355-362, 2002.
4. Duchaineau M., Wolinsky M., Sigeti D., Miller M., Aldrich C., and Weinstein M., ROAMing Terrain: Real—Time Optimally Adapting Meshes, in *Proc. Visualization '97*. Oct., pp.81-88, 1997.
5. Dutton G., Modeling Locational Uncertainty via Hierarchical Tessellation. In Goodchild M.F. and Gopal S., editors, *Accuracy of Spatial Databases*, Taylor & Francis. pp125-140, 1989.
6. Dutton G., A hierarchical Coordinate System for Geoprocessing and Cartography, *Lecture Notes in Earth Sciences*, Springer-Verlag, 230pp, 1999.
7. Faust N., Ribarsky W., and Jian g T.Y., Real-Time Global Data Model for the Digital Earth. http://www.ncgia.ucsb.edu/globalgrids/papers/faust.pdf., 2000.
8. Fekete G., Rendering and Managing Spherical Data With Sphere Quadtree. *Proceedings of Visualization '90*. IEEE Computer Society, Los Alamitos, CA. 176-186, 1990.
9. Gerstner T., Multi-resolution Visualization and Compression of Global Topographic Data. *Geoinformatica*. 7(1): 7-32, 2003.
10. Gold C.and Mustafavi A., Towards the Global GIS. *ISPRS Journal of Photogrammetry & Remote Sensing*, 55(3): 150-163, 2000.
11. Goodchild M.F., and Yang, S.R., A Hierarchical Data Structure for Global Geographic Information Systems. *Computer Vision and Geographic Image Processing*, 54(1):31-44, 1992.
12. Hoppe H., Progressive Meshes. *SIGRAPH 96 Conference Proceedings*, pp99-108, 1996.
13. Kolar J., Representation of The Geographic Terrain Surface Using Global Indexing. *Proceeding of 12th International Conference on Geoinformatics*. Sweden, 321-328, 2004.
14. Lee M. and Samet H., Navigating through Triangle Meshes Implemented as Linear Quadtree, *ACM transactions on Graphics*, 19(2): 79-121, 2000.
15. Lindstrom P., Koller D, Faust and Gregory., A Real-Time Continuous Level of Detail Rendering of Height Fields. *SIGGRAPH'96 Conference Proceedings*, pp109-118, 1996.
16. Lindstrom P. and Pascucci V., Terrain Simplification Simplified: A General Framework for View-Dependent Out-of-Core Visualization. *IEEE Transactions on Visualization and Computer Graphics*, July-September 8(3):239-254, 2002.
17. Lukatela H., A Seamless Global Terrain Model in the Hipparchus System, Http://www.geodyssey.com/global/papers, 2000.
18. NIMA, Digital Terrain Elevation Data, http://www.niama.mil/, 2003.
19. Sahr K. and White D., Discrete Global Grid Systems. *Computing Science And Statistics*, Interface Foundation of North America. Inc., 30pp, 1998.
20. Sahr K., White D. and Kimerling A., Geodesic Discrete Global Grid Systems, *Cartography & Geographical Information Science*, 30(2): 121-134, 2003.
21. White D., Global Grids From Recursive Diamond Subdivisions of The Surface of an Octahedron or Icosahedron. *Environmental Monitoring and Assessment*, 4(1):93-103, 2000.

Photographs Alignment and High Dynamic Range Image Composition Based on Varying Exposure Levels

Shungang Hua and Lidan Wang

Key Laboratory for Precision and Non-traditional Machining Technology of Ministry of Education, Dalian University of Technology, Dalian 116024, P.R. China
hsgang02@dlut.edu.cn, wanglidan2000@sina.com

Abstract. An approach is proposed in this paper for aligning the photographs, which are taken with varying amounts of exposure towards the same scene, and fusing into a high dynamic range image. Firstly, the median threshold images of the photograph-sequence are computed, and their image pyramids are constructed using multi-scale techniques. Comparing the image pyramids level-by-level completes shift-alignments of photographs. Based on the shift-alignments, rotation-alignments of photographs can be achieved. According to least-squares principle, the response function curve of the imaging process can be recovered; the mapping relationship between pixel values and exposures is acquired with the sample pixels from the aligned photograph-sequence. A satisfactory high dynamic range image can be constructed from the photographs. The experimental results show that the proposed approach is fast and efficacious.

Keywords: image alignment, high dynamic range image, image pyramid, response curve, irradiance.

1 Introduction

In contrast to common digital image, high dynamic range image (HDRI) [1], whose pixel values are in proportion to the radiance values in the scene, can represent the varying dynamic range of the scene. Because HDRI is usually stored with mantissa and exponent, the confine of gray-levels is broken. The details in dark or bright regions of the scene can be displayed clearly. Therefore HDRI can be applicable to areas such as image-based modeling, rendering, and lighting, physically-based rendering, virtual reality, augmented and mixed reality, motion blur, and so on [2][3][4][5].

Although a few special digital cameras can be used to capture HDRI directly, it is expensive and not prevalent. Most researchers and photographers still employ a standard digital camera and composite HDRI from differently exposed photographs of the same scene. One of the limitations of this method is that the camera should be still among photographs. If there are some slight shifts or rotations among images, the constructed HDRI will be blurry. However camera's dithering is inevitable during shoot. For this, Greg Ward [6] presented a method of photographs registration for compositing HDRI. But the method was only for shift alignment, and didn't take rotation into account.

Z. Pan et al. (Eds.): ICAT 2006, LNCS 4282, pp. 1146–1155, 2006.

In this paper, an approach is presented for shift and rotation alignment among photographs, then the HDRI is constructed from varying exposed photographs of the same scene.

2 Image Alignment

In order to obtain a HDRI, we should take multiple photographs towards the same scene with varying exposures. We ought to take photographs on a fixed position ideally, but it is difficult to keep the camera still strictly, even using tripod mounting. Since the dithering errors will have a great impact on recovering the response curve of the imaging system, we must register them at first.

Our strategy of image alignment is that choosing one image from the image sequence as a reference (generally, we select the mid-exposed one for better effect), then registering the others with it respectively and computing offsets among them.

2.1 Binarization and Noise-Exclusion

A direct method of image alignment is comparing the outlines of the objects in the images. However, conventional edge detection is sensitive to exposure time. When the exposure time of photographs is different markedly, outlines of corresponding objects will appear differences obviously (see Fig. 1). So it isn't applicable to alignment between varying exposure images.

If we choose the median value of the image as a threshold, we can partition the pixels into two equal populations, one brighter and one darker than the threshold, and create the binary image (threshold image). Theoretically, the same scene will produce the same binary image at any exposure level by the median value.

Hence, for gray-scale images, we can compute histograms and partition the pixels by the median value M. The threshold images can be created using below equation:

$$V_1 = \begin{cases} 0, & V < M \\ 1, & V \geq M \end{cases}. \tag{1}$$

where V_1 is pixel value after image binarization, V is pixel value in original gray-scale image, M is the median value of gray-scale image.

For the color images, we should transform them into gray-scale images before binarization process. There are several methods for gray-scale transform. Fig. 1 shows the results of edge detection and median threshold binarization for two differently exposed images, which have been transformed from color into gray-scale firstly. Two median threshold images are consistent with each other as shown in Fig. 1(c) and (d), but the results by edge detection have great distinction as shown in Fig. 1(e) and (f). This example shows the advantage of median threshold binarization for differently exposed images.

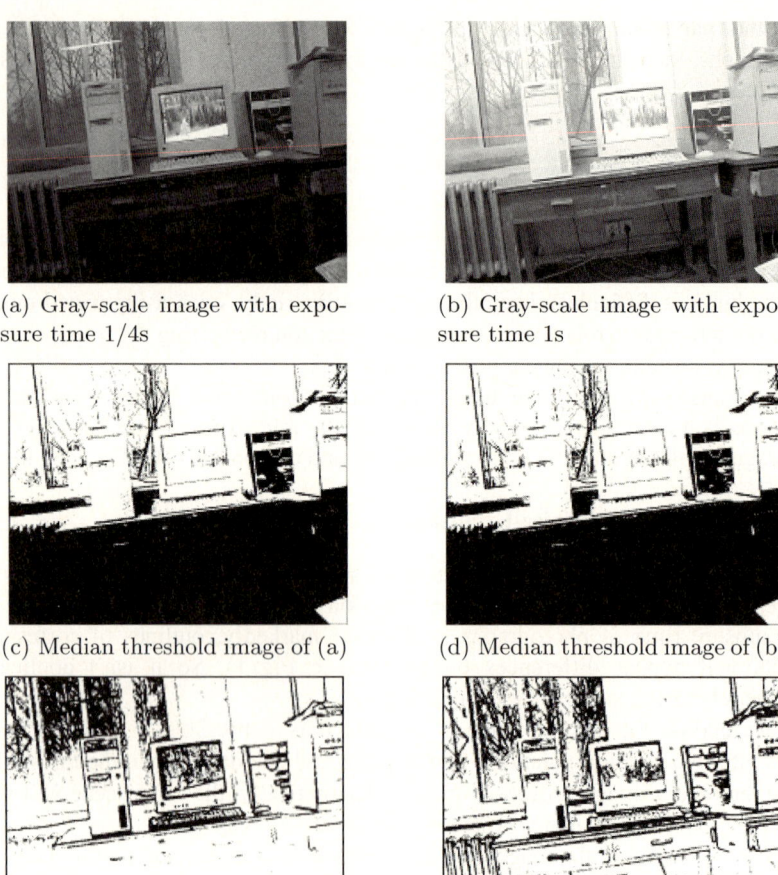

(a) Gray-scale image with exposure time 1/4s

(b) Gray-scale image with exposure time 1s

(c) Median threshold image of (a)

(d) Median threshold image of (b)

(e) Edge image of (a)

(f) Edge image of (b)

Fig. 1. Results of median threshold binarization and edge detection

Alignment between images is sensitive to the noises, especially near the median M, which will destabilize difference computation. For instance, the pixels, which should be a little darker than (brighter than or equal to) the median pixels, because of noise, appear to be a litter brighter than or equal to (darker than) the median, then we will assign value 1 (0) to it by mistake. For the pixels far away from the median, the influence of noises is relatively less. We should throw these noises away before comparing computation.

In order to eliminate the influence of noises near the median, we can assign value 0 to the pixels, which are within ± 4 of the median value, and keep other pixels original values:

$$V_2 = \begin{cases} 0 \ , & |V - M| \le 4 \\ V_1 \ , & |V - M| > 4 \end{cases} . \tag{2}$$

where V_2 is pixel value in noise-exclusion binary image; V_1 is pixel value in original binary image by equation (1); V, M are the same as in equation (1). After noise-exclusion, we can take the differences of these two binary images with an exclusive-or (XOR) operator to get shift and rotation offsets between images.

2.2 Shift Alignment

There are not only shift offsets but also rotation offsets between images. We compute all the shift offsets firstly, and then carry out the rotation alignment base on the shift offsets. After binarization and noise-exclusion, we can facilely find the aligning location corresponding to the minimum XOR difference by moving an image and comparing it with the reference image continually.

However, for high-resolution images, because all pixels must be computed every time, moving and comparing directly will expend much time. Therefore this method is not applicable to multiple high-resolution images, especially in real-time system.

To accelerate comparing (computing) process, we take the following strategies.

1) We construct the image pyramids [7] for binary images by multi-scale technique. For each lower level in an image pyramid, we take the previous binary image and filter it down by a factor of two in each dimension. The number of the pyramid levels depends on the less one between the height and the width of the original image, and besides, the lowest level must be resolvable. In this paper, we shrink the less dimension to 17~32 pixels. A five-level pyramid, which has been shrunk 4 times, is shown in Fig. 2.

Fig. 2. Image pyramid

In order to get the overall shift offset for alignment, we begin with the lowest level (binary) image pair. Move a unaligned binary image within a range of ±1 pixel in each dimension (contains 9 locations: Up, down, left, right, left-up, left-down, right-up, right-down and center), and then compare it with the reference binary image by

XOR operator. If the corresponding pixel values are not equal to each other, the result of XOR is 1, else is 0. We can get the shift offset corresponding to the minimum XOR difference, which is the sum of value 1. The location with the minimum difference is the optimum aligning position of this level. At the next level, multiply the previous offset by 2, and compute the minimum difference offset within a ±1 pixel range of this double previous offset. Repeat this operation until to the highest level (original image). Thus we can get the final shift offset.

2) We divide the pixels into groups, which have 16 or 32 pixels, and apply bitwise operations on 16-bit or 32-bit words for moving and XOR operation. It can speed up the computation, not only because 16 or 32 pixels can be disposed in one process, but also the speed of bitwise operation is far faster than byte-wise operation.

2.3 Rotation Alignment

Based on the shift offsets, we get a shift-aligned image sequence with the overlapped parts. For Rotation alignment, we take a circle in image whose center locates at the center of the image and diameter is the less one of the height and the width. We compare the pixels on the circumferences between images to search the optimum matching location within a range (the range of ±5° in this paper).

Rotate the circumferential all pixels of the unaligned image pixel by pixel, and compare it with the reference image by XOR operator. Count the result of XOR to find out the minimum difference corresponding to the optimum aligning location. And then relative to the reference image, rotate the image in terms of the rotation offset. After rotation alignment, we cut images to keep the overlapped parts.

Because of coupling between shifts and rotation, if the rotation angle is too large, the result of shift alignment may be inaccurate. In order to obtain an accurate result, we should repeat above operation. Namely, shift alignment → rotation alignment → shift alignment → rotation alignment →..., until the rotation offset is 0. During this process, we should not really cut out the no-corresponding pixels after shift alignment. Instead, we just extract the overlapped pixels for the next rotation alignment, lest the images should be cut excessively. We just cut the white margin after rotation alignment until the last rotation offset is 0.

3 HDRI Composition

HDRI Composition is to recover and record the true lighting information of the scene. For this, we ought to recover the response curve of the imaging system from the aligned images with different exposures, and get the mapping relation between exposure and pixel value, then fuse the images into a HDRI of the scene.

3.1 Recovering the Response Curve

The response curve of the imaging system represents the relation between the exposure H and the pixel value V (As to color image, red, green, blue channels should be deal with independently). Generally, the irradiance E accepted by camera is proportional to the radiance I in the scene. In regular exposure latitude (exposure time

Δt <10s and Δt >1/1000s), the exposure H is equal to the product of the irradiance E and the exposure time Δt (i.e. $H = E\Delta t$).).

In most cases, the absolute radiance I is not necessary. The relative radiance (or irradiance E) is enough to represent the lighting information of a scene. Hence, we have to work out the relation between pixel value V and exposure H or irradiance E. in other words, we should recover the response curve.

1) Recovery principle

According to literature [1], we can recover the response curve of the imaging system. We sample some corresponding points from the differently exposed images. As to these points, we assume that the pixel value V is a function of the exposure H (Capital letter V represents discrete variable, and small letter v represents continuous variable in this paper). So we can write an equation as below:

$$V_{ij} = f(H_{ij}) . \tag{3}$$

where f is a nonlinear function; i=1~N indicates the index of sample pixel location (N is the number of sample pixels in each image); j=1~M indicates the index of image (M is the number of images); V_{ij} represents the pixel value on location i in image j; H_{ij} represents the exposure on location i in image j. Generally, the pixel, whose exposure H is larger, has bigger pixel value V, thus we make the reasonable assumption that the function f is monotonically increasing.

As shown in Fig. 3, ordinate V represents pixel value, and abscissa ln$H$ is natural logarithm of exposure. There are $M = 5$ differently exposed images, from which we sample $N= 4$ groups of the pixels. Because we don't know the irradiance E_i, the horizontal position of the response curve can't be defined. Thereby E_i is assumed to be 1 unit temporarily. Different symbols in Fig. 3 mean different groups, and each group of the sample pixels has a sample curve. What we have to do is to move these curves horizontally until they line up to a smooth monotonic curve. But the horizontal position of the response curve is unknown, and need to be defined artificially. The response curve shows the nonlinear characteristic in dark and bright regions.

2) Implementation

Usually, the pixel values in common digital image are finite integer from 0 to 255, so we care the mapping relation between 256 pixel values and exposures rather than the expression of function f.

Because f is monotonic, we take inverse function and natural logarithm for equation (3), then:

$$F(V_{ij}) = \ln E_{ij} + \ln \Delta t_j \tag{4}$$

where, $F(V_{ij}) = \ln f^{-1}(V_{ij})$, and i, j are the same as in equation (3).

In order to let the sample pixels satisfy equation (4) in a least squares sense, we transform equation (4) to objective function as follows:

$$\sum_{i=1}^{N} \sum_{j=1}^{M} [F(V_{ij}) - \ln E_i - \ln \Delta t_j]^2 = o \tag{5}$$

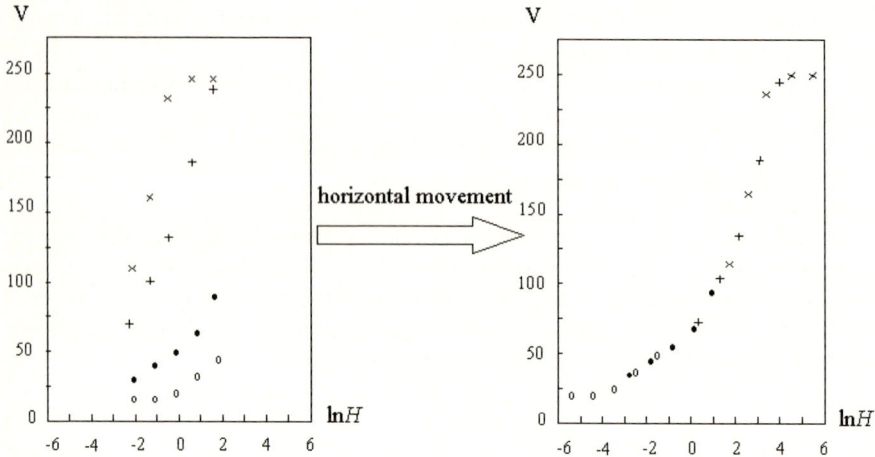

Fig. 3. Process of recovering the response curve

In order to reduce the influence of the nonlinear characteristic, we can bring a weighting factor $w(V)$ into equation (5). $w(V)$ has minimum value when $V = 0$ and 255, and increases gradually when V approaches 128. For smoothing the curve, smoothness term $F''(v) \approx F(v-1) - 2F(v) + F(v+1)$ is introduced too, so we can get following equation:

$$\sum_{i=1}^{N}\sum_{j=1}^{M}\{w(V_{ij})[F(V_{ij}) - \ln E_i - \ln \Delta t_j]\}^2 + \eta \sum_{V=1}^{254}[w(V)F''(V)]^2 = o. \qquad (6)$$

where η is smoothness factor, which is assigned experimentally. The weighting factor in smoothness term is also for reducing the effect of the nonlinear characteristic. In above equation, Δt_j and $w(V)$ are known, while $\ln E_i$ and $F(V_{ij})$ are what we want to get. We have $N \times M$ equations about the N groups of the pixels. Besides we add $F(128) = 0$ to confirm the horizontal position of the curve. Thus the $N \times M + 1$ equations compose the solving system for the N values of $\ln E_i$ and 256 samples of $F(V)$. In order to ensure that the solving system is overdetermined, we should let $N \times M + 1 \geq 256 + N$, i.e. the pixel groups $N \geq 255/(M-1)$. Equation(6) can be robustly solved using the singular value decomposition (SVD) method, so the response curve can be recovered.

3.2 Constructing HDRI

Based on the recovered response curve, we can derive a HDRI from the image sequence. $\ln E_i$ can be obtained directly by equation (4), but we compute $\ln E_i$ using all the images to reduce the errors as below equation:

$$\ln E_i = \frac{\sum_{j=1}^{M} w(V_{ij})[F(V_{ij}) - \ln \Delta t_j]}{\sum_{j=1}^{M} w(V_{ij})} . \tag{7}$$

where i is the index of each pixel location in image; j is the index of image. The E_i calculated by equation (7) is proportional to the radiance of the scene, and is just what we want. For color image, we will deal with red, green, blue channels respectively.

4   Experiment of Alignment and HDRI Composition

Using the approach proposed in this paper, we have aligned an image sequence with varying exposure levels, recovered the response curve of the camera, and then constructed the HDRI of the scene. We have developed an alignment and HDRI composition system using VC++ 6.0 programming environment. The HDRI is saved as Radiance's RGBE format [8].

Fig. 4 is an image sequence with 6 photographs (resolution: 650×520) taken from Kodak Z7590 digital camera, whose shutter speeds are 1/16, 1/8, 1/4, 1/2, 1 and 2s. During shooting, camera has some shift and rotation offsets. We recover response curve by 150 groups of the sample pixels from the image sequence. The random sample pixels are chosen automatically.

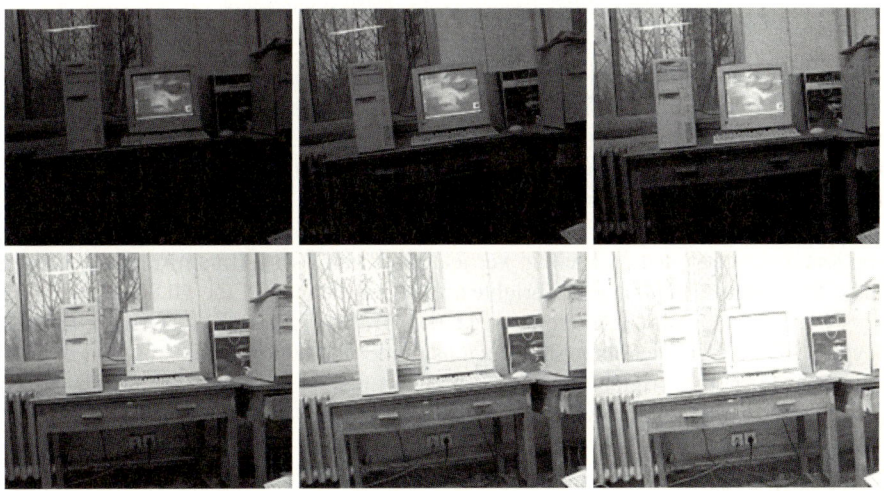

Fig. 4. Digital Photographs with different exposures

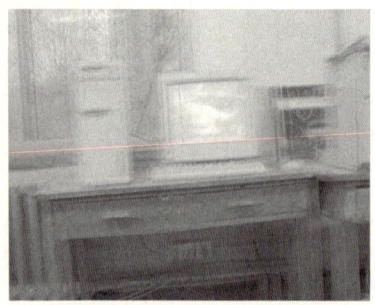

(a) Constructed HRDI with an un-aligned sequence

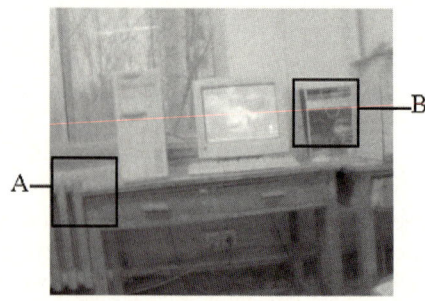

(b) Constructed HRDI with a shift-aligned sequence

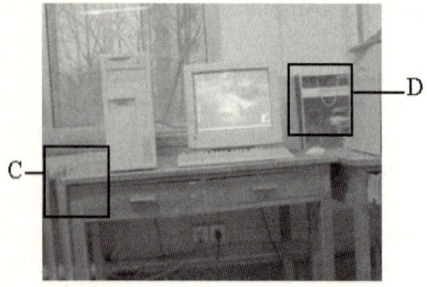

(c) Constructed HRDI with a shift-and-rotation-aligned sequence

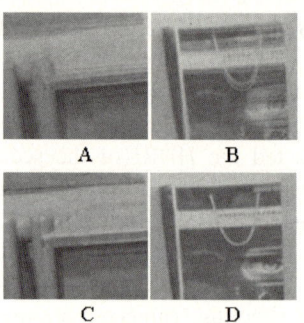

(d) Amplified details

Fig. 5. High dynamic range image composition

Fig. 5(a) is a constructed HDRI with original unaligned sequence, and the HDRI is blurry in the whole image. Fig. 5(b) is with a shift-aligned sequence. It is clear in the center of the image, but blurry near the edges. Fig. 5(c) is with a shift- and rotation-aligned sequence, and the constructed HDRI is clear in the whole image. Fig. 5(d) is amplified details of the panes in Fig. 5(b) and 5(c).

This image sequence is aligned two times. Its maximum shift offset is 30 pixels in horizontal direction and 5 pixels in vertical direction. Its maximum rotation offset is $3.2°$. As shown in Fig. 5(c), the brightest relative radiance in the HDRI is (97.9635, 32.8506, 24.6320), and the darkest one is (0.0261, 0.0272, 0.0281). Dynamic range is beyond 3.7×10^3. The details in dark regions (under the table) are clearer than the first four images in the original sequence, and the details in bright region (computer screen) are clearer than the last three images.

5 Conclusion

In contrast to edge detection, median threshold binarization is more suitable for aligning the differently exposed images of the same scene. In this paper, we construct image pyramids for the binary images, and get the shift offsets and rotate offsets among the images. The response curve of the camera is recovered from aligned images by least square method. The irradiance (relative radiance) of every point in the scene can be calculated, and the HDRI is constructed. The experimental results show that the proposed approach is effectual and the constructed HDRI is satisfactory.

References

1. Debevec, P.E., Malik, J.: Recovering high dynamic range radiance maps from photographs. Proc. of ACM SIGGRAPH '97. ACM Press, New York (1997) 369-378
2. Debevec, P.E., McMillan, L.: Image-Based Modeling, Rendering, and Lighting. IEEE Computer Graphics and Applications 22 (2002) 24-25
3. Debevec, P.E.: HDRI and Image-Based Lighting. Proc. SIGGRAPH (2003), Course 19,San Diego,July (2003).
4. Debevec P.E.: Image-Based Lighting. IEEE Computer Graphics and Applications 22 (2002) 26-34
5. Agusanto, K., Li, L., Zhu, C.G., Sing, N.W.: Photorealistic rendering for augmented reality using environment illumination. Proceedings of the Second IEEE and ACM International Symposium on Mixed and Augmented Reality (ISMAR '03). Tokyo, Japon, October (2003) 208-216
6. Ward, G.: Fast, Robust Image Registration for Compositing High Dynamic Range Photographs from Handheld Exposures. Journal of Graphics Tools 8 (2003) 17-30
7. Li, J.Y.: Centroid-based approach to multiscale representation of binary images. Journal of Zhejiang University (Sciences Edition) 30 (2003) 284-288
8. Ward, G.: High Dynamic Range Image Encodings.
9. http://www.anyhere.com/gward/hdrenc/hdr_ encodings.html (2002)

Elastic Algorithm: A New Path Planning Algorithm About Auto-navigation in 3D Virtual Scene

Yong Chen, Ke-qin Wu, Dong Wang, and Ge Chen

College of Information Science and Engineering ,Ocean University of China,
Qingdao 266071,China
chenyong@ouc.edu.cn

Abstract. Elastic Algorithm proposed in this paper is a new and fast path planning algorithm to solve the problem of auto-navigation in 3D virtual scene. First, with a grid model based representation of virtual environments, different obstacles are assigned different color in the projection map of scene and their encasing boxes are stored to provide local path. Then, Elastic Algorithm is designed to optimize the basic path. It can be applied to complex condition and moving object, and has high stability and efficiency in solving the path planning problem.

Keywords: Path Planning; Grid model; collision-free; Navigation.

1 Introduction

Navigation in virtual environment plays an important role in Virtual Reality and Computer Animation. In virtual 3D scene, users can observe and investigate 3D objects from different angles of view by means of navigation to get more useful information [1]-[2].

There are two chief ways of navigation for user to explore the virtual scene. The first is interactive navigation. This kind of method is very agile, users can totally control the navigation position and view direction as their wish, by means of operating the mouse or the keyboard, but the users got lost easily when they enter an unfamiliar virtual scene. Another way is selected navigation. Users can visit the virtual scene according to the prearranged path. This prearranged path is always recorded by the producer before use. This method is easily realized but produces inconvenience. Especially in the condition of complex scene, if the aim of the users cannot be predicted, the task is hard to be accomplished.

This paper addresses automatic path finding problem. According to the user's destination, an optimized path is produced by our algorithm.

2 Previous Works

Path Planning is also called Obstacle Avoidance or Collision-free Path Planning, it aims at producing a Collision-free path from a start position to a target position in the environment which contains obstacles, according to a certain criterion (e. g. the

Z. Pan et al. (Eds.): ICAT 2006, LNCS 4282, pp. 1156–1165, 2006.

shortest distance)[3]-[4]. The current auto-navigation path planning algorithm in 3D virtual scene is mainly developed from Robot Path Planning Algorithms and Path Finding Methods in Geography Information System (GIS).

Path Planning is a very important task in the Robotics. Since the invention of the first manipulator arm in American in the late 1940's, the related research and application developed rapidly in occident and Japan. Accordingly, the research on Robot Path Planning and related algorithms sprung up. A lot of effective algorithms have been introduced to solve the Path Planning problem, such as geometry method, space decomposition method, potential field method, mathematical analysis method, etc. In the area of Robot, we hope the Robot can detect the unknown or partly unknown surroundings with all kinds of sensors, and then use the acquired information to make decision of marching forward. So the Path Planning problems we concerned are always based on the unknown or partly unknown surroundings [5]-[11].

Path Planning is also a research hotspot in GIS. Researchers often describe the Shortest Path problem as the Meshwork problem of graph theory. This method can solve the problem such as traveling on cities and highways, but it complicates the problem when dealing with 3D virtual scene containing large non-obstacle area.

Comparing with Robotics and GIS, the initial condition in solving Path Planning of Virtual Reality, Computer Animation, Game and Driver Exercitation is much simpler. Before the 3D scene is rendered, information of all objects has to be known, such as the size and position of the static objects, the original position, speed, outside force of the moving objects. So, when complete environment information is known, the main task of Path Planning in 3D scene is to find the optimized path from the start position to the target position.

3   Information Representation of 3D Scene

Before the calculation of collision-free path in 3D scene, we must represent all information of the environment, such as obstacle, collision-free area, etc. There are 4 basic methods to represent virtual scene [11]:

(1) Representing obstacle by polygon;
(2) Representation of collision-free area;
(3) Uniform grid method;
(4) Route map method.

Method (2) and (3) are not applicable to complex 3D environment. And method (1) is time-consuming, so encasing box is often used to simplify complex 3D obstacle, resulting in imprecise collision detection. In our algorithm, we make full use of adjacency relation among objects, thus the projection map of 3D scene, similar to method (3), is selected to represent environment information.

3.1   Represent of Environment Information Based on Projection Map

When the 3D scene is modeled, the Layout Plan of collectivity building is often used to ensure the precision of modeling. The obstacles projection map of 3D scene is produced based on it. We project the obstacles of 3D scene which cannot be passed through to a raster plane, resulting in 2D projection map in uniform grid format. Fig. 1 shows a sample of 3D scene. According to it, Fig. 2 is produced to present the discrete obstacle information with size 1024×800. For static environment, the rasterization only needs to be performed once.

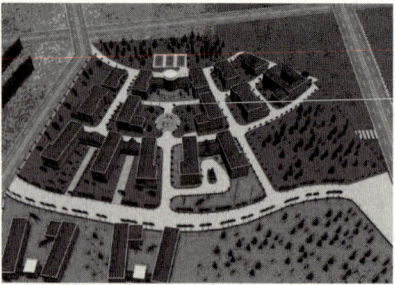

Fig. 1. The sample 3D scene

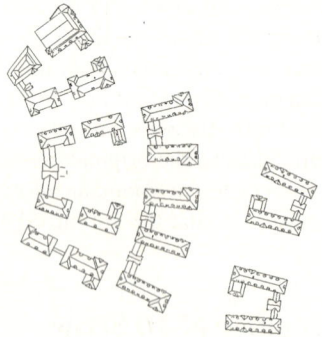

Fig. 2. The obstacle's projection map of 3D scene

3.2   Representation of Obstacles

In order to distinguish Obstacles in 3D scene, we fill the Obstacles with different color in the obstacles projection map as shown in Fig.3. This projection map will be represented by a matrix called the Scene Projection Map Matrix (SPMM).

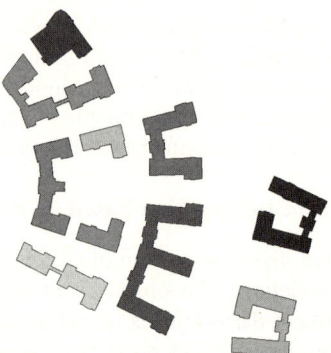

Fig. 3. Representing Obstacles with different color

Definition 1: Obstacle Point and Non-Obstacle point

In the SPMM, when Map $(u_i, v_i) = 0$, there is no obstacle on the site (u_i, v_i) in the 3D scene, so this site is called Non-Obstacle Point; otherwise the site is called Obstacle Point, the value of Map (u_i, v_i) corresponds to a certain obstacle in the 3D scene.

$$map_i(u,v) = \begin{cases} 0 & \text{Non-Obstacle Point} \\ C & \text{Obstacle Point} \end{cases}$$

4   The Elastic Algorithm for Path Planning

In this section, we give an overview of our approach and then introduce our algorithm in detail.

4.1   Algorithm Overview

When walking in a unfamiliar environment of the real world, the walker will chooses his direction toward his destination, as shown in Fig.4.a, S->T; if he meets an obstacle, he may try to round it first, and then newly follows his direction toward his destination, as shown in Fig.4.a, S->A->B->C->D->T, point S represents the start point and point T represents the target. More likely, the walker will choose the shorter route which is approximately tangent to the obstacle, as shown in Fig.4.b, S->B->C->T.

This idea quite likes using elastic to connect the start point and the target point. When there is an obstacle in its way, the elastic will be pulled, along the boundary of the obstacle, since it cannot pass through directly the obstacle. It is the elasticity of the elastic that make the length of the path to be the shortest. Based on this idea, we designed this elastic algorithm to solve the automatic path finding problem.

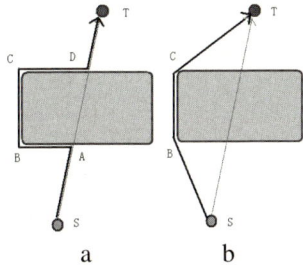

a   b

Fig. 4. Main algorithmic idea inspired by elastic

4.2   Algorithm Description

In this elastic algorithm, we should pretreat the obstacles in the SPMM and get the route surrounding them, then perform two stages disposal: first, create the basic path and record it as a linked list build with a series of linked nodes (e.g. S->A->B->C->D->T); second, use the elastic algorithm to get an optimized navigation path.

4.2.1 Algorithm Introduction

Definition 2: Surrounding Route of Obstacle and Boundary Point

A Surrounding Route of Obstacle (SRO) is composed of its Boundary Points and these Boundary Points are stored in its corresponding circular linked list; Boundary Points are such nodes that have and at least have one neighboring node which represents the obstacle, as the points composing the green line surrounding the quadrangular obstacle in Fig.5.

Fig. 5. Surrounding Route of Obstacle

SRO can be produced by scanning the SPMM, after all the Boundary Points have been founded, we can store them in a circular linked list of the corresponding obstacle. In this way, if the path meets one obstacle, its color in projection map will show us which obstacle it is, the SRO will be cut into two parts, the shorter one will be selected as the local basic path.

4.2.2 Creating Basic Path

The main task of this stage is to create a basic path in the SPMM to prepare for the optimization stage.

```
Begin
    Step1: read S,T; S->PL; // S is start point;
                            // T is target point;
                            // PL is Path Link List and empty at first;
    Step2: current point= next point on line S-T, temp= Map (current point);
        If current point ≠ T then
            Goto Step 3;
        Else
            Goto Step 5;
    Step3: If temp=0 then
            Goto Step 2;
    Step4: If temp=C then
                Find two Boundary Point; // Like A and D in Fig.4.a
                Find Local Path according to C; // Like ABCD in Fig.4.a
                //Note that the Local Path is composed of many points more
                //than 4 points, A, B, C and D
        Local Path->PL;
    Step5: T->PL; //Add T into PL
End.
```

Algorithm 1. Creating Basic Path

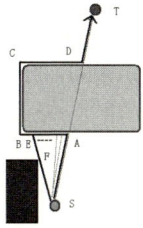

Fig. 6. Elastic Algorithm demonstration

Begin
    Step1: the first node in PL->front, the second node in PL-> mid;
      If mid = Destination Then
          Goto Step 6;   // Algorithm end;
    Step2: the next nodes of PL->temp;
      If temp = Destination Then
          Goto Step 6;
      Else
          Temp->back;
    Step3: If mid is in the line of front to back Then
          {
                   Delete mid from PL;
                   Back->mid;
                   Goto Step 2;
          }
    Step4: If (mid is not in the line of front to back) and (no obstacle is in the
          line of front to back) Then
             {
                   Delete mid from PL;
                   Back->mid;
                   Goto Step 2;
             }
    Step5: If (mid is not in the line of front to back) and (there are obstacles in
          the line of front to back) Then
             {
                   Add the new obstacles' local path into PL between
                   front and mid;
                   The first node of local path->mid;
                   Goto Step 2;
             }
    Step 6: End.

Algorithm 2. Elastic Algorithm for optimizing basic path

Basic method: draw a line between the start point A and the target point B, check the value of the point on the line one by one. If the point being checked is a Obstacle Point, find two Boundary Points A and D, then read corresponding SRO to find the local basic path, add the local path A->B->C->D into the path linked list; if the point is Non-Obstacle Point, just check the next point; if the point is target point, end the algorithm.

4.2.3 Elastic Algorithm for Optimizing Basic Path

The Basic Path can meet the demand of collision-free, but it is not the optimal path we want. And some parts of the Path Linked List are composed of Local Path which is created by too many points, so we have to predigest it. The Elastic Algorithm is designed for this purpose.

Basic Method: after obtaining the Basic Path Linked Line PL, as SABCDT in Fig.4.a, we perform elastic algorithm: drag SA along A->B until it meet B or another obstacle's point F. if it meet B, remove A from PL; if F, remove A and add F into the path linked list PL between S and B, take F as S. Repeat the above step until reach T.

4.2.4 Applying Elastic Algorithm Inside Tier Building

In this Elastic Algorithm, we project the 3D obstacles to 2D plane, so when the start point and the destination are on different floors of a building, the Elastic Algorithm should be adjusted.

To find a path between two positions on different floors,we perform the algorithm in different floors respectively: first, marks two ends of the stairway on the two floors as two midway node, then, find the path between start point and one midway node in the same floor and the path between target point and another midway node respectively, and connect the two path with the mid path between the two midway nodes to build a complete path from the start to the destination (see Fig.7).

Fig. 7. Elastic Algorithm for Tier Building

5 Algorithm Analysis

5.1 Flexibility

Excellent flexibility is achieved because the projection map of scene is adopted in the elastic algorithm.

5.1.1 Complex Obstacle Avoidance

The obstacle avoidance method based on encasing box of 3D object, proposed by [12], is more applicable to convex obstacles, but relatively incapable of processing complex obstacles, such as the parterres shown in Fig.8.

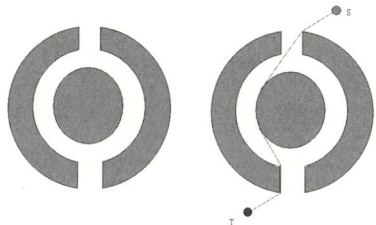

Fig. 8. Finding path through parterres

The encasing box based method may fail to find a path through complex obstacles sometimes or has to divide them into several pieces. But the Elastic Algorithm can deal with any concave obstacles easily. As shown in Fig. 8, a collision-free path form S to T is quickly found by the algorithm. Theoretically, any environment, even the one as complex as labyrinth, can be processed by this algorithm.

5.1.2 Real-Time Obstacle Avoidance for Moving Objects

Some applications such as computer game and virtual training require an ability of real-time obstacle avoidance. In these applications, moving objects are controlled by mouse or keyboard. Genetic methods often have difficulty in real-time obstacle avoidance [13, 14]. But by comparing the projection position of the object with the projection map of the scene, the Elastic Algorithm solves this problem easily.

5.2 Efficiency

Because the algorithm is based on the Scene Projection Map Matrix, the adjacency relationship between pixels can be utilized conveniently. Therefore, the local collision-free paths are quickly found by reading the precomputed encasing boxes of obstacles.

Two main factors affect the efficiency of finding a collision-free path: the distance between the start node S and target node T, and the number of obstacles in a virtual scene. On the one hand, the efficiency of finding the basic path from S to T is directly affected by the number of nodes in the path. On the other hand, the efficiency of optimizing the basic path by the Elastic Algorithm is directly affected by the number of obstacles in the path. Therefore, in general, for the scene with a lot of little obstacles, this algorithm is more efficient than others.

6 Test and Result

We apply this algorithm to a virtual walkthrough environment. All objects in the environment are 3D objects which were modeled by 3D Max software and stored in user-defined format. A scene of the environment is shown in Fig.9. In the test, the algorithm can quickly find the optimal path form any start position to target position. Fig. 10 gives 4 examples to show its ability to deal with different complex cases.

Fig. 9. An example of 3D virtual walkthrough environment

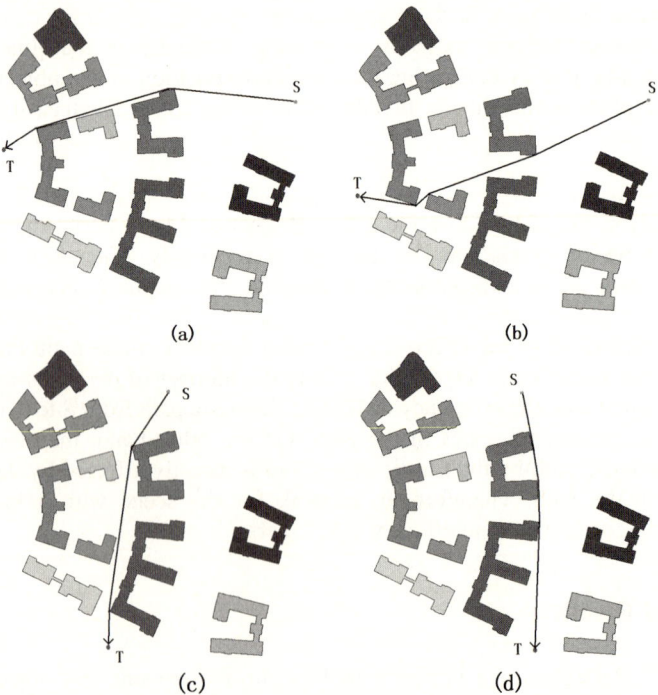

(a)   (b)

(c)   (d)

Fig. 10. Four examples of path finding in the 3D virtual walkthrough environment

7   Conclusion

This paper proposes a new algorithm based on Scene Projection Map Matrix, called Elastic Algorithm, to address the problem of automatic path planning and obstacle avoidance in 3D virtual navigation. First, local collision-free paths are detected based on the encasing boxes of obstacles which are precomputed with well known environment information. Then the Elastic Algorithm was employed to optimize them. The excellent efficiency and flexibility of the algorithm was analyzed, and an experiment in applying this algorithm to 3D virtual scene verified its effectiveness and practicability.

References

1. P Jansen-Osmann. Using Desktop Virtual Environments to Investigate the Role of Landmarks. Computers in Human Behavior, 2002.18: 427~436
2. Zhigeng Pan, A.D.Cheok, Hongwei Yang, Jiejie Zhu, Jiaoying Shi, Virtual reality and mixed reality for Virtual learning environments, Computers & Graphics. 2006.30(1): 20~28
3. C. Latombe, Robot Motion Planning. Norwell: Kluwer, 1991. 143~176
4. Mingming Zhang, Zhigeng Pan, Pingan Wang, Time-critical rendering algorithm with incorporation of LoD,visibility culling and object impostor, Journal of Visualization and Computer Animation, 2003.14(4): 211~223
5. J.T.Schwartz, M.Shair, A Survey of Motion Planning and Related Geometric Algorithms. Artificial Intelligence, 1998, 37(1): 55~67
6. R.A.Brooks, T. Lazano-Perez, A Subdivision Algorithm in Configuration Space for Find Path with Rotation. Proc. Of the 8th Int. Conf on Artificial Intelligence. Karlsruhe, FRG. 1983: 366~380
7. Y.K.Hwang, N. Ahuja, A Potential Field Approach to Path Planning. IEEE Trans. Robot. & Autom, 1992,8(1): 23~32
8. Z. Ma, Z. Yuan. Real-time Navigation and Obstacle Avoidance Based on Grid Method for Fast mobile Robot. Robot, 1996, 18(6): 344~348(in Chinese)
9. Z. Yuan, M. Gao. A New Method of Real-time Navigation and Obstacle Avoidance for Mobile Robot in Dynamic Environment. Robot, 2000, 22(2): 81~88(in Chinese)
10. Yunfang Ge, Zhigeng Pan, Weiwei Xu, Vision-based Path Planning in Intelligent Virtual Environment, 6th International Conference on Computer Graphics and Artificial Intelligence, Limoges, FRANCE, 2003: 25~34
11. Weiwei Xu, Zhigeng Pan, Yunfang Ge, Novel Method for Curved Path Human Walking Animation, in Proceedings of Second International Conference on Images and Graphics, Hefei, China, 2002: 993~999
12. A. Du, G. Zhai. Design of Moving Path Based on Simplified Terrain. Computer Engineering and Application, 2005.18: 45~48.(in Chinese)
13. Q. Li, L. Lin, G. Yan. A Evolutionary Algorithm for Path Planning of Mobile Robot. Proceedings of the 3rd world congress on intelligent control and automation. Hefei, China, 2000, 28(2): 1206~1209(in Chinese)
14. G. Chen, L. Shen. Genetic Path Planning Algorithm for Complex Environment Path Planning. Robot, 2001, 23(1): 40~45.(in Chinese)

Mental Representation of Spatial Structure in a Virtual Room-Sized Space

Zhiqiang Luo and Henry Been-Lirn Duh

Centre for Human Factors & Ergonomics, School of Mechanical & Aerospace Engineering,
Nanyang Technological University, Singapore
peterluo@pmail.ntu.edu.sg, mblduh@ntu.edu.sg

Abstract. To keep spatial awareness in virtual multilevel building, navigator should understand the spatial structure of space. Mental representation of spatial structure in a virtual cylindrical room was investigated in present experiments. Participants first observed two static views of space in which the two viewpoints were on the same vertical plane but with different heights, and then either judged the relative direction of object in the first experiment or egocentrically pointed out the direction of object in the second experiment. The results suggested that the orientation-dependent representation of spatial structure was created even though participants could learn the space from two different viewpoints lying on the vertical dimension of space.

Keywords: virtual reality, spatial cognition, navigation.

1 Introduction

Understanding the structure of space is a natural activity when people explore a three-dimensional (3D) space. Navigation is a necessary component of task performed in simulated buildings. Previous studies demonstrated that people poorly performed navigation task in virtual buildings, especially when the vertical traveling was involved [1]. Soeda et al [2] suggested that, after traveling the stairwell, people could keep the orientation by environmental information. One intuitive way to realize this method is to give visual access to different floors so that individual can know spatial features on the target floor before vertical traveling [3]. Thus, mental representation created by observing the spatial layout on both the upper floor and the target floor is assumed to better help individual to keep high spatial awareness in building.

Mental representations of room-sized space are orientation dependent when the space is learned from single viewpoint on both the horizontal and vertical dimensions of the room-sized space [4, 5]. After subjects experienced one of five perspectives lying on the vertical dimension of virtual space, Luo [4] found that subjects who observed 45-degree view performed best in judging the relative direction among objects, whereas participants observing 0-degree perspective could best point out the direction of object with respect to the egocentric reference. In Shelton and McNamara's study [5], subjects who stood on the ground observed the spatial layout from one position in the room. Performance in judging the relative direction was more

Z. Pan et al. (Eds.): ICAT 2006, LNCS 4282, pp. 1166–1174, 2006.

accurate for imagined heading parallel to study view than for imagined headings parallel to novel views.

The effect of viewpoint elevation was systematically investigated in designing the aviation display. Wickens and colleagues [6, 7, 8, 9, 10] suggested that the display showing the egocentric view better supports the local guidance in which the egocentric reference is required, and the display showing the exocentric view, especially when the degree of elevated viewpoint was 45^0 , enhances the understanding of structure of space in which the exocentric reference takes main function. Further, they investigated the function of split-screen display that showed both egocentric and exocentric views in the same display and found this display provided the best support for the continuous task of local awareness and guidance and poor support for some of global situation awareness (SA) tasks [8].

The goal of present study was to investigate the effect of dual views on the mental representation of the spatial structure in a virtual room-sized space. Two views, 0-degree (egocentric) view and 45-degree (exocentric) view, were considered in present experiments. The egocentric view was presented from the perspective of the individual standing on the floor of room, and the exocentric view was presented from the perspective of the individual viewing the spatial structure from a higher position (for example the upper floor). Previous studies found that mental representation to spatial layout in room was orientation-dependent even though people could experience three static views on the floor [5]. The design of dual views in aviation display also suggested that the combination of egocentric and exocentric views could not improve the understanding of global structure of space [8]. Thus, it was hypothesized that the mental representation created by observing two views, the egocentric and exocentric views, was orientation dependent.

Two tasks, the judgment of relative direction (JRD, "Imagine you are at the position of A object and facing B object, Point C object" in Experiment 1) and egocentric pointing task ("Imagine you are facing object A, Point B object" in Experiment 2), were adopted to test the representation of space in mind. JRD task was primarily sensitive to object-to-object spatial relations represented in memory, whereas the egocentric pointing task was sensitive to self-to-object spatial relations in memory [11, 12].

2   Experiment 1

There were 24 student, 12 males and 12 females, from Nanyang Technological University participating the experiment. They received 10 dollar for participantion.

The virtual scene was constructed in EON (Eon Reality Company, 2004), and showed on the i-glass HMD (i-O Display Systems, LLC) with the 26.5^0 diagonal field of view. The room was cylindrical shape and measured 8 m diameter and 6 m height in virtual space. There were 7 objects located on the floor. Three of objects had heights (2 meters) greater than observer's eye height (1.7m) on the floor. When taking the tests, participants would point out the target direction in front of a board via a laser pointer.

2.1 Experiment Design

Participants experienced both 0-degree and 45-degree views. The distance between the viewpoint and the center of layout was 4m in virtual space. Two orders of viewing were designed: one was beginning at 0^0 and then at 45^0 while another one was first beginning at 45^0 and then at 0^0. Participants spent the same time on observing the spatial layout in each view. The direction between any two objects was defined, where 0^0 direction was defined from Stoneware to Lamp, and the degree of direction increased counterclockwise (see Fig. 1). The 0^0 direction paralleled with the orientation of subject in the egocentric view. Further, the room was constructed with the cylindrical shape in order to minimize the extra disturbance on representation caused by linear walls [5].

JRD was adapted to test the mental representation in memory. Specifically, participants were required to point out the direction of the top of target. When performing the task, participants stood at the mark in front of a board, and used the laser pointer to point out the direction required in the task. The experimenter recorded the response time and the coordinates of both the laser point on the board and participant's eyes. When these two coordinates were known, the horizontal and vertical angles from eyes to the red point on the board could be calculated.

The principle independent variable was the imagined heading and the order to viewing. Six unequally imagined headings were used, ranged from 72^0 to 325^0. The dependent variables were the angular error and the pointing latency. The angular error was measured as the angular difference between the actual direction of target and the pointing direction. The pointing latency was measured as the time from the presentation of question to the end of response.

2.2 Procedure

There were three phases in experiment. First, participants took the following memory test. They were required to scan 9 objects printed on a paper for 30 seconds and then generate these objects at the corresponding positions on a blank paper with same size. These 9 objects were not used in the virtual room. Participants who correctly recalled more than 5 objects were allowed to proceed to the next phase. All participants could recall more than 6 objects in this test. Second, participants observed the 7 experimental objects printed on a paper. After they were familiar with the objects, they wore HMD and were instructed to watch an empty virtual room viewed from the assigned viewpoint. The room size was the same with the experimental room containing the objects. Then the experimenter displayed the experimental virtual room containing 7 objects viewed from the same viewpoint. Participants spent 2 minutes learning the location and size of each object. During this time the experimenter helped them to recognize the virtual objects if necessary. After experiencing the first view, participants would watch the previous empty room from the second viewpoint. They also spent 2 minutes observing the experimental spatial layout from the latter viewpoint. Last, participants began to take spatial test in front of the testing board.

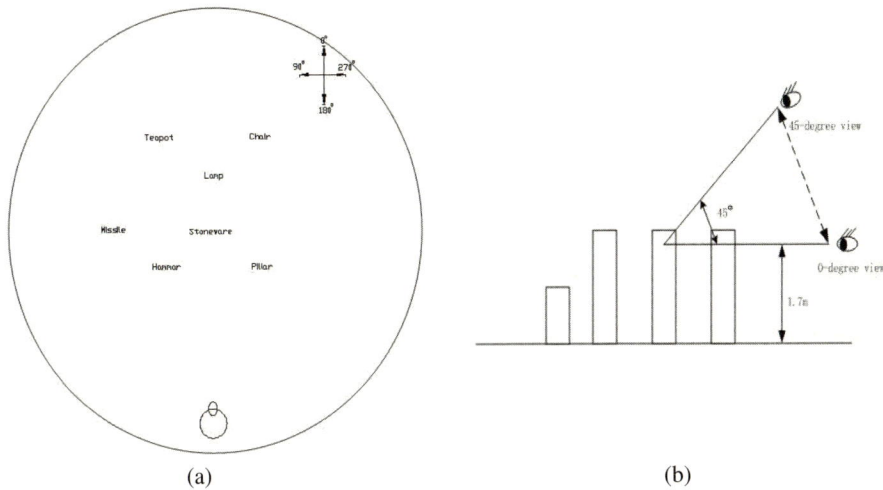

(a)   (b)

Fig. 1. (a) The spatial layout of room and the arrow with degree presenting the direction; (b) viewpoint locations, the dashed line with two arrows presenting the two orders of viewing

2.3   Result and Discussion

All dependent measures were analyzed using a split-plot factorial ANOVA with terms for order of viewing, gender, imagined heading. Order of viewing and gender were between-participants; imagined heading was within-participant. An α level of .05 was used.

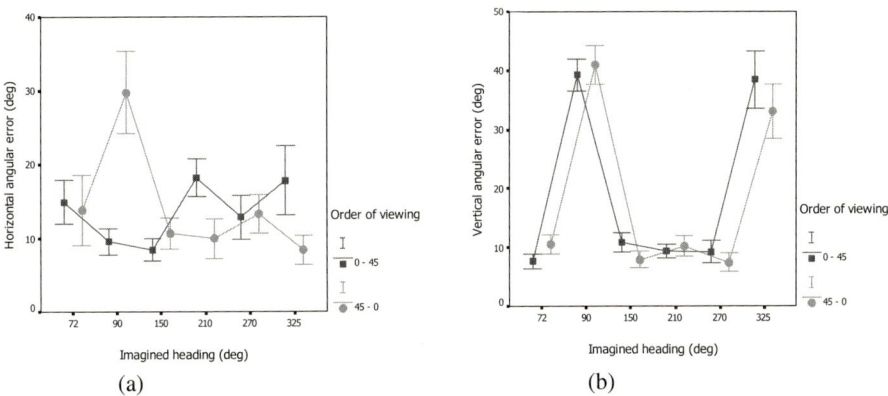

(a)   (b)

Fig. 2. (a) Angular error in judgments of relative horizontal direction and (b) angular error in judgments of relative vertical direction in JRD task. Error bars represent ±1 standard error of the mean (SEM).

To the performance on judging the horizontal direction, the interaction between the imagined heading and order of viewing was significant, $F(5, 110) = 5.602, p = .002$

(see Fig. 2(a)). Further, the significant effect of imagined heading was not found in the order of viewing from 0^0 to 45^0, while in the order of viewing from 45^0 to 0^0, the effect of imagined heading was significant, F(5, 55) = 5.08, p = .016. The data suggested that the mental representation presented the orientation-dependent property if the egocentric view was learned lately, but this property was weak in memory if the exocentric view was learned lately. The larger viewing angle in the exocentric view seemed to be an important determinant of orientation-free performance in JRD test [12]. The reason could be that subjects better remembered the global property, especially the depth, of array distributed on the floor if they observed the exocentric view lately. The global environmental information was assumed to facilitate the generation of judging horizontal direction [6].

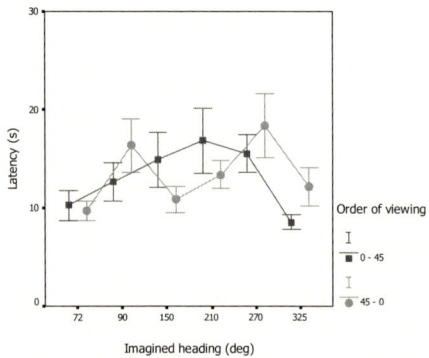

Fig. 3. Latency to perform JRD tasks in JRD task. Error bars represent ±1 standard error of the mean (SEM).

The effect of imagined heading on the judgment of vertical direction was significant, F(5, 110) = 64.348, p < .001, see Fig.2(b). Further the pos hoc analysis found the performances for each heading of 90^0 and 325^0 was substantially worse than performances for the other four imagined headings (72^0, 150^0, 210^0, 270^0), with p < .001 in each level. The data indicated that judging vertical direction might require different knowledge from that needed in judging horizontal direction. For example, the height of object should be considered in judging vertical direction but not in judging horizontal direction. Height of object was observed more efficiently in the egocentric view than the exocentric view. No effect of order of viewing suggested two groups acquired the same representation for the vertical direction.

Fig. 3 plotted the pointing latency to perform the task under two orders of viewing. The effect of imagined heading was significant, F(5, 110) = 4.585, p = .004. But in each order of viewing, the function of imagined heading might be different. In the order from 0^0 to 45^0, the time for the heading 325^0 was significantly faster than time spent for headings 150^0, 210^0 and 270^0. In the order from 45^0 to 0^0, the time spent for heading 270^0 was longer than time for headings 72^0, 150^0, and 325^0. The time difference in the condition of order of viewing from 0^0 to 45^0 seemed to stem from increased difficulty in mentally translating to the required position that was far from viewpoints. The time difference in the condition of order of viewing from 45^0 to 0^0 showed a different pattern. The increased mental rotation departing from the front-back (0^0-180^0) dimension delayed the reaction time in task.

3 Experiment 2

There were 20 student, 10 males and 10 females from Nanyang Technological University, participating the experiment for the pay 10 dollar per one hour.

The materials and procedures were similar to those used in the first experiment. But participants would perform the egocentric pointing task. In addition, participants were required to imagine standing at the position where they observed the spatial layout from 0-degree perspective in the virtual room. Participants were also required to point out the direction of the top of target. The dependent measures were the same as those in first experiment But the imagined heading was now defined between the participant and object faced in virtual room. Only five imagined headings which lied around the 0^0 direction were considered in this task.

The effect of imagined heading on the vertical angle is significant, $F(5, 90) = 79.504$, $p < .001$ (see Fig. 4(a)). Performance on the imagined heading of 0^0 was substantially better than performance on the other headings, $F(1, 98) = 15.610$, $p < .001$. It was noteworthy that the performance on the imagined headings (25^0 and 340^0) departed farthest from the 0^0 direction was worse than performance on other three imagined heading, $F(1, 98) = 122.288$, $p < .001$. The data suggested that the likelihood of slippage in vertical information increased with increasing mental process. It also indicated that subjects could better represent the spatial vertical information around the 0^0 direction.

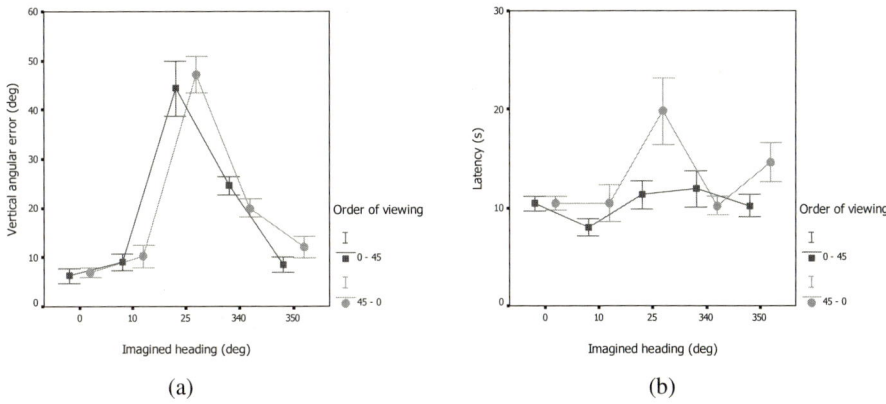

(a)   (b)

Fig. 4. (a)Angular error in judgments of vertical direction and (b) latency in egocentric pointing task. Error bars represent ±1 standard error of the mean (SEM).

The effect of imagined heading on the response latency was significant, $F(5, 90) = 6.932$, $p < .001$ (see Fig. 4(b)). The interaction between the imagined heading and order of viewing also showed significant effect on the response latency, $F(5, 90) = 4.247$, $p = .009$. Further, there was no difference between any imagined heading in the order of viewing from 0^0 to 45^0; while in the order of viewing from 45^0 to 0^0, the effect of imagined heading was significant, $F(4, 49) = 4.33$, $p = .005$. To some extent, the data indicated the dynamic property of mental representations created by observing two views, which would be discussed in detail in General Discussion.

4   General Discussion

The principle goal of experiments was to determine the role of dual views on the mental representation for the spatial structure of virtual room. The two experiments tested two different spatial relations, object-to-object and self-to-object relations, in memory. The results mainly showed the orientation-dependent performance which supported the hypothesis of present study. We explained the performance in the context of spatial references created by both observer and objects in environment.

In the context of virtual room-sized space, the 0-degree and 45-degree views were different with respect to the perception and task supported. The 45-degree view provided more global information of environment and visual cues creating the depth dimensionality of layout, whereas the egocentric view gave more visual cues describing the characteristics of objects, especially the height information [14]. Second, the exocentric reference was the natural choice to code spatial relationship among objects in the 45-degree view, which was appropriated for the exocentric task involving geographical directional judgments [13]. Egocentric reference was usually adapted in the egocentric view to code spatial relations, which supported the egocentric task involving the orientation [7]. The intention to combine these two views was that subjects could integrate the different spatial information provided in each view in order to effectively enhance the understanding of structure in space. The experimental data in present study revealed that this objective was partially achieved by this design.

When subjects were performing JRD task, they needed to construct exocentric retrieval coordinates over the reference object to retrieve position of object [11]. The efficiency of constructed coordinates was determined by both the perceived properties of structure and the egocentric view. Mental transformations were involved to mediate the conflict between the constructed reference for retrieval and the coding reference. Further, errors (in terms of pointing accuracy and latency) were produced in the process of mental transformation. When judging the spatial vertical direction, subjects required to retrieve the relative distance between the tested location and target's position, and the relative height of target. Much mental process should be involved to interpret the depth and height in the context of exocentric reference. One possible way was to recall the representation created in exocentric view to determine the depth and pick up the height information mainly from the representation got in the egocentric view. The whole performance on judging vertical direction indicated that participants could better represent the spatial vertical information in the direction they ever orientated than the novel directions they never faced.

Regarding the judgment of spatial horizontal direction in JRD task and reaction time in egocentric pointing task, both the imagined heading and order of viewing could influence the performance. Specifically, the effect of imagined heading on representation was not observed when the exocentric view was observed as the second view. From the point of view of memory update, the data suggested that the spatial knowledge learned by observing each view was integrated with each other. One possible explanation of the integration of spatial knowledge was that the representation in the first point of view might be normalized to coincide with the new representation by the way that the old representation was interpreted or inferred by the updated reference system defined in the second point of view. The performance suggested that the fidelity of scene in the egocentric view played strong role on orientation-specific representation, which brought bias to the reference to code spatial relations in memory.

5 Conclusion

In summary, individuals can not construct view-invariant representation of virtual room space after observing from two viewpoints that lied in different heights of space. However, there were a few evidences that the experience of dual views can partially improve the understanding of spatial layout. If the egocentric view is learned first and then the exocentric view is observed, the representation of relative horizontal direction shows the orientation-free property.

References

1. Richardson, A. E., Montello, D. R., Hegarty, M.: Spatial knowledge acquisition from maps and from navigation in real and virtual environments. Mem. & Cog. 27 (1999) 741-750.
2. Soeda, M., Kushiyama, N., Ohno, R.: Wayfinding in cases with vertical Motion. In: Proceedings of MERA97: Int. Conf. on Environment-Behavior Studies (1997).
3. Passini, R.: Wayfinding in architecture. New York: Van Nostrand Reinhold (1984).
4. Luo, Z.: Effect of perspective elevation and environment features on representation of a virtual room space. Virtual Reality (submitted, 2006).
5. Shelton, A. L., McNamara, T. P.: Systems of spatial reference in human memory. Cog. Psy., 43 (2001) 274-430.
6. Hickox, J.C., Wickens C.D.: Effects of elevation angle display, complexity, and feature type on relating out-of-cockpit field of view to an electronic cartographic map. J. Exp. Psy.: Applied 5 (1999) 284-301.
7. Wickens, C. D., Hollands, J. G.: Engineering psychology and human performance (3rd ed). Englewood Cliffs, NJ: Prentice Hall (2000).
8. Wickens, C. D., Olmos, O., Chudy, A., Davenport, C.: Aviation display support for situation awareness (No. ARL-97-10/LOGICON-97-2). Savoy, IL: University of Illinois, Aviation research Lab. (1997).
9. Wickens, C. D., Prevett, T. T.: Exploring the dimensions of egocentricity in aircraft navigation play. J. Exp. Psy.: Applied 1 (1995) 110-135.

10. Wickens, C. D., Vincow, M., Yeh, M.: Design application of visual spatial thinking: The importance of frame of reference. In: Shah, P., Miyake, A. (eds.): The Cambridge handbook of visuospatial thinking. New York, USA: Cambridge University Press (2005) 383-425.
11. Easton, R. D., Sholl, M. J.: Object-array structure, frames of reference, and retrieval of spatial knowledge. J. Exp. Psy.: Learning, Memory, and Cognition 21 (1995) 483-500.
12. Sholl, M. J., Nolin, T. L.: Orientation specificity in representations of place. J. Exp. Psy.: Learning, Memory, and Cognition 23 (1997) 1494-1507.
13. Howard, I.: Spatial vision within egocentric and exocentric frames of reference. In Ellis, S., Kaiser, M., Grunwald, A. (eds.): Pictorial communication in virtual and real environments. Bristol, PA: Taylor & Francis (1991) 338-358.
14. Morar, S. S., Macredie, R. D., Cribbin, T.: An investigation of visual cues used to create and support frames of reference and visual search tasks in desktop virtual environment. Virtual Reality 6 (2002) 140-150.

A Novel Planar Walking Algorithm
for Virtual Walking Machine

Jangwoo Park[1], Jungwon Yoon[2], Yo-An Lim[1], and Jeha Ryu[1]

[1] Human-Machine-Computer Interface Lab.,
Dept. of Mechatronics, Gwangju Institute of Science and Technology, Gwangju, Korea
{jw7912, yo-anl, ryu}@gist.ac.kr
[2] School of Mechanical & Aerospace Engineering,
Gyeongsang National University, Jinju, Korea
jwyoon@gnu.ac.kr

Abstract. This paper proposes a novel planar walking algorithm for the Virtual Walking Machine (VWM), which is a dual foot platform type locomotion interface. Unlike existing algorithms used for VWM, the proposed algorithm utilizes a constraint relationship between two platforms as well as position control. Experiments on the VWM show that the proposed planar walking algorithm can generate straight and turning motions which are smoother and collision-free.

Keywords: Locomotion Interface, Walking Algorithm, Navigation.

1 Introduction

Several kinds of locomotion interfaces for walking in a virtual environment have been developed. Among them, the types of treadmill and foot platforms are typical configurations considering human walking patterns. Although these types of locomotion interfaces can easily generate straight walking motion, it is difficult for them to make natural turning motions mainly because of their mechanical restrictions [1]. For example, the treadmills that have 1-DOF (degree of freedom) belt motion can not make the natural turning motion. The Sarcos Treadport does not have any turntable that rotates the whole system, so it uses the gesture-based rate control [1]. ATLAS measures lateral position of a leg to determine a turning angle of the turntable and makes physical turning motion by the turntable [2]. However, the user cannot get feelings of natural turning due to the limitation that it has only 1-DOF belt motion. In order to solve the problem, 2-DOF treadmills were developed [8, 9]. However, they have problems in implementing the turning motion such as generation of lateral force and mechanical complexity. Similarly, many devices with foot platforms were also developed. In the case of the Gait Master [3], they make X, Y, Z stages and put plates for yaw motion on the stages. While this mechanism allows more walking degrees of freedom then treadmills does, its walking motion is limited and is not smooth. Lately, a new type of locomotion interface called 'CirculaFloor' was developed. It uses four mobile robots in order to make omni-directional walking, but it cannot generate uneven terrain and the available walking speed is slow [4]. In view of mechanical

Z. Pan et al. (Eds.): ICAT 2006, LNCS 4282, pp. 1175–1185, 2006.
© Springer-Verlag Berlin Heidelberg 2006

characteristics, the VWM [5] is a foot platform type locomotion interface. The previous walking algorithms for VWM let a user for straight walking only. This paper proposes a novel planar walking algorithm which allows straight walking and turning motions simultaneously. First, we will explain the existing straight walking algorithm. Then, we will modify and extend it to develop the planar walking algorithm.

2 Position-Based Straight Walking Algorithm

Human gait cycle consists of a stance phase, when a foot contacts the ground, and a swing phase, when a foot is in the air. When both feet are in the stance phase, it is called double stance phase. The existing straight walking algorithm for the VWM [5] was developed considering the double stance phase, which increased the natural walking feeling on the VWM. During the double stance phase, both feet contact ground (platforms), so there should be no relative motion between them. This is called *double stance condition*.

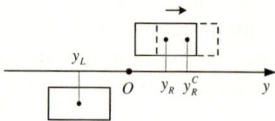

Fig. 1. Foot Platform Coordinates for Straight Walking

In Fig. 1, y_R and y_L are the current center positions of each foot platform on straight walking line, the superscript C is command for next control step, y_R^C is right platform's command position. The existing straight walking algorithm on the VWM is based on the command velocity and can be summarized as follows:

For Swing Phase, $\dot{y}_i^C = \dot{y}_i^{track}$

For Stance Phase,

  (i) For Single Stance Phase, $\dot{y}_i^C = -v_{avg,i}^{sw}$ (1)

  (ii) For Double Stance Phase,

  $$IF\,(y_R + y_L)/2 > 0,\ \dot{y}_i^C = -K(v_{avg,R}^{sw} + v_{avg,L}^{sw})/2$$

  $$IF\,(y_R + y_L)/2 < 0,\ \dot{y}_i^C = K(v_{avg,R}^{sw} + v_{avg,L}^{sw})/2 \qquad (i = R, L)$$

Where, $\dot{y}^C$ is the command velocity of a platform, $\dot{y}^{track}$ is the velocity of the tracker, K is the velocity gain, and v_{avg}^{sw} is the average velocity during the previous swing phase, defined as

$$v_{avg}^{sw} = \frac{1}{T_{sw}} \int_{t}^{t+T_{sw}} \dot{y}^{sw} dt \qquad (2)$$

Where $\dot{y}^{sw}$ is the velocity of the platform during the swing phase, and T_{sw} is the time of swing phase. Through this velocity-based algorithm, the distance moved during the previous swing phase is compensated in the current stance phase. During the double stance phase, this algorithm makes the velocity of both platforms equal resulting in zero relative motion. But this algorithm has some problems; During every single stance phase, the velocity of the platform in the stance phase is always constant. However, the velocity of the platform in the stance phase change abruptly when the phase changes, from single stance phase to double stance phase or vice versa, or when the average of the position of two platforms meets the center of VWM. This makes the user unstable while walking on VWM. To solve this problem, we propose a position-based walking algorithm as follows;

For Swing Phase, $y_i^C = y_i^{track}$

(3)

For Stance Phase, $y_i^C = y_i - K_y y_{avg}$ $(i = R, L)$

Where y^C is command position of a platform, y_{avg} is the average position of two platforms, calculated as $y_{avg}=(y_R+y_L)/2$, and K_y is the position gain. In this algorithm, the platform in the swing phase follows the tracker position like the previous one. However, in the stance phase, the proposed algorithm uses the average position y_{avg}. If y_{avg} is zero, we can assume that the center of user's body is on the center of the device. If y_{avg} is not zero, the platform of the stance phase moves towards the direction to make y_{avg} zero, i.e., the proposed algorithm compensates user's position by making y_{avg} zero, which ensures that the velocity of the platform in the stance phase changes smoothly because y_{avg} does not change abruptly. Note that the proposed algorithm satisfies the double stance condition because the changes of the positions of both platforms are equal in the double stance phase. Fig. 2 compares the command velocity profiles of two algorithms (right platform). Fig. 2 (a) shows that the command changes abruptly when the phase changes, while Fig. 2 (b) shows the command velocity changes smoothly during the stance phase.

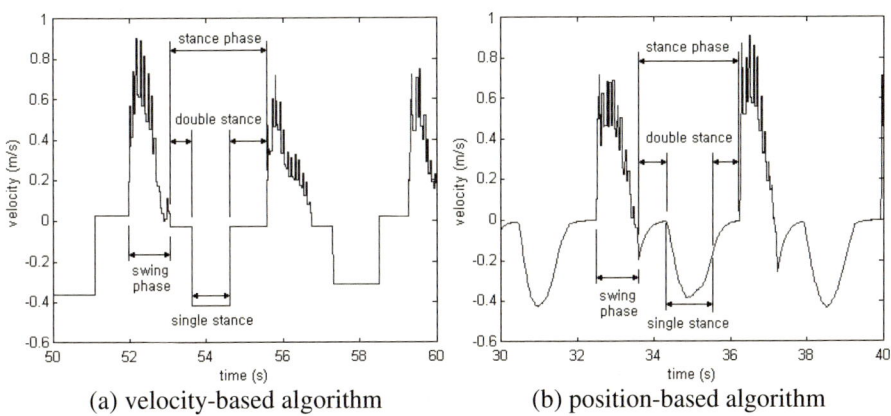

(a) velocity-based algorithm   (b) position-based algorithm

Fig. 2. Command Velocity Profile of a Platform

Fig. 3 shows the experimental results of the platform. The dotted line is the command, and solid line is the actual velocity of the platform. It can be seen that the position-based algorithm follows the command velocity better then the velocity-based algorithm. Note that the proposed algorithm can be extended easily to more general planar walking algorithm, which will be explained in the next section.

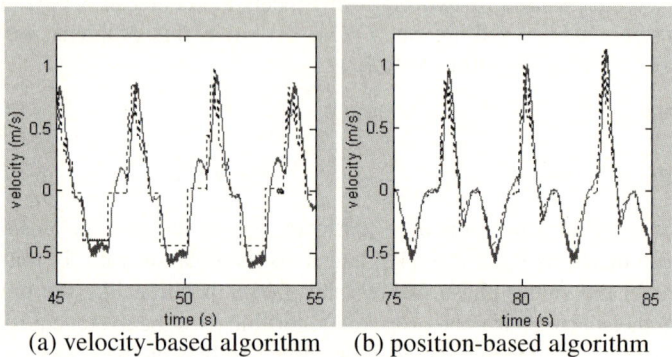

(a) velocity-based algorithm   (b) position-based algorithm

Fig. 3. Velocity Profile of a Platform

3 Planar Curved Path Walking Algorithm

Planar walking means any kind of walking on a plane, such as straight walking, turning, side step etc. However, the most frequently occurring walking patterns are straight walking and turning [6]. To let a user walk on the plane as naturally as possible by using a locomotion interface, a reliable walking algorithm is important.

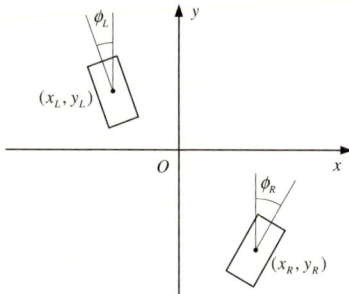

Fig. 4. Foot Platform Coordinate for Planar Walking

Fig. 4 shows the posture of two foot platforms in the walking plane x-y. The origin O is the center of the locomotion interface. Basically, the proposed position-based straight walking algorithm in the previous section can be independently applied to each variable x, y, ϕ in order to make the planar walking scenario as follows:

For Swing Phase, $X_i^C = X_i^{track}$ ***and*** $\phi_i^C = \phi_i^{track}$

For Stance Phase, $X_i^C = X_i - K_X X_{avg}$ ***and*** $\phi_i^C = \phi_i - K_\phi \phi_{avg}$ ($i = R, L$)

$$(4)$$

Where X is the position vector (x,y), $X_{avg}=(X_R+X_L)/2$, $\phi_{avg}=(\phi_R+\phi_L)/2$, K_X is a position gain matrix, and K_ϕ is orientation gain. If applied to each variable x, y, ϕ independently, the algorithm in Eq.(4) faces two important problems: (i) collision between the two platforms (ii) the algorithm does not satisfy the double stance condition, that is, there occurs a relative motion between the two platforms during the double stance phase. We need, therefore, the additional constraint conditions for solving these problems. Many biomechanics researchers studied human turning motion with constant curvature, and reported that path curvature is an important factor of human walking [6, 7]. The concept of path curvature can be used to solve the above two problems.

3.1   Radius(ρ) and Angle(θ) of Path Curvature

In order to use the concept of path curvature, we need to estimate the radius of path curvature. Fig. 5 shows how to estimate the radius when the right foot is in the swing phase. There are three curved paths; the right line is for the right platform, the left line is for the left platform, and the center line is the user's walking path. If the position of the right foot in swing phase is (x_R^{track}, y_R^{track}), then we can find a circle which passes through initial reference point $(L,0)$ (■ point in Fig.5) and (x_R^{track}, y_R^{track}) (● point in Fig.5), and the center of the circle is on the x-axis. The point $(O_C, 0)$ is the center of the circle, and L is dependent on the distance between both feet when the user stands upright. Then, the radius of path curvature satisfies the following equation;

$$\rho = O_C = \frac{(x_R^{track})^2 + (y_R^{track})^2 - L^2}{2(x_R^{track} - L)} \qquad (5)$$

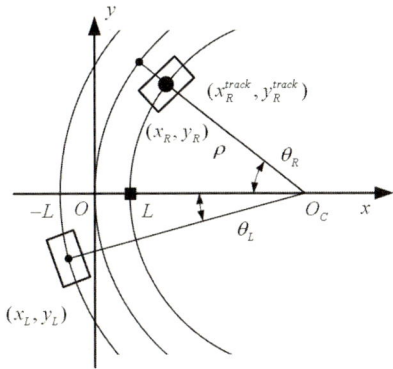

Fig. 5. Path Curvature Estimation

Generally, the curvature radius ρ is always positive. However, we use the sign of the radius to distinguish the direction of turning. If the path is curved towards the right, then the sign is positive, otherwise, the sign is negative. In the case that the left foot is in swing phase, we can use Eq. (5), after substituting L for $-L$. We define another important variable θ, the angle of path curvature, as the angle between x axis and the line passing through the center of a circle O_C, and the position of the platform (x, y).

$$\theta_R = \sin^{-1}(\frac{y_R}{\rho - L}),\ \theta_L = \sin^{-1}(\frac{y_L}{\rho + L})\quad (-90 < \theta \le 90) \tag{6}$$

Because of mechanical characteristics of VWM, θ can vary between -90 and 90. By using radius ρ and angle θ, a planar walking algorithm can be developed.

3.2 Planar Curved Path Walking Algorithm

Basic concept of the planar curved path walking algorithm is that the swing phase platform follows the tracker position and the stance phase platform compensates user posture, which is the same as the straight walking algorithm. However, additional constraint condition that two platforms should have the same center of curvature must be satisfied in the planar curved path walking algorithm i.e.:

For Swing Phase, $\rho(x_i^{track}, y_i^{track})$ **and** $\theta_i^C = \theta_i^{track}(x_i^{track}, y_i^{track})$

$$\tag{7}$$

For Stance Phase, $\theta_i^C = \theta_i - K_\theta \theta_{avg}$ $\qquad (i = R, L)$

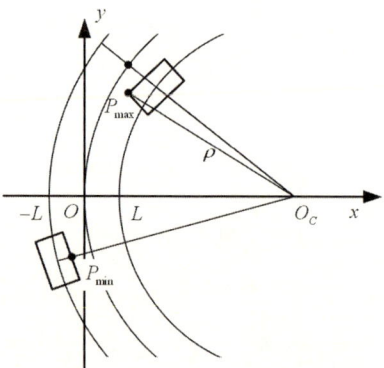

Fig. 6. Avoidance of Collision

Where $\rho(x_i^{track}, y_i^{track})$ is the curvature radius and $\theta^{track}(x_i^{track}, y_i^{track})$ is the curvature angle of tracker, and $\theta_{avg} = (\theta_R + \theta_L)/2$ is the average angle. The curved paths of both platforms are changed by the estimated curvature radius in real-time. However, the curvature radius does not change during the double stance phase. Using curvature radius and curvature angle, we can get the actual platform postures (x, y, ϕ) as

$$x_R = \rho - (\rho - L)\cos(\theta_R), \quad y_R = (\rho - L)\sin(\theta_R), \quad \phi_R = -\theta_R$$
$$x_L = \rho - (\rho + L)\cos(\theta_L), \quad y_L = (\rho + L)\sin(\theta_L), \quad \phi_L = -\theta_L \qquad (8)$$

Note only two variables ρ and θ are needed to represent three variables x, y, ϕ. The above planar curved path walking algorithm can avoid collision between two platforms and can satisfy the double stance condition. Fig. 6 shows the case of the right turn. P_{max} is the point on the right platform which has maximum distance from the center of curvature O_C. P_{min} is the point on the left platform which has minimum distance from the center of curvature O_C.

The collision avoidance condition for two platforms can be satisfied if

$$\overline{O_C P_{min}} > \overline{O_C P_{max}} \Leftrightarrow \overline{O_C P_{min}} - \overline{O_C P_{max}} > 0 \qquad (9)$$

The geometric factors in Eq. (9) are the shape of platform which can be assumed to be a rectangular plate for simplicity, the distance between centers of two the platforms, $2L$, determined by anthropometric parameters, and the curvature radius ρ. Given the shape of platform and L, we should find available radius of curvature which satisfies the collision avoidance condition.

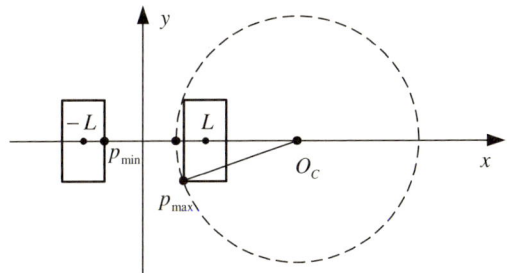

Fig. 7. Condition of Collision Avoidance

Fig. 7 shows that $\overline{O_c P_{min}} - \overline{O_c P_{max}}$ is getting smaller as the curvature center O_c move towards the origin. This means that we should find the minimum of O_c satisfying the condition, and we should use ρ which is not less than the minimum. After these considerations, we have found that the minimum of ρ is 1m for the VWM [5].

Note that the double stance condition can be verified easily. During the double stance phase, there is no change of the curvature radius, and the curvature angle changes for both the platforms are the same.

$$\rho = const. \text{ and } \dot{\theta}_R = \dot{\theta}_L \qquad (10)$$

So there is no relative motion between two platforms. For no relative motion between two platforms, all coordinates of the right platform with respect to the left platform frame should be constants.

$$\dot{x}_{R/L} = 0 \quad and \quad \dot{y}_{R/L} = 0 \quad and \quad \dot{\phi}_{R/L} = 0 \tag{11}$$

4 Navigation in Virtual Environment

We interface VWM with a virtual environment for applying the proposed planar walking algorithm for navigation in VE. VWM supplies user's posture information to VE. Using this information, VE can change posture of view. A large screen is installed in front of VWM for navigation experiment. During navigation, a user feels that scene is changing with his movement. OpenGL® is used for implementing the virtual environment. It uses modelview transformation method for coordinate transformation. The most important problem of navigation in VE is to move the ground of VE according to user's movement. To solve the problem, we make the ground movement in VE equal to the stance phase platform movement which user considers as the ground. As discussed earlier, the two important factors of stance phase platform's movement are curvature radius and curvature angle. With these two variables, we can generate the ground movement in VE.

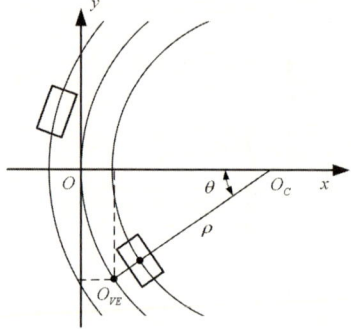

Fig. 8. Movement of the Ground in VE

Fig. 8 shows the movement of ground in VE according to the movement of the stance phase platform. At the initial time, the origin of ground in VE, O_{VE}, and the center of VWM, O, are same. If a user walks along a constant path curvature radius ρ, movement of curvature angle θ_{local} is as follows:

$$\theta_{local} = \theta - \theta_{initial} \tag{12}$$

Where $\theta_{initial}$ is the initial curvature angle in the stance phase (Fig. 8 shows the case that $\theta_{initial}$ is equal to 0). With θ_{local} and ρ, the ground movement can be represented as

$$x_{local} = \rho(1 - \cos\theta_{local}), \quad y_{local} = \rho\sin\theta_{local}, \quad \phi_{local} = -\theta_{local} \tag{13}$$

However, above equations can be applied for one step only. For a user to walk many steps, we need additional algorithm to take care of accumulation of steps. For this, we define the walking reference points x_o, y_o, ϕ_o.

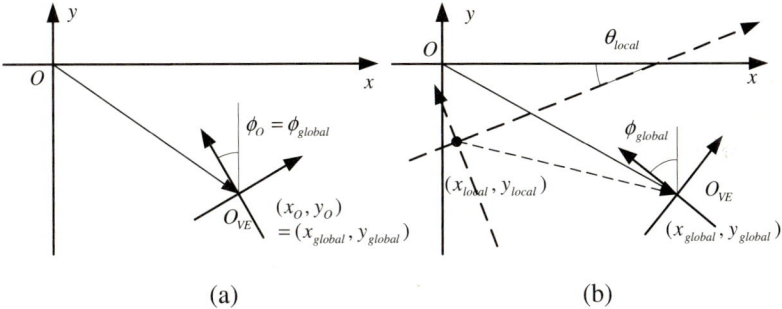

Fig. 9. Transformation Algorithm for Accumulation of Steps

Fig. 9 (a) shows the moment when the phase changes. The walking reference points are updated by the posture of O_{VE}. Fig. 9 (b) shows how to change the ground origin O_{VE} after updating. The vector (x_o, y_o) will be changed in the view of the global coordinates as θ_{local} changes. $(x_{global}, y_{global}, \phi_{global})$ is the actual posture of the ground in VE. By using the walking reference points x_o, y_o, ϕ_o, we can implement the effect of step accumulation. The additional algorithm is as

IF Phase_change ==FALSE,

$$\begin{bmatrix} x_{global} \\ y_{global} \end{bmatrix} = \begin{bmatrix} x_{local} \\ y_{local} \end{bmatrix} + \begin{bmatrix} \cos\phi_{local} & \sin\phi_{local} \\ -\sin\phi_{local} & \cos\phi_{local} \end{bmatrix} \begin{bmatrix} x_o \\ y_o \end{bmatrix}$$

$$\phi_{global} = \phi_o + \phi_{local}$$

(14)

IF Phase_change == TRUE,

$$x_o = x_{global}, \quad y_o = y_{global}, \quad \phi_o = \phi_{global}, \quad \theta_{initial} = \theta$$

where $x_{global}, y_{global}, \phi_{global}$ are actual posture of O_{VE}, which are transformed by x_o, y_o, ϕ_o, and $x_o, y_o, \phi_o, \theta_{initial}$ are updated when phase changes.

5   Experimental Results

The proposed planar curved path walking algorithm can implement straight walking and turning simultaneously. We performed simple navigation experiments to verify the effectiveness of the proposed planar walking algorithm. To test the performance of straight walking and turning at the same time, we developed virtual environment for experiment. The available minimum radius of curvature in the VWM[5] is about 1m because of many mechanical constraints. So, we made three types of path curvature such as 2m, 1m, 0.5m in VE. We selected three subjects, and trained them for two hours. After training, we let them walk all the paths at once per each subject. Walking trajectory can be computed by using $x_{global}, y_{global}, \phi_{global}$. The results of the experiments are shown in Fig. 10. The dotted line is the desired path in VE, and solid line is the actual walking trajectory of each subject. As shown, subjects followed the 2m and 1m curvature paths well (Fig. 10 (a)), but could not follow 0.5 m curvature path well (Fig. 10 (b)). Considering that the limitation of available radius of curvature is 1m, we can think that path which has smaller curvature than the available minimum radius of curvature is difficult for user to follow. In conclusion, both straight walking and smoother large curvature turning without any collision are possible with the proposed planar curved path walking algorithm.

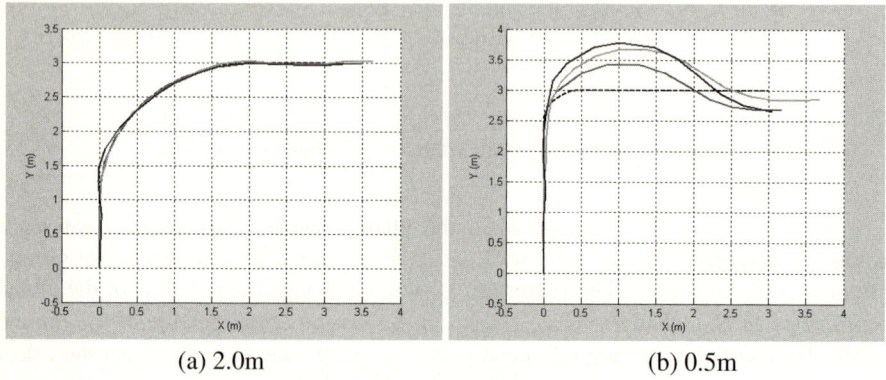

(a) 2.0m   (b) 0.5m

Fig. 10. Experimental Result

6 Discussions and Conclusion

As shown in the Fig.10, the proposed planar curved path walking algorithm can be used to implement the straight walking and turning simultaneously. Actually, the proposed algorithm can be applied not only to VWM, but also to any locomotion interface that can be classified into dual foot platforms.

In the proposed algorithm, we assume that the factors to determine the curvature of walking path is the foot position in the swing phase. However, turning is very complex action, and there are many other factors determining walking path curvature, besides swing phase foot position. There is no report which defines the functional relationship between walking path curvature and kinematical parameters exactly. So, for more accurate human-like natural walking, we will have to study walking motion in the view of the biomechanics, to find functional relationship about turning motion.

Acknowledgments

Research reported here was supported by a grant (No. R01-2002-000-00254-0) from the Basic Research Program of the Korea Science & Engineering Foundation and by the Korea Research Foundation Grant funded by the Korean Government (MOEHRD) (KRF-2005-005-J09902).

References

1. J. M. Hollerbach, "Locomotion interface,"in: Handbook of Virtual Environments Technology, K.M. stanney, ed., Lawrence Erlbaum Associates, Inc. 2002, pp. 239-254.
2. H. Noma, T. Miyasato, "A New Approach for Canceling Turning Motion in the Locomotion Interface, ATLAS," ASME DSC - Vol.67, 1999, pp. 405 – 407.
3. H. Iwata, H. Yano, F. Nakaizumi, "Gait Master: a versatile locomotion interface for uneven virtual terrain,"Virtual Reality, 2001. Proceedings. IEEE 13-17 March 2001, pp. 131 - 137.
4. H. Iwata, H. Yano, F. Nakaizumi, H. Noma, "CirculaFloor," Computer Graphics and Applications, IEEE Volume 25,Issue 1,Jan.-Feb. 2005, pp. 64 – 67.
5. Jungwon Yoon, Jangwoo Park and Jeha Ryu, "Walking Control of a Dual-Planar Parallel Robot for Omni-directional Locomotion Interface" IROS 2005. IEEE/RSJ International Conference on 2-6 Aug. 2005, pp. 1151 - 1156.
6. Micheal S. Orendurff, Ava D. Segal, Jocelyn S. Berge, Kevin C. Flick, David Spanier, Glenn K. Klute, "The kinematics and kinetics of turning: limb asymmetries associated with walking a circular path", Gait & Posture 23, pp. 106 - 111.
7. Gregoire Courtine and Marco Schieppati, "Turning of a Basic Coordination Pattern Constructs Straight-Ahead and Curved Walking in Humans", Journal of Neurophysiology Vol 91 April 2004, pp. 1524 - 1535.
8. R. Darken, W. Cockayne, D. Carmein. "The Omni-Directional Treadmill: A Locomotion Device for Virtual Words," Proc. of User Interface Software Technology (UIST 97), pp.213-222.
9. H. Iwata, "The Torus Treadmill:Realizing Locomotion in VEs," IEEE Computer Graphics and Applications, Vol. 19, No. 6 1999, pp. 30-35.

An Interactive System of Virtual Face Pose Estimation

Zheng-yi Wu[1], Jian Shi[1], Xiaoming Tong[2], and Zheng Tan[1,2]

[1] Department of Information and Control Engineering, Changshu Institute of Technology,
Jiangsu 215500
[2] Institute of Information Engineering, Xi'an Jiaotong University, Xi'an 710049
{wwzzyy, shijian}@cslg.edu.cn

Abstract. On the basis of an established individualized face 3D model, this paper implements a new facial pose detection based on face model plane. The new method, by utilizing the feature point correspondence between model plane and model image, can compute the three parameters of face pose angle and effect model display, representing a simple interactive system of virtual face pose estimation. Experiments show that proposed algorithm, simple and highly automated, can accurately and effectively detect facial pose information and display pose changes of virtual models.

Keywords: face pose estimation; face 3D model; homography.

1 Introduction

Virtual reality has been received growing attention in the field of film, game and cartoon design as well as intelligent human-computer interaction, model-based video coding, and intelligent monitoring. As the face carries the most important information about the subject, it is necessary to individualize facial models and describe the changes of facial pose and expression.

Virtual reality, human-computer interaction, multi-pose estimation, and expression recognition are all based on facial pose information. Given the homography between coplanar facial features and video frame pixels, this paper develops a virtual reality system to estimate facial pose in video sequence based on the individuation of facial models and face detection algorithm.

As 2-D images cannot fully show the position of facial feature points, we need prior knowledge to estimate the facial pose. Most algorithms use image features (such as grayscale, color and image gradient) to detect facial pose, but that will necessitate a large number of training samples to establish the correlation between facial pose and image features[1]. Recently, thanks to the fast development of 3-D modeling technology, the acquisition of individualized 3-D face has been made much easier, and the estimation algorithm based on such models [2,3,11] has attracted wide attention. By establishing accurate geometrical information, model-based methods lead to even more precise and robust results, demonstrating their potential for wide application.

Based on the homography of feature points obtained from models and video sequence, our pose estimation algorithm computes the three parameters for facial pose angle. Experiments have shown the validity of the method. The virtual reality system

Z. Pan et al. (Eds.): ICAT 2006, LNCS 4282, pp. 1186–1192, 2006.

can real-time detect the position of feature points by following the algorithm, thus realizing facial pose interaction.

2 Basic Algorithm

We assume that a 2D point is denoted by $\mathbf{m} = (u,v)^T$, and a 3D point by $\mathbf{M} = (X,Y,Z)^T$.   The   corresponding   augmented   vectors   are $\tilde{\mathbf{M}} = (X,Y,Z,1)^T$ and $\tilde{\mathbf{m}} = (u,v,1)^T$, respectively. The relationship between a 3D point $\tilde{\mathbf{M}}$ and its image projection $\tilde{\mathbf{m}}$ is given by

$$s\tilde{\mathbf{m}} = \mathbf{A}[\mathbf{R} \quad \mathbf{t}]\tilde{\mathbf{M}} \tag{1}$$

where s is an arbitrary scale factor, the extrinsic parameters $[\mathbf{R} \quad \mathbf{t}]$ is the rotation and translation which relates the world coordinate system to the camera coordinate system [4], and $\mathbf{A}$ is called the camera intrinsic matrix.

Without loss of generality, we assume the model plane is on $Z = 0$ of the world coordinate system. We denote the ith column of the rotation matrix R by $\mathbf{r}_i$. According to Eq.(1), we have

$$s\begin{pmatrix} u \\ v \\ 1 \end{pmatrix} = \mathbf{A}[\mathbf{r}_1 \quad \mathbf{r}_2 \quad \mathbf{r}_3 \quad \mathbf{t}]\begin{pmatrix} X \\ Y \\ 0 \\ 1 \end{pmatrix} = \mathbf{A}[\mathbf{r}_1 \quad \mathbf{r}_2 \quad \mathbf{t}]\begin{pmatrix} X \\ Y \\ 1 \end{pmatrix} \tag{2}$$

Therefore, the relation between the model point $\mathbf{M}$ and its image $\mathbf{m}$ are constructed by a homography matrix $\mathbf{H}$:

$$s\tilde{\mathbf{m}} = \mathbf{H}\tilde{\mathbf{M}} \quad \text{with } \mathbf{H} = \mathbf{A}[\mathbf{r}_1 \quad \mathbf{r}_2 \quad \mathbf{t}] \tag{3}$$

As is shown that the 3×3 matrix $\mathbf{H}$ is also determined by a scale factor.

Given an image of the model plane, a homography matrix can be estimated. According to Eq.（3）, we have

$$\mathbf{H} = \begin{pmatrix} h_{11} & h_{12} & h_{13} \\ h_{21} & h_{22} & h_{23} \\ h_{31} & h_{32} & 1 \end{pmatrix} = \lambda \mathbf{A}[\mathbf{r}_1 \quad \mathbf{r}_2 \quad \mathbf{t}] \tag{4}$$

$$[\mathbf{r}_1 \quad \mathbf{r}_2 \quad \mathbf{t}] = \frac{1}{\lambda}\mathbf{A}^{-1}\mathbf{H} \tag{5}$$

where the intrinsic matrix $\mathbf{A}$ could be determined previously according to the camera standardized algorithm.

Using the knowledge that $\mathbf{r}_1$ and $\mathbf{r}_2$ are orthonormal, we can calculate $\mathbf{r}_1$, $\mathbf{r}_2$ and $\mathbf{t}$, as well as $\mathbf{r}_3 = \mathbf{r}_1 \times \mathbf{r}_2$.

By the above presentation, the pose estimation can be ascribed to the calculation of homography matrix $\mathbf{H}$, which can be obtained by Eq.(3). The coplanar facial features illustrated in Fig. 1 are selected for the computation.

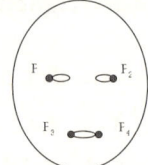

Fig. 1. Facial features

3   System Structure

As shown in Fig. 2, the system consists of 5 modules, i.e., modeling, video sampling, feature orientation, pose estimation and model display. The 3-D face modeling is carried out off-line, while the others are real-time.

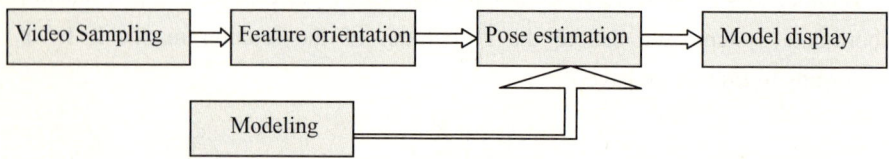

Fig. 2. System structure

3.1   3-D Face Modeling

Firstly, we obtain face model based on single obverse face image [5], which uses coplanar facial features of the image to adjust the positions of a general 3-D grid face model. Then we establish the individual face model according to the statistical information of face features. Finally, we store the coordinates of the feature points on the plane as the model information.

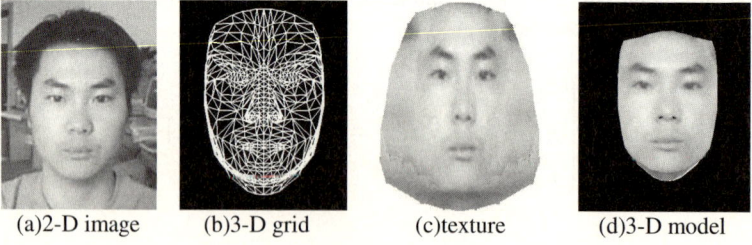

(a)2-D image   (b)3-D grid   (c)texture   (d)3-D model

Fig. 3. 3-D face model

3.2 Facial Features in Video Sequence

The feature orientation algorithm for initial frame differs from that of continuous frames. For initial frame, we get possible skin area by target extraction and color detection, and obtain candidate area through trough detection. Then the precise feature position is derived by feature verifying technology. While for continuous frames, we predict the feature area according to the relativity between frames and determine the feature position of current frame according to the previous frame.

As video sample system is usually fixed on desktop, we can remove the background by target extraction. Though the detection steps increase, this measure will effectively remove the noise in images with complex background, which will improve the running speed.

As skin color is distributed centrally in color space (Cr, Cb), and is not much affected by changed lighting condition, the color area thus derived is made more robust. After removing noise, we get the candidate face area set [5].

As arms and some other areas will cause interference, we need to test the candidate area of face by detecting the two troughs of the face area grayscale --- the two troughs form two eyes, lending to the construction of a tentative face. This tentative face can be verified by being projected on to the original face space [6].

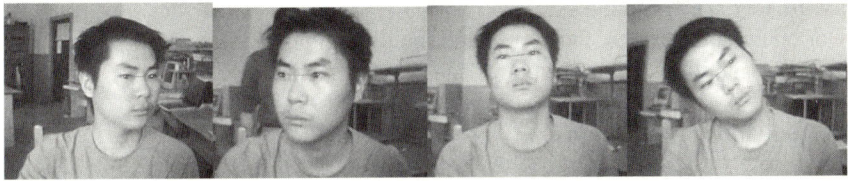

Fig. 4. Face detection

When we get the position of eyes, the information of eyes' edge is used to determine the position of canthus. First, we obtain such information through detection in the eyes' region. Then the noise in eyes' region is morphologically eliminated, and the precise position of canthus is obtained by canthus detection in the binary map of eyes' region. In this paper, only the outside canthus is used for pose estimation.

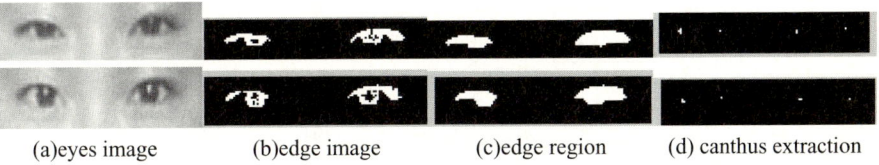

(a)eyes image   (b)edge image   (c)edge region   (d) canthus extraction

Fig. 5. Canthus detection

The mouth region contains more red component and less blue component than other facial regions. Hence, the detection of mouth region is fulfilled by enhancing the lip color chromatism [7].

The chrominance component Cr is enhanced to $(Cr)^2$. By adding the reverse sum of the brightness component Y, the mouth area is obviously enhanced as shown in Fig. 6(b). Then we subtract the enhanced blue components $(Cb)^2$, and the mouth region is finally obtained.

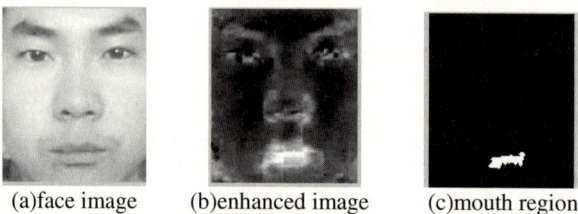

(a)face image   (b)enhanced image   (c)mouth region

Fig. 6. Mouth detection

After the detection of the mouth region, the corners of the mouth are obtained in the same way as the canthus.

For continuous frames, face, eyes and mouth regions are derived by area tracking technology and then the feature points can be determined.

3.3 Derivation of Facial Pose

When we get the positions of feature points, the pose parameters can be derived by computing the homography matrix according to the position of face feature points and face models, just as mentioned in Section 2.

3.4 Model Display

The object can be rotated and translated by adjusting the camera position in OpenGL. After we get the parameters of facial pose, we can display the model's pose changes ,which should match the poses in the video frame. The algorithm diagram is shown in Fig. 7.

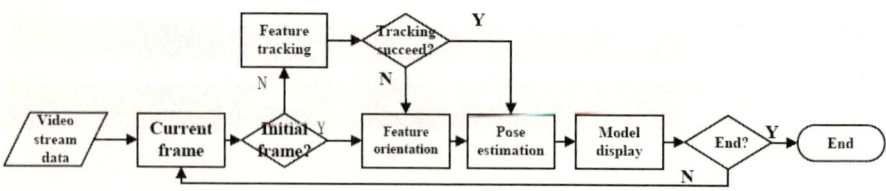

Fig. 7. Estimation flowchart

4 Experiments and Results

The virtual reality system is run on PC, which adopt a common CCD camera and the video data form is YCrCb, which can directly used in image process. Fig.8 shows parts of the research results. The video frame lies on the top left corner, below which is shown the value of the three rotation angels of the facial pose, and our model results are displayed on the right side. The results demonstrate that our algorithm can estimate facial pose in video sequence effectively. According to the experiment analysis, the pose estimation errors mainly come from the model-inherent errors and feature position errors. The error is conspicuous when the rotation angel is so large that the feature points are covered. Therefore, the method can only guarantee the estimation accuracy in the case of the facial features being uncovered. However, this problem could be tackled by considering more facial feature points and selecting the most appropriate facial feature points.

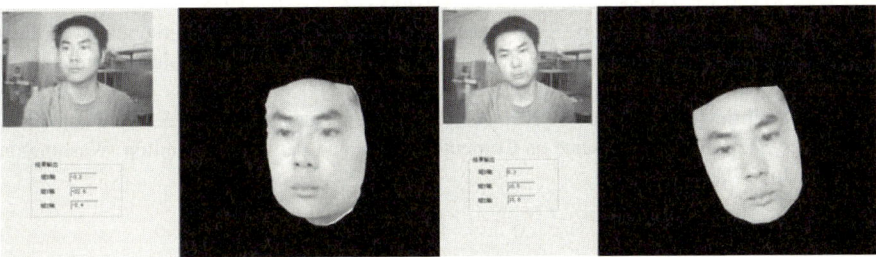

Fig. 8. Pose estimation results

5 Conclusions

In this paper a facial pose estimation algorithm based on video sequence is proposed, and a real-time virtual facial pose interface system is developed. Research result shows that this method can estimate video facial pose effectively. Our further research will focus on the selection of facial features so as to eliminate the influence of expression changes and make pose information more robust. On the other hand, the improvement of feature estimation algorithm could enhance the model's sensitivity to facial expression change, thus making help to reconstruct the expression of a virtual face.

References

[1] Q. Chen, H. Wu, T. Fukumoto, M. Yachida, 3D head pose estimation without feature tracking, In: Proceedings of Third IEEE International Conference on Automatic Face and Gesture Recognition, 88-93,1998.
[2] P. Yao, G. Evans, A. Calway, Using affine correspondence to estimate 3-D facial pose, In: Proceedings of IEEE Int. Conf. on Image Processing, 3: 919-922, 2001.

[3] I. Shimizu, Z. Zhang, S. Akamatsu, K. Deguchi, Head pose determination from one image using a generic model, In: Proceedings of IEEE International on Image and Graphics, 290 – 293, 2004.

[4] Z. Zhang. A Flexible New Technique for Camera Calibration, IEEE Transactions on Pattern Analysis and Machine Intelligence, Vol. 22, No. 11,1330-1334, Nov, 2000.

[5] T. Zheng, C.X. Guo, Y.C. Xing, 3-D face modeling and emotion computing based on single obverse face image, The 1st conference on emotion computing and intelligent interface, China,2003.

[6] Y.C. Xing, C.X. Guo, T. Zheng, Accurate face estimation based on trough in complex background, The 4th conference on biologic recognition, China, 2003.

[7] Rein-Lien Hsu, Abdel-Mottaleb M., Jain A.K., Face Detection in color images, IEEE Trans. On Pattern Analysis and Machine Intelligence, 2002, 24(5): 696~706.

[8] T. Darrell, G. Gordon, M. Harville, J. Woodfill, Integrated person tracking using stereo, color, and pattern detection, In: Proceedings of IEEE Computer Society Conference on Computer Vision and Pattern Recognition, 601 – 608, 1998.

[9] R. Rae, H.J. Ritter, Recognition of human head orientation based on artificial neural networks, IEEE Transactions on Neural Networks. 9:257-265, 1998.

[10] R. Newman, Y. Matsumoto, S. Rougeaux, A. Zelinsky, Real-time stereo tracking for head pose and gaze estimation, In: Proceedings of Fourth IEEE International Conference on Automatic Face and Gesture Recognition, 122-128, 2000.

[11] M. Dimitrijevic, S. Ilic and P. Fua, Accurate Face Models from Uncalibrated and Ill-Lit Video Sequences, Conference on Computer Vision and Pattern Recognition, Washington, DC, June 2004

An Efficient Manipulation of Game Contents on Heterogeneous Platforms Using MR Interface

Gi Sook Jung, Seung-Dae Jeong, Kyung Ho Jang, and Soon Ki Jung

Virtual Reality Laboratory, Department of Computer Engineering,
Kyungpook National University, 1370 Sankyukdong, Bukgu, Daegu, 702-701, Korea
{gsjung, sdjeong}@vr.knu.ac.kr, {khjang, skjung}@knu.ac.kr

Abstract. In this paper, we propose a prototype system, which deals with dynamic and huge graphic data on heterogeneous platforms, thus enabling clients to manage their shared virtual world in their hardware/software environment. Through the proposed system, users can experience the same virtual world in different interface metaphors: the keyboard of PC, a virtual control using a handheld MR (Mixed Reality), and the key button/stylus of PDA. Since we consider various service styles to various clients, first of all, we need to adjust the system's service level to low-end devices having lower performance. Therefore, we processed two kinds of considerations, data simplification, and the virtual control interface using handheld MR method to overcome limitations related to data transmission and data input.

Keywords: handheld augmented reality, handheld mixed reality, graphic streaming, virtual control, heterogeneous platform.

1 Introduction

Efficient manipulation of multimodal massive data, which plays an important role in the fields such as entertainment, medical applications, education, and scientific applications, is an emerging interdisciplinary research field. Through PC-based 3D network games or networked virtual reality, we can experience a remote manipulation of a huge body of dynamic data. Since both the user and the system must effectively deal with that kind of data set, we need to develop a versatile system that considers efficient data simplification and that provides effective interface for heterogeneous platforms including low-end devices.

For this reason, we have developed a prototype system built on existing 3D network game, and then examined efficient handling of a massive body of graphic data and the usability of optional MR (Mixed Reality) interface. From these experimental results, we propose not only efficient data simplification methods including hierarchical geometry hashing, visibility culling, and NPR (Non-Photorealistic Rendering), but also an effective MR interface as a client's ability. Fig. 1 shows tablet PC and PDA users playing Quake II[10] demo game in a new rendering style, with handheld MR and key button/stylus interface, respectively.

Z. Pan et al. (Eds.): ICAT 2006, LNCS 4282, pp. 1193–1203, 2006.

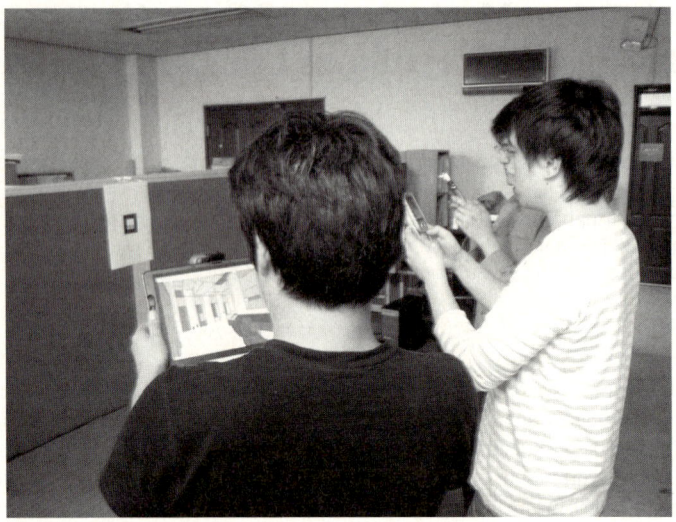

Fig. 1. Heterogeneous clients with different interfaces

In this paper, we describe the unique properties of our system focused on efficient graphic data simplification and intuitive virtual game control, after outlining related work and system overview. Finally, we analyze the experimental results, and then conclude by mentioning future work.

2 Related Work

Our related work can be classified as 3D graphic streaming, handheld AR interface, and virtual game control.

2.1 3D Graphic Streaming

Several methods, especially related to remotely navigating large virtual world, have been proposed in the form of streaming 3D scene on the server by E. Teler and D. Lischinski[14], M. Hosseini and D. Georganas[5], and G.S. Jung, et al.[6,7].

E. Teler and D. Lischinski[14] presented a 3D scene streaming approach for remote walkthroughs, which allows a user on a client machine to interactively navigate a remote 3D scene. M. Hosseini and D. Georganas[5] used the MPEG-4 standard for streaming 3D worlds and the corresponding animation over the web while users navigate and manipulate the content on server. Whereas both systems dealt with static and predefined virtual world on server, G.S. Jung, et al.[6,7] managed a dynamic game data, which could be streamed after graphic data simplification and simple compression, and which considers heterogeneous clients' various computing power and network bandwidth.

2.2 Handheld AR Interface

Recently, a number of handheld AR (Augmented Reality) systems using marker tracking have been developed. These systems use various interface styles to overcome input limitation of handheld devices, as well as to provide a new sense of game playing. We can discern the research trend through several prototype games based on visual code system[11,12,13], AR Tennis[4], the first stand-alone Handheld AR[16], and Invisible Train[15].

M. Rohs[12] used camera-equipped mobile devices and marker-based interaction for gesture-based control of games that incorporate physical and virtual aspects. They developed several prototype games using visual code system[11], which generates pose-related information such as distance, tilt, rotation, and world coordinate system with respect to the marker, and adapts marker-based interaction techniques with well-defined interaction primitives[13].

A. Henrysson[4] introduced AR Tennis as a prototype system to support face to face collaborative AR gaming. They adapted the ARToolKit library[1] to the Symbian mobile phone operating system and then developed a sample collaborative AR game, AR Tennis. They considered the mobile phone as a tangible input device and exploited its motion as a primary interaction method, unlike traditional AR interfaces in which the display and input devices are separated.

D. Wagner and D. Schmalstieg[16] proposed what they call the first stand-alone AR system for a PDA with a commercial camera. The application provides users with a three-dimensional augmented view of the environment, at a good accuracy of overlay registration by using ARToolkit[1], the tracking code of which is ported to the PDA. In addition, they introduced an optional client-server architecture that is based on wireless networking and is able to dynamically and transparently offload the tracking task in order to provide better performance in select areas.

D. Wagner, et al.[15] presented a system architecture for interactive, infrastructure-independent multi-user AR applications running on off-the-shelf handheld devices. They implemented a four-user interactive PDA game, Invisible Train, as an evaluation setup to encourage playful engagement of participants in a cooperative task.

Originally, the term AR was used in the context of a RV (Reality-Virtuality) continuum which also includes AV (Augmented Virtuality) [9]. In the RV continuum, real environment consists of only real objects, and virtual environment consists of only virtual objects. Generic MR environment is defined as one in which real world and virtual world objects are presented together within a single display, that is, anywhere between real and virtual environments which are the extremes of the RV continuum. Even though our system referenced existing AR techniques, it is more AV-like and can be fully adapted to the RV continuum. As a result, we use the term MR.

2.3 Virtual Game Control

Studies of virtual game control by [3][8]. R. Headon and R. Curwen[3] have described a sensing system for recognizing and characterizing human movements, which can be applied to an ubiquitous game environment. They considered the control of computer games through players interacting with the physical environment in a natural and appropriate manner. This virtual game control results in bidirectional influences between virtual game world and real game world. They demonstrated a system in which actions in the game are mapped to similar actions in the real world, with a 3D first-person game, Quake[TM].

D.H. Lee and S.K. Jung [8] presented a method to integrate a more flexible user interface into X3D using computer vision-based techniques. The proposed method allows navigation of a virtual environment on the WWW using only a USB camera and client program, without the need for a mouse or keyboard interface, specific equipment, or environmental setup.

3   System Overview

The current study have advanced our previous 3D streaming engine, which can extend existing PC-based network games onto heterogeneous mobile platforms without modifying the original software[6,7], adding an intuitively playable MR interface. In order to play a network game, all kinds of client events including keyboard, mouse, stylus, and key pad button, can be transmitted to the server after translating those events into the game events on the server. Additionally, for a multimodal game interface, we use the camera's posture with respect to the base marker. This kind of MR interface provides a tangible metaphor to manipulate intuitively the game contents.

3.1   Conceptual System Diagram

Our system has been developed on WLAN; a conceptual system diagram is shown in Fig. 2. The system consists of multiple servers on a PC and clients on a PC or handheld device. We can execute a game on the PC server in the form of MR interface as well as the original game interface. The execution process is as follows. First, a client connects with the invoke manager on the PC server that can play a 3D network game. Second, the invoking manager executes a game server to establish a one-to-one connection between the client and the game server. Lastly, the first connection between the invoking manager and the client is closed. The next connections between another clients and game clients follow the same process.

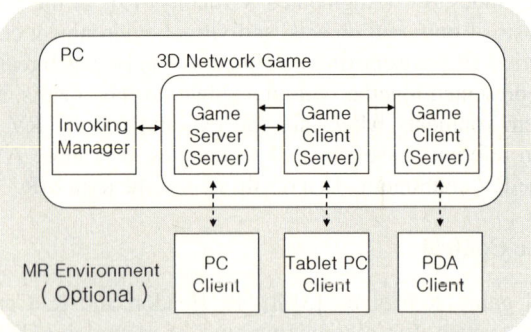

Fig. 2. Various clients on heterogeneous platforms

3.2 Client-Server Structure

Through the client-server connection between a client and PC server, our system performs two tasks: graphics streaming from server to client, which is processed by event transmission from client to server, and virtual game control that maps camera pose on client into game events on server(Fig. 3).

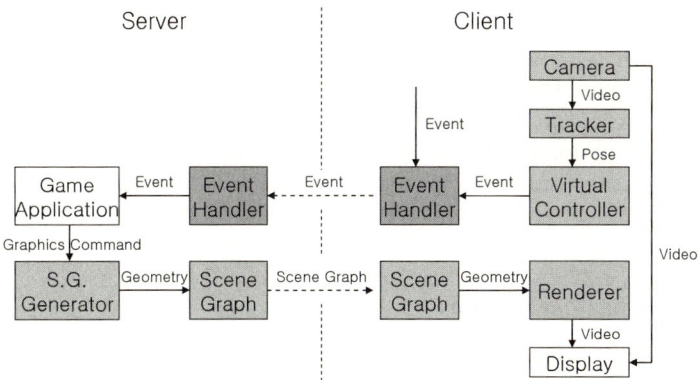

Fig. 3. Client-server structure

For graphics streaming, as described in our previous papers[6,7], we developed a middle-ware streaming engine that make it possible to play existing OpenGL-based 3D network games on PDA. The server side engine processes OpenGL command stream capture, scene graph reconstruction, data simplification, compression, and transmission. To reduce the amount of transmission, we use a client-server scene graph, hierarchical geometry hashing, visibility culling, and a simple NPR (Non-Photorealistic Rendering) technique. The client-side engine simply renders the scene graph after updating it with received geometry and view information.

In order to control a game application on a server in a tangible and intuitive method, we chose an MR interface composed of camera, tracker, and virtual controller on a client. After a tracker detects markers from camera images to calculate camera pose, the virtual controller generates pose-related information, for example, distance, tilt, roll, speed, world coordinates with respect to a marker, and maps those values to specific game events capable of playing the game naturally.

4 Effective Graphic Data Simplification

In our client-server connections, the clients not only can be implemented on heterogeneous platforms including PC and PDA, but also can be fully extended to other upcoming mobile platforms. To have heterogeneous clients choose the rendering style as their processing power and network bandwidth, we proposed a data simplification technique for dynamic and huge graphics data on server.

4.1 Dynamic Massive Graphic Data

Unlike other usual graphic systems, our system has some important differences in terms of generating graphic data on a server. The first thing is that our system uses un-expectable geometry information dynamically and irregularly captured by GLIntercept[2], while other systems usually deal with the preprocessed and static graphic data. The second thing is that we can know not the whole world, composed of primitives, but only a small part at rendering point of time.

Acquainted with specific application, for example Quake II[10], we can know and preprocess the whole rendering information, and may not reorganize total geometry structure every frame. However, we assume that the application-specific rendering information is not known in advance, because we want our method to be extended more generalized prototype system dealing with dynamically inserted and deleted massive graphic data. Therefore, we implemented our system in the form of reconstructing and updating a scene graph every frame from command stream about graphics library.

4.2 Data Simplification Methods

To simplify dynamic and massive data on a server, which cannot even be transmitted to the clients, we use three techniques: hierarchical geometry hashing, visibility culling, and NPR[6,7]. We designed a hash function for Vertex, Primitive, and Object, which are the nodes of the scene graph, to decrease geometry redundancies generated in intra-frame and inter-frames during the animation. With the results of hierarchical hashing, we can dynamically reconstruct client-server scene graph in inserting, deleting, and updating for captured geometry nodes. In addition, we can use the hash keys to deliver the change of the scene to the client.

The reconstructed scene includes both visible and invisible Objects. In order to transmit only visible Objects, it is important to find visible ones through view frustum culling and occlusion culling. In our system, we use the glViewFrustum( ), one of OpenGL functions as the view frustum culling, and the Z-Depth test of graphic card as the occlusion culling, to find visible Objects and Primitives in the current frame. Occlusion culling using Z-Depth test is processed as follows. First, the system gives a number to each Object. Second, the system renders the scene graph after translating the given number into RGB value. Finally, we extract visible Object IDs, Primitive IDs, and Vertex IDs from the rendered results of frame buffer.

We use simple NPR instead of texture mapping, because the performance on various platforms is limited to low-end devices and the transmission amount should be reduced for real time rendering. The server calculates the average of texture color, which is mapped to each primitive, to send it to the client. The client renders Objects, which are filled with the received color, in line drawing style.

5 Virtual Game Control Using MR Interface

We use the term "virtual game control" in terms of using sensing information achieved from a camera sensor, instead of a general keyboard or mouse input, in playing games.

The ideal virtual game control system is, from our point of view, one in which various sensing information from the real world is suitably mapped into virtual events in the virtual world using a similar metaphor. Although the similarity of interface metaphors is one of the most important elements that effects the usability, intuitiveness, and eventually immersion to a game, we usually compromise between the cost and efficiency. Related to our virtual game control system, therefore, we have found common ground from the previous two researches[3][11,12,13].

R. Headon and R. Curwen[3] defined (Condition, Action, Key event) mapping table to implement virtual Quake^{TM} control system, in which Condition is determined by floor tiles used in determining direction and EMG sensor worn on the player's forearm to detect fist-making action that simulates shooting. While they use special equipment such as a floor and an EMG sensors to design a Condition, we use only a camera sensor to define it from handheld device's pose with respect to a marker.

When determining our Condition, we referenced the orientation parameters used in M. Rohs[11,12,13]'s visual code system for mobile phone and its applications. However, the way of calculating our orientation parameters is totally different from his system. Our orientation parameters, their generation algorithm, and Condition mapping table are shown in Fig. 4, Fig. 6, and Table. 1. In order to more clearly show the concept of real and virtual worlds, we changed the name of mapping table items from (Condition, Action, Key event) into (RealCondition, GameAction, KeyEvent). The only difference between the two mapping tables is in the Condition/RealCondition depending on what we sense is whether human movements in ubiquitous computing environment or handheld device's pose in MR environment. The scene of playing our handheld MRQuake is shown in Fig. 5.

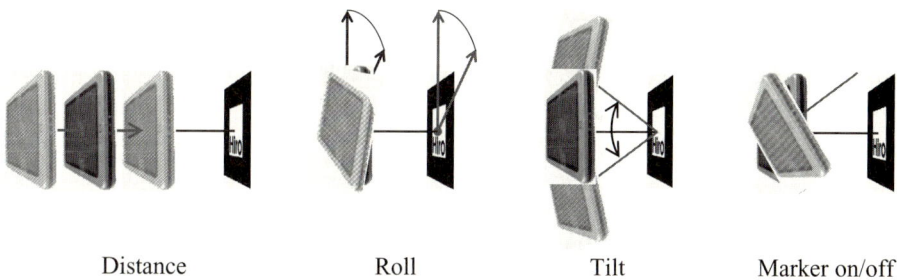

| Distance | Roll | Tilt | Marker on/off |

Fig. 4. Orientation parameters

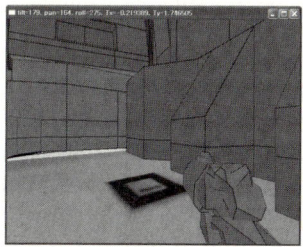

Fig. 5. Handheld MRQuake on tablet PC

Table 1. Virtual control mapping table for Handheld MRQuake

Real Condition	Game Action	Key Event
200 < Tilt < 270	Forward	Up
90 < Tilt < 160	Backward	Down
30 < Roll < 90	Turn left	Left
270 < Roll < 330	Turn right	Right
Marker on/off time > 200 ms	Jump	Space
160 < Tilt < 200 and (0 < Roll < 30 or 330 < Roll < 360)	Stay	NOT
Scale factor to marker size > 1.3	Shoot	Control_L

```
ControlThread( )
{
      loop
      {
            Marker recognition processed by ARToolkit
            Marker pose calculated by ARToolkit
            Tilt and Roll from pose matrix
            Scale factor from pose matrix
            switch ( RealCondition )
            {
                  Post KeyEvent as GameAction
            }
      }until( end )
}
```

Fig. 6. The algorithm of virtual game control

6   Experimental Results

Using Quake II[10] demo program, we tested our prototype system, and analyzed it in graphic data simplification and usability evaluation.

6.1   Graphic Data Simplification

For the first 115 frames of Quake II demo, we examined two kinds of data simplification techniques, hierarchical geometry hashing by special hash keys and occlusion culling using Z-Depth test; the results are shown in Fig. 7 and Fig. 8. The reason why we should transmit the small part of the whole world after simplifying geometry data is that current low-end devices generally use software rendering technique and don't have memory enough to save and process the whole world.

Whenever capturing the basic geometry nodes, Vertices, Primitives, and Objects, as defined in our previous studies[6,7], the proposed system always queries each node's existence to Scene Graph with its hash key. Fig. 7 shows that most of geometry nodes, whether they are intra-frame or inter-frames, are redundant because of their spatio-temporal coherence. The higher the rate of captured nodes and hit numbers to Scene Graph is, the higher the redundancy is. Therefore, vertex hashing is one of the most critical consideration to reduce redundancy and transmission to the client. Even if the hit rate of Primitives and Objects is lower than Vertices, we must consider their hashing because they have huge vertices as their child nodes.

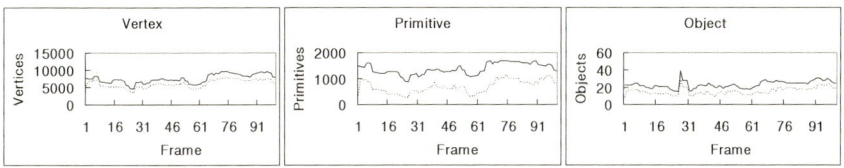

Fig. 7. Hierarchical geometry hashing. dashed line: the number of captured nodes, dotted line: the hit number resulted from the queries to Scene Graph.

Occlusion culling using Z-Depth test is processed for current frame's nodes of the Scene Graph, which means occlusion culling is processed after geometry hashing. From the results in Fig. 8, we can know a transmission to a client can be limited to the visible child nodes of the Scene Graph. For example, when the system determines the nodes to be transmitted to the client, the search range and transmission data can be decreased efficiently. We hierarchically search and transmit the visible nodes with their related index information.

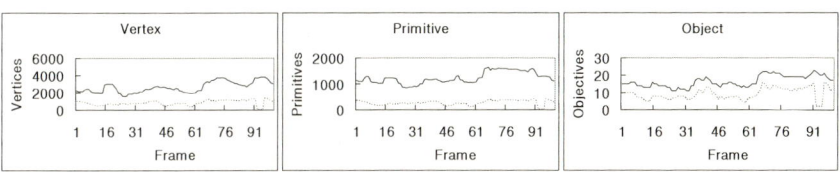

Fig. 8. Occlusion culling using Z-Depth test. dashed line: current frame's nodes in Scene Graph, dotted line: current visible nodes of Scene Graph.

At this point, we don't deal with the size and efficiency of index structure in order to focus on only geometry itself. However, in transmission, balancing index structure and geometry data, the network bandwidth, client's capacity and processing power are all related to the efficiency of graphic streaming system.

6.2 Usability Evaluation

After developing our prototype system, we evaluated the usability of the three interfaces to PC, tablet PC, and PDA: keyboard, virtual control using MR, and key button, in terms of mobility, ease of input, novelty, excitement, and time to become skilled. From six volunteers consisting of five males experienced in several PC based network games and one female unfamiliar with games, we achieved the results shown in Table 2, in which the lowest and highest figures are 0 and 10 respectively, and the time unit is a minute.

Table 2. Usability Evaluation of three different platforms

Platform	PC	Tablet PC	PDA
Interface	Keyboard	Virtual control using MR	key button
Rendering style	Simple NPR	Simple NPR	Simple NPR
Mobility	0.0	5.3	9.5
Ease of input	9.3	5.7	6.7
Novelty	3.3	8.8	6.0
Excitement	4.2	6.3	5.7
Time to become skilled	3.6	13.7	6.5

Since the mobility is limited to the effective area of keyboard input, marker recognition, or wireless LAN, we can take it for granted that the order is PC, tablet PC, and PDA. On the contrary, the easiest input interface is a PC keyboard because users are fully experienced with keyboard input, and also exposed to various PC games. For novelty meaning the sense of new experience, the virtual control of tablet PC results in the highest average that may be cased by curiosity with a different unique interface from their usual one when they play a game. In the case of excitement, users evaluate a virtual control of tablet PC is the most exciting thing, but the order partially resulted from novelty as well as the fact that it is a more tangible interface. As for the final item, the time needed to become skilled, users spent the longest time on learning how to control the game under the virtual control interface.

Virtual control interface using MR ranked lower in mobility, ease of input, time to become skilled, whereas higher in novelty and excitement. Interpreting these results, the first reason is that users were not familiar to the virtual control interface; the second is that the interface design was not optimized to the game yet, that is, the real actions of users are not appropriately mapped to the physics in the game, and the third is that they respond to the game with lower sensitivity caused by network delay and marker tracking.

Despite the lower ranks of virtual control using MR in mobility, easiness of input, and time to become skilled, we still have a prospect for that interface especially in the situation where users have some difficulties to freely use a keyboard, key button, and stylus. In addition, for users who want more exciting entertainment related to real physical actions, it could provide a good interface under the guarantee of registration accuracy, delay limit, and processing power. Therefore, in the case of more powerful handheld devices than now, we can fully expand it to effective interface of a new game.

7 Conclusions and Future Research

In this paper, we proposed a test-bed prototype system to deal with dynamic and huge graphic data on heterogeneous platforms. The system presented a possibility or a paradigm to enable various clients to manage their shared virtual world in their hardware/software environment. Recently, we have considered an environment in which a PC user playing a game in photorealistic rendering style and with multiple-key combinations, a tablet PC user on handheld MR interface with limited mobility, and a

PDA user with a simple NPR interface in mobile environment are sharing their game world by more natural interaction metaphor.

Although we have implemented the cooperated prototype system as well as each client-server connections, the system still has some limitations in scalability, usability, and performance. Therefore, in the near future, we will improve the proposed system into more effective system, with a natural interaction metaphor and using the visibility of the game configuration.

Acknowledgment. This work was supported by the *Brain Korea 21* Project in 2006.

References

1. ARToolKit : http://www.hitl.washington.edu/artoolkit
2. GLIntercept : http://glintercept.nutty.org
3. Headon, R., Curwen, R.: Movement Awareness for Ubiquitous Game Control. Personal and Ubiquitous Computing 2002. Vol.6. No.5-6. Springer-Verlag, London (2002) 407-415
4. Henrysson, A., Billinghurst, M., Ollila. M.: Face to Face Collaborative AR on Mobile Phones. Proc. of ISMAR 2005 (2005)
5. Hosseini, N., Georganas, D.: MPEG-4 BIFS Streaming of Large Virtual Environments and Their Animation on The Web. Proc. of Web3D (2002) 19–25
6. Jung, G.S., Jung, S.K.: A Streaming Engine for PC-based 3D Network Games onto Heterogeneous Mobile Platforms. Edutainment2006. LNCS. Vol. 3942. Springer-Verlag, Berlin Heidelberg (2006) 797-800
7. Jung, G.S., Kwon, S.I., Park, M.W., Won, K.H., Jung, S.K.: A New Dynamic Client-Server Scene Graph for Mobile NPRQuake on Heterogeneous Frameworks. Proc. of CASA2005. (2005) 37-42
8. Lee, D.H., Jung, S.K.: Computer Vision-Assisted Interaction in X3D Virtual Environment on WWW. LNCS. Vol. 2713. Springer-Verlag, Berlin Heidelberg. (2003) 332-340
9. Milgram, P., Takemura, H., Utsumi. A., Kishino. F.: Augmented Reality: A class of displys on the reality-virtuality continuum. SPIE: Telemanipulator and Telepresence Technologies, (1994)
10. Quake II. Id Software : http://www.idsoftware.com
11. Rohs, M.: Real-World Interaction with Camera Phones. 2nd International Symposium on Ubiquitous Computing Systems (UCS 2004). LNCS. Vol. 3598, Springer. (2005) 74–89
12. Rohs, M.: Marker-Based Embodied Interaction for Handheld Augmented Reality Games. Proc. of PerGames at PERVASIVE 2006 (2006)
13. Rohs, M., Zweifel, P.: A Conceptual Framework for Camera Phone-based Interaction Techniques. PERVASIVE 2005. LNCS. Vol. 3468. Springer. (2005) 171–189
14. Teler, E., Lischinski, D.: Streaming of Complex 3D Scenes for Remote Walkthroughs. Proc. of EUROGRAPHICS 2001 (2001) 17-25
15. Wagner D., Pintaric T., Ledermann F., Schmalstieg D.: Towards Massively Multi-User Augmented Reality on Handheld Devices. Proc. of PERVASIVE 2005
16. Wagner, D., Schmalstieg, D.: First Steps towards Handheld Augmented Reality. Proc. of ISWC2003. White Plains. IEEE Computer Society, NY USA. (2003) 127–137

Manipulation of Field of View for Hand-Held Virtual Reality

Jane Hwang[1], Jaehoon Jung[1], and Gerard J. Kim[2,*]

[1] Dept. of Computer Science and Engineering
POSTECH
Pohang, Korea
jane@postech.ac.kr
[2] Dept. of Computer Science and Engineering
Korea University
Seoul, Korea
gjkim@korea.ac.kr

Abstract. Today, hand-held computing and media devices are commonly used in our everyday lives. This paper assesses the viability of hand-held devices as effective platforms for "virtual reality." Intuitively, the narrow field of view of hand-held devices is a natural candidate factor against achieving an effective immersion. In this paper, we show two ways of manipulating the visual field of view (perceived or real), in hopes of overcoming this factor. Our study has revealed that when a motion-based interaction was used, the FOV perceived by the user (and presence) for the small hand-held device was significantly greater than the actual. The other method is to implement dynamic rendering in which the FOV is adjusted depending on the viewing position and distance. Although not formally tested, the second method is expected to bring about higher focused attention (and thus immersion) and association of the visual feedback with one's proprioception. The paper demonstrates the distinct possibility of realizing reasonable virtual reality even with devices with a small visual FOV and limited processing power through multimodal compensation.

Keywords: Computer Interface, Human Factors, Virtual Reality, Hand-held.

1 Introduction

The performance and functionalities of hand-held computing and media devices have advanced dramatically in recent times. Hand-held devices are those computer embedded systems that are small and light enough to be held in one hand such as personal digital assistants (PDA), cell phones, ultra mobile computers, and portable game consoles. Today's hand-held computers are equipped with processors approaching 1GHz performance with graphics accelerating chips, sound/signal processing modules and a sleuth of sensors (e.g. camera, gyros, light sensors) and multimodal displays (e.g. vibrators, auto-stereoscopic display). Nevertheless, one can be skeptical whether such devices can be used for "virtual reality," e.g. to the extent

---

* Corresponding author.

Z. Pan et al. (Eds.): ICAT 2006, LNCS 4282, pp. 1204–1211, 2006.
© Springer-Verlag Berlin Heidelberg 2006

of eliciting immersive feelings (not just for 3D contents viewing). One obvious reason is the very narrow field and small absolute size of the visual display in hand-held devices. It is not obvious whether interactivity alone can sufficiently enhance the virtual experience to achieve reasonable "VR."

In this paper, we propose two ways of manipulating the visual field of view (perceived or real) in hopes of overcoming this factor, and show the feasibility of the hand-held VR. We conducted an experiment comparing the perceived field of view (FOV), the level of immersion and presence among the users' of various VR platforms including the hand-held device. That is, the VR platforms were varied in their sizes of physical/software FOV and in styles of interaction. In this comparative study, we considered the use of a motion based interaction as the factor for the style of interaction. Motion based interaction (e.g. gesture, direct interaction) is already considered a desirable style of interaction for virtual reality systems [1]. This is because it involves many parts of our body (if not the whole) and leverages on one's sense of proprioception, improving the overall user felt presence and immersion (and even task performance) [9]. In the case of hand-held devices, the motion based interaction also becomes coupled with the visual display/head (a situation unique to the hand-held device) because the sensors and the displays are all physically integrated (and moving) together. Currently, interaction in the handheld devices is still mostly button and finger-based and naturally, one way is to enrich the user experience is to provide the body-based and motion based. The paper hopes to demonstrate the distinct possibility of realizing reasonable virtual reality even with devices with a small visual FOV and limited processing power through multimodal compensation.

The other method is to implement dynamic rendering in which the FOV is adjusted depending on the viewing position, and distance. For instance, the user can move the device in and out to widen or reduce the FOV (i.e. window metaphor). Although not formally tested, the second method is expected to bring about higher focused attention (and thus immersion) and association of the visual feedback with one's proprioception. For both methods, sensors (but inexpensive) are required to approximately detect user motion and track one's head (or view) position and direction.

2 Motion-Based Interaction and Perceived FOV

The main purpose of this study was to assess the feasibility of virtual reality with relatively small screens (as in the hand-held devices) by taking advantage of other system factors, such as multimodal interaction, especially motion based interaction. The basic approach was to have the subjects navigate through a given virtual environment (Experiment I) and search and select objects (Experiment II) using VR platforms differing in their screen sizes and software (geometric) FOVs (SFOV). The software FOV (SFOV) differs from the actual physical FOV (PFOV) in that it refers to the angle encompassing a given scene in its original scale.

2.1 Experiment Design and Procedures

There were five conditions for the two experiments as shown in Table 1. The primary condition represents the motion based hand-held platform, and as comparison groups there were four others. The button-based hand-held platform represents the current form of the hand-held devices. To see the effects of "hand grasping" (whether the mere hand grasping contributes to a possible immersion or sustained attention), a small (same as the hand-helds) screen platform condition was also added. The desktop monitor and large PDP (Plasma Display Panel) display based platforms represent the nominal VR platforms with larger display sizes (larger PFOV and SFOV).

The motion-based interface was implemented by attaching a USB camera to the hand-held computer (VGN-U71P from SONY) and using the optical flow information to estimate the amount and direction of the movement in mainly three directions (right/left, up/down, forward/backward). For details, see [4].

Table 1. Six test conditions in the experiment. Asterisks denote average values.

Platform Characteristics / Test Groups	Screen Size: width x height	Viewing Distance / Physical FOV	Software FOV
Hand-held / Motion based	10cm x 7.5cm	37.97cm* / 15°	30° (200%)
Hand-held / Button based	10cm x 7.5cm	37.97cm* / 15°	30° (200%)
Small Screen / Keyboard & Mouse	10cm x 7.5cm	37.97cm / 15°	30° (200%)
Desktop Monitor / Keyboard & Mouse	34cm x 26cm	63.44cm / 30°	45° (150%)
Large PDP / Keyboard & Mouse	68cm x 51cm	58.88cm / 60°	60° (100%)

We performed two experiments. In Experiment I, the users were questioned for presence, system usability, enjoyment and perceived field of view after navigating through the virtual environment in the given platform. In Experiment II, the task (navigating and selecting objects) completion time was measured. A one factor within-subject experimental design was for both experiments. In both cases, the independent variable was the type of the VR platform. The major dependent variables for Experiment I were the level of presence/immersion, various usability, and perceived FOV, and for Experiment II, the task completion time.

As the first experiment assessed presence and immersion, the respective subjects had to fill out an immersive tendency questionnaire which was adapted from the work by Witmer and Singer [11] and Slater [8]. As for assessing the perceived FOV, the questionnaire included a question of whether the display of the given VR platform provided sufficient FOV. In another assessment, the user was asked to mark on a

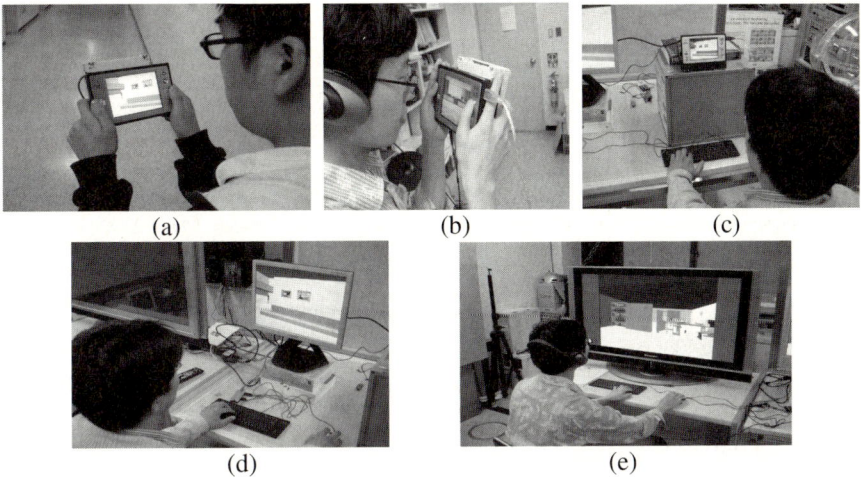

Fig. 1. The VR platforms tested: (a) Hand-held / Motion based (b) Hand-held / Button based
c) Small Screen / Keyboard & Mouse (d) Desktop Monitor / Keyboard & Mouse (e) Large
PDP / Keyboard & Mouse

pictorial snapshot of the virtual environment the extent to which one felt one could
see through the display. Fig. 1 shows snapshots from the experiment. Twenty-five
subjects participated in each of the experiment. We omit further details of the
experiment due to lack of space.

2.2   Results

We used the ANOVA to verify the significance of the conditions and the Student-
Newman-Keuls test for grouping the test conditions with respect to the statistical
results. We give a report to the major findings of our study with regards to the
perceived FOV, presence, immersion, usability, task performance, enjoyment and
cyber-sickness. Due to the limitation of the space, we will show the benefits to the
perceived FOV, presence and immersion.

   Fig. 2 shows the ANOVA results for the case when subjects marked the extent of
their perceived FOV, and it suggests that the perceived FOV is significantly widened
compared to the PFOV ($F_{4,96} = 12.72$, $p < 0.0001$ in marking). In addition to the
support by the existing literatures [6][8], the perceived FOV, in our study, also had a
strong correlation with immersion and presence (Pearson correlation value was 0.301,
$p = .001$ with immersion, correlation value was 0.475, $p < .0001$ with presence).
Presence and immersion significantly improved with the motion based interaction
(immersion: $F_{4,96} = 5.38$, $p = .0005$, presence: $F_{4,96} = 17.43$, $p < .0001$) (See Fig. 2).
Note that the perceived FOV of the hand-held with the motion-based interface is
almost twice that of the actual, while the presence level is comparable to those with
the desktop and large projection screens.

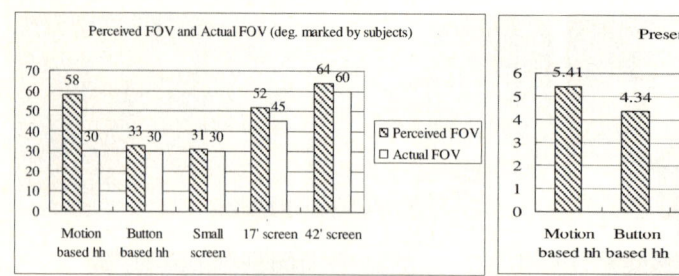
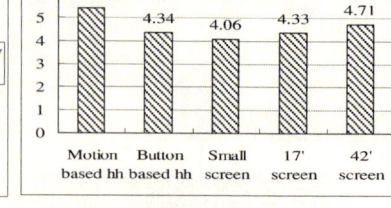

Fig. 2. Perceived FOV / Presence vs. various VR platforms

3 Dynamic FOV Adjustment for Hand-Held Display

3.1 Manipulating Software FOV

As already described, the narrow FOV and small size of the hand-held display (without any other provision) can cause lowered immersion in the hand-held VR. In addition, we claim that the fixed FOV despite changing viewing distance is also unnatural and can bring about similar effects (See Fig. 3(a)).

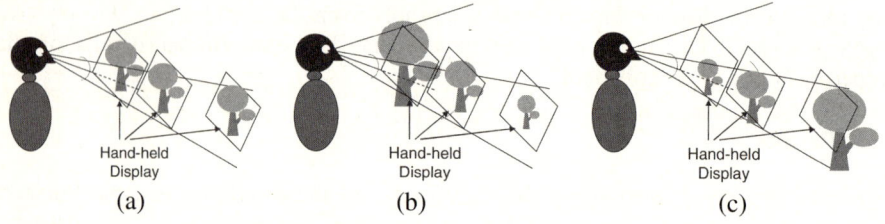

Fig. 3. Considering eye-display distance in hand-held VR: (a) Nominal Hand-held VR, (b) Hand-held VR as a magnifying glass, (c) Hand-held VR as a see-through window into VE

Therefore, to alleviate this problem, we suggest two different software FOV manipulation techniques using an approximate measurement of the eye (or head) position relative to the hand-held device. We attached and interfaced the SRF10 ultrasonic range finder to the hand-held device, and it can detect obstacles in the range of 3 cm to 6 m from the hand-held device screen.

The first proposed FOV technique is to adjust the visual FOV to mimic the behavior of a magnifying glass (see Fig. 3 (b) and Fig. 4). The FOV becomes narrower as the view distance is reduced. This method is useful for the applications in which the detailed views of the object are important but size perception is not.

The second proposed FOV technique is to use the hand-held device in an opposite way, as a see-through window into the virtual environment (see Fig. 3(c) and Fig. 5). As the head gets closer to the screen (or window), there are more parts of the virtual environment visible, thus the FOV widens (and objects are drawn smaller). As you can see in Fig. 5, the size of the virtual object "perceived to the user" is kept the same regardless to the eye-display distance. This approach is better suited for applications in which size or spatial perception is important such as medical training VR systems.

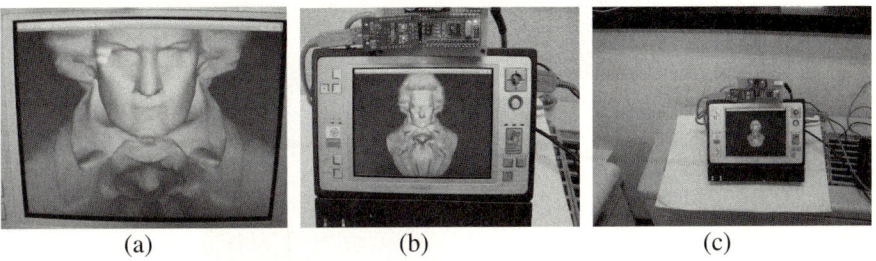

(a)   (b)   (c)

Fig. 4. Hand-held VR as a magnifying glass; the size of the virtual object looks bigger when the hand-held display is close to the eyes: (a) close (15 cm), (b) medium range (30 cm), (c) far range (60 cm)

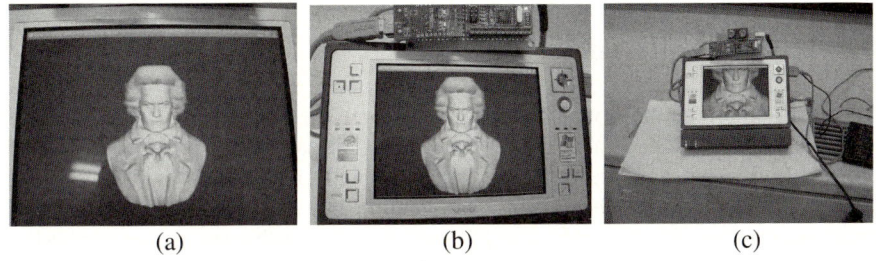

(a)   (b)   (c)

Fig. 5. Hand-held VR as a see-through window; the size of the virtual object looks same because we adjusted the software FOV using the eye-display distance: (a) close (15 cm), (b) medium range (30cm), (c) far range (60cm)

3.2 Model Simplification Considering Visual Perception of User

Hand-held devices are still not as powerful in terms of their graphic capabilities compared to the desktop environments that most users are accustomed with. View dependent simplification can be applied along with the varying the FOV to enhance the perceived quality of the target model and the system performance at the same time. In the case of a magnifying glass hand-held VR, as the view distance becomes larger and the FOV widens (objects smaller), the mesh can be simplified because the user's detail perception will be trivial (See Fig. 6). In the case of the see-through hand-held VR, the opposite rule is applied. This technique can provide more visual detail and realism given the same amount of system resource. Such a system optimization is important for a reduced platform such as hand-held devices.

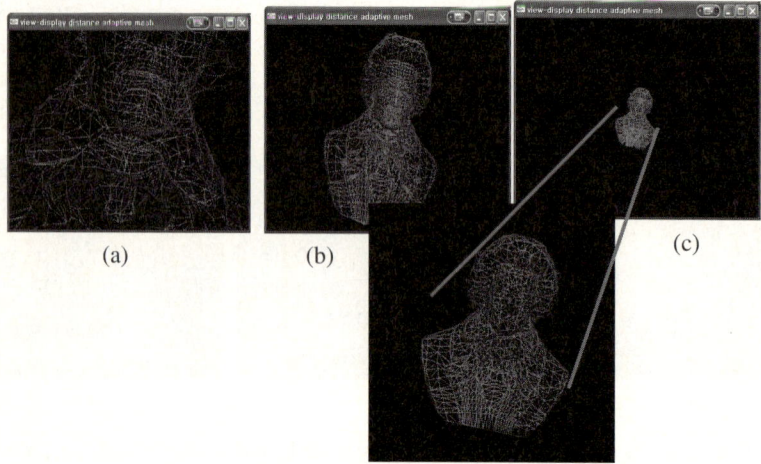

Fig. 6. Simplifying the mesh with the changing eye-display distance. The case of hand-held VR as a magnifying glass: (a) close (15 cm), (b) medium range (30cm), (c) far range (60cm).

4 Discussion and Conclusion

This paper presented the several ways to manipulate the perceived and software FOV of the hand-held display in hopes to realize the virtual reality providing sufficient realism, immersion and presence on a reduced and small platform like hand-held devices. The FOV was chosen for manipulation because it was expected that the screen size was the most negative factor toward realizing the true meaning of VR on hand-held devices. The results have shown that the motion-based interaction, a unique characteristic of hand-held devices, can help improve the perceived FOV and presence/immersion up to a level comparable to the nominal VR platforms. We believe the widely perceived FOV is due to the similarity of the motion-based interaction to how humans obtain a wide FOV through one's eye ball movement (saccadic movement) and neck movement.

In addition, the software FOV can be adjusted with view dependent mesh simplification to provide more realistic or practical display conditions and improve the perceived quality and focus to the user. Because the device is held in user's hand, this means that the size, quality and spatial perception is inherently tied to one's proprioception to be even more effective.

In the process of the study, a camera/accelerator based relative tracking technique has been developed to realize the motion based interaction on the hand-held device, and an inexpensive ultrasonic range sensing was developed for an approximate tracking of the user's head relative to the display screen.

With these results alone, it is plausible to claim that hand-held VR has a distinct potential to provide sufficient detail and immersion for high presence (e.g. comparable to nominal VR systems). This can be even furthered with other added elements such as multimodality (e.g. voice, tactile/haptic feedback, stereo display, etc), and environment binding/interaction (e.g. playing motion based golf on a grass field).

We are currently working on adding more multimodal sensing and displays for hand-held VR such as multiple vibro-tactile displays and 3D sound. At the same time, we are continually improving the accuracy of the camera based motion-based interaction and ultrasonic sensor based user tracking. Further validation is needed through exploration of various hand-held VR applications and usability studies as well.

Acknowledgement. Parts of this paper was submitted to ACM VRST '06 and Springer Virtual Reality. This work was supported by the grant from the Virtual Reality and Computer Graphics ITRC program by the Korean Ministry of Information and Communication.

References

1. Bowman, D. A., et al. A Survey of Usability Evaluation in Virtual Environments: Classification and Comparison of Methods. Presence: Teleoperators and Virtual Environments, 11, 4, (2002) 404-424
2. Bowman, D. A. and Hodges, L. F. An evaluation of techniques for grabbing and manipulating remote objects in immersive virtual environments. In Proceedings of the symposium on Interactive 3D graphics, Rhode Island, United States, (1997)
3. Cohen, J., Duca, N., Luebke, D., Schubert, B. GLOD: A Geometric Level of Detail System at the OpenGL API Level. IEEE Visualization 2003, Seattle, WA (2003).
4. Hwang, J., Jung, J., Kim, G. J. Hand-held Virtual Reality: A Feasibility Study, In Proceedings of ACM Virtual Reality Software and Technology 2006, (2006) (to be appeared).
5. Lee, S., et al. Formation of spatial presence: by form or content?. In Proceedings of 7th Annual International Presence Workshop, Valencia, Spain, (2004)
6. Lin, J. J.-W., et al. Effects of field of view on presence, enjoyment, memory, and simulator sickness in a virtual environment. In Proceedings of IEEE Intl. Conf. on Virtual Reality (VRST '06), (2002)
7. Maringelli, F., et al. The Influence of Body Movement on Subjective Presence in Virtual Environments. Human Factors, 40, 3, (1998) 469-477
8. Polys, N. F., et al. Effects of information layout, screen size, and field of view on user performance in information-rich virtual environments. In Proceedings of ACM Virtual Reality Software and Technology (VRST '05), Monterey, California, USA., (2005)
9. Slater, M. A Note on Presence Terminology. Presence-Connect. 3, Jan. (2003)
10. Slater, M. Measuring Presence: A Response to the Witmer and Singer Presence Questionnaire. Presence: Teleoperators and Virtual Environments, 8, 5, (1999) 560-565
11. Witmer, B. G. and Singer, M. J. Measuring Presence in Virtual Environments: A Presence Questionnaire. Presence: Teleoperators and Virtual Environments, 7, 3, (1998) 225-240

Hierarchical 3D Data Rendering System Synchronizing with HTML

Yousuke Kimura[1], Tomohiro Mashita[2], Atsushi Nakazawa[1,2],
Takashi Machida[1,2], Kiyoshi Kiyokawa[1,2], and Haruo Tamekura[1,2]

[1] Graduate School of Information Science and Technology, Osaka University
[2] Cybermedia center, Osaka University

Abstract. We propose a new rendering system for large-scale, 3D ge-
ometic data that can be used with web-based content management systems (CMS). To achieve this, we employed a geometry hierarchical encoding method "QSplat" and implemented this in a Java and JOGL
(Java bindings of OpenGL) environment. Users can view large-scale geometric data using conventional HTML browsers with a non-powerful
CPU and low-speed networks. Further, this system is independent of the
platforms. We add new functionalities so that users can easily understand
the geometric data: Annotations and HTML Synchronization. Users can
see the geometric data with the associated annotations that describe the
names or the detailed explanations of the particular portions. The HTML
Synchronization enables users to smoothly and interactively switch our
rendering system and HTML contents. The experimental results show
that our system performs an interactive frame rate even for a large-scale
data whereas other systems cannot render them.

1 Introduction

The widely used World Wide Web provides many types of information including
texts, sounds and 2D images for various purposes. These sorts of multimedia
data are very helpful to enrich contents and enhance users' experiences.

Use of 3D geometric data is an effective method for understanding contents
because users can browse them from arbitrary viewpoints. Our goal is to develop
a 3D geometric data browser along with user interfaces for the purpose of web-
based contents management systems (CMS) into World Wide Web. Our browser
can render large-scale geometric data very quickly even on not so powerful user
terminals. We designed this system to compensate for three issues.

First, this software should work independently of users' hardware and software environments. Previous solutions have needed additional plug-in software
to render 3D geometric data, thus users had to install the software in advance.
Additionally, this sorts of plug-in software can not always be ported to all platforms. To resolve this issue, we developed our software as a Java applet so that
it would work on any platform including mobile terminals.

The next issue is the rendering performance. Compared to texts or images,
rendering 3D geometry requires much computation cost, in particular for rendering large-scale geometric data. Further, our rendering system must work at

Z. Pan et al. (Eds.): ICAT 2006, LNCS 4282, pp. 1212–1222, 2006.

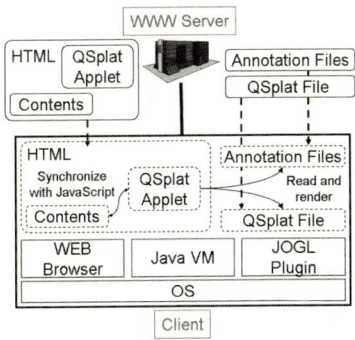

Fig. 1. Architecture of Our Rendering System

an interactive frame rate in any environment - from desktop PCs to mobile terminals. For this issue, we introduce a hierarchical geometry encoding method "QSplat[1]" as a 3D geometry description format. With the QSplat rendering system, we can adjust the image quality of the rendered 3D model and its frame rate according to the terminal's environment and users' interactions.

The third issue is the synchronization between the geometric data and other data in CMS. Because we want to use 3D geometric data as multimedia data in web-based CMS, the objects' locations or objects' portions in the data should be associated with other information, such as texts or sounds in the CMS database. Therefore, we develop a method to draw annotations at the particular positions of the objects, and for HTML synchronization functions. Annotations show names and details onto the geometric data, and HTML synchronization offers user's much interactive browsing experience between the 3D object and the HTML browsers. If users click the links in the HTML browser, the viewing position in the 3D geometric data browser smoothly moves to the particular position. On the other hand, when annotations in the 3D geometric data browser are clicked, the associated HTML or other multimedia data are activated and users can smoothly see and hear a detail description of the portion.

Several solutions, such as VRML, have been proposed to show 3D data in web browsers, called Web3D. But these usually cannot be applied when the objects are complicated, because the size of such data is enlarged by a complicated 3D geometric object and it is hard to render in an interactive frame rate. Several commercial Web3D technologies, such as Cult3D[2], Viewpoint[3], Shockwave 3D[4] solve the data size problem and have various functions for more effective rendering or animation.

Point-based rendering is more useful than polygon-based rendering in cases where the shape of the 3D object is complex[5]. Here, the model is assumed to be of a lot of points of various sizes. This sorts of rendering method can easily introduce multiresolution rendering, which enables dynamic changes in the resolution of models while the rendering procedure proceeds. QSplat, Surfels[6], and several other systems[7][8][9] are examples of point-based rendering methods. On our approach, we employed the QSplat method for rendering and data transmission.

In the reminder of this paper, we first give an overview of our systems in Sect. 2. Next, we describe QSplat, on which we base our rendering system, in Sect. 3. We explain the way of storing and rendering annotations in Sect. 4. In Sect. 5, we present an example of synchronization of object rendering and HTML browsers. The experimental results are shown in Sect. 6. Finally, we show applications of our method and give conclusions in Sect. 7 and Sect. 8 respectively.

2   System Overview

The architecture of our system is shown in Fig. 1. This system works on a web browser, Java Virtual Machine (JVM) and JOGL (Java Bindings for OpenGL) [10]. First, the web browser downloads the html file and applet. The applet loads the 3D data (QSplat file) and annotation files from the server, then it renders the 3D model using JOGL.

The annotation files manage information such as annotation IDs and descriptions, or relationships to the 3D model. Annotation IDs are used in both HTML (JavaScript) and the Java applet for HTML synchronization. The description can contain various information including words, sentences, hyperlinks or numerical data. The field is used not only for text but also for hyperlinks of sound data or viewing position and directions.

3   QSplat Rendering

QSplat is a kind of point-based rendering system. The object is expressed as a set of the points (SPLATs) of various sizes.

Each splat is defined by the parameters of; center position, radius, normal, normal cone, and optionally color. Further, the whole object geometry is constructed as a tree structure (Fig. 2). Here, one node corresponds to a splat. One parent node has up to 4 child nodes. Higher level nodes correspond to a rough geometric structure, and lower level nodes correspond to the details. In the QSplat file, each splat's parameters are quantized so that one splat data is encoded to 4 bytes (if color data, 6 bytes).

On the rendering stage, the tree is searched from high-level to low-level nodes. Tree traversal is stopped at the appropriate level and the nodes of that level are rendered. Here, the visibilities of the nodes are also considered. As the target nodes are at a lower level, the result becomes finer and more time is necessary for rendering. Thus, if the processing power is limited, the program draws higher level nodes and keeps interactive frame rates (Fig. 3).

The system can draw the data while the data file is being loaded from server, because the QSplat data are stored from high-level to low-level data in the file. Thus, the user doesn't have to wait until the system loads all the QSplat data from the server. This is a good feature for low bandwidth environments and

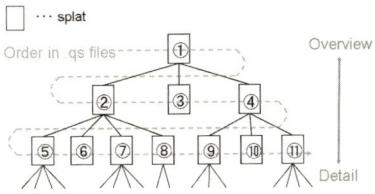

Fig. 2. QSplat Tree

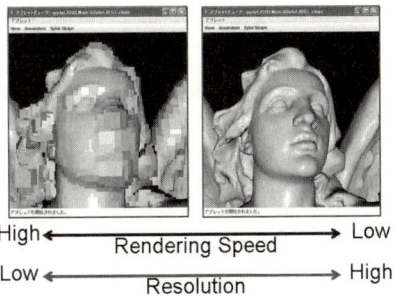

High ← Rendering Speed → Low

Low ← Resolution → High

Fig. 3. Trade-off between Rendering Speed and Resolution

reduces user irritation. For the same reason, our system draws low resolution (high level) data while a user is changing viewpoints in the browser. During this operation, a quick and interactive response is achieved for user operations.

4   Annotation

Annotations show names or explanations of 3D models or portions of 3D models, and are rendered with the 3D model. Each annotation has a unique ID (annotation ID). Annotation IDs are commonly used in rendering systems and HTML. How to use annotation ID is described in detail in Sect. 5.

4.1   Annotation Files

Annotations are related to the nodes or leaves in a QSplat tree. If the associated QSplat nodes are visible and rendered, the annotation is also rendered near the splats.

In most cases, one annotation corresponds to multiple nodes. In such cases, we associate the annotation and the root-nodes of the highest subtrees. Figure 4 shows the case that the annotation "Head" is related to the 3 splats indicated by arrows.

Because the annotation and the splat nodes are not in a one to one correspondence, we used two files to describe the annotation: annotation and association files. An annotation file describes unique annotation IDs, view information (position, rotation, rotation axis, field of view) and descriptions. The view information

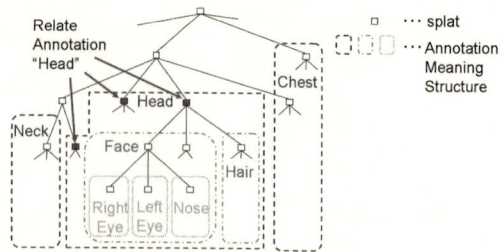

Fig. 4. Relating Annotations to a QSplat Tree

Index	ID	View	description
1	REye	1.0E9 1.5E9 -5.7E8 ...	Right_Eye
2	LEye	1.0E9 1.4E9 -6.3E8 ...	Left_Eye
3	Nose	1.0E9 9.6E8 4.2E8 ...	Nose
4	Hair	8.1E8 1.2E9 -3.0E8 ...	Hair

Annotation File

Index	Parent	Annotation
183	52	2
184	52	2
196	56	4
...		

Association File

Fig. 5. Samples of Annotation and Association Files

is used for the HTML synchronization function. When a user wants to see a particular portion of the 3D data that accords with the annotation name, this view information is used to set the correct viewpoint.

The association file contains the relationship between the annotation and the splat indexes. Here, one annotation may correspond to multiple Splats. Figure 5 shows an example.

To make annotation and association files, we developed the editing tool shown in Fig. 6. Designers can easily create and edit annotations by clicking the splats of 3D data and writing texts or other descriptions.

4.2 Drawing Annotations with a 3D Model

Annotations must be drawn at the "free space" of the 3D model or other annotations; arrows indicate correspondences between annotations and corresponding splats (Fig.7). Here, two issues need considering; 1. how to find the "free space," and 2. how to avoid "crossing" of the arrows. We describe the algorithm below.

First, we find the rectangular region where the 3D model is rendered. We call this region the "model-rendered area" (Fig. 7(a)). The model-rendered area is then split into 4 areas (Fig. 7(b)). The position of the annotation is decided by which area the target splat is located in (Fig. 7(b)). For example, if the splats are rendered in area 1, the annotation is located in the right side of the model-rendered area.

If multiple sets of annotated splats are located in the same area, the vertical order within the area is used for the arrangement of the annotations. Namely, if three sets of annotated splats are rendered in an area in a particular order, the

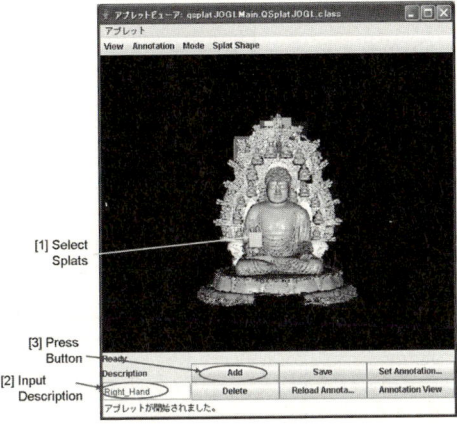

Fig. 6. Annotation Editing Tool

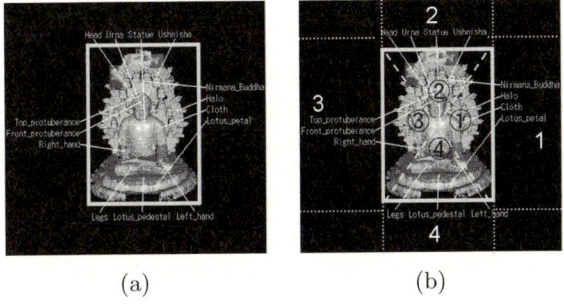

(a)   (b)

Fig. 7. Locating Annotation. (a) Compute model-rendered area. (b) Divide model-rendered area and locate annotations.

three annotations are drawn in the free space of the area with the same vertical order of the splats. Finally, arrows are drawn to connect the annotations and the splats.

5   Synchronization with HTML

Our applet can interact with other HTML contents thorough JavaScript, which can call methods of the Java applet, and the Java applet can call functions of JavaScript. We utilize these features. In our applet, some methods are defined for interacting with JavaScript. The HTML synchronization is realized by JavaScript functions calling these methods and controlling the HTML contents.

The architecture of synchronization is shown in Fig. 8. If the user clicks a content (Fig. 8 [A]), the associated JavaScript function is called with an annotation ID as an argument (Fig. 8 [B]), where the annotation IDs are predefined to

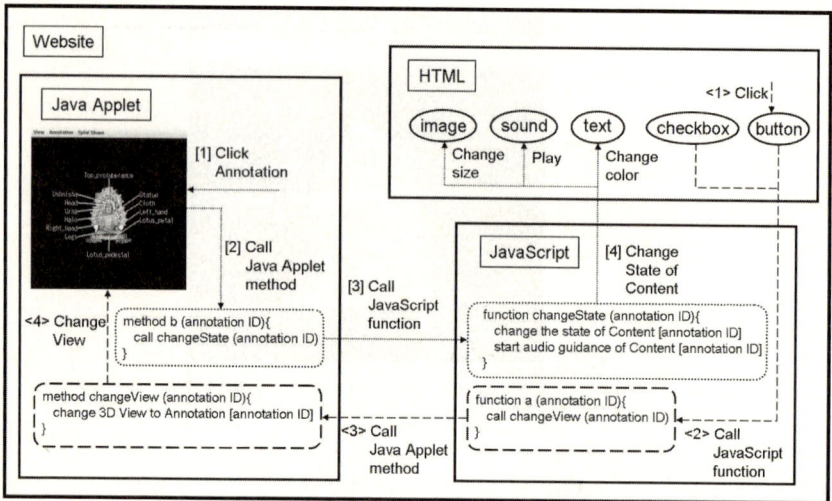

Fig. 8. Architecture of Synchronization with HTML Contents

identify annotations and contents associated with a particular annotation. This function calls the applet method with the same annotation ID (Fig. 8 [C]), and the view of QSplat is changed to a predefined one according to the annotation ID (Fig. 8 [D]). On the other hand, if the user clicks an annotation in the applet (Fig. 8 [a]), the predefined method is called with an annotation ID (Fig. 8 [b]), Then the predefined method calls the JavaScript function with an annotation ID (Fig. 8 [c]), and these functions control particular contents corresponding with the annotation ID(Fig. 8 [d]).

We have made a sample website that expounds on the Great Buddha, as shown in Fig. 9. In this site, our applet is located on the left, and the descriptions of each part of the Great Buddha are located on the right. These descriptions correspond to each annotation in the applet. If headings of the descriptions are clicked, JavaScript functions are called to change the view of QSplat and to show the detailed description. If the user clicks an annotation in the applet, a predefined JavaScript is called, and a detailed description is shown on the right side of web page and the voice guidance is played.

6   Experiments

Two experiments were conducted to verify the usefulness of our rendering system in terms of rendering performance.

6.1   Experiment 1: Comparing Existing Rendering Systems

We compared the rendering speed of our system and that of a VRML viewer, the Cortona VRML Client[11]. VRML viewers are widely-used 3D rendering

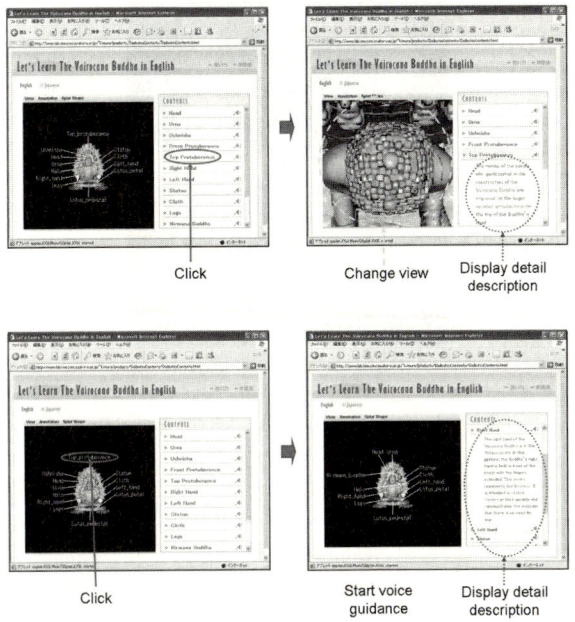

Fig. 9. Sample Website with Our Applet Synchronizing with Other Contents

systems that can be executed on web browsers. In Experiment 1, we prepared 4 kinds of VRML data and corresponding QSplat data (Fig. 10) and located them on a server. Then, we downloaded them with a client PC (Intel Pentium 4 2.5 GHz, 768MB memory, NVIDIA GeForce4 Ti4200, Internet Explorer 6.0, JRE 1.5.0.07) through a wired LAN (about 85 Mbps), rendered them with Cortona or our system, and measured their execution time.

Table 1 shows the results of Experiment 1. First, our system's executing time to finish rendering was much shorter. Specifically, the larger the data size, the larger the difference between the execution times. In the case of data 4, Cortona could not finish execution because the data size was too large. When a viewer renders VRML data, a scene graph is made, thus if the data size is large, execution time increases explosively. On the other hand, with QSplat, a scene graph is not made, so even if the data size is large, execution time increases only linearly. Next, because our system renders from lower to higher-resolution data sequentially, users can reasonably quickly see the first view as the time to first view depends on the lowest data. In VRML, users have to wait until all data are rendered. This waiting time gets longer proportional to the data size. In terms of frame rate, the frame rate of the VRML viewer in changing the view was smaller than that of our system for each data size. These experimental results show that users can not smoothly browse large size 3D geometric data with a VRML viewer. However, using our system, the resolution of the image is adjusted to maintain the frame rate so that users can browse even large size 3D geometric data.

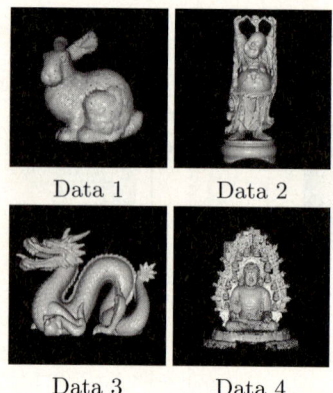

Data 1   Data 2

Data 3   Data 4

Fig. 10. Experimental 3D Geometry Data

Table 1. Comparison of Our Rendering System with a VRML Viewer

	Data Size [MB]		Number of Polygons [thousands]	Number of Splats [thousands]	Time to Begin Displaying Image [sec.]		Time to Finish Rendering [sec.]		Frame Rate While Changing View [fps]	
	VRML	QSplat	VRML	QSplat	VRML	QSplat	VRML	QSplat	VRML	QSplat
Data 1	4.4	0.2	69	58	2	1	2	2	*1	8.0
Data 2	71.2	6.7	1087	1757	71	1	71	4	1.2	8.0
Data 3	56.8	8.1	871	2129	51	1	51	5	1.2	8.0
Data 4	142.5	9.9	3109	2591	*2	1	*2	6	*2	8.0

*1 Enough high speed.
*2 The system can't render the model because the data sizes are too large.

6.2   Experiment 2: Executing Our System in Several Environments

We executed our systems on a desktop PC (same one used in Experiment 1) thorough a wired LAN (about 85 Mbps), on a mobile PC (Intel Pentium M 1.1GHz, 504 MB memory, Intel 82852/82855 GM/GME Graphics Controller, Internet Explorer 6.0, JRE 1.5.0.07) through a wired LAN, and on a mobile PC through wireless LAN (about 8Mbps), and measured and compared their execution times.

Table 2 shows the results of Experiment 2. The difference of terminal doesn't materially affect the execution time. It shows that our system has the potential to be used on any terminal. On the other hand, network speed enormously influences execution time. In the case of a wireless LAN, execution time increases in proportion to data size. In actual use, if the data size is too large, our system stops downloading at a proper resolution level and renders the model at that level.

Table 2. Comparing Execution on a Desktop Terminal with on a Mobile Terminal, and Comparing Execution through a Wired LAN with through a Wireless LAN

	Data Size [MB]	Number of Splats [thousands]	Download + Rendering Time [sec.]			Re-rendering Time After Changing View [sec.]	
			Desktop/ Wired	Mobile/ Wired	Mobile/ Wireless	Desktop	Mobile
Data 1	0.2	58	1.4	1.6	6.1	-	0.2
Data 2	6.7	1757	4.2	4.8	59.8	3.0	3.6
Data 3	8.1	2129	4.4	5.4	70.2	3.1	3.9
Data 4	9.9	2591	5.3	6.2	86.4	4.0	4.5

7   Applications

We designed this rendering system to use with content management systems. For example, e-learning systems such as those involving biology, art or history need this sort of geometric data. Also, applications for digital archive systems need this sort of rendering system.

We are now designing a new CMS that can deal with QSplat data and their annotations. Our rendering system is also included in this CMS. The architecture of this CMS is shown in Fig. 11. The system consists of contents registering, website editing, and 3D data rendering systems. The contents registering system manages data including texts, images or other multimedia files. The website editing system generates HTML files from source scripts that users edit with a special markup language. The 3D data rendering system is downloaded with HTML files and renders 3D geometric data on a HTML browser. Our applet is used as the 3D data rendering system.

Using this CMS, a user can design websites with various contents including 3D geometric and annotation data, even if the user doesn't have detailed knowledge of HTML or the architecture of the CMS.

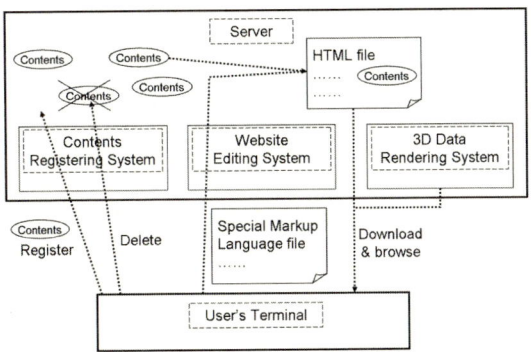

Fig. 11. CMS We Design

8   Conclusion and Future Work

We proposed a new 3D geometric data rendering system that can be used in conventional Web browsers or Content Management Systems. We implemented QSplat rendering as a Java Applet so that it can quickly and precisely render large scale 3D geometric data. Our rendering system can dynamically control the rendering frame rate and the preciseness of the rendering. Thus, it can be used in a wide variety of hardware/ software/network environments such as powerful desktop PCs or mobile wireless terminals. The HTML synchronization technique enables users to smoothly view 3D geometry contents.

We will extend this system for use with the Content Management System. We are now trying to implement a website editing system that allows users to make a website with registered 3D geometric data and synchronizing functions. We are also going to implement a content registering system that users can register 3D geometric data through a web interface. For this, we are presently designing a markup language and implementing functions to convert it into HTML.

References

[1] S. Rusinkiewicz, M. Levoy, "QSplat: A Multiresolution Point Rendering System for Large Meshes," Proc. ACM SIGGRAPH 2000, pp.343-352, 2000.
[2] "Cult3D," http://www.cult3d.com/
[3] "Viewpoint," http://www.viewpoint.com/pub/
[4] "Adobe Shockwave Player,"
    http://sdc.shockwave.com/products/shockwaveplayer/
[5] T. Fujimoto, K. Konno, N. Chiba, "Introduction to Point-based Graphics," The Journal of the Society for Art and Science Vol.3 No.1, pp.8-21, 2004.
[6] H. Pfister, M. Zwicker, J. Baar, M. Gross. "Surfels: Surface elements as rendering primitives," Proc. ACM SIGGRAPH 2000, pp.335-342, 2000.
[7] F. Duguet, G. Drettakis, "Flexible Point-based Rendering on Mobile Devices," IEEE Computer Graphics and Applications, Vol.24, No.4, pp.57-63, 2004.
[8] Y. Okamoto, S. Yamazaki, K. Ikeuchi, "Efficient Point-based Rendering Method for Huge 3D Models using Sequential Point Clusters," Proc. Meeting on Image Recognition and Understanding 2004 (MIRU 2004), Vol.1, pp.207-212, 2004.
[9] Q. Peng, W. Hua, and X. Yang, "A new approach of point-based rendering," Proc. Computer Graphics International 2001, pp.275-282, 2001.
[10] "Java Bindings for OpenGL," https://jogl.dev.java.net/.
[11] "Cortona VRML Client," http://www.parallelgraphics.com/products/cortona/.

Fragment Indexing of XML-Based Metadata for Digital TV Contents*

Hyoseop Shin[1], Minsoo Lee[2],**, and Seokhyun Son[1]

[1] Dept. of Internet and Multimedia Engineering,
Konkuk University, Seoul, Korea
hsshin@konkuk.ac.kr, myviki@konkuk.ac.kr
[2] Dept. of Computer Science and Engineering,
Ewha Womens University, Seoul, Korea
mlee@ewha.ac.kr

Abstract. TV-Anytime metadata is being widely accepted as a metadata standard format that describes digital TV contents. It provides a wide spectrum of information of TV programs such as program information, program groups, program schedules, program reviews, program segments, user preferences, etc. These metadata are structured in a large hierarchical XML document. For efficiency, the metadata is split into a set of smaller pieces of metadata fragments that can be transmitted and accessed independently over a broadcast network. In this paper, we propose a fragment-based XML data indexing and querying scheme for efficient processing of TV-Anytime metadata. The experimental results show that the proposed scheme performs better than the generic XML data indexing and querying methods.

Keywords: TV-Anytime metadata, XML indexing, metadata fragment.

1 Introduction

As an emerging standard for data representation and exchange on the Internet, XML is being adopted and used in more and more industry area. Although many methods of storing and querying XML data have been proposed in the literature [1,2,3,4,5,7,8,9,10,11], they are often not optimal or adequate for a system with domain-specific requirements. While systems in a special domain may be more restrictive in computing power, main-memory size, and secondary disk spaces, they also pose new chance of customization and optimization in storing and retrieving XML data. This is because the characteristics and behaviors of the XML data in a specific domain are likely to be known a priori.

TV-Anytime metadata[6] is being widely accepted as a metadata standard format that describes digital TV contents. It provides a wide spectrum of information of TV programs such as program information, program groups, program schedules, program reviews, program segments, user preferences, etc. These metadata are structured in a

---

* This work was supported by Korea Research Foundation Grant funded by Korea Government(MOEHRD, Basic Research Promotion Fund) (KRF-2005-003-D00281).
** Corresponding author.

large hierarchical XML document and thus for efficiency reason, the metadata is split into a set of smaller pieces of metadata fragments that can be transmitted and accessed independently over a broadcast network. In this paper, we propose a fragment-based XML data indexing and querying scheme for efficient processing of TV-Anytime metadata.

The remainder of the paper is organized as follows. Section 2 describes the background of TV-Anytime metadata. Section 3 explains the querying model of TV-Anytime metadata. Section 4 presents fragment-based indexing scheme. Section 5 describes the process of the query processing of TV-Anytime metadata. Section 6 gives performance evaluations and our conclusion is given in Section 7.

2   Background: TV-Anytime Metadata

The TV-Anytime metadata [6] is conceptually categorized into four areas: the content description metadata which describes the contents, the instance description metadata which describes the broadcasted instances of the contents, the consumer metadata which describes the consumers, and the segmentation metadata which describes the segments of the contents. The metadata deal with the different aspects of the content and the consumers in broadcast environment.

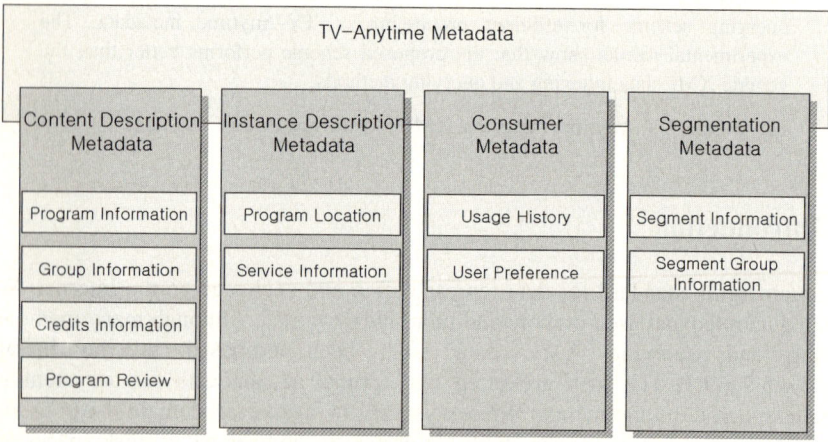

Fig. 1. Outline of TV-Anytime Metadata Specification

Each metadata is further classified into sub-categories as illustrated in Fig. 1. The content description metadata consists of the program information, group information, credits information, and program review information. Each program and program group is given an identifier called *CRID* (content referencing identifier) which is used for referring to a content in the other parts of the metadata (e.g. within the instance description metadata or segmentation metadata). The instance description metadata consists of the program location information and service information. Instances are divided into the scheduled events and the on-demand events each of which is described in the program location information. The service information describes the broadcast channels.

```
<TVAMain>
<ProgramInformationTable>
 <ProgramInformation programId="PROG-123">
    <BasicDescription>
        <Title>Sunrise News</Title>
        <Synopsis>Morning News</Synopsis>
        <Keywords>
            <Keyword>politics</Keyword>
            <Keyword>economy</Keyword>
        </Keywords>
        <Genre>News</Genre>
        <CreditsList>
            <CreditsItem>
                <Role>Reporter</Role>
                <Agent>Richard Perry</Agent>
            </CreditsItem>
            <CreditsItem>
                <Role>Producer</Role>
                <Agent>Tom Martin</Agent>
            </CreditsItem>
        </CreditsList>
    </BasicDescription>
 </ProgramInformation>
</ProgramInformationTable>
<ProgramLocationTable>
 <BroadcastEvent serviceIdRef="NBC">
    <ProgramIdRef>PROG-123</ProgramIdRef>
    <PublishedStartTime>
        2003-04-29T09:40:00</PublishedStartTime>
    <PublishedEndTime>
                2003-04-29T10:30:00</PublishedEndTime>
 </BroadcastEvent>
</ProgramLocationTable>
<ServiceInformationTable>
 </ServiceInformation serviceId="NBC">
  <Name>NBC</Name>
  <ServiceURL>www.nbc.com</ServiceURL>
 </ServiceInformation>
</ServiceInformationTable>
</TVAMain>
```

Fig. 2. An Example of TV-Anytime Metadata

In Fig. 2, regarding a program identified as 'PROG-123', its program information, program location, and service information are described. The program information and the broadcast event are interconnected via the identifier 'PROG-123'.

The consumer metadata describes the consumers rather than the contents, thus this metadata is not usually transmitted from the broadcasters to the consumers. The consumer metadata consists of the usage history and user preference. The segmentation metadata describes information regarding the concept, '*segment*' which represents a continuous part of a program. The segmentation metadata consists of the segment information describing segments and segment group information describing group of segments. Each segment group enables non-linear play of contents (e.g. highlights, table of contents, bookmarks, preview, etc).

2.1 Carriage of TV-Anytime Metadata

As a TV-Anytime metadata document consists of the various parts as mentioned above and is described in a large hierarchical XML document, it is not efficient to transmit the document in the original format in the broadcast transport layer. The pre-processing of the TV-Anytime metadata for transmitting over uni-directional broadcast streams like MPEG-2 TS consists of fragmentation, encoding, and encapsulation steps.

In fragmentation step, the metadata is split into a set of fragments that can be transmitted and updated independently. The standard fragment types defined in TV-Anytime metadata includes TVAMain, ProgramInformation, GroupInformation, OnDemandProgram, OnDemandService, BroadcastEvent, Schedule, ServiceInformation, CreditsInformation, PersonName, OrganizationName, Review, ClassificationScheme, CSAlias, SegmentInformaton, SegmentGroupInformation. For example, in Fig. 2., the ProgramInformation (which contains title, genre, etc. of a program), the BroadcastEvent (which contains publishedtime and endtime, etc. of an event), and the ServiceInformation are independently transmitted as differenet fragments. Fig. 3. illustrates the fragmentation of the TV-Anytime metadata documents.

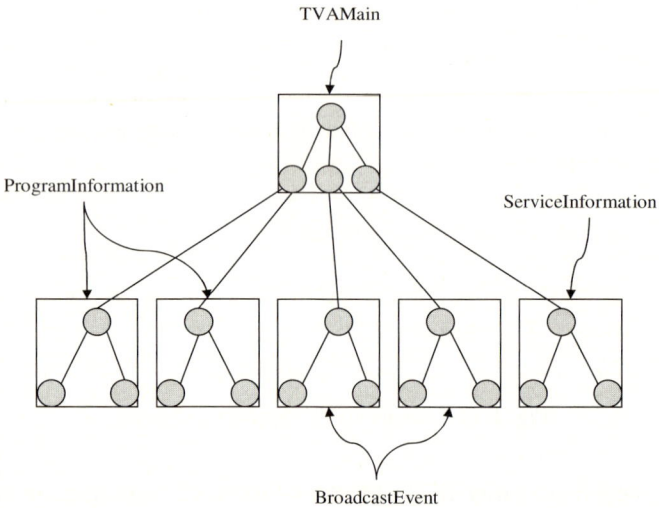

Fig. 3. Fragmentation of TV-Anytime Metadata

After the fragmentation step, the resulting fragments can be encoded into a binary format for space efficiency and then be encapsulated with additional information such as version number and fragment identifier. After the encapsulation step, the resulting metadata stream is inserted into the transport stream as appropriate.

3 TV-Anytime Metadata Querying Model

In querying TV-Anytime metadata, the target of users' queries is metadata fragments that match query conditions which are based on the values of sub-elements of the target fragment type. The typical target fragment types are ProgramInformation, GroupInformation, BroadcastEvent, Schedule, ServiceInformation, CreditsInformation, PersonName, SegmentInformaton, SegmentGroupInformation. The typical examples of sub-elements used for specifying query conditions against tartget fragment types are title, actor, genre, program start/end time etc. The query conditions are represented by conjunctive forms of atom boolean expressions each of which is formed as '*element-name binary-operator literal*'.

Assume that a TV-Anytime metadata document D and its tree representation T_D are given and a target fragment type is specified by T_F, a sub-tree of T_D and the query condition q_F of which all the *element-name*s exist within the sub-tree T_F. The TV-Anytime metadata querying model is defined as:

$$Q(T_F, q_F) = \{ \text{ f} \mid \text{type(f)} = T_F \wedge q_F(\text{f}) = \text{true } \}$$

For instance, consider a query for the TV-Anytime metadata document in Fig. 2 that requests "the information of programs of which genre is 'News'". In this query, the target fragment type is 'ProgramInformation' and the query condition is 'Genre = News'. The result of the query is the 'ProgramInformation' metadata fragments whose 'Genre' is 'News'. In general, the target fragment type and the query condition can be expressed in an XML path language such as XPath. The target fragment type is expressed in an absolute path from the root and the sub-elements within the query condition in a relative path from the node that represents the target fragment type. Regarding the query above, the target fragment type is '/TVAMain/ProgramInformationTable/ ProgramInformation', and the sub-element tied with the query condition is 'BasicDescription/Genre'. Alternatively, the query can be expressed in XPath as :

```
/TVAMain/ProgramInformationTable/ProgramInformation
[ BasicDescription/Genre = 'News' ].
```

The naive method of processing the TV-Anytime queries is to uncover every target fragment and to check if it matches the given query condition. However, as the entire TV-Anytime metadata is broken up into many fragments of small size, the method suffers from the performance degradation. In the following section, we propose an indexing mechanism for speeding up searching among a large number of fragments.

4 Fragment Indexing of TV-Anytime Metadata

It is not efficient to look into the content of every fragment delivered over the broadcast network only to find some fragments that match the query conditions specified by the values of certain nodes of a fragment type. To avoid this overhead, fragment indexing is required so that the system is able to find fragments efficiently. From the TV-Anytime querying model in the previous section, we propose the indexing method that frequently referred nodes in query conditions are indexed in advance. Indices are defined on a fragment type using single or multiple nodes within a fragment type as the key. For the XML example in the previous section, an index can be defined on 'ProgramInformation' fragments using the element 'Genre' to accelerate searching the information of the programs of specific genres.

An index consists of a set of entries each of which is formatted as key_value, fragment_id. The key_value represents the value of the index key. If an index key is a composite type, the key_value consists of multiple fields. The fragment_id is the identifier of a fragment. An index of XML fragments can be built in common access methods like B+-trees. As there can be more than one index in the repository, two supplemental structures are provided to assist selecting indices for user-given queries:

IndexDictionary, IndexKeyfield. The IndexDictionary maintains the information of each index available in the repository. The structure of the IndexDictionary is <index_id, fragment_type, num_key_field, key_field_list >. The index_id identifies an index. The fragment_type represents the type of fragments on which an index is built on. The num_key_field is the number of key fields which constitute the index key and the key_field_list lists the key fields of an index. The IndexKeyfield describes the information of the key fields used in the index keys. The structure is <field_id, field_path, field_type>. The field_id is the identifier of a key field. The field_path represents the absolute path from the root node to the designated node. The field_type is the type of the node in the repository.

5   Processing of TV-Anytime Metadata Queries

The TV-Anytime metadata stored in the repository are retrieved in the fragment basis. A fragment type is specified as the query target and query conditions are specified against the values of the nodes within the fragment type. For example, the fragments in the fragment type *'Program Information'* can be filtered on their genres. After the matching fragments are fetched from the fragment repository, they get parsed into a form as desired in the applications.

The retrieval process consists of four steps:

1) **Selecting Indices** select the suitable indices to process the user-given query by looking into the *IndexDictionary* and *IndexKeyfield* structures.
2) **Filtering Fragment Identifiers** filter the identifiers of the fragments that match the query condition by looking into the relevant indices.
3) **Retrieving Fragments** retrieve the content of the fragments indicated by the fragment identifiers by looking into the fragment repository.
4) **Parsing Fragments** parse the content of the fragments which are returned as the query result.

6 Performance Evaluations

In this section, we examine the performance of the proposed fragment-based indexing scheme (*fragment*) in the aspects of data loading, reconstruction, and querying, by comparing with the other approaches such as the node numbering scheme (*numbering*) plus structural joins[10,11] and the attribute inlining scheme[9] (*inlining*).

In the node numbering scheme[10], each element or attribute in the XML document is separately stored as a tuple within a table. Each tuple has the structure of < doc_id, begin_pos, end_pos, level >, where *doc_id* is a document identifier, and *begin_pos* and *end_pos* are the beginning and ending word positions of a tag within the document, and *level* is the depth of a tag when the XML document is represented as a tree. Under this node numbering scheme, the ancestor-descendant and parent-child   relationships between nodes can be verified by examining the tuple values. If a node 'A' is an ancestor of a node 'B'(i.e., A//B), the conditions 'A.doc_id == B.doc_id, A.begin_pos <= B.begin_pos, A.end_pos >= B.end_pos' are satisfied. If a node 'A' is the parent of a node 'B' (i.e., A/B), the condition 'A.level == B.level - 1' is added to the conditions above. According to these properties, to obtain node pairs that satisfy the 'A//B' or 'A/B' relationships, a structural join operation on the node table is performed using the join conditions above.

The attribute inlining scheme[9] handles excessive fragmentation of XML documents by assembling multiple XML elements into attributes of a same relational table. The method inlines as many descendants of an element as possible into a single relation unless a descendant node has an in-degree greater than oneor zero. Otherwise, plural descendants will create another relations. The attribute inlining scheme can automatically generate a relational database schema for XML documents based on a given DTD or XML Schema. Also, it may suffer less from several joins in processing path expression queries than the node numbering scheme. In practice, however, the resulting schema may not be considerably different from that of the node numbering scheme, especially when many of nodes in a DTD specification have in-degree greater than one. In our applications, it turned out that the TV-Anytime metadata contains about 80% plural XML tags. Another serious problem with the attribute inlining scheme in our application is that the approach is so sensitive to the XML data schema that a change of a node would trigger the rebuilding of the database. Meanwhile, the proposed fragment-based approach does not have to rebuild the database unless a fragment type is deleted or a new fragment type is added.

We implemented these schemes on top of a relational database engine in a linux computer which has 1GMhz CPU, 512 mega byte main memory and a hard disk installed. Two different datasets were used for the experiments: small synthetic data set which includes 12,000 fragments (i.e., about six mega byte) and large real data set that represents 14 days program data for 100 channels which is equal to 210,000 fragments (i.e., 70,000 for each one of three fragment types or about 30 mega byte).

The experiment was performed in two categories: data loading and reconstruction and data querying. In the loading and reconstruction experiments(Fig.4-(a), (b)), the *fragment* method was faster than the other methods. Especially, the reconstruction of the proposed method was faster by up to 20 times. This is because the *fragment* method suffers less from the overhead of splitting and restructuring of XML data.

In the querying experiments(Fig. 4-(c), (d)), we tested two different queries. The simple query has single filtering condition and single return field. The complex query has multiple filtering conditions and multiple return fields. The *numbering* scheme was the worst as in the previous experiments. For the simple query, the *inlining*

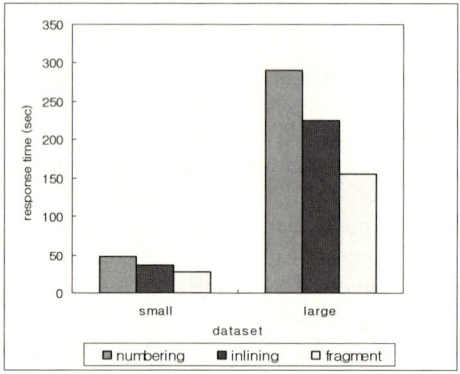

(a) metadata loading

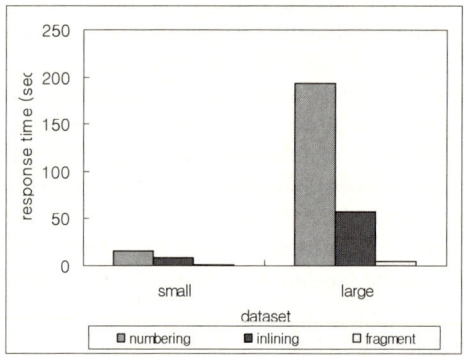

(b) metadata reconstruction

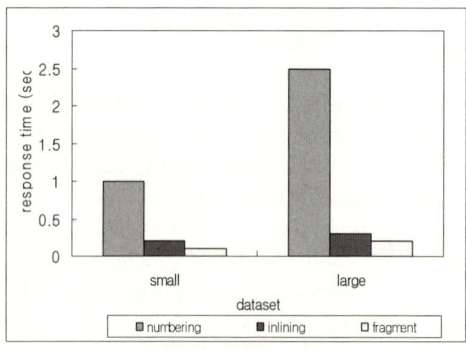

(c) simple query

Fig. 4. Performance Evaluations

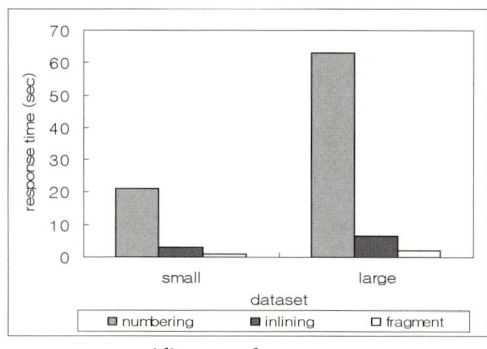

(d) complex query

Fig. 4. (*Continued*)

scheme showed similar performance to the *fragment* scheme, but the performance gap became wider for the complex query. This is because the *inlining* scheme is required to join many normalized tables to perform the complex query.

7   Conclusion

TV-Anytime metadata as a standard metadata format for describing digital TV programs is getting more and more attention from the industry standard bodies such as ATSC[12] and DVB[13]. TV-Anytime metadata can provide rich descriptions about TV contents. As the metadata is orgarnized in a large hierarchical XML document, it is necessary for the document to be split into smaller pieces called fragments. In this paper, we proposed the fragment-based indexing scheme to accelerate the processing of the typical TV-Anytime metadata querying model. In the experiments, the proposed method outperformed the well-known generic XML data indexing and querying methods.

References

1. Shu-Yao Chien, Zografoula Vagena, Donghui Zhang, Vassilis J. Tsotras, and Carlo Zaniolo, Efficient structural joins on indexed XML documents, In Proc. of VLDB 2002, pages 263-274, Hong Kong, China, August 2002.
2. B. F. Cooper, N. Sample, M. J. Franklin, G. R. Hjaltason, and M. Shadmon, A fast index for semistructured data, In Proc. of VLDB 2001, pages 341-350, Roma, Italy, September 2001.
3. A. Deutsch, M. F. Fernandez, and Dan Suciu, Storing semistructured data with STORED, In Proc. of ACM SIGMOD 1999, pages 431-442, Philadelphia, USA, June 1999.
4. M. Fernandez and D. Suciu, Optimizing regular path expressions using graph schemas, " In Proc. of ICDE 1998, pages 4-13, Orlando, Florida, February 1998.
5. R. Goldman and J. Widom. Dataguides: Enalbing query formulation and optimization in semistructured databases, In Proc. of VLDB 1997, pages 436-445, Athens, Greece, August 1997.

6. TV-Anytime Metadata Working Group, Specification Series: S 3 on Metadata Version 1.3, TV-Anytime Forum, January 2003.
7. Torsten Grust, Accelerating XPath location steps, In Proc. of ACM SIGMOD 2002, pages 109-120, Madison, Wisconsin, USA, June 2002.
8. Quanzhong Li and Bongki Moon, Indexing and querying XML data for regular path expressions, In Proc. of VLDB 2001, Rome, Italy, September 2001.
9. J. Shanmugasundaram, K. Tufte, C. Zhang, G. He, D. J. DeWitt, and J. F. Naughton, Relational databases for querying XML documents limitations and opportunities, In Proc. of VLDB 1999, pages 302-314, Edinburgh, Scotland, September 1999.
10. D. Srivastava, S. Al-Khalifa, H.V. Jagadish, N. Koudas, J. M. Patel, and Y. Wu, Structural Joins: a primitive for efficient XML query pattern matching, In Proc. of ICDE 2002, San Jose, USA, February 2002.
11. C. Zhang, J. F. naughton, Q. L. David, J. DeWitt, and G. M. Lohman, On supporting containment queries in relational database management systems, In Proc. of ACM SIGMOD 2001, Santa Barbara, CA, USA, May 2001.
12. Advanced Television Systems Committee, http://www.atsc.org.
13. Digital Video Broadcasting, http://www.dvb.org.

Using a MyoKinetic Synthesizer to Control of Virtual Instruments

Duk Shin[1], Atsushi Katayama[2], Kyoungsik Kim[2,3], Hiroyuki Kambara[2,3], Makoto Sato[1], and Yasuharu Koike[1,3]

[1] Precision and Intelligence Laboratary, Tokyo Institute of Technology
[2] Department of Intelligence and Systems Science, Tokyo Institute of Technology
[3] CREST, Japan Science and Technology Agency
{shinduk, akatayama, kyoungsik, hkambara}@hi.pi.titech.ac.jp,
{sato, koike}@pi.titech.ac.jp

Abstract. We have been developing a new type of human-computer interface, myokinetic synthesizer (MyoKinSynthesizer), using electromyography (EMG) signals. It enables a user to select virtual instruments and to control its properties such as volume and tone without any position or force sensors. The virtual marimba system emulates the basic properties of the real instrument by producing a sound depending on in which of eight zones and how hard the user is hitting. The virtual drum set is composed of 4 different virtual drums controlled by arms and legs. We used a three-layer neural network to estimate position and force of the forearm from EMG signals. After training the neural network and obtaining appropriate weights, the subject was able to control the movement of virtual avatar and to play virtual instruments. The system was destined to be used as a demonstration of VR entertainment and music therapy rehabilitation.

1 Introduction

Muscle contraction is the fundamental unit of body motion and posture control. Coordinated contractions by several muscles allow for various movements of human limbs. Human limb movements are controlled by the central nervous system (CNS). The CNS controls muscle contraction using electrical impulses. Surface EMG signals captured by sensors attached to the skin above the muscle typically contain superpositions of those impulses and these signals connotes the fact that these signals are related to the amount of contraction. By measuring EMG signals, it is possible to predict the next stage of movement or force before motion [1]. Therefore, it is also possible to use EMG signals as an input signals for a human interface system and robot control. There are some approaches to using EMG signals for control of prosthetic arm or robotic hand and control command of human interfaces [2, 3]. The EMG signals in these studies, however, were used just on/off control.

NASA scientists have used EMG signals to substitute for mechanical joysticks and keyboards [4]. They demonstrated the ability to control and land

Z. Pan et al. (Eds.): ICAT 2006, LNCS 4282, pp. 1233–1242, 2006.

a computer-simulated airplane using only EMG signals from the forearm. The commands were corresponding to the gesture for controlling the joystick. They also succeeded to recognize typing on a numeric keyboard from EMG signals. These techniques were developed in the field of biomedical engineering such as prosthetic arm. However, in these approaches, the command was corresponded to the specific gesture for controlling the joystick or the keyboard, not continuous motion. The BioMuse has been demonstrated as an interface to music synthesizers [5]. The BioMuse translated the amplitude of EMG signals to MIDI signals directly. However, it takes time for beginners to generate the desired sound.

Resently, we proposed that the MyKinSynthesizer approximates the 3D motion and force of the user's hand based on a musculo-skeletal model synthesized from EMG signals [6]. Here, we have created virtual instruments using MyKinSynthesizer. The proposed system enables a user to control and play virtual instruments continuously using his arms and legs. The user manipulates the instruments in free space and a computer generates the appropriate sound. There is also a computer which is rendered virtual representation of the user and the instruments. The instruments can be controlled in the same way as normal instruments but the technique offers great freedom when engineering the interface since there are no physical or acoustic constraints.

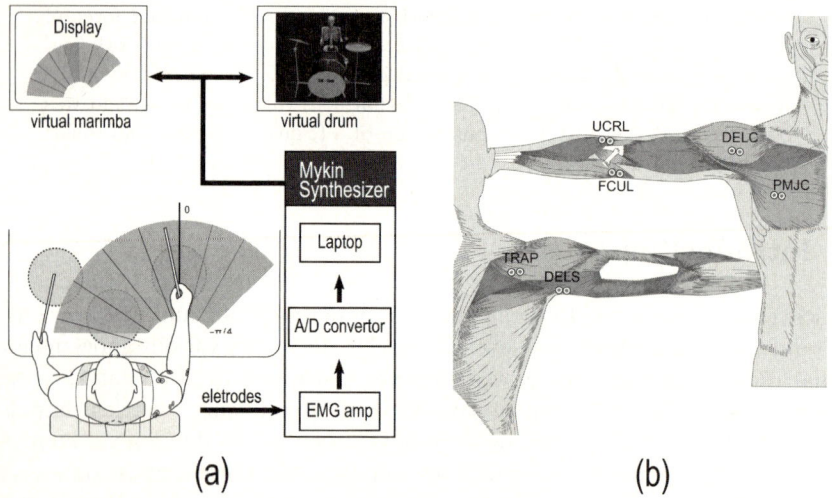

Fig. 1. The experiment's configuration (a) and The electrode positions in EMG measurement for marimba (b)

2   Methods

As an application of this technology we have created a virtual marimba and a virtual MIDI sound player as shown in figure 1 (a). The subject sat on a chair in front of the desk. The subject hit a specified position on a paper marimba or a drum-set with stick. The arm posture of the subject (the choice of a drum or a marimba bar) was calculated from the EMG signals of shoulder muscles. The timing and magnitude of the hit force was also calculated from the EMG signal of elbow muscles or leg muscles. A monitor in front of the subject displayed the virtual avatar and virtual instrument.

To create the system a series of experiments aimed at data collection used for algorithm prototyping in MATLAB were first carried out and the creation of a standalone application was implemented using C++. The stand-alone application fetches data from a PC Card A/D-converter and uses a software MIDI device for sound output. To make the interaction more intuitive a 3D graphical representation was also implemented.

2.1   EMG Signals

During the experiment, surface EMG signals were recorded from 6 (virtual marimba) or 12 (virtual drum) muscles as shown in figure 1 (b). For the shoulder posture detection, pectralis major clavicular head (PMJC; drum and marimba), deltoid- scapular part (DELS; drum and marimba), deltoid- clavicular part (DELC; marimba only), Trapezius (TRAP; marimba only) were measured. For the hit detection, the flex. carpi ulnaris (FCUL; drum and marimba), ext. carpi radialis longus (ECRL; drum and marimba), triceps lateral head (TRIA; drum only), Tibialis Anterior (TIBA; drum only) were measured.

We recorded EMG signals by using pairs of Ag-AgCl surface electrodes in bipolar configuration. Each signal was sampled at 2 kHz with 16-bit resolution. The signal was digitally rectified, integrated for 0.5 ms, sampled at 200Hz, and finally filtered with a cutoff frequency of 3Hz. If one rectifies, integrates and passes the raw signal through a low-pass filter, the output is a signal proportional to the muscle force. We called the signal gQuasi-tensionh due to their similarity to true muscle tensions [7]. The preprocessing algorithm is visualized in figure 2. Using pairs of silver-silver chloride surface electrodes, EMG activity was recorded. After the raw EMG signal has been sampled at 2 kHz with 16-bit resolution, it is then rectified, integrated over 10 ms and passed through a low-pass FIR filter (finally producing a signal from on referenced as EMG_q) with an impulse response of the following form:

$$h(t) = 6.44 \times (\exp^{-10.80t} - \exp^{-16.52t}) \tag{1}$$

(the sampled filter's coefficients were normalized by dividing them with the sum of the unnormalized coefficients)

2.2   Position Estimation

For a very rough classification of the horizontal position of a stick held by the user (i.e. three zones indicating only left, center or right), the similar thresholding algorithms could be used to solve problem 2. However, if one needs a more fine-grained classification a different approach of using a neural network combining

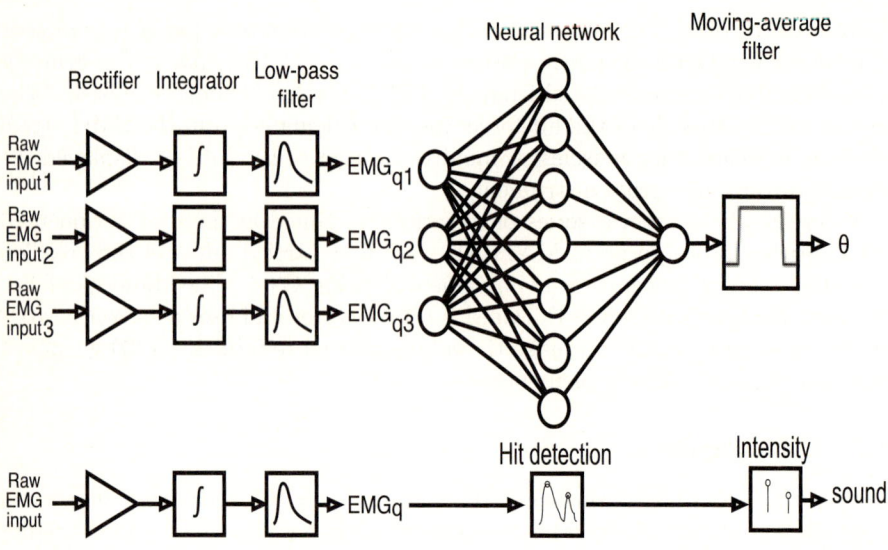

Fig. 2. Block diagram of the signal preprocessing

input from several muscles can be used to estimate a parameter that is related to the position. With the aim of making the relationship between the network inputs and outputs less complex (as well as having the added benefit of better ergonomics) marimba's horizontal bars (or drum set) structure was used by an arc of length π divided into discrete zones. A three-Layer neural network, shown in figure 2, was used to identify the input EMG signals as associated shoulder posture, i.e. marimba's bar detection. The first layer of the neural network consists of the EMG input signals from each muscle. The second layer is the middle layer, and third layer is the output shoulder posture for each bar. The position estimation of the stick used for hitting is performed by using EMG_q from three muscles related the horizontal movement of the shoulder (see figure 1(b)) as inputs to a neural network trained using a back-propagation algorithm. The back-propagation is a supervised training method in which a training session allows the system to learn the relationship between EMG_q and the position of the stick. Because of various muscle activation patterns between the left and right shoulder separately trained networks are used for each shoulder. Since it was desired to minimize reliance on external equipment (such as a motion capture system) to keep the system portable a heuristic training is used: The user is instructed to perform static co-contractions followed by hit movements in predefined zones designated on a screen. An angle θ located in the middle of the zone is then used to represent the target output used for network training.

Apart from the input layer the neural network is composed of a 7-node hidden layer (using sigmoid transfer functions) and a single-node output layer (linear transfer function). To increase the precision of the network the number of zones used for training (12) were twice of that used when playing (6 per shoulder with

4 overlapping resulting in a possible spectrum of 8 tones). Because the network output often was found to oscillate around the desired value a moving average filter was placed at the network output to dampen this effect. The network performance was rather poor for extreme outward rotations (i.e. to the extreme right for the right shoulder) and for this reason θ was limited to the the interval $[\frac{\pi}{2}, \frac{-\pi}{4}]$ for the right shoulder and $[\frac{\pi}{4}, \frac{-\pi}{2}]$ for the left ($\theta = 0$ located right in front of the user). This means that zones to the extreme left can only be accessed by using the right hand and vice versa. The algorithm used for the position estimation is visualized in figure 2. Capture of training data takes about one minute and the actual weight adaption calculations (incorporating various measures to prevent over-learning) takes less than one minute on an IBM Thinkpad laptop equipped with a 1.6 GHz Pentium M processor.

2.3   Hit Detection and Intensity Estimation

By capturing data from a lower-arm muscle involved in the hit movement we can find satisfying solutions to the problems by only regarding the amplitude and derivative of the filtered signal. In particular, comparing the signal to a threshold value and monitoring when the derivative of the signal changes from positive to negative provides a good estimate of when the user is hitting. Since the filtered EMG signal is a measure of the force used when hitting one way to estimate the intensity is to make it a function of the maximum value seen during the hit movement.

Detection of when the user has performed a hit movement is carried out with thresholds being computed from the training data considering only the relationship between the maximal and minimal values of EMG_Q (see figure 2). Because multiple local maxima sometimes occurs after the main peak of a hit no new hits are detected until 250 ms has passed since the last detection. The intensity of the sound (as represented by the parameter *velocity* in MIDI terminology) is calculated according to equation (2)

$$v = a \ln(x - b) \tag{2}$$

with x being the value of EMG_q immediately after the derivative changes from positive to negative and a and b is calculated to match the function's range to the available intensity levels according to the hit threshold and maximum value seen during training.

3   Results

Using data from EMG sensors attached to the user's skin we can estimate the user's muscle tension, joint stiffness and posture giving us many degrees of freedom to use when creating the interface. The instruments we have created to illustrate the technology are a virtual marimba and a virtual drum set. The marimba is controlled with the arms and has virtual bars laid out in a horizontal fashion like a real marimba. According to the applied force and at which virtual bar (which can be marked out in an arbitrary way) the user aims the appropriate sound is played. The drum set is composed of 4 different virtual drum controlled by arms and legs. As for the arms, according to where the user is aiming (to the left, center or right) and the force used the proper drum sound is generated.

Because of the fact that EMG signals are roughly 100 ms ahead of the actual movement they evoke we can make highly responsive systems (with very good synchronization of sound and computer graphics) compared to other approaches of realizing similar systems (using video camera, motion capture etc). Moreover the system is more portable, easier to set up and could be fabricated to a lower cost.

3.1 Virtual Marimba

The virtual marimba system is controlled with the right arm and has virtual bars laid out in a horizontal fashion like a real marimba. According to the applied force and at which virtual bar (which can be marked on a paper) the user aims the appropriate sound is played. The proposed virtual marimba system used 6 muscles (for hit detection and intensity; FCUL and ECRL, for posture detection; PMJC, DELC, DELS, TRAP see figure 1(b)). Figure 3 shows that the user play the virtual marimba. In this section we analyze two aspects related to the performance of the system. In figure 5, EMG_q is plotted together with the detected hits. As can be seen, although multiple local maxima occurs after the main peak of a hit, the hit detection algorithm performs very well.

And also the hit detection algorithm performs well although the threshold level used for detection is mostly a matter of personal preference as long as it is sufficiently elevated to ignore background noise present in the signal.

Figure 6 shows the system's estimation of the position (as represented by the zone number). One can see that the system has problems performing the correct classification just after user's hand moves between zones. During this time the stick is close to the borders of a zone but since the user typically aims for the middle of a zone this does not lead to problems in practice.

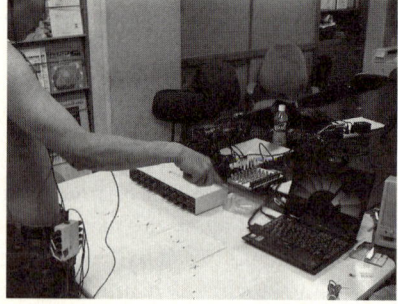

Fig. 3. Virtual marimba system

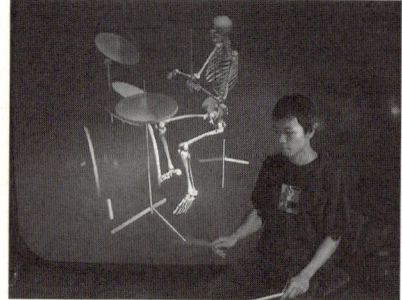

Fig. 4. Virtual drum system

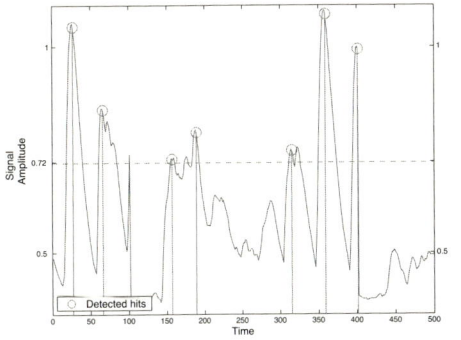
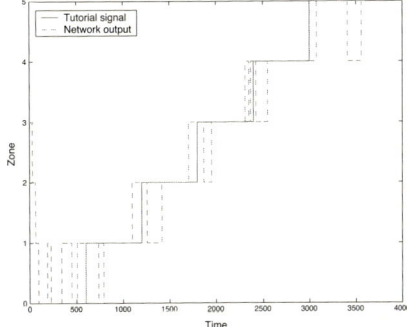

Fig. 5. Example of detected hits (dotted lines with circles) in the case of a threshold of about 0.72 (dashed line)

Fig. 6. The estimated zone (dashed line) compared to the correct zone (solid line) associated with the right arm

We have created a system for virtually playing instruments. The user manipulates the instruments in free space and the approriate sound is generated by a computer. There is also a computer rendered virtual representation of the user and the instruments. The instruments can be controlled in the same way as normal instruments but the technique offers great freedom when engineering the interface since there are no physical or accoustical constraints.

3.2   Virtual Drum

The proposed virtual avatar system used 2 muscles of legs and 10 muscles of arms. For the shoulder posture, EMG signals of PMJC and DELS were measured. These muscles also used to select virtual drum (snare drum, hi-hat cymbal and crash cymbal). EMG signals of FCUL, ECRL and TRIA were also measured for the elbow hit movement. TIBA of left leg used to hit the hi-hat pedal and TIBA of right leg used to step on base drum pedal.

The virtual drum set is composed of 4 different virtual "drums"; crash/ride cymbal, snare drum, hi-hat and bass drum.

1. Cymbal : The cymbal is played by 4 EMG signals of the right arm corresponding to the beat.
2. Snare-drum : The snare drum is controlled by 8 EMG signals in both arms.
3. Hi-hat : A user can control Hi-hat with two arms. The opening and shutting of Hi-hat is adjusted by On/Off signal from an EMG activity of the left-leg.
4. Bass drum : The bass drum is controlled by EMG signals from the right leg.

Virtual drum can generate sound without time delay. Because an EMG is about 100ms ahead of movement, we can discriminate the next posture prior to movement. Based on that the estimation is quicker than the movement, we can generate the appropriate sound and volume of the virtual drum while synchronizing the motion of a virtual skeleton. We perform calibration prior to playing

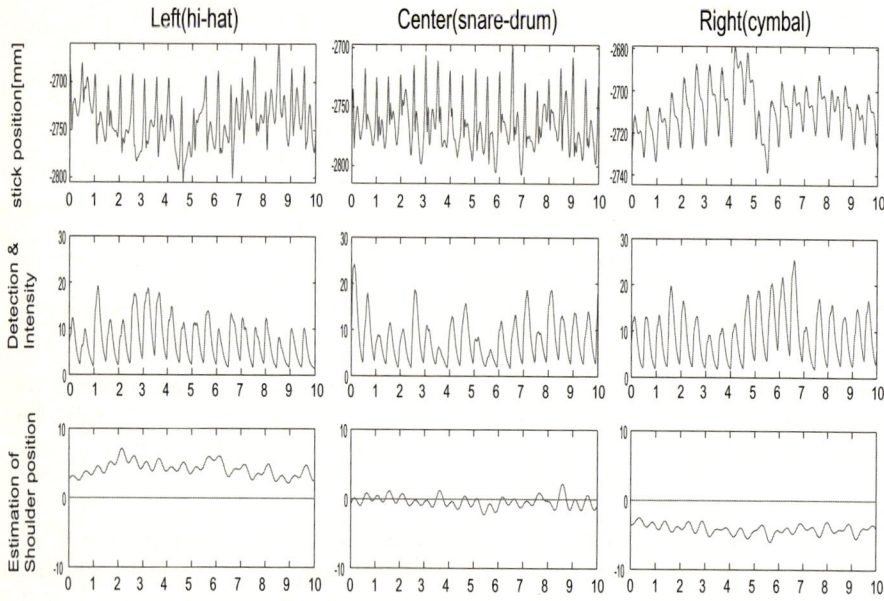

Fig. 7. Detection and Intensity of a virtual drum set

because there are personal differences on EMG activities. We show in figure 4, a subject plays the virtual drum system. The player throws his arms on the air as if he beats a drum, but the sound of drum is heard. In figure 7, we show some plots of hit detection and intensity during tasks of experiment. Each first plots shows the end postion of the stick. The stick posture of the subject was measured by an OPTOTRAK. Each second plots show the detection of timing and the intensity of sound from EMG signals processing algorithm (see figure 2). The bottom plots show the estimation of shoulder posture (see also figure 2). The data of the plot was sampled at 200Hz. As can be seen at center plots, whether the subject hit quickly or not, the hit detection algorithm performs very well.

And the stick movement was always the same but the sound (force) was different. By using an external measurement sensor, such as camera, it is impossible to measure an intrinsic time-varying force. This intrinsic force works as an input variable provided for the human interface resulting in an intuitive operation. we can estimate intrinsic forces and the posture of the limb prior to movement, and then these variables are used as input for the human interface.

4   Conclusions

There are many application to interactive music performance systems in a virtual environment [8, 9, 10, 11, 12]. Most conducting systems use gesture recognition for use by professional conductors, but play back only synthesized audio (MIDI).

However, it is impossible to measure an intrinsic time-varying force by using an external measurement sensor, such as camera or motion capture. We proposed a novel method to describe the design and implementation of a virtual system emulating a pulsatile instrument using EMG measurement. We have also investigated the feasibility of using MykinSynthesizer for human interfaces. Since EMG activities are different depending on the posture and intensity, we can discriminate diverse posture and control the volume corresponding to the amplitude of muscle tension. This intrinsic force works as an input variable provided for the human interface resulting in an intuitive operation.

In our syatem, human beings use a diverse combination of muscles to take pose. The avatar posture and the sound selection is controlled by the presence of the user's hand in different zones as estimated by a neural network and thresholding algorithm. The intensity of the sound is related logarithmically to the amplitude of the filtered EMG signal. Since the system is based on a neural network architecture it is very flexible. Although the usage scenarios described here emulates the traditional style of interfacing with a marimba (or drum) any muscles whose activity can be measured using surface EMG can be used. Sujects will be able to experience what it is like to use virtual instruments and realize the potential of virtual user interfaces that could be controlled by almost any muscle of the body.

Since the instruments are virtual not much space is needed. The equipment used are laptop computers, EMG sensors attached on the users skin and a screen showing the computer generated graphics. These virtual pulsatile instrument systems are not aware by the users, so the users would feel that they control the instrument directly by their arms and legs. Because the intensity of the sound is proportional to the degree of his muscle activity. This portable virtual system that could be used at conferences (for technology demonstration purposes) or hospitals (for music therapy rehabilitation).

Acknowledgment

This work was supported by grants from the Ministry of Education, Science, Sports and Culture, Grant-in-Aid for Scientific Research (B), 16360169 and JST CREST Program to Y. Sakurai.

References

1. Koike, Y. and Kawato, M. : Estimation of arm posture in 3D-space from surface EMG signals using a neural network model. IEICE Transactions Fundamentals D-II(4), (1994) 368-375.
2. Jacobsen, S.C., Wood, J.E., Knutti, D.F., and Biggers, K.B. :The Utah/MIT dexterous hand: work in progress. Int. J. Robotics Research, vol. 3, no. 4, (1984) 21-50
3. Meek, S.G., Jacobsen, S.C., and Straight, R. : Development of advanced body-powered prosthetic arms. Journal of Rehabilitation Research and Development, vol. 26, (1989)

4. Bluck, J. : Nasa scientists use hands-off approach to land passenger jet. http://amesnews.arc.nasa.gov/releases/2001/01 08AR.html.
5. Tanaka, A. : Musical technical issues in using interactive instrument technology with application to the BioMuse. in eICMC Proceedingsf (2001) 124-126.
6. Koike, Y. : Tele-Kinesthetic Interaction: Using Hand Muscles to Interact with A Tangible 3D Object, SIGGRAPH2006. (2006)
7. Koike, Y. and Kawato, M. :Estimation of dynamic joint torques and trajectory formation from surface electromyography signals using a neural network model. Biological Cyberbetics, vol. 73 (1995) 291-300
8. Mathews, V. : The Conductor Program and Mechanical Baton, in Max V. Mathews and J. R. Pierce, eds.: Current Directions in Computer Music Research, MIT Press, Cambridge, (1991)
9. Pogue, D. : The dangers of the Digital Orchestra. New York Times Direct, Apr 5, (2001)
10. Borchers,O. : WorldBeat: Designing a baton-based interface for an interactive music exhibit. Proc. CH197, ACM, (1997) 131-138
11. Lee, M., Garnett, G., and Wessel , D. : An Adaptive Conductor Follower. Proc. International Computer Music Conference, ICMA, San Francisco, (1992)
12. Kragtwijk M., Nijholt A., and Zwiers J. : Implementation of a 3D Virtual Drummer. Computer Animation and Simulation, N.Magnenat-Thalmann and D. Thalmann, eds., Springer Verlag Wien, (2001) 15-26.

View-Dependent Simplification of Complex Urban Scenes Using Weighted Quadtrees

Bum-Jong Lee, Jong-Seung Park, and Mee Young Sung

Department of Computer Science & Engineering, University of Incheon,
177 Dohwa-dong, Nam-gu, Incheon, 402-749, Republic of Korea
{leeyanga, jong, mysung}@incheon.ac.kr

Abstract. This article describes a new contribution culling method for the view-dependent real-time rendering of complex huge urban scenes. As a preprocessing step, the view frustum culling technique is used to cull away invisible objects that are outside the view frustum. For the management of the levels-of-detail, we subdivide the image regions and construct a weighted quadtree. The weight of each quadtree node is defined as the sum of weights of all objects contained in the node or its child nodes. The weight of an object is proportional to the view space area of the projected object as well as the distance from the viewpoint. Hence, large buildings in the far distance are not always culled out since their contributions to the rendering quality can be larger than those of near small buildings. We tested the proposed method by applying it to render a huge number of structures in our metropolitan section which is currently under development. Experimental results showed that the proposed rendering method guarantees real-time rendering of complex huge scenes.

1 Introduction

When rendering a large scene, a huge number of objects can reside in the viewing frustum. Urban environments present challenges to interactive visualization systems, because of the huge complexity. Many previous works have been focused on high quality interactive visualization of complex urban environments [1]. A huge number of objects should be drawn to ensure the high quality rendering. However, it slows down the rendering speed, which is not acceptable for real-time rendering. Some insignificant objects need not be drawn and they should be culled away from the set of objects in the scene. Such a culling process should be performed for each rendering cycle and it should be proceeded fast enough to satisfy the real-time requirement. A suitable spatial data structure is required for the fast culling.

Visibility culling reduces the number of polygons sent to the rendering pipeline by excluding faces that need not be drawn. There are several different stages of culling[2]: *backface culling*, *view frustum culling*, *portal culling*, and *occlusion culling*. For the real-time rendering for complex scenes, the use of *levels-of-detail* (LODs) is necessary. The LOD management involves decreasing the details of

Z. Pan et al. (Eds.): ICAT 2006, LNCS 4282, pp. 1243–1252, 2006.

an object as it moves away from the viewer. The use of LOD increases the efficiency of rendering by reducing the number of polygons to be drawn. An appropriate level of the LOD should be determined automatically to provide the unnoticeable change of the rendering quality. The LOD selection techniques can be classified into three categories: *ranged-based method*, *projected area-based*, and *hysteresis method*[2]. The ranged-based method is to associate the different LODs of an object with different ranges. The projected area-based method uses the projected area of the bounding volume to associate the LODs. The projected area-based method uses the number of pixels of that area, called the screen space coverage. If the LOD varies around some transition value, there is a risk to switch back and forth between two levels from frame to frame. The hysteresis method prevents the LOD flickering by distinguishing between upwards translations and downwards transitions.

This paper describes a weighted quadtree structure for fast rendering of complex huge urban scenes. Objects that are far away from the camera do not contribute significantly to the rendering quality. We throw away objects whose projected areas into the screen space are below a given threshold. This is called the *contribution culling*. The weighted quadtree structure supports both the fast view frustum culling and the contribution culling well.

In Section 2, we describe general rendering methods of complex scenes. In Section 3, the proposed weighted quadtree structure is described. In Section 4, experimental results for complex urban scenes are presented. Finally, concluding remarks and future works are described in Section 5.

2   Rendering Complex Scenes

Geometry-based rendering has been actively studied to satisfy the requirement of real-time computation in drawing large complex scenes. The view frustum culling is the most obvious visibility culling[3]. It is based on the fact that only the objects in the current view frustum need to be drawn. A view frustum is usually defined by six planes, namely the front, back, left, right, top, and bottom clipping planes, which together form a cut pyramid. The six bounding planes are represented by $\pi_i : \mathbf{n}_i \cdot \mathbf{x} + d_i = 0$ for $i = 1, \ldots, 6$, where $\mathbf{n}_i$ is the normal of the plane π_i, d_i is the offset of the plane π_i, and $\mathbf{x}$ is an arbitrary point on the plane. Whether an object is in the frustum is determined by an intersection test of the object and the six planes. If the left side of the plane equation is greater than zero, then a point $\mathbf{x}$ is outside the plane. If the value equals to zero, then the point is on the plane. If the point $\mathbf{x}$ is inside all planes, then the point is inside the view frustum.

As well as the simple intersection test method, there are several optimization methods for the view frustum culling. The octant test reduces the number of intersection tests that should be done. The view frustum is split in half along each axes, resulting in eight parts. Then, if the bounding sphere is inside the three nearest planes, it must also be inside all planes of the view frustum. There is another way to reduce the number of intersection tests. If the bounding volume

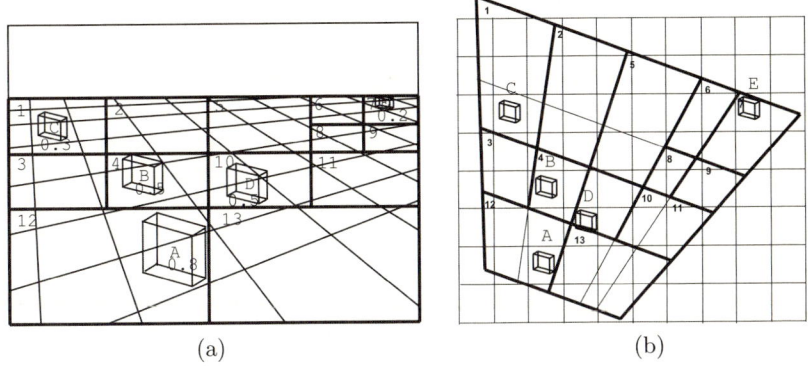

Fig. 1. Terrain cells in the screen space (a) and corresponding regions in the world space (b)

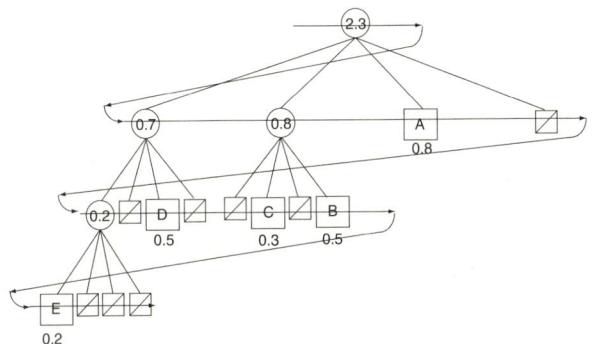

Fig. 2. A quadtree for the objects in Fig. 1

of a node is completely inside one of the plane of the view frustum, then the bounding volumes of the node's children also lie completely inside that plane. Hence it is not required to test the plane for the child nodes of the node.

The temporal coherence and the camera movement coherence can be exploited to reduce the intersection tests. The temporal coherence is based on the fact that if a bounding volume of a node is outside of a view frustum plane at the previous frame, then the node is probably outside of the same plane. The camera translation and rotation coherency exploits the fact that, when navigating in a 3D space, only one of a rotation around an axis and a translation is commonly applied to the camera. In that case, many objects that were outside the plane at the last frame still remain outside. The fact inspires us to use a hierarchical structure for the view frustum to speed up the culling process [1][4].

As an effective view frustum culling implementation, we use a quadtree data structure. The classical quadtree can be used for the view frustum culling to remove many objects at once from the graphics pipeline [5][6]. The terrain area is divided into cells of regular squares. A bounding box centered at the camera position is managed during the camera movement. The quadtree structure is recomputed only when the camera crosses the bounding box. When cells are on a frustum boundary, low level quadtree nodes are used to refine the areas in order to reduce the number of objects to be sent to the rendering pipeline. Gudukbay[7] presented a view frustum culling algorithm that traverses the quadtree in a preorder traversal. The frame coherency property simplifies the view frustum culling algorithm. Yin[8] introduced a method which constructs a static quadtree in a preprocessing step and culls out invisible objects by view frustum culling using the quadtree.

From the next section, we describe a hierarchical weighted quadtree structure for the efficient implementation of the view frustum culling and the contribution culling. When rendering a complex environment containing a huge number of objects, the rendering speed should not be slowed down. To avoid such dependency on the number of visible objects, we investigate a criteria to choose the most contributive objects for high quality rendering. Small objects in the screen space are culled out even though they are near to the camera position.

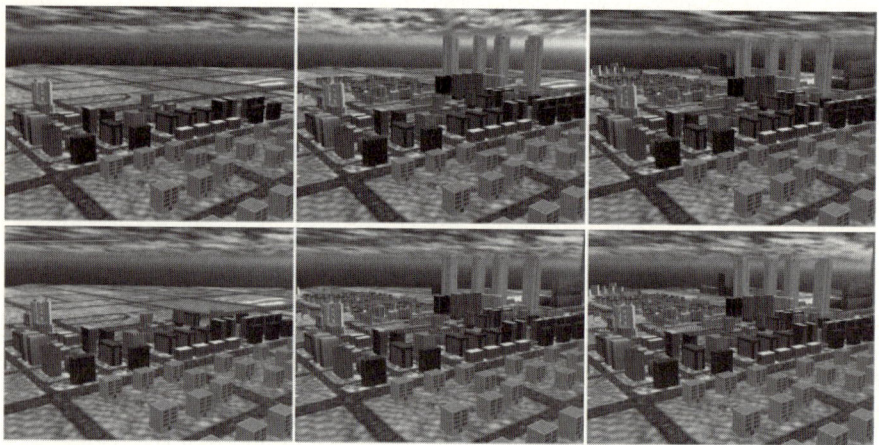

Fig. 3. Rendered scenes using simple methods: culling by the distance measure (upper), culling by the number of polygons (lower)

3   Contribution Culling Using Weighted Quadtree

Drawing all visible objects is too slow and inappropriate to real-time rendering systems. Rendering only the most important visible objects is necessary and, hence, appropriate LOD techniques for urban objects are essential. If small details contribute little to the scene then it should be discarded. The contribution of each object is measured as the area of the projection in the screen space. When computing the contribution measure, we consider only the bounding volume of the object. The bounding volume is projected onto the projection plane and the area of the projection is then estimated in pixel units. If the number of pixels in the area is smaller than a given threshold value then the object is culled away from the rendering pipeline.

Our contribution culling method uses a weighted quadtree structure for the rendering of complex urban scenes. We denote the j'th coordinate vector of an object in the world space by $\mathbf{X}_j = (x_j, y_j, z_j)$ and the coordinates in the screen space by $\mathbf{x}_j = (u_j, v_j)$. The overall steps of the proposed algorithm are as follows:

Step 1 (Initialization):
1. Compute C_1, the quadrilateral region corresponding to the overall terrain in the screen space.
2. Create an empty quadtree with a root node n_1 and associate the node to C_1. Set w_1 (the weight of n_1) to zero.

Step 2 (Computing object weights): For each object obj_i ($i = 1 \ldots N$), where N is the number of total objects, perform the following steps.
1. Compute $\mathbf{x}_j$, the projection of the object point $\mathbf{X}_j$ to the screen space.
2. Compute A_i, the area of the bounding rectangle of the object.
3. Compute the weights w_i using $\mathbf{A}_i$.

Step 3 (Inserting objects to the quadtree): Initialize the node index k to zero and perform the following recursive quadtree construction process.
1. If there are no objects in C_k, goto Step 4.
2. If there is a single object in C_k, set w_k to the weight of the node and goto Step 4.
3. If there are more than one objects in C_k, split the associated region C_i into four subregions and create corresponding four child nodes. Set w_k to the sum of all object weights inside the quadrilateral region.
4. Repeat Step 3 for the four child nodes.

Step 4 (Culling): Choose a fixed number of the most significant objects from the quadtree using the node weights.
1. The sum of the weights of the chosen objects is maximized while traversing the quadtree in the breath-first-order.

We describe the above steps in more detail. In Step 1, C_1 is the quadrilateral region of the entire terrain, as shown in Fig. 1(a). To split the region into four subregions, we calculate four corners of the region e_k ($k = 1, \ldots, 4$). If the four corners of the terrain in the world space are E_k ($k = 1, \ldots, 4$), the corresponding corners in the screen space can be calculated by projecting each E_k onto screen space using the projection matrix. In Step 2, the projection $\mathbf{x}_i$ of each object point $\mathbf{X}_i$ is computed by projecting the point in the world space into the screen space. Then, we calculate A_i, the area of the bounding rectangle of the i'th object, using Eq. (1):

$$A_i = (\mathbf{max}(u_j) - \mathbf{min}(u_j))(\mathbf{max}(v_j) - \mathbf{min}(v_j)) \qquad (1)$$

where u_j and v_j are the screen coordinates of the i'th object. The weight is set to A_i, the area of the bounding rectangle in the screen space.

The quadtree is constructed in Step 3. Each object is inserted to the quadtree together with its weight. The weight is the sum of the weights of all objects in the node and its child nodes. The associated quadrilateral screen region for a node is split into four subregions if the node has more than one object. In Step 4, a fixed number of significant objects are selected. We traverse the quadtree in a breath-first-order as shown Fig. 2 and choose the fixed number of the most significant objects. Let M be the desired number of objects to be drawn. Then, we try to choose M objects starting from the root node n_1. It is equivalent to choose M objects from the four subnodes of n_1. For each subnode n_k $(k = 2, \ldots, 5)$, we try to choose $(M * w_k/w_1)$ objects from the node. The selection process is repeated recursively until the desired number of objects are actually chosen. It is possible that the number of the selected nodes is less than the desired number of nodes since some internal nodes and their subnodes have no significant nodes at all or they have fewer significant nodes than expected.

Fig. 1(a) shows terrain cells and their associated objects. Each cell region is marked with an identification number and a capital letter. A number for each object indicates the weight of the object. Fig. 1(b) shows the corresponding terrain cells in the world space. Fig. 2 shows the quadtree for the scene in Fig. 1. A circled node is either the root node or an internal node and the squared node is a leaf node. Each non-empty node has a number that is the weight of the node. After constructing the quadtree, the quadtree is searched in the breath-first-order. For example, if we want to render only two objects, then the second node and the third node are chosen since they have two highest weights in the second level. Then, since the third node has no child nodes, object A is chosen. Then, in the third level, object B is chosen among the four child nodes of the second node in the second level.

4   Experimental Results

To demonstrate the effectiveness of the proposed method we have implemented a rendering engine using C++ and DirectX 9.0 on the Windows platform. We tested on a 2.8GHz Pentium 4 PC with 512MB DDR RAM and an ATI RADEON 9200 GPU with 64MB DRAM.

For the comparison purpose, two simple methods of LODs are implemented. The first method limits the number of polygons and only the fixed number of the nearest polygons are rendered. The first row of Fig. 3 shows rendered urban scenes using the method. The number of rendered polygons for the images at the upper row of the figure are 960, 3,000, and 5,040, respectively, from left to right order. The second method limits the the visibility range. All the polygons outside the visibility range are culled away. The images at the second row of Fig. 3 are the rendered urban scenes using the method. The visibility ranges are 300, 1,000, and 2,750 meters, respectively, from left to right order.

As well as the rendering quality, the rendering frame rate should also be stable when the viewer is navigating in a virtual world. The proposed method has provided almost the same quality of rendering with the same frame rate. The

Fig. 4. Rendered scenes using our method when the camera is walking forward (upper) and looking around at a fixed position (lower)

view magnification experiments and camera rotation experiments are shown in Fig. 4. When the scene is magnified, small objects at far distances are gradually scaled larger, as shown in the upper six images of Fig. 4. The lower nine images of Fig. 4 show the rendered scenes when the camera is rotated 0, 40, 80, 120, 160, 200, 240, 280, and 320 degrees, respectively, at the fixed camera position. During the rotation, the number of rendered polygons and the variation of the rendering frame rate are shown in Fig. 6.

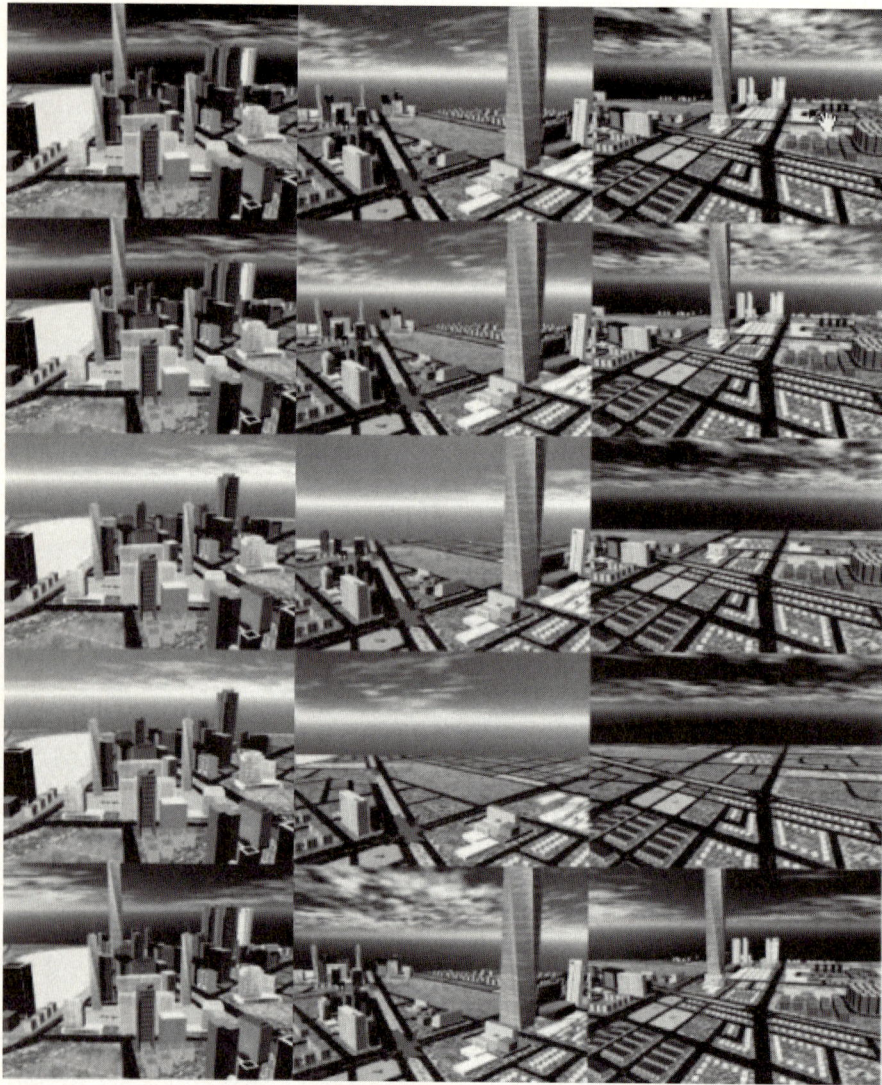

Fig. 5. Comparison of rendered scenes: using no LODs, using view frustum culling, using constant distance, using constant number of polygon, using proposed method

The proposed method has kept high-quality rendering without significant performance depreciation. We compared the rendering quality of five different methods: a simple method without using LOD, the view frustum culling method, the fixed visibility range method, the fixed number of polygons method, and the proposed method. The rendered scenes using those five methods are shown in Fig. 5. The images in the first row are the rendered scenes using the

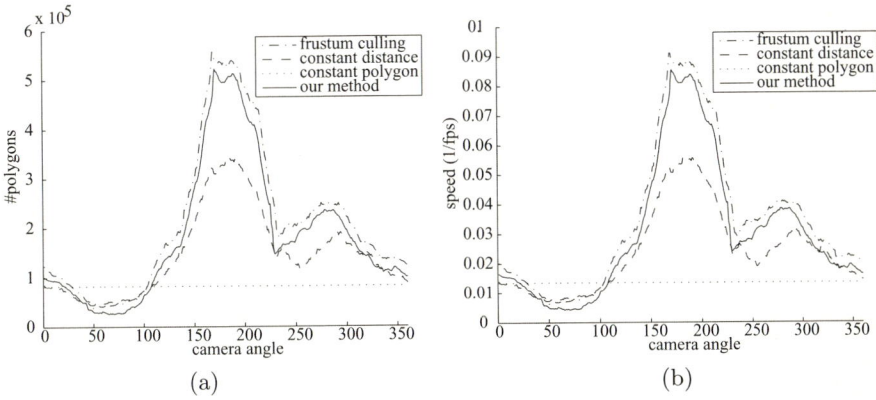

Fig. 6. Comparison of rendering performance for the 360° rotating camera: (a) the number of polygons, (b) the rendering speed

novice method without using LOD, which means all the objects are sent to the rendering pipeline. The images in the second row are the rendered scenes using the view frustum culling method. The method renders only the objects that are inside the view frustum and the rendering frame rate is much faster than that of the first method. The images in the third row are the rendered scenes using the fixed visibility range method. The objects that are placed outside the distance over 900 meters do not be rendered. Though the fixed visibility range method provides faster frame rate, the rendering quality is not satisfied. The images in the fourth row are the rendering results using the fixed number of polygons method. The number of polygons was set to 82,720 polygons. Significant objects in far distances were disappeared and the quality is bad. The images in the last row are the rendering results using our proposed method. The number of polygons is always equal to or less than that of the view frustum culling method. However, the rendering quality is as good as that of not using any LOD method. In our methods, both the huge number of tiny objects and the mostly occluded objects are not drawn.

We measured the performance when the camera is turning around 360 degrees at a fixed position, whose rendered scenes are shown in lower side of Fig. 4. The camera is rotated with respect to Y-axis at a fixed position. The measurements are shown in Fig. 6. Fig. 6(a) and Fig. 6(b) show the number of polygons and the rendering frame rate, respectively, for the corresponding camera angle. Two graphs are similar since the rendering frame rate is proportional to the number of polygons. The figure indicates that the proposed method reduces the number of polygons by about 50,000 and it is faster than using the view frustum culling by about 0.005sec. The rendering speed is 0.008sec when the camera angle is around 75 degree and the rendering speed is 0.093sec when the camera angle is around 175 degree. The variation is due to the fact that the number of significant objects is varying, as you can check it in lower side of Fig. 4.

5 Conclusion

This article has presented a novel contribution culling method for the real-time rendering of complex urban scenes using the weighted quadtree structure. Objects are culled away from the rendering pipeline when their screen projected areas are too small to contribute to high-quality rendering. Contributions of objects are represented by weights on nodes of the created quadtree. By traversing the nodes, a fixed number of significant nodes are selected to be drawn. The rendering speed is determined by the number of significant objects to be drawn.

The proposed method has applied to our new metropolitan region which is currently under development. Experimental results showed that the proposed rendering method guarantees real-time rendering of complex huge scenes. We compared the rendering quality of five different methods and found that the rendering quality of the proposed method is significantly better than those of classical LODs methods at the same rendering frame rate.

Acknowledgements. This work was supported in part by grant No. RTI05-03-01 from the Regional Technology Innovation Program of the Ministry of Commerce, Industry and Energy(MOCIE) and in part by the Brain Korea 21 Project in 2006.

References

1. Tsuji, T., Zha, H., Kurazume, R., Hasegawa, T.: Interactive rendering with lod control and occlusion culling based on polygon hierarchies. In: Proceedings of the Computer Graphics International (CGI'04). (2004) 536–539
2. Akenine-Möller, T., Haines, E.: Real-Time Rendering. A. K. Peters, Ltd., Natick, MA, USA (2002)
3. Assarsson, U., Moller, T.: Optimized view frustum culling algorithms for bounding boxes. Journal of Graphics Tools **5**(1) (2000) 9–22
4. Samet, H., Webber, R.E.: Hierarchical data structures and algorithms for computer graphics. i. fundamentals. IEEE Computer Graphics and Application **8** (1988) 48–68
5. Falby, J.S., Zyda, M.J., Pratt, D.R., Mackey, R.L.: Npsnet: Hierarchical data structures for real-time three-dimensional visual simulation. Computers and Graphics **17**(1) (1993) 65–69
6. Pajarola, R.: Large scale terrain visualization using the restricted quadtree triangulation. In: Proceedings of IEEE Visualization'98. (1998) 19–24
7. Gudukbay, U., Yilmaz, T.: Stereoscopic view-dependent visualization of terrain height fields. IEEE Transactions on Visualization and Computer Graphics **8**(4) (2002) 330–345
8. Yin, P., Shi, J.: Cluster based real-time rendering system for large terrain dataset. Computer Aided Design and Computer Graphics (2005) 365–370

Indoor Environment Modeling for Interactive VR – Based Robot Security Service

Sangwoo Jo[1,2], Yong-Moo Kwon[1], and Hanseok Ko[2]

[1] 39-1 Hawolgok-dong, Sungbuk-ku Imaging Media Research Center
Korea Institute of Science and Technology, Seoul, 136-791, Korea
[2] 5ka-1 Anam-dong, Seongbuk-Gu, Eng. Bldg. Room 419 or 439, Dept. of Electronics and
Computer Engineering, Korea University, Seoul, 136-713, Korea
tiny@imrc.kist.re.kr, ymk@kist.re.kr, hsko@korea.ac.kr

Abstract. This paper presents our simple and easy to use method to obtain a 3D textured model. Our algorithm consists of building a measurement-based 2D metric map which is acquired by laser range-finder, texture acquisition/stitching and texture-mapping to corresponding 3D model. The algorithm is applied to 2 cases which are corridor and space that has the four walls like room of building. The proposed algorithm can be applied to 2D/3D model-based remote surveillance system through WWW. The application terminals of this environment model for interactive VR that we consider are PC, PDA and Mobile phone. Especially, this paper introduces a case of service on WIPI-based mobile phone.

Keywords: Indoor environment modeling, Surveillance robot, 2D and 3D model, Human robot interface.

1 Introduction

In large scale environments like airport, museum, large warehouse and department store, autonomous mobile robots will play an important role in security and surveillance tasks. Robotic security guards will give the surveyed information of large scale environments and communicate with human operator with that kind of data such as if there is an object or not and a window is open. In view of visualization of information and human machine interface, a 3D model can give much more useful information than the typical 2D maps used in many robotic applications. It should be also noted whether windows and doors are opened or closed can be rendered with 3D model, while 2D map specifies only the location of window or door.

VR (Virtual Reality) technology can provide several advantages in view of intuitive understanding, real-time interactivity and virtual experience based on simulation model. This paper aims to achieve the technology fusion between VR and robot technologies. The research goal includes intuitive interaction between user and robot based on virtual robotic space that corresponds to physical space and robot.

Several research results have been reported for 2D and 3D modeling of indoor environment for robot application. 3D modeling techniques are typically divided into two groups. The first one is composed by active techniques based on rage sensors

Z. Pan et al. (Eds.): ICAT 2006, LNCS 4282, pp. 1253–1262, 2006.
© Springer-Verlag Berlin Heidelberg 2006

measuring directly the distance between the sensor and points in the real world. Researches in the group are generally implemented with 2D or 3D laser scanner for geometry and cameras for texture [1-7]. Techniques in the second group are passive and get the 3D information from several 2D digital photographs or video sequences (such as in stereo or photogrammetry) [8-10]. This approach use only camera device and get 3D information using image processing. Each one of these techniques has advantages and limitations. However, in view of accuracy of model, we use both the range-sensor and camera and simplify the modeling method in terms of interactive virtual reality.

In this paper, we present our simple and easy to use method to build both of 2D map and 3D textured model. Here, we build 2D map using 2D laser scanner while acquiring texture images at the corresponding position. Our researches on the virtual indoor environment modeling can be used for the application of remote surveillance, game contents, museum indoor modeling and so on. The developed indoor 2D/3D map is based on standard format, SVG (Scalable Vector Graphics) format for 2D map and VRML(Virtual Reality Modeling Language) format for 3D map. For interactive VR application, we will present mobile phone for remote access. Our 2D map can be accessed with WIPI [13] (Wireless Internet Platform for Interoperability) based mobile phone which is Korean Standard Wireless Internet Platform for mobile device.

2   System Overview

This section gives an overview of our method to build a 3D model of an indoor environment. Fig. 1 gives an overview of the indoor map modeling method. In Fig. 1, M, A, and SA stand for manual, automatic and semi-automatic respectively.

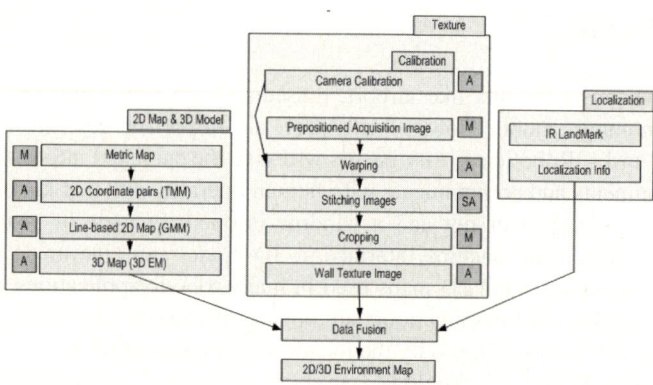

Fig. 1. An overview of our method to build 2D/3D model of an indoor environment

In 2D map & 3D model, the geometry data is acquired with 2D laser scanner manually. Based on these geometry data, TMM (Table Metric Map), GMM (Graphic Metric Map) and 3D EM (Environment Map) is generated automatically. The TMM,

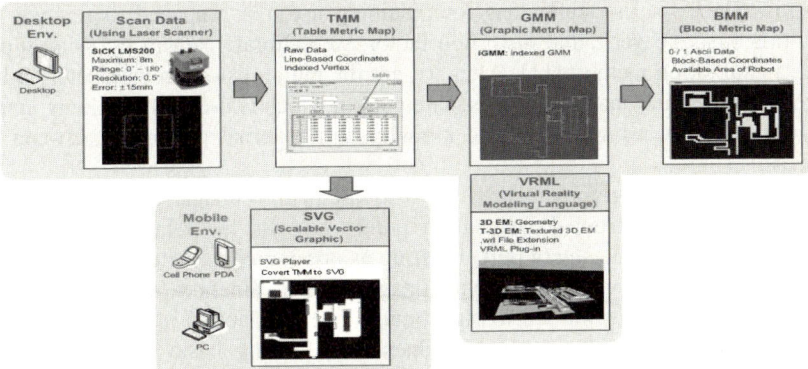

Fig. 2. Data flow of building 2D and 3D model for indoor environment

GMM procedure will be explained in detail in Section 4. Fig. 2 shows the presented method for building 2D and 3D model for virtual indoor environment.

Fig. 3 shows our indoor modeling system using LMS200 laser scanner and two IEEE-1394 cameras. LMS200 laser scanner has 180° scan range and 1.5cm accuracy in 8m apart. Two cameras are set up like Fig. 3(right) in order to get wide view of texture.

In our research, we use two approaches for localization of device. One is using an automatic IR landmark-based localization device, named as starLITE [12] which is developed in ETRI, the other is using dimension of floor square tile (DFST) manually. The DFST approach is applied when starLITE is not installed. The DFST method can be used easily in the environment that have reference dimension without the additional cost for the localization device. In our indoor environment, there are a 0.6m square size tiles on the floor. We can use these tiles for localizing the kart position when automatic localization is not available.

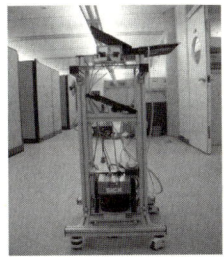

Fig. 3. Laser scanner and IEEE-1394 dragonfly camera pair are set up in moving kart

3 Calibration

Camera calibration process consists of two steps. First calibration is for getting radial distortion parameter and the last one is for obtaining external parameter between two cameras. Since we use 2mm lens for obtaining textures, we need to remove lens distortion first. To get radial distortion factor, we calibrate camera by using typical camera calibration method [11]. After we get the radial distortion parameter and get rid of it, we acquire image that has square pattern which is used for obtaining camera information. Now we would like to know camera external parameter between two cameras.

Here we use homography method. Two square pattern images are taken from two camera respect and from 4 correlation points give us the relation between two cameras. In Fig. 4, one camera (left) is set up as orthogonal to pattern plane and from the homography matrix we can warp the image of other camera to left one.

After right image is warped to right image, the overlapped region is blended in weighted averaging with two pixel values in following basic equation (1). The notation R and L mean that corresponding Right and Left camera pixel each other. Alpha and beta values are determined by the horizontal distance between correspondence pixel point and the edge of left or right image.

Calibration pattern and camera distance is 70cm so that if the sharpness of object image which is located far or near than 70cm may be not as good as object near the 70cm because of incorrect homography matrix value. So when we calibrate the two cameras, we get the different homography matrix by setting unit distance between object and camera as 30cm from 70cm to 190cm.

$$Color = \frac{\alpha \cdot R + \beta \cdot L}{\alpha + \beta} \tag{1}$$

Fig. 4. Radial distortion removed image. (left) Two camera images that has pattern (right) Right camera image is warped to left camera by homography matrix.

The external calibration between camera and laser scanner is done by matching at center point in vertical direction. As we can see in Fig. 3, the center points of entire devices are set up as in one vertical line. From this external calibration, we can get the data from LS and camera consistently according to localization data.

4   Indoor Modeling

4.1   2D Modeling

A 2D map is the basis of our algorithm because an accurate 2D map could build an accurate 3D model. Typical approach of 2D map building method using laser scanner is scan matching. To use scan matching method, the system needs to have moving vehicle with odometry equipment like robot. Robot platform with laser scanner equipment can solve the problem of pose and position but it is quite complicate. In our case, we use metric map which is generated by laser scanner with known orientation. We use DFST method or StarLITE system to get orientation of 2D metric map data so that we do not have to worry about pose and position problem of camera or data gathering device. If we use the 2D map data from 2D flat drawing, we just need to process that kind of data to be converted into line-based presentation data which represent the basic wall plane. We use user interface program is shown in Fig. 5(left) and the graphical 2D map is shown in Fig. 5(center).

Here, we define line-based 2D map as shown in Fig. 5(left). We use two points' coordinates for specifying one line and each line is connected to 2D map model. Because each line is specified in two point data and it is shown in table-like display, so we call it as TMM. Fig. 5(center) shows a graphic version of TMM that we made in order to view the line-based data in visualization by the base coordinate, so we call it as GMM. Lastly Fig. 5(right) shows converted 2D metric map which is a SVG format. By converting into this format, we can see our 2D map in any internet explorer browser just with SVG plug-in and interact with robot in remote environment through 2D map.

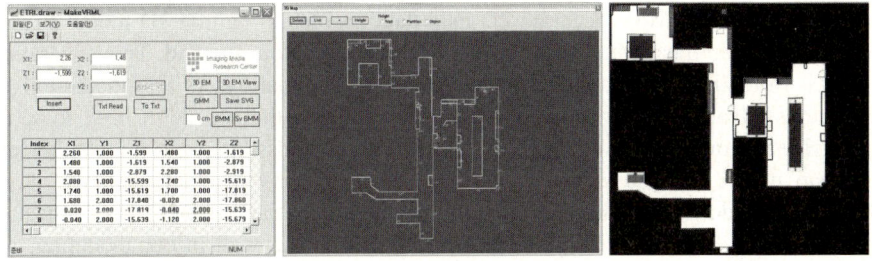

Fig. 5. 2D metric map. (left) Tabled metric map (TMM) data and user interface (center) Graphical metric map (GMM) (right) 2D Map in SVG format.

The laser scanner is positioned in the same center point of camera in vertical direction. And then we can determine the laser scanner pose by doing that set the laser scanner orthogonal to wall. Now we know the laser position information so that we could know the part of shape in environment from laser scanner. We gather the geometric data twice in 1 location by rotating the laser scanner in 180° to scan the opposite side. We can finally generate total 2D metric map by gathering and merging these geometric data. Since we use a line (wall plane) - based raw data format, we can extend the 2D map data to various standard file format like SVG.

A SVG based 2D model is generated from TMM automatically. SVG file can be rendered with internet explorer browser. We also implement SVG browser for cellular phone application with WIPI based mobile phone. Fig. 6 shows the rendering of 2D map model with mobile phone.

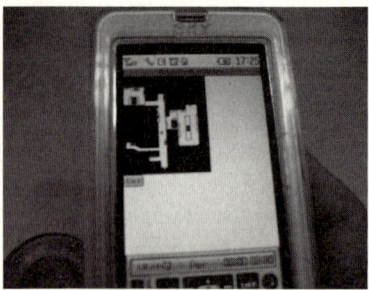

Fig. 6. 2D map model in WIPI based phone

4.2 3D Modeling

Here is a basic idea of building a 3D model. We assume that wall plane is orthogonal to floor plane. This assumption is quite very adequate for indoor environment because in most case of indoor environment a wall is basically orthogonal to a floor in most case of building. The geometry of the 3D model consists of two parts: the floor and the walls. The floor is modeled by a single plane and the walls are the main model of the 3D model.

Since we use the 2D metric map data, we just need to show the wall and floor plane in 3D model. More accurate 2D map data enables to build a 3D model so that accurate 2D map measuring is very important process in our method. This generation which is from 2D map data to 3D model is a full of automatic step. This method gives us various advantages. First of all, it is very simple so that we don't need to setup expensive equipment like moving platform. And if it is possible, we can make 2D and 3D map model using a 2D flat drawing which is easily available in these days. Secondly, we do not consider if doors might open or not and if there is an object in front of walls. Since we focus on the presentation of the wall in our modeling, we basically do not want the temporarily changing objects and linear features which occlude the walls. By omitting the front object of walls, a 2D map and 3D model depends only on measuring exactitude so our method has good advantage in terms of simplification.

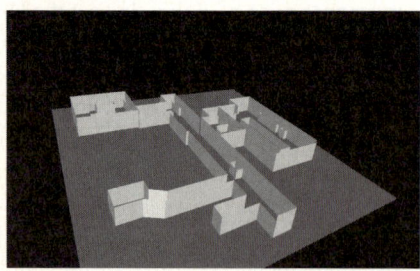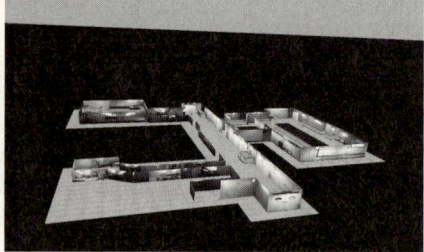

Fig. 7. 3D Map Model and textured 3D Model

Our 3D model is generated in VRML format as shown in Fig. 7(left) and the final 3D model combined with processed texture is shown in Fig. 7(right). Since we use a raw data which is line-based table metric map data from 2D metric map, we can render the 3D model in other 3D renderer such as OpenGL which means easy data conversion is available.

5 Texture Generation

In this paper, the texture generation is focused on the walls. First, the images which are gathered from walls are stitched in one image automatically. And then, we process the image by cutting to represent different depth part. Finally, we acquire textures for the 3D model to match especially for walls.

The camera pose and position is known when we gather textures of walls. Both floor and walls are given by known planes in 3D: the floor is simply the ground plane, and a walls' plane is given by assigning the respective wall of the 2D map. Instead of using moving platform like robot, we use the known point of texture acquisition device and pose of device that is very still when it moves to other point. There are 2 types shape in indoor environment which is the corridor and room-like shape. The former looks like just as corridor. It has long sequence walls and we have to gather part of it at one time and merge them to get the whole texture the wall. The latter is enclosed area with wall like room. In this case we gather the images in the 4 directions of room orthogonal to walls. In these two gathering method, we can generate whole texture of indoor environment easily.

To get wide area of texture in one time, we use small value of focal length. As we use small value of it, we have to remove radial distortion of images firstly. There is a demerit of using small value of focal length lens that image resolution is lowered due to distortion removed image. We omit the image warping process because we know the camera pose is orthogonal to wall plane. The stitching process is processed semi-automatically. We basically find the correspondence points between two input images and we stitch two sequence images just like in calibrating two cameras by these corresponding points. So after we take images for both sides of wall, we can get stitched two big images for both walls respectively. Finally we cut stitched images for fitting to the 3D model for walls. If the wall plane of indoor environment is one plane and there is no disparity, we do not need to make a 3D model in different depth or cut stitched images for texture generation. However, there are several doors and other different depth object in our wall plane and we already build a 2D map considering the depth. So, we process images taking the different depth into account to produce individual texture for the 3D model for walls each other. Fig. 8 shows the processed image in each step. Acquired images are stitched by homography method and applied to basic blending processing which is mentioned in chapter 3. Fig. 8(upper) shows acquired radial distortion free images respectively and Fig. 8(down) shows the stitched image of Fig. 8(upper). There is different depth in stitched image so that we cut stitched image in different depth plane. Also image might have the ceiling or floor plane so we cut those kinds of plane after stitching all images.

Because most people get the idea of environment through wall than floor, we apply the simple way to the floor plane texture generation. We use one pictured tile image for floor texture and duplicate it to floor plane.

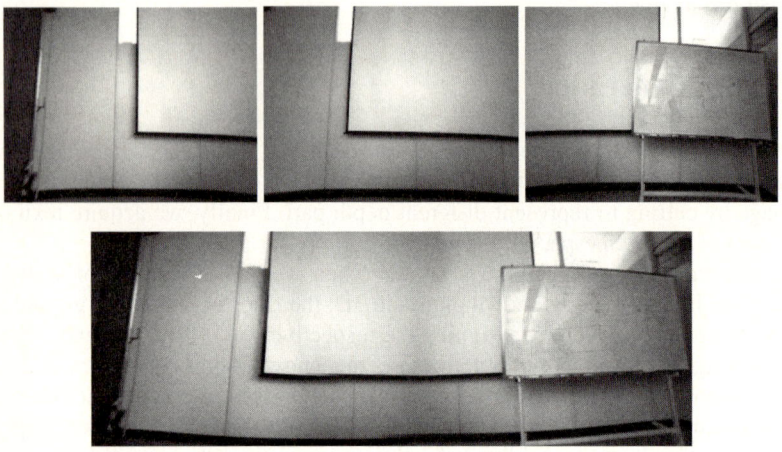

Fig. 8. Texture Processing

6   Interactive VR – Based Robot Security Service

As we shortly mentioned in chapter 4, we would like to control the remote robot and recognize the circumstance of that environment from robot using our result which is 2D and 3D map. The 2D and 3D map which we see are the VR space and in VR space, we can interact with real object which is robot. In order to that, the user has to have the 2D and 3D map to control the robot and there has to be somewhat connection between user device terminal and robot. Following Fig. 9 shows the network connection for each user device between user and robot. The robot position and viewing angle are continuously updated to web server and user get that information from server and see that in map that user has. When user wants to move the robot to check the status of some point, user designate the desire point using map and that information is passed on to robot trough web server. Finally user can see that robot reaction in the map and get the required status of environment using robot.

We take the PC, PDA and Mobile phone as the terminal of our interactive robot service into account. In case of PC, the resource is much more abundant than PDA or mobile phone so that it is comparatively easy to implement. However, in case of PDA or mobile phone, we firstly have to consider the platform in view of computing resource. We develop in Window CE and WIPI platform for PDA and mobile phone respectively and those terminals including PC give interactive robot service to user according to upper network concept. WIPI platform for mobile phone especially support the C and Java language in implementation. This is one of the important reasons why we choose the WIPI platform in case of mobile device.

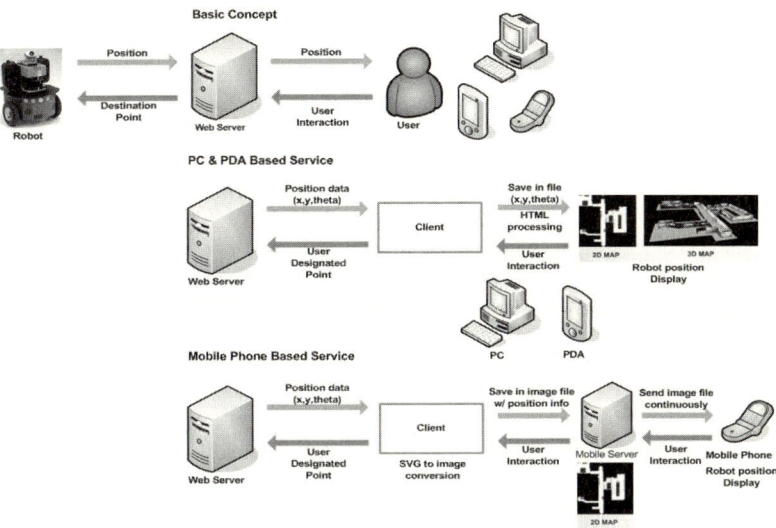

Fig. 9. Network concept between map and robot

7   Conclusion and Future work

This paper presents the 2D and 3D modeling method for interactive virtual reality taking robot security into account and mobile phone application of it. As a real application of the presented algorithm, data set of 83 images and 2D metric map data was recorded at ETRI 7th building 1st floor, covering parts of a region of about 25 × 25 meters. The 2D map data that we generate are 112 wall planes. The 2D and 3D map is generated using those data. The model is generated as SVG and VRML format and it can be viewed in a web browser with a SVG and VRML plug-in. We see our technique as a successfully easy and simple method to generate 3D model. The big advantage of our method is in vivid described model that is texture of model is very realistic.

In order to communicate with robot and human through virtual model, it needs to be very accurate and realistic. We are confident to build a 3D model simply and easily in human's wants that is realistic enough to interact with robot. Moreover, in real application, we can easily see the whole environment, understand the situation and interact with the robot by using user friendly device like Mobile Phone.

Regarding our future work, we will develop our algorithm in terms of more automatic processing of 2D map generation and texture matching. And by modeling the object in environment, we will be able to get more intuitive and understandable 2D and 3D model to interact with robot in remote distance. Moreover, interacting information that we use now are just robot position and rotation. The user might have more immersed feeling through additional environment information like sensor status in that environment.

Acknowledgments. This work was supported in part by MIC & IITA through IT Leading R&D Support Project.

References

1. Y. Liu et al, "Using EM to Learn 3D Models of Indoor Environments with Mobile Robots", *18th Int'l Conf. on Machine Learning, Williams College*, June 28-July 1, 2001.
2. D. Hanel, et al., "Learning Compact 3D Models of Indoor and Outdoor Environments with a Mobile Robot", Elsevier Science, *Robotics and Autonomous Systems*, Vol. 44, No. 1, pp. 15-27, 31 July, 2003.
3. O. Wulf, et al., "2D Mapping of Cluttered Indoor Environments by Means of 3D Perception", *Proceedings of the 2004 IEEE, Int'l Conf on Robotics & Automation*, New Orleans, Apr. 2004.
4. B. Peter, et al., "3D Modeling of Indoor Environments by a Mobile Robot with a Laser Scanner and Panoramic Camera", *IEEE/RSJ International Conference on Intelligent Robots and Systems (IROS 2004)*, 2004.
5. Kai Pervölz, et al., "Automatic Reconstruction of Colored 3D Models", Robotik 2004, Munich, Germany, June 2004.
6. D. Paulo, et al., "Registration and fusion of intensity and range data for 3D modeling of real world scenes", *Fourth International Conference on 3-D Digital Imaging and Modeling*, 2003.
7. I. Stamos, P. K. Allen, "3-D Model Construction Using Range and Image Data", *IEEE International Conference on Computer Vision and Pattern Recognition*, pages 531-536(volumn I), South Carolina, June 2000.
8. D. Aliaga, D. Yanovsky, and I. Carlbom, "Sea of images: A dense sampling approach for rendering large indoor environments", *IEEE Computer Graphics & Applications, Special Issue on 3D Reconstruction and Visualization*, pp. 22-30, Nov/Dec 2003.
9. Faugeras O.D., *Three-Dimensional Computer Vision: A Geometric Viewpoint*, Cambridge, MA: Mit Press, 1993.
10. P. Debevec, "Reconstructing and Augmenting Architecture with Image-Based Modeling, Rendering and Lighting", *Proceedings of the International Symposium on Virtual Architecture (VAA' 01)*, pp.1-10, Dublin 21-22 June 2001.
11. Zhang. Flexible Camera Calibration by Viewing a Plane from Unknown Orientations. *ICCV99*.
12. Heeseoung Chae, Jaeyeong Lee and Wonpil Yu, "A Localization Sensor Suite for Development of Robotic Location Sensing Network," *International Conference on Ubiquitous Robots and Ambient Intelligence (ICURAI 2005)*, 2005.
13. www.wipi.or.kr

Research on Mass Terrain Data Storage and Scheduling Based on Grid GIS[*]

Zhang Jing[1] and Huang Hai[2]

[1] College of Resources Environment and Tourism
The Capital Normal University, Beijing 100037, P.R. China
zhangjings@mail.cnu.edu.cn
[2] School of Computer Science and Engineering
Beihang University, Beijing 100083, P.R. China
huanghai@vrlab.buaa.edu.cn

Abstract. In order to meet the need for 3D real-time dynamic visualization of mass terrain data, the spatial database in Grid GIS is taken as the data source of large-scale terrain scenes. Mass terrain data from distributed heterogeneous GIS spatial database are integrated, and their storage and access methods are designed on the basis of grid concept, ensuring that 3D terrain scene from any spatial information source can serve users on demand anywhere at any time. In addition, according to the requirements for low delay and high throughput of terrain data transmission, both the filtering mechanism of terrain data and multi-path data transport service are proposed so as to achieve the best possible viewing experience under the current network conditions. The experimental results show that the proposed mechanism is effective.

1   Introduction

Large-scale terrain visualization has been widely used in GIS, virtual reality, games and simulation, etc. In particular, the virtual battlefield simulation environment requires for real-time display of large-scale terrain model. In this process, two problems occur.

The first problem is the source of 3D terrain mass data. Currently, the high-precision terrain data storage and processing system is mainly GIS (Geographical Information System). A large number of GIS systems have been established with extensive and in-depth GIS application. These GIS systems are mostly designed for special GIS data sources and applications. With the development of network technology and practical demands, people not only access local geographical information, but also access wide area distributed geographical information. The focus of GIS research has transferred from the traditional data structure and algorithm to WebGIS [12]. However, utilizing WebGIS a user can only visit a spatial information system at a time. If he/she wants to access the data in other

---

[*] This paper is supported by the Beijing Natural Science Foundation of China under the grant No. 4042011.

spatial databases simultaneously, it is very difficult or even impossible to integrate these data in different databases. Therefore, research & development of Grid GIS based on grid computing technique have become one of the focuses in GIS field [2], [4], [7]. A key problem that Grid GIS should resolve is to collect and share distributed spatial information resources, implement integrated organization and processing for spatial information data, and provide services on demand.

The second problem is transport and display of 3D terrain scene data, which involves elaborate models and high-resolution texture data. Even through the wide band network, scene transport also requires for a longer time, and the user has to wait for a long time to observe the scene. Therefore, real time and display fidelity have to be balanced in 3D terrain scene transport, such as adoption of simplified scenes (rough model and low-resolution texture) or reservation of more bandwidth for scene transport. However, the more vivid and more refined scene display requirements of mass terrain elevation data constantly expand the scale of scenes. Simply relying on rapid drawing technology of hardware acceleration cannot meet the requirements for drawing speed in practical applications. Especially for the terrain, the number of triangles increases four times of the increase of terrain size. It is necessary and inevitable to design the rapid drawing algorithm primarily irrelevant to or weakly relevant to the scene scale [1], [3], [6].

In this paper, based on previous research, the spatial databases in Grid GIS are taken as data source of large-scale terrain scenes. 3D terrain mass data from distributed and heterogeneous GIS spatial databases are integrated and organized according to grid concept. In addition, the progressive transmission mechanism, which takes not only transport delay but also throughput into account, is studied. As a result, 3D terrain scene from any spatial information source can be transported at any time after process and can serve the spatial information user with the corresponding authority at any location on demand.

2   Terrain Data Processing and Storage

The sources of terrain data in Grid GIS are distributed geographically with heterogeneous data formats and storage mediums. There are three traditional spatial data storage mediums: spatial data documents, object-oriented database, and spatial database. The middleware able to access different spatial data directly is first established in order to eliminate the differences in grammatical structure of spatial data, i.e., the connector able to access spatial data documents, object-oriented database, and spatial database directly is developed. The heterogeneous spatial data are accessed through spatial data connector, and the diversity of original GIS data formats and access ways is shielded. However, in addition to the grammatical heterogeneity, there is also semantic heterogeneity in spatial data [5]. In order to resolve the problem of semantic heterogeneity, mass data storage and management capacity of Grid GIS are fully utilized in this paper to map terrain data in every source to the uniform data organization formats at the preprocessing stage. The method proposed in [8] is adopted to divide elevation data and texture data in terrain data into regular terrain pieces, which will further adopt embedded zerotree coding to obtain progressive compression code stream [10], [13]. Elevation data, texture data, and location name identifiers in terrain data are associated through the coordinates. The progressive compression code streams, location name identifiers, and center coordinates of every terrain piece are stored in terrain database as the final existence. At the same time, the metadata of the database are stored in IS (Index Service). The client can access IS through RB (Resource Broker) to obtain the storage information of the required data, and the data will be transported to and displayed at the client in the form of stream media. In the process of data display, the client can also locate and search for the geographical position through name identifier or the coordinates interactively (see Fig. 1).

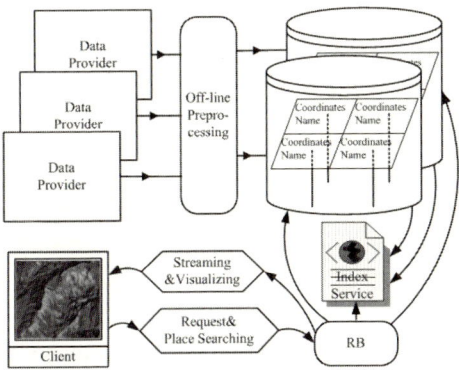

Fig. 1. Terrain data storage and scheduling based on Grid GIS

We may suppose D as large-scale terrain mass data which will be stored at n Grid GIS nodes in distributed way. D_i is stored at node i, and $D_i \subseteq D(i = 1, 2, \cdots, n)$, then the logic view of D stored in Grid GIS is shown as Fig. 2, in which terrain data storage system is mainly composed of RB Service, IS, etc. RB Service provides the user with data access, storage and management functions. It adopts distributed structural design with each LAN (Local Area Network) domain owns a RB server providing data access service independently. When the user makes a request, RB will provide various data operation services for the user. The distributed RBs are able to work together to provide WAN (Wide Area Network) data services. RB is able to analyze user's request and find the suitable storage resources to provide the user with data operation and management services. After RB obtains the data, it will adopt streaming media transport protocol to transmit the data to the client directly.

IS is a hierarchical distributed service structure composed of local IS and central IS, with every local IS responsible for the corresponding local resource & metadata information and central IS responsible for establishing index of every local metadata information & data buffer to provide global metadata view.

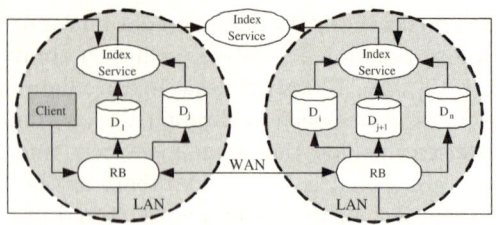

Fig. 2. Logic view of terrain data storage and accessing

IS and RB are designed and realized independently with the service relation established through system deployment and configuration.

A kind of important metadata stored in IS is the boundary coordinates of $D_i(i = 1, 2, \cdots, n)$. Suppose when D is stored in a distributed way, D_i and D_j are adjacent terrain scenes, then when the terrain scenes displayed at the client change from D_i to D_j, RB will access IS to search for the boundary coordinates of D_j to determine the storage node of D_j, read D_j data, and then transport the data to the client so as to ensure the smoothness and continuity of scene display at the client. Notice the boundary coordinates here are those of D_i boundary points, and are different from those of central points of terrain pieces stored in the database when D_i is divided into terrain pieces at the storage node.

3   Terrain Data Scheduling and Transport Mechanism

Given the current network conditions, in order to achieve the best possible viewing experience, it is necessary that data should be transferred in a timely way; and at the same time, high throughput is preferred. In this paper, we leverage the scheduling method of terrain data to achieve this purpose. The scheduling method is based on two techniques. One is the data filtering method based on viewing volume projection. The original intention of this method was only to transport most "useful" terrain data to the client and filter the non-essential data so as to reduce the overall transport time and bandwidth occupation. The other is Multi-path Data Transport Service, which will select multiple paths with less transport delay to transport terrain data so as to obtain high throughput.

3.1   Data Filtering Mechanism Based on Viewing Volume Projection

This method is based on the following fact: when the user observes a scene, he/she will not notice every terrain piece in the scene, and cannot see clearly all the visible terrain pieces. Less data are required to be transported for the more distant terrain pieces. Therefore, in this paper, only the visible terrain pieces are selected to be transported and more code stream data are transported for the nearer terrain pieces so that the scene transport time is reduced. When the user has changed the view point, new terrain pieces can be transported. Terrain piece is used as the unit for visibility determination. And the view points are divided into low view points and high view points to be handled separately.

If the view point is low, the viewing volume is projected to x-y plane according to the algorithm in [9], i.e. the upper, lower and near clipping planes are ignored, as shown in Fig. 3(a), among which the triangle represents the projection of the cone on $x - y$ plane, the grey panes represent the visible data pieces, and V represents the projection point of view point on $x - y$ plane. Suppose the side of terrain piece on $x-y$ plane is a; there are $n_k(k = 0, 1, \cdots, \lceil \frac{x_2-x_1}{a} \rceil)$ terrain pieces with the x-coordinate of $x_1 + ka$; if the x-axis distance between the terrain piece and V increases a, the data to be transported from this terrain piece will decline λ times; the bandwidth available for terrain data transport is B; transport of the terrain piece where V is located in requires for the network bandwidth of β. Then:

$$\sum_{k=0}^{\lceil (x_2-x_1)/a \rceil} n_k \lambda^k \beta = B.$$

Therefore, the network bandwidth required to be allocated for every terrain piece with the x-coordinate of $x_1 + ka$ is:

$$\lambda^k \beta = \lambda^k B / \sum_{k=0}^{\lceil (x_2-x_1)/a \rceil} n_k \lambda^k. \tag{1}$$

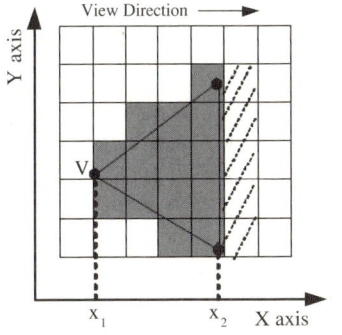 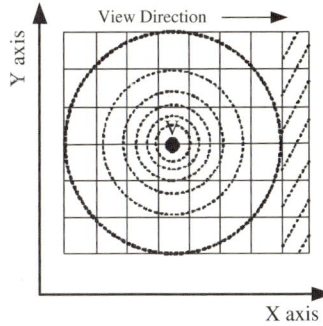

(a) Visibility determination of the terrain piece with low view point

(b) Visibility determination of the terrain piece with high view point

Fig. 3. Visibility determination of the terrain piece with different view point

If the view point is high, the viewing volume is projected to $x - y$ plane. As shown in Fig. 4, after the terrain data are divided into pieces, viewing point V will always be located near the center of the scene. The closer the terrain piece is to V, the more data of the terrain piece are required to be transported through the network so as to obtain clearer visualized results; The farther away the terrain piece is to V, the less data of the terrain piece are required to be transported. The density of concentric circles of dotted line in Fig. 3(b) represents the contrast of required data transport volumes of terrain pieces in the visible area. Similarly, if the view point is high, the network bandwidth can also be computed for every terrain piece in the visible area similar to the low view point. The description is omitted here due to space limitation.

No matter the view point is low or high, only the terrain pieces in the visible area are required to be transported with the motion of view point. However, part of invisible terrain data in the view direction are transported in advance in order to increase the real-time nature of terrain display, as the terrain pieces covered by dotted lines shown in Fig. 3(a) and Fig. 3(b).

3.2   Multi-path Data Transport Service

In order to obtain high throughput, the most direct way is to broaden the bandwidth. However, the grid is established on the basis of the current Internet infrastructure, so it is unfeasible to obtain high throughput simply by broadening the bandwidth. In this paper, we utilize multiple concurrent paths through the Internet to improve the throughput [11]. Where standard Internet routing protocols try to find the single shortest path route from source to destination, we try to discover multiple routes across the Internet. Although the discovered routes may have higher latency than the shortest path, the ensemble of path(s) can offer higher throughput. However, when using paths with length (hop counts) greater than the shortest path, no matter how the flow rates are distributed across the paths, not only the total utilization but also the transfer delay is greater than that used by shortest path routing. In order to trade off between high throughput and low delay, we should restrict length of any selected path within q times length of shortest routing path.

The underlying communication network is modeled by a directed graph $G = (V, E)$, which is a structure consisting of a finite set of vertices $V = \{v_1, v_2, \cdots, v_n\}$ and a finite set of edges $E = \{(v_i, v_j)|v_i, v_j \in V, v_i \neq v_j\}$, where each edge is an ordered pair. V corresponds to the set of routers and E to the set of physical links between them. Without loss of generality, let v_1 be the source node, v_n destination node. Also, let $P(v_1, v_i, \cdots, v_k)$ denote a path formed by $v_1, v_i, \cdots, v_k$ connected in sequence. $P = \{P(v_1, v_i, \cdots, v_k)|i, k \in \mathcal{I}, 1 < k \leq n\}$ is a group composed of paths; A is a linear list, the data elements in which are vertexes in graph G; the length of the shortest path routing between v_1 and v_n is h. Table 1 shows the operations used in path selection.

Based on the assumptions and definitions above, the path-selection algorithm is given in Table 2. After the path-selection approach is carried out, the final remaining paths in group P are those connecting the source node v_1 and the destination node v_n. All these paths are disjointed, so that the bottleneck link is avoided. However, although none of the paths in P is longer than q times the length of shortest routing path, there may be major differences in actual transmission delay of these paths due to the uncertainty of network performance. Therefore, we further select N paths with minor differences in actual

Table 1. Operations used in path selection

Operation	Description
Length(P(v1, vi, , vk))	Return the link number of path P(v1, vi, , vk).
Neighbor(vi)	Return the next adjacent node to vi; when Neighbor(vi) is called for the 1st time, return the 1st adjacent node to vi; when Neighbor(vi) is called for the 2nd time, return the 2nd adjacent node to vi, and so forth; if there is no subsequent adjacent node to vi, return NULL.
P(v1, vi, , vk)+vm	Return P(v1, vi, , vk, vm).
Append(A,vi)	Append vi to linear list A.
Delete(A,vi)	Delete vi from linear list A.
Get(A)	Return a data element in linear list A randomly; if there is no data element in linear list A, return NULL.
Get(P,vi)	Return a path in P with the last node of vi.
Add(P, P(v1, vi, , vk))	Add path P(v1, vi, , vk) to Group P.
Remove(P, P(v1, vi, , vk))	Remove path P(v1, vi, , vk) from Group P.

Table 2. Path-selection algorithm

```
Algorithm: Path selection
[BEGIN]
P = {P(v1)}; A = (v1); Vertex=Get(A);
WHILE (Vertex != NULL)
    {Temp = Neighbor(Vertex);
     WHILE (Temp != NULL)
        {IF (Temp = = vn)
            {Add(P, Get(P, Vertex)+Temp); Temp = NULL;}
         ELSE IF (Length(Get(P,Vertex)+Temp) < q*h )
            {Add(P, Get(P, Vertex)+Temp); Append(A, Temp);}
         ELSE
            Temp = Neighbor(Vertex);
        }
     Remove(P, Get(P, Vertex)); Delete(A, Vertex);
     Vertex = Get(A);
    }
[END]
```

transmission delay from Group P as the transmission paths for terrain data. More specifically, we calculate weight w_i for every path I in Group P according to Formula (2), and select N paths with higher weights:

$$w_i = Min(\lceil \frac{Max(RTT_k)}{RTT_i} \rceil, F) \times G, \tag{2}$$

among which $k = 1, 2, \cdots, n$; $F = 6$; $G = 5$, and RTT_i represents RTT of path i.

Formula (2) shows the higher the weight of the path, the smaller the RTT. Therefore, the transmission delays of N paths selected are minor.

3.3   Scheduling Method of Terrain Data

Suppose the bandwidths of N paths selected according to Formula (2) are $B_1, B_2, \cdots, B_N$, respectively, then $B = \sum_{i=1}^{N} B_i$. Suppose the size of data packet in network transmission is S, the frame rate is f, then once a frame is drawn, the number of data packets to be transmitted in the network is $\frac{B}{f \times S}$.

Combining the interlacing transmission method for code stream data proposed in [8], we can build the running logics for client and server respectively. The differences lie in how to calculate how many bits of terrain pieces should be coded into a data packet; meanwhile, load balance should be realized among the selected paths, so in the running logics packets should be allocated to different paths for transmission according to the bandwidth residual of every path.

On the basis of the interlacing transmission method for code stream data, according to Formula (1), every data packet should contain $\lambda^k S / \sum_{k-0}^{\lceil (x_2 - x_1)/a \rceil} n_k \lambda^k$ bits of every terrain piece with the x coordinate of $x_1 + ka$ in Fig. 3. In order to realize load balance of transmission data volume among the paths, $\frac{B}{f \times S}$ data packets to be transmitted for every frame should be allocated to the selected N paths reasonably. Therefore, $\frac{B}{f \times S} \times B_i / \sum_{i=1}^{N} B_i = \frac{B_i}{f \times S}$ data packets should be transmitted through path i.

4   Experimental Results

According to the method above, we have implemented preliminary performance test. The testing environment is 100M Ethernet. There are two grid storage nodes. The host configurations are P4 2.8, 512M memory, and P4 2.4G, 512M memory. The client host configuration is P4 2.4G, 512M memory. The video card is GeForce FX 5200. At the pre-processing stage, terrain data are divided into 16*16 pieces and compressed into code streams to be stored in SQL Server 2000 database of grid nodes. Testing by adjusting the available bandwidth B of data transmission path, we find that when the available bandwidth B=700K, the real-time frame rate may exceed 20fps (see Fig. 4), and the smooth dynamic visualization effect is obtained.

Meanwhile, we have implemented simulation test for throughput of multi-path data transport service. The simulation network environment is the complete graph composed of 5 nodes (see Fig. 5(a)). We chose uniform link bandwidth and uniform link delay in this simulation. The bandwidth of every link is 1M. The source node is s, and the destination node is d. Let $q = 2$, then the changes

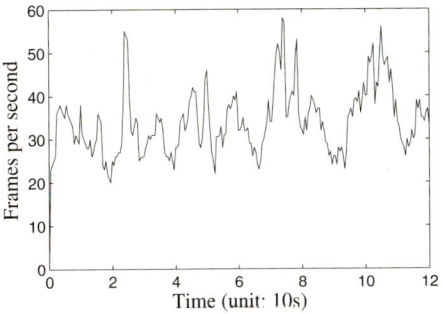

Fig. 4. Record of frame rates

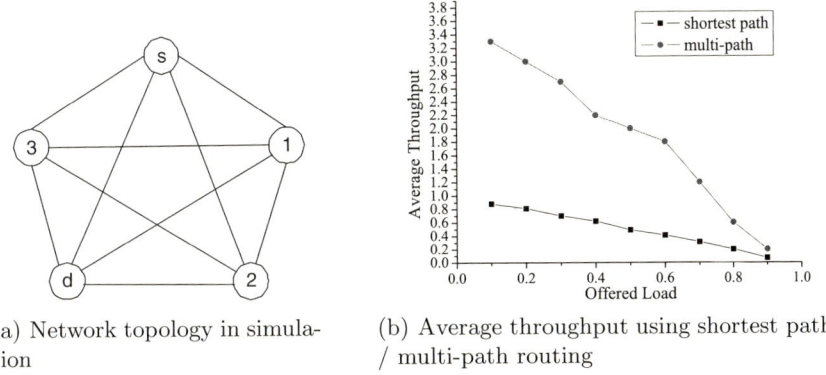

(a) Network topology in simulation

(b) Average throughput using shortest path / multi-path routing

Fig. 5. Experimental results

of throughput with the changes of network load under the shortest path routing and multi-path routing are shown in Fig. 5(b).

We can see in Fig. 5(b) that under the same network load conditions, adopting multi-path routing is able to increase the throughput of mass terrain data transmission significantly in comparison with adopting the shortest path routing.

5   Conclusions

Real-time visualization of large-scale terrain scene is of great significance. In this paper, the storage and access methods for mass terrain data are designed on the basis of grid concept by integrating mass terrain data from distributed heterogeneous GIS spatial database. The distributed heterogeneous IS provides the users with global terrain data resource view. RB provides the users with various data operation services. And the users can access terrain data anytime anywhere. Also, the existing terrain data stream media transmission technologies are leveraged. Then the requirements for delay and throughput of mass terrain data in network transmission are integrated to propose the filtering mechanism to reduce unnecessary data transmission and the multi-path data transmission services to fully utilize the existing network infrastructure to increase throughput of data transmission. This experiment demonstrates the proposed methods can realize real-time online display of large-scale terrain scene on PC.

References

1. Zhuo, Y.F., Zhao, Y.B., Shi J.Y.: A Survey of Real-time Terrain Rendering Algorithms. Computer Simulation, Vol. 22, No. 3 (2005) 4–7
2. Jiang, Y.F., Lv, G.N.: Grid computing and infrastructure and key technology of grid GIS. Science of Surveying and Mapping, Vol. 30, No. 4 (2005) 16–19
3. Bo-Yin Li, Horng-Shyang Liao, Chang, C.H., San-Liang Chu: Visualization for HPC data - large terrain model. Proceedings of the Seventh International Conference on High Performance Computing and Grid in Asia Pacific Region, (2004) 280–284
4. Shen, Z.F., Luo, J.C., Cai, S.H., Zheng, J., Chen, Q.X., Sun, Q.H.: Architecture of Grid-GIS and Its Key Techniques. Geo-Information Science, No. 4 (2003) 57–62
5. Deng, S.J., Wu, C.H., Meng, L.K., Xu, L.: Spatial Data Integration Services for Grid GIS. Computer & Digital Engineering, Vol. 34, No. 2 (2006) 39–43
6. Ng, C.M., Nguyen, C.T., Tran, D.N., Tan, T.S., Yeow, S.W.: Analyzing pre-fetching in large-scale visual simulation. Proceedings of Computer Graphics Intemational 2005, (2005) 100–107
7. Sun, Q.H., Chi, T.H., Wang, X.L., Zhong, D.W.: Design of middleware based grid GIS. Geoscience and Remote Sensing Symposium, (2005) 854–857
8. Ma, Z.G., Zhang, K., Wang, G.P., Dong, S.H.: Streaming 3D Terrain over Network. Acta Scientiarum Naturalium Universitatis Pekinensis, Vol. 42, No. 1 (2006) 116–120
9. Zhao, Y.B., Shi, J.Y., Zhou, J., Pan, Z.G.: A Fast Algorithm for Large Scale Terrain Walkthrough. Journal of Computer-Aided Design & Computer Graphics, Vo l. 14, No. 7 (2002) 624–628
10. Nagatomo, K., Yoshikai, D., Okuda, M.: Progressive coding of textured 3D models. Multimedia and Expo, No. 1 (2002) 357–360
11. Shi, S., Wang, L.L., Calvert, K.L., Griffioen, J.N.: A multi-path Routing Service for Immersive Environments. 2004 IEEE International Symposium on Cluster Computing and the Grid, (2004) 699–706
12. Rishe, N., Sun, Y., Chekmasov, M., Selivonenko, A., Graham, S.: System architecture for 3D terrafly online GIS. Proceedings of the IEEE Sixth International Symposium on Multimedia Software Engineering, (2004) 273–276
13. Zhang, L.B., Wang, K.: An Image Compression Algorithm Based on Integer Wavelet Transform. Journal of Software, Vol. 14, No. 8 (2003) 1433–1438

Multi-touch Interaction for Table-Top Display

Song-Gook Kim, Jang-Woon Kim, Ki-Tae Bae, and Chil-Woo Lee*

Department of Computer Engineering, Chonnam National University
Yong-bong Dong 300, Gwang-Ju, South Korea
uaini@image.chonnam.ac.kr, woon418@image.chonnam.ac.kr,
bkt2002@image.chonnam.ac.kr, leecw@chonnam.ac.kr

Abstract. In this paper, we describe a system of multi-touch tabletop display and its control algorithm for Google-earth^{TM} that utilizes hand gesture as mouse free interaction. The system adopts well known FTIR technique. The hand gesture of necessary instruction is predefined according to the number, position, and movement of the fingertips which are obtained from multi-touch of a single user. The system consists of a beam-projector and an acrylic screen attaching infrared LED as light source, and an infrared camera for capturing the fingertip image. Input image is preprocessed with simple morphological method to remove the noise and to determine the fingertip region. In recognition process, gesture commands are recognized by comparing the preprocessed image with predefined gesture model of fingertips. In detail, firstly the number of the spot; fingertip mark, angles among the spots, and Euclidean distance between two spots are calculated, and then the values are compared with the information of the model. The effectiveness of the system can be proved through the experimental results.

Keywords: Multi-touch, Tabletop display, FTIR (Frustrated Total Internal Reflection), human computer interaction.

1 Introduction

Recently, according as frequent use of information system in daily life, the research on understanding user intention and action awareness is being popular because if the system understands it we can construct the user-friendly interaction easily. There are many methods to establish the purpose, and hand touch is considered as the most intuitive and convenient method for controlling the system. So, constructing multi-touch screen and hand gesture recognition for display are receiving much attention as core technologies for advanced information system in the human interface research field. Therefore, the researches about tabletop display with large screen installed on table are very popular [1].

Generally, in designing a tabletop display, we have to consider five key aspects in order to make an ideal system; (1) multi-touch interaction using bare hands, (2) implementation of collaborative work, (3) direct touch interaction, (4) the use of physical objects as interaction tool, (5) not expensive for the public large display. And with these aspects, tabletop display ultimately integrates

---

* Corresponding author (Tel.: 82-62-530-1803).

Z. Pan et al. (Eds.): ICAT 2006, LNCS 4282, pp. 1273–1282, 2006.

interaction of three elements; Computer, physical objects and displayed objects, to human user as the central figure very easily. Additionally, tabletop display can help cooperative interaction of multi-users as medium of communication. However until now most of displays are generally recognize only a single point touch. Multi-touch recognition has many difficulties to be implemented, so rich interaction for the system is limited. The design of multi-touch tabletop user interfaces is still in its infancy and is not yet well understood.

In this paper, we will describe a system of multi-touch tabletop display and its control algorithm for Google-earth^{TM} that utilizes hand gesture as most intuitive tool of human computer interaction. Also, we are going to describe the technologies which include multi-touch sensing technique in the previous researches.

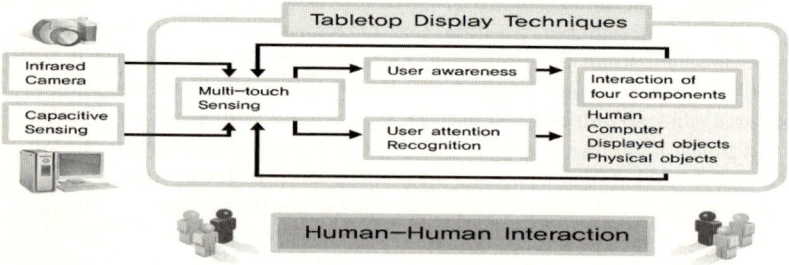

Fig. 1. The outline and the goal of tabletop display

2   Related Work

Myron Kreuger can be considered as one of the pioneers in interactive computer based art. His focus was to create unencumbered, artificial realities where the humans could participate with their entire body without wearing any special instruments in an experience created by the computer. His works have affected many things to tabletop display researches.

In the section of "Emerging Technologies", SIGGRAPH 2006' we can see various multi-touch technologies which are being developed in the world [1]. From having experience of the technologies we can see that the terminology called "table" becomes interface of synthetic device that both sensing and output means are integrated.

Most of the researches about tabletop display are classified into several types according to system configuration and sensing method. We are going to explain the types as follows.

2.1   Capacitive Sensing Based Interaction

There are a number of systems which embed electronic capacitive sensing device into the surface itself such as SmartSkin [5] and DiamondTouch [2]. These systems typically result in very fast and precise detection of touch compared to the following vision based approaches. However, these systems still require very complicated hardware configuration with low resolution.

Also the systems usually rely on top-down projection. So occlusion can frequently occur between hands and displayed images and also the distortion of image can occur. As a result, a user frequently tries to see the distorted images on their hands and tries to move it away from screen. Consequently, it disrupts the focus of attention. Especially, SmartSkin [5] analyzes sensor value of two dimension called "proximity pixels" using the capacitive sensing method. Therefore, the recognition of hand shape and the discrimination of hand proximity are available with the very fast speed.

2.2   Vision Based Interaction

Computer vision based method has capable of sensing capabilities including detection and recognition of objects placed on the screen itself.

Previously, the AugmentedDesk [6] uses a thermo-infrared camera mounted above the table to extract the shape of hands from the background. And also template matching method used to detect the 2D positions of all the fingertips of both hands for such tasks as two-handed drawing and GUI navigation. But their single camera setting cannot determine whether a finger is touching the table surface or not. Lumisight Table [4] is based on the optical design of a special screen system composed of a building material called Lumisty and a Fresnel lens. This system combines films and a lens with four projectors to display four different images, one for each user's view. Thus, a method for a mixed and integrated display of shared and private information on a single screen could become a new paradigm in human-computer interaction. Therefore, the Lumisight Table [4] is physically single device but can be visually used multiple person. Recently, New York University announced the multi-touch sensing display [3] using FTIR (Frustrated Total Internal Reflection) technique to the public. Because such methods use all video cameras, there are many advantages to get image data of high resolution inexpensively and so on.

In vision based method, both top-down and rear projection methods have been used but latter one becomes main approaches to many systems. Because the discrimination of fingers touch is difficult and inexact on screen in top-down method. Additionally, rear mounting configuration can gradually expand into implementation of augmented reality using physical objects.

2.3   Display System of Top-Down Projection

One popular approach is to mount a camera and projector high on a shelf or on the ceiling [2, 5, 6]. Such mounting configurations are typically necessary because of the throw requirements of projectors and the typical focal length of video cameras. Such a configuration has the following drawbacks. Ceiling installation of a heavy projector is difficult, dangerous, requires special mounting hardware. Once the installation is complete, the system and projection surface cannot be moved easily. Often minor vibrations present in buildings can create problems during operation and make it difficult to maintain calibration. The user's own head and hands can occlude the projected image as they interact with the system.

2.4 Display System of Rear Projection

A second approach is to place the projector and camera behind a diffuse projection screen [3, 4]. While this enables the construction of a self-contained device, allows the placement of codes on the bottom of the objects, and eliminates occlusion problems, this approach also has drawbacks. It is difficult to construct such a table system with large display area which also allows users room enough to put their legs under the table surface. Because the camera is looking through a diffuse surface, the imaging resolution is limited. High resolution capture of documents, for example, is impossible. A dedicated surface is required, and the resulting housing for the projector and camera can be quite large. This presents manufacturing and distributing problems for a real product.

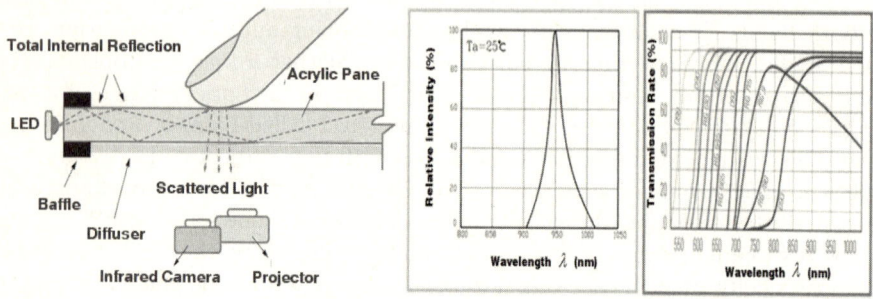

Fig. 2. The principle of FTIR (left). Detailed specification of infrared LED and infrared pass filter (right).

3   System Overview

3.1 FTIR (Frustrated Total Internal Reflection) Sensing Technique

Our tabletop display makes use of FTIR (frustrated total internal reflection), which is a phenomenon that accompanies total internal reflection in a waveguide medium. When the fingertips touch the surface of a waveguide medium, the condition of the total internal reflection is disturbed. Therefore, a scattering occurs along the surface where FTIR happens. Consequently, the infrared camera with IR pass filter placed below the screen can capture the scattering as a bright spot on the homogenous surface. Infrared LED used in our system has peak emitting power at 950nm in wavelength. So we have utilized the B+W infrared pass filter of the Schneider 093 version See Fig 2.

3.2 Hardware Configuration

We adopted the multi-touch display concept developed by NewYork University using two rows of infrared LED as light sources on either side of an acrylic screen, which acts as a waveguide. In our prototype, we used a 660mm (wide) × 510mm (high) × 8mm (thick) sheet of acrylic, whose four edges have been polished clearly Fig 3. This acrylic sheet is four edges-lit by infrared LED which is placed directly against the polished four edges so as maximize coupling efficiency into total internal reflection, while the infrared camera with the infrared pass filter is mounted orthogonally to the screen. The screen is covered by a special film and rear-projection composition that acts as a diffuser and prevents the light from escaping. And the gradient of acrylic screen is 30 degrees for an arrangement of equipment. Tabletop display also has the air-cap of only 2mm between screen and special film for preventing light spreads.

Fig 3 shows the prototype of our table-top display, which includes a projector, a infrared camera attached the infrared pass filter and infrared LEDs. The infrared camera can capture 320*240 images at 30 frames per second on a Pentium IV 3.0GHz.

Fig. 3. The acrylic screen attaching infrared LED (left). The inside of the prototype system, and the configuration of camera and projector (right).

4 Interaction Techniques

The recognition system of multi-touch interaction was developed by using the Microsoft Visual C++ compiler with the Image Processing Libraries (IPL) and Open Computer Vision library (OpenCV) offered from Intel. These libraries contain special image-processing functions optimized for the Pentium architecture to ensure efficient computational performance.

Our table-top display is capable of tracking fingertip movement and counting the number of fingertips that the user is using for interaction. The only one time calibration is required, in the process the view of the camera has to be

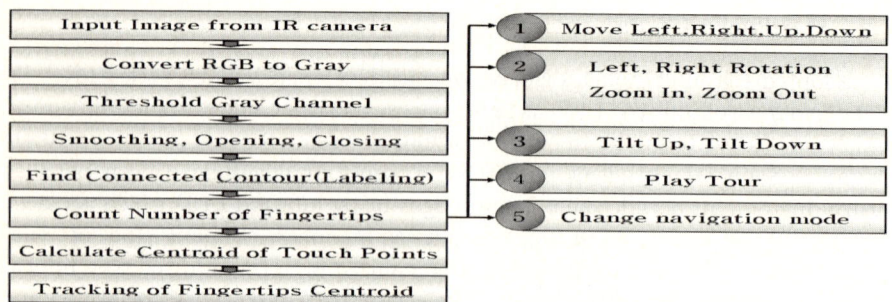

Fig. 4. The algorithm flowchart of our tabletop display system

adjusted to the maximum width of X axis (660mm) and the maximum height of Y axis (510mm). The captured image is successively processed through a series of pipelined stages shown in Fig 4.

The system uses acquired images to process the image through a series of pipelined stages, successively refining the information about the position of the fingertips by removing noise and segmenting the touch points from the background. Once the position of the hands is known, the system then counts the number of bright spots where the user is touching on the screen. Each stage of this flowchart is discussed in the followings. The Fig 5 shows the segmentation result of touched fingertips.

Firstly, the RGB color images obtained from infrared camera are converted to the Gray scale images. And then binary image is obtained by using appropriate threshold value. Continuously, we conduct noise reduction process of smoothing, opening, closing in consecutive order for detecting touch points. In the next process, we also apply the labeling for counting the number of touched fingertips. And then related commands (shown in Table 1) ;Click or Pointing, Move, Left Rotation, Right Rotation, Zoom-In, Zoom-Out, Tilt-Up, Tilt-Down ,and Play Tour, are executed according to the number of bright spots. We are going to describe interaction techniques for controlling Google-earth ^{TM} via one hand or both hands.

The instructions are divided into four major categories; static gesture, spatial dynamic gesture, temporal dynamic gesture, and (spatial+dynamic) gesture.

4.1   One-Handed Interaction

In case of using only one hand, a user can use the move, zoom-in, zoom-out, left-rotation, right-rotation instructions for controlling of Google-earth ^{TM}. When the user is contacting on the screen, she/he is apts to use more than one finger. If the bright spot is one, the click event of left button of mouse happens and acts as role of catch. So, by moving the fingertip to forward, backward, left, right or arbitrary direction the user is able to explore of satellite picture. And, if the

Fig. 5. Segmentation results of touched the fingertips

fingertip is contacted at arbitrary position, the instruction of movement happens in relation to the contacted direction. If the contacted fingertip recedes from the center of the screen, it is possible to explore the satellite picture with the faster speed. If the user selects arbitrary two places on screen with click command, then the system shows the shortest route between the two places. A user can additionally select arbitrary area in the mini-map of the Google-earth^{TM} at the right side top portion for direct movement. When a user touches on screen using a thumb and a forefinger, namely it has two touch points, zoom-in and zoom-out instructions are achieved. If the user does not move in the state that the thumb and the forefinger are touched, any reaction will not occur. But if the distance between two fingers becomes closer, the zoom-out instruction is achieved. On the other hand the distance of two fingers become away, the zoom-in instruction is executed. Both left-rotation and right-rotation instructions are also controlled by using the thumb and the forefinger. At this time, the moving index finger indicates rotation amount and direction while the thumb is fixed as principal axis. That is, the differences of zoom instruction from rotation instruction are caused by variation of angle and Euclidean distance of two bright spots. In detail, angles among the bright spots and Euclidean distance between two bright spots are calculated, and then the values are compared with the information of the model. Also, contacted points are initially stored to buffer and continuously observed to check the variation. Fig 6 shows the instruction set that use one hand motion.

4.2   Two-Handed Interaction

In case of using both hands, other instructions ;zoom-in, zoom-out, tilt-up, tilt-down, and play-tour, can operate the system depend on the number of fingertips that are contacted on the screen. If the distance of two fingertip spots made by one finger of both hands become away from each other, zoom-in instruction is executed, and in the opposite case, zoom-out instruction is achieved. In this case, we can use faster and more dynamic command than one handed instruction. We detected the center of two fingertips and calculated the Euclidean distance between two bright spots in this case. Also the user can execute tilt-up and

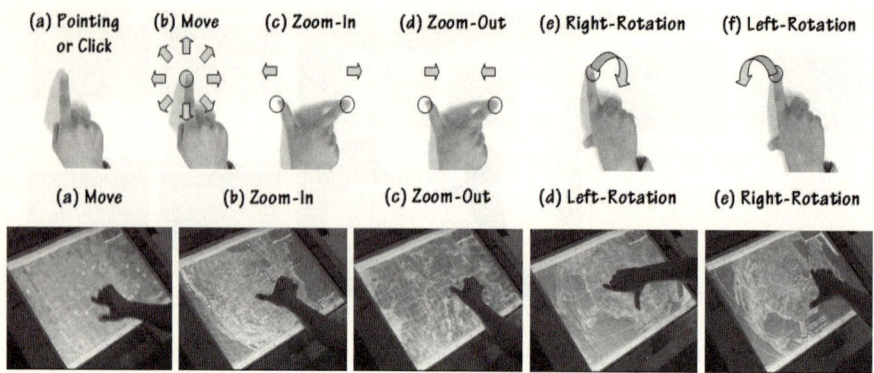

Fig. 6. One handed instruction set. (a)Pointing or Click: single point touch. (b)Move: move to arbitrary direction. (c)Zoom-In (d)Zoom-Out (e)Right-Rotation: the thumb is fixed. (f)Left-Rotation: the thumb is fixed.

tilt-down instruction. For the instruction, the user activate the tabletop display with two fingers of left hand which are fixed on the screen, on the contrast to the fingers, one finger of right hand determines the amount of tilt variation by moving the finger position. To performed instruction predefined information are continuously compared with the calculated information from input image. This instruction permits exploring 3D shape of buildings and outdoor scenery with solid model. The last instruction of Google-earth^{TM} is play-tour command for traveling the historic and famous places. A user contacts four fingertips of both hands on screen and wait for few seconds. This instruction is peculiar and special

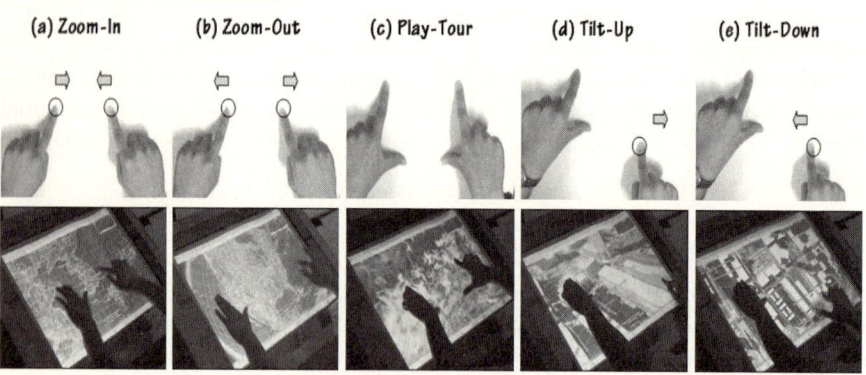

Fig. 7. Two handed instruction set. (a)Zoom-In (b)Zoom-Out (c)Play-Tour: both hands are fixed for a few seconds. (d)Tilt-Up: fingers of Left hand are fixed. (e)Tilt-Down: fingers of Left hand are fixed.

Table 1. The control commands for the Google-earth^{TM}

Command	Control result of Google-earth
Move	Moves the viewer in the direction of the arrow.
Rotate Clockwise	Rotates the view clockwises. The earth spins counter-clockwise.
Zoom-In	Zooms the viewer in.
Zoom-Out	Zooms the viewer out.
Tilt-Up	Tilts the viewer toward "top-down" view.
Tilt-Down	Tilts the viewer toward "horizon" view.
Play Tour	Plays the tour mode for all selected items in the Places pane.

instruction of Google-earth^{TM}. Fig 7 shows instruction set that consists of using both hands.

5   Concluding Remarks and Future Work

In this paper, we describe a unique tabletop display system which adopts FTIR (Frustrated Total Internal Reflection) sensing technique and its control command for well-known Google-earth^{TM} system. In the system we develop very simple instruction set which used variation of the number of finger spots and location. The recognition algorithm is very simple so that the system implemented in real-time by using ordinary personal computer.

However the system has some drawbacks which should be improved in the next version. The first one is to develop more sensitive technology for capturing light tap gesture on the screen since usually the users want to use light touch. Also, if we can develop the technique it may be used for recognize the pressure of the touch. The second thing is to construct more reliable technologies which can avoid the interference of surrounding illumination. Since the system uses the infrared light source, it is so sensitive to the brightness of ambient light. This drawback makes the system not to be used in usual indoor environment. The next one is to have algorithm which can identify owners of fingers in multi-user interaction. If we realize the algorithm we can develop many interesting application software.

Acknowledgments

This research has been supported by research funding of "Culture Technology Research Institute", and "Center for High-Quality Electric Components and Systems", Chonnam National University, Korea.

References

[1] In the section of "Emerging technologies" of ACM SIGGRAPH 2006 Full Conference.

[2] Dietz, P. and Leigh, D. "DiamondTouch: A Multi-User Touch Technology." In Proceedings of the 14th Annual ACM Symposium on User Interface Software and Technology (Orlando, Florida, November 11 - 14, 2001). UIST '01. ACM Press, New York, NY, pp. 219-226.

[3] Han J. Y. "Low-Cost Multi-Touch Sensing through Frustrated Total Internal Reflection." In Proceedings of the 18th Annual ACM Symposium on User Interface Software and Technology, ACM Press, New York, NY, 2005, 15-118

[4] Matsushita, M., Iida, M., Ohguro, T., Shirai, Y., Kakehi, Y., and Naemura, T. 2004. Lumisight Table: A Face-to-face Collaboration Support System That Optimizes Direction of Projected Information to Each Stakeholder. In Proceedings of the 2004 ACM Conference on Computer Supported Cooperative Work (Chicago, Illinois, USA, November 06 - 10, 2004), CSCW '04. ACM Press, New York, NY, pp. 274-283.

[5] Rekimoto, J. 2002. SmartSkin: An Infrastructure for Freehand Manipulation on Interactive Surfaces. In Proceedings of the SIGCHI Conference on Human Factors in Computing Systems. CHI '02. ACM Press, New York, NY, pp. 113-120.

[6] K. Oka, Y. Sato, and H. Koike, "Real-Time Tracking of Multiple Fingertips and Gesture Recognition for Augmented Desk Interface Systems," Proc. IEEE Int'l Conf. Automatic Face and Gesture Recognition (FG 2002), IEEE CS Press, 2002, pp. 429-434.

Reliable Omnidirectional Depth Map Generation for Indoor Mobile Robot Navigation Via a Single Perspective Camera

Chuanjiang Luo[1,2], Feng Zhu[1], and Zelin Shi[1]

[1] Optical-Electronic Information Laboratory, Shenyang Institute of Automation,
Chinese Academy of Sciences, Shenyang, China
{lcj0603, fzhu, zlshi}@sia.cn
[2] Graduate School of the Chinese Academy of Sciences, Beijing, China

Abstract. This paper deals with the problem of finding the largest navigable areas around a mobile robot, which is important for navigation and action planning. We propose a method to obtain reliable dense 3D maps using a novel omnidirectional stereo vision system. The vision system is composed of a perspective camera and two hyperbolic mirrors. Once the system has been calibrated and two image points respectively projected by upper and below mirrors are matched, the 3D coordinate of the space point can be acquired by means of triangulation. To achieve the largest reliable dense matching, our method are divided into three steps. First reliable FX-dominant matching; then feature matching and ambiguous removal; finally the remaining points between features are matched using dynamic time warping(DTW) with modified energy functions adapted well to our system. Experiments show that this proposed vision system is feasible as a practical stereo sensor for accurate 3D map generation.

1 Introduction

Obtaining panoramic 3D map information for mobile robots is essential for navigation and action planning. Although there are other ways to fulfill this task, such as ultrasonic sensors or laser range finders, stereo vision system, especially catadioptric vision system excels them in its precision and wide angle of view without energy emission.

Mobile robot navigation using binocular omnidirectional stereo vision has been reported in [1], [2], [8]. Such two-camera stereo system are costly and complicated compared to single camera stereo system. Omnidirectional stereo based on a double lobed mirror and a single camera was developed in [3], [4]. A double lobed mirror is a coaxial mirror pair, where the centers of both mirrors are collinear with the camera axis, and the mirrors have a profile radially symmetric around this axis. This configuration has the merit to produce two omnidirectional scene in a single image. However, the effective baseline is quite small due to the closeness of the two mirrors. To overcome this drawback, we have developed a large baseline panoramic vision system to be described in Section 2.

To build a depth map for mobile robot navigation, the most important and difficult process is omnidirectional stereo matching. Once two image points respectively

Z. Pan et al. (Eds.): ICAT 2006, LNCS 4282, pp. 1283–1292, 2006.

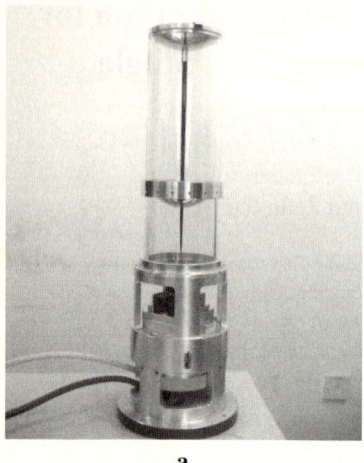

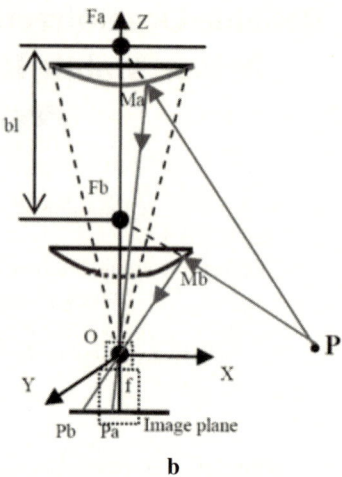

a   b

Fig. 1. a: The appearance of the stereo vision system. b: The configuration of the system.

projected by upper mirror and below mirror are matched, the 3D coordinate of the corresponding space point can be obtained by triangulation. State of the art algorithms for dense stereo matching can be divided into two categories:

Local method: These algorithms calculate some kind of similarity measure over an area [11]. They work well in relatively textured areas in a very fast speed, while they cannot gain correct disparity map in textureless areas and areas with repetitive textures, which is a unavoidable problem in most situations. In [13] a method of finding the largest unambiguous component has been proposed, but the density of the disparity map varies greatly depend on the discriminability of the similarity measure in a given situation.

Global method: These method make explicit smoothness assumptions and try to find a global optimized solution of a predefined energy function that take into account both the matching similarities and smoothness assumptions. The energy function is always in the form of $E(d) = E_{data}(d) + \lambda \cdot E_{smooth}(d)$, where λ is a parameter controlling the proportion of smoothness and image data. Most recent algorithms are belong to this category [9], [10]. The biggest problem of global method is that the data term and the smoothness term represent two process competing against each other, resulting in incorrect matches in areas of weak texture and areas where prior model is violated.

Although numerous methods exist for stereo matching, they are designed towards ordinary stereo vision purpose. As there are some particularities in the catadioptric images and the high requirement of reliability for navigation, we propose a three step algorithm that combines the advantages of feature matching and dense global matching. The rest of the paper is organized as follows: in Section 2, we briefly describe principle of our catadioptric stereo vision system; a full model of calibrating the system is presented in Section 3; in Section 4, we detail the omnidirectional stereo matching and depth map generation; our experimental results are shown in Section 5 and in Section 6 we conclude the paper.

2   Principle of Our Vision System

The system we have developed [5] is based on a common perspective camera coupled with two hyperbolic mirrors, which are separately fixed inside a glass cylinder (Fig.1a). The two hyperbolic mirrors share one focus which coincides with the camera center. A hole in the below mirror permits imaging via the mirror above. As the separation between the two mirrors provides much enlarged baseline, the precision of the system has been improved correspondingly. The coaxial configuration of the camera and the two hyperbolic mirrors makes the epipolar line radially collinear, thus making the system free of the search process for complex epipolar curve in stereo matching (Fig.2).

To describe the triangulation for computing 3D coordinates of space points, we define the focal point O as the origin of our reference frame, z-axis parallel to the optical axis pointing above. Then mirrors can be represented as:

$$\frac{(z - c_i)^2}{a^2} - \frac{(x^2 + y^2)}{b^2} = 1 \ . \qquad (i = a, b) \tag{1}$$

Only the incident rays pointing to the focus $F_a(0, 0, 2c_a)$, $F_b(0, 0, 2c_b)$ will be reflected by the mirrors to pass through the focal point of the camera. The incident ray passing the space point $P(x, y, z)$ reaches the mirrors at points M_a and M_b, being projected onto the image at points $P_a(u_a, v_a, -f)$ and $P_b(u_b, v_b, -f)$ respectively. As P_a and P_b are known, M_a and M_b can be represented by:

$$\frac{x_{M_i}}{u_i} = \frac{y_{M_i}}{v_i} = \frac{z_{M_i}}{-f} \ . \qquad (i = a, b) \tag{2}$$

Since point M_a and M_b are on the mirrors, they satisfy the equation of the mirrors. Their coordinates can be solved from equation group (1) and (2). Then the equation of rays $F_a P$ and $F_b P$ are:

$$\frac{x_p}{x_i} = \frac{y_p}{y_i} = \frac{z_p - 2c_i}{z_i - 2c_i} \ . \qquad (i = a, b) \tag{3}$$

We can finally figure out coordinate of the space point P by solving the equation (3).

3   Calibrating the Camera and Mirrors

Camera calibration is a vital process for many computer vision jobs. In using the omnidirectional stereo vision system, its calibration is also important, as in the case of conventional stereo systems. Compared with the present calibrating techniques only concerning the camera Intrinsics [7], our calibrating algorithm presents a full model of the imaging process, which includes the rotation and translation between the camera and the mirror, and an algorithm to determine this relative position from observations of known points in a single image. We divide the calibration into two steps. Firstly we calibrate the camera's intrinsics without the mirrors in order to reduce computational complexity. Once the camera intrinsics are known, we estimate the pose parameters of the CCD camera with respect to the mirrors by LM algorithm. The function to be optimized is the sum of squared difference between coordinates of targets and the locations calculated from the targets' image points from the projection model.

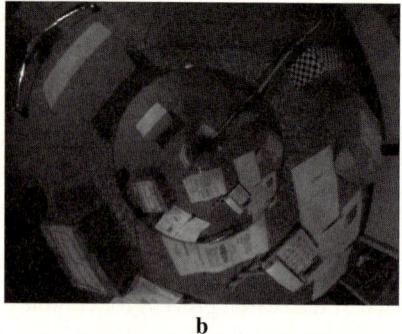

a   b

Fig. 2. a: A calibration image used in our experiment. b: Real indoor scene captured for depth map generation.

Table 1. Calibration results with real data

	α	β	γ	t_x	t_y	t_z
value	$-0.9539°$	$0.1366°$	$0.1436°$	$-0.0553mm$	$-0.1993mm$	$1.8717mm$

Fig.2a shows one example of the calibration image in our experiment. The calibration was performed using a set of 81 points equally distributed on a desk with different heights from 0 to 122mm around the vision system. The calibration results with real data are listed in Table 1. The calibration result was verified using a new set of 40 untrained points, the average square error of the set points is 34.24mm without considering the camera-to-mirror transformation while 12.57mm with the calibration result. For more details about the calibration process, see [6].

4   Stereo Matching

4.1   Overview

The images acquired by our system(Fig.2b) have some particularities in contrast to normal stereo pairs as follows, which may lead to poor result using traditional stereo matching methods: (1) The upper mirror and below mirror have different focal length that the camera focal length has to compromise with the two, thus causing defocusing effect. As a result, similarity measures take on much less discriminability. (2) Indoor scene has much more weak textured and textureless areas than outdoor scene. (3) The resolution gets lower when moving away from the image center. The result is the farther off the center, the more unreliable the matching result is.

To solve problem (1), we propose a three-step method that allows matching distinctive feature points first and breaks down the matching task into smaller and separate subproblems. For (2) we design a specific energy function used in the third step DTW, in which different weights and penalty items are assigned to points of different texture level and matching confidence. Then we throw away the matching result of the most indiscrminable points, replacing it with interpolation. For (3), we regard points farther

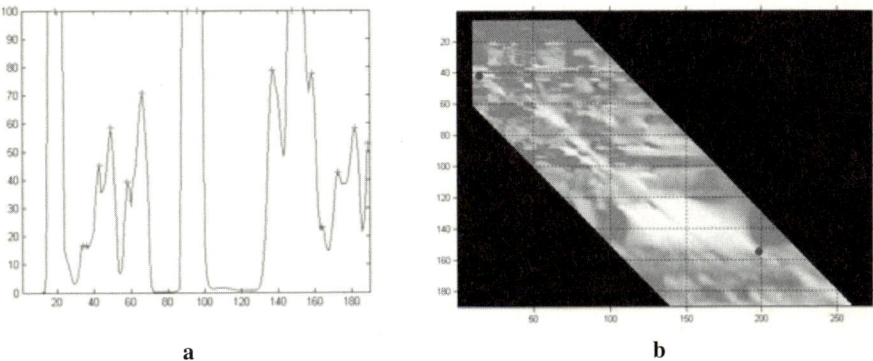

a   b

Fig. 3. a: The curve of texture intensity along the epipolar line. To show it clearly, we removed the part the curve is higher than 100 only labeling the detected feature points. b: Detected reliable FX-dominant matching result in the MZNCC matrix. The black region of the matrix is formed since it is out of the disparity search range.

than the most farthest matched feature point off the center as unreliable, leaving them as unknown areas. This is also required by DTW.

Epipolar geometry makes the stereo matching easier by reducing the 2D search to a 1D search along the same epipolar line in both images. To handle epipolar property conveniently, we unwrapped the raw image to two panoramic images which corresponding to images via below and upper mirrors respectively(Fig.7 a,b). The matching process is done on every epipolar pair respectively. The red line labeled in the two panoramic images are the same epipolar line for the subsequent illustration of our proposed method, of which the one above has 190 pixels and the one below 275 pixels.

4.2   Similarity Measure and Defined Texture Level

The similarity measure we choose here is zero-mean normalized cross correlation (ZNCC), since it is invariant to intensity and contrast between two images. But directly using this measure would result in low discriminability. Chances exist that two templates with great difference in average gray-level or standard deviation which cannot be deemed as matched pair may have high ZNCC value. To avoid this possibility, we modified ZNCC(called MZNCC) by multiplying a window function as follows:

$$C(p,d) = \frac{\sum (I_a(i, j + d) - \mu_a) \cdot (I_b(i, j) - \mu_b)}{\sigma_a \cdot \sigma_b} \cdot w(|\mu_a - \mu_b|) \cdot w(\frac{max(\sigma_a, \sigma_b)}{min(\sigma_a, \sigma_b)} - 1) , \quad (4)$$

where $w(x) = \begin{cases} 1, & x < \lambda \\ 1 - (x - \lambda), & x \geq \lambda \end{cases}$, μ_a, μ_b are the average gray-level of matching window, σ_a, σ_b are the standard deviation. For every epipolar line, all MZNCC value are stored as a matrix(Fig.3b) to be used in the next step. The y-axis represents the pixel number in the epipolar of Fig.7a, while x-axis represents the number in Fig.7b.

We define our texture level by the sharpness of the autocorrelation curve. For a given pixel and a given template centered in the pixel, we slide the template one pixel at a

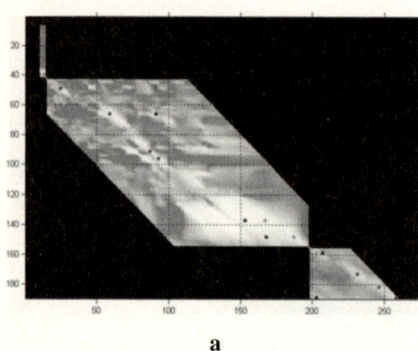 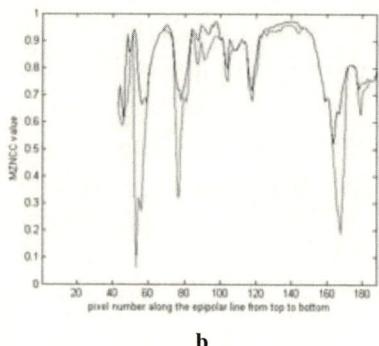

a   **b**

Fig. 4. a: Result of feature matching. All points labeled in the graph mean candidate match for detected features, red and green are the results chosen by maximization of sum of MZNCC and then green are removed for uneliminated ambiguous. b: the global maximum MZNCC value in this epipolar(blue) and MZNCC value along the matching route chosen by our algorithm(red).

time in the two opposite directions along the epipolar line and stop at the location the MZNCC value of the shifted template with the primary one decrease below a certain threshold for the first time. Let l be the distance between the two stop points, which is inverse proportional the texture level. The texture intensity can be formalized as:

$$T(u, v) = \sum_{-r \leqslant (i, j) \leqslant r} (I(u + i, v + j) - \bar{I})^2 / l^2 , \qquad (5)$$

where r is the radius of the template. The texture intensity curve of the red labeled epipolar is shown in Fig.3a. Using this definition and two threshold, the whole image can be divided into three regions: strong textured, weak textured and textureless regions.

4.3   Reliable FX-Dominant Matching

This step follows the notion of FX-dominant defined by Sara [12]. The key of this notion is the uniqueness constraint which means each point may be matched with at most one point in the other image, and the ordering constraint which states the order of the matched points in the two epipolar line is the same. The latter one is not always true, but it is reasonable for most cases, especially indoor scene. The FX-region of a certain matched pair (i, j) in the MZNCC matrix is defined as the set of pairs that cannot coexist with (i, j) without violating these two constraint:

$$FX(p) = \{q = (k, l) | (k \geqslant i \wedge l \leqslant j) \vee (k \leqslant i \wedge l \geqslant j) \wedge q \neq p\} . \qquad (6)$$

It is formed by two opposite quadrants around (i, j) in the MZNCC matrix. And FX-dominant matching is to find pairs that has higher value than any pair in the FX-region.

However, due to noise and distortion, the selected FX-dominant pairs still can not ensure its reliability. We only choose pairs from the FX-dominant results which satisfy the condition that the difference of the MZNCC value of the pair and the second local maximum MZNCC of $FX(p) \cup p$ is higher than a threshold(we choose 0.15). The number

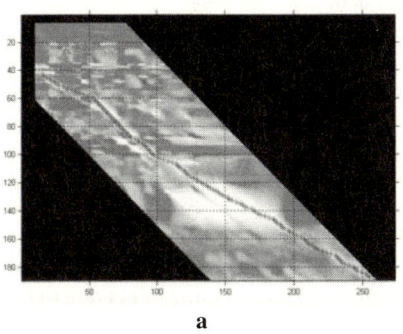

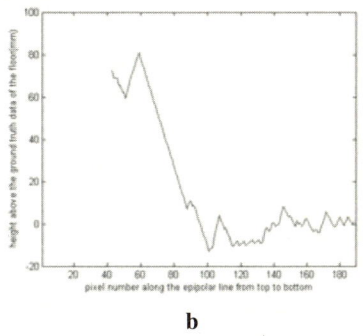

a   b

Fig. 5. Matching route in the MZNCC matrix via DTW(a) and depth curve for this epipolar(b)

of pairs chosen by such strategy is quite small(2–8 in our case), but it does make sense because FX-region of these pairs can be removed that the matching problem is divided into subproblems. Without this step, the next step of feature matching will find much less number of reliable matched features. The result of reliable FX-dominant matching is shown in Fig.3b, and the matrix with FX-region cut is shown in Fig.4a.

4.4   Feature Matching and Ambiguous Removal

In this step, firstly we plot the curve of the texture intensity for a given epipolar line and choose all local maximum as feature points(Fig.3a all points labeled red cross). For every feature point every matching pair with local maximum MZNCC higher than 0.7 is labeled as a candidate match(Fig.4a all labeled points). Then we select a combination of candidate matching pairs that obey uniqueness constraint and ordering constraint and has the highest sum of MZNCC(A feature point can be left unmatched with a zero contribution to the sum of MZNCC). The selected combination of illustrating epipolar shown in Fig.4a is labeled red and green. In this selected combination, still some ambiguous match candidates exist. We mean a selected candidate is unambiguous if it is the only choice without altering other matched feature points under uniqueness and ordering constraint, otherwise it is ambiguous. We will then remove all ambiguous feature points until no matched feature is ambiguous. In Fig.4a, the ambiguous match candidates are labeled green and they are to be removed from the feature matching result.

4.5   Dense Matching Via DTW

The remaining correspondences can be determined by dynamic time warping(DTW)[9]. A starting and an ending point should be known at first to use DTW. The matched feature points in the last step can naturally perform this role. Therefore, DTW can be applied to every range between adjacent matched feature points. This objective of DTW is achieved by finding a path with optimized energy function in a search space defined by the search range. The path is also restricted by the starting and ending point as well as the uniqueness and ordering constraint. The most important part is the definition

Table 2. The penalty item

	strong textured	weak textured	textureless
A	$-\lambda \cdot \mu \cdot max((0.7 - MZNCC), 0)$	$-\mu \cdot max((0.7 - MZNCC), 0)$	0
B	$-\sigma \cdot \lambda \cdot \mu \cdot max((0.5 - MZNCC), 0)$	$-\sigma \cdot \mu \cdot max((0.5 - MZNCC), 0)$	-MZNCC
C	-MZNCC	-MZNCC	-MZNCC

of the energy function. Unlike others straightforwardly use sum of intensity difference [9] or define the energy function with smoothness item(most formulation of smoothness cannot be directly used in our case because of the strong foreshortening effect due to the large baseline), we define our energy function in the form of sum of MZNCC value plus a penalty item aim to assign different weights to different points based on the texture level and matching confidence:

$$E = \sum MZNCC(i, j) + \sum penalty(i, j) . \tag{7}$$

where (i, j) is in the matching route. To define the penalty item, we make another classification of all points. A point is belong to Class A(high confidence) if the global maximum MZNCC value is higher than 0.7, Class B(low confidence) if the global maximum MZNCC is between 0.5 and 0.7, otherwise Class C(noise). Then the penalty item is defined as Table 2, where λ is the strong texture weight, μ is penalty level and σ low confidence weight(in our case, $\lambda = 4$, $\mu = 4$, $\sigma = 0.4$).

The result of DTW performed in the red labeled epipolar is shown in Fig.5a, the computed depth curve in Fig.5b. Fig.4b shows the MZNCC curve along the matching route and the global maximum MZNCC curve for the epipolar. From Fig.3a and Fig.4b, we can see the result route only deflect the global maximum MZNCC curve in textureless points and points belong to low confidence or noise, which is an expected result.

4.6   Post-processing

A postprocessing step replacing textureless match with interpolation is applied to get smooth surfaces. As in the textureless areas, the similarity value is ambiguous that the

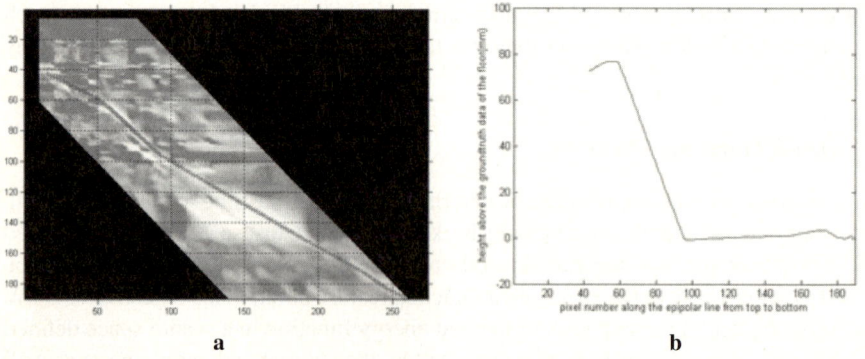

a   b

Fig. 6. Matching route after post-processing(a) and computed depth curve for this epipolar(b)

matching route can vary greatly with small energy variation. The result is the maximization of energy function does not necessarily correspond to the correct match, causing jagged depth map(Fig.5b). Easily observed, the textureless regions almost correspond to flat areas, we use two nearest textured(strong or weak) match to interpolate the textureless point. Fig.6 shows the matching route and depth curve after postprocessing.

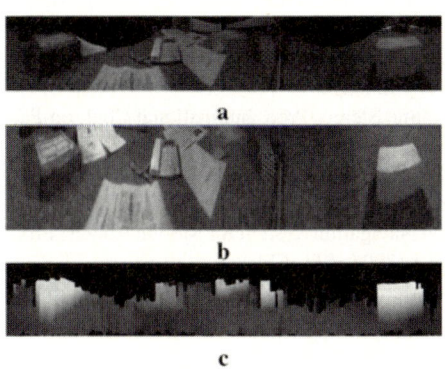

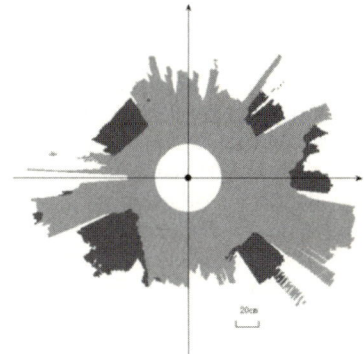

Fig. 7. Panoramic images unwrapped from the raw images of Fig.2b(a and b are converted by images via the below and upper mirrors respectively) and the detected depth map(c) corresponding to a

Fig. 8. Omnidirectional scene information obtained by our system, of which green represents navigable areas, red detected obstacle areas

5   Experimental Result

Fig.7c shows the result of the generated depth map via the proposed method. This depth map measures the height above the floor. The brightness of the map is proportional to the height, while black represents unknown areas. Although the ground truth map is unavailable, the real height can be surveyed accurately for most points. We randomly selected hundreds of points that can be measured and checked the error, found that most(about 95%) are smaller than 15mm, only slightly higher than the calibration error. We set the threshold of navigable areas as 25mm above the floor and get the navigable map in Fig.8.

6   Conclusion

We have developed a complete framework of automatically generating omnidirectional depth maps around a mobile robot using a novel designed panoramic vision sensor. We have presented the combination of feature matching and global matching for computational stereo. The experimental result is quite convincing. Although this method uses some thresholds and parameters, the matching result does not critically rely on them. However, the proportion of detected areas is a bit small in a few epipolar lines, we will try to improve on this problem using inter-epipolar consistency in our future work.

Acknowledgement. This work is supported by National Science Foundation of P.R. China under granted number 60575024.

References

1. Gluckman, J., Nayar, S.K., Thoresz, K.J.: Real-time Omnidirectional and Panoramic Stereo. Proc. DARPA Image Understanding Workshop (1998) 299–303
2. Ma, J.: Omnidirectional Vision Based Localization and Path Planning for Mobile Robots. Doctor Thesis of Beijing Instititue of Technology (2003)
3. Southwell, M.F.D., Basu, A., Reyda, J.: Panoramic Stereo. Proc. International Conf. on Pattern Recognition (1996) 378–382
4. Cabral, E.L.L., de Souza Jr., J.C., Hunold, M.C.: Omnidirectional Stereo Vision with a Hyperbolic Double Lobed Mirror. Proc. International Conf. on Pattern Recognition (2004) 1–4
5. Su, L., Zhu, F.: Design of a Novel Stereo Vision Navigation System for Mobile Robots. Proc. IEEE Conf. on Robotics and Biomimetics, Vol.1 (2005) 611–614
6. Luo, C., Su, L., Zhu, F., Shi, Z.: A Versatile Method for Omnidirectional Stereo Camera Calibration Based on BP Algorithm. Lecture Notes in Computer Science, Vol.3972 (2006) 383–389
7. Geyer, C., Daniilidis, K.: Conformal Rectification of Omnidirectional Stereo Pairs. Proc. IEEE Workshop on Omnidirectional Vision and Camera Networks 7 (2003) 1–6
8. Koyasu, H., Miura, J., Shirai, Y.: Mobile Robot Navigation in Dynamic Environment using Omnidirectional Stereo. Proc. IEEE Conf. on Robotics and Automation (2003) 893–898
9. Lee, Y., Kim, D., Chung, M.: Feature Matching in Omnidirectional Images with a Large Sensor Motion for Map Generation of a Mobile Robot. Pattern Recognition Letters, Vol.25 (4) (2004) 413–427
10. Felzenszwalb, P.F., Huttenlocher, D.P.: Efficient Belief Propagation for Early Vision. International Journal of Computer Vision, Vol.70, No.1 (2006) (to appear)
11. Devernay, F., Faugeras, O.: Computing Differential Properties of 3-D Shapes from Stereoscopic Images without 3-D Models. Proc. CVPR (1994) 208–213
12. Sara, R.: The Class of Stable Matchings for Computational Stereo. Research Report CTU-CMP-1999-22, Center for Machine Perception, Czech Technical University (2001)
13. Sara, R.: Finding the Largest Unambiguous Component of Stereo Matching. Proc. 7th European Conf. on Computer Vision, Vol.2 (2002) 900–914
14. Manduchi, R., Tomasi, C.: Distinctiveness Maps for Image Matching. Proc. International Conf. on Image Analysis and Processing (1999) 26–31

Enhanced 3D Interaction with Augmented Visual Information

Dongwook Lee and Jinah Park

Computer Graphics and Visualization Lab,
Digital Media Lab
Information and Communications University,
119 Munji-ro Yusong-gu Daejeon, Korea
{aalee, jinah}@icu.ac.kr

Abstract. As 3D graphics environment becomes the standards for most computer systems, it is natural to seek a 3D input device for manipulating an object in a 3D virtual world. Unlike 2D interface, however, 3D interface creates perceptual mismatches including depth perception problem. The objective of our research is to enhance the depth perception and 3D interaction by providing additional information based on the pictorial depth cues and interaction cues. In this paper, we investigated how to incorporate such cues. We designed two kinds of additional viewport that are to be placed on the top of the interaction window. One is a basic additional view with a different FOV, and the other is a compound view made up with 9 small sub-views with varying viewing direction. We also implemented two behaviors of the augmented view with respect to user interaction: Interactive Resizing and Holding-Z. Through a set of user performance tests, we have concluded that the basic additional view with Interactive Resizing and the additional compound view made statistically significant improvement on the performance of 3D interaction with a 3D input device.

Keywords: Virtual Environment, Human Computer Interaction.

1 Introduction

We live in a 3D world and interact with 3D objects in 3D environment using a tool in 3D space. Therefore, it should be natural for us to use a 3D input device for 3D virtual world. As a matter of fact, there are many 3D input devices available these days as an interaction medium of the virtual environment. However, use of 3D devices causes some perceptual problems that are not present when a 2D input device is applied. As contrary to our expectation that it is easier to interact with objects using a 3D input device, it takes an extra effort to pinpoint with the 3D input device in the 3D virtual space.

The visual environment in the real-world provides many sources of information about 3D space. These sources are usually called 'depth cues' and human perceives 3D space with these cues. Virtual environment also creates and provides these depth cues to a user. However, when we use a 2D display to depict the 3D virtual

Z. Pan et al. (Eds.): ICAT 2006, LNCS 4282, pp. 1293–1304, 2006.
© Springer-Verlag Berlin Heidelberg 2006

environment, there are critical differences between the depth cues created in real world and virtual environment.

The most distinguish one is the size of the area where the visual information gets displayed. The size of the visual field generated from regular virtual environment is limited to the size of the 2D physical display, and this size of the area is usually small, compared to the human's real visual field. To provide visual information more realistically, in this small area, the virtual environment must provide perspective viewing frustum which has the field of view (FOV) ranged from 40 to 60 degree. Compared to the human's FOV, which is about 150 degree with binocular vision, the FOV of virtual environment is very narrow, and it can limit the visibility and linear perspective. Due to the limited display size, the virtual environment assumes that the direction of the user's visual field is always placed at the center of the screen. Therefore, if a user wants to move or rotate his or her way of direction, he or she needs to do some additional action to accommodate the change explicitly. Otherwise, in the sense of interaction, it may affect against user's performance.

In this paper, we address these limited visual representations as the reason to the depth perception problem and reduced interaction. To solve the problem, we tried to correct the visual representation by providing additional visual information. The additional visual information was generated based on the depth and interaction cues which were poorly represented by the differences mentioned before.

Our target environment is arm-ranged virtual environment where the objects in the world are reachable by moving his or her arm or hand. This environment is one of the most vigorously researched areas among the virtual environment using 3D input devices. There are various types of 3D input device categories: Mouse Based 6 DOF (Degree of Freedom) Input, Flying Mice, Desktop Devices and Multi-DOF Armatures [2]. In our research, we focused on the multi-DOF armatures which provide a stylus based on joint and arm.

2   Related Work

There have been many research works on the depth perception of human. As an example, Geoffrey [6] showed how shadows, stereoscopic and other visual cues affect human depth perception by experimenting spatial tasks.

One of the most important components of the depth cues is related to FOV, which has been examined by many researchers for its effect on virtual environment. Mainly, there are two different approaches about FOV: regular 2D display [13] and Head Mounted Display (HMD) [14]. Because FOV is one of the main components for the viewing frustum, it is important to find out the optimal FOV and display pixel size for the specific display or application. Generally, like the FOV of human, higher FOV makes better performance. However, due to the minimization effect which is caused by the limited size of display, regular virtual environment has also limited degree of FOV [13]. It is possible to reduce problem of depth perception, by modifying, enhancing or adding one or more depth cues. Shumin et al. [3] adapted semi transparency to a cursor in 3D space to recognize the position of other objects in 3D space more efficiently. Adding a shadow to the 3D cursor also notably enhances depth perception of a user [4]. Jodie et al. [7] studied the depth perception of real world and virtual world, and they showed that a large screen immersive display is better than HMD about the human depth perception. Non-photorealistic Rendering (NPR) technique of computer graphics can be enhancement method for depth perception. By applying NPR to virtual or real scene, the visual characteristics of depth cues can be enhanced, and consequently help human depth perception [5]. The position and direction of a camera also considered as a research topic. Camera in hand metaphor, adapting the cursor position as the position of a camera, was suggested by Joan and Karin [9]. Unlike our approach, there was only one viewport in Camera in hand metaphor. We considered their approach may useful for the interaction method. However, it is not enough to enhance depth perception, together. Karan et al. [8] proposed to produce visual information by data mining of the camera position. By applying the data mining method to collecting the position of camera, they suggested various scene making schemes.

We can also relate our research with information visualization field as it creates a way to display the produced visual feedback to a user. Fisheye view, which is also known as Focus+Context method, was mainly studied to produce both detail and context of visual information. [10]. Scott [11] tried to reinforce navigation performance of a user by distorting 3D information. Information visualization is also concerned with user's ROI. Focus+Context method distorts the information area according to the user's input which is considered as user's ROI. By interactively changing the area size of distortion, Carl [12] improved fisheye view. He adopted the velocity of a user's cursor as the criterion of the interaction.

3 Method

The objective of our research is to enhance the depth perception and 3D interaction by providing additional information based on the pictorial depth cues and interaction cues. The additional visual information that we try to provide a user consists of four main features: depth context, minimizing distortion, 2D context and realistic interaction. Based on pictorial depth cues, we applied higher FOV and compounded FOV to bring more depth context while minimizing distortion. Two dimensional context and realistic interaction were achieved by implementing Focus+Context method and fixing view position, respectively.

The additional visual information was implemented with OpenGL, and PHANToM® Omni™ haptic device was used as a 3D input position device. We implemented two additional views: Basic Additional View and Compound View, and two behaviors of the view: Holding Z and Interactive Resizing.

3.1 Additional Views

Instead of using just one viewing frustum focused at the center of the screen, we attached another viewport to the virtual environment which already has its own viewport. By doing this we can obtain two different scenes of virtual environment at the same time. One of the advantages of having this additionally created scene is that the user performance of interaction can be enhanced when a user interacts with the virtual environment displayed towards the edges of the screen.

If a user interacts with virtual environment at the peripheral region of the screen, the tasking can be disturbed by the far distortion of the perspective viewing frustum. Therefore, when a user should perform some tasks at the edges of the screen, he or she has to move or rotate the viewport or virtual environment. However, by applying another viewport to the virtual environment, we can change the center of viewport in the screen. This makes a user can freely remove perspective distortion caused by far peripheral vision, which is positioned at the edges of the viewport.

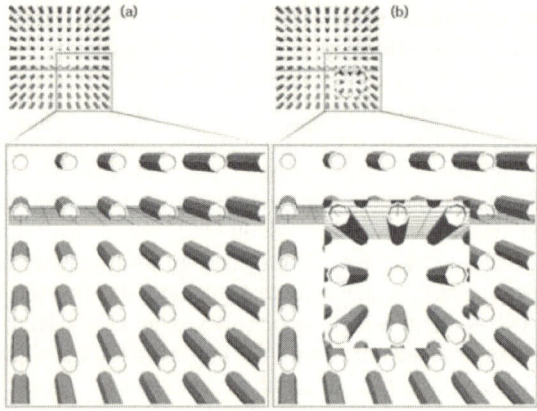

Fig. 1. The distortion of far peripheral vision (a) and two different viewports in one image (b)

Fig.1 shows the effectiveness of additional view. In Fig.1, arrays of stick shaped objects arranged parallel to z-axis. The right-lower side is shown in magnified scale. The perspective distortion gains strength as the pixel position of the projected image moves towards the edges of the screen as shown in Fig.1(a). Fig. 1(b) shows the additional view, which corrects the distortion, is overlaid on the top of the window.

In the aspect of depth cues, we want to create more realistic depth context than regular virtual environment. The depth context, what we are mentioning here, is the continuous visual information of the environment about z-axis.

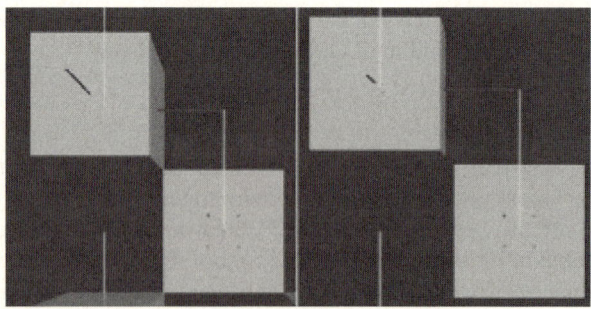

Fig. 2. Different depth context from 60 degree of FOV (left) and 20 degree of FOV (right)

Fig.2 indicates the differences of depth context caused by different FOVs. In this figure, we can see more information about z-axis when we use bigger degree of FOV. Therefore, if we want more the depth context from the virtual environment, we need to apply higher degree of FOV.

The depth context is two-edged blade, because of its peripheral vision and perspective distortion. As we mentioned it before, far peripheral vision creates perspective distortion, which can lead performance reduction and depth context at the same time. To obtain the depth context and to minimize distortion at the same time, we subdivided the viewing area of the additional view. Each smaller viewport has lower FOV so that the distortion is reduced. These smaller viewports are combined into one view which we call *a compound view*. Then the compound view adds up FOV of its component viewport, creating bigger FOV to provide better depth context.

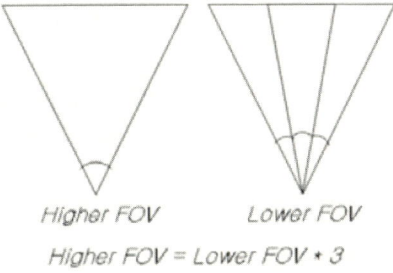

Higher FOV   *Lower FOV*

*Higher FOV = Lower FOV * 3*

Fig. 3. Concept of the compound view

Fig.3 shows the basic concept of a compound view. By placing the viewing frustums which have identical FOV at the same position and rotating them about their FOV, we can achieve higher depth context.

The Additional Views are implemented based on the depth cues. Therefore, the purposes of the Additional Views are more focused to enhance depth perception.

Basic Additional View is the most fundamental implementation of additional view. The purpose of this view is to obtain the depth context of the scene, and we applied

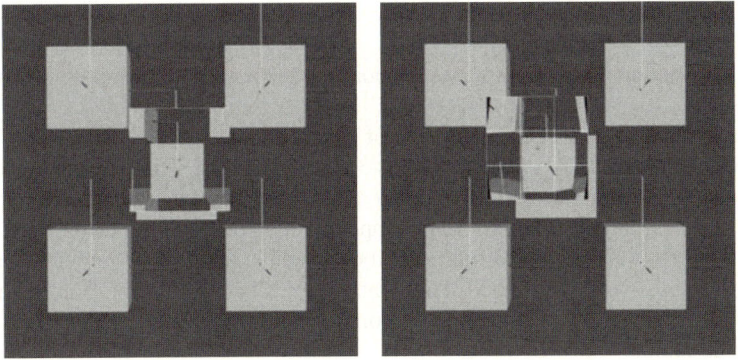

Fig. 4. Screenshot of Additional View (left) and Compound View (right)

multiple FOV. The FOV of virtual environment is 20 degree, and the FOV of Additional View is 60 degree. The left side of Fig.4 is a snapshot of the application using Basic Additional View. We can see the far peripheral vision at the edges of the screen have reduced by overlapping the image created by Basic Additional View.

Our next additional view is the Compound View which is specialized to obtain the depth context while minimizing the distortion. The right side of Fig.4 shows a snapshot of the window applied a compound view.

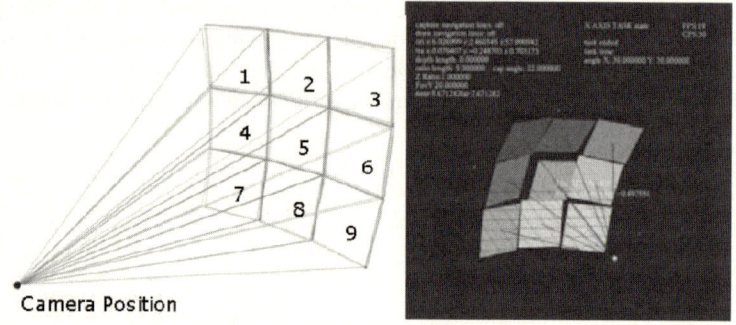

Fig. 5. Camera arrangement of Compound View

As shown in Fig.5, the compound view consists of nine cameras and projected images. The positions of camera for each compound views are same; they are all placed at the right behind of the cursor, while the viewing directions are rotated about x-axis and y-axis to create depth context of higher FOV.

The rotated angle for each views of compound view is based on the degree of FOV and the compound number. Equations (1) through (4) show how to calculate the rotation angles as follows.

$$n = \frac{HigherFOV}{CompoundFOV} \tag{1}$$

$$\text{Compound Number: from 1 to } n^2 \tag{2}$$

$$\text{Rotation by x-axis: ((Compound Number–1)\%n–n/2)*CompoundFOV} \tag{3}$$

$$\text{Rotation by y-axis: (n/2–(Compound Number–1)/n)*CompoundFOV} \tag{4}$$

Compound View shown in the right side of Fig.4 has 60 degree of HigherFOV and 20 degree of CompoundFOV. Therefore, n is 3 and Compound Numbers are from 1 to 9. Rotation of x-axis for Compound Number 1 is -20 degree and can be calculated with (3). Likewise, rotation of y-axis for Compound Number 1 is 20 degree and can be calculated with (4). Due to the rotation process, some parts of the projection areas of additional views were overlapped. To maintain the 2D context in the Compound View, we need to remove this overlapped region. By shifting pixels, we can remove the overlapped region.

3.2 Behaviors of Additional Views

The additional view is created at the tip of the 3D cursor, and is placed at the cursor position on the display window. When user moves the 3D cursor, the additional view shows corresponding view as if the 'eye' is placed at the tip. Apart from the construction of additional view, we also defined the behavior of the additional view. Differing from the traditional fixed view which is fixed in place, the additional view has its own position and size in the display. Therefore, we need to form the scheme for position and size of additional view. The interaction cues for our solution: 2D context and realistic interaction were applied to set the behavioral scheme of additional view.

We first explain the placement of images. As the viewport of virtual environment creates the image of the scene, the additional view also creates the image of the scene. We need to find out the proper location where this image will be placed. Because the user's ROI is where the user is focusing and interacting, we want to position the image of additional view at the user's ROI. And we adopted the position of 3D input device as the user's ROI. Generally, a user's ROI is considered as a spot where a user is seeing, and this spot can be extracted through the method like gaze tracking. However, the cursor of 3D input device can also be considered as a user's ROI due to the directness between a user and the 3D input device. Furthermore, using the position of a cursor as user's ROI is widely used in various fields like information visualization [10][11][12] and interaction [9]. Therefore, we applied the 2D projected position of the 3D input device as a user' ROI to enhance the interaction between virtual environment and the 3D input device. One another interaction cue we applied to create additional visual information is the speed of the user's cursor. When a human focuses to something or somewhere, he or she barely moves his or her sight. If a human find something or somewhere, the velocity of his or her sight increases. This basic human behavior was implemented as the size for the image of the additional view. If the velocity of user's cursor gets fast, the size for the image of the additional view gets smaller. Conversely, if the velocity gets slow, the size gets larger.

This feature of interactivity was implemented by Interactive Resizing. Interactive Resizing, here we implemented, is literally the rule for the size of the additional view. As like human behavior for the interaction and ROI, our Interactive Resizing controls the size of additional view according to the user's interaction behavior.

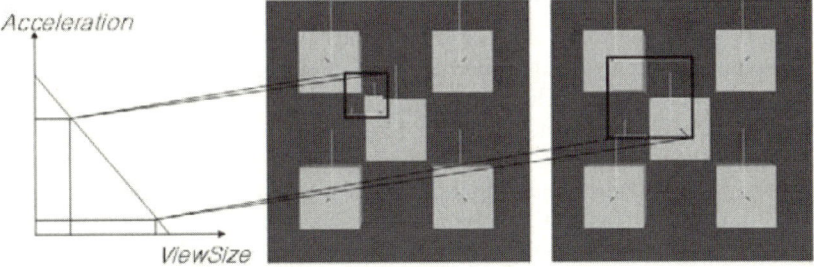

Fig. 6. Construction of Interactive Resizing

Fig.6. shows the Interactive Resizing scheme. It changes the size of additional view according to the acceleration of the cursor which is moved by user. The size of additional view and the acceleration of the cursor are in inverse proportion.

As we tried to obtain the depth context from viewport, we need to maintain 2D context of a scene for the enhancement of interaction. Like depth context, 2D context is the continuous visual information about x and y-axis. If the additional image from additional view overlapped to the user's ROI, the position of the cursor, it may conceal the image from the viewport of virtual environment and create discontinuity about 2D image. To prevent the discontinuity and recover the 2D context, we need to make the 2D image of additional view looks similar to the image of virtual environment. By holding the position about z-axis of the additional view, we can create the similarity about 2D image and maintain 2D context.

By fixing the z-position of additionally mounted viewport, we can obtain 2D context. To fix the position of viewport, we need to calculate the optimal z-axis position according to the position of the view for the environment and the size of the display.

4 Experiments

We address that additional information based on the pictorial depth cues and interaction cues would enhance the depth perception and 3D interaction, and we suggested to augment views and to define interaction behavior. To prove the advantage of our solution about to the problems, we set and performed some user tasks. The objective of user tasks is to evaluate either our suggested additional visual information can reduce depth perception problem and enhance the 3D interaction or cannot. Therefore, the user tasks are based on two aspects. First one is to evaluate depth context performance, and second one is to evaluate interaction performance. To evaluate our additional visual information, we compared the performance of tasks with and without additional visual information. Without additional visual information, the virtual environment has only one viewing frustum with 20 degree of FOV, and this will be called as 'Regular Virtual Environment'.

The performance of the tasks under the condition of Regular Virtual Environment was compared with 'Added View Virtual Environment' which is the virtual environment with additional visual information. Added View Virtual Environment consists of five different views: Basic Additional View (View #1), Basic Additional View + Interactive Resizing (View #2), Basic Additional View + Holding Z (View #3), Basic Additional View + Interactive Resizing + Holding Z (View #4) and Compound View (View #5). The Basic Additional View had 60 degree of FOV, and the behaviors of view were applied to Basic Additional View to evaluate their performance enhancement. The CompoundFOV and HigherFOV for the Compound View were set to 20 degree and 60 degree, respectively.

Our first task is ABT (Axis Based Task) which has the purpose of evaluation of the depth perception. During the tasking time, a user touched the start point and end point with 3D input device, as fast and precise he or she can. The distance between start point and end point is 150 millimeter in real world, and their positions are in same axis: x, y or z. Box-shaped reference objects were placed at the side of each point and the center of the screen for the user's positioning.

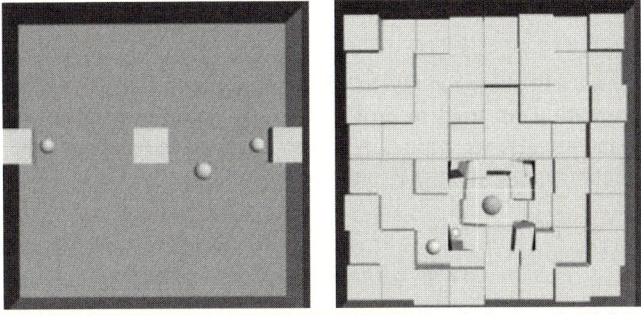

Fig. 7. Screenshot of ABT (left) and HCT (right)

The left figure of Fig.7 shows the snapshot of ABT. The red sphere on the right side of picture and the blue sphere on the left side of picture indicates the start point and end point, respectively. Another blue sphere near the center is the position of cursor. The white box-shaped reference object can be seen at the side of the points and center of the screen.

HCT (Height Choice Task) is similar to the ABT at the aspect of pointing. Using 3D input device, a user touched the goal point on the screen as fast and precise he or she can. Once a user touched the goal point, next goal point appeared at the different position. The distance between current goal point and next goal point is over 150 millimeter in real world. There are eight different x and y positions and three z positions for the goal point, and box-shaped reference object is placed behind of goal point. However, unlike the ABT, the goal points of HCT do not aligned to the axis. Therefore, the track of 3D input device is not dependent on the specific axis. This makes the HCT be more real-like task than ABT. We set the HCT to evaluate the additional visual information in the circumstance of real-like tasks. The right figure of Fig.7 is snapshot of the HCT. Blue sphere and red sphere indicate the goal point and cursor point, respectively. The white box-shaped reference object let the user know the approximate depth position.

There were four subjects who are all males and have no deficiency in 3D perception. Before start the tasks, all subjects had training time for every circumstances. For every tasks subjects performed we collected the elapsed time and distance error. The elapsed time is the time amount to perform each task in second, and distance error is the distance between goal object and cursor in millimeter. We gathered elapsed time to evaluate the efficiency of interaction and measured distance error to evaluate the correctness of interaction.

To evaluate the result more statistically, we applied t-Test to analyze the results. There are six main components for the t-Test: Null Hypothesis, Alternative Hypothesis, t-statistic, P value, critical value and level of significance. While, null hypothesis is the general knowledge what we try to decline, alternative hypothesis is the hypothesis what we want to prove. If t-statistic is bigger than critical value and P(T<=t) value is smaller than the level of significance whose value is 0.05, than we adopt alternative hypothesis.

5   Results

In this section, we will show the results of our experiments and the analysis of on the additional information we tried to provide. To evaluate the result of user task more correctly and statistically, we applied t-Test to evaluate the elapsed time and distance error. After briefly representing the statistical results, we will discuss the meaning of them.

Table 1. The Adoption of t-Test

		View #1	View #2	View #3	View #4	View #5
Elapsed Time of ABT		Null	Alternative (0.230611)	Null	Null	Alternative (0.047419)
Distance Error of ABT		Null	Null	Null	Null	Alternative (0.165443)
Elapsed Time of HCT		Alternative (0.633421)	Alternative (0.982212)	Alternative (1.204267)	Alternative (1.484923)	Alternative (0.545589)
Distance Error of HCT		Null	Alternative (0.258802)	Null	Null	Null

Table 1. is the brief results of t-Test. The view numbers were represented and explained at the Experiments section. While 'Null' of the table means the t-Test adopted null hypothesis, 'Alternative' means the t-Test adopted alternative hypothesis. Numbers followed after 'Alternative' show how the additional views were strongly affected. We used these values as the power of degree.

We expected that the Basic Additional View, which was constructed based on the depth context, will enhance the depth perception. However, the results show that applying Basic Additional View without other interaction cues (View #1) does not enhance the depth perception. Basic Additional View itself was effectively activated only with HCT which is more real-like task. This is because of the number of the reference objects shown in the screen, we assumed. As the number of the reference objects grows, the additional view can provide more depth context. And this leads user performs better, as we intended. However, it is true that applying mere Basic Additional View is incomplete to enhance depth perception and 3D interaction.

By applying Interactive Resizing which is one of our interaction cues, we expected the enhancement of 3D interaction. As the table shows, the results of applying Interactive Resizing (View #2) increased user performance highly. In the aspect of power of degrees, View #2 shows most successful results among the additional visual information. However, t-Test for Distance Error of ABT did not adopted alternative hypothesis, which means the Interactive Resizing is not enough to convince at the view of correctness. We assume that this adoption was caused by the distortion of the depth, which was not covered by depth context.

The t-Test of ABT using Basic Additional View with Holding Z (View #3) adopted Null hypothesis, which means performed poorly than Regular Virtual Environment. This unexpected results are because by the characteristics of Holding Z interaction. By applying Holding Z to Basic Additional View, we fixed the position of z-axis of the additional view, and hindered far peripheral vision, at the same time. And this combination made the additional view looks like Regular Virtual Environment. The actual decrease of performance was occurred when the objects were aligned on the z-axis and concealed the additional view. However, the purpose of Holding Z interaction was significantly proved on the results of HCT which is more real-like task. t-Test result of Elapsed Time of HCT is alternative and its power of degree was very strong. This is caused by the purpose of Holding Z, to acquire 2D context.

The result of Basic Additional View with Interactive Resizing and Holding Z (View #4) at the same time are similar to the before ones, because of the effectiveness of Holding Z.

t-Test for Compound View (View #5) shows another successful results of the Added View Virtual Environment. According to the results of user task, Compound View is most useful for the depth perception and 3D interaction. These results of Compound view are caused by its characteristic: Bigger peripheral vision with minimizing distortion. With wide peripheral vision the view can provide more depth context to a user. By reducing the problem of wide peripheral vision with multiple views with lower divided viewing angles, we can enhance the depth perception and 3D interaction at the same time.

6   Discussion and Conclusion

In this paper, we addressed that the source of the depth perception problem and reduced 3D interaction was the limited visual information of the virtual environment. To solve this problem, we considered two different aspects: human's depth perception and interaction. In the aspect of depth perception, we tried to apply depth context and minimizing distortion which are caused by the far peripheral vision. From the interaction cues, realistic interaction and 2D context were adopted. In the implementation, the depth cues were applied as the additional view which has more depth context and the interaction cues were adopted to control the behavior of the additional view. To evaluate the necessity of the additional visual information, we performed several experiments which are related to the depth perception and 3D interaction. As a result, we can find out that the additional visual information aids human's depth perception and 3D interaction.

One of the contributions of our research is that it is based on both depth perception and 3D interaction. Compare to other related work, our research applied two different regions to enhance depth perception and 3D interaction at the same time. Consequently, the experimental results of the additional visual information proved the effectiveness of our approach. Another contribution is the development process of the additional views. The advantage of applying additional view does not only proper to the enhancement of the 3D interaction, but also aid other region like information visualization.

Our next research will be focused on the acquisition of 2D context and depth context at the same time. We already tried to obtain 2D context and depth context at the same time by using Holding Z method. However, the result of simple 'holding z-axis' procedure limited the visual information. We assumed the relational distance between the additional view and the objects of virtual environment should be considered for the 2D context, and by applying this approach, we can acquire more precise 2D context and depth context at the same time for the enhancement of the 3D interaction.

Another future work is to deal with large-scale VE using stereoscopic. We did not include stereoscopic as our depth cues, because it is binocular depth cue, not pictorial depth cue. In the next research we have a plan to extend the range of depth cues to the binocular, using stereoscopic. We also have a plan to apply the additional visual information to the large-scale VE. Because of the mechanism of the human perception, we expect our approach will increase the 3D interaction of the large-scale VE.

Acknowledgments. This research was supported by the MIC (Ministry of Information and Communication), Korea, under the Digital Media Lab. support program supervised by the IITA (Institute of Information Technology Assessment).

References

1. Colin Ware, Information Visualization (Second Edition), Morgan Kaufmann Publisher 2004
2. Shumin Zhai, User performance in relation to 3D input device design, ACM SIGGRAPH Computer Graphics 1998
3. Shumin Zhai, William Buxton, Paul Milgram, The Partial-Occlusion Effect: Utilizing Semitransparency in 3D Human-Cumputer Interaction, Proceedings of ACM Transactions on Computer-Human Interaction, Volume 3, Issue 3, September 1996, pp. 254 – 284
4. Scott E. Hudson, Adding Shadows to a 3D Cursor, ACM Transactions on Graphics Volume 11, Issue 3, July 1992, pp. 193 - 199
5. Amy Ashurst Gooch, Peter Willemsen, Evaluating Space Perception in NPR Immersive Environments, Proceedings of 2nd International Symposium on Non-Photorealistic Animation and Rendering, 2002, pp. 105 - 110
6. Geoffrey S. Hubona, Gregory W. Shirah, Darniet K. Jennings, The Effects of Cast Shadows and Stereopsis on Performing Computer-Generated Spatial Tasks, IEEE TRANSACTIONS ON SYSTEMS, MAN, AND CYBERNETICS, 2004
7. Jodie M. Plumert, Joseph K. Kearney and James F. Cremer, Distance Perception in Real and Virtual Environments, APGV 2004
8. Karan Singh, Ravin Balakrishnan, Visualizing 3D Scenes using Non-Linear Projections and Data Mining of Previous Camera Movements, AFRIGRAPH International conference on Computer graphics, 2004
9. Joan De Boeck, Karin Coninx, Haptic Camera Manipulation: Extending the "Camera In Hand Metaphor", EuroHaptics, 2002
10. Manojit Sarkar, Marc H. Brown, GRAPHICAL FISHEYE VIEWS OF GRAPHS, Human Factors in Computing Systems, CHI'92 Conference Proceedings, 1992
11. Scott Vallance, Paul Calder, Context in 3D Planar Navigation, Australian Computer Science Communications, 2001
12. Carl Gutwin, Improving Focus Targeting in Interactive Fisheye Views, CHI'02 conference Proceedings, 2002
13. Michael Keller, Thomas Schenell, and Katherine Lemos, Pilot Performance as A Function of Display Resolution and Field of View in a Simulated Terrain Following Flight Task using a Synthetic Vision System, Digital Avionics Systems Conference, 2003
14. Kevin Arthur, 1996. Effects of Field of View on Task Performance with Head-Mounted Displays, CHI 1996, pp 29-30, 1996

Research and Application of Virtual Reality in the Field of Web-Based Education

Zhao Chengling and Zhang Zhaohua

Information Technology Dept. Central China Normal University,
Wuhan, Hubei, 430079, China
zzhua@163.com

Abstract. Virtual Reality is an artificial environment created with computer hardware and software. Because it can create an environment that it is similar with the real world, thus it can solve the request of the study media. Now there are four types of VR systems: immersion VR, desktop VR, Unencumbered VR and Telepresence. This article introduced the four types and discussed the application of every type in the field education. And also point out what education benefits from using Virtual reality. What's more, three main applications of VR in the field of network education were discussed. They are VR environment, VR laboratory and VR schooling. The emergence of VR would bring a profound influence VR to the education, and has a huge application prospect in the education domain.

Keywords: virtual reality; network education; virtual environment.

1   Introduction

Wbster's defines Virtual as "being such in essence or effect though not formally recognized or admitted" and Reality as "the quality or state of being real". Yet, the Virtual Reality is a computer simulation of a real 3-dimensional world, often supplemented by sound effects. People often associate virtual reality with a body suit and head gear that inclues an internal screen. The suit measures your body's movements and displays them on the screen. These computerized images can be simulated in any environment making you feel like you're really there. This is one interface; a more common use for VR is seen in many 3D computer games. Nowadays, VR is used in many fields, such as architecture, manufacturing, museums, visualization, medical, education and training. The emergence of VR would bring a profound influence to the education. This article mainly discussed the character and the types of VR, and the application of VR in the field of education.

2   Characteristic and Types of VR

Computer visualization is reshaping how scientists evaluate and explore their data and promises to transform how students learn. Within the past four decades,

Z. Pan et al. (Eds.): ICAT 2006, LNCS 4282, pp. 1305–1309, 2006.

dramatic advances in graphic display and high-end computing have made it possible to transform billions of bits of data into interactive, three-dimensional images that you can manipulate in real time. Here, all the display and feedback devices that make this possible are collectively termed "Virtual Environments." Grigore Burdea point that VR has three main characteristics in his book "Virtual Reality Technology. They are three "I"-Immersion, Interactivity and Imagination. There are four types of VR systems: immersion VR, desktop VR, Unencumbered VR and Telepresence.

2.1 Immersion VR

Immersion VR uses head mounted displays with one monitor for each eye, sound and position trackers to place the participant inside a virtual environment. The virtual world appears to respond to head movement in a familiar way (the way the natural world does: not at all) and in a way which differentiates self from world. You move and the virtual world looks like it stays still. The sense of inclusion within a virtual world, which this technology creates, has a powerful personal impact.

2.2 Desktop VR

Some systems, which call themselves VR, show 2-D or 3-D displays on a computer screen rather than using a head mounted display. Although they lack the immersion quality, they consist of computer-generated environments, which exist, in 3 dimensions (even if they are shown on a 2-D display). Because the worlds exist in 3 dimensions, users can freely navigate in 3 dimensions around in the worlds. Examples are BattleTech in Chicago, where users climb into cockpits and drive BattleMech robot warriors around a virtual world shown on their cockpit screen, blowing each other up. Another example of desktop VR is CAD packages like Virtus Walkthrough, which allow users to navigate around the 3-D worlds they have modeled. These forms of VR are less expensive and therefore more common than most of the other types. Flight simulators are another example, where participants "fly" though models of real or fantasy worlds, watching the world on a 2-D screen. FighterTown uses real Navy fighterplane cockpits with 2-D displays.

2.3 Second Person/Unencumbered VR

Unlike immersion VR, "unencumbered" VR systems involve real-time perceptions of and response to the actions of human unencumbered by helmets or gloves, wires or any other intrusive sensors or displays. Immersion VR simulates real world perceptions. You know you are "there" because sounds and images in the virtual world respond like the real world to your head movements. An alternative approach is what Michael Miller calls "second person VR," exemplified by some of the work of Myron Krueger (Kruger, 1991), Vivid Effects, and ENTER Corporation. In second person VR, you know you are there because you see yourself as part of the scene. On one side of the room, you stand in front of a blue background. You face a monitor and TV camera. On the monitor you see yourself, but instead of being in front of the blue background, the self you see is inside of a graphic or combined video/graphic virtual world. Edge detection software keeps track of your location and movement and allows you to interact with graphical objects on the screen. Rather than mimicking real world sensations, second person VR changes the rules, and relies strongly on a "seeing is believing" argument to induce a sense of being there.

2.4   Telepresence

Telepresence is a fourth major embodiment of VR. Telepresence VR uses cameras, microphones, tactile and force feedback and other devices linked to remote control capabilities to allow a participant at one site (e.g., an office building) to move their head or hands to control robots and sensors at a remote location (e.g., undersea or in space), experiencing what they would experience at that remote site. "Microteleoperation" uses a microscope and micromanipulator to give the operator a sense of presence and the ability to act in a microscopic environment (Robinett, 1992). Telepresence and other forms of VR sometimes are accomplished using "heads up displays" which superimpose the virtual display over real world sensory input.

3   VR-Related Technologies

Other VR-related technologies combine virtual and real environments. Motion trackers are employed to monitor the movements of dancers or athletes for subsequent studies in immersive VR. The technologies of 'Augmented Reality' allow for the viewing of real environments with superimposed virtual objects. Telepresence systems (e.g., telemedicine, telerobotics) immerse a viewer in a real world that is captured by video cameras at a distant location and allow for the remote manipulation of real objects via robot arms and manipulators.

4   Educational Benefits of Using Virtual Reality

In the premier edition of the VR in the schools newsletter published by the East Carolina University Virtual Reality and Education Laboratory (June 1995), Dr. Veronica Pantelidis gives a "top-ten" list for the reasons to use graphic-based VR in education. She also lists ten reasons for using text-based (network-based) VR, which at the time was all that was available prior to the now readiliy accessable VRML capabilities. The graphic-based benefits:

1. Provides motivation.
2. Can more accurately illustrate some features, processes, etc. than by other means?
3. Allows extreme close-up examination of an object.

4. Allows observation from a great distance.
5. Allows the disabled to participate in an experiment or learning environment when they cannot do so otherwise.
6. Gives the opportunities for insight.
7. Allows the learners to proceed through an experience at their own pace.
8. Allows the learner to proceed through the experience during a broad time period not fixed by a regular class schedule.
9. Provides experience with new technologies through actual use.
10. Requires interaction. Encourages active participation rather than passivity...

The text-based (network-based) VR benefits:

1. Encourages creativity
2. is motivating
3. Highly interactive
4. Provides social atmosphere
5. Allows passive student to become active
6. Allows student to experiment with different personalities
7. Allows student to take on role of persona in different cultures
8. Provides equal opportunity for communication with students in other cultures
9. Teaches computer skills
10. Builds keyboarding skills In all, when the technology of VR appears, it brings a great change to the education. Now we can realize Virtual space-time, Virtual content, Virtual study-equipment and Virtual character.

5   Application of VR in the Field of Network Education

5.1   Virtual Study Environment

With the technology of VR, we can build a study environment that is virtual. It is the same for this VR study environment, in which the studies are carried out fully or partly at a distance. It is in the virtual study environment where the participants of the study circle or the course "meet", that is where you work together on your impressions and experiences, test ideas and theories, get help to see the context etc. It is where you meet the experiences, interpretations, values and opinions of others. It is in this virtual study environment where you together transform more or less fragmentary information into meaningful knowledge.

5.2   Virtual Laboratory

The Virtual Laboratory is a platform where we can publish and discuss our research on experimentation in the life science, art, and technology. The shared virtual laboratory can be many things–part of a car design; the interior of an ancient cultural shrine that has fallen into ruin; the eye of a storm; or, some three-dimensional environment that does not physically exist. Collaborators enter the environment as "avatars"–life-like computer-generated representations. The environment transmits gestures as well as audio and video, so users have a greater sense of presence in the shared space than they would with other collaborative media. This adds a new dimension to virtual collaboration. In tele-immersion, participants are not talking about a molecule; they are standing inside it. They are not looking at a scale model of a car design; they are sitting in the driver's seat. They are not using telescopes to observe astronomical phenomena; they become bigger than our galaxy. Participants can change their size, can interactively change parameters on a supercomputing calculation, and can get "inside" their data. With tele-immersion, they can then work with colleagues to collectively study the impact of those changes. Enhanced with these capabilities, collaborators may choose to work virtually even if more traditional face-to-face meetings are possible.

5.3   Virtual Schooling

The term "Virtual Reality" is broadly used and widely interpreted. (Isdale 1993) On the Internet, VR is generally interpreted as artificial spaces that can be navigated in three dimensions and "feels" real. Virtual School is a school without gate and wall. It creates a virtual school that real school can share their resources and students can use them freely. In virtual school, an architect could "tour" a building he/she just created. An archaeologist could walk through a village that existed thousands of years ago. A geography student could visit the Gobi Desert, the Himalaya Mountains or perhaps the gulf coastal plains of Louisiana and "experience" the differences among environments.

6   Conclusion

VR cannot replace a field experience. It cannot infuse a student into an environment that has all the sights, smells and feeling the real location has, What now VR can do is create an experience that helps students better understand a place, a people, a process. But with the time pass by, the technology is advancing at such a rate that the entire real environment has the VR environment will be possible has! It will be a bran-new revolution to the education field!

References

1. Gail S. Ludwig (1996) "VIRTUAL REALITY: A New World for Geographic Exploration"
2. Grigore C. Burdea, Philippe Coiffet. Virtual Reality Technology [M]. Wiley -IEEE Press, 2003. 129 -135.
3. Carrie Heeter, Ph.D. The Thin Line: Hypermedia meets Virtual Reality. By Glenn Russell ? 2001, Glenn Russell.

Indoor/Outdoor Pedestrian Navigation with an Embedded GPS/RFID/Self-contained Sensor System

Masakatsu Kourogi[1], Nobuchika Sakata[1,2],
Takashi Okuma[1], and Takeshi Kurata[1,2]

[1] National Institute of Advanced Industrial Science and Technology (AIST),
Umezono 1–1–1, Central 2, Tsukuba, Ibaraki, 305–8568, Japan
m.kourogi@aist.go.jp
http://itri.aist.go.jp/rwig/ari/
[2] Tsukuba University, Tenodai 1–1–1, Tsukuba, Ibaraki, 305–0006, Japan

Abstract. This paper describes an embedded pedestrian navigation system composed of a self-contained sensors, the Global Positioning System (GPS) and an active Radio Frequency Identification (RFID) tag system. We use self-contained sensors (accelerometers, gyrosensors and magnetometers) to estimate relative displacement by analyzing human walking locomotion. The GPS is used outdoors to adjust errors in position and direction accumulated by the dead-reckoning. In indoor environments, we use an active RFID tag system sparsely placed in key spot areas. The tag system obviously has limited availability and thus dead-reckoning is used to cover the environment. We propose a method of complementary compensation algorithm for the GPS/RFID localization and the self-contained navigation represented by simple equations in a Kalman filter framework. Experimental results using the proposed method reveals that integration of GPS/RFID/dead-reckoning improve positioning accuracy in both indoor and outdoor environments. The pedestrian positioning is realized as a software module with the web-based APIs so that cross-platform development can easily be achieved. A pedestrian navigation system is implemented on an embedded wearable system and is proven to be useful even for unexperienced users.

1 Introduction

Wearable computing systems can be highly useful if the position and direction of the users are provided, which are one of the most essential pieces of contextual information. This paper aims at gaining the position and direction of pedestrians and providing personal navigation services.

In outdoor environments, the GPS is the most promising technology to acquire the position. However, the precision of the position can be degraded by several conditions and is sometimes unavailable since the GPS signals can be easily blocked by structures such as buildings. It is also difficult for the GPS

Z. Pan et al. (Eds.): ICAT 2006, LNCS 4282, pp. 1310–1321, 2006.

to achieve stride level precision for wearable systems which has strict limitation in size and weight of the hardware. We use a method of dead-reckoning [1] to complement precision and availability of the GPS. Dead-reckoning measures and analyzes human walking locomotion by self-contained sensors to estimate relative displacement.

In indoor environments where the GPS is unavailable, RFID technology is used to locate persons equipped with the active RFID tags. RFID tag readers are placed in key spots such as entrances and hallways so that the reader can acquire the position of each wearable system by detecting the ID signal from the tag. The wearable system will be notified of the position via wireless network. And combinational method of active RFID tag localization and dead-reckoning is described.

Ladetto et. al. proposed dead-reckoning method combining the GPS, digital magnetic compass and gyrosensors [3]. However, the method assumes that azimuth computed by differentiating two GPS results are available if needed. The GPS will easily become unavailable even in outdoor environments, especially on urban area where high-rise buildings block the signals from the satellites. The method also assumes that the earth magnetic field can be acquired at relatively high accuracy. However, if the user is equipped with many electronic devices that cause magnetic disturbance locally and dynamically, the magnetic compass will not give a good estimation of the user's azimuth. Schwartz et. al. proposed an indoor localization system based on an active RFID tag system and infrared beacons [4]. Although the proposed system works well in indoor environments, many IR beacons and RFID tags are required to cover the environments. Lee et. al. proposed a dead-reckoning method based on wearable inertial sensors [5]. The method, however, requires fine tuning for several thresholds most of which are experimentally acquired by repetitive trails, and thus has difficulty to exploit multiple external sources of information to be theoretically integrated.

We implement the proposed method as an embedded system to output position and azimuth of a user. A pedestrian navigation system for indoor/outdoor environments is constructed by coordination with the embedded system and external navigation applications. The first key contribution of this work is to propose a method to integrate estimation of position and direction by dead-reckoning, the GPS and the RFID tag system with a Kalman filter framework so that the method can be combined with other source of information as for user's position and direction. The second is to provide implementation of the method which realizes pedestrian navigation system usable both indoors and outdoors with an wearable embedded computing system. The implementation is built from software modules connected with each other by the web-based APIs and thus easily to be cooperated with other web-based applications.

2   Pedestrian Positioning in a Kalman Filter Framework

The pedestrian positioning can be achieved by detection and measurement of human walking locomotion characterized by its stride and azimuth, and updating the current position incrementally. We proposed a method of dead-reckoning in the Kalman filter framework [1]. In this method, the state vector s_t is written in the equation below:

$$s_t = [x_t, y_t, v_{x_t}, v_{y_t}]^T, \tag{1}$$

where (x_t, y_t) is the position of a user at discrete time t and (v_{x_t}, v_{y_t}) is its time derivative, that is the velocity vector. By analyzing acceleration vector (a_x, a_y, a_z) and angular velocity vector $(\omega_x, \omega_y, \omega_z)$ observed near the center of gravity of human body, its walking locomotion can be detected and measured. We proposed the method to detect walking locomotion and estimate the walking stride l_t [1]. Walking direction (azimuth) θ_t can be estimated by time integration of the angular velocity $(\omega_x, \omega_y, \omega_z)$ with adjustment of its cumulative errors by sensing the earth magnetic vector (m_x, m_y, m_z). We proposed the method in our past research [2].

It is supposed that the position and the velocity of the state vector can be observed, we obtain Kalman filter equations by the following:

$$s_{t+1|t} = s_t + K_t(O_t - s_t) \tag{2}$$

$$K_t = P_t(P_t + R_t)^{-1} \tag{3}$$

$$P_{t+1|t} = P_t - K_t P_t \tag{4}$$

where K_t is a Kalman gain, O_t is an observation vector, P_t is the error covariance matrix for the state vector, and R_t is the error covariance matrix for O_t. While no observation is acquired, the state vector s_t and its covariance matrix P_t are projected by the equations below:

$$s_{t+1} = F(\Delta t)s_t, \tag{5} \qquad F(\Delta t) = \begin{bmatrix} 1 & 0 & \Delta t & 0 \\ 0 & 1 & 0 & \Delta t \\ 0 & 0 & 1 & 0 \\ 0 & 0 & 0 & 1 \end{bmatrix}, \tag{7}$$

$$P_{t+1} = F(\Delta t)P_t F(\Delta t)^T + Q, \tag{6}$$

and Q is the error covariance matrix for the projection in the equation (5), and Δt is a discrete time interval between t and $t+1$.

If the observation vector O_t and its error covariance matrix R_{O_t} are obtained, these observation can be integrated into the estimation in the Kalman filter equations represented by (2), (3) and (4). In this paper, we will use dead-reckoning, the GPS and an active RFID tag system as sources of positioning information. Section 3 describes error model of the GPS and dead-reckoning and how these models are used to fuse the GPS into the proposed positioning method. In the section 4, we will introduce an error model of positioning by the active RFID tag system and describe how to use the positioning results in updating estimation in the proposed framework.

3   Error Models of the GPS and Dead-Reckoning

To construct error models for the GPS and dead-reckoning, we first categorize the positioning error in the GPS by the causes and then construct an error model for each source of error. Meanwhile, estimation error of relative displacement by dead-reckoning is modeled separately into direction and stride error.

3.1   Error of the GPS Positioning

Positioning error in the GPS is mainly caused by three factors: (A) error caused by multipath effect, (B) biased error caused by signal propagation delay, (C) unbiased random error [6][7]. GPS signals are degraded by multipath effect such as signal reflection and diffraction. Since the multipath effect has very localized cause it is difficult to construct a generalized model.

We determine if a positioning result of the GPS is degraded by multipath effect so as to be able to discard such degraded results. The determination of multipath effect is realized in combination with the dead-reckoning as described in section 3.3.

GPS signals are delayed when passing through ionosphere and convection sphere. Delayed signals increase pseudorange and thus cause biased error. The biased error is known to be constant locally if measured by the same set of satellites. Thus, any GPS positioning results can be compensated by observing the biased error at fixed known point where all of GPS satellites in the sky can be monitored. DGPS is bias monitoring and broadcasting service to provide the bias error and thus achieves more accurate positioning.

The remaining error can be considered as unbiased random error, which is white noise. Error variance σ_r^2 can be determined by the Horizontal Dilution of Precision (HDOP) value on geometrical arrangement of the satellites.

Therefore, a GPS positioning result $p_{gps}(t)$ free of multipath error can be described as follows:

$$p_{gps}(t) = p(t) + e_b(t) + e_r(t), \tag{8}$$

where $p(t)$ is the true position, $e_b(t)$ is the biased error, and $e_r(t)$ is the unbiased random error. Since $e_b(t)$ can be estimated at the fixed observation point, $p_{gps}(t)$ is handled using the Kalman filter framework.

3.2   Error of Dead-Reckoning

The dead-reckoning detects and measures relative displacement stepwise by analyzing human walking locomotion using self-contained sensors (accelerometers, gyrosensors and magnetometers). The process is shown below:

1. Estimate the moving vector d_i and the walking stride l_i.
2. Compute the i-th relative displacement vector $m_i = l_i d_i$.

By accumulating the relative displacement vector, the current relative position from the basis point can be computed.

To fuse the observation into the Kalman filter framework, the observation as for the position and the velocity are required. If user's walking locomotion is detected and its stride l_t, its time interval T required for walking and walking azimuth θ_t are obtained, we update the state vector and its covariance matrix by setting the observation $O_t = [\hat{x}_t, \hat{y}_t, \hat{v_{x_t}}, \hat{v_{y_t}}]^T$ is shown below:

$$O_t = [x_t + l_t \cos\theta_t, y_t + l_t \sin\theta_t, \frac{l_t \cos\theta}{T}, \frac{l_t \sin\theta}{T}]^T. \tag{9}$$

If no walking locomotion is detected within a fixed length of time, an observation that no movement has been made is obtained. Thus, the observation vector O_t can be written in the following equation:

$$O_t = [x_t, y_t, 0, 0]^T. \tag{10}$$

The estimated position has two types of error caused by dead-reckoning: error in estimation of moving direction d_i and error in stride l_i. The error model of positioning result in dead-reckoning is constructed in the following section.

We use a method of estimating the walking stride l_i and the moving direction d_i [1]. The error of l_i is known to have the normal distribution and the variance is proportional to the stride. The error of directional angle of d_i similarly is Gaussian and the variance σ_d^2 has already been determined by the repetitive experiments using the attitude reference system with high accuracy.

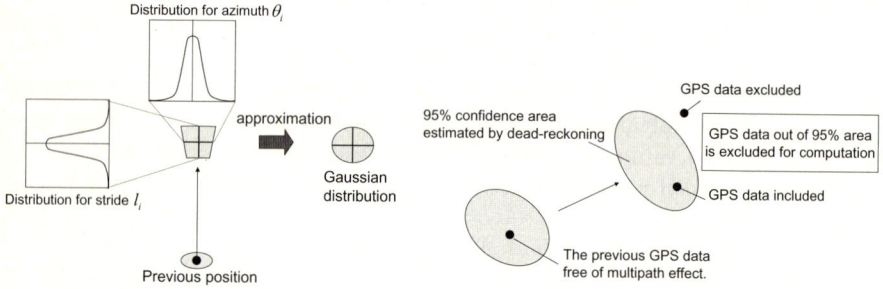

Fig. 1. Error distribution and its approximation by the normal distribution

Fig. 2. Sorting out GPS data with dead-reckoning

Considering the i-th walking step, the position after movement p_i has complex distribution as shown in Fig. 1. Since the standard deviation σ_d of moving direction is known to be 0.2–0.4 [deg], the arc region generated by the error of direction can be approximated to the tangent line. Therefore, the composition of the two types of error can be approximated by the Gaussian distribution whose axes are the tangent line and the radial line.

Suppose the i-th position (x_i, y_i) has the normal distribution whose mean vector is m_i and the covariance matrix is C_i, and the i-th moving unit vector (d_{x_i}, d_{y_i}) have Gaussian distribution whose mean direction is θ_i and variance is $\sigma_{\theta_i}^2$. The error of moving direction e_i can be approximated as Gaussian distribution along with the tangent line when the variance of direction $\sigma_{\theta_i}^2$ is small enough. This is equivalent to the approximation shown in Fig. 1. The mean vector of moving displacement vector (d_{x_i}, d_{y_i}) is $(\cos\theta_i, \sin\theta_i)$, and the error of direction e_i can be regarded as Gaussian whose mean vector is zero and variance is $(l_i \tan\sigma_{\theta_i})^2$.

The $i+1$-th position (x_{i+1}, y_{i+1}) can be written as a linear combination of these variables as shown below:

$$\begin{bmatrix} x_{i+1} \\ y_{i+1} \end{bmatrix} = \begin{bmatrix} x_i + l_i \cos\theta_i - e_i \sin\theta_i \\ y_i + l_i \sin\theta_i + e_i \cos\theta_i \end{bmatrix} = A_i \begin{bmatrix} x_i \\ y_i \\ l_i \\ e_i \end{bmatrix}, \tag{11}$$

where $A_i = \begin{bmatrix} 1 & 0 & \cos\theta_i & -\sin\theta_i \\ 0 & 1 & \sin\theta_i & \cos\theta_i \end{bmatrix}$.

If (x_i, y_i, l_i, e_i) is considered to have the normal distribution, the $i+1$-th position (x_{i+1}, y_{i+1}) is also Gaussian whose mean vector m_{i+1} and the covariance matrix C_{i+1} are expressed as the following equations:

$$\mathrm{m}_{i+1} = \mathrm{m}_i + l_i \boldsymbol{d}_i, \tag{12}$$

$$\mathrm{C}_{i+1} = A_i R_i A_i^T, \tag{13}$$

where R_i is the covariance matrix of $\begin{bmatrix} x_i & y_i & l_i & e_i \end{bmatrix}^T$. Since (x_i, y_i), l_i and e_i are independent with each other, the covariance between each variable is zero and R_i can be expressed as follows:

$$R_i = \begin{bmatrix} \mathrm{C}_i & 0 & 0 \\ 0 & \sigma_{l_i}^2 & 0 \\ 0 & 0 & (l_i \tan\sigma_{\theta_i})^2 \end{bmatrix}. \tag{14}$$

Therefore the estimated position (x_i, y_i) by dead-reckoning has Gaussian distribution whose mean vector m_i and its covariance matrix C_i are expressed in Equations (12)(13).

As for estimated velocity, the proposed method [1] gives Gaussian uncertainty of each estimation by the standard deviation σ_v on statistical basis. The error covariance matrix R_{DR} in equation (3) can be written in the following equation:

$$R_{DR} = \begin{bmatrix} \mathrm{C}_i & 0 & 0 \\ 0 & (\sigma_v \cos\theta_i)^2 & 0 \\ 0 & 0 & (\sigma_v \sin\theta_i)^2 \end{bmatrix} \tag{15}$$

3.3   Integration of the GPS and Dead-Reckoning

GPS estimation free of multipath effect shown in Equation (8) is Gaussian, and relative displacement estimated by dead-reckoning is Gaussian with Equations (12) and (13). Therefore, estimation by the GPS and dead-reckoning can be fused together in the Kalman filter framework.

As described earlier, GPS estimation degraded by multipath effect is not Gaussian. We therefore exclude GPS data out of the 95% confidence region estimated by dead-reckoning as outliers to reduce influence caused by multipath effect shown in Fig. 2.

The GPS estimation can be used in two ways: single positioning mode and differentiating mode of two positioning results (two positions and its elapsed time), which are required to be included in the 95% confidence region. In the former mode, a single GPS estimation is used to update the position by observation vector $O_{G_S} = [x_{gps}, y_{gps}, 0, 0]^T$, but not used to update the velocity. The variance of position σ_{G_S} is determined by HDOP (Horizontal Dilution of Position) value of the estimation. We therefore obtain the error covariance matrix R_{G_S} by the following equation:

$$R_{G_S} = \begin{bmatrix} \sigma_{G_S}^2 & 0 & 0 & 0 \\ 0 & \sigma_{G_S}^2 & 0 & 0 \\ 0 & 0 & \sigma_\infty^2 & 0 \\ 0 & 0 & 0 & \sigma_\infty^2 \end{bmatrix}. \tag{16}$$

The latter mode does not give absolute position but its moving direction θ_G and the speed v_G with lesser influence of biased error of the GPS than the former mode. The observation vector can be written below:

$$O_{G_D} = [(x_t + v_G \cos \theta_G), (y_t + v_G \sin \theta_G), v_G \cos \theta_G, v_G \sin \theta_G]^T. \tag{17}$$

Error of differentiation of two positioning results has same error characteristics as unbiased random noise explained in Section 3.1 since the differentiation cancels the biased error. Since error of moving direction θ_G is assume to be small,

$$R_{G_D} = \begin{bmatrix} (\sigma_{G_D} \cos \theta_G)^2 & 0 & 0 & 0 \\ 0 & (\sigma_{G_D} \sin \theta_G)^2 & 0 & 0 \\ 0 & 0 & c(\sigma_{G_D} \cos \theta)^2 & 0 \\ 0 & 0 & 0 & c(\sigma_{G_D} \sin \theta)^2 \end{bmatrix}, \tag{18}$$

where c is constant representing uncertainty of measurement of time T. However, it is noticed that two positioning results are required to be not so far to accurately estimate its velocity since it assumes linear movement of a user during the measurement.

4   Positioning by Active RFID Tag System

In indoor environments where the GPS is not available, we deploy an active RFID tag system of which each tag is held by user and RFID readers are placed on fixed position so that user's location can be determined by detecting the ID signal from the tag. A design for reachable distance of ID signals is especially important since the distance determines the ability to narrow down the range of location.

We assume the active RFID tag is attached at hip height (around 0.6m) and RFID tags and readers are designed to be detected within 1.5m. This design allows the RFID location system to acquire the position to a precision of 1.3m. Preliminary experiments reveal positioning error of the RFID location system has the normal distribution with standard deviation $\sigma_{tag} = 0.4$ [m].

Since the implementation of the RFID tag system allows the ID signals to reach too far to accurately estimate velocity of the user. Thus the observation vector O_t does not specify the velocity of a user but its position only. Then, the observation vector is provided if the ID signal is received by the reader placed at fixed position (x_{tag}, y_{tag}) and is written in the following equation:

$$O_t = [x_{tag}, y_{tag}, 0, 0]^T, \qquad (19) \qquad \mathrm{R}_{tag} = \begin{bmatrix} \sigma_{tag}^2 & 0 & 0 & 0 \\ 0 & \sigma_{tag}^2 & 0 & 0 \\ 0 & 0 & \sigma_{\infty} & 0 \\ 0 & 0 & 0 & \sigma_{\infty} \end{bmatrix} \qquad (20)$$

and the error covariance matrix R_{tag} is given by experimentally measured deviation σ_{tag} of reachable location.

5   Experiments

5.1   Implementation

We implemented the proposed method on an embedded computing system composed of a GPS module, self-contained sensors and a RFID tag as for sensory parts. The system outputs estimation of position and azimuth in the standard format called NMEA-0183 used by many of GPS receivers so that commercial navigation software can work with the output immediately. We use Google Earth for this purpose.

An outlook of our navigation system is shown in Fig. 3, and the schematic diagram of the system in shown in Fig. 4. We use ViewRanger (OS: NetBSD) from Japan SGI as an embedded computing system whose size is 95mm x 65mm x 33mm and weight of 130g. The GPS module in the system is a standard receiver using the L1 band and C/A coding by stand alone positioning with 12 channels. We use active RFID tags and readers (which use 303.2MHz band and provide 2400bps communication link) from Y-matic Inc, and 3DM-GX1 (3-axes accelerometers, gyrosensors and magnetometers) from MicroStrain Inc for self-contained sensors.

Our implementation is composed of software modules which are connected with each other by the web-based APIs so that cross-platform development can be easy to be achieved.

5.2   Experimental Results

We have conducted experiments on five users collecting sensory data from the self-contained sensors, the GPS receiver and the detecting log of the ID signal from the user's tag by the active RFID tag readers placed in the building where the users are passing through. In this experiment, each user equipped with the system walked outdoors and then went into the building, took an elevator from ground to the 3rd floor and entered to a room which is the destination. Total distance of walking path is 368.1 meter (outdoor: 247.2 meter, indoor: 120.9 meter). Two RFID readers are placed at the entrance (a windbreak room) to the building and the elevator hallway at the ground floor.

First, overall trajectories generated by the dead-reckoning only, GPS only and the proposed method (GPS/RFID/dead-reckoning integrated) and the ground truth data on one of the users are shown in Fig. 5.

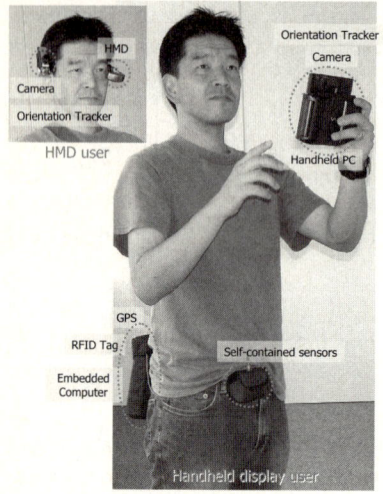

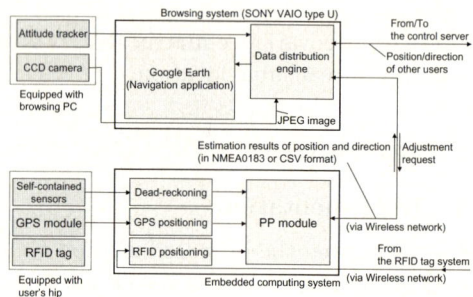

Fig. 3. Outlook of the pedestrian navigation system

Fig. 4. Diagram of the pedestrian navigation system

In this run of experiment, the GPS firstly gives stable positioning results with constant offset errors. Then dead-reckoning was severely degraded in the middle of experiments because of drift errors in gyrosensors. However, differentiation of GPS estimation fairly adjusted the bias and prevented the estimated position from far more deviation. The GPS signal has been useless at the half of walking distance outdoors because of multipath effect caused by the high-rise building. After the signal was lost, dead-reckoning and the RFID tag system adjusted and updated estimation of the position and the direction. Fig. 7 shows two positions where the RFID readers are placed and estimated position is appropriately adjusted by the RFID tag system. The trajectories in the 3rd floor is depicted in Fig. 8.

Averaged error of distance across the five users estimated by dead-reckoning (DR) only, GPS only and the proposed method are shown in Fig. 6. It is noticed that in outdoor environments GPS estimation improved positioning accuracy although the stand-alone GPS positioning has given less accurate positioning results since differentiation of GPS results were used to adjust errors in position and direction. In indoor environments, the RFID positioning pinpointed each user's location and drastically reduced errors in positions.

5.3   Practical Usage of the System in an Openhouse Situation

We have constructed the pedestrian navigation system for multiple users and a control center system which acts as a data exchange server for each user's location/direction. On the control center side, the real-time location of participants can be monitored and be intervened for adjustment if necessary. We deployed our

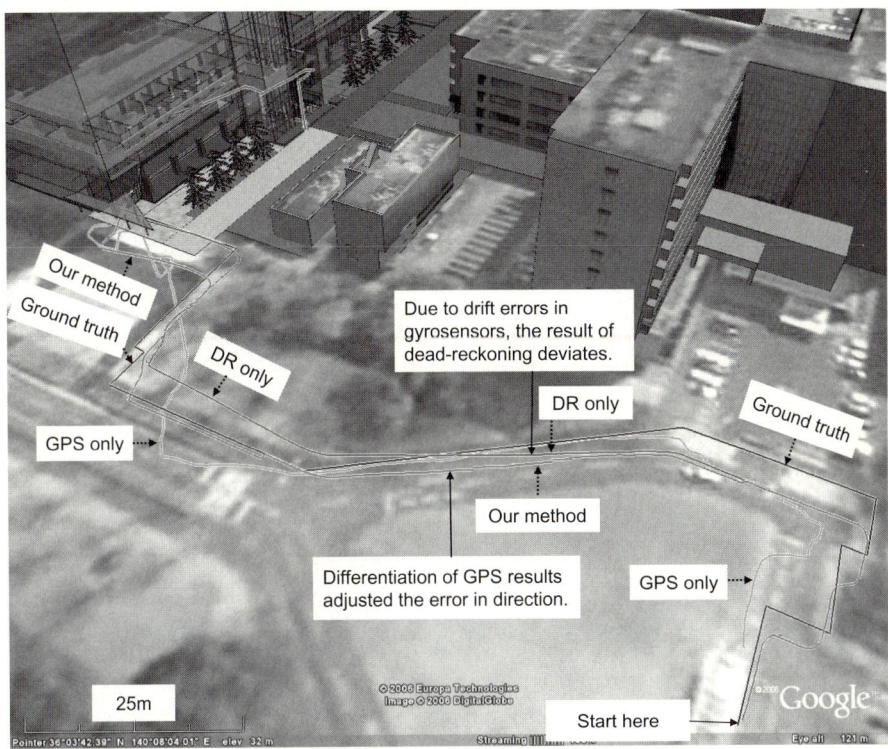

Fig. 5. Overall trajectories and surrounding environments

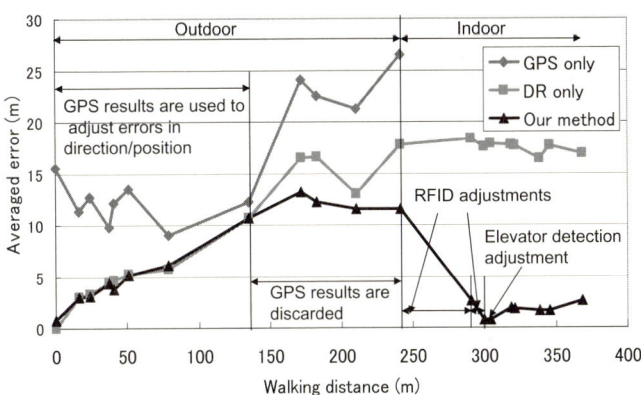

Fig. 6. Averaged errors across the five subjects in distance

system in a practical situation of the laboratory's openhouse with which many children participated. They were provided with our wearable systems with no prior experiences and very few adjustment (User's height is the only parameter

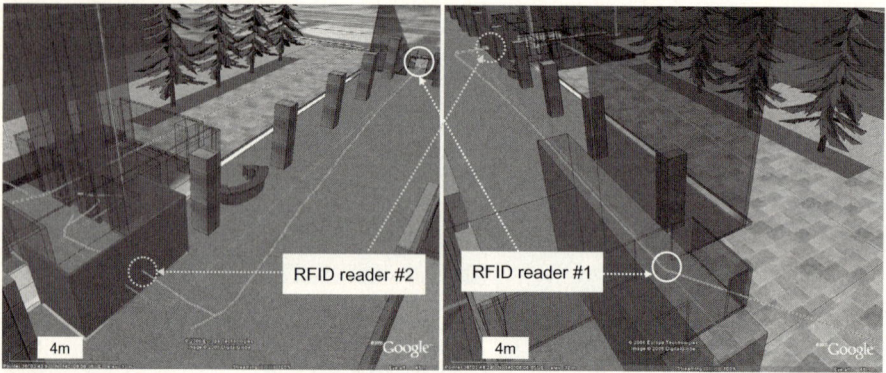

Fig. 7. Trajectories adjusted by the RFID tag system

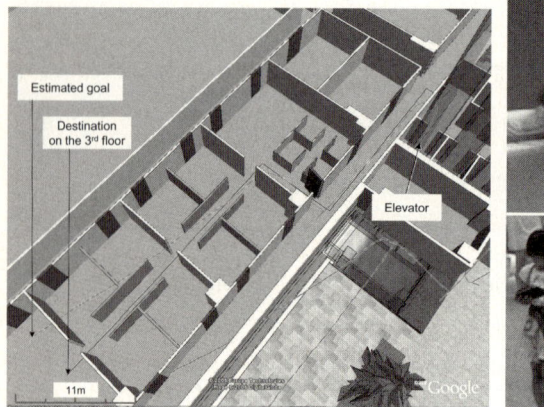

Fig. 8. The trajectories in the 3rd floor

Fig. 9. Kids playing with our pedestrian navigation system in the open-house

provided to the system). There were 23 participants (most of them are aged under 12 years) for this trial. Even with this situation, our systems have provided fair estimation (2–6m of error in position) of their location and direction. In this run of practice with some trouble of wireless network, our systems were forced to work in dead-reckoning-only mode. But good estimation has been obtained mainly because each participants has experienced with the system for limited span of time. Fig. 9 shows appearance of kids playing with our system.

The participants were interviewed shortly after the experiences and asked for comments on our system. Most of them noticed slight deviation from the ground truth since the detailed CG within the buildings were provided to comparison, but also commented that the deviation were not fatal for navigation. They also reported that the map heading-up function made their location easy to be recognized.

6   Conclusion

This paper describes the pedestrian positioning method to fuse dead-reckoning, GPS and RFID positioning within the Kalman filter framework. Error models of each positioning method are described in the simple equations that can be applicable to other sources of information as for location and direction to be integrated. The proposed method is implemented as software module with the web-based APIs on an embedded (and wearable) computing system. Experimental results show that GPS and the active RFID tag system seamlessly and effectively adjust estimation errors in dead-reckoning. The pedestrian navigation and control system are realized for multiple users and used in relatively practical situations where kids can play by the system without prior experience or complicated calibration.

References

1. M. Kourogi and T. Kurata, "Personal positioning based on walking locomotion analysis with self-contained sensors and a wearable camera," in *Proc. of IS-MAR2003*, pp. 103–112, 2003.
2. M. Kourogi and T. Kurata, "A method of personal positioning based on sensor data fusion of wearable camera and self-contained sensors," in *Proc. IEEE Conference on Multisensor Fusion and Integration for Intelligent Systems (MFI2003)*, pp. 287–292, 2003.
3. Q. Ladetto et. al, "Two Different Approaches for Augmented GPS Pedestrian Navigation," in *LOCELLUS2001*, 2001.
4. T. Schwartz, B. Brandherm and D. Heckmann, "Calculation of the User-Direction in an Always Best Positioned Mobile Localization System," in *Proc. AIMS2005*.
5. S. W. Lee and K. Mase, "Activity and Location Recognition Using Wearable Sensors," in IEEE Pervasive Computing, Vol. 1, No. 3, pp. 24–32, 2002.
6. B. W. Parkinson and J. J. Spilker, "Global Positioning System: Theory and Applications," American Institute of Aeronautics and Astronautics, Inc., 1996.
7. B. H. Wellenhof and H. Lichtenegger and J. Collins, "Global Positioning System, 5th edition," Springer-Verlag, 1992.

A Communication Model of Scents Mediated by Sense-Descriptive Adjectives

Yuichi Bannai[1,2], Masayuki Ishizawa[2], Hiroshi Shigeno[2], and Kenichi Okada[2]

[1] Canon Inc.
[2] Department of Computer Science and Informatics, Keio University

Abstract. Studies on olfactory communication using scents in addition to audio/visual information have recently become active. In a scent communication system, no representation scheme of scent information has been established due to lack of a basis for the smell. We introduced background scents that provide the ambience of image contents, and proposed a communication model for the background scents using sense-descriptive adjectives for association. The results of our experiments showed that the communication model is effective for enhancing the image contents.

1 Background

The five senses remote communication network, which exchanges messages through information obtained from the five senses, i.e. vision, hearing, touch, smell, and taste, has lately attracted much attention. The information recognized by the olfactory organs differs from that by the other four senses. The sense of smell powerfully affects humans since it is directly transmitted to the cerebral limbic system that governs emotions.

Although the information we acquire through the nose is much less than that through the eyes or ears, scent information has a major influence on how people feel. For example, feelings are intensified by adding a scent to images and sound, or a feeling of relaxation is produced by scents used in aromatherapy. Therefore, scent information is expected to further enrich communication media.

As scent information has no basis such as the RGB for image information, no scheme for representing scent information has been established. In open systems, the sender may find it difficult to describe a specific scent, and the receiver may not always get the desired scent due to the limitation of his/her diffuser. Consequently, it is necessary for both the sender and receiver to have an agreement on the scent information before communication.

We focus on the sensory impressions of scents instead of the precise reproduction of scents, and propose a model for communicating scents mediated by sense-descriptive adjectives (SDA).

In our model, we built a database containing SDA and their relation to the scents, and placed it on the Internet so that we could retrieve the scent information associated with the SDA. A contents creator can add a scent to an image using the SDA instead of putting the specific scent name. On the other hand,

Z. Pan et al. (Eds.): ICAT 2006, LNCS 4282, pp. 1322–1332, 2006.

Table 1. Usage of auditory and olfactory information

	Type A	Type B
Auditory information	Sound effects, imitation sounds	Background music
Olfactory information	Material scent	Background scent
Description	Noun	Adjective

a contents viewer can generate a preferred scent depending on his/her diffuser data on the relation between the SDA and the scent.

2 Representation of Scent Information for Telecommunication

2.1 Classification of Scent Information

Upon receiving information via the five senses, the human brain processes much more visual information than audio and olfactory information. Table 1 shows the usage of audio and olfactory information accompanying visual information such as a movie. The first type (Type A) offers information by expressing an object as precisely as possible. The other one (Type B) expresses an ambience of the images and presents it psychologically and sensorily rather than specifically.

In the case of audio communication, generating imitation sounds or sound effects such as a knocking sound or an engine sound is categorized as Type A, while playing background music is classified as Type B. When information is provided using Type B, the viewer can gain an impression of the environment even when it is not actually shown, or can recognize the subject of the image as an ambience. Let us apply this classification to scent information.

We define a scent as a material scent when it clearly corresponds to an object or an event such as the smell of coffee on the table or the smell of fire in the battlefield. A material scent can be described by a noun because we can imagine the specific object or event when we smell it.

On the other hand, a scent is defined as a background scent analogous with background music when we intend to present its impression psychologically and sensorially. Therefore, it can be expressed by adjectives like 'romantic' or 'soft'.

This concept makes the interface highly useful since everyone can easily specify the desired scent using nouns or adjectives without having a special knowledge of scents.

2.2 Previous Research on Scent Information Systems

Trial runs on transmitting scent information with audio/visual information has being conducted in the field of virtual reality (VR).

Sensorama [7] developed by Heilig in the 1950s was the first VR system that displayed scent information with audio/visual information. In Friend Park [8], the "aroma" of a virtual object or environment is defined as an area that a scent can reach. The aroma provides users in the area with an increased sense of reality by generating the scent.

Some systems that add a scent to Web contents are referred to in Kaye's article [3]. Computer controlled olfactory displays such as iSmell [2] or Osmooze [6] are used in these systems. Another type of diffuser "air cannon olfactory display" that generates toroidal vortices of scent airs in order to display the scent in restricted space is proposed in [9].

Adding a scent to image media such as movies has been proposed by a number of researchers. Okada et al. [5] measured the viewer's mental condition by his/her brainwaves, and analyzed the relation between the scent and the viewer's feelings during a movie.

A smell synthesis device that aims to present the scent of an object in a remote place has being developed. Nakamoto et al.'s system [4] analyzes the smell to be transmitted and presents the analyzed data as the composition ratio of the scent elements. On the receiver side, a feedback control changes the ratio of the scent elements owned by the receiver to reproduce the target scent.

A wearable olfactory display with a position sensor has also been developed [10]. By controlling the density of olfactory molecules, it can present the spatiality of olfaction in an outdoor environment. An olfactory information transmitting system consists of the display mentioned above, a sensing system using three gas sensors and matching database. A user can experience a proper sense of smell through the system by translating obtained olfactory information.

AROMA [1] tries to introduce the olfactory modality as a potential alternative to visual and auditory modalities for providing messaging notifications. The experiment shows that the olfactory modality was shown to be less effective in delivering notifications than the other modalities, but produced a less disruptive effect on user engagement in the primary task.

However, no communication model for open systems has been established yet, and only a limited number of scents can be handled in the above systems.

This paper proposes a scent communication model mediated by sense-descriptive adjectives, and examines its effectiveness by some experiments.

3   Scent Communication Model Using Sense-Descriptive Adjectives

3.1   Scent Communication Model

As mentioned above, we focus on the background scent, which accompanies the movie (visual and auditory information) to emphasis the ambience or impression of the scene.

In Figure 1, a contents creator makes his/her image based on a script on a creator's site. When he adds a scent to the content, he might use an ambiguous sense descriptive adjective such as "fresh scent" and/or "romantic scent" in a scene: i.e., he wants to use effective scents for his production without having special knowledge of scents. SDA instead of the scent name is then transmitted to the viewer's site accompanying the coded audio/visual data.

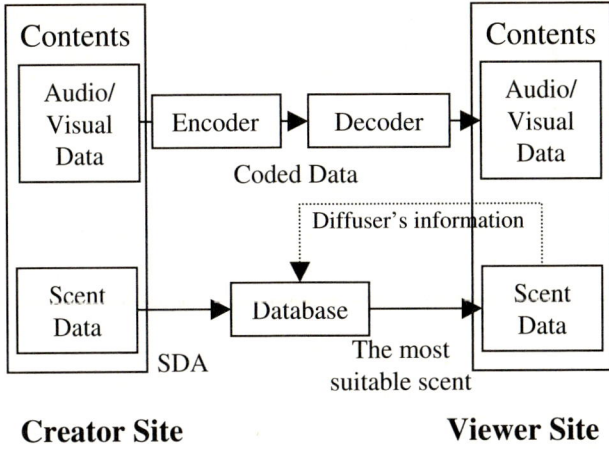

Fig. 1. Scent communication model

On the viewer's site, SDA must be replaced by a specific scent name that is contained in his diffuser. As the number of scents in the diffuser is limited, the list of the scents must be sent to the database beforehand. The database contains a table that is used to transform SDA to the most suitable scent for the viewer. This scent is diffused from the diffuser synchronizing with audio/visual data. The database may be located in either site or another site on the Internet.

3.2   Protocol for Scent Communication

Figure 2 shows the protocol for scent communication. The system consists of three sites: a viewer site consisting of a client PC with a diffuser, a creator site containing a contents server, and a database site with a database server that translates the SDA to background scents. The viewer plays back the contents with the background scents by the following process.

1. The viewer site sends a request to the creator site for the SDA contained in the contents.
2. The creator site sends the SDA to the viewer site.
3. The viewer site sends both the SDA and the list of scents, which the diffuser contains, to the database site.
4. The database site translates the SDA and selects the appropriate background scents, then sends them back to the viewer site.
5. After receiving the background scent, the viewer site sends a request to the creator site for the contents.
6. The creator site transmits the contents to the viewer site.
7. The contents are downloaded and played with diffusion of the background scents.

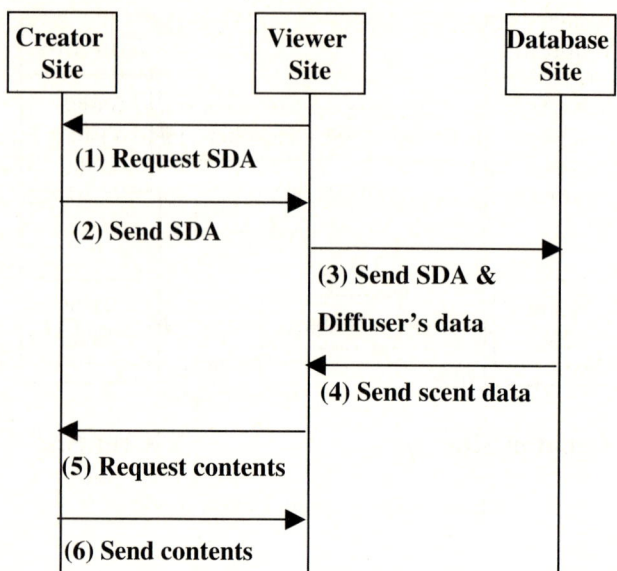

Fig. 2. Protocol for scent communication

Table 2. Membership values between sense-descriptive adjectives and background scents

Adjectives	Grape-fruit	Rose-mary	Rose	Jas-mine	Pepper-mint	Vani-lla	Ylang-ylang	Laven-der	Sandal wood	Chamo-mile	Berga-mot
romantic	.39	.37	.58	.62	.43	.68	.44	.46	.31	.35	.49
attractive	.42	.38	.62	.60	.36	.68	.48	.37	.36	.32	.45
passionate	.44	.32	.42	.49	.32	.6	.36	.39	.32	.32	.51
stimulative	.60	.64	.5	.38	.61	.3	.38	.64	.5	.64	.54
warm	.46	.38	.44	.55	.32	.75	.44	.52	.46	.32	.65
soft	.39	.21	.48	.54	.25	.77	.46	.35	.38	.18	.43
comfortable	.35	.19	.5	.5	.25	.65	.45	.29	.3	.21	.37
relaxed	.6	.38	.44	.49	.64	.62	.46	.49	.35	.26	.42
tense	.33	.49	.31	.2	.45	.14	.27	.43	.37	.58	.48
dynamic	.33	.39	.25	.2	.32	.26	.27	.33	.33	.51	.43
active	.49	.33	.26	.35	.43	.25	.31	.43	.39	.45	.52
vivid	.67	.39	.33	.35	.51	.33	.4	.52	.44	.44	.57
clean	.74	.6	.44	.5	.82	.4	.5	.57	.45	.35	.6
refreshing	.8	.48	.46	.57	.83	.39	.49	.6	.4	.32	.69
pleasant	.67	.3	.36	.5	.58	.67	.43	.46	.31	.21	.58
natural	.61	.38	.4	.42	.54	.43	.52	.52	.45	.25	.5

3.3   Database of SDA and Background Scents

The database converts the SDA to the background scents. It is impossible to uniquely map the SDA to the background scent because of their ambiguity. The relationship between a member of SDA and that of the background scent is measured as a membership value $[0, 1]$ of fuzzy functions. Membership values are predetermined by an experiment such as Experiment 2, and stored in a table as shown in Table 2. For each received SDA, the database searches the scents in the corresponding row of the table, and sorts them in descending order based on the membership value.

We define the scent having the highest membership value as the most suitable scent and the other scents as alternative scents. In Table 2, underlined numbers show the highest membership values on each row. The corresponding scents are the most suitable scents for the adjectives. Appropriate scent data is sent to the viewer site in response to its request.

4   Evaluation

4.1   Scent Diffuser

Figure 3 is FUKUHARA scent diffuser we used in Experiment 3. The diffuser is 253mm wide, 550mm deep, and 408mm high, and is equipped with five scent tanks and an air compressor. The diffuser controls scent output by start/stop commands via RS232C interface. The user can sniff the scent air from top of the tube connected to the scent tank.

4.2   Experiment 1: Selection of SDA

We selected 45 words as SDA candidates from the scent evaluation terms appearing in previous researches. Synonyms such as "refreshing" and "crisp",

Fig. 3. Scent diffuser

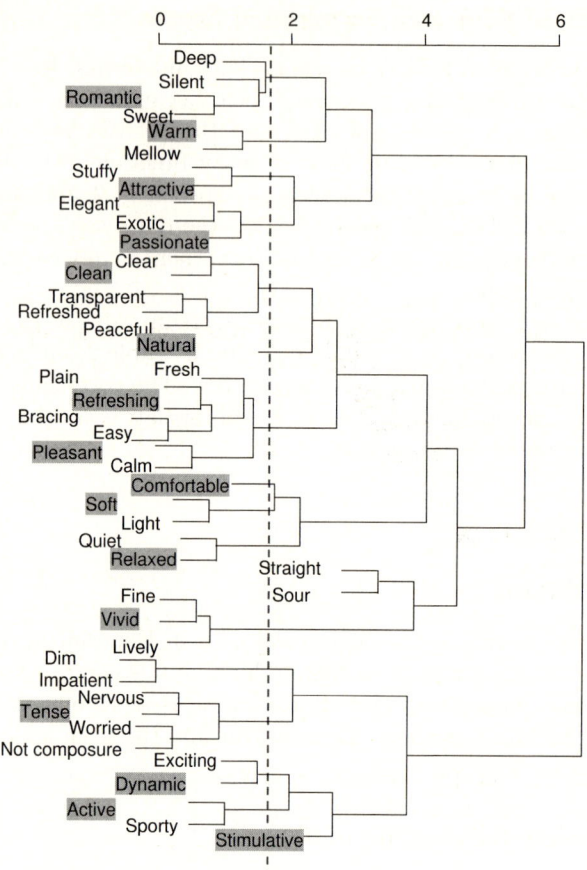

Fig. 4. Dendrogram of sense-descriptive adjectives

"peaceful" and "calm" are united, and adjectives associated with unpleasant smells are excluded.

If the list is too big, it will be difficult for the contents creator to pick up a SDA, while if the list is too small, it will be impossible to select an appropriate SDA. We conducted the following experiments in order to sum up less than 20 words of SDA that are frequently used in movies.

Ten scenes (2 minutes per scene) from 6 movies were shown to 20 participants (16 males, 4 females, aged 20 to 25). They were asked to select an arbitrary number of SDA that is appropriate to the scene from the list of 45 words. They were allowed to add an appropriate word if the necessary words were not on the list. The proximity of SDA was calculated by hierarchical clustering analysis (complete-link method), and a dendrogram shown in Figure 4 was obtained.

Finally, we chose the 16 words that appear in the first column of Table 2 from different clusters considering frequency of selection by the participants. The boxed words in the dendrogram of Figure 4 were selected as SDA.

4.3   Experiment 2: Mapping SDA to Background Scents

Since both SDA and background scents are ambiguous, it is difficult to uniquely map one to another. Eleven scents that are widely used for aromatherapy and research activities are shown in the first row of Table 2. We define the relation between the set of SDA (16 adjectives) and the set of background scents (11 scents) using the membership value of the fuzzy set. The higher the membership value that ranges from 0 to 1, the closer the relation of elements from each set.

Experiment 2 aims to determine the membership value. The same participants as in Experiment 1 sniffed each of the 11 background scents and rated each of the 16 words of the SDA on a scale of 1 (disagree) to 5 (agree). The mean values of the scale were calculated, and converted into a range from 0 to 1. The converted values were stored as the membership values between the SDA and the background scent as shown in Table 2.

4.4   Experiment 3: Alternative Scents

We defined the most suitable scent as the scent having the highest membership value of the column corresponding to the specified SDA in Table 3.3. The other scents are defined as the alternative scents. If the most suitable scent does not exist in a client's diffuser, a scent having the next highest value is searched until a scent that the client owns is found.

The aim of Experiment 3 is to investigate whether or not the alternative scent provides the same effect as the most suitable scent. Forty participants (85% male) were divided into 10 groups. Each participant watched four movies in a different order under the following conditions.

- movie only
- movie with the most suitable scent
- movie with an alternative scent
- movie with an irrelevant scent.

Scenes from the four different movies were selected for the experiment. Four members in each group are assigned as shown in Table 3. For example, member A watched scene 1 without smell, scene 2 with the most suitable scent, and so on. Note that each member sees the same scene once. An evaluation sheet that used a 5-grade scale where 0 is anchored to 'I did not feel like the SDA with the scent at all' and 4 to 'I felt like the SDA with the scent very well' was filled out by the participants on the basis of their impression. Table 4 shows the scenes, SDA, and scents used in Experiment 3. The numbers in parentheses are membership values of the scent.

Figure 5 shows the results of the experiment. In Figure 5, the first two movies without smell have a higher value than the last two movies without smell, presumably because they convey strong messages and thus give a strong impression to the viewers only by audio/visual data. The value of impression in all scenes increases by adding the most suitable scent. The same trends are shown in the case of adding the alternative scent, except for the action movie.

Table 3. Assignment of members for each group

Scene	Movie only	Movie with the most suitable scent	Movie with the alternative scent	Movie with the irrelevant scent
1	A	B	C	D
2	D	A	B	C
3	C	D	A	B
4	B	C	D	A

Table 4. Scenes, sense-descriptive adjectives, and background scents in Experiment 3

Scene	Adjective	Most suitable scent	Alternative scent	Irrelevant scent
1 Action (Mission impossibleII)	Active	Bergamot(.52)	Grapefruit(.49)	Vanilla(.25)
2 Horror(Ring)	Tense	Camomile(.58)	Rosemary(.49)	Vanilla(.14)
3 Animation(Raputa)	Clean	Peppermint(.83)	Grapefruit(.80)	Chamomile(.32)
4 Romance(Titanic)	Attractive	Vanilla(.68)	Rose(.62)	Sandal wood(.31)

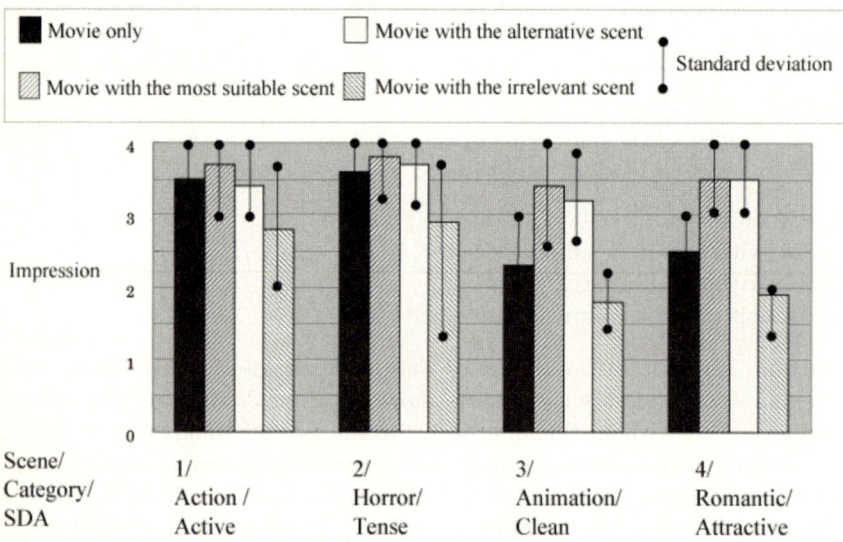

Fig. 5. Score of impressions of sense-descriptive adjectives for the movies with different conditions

4.5   Consideration

It is believed that the scenes conveying strong messages such as in action and horror movies give a strong impression with images alone, whereas adding a scent is effective for neutral scenes in animation and romantic movies.

We tested the difference of mean scores of each scene between the following three cases by Student's t-test, i.e., between the cases of

1. "with the most suitable scent" and "with the alternative scent"
2. "with the alternative scent" and "with the irrelevant scent"
3. "movie only" and "with the irrelevant scent".

Table 5. Results of t-test

Scene	Most suitable scent vs. Alternative scent	Alternative scent vs. Irrelevant scent	Movie only vs. Irrelevant scent
1	0.20	2.21*	2.27*
2	0.46	1.86*	1.86*
3	0.63	5.53**	2.34*
4	0	7.8**	2.93**

* 5% level   ** 1% level

Table 5 shows T values in each case using four scenes. We found no statistical differences in the first case, whereas statistical differences were found in the second and third cases. Therefore, we derive the following facts.

1. The impression of scene increases by adding the scents that correspond to the SDA fitting the scene.
2. Since there exist no statistical difference in the first case of t test, the alternative scent is as effective as the most suitable scent. This implies that more than one alternative scent could be used with the same SDA.
3. The impression decreases by adding the scents that are irrelevant to the SDA fitting the scene.

5   Conclusion

In order to exchange scent information, it must have a unique representation between the sender and receiver sites. However, no representation scheme has been existed due to lack of a scent information basis.

We introduced a background scent that is used as the background of the images analogous with background music, and proposed the concept of background scent communication mediated by SDA that presents the ambience of the images. The membership values between the 16 SDA and the 11 background scent were calculated, and the most suitable scent and an alternative scent for each SDA were selected based on the membership value.

The experiments showed that the alternative scent as well as the most suitable scent effectively reinforce the movie contents. This result means that communication partners do not necessarily possess the exactly the same kind of scents in each site, and suggests the possibility of scent communication in open systems.

References

1. Bodnar A., Corbett R., Nekrasovski D. : AROMA: Ambient awareness through olfaction in a messaging application, *ICMI '04 Proceedings*, pp. 183- 190, (2004).
2. Edge Review: DigiScent Ismell,
   http://www.edgereview.com/ataglance.cfm?category=Edge&ID=136.
3. Kaye J.: Making scents, *Interactions* Jan/Feb, pp. 48–61(2004).
4. Nakamoto T., Nakahira Y., Hiramatsu H. and Moriizumi T.: Odor recorder using active odor sensing system, *Sensors and Actuators B*, 76 465, (2001).
5. Okada K. and Aiba S.: Toward the actualization of broadcasting service with smell information, *Institute of Image information and Television Engineering of Japan Technical Report* (in Japanese), Vol. 27, No. 64, pp. 31-34, (2003).
6. http://www.osmooze.com/osmooze/osmooshop_gb.html
7. Retrofuture: Sensorama's pre-virtual reality,
   http://www.retrofuture.com/sensorama.html
8. Shigeno H., Honda S., Osawa T., Nagano Y., Okada K. and Matsushita Y.: A virtual space expressed the scent and wind -A virtual space system "Friend Park", *Journal of Information Processing Society of Japan* (in Japanese), Vol. 42, No. 7, pp. 1922-1932, (2001).
9. Yanagida Y., Noma H., Tetsutani N., and Tomono A.: An unencumbering,localized olfactory display, *CHI '03 Extended abstracts*, pp. 988–989, (2003).
10. Yokoyama S., Tanikawa T., Hirota K. and Hirose M.: Olfactory field simulation using wearable olfactory display, *Tans. of Virtual Reality Society of Japan* (in Japanese), Vol. 9, No. 3, pp. 265-274, (2004).
    http://www.cyber.rcast.u-tokyo.ac.jp/project/nioi_e.html.

Hand Shape Recognition Using a Mean-Shift Embedded Active Contour (MEAC)

Eun Yi Kim

Dept. Of Internet and Multimedia Eng., Konkuk Univ., Seoul, Republic of Korea
eykim@konkuk.a.kr

Abstract. This paper presents a hand shape recognition system using an active contour model (ACM) and applies it to an HCI to control a mobile robot. For the recognition of hand shapes, the technique should be developed to accurately track variously changing hands in real-time. For this, we develop a mean-shift embedded active contour (MEAC) which can improve the convergence speed and the tracking accurracy than the standard ACM. The proposed recognition system consists of four modules: a hand detector, a hand tracker, a hand shape recognizer and a robot controller. The hand detector locates a skin color region with a specific shape as a hand in the first frame. Thereafter, the detected region is accurately tracked through the whole video sequence by the hand tracker using a MEAC, and its shape is recognized using Hue moments. To assess the validity of the proposed system, we tested the proposed system to a walking robot, *RCB-1*. The experimental results show the effectiveness of the proposed system.

Keywords: Active contour model, mean-shift procedure, human-computer interface, object tracking, hand shape recognition.

1 Introduction

Recently, a hand gesture has been one of the most common and natural communication media between human and computer system. A hand gesture recognition research has gained a lot of attentions because of its applications for interactive human-machine interface and virtual environments. Most of the recent works can be classified into two groups: device-based techniques and vision-based techniques [1-3]. Device-based techniques use the additional devices such as a glove. Meanwhile, vision-based techniques detect the user's hand by processing images or videos obtained via a camera, making them less intrusive and more comfortable for users, as well as inexpensive communication devices. Accordingly, there have been an increasing number of gesture recognition researches using vision-based methods.

However, the practical use of vision-based recognition system requires the automatic detection and tracking of the hand shapes in real-life situation. To extract hand region, Freeman et al. [1] detected a hand in every frames. It is so time consuming and sensitive to the clustered background. In [3], a method using Kalman filter and an affine contour deformation model was used for accurately tracking the

Z. Pan et al. (Eds.): ICAT 2006, LNCS 4282, pp. 1333–1341, 2006.
© Springer-Verlag Berlin Heidelberg 2006

hand shapes. Although it is effective to detect change of predefined hand shapes, it is difficult to track variously changing hands accurately.

To solve the abovementioned problems, this paper presents a hand shape recognition system using an active contour model (ACM). The ACM is successfully used for non-rigid object tracking because of their ability to effectively descript curve and elastic property [4]. A key component of a successful tracking is its ability to search efficiency for the target, then the search efficiency is determined by the location of the initial curve. When the initial curve is near the object, the convergence on the object boundary is invariably fast and accurate. Conversely, when the initial curve is far from the object, convergence involves a much heavier computational cost and errors are induced, such as noise and holes that have similar features to object boundary. Moreover, highly active objects with large movements can be lost. Consequently, the initial curve should be localized nearby the target object for search efficiency and accurate results.

For this, a mean-shift embedded active contour (MEAC) is developed for real-time object contour tracking robust to the location of the initial curve. The MEAC performs by two steps: curve localization step and curve deformation step. The initial curve is re-localized nearby the object using a mean shift algorithm. Thereafter the curve is deformed using a level set method.

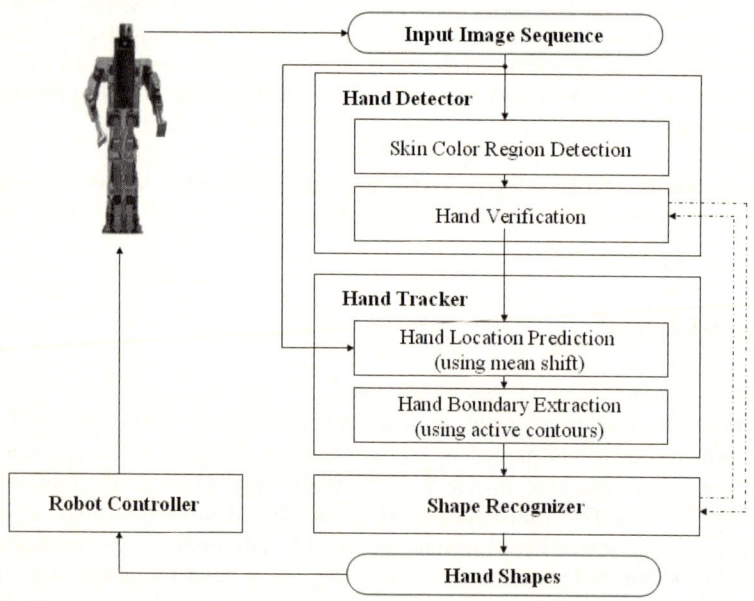

Fig. 1. Overview of the proposed system

Fig. 1 shows the overview of the proposed recognition method, where it is composed of a hand detector, a hand tracker, a hand shape recognizer and a robot controller. The hand detector detects a skin color region, which has a specific shape, as hand in an image. Then, the hand tracking is performed using the MEAC. Thereafter the hand shape recognition is performed using Hue moments.

To assess the validity of the proposed recognition method, it is applied to control a walking robot, *RCB-1*. Then five different gestures were selected to control a robot. The gestures were stop, go-forward, shrink, turn-left and turn-right. The experimental results show the effectiveness of the proposed system.

2 Hand Detector

In this section, we describe the method for extracting hand region from a color image. The proposed method detects a hand using skin color information described by 2D Gaussian model in chromatic color space. In the RGB space, color representation includes both color and brightness. Therefore, RGB is not necessarily the best color representation for detecting pixels with skin color. Brightness can be removed by dividing the three components of a color pixel (R, G, B) according to intensity. This space is known as chromatic color, where intensity is a normalized color vector with two components (r, g). The skin-color model is obtained from 200 sample images. Means and covariance matrix of the skin color model are as follows:

$$\mu = (\bar{r}, \bar{g}) = (117.588, 79.064),$$

$$\Sigma = \begin{bmatrix} \sigma_r^2 & \rho_{X,Y}\sigma_g\sigma_r \\ \rho_{X,Y}\sigma_r\sigma_g & \sigma_g^2 \end{bmatrix} = \begin{bmatrix} 24.132 & -10.085 \\ -10.085 & 8.748 \end{bmatrix}.$$

The proposed method detects skin color pixels from a color image using the skin color model. Thereafter, the connected-component analysis is performed on the binary image.

The generated components are considered as the candidates of the hand, and recognized by a hand shape recognized which will be introduced in Section 4. If the shape of a component is recognized as "stop," it is verified as a hand

3 Hand Tracker

After a hand is detected, instead of detecting hand in every frame, the proposed system tracks the hand to save computation cost and make the temporal correspondence between the successive frames. To track hand, we use a MEAC. In the MEAC, the tracking process is achieved by two steps: the curve localization step and curve deformation step. In the first step, a mean shift algorithm is used to move the initial curve without changing the shape and scale of the curve. Then, a level set method is used to deform the curve toward the object contour.

3.1 Curve Localization

The objective of this step is to move the initial curve near the object of interest without changing the shape and scale of the curve. For this, a mean-shift algorithm is used.

The mean shift algorithm iteratively replace the search window location (the centroid) with a hand probability distribution $\{P(I_{ij}|\alpha_o)\}_{i,j=1,...,IW,IH}$ (IW: image width, IH: image height) which represent the probability of a pixel (i,j) in the image being part of hand, where α_o is its parameters and I is a photometric variable. In this paper, the skin color model is used as hand probability distribution. The search window location is simply computed as follows [5]:

$$m_x = M_{10}/M_{00} \quad \text{and} \qquad m_y = M_{01}/M_{00,} \tag{1}$$

where M_{ab} is the $(a + b)th$ moment as defined by

$$M_{ab}(W) = \sum_{i,j \in W} i^a j^b P(I_{ij} \mid \alpha_o).$$

The hand location is obtained by successive computations of the search window location (x,y). The center of search window W is initialized with the center of the bounding box of the initial curve, B. and its size is updated in proportional to the amount of object's motion at each frame as follows:

$$W^t_{width(height)} = \max\left(\alpha\left(\left|m_y^{(t-1)} - m_y^{(t-2)}\right| - B_{width(height)}\right), 0\right) + \beta B_{width(height)} \tag{$t>2$},$$

where α and β is a constant, and the t is the frame index.

3.2 Curve Deformation

After the initial curve is localized, the curve is deformed until it matches the object boundary using region competition based active contours.

Region competition is proposed by Zhu and Yuille as a hybrid approach to image segmentation [6]. Their basic functional is as follows:

$$E[\Gamma,\{\alpha_i\}] = \sum_{i=1}^{M}\left\{\frac{\mu}{2}\int_{R_i} ds - \log P(\{I_s : s \in R_i\}\mid \alpha_i) + \lambda\right\}, \tag{2}$$

where Γ is the boundary in the image, $P(\cdot)$ is a specific distribution for region R_i, α_i is its parameters, M is the number of the regions, s is a site of image coordinate system, and μ and λ are two constants.

To minimize the energy E, steepest descent can be done with respect to boundary Γ. For any point $\vec{v}$. On the boundary Γ we obtain:

$$\frac{d\vec{v}}{dt} = -\frac{\delta E[\Gamma,\{\alpha_i\}]}{\delta \vec{v}}, \tag{3}$$

where the right-hand side is (minus) the functional derivative of the energy E.

Taking the functional derivative yields the motion equation for point $\vec{v}$:

$$\frac{d\vec{v}}{dt} = \sum_{k \in Q_{(\vec{v})}}\left\{-\frac{\mu}{2}k_{k(\vec{v})}\vec{n}_{k(\vec{v})} + \log P(I_{(\vec{v})} \mid \alpha_k)\vec{n}_{k(\vec{v})}\right\}, \tag{4}$$

where $Q_{(\vec{v})} = \{k \mid \vec{v} \text{ lies on } \Gamma_k\}$, i.e., the summation is done over those regions R_k for which $\vec{v}$ is on Γ_k. $k_{k(\vec{v})}$ is the curvature of Γ_k at point $\vec{v}$ and $\vec{n}_{k(\vec{v})}$ is the unit normal to Γ_k at point $\vec{v}$.

Region competition contains many of the desirable properties of region growing and active contours. Indeed we can derive many aspects of these models as special cases of region competition . Active contours can be a special case in which there are two regions (object region R_o and background region R_b) and a common boundary Γ as shown in follows:

$$\frac{d\vec{v}}{dt} = -\mu k_{o(\bar{v})} \vec{n}_{o(\bar{v})} + \left(\log P(I_{(\bar{v})} \mid \alpha_o) - \log P(I_{(\bar{v})} \mid \alpha_b) \right) \vec{n}_{o(\bar{v})} \tag{5}$$

The active contour evolution was implemented using the level set technique. We represent curve Γ implicitly by the zero level set of function $u : \mathscr{R}^2 \rightarrow \mathscr{R}$, with the region inside Γ corresponding to $u > 0$. Accordingly, Eq. (5) can be rewritten by the following equation, which is a level set evolution equation [4]:

$$\frac{du(s)}{dt} = -\mu k_s \|\nabla u\| + \left(\log P(I_s \mid \alpha_o) - \log P(I_s \mid \alpha_b) \right) \|\nabla u\| \tag{6}$$

where

$$k = \frac{u_{xx} y_y^2 - 2u_y u_x u_{xy} + u_{yy} u_x^2}{(u_x^2 + u_y^2)^{3/2}}.$$

4   Hand Shape Recognizer

The shape of an extracted hand region is recognized by comparing with templates. Then, to describe hand shapes, we use moment invariants proposed by Hu [7], since the invariants are independent of position, size and orientation.

Let $f(x,y)$ denote the binary image which indicates a pixel belong to hand region or not. Then, the two-dimensional $(p+q)$th order moments for $f(x,y)$ are defined as follow:

$$m_{pq} = \int_{-\infty}^{\infty} \int_{-\infty}^{\infty} x^p y^q f(x, y) dx dy \tag{7}$$

where $p,q=0,1,2\cdots$.

In digital image, Eq.(7) can be described as

$$m_{pq} = \sum_x \sum_y x^p y^q f(x, y) \tag{8}$$

The central moments are defined as

$$\mu_{pq} = \sum_x \sum_y (x-\bar{x})^p (y-\bar{y})^q f(x, y) \tag{9}$$

where

$$\bar{x} = \frac{m_{10}}{m_{00}} \quad and \quad \bar{y} = \frac{m_{01}}{m_{00}} \tag{10}$$

The normalized central moments, denoted η_{pq}, are defined as

$$\eta_{pq} = \mu_{pq} / \mu_{00}^\gamma \tag{11}$$

where $\gamma=(p+q)/2 + 1$ for $p+q=2,3, \cdots$.

A set of seven invariants moments can be derived from the second and third moments.

$$\phi_1 = \eta_{20} + \eta_{02}, \quad \phi_2 = (\eta_{20} - \eta_{02})^2 + 4\eta_{11}^2$$

$$\phi_3 = (\eta_{30} - 3\eta_{12})^2 + (\eta_{03} + \eta_{21})^2, \quad \phi_4 = (\eta_{30} + \eta_{12})^2 + (\eta_{03} + \eta_{21})^2$$

$$\phi_5 = (3\eta_{30} - 3\eta_{12})(\eta_{30} + \eta_{12})[(\eta_{30} + \eta_{12})^2 - 3(\eta_{21} + \eta_{03})^2]$$

$$+ (3\eta_{21} - \eta_{03})[3(\eta_{03} + \eta_{12})^2 - (\eta_{21} + \eta_{03})^2]$$

$$\phi_6 = (\eta_{20} - \eta_{02})[(\eta_{30} + \eta_{12})^2 - (\eta_{21} + \eta_{03})^2] + 4\eta_{11}(\eta_{30} + \eta_{12})(\eta_{21} + \eta_{03})$$

$$\phi_7 = (3\eta_{21} - \eta_{03})(\eta_{30} + \eta_{12})[(\eta_{30} + \eta_{12})^2 - 3(\eta_{21} + \eta_{03})^2]$$

$$+ (3\eta_{12} - \eta_{30})(\eta_{21} + \eta_{03})[3(\eta_{30} + \eta_{12})^2 - (\eta_{21} + \eta_{30})^2]$$

$$(12)$$

This set of moments is invariant to translation, rotation, and scale change [7].

To recognize the hand shape, Euclidean distance between moment invariants of hand in current frame and templates is used.

5 Application to a Robot Control

User can control the mobile robot with predefined hand shapes in front of camera without any hand-held device. The distance between user and camera is about a miter. The system was implemented using a PC and a web cam without additional devices such as data gloves and frame grabber boards.

In the proposed system, the mobile robot is controlled by right hand shapes. For the purpose of experiment we selected five different hand shapes. These were logically associated with five different commands needed for robot motion. Fig. 3 shows the five predefined hand shapes and corresponding commands.

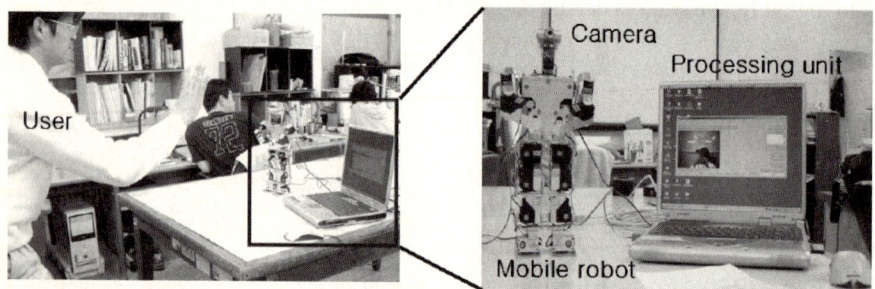

Fig. 2. System Environment

| (a)Stop | (b)Go forward | (c)Shrink | (d)Turn left | (e)Turn right |

Fig. 3. Predefined hand shapes and commands

If the system finds the hand whose shape is "stop," the tracking process is started and the tracked hand is recognized. When a hand shape is recognized in successive three frames, the corresponding command is performed. Command "stop" makes robot stop their action and maintain standing pose. And other commands make robot take corresponding actions.

6 Experimental Results

The proposed system was implemented using MS Visual C++ 6.0 and OpenCV beta3.1 to get 320×240 and 24-bit color images captured 3 frames/s from camera mounted mobile robot without an additional frame grabber board. The used robot is *KHR*-1 which can controlled servo motor, *KRS*-784.

6.1 Results of Tracking

The proposed system was evaluated through testing 529 frames for 4 persons. Each person tried many times to change hand shapes. And to show the effectiveness of the proposed hand tracking method, we compare the results between the proposed method using mean shift and the method only using active contours without mean shift. Fig. 4 shows the tracking results of the hands.

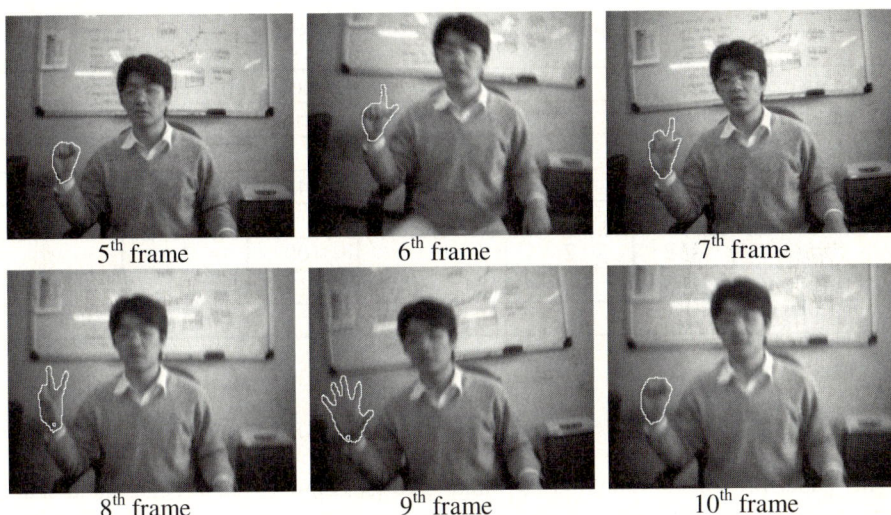

5th frame 6th frame 7th frame

8th frame 9th frame 10th frame

Fig. 4. Results of the hand tracking

The quantitative comparison in term of convergence speed is shown in Fig. 5. In the proposed method, because initial curve is re-localized neared the hand using mean shift, iteration of curve evolution is fast converged. Due to it, the method only using active contour model takes lager time to track the object than the proposed method as shown in Fig. 5.

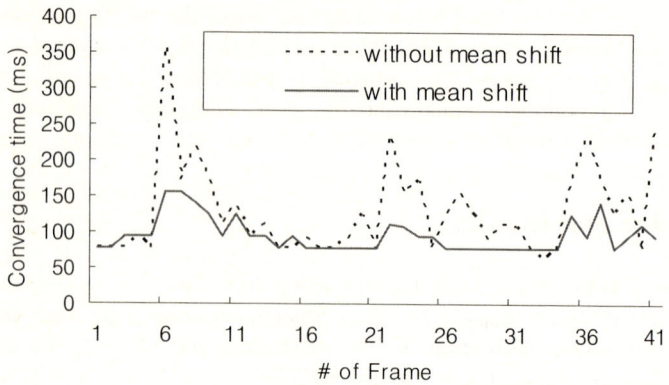

Fig. 5. Comparison of two methods in term of convergence time

6.2 Results of Static Shape Recognition

Table 1 shows the hand shape recognition results using moment invariants. Overall, the approach classified 96.8% of the examples correctly and erred in 17 of the 529 testing frames.

Table 1. Hand shape recognition results

		Shape recognized				
		Stop	Go forward	Shrink	Turn left	Turn right
Shape given	529					
Stop	107	101	2	4		
Go forward	103	2	101			
Shrink	112	2		109	1	
Turn left	106			1	103	2
Turn right	101		2		1	98

7 Conclusions

This paper presents a vision based walking robot control system using hand shape recognition. The proposed system proposed of four modules: a hand detector, a hand tracker, a hand shape recognizer and a robot controller. The hand detector detects a skin color region, which has a specific shape, as hand in an image. Then, the hand tracking is performed using an active contour model with mean shift. Thereafter the hand shape recognition is performed using Hue moments. To show the effectiveness of the proposed system, we tested the proposed system to a walking robot, *RCB-1*.

Acknowledgments. This paper was supported by Konkuk University in 2004.

References

1. William T. Freeman, and Craig D. Weissman.: Television control by hand gestures. IEEE International. Workshop. on Automatic Face and Gesture Recognition. (1995) 179-183
2. Hyeon-Kyu Lee and Jin H. Kim.: An HMM-Based Threshold Model Approach for Gesture Recognition. IEEE Transactions on Pattern Analysis and Machine Intelligence. Vol. 21, No. 10 (1999) 961-973
3. Min C. Shin, Lenonid V. Tsap, and Dmitry B. Goldgof.: Gesture Recognition using Bezier curves for visualization navigation from registered 3-D data. Pattern Recognition. Vol. 37, No. 5 (2004) 1011-1024
4. Freedman, D., and Zhang, T.: Active Contours for Tracking Distributions. IEEE Transactions on Image Processing. Vol. 13, No. 4 (2004) 518-526
5. Kim, K. I., Jung, K., and Kim, J. H.:Texture-Based Approach for Text Detection in Image Using Support Vector Machines and Continuously Adaptive Mean Shift Algorithm. IEEE Transactions on Pattern Analysis and Machine Intelligence. Vol. 25, No. 12 (2003) 1631-1639
6. Zhu, S. C., and Yuille, A.: Region Competition: Unifying Snakes, Region Growing, and Bayes/MDL for Multiband Image Segmentation. IEEE Transactions on Pattern Analysis and Machine Intelligence. Vol. 18, No 9 (1996) 884-900
7. Gonzalez, R. C., and Woods R. R., *Digital Image Processing*, Prentice Hall, New Jersey, 2002

Author Index

Printing: Mercedes-Druck, Berlin
Binding: Stein+Lehmann, Berlin